Javanese
English
Dictionary

Javanese English Dictionary

by Stuart Robson and Singgih Wibisono
with the assistance of Yacinta Kurniasih

PERIPLUS

Published by Periplus Editions (HK) Ltd
Copyright © 2002 Periplus Editions (HK) Ltd

ISBN 0-7946-0000-X
Printed in Singapore

Distributed by:

Asia Pacific
Berkeley Books Pte Ltd
130 Joo Seng Road
#06-01/03
Olivine Building
Singapore 368357
Tel (65) 280 1330; Fax (65) 280 6290

Japan & Korea
Tuttle Publishing
RK Building, 2nd Floor
2-13-10 Shimo-Meguro
Meguro-ku, Tokyo 153 0064
Tel (03) 5437 0171; Fax (03) 5437 0755

Indonesia
PT Java Books
Kelapa Gading Kirana
Blok A 14/17, Jakarta 14240
Tel (62) 21 451 5351; Fax (62) 21 453 4987

North America
Tuttle Publishing
Distribution Center
Airport Industrial Park
364 Innovation Drive, North Clarendon, VT 05759-9436
Tel (802) 773 8930; Fax (802) 773 6993

Contents

Preface

This dictionary is a pale reflection of the linguistic reality that is the Javanese language. The description to be found here fails to do justice to the richness of expression of the speech of ordinary people as they go about their daily lives, or of the dalang as he weaves his wonderful tales through the night, not to mention the wealth of the literary classics. It only scratches the surface.

Quite apart from the task of sharpening the definitions of words already listed, there is also a vast amount of work waiting to be done by students in the field and in the libraries, so that in due time a more complete tool can be offered to those who wish to become better acquainted with the civilization of Java in its various aspects.

When the idea of a new dictionary of Modern Javanese was mentioned in the presence of Romo Zoetmulder one day in his library at the Pasturan Kumetiran, he warned that it would be a very difficult project to complete. But his warning went unheeded. The needs of students with little or no Dutch had always impressed themselves, and it seemed not too difficult to use the existing works—reviewed, refined and added to—in order to produce a work sufficiently broad and practical.

Now that this tool is ready, we can only offer it to the public in the hope that it will prove useful and fulfil a need.

Grateful record is made of the contributions of:

- Romo P.J. Zoetmulder, for upholding a high ideal of scholarship in Javanese lexicography;
- Th. Pigeaud, for providing a solid basis with his dictionary that has stood the test of time, and
- Elinor C. Horne, for being the first to attempt the task of creating a Javanese-English dictionary;
- The families of Bapak B. Suhardjo in Muntilan, and of the late Bapak S. Kibat Notowihardjo in Sleman, for their loving acceptance of someone interested in all kinds of Javanese words;
- Pak Singgih and Bu Titiek, for being willing to spend three years of their lives in Melbourne on the project;
- The Australian Research Council, for its generous funding, without which nothing would have been possible;
- Raymond Weisling, for showing a sincere interest and giving encouragement to publish;
- Yacinta Kurniasih, whose excellent help has substantially improved the quality of the work and whose feeling for Javanese is quite remarkable;
- Eric Oey, for being willing to take on the publication of a Javanese dictionary;
- And all the others who have assisted with information or advice.

Mugi-mugi wonten kasilipun.

Introduction

1. The Javanese Language

Javanese is the language of the island of Java, located in Southeast Asia within the Republic of Indonesia. It is a member of the Austronesian family of languages, and is thus closely related to, but distinct from, the other languages of its region. It is spoken mainly in the provinces of Central and East Java, including the Special Area of Yogyakarta; its immediate neighbours are Sundanese (spoken in West Java), Madurese (spoken on the island of Madura and adjacent parts of East Java), and Balinese (spoken in Bali and western Lombok).

The exact number of speakers of Javanese is unknown, as census data are not broken down by language, but it is estimated that up to half of the total population of Indonesia are Javanese-speaking; if this is so, then there may be 100 million speakers. In this connection, it should be noted that Javanese is not restricted to the regions mentioned, because the Javanese have moved into many other areas, and have taken their language with them. Historically, the sultanates of Cirebon and Banten (founded in the 16th century and located in West Java) were Javanese, and the process of transmigration in the 20th century has brought Javanese into Lampung in southern Sumatra, Kalimantan, Sulawesi and other islands. Furthermore, a large proportion of the present population of the capital, Jakarta, is of Javanese origin. Hence, as well as being an Indonesian regional language in the strict sense, Javanese can also be called an ethnic language, that is, one spoken by and defining the ethnic group of the Javanese. For the sake of completeness, one should also note that there has been a Javanese-speaking group in Surinam in South America for more than a century, as well as a smaller one in New Caledonia.

The above description of Javanese will help to define its relation to Indonesian, the national language of Indonesia. Indonesian is a variety of Malay, another important member of the Austronesian language family, originating from the western part of the Indonesian Archipelago. In its function of national language, Indonesian is taught and used over the entire territory of Indonesia. This means that those whose mother tongue is Javanese will also (in greater or smaller measure) become familiar with it and use it, thereby creating a significant interface between the two—in essence the same as that between any other regional-ethnic language and Indonesian, except that Javanese does tend to exert a rather strong influence on Indonesian. There is a mutual influence between the Javanese and Indonesian languages, which deserves further study.

Apart from the sheer weight of numbers, there are social and historical reasons for the dominance of Javanese. These relate to the position of the Javanese in the archipelago over many centuries. An example is the "borrowing" of the system of language levels by the neighbouring languages, Sundanese, Madurese, Sasak (in

Lombok) and Balinese. History tells us of a high degree of political and cultural development on the part of the successive kingdoms of Java. The descendants of Javanese royalty are still to be found in four courts in Central Java, namely the Kasunanan and Mangkunegaran in Surakarta (Solo), and the Kasultanan and Pakualaman in Yogyakarta. It is these courts that carry prestige for many Javanese in cultural and social matters. However, there are two more courts, the Kasepuhan and Kanoman in Cirebon, as well as historical traditions of yet another in Blambangan at the extreme eastern end of the island opposite Bali, and finally two more in Madura, at Sumenep and Bangkalan.

Having mentioned courts, however, it is by no means true that at the present time the Javanese language of Surakarta and Yogyakarta is accepted by all Javanese as standard or the most prestigious variety. There exist many regional variants, best termed dialects, as well as socially determined variants across the regions. Roughly speaking, the dialects correspond to former Residencies, broad geographical areas sharing the same cultural and social traditions. However, there also exist variations on a smaller scale, in some cases even down to the village level, which are of interest. Unfortunately, there has never been a complete dialectological description of Javanese.

Javanese is the language of everyday communication for those who call themselves Javanese, or who have been brought up within this speech community. It is used for all the functions for which Indonesian is not required or appropriate. Javanese is famous for possessing a system of language levels. It is definitely not the case that it is two languages in one, as some like to assert. Our approach here is that there is one basic "level" of Javanese, termed Ngoko, which is the one that is used when talking to oneself or to intimates. The other main level, termed Krama, is a "ceremonial" variant on this, whereby a number of high-frequency Ngoko words have Krama equivalents, and its use corresponds to speech situations calling for respect, including not only hierarchical differences but also social distance. This is a clear example of how language responds to and expresses the structure of society. The system of language levels found in Javanese is not unique, and that of Balinese is perhaps equally elaborate, also reflecting its social differences.

Having its basis in the nature of social relations, it is true to say that the use of language levels is not optional—one cannot choose to use just one or another. But the correct use of the levels, that is, the selection of the proper variant, does depend on a feeling for the relations that exist within a given speech-situation. To complete the picture, we should add that there is another level, called Madya, which represents a sort of compromise between Ngoko and Krama. Together, Krama and Madya are often termed simply "Basa" by native speakers. The norms for the use of Basa vary between urban and rural settings, and in practice there is no watertight division between the levels, but instead a continuum, or range of choices, the mixture varying according to the speaker's perception of the needs of the moment. Some Javanese scholars have developed technical terms for the different mixes, but we are not concerned with these here, except to point out that Krama Inggil ("High Krama") and Krama Andhap ("Low Krama") are in fact not language levels at all, but restricted honorific and humble vocabularies respectively, which as such can be fitted into whatever level is being used, be it Ngoko or Krama. Krama Inggil expresses respect for the person being addressed or spoken about, and hence can never be used of oneself, and Krama Andhap on the other hand can be used only of oneself, as it expresses humbleness.

Alongside its use for everyday communication, Javanese has another dimension, which can be called "literary", covering not only written literature but also forms of theatrical performance. A description of Javanese without reference to this would be incomplete. Literary forms are to be found in the vast poetical literature of the 19th century, for example, and these in their turn have their roots even further back in time, dating from the Hindu-Buddhist period of Java's history, when the earliest literature arose. For the sake of clarity, one should mention that the term Old Javanese is used only for this ancient literature, written from the 9th up to the 15th century in Java, and continued and preserved in its purest form in (Hindu) Bali. The literature produced after the coming of Islam in Java in the 16th century is all termed Modern Javanese by Javanists. The term Kawi, as used in Java (as opposed to Bali), refers to classical Modern Javanese, as found in premodern poetical works. Such archaic forms are found in spoken Javanese only in rare, stereotyped expressions. The language of the wayang performance is not just one style or idiom, but ranges from the everyday, often coarse, language appropriate to the popular dialogues of the clown-servant figures to its passages of description, audience scenes, and poetical interludes. Suffice it to say that the language used by the performer (dhalang) is not Old Javanese, with the exception of the suluk (stanzas used to create mood), although there do exist turns of phrase specific to the wayang, and the dhalang must also master the use of the special language of the court (Basa Kedhaton).

Further, Javanese possesses a modern literature, which arose in the 20th century, expressed in the forms of the novel (roman), free verse (geguritan) and short story (cerita cekak). This literature runs parallel to modern Indonesian literature, and is similar to that in its personal expression and realism. The earliest examples were written in Krama, but all recent Javanese literature is in Ngoko. At present little is being printed in Javanese, the main vehicles being periodicals.

Finally, one should not omit to mention that Javanese has its own writing-system, which derives ultimately from the Pallava script of early South India. This was adapted for writing Javanese. Palm leaves (lontar) were used as material, the letters being engraved with a sharp knife; this method is still used in Bali for creating manuscripts. (Balinese script is closely related to Javanese.) Later, European paper came to be used, and this is the main material found in the thousands of Javanese manuscripts kept in libraries in Indonesia and overseas. The Javanese script is still known in Java, being taught in schools, but is little used in practice. There is a printed form of the letters which was used in the colonial period for Javanese-language publications, but gradually its place was usurped by the Roman script. Javanese script embodies part of the Javanese cultural heritage, and it carries overtones of the power of the written word that Roman script does not. The written word, and all traditional forms of literature, were regarded as serious subjects, and hence appropriate for conveying messages of a didactic or edifying nature, alongside quite mundane uses. A knowledge of the script is recommended for those who need to read original historical or literary sources dating from the pre-modern period, not to mention the two-volume dictionary of Gericke and Roorda of 1901.

The study of Javanese by Europeans did not begin until the 19th century. Prior to this, the Dutch East India Company (VOC) conducted its contacts with native rulers through Malay. Credit for the first scholarly interest in Java must go to Thomas Stamford Raffles, who was Lieutenant-Governor of Java during the British Interregnum (1811–16). The results of his investigations are to be found in his two-volume *History of Java* (1817, second edn 1830), and these include the first exploration of Javanese language and literature, to which more than 100 pages are devoted.

Following the end of the Java War and the beginning of the colonial period proper in 1830, there was a growing awareness on the part of the authorities of the usefulness of a knowledge of Javanese language and customs, leading to the inclusion in 1842 of Javanese alongside Malay in the training of aspirant civil servants at Delft in The Netherlands. This tradition has been continued by a line of professors of Javanese at the University of Leiden down to the present day. In this sense it can be seen that the study of Javanese was a product of the colonial relationship, and it is understandable that it was a Dutch monopoly at that time. Considerable advances were made, due to the efforts of Dutch scholars who devoted themselves to the study of Javanese, often deeply impressed by the sophistication of the traditions which they found preserved among the literate classes in the Principalities, i.e. the court-cities of Central Java. It would not be until after the departure of the Dutch in 1949 that Javanese would receive much attention from the international community, fortunately coupled with a gradually growing awareness of the inestimable value of the collections assiduously assembled by earlier generations in Leiden.

2. Existing Dictionaries of Javanese

It may not be unfair to say that the lexicography of Javanese has had a somewhat chequered career. It represents a long series of attempts to explore the Javanese language and make it accessible, primarily to non-Javanese students, with varying degrees of success. A short account of earlier publications may serve to illustrate this point.

The first dictionary of Javanese, the *Algemeen Nederduitsch en Javaansch Woordenboek* (General Dutch and Javanese Dictionary), was published by P.P. Roorda van Eysinga (using Roman characters) in 1835. Although this work was clear and practical, it is normally ignored, and was apparently not used by others.

The second in line was the *Javaansch-Nederduitsch Woordenboek* (Javanese-Dutch Dictionary) compiled by J.F.C. Gericke and published by T. Roorda in Amsterdam in 1847.

Next came the *Dictionnaire Javanais-Français* (Javanese-French Dictionary) of L'Abbé P. Favre, published in Paris in 1870—also completely forgotten by later scholars.

As the next step, the *Javaansch-Nederduitsch Handwoordenboek* (Concise Javanese-Dutch Dictionary) of 1875 was a new version of Gericke and Roorda's dictionary, prepared by A.C. Vreede. This incorporated an unpublished dictionary compiled by C.F. Winter and J.A. Wilkens, not to mention additional materials published by P. Jansz in Semarang in 1869 and 1871.

meanings given apparently differ, either in emphasis or totally, or the word is missing in one but present in the other. What is going on here? Is this the same language? Was one lexicographer right and the other wrong?

I prefer to believe that they were equally competent, but had an unavoidably limited view of the whole picture. The first factor to be noted is a relatively weakly developed notion of a standard language (compared with English, for example). In the prewar period, it was claimed, for example by Pigeaud, that the idiom of Surakarta was standard, and thus all else was dubbed *gw* (gewestelijk = regional); Jansz may not have been equally convinced of the validity of such claims, or he may have used a different network of informants. In particular for items which do not occur in written sources, one is dependent on informants, who report only that part of the meaning of an item they are familiar with and use regularly. Informants from Central Java, for instance, when confronted with an unfamiliar word, have a tendency to say, "Oh, that's East Javanese dialect!". It may or may not be; after all, they are not in a position to go and check.

So the first complication to be noted is regional variation, the "dialect" factor. This may well explain why different meanings are attributed to the same form: both are right, but used by different people. But are we really looking at the same word, or at homonyms? One has to make a choice here, and if there is no apparent link (semantically or historically), then they are probably separate words. While it is relatively easy to identify a generally accepted ("standard") form, the rest have to be given the blanket term *reg* (regional = dialect), although so far we have no way of telling to which dialect or sociolect the word belongs—obviously a highly unsatisfactory state of affairs.

The second complication is change through time. As we know, every language is changing, and this applies also to Javanese. There are shifts in meaning, including new meanings added to old ones, there are words which have dropped out of use, and there is the possibility of new words being added. These are interesting questions that need to be considered.

When a new meaning has been added, this may represent a genuine extension of the old meaning, or perhaps one that already existed but was missed by older dictionaries. In either case, we should attempt to arrange the meanings as a succession from a basic, literal or physical one to extended, figurative ones. When a word appears to have dropped out of current use, we still have to be cautious, as some listed by Pigeaud as *vo* (verouderd = obsolete) have turned out to be in regular use in the countryside and not obsolete at all. Seemingly obsolete words do need to be listed, on the assumption that they may occur in older published sources, even if people no longer use them in daily speech.

This is in turn connected with the huge changes that have taken place in Javanese culture during the past 100 years: all sorts of objects and customs that were once well known, both in the countryside and at court, have now disappeared. And yet one still has to be careful in case they survive in some isolated spot after all. In any case their historical value is undoubted. For example, much of what is provided in L. Th. Mayer's *Een Blik in het Javaansche Volksleven* (A Glimpse into the Life of the Javanese), dating from 1897 and replete with terminology and sketches, is no longer generally known, but as a record it does have considerable interest.

Completely new words do not seem to occur very often in Javanese, probably because the innovation accompanying modernisation and the development of language to meet the needs of technology, politics and government have been concentrated on Indonesian as national language. The speaker of Javanese switches to Indonesian vocabulary in order to express such things. It may be more correct to say that the Indonesian term is borrowed and becomes Javanese, even though the phonological rules of Javanese do not (yet?) apply. In any case, where the term is normal Indonesian and is to be found in the Indonesian dictionaries, we have not done double work and listed them as Javanese as well. The reader is referred to the Indonesian dictionaries, in the hope that no misunderstandings will occur, as it can safely be assumed that the majority of students of Javanese will also have studied Indonesian, and will be aware of the difference between the two languages.

A third, less tangible, aspect of the "moving target" is what may be called "individual variation". This occurs at the opposite end of the spectrum from formal, standard or fixed written forms, that is, the kind of speech in which people give expression to their emotions in a spontaneous and lively way. Their attitude to the language seems to be one of a good friend, someone we can make jokes with, without fear of causing offence. The variation occurring here involves changing the shape of a common word, in such a way as to convey some heightened feeling. The basic lexical meaning remains the same, but the word gains an added nuance by virtue of the variation.

There are three kinds of variation to be distinguished here. The first is the intensive, where a change in sound conveys an intensification of the meaning. This is restricted to spoken Javanese, and to Ngoko. The second is harder to define; it appears to heighten the familiar or jocular quality of the word, and the selection of variants here is very much a matter of individual choice within the idiosyncratic style of each person. An extension of this is the situation where speakers create playful variants on existing words as a kind of game—they feel free to change the sound in order to imply another meaning, often humorous or suggestive. Words of this third type are unlikely to find general currency or become incorporated into the lexicon of Javanese, although the factor of creativity must never be underestimated in linguistic innovation. The whole area of ephemeral slang and secret in-group codes is not touched upon here, due to a lack of data.

Finally, in order to be complete one should include the description of those items which speakers feel to be crude and would not use in polite society. Javanese has its fair share of these, and a number have been included here, as they represent an essential, intimate, part of the lexicon, although speakers may disagree about the degree of acceptability of such words.

4. This Dictionary

Having lived in Yogyakarta in 1972–3 (as assistant to Professor P.J. Zoetmulder, working on his Old Javanese dictionary), and again for shortish periods in 1983 and 1985 in Muntilan and Sleman (under the Indonesian Studies Program of Leiden University), I had felt a certain measure of frustration trying to work with the existing dictionaries, because of their various shortcomings, alluded to above. At the same time, experience in the field showed what a difficult subject of study the Javanese language is. Again and again words were not to be found: sometimes apparently very common, simple ones, and sometimes terms pertaining to the realities of everyday life in the countryside. There is no doubt that there is a long way to go before our coverage is even moderately complete. Well aware, then, of the dangers, I had toyed with the idea of a concise dictionary of Modern Javanese that might replace Pigeaud and Horne, for the benefit of foreign students of the language.

After departure from the University of Leiden early in 1991 and a hurried application for funding to the Australian Research Council, the die was cast when, unbelievably, the project was funded. This made it possible to recruit a native-speaker, Drs Singgih Wibisono, as full-time Research Associate, freed from his position at the University of Indonesia in Jakarta for a three-year period to work at Monash University on compiling a Javanese-English dictionary.

The aim of the project was very modest—it had to be, given that the team consisted of only two, and the funding would last only three years. The aim was to compare the existing dictionaries, and on this basis to combine data and compile a new one. At the same time, bearing in mind the limited scope, certain rare or very specialised items would be dropped, and replaced with a small number of new items, drawn from the authors' own experience of the language. The intention was consciously to do justice to the cultural content of words, in particular drawing on Singgih Wibisono's insider knowledge of wayang and dance. There was, however, no attempt to analyse fresh materials in a systematic way, and the computer was used only for word-processing. To be specific, the sources were the dictionaries of Pigeaud, Poerwadarminta and Horne, supplemented with Gericke-Roorda and Jansz. We acknowledge our debt to these predecessors, without whom it would have been impossible to come as far as this.

Scope

This dictionary does not intend or pretend to be complete. In order to be reasonably complete, much more research, both in written sources and in the field, would be needed, but then the result would be huge. So we beg the reader's indulgence if a particular word or shade of meaning is not listed.

On the other hand, some words are likely to be found that are unfamiliar to some native speakers, perhaps because they are taken from a certain dialect or are now obsolete. We may even have erred on the generous side, out of an interest in the historical, bearing in mind the developments that have occurred over time. For comparison with earlier phases of the Javanese language, readers are invited to consult P.J. Zoetmulder's *Old Javanese-English Dictionary* of 1982, which covers both Old and Middle Javanese and is based on a wide range of sources, with examples from them arranged chronologically for convenience.

This dictionary aims firstly to be moderately complete for contemporary Javanese in order to include vocabulary needed for communication and for using published materials. The choice of items for inclusion does contain a subjective element, but has been guided by a native speaker's feeling for what is useful. The dictionary lists a large number of items marked as *reg*; these are words which are felt to be non-standard, in the sense of being either restricted to a particular area

15

(dialectal) or to a certain social group (sociolectal). The dictionary aims secondly to take account of a time dimension, in that it contains items which are possibly no longer current in spoken Javanese. No mark has been given to these, in view of the difficulty of identifying them, as mentioned above. However, words which are unlikely to be found in the spoken language but are important for literary sources are marked with the sign *lit*.

It goes without saying that each language level is represented. The marks *kr* (Krama) and *k.i.* (Krama Inggil) are only provided when these forms differ from Ngoko. In other words, if there is no indication the word is common to all levels. Where both Ngoko and Krama forms exist, the full description is given under the Ngoko, and only a concise one under the Krama, so that the reader should also refer to the Ngoko.

There has been no attempt to provide etymologies for loanwords, despite the special interest of this subject, due to a lack of research, and it has not been possible to include example sentences, due to a lack of space. One hopes that the definitions will be clear enough to speak for themselves.

The present dictionary will be found to rely heavily on both Pigeaud and Horne, but will contain a little more than either of these, although there are also words from both that have been deliberately omitted as being unnecessary for the non-specialist user.

The greatest challenge has been to provide meanings in clear English that come as close as possible to covering the areas of meaning of the Javanese words. In this respect it is hoped that this dictionary constitutes an advance on both Pigeaud and Horne. It was felt particularly important to be accurate with items that have a special cultural content, e.g. beliefs, the arts, or religion. With other items it was not possible, for reasons of space, to go into much detail, for example with the names of plants; for the Latin names, the reader should consult F.S.A. de Clerq's *Nieuw Plantkundig Woordenboek voor Nederlandsch Indië* (New Botanical Dictionary for the Netherlands Indies) of 1909. For fields such as animals, including insects, no source was available to us, while John MacKinnon's *Field Guide to the Birds of Java and Bali* (1988) was useless, as it gives the Latin, English and Indonesian names for the birds, but not the Javanese and Balinese—surely the most relevant ones for the people concerned!

5. Arrangement

Homonyms are indicated with roman numerals: e.g. I, II, III.
Items are listed under their base-word, not their derived forms. Javanese has an interesting morphology, whereby a range of derived forms can exist based on one base-word. It is useful to be able to compare these under one heading.

This means that in such cases the user has to be able to "deconstruct" a derived form, in order to find it. This applies mainly to the verbal system, but also to a lesser extent to some nouns and adjectives. The commonest difficulty occurs with nasalised forms, and sometimes it has not been possible to decide which form is the real base-word; in such instances a cross-reference will assist.

It will not be necessary to give a full account of Javanese grammar here, as students of Javanese will already be familiar with it. The following descriptions can be used for reference in conjunction with the dictionary:

Horne, E.C.: *Javanese-English Dictionary.* 1974, pp. xix–xxvii.
Robson, Stuart: *Javanese Grammar for Students.* Monash Papers on Southeast Asia No. 26, 1992.
Sudaryanto (ed.): *Tata Bahasa Baku Bahasa Jawa.* Duta Wacana U.P. 1991.
Suharno, Ignatius: *A Descriptive Study of Javanese.* Pacific Linguistics Series D No. 45. 1982.

Below are some notes which will help to clarify the arrangement of forms, and the meanings associated with them.

Verbs

Some verbs have a simple form, but many feature nasalisation, i.e. a nasal sound in initial position, often in combination with a suffix. The rules for formation are:

Initial letter	Form of nasal	Example
any vowel	ng-	aku - ngaku
p	replaced by m	pinggir - minggir
b	m- prefixed	bali - mbalèni
t	replaced by n-	tengen - nengen
d	n- prefixed	dangu - ndangu
th	replaced by n-	thuthuk - nuthuk
dh	n- prefixed	dhalang - ndhalang
c	replaced by ny-	cantrik - nyantrik
j	n- prefixed	jaluk - njaluk
k	replaced by ng-	kiwa - ngiwa
g	ng- prefixed	gawa - nggawa
r	ng- prefixed	ragad - ngragadi
l	ng- prefixed	lair - nglairaké
s	replaced by ny- or n-	silih - nyilih
w	replaced by m-	weruh - meruhi
n	no change	nastiti - nastitèkaké
m	no change	masalah - masalahaké
ng	no change	ngéné - ngénèkaké

Notes:
1. In the case of initial vowels and n-, m- and ng-, there will be ambiguity regarding the possible base-word, so the user may have to look in two places in order to find the correct form.
2. There are some irregularities in the application of these rules, for example with monosyllabic base-words, which often are extended with an initial e-.
3. There are a number of words beginning with nga- or nge- for which a base-word beginning with a-, ka- or ke- is not clearly indicated, especially with intransitive verbs (that is, verbs without a corresponding passive form, in which the base-word can be seen).

In such cases it is best to look under ng-, where a cross-reference (if necessary) will be found. In a few instances, the base-word itself begins with an initial ng-.

Function:
1. A nasalised form may be either intransitive or transitive. If the latter, then it is always active. Passive forms are never nasalised, but have their own forms which are predictable and therefore not listed. Example:

> active *njupuk* to take (takes, took, etc.)
> passive *dijupuk* taken; *tak jupuk* taken by me; *kok jupuk* taken by you.

2. In combination with suffixes, the nasalised form is again active, but with a range of possible extra meanings.

Suffix -i
If this form exists, its specific meaning is not completely predictable and is therefore defined. Many have a locative meaning, some are causative, and all but a small group are transitive. For rules of formation, refer to a grammar.

Suffix -aké (Krama -aken)
Where this form exists, the specific meaning is not completely predictable, and is therefore defined. Some are causative, occasionally benefactive, and all but a small group are transitive. For rules of formation, refer to a grammar.

The passive forms of these verbs are predictable. Similarly the imperatives, irrealis and propositives, which are therefore not listed.

Two special verbal categories
These forms serve to modify a verb in a particular way, in order to provide another element of meaning.
pating:
A word listed in combination with *pating* conveys the meaning of a state or action characterised by "plurality" (otherwise marked with *pl*), suggesting that a number of actors are present or that the action is carried out in a dispersed way (all over the place, everywhere).
mak:
The mark *repr* indicates that the word listed is preceded by *mak* in order to suggest that the sound, action or feeling occurs in a sudden or unexpected way. These expressions contain a "representative" or onomatopoeic element, and Javanese is especially rich in them.

Adjectives

Alongside the usual form of an adjective, there also exists a derived form using the prefix ke- and suffix -en in combination to convey an "excessive" meaning, e.g. from *dawa* (long), *kedawan* (too long). As these are predictable they are generally not listed separately. For rules of formation, please refer to a grammar.

Words belonging to more than one grammatical category

It sometimes happens that the one form belongs to more than one category (part of speech), and hence can function quite differently in a sentence. These separate meanings are carefully distinguished in the dictionary. A simple example is:

kembang 1. flower; 2. to flower.

In order to clarify this distinction, all verbs are listed in their infinitive form in English, viz. "to…".

The prefixes a- and ma-, which occur with words in some literary sources and are archaic, have been deliberately omitted from this dictionary.

Spelling

The spelling used for Javanese is the one officially accepted in Indonesia, with the exception that we use two simple diacritical marks, namely é and è, as these are considered essential to distinguish these two sounds from the mute e or schwa (without mark; in Javanese called pepet).

The current spelling is thus different from the one used in Horne's dictionary, which was published before the new system was introduced. Users should note in particular the spellings th and dh (instead of the earlier t and d with a dot below), representing the retroflex stops, unvoiced and voiced respectively, which must be clearly distinguished from t and d, the unvoiced and voiced dental stops.

The letter k represents both the guttural and glottal stops. The letter q is not used for the latter. In some positions, the glottal stop is not customarily written at all, e.g. saiki [sa'iki], 'now'.

In the antepenultimate syllable of Javanese words, the vowel tends to be weakened, so that for example an a is pronounced as e; for the purposes of the dictionary, however, in such cases the spelling with a is kept.

Similarly, with the prefixes ka-/ke-, pa-/pe-, and sa-/se- (where these spellings are equivalent), the forms ka-, pa- and sa- have been preferred, but readers should also check under the alternative.

In the case of the final consonants -t and -d, and -p and -b, it was observed that there is some confusion, even in Javanese script and amongst native speakers, probably because a voiced consonant becomes unvoiced in final position. Even so, we believe that it is an important distinction and have tried to follow the most original spelling.

Stuart Robson

List of Abbreviations

adr	term of address
chld	children's word
coll	colloquial
cr	crude
esp	especially
excl	exclamation
fig	figurative
gram	grammatical term
idiom	idiomatic expression
inf	informal
intsfr	intensifier
k.a.	Krama Andhap (see Introduction)
k.i.	Krama Inggil (see Introduction)
kr	Krama (high language level)
lit	literary
md	Madya (middle language level)
ng	Ngoko (low language level)
opt	optional
o.s.	oneself
pass	passive
pl	associated with a plural subject
pron	pronounced as, pronunciation
prov	proverb
reg	regional, i.e. dialectal or non-standard
repr	imitative verb adjunct with *mak*, see Introduction
shtc	shortened compound
shtf	shortened form
s.o.	someone
s.t.	something
subst	substitute
s.w.	somewhere
usu	usually
var	variant
way	term associated with the wayang (shadow theatre)

A

aba 1 sign, sound; 2 order, command; to order, command; 3 spoken word; to say, speak;
  ngabani 1 to give a signal, give a command; 2 to quote (a price). *See also* aban.

abab 1 breath; 2 *fig* hot air;
  ngababi to breathe on s.t.;
  kababan to get blown on; to feel a rush of air, *e.g.* from a passing vehicle or a gunshot.

abad 1 century; - kepungkur the last century; 2 age, era; - modhèren the modern age (era);
  maabad-abad for centuries.

abadi eternal, eternity.

abadiyah eternal.

abah I ngabah-abahi *lit* to scold.
  II abahan 1 timber; 2 wooden block for cutting off the head;
  kumurep ing abahan to lie face down on a wooden block, *fig* to put fate in s.o.'s hands.

abah-abah I tool, instrument; - tenunan loom.
  II saddle. *See also* lapak.
  ngabah-abahi to saddle.

aban, aban-aban 1 orders for drill; 2 *reg* loud noise. *See also* aba.

abang *ng*, abrit *kr* 1 red, reddish-brown; 2 ripe (of ripe product); - biru *fig* circumstances, fate; - dluwang very pale: even white paper is redder; - mbranang *or* abing bright red; - tuwa dark red;
  abang-abang s.t. red;
  ngabang to redden; - bironi to cause s.o. to be ashamed;
  ngabangi 1 to redden s.t.; 2 to make the colour redder than before; 3 to become red;

ngabangaké to cause s.t. to be red; - kuping (rai, mata) *fig* to cause s.o. to be angry;

abangan one who does not adhere strictly to the precepts of Islam;

abang-abang lambé 1 to make the lips red; 2 *fig* what the listener wants to hear; 3 *fig* to play up to s.o.; small talk; gossip. *See also* bang.

abar I no longer effective, powerless;
  ngabar 1 to evaporate, vaporise; 2 to lose effectiveness; 3 to default on an obligation (of bet); 4 to excite the gamecocks before fighting by facing them to each other;
  ngabaraké to cause s.t. to be powerless;
  pangabaran magical formula for destroying the enemy's power;
  kabar to lose the best essence; santen - thin coconut milk (*see also* santen); prawan - non-virginal girl (*see also* prawan);
  abaran *or* abar-abaran (of gamecocks) to face each other excitedly before fighting. *See also* aber I.
  II ngabar-abar to threaten by brandishing a sharp weapon. *See also* agar.

abas I ngabas to act indiscriminately, without basis.
  II ngabas *var of* ngabar, *see* abar I.

abdas to cleanse o.s. ritually before prayer;
  pabdasan *or* padasan a large earthen vessel with a tap, containing well water for ritual ablution before prayers.

abdi *k.i.* (batur, réwang *ng*, réncang *kr*) servant; - dalem 1 servant at court; 2 I, me (when addressing o.s. to royalty); - dalem jaba palace officials

under the vice regent; - **dalem juru** palace soothsayer; - **dalem garap** clerk in a Surakarta regent's office; - **dalem prajurit** palace guard; - **dalem silir** court official in charge of the palace lamps;
ngabdi to live in s.o.'s home as a servant, *fig* to give good service to s.o.;
ngabdèni to be s.o.'s servant;
ngabdèkaké 1 to have s.o. live in s.o.'s home as a servant; 2 to take s.o. as a servant;
kaabdèkaké *ng*, **kaabdèkaken** *kr*, to be appointed as a servant at court;
pangabdi *or* **pangabdèn** service.

aben I to compete; competition, confrontation (*kr for* **adu**).
II each, every (*coll var of* **saben**);
abené usually;
aben-aben from time to time, again and again.

aber I to lose its magic power; no longer effective (of magic formula *etc*) (*var of* **abar**);
ngaber-aberi to cause s.t. to be powerless.
II to fly (*var of* **iber**);
aber-aberan *or* **iber-iberan** flying creatures.

abet, ngabet *or* **mangabet** *lit* to be a servant;
kabet to be framed;
abet-abet 1 frame; 2 *lit* a female servant in a hermitage.

abing bright red. *See* **abang**.

abipraya intention, purpose;
saabipraya harmonious, to make an agreement.

abir long-handled Chinese sword.

abiséka 1 consecration of a king; 2 king's name given at a consecration.

abjad 1 alphabet (Arabic or Latin); 2 alphabetical order.

ablah, ngablah-ablah 1 wide open; 2 to sleep sprawled on one's back.

ablak, ngablak 1 to open the mouth wide;
2 to blab; 3 to talk senselessly;
ngablak-ablak wide open;
ngablakaké to leave s.t. wide open. *See* **blak, eblak**.

abon I shredded meat that has been boiled and fried.
II s.o. who is paid as part time labour (of cigarette home industry).
III *reg* offering; **kebo** - buffaloes offered for ritual ceremonies (*see also* **kebo**); **yatra** - money to buy a buffalo for religious offering (*see also* **yatra**).

abon-abon variety of side-dishes for ceremonial meals.

abong-abong *reg* just because.

abor rotten (of egg).

abot *ng*, **awrat** *kr*, heavy, hard, weighty; - **ènthèng** degree of weight; - **sangganè** *fig* to be unable to oppose s.o. (of competition *etc*); to have difficulty supporting s.o.; **tembako** - strong tobacco (*see also* **tembako**); **lakon** - a profound drama (*see also* **lakon, laku**); **ngabotaké** to consider (more) important.
See **bot, bobot**.

abra glittering, sparkling.

abrag *or* **abrag-abrag** 1 household articles, utensils; 2 lumber, junk;
diabrag (of clothing, shoes *etc*) intended for everyday or ordinary use;
abragan 1 household utensils; 2 junk, worn-out articles.

abreg plentiful;
abreg-abregan to be piled up;
saabreg-abreg in heaps.
See also **ambreg** II.

abrik, ngobrak-abrik to turn upside down;
mobrak-mabrik in disarray; in utter disorder.

abrit red (*kr for* abang).

absah 1 valid; 2 paid up.

absara god, deity.

absari goddess, female deity.

abuh swollen, puffy;
ngabuh-abuhi to be swollen (of wound, corpse).

abuk I 1 power (*reg var of* bubuk); 2 manure, fertiliser (*reg var of* rabuk).
II ngabuk 1 to claim possession of s.t. one does not own; 2 to obtain merchandise without paying for it.

abul, ngabul-abul *or* ngobal-abul to scatter;
mabul-mabul *or* mobal-mabul scattered all over the place.

abur flight through the air;
ngaburaké 1 to let s.t. fly away; 2 to fly (an aeroplane);
mabur to fly up, fly away; montor - aeroplane.
See also bur.

abyagata, ngabyagata *lit* to set to work.

abyor to twinkle;
mabyor twinkling, sparkling, shining.

acak, ngacak 1 *reg* to try, make an effort (*var of* cacak); 2 begin to do s.t.; 3 to flood;
kacakan 1 to be flooded; 2 to get (what others get).

acala *lit* mountain.

acar I pickles; - bawang garlic pickles; - bening uncooked pickles; - mateng cooked pickles; ngacar 1 to make (into) pickles; 2 to become pickles.
II ngacar 1 to thrust, lunge; 2 to make preparations for; 3 to share. *See also* ancar.

acara 1 programme; 2 item of a programme;
ngacarani to welcome with s.t.;
pangacara master of ceremonies.

aceng, ngaceng to have an erection;
ngacengan lascivious, lustful.

acir, ngacir 1 to stand alone and look high (of tree); 2 to run away;

ngocar-acir 1 to scatter around untidily; 2 to squander;
kocar-kacir strewn all about, in disarray.

aco, ngaco to talk claptrap, talk without knowing what one is talking about.

acuk *var of* aceng.

acum pale in the face (because of illness). *See also* celom.

acung, acung-acung to point at, point out;
ocang-acung to point out repeatedly, to keep raising one's hand;
ngacung to raise the hand;
ngacungi *or* ngecungi 1 to point at/to s.t.; 2 *cr* to offer s.t.;
ngacungaké 1 to raise, lift; 2 to appoint s.o. as a representative;
acungan 1 substitute, representative; 2 act of raising the hand.

ada I time of scarcity;
ngadani 1 to start first; 2 to originate, initiate; 3 to inspect, direct, maintain.
II palm leaf rib (*var of* sada).

ada-ada 1 central vein of leaf or feather; 2 support, prop; 3 a certain Javanese script punctuation mark used at the beginning of a sentence (*see also* adeg-adeg); 4 a certain kind of song in a wayang performance to create atmosphere in a scene; to sing a song as above; 5 to initiate;
mangada-ada *lit* to stand on end like palm leaf ribs.

adab good manners, civilised conduct.

adabiyah *var of* adangiyah.

adaini a major artery in the neck, arms or legs.

adan I a call to prayer; to recite the call to prayer.
II ngadani 1 to inspect, organise (of work); 2 to maintain. *See also* dandan.

adang to cook rice by steaming;
ngadangaké to steam rice for s.o.;
adangan *or* dang-dangan cooked rice or other kinds;

padang cook (*specifically for rice*);

padangan kitchen, specially for cooking rice;

saadang sapanginang *fig* in as short a time as it takes to cook rice or chew betel;

Pandhawa madangaké sibling combination, consisting of five brothers and one sister. *See also* **dang**.

adangiyah opening salutation of a letter.

adas fennel; **lenga -** fennel oil, sometimes used for stomachache;

sembur-sembur adas *fig* blessing conveyed by old people to a child by blowing on the head (*see also* **sembur**).

adat 1 traditional patterns of behaviour; **2** (*or* **adaté**) usually, customarily; **- kalumrahan** traditional custom; **- pakulinan** habit, usage; **- saben** usual, customary;

- tatacara social norms, customs and manners; **- waton** traditional law *or* custom, social norms;

ngadat 1 *var of* **adat**; **2** to make a habit of, do customarily; **3** troublesome, to keep giving the same problem;

padatan 1 habit, usage, custom; **2** usually, customary.

adawiyah *var of* **adangiyah**.

adeg 1 founding; **2** act of setting up; **3** standing; **4** (*or* **adegan**) scene (in a play);

adeg-adeg 1 mainstay, supporting prop; **2** a Javanese script punctuation mark at the beginning of a sentence; **- antep** (**kantep**) (of babies) to keep falling when trying to stand;

saka 1 to stand motionless as a pillar; **2** (of tops) to spin on one spot and look motionless;

ngadeg, jumeneng *k.i.* to stand;

ngadegi *or* **ngedegi 1** to build s.t. onto s.t. else; **2** (**njenengi** *k.i.*) to be present at; **3** to take part;

ngadegaké *or* **ngedegaké 1** to set up, to build; **2** to hold; **3** to appoint, install;

madeg *ng, kr,* **jumeneng** *k.i.* **1** to become; **2** to stand (up), to be established; **- kraman** to carry out a rebellion;

adegan scene (in a play);

adeg-adegan 1 jumenengan *k.i.* in a standing position; **2** formal appointment, installation (of an official);

pangadeg 1 (*var of* **piadeg**) stature (*see also* **dedeg**); **2** measure of height;

mangadeg *lit* to stand up;

sadeg sanyet an instant, just for the moment.

adha a small dam.

adhag, ngadhag-adhag *or* **ngedhag-edha 1** to lie face up; **2** to lie openly;

ngadhagaké *or* **ngedhagaké** to let s.t. lie openly.

adhah container; **- awu** ashtray;

ngadhahi *or* **madhahi** to accommodate, put in. *See also* **wadhah**.

adhak, adhakan 1 within easy reach, close to things, handy; **2** usually, customarily.

adhang, adhang-adhang *or* **ngadhang-adhang** to wait s.w. for people/things to go past;

ngadhang to wait s.w. for people/things to go past;

ngadhangi *or* **ngadhang-adangi** to block the passage of;

ngadhangaké to stop s.t. for s.o. else;

adhangan 1 waiting place for s.t. passing by; **2** passing vehicles which can give a lift.

adhèg on heat (of animals).

adhèh, ngadhèhaké to cause (a horse) to gallop;

adhéhan *or* **adhéyan** act of galloping, gallop of a horse.

adhèk *reg* younger brother/sister. *See also* **adhi, adhik**.

adhem *ng*, **asrep** *kr* 1 cool; 2 calm, to keep control of o.s., peaceful; 3 short in weight; - **anyep** 1 cold and tasteless; 2 *fig* apathetic; - **ayem** 1 calm, peaceful, comfort; 2 apathetic; - **njekut** intensely cold;
ngadhem to cool o.s., to escape from the heat;
ngadhemi to make s.t. cooler;
ngadhemaké to let s.t. become cold;
kadhemen 1 excessively cold/cool; 2 to have/get a chill;
adheman 1 a shady place; 2 a special night for considering a number value of days *e.g.* before a ceremony;
adhem-adheman to execute s.t. quietly.

adhèng to have no more trouble from, to be better (illness).

adhep *ng* **ajeng** *kr*, 1 the front part of s.t.; 2 what one focuses on or keeps in mind (*e.g.* a belief);
adhep-adhep *reg* to stand in front of s.o. who is eating in order to get a part of the meal;
ngadhep *ng*, *kr*, **sowan** *k.i.* appear before s.o.;
ngadhepi 1 to appear before s.o.; 2 to face, confront; 3 to sit in front of s.t.;
ngadhepaké *ng*, **ngajengaken** *kr* 1 to face, front, look on to; 2 to lay s.t. in front of s.o., to bring s.o. up before the authorities;
madhep 1 to face (toward); 2 to be steadfast; - **mantep** fixed, determine;
adhep-adhepan face to face.

adhi *ng*, *kr*, **rayi** *k.i.* 1 younger sibling; 2 smaller (of the same things); 3 wife; - **ipé** younger brother/sister-in-law; **kakang** - older-younger sibling relationship (*see also* **kakang**);
ngadhi to address s.o. or regard s.o. as one's own younger sibling;
adhimas *or* **dhimas** *polite term of address for younger brother or male relatives*;

adhiajeng *or* **dhiajeng** *polite term of address for younger sister or female relatives*;
adhi ketemu gedhé fiancée, girl friend.

adhik *var of* **adhi**.

adhong a kind of bamboo sieve for catching fish;
ngadhong to catch fish by putting a bamboo sieve in a small stream.

adhu planted during the dry season, *var of* **gadhu**.

adhuh *excl of pain, joy*; - **biyung** *or* - **mbok** *excl of pain*; - **laé** *lit, excl* my goodness, oh dear!
ngadhuh *or* **ngadhuh-adhuh** to exclaim in pain, lament, moan, groan. *See also* **dhuh**.

adhuk, **ngadhuk** to stir, mix, plough through, stir up s.t. from the bottom;
ngadhuk-adhuk to plough through;
ngadhuki to stir up s.t. continuously;
adhukan mixture;
campur adhuk mixed up.

adhul, **ngadhul-adhul** *or* **ngodhal-adhul** 1 to mess things up, scatter things about; 2 to unravel a mystery, disclose a secret; 3 to spend (money) foolishly;
madhul-madhul *or* **modhal-madhul** unkempt, dishevelled; scattered about untidily.

adhum I shady, leafy. *See* **édhum**, **éyub**.
II **adhum-adhuman** to discuss (*esp* private matters), to talk secretly to each other.

adi I fine, beautiful; - **aèng** valuable and rare; - **éndah** splendid; - **luhung** highly valued quality;
ngadi to beautify o.s.;
- **busana** to beautify one's dress; - **sarira** to beautify one's appearance;
ngadi-adi to make s.t. beautiful, value highly, adorn;
adèn-adèn s.t. valued highly;
ngadèn-adèni 1 to value highly; 2 to

take solicitous care of, to pamper affectionately. *See also* **èdi**.

II **ngadi-adi** to demand s.o.'s attention; **ngadèn-adèni** to spoil.

adigang (to make) an arrogant display of one's superior power.

adiguna (to make) an arrogant display of one's superior knowledge.

adigung (to make) an arrogant display of one's superior status.

adil just, impartial, equitable; - **paramarta** righteous and noble; **Ratu** - the just king, legendary figure (*see* **ratu**);
ngadili 1 to judge; 2 to put s.o. on trial, bring to justice;
pangadilan law court.

adilaga *lit* battle, war.

adiningrat 'the best in the world': honorific used after the city names Surakarta and Yogyakarta (sites of royal courts). *Also* **hadiningrat**.

adipati 1 king, regent, ruler, sovereign; 2 title used by princes;
kadipatèn residence of the Crown Prince;
pangéran adipati anom Crown Prince, prince royal (*see* **pangéran**).

adiraga, ngadiraga *lit* to beautify one's appearance.

adoh *ng*, **tebih** *kr* far, distant; **sedulur** - distantly related family (*see also* **sadulur, dulur**);
ngadoh *or* **ngedoh** 1 to move away; 2 to be at a distance;
ngedohi to keep at a distance from, to move away from;
ngedohaké to put at a distance;
kadohan 1 afar, the distance; 2 (*or* **kadohen**) excessively far;
adoh cedhaké comparative distance;
adoh ngaluk-aluk *or* **adoh nyamut-nyamut** *or* **adoh nglangut** far off, at a great distance.
See also **doh**.

adol *ng*, **sadé** *kr* 1 to sell; 2 *var of* **dodol** to sell for a living; - **adab** to persuade s.o. to buy s.t. which one can not deliver; - **ayu/bagus** to show off one's good looks; - **awak** *or* - **gembès** to engage in prostitution; - **bau** to offer one's services for hire; - **bokong** to get paid for occupying s.o.'s seat as a way of holding it in a bus or train; - **gadhé** *or* - **séndhé** to sell a ricefield temporarily; - **gawé** to hire o.self out; - **gendhung** to boast; - **karya** to serve for pay; - **sanggup** to make empty promises. - **sengung** boastful; - **supata** to disavow with an oath; - **swara** 1 to show off one's singing; 2 to cheat people by lying; **tuwa** to sell one's ripened rice before it is harvested; - **umuk** to boast; - **taunan** to hire out land for a long period; **ngadol** *or* **ngedol** to sell; **ngedoli** *ng* **nyadèni** *kr* 1 to serve customers; 2 to sell many objects; **ngadolaké** *or* **ngedolaké** *ng* **nyadèkaken** *kr* to sell s.t. on behalf of s.o. else; **madolaké** attractive to buy; **kulak warta adol prungon** *see* **kulak**; **adol awèh tuku arep** *trading idiom*, to agree on a price.
See also **dol, dodol**.

adreng strong, firm, eager.

adres *lit* hard, heavy (*var of* **deres**).

adri *lit* mountain.

adu *ng*, **aben** *kr* 1 in contact, in confrontation - **arep** face to face; - **cukit tepung taritis** *lit* 'matching of roofs', very crowded (of houses); - **geger** back to back; - **manis** 1 to take account of other's feelings in a friendly manner; 2 to engage in social niceties; - **sèrèt** 1 (of floor tiles *etc*) fitted together checkerboard style; 2 (of stripes) to set in a zigzag herringbone pattern; 2 to compete; - **jago** *ng*, **aben sawung** *kr*, 1 cockfighting; 2 *fig* competition among candidates; - **karosan** to have a confrontation of strength; - **kasektèn**

to compete in magic power; - **kumba** to knock together the heads of the combatants; - **sungut** 'to link feelers', a clash, conflict; to clash; - **swara** 1 quarrels; 2 song contest; **ngadoni** 1 to confront, face up to; - **perang** to go to war; 2 to mix, combine with; - **jamu** to mix medicine; **ngadon-adoni** to incite, instigate; **adon** 1 contestant; **jago** - fighting cock (*see also* **jago**); 2 ingredient: - **tamba watuk** cough medicine ingredient; **adonan** mixture.

adul, adul-adul to tell tales;
  ngaduli *or* **ngadul-aduli** to tell s.o. bad things about s.o. else;
  ngadulaké to tell tales about s.o. to s.o. else;
  adul-adulen to tell tales habitually;
  pangadul-adul tale-telling. *See also* **wadul**.

adus *ng, kr* **siram** *k.i.* to take a bath; - **getih** bleeding from wounds all over the body; - **kringet** *fig* to do physical labour; - **grujug** to bathe by pouring water over the head with a dipper; - **kramas** to bathe and wash hair before a ritual activity; - **kungkum** to take a tub bath; - **nipas** ritual bath 40 days after giving birth; - **sibin** to take a quick bath by using a small wet towel; - **wuwung** to bathe over the head;
  padusan *ng, kr* **pasiraman** *k.i.* 1 bathing-place; 2 the day before the beginning of the Fasting Month when people cleanse themselves ritually. *See also* **dus**.

adzan *var of* **adan**.
aé just, only (*reg var of* **baé, waé**).
aem to eat (*chld, var of* **maem**).
aèn, ngaèn bound to happen, beyond any doubt;
  ngaènaké *or* **ngaèkaké** to prove s.t. is real.
aèng strange, peculiar, out of the ordinary;

ngaèngaké to regard s.t. as strange;
  ngaèng-aèngi to behave in an odd or unusual way.
aès make up, dress (*var of* **paès**);
  ngaèsi *reg* to make up s.o., dress s.o.
agag, agag-agag to brandish a weapon;
  ngagag-agagi to threaten s.o. by brandishing or pointing a weapon;
  magag uncertain, reluctant.
agahan eager.
agama *ng,* **agami** *kr* religion, sacred or spiritual tradition; - **Hindhu** Hinduism; - **Katolik** Catholicism;
  agama ageming aji the spiritual tradition adhered to by kings.
agar I ngagar to rub; - **geni** to make fire by rubbing wood;
  agaran 1 wooden tools for making fire; 2 way of rubbing; **agar-agar** a threat, deterrent.
  II ngagari *or* **ngagar-agari** to threaten s.o. by pointing a weapon; **ngagar-agaraké** to point a weapon to threaten s.o.
agé *ng,* **énggal** *kr* quick, right away; **agé-agé** in a rush, hurried. *See also* **gé**.
agèh I *reg* come on!
  II diagèhi *reg* to get a portion, share. *See also* **bagé**.
agèk *coll for* **lagi**.
agel 1 fibre taken from the upper part of a palm; 2 rope woven from this material.
agem I bundle of newly harvested rice.
  II to use (*root form k.i. for* **anggo**).
ageng large, big, great (*kr for* **gedhé**).
agep will, shall *reg var of* **arep**.
ager *or* **ager-ager** 1 a kind of seaweed; 2 a kind of food made from seaweed.
agi *coll for* **lagi**.
agik, ogak-agik *var of* **oglak-aglik** unstable, wobbly (of teeth, table legs *etc*).
agil, ogal-agil to teeter, sway precariously.
agir, ngagir to lie flat on one's stomach with lifted head;
  ngagiri to lie flat on s.t.

agla, ngagla (to return) empty-handed.

aglag, ngaglag-aglag *cr* to eat.

aglah, ngaglah 1 to block the way by standing with legs wide apart (rudely); 2 clear, obvious.

aglar *lit* spread out. *See also* gelar.

aglèg, oglag-aglèg *reg var of* aglig.

aglig, oglag-aglig unstable, wobbly; moglag-maglig (coming) loose.

aglik, ngaglik to teeter on the edge in a high place.

aglis speedy, quick (*lit var of* gelis).

agni 1 *lit* fire; 2 the name of the God of Fire.

agnya 1 order; 2 *gram* imperative.

agol, ngagol-agoli to cause s.o. to stop doing s.t. *See also* kagol.

agop, tan agop *lit* without a break; ceaselessly.

agor deep and hoarse (of voice); ngagor-agori to break (of voice).

agra *lit* top, peak, point.

agrang, ngagrang *var of* nganggrang 1 leaning against s.t.; 2 left unfinished; ngagrangaké 1 to lean s.t. against s.t.; 2 to leave s.t. unfinished.

agrèh, ngograh-agrèh to disturb, irritate.

agrèk, ngograk-agrèk to prod with a stick.

agreng thick and dark. *See* greng.

agring *lit* sick, ill.

agro, ngagro-agro *or* ngagru-agru to pester, bother, disturb.

agrong I steep, precipitous, jurang - a steep chasm.

II *see* magrong.

agru *var of* agro.

aguk *reg* to put on airs.

agul, agul-agul 1 bulwark; 2 champion.

agung 1 *lit* high, exalted, great, large; 2 to be high, full (of water level, *also* megung).

agus *var of* bagus: *used as a male name.*

Ahad *or* Ngahad Sunday.

ahyun *lit* to want, desire.

ai *reg excl of incredulity or deprecation.*

aib *var of* gaib.

ail weary (of the mouth).

ain *var of* aèn.

aing I but (*reg coll of* nanging).

II *reg* I, me.

ait, ngait 1 to pull, jerk; 2 to put away, put aside. *See also* sait.

aja *ng* sampun *kr* don't; - dhisik not now, not too soon; - dumèh *var of* - dupèh don't show off; - kongsi (*var of* - nganti) don't let it happen that; - manèh (sampun malih *kr*), let alone, much less; - nganti 1 don't let it happen that; 2 (to tell s.o.) not to; 3 (in order) not to, so that not; - pisan-pisan don't by any means; - olèh (*coll*: - éntuk) don't allow; - silih (*var of* - manèh); - sok don't ever; - ta (*reg* aja si) please don't. - manèh-manèh never again; - tan ora don't fail to;

ajaa if it were not for the fact that.

ajab, ngajab to hope, wish; ngajabi to wish for; ngajab-ajab to hope (for), look forward to, anticipate; pangajab hope, anticipation.

ajag I *or* asu ajag jackal, hunting-dog; ngajagi to hunt (of people or animal) by using a dog.

II ngajag to intersperse; ngajagi to plant (an area) with additional plants; ajagan plants planted between others.

ajah, ngajahi to train (animals); ngajahaké to have trained; ajahan a trained animal.

ajaib *or* ngajaib astonishing, amazing; marvellous, miraculous.

ajak, ajak-ajak *or* ngajak to ask s.o. to come along, join one; ngajaki to ask others to join one; ajakan invitation, a suggestion to join in s.o.'s activity;

ajak-ajakan to ask each other to join in an activity;
pangajak act of inviting. *See also* **jak**.
ajal I *coll var of* **jajal** to try to do;
ajalé *excl* try!;
ajal-ajal to try to do s.t.
II 1 origin, source; 2 limit, boundary, dividing-line; - **kamulan** origin, beginning;
ngajali 1 to form a boundary, dividing-line for; 2 to set a time limit (on);
ngajal ulihan (**pulihan, mulihan**) to return to where one came from.
III (*or* **ngajal**) to pass away.
ajan I a call to prayer; to recite the call to prayer (*var of* **adan, azan**).
II **ngajani** to urge or persuade s.o. to do wrong;
pangajan persuasion, urging;
kèlu ing pangajan to go along with an evil urging.
ajang 1 (**ambeng** *k.i.*) a dish from which food is eaten; 2 site of an activity;
ngajangi 1 to dish up s.o.'s food; 2 to organise, hold an activity; 3 to serve as a place for; 4 line of work;
ajangan 1 (**ambengan** *k.i.*) a serving of food; 2 site of an activity.
ajap *see* **ajab**.
ajar I to learn, exercise, receive training;
- **kenal** to make one's acquaintance;
- **mlaku** to exercise walking; 2 teacher of spiritual knowledge; **ki** - *adr* teacher; **kurang** - 1 impolite, rude; 2 (*or* **kurang asem**) *excl of dislike, see also* **kurang**;
ajar-ajar to start to learn, to try to make s.t.;
ngajar 1 to teach, train; 2 to punish;
ngajari to teach s.o. to (do);
ngajar-ajari to try to teach s.o. to do wrong;
ngajaraké to teach a subject;
ajaran 1 teaching, a lesson; 2 in the learning stage;

ajar-ajaran 1 teaching(s), act of teaching; 2 to teach each other;
pangajaran instruction, training, education.
II section of a citrus fruit;
ngajari to divide (citrus fruit) into sections;
ajaran s.t. divided into sections (of citrus fruit).
ajat 1 a need; 2 (*or* **kajat**) religious offering or sacrifice; 3 extra Islamic prayer said at midnight; 4 public prayer meeting;
ngajati to wish for, plan, intend;
ngajataké to wish for (an objective). *See also* **kajat**.
ajeg constant, steady, fixed, regular;
ngajegi to do steadily or as a regular practice;
ngajegaké to have/make s.o. do steadily; to accustom s.o. to (doing s.t.);
ajeg-ajegan constantly, frequently;
pangajeg consistency (of law).
ajèr to melt, dissolve; *fig* to relent;
ngajèri to melt, dissolve s.t.;
ngajèraké to melt for s.o.; to have s.t. melted;
pangajèran 1 act of melting; 2 place of melting.
See also **jèr**.
ajeng I facing (*root form: kr for* **adhep**).
II progress, forward movement (*root form: kr for* **aju**).
III front (*root form for* **arep**).
IV will, want (*md for* **arep**).
V younger female. *See also* **jeng**.
aji I *ng*, **aos** *kr* value, worth; - **pumpung** *or* - **mumpung** opportunistic, to take the opportunity to enjoy o.s.;
ngajèni 1 to respect, honour; 2 to value;
ngaji-aji to esteem or value highly;
ajèn-ingajènan to respect each other;
pangaji *or* **pengaji** at the price of; to the amount of.
II king.

III *or* **aji-aji** magic formula, amulet.
IV *var of* **kaji II**;
ngaji *ng*, **ngaos** *kr* to recite the Quran;
ngajèkaké 1 to send s.o. to study and recite the Quran; 2 to recite the Quran for others.

ajrih fear, afraid, scared; awe, respect (*kr for* **wedi**); - **asih** respectful and devoted;
ngajrih-ajrihi 1 fearsome; 2 to threaten s.o. (*kr for* **ngedèn-dèni**).

aju *ng*, **ajeng** *kr* forward movement; - **undur** vicissitudes, ups and downs;
ngajoni 1 to approach s.o. by moving forward; 2 to take part in;
ngajokaké 1 to put forward; to (cause to) move forward; submit; 2 to remand;
maju 1 to go forward, advance; 2 to face, confront; to go to war.
See also **maju**.

ajug, **ajug-ajug** 1 tray or pedestal for an oil lamp; 2 *reg* handle of a harrow.

ajun *or* **ajung** assistant; - **jeksa** deputy of a prosecutor.

ajur 1 severely damaged, crushed; 2 to dissolve, disintegrate, digest; - **kumur-kumur** wrecked; - **luluh** 1 dissolved; 2 smashed; - **memet** completely crushed; - **mumur** pulverised.

Akad Sunday. *See also* **Ahad**, **Ngahad**.

akal idea, scheme, thought; **akal-akal** to have a foolish idea, to try a trick;
ngakal to find (a solution);
ngakali 1 to deceive; 2 to take advantage of s.o., cheat s.o.;
ngakal-akali to cheat others again and again;
akal-akalan manipulation, machination;
kalah okol menang akal *prov* 'the brain is mightier than the bone'.

akas hard and dry, crusty.

akasa *lit* the sky, the heavens.

akèh *ng*, **kathah** *kr* much, many, plenty;
ngakèhi to make s.t. more;

ngakèhi-ngakèhi to cause to be too much;
kakèhan (*or* **kakèhen**) too much; excessively much/many; - **cangkem** 1 (to engage in) too much talk (and too little action); 2 (to do) too much grumbling;
akèh-akèhan to compare or compete for most;
akèh-akéhé *or* **kèh-kèhé** at most.

akèn to tell s.o. to do s.t. (*kr for* **akon**).

akep, **ngakep** to hold between the lips; - **pipa** to smoke a pipe.

akérat the hereafter, the next life; **donya** - eternal (*see also* **donya**).

akik agate; **akik-akikan** 1 all kinds of agate; 2 imitation agate.

akil-balèg of age, adult (in Islam, able to undertake religious duties).

aking 1 dry (*kr for* **garing**); 2 *ng*, *kr*, to dry out; **sega** - dried rice (*see also* **sega**).

akir the end; - **taun** the end of the year;
akir-akir lately, recently;
ngakiri to end, close;
akir(-akir)é finally.

akon to tell s.o. to do s.t.;
akon-akon to hand out orders (to many);
ngakon to order, have s.o. do s.t.

akrab close relatives; intimate, chummy;
ngakrabi to be close to;
ngakrabaké to bring close, strengthen (friendships *etc*).

aksama *or* **pangaksama** *lit* forgiveness, pardon; **nyuwun** - to ask forgiveness (*see also* **suwun**).

aksami *var of* **aksama**.

aksara 1 letter of an alphabet; 2 written character; - **gedrik** printed characters; - **murda** capital (Javanese) letters; - **rékan** Javanese characters to accommodate foreign sounds; - **swara** vowel letters.

aksi *lit* eye (*var of* **èksi**).

aku 1 *ng*, **kula** *kr*, **dalem** *k.i.* I, me; - **kowé** we, us; - **kabèh** all of us;
ngaku *ng*, **ngaken** *kr* **1** to adopt s.o. as a member of the family; **2** to acknowledge, admit, confess;
ngakoni to admit;
diakokaké 1 to pass s.o. off as a relative; **2** to say that s.t. belongs to s.o. when it doesn't;
ngaku-aku to claim falsely;
pangakuan dosa confession (Roman Catholic);
wong kaya aku kowé people like us.

akur harmonious, congenial, agreeable;
ngakuraké 1 to synchronise (of watch, scale); **2** to appease, bring about peace;
akuran 1 mutually agreed; **2** to compromise; **2** verification, collation.

ala *ng*, **awon** *kr*, **èlèk** *coll*, bad, evil, nasty, ugly; - **atiné** bad character; - **becik** quality; - **meneng** *or* - **nganggur** to pass the time in a better way than doing nothing; - **duluné** indecent, improper; - **tanpa rupa** unattractive looking;
ala-ala bad though one may be;
ngala-ala to sully s.o.'s name, to speak ill of s.o. behind their back;
ngalani to do bad things to s.o.; to bring harm to; to make s.o. bad;
ngalan-alani to make s.t. bad;
ngalakaké 1 to make s.t. or s.o. look bad; **2** to treat as bad;
ingalan *lit* to be treated badly;
alané 1 what is bad; **2** rather than;
ala-alané (*or* **alané ala**) worst of all;
alan-alan scapegoat;
alan-alanan *ng*, **awon-awonan** *kr*, **1** of inferior quality; **2** to do bad things to each other;
saala-alané as bad as possible;
piala evil, wickedness, felony, misdeed, crime;
miala *or* **mialani** to bring harm to;
pangala-ala evil talk;

ala belo becik jaran *prov* a bad child of good parents;
becik ketitik ala ketara *prov* good deeds will make themselves known and evil will out.

alab, **ngalabi** to inundate.
mangalab-alab *lit* to overflow. *See also* **lèb, elèb; leb, eleb**.

alad flame;
ngalad-alad *or* **malad-malad** (*lit* **mangalad -alad**) to flare up, *fig* to burn with desire.

alah *excl of disbelief*; - **déné** in vain; - **ora** reluctant, half-hearted.

alal behalal *or* **alal bihalal** *or* **halal bihalal** **1** to ask and give forgiveness at the end of the Fasting Month; **2** a gathering of a social group (workers at same office, people of same ethnic origin *etc*) soon after the Fasting Month for such a purpose. *See also* **halal**.

alam 1 world, universe; - **akir** the next world, life after death; - **arwah** world of ancestral spirits; - **donya** world, universe; - **kabir** world of mortals; - **sahir** the eternal world; - **saisiné** the universe and all its contents; **ngèlmu** - physics (*see also* **ngèlmu**); **ora** - unnatural, out of the ordinary; **2** era; - **modhèren** modern era;
ngalami to experience;
alam-alaman 1 period; **2** role-playing;
pengalaman an experience; to have experiences; **wallahu'alam**. God knows best; I don't know. *Also* **ngalam**.

alamat I address of a letter, of one's residence;
ngalamati to write an address on;
ngalamataké to address (a letter) for s.o. *Also* **ngalamat**.
II sign of a coming event, portent; to omen, indicate;
ngalamati *or* **ngalamataké 1** to symbolise; **2** to portend, indicate.

alang I crosswise dimension; **-ujur 1** dimensions (length and width); **2** location, position; **3** the real facts;
ngalangi 1 (*or* **ngalang-alangi**), **mambengi** *kr* to impede, obstruct; **2** to break payment (of installment);
ngalangaké to place s.t. crosswise or in such a way as to be an obstacle;
malang in a crosswise position; *fig* unlucky; **- mégung** crisscross; **- mujur** lengthways and crossways;
kalangan (*or* **kalang-kalangan**) blocked, impeded; to run into obstacles;
alangan 1 hindrance, obstacle; **2** accidental damage, mishap;
alang-alangan to obstruct each other.
alang-alang tall coarse grass;
alang-alangan a place where such grass grows in abundance.
alap, ngalap 1 to take, put to use, take advantage of; **2** to seek possession of; **- ati** to entice, charm s.o.; **- berkah** to seek s.o.'s blessing; **- dho 1** to take two masters; **2** married to two women; **- gawé** to look for a job as a blue-collar worker; **- menang** to gain victory, strive for victory; **- nyaur 1** to sell (merchandise) on consignment; **2** pale and wan from malnutrition; **- opah** to earn a wage; **- putih** to want revenge; **- reruba** *or* **- besel** to be open to bribes;
kalap taken by spirits (in a river, ocean or forest); **alap-ingalap** to cross-marry; **alap-alapan** *way* struggle to get possession of a princess;
pangalapan a haunted place.
alap-alap a variety of hawk.
alas I *ng*, **wana** *kr* **1** forest; **2** *reg* fields, area outside the village; **- greng** dense jungle; **- gung liwang-liwung** extensive and dense jungle; **asu -** *or* **asu ajag** jackal, wild dog (*see also* **asu**); **ayam -** jungle fowl (*see also* **ayam**); **- alas 1** an evil spirit of the forest; **2** *term of abuse* (*see also* **sétan**);

ngalasaké 1 to exile s.o. into the jungle; **2** to allow (land) to revert to jungle;
alasan 1 wild; **2** uncultivated; **lemah -** uncultivated land (*see also* **lemah**); **wong -** forest dweller, aboriginal people living in the forest (*see also* **wong**);
alas-alasan 1 replica of a forest; **2** dramatic forest scene of a (wayang) play;
pangalasan former official in forest affairs;
ngayam alas to wander around in the forest (like a jungle fowl).
II **alasan** *or* **alesan** reason, excuse.
alat *var of* **walat** suffering caused by a holy person as punishment. *See also* **walat**.
aldaka *lit* mountain.
aleb I *or* **alep** very beautiful, fine.
II **ngalebi** to flood s.t., inundate.
kaleban *or* **keleban** to get flooded, inundated. *See also* **leb**.
alem praise, compliment;
ngalem *or* **ngelem** to praise;
aleman 1 to ask for affection; **2** to be attached;
pangalem high praise;
pangaleman a public figure of great stature;
golèk alem to seek s.o.'s praise or sympathy. *See also* **lem**.
alembana praise, compliment;
ngalembana to praise.
alèn-alèn imitation ring, small ring, toy ring. *See also* **ali-ali**.
aleng preferable (*coll of* **aluwung**).
alep very beautiful, fine. *See* **aleb**.
alès *lit* to go away.
alesan reason (*var of* **alasan**).
ali-ali *ng*, **sesupé** *kr*, *k.i.*, finger-ring;
ngalèn-alèni to put a ring on s.t.;
alèn-alèn imitation ring, small ring, toy ring.

alih, **ngalih** *ng*, **pindhah** *kr* **1** to move, change residence; **2** to change (places); **lintang -** a shooting star;
ngolah-ngalih to keep moving around;
alihan *or* **ngalihan** to have a tendency to move (house, job).

alik, **I ngolak-alik** to turn s.t. repeatedly. **II ngalik-alik** (*var of* **galik-galik**) high-pitched and melodious. *See also* **galik**. **III alika** *reg* preferable.

alim 1 pious, religious, well-behaved, peace-loving; **2** forgiveness; **3** learned (of poets, scholars *etc*);
ngalimi to behave like a pious person;
aliman 1 forgiveness; **2** forgive me (for not giving anything: said when refusing a beggar);
kaliman *or* **nyuwun alim** (**ngalim**) *lit* forgive me;
paliman forgiveness;
pasang aliman tabé *lit* forgive me (a greeting).

aling, **aling-aling** cover, concealment, protective shield;
ngalingi to conceal;
ngaling-alingi to cover up with a concealment;
kalingan *or* **kaling-kalingan** shielded by, covered by;
aling-alingan shielded, concealed from view; **- katon** to reveal s.t. inadvertently;
tanpa tèdhèng aling-aling unprotected, uncovered, *fig* to say straight out.

alis *ng*, *kr*, **imba** *k.i.* eyebrows;
saalis a hair's breadth.

alit small, tiny (*kr. for* **cilik**);
kalitan (*or* **dalem kalitan**) residence of the youngest son of the king of Surakarta.

aliyas also known as.

Allah God (term used by both Muslims and Christians);
Allahu akbar 'God is the greatest', God Almighty;
Allahu tangala God the most high;
ka-Allahan Godlike;
kersaning Allah God's will;
wallahu alam God knows (*see also* **alam**);
ya Allah ya robbi *excl of surprise*; oh, my God!

almarhum the late, the deceased.

alok 1 a yell, shout; **2** to call out, cheer; **- kélangan** to call out as a result of losing s.t. *See also* **lok**.

alon slow, soft;
alon-alon slowly, softly, cautiously;
alon-alonan *or* **lon-lonan** slowly, at a leisurely pace;
alon-alon waton kelakon *prov* 'slow and steady wins the race'.

along preferable (*coll var of* **aluwung**).

alu pestle for pounding things in a mortar;
ceblok alu *fig* to take turns at working;
nyagak alu *prov* unreliable talk.

alualah I ngalualah 1 to wail; **2** to ask for help.
II ngalualah to leave it, do nothing about it.

aluamah, *see* **ngaluamah**.

alub, **ngalub 1** to bark (of dog), regarded as a sign of s.t. unfortunate; **2** to bring about s.t. unfortunate by mentioning it; **3** to express a feeling of desperation.

aluk, **ngaluk-aluk** very far away.

alum 1 withered, limp, drooping (of leaf, plant *etc*); **2** *fig* faint, languid; **3** in the process of healing (of wound);
ngalumaké to cause to droop.

alun wave;
ngalun to undulate.

alun-alun broad grassy square in front of a palace or regent's residence.

alur kinship relation;
aluran 1 relationship in kinship system; **2** traces (of events, trail or track on the ground).

alus 1 fine, smooth; 2 incorporeal, invisible; 3 refined; - budiné (or bebudèné) refined character;
ngalusi to treat courteously;
ngalusaké to refine s.t.; to make smooth;
alusan fine type of male classical dance, of fine quality (of batik, fabric etc)

aluwung preferable. Also luwung.

ama insect pest, plant disease, fig public nuisance; - menthèk rice-plant disease.

amad female servant at the court; - dalem one in service at a royal grave.

amah, ngamah-amah 1 very angry; 2 to be passionate, desirous;
ngamah-amah mangsa daging to be desirous of devouring meat.

amal good deed, charity, charitable donation; - kadonyan worldly goods donated for charitable purposes; - karun hidden (buried) treasure;
ngamal to give to charity;
ngamali to give to (a charitable cause);
ngamalaké to put into practice, apply.

aman safe, secure;
ngamanaké to protect from threatened danger.

amat I var of amad.
II ngamati or ngamat-amati to watch over, keep a sharp eye on;
ngamataké to keep track of, examine.

amanat 1 an entrusted task; 2 a speech conveying a message to people.

amarga ng because (var of marga).

amargi kr because (var of margi).

amba I, ng wiyar kr 1 wide, broad, spacious; 2 width, breadth; - ciyut width;
ngambani to (do) on a wide scale;
ngambakaké to widen s.t.;
kamban or kekamban too wide;
saambané the same size as.
II (pron as: am-ba) lit 1 servant; 2 I, me.

ambah, ambah-ambah an epidemic;
ngambah 1 to traverse; - gegana to fly through the air; 2 to get involved in;
ngambahaké to let a baby's feet touch the ground;
kambah to get traversed (by);
ambah-ambahan 1 act of traversing; 2 place frequently traversed; 3 an epidemic (var of ambah-ambah).

ambak I or ambak-ambak, ambakna, ambakné, ambaknéa even though.
II or ambak ambing of course, I know.
III ambakna or ambak-ambakané(a), ambakpuna how come, it's ridiculous that…

ambal I 1 one stair in a flight;
ambal-ambalan a flight of stairs.
II (number of) times; - pindho twice;
ngambali to repeat, to do again;
ambal-ambalan to do repeatedly;
surak - to cheer again and again;
mangambal-ambal lit to do again and again.

ambar fragrance;
ngambar 1 to give off fragrance; 2 fig famous, renowned;
ngambar-ambar to give off fragrance everywhere.

ambara lit sky;
ngambara 1 to fly through the sky; 2 to wander around.

ambaro breakwater in a harbour.

ambawang reg a young mango.

ambeg, ambegan 1 breath, breathing; to breath; 2 fig to relax.

ambek 1 character, (having) a character trait; - adil paramarta (having) a just and noble character; - darma helpful character; - siya (having) cruel treatment to others; - sura or - wani (having) a bold character; - welas (having) a compassionate character; - pati (having) contempt for death; 2 assumption, opinion, feeling (var of anggep); 3 conceited, arrogant;
ngambeki 1 to act snobbishly; 2 to snub s.o.;

pambekan 1 character, temperament; **2** *reg* conceited, snobbish.

ambèk and, with (*reg var of* **karo**).

amben I 1 belly-band for a horse; **2** woman's sash.

II every time (*coll var of* **saben**).

ambèn low wooden or bamboo bench for sitting or sleeping on;
ambèn-ambènan bamboo coffin.

ambeng I 1 (*or* **ambengan**) rice and various foods in dishes or in a bamboo tray as a ritual meal; **2** dish, plate (*k.i. for* piring).
II ambengan to sit around while guarding.

ambeng-ambeng *reg* jungle grass (*kr for* **alang-alang**).

ambèr to overflow.

ambet smell, odour (*kr for* **ambu**);
ambetan durian fruit (*kr for* **durèn**).

ambi *or* **ambik** (together) with, and (*reg var of* **karo**).

ambil, ngambil *lit* to take, get, pick up;
ngambil-ambil to try to win over or to reconcile;
ngombal-ambil *reg* to rake up the past.

amblas lost, gone, vanished.

ambleg 1 to give way, collapse; **2** bankrupt.

ambles 1 to sink below the surface; - **bumi** to enter into the earth; **2** recessed, set in(ward).

amblong to give way, cave in.

ambo, ngambo to hoist; - **layar** to hoist sail.

ambok I *var of* **mbok**.
II ambokna even though (*var of* **ambakna**).

ambon *ng*, **ambetan** *kr* nickname for the (strong smelling) durian fruit;
ambon-ambon (**ambet-ambetan** *kr*) odour. *See* **ambu**.

ambra, ngambra-ambra 1 widespread, commonplace; **2** to scatter, strew; **3** to digress; **4** (of talk) desultory.

ambrah, ngambrah widespread, common, popular.

ambral *var of* **amral** admiral.

ambreg I to collapse;
ngambregaké to cause s.t. to collapse.
II ngambreg *or* **ngambreg-ambreg** to pile up, accumulate;
ambreg-ambregan heaped untidily.

ambrih *reg var of* **amrih**.

ambrik *var of* **amrik**.

ambril *var of* **amril**.

ambring *reg* very quiet.

ambrol to give way, collapse;
ngambrolaké to cause s.t. to collapse.

ambruk to fall down, come down, collapse;
ngambruk to lie down;
ngambruki *or* **ngembruki** to fall on(to);
ngambrukaké to cause s.t. to collapse. *See* **bruk**.

ambrung I *lit* buzzing *or* humming sound.
II *reg var of* **ambyuk**.

ambu *ng*, **ambet** *kr* odour;
ngambu to smell;
ngamboni to offer s.t. for smelling;
ngambokaké to cause s.o. to smell;
kambon to get a whiff of, get touched lightly by; - **getih** to get touched by the smell of blood;
pangambu sense of smell;
mambu 1 to have an odour; **2** to perceive an odour; **3** to spoil, spoiled; **4** (of news) out of date, stale; - **ati** one who has been loved; - **getih 1** (a weapon that) has been used for killing people; **2** to want to kill s.o.; - **ilu** to have learned one's lesson;
- **kulit daging** a relative, one's flesh and blood;
mambu-mambu a relative, distantly related;
ora mambu bocah (of a child) old beyond one's years;

ora mambu énthong irus *or* ora mambu sega jangan not a blood relation;

ora mambu wong Jawa (a Javanese who) lacks the essential Javaneseness;

ora mambu wong lanang 1 unmanly; a female virgin;

ora mambu wong wadon 1 unwomanly; 2 a male virgin;

kaselak mambu angin (of food) on the verge of losing its taste, *fig* on the verge of losing a good chance.

ambuda *lit* cloud.

ambul *reg* irresponsible, unmannerly.

ambulung *reg* a palm tree.

ambung *ng, kr,* aras *k.i.* a kiss;

ngambung *ng, kr,* ngaras *k.i.* to kiss; - dhengkul to kiss the knee, *fig* to show esteem and humility toward s.o.;

ngambungi to kiss s.o. repeatedly;

ngambungaké to have s.t. kiss s.o.;

ambung-ambungan to kiss each other.

ambur *reg var of* ambus.

ambus, ngambus to sniff;

ngambus-ambus to sniff continuously;

ngambusi to sniff repeatedly.

ambyah, ngambyah *or* ngambyah-ambyah commonplace, abundant, affluent.

ambyak, ambyak-ambyakan to disperse.

ambyang I *reg* dry grass for kindling.

II ngambyang-ambyang to wander everywhere restlessly.

ambyar to fall to pieces, burst into fragments.

ambyog, ngambyog *or* ngambyug to move in with s.o. temporarily; to stay at s.o.'s home.

ambyong, ngambyong *reg* to assemble together.

ambyuk to flock, move in a swarm. *See also* byuk.

ambyur 1 to plunge, splash, jump into water; 2 *fig* to plunge into activities.

ngambyuri to jump into water;

ambyur-ambyuran to jump into water repeatedly (for fun).

amé I *reg* to dry out. *See* pé II mé.

II ngamé to rave, be delirious;

ngamèkaké to talk about s.t. or s.o. while sleeping or delirious.

amèk *ng,* mendhet *kr* to go and get, pick (up); - iwak fishing;

ngamèk to pick up;

ngamèkaké to pick s.t. up for s.o. else. *See also* mèmèk.

amel, ngamel very fond of (food);

ngamel-amel to eat s.t. again and again.

amem taciturn, close-mouthed.

amèn I *coll* always, constantly.

II *or* ngamèn *or* amèn-amèn to perform (a show) publicly.

ameng I only (*reg var of* amung, mung).

II to have a foul odour.

III *or* ameng-ameng to engage in recreation (*k.i. for* dolan-dolan);

ameng-amengan pastime, source of amusement, hobby.

amèr, omar-amèr mushy, beginning to go off (cooked rice).

amet measuring unit for rice plants: 25 bunches or *ca* 154 kg.

amik I to get (*reg var of* amèk).

II only (*reg var of* amung, mung).

amin amen;

amin-amin religious ceremony at which food blessed by a religious man is served;

ngamini 1 to say amen frequently during a prayer; 2 to approve of, concur with.

aming only (*coll var of* mung).

amis to smell fishy;

ngamis-amisi to make s.t. smell or taste fishy;

amis bacin fishy and rotten, *fig* difficulties, troubles.

amit 1 to ask permission to leave; 2 (*or*

amit-amit) I beg your pardon; - **sèwu** excuse me;

amit-amit *excl* God forbid!

amlang *lit* bright, shining, gleaming.

amlas, **amlas asih** *lit* inspiring pity (*see also* **welas** I);

sambat amlas asih to wail pitifully (*see also* **sambat**).

amleng to go away without explanation.

amoh in rags, ragged, worn out: *esp* clothing;

ngamohaké to make s.t. ragged, wear out.

among 1 to take care of, handle, protect; - **asmara** to be in love with each other; - **beksa** an organisation that maintains Javanese classical dances; - **geni** *reg* to tend the fire (sit in front of the brazier); - **karsa** to follow one's own wishes; - **raga** *or* - **slira** to control o.s.; - **tamu** to receive (or those who receive) guests at a gathering; 2 to engage in, handle;

- **dagang** businessmen, merchants; - **tani** peasants; **kaki** - godfather; male good spirit that (protects human beings (*see also* **kaki**); **nini** - godmother; female good spirit that protects human beings (*see also* **nini**); **pamong** 1 public official; - **désa** village official; - **praja** civil servant; person in charge of a certain territory; 2 guardian; **Sang Pamong Agung** the Great Guardian, God.

amor 1 to mingle (with others); 2 mixed, combine with;

amor turu 1 to sleep in the same bed with; 2 to have sexual intercourse. *See* **awor**, **wor**, **mor**.

amot 1 to hold, accommodate; loaded with; 2 *fig* rich in forgiveness; patient and wise;

ngamot *or* **ngemot** 1 to contain, hold; 2 to be loaded with;

ngamotaké to load s.t.;

kamot 1 to hold, accommodate; 2 to get contained;

pamotan 1 loading-place; 2 a load. *See also* **momot**, **mot**.

ampad I leaning, aslant.

II **ngampad** to whip, throw.

III **ampadan** the lowest leaf of a tobacco plant.

ampah I *reg* valley.

II **ngampah** to restrain, hold in check.

ampak, **ampak-ampak** mountain mist;

ngampak-ampak to form large groups like heavy clouds;

ampak-ampakan moving forward in large groups.

ampal beetle.

ampang 1 light (weight); 2 weak; **tembako** - light tobacco (*see also* **tembako**); **swara** - light voice (*see also* **swara**);

ngampangaké 1 to cause to be light; 2 to belittle, disparage.

ampar I floor;

ngampar to sit or to sleep on a floor; **amparan** 1 a mat to sit on; 2 a kind of chair (without back).

II *or* **ngampar-ampar** to hit; **gelap** - the lightning strikes (*see also* **gelap** II).

ampas 1 residue after the essence has been removed; - **krambil** shredded coconut from which the milk has been pressed; 2 pieces left in a pan after the broth has been finished.

ampeg 1 strong; **tembako** - strong tobacco (*see also* **tembako**); 2 oppressed, constricted (of breathing).

ampèk *or* **sampèk** *reg* until.

ampel, **ngampeli** to insert kindling for making a fire.

ampèl a variety of bamboo. *See* **pring**.

amper, **ngamper** to throw at/to *var of* **ngampar**.

amperu *or* **peru** gall.

ampet, **ngampet** to restrain, check.

ampéyan (*k.i. of* **selir**) minor wife of aristocrat, royalty.

ampil, **garwa** - a wife other than the queen (*k.i. for* **selir**);
ngampil 1 to carry, bring, take (*k.i. for* **nggawa**); 2 to borrow (*k.i. for* **nyilih**);
ampilan royal insignia carried in procession in front of the ruler.

amping, **amping-amping** *or* **amping-ampingan** to hide behind s.t.;
ngampingi *or* **ngamping-ampingi** 1 to guard s.o. at a side; 2 to flank, stand beside; 3 to block s.o. from view by standing in front of him/her;
amping-amping wong gedhé *fig* to engage an elite person as one's protector.

ampir I ngampiri to call for s.o., pick up s.o.;
ngampiraké to ask s.o. to drop in;
ampiran place for stopping.
mampir *or* **kampir** to stop off, drop in.
II **ampir-ampir** front porch.

amplèk a certain vest, sleeveless shirt;
ngamplèk (of clothing: *esp* shirt) too small.

amplik, **amplik-amplik** *or* **ngamplik** balanced precariously near the edge of s.t.

amplok, **ngamplok** to cling to s.o. with arms and legs.

amplop envelope;
ngamplopi to put into an envelope;
amplopan placed in an envelope.

ampo high-calcium baked clay tablet eaten *esp* by pregnant women;
ngampo 1 resembling such a tablet; 2 to make clay tablets.

ampoh I endowed with supernatural power (*reg var of* **ampuh**).
II to restrain (*reg var of* **ampah**).

ampok *reg* roofed verandah-like extension to a house.

ampok-ampok *reg* wearing only a loincloth.

ampuh I 1 to possess special (supernatural) power (weapon, words); 2 strong (coffee, tobacco, medicine).
II **ampuhan** a gale with mist and rain in the mountains.

ampun I don't (*md for* **aja**); - **ngoten** don't do that.
II to have (done) (*reg md for* **wis**).

amput, **ngamput** *cr* to copulate with (a female);
diamput *excl* darn! (mild disgust or displeasure);
dudu amput-amputé no match for; far below.

ampyak I, **ngampyak** to act blindly; - **awur-awur** to act recklessly.
II **ngampyaki** to speak angrily to a group of people;
ampyak-ampyakan to walk together in throngs.

amral admiral.

amrèh *reg var of* **amrih**.

amrih so that, in order to. *See also* **mrih**, **pamrih**.

amrik fragrant, to give off an odour.

amril sandpaper;
ngamril to rub with sandpaper.

amring quiet. *See* **mamring**.

amud *see* **amut**.

amuk I blind attack; **mbarang** - *or* **soroh** - to attack violently (*see also* **soroh**);
ngamuk to attack blindly; - **punggung** to attack blindly;
pangamuk *or* **amukan** act of raging;
amuk-amukan to fight each other vehemently;
ngamuk kaya banthèng ketaton to attack with great violence.
II *or* **muk** only (*coll var of* **amung**, **mung**).
III preferable (*reg var of* **angur**).
IV **amuk-amuk** *reg* (to eat) with the mouth stuffed, chewing on.

amun, **amun-amun** fog;
dadi endhog amun-amun *fig* totally smashed.

amung only (*var of* **mung**).

amut, ngamuti to hold in the mouth, suck on. *See also* mut.

ana *ng*, wonten *kr* 1 to exist; - temenan to really exist; 2 to have; 3 to be equal to; 4 there is; 5 (*or* - ing) at, in, on, to be/stay in;

nganani to create, establish, bring about;

nganakaké 1 to bring about, create; 2 to hold, organise, arrange, make; 3 to cause;

nganak-anakaké to go to a lot of bother fixing s.t.;

anané the existence (of);

kaanan *or* kahanan conditions, circumstances, situation;

ana déné *ng*, wondéné *or* wondéning *kr* 1 now, while, and; 2 it so happens;

ana pisan it certainly exists;

anaa kaé even if there were…

ana-ana waé 1 *excl suggesting that words fail one*; kok - there is always s.t.;

ana gula ana semut 'where there is sugar there are ants', *prov* people go where s.t. is to be had;

ana catur mungkur to disregard whisperings.

anacaraka *see* hanacaraka.

anak *ng*, *kr*, putra *k.i.* offspring; - angkat adopted child; - anung outstanding *or* adopted child; - bojo wife and child(ren); - jadah illegitimate child; - kumpeni soldier; - kuwalon stepchild; - lanang *ng* (-jaler *kr*, putra kakung *k.i.*) son; - mas favourite child; - ontang-anting an only child; - Pandhawa sibling combination consisting of 5 boys; - prabu title by which a king is addressed by his father (in law) or uncle; - pujan *lit* a child created magically; - pupon a child adopted in babyhood; - wadon *ng* (- èstri *kr*, putra putri *k.i.*) daughter;

anak-anak (peputra *k.i.*) to have children;

nganak to call s.o. (or regard s.o.) as one's own child;

nganaki 1 to provide interest; 2 to father (an illegitimate child); 3 to provide for (one's children); 4 to produce a copy or imitation of;

nganakaké to give birth to; to be the parent (of);

nganak-anakaké to raise (a child) to adulthood;

manak to reproduce (of animals; *cr* of people);

anakan 1 the young of an animal; 2 doll; 3 small (of natural phenomena); 4 duplicate, copy; 5 drawer, section, compartment; gunung - hill; segara - small sea, bay;

anak-anakan doll, puppet; - timun cucumber used as a doll; adopted person who later marries the adoptive parent;

nak-kumanak to multiply, flourish (of people, animals, plants);

anak molah bapa kepradhah *prov* the father has got into trouble because of the son's attitude.

anal, nganal to walk fast, hasten.

anam, nganam to weave; - képang 1 to make woven bamboo; 2 resembling woven bamboo;

nganam-anam to weave in and out; *fig* to work out a plan, think over;

nganami to weave s.t. into (an article);

anaman woven; - klasa woven mat.

anapun *lit* it so happened.

anapi but, *reg var of* nanging.

ancab, ngancab to attack viciously.

ancak woven bamboo mat on which offerings to the spirits are placed.

ancal the flower of certain tuberous plants.

ancala *lit* mountain.

ancam, ngancam *or* ngancam-ancam to threaten verbally;

ancaman a threat;

ancam-ancaman to threaten each other; **pangancam** *or* **pangancam-ancam** threatening.

ancang, ngancangi *or* **ngancang-ancangi** to get set for doing s.t.; to be ready to do;
ancang-ancang to get ready.

ancar, ngancari to stab with a spear.

ancara *var of* **acara**.

ancas goal, ambition, ideal;
ngancas 1 to strive toward an ideal; 2 to take a short cut; 3 with a single stroke;
ngancasaké to direct s.t. at/toward;
ancasing sedya definite intention.

anceb sticking, stuck (into).

ancel, nganceli *or* **ancel-ancelan** *cr* to copulate with s.o.

ancer, ancer-ancer 1 mark(er); 2 the approximate location;
ngancer-anceri 1 to place a mark(er); 2 to give s.o. directions.

ancik, ngancik to reach; **- diwasa** to come of age;
ancik-ancik 1 to stand on s.t.; 2 *or* **ancikan** s.t. stood on;
ancik-ancik pucuking eri *prov* in a critical situation, in a precarious position.

anco a long-handled net.

ancog, ancog-ancogen doubtful about; not quite sure what one wants.

ancok, ancok-ancok *reg* 1 a small hut (in a ricefield); 2 roofed verandah-like extension to a house.

ancol, ancol-ancolen lacking in good manners.

ancug I ngancug *or* **ancug-ancug** to walk with an ungainly gait (*e.g.* of a tall thin person).
II *see* **ancuk**.

ancuk *cr* to copulate with s.o.

ancul 1 *var of* **ancug**; 2 *or* **anculan** equipment for scaring birds away from ripening rice plants.

ancung a variety of children's game;
rebut ancung to compete to obtain a goal;
mancung *reg* to climb in a tree.

ancur I (to get) broken, smashed; **- lebur** totally destroyed;
ancur-ancuran completely smashed.
II 1 material for making glue; 2 powdered glass melted into glue (for coating kite strings);
ngancur-ancuri 'to apply glue to'; 1 to follow s.o.'s wishes because of their flattery; 2 to inflame a quarrel to make it worse.

andak *excl of disbelief*; **- iya** I don't believe it (*var of* **apa iya**).

andaka *lit* bull, wild ox.

andakara *lit* sun.

andam a variety of fern.

andana, andana warih *lit* noble;
trahing andana warih of noble descent.

andané *reg, excl of surprise*.

andang *var of* **endang**, **énggal** *kr*, quick, soon, immediate. *See also* **dang II**.

andaru *or* **daru** falling star bearing an omen.

andel 1 believer; 2 one who trusts;
ngandel to believe (in), trust;
ngandeli *or* **ngandelaké** 1 to rely on; 2 to trade on;
ngandelan gullible, over-trusting;
andel-andel 1 mainstay, one who can be depended upon; 2 trustworthy commander;
ngandel-andelaké *or* **ngendel-endelaké** to depend too heavily on (the wrong values);
kumandel to be convinced of;
piandel 1 belief, superstition; 2 s.t. or s.o. whom one can rely on.

ander upright roof-supporting beam in a house frame.

anderpati *lit* to be determined to die, ready to be killed (in battle).

andha ladder, ladderlike steps; - **jagang** or - **jagrag** stepladder with steps on both sides; - **junjang** latticed bamboo poles forming a trellis for vines; - **lanang** ladder consisting of a pole with rungs projecting on each side; - **pengantèn** or - **mantèn** stepladder; - **widadari** rainbow;
ngandhani to lean a ladder against;
andhan-andhan 1 a short flight of ladderlike wooden steps; 2 drying rack of bamboo poles; 3 stairs, steps;
ngandhan-andhan falling in loose waves (of hair).
andhah, andhahan 1 subordinate, underling; 2 *gram* affixed; tembung - derived word, affixed form (*see also* tembung I);
ngandhahi to subordinate, subjugate o.s. (to);
ngandhahaké to supervise (one's subordinates), be in charge.
andhap 1 below, under (*root form: kr for* isor); 2 short, low (*kr for* cendhèk); 3 to descend (*root form: kr for* dhun); andhap asor humble, self-effacing.
andhapan wild boar (*kr for* cèlèng).
andhar, ngandharaké to explain, tell;
ngandhar-andhar excessively long (of speech or writing);
andharan 1 speech, narration, account; 2 a long-winded account.
andhé, andhéné, andhé-andhéné or saandhéné *reg* if, supposing that.
andheg *ng*, èndel *kr* act of stopping;
ngandheg 1 to stop s.t.; 2 to have no menstrual periods, pregnant (*var of* meteng);
ngandhegi or ngendhegi 1 to stop s.o. or s.t. that is passing through; 2 to stop (in) at;
ngandhegaké or ngendhegaké to stop s.t.;
mandheg *ng*, kèndel *kr* to come to a stop;
kandheg to get stopped.

See also endheg I.
andhèk, andhèkané, andhèkna or andhèkné *reg var of* andhé; andhèkpuna *lit var of* andhé.
andhel *var of* andel.
andhem I ngandhemi 1 to commit o.s. to; - tékad to stand by one's resolve; 2 to acknowledge freely.
II andheman indentation in an animal's chest (where the heart is).
andheng, andheng-andheng skin blemish, mole.
andhèr to gather, form a crowd.
andhih *var of* endhih.
andhil 1 a share of ownership; 2 scale for weighing opium. *See* ondhal-andhil.
andhok 1 to sit and eat in a foodshop; 2 (*or* ngandhok, mandhok) to stay (stop) s.w.;
ngandhokaké to have s.o. stay s.w.
andhong I horse-drawn cab (four wheels, two horses);
ngandhong 1 to ride in a cab, go by cab; 2 to transport passengers as one's job;
ngandhongaké 1 to use as a cab, or have it used for profit; 2 to have s.o. or s.t. carried by a cab.
II ngandhongi to change places with, replace, substitute for.
andhuk towel;
ngandhuki to dry s.o. with a towel;
andhukan to use a towel.
andik I *lit* severe, harsh; - angatirah severe and burning.
II *reg* somewhat, rather; - réné somewhat closer.
andika I *lit* you.
II ngandikani *k.i.* to tell s.o., say to;
ngandikakaké *k.i.* to state s.t.;
andikakaké, dikakaké *k.i.* to have received orders to. *See also* ngendika.
andir *reg* road worker (*var of* anjir).
andon to carry on, engage in; - asmara to engage in love; - jurit *or* - perang to fight

a war; - **gawé** to go out for a job; - **laku** *or* - **paran** to travel; - **lelana** to wander, ramble; - **tuwa** older brother/sister-in-law;

ngandonaké to have/make s.o. (do) steadily.

andong a certain plant used to weave mat, hat, bag *etc*.

andrawina *lit* feast, banquet;
kembul bojana andrawina to dine together at a large dinner party.

ané how… ! what… ! (*stressing the preceding word*); **édan** - how crazy that is!

anèh strange, odd, peculiar;
nganèhaké 1 to regard s.t. as odd; 2 to cause s.t. to be strange;
nganèh-anèhi very much out of the ordinary;
anèh-anèh s.t. strange.

anéka *lit* variety; - **warna** of many kinds, multicoloured. *Also* **manéka**.

anèm young (*kr for* **anom**).

anèng, at, on, in (*coll for* **ana ing**). *See* **nèng, ana**.

angabèhi *see* **ngabèhi**.

angad *var of* **ongod**.

angah, angah-angah greedy, selfish;
ngangah-angah to be passionate, selfish.

angap an open mouth;
mangap open(ed) (of the mouth);
ngangapaké to open (one's, s.o.'s) mouth.

angas one who seems brave but actually is afraid;
ngangasi to bluff s.o.

angèl hard, difficult;
ngangèli *or* **ngangèlaké** to make s.t. difficult;
ngangèl-angèl *or* **ngengèl-engèl** to complicate s.t.;
ngangèl-angèli *or* **ngengèl-engèli** to cause difficulties for s.o.;
kangèlan to have difficulties;

angèl-angèlan s.t. difficult, difficult things;
angèl-angèlé the most difficult. *See also* **ngèl**.

angen, angen-angen thought, idea;
ngangen-angen 1 to keep thinking about s.o.; 2 to hope to meet s.o.;
kangen to long for, miss s.o.;
pangangen-angen thought, expectation.

angèn to herd, tend (*kr for* **angon**).

anges *reg var of* **angus**.

anget 1 warm, hot, lukewarm; 2 feverish; 3 secure, safe; 4 more in weight;
ngangeti *or* **ngangetaké** to make warm;
manget-manget lukewarm;
anget-angetan s.t warm (of food, drink).

angga 1 *lit* body; 2 bundles of newly harvested rice.

angga-angga *or* **anggang-anggang** water-spider.

anggak *reg* boastful, conceited;
anggak-anggakan to show off, boast, brag.

anggal *reg* light (not heavy);
nganggalaké to make light(er).

anggana *lit* 1 alone, by o.s.; 2 *lit* woman, girl.

anggang-anggang I water-spider (*var of* **angga-angga**).
II 1 with soft and slow, easy movements; 2 *reg* scarce, distantly spaced;
nganggang-anggang to treat s.t. cautiously.

anggaota *or* **nggaota** to earn for a living;
panggaotan occupation, work, job.

anggar I the sport of fencing;
nganggar to carry a sword or sharp weapon in a sheath or scabbard at the side;
anggaran sheath, scabbard.
II **nganggar** 1 to buy on credit; 2 to borrow (money) without security;

anggaran 1 a loan; 2 earmarked funds.

anggara *lit* Tuesday; - **kasih** *alternative name for* **Selasa Kliwon**.

anggé to use, wear (*root form: kr for* **anggo**).

anggé-anggé mole-cricket found in a ricefield.

anggel I **anggelan** *or* **anggel-anggel** small wooden dam used to control the flow of water in a ricefield; **nganggeli** to dam up, hold back.

II **anggel-anggel** *reg* s.t. saved for future use.

anggep opinion, assumption;
nganggep 1 to consider, regard as; 2 to pay attention;
anggep-anggepan to look down on (people, things); to consider s.t. or s.o. unworthy;
kanggep to be appreciated;
panganggep *or* **pianggep** opinion, thought, attitude.

angger I 1 each, every; 2 every (time, whenever);
angger-angger every time, always.

II 1 (*or* **anggeré**) if, provided that; 2 (*or* **anggeré**) to do s.t. for no good reason other than just doing it; 3 (*or* **anggeré**) just be able to do the most important, basic thing and no more;
angger-angger rule, regulation;
ngangger-anggeri to apply rules (to); to furnish regulations (for).

anggèr *adr* young man.

anggi, anggi-anggi a certain medicinal herb.

anggit thought, creation, idea;
nganggit 1 to arrange (flowers); 2 to invent, think up; 3 to compose, write (literary works);
anggitan 1 composition, invention; 2 quick to catch on, smart;
nganggitaké to compose for s.o.

angglong 1 reduced to a small amount (of the contents of a container); 2 dis-

appointed and grieving.

anggo *ng*, **anggé** *kr*, **agem** *k.i.* the way to use;
nganggo 1 to use, by means of; 2 to have s.t. attached or accompanying it; 3 to misuse, misappropriate (funds); 4 to wear, *i.e.* use (apparel); 5 to consider, regard as;
nganggoni 1 to dress s.o. (in), have s.o. wear; 2 to wear, put on many items;
nganggokaké to help s.o. dress, dress s.o.;
nganggo-anggo to wear jewelry, be well-dressed;
nganggon-anggoni to dress s.o. (in);
kanggo for; useful;
anggon-anggon *ng*, **anggèn-anggèn** *kr*, **agem-ageman** *k.i.* s.t. to be worn;
kanggonan to get s.o. or s.t. put in one's place.

anggon *ng*, **anggèn** *kr*, 1 act of doing, the way to act; 2 place; **salah** - misplaced (*see also* **salah**); 3 *reg* usual, ordinary, not unexpected;
manggon *ng*, **manggèn** *kr*, **lenggah** *k.i.* 1 to live, stay; 2 to settle;
panggonan place.
See **nggon, enggon**.

anggong to pant because of a heavy burden.

anggop *see* **agop**.

anggota 1 a body part, limb; 2 member of a group or organisation.

anggrah, anggrah-anggrah 1 twigs used to block the way; 2 s.t. worthless.

anggrak, nganggrak to stop s.o. by pointing a weapon and threatening (of robber *etc*).

anggrang, nganggrang 1 to stand in a high place; 2 left unfinished;
nganggrangaké 1 to lean s.t. against; 2 to leave work unfinished.

anggras, nganggras to threaten s.o. by bluffing.

anggreg, anggreg-anggreg *or* onggrag-anggreg not flowing freely, to proceed haltingly;

nganggreg-anggregi to slow s.t. down, cause to proceed haltingly.

anggrèk orchid.

anggrem *reg var of* angrem.

anggreng *lit* to roar, groan in pain. *See also* gereng.

anggrik, nganggrik-anggrik thin as a rake.

anggris 2½ guilders' worth in coin or notes (*var of* ringgit).

anggrok, manggrok to stay s.w. temporarily, stop (over);

nganggroki to occupy a place temporarily;

nganggrokaké to have s.o. stay s.w. *See also* enggrok.

angguk 1 a horse-riding dance performed by boys or young men; 2 a children's singing and dancing game.

anggung I *lit* constantly, always.

II a cooing sound;

manggung to coo.

anggur I grape, grape vine, wine.

II *or* angur *reg* preferable.

III nganggur free, at leisure, not working, not to be used;

nganggguraké to neglect, leave s.t. untouched;

angguran 1 unemployed; 2 *reg* a certain tax in the village;

anggur-angguran idle, with nothing to do.

anggut, manggut-manggut *or* monggat-manggut to nod the head again and again.

angi to cool newly cooked rice by spreading and fanning it;

angèn cooked rice that has been cooled.

angin 1 wind, breeze, draft; 2 air; - becik *fig* a change for the better; - dharat offshore night wind; - dhudhuk internal 'wind' that can be fatal; - dombang south wind common during the dry season; - gendhing strong east wind that brings illness with it; - laut daytime onshore wind; - lésus hurricane, typhoon;

angin-angin to expose o.s. to drafts, get in a draft;

ngangin-angin 1 to get some fresh air; 2 to go out to hear the news;

ngangin-anginaké to dry s.t. in the wind;

kanginan to be exposed to, be affected by wind, get blown;

anginen (of stomach) to ache, feel bloated;

angin-anginan to behave erratically, work in spurts;

masuk (*or* mangsuk) angin to have/get a cold (*see* masuk, mangsuk);

bisa njaring angin 'to be able to snare wind'; very powerful.

angka I 1 number, digit, numeral; - Arab Arabic numeral; - taun year in digits; 2 mark, grade; 3 grade level; 4 a number in ordinal series;

ngangkani to number.

II *var of* angkah;

ngangka-angka to expect, imagine.

angkah intention, expectation;

ngangkah to intend, expect;

pangangkah intention, expectation, goal.

angkang, ngangkang to echo, sound clearly in the distance (gamelan music);

angkara (*or* angkara murka) *lit* selfish, greedy;

angkas, ngangkas-angkas 1 to concentrate on, await eagerly; 2 to look forward to.

angkasa *lit* the sky, the heavens;

tumenga ing angkasa to look up into the sky.

angkat 1 adopted; adoptive; anak - adopted child (*see also* anak); bapak - adoptive father (*see also* bapak);

angkat-angkat to lift s.t. heavy; 2 to lift; - junjung hard physical work; 3 departure;

ngangkat 1 to lift; 2 to promote, elevate;

mangkat to leave, depart (*see also* pangkat II);

angkatan *or* angkat-angkatan 1 act or way of lifting; 2 class group; 3 a generation (of people); group of people constituting a movement; 4 moment to start (of song, dance *etc*).

angkel, angkel-angkel to sit and be disinclined to stand up;

angkel-angkelan *reg* resentful;

mangkel annoyed, irritated (at), resentful.

angker 1 haunted, eerie, bewitched; 2 dignified.

angkil 1 payment for greasing the palm; 2 to work as a coolie or become a soldier by contract.

angkin coloured chintz worn by women for covering wide wrapped sash.

angklah *reg* 1 enervated, weak, tired; 2 in a difficult situation. *See* anglah.

angklé tired, weary.

angklek *or* ngangklek *or* ongklak-angklek *reg* to proceed at a slow, laborious pace.

angklèk to hop on one foot (*var of* èngklèk);

ngangklèk *or* ngèngklèk to wear (a sheathed kris) at the back.

angkleng, ngangkleng *reg* to have a long, tiresome wait.

angklik, angklik-angklik to stand or sit in a high precarious position;

mangklik-mangklik balanced precariously in a high position. *See also* angkrik-angkrik.

angklung 1 a musical instrument consisting of suspended bamboo tubes which sound against each other when shaken; 2 an ensemble of such instruments;

ngangklung to play this instrument.

angkrah, angkrah-angkrah waste material, refuse, flotsam in a stream.

angkreg *var of* anggreg.

angkrèk I child's toy: a small wooden or cardboard puppet that moves up and down on a stick when the string is pulled. *Also* angkrok.

II *var of* anggrèk.

angkrik, angkrik-angkrik *or* mangkrik-mangkrik to sit in a high place.

angkring long carrying shoulder pole with containers of food, drinks, and utensils on either end;

angkringan food or drink sold by peddlers in such containers.

angkrok *var of* angkrèk.

angkruk, angkruk-angkruk *or* mangkruk-mangkruk to sit perched in a high place;

ngangkruk-angkrukaké to put s.t. (large) in a high place.

angkud, ngangkud to transport, haul. *Also* angkut.

angkuh I arrogant, complacent, self-satisfied;

ngangkuhi to treat arrogantly;

piangkuh arrogance, conceit.

II ngangkuh to regard, think of (as). *See also* rengkuh.

angkul, angkul-angkul 1 peg for hanging a pair of scales; 2 the part of a yoke that encircles the ox's neck.

angkup unopened sheath of fruit or flower bud.

angkur reinforcing corner brace for a wall.

angkus 1 a short spear; 2 long hook used on fire.

anglah *or* angleh 1 enervated, weak, tired; 2 sick, ill. *Also* angklah.

anglang, nganglang to travel around, do the rounds of. *See also* langlang.

anglek I cloying.

II *lit* grief, profound sorrow.

angleng I *reg* preferable, rather than; 2 *reg* eccentric, deranged.

anglèng I *lit* to live in, enter a hole (cave *etc*).
II clear (of hearing, meaning);
nganglèngaké to listen carefully to, figure out, comprehend (the meaning of).

angler 1 pleasantly smooth, gentle (without jerks); **turu -** to sleep soundly; 2 to hold steady in flight (kites).

anglèr to harrow a field for the last time, before planting.

angles 1 *var of* **angler**; 2 to go away without saying goodbye to anyone;
3 to feel profound sorrow.

anglih I *lit* to move s.t.
II *lit* hungry. *See* **ngelih**.

angling *lit* to speak, say;
onglang-angling to converse, chat. *See also* **ling**.

anglir *lit* like, as. *See* **lir I**.

anglo charcoal brazier; **- padupan** covered incense burner.

anglong I to ebb, reduced; **- jiwa** to waste away *e.g.* from sorrow.
II **manglong** to stoop, dangle;
nganglongaké to dangle s.t. *See* **anglung**.
angluh, ngangluh to complain;
panganlgluh complaint. *See also* **keluh II**.

anglung, manglung to stoop, bend, bow, lean (toward); bent downward;
nganglungaké to bend s.t. downward (*var of* **nganglongaké**).

angob a yawn, yawning; to yawn.

angok to recede, ebb.

angon *ng*, **angèn** *kr*, to herd, tend; **- angin** to have a proper regard for time; **- kedhap** to keep an eye on what others are doing; **- iriban** to keep an eye open for an opportunity; **- mangsa** (*var of* **- angin**); **- ulat** (*var of* **angon iriban**);
ngangon 1 to herd, tend; 2 *fig* to care for, have regard for;
pangon boy who tends livestock; *fig* supervisor;
pangonan grazing field for livestock;
angon ulat ngumbar tangan *prov* on the lookout to steal or pick pockets. *See also* **ngon**.

angot to refuse to do anything, be in a bad mood;
angot-angotan 1 according to one's mood; 2 recurrent. *See also* **ngot**.

angrang a large red tree ant. *See also* **ngangrang, kemangrang**.

angrèh *or* **mangrèh** *lit* to rule, hold sway over. *See also* **rèh**.

angrem 1 to sit on eggs; 2 *fig* to stay in one place; 3 to rise late (of moon);
ngangremi *or* **ngengremi** to sit on eggs to hatch them;
ngangremaké *or* **ngengremaké** to put eggs in a nest to be hatched by a hen;
angreman 1 nest where eggs are being hatched; 2 *fig* hideout, hiding-place;
pangreman *or* **pangangreman** *var of* **angreman**.
See also **rem II**.

angrob *lit* to rise (of water level). *See* **rob**.

angrog *lit* (to speak, sing) in unison. *Also* **angrug**.

angsa I 1 *lit* goose.
II *or* **wangsa** *lit* family, dynasty.
III *lit* share, portion.
IV **ngangsa** *or* **ngangsa-angsa** greedy, covetous; excessively ambitious.

angsab *var of* **asab**.

angsag *var of* **asag**.

angsah *lit* advance, attack;
mangsah to advance, go forward bravely; **- prang** to go into battle;
ngangsahaké to send off to war.

angsal 1 to receive, accept (*kr for* **olèh**); 2 s.o.'s act of (do)ing (*md for* **olèh, anggon**).
II if, provided (*var of* **waton**).
III origin (*var of* **asal**).

angsang 1 gill (fish's breathing apparatus); 2 grate for holding coals in a brazier; 3 base/foot of a receptacle; 4 big receptacle on a base; 5 closet or cupboard shelf.

angsar or ngangsar magic power of amulet;
ngangsari to give spiritual power to s.o.

angseg act of pushing or pressing;
ngangseg to push, press (forward);
ngangsegaké to press s.t. forward; to quicken the pace of work.

angslep or mangslep to enter, insert. See aslep, angslup.

angsli var of asli.

angslup 1 to set (var of angslep); 2 (or mangslup) to enter, insert;
ngangslupaké to insert s.t.

angso var of aso.

angsog beached (of small boats).

angsoka a flowering tree. See soka.

angsring var of asring.

angsrog var of asrog.

angsu, ngangsu 1 to draw water for household use; 2 fig to learn, study; - kawruh to seek knowledge;
ngangsoni to draw water from;
ngangsokaké to draw water for s.o.;
pangangsu 1 one who draws water; 2 a matter of learning;
pangangson 1 place where household water is obtained, fig source of knowledge; 2 container for drawing water;
ngangsu banyu apikulan warih prov having a basic knowledge before learning s.t.;
ngangsu banyu ing kranjang prov to learn s.t. but fail to apply it.

angsuk or angsukan a harmonious match;
mangsuk 1 to enter; 2 to match;
mangsuk angin to have/get a cold.

angsul reg kr for bali;

angsul-angsul gift to a guest departing from a ceremonial meal.

angsung lit to give; - pangapura to forgive; - dhahar reg to place an offering for the spirits; to offer flowers, burn incense etc at s.o.'s grave; - pambagya to welcome;
ngangsungaké lit to give, hand up s.t.

angsur I ngangsur to pay by installments;
ngangsuri to buy s.t. by installment for s.o.;
ngangsuraké to sell s.t. on credit; to pay by installments for s.o.;
II ngangsur or ngangsur-angsur heavy and long breathing.
III mangsur or mangsur-mangsur diarrhoea.

anguk I coll var of angur.
II anguk-anguk or manguk-manguk to keep putting one's head out of (a door, window etc);
ongak-anguk or mongak-manguk to put one's head out of (a door, window etc) repeatedly.

angun, angun-angun I bull.
II law upholder.

angur preferable; rather than.

angus soot, lampblack;
ngangus 1 to produce soot; 2 to blacken with soot.

ani, ani-ani 1 a small palm-held reaping knife for cutting rice stalks; 2 to harvest rice with such a knife;
ngenèni to harvest rice with a special knife.
See also panèn.

aniaya cruelty, ill treatment;
nganiaya to maltreat, beat cruelly, torture;
kaniaya or kaningaya to be maltreated, to get bad treatment;
panganiaya maltreatment, cruel treatment.

anila *lit* wind.

anindita esteemed, revered, distinguished.

anindyamantri *lit* chief minister.

aning but, however (*reg var of* nanging).

anis *lit* gone away.

anja, nganja-anja 1 to become emotional; 2 to walk on one's hands; 3 to take a run before jumping; 4 to have a good time, enjoy o.s.;
  anja-anja 1 a variety of spider; 2 a dwarf demon with a red tongue who can cause skin diseases (traditional belief);
  anja-anjanen *or* anjan-anjanen to have a distaste for; to be disinclined.

anjali *lit* a gesture of respect;
  manganjali *lit* to make an obeisance;
  panganjali respectful greeting (with palms together touching the forehead).

anjang, anjang-anjang bamboo latticework used as a support for climbing vines;
  nganjang-anjangi to set up lattice work for climbing vines.

anjat *reg* steeply sloping mountain side;
  nganjat to slope upward;
  nganjati *reg* to climb a sloping mountain side;
  manjat *reg* sloping steeply;
  panjatan *reg* ascent.

anjèng *reg* 1 to go out for pleasure; 2 to go to a ceremony.

anjel, nganjelaké to set forward.

anjer *var of* anjir.

anji, anji-anjinen *or* kanji to learn one's lesson.

anjing entering;
  nganjingi to enter into s.o.'s body or s.t.;
  nganjingaké to have s.t. enter into;
  anjing-anjingan mortice joint, dovetailed joint;

manjing 1 to enter into; 2 to enter and become one with;
  manjing ajur ajèr 1 having the (magical) power to penetrate any substance; 2 easy to communicate with all levels of people. *See also* panjing.

anjir I 1 stake or pole used as a marker; picket pole; 2 to stand on one's head. II road repair worker;
  nganjir to repair roads.

anjleg *or* anjreg *reg* to live or to be located in/at.

anjlog 1 to jump down; 2 to descend sharply;
  nganjlogi to jump down onto, pounce on;
  nganjlogaké to cause s.t. to fall down;
  anjlog-anjlogan to jump down again and again. *See also* jlog.

anjog having arrived at, leading to/into;
  nganjogaké to cause to arrive at. *See also* jog.

anjrah present everywhere, ubiquitous; to spread throughout.

anjrak to settle.

anjrit *lit* to scream. *See* jerit.

anjrum *lit* lying at ease (of cattle, *e.g.* while chewing the cud). *See also* jerum.

anjuk, nganjuk to buy on credit.

anjum to extend the hands; - tangan to extend both hands in a greeting (Muslim style).

anjun I earthenware water crock; tukang - potter, maker of earthenware. II *or* anjung *or* ajun adjunct.

anjur I and then, after that (*coll of* banjur). II nganjuraké to suggest, advise; anjuran advice, suggestion(s).

anom *ng*, anèm *kr*, timur *k.i.* young. *See also* nom.

anon *lit* to see, know. *See* ton.

anor low, humble, inferior; - raga modest, humble;

nganoraké or **ngasoraké** to efface o.s., to conduct o.s. modestly. *See also* **anuraga**.

anrang *lit* to attack; - **wèsthi** to attack the enemy. *See also* **serang**.

anrus *lit* right after that, continuously, again and again, straight. *See also* **terus**.

anta I stale tasting, taste of fresh water, tasteless.

II **nganta-anta** to demand revenge (against); to be exasperated, out of patience.

antah *var of* **wantah**.

antak, ngantak-antak 1 to expect s.o. impatiently; 2 to be choked.

antaka *lit* death, dead; to die;
kantaka unconscious.

antakusuma 1 name of a special vest; 2 *way* flowered fabric for certain costumes.

antal or **antal-antalan** slow in tempo, of gamelan music;
ngantali or **ngantal-antali** to allow plenty of time (for);
ngantalaké to slow (the music) down.

antan, antan-antan 1 to keep trying to walk (of a child); 2 preparation;
tanpa antan-antan impatient.

antang I *var of* **tantang**.
II **ngantang** to dry s.t. (*e.g.* maize) in a high place.

antar I long stick (*var of* **gantar**).
II loud;
ngantaraké to make louder;
ngantar-antar to speak loudly; to glow, burn brightly; *fig* very angry. *See also* **kantar**.

antara *ng*, **antawis** *kr* 1 between, among, within; 2 (*or* **antarané**) approximately; 3 some, a certain amount (of time);
ngantarani to increase the space or time, put space between;

ngantarakaké to estimate approximately;
ora antara suwé not long afterwards, before long.

antariksa *lit* sky, firmament.

antawacana *way* characteristic speech style of a character.

antawis between, among (*kr for* **antara**).

anteb 1 firm, steadfast; 2 heavy, weighty;
manteb 1 steadfast, dedicated (as a servant); 2 fulfilled, gratified;
antebing tékad firm will, resolution.

antem a blow with a fist;
ngantem 1 to hit, punch; 2 to charge more than a normal price;
pangantem a punch;
anteman or **antem-anteman** a punch;
antem-anteman to hit each other, have a fistfight.

anteng steady, tranquil;
- **kitiran** or - **tlalé** to wriggle, squirm;
- **kreneng** to pretend to be nice.

anter *var of* **antar**.

antèr 1 quiet, serene; 2 calm and even-tempered (of child).

anthèk 1 helper to a tradesman or labourer; 2 sycophant, yes-man;
nganthèk 1 to be(come) a helper; 2 to be a lackey.

anthuk, nganthuki to nod at (as a sign);
manthuk to nod;
manthuk-manthuk, monthak-manthuk to keep nodding;
manthukan to always agree, never say no.

anti I **nganti** *ng*, **ngantos** *kr* 1 to wait; 2 till, up to the point that, for (length of time); **aja nganti** don't let it happen that...
II **anti-anti** *ng*, **antos-antos** *kr*, **nganti-anti** to look forward to, long for;
panganti-anti hope, expectation. *See also* **kanti**.

antiga *lit* egg.

antih, ngantih to spin (thread).

anting I 1 sliding weight on a scale beam; 2 metal pieces holding car springs to the frame.

II anting-anting dangling earrings.

III ontang-anting an only child; a child without relatives; alone in the world.

IV a swing;

montang-manting 1 to sway; 2 to exert o.s.;

ngontang-antingaké to sway s.o. or s.t.

antob a belch; to belch;

ngantobaké to cause s.o. to belch. *See* atob.

antol a supporting brace;

ngantoli to attach a brace to; to brace or support s.t.

antos to wait (*root form: kr for* anti).

antrakusuma *see* antakusuma.

antri to queue up, stand in a line.

antrog *var of* entrog;

kantrog to get shaken up.

antru I 1 tool for prying; 2 equipment for drawing water from a well.

II *reg* a platform hut.

antu *var of* anti.

antuk I *lit* to get, receive.

II *root form: kr for* ulih.

III ngantuk sleepy;

ngantukan always sleepy, sleepy by nature.

antyabasa *gram* a variety of humble Ngoko.

anu 1 representing a pause to collect one's thoughts; 2 substitution for a word that has slipped the mind; 3 expressing vagueness rather than definiteness; 4 *euphemism* sex organ;

nganu 1 to do s.t. naughty to s.o.; 2 *substitution for a word that means doing s.t.*;

anua otherwise, had s.t. happened.

anugraha *see* nugraha.

anuswara *gram* nasal consonant.

anyag 1 nganyag to keep walking without stopping; 2 to walk rudely in front of s.o. without excusing o.s.;

anyag-anyag *or* anyag-onyog *var of* nganyag.

anyam *var of* anam.

anyang I *ng*, awis *kr*, nganyang to bargain for (an item);

anyang-anyang to bargain, haggle;

anyang-anyangan *or* nyang-nyangan haggling over the price (between the seller and the buyer);

panganyang act or way of bargaining. *Also* nyang II.

II anyang-anyangen (to have) dysuria.

III dried out; enjet - dried lime (*see also* enjet).

anyar *ng*, énggal *kr* new, recent; - grès brand new;

nganyari to use s.t. or to do for the first time;

nganyar-anyari strange, unusual;

nganyaraké to make s.t. (or to have s.t. made) like new;

anyaran new (at);

anyar-anyaran 1 new (at); 2 to compare or compete in newness.

anyawar a certain plant.

anyèh *var of* anyih.

anyel annoyed, irritated (at);

nganyelaké annoying, irritating;

anyelan (atèn) easily irritated.

anyep 1 flat, insipid (of food flavour or aroma); 2 cool(er than normal), cold; 3 *fig* apathetic;

nganyep to use no salt on one's food, as a form of self-denial;

anyep-anyepan unsalted food.

anyer, nganyer *var of* nganyur, *see* anyur.

anyes damp and chilly, ice-cold.

anyih, nganyih-anyih finicky, hard to please. *Also* anyèh.

anyir 1 cloyingly rich-tasting; 2 rancid, rank, putrid.

anyleng excessively sweet, cloying.

anyles *var of* **anyes**.

anyur, nganyur to stand (up);

nganyur-anyur *or* **ngonyar-nganyur** to stand in a disrespectful attitude near s.o.

anyut, nganyut to get carried away by the current; - **jiwa** *or* - **tuwuh** *or* - **urip** to commit suicide;

nganyut-anyut melodious and touching the heart;

nganyutaké to cause s.t. to be carried away by the current circumstances.

aoliya religious disciple, holy person.

aor having a bad taste in the mouth.

aos 1 well filled (ear of rice); **2** value (*kr for* **aji**).

apa *ng,* **punapa** (*also pron as:* **menapa**) *kr* **1** what; **2** or; **3** is it the case that…?; **4** that which; **5** whatever; anything; **6** something; **7** *expl pointing out s.t., or holding s.t. up to derision;* - **iya** isn't it true? - **manèh 1** what else?; **2** furthermore; especially; **3** to a much greater degree; - **waé 1** what (sort of) things?; **2** whatever; anything;

apa-apa something; anything; everything;

ngapa 1 to do what?; **2** why?; **3** what? (*var of* **apa**);

ngapakaké to do what to (s.o., s.t);

apaa why on earth?;

apané it's what?

apa-apané everything/anything belonging to or connected with s.t.

apah squeezed out, wrung dry.

apal to know by heart, memorise;

apalan 1 material to be memorised; **2** to learn by rote;

ngapalaké to learn by heart;

diapali to be memorised;

apal-apalan more or less memorised.

apan *lit* for, as.

apé will, to want (*reg var of* **arep**).

apeg *or* **apek** musty, mouldy, sweaty;

gundhulmu apeg bother you! (*see also* **gundhul**).

apem a rice flour cake usually served as a ceremonial food; - **domba** *or* - **dombong** a large rice flour cake;

ngapem to make a rice cake.

apes unlucky; to have bad luck; - **mblebes** (*or* - **pepes**) **1** (to have) extremely bad luck; **2** if the worst comes to the worst;

ngapesaké to cause to be unlucky;

kapesan bad luck, ill-fated;

apesé *or* **apes-apesé** at least;

pangapesan weakness; Achilles heel.

api I steam; **kapal** - steam boat (*see also* **kapal**); **gaman** - firearms (*see also* **gaman**);

api-api to warm o.s. by the fire;

prapèn fireplace, brazier, furnace.

II api-api *or* **apèn-apèn** to pretend, act as if.

III ngapèn-apèni to exert o.s., help s.o. holding a ceremony.

apik *ng* **saé** *kr* good, nice, attractive;

ngapiki to be nice to s.o.;

ngapikaké to make better, improve;

ngapik-apik to fix up, to take care of s.t.;

apikan better than;

apik-apikan *ng,* **saé-saénan** *kr* **1** to compete in beauty; **2** to be nice to each other; **3** something good/nice;

apik kemripik nancang kirik *prov* to look good on the outside but have an evil heart.

apit 11th month of the Islamic calendar, Dulkangidah; **mangsa** - a period during 11th and 12th month of the Javanese calendar (*see also* **mangsa I**);

ngapit 1 to flank; **2** to lay odds of 2-to-1 against;

kapit to be flanked;

apitan odds;

pancuran kapit sendhang *see* **pancuran**;

sendhang kapit pancuran *see* **sendhang**.

aplik, ngaplik tiny (compared with its surroundings).

aplo nothing;

ngaplo to have nothing, produce nothing.

apor *reg* exhausted.

apu *kr* (**enjet** *ng*) slaked lime (for betel chewing).

apuh wrung out, dry (clothing).

apura *ng*, **apunten** *kr* forgiveness;

ngapura to forgive, pardon; **panga-pura** the act of forgiving; **ngapunten** 'excuse me', 'pardon'.

apurancang, ngapurancang (to sit or stand) in a humble attitude, with fingers joined and thumbs touching.

apus I deceit;

ngapusi to deceive/outwit s.o.;

apus-apus deceiving habitually;

apus-apusan fake, swindle;

kapusan to get cheated, taken in;

apus krama *lit* to deceive with smooth talk.

II horse's trapping.

III lame, crippled (in arm or leg).

ara *var of* **hara**.

ara-ara large field, uncultivated grass-land; playing field for sport.

Arab Arab; **bangsa -** Arabian (*see also* **bangsa**); **tulisan -** Arabic characters (*see also* **tulis**); **negara -** Arabia (*see also* **negara**);

ngarabi to have an Arabic style;

ngarabaké 1 to make s.t. in an Arabic way; **2** to translate into Arabic;

arab-araban not a real Arabian/Arabic.

arad *reg* a kind of fishnet;

ngarad 1 to pull, drag; **2** to subject to forced labour;

aradan 1 one forced into labour; **2** forced labour, slavery; **3** victim sacrificed to the spirits.

arag, ngarag 1 to sieve, sift; **2** to sort (sand, gravel);

ngarag-aragi 1 to sort (pebbles, gravel) according to size by screening; **2** to clean weeds and debris after harrowing a rice-field.

arah I 1 direction; **2** plan, aim;

ngarah 1 to aim (toward), reach to/for intend; **- pati** to plan on killing; **2** to aim s.t in a certain direction;

ngarah-arah to attain a certain aim;

ngarahaké to aim, direct, point;

pangarah expectation, aim. *See also* **angkah**.

II arahan *obs* temporary worker; **- prajurit** irregular soldier.

arak I 1 rice wine, alcoholic beverage made of distilled sap; **2** liquor (brandy, whisky, gin *etc*);

ngarak to ferment (of ripe fruits, sticky rice).

II ngarak to take s.o. around in public; **- pengantèn** to form a procession which accompanies the bride and groom publicly;

arak-arakan a parade, procession, review;

pangarak 1 act of parading or forming a procession; **2** people who take part in a procession.

III *or* **harak** *excl inviting agreement or confirmation, var of* **rak I**.

aral obstacle.

aran 1 *ng*, **nama** *or* **nami** *kr*, **asma** *k.i.* personal name; **2** name (what s.t. is); **dadi -** *or* **kari -** dead (*see also* **dadi**, **kari**); **- aran** *gram* noun (*see also* **tembung**);

ngarani *ng* **mastani** *kr*, **1** to call, name; **2** to regard, consider; **3** to accuse;

karan what s.o. or s.t. is called or known as;

aran-aran mockery, ridicule; **dadi - to be a laughing-stock** (*see also* **dadi**);

ngaran-arani to try to accuse s.o.

arang I *ng*, **awis** *kr* **1** (*or* **arang-arang** *ng*,

awis-awis *kr*) scarce, infrequent, rare, seldom; **2** widely spaced; **- kerepé** comparative space, frequency; **- kranjang** very closely spaced, 'even a closely woven basket is more spacious';
ngarang to become less numerous/scarcer;
ngarangi to make/become less numerous/frequent; to space out;
ngarangaké to thin out;
arang wulu kucing *prov* very closely spaced, 'even a cat's fur is more widely spaced'.
II mangarang *lit* sad, pining, languishing.

aras I 1 a kiss (*k.i.* for **ambung**); **2** seat, place to sit, throne; **- kembang** a favourite among one's superiors;
ngaras to kiss (*k.i. for* **ngambung**);
pangarasan cheek (*k.i. for* **pipi**).
II aras-arasen listless, enervated.

arcapada *or* **ngarcapada** *lit* world, earth; **titah** - creatures (*see also* **titah**).

arda *see* **harda**.

ardana *lit* money. *See also* **redana**.

ardacandra 1 *lit* crescent (moon); **2** *way* name of a magic arrow with crescent-shaped point.

ardawalépa *way* ill-bred, failing to follow rules of proper conduct by answering back; impudent, impertinent.

ardawalika name of a dragon-shaped item of regalia.

ardaya heart, mind. (*var of* **wardaya**).

aré 1 *or* **ngaré** valley, lowland; **2** *coll var of* **jaré(né)**.

arèh coconut milk that has been simmered until thick;
ngarèhi to put such milk on s.t.

arèk *reg* **1** child; **2** a native of.

arem, arem-arem 1 s.t. that soothes; **2** name of a food made of rice with mincemeat in it;
marem satisfied, content;
ngarem-aremi to soothe s.o.;

pangarem-arem s.t. that soothes; **sawah** - ricefield turned over to a retired village official as a pension (*see also* **sawah**).

areng charcoal; **- bathok** charcoal made from coconut shell; **- stingkul** *or* **- watu** coal;
ngareng 1 to make charcoal; **2** to become charcoal;
pangareng-areng s.t. used to produce charcoal;
asok glondhong pangareng-areng *way* to offer logs for fuel, *fig* tribute paid to a sovereign power.

arep I *ng*, **badhé** *kr*, **arsa**, **karsa** *k.i.* **ajeng** *md*, to want, intend to; going to, in order to;
arep-arep gambling stakes;
ngarepi 1 to want, covet; **2** *reg* to be willing to pay (a certain price);
ngarepaké to wish, desire;
arepan 1 to want everything one sees, covetous; **2** *reg* to be willing to do (go);
ngarep-arep 1 to expect; **2** to look forward to;
pangarep-arep 1 hope; **2** expectation.
II ngarep 1 in front; **- (m)buri** in front and behind; **2** earlier, before; **3** the coming (time, period); **taun** - next year (*see also* **taun**);
ngarepaké 1 before; to precede; **2** to face (toward), face s.t. toward;
ngarepan 1 the front; **2** front section of a Javanese house, where guests are received;
pangarep *ng*, **pangajeng** *kr*, **pangarsa** *k.i.*, leader, one who presides, chairman;
kasebut ing ngarep mentioned before/above;
arep jamuré emoh watangé to want the advantages but avoid the difficulties.

arès I inner part of banana stalk.
II arès-arèsen *reg* to have a certain disease of the fingernails or toenails.

arga *lit* mountain.

ari I *lit* 1 day; 2 sun.

arian *or* arèn paid by the day; kuli -
day labourer (*see also* kuli).

II *lit* enemy.

III *lit* younger sibling.

IV *reg* if, whenever.

ari-ari, aruman *k.i.* afterbirth.

ariaya *var of* riyaya.

arih I *var of* arèh.

II ngarih-arih 1 to cheer up or comfort
s.o.; 2 to coax, wheedle, persuade;

pangarih woman who assists the bride
during the wedding ceremony;

pangarih-arih comfort, solace;

tan lilih saka pangarih-arih *lit* any
comfort is in vain.

arik, orak-arik a name of food made of
scrambled egg and sautéed vegetables;

ngorak-arik 1 to make such a food;
2 to disarrange, mess up, scratch
around;

morak-marik messed up, in disarray.

aring I having recovered (from, calm); -
napasé recovered one's breath;

ngaringaké to bring about recovery in;
to restore s.o. to calmness;

ngaring-aring to play around happily;

ngaring-aringi to comfort s.o. to stop
them crying;

pangaring wedding attendants;

kakaring to get a breath of fresh air;

pakaringan balcony;

pangaring-aring comfort, solace.

II aring-aring *or* orang-aring a certain
plant the leaves of which produce oil; a
certain plant used as a medicine for
children.

III *or* ring in, at, on (*reg var of* ing).

arip sleepy; - arip s.t. to keep one awake
(*see* tamba);

arip-arip contribution paid by villagers before Mulud ritual ceremony for
buying mats which will be used in the
mosque;

ngaripi *or* ngaripaké to make s.o.
sleepy;

ngarip-aripi *or* ngarip-aripaké causing drowsiness;

karipan 1 sleepy from staying up too
late; 2 to oversleep.

aris I soft and calm, composed, under
control.

II boundary line marked with a rope.

III chairman of village, district head;
mantri - assistant district chief (*see
also* mantri).

IV, arisan social gathering usually held
monthly by neighbourhood wives with
a lottery.

arit I sickle;

ngarit 1 to cut grass with a sickle; 2 to
work by cutting grass;

ngariti *or* ngeriti to cut grass
everywhere;

ngaritaké to cut grass for s.o; to have
s.o. mow grass with a sickle;

aritan act of cutting with a sickle; the
result of cutting with a sickle;

pangarit (one who has a job as)
grasscutter.

II ngarit-arit *or* ngorat-arit 1 to scatter
untidily; 2 to squander;

korat-karit scattered, in disorder;

morat-marit confused, disorganised.

ariwarta daily newspaper.

arka *lit* sun.

aron *coll for* karon (rice which is) half
cooked. *See* karu.

arsa *k.i. for* arep, 1 *lit* to intend to, willing
to, going to; 2 (*or* ngarsa) in front of;

ing ngarsa sung tuladha to set an
example for others.

arsi *lit var of* arsa.

arta money (*kr for* dhuwit).

artaka *lit* 1 treasure; 2 money. *See also*
hartaka.

artati *lit* sugar, sweet. *See also* hartati.

artawan wealthy person.

arti *ng*, artos *md*, meaning, idea conveyed;

pangarti *or* **pangerti** comprehension, grasp. *See also* **ngerti**.

artos *kr for* **arti**.

aruara *or* **ngaruara** to make a big fuss; turmoil, distress, agitation. *See also* **haruhara**.

arubiru 1 to disturb, upset; 2 to interfere in other people's business.

aruh, **aruh-aruh** to speak to in greeting; **ngaruh-aruhi** to greet or speak with in a friendly way.

arum I 1 fragrant, *fig* favourably known; 2 (of sounds, *esp* voices) sweet and pleasant.
II **aruman** *k.i.* afterbirth.

arungan busy, preoccupied (with).

arus rank (of odours, *esp* blood, the riverbank).

arwah soul, spirit, of the departed.

arya title of male nobility.

asab I **ngasab** to smooth s.t. by rubbing, *esp* with sandpaper.
II *or* **angsab** *reg* worthwhile.

asag, **ngasag** to glean, go over a field after the harvest.

asah, **asah-asah** to do the washing-up; **ngasah** 1 to sharpen, whet; 2 to grind; - **pikir** to exercise the power of thinking;
ngasahi to wash (things, *esp* dishes); **ngasahaké** to sharpen for s.o.;
asahan 1 whetstone; 2 having been sharpened; 3 having been washed; **asah-asahan** s.t. used for washing.

asal I (place of) origin, source; - **usul** ancestral origin; - **dunung** place of origin.
II if, provided.

asantun, **tan asantun** *lit* after that, without delay (*var of* **asari**).

asar *or* **ngasar** afternoon prayer (about 4 p.m.); - **dhuwur** prayer time about 3–4 p.m.; - **endhèk** prayer time about 4–5 p.m.;
ngasar to observe the afternoon time

of prayer.

asari *lit*, **tan asari** after that, without delay. *See also* **asantun**.

asas 1 foundation, base, basis; 2 principle; 3 goal, purpose.

asat dried, to become dry;
ngasataké 1 to drain s.t.; 2 to dry s.t. up;
kasatan to have run out of water, *fig* having a scarcity of wealth, broke. *See also* **sat**.

ascarya *lit* amazement. *See also* **kascaryan**.

asé fried transparent bean flour vermicelli mixed with fried potatoes.

asem 1 tamarind; 2 sour, *fig excl* expressing a sour reaction; **gula** - sugar-coated tamarind (eaten in a confection) (*see also* **gula**); **uyah** - salt and tamarind for seasoning fish or for use as a compress (*see also* **uyah**); 3 *term of abuse*: damn it!
ngasem to become sour;
ngasemi to put tamarind into s.t.;
masem 1 sour; 2 unripe; 3 (of clothing) old and faded but still nice-looking.

asèng *reg* to invite s.o. to come along.

asep smoke, steam.

asèp *reg* a belch; to belch. *See also* **atèb**.

asih love, compassion; to feel loving kindness; - **tresna** loving affection;
ngasihi to love;
ngasih-asih to plead for compassion;
mangasih-asih *lit* to flatter, plead for compassion;
kinasih beloved;
kasihan a beloved; **kecubung** - amethyst that can cause s.o. to fall in love (*see also* **kecubung**);
pangasihan a magic formula used for inspiring love (*see also* **aji III**).

asik, **ngosak-asik** to put into disarray, mess up;
mosak-masik in disorder, in a mess.

asil 1 result; 2 product; 3 income;
ngasili income producing;

ngasilaké to produce;

kasil to succeed, produce results;

pangasilan income, earnings. *See also* kasil.

asin 1 salty; 2 prepared by a salting process (of fish, egg *etc*); endhog - salted egg (*see also* endhog); iwak - salted fish (*see also* iwak);

ngasin to treat (foods) by a salting process;

ngasini to make foods saltier; to salt foods too much;

ngasinaké to make s.t. (*e.g.* foods) saltier;

masin in a salting process (of egg, fish);

asinan salted vegetables or fruits, pickles;

pangasinan salting industry, salting-place.

asing 1 foreign; 2 unfamiliar.

asistèn assistant (Wadana, Resident).

aslep to enter, insert (*see also* angslep, mangslep).

asli 1 source, origin; 2 pure, original; 3 native, indigenous, autochthonous; 4 genuine, authentic;

ngaslèkaké to restore the original form (of).

aslup *var of* angslup.

asma personal name (*k.i. for* aran, jeneng);

ngasmani 1 to sign; to write one's name on s.t.; 2 to give a name to s.o.

asmara *lit* romantic love;

kasmaran to be in love, affected by passionate feelings.

asmaradana *or* asmarandana a certain classical verse form.

asmaratura *lit* to fall in love, be infatuated with.

aso *or* ngaso to rest, take a break;

ngasokaké to rest s.t.; to have/let s.o. rest.

asoh *var of* asuh.

asok 1 to pay (tax, tribute *etc*); 2 to pour (into, out);

pasokan supply, money paid (*e.g.* taxes, fines).

See also sok II.

asor 1 low, inferior; 2 contemptible; 3 to lose; - perangé to be defeated in a war; - unggul win or lose;

ngasoraké 1 to defeat; 2 to cause to be inferior; 3 to humble;

kasoran to be defeated;

asor (ing) timbang 1 having the same level with others' knowledge but not in a certain ability.

asrama *or* pasraman *lit* monastery, hermitage.

asreng *lit* stern, harsh; angry, displeased.

asrep cold, cool (*kr for* adhem);

ngasrep to eat only unsalted food as a form of self-denial.

asri beautiful, attractive;

asrèn-asrèn *or* pasrèn decorations.

asring often, many times (*kr for* kerep).

asrog *var of* angsrog.

asru *lit* 1 loud; 2 fast, speedy. *See also* seru.

assalam(u)alaikum peace be upon you (Muslim greeting). *See* salam I.

asta hand (*k.i. for* tangan); - candhala to hit each other cruelly;

ngasta 1 to bring, take, carry (*k.i. for* nggawa); 2 to do, work (*k.i. for* nyambutgawé); 3 to hold, grasp; to handle (*k.i. for* nyekel).

astafirlah may God forgive me! (uttered when one is shocked).

astaga *excl* oh God!

astana 1 *lit* palace, court; 2 burial place of a revered or high-ranking person.

astapirlah *var of* astafirlah.

astha *lit* eight; -brata the eight precepts (for governing).

astra *lit* 1 weapon; 2 arrow.

astu *lit* amen; awignam - may there be no

obstacle (*see also* **awignam**).

asu *ng*, **segawon** *kr* dog; - **ajag** jackal, hunting dog (*see also* **ajag** I); - **belang** 1 spotted dog; 2 mongrel; - **buntung** 1 *term of abuse*, 'tailless dog!'; 2 to control others by virtue of one's wealth or power; - **kikik** a small long-haired dog;

asu arebut balung *prov* to fight over s.t. trivial;

asu belang kalung wang *prov* 1 a nouveau-riche person; 2 an ugly person who is popular for his riches;

asu gedhé menang kerahé *prov* to get the credit earned by one's inferiors;

asu munggah ing papahan *prov* married to an older brother's ex-wife;

rindhik asu digitik quickly, instantly.

asuh *or* **asoh** *var of* **aso**.

asuk *var of* **angsuk**.

asung *var of* **angsung**.

asup *lit* to enter, set (of sun).

asut I **ngasut** to shuffle (of cards).

II **ngasut** to agitate.

aswa *lit* horse;

aswaméda *way* great annual sacrifice made by a king.

asya *lit* 1 to laugh; 2 mouth.

ata *see* **sapi**.

atag, **ngatag** to threaten or pressure s.o. to do s.t.;

atag-atagan 1 to force each other to do s.t.; 2 forced, compelled;

pangatag a threatening suggestion.

atak I **atak-atak** *reg* to start doing s.t.

II **atak-atakan** *reg* election for village head.

III **ngataki** to heap and wrap (coins);

atakan roll of wrapped coins.

IV **atakan** tray (*var of* **tatakan**).

atal yellow ochre used as a cosmetic application for the skin;

ngatali 1 to apply yellow cream to the body; 2 yellow coloured like ochre.

atap I *lit* neatly arranged or conducted;

atap silaning akrami etiquette, precise behaviour, proper social conduct. *See* **tap** I, **atrap**.

II *reg* roof; thatched roof (*var of* **atep**);

ngatapi to put a roof on.

atas I 1 upon; - **angin** foreign country; **atas karsaning Pangéran** because of God's will.

II **ing** (**ng**)**atasé** *or* **saatasé** not to mention the fact that, furthermore.

III **ngatas** 1 to inform one's superior; 2 to go up;

ngatasi to handle, cope with;

atas-atasan to compete for supremacy.

atat parrot-like bird.

atawa *lit* or (*var of* **utawa**).

até *reg* to want (*var of* **arep**).

atèb a belch; to belch (*var of* **atob**, **antob**).

atéla(h) men's short buttoned-up jacket.

atep thatched roof;

ngatep *or* **ngatepi** to put a thatched roof on.

ater to carry; - **pangan** to convey food;

ater-ater 1 *gram* prefix; 2 preface, foreword, introduction; 3 ritual meal sent to neighbours;

ngateri *or* **ngeteri** to bring food to;

ngater-ateri 1 to add a prefix to; 2 to give an introduction to;

ngateraké *or* **ngeteraké** to accompany, take. *See also* **ter**.

atèr 1 quiet, serene; 2 calm and even-tempered (*reg var of* **antèr**).

athèng *var of* **gathèng**.

athi, **athi-athi** locks of hair worn in front of the ears (*esp* women).

athuh *excl expressing a rush of feeling: var of* **adhuh**.

athuk I 1 a match; 2 to get on well together;

mathuk 1 to agree; 2 compatible;

dudu athuké it does not match.

II *coll* preferable;

athuka *coll var of* **anua**; 1 otherwise;

2 supposing that. *See* **luwung**, **aluwung**.

III **athuk-athèng** *reg* to take chances.

athung, athung-athung to raise the hand to attract attention;

ngathung 1 to raise the hand; 2 to hold the hand out asking for s.t.;

ngathungi *or* **ngethungi** to raise the fist or weapon in the hand to threaten s.o.;

ngathungaké 1 to give, hand over to; 2 to raise the hand for receiving s.t.;

kathung-kathung empty-handed.

See also **thung II**.

ati I *ng*, **manah** *kr*, 1 (**pang**)**galih** *k.i.* heart; mind; 2 core, pith;

atèn-atèn 1 character; 2 soft inner pith of a stalk;

aja dadi atimu don't take it to heart;

entèk atiné scared to death;

karepé ati wish, heart's desire;

mantep atiné to be sure of what one wants;

ora dilebokaké ing ati not taken seriously.

II **ati-ati** *or* **ngati-ati** *ng*, **atos-atos** *or* **ngatos-atos** *kr* to be careful, watch out (for);

pangati-ati care, caution.

atis cold, chilly;

katisen to suffer from cold.

See also **tis, tistis**.

atiti *lit* guest.

atma 1 soul, spirit; 2 *lit* child, offspring.

atmaja *lit* child, offspring.

atmaka *lit* child, offspring.

atob a belch; to belch, (*var of* **antob**).

aton, aton-aton *lit* to keep looking (at). *See also* **ton**.

atos I 1 hard, firm; harsh; 2 powerful;

ngatosi 1 to become hard; 2 to make harder (than it was);

ngatosaké to make s.t. hard.

II **atos-atos** *or* **ngatos-atos** careful (*kr* for **ati-ati**).

atrap *lit* to put in place, arrange (*var of* **atap**).

atub lush, luxuriant (of leaves, fruits).

atul well acquainted with.

atur I 1 saying (*k.i. for* **kandha**); 2 advice;

ngaturi 1 to ask s.o. to do (*k.a. for* **akon, ngongkon**); 2 to call (*k.a. for* **ngundang**); 3 to invite (*k.a. for* **ngulemi**); 4 to give (*k.a. for* **mènèhi**); - **uninga** to inform;

paturan 1 written or oral report delivered to a superior; 2 *reg* female servant.

II **ngatur** to organise, arrange, regulate;

aturan 1 regulation, rule; 2 etiquette, manner.

atus I hundred;

atusan 1 hundreds; 2 a currency note or coin with the value of 100; 3 digit occupying the hundreds' place;

satus 100;

nyatus 100 each;

satusan 1 about one hundred; 2 (*or* **nyatusan**) 100 each.

II dried out thoroughly;

ngatus *or* **ngetus** to let dry out, drain, drip dry;

ngatusaké 1 to dry out; 2 to dry out for s.o.

See also **tus II**.

atut peace and harmony (of a married couple); - **runtut** harmonious marriage;

patutan (a child) who is procreated (by...); to have child(ren).

atyanta *lit* exceedingly.

aub shady, sheltered;

ngaub 1 to take shelter; 2 *fig* to be under the protection of;

ngaubi to provide shelter, protect;

pangauban 1 shelter, shade, protection; 2 protector, patron;

ngaub awar-awar to lack authority.

See also **éyub**.

aut *reg* small, narrow.

awa I *var of* **hawa**.

II *lit* light, clear.

III to tease, treat with disrespect.

awad pretense;

awad-awad to pretend, act as if;

awadan *or* pawadan a pretext; to claim that.

awag, ngawag to mention s.t. arbitrarily;

awagan to act randomly or without regard for regulations or propriety.

awak *ng*, badan *kr*, salira, sarira, slira *k.i.* body;

awak-awak 1 main part, main body; 2 to bathe quickly only from the waist up; 3 a representative, substitute;

awakku I;

awakmu you;

awaké he/she, you;

awaké dhéwé we, us;

ngawaki to do by o.s.;

pawakan 1 shape (of the body); 2 figure; 3 nature;

pangawak character, nature; manungsa - déwa a human being of divine nature;

awak-awakan a manufactured body.

awal beginning, initial stage;

ngawal to prance (of horses);

ngawali to begin to do s.t.;

ngawalaké to put forward;

awal-awal a kind of a pancake turner.

awan *ng*, siyang *kr*, 1 the middle part of the day when the sun is at its height: from *ca* 11 a.m. to 4 p.m.; 2 daytime;

kawanen *or* kawanan 1 too late; 2 too early (depending on the reference point);

awan-awan in broad daylight;

awan-awanan late in the day.

awang, ngawang 1 vague, hazy;

awang-awang the sky; (up in) the air;

awangan without recourse to written notation;

awang-awangen 1 to feel dizzy when looking down from a height; 2 to feel unsure.

awang-uwung *lit* the sky.

awar, awar-awar a certain plant, the leaves and roots used for medicinal purposes;

ngaub awar-awar *prov* 'to take shelter under the shrubs'; to seek protection from an ordinary person.

awas 1 able to see, sighted; 2 having sharp eyesight; 3 alert, on the lookout; 4 clairvoyant;

ngawasi to supervise;

ngawasaké to keep a sharp watch on. *See* wawas.

awat, ngawat-awati *or* ngawat-awataké to supervise, keep an eye on.

awé, ngawé to call s.o. by waving;

awé-awé *or* ngawé-awé to wave to s.o.;

pangawé 1 act of waving; 2 holding the hand high above the head;

sapangawé *or* sadedeg sapangawé the height of a standing man's upstretched hand.

awèh 1 to have permission; 2 to give;

- pambagé to welcome; - pangapura to excuse; - salam to send regards; - slamet to congratulate; - urmat to salute; - weruh to convey information;

pawèh gift, thing given.

See wèh I, wèwèh.

awèl, awèl-awèl *reg* to mutter.

awer, awer-awer 1 s.t. used to cover one's nakedness; 2 string used as a fence or border;

ngawer-aweri to use string for fencing or bordering a spot or space.

awèt long-lasting, durable, unchanged over a period of time;

ngawètaké to preserve, stuff;

ngawèt-awèt to make s.t. last a long time.

See also wèt.

awi I 1 let's... ! (*md for* ayo); 2 please help yourself (*md for* mangga). *See also* suwawi.

II *reg* may be (*md for* manawi).

awicarita expert in telling stories.

awig 1 skilful, skilled; **2** skilfully crafted, finely wrought (of handicraft).

awignam astu *lit* may there be no obstacle. *See also* **astu**.

awil, awil-awil *or* **owal-awil** to move loosely or aimlessly.

awin, ngawin to hold (a chicken) tightly by the head and feet preparatory to slaughtering it.

awir *or* **awiran** river flotsam;
ngawir-awir attached loosely so as to move freely. *See also* **kowar-kawir**.

awis I 1 sparse (*kr for* **arang**); **2** expensive, scarce (*kr for* **larang**).
II to bargain (*kr for* **anyang**).
III ngawisi to forbid (*kr for* **nglarang**); **awisan** forbidden (*kr for* **larangan**).
IV awisan arsenic (*kr for* **warangan**).

awit 1 since, beginning from; **2** to start.

awiyat *lit* sky, (up in) the air.

awoh 1 to bear fruit; **2** to have results. *See* **woh**.

awon bad (*kr for* **ala**).

awor mixed, combined, mingled;
kaworan mixed with.
See also **wor, mor**.

awra scattered everywhere.

awrat 1 heavy, weighty (*kr for* **abot**); **2** to hold, accommodate (*kr for* **amot**).

awu I ash; **udan** - a rain of ash (*see also* **udan**); - **blarak** cleansing powder (of burnt coconut frond);
ngawoni to put ashes on;
pawon kitchen.
II family ranking according to the order in which members of preceding generations were born;
ngawu-awu to trace a genealogy.

awud, ngawud to act senselessly;
ngawud-awud 1 to scatter, strew; **2** to waste, squander;
mowad-mawud spread about carelessly.

awug, awug-awug a kind of cake made from cassava, sugar and grated coconut;

ngawug to crumble (soil);
mawug crumbled fine (of soil, preparatory to planting).

awuh *lit* to scream.

awul *var of* **abul**.

awun, awun-awun dew (*var of* **bun**).

awur, ngawur to do s.t. haphazardly or without basis;
mawur 1 loose(ned), not sticking together; **2** scattered;
ngawur-awur to scatter;
ngawur-awuri to sprinkle s.t.; to sprinkle onto;
ngawur-awuraké to sprinkle/scatter s.t.;
awur-awuran 1 randomly; **2** scattered at random.
See also **wur**.

aya (to have) trouble, difficulty;
ngaya to work hard with a lot of difficulties;
ngaya-aya to act enthusiastically; to do with trouble;
éwuh aya ing pambudi to have difficulty attempting, in a dilemma, torn between alternatives.

ayab I a large long-handled fishnet;
ngayab to catch fish with such a net.
II ngayab to escort.
See **ayap**.

ayah I time (*var of* **wayah**).
II *excl of incredulity*: I don't believe it!
III ngayahi to carry out, perform; - **wajib** to carry out a duty;
ayahan community or official task.
IV ngayah *reg* to do senselessly.

ayak I ayaké probably, perhaps, maybe.
II ngayak to strain, screen, sieve;
ayakan sieve.
III ngayaki to call people to work.
IV ayak-ayakan name of a Javanese melody.

ayam I chicken (*kr for* **pitik**); - **alas** woodcock, jungle fowl;

ayam-ayaman 1 waterfowl; 2 a certain grass;

nusup ngayam alas 'to enter the forest as a jungle fowl'; to wander around incognito.

II ngayam-ayam to expect, look forward eagerly to.

III ngayam-ayam to threaten s.o. by pointing a weapon.

IV ngayam-ayam to prance.

ayan epilepsy;

ayanen to have/get epilepsy.

ayang I ayang-ayangan shadow. *See also* **wayang**.

II ngayang to help, aid.

III ayang-oyong *reg* to keep moving around with all one's baggage.

ayap *see* **ayab**.

ayar, ngayar 1 to tear up; 2 to weave a certain grass; 3 to spread s.t. (*e.g.* rice bundles) to dry in the sun.

ayat I a verse of the Quran.

II ngayati 1 to carry out, perform; 2 to bend (a bow) before releasing the arrow; 3 to set to work.

ayeg, mayeg-mayeg *or* **ngayeg-ayeg** 1 unsteady, threatening to topple; 2 extreme, in a high degree (far, high, much).

ayem untroubled, peaceful, comfortable;

ngayem-ayem to relax, make o.self comfortable;

ngayem-ayemi to make s.o. calm;

ngayem-ayemaké to cause to feel happy;

ayeman peaceful by nature;

ayem-ayeman remaining calm.

ayeng, mayeng *or* **mayeng-mayeng** to wander around.

ayer I supervisor, overseer;

ngayer to supervise;

ayeran 1 a community task; 2 security *e.g.* for a loan.

II *see* **anyer, anyur**.

ayid 1 sticky, gluey; 2 rancid, spoiled.

ayo *ng*, **mangga** *kr*, **sumangga** *k.i.* come on, let's, please (invitation to do s.t.);

ayon to make an agreement (to do s.t. bad together).

ayom shady, shaded, protected;

ngayom to seek protection, take shelter;

ngayomi to protect, shade.

ayon to challenge, rebel against;

ngayoni 1 to recheck the weight; 2 to oppose (the enemy).

ayu 1 beautiful, pretty; 2 *or* **hayu** peaceful and prosperous;

ayon-ayon *or* **ayu-ayunan** 1 cosmetics; 2 s.t. used to make up.

ayub, ngayub-ayub to look pale and listless;

ayub-ayuben still half asleep.

ayubagya, mangayubagya to congratulate, offer best wishes;

pangayubagya congratulations, best wishes.

ayuh *or* **ayuk** *coll var of* **ayo**.

ayum, ngayumi to patch, mend.

ayun I swing;

ngayun to swing s.o.;

ayunan *or* **ayun-ayunan** children's swing, baby's swing;

ayun-ayunan to swing (on a swing, hanging tree roots *etc*).

II *lit* to want;

ngayunaké to long for, desire, yearn for;

kayun *lit* a wish, desire.

III front; **ing (ng)-** in front;

mangayun to appear before s.o.;

ayunan presence;

ayun-ayunan facing each other;

pangayunan presence;

marak ing pangayunaning Pangéran to appear before God; deceased.

ayur *see* **anyur**.

ayut, ngayut to tie up into a single bundle.

aywa *lit* do not!

azan *see* **adan I**.

B

bab 1 about, concerning, on (the subject of); **2** subject matter; **3** chapter (of book);
ngebabi to group into chapter headings on;
ngebabaké to explain the cause of a happening.

babad I history, chronicle;
mbabad to record the history of.
II *or* **mbabad** *or* **mbabadi** to clear land by cutting growth;
babadan 1 land where the trees have been felled; cleared land; **2** mown; **3** *reg* inherited land or field.
III *see* **babat**.

babag I the equal of; a match for;
sababag of the same age or quality.
II babagan 1 field, area; **2** landing-place on a river bank.

babah I 1 Indonesian-Chinese male; **2** (*or* **bah**) title, reference term for Indo-Chinese male; - **buyut** *adr* elderly Chinese person; **3** *or* - **njengkelit** *or* - **njungkir** to do a somersault (children's game).
II *or* **babahan** *reg* occasion;
mbabah to make a hole under a wall (of thief);
babahan 1 a hole through the wall foundation; **2** *lit* opening of the body;
nutupi babahan nawa sanga to close the nine body openings, *fig* to restrain all carnal desires.

babak I skinned, bruised, scratched; - **belur**, - **bundhas** *or* - **bunyak** black and blue; skinned and bruised;
mbabak 1 to peel a tree (trunk); **2** *reg* to rub with pieces of bark, to anoint with tree bark oil;
babakan 1 bark, peel; - **kayu** wood shavings.
II (*or* **babakan**) scene from a play or stanza from a song, performed for hire by travelling entertainers;
sababak a part of a play; one scene.
III babakan *reg* a new settlement.

babak-salu a certain large centipede.

babal I (*or* **mbabal**) to get loose, slip out.
II a very young jackfruit.

babar I 1 birth (*k.i. for* **lair**);
mbabar *or* **babaran** to give birth (*k.i. for* **nglairaké**);
babaran birth; to be born (*k.i. for* **lair**).
II to proliferate.
III unfolding; opening out; - **layar** billowing sail;
mbabar 1 to unfold, open out, uncover;
- **wadi** to reveal a secret; **2** to print, distribute (newspaper, book *etc*);
babaring lelakon the unfolding of a life story;
babaran product, output.
IV mbabar to dye batik;
babaran dyeing of batik;
pambabar the way of dyeing batik.

babar pisan altogether, completely;
mbabarpisani to do s.t. all at once;
mbabarpisanaké 1 to do more than one thing at a time; **2** to finish s.t. off completely.

babat I tripe (as food); - **galeng**, - **sumping**, - **tawon** various portions of the animal intestine, producing various forms of tripe.
II wingka babat a cake made from sticky rice flour (*see also* **wingka**).

babi 1 pig; **2** name of one of the small playing-cards (*kertu cilik*);

babèn pig husbandry.

babit, mbabit to swing/slash at;
   mbabitaké to swing s.t.;
   kebabit to get slashed off;
   babitan act of swinging s.t.

bablas 1 gone, vanished; **2** direct, unswerving; **3** accomplished; **4** advanced;
   mbablasaké to send forward, continue, pass on;
   kebablasen to go too far inadvertently.

babo *excl of anger or defiance*; **- majua** oho, come on!

babon I 1 female animal mate; animal that has reproduced, *esp* a hen; mother hen (*see also* **babu**); **- angrem** a certain batik pattern.
   II manuscript; original.
   III capital (to be invested).

babrag I mbabrag (of males) having become mature.
   II babragan rack for storing earthenware.

babrah, mbabrah to expand, increase.

babrak, mbabrak to spread, widen.

babral, mbabral to trim, cut off, prune (plants).

babu 1 female servant to a (foreign) family; **2** *lit* mother; **- Hawa** Eve (mother of mankind).

babud *see* **babut**.

babuh *var of* **babo**.

babuk, mbabuk *reg* **1** to chase (of animals); **2** to butt with the horns.

babut I mbabut *reg* to extract, pull out.
   II carpet, mat.

bacek muddy; boggy;
   kebaceken waterlogged.

bacem *or* **baceman** food partly steamed, then finished by frying; **tahu -** soybean cake cooked as above (*see also* **tahu**);
   mbacem to cook as above.

bacin foul-smelling, rotten; **amis -** s.t. wrong, trouble (*see also* **amis**);
   mbacin-mbacini to cause s.t. to be foul-smelling;

bacin-bacin iwak, ala-ala sanak (*traditional rhyme*) even though he's no good, he's still a relative.

bacira *lit* open field, plain, raised floor.

bacok a jab (with sharp tool);
   bacok-bacok to strike or chop at repeatedly;
   mbacok to strike, slash;
   mbacoki to hit with sharp tool; to slash many objects;
   mbacokaké to use s.t. sharp for hitting;
   bacokan gash; gashing; act of hitting with s.t. sharp;
   bacok-bacokan to hit each other with a sharp weapon.

bacot *cr* mouth;
   mbacot *cr* to speak, talk.

bacuk *reg var of* **bacok**.

bacut 1 *var of* **banjur**; **2** *var of* **bacot**;
   mbacut straight ahead;
   mbacutaké to continue;
   kebacut (now that it's) too late;
   kebacuten to go too far inadvertently.

bada I *var of* **bakda**.
   II bebada (of babies in the womb) to begin to be born.

badal I 1 one who has made the pilgrimage to Mecca; **2** *reg* representative, substitute.
   II mbadal *or* **mbadali** to disregard; **- préntah** to avoid an order.

badalah *excl* boo! hallo!

badan I 1 body (*kr for* **awak**); **- alus** ghost, spirit; **- sepata** all alone in the world; **- wadhag** body, physical embodiment; **bebadan** corporation, agency, executive body, institute.
   II *var of* **bakdan**.

badhar 1 disclosure, revelation; **2** to return to one's original form;
   mbadharaké 1 to cause to fail; **2** to restore magically to one's original form;
   kebadharan to have one's intention discovered; to be caught out.

badhé I 1 will, want (to) (*kr for* **arep**);
2 going to (do) (*kr for* **bakal**);
3 material (*kr for* **bakal**).
mbadhèni *or* mbebadhé to prepare s.t.
for the future; to educate or train s.o.
to become; to work for the first time.
II 1 mbadhé to guess (at) (*var of*
bedhèk); 2 to predict;
binadhé *lit* expected to become.
III badhé-badhé *reg* bridal chair.

badheg 1 smelling bad; 2 to have spoiled;
3 *reg* ill-bred.

badhèg an intoxicating beverage made
from fermented coconut-palm juice
(cassava, rice *etc*).

badhèk *var of* badhé, bedhèk.

badhel, mbadhel underdone (of rice,
cake *etc*).

badhèr a kind of a freshwater fish.

badhigal I cocoon.
II mbadhigal ill-mannered, ill-bred,
strange-acting.

badhigas, badhigasan *or* bedhigasan ill-
mannered, boorish.

badhigul stupid, ignorant; to put on airs.

badhik *reg* dagger.

badhil, bodhal-badhil *reg* frayed, fraying;
pating bradhil *pl* frayed (*see also*
bradhil).

badhog, mbadhog *cr* to eat.

badhol a certain edible freshwater fish.

badhong 1 breastplate (men's dance,
horse); 2 a wing-like ornament between the shoulders (kings in theatre);
3 (*k.i. for* **kewadonan**) female genitals; 4 *reg* a large fish trap; 5 *reg* a
groin to protect a dyke.

badhud *see* badhut.

badhur I a certain tuberous plant.
II badhuren *or* badhur-badhur 1 (of
skin) rough; 2 (of silver coins)
tarnished.

badhut I clown, comedian, joker;
mbadhut to joke, clown around;
mbadhuti to act like a clown;

badhutan 1 joking; 2 to act as a clown;
3 a scene in a play where the clowns
are in action; 4 laughing-stock.
II a certain kind of pliers.

badir to waste s.t. by leaving it (*inf var of*
mubadir).

badra I bebadra 1 to clear jungle for
settling; 2 to begin life again in a new
place;
badran established as a settlement.
II *lit* moon;
kèmengan badra irawan *lit* grieving
like a clouded moon, *fig* very sad.
III *lit* good fortune; (good) luck.

baduwi a nomad; desert-dweller.

baé I (*pron as:* waé) *ng*, kémawon *kr*, 1
only, just (*referring to preceding word*);
2 *emphatic word, e.g.* saiki baé now
(not some other time); 3 *indefinite, with
interrogative word, e.g.* apa baé anything; sapa baé anybody; 4 even, *e.g.*
aku baé ora ngerti even I don't know.
II baèn-baèn (*only ng*) usual; ora - *or*
dudu - not usual;
sebaéné weird, unnatural, extraordinary.

baem I a certain freshwater clam.
II molar (*var of* bam).

baèn *var of* baé.

baga I *lit* 1 womb; 2 vagina.
II share, portion.

bagal ear of corn.

bagas healthy-looking, health; - waras *or*
- kuwarasan healthy, in excellent
physical condition.

bagaskara *lit* sun.

bagaspati *lit* sun.

bagawan *or* begawan holy man, hermit;
mbagawan *or* mbegawan *or* megawan
to live as a hermit.

bagé I mbagé to share, distribute;
mbagèni (*reg* mbagèhi) to give a
portion/part/share;
kebagéan to be alloted (a share, a
part);

bagéan part, portion, share;
  pambagé act of sharing.
  II **mbagèkaké** to greet, welcome;
  bagéa *lit* a greeting; - **sapraptanira** (I)
  welcome (your arrival);
  bagé-binagé to greet each other.
bagèh *var of* **bagé** I.
bagel I a piece of wood;
  mbagel to throw a piece of wood at.
  II unripe (for fruits) (*var of* **magel**).
bagèn *reg* so that; to let s.t. happen (*var
  of* **karebèn**).
bagéndha *title for addressing a king.*
bagi *var of* **bagé**.
bago 1 inner bark of the *so*-tree; 2 sack
  made of *so*-tree bark.
bagol I **mbagol** to deceive people
  habitually.
  II **bagolan** a medicine for stomachache.
Bagong I name of a wayang clown (son
  of Semar).
  II *reg* gold coin attached to a chain of
  a pocket watch *etc.*
  III **bagongan** speech style prescribed
  for use by palace retainers.
bagor 1 woven material made of a certain
  tree bark; 2 sacks made of woven bark.
bagowong total lunar or solar eclipse.
bagrègan broken-down, not in working
  order.
bagya *lit* 1 happy; 2 well-being, happiness;
  kabagyan happiness;
  pambagya *lit var of* **pambagé**.
bah I *adr* Indonesian-Chinese male. *See*
  babah I.
  II *or* **bah-bah** *reg* let (it go)!; I don't
  care!
  III (*pron as:* mbah), **éyang** *k.i.* 1 grandparent; - **kakung** grandfather, - **putri**
  grandmother; - **buyut** great-grandparent; 2 *adr for old person.*
bahak I hawk-like predatory bird.
  II **mbahak** *or* **mbahaki** *or* **mbebahak**
  to take others' possessions arbitrarily;
  bahakan things acquired by looting.

bahan wooden materials for building a
  house, *var of* **abahan**.
bahar *lit* ocean, sea.
bahem *see* **baem**, **bam**.
bahni *lit* fire.
bahu *var of* **bau**.
bain *reg var of* **baé**.
baita boat (*kr for* **prau**).
bajag I pirate;
  mbajag to carry out piracy, plunder;
  bajagan 1 s.t. to be plundered; 2 result
  of plundering.
  II **mbajag** to go forth to fight.
bajang stunted in growth; - **kerèk** a kind
  of grasshopper; **bocah** - a stunted child;
  a child whose hair was never been cut
  (*see also* **bocah**);
  buta - a stunted giant (*see also* **buta**);
  bajangan 1 *var of* **bocah bajang**; 2 *reg*
  young mango;
  mbajangaké to leave uncut (of the
  hair of a last surviving boy in the
  belief that his feminine appearance
  will enable him to survive).
bajeng I **mbajeng** firstborn (*kr for*
  mbarep).
  II **mbajeng** *or* **bajengan** in an orderly
  row, lined up. *See* **banjeng**.
baji I *reg, coll* isn't it!
  II round-headed nail for a tambourine-
  like musical instrument. *See* **bèji** II.
bajigur 1 a certain coconut drink served
  hot; 2 *term of abuse*: damn it!
bajing I squirrel.
  II 1 cotton apron with a tool pocket;
  2 bundle of tied grass for roof
  thatch.
  III **mbajing** to drive an ox-cart.
  IV **mbajing** to rob, to steal;
  bajingan 1 scoundrel, gangster;
  2 thief, crook; 3 *term of abuse.*
bajisan *reg* hostility, enmity.
bajo *lit* pirate.
bajong I **mbajong** to splash water, *esp* by
  stamping in a puddle;

mbajongi to wet s.t. by stamping in a puddle;

bajongan a splash by stamping in a puddle.

II **bajongan** to chip in to buy s.t.

bajra *lit* 1 jewel; 2 5-pointed spear; 3 lightning, thunderbolt.

bajug, mbajug ill-mannered.

bajul crocodile; - **buntung** 1 playboy, womaniser, molester of women; 2 *term of abuse*; - **dharat** 1 woman-chaser, wolf; 2 crook, criminal;

mbajul to chase women, womanise, flirt;

bajul lali marang salirané *prov* to forget one's humble origins.

bak I *or* **baké** *reg* I'll..., let us, come on!

II **ngebak** to dig over, clean up.

III *reg* strip of ground into which a field of sugarcane is divided.

IV 1 trough, watertank; 2 box (seat for coachman); 3 seat (in an **andong**); 4 shelf.

V Chinese ink.

VI (*pron as:* **mbak**) 1 elder sister; 2 *adr* for girl or lady older than o.s.

bakar cooked by roasting;

mbakar 1 to burn; 2 to set on fire; 3 to roast s.t. over coals;

mbakari to burn up;

bakaran 1 roasted, burned; 2 roaster, roasting equipment;

pambakar act of roasting;

kebakaran to get burnt accidentally.

bakaran to play baccarat; baccarat.

bakat strong. *See* **bangkat**.

bakbakan distraught.

bakda 1 after; 2 day of celebration at end of the Fasting Month; 3 ended, finished (of work); - **dheng** the first moment after the Fasting Month signalled by mosque drums; - **mulud** 4th month of the Islamic calendar;

bakdan to celebrate at end of the Fasting Month; to wear new clothing on that day;

sabakdané after.

baken main, essential, basic (*opt kr for* **baku**).

baki serving-tray.

bakmi a Chinese dish made with noodles.

bakmoé a Chinese dish made with rice and beancake.

bakmoi *var of* **bakmoé**.

bako, mbako tobacco (*shtf of* **tembako**).

bakoh *reg var of* **bakuh**.

bakon *see* **baku**.

baku 1 main, essential, basic; 2 ricefield given to a village head instead of salary; - **karang** villager who owns a house and yard but no ricefields; - **kebo** one who carries out his job with his buffalo; - **omah** home owner; - **pajeg** land tax; - **sawah** 1 one who has part ownership of a ricefield; 2 portion of a ricefield subject to tax; **wong** - home owner, permanent resident;

mbakoni 1 to back financially; 2 to be the responsible person behind (s.t.); to supply s.o.'s basic needs;

bakon having the right to own a ricefield in a village;

bakuné basically, normally;

bebaku basis, foundation.

bakuh 1 solid, sturdily built; 2 *reg* determined.

bakul 1 market seller; 2 trader in agricultural products; 3 basket (*reg var of* **wakul**); - **ojogan** itinerant peddler; - **rombèng(an)** old-clothes man, second-hand dealer; - **tikus** peddler unlucky from not having enough capital; - **timpuh** sedentary market seller; - **wadé** batik goods seller; **mbakuli** to buy (goods) from a middleman to sell retail;

mbakulaké to have s.o. sell (goods handled by a middleman) retail;

bakulan 1 *or* **bebakulan** act of selling in the marketplace; **2** to play solitaire.

bakula a certain flower.

bakung a certain flower.

bakwan a cornfritter-like food, made with shrimp added.

bakyak a type of wooden sandal.

bakyu (*pron as:* **mbakyu**) **1** elder sister; **2** *adr* for girl or lady older than o.s.

bal I 1 ball;- **blèter** a soccer ball; **2** light bulb;

bal-balan (to play) soccer; a soccer game or match.

II roll, bolt (of fabric); bale (of tobacco *etc*);

ngebali to pack in bolts/bales;

balbalan in the form of bolts/bales.

III railway warning signal.

bala I 1 army, troops; **2** team-mate; one on the same side; **-koswa** *lit* army, troops; **-pecah** breakable things: crockery, dishes and glasses; **-srèwu** *way* magical power to transform o.s. into a huge giant with a thousand heads;

mbala to take sides with.

II name of the 25th **wuku**.

balabag *lit* **1** board; **2** one who is responsible for s.t. *See* **blabag**.

balabak name of a metre and melody of a classical song (*tembang tengahan*).

balabar, mbalabar *lit* to overflow. *See* **blabar II**.

Baladéwa elder brother of Kresna;

Baladéwa ilang gapité 'B. has lost his clamp'; to lose one's power or authority; totally powerless.

balak I (of fruit) to fall from the tree before ripening;

mbalak to cancel, avoid, reject, send s.o. back.

II a domino with an equal number of dots.

balang thrown;

mbalang to throw; **- tingal** *or* **- liring** to cast a glance, flirt;

mbalangi to throw to/at;

mbalangaké to throw s.t.;

balangan 1 the act of throwing; **2** part of wedding ceremonies in which small bunches of betel leaves held by bride and groom are thrown to each other at the moment they meet: whoever throws first will be the dominant partner;

balang-balangan to throw to each other;

bebalang *lit* messenger;

pambalang 1 the act of throwing; **2** a measure of distance;

sapambalang a stone's throw.

balap racing; **montor -** racing car;

mbalap to speed;

mbalapaké to make s.t. go fast;

balapan a race, a racecourse; to race.

balas a weight for holding or steadying s.t.; ballast.

balé 1 hall, public building; **- désa** village administration building; **- kambang** an artificial island with a pavilion (reached by a bridge or walkway) in the centre of a pool surrounded by gardens; **2** front hall of a residence, used for entertaining; **- agung** a large front hall; **- sigala-gala** fire-trap, house like a tinder box (referring to a wayang episode in which the Pandhawas were to be burned alive in a house of lac).

balèg 1 to become an adult (*see* **akil**); **2** to have become accustomed, to know best;

mbalèg mature.

balèk *reg var of* **balik**.

baléla rebellion;

mbaléla to resist authority, rebel.

bales I *reg* steamroller.

II **mbales, mbalesi** to answer (a letter).

III ballast (*var of* **balas**).

IV *var of* **wales**.

bali *ng*, wangsul *kr* 1 to return, come back; 2 to be or go home;
mbalèni 1 to repeat, do over; 2 to return to (a subject);
mbalèkaké 1 to return s.t.; 2 to refuse to accept;
balèn 1 a ride home/back; 2 to remarry (a divorced spouse);
bola-bali *ng*, wongsal-wangsul *kr* 1 to move back and forth; 2 to do again and again; mbolan-mbalèni to do over and over.

balig *see* akil, balèg.

balik 1 on the contrary, on the other hand, the other way around; 2 *var of* bali; mbalik 1 to turn over or upside down, flip over; to turn around; 2 to change, take a different course; 3 to turn back; 4 to reflect (of rays);
bolak-balik *var of* bola-bali;
mbolak-mbalik to keep turning, keep returning.
See also walik.

balila *var of* baléla.

baliswara a technique of composition in classical poetry, whereby words are placed in reverse order for metrical purposes.

balok 1 log, beam; 2 pieces of fried cassava.

balon I 1 balloon (child's toy; aerial conveyance); 2 light bulb.
II *reg* prostitute.

balong 1 a pool for keeping fish; 2 a depression in the ground which is flooded.

balowarti *var of* baluwarti.

balsem balm, ointment.

baluh 1 weight used to submerge a fishnet; 2 fishing-tackle;
mbaluhi 1 to weight s.t. down; 2 *or* mbebaluhi to band together with s.o. in stirring up trouble.

baluk I *reg* market seller (*var of* bakul).
II mbaluk 1 *reg* to return (*var of* mbalik); 2 *or* mbaluki *reg* to turn over (*var of* malik *or* maliki).

balunan *or* balonan *reg* shifty, unreliable.

balung *ng*, tosan *kr*, *k.i.* bone; - nom cartilage; - pakèl mango stone; - sungsum bone with marrow; - tinumpuk double wedding; - tuwa old, aged; - wesi very strong;
mbalung resembling bone(s); - sungsum 1 to be second nature; 2 to be thoroughly inculcated; - usus to waver in one's determination or devotion to ideals;
balungan frame; skeleton; - gendhing basic melody; - omah (wooden) house frame; - lakon outline of the story;
bebalung bones, skeleton (*lit var of* balung);
bebalungan *lit var of* balungan;
ngumpulaké balung pisah *prov* 'to collect the scattered bones'; to join two relatives in marriage (thus making family ties closer);
nututi balung wis tiba *prov* 'to catch the fallen bone'; to correct a wrong utterance that has been pronounced;
rebut balung tanpa isi *prov* 'to struggle for possession of an empty bone'; to struggle to obtain s.t. trivial.

balur I a certain freshwater fish, sold dried and salted.
II *var of* belur.

baluwarti brick wall surrounding a palace.

bam molar; - wekas(an) wisdom tooth.

bamban to repeat from the beginning.

bambang I *way* a young knight; son of a holy man;
bambangan *way* figures of fine young knights;
mbambang 1 resembling a young knight; 2 (having) a slender body (of men).
II a disease of rice plants.

bambet bamboo (*md for* bambu, pring).

bambing or **bambingan** steep riverbank or mountainside;
  mbambing 1 in a precarious position; **2** slanting, sloping (of boats, road on a mountainside).

bambon 1 opium den; **2** room in the inner part of a Javanese-style house.

bambu *ng*, **bambet** *md*, bamboo.

bambung, mbambung unwilling to conform to proper standards of behaviour;
  bambungan or **mbambungan** characterised by such behaviour.

ban 1 tyre; **2** sash, fabric belt; **3** track; - **sepur** railway track.

bana I *reg* it does not/cannot exist.
  II *reg* open area.
  III bebana *lit* demand, requirement;
  mbebana or **mbebanani** to request, demand.

banar bright(ly lit);
  banaran open and bright place.

banarawa marsh, swamp; **sawah** - lowlying ricefield that becomes a swamp during the rainy season.

banaspati *way* fire demon.

banat a kind of fishnet;
  banatan sling.

banawa *lit* boat.

banawasa *lit* jungle, forest. *See also* **wana, wanawasa.**

banawi or **benawi** *lit* river.

bancak I woven bamboo food container for a cone of rice and other dishes;
  mbancaki to hold a ritual marking a special event in a child's life;
  bancakan a ritual held to mark a special event in a child's life.
  II name of a clown-servant in a Panji story.

bancana *lit* obstacle, hazard.

bancang (to do) concurrent jobs; - **telu** to hold three jobs concurrently;
  mbancang to tie s.t. to two or more objects.

bancar copious and free-flowing.

bancèr, mbancèr *reg* (to go) dancing with a female dancer.

bancèt a certain small tree frog.

banci I 1 an effeminate man; **2** an asexual person;
  kebancèn (of garment) too small or short.
  II a plant the leaves of which are used in folk medicines.

bancik I base; a bench used as a base. *See also* **ancik.**
  II mbancik in trance.

bancot *cr* mouth (*var of* **bacot**).

banda I cord for tying s.o.'s hands;
  mbanda to tie s.o.'s hands, usually behind the back;
  bandan 1 or **bebandan** with hands tied, *fig* to be caught; under arrest; **2** a show where the performer is tied tightly and releases himself with his magic power.
  II *lit* body.

bandakala, mbandakalani *lit* dangerous; to oppose bravely.

bandar I harbour, port.
  II person acting as banker at the gambling table; croupier.

bandara *see* **bendara.**

bandawala a duel; - **pati** a duel to the death.

bandawasa *lit* strength.

bandayuda *lit* to fight hand-to-hand.

bandel I 1 (of children) brave, not prone to crying; **2** (of children) undisciplined, disobedient; **3** obstinate, stubborn.
  II bird used as live bait.

bandeng an edible fish that is born in the sea and later migrates to rivers; kind of milk-fish.

bandha 1 wealth, fortune, property; **2** capital investment; - **abab** to engage in business with only talk as capital - **bandhu** to have a wealth of relatives as well as money; - **bau** all brawn and no brains; - **béya** expenses;

mbandha wealthy;

mbandhani 1 to finance s.t.;

bandhan 1 to contribute money to a cause; **2** contribution to a cause.

bandhang I basket for carrying sugar-cane seedlings.

II banjir - flash flood;

mbandhang to bolt (horse);

mbandhangaké to make s.t. go fast;

bandhangan 1 to do things fast; **2** carried off from where it belongs.

bandhel stubborn, wilful, obstinate (*var of* **bandel**);

mbandhel to act defiantly, obstinate.

bandhem missile, object hurled;

mbandhem to throw at, hurl (missile) at.

bandhil sling for hurling missiles;

mbandhil to shoot (at) with a sling;

mbandhilaké to hurl (missiles) at.

bandhing, mbandhing to compare;

mbandhingaké to compare s.t. with;

bandhingan comparison;

pambandhing standard of comparison.

bandhol 1 impolite, insolent; **2** (of horses) wild, untamed; **3** bandit chief; **4** *reg* irresponsible, joker;

mbandhol to behave like a bandit chief; to act insolently;

bandhol ngrompol a gathering of criminals.

bandhosa a covered wooden or bamboo bier.

bandhot 1 ram, male sheep or goat; **2** lascivious old man; **3** womaniser, ladies' man;

bandhotan a certain snake.

bandhu relatives. *See also* **bandha**.

bandhul 1 iron ball used as a weight; **2** hanger;

mbandhuli to weigh s.t. down; to attach a weight to s.t.;

bandhulan *or* **bandulan 1** children's swing; **2** a swinging baby bed.

bandrèk I skeleton key, master key;

mbandrèk to open with a skeleton key. **II** adultery.

bandreng, mbandreng *or* **bandrengan** *reg* to work assiduously (at).

bandring *reg* sling for hurling missiles (*var of* **bandhil**).

bandul, mbandul to swing;

bandulan children's swing (*var of* **bandhulan**).

bané *var of* **banèn**.

banèh different (*var of* **bènèh**).

banèk *var of* **banèn**.

banèn sound, voice.

bang I red (*shtf of* **abang**); **bangjo** traffic light (*shtf of* **abang ijo**);

bangbang wétan sunrise (when the sky looks red);

bang-bangan batik with predominantly red colouration.

II region; - **wétan** eastern region.

III bank;

ngebangaké 1 to put money in the bank; **2** to put up s.t. as security for the bank.

IV mbang (*shtf of* **kembang**); - **mlathi** jasmine.

V bangbang alum-alum *way* backbone of the state/country.

bangah a certain plant with a bad smell.

bangbang I disease of rice plants (*var of* **bambang II**).

II bangbang alum-alum *see* **bang**.

banger fetid.

banget *ng*, **sanget** *kr* **1** very, very much, extremely; **2** serious, intense; **3** emphatic;

mbangeti excessive;

mbangetaké 1 to make s.t. worse; **2** to intensify;

kebangeten excessively, terribly, overly.

bangga 1 to resist (*e.g.* the police); disobey; **2** to refuse.

banggal 1 very hard (of roasted food, swollen skin *etc*); **2** stump of tobacco plant; **3** object thrown;

mbanggal to throw s.t. at.

banggel, mbanggel undercooked, raw inside.

banggèl, mbanggèl 1 to snap at (as though to bite); **2** to give a rebuttal (in debating);
mbanggèlaké to have s.o. sell (merchandise, usually fabrics) on commission. *See* **bangkèl**.

banggèn I shared, common cowstall.
II mbanggèni *or* **bebanggèn** *reg* to accompany music by singing.

banggi I *reg* to resist (*kr for* **bangga**).
II *reg* cost, charge (*kr for* **béya**).
III *shtf of* **ubanggi**, promise, commitment (*kr for* **ubaya**).
IV (good) luck (*kr for* **bara**);
pinten banggi luckily (*kr for* **pirabara** *or* **pirangbara**).

bangir, mbangir long and tapering (the finest nose shape);
mbangiri to make (the nose) pointed;
mbangiraké to make (the nose) more tapered.

bangka 1 hard (of unriped fruit); **2** coarse; **klasa -** a hard (in texture) mat; **3** *cr* dead; **4** *or* **bangkan** hard (of soil).

bangkak 1 hard (of body, soil, lump, cake); **2** crop disease.

bangkal, mbangkal *reg* to say in disagreeent, object.

bangkang I a certain hard-shelled snail.
II mbangkang to disobey, resist.
III mbangkang to renew the colour of batik cloth.

bangkar 1 unfinished work; **2** unslaughtered dead cattle.

bangkat *reg* strong;
mbangkat *or* **kebangkat** strong enough to do s.t.

bangké *cr* corpse, carcass (of animals).

bangkèk, mbangkèk narrow at the midsection, small waist;
bangkèkan *ng*, **pamekak** *k.i.* waist-(line).

bangkèl I *reg* quarrelsome person.
II mbangkèl 1 to pack fabrics to be sent; **2** to buy (up) for resale;
mbangkèlaké *or* **mbanggèlaké** to sell on commission, sell to middleman;
bangkèlan 1 (merchandise) sold on commission; **2** one who sells fabrics on commission; **3** trade by selling on commission.

bangkit *lit* can, to be able.

bangkok *or* **bangkokan** large and old (of animals; *cr* of people).

bangkol *or* **bangkolan** a wooden peg fitted onto a shoulder carrying pole to prevent the rope that holds the burden from slipping.

bangkong *or* **bangkongan** large old frog;
mbangkong 1 resembling a large old frog; **2** to sleep too late in the morning; to get up quite late.

bangkrah 1 damaged, broken, wrecked; **2** decayed (because of suffering disease).

bangkrèh, bongkrah-bangkrèh *or* **bungkrah-bangkrèh** in disorder, strewn with scattered items.

bangkrong, mbangkrong *or* **mbangkrung** bent, curved (of the human or horse's back).

bangkrung *var of* **bangkrong**.

bangkrut bankrupt;
mbangkrutaké to liquidate (a business).

bangku I short-legged bench or table; low bench used as a seat; **- dhépok** short-legged (square or round) table used for playing cards.
II *or* **bangkon 1** having the right to possess a ricefield of the village; **2** ricefield given to officials instead of salary.

bangkyak var of **bakiyak**.

bango I a variety of stork; **- thonthong** a certain large stork with a long beak; **- buthak** an old such stork.
II small roadside shop dealing in goods or refreshments.

bangsa 1 (member of a) nationality; ethnic group; nation; **2** (member of a) category, class;
- **seger-segeran** kinds of refreshments; - **mas inten** sorts of jewelry.

bangsal large assembly hall; - **pangrawit** a finely carved palace hall.

bangsat 1 crook, outlaw; **2** *term of abuse*.

bangsawan aristocrat.

bangsul *reg* to return (*var of* **wangsul**).

bangun I *lit* to wake up, get up; - **ésuk** *ng*, - **énjing** *kr*, dawn, daybreak, crack of dawn;
mbangun 1 to build up; **2** to perform; - **tapa** to seclude o.s. for meditation; - **tresna** to be in love with each other; - **turut** to obey; - **alin-alin** *lit* to worry about s.o.; - **ni(ng)kah** to hold a second wedding ceremony as a necessity for having a child; - **wecana** to make a follow-up accusation.

banjar row, rank; - **pakarangan** house and yard;
mbanjari to plant in rows;
banjaran 1 in rows (trees, plants, houses); **2** row.

banjel 1 replacement, assistance (for another worker); **2** substitute (for usual food during shortage);
mbanjel to step in and help;
mbanjeli to provide s.o. with assistance.

banjeng a long row, line (people or houses);
mbanjeng, (be)banjengan to form an unbroken line.

banjir 1 flood; **2** to be in flood;
mbanjiri 1 to flood (land); **2** to provide an abundance;
kabanjiran to get flooded;
banjiran to be under water, flooded.

banjur *ng*, **lajeng** *kr* then, after that;
kebanjur to go too far, further than intended;
mbanjuraké to continue, go on with s.t.;

sabanjuré 1 after that, subsequently; **2** and so forth.

banjut I *coll var of* **banjur**.
II *lit* **mbanjut** to take away (and make disappear); - **nyawa** to take life away, *i.e.* cause to die.

banor *reg* having defective vision.

bantah *or* **bantahan** to debate, quarrel, dispute, argue over;
mbantah *or* **mbantahi** to argue (over), oppose, refute;
bantah-bantahan *or* **bebantahan** to argue/debate/dispute with each other.

bantal pillow; - **dawa** Dutch wife, bolster (*see also* **guling I**);
mbantali to equip s.t. with a pillow;
bantalan 1 to use a pillow; to use s.t. as a pillow; **2** railway sleeper; **3** pincushion; **4** (*or* **bantal susun**) dam in a sugarcane field.

bantala *lit* earth, ground.

bantas 1 loud and clear (of gunshot, fireworks); **2** high quality (of woven cloth).

bantat swollen and hard (of pimple, boil); partially cooked (of bread, cake *etc*).

banten *or* **bebanten** *lit* offering, human sacrifice, *esp* in war.

banter 1 fast; **2** hard; **3** loud;
mbanteraké 1 to make faster; **2** to make harder; **3** to make louder.

banting, mbanting to throw down forcefully, hurl, fling down;
mbantingi to throw down repeatedly;
kebanting 1 to get hurled; **2** at odds with;
bantingan 1 s.t. to be flung; **2** energetic.

bantu 1 help, assistance; **guru** - elementary-school teacher; **2** auxiliary troops, reinforcements;
mbantu 1 to help, aid, assist; **2** to back up, support;
mbantoni to help s.o.;
mbantokaké to have s.o. help;

bebantu *or* **bebanton** help, aid, assistance;

bantuan help, aid, assistance;

bantu-binantu to help each other;

pambantu 1 help, aid, assistance; 2 helper, assistant.

banyak goose, swan; - **angrem** 1 a certain nebulous spot near the Southern Cross; 2 heaped-up rice with an egg inside (for ritual meal); - **dhalang** item of regalia in the shape of a goose, carried in court ceremonial; - **patra** a certain wild bird resembling a duck or goose;

mbanyaki *cr* to act hastily and ineffectually;

banyakan *or* **bebanyakan** breakers, white horses (in the sea).

banyar a herring-like fish.

banyol joke; **juru** - joker (*see also* **juru**); **mbanyol** to joke around;

banyolan 1 to make jokes, clown around; 2 a joke.

banyu *ng*, **toya** *kr*, 1 water, fluid; - **bening** *fig* 1 spiritual knowledge; 2 medicine, spiritual guide; - **daging** meat broth; - **gégé** water for bathing a baby to make it grow faster; - **godhogan** *or* - **mateng** boiled drinking water; - **kawah** forewater, amniotic fluid; - **keras** spirits; - **landa** soda water; - **landha** lye, water in which burnt rice stalks have been soaked (used as shampoo); - **ledheng** tap water; - **leri** water in which rice has been washed prior to cooking; - **mas** gilding fluid used in embroidery; - **panguripan** water having the power to revive the dead; - **pinerang** inseparable: *fig e.g.* brothers who often quarrel with each other but finally get along well again; - **rasa** quicksilver, mercury; - **susu** mother's milk; - **tangi** warm water for bathing children and invalids; - **tawa(r)** fresh water; - **tumètès** sound effect produced by the puppeteer tapping with slow steady beats on the puppetbox; - **wantah** (unboiled) fresh water; - **wayu** water that has been kept overnight; - **windu** water kept for several days used for a ritual bath; - **wisuh(an)**; - **wijikan** *k.i.* water in finger bowls placed on the dining table; - **wulu** water for washing face, hands and feet ritually before praying;

mbanyu 1 resembling water; to liquefy, melt; 2 to bath, wash down; 3 aqueous;

mbanyoni 1 to supply with water; 2 to break, of the waters (before giving birth);

banyon 1 a mouthwash for blackening the teeth; 2 the bathing of a fighting cock; 3 the number of times a fighting cock is bathed;

bebanyu *ng*, **tetoyan** *kr*, to urinate;

banyunen to have diarrhoea;

mbanyuwara to avoid touching water as an ascetic practice;

caruk banyu to estimate s.o.'s treasures all in all;

dadia banyu suthik nyawuk (of relationship) completely broken;

dom sumurup ing banyu *prov* (to be) in disguise in order to investigate s.t.;

kaedus banyu sasiwur 'to be bathed with one scoop of water'; to get a very small share;

kaya banyu karo lenga 'like water and oil'; to be hostile to each other, unable to get along well with each other;

kena iwaké aja nganti buthek banyuné *prov* to take a problem in hand very carefully; to gain a goal without any conflict;

lebak (ledhok) ilining banyu *prov* the underlings are always blamed for any affair;

ngangsu banyu ing kranjang *prov* 'to draw water with a basket'; wasted effort; to do s.t. futile, in vain (*see also* **angsu**);

ngangsu banyu apikulan warih *fig* to possess basic knowledge before studying s.t. difficult;

nggarap banyu to have a menstrual period;

ngubak-ubak banyu bening *prov* 'to stir up clean water'; to cause quite a stir;

sedulur tunggal banyu *prov* a pupil of the same teacher (regarded as a brother);

suwé banyu sinaring *prov* to do s.t. easily.

bapa father; - babu revered ancestor(s); - biyung parents; - paman uncle (parent's younger sibling); Bapa, Putra lan Roh Suci Father, Son and Holy Ghost (*see also* bapak);

mbapa to call s.o. father; to regard s.o. as a father;

kebapan resembling one's father in nature;

anak molah bapa kepradhah *prov* the father in trouble because of the conduct of his son.

bapak *ng, kr,* rama *k.i.* father; 2 *adr, title* older and/or higher-ranking male; - angkat foster father; - cilik uncle (parent's younger sibling) (*see also* paklik); - gedhé uncle (parent's older sibling) (*see also* pakdhé); - kuwalon stepfather; - pocung a tiny red beetle;

mbapak to call s.o. father; to regard s.o. as a father;

bapak(n)é *adr* husband (if the couple have children);

bapak(n)é gendhuk/tholé my husband (oblique reference term);

bapaké (bo)cah-(bo)cah *ng,* bapa-kipun laré-laré *kr,* my husband.

bapang 1 signpost, signboard; 2 a certain classical dance performed by males; 3 obstacle;

mbapang to stretch arms sideways;

bapangan winged kite.

bapem a small round metal badge, formerly used by village officials.

baptis baptism;

mbaptis to baptise;

baptisan ceremony of baptising, baptism.

bapuh *reg* solid, sturdily built (*var of* bakuh).

bar *shtf of* bubar; 1 after; 2 finished, over;

ngebaraké to finish;

bar-baran completely finished;

barji barbèh (*shtf of* bubar siji bubar kabèh) if one quits we all quit;

ora bar-bar to keep on doing.

bara I fringe hanging on either side of the belt buckle;

mbara to attach a fringe to.

II mbebara to travel around in search of a livelihood;

mbara gawé *ng,* mbara damel *kr,* holding a feast (*e.g.* wedding ceremony *etc*).

III (banggi *kr*) (good) luck.

IV a hundred million.

V a certain type of fishing gear;

pirangbara happily and unexpectedly;

pecruk tunggu bara *prov* to be entrusted with s.t. of which one is very fond.

bara-bara I ornamental fringe hanging on a belt worn by classical dancers.

II *reg* do not expect even that much (s.t. less is likely).

barah leprosy.

barak I age (group);

barakan a contemporary;

sabarakan of the same age group.

II 1 temporary quarters for large numbers of people; 2 a house where ill people are quarantined.

mbarak to quarantine (people).

III mbarak to stand in a line/row;

barak-barak in array, lined up.

barang I 1 thing, goods, stuff; 2 article, object, ware; - dagangan merchandise; - larangan prohibited objects; 3 matter; 4 baggage, goods.

II 1 basic gamelan scale; **2** certain notes of the 5 (sléndro) and 7 (pélog) note scale; **- miring** gamelan scale, combining the 5 and 7 note scales; **- gedhé** gamelan octave.

III mbarang to perform publicly for a living; **- amuk** to go on the rampage; **- gawé** to hold a party, *usu* to celebrate a wedding or circumcision; (*or* **mbebarang**) **wirang** *fig* to make a show of being embarrassed;

barangan entertainment performed by travelling players.

IV and things like that, and all that; **ora barang**... or anything; **ora barang-barang** it's nothing.

V sabarang, sabarangan anyone, anything (see also **sembarangan**).

barat I strong west wind occurring *usu* during the rainy season.

II baratan *reg* common property (of village ricefields).

barbèh *see* **bar**.

barèh I borah-barèh in disorder, disarranged, scattered.

II mbarèhi *reg* to become more serious (of disease, pain).

III barèhan friend about the same age. *See also* **barakan I**.

barèk 1 *reg* (together) with; **2** while. *See also* **bari**.

bareng 1 together; **2** when, as soon as; **3** whereas, while;

mbarengi 1 to accompany. **2** to coincide with;

mbarengaké 1 to cause s.t. or allow s.o. to accompany; **2** to cause s.t. to coincide with;

barengan 1 *or* **bareng-bareng** *or* **bebarengan** together (with); **2** a companion;

kebarengan to come together unintentionally.

barèng *reg* a small gong (*var of* **bendhé**).

barep, mbarep *or* **pambarep** *ng*, **mbajeng** *or* **pambajeng** *kr*, **pambayun** *k.i.* first-born child, oldest child; **- urip** oldest living child.

barès 1 simple, plain, unaffected; **2** straightforward, without airs or embellishments;

- kurès plain and honest; (to say) straightforwardly;

mbarèsi to tell s.t. plainly.

bari *or* **mbari** *var of* **barèk**;

barinan *reg var of* **barengan**.

baribin *lit* assault on the ears (*var of* **bribin**).

barih, mbarihi to change for the worse (of disease, pain). *See also* **barèh II**.

barik *var of* **barèk**.

baring *reg* **1** a fool; **2** rude.

baris I 1 to march; **2** marching people or soldiers; **- pendhem** (to make) a secret march; **- baris** *see* **pacak**;

mbarisi to guard with a line of marchers;

mbarisaké to have (people) line up;

barisan ranks, line of marchers, brigade, troops.

II rooster feather from the neck or tail.

III package to be carried by hand.

barji *see* **bar**.

barkah *or* **berkah** blessing, good wishes, prayers.

barkat *var of* **berkat**.

barkas, barkasan wrapped bundle. *See* **berkas**.

barlèn 'Berlin silver', white metal, pewter.

barléyan 1 diamond; **2** a variety of timber of good quality.

barlin *var of* **barlèn**.

barliyan *var of* **barléyan**.

baro, baro-baro a white rice porridge with coconut sugar and grated coconut in the middle, served at ceremonies.

baron *see* **baru**.

barong 1 name; **2** tassel, fringe; **3** a giant-king character type;

barongan 1 thorny bushes growing

around bamboo stalks; **2** a show featuring a man dressed as a monster; the performer in such a show; **3** fringed; having tassels; **4** having a mane;

barong asépak 1 a certain batik design; **2** figure painted on a saddle flap;

parang barong batik design reserved for the royal family's garments (*see also* **parang III**;

singa barong 1 male lion; **2** man in a street show dressed as a monster with the head of a lion (*see also* **singa**);

yuyu rumpung mbarong rongé *see* **yuyu.**

baros a variety of large tree.

baru new;

mbaroni to plant (a field) with a new or unusual type of rice;

baron young plant (*esp* coffee).

barubah *lit* **1** to move; **2** dizzy, headachy, groggy. *See also* **brubah.**

barud *see* **barut.**

baruna the God of the Sea.

barung 1 *lit* together; to accompany; in time with or simultaneous with (a gamelan beat);

mbarung to do s.t. in time with; - **sinang** (two events) occurring at the same time;

mbarungi 1 to accompany; **2** to disturb, bother;

binarung to be accompanied.

barus, mbarus *or* **mbarusan** *reg* **1** straight away; **2** just now;

kapur barus *see* **kapur.**

barut a cut, scratch;

mbarut to scratch;

kebarut-barut to be scratched.

bas I leaf stalk from a certain palm tree, used for making rope.

II *shtf of* **tebas** to buy up the entire stock; - **mentah** money received as a substitute for meal that must be consumed;

bas-basan 1 contracted job; **2** a certain children's game played by moving pieces on a diagram of squares.

basa I 1 language, speech; - **antya** a variety of humble Ngoko (*see also* **antya**); - **bagongan** speech style used by palace retainers; - **gancaran** prose; - **kedhaton** speech style used by the king and court officials during a ceremonial court meeting; - **lésan** oral language; - **paguneman** colloquial speech; - **pedinan** everyday speech; - **(pe)pernèsan** flirtatious expressions for flattering a person of the opposite sex; - **rinengga** stereotype literary expression; **2** (to speak) Krama; **3** to have (a certain) kin relationship;

mbasani to speak Krama to s.o.;

mbasakaké 1 to put (translate) into Krama; **2** to express in the form of a saying; **3** to use the words the listener would use on s.o.'s behalf;

basan-basanan *or* **basan-binasan** to speak Krama to each other;

bebasan a saying, set expression.

II basan, mbasan *reg* when, whenever.

III *reg* only, just, because of.

basang *var of* **basan II.**

basèh *var of* **basik.**

baseng to have a rotten or putrid odour.

basi large glazed earthenware dish for serving food.

basih *var of* **basik.**

basik, bosak-basik disorderly.

basin a foul odour.

baskara *lit* sun, name of the Sun God.

baskom washbasin.

basmi *or* **besmi** to burn (*root form: kr of* **obong**).

basuh *var of* **wasuh.**

basuki I to prosper, flourish.

II name of the dragon-shaped Ocean God.

bata *ng*, **banon**, *kr*, **1** brick, brick wall; **2** cube, brick-shaped block; - **bumi**

brick wall; - **luluh** bricks being processed;

mbata brick-shaped, brick-like;

mbata rubuh 'like falling bricks'; thunderous (applause);

mantu mbata rubuh to celebrate a wedding ceremony on a large scale;

mbata sarimbag squarish (of handwritten Javanese script);

batan 1 in the shape of a brick or block; 2 built with bricks.

batal invalid;

mbatalaké to cancel, render invalid.

batang I mbatang to guess (the answer) to;

batangan 1 the answer to a riddle, the meaning of a dream; 2 a certain pattern of drumbeats.

II to beat a certain drum (**kendhang**).

batèh *reg var of* **batih**.

batek, mbatek 1 to pull (at), tug (on); 2 eager.

bates *var of* **wates**.

bathang 1 *cr* dead body; 2 carrion; - **lelaku** person making a solitary journey; - **ucap-ucap** two persons journeying together;

mbathang to float on one's back (as a form of swimming); - **kèli** *fig* to be carried along by the current;

nyundhang bathang banthèng *prov* to promote an unlucky, formerly prominent person.

bathara male mythological deity; **asoca** - wise, clairvoyant;

binathara god-like;

ratu agung binathara a great revered king.

bathari female mythological deity.

bathi 1 profit, benefit, gain; - **kesel** to work hard but in vain; 2 to produce children;

mbathi to make (a certain) profit; to swindle for gain;

mbathèni to make a profit on (a transaction);

mbathèkaké to create a profit for, be beneficial to;

bathèn *or* **bebathèn** amount of profit;

kebathèn profitable, having a profit.

bathik *ng*, **serat** *kr*, fabric worked by the batik process; - **cap** *or* - **cap-capan** printed batik; - **tulis** hand-worked batik;

mbathik to do batik work;

mbathikaké to make batik for s.o.; to have batik made; to have fabric worked in batik;

bathikan batik work; batik-making;

pambathik the working of batik.

bathok 1 coconut shell; 2 skull; - **bolu** half-coconut shell with three eyes;

mbathok resembling a coconut shell;

mbathok mengkureb hemispherical shape (like a face-down half-coconut shell);

bathok bolu isi madu a person of low background but high intelligence.

bathu *or* **mbathu** 1 to eat together from one plate; 2 to contribute capital to an enterprise; to buy a share in an enterprise;

bathon *or* **bathonan** 1 to pool capital for a business enterprise; to pool money for a certain purpose; 2 to eat together from one plate.

bathuk *ng*, *kr*, **(pa)larapan** *k.i.* forehead; - **banyak** *or* - **nonong** a bulging forehead;

bathuk nyéla cendhani a classic ideal forehead ('forehead like marble').

batih 1 one's household; 2 (nuclear) family;

mbatih to feel as close as a member of the family;

batihan *or* **bebatihan** in the neighbourhood.

batin *ng*, **batos** *kr*, 1 inward (feeling); 2 one's inner self;

mbatin to ponder inwardly;

kabatinan *or* **kebatinan** 1 pertaining to

the inner self; 2 mysticism, spiritualism.

batos inward (feeling), inner self (*kr for* **batin**).

batu 1 stone, rock (*see also* **watu**); 2 battery.

batur I *ng*, **réncang** *kr*, **abdi** *k.i.* servant;
- **tukon** slave;
mbatur to be a servant.
II *or* **bebatur** low brick or stone wall which keeps moisture back from the foundations of a house;
mbaturi to provide (a house) with a wall as above.

bau I 1 upper arm; 2 labour, manpower;
- **dhanyang** supporting beam in a house frame; - **kapiné** *or* - **kapini** partial attitude; - **kiwa tengen** one's total strength; - **lawéyan** 1 s.o. whose last two (or more) spouses have died; 2 s.o. with a dimple on the shoulder; - **tengen** right-hand man, trusted person; -**dhendha** very powerful; -**sastra** dictionary; -**suku** village worker in the ricefield given to the village head;
mbaoni to do (a job);
bebau 1 head of a village area; 2 village worker; 3 one who performs a job;
pambaon 1 ship's mast; 2 support pole;
baudhendha nyakrawati powerful, rich and respected.
II a measure of area: *ca* 1.75 acres;
baon *or* **bebaon** many bau's.

baud skilled (in), expert (at).
See also **baut**.

baung 1 bear; 2 *chld* dog; 3 a certain freshwater fish; 4 menthol liniment;
mbaung 1 (of dog) to howl, whine; 2 *cr* to sing, cry.

baureksa 1 guardian spirit of a certain place; 2 one who has long held sway in a certain place;
sing mbaureksa guardian spirit of a house, tree *etc.*

baut bolt, screw.

bawa I situation, circumstances; character.
II to build s.t. on one's own efforts;
- **leksana** to fulfil any promise; to put one's words into action; - **rasa** to engage in discussion about the inner meaning of life;
mbawani 1 to hold sway over; 2 *reg* to hold a celebration (of wedding or circumcision).
III 1 vocal prelude to a piece of music; 2 sound, voice; - **swara** song prelude;
mbawani to sing a prelude to a musical piece.
IV *gram* affix.

bawah I domain; within the area of;
mbawahi *or* **mbawahaké** to have authority over;
kebawah under the authority of;
bawahan (person, place) under the authority of.
II celebration of wedding ceremonies *etc.*

bawak wooden blade-holder for a hoe.

bawal a certain freshwater fish.

bawana *var of* **buwana**.

bawang I garlic; - **kothong** *or* **pupuk** - person who cannot contribute a full share (*usu* referring to a child in a game with older children)(*see also* **pupuk**);
mbawang to season with garlic.
II rice ready to be planted in the ricefield.
III *or* **mbawang** *reg* a variety of mango.

bawasir haemorrhoids.

bawat long-handled ceremonial umbrella.

bawèl always nagging;
mbawèli to nag or carp at s.o.

bawéra spacious, broad.

bawi *reg kr for* **bawa**.

bawon 1 a share of the rice harvest received for one's services during harvesting; 2 a certain measure of newly harvested rice (a sheaf of eight bundles);
mbawoni to give s.o. their earned

portion of the harvest;

mbawonaké to give a portion of the harvest to the harvesters;

bawonan a bundle of rice as a payment given to the harvester.

bawuk I 1 dark grey; **2** (of clothing) faded, worn.

II 1 female genitals; **2** *term of endearment applied to little girls.*

bawur 1 mixed (together); **2** (of vision) blurred, hazy;

mbawuraké 1 to mix (a variety of things) together; **2** to confuse; **3** to cause (vision, view) to be blurred or unclear.

baya I crocodile; - **dharat** wolf, woman-chaser;

binaya mangap surrounded by danger;

nglangèni tai baya *prov* to go to a lot of trouble without any repayment.

II *or* **babaya** *or* **bebaya** danger, hazard;

mbebayani dangerous;

sabaya pati together in life and death.

III 1 perhaps, possibly; **2** *lit* is it so (that…)?; **3** even if, even though; **4** (not) anything; **5** *with interrogative word how* (*etc*) on earth…!

IV reciprocal promise, commitment (*shtf of* **ubaya**).

bayah I duckling (young of the **bèbèk**).

II mbayahi in a critical condition.

bayak I woman's blouse pinned in front (*shtf of* **kebayak**).

II bayak-bayak *or* **bebayakan** crowded, jammed.

bayaka *reg* perhaps, probably (*var of* **ayaké**).

bayakna *var of* **bayaka**.

bayan I parrot; parakeet.

II messenger, errand-runner; village official in charge of security (*shtf of* **kebayan**).

bayang I bamboo bed.

II bayangan image, shadow;

mbayangaké to imagine, visualise.

III mbayang *or* **mbayang-bayang** to support or carry (a patient who cannot walk);

bayangan a patient being supported and helped to walk.

IV bayangan prey.

bayangkara 1 palace guards; **2** police.

bayangkaré ladies-in-waiting, *var of* **bayangkara**;

binayang bayangkaré *lit* escorted by ladies-in-waiting.

bayangkari *var of* **bayangkara**.

bayar pay, salary, wages; - **jrèng (kencrèng)** to buy for cash (rather than on credit);

mbayar to pay;

mbayari to pay for;

mbayaraké to pay (a price), pay out, expend, disburse;

bayaran payment, wages;

pambayar payment; act of paying.

bayas a certain freshwater fish.

bayawara proclamation. *Also* **byawara**.

bayèk *coll* baby.

bayem spinach.

bayi baby; - **abang** a newborn baby;

bayèn to give birth to a baby;

mbayèni to deliver s.o.'s baby.

bayonèt bayonet.

bayong, mbayong *reg* to come together in a place.

bayor a certain fish.

bayu I *lit* wind; - **bajra** wind and thunder storm.

II (*or* **bebayu**) blood vessel; *fig* strength; **bebayon** amulet having the power to harm others.

bayun firstborn (*k.i. for* **barep**);

pambayun 1 firstborn child; **2** *lit* female firstborn child; **3** breast (*k.i. for* **susu**).

bayur a kind of tree.

bé I to fall through.

II to guess, bet (*coll for* **bedhé**).

III name of the 6th year in the **windu** cycle.

bebada *see* bada.

bebadra *see* badra.

bebah task, responsibility (*root form: kr for* bubuh)

bebak, mbebak to pound in order to peel the husk from (as the first step in processing coffee, rice *etc*); bebakan the result of pounding; s.t. to be pounded. *See also* bebeg II.

bebana *see* bana.

bebandan *see* banda.

bebara *see* bara.

bébas 1 free(d), unhampered, unimpeded; 2 free of charge; mbébasaké to release, set free, liberate.

bebasan *see* basa.

bebaya danger (*see* baya).

bebed *ng, kr,* nyamping *k.i.* batik garment worn by men; - (sabuk) wala child's garment worn with one end wrapped below the waist to form a sash; mbebedi to help s.o. dressing in a bebed; bebedan to put on or wear a bebed; nanggung bedhahé bebedé, gempalé warangkané to bear undesirable consequences.

bebeg I 1 clogged, stopped up; 2 overstuffed; overburdened; 3 to feel bloated; mbebeg 1 to dam up; 2 to restrain; bebegan a dam.
II to pound (*var of* bebak).

bebeh apathetic, listless.

bèbèk duck; cocor - a certain plant with beautiful flowers (*see also* cocor); mbèbèk 1 resembling a duck; 2 to follow unthinkingly; bèbèk diwuruki nglangi *prov* to do s.t. unnecessary, futile; bèbèk mungsuh mliwis competition between two persons of the same level; opor bèbèk mentas awaké dhèwèk *a rhyme referring to someone who is successful at being self-supporting.*

bebel dull-witted, mentally sluggish, stubborn; bebelen *or* kebebelen constipated.

bebeng, kebebeng 1 to get stuck; 2 stillborn; 3 impeded.

bèbèr spread, opened out; wayang - performance using a picture-roll (*see also* wayang); mbèbèr to spread, open out, display; mbèbèri to spread out; mbèbèraké 1 to explain; 2 to spread s.t. out for s.o.

bebet *see* bebed.

bèbèt 1 descendant, lineage; 2 unblemished in character and lineage (as recommended to the groom). *See also* bibit.

bebreg overwhelming (quantity, supply).

bèbrèk, mbèbrèk to widen, change for the worse (of wound).

bebrel, mbebrel flimsy.

bèbrèl *var of* bebrel.

bebret, mbebret flimsy, easily ripped.

bèbrèt I *var of* bebret.
II mbèbrèt to make a tearing sound (*e.g.* cloth ripping, fart, leaky muffler *etc*).

bécak pedicab; mbécak 1 to ride in a pedicab; 2 to operate a pedicab as one's livelihood; mbécakaké 1 to send s.o. in a pedicab; to pay s.o.'s pedicab fare; 2 to transport s.t. by pedicab; bécakan pedicab fare; bécak-bécakan 1 imitation or toy pedicab; 2 sightseeing by pedicab.

bècèk I muddy.
II 1 a certain meat stew served at ritual feast; 2 *reg* meat curry.

becici wild banana.

becicing 1 above-ground tuberous root; 2 banana cluster at lower end of stalk.

becik *ng,* saé *kr,* good, kind, fine; mbeciki 1 to treat kindly; 2 to make better;

mbecikaké to improve s.t.;

kabecikan kindness, goodness;

becik-becikan 1 to be on good terms with each other; 2 to compete in quality;

beciké it would be better;

becik ketitik ala ketara *prov* the good will make itself known, along with the bad.

becira raised floor.

becokak or becokakan *reg* mischievous, reckless, unruly.

bècu, mbècu to scowl with anger;

béca-bècu to keep scowling.

becus *cr* capable, competent. *See also* pecus.

béda I *ng*, bènten *kr* different;

mbédakaké 1 to distinguish, differentiate; 2 to discriminate against;

prabéda *lit* different.

II mbéda to irritate;

mbebéda to keep teasing, annoying, irritating s.o.

bédang, mbédang having a flared rim (*shtf of* lambé dandang).

bedaringan *var of* pedaringan.

bededeng or mak bededeng *repr* sounding long and hard;

mbededeng 1 to become long and hard; 2 to exert all one's strength.

bedèdèng, bedédang-bedèdèng to walk with an arrogant swagger.

bedèndèng *var of* bedèdèng.

bedhad detached, loose.

bedhadhag, mbedhadhag flabby (of belly etc).

bedhadhok I *reg* a certain large basket.

II mbedhadhok *reg* careless, ill-mannered.

bedhag 1, mbedhag or mbebedhag to hunt; to go hunting; 2 to chase; 3 to seek a job; 4 to win at gambling;

bedhagan 1 hunted game animal; 2 wage for hired worker;

pambedhagan hunting ground.

bedhagal *cr* abusive term; damn!

mbedhagal 1 to coerce into (do)ing.

bedhah 1 broken through, ripped open; 2 to be overcome by force; - bumi 1 price of burial plot; 2 gravedigger's fee; 3 wages of one who looks after graves;

mbedhah 1 to conquer; 2 to drain (water) from a dam; 3 to break through; 4 to cut out; 5 *or* mbebedhah to start ploughing a ricefield; 6 to become fatter and fatter;

bedhahan 1 a ripped piece, a scrap; 2 cut (of clothing); 3 small drainage ditch in a ricefield;

mbedhahi to cut out;

mbedhahaké 1 to cause s.t. to break accidentally; 2 to rip s.t. open for s.o.

bedhal, mbedhal 1 to break loose from a tether or stall; 2 to leave (companions) against one's will.

bedhama 1 a certain archaic weapon; 2 a type of axe; 3 *reg* appointment.

bedhami or bedhamèn to enter into an agreement, *esp* a peace treaty;

bedhamèn cessation of hostilities; ceasefire agreement.

bedhandho, mbedhandho hesitant, undecided.

bédhang, mbédhang to love illicitly;

bédhangan 1 to have an extramarital affair; 2 *cr* beloved man/woman.

bedhati *reg* ox-cart (*var of* pedhati).

bedhawang *lit* land tortoise.

bedhaya 1 a certain court dance performed by females; 2 performer of this dance.

bedhé to guess (*var of* badhé *or* badhèk).

bedhedheg, mbedhedheg 1 mushy, soggy; 2 swelling with pride.

bedhèdhèh, mbedhèdhèh flabby, paunchy.

bedhegel, mbedhegel to feel resentful.

bedhegud *reg* vigorous, energetic.

bedhegus or mak bedhegus suddenly popping into view.

bedhèk, mbedhèk to guess (at), *var of* badhé, badhèk, bedhé;
  mbedhèki to have s.o. guess;
  bedhèkan 1 riddle, guessing-game; 2 the answer to a riddle; 3 (*or* bedhèk-bedhèkan) to ask each other riddles; to play guessing-games;
  pambedhèk guessing.

bedhel, mbedhel to crack or snap easily.

bedhèl, mbedhèl 1 to operate (surgically); 2 to disembowel; 3 to divert (a stream);
  mbedhèli to keep lancing;
  bedhèlan incision, wound.

bèdhèng *or* bèdhèngan seedbed consisting of heaped up soil between irrigation ditches;
  mbèdhèngi to make a seedbed in a ricefield;

bedhenguk *var of* bedhengus.

bedhengul *var of* bedhengus.

bedhengus *or* mak bedhengus *repr* a sudden appearance, heaving into view.

bedhès 1 *reg* monkey; 2 *cr, excl* 'my god'.

bedhidhèt to grow well (of plants).

bedhidhing chilly, chilled; mangsa - a night-time chill in the dry season.

bedhigal, mbedhigal 1 eccentric, strange acting; 2 ill-mannered.

bedhigas, bedhigasan *or* pating bedhigas having ill-mannered actions.

bedhil *ng*, senjata *kr* gun, rifle; - angin air rifle; - lantakan breech loader; - pacar wutah shotgun;
  mbedhil to shoot;
  mbedhili to shoot s.t. repeatedly;
  bedhil-bedhilan 1 toy gun; 2 to exchange gunfire;
  pambedhil the act of shooting;
  sapambedhil distance travelled by a bullet, a rifle-shot away.

bedhiyang 1 a fire built for warmth; 2 to warm o.s. at a fire.

bedho a draw; to be called off;
  mbedhokaké 1 to make a draw; 2 to fail, call off.

bedhodhog, mbedhodhog 1 to swell out (of water-soaked seeds); 2 ruffled, fluffed up (of bird's feathers); 3 swelling with pride (*var of* mbedhedheg);
  mbedhodhogaké to cause (feathers) to be ruffled.

bedhodhok *var of* bedhodhog.

bedhog I short-handled axe, *esp* for digging out tree stumps;
  mbedhog to dig out (stumps);
  bedhogan a hacked-out stump.
  II 1 to steal a fowl; 2 *lit* to kidnap;
  bedhogan 1 a stolen fowl; 2 *lit* kidnapped woman.

bedhol pulled out, uprooted; - désa to move an entire village to a new settlement; - gendéra to withdraw a military force; - jangkar to weigh anchor; - songsong traditional court ceremony held after the rice mountain ceremony (grebeg);
  mbedhol to pull out, uproot;
  mbedholi to pull out many objects;
  bedholan 1 s.t. that has been pulled out; 2 technique of removing puppets from the banana log where they are kept; 3 alumnus.

bedhu *reg var of* bedho.

bedhudhak a certain venomous snake.

bedhudhug, mbedhudhug bloated, swollen.

bedhug 1 mosque drum; gamelan drum resembling a mosque drum; 2 sounding of the mosque drum at noon to summon Muslims to prayer; 3 noon; 4 *lit* o'clock; - awan noon; - bengi *or* - dawa midnight; - telu about 3:30 a.m.;
  mbedhug 1 to beat a gamelan drum; 2 (to fast) only until noon (rather than sundown);
  sabedhug 1 the same size as a mosque drum; 2 time period from 6 a.m. to 12 noon.

bedhugul not dressed properly; not wearing a kris.

bedhul *var of* **bedhol**.

bedhungul *repr* a sudden appearance, to pop up.

bedhungus *or* **bedhengus** *var of* **bedhungul**

bedinan *ng*, **bedintenan** *kr*, daily (*var of* **pedinan** *ng*, **pedintenan** *kr*). *See* **dina**.

bedodok, mbedodok 1 boastful; **2** to talk too much.

bedodong, mbedodong 1 bloated, stiff and swollen; **2** *cr* dead.

bedondi to quarrel. *See* **perdondi**.

bedor name of one of the small playing-cards (*kertu cilik*).

bedud I mbedud headstrong, obstinate. **II bedudan** opium pipe.

bedudung, mbedudung stuffed, bloated (from overeating).

beg *or* **mak bleg** *repr* of a sudden fall, splat!

bèg *or* **mak bèg** *repr* falling; **bag-bèg** to fall repeatedly.

bega to have a speech difficulty; to stammer.

begadad, mbegadad to steal domestic animals.

begadag *var of* **begadad**.

begagah, mbegagah to stand with the legs wide apart.

begajagan to exhibit crude behaviour; to have bad manners (of female servants).

begajul playboy, wolf; **mbegajul** to chase after women; **begajulan 1** playboy; **2** to chase after women.

bégal bandit, robber; **mbégal** to rob, hold up; **bégalan 1** robbery, holdup; **2** loot; **3** *reg* certain part of a traditional wedding ceremony; **ambégal sambi angajang** to intend to steal s.t. by pretending to help the owner.

begandring *or* **begandringan** gathering; to engage in discussion.

beganjok a building in the style of a mosque; **mbeganjok** to have a strange character; out of the ordinary.

begar pleased, delighted.

begawan holy man, hermit (*var of* **bagawan**).

begeblug *var of* **pageblug**.

begedèl *var of* **bergedèl**.

begedud, mbegedud wilful, obstinate.

begegeg, mbegegeg to remain motionless.

begègèh, mbegègèh to stand with the legs moderately far apart.

begèjègan ill-mannered, insolent.

begejil (of children) obstreperous.

begènggèng, mbegènggèng to improve in one's condition (physically, materially).

begèr delighted, pleased.

begigih, mbegigih 1 to stand with the legs slightly apart; **2** adamant in one's refusal to help.

begja 1 (good) luck; fortunate; at peace with one's environment; **2** *fig* bad luck; - **cilaka** fate; - **kemayangan** great good luck; **begja(n)-begjan** to try one's luck; **begja-begjané** at best; **begjan** *or* **begjan-begjan** to do s.t. just for luck; **kabegjan** (good) luck; **kabegjan kebrayan** a man of fortune.

begledhug the low rumbling sound of an active volcano.

bégod, mbégod stubbornly disobedient.

begog stupid person; **mbegog** to act stupidly, *i.e.* sit around staring blankly into space.

begogok, mbegogok to sit completely motionless.

begok a variety of bird.

begondhal *var of* **begundhal**.

begu to have a speech difficulty; to stammer (*var of* **bega**).

beguguk, mbeguguk to stand one's ground, refuse to give in;

mbeguguk ngutha waton to defy authority.

begundhal yes-man, sycophant. *Also* **begondhal**.

begupon pigeon-house (*var of* **pagupon**).

beguron institution for religious and mystical training (*var of* **paguron**).

bèh all (*shtf of* **kabèh**). *See also* **barbèh**.

bèhèl *reg* very rich.

bèi *shtf of* **ngabèhi**.

beja *var of* **begja**.

béja to say (*subst kr for* **kandha**);
  mbéjani to say to s.o.;
  bebéjan to speak to each other.

bejaji, mbejaji to have worth.

bejad 1 damaged, spoiled; 2 depraved, socially unacceptable;
  mbejad *or* **mbejadi** to wreck, tear to pieces;
  mbejadaké to cause s.t. to be wrecked.

bejèr an eye disease, inflamed eyelids.

bèji I pool, pond (for swimming or boating).
  II large-headed nail.
  III **bèjèn** jewelled.

béjos capable, can, to be able.

bejud, mbejud *reg* stubborn, headstrong.

bejujag, mbejujag to please o.s., follow one's own ideas, not obey custom.
  See also **jujag**.

bèk I *adr* aunt (*var of* **bi**).
  II back (football position).
  III *reg* headman of a residential area in town.
  IV *reg* maybe.
  V (*pron as:* **mbèk**) 1 possession, belonging (*coll var of* **darbèk**); 2 together with. *See also* **ambèk**.
  VI (*pron as:* **mbèk**) to give up.
  VII (*pron as:* **mbèk**) *chld* sheep.

béka (to be) a nuisance/hindrance;
  mbéka *or* **mbékani** fussy, hard to handle.

bekakak 1 roasted chicken/duck; 2 sacrificed animal.

bekakas 1 equipment, necessities; 2 parts/materials of which s.t. is made.

bekakrah, mbekakrah *or* **pating bekakrah** in disorder; scattered in a mess.

bekakrak *var of* **bekakrah**; **bekakrakan** confused or disordered action.

bekamal *reg* salted (*var of* **kamal**).

bekangkang, mbekangkang to stand or lie with the legs spread wide apart.

bekasakan 1 boorish behaviour; 2 jungle demon, evil spirit of the forest.

bekatul very fine chaff produced by pounding rice. *See also* **katul**.

bekecek, mbekecek to chatter, to talk copiously.

bekécot a tree snail (*var of* **bekicot**).

bekel 1 low-ranking official at court; 2 village head.

bèkel jacks, knucklebones;
  bèkelan to play jacks.

bèkèl 1 protrusion of the stomach; 2 a variety of fish.

bekem, mbekem to clutch in the hand.

bekeneng, bekenengan to engage in heated argument.

bekengkeng, mbekengkeng unyielding, stubborn.

bekèngkèng, mbekèngkèng to sit with the legs spread wide apart;
  mbekèngkèngaké to spread the legs wide apart. *Also* **pekèngkèng**.

bekès, mbekès to spit (of cats).

bekètrèk *var of* **blekètrèk**.

bekicik, mbekicik 1 to quibble, *fig* talkative; 2 to argue habitually; 3 to cheat at cards.

bekicot a tree snail.

bekik, bekak-bekik to shriek repeatedly;
  mbekik to shriek;
  pating bekik *or* **pating brekik** *pl* to shriek.

bekikuk crossbreed between a domestic chicken (**pitik**) and a certain hybrid chicken (**bekisar**).

bekingking I a certain snail.

II **mbekingking** very thin, emaciated.

bekis, mbekis to spit (of cats) (*var of* **bekès**).

bekisar crossbreed between a domestic chicken (**pitik**) and a wild chicken (**ayam alas**).

bekisik, mbekisik (of skin) dried, cracking.

bekita-bekitu *or* **bekituan** *reg* to rant in anger.

bekiwit, mbekiwit to cheat at cards.

bekok, mbekok 1 addicted (to), *esp* smoking; **2** (of tobacco leaves) badly formed; **3** ill-mannered.

bekokrok, mbekokrok 1 loose, coming unbound; **2** worthless.

bekong *reg* a measure, *esp* for raw rice or oil;

mbekong to measure out (rice, oil).

bekongkong, mbekongkong 1 to sit idly loafing; **2** to sit improperly with the legs apart on a chair; **3** *var of* **bekungkung**.

bekos, mbekos to snort.

beksa *k.i. for* **jogèd**.

bekta to carry, bring, take (*root form: kr for* **gawa**).

bekti 1 to have great respect/esteem (for); **2** one's respects (in opening or ending phrase of letters); **3** money or things given to a village head or in acknowledgement of his kindness;

mbektèni to pay one's respects to, esteem for s.o.;

ngabekti to pay one's respects to s.o.;

ngabektèn occasion for showing one's respect by kissing the knee of an older person;

pangabekti one's respects.

bekucuk, mbekucuk to rinse one's mouth out.

bekuh, mbekuh to complain by moaning;

bekah-bekuh to keep complaining and moaning.

bekuk, mbekuk 1 to bend; **2** to break a neck; **3** to capture, arrest;

mbekuki to get s.o.'s money/property away from them.

bekungkung I *var of* **pekungkung**.

II cage-like tiger trap.

bekunung, mbekunung stubborn, unwilling to defer to others.

bekur, mbekur to coo.

bekus *var of* **bekis**.

bekusuk, mbekusuk old and faded.

bektos *subst kr for* **bekti**.

bektya *lit var for* **bekti**.

bel *repr* puffing/flaring up.

béla 1 to sacrifice o.s. in defence of s.o. or s.t.; **2** to have a joint circumcision (with another boy); **- pati 1** to sacrifice one's life; **2** to join (another) in death; **ndhèrèk - sungkawa** to offer one's condolences;

- tampa misunderstood;

mbélani to defend, support;

mbélakaké to sacrifice one's life as a means of solidarity;

pambéla defender, defence.

belah I 1 *lit* split; **2** a measure of harvested rice: one bundle, half a sheaf;

mbelahi 1 *lit* to split; **2** to bundle into sheaves;

karo belah 150, **telu belah** 250 *etc* (*market terms*); **- Banten** a style of jacket with split sleeves.

II **wong belahan** fisherman (at sea), boatman.

belak disease of the soles of the feet;

belaken to have/get such a disease.

belang 1 blemish (skin, cloth); **2** white spot(s) on an animal's coat.

belas -teen; **pat-** fourteen, **nem-** sixteen.

belèh I *reg* no, not (*var of* **beli(h)**).

II **mbelèh** to slaughter, butcher;

mbelèhi to slaughter frequently;

mbelèhaké to have a domestic animal slaughtered;

belèhan 1 slaughtering-place; **2** animal to be slaughtered;

pambelèhan slaughtering-place.

belek crowded, piled up (people, work).

belèk I mbelèk to cut (off), make a slit (in).

II chicken droppings (*var of* tembelèk).

bèlèk an eye disease, conjunctivitis;
bèlèken to have/get such a disease.

belem, mbelem to roast (*esp* cassava, corn) in a bed of hot coals and ash;
beleman 1 brazier for roasting foods in hot ash; 2 roasted foods (*esp* cassava, corn).

bèlèng, mbèlèng *reg* hard to handle, refractory.

beler, mbeler 1 persistently annoying (of child, a stray chicken); 2 to neglect repaying a debt; 3 negligent.

belèr, mbelèr to cut;
mbelèri able/liable to cut;
kebelèr to get cut by s.t. other than a cutting implement.

bèlèr, mbèlèr *reg var of* mèlèr.

bèlès inflamation of the eye. *See also* jèlès, jèlèh.

belet I *reg* mud, muck.

II indigo leaf (*kr for* nila).

III foal, colt (*subst kr for* belo).

IV, kebelet to need to go to the toilet; to feel an urge to do s.t.

beli(h) *reg* no, not. *See* belèh.

belik I a small natural pool, a spring at the side of a river.

II *or* mbeliki to begin bearing fruit in season.

beling I 1 shards of glass; 2 porcelain.

II mbeling hard to handle.

belis devil, bad spirit. *See also* iblis.

belit I a card game with the small cards (*kertu cilik*).

II mbelit 1 to be a glib talker; 2 to sneak away from work; 3 (of debts, bills) hard to collect.

belo foal, colt;
belo mèlu seton *prov* to follow the crowd unthinkingly.

belok stocks, fetters.

bélok, mbélok to turn.

belong *reg* flooded spot in a ricefield. *See also* balong.

bélong unevenly pigmented (of face skin).

belor glasses, sunglasses.

bélot, mbélot to disregard the orders of s.o. in authority.

beluk I 1 steam, mist; 2 *reg* smoke.

II *or* kokuk-beluk a kind of owl; -ananjak to do as one likes, without regard for others' advice.

III a certain caterpillar.

IV *reg* to call to, yell at.

V mbeluk to turn (*reg var of* bélok).

belung (of soil) soggy, heavily moist.

belur *or* babak belur black-and-blue. *See also* babak.

bem (musical) mode (for gamelan ensemble or gamelan drum (kendhang)).

béma 1 (to be) a nuisance/hindrance; 2 danger, hazard; 3 frightening; tundha - helter-skelter, disorganised (*see also* tundha).

bembeng, mbembeng big around, thick (of cylindrical shapes).

bèmbrèng, mbèmbrèng to spread (out), stretch (open).

bémo three-wheeled motor vehicle (*shtc from* bécak-motor).

ben I contact, confrontation (*root form: kr for* du). *See* aben.

II every (*shtf of* saben).

bèn 1 (kajengipun *kr*) so that; 2 let it...; 3 okay (it's up to you), have it your own way.

bena flood (*kr for* banjir).

béna *or* bénah *reg var of* béda.

benah, bebenah to straighten up, clean up.

benak, mbenakaké to fix up, set right.

benampéyan you (*reg var of* sampéyan).

benang thread, string, yarn (*kr for* bolah); - gelasan string onto which ground glass has been stuck for kite fighting; - gulung ball of string; - kelos spool of thread; - **layangan** kite string; - **mas** golden string.

benangpéyan *var of* **benampéyan**.

benawi large river (*kr for* **bengawan**).

béncak name of a children's game.

bencana disaster, calamity, debacle, havoc.

bencé the male of a kind of quail (**gemak**).

bencélung *var of* **bencilung**.

bèncèng 1 different (of will, conduct); 2 not well matched, not fitting properly; - **cèwèng** always disagreeing.

bencèt I sundial.

II **mbencèt** to bully s.o. in an unguarded moment.

béncok tree frog.

bencilung, **mbencilung** *reg* to cheat.

bencolèng, **mbencolèng** ill-mannered, uncouth, tough;

bencolèngan to act uncouthly.

bendana I *lit* string, rope.

II a nervous habit (head-shaking, facial tic *etc*).

bendara 1 master, mistress; 2 title for the nobility;

Bendara Pangéran Harya (**B.P.H.**) title for brothers of the Sultan of Yogyakarta; **Bendara Radèn Ayu** (**B.R.A.**) title for a married princess; **Bendara Radèn Mas** (**B.R.M.**) title for an unmarried prince.

bendha a certain variety of **kluwih** tree.

béndha a certain dark brown hard-shelled fruit.

bendhalit, **bendhalitan** *or* **pating bendhalit** to twist and turn, fidget.

bendhalungan to talk incorrectly in speech etiquette.

bendhé small copper or bronze gong, *esp* used to call attention;

sasoré - throughout the evening (*see* **soré**).

bendhéga ship's crew, voyage companion.

bendhel a bound volume;

mbendhel to bind (books, papers); **mbendheli** to bind (papers) in a file;

mbendhelaké to have s.t. (books, magazines) bound;

bendhelan a file of bound papers.

bendhèl to talk or argue habitually; to nag.

bèndhel *var of* **bendhel**.

bendhèng, **mbendhèng** to stretch (fabric) to its widest dimension by pulling from opposite sides.

bèndheng *reg* 1 large rope; 2 electric wiring;

mbèndheng 1 to tie with large rope; 2 to connect up (electrical wiring).

bèndher (book) binding; **tukang** - bookbinder (*see also* **tukang**).

bendhèt, **mbendhèt** to open s.t. by making space between; to hold s.t. open by pressing the edges apart.

bendhéyot, **mbendhéyot** (of burdens) many and heavy to carry;

bendhéyotan weighted down.

bèndhi gig, two-wheeled carriage drawn by one horse.

bendho large-bladed knife for cutting wood;

mbendho to slash with a bendho.

bendhol, **mbendhol** 1 having a knob or bump on it; 2 *or* **mbendholan** boastful, arrogant;

bendholan a knob or bump; **mbendhal-mbendhol** having knobs at some places on it.

bèndi *var of* **bèndhi**.

béndra *lit* frisky, frolicsome; to be infatuated (with).

béndrang a tasty soup prepared a day or longer ahead of eating (*var of* **bléndrang**).

béndrong I rhythmic beats produced by pounding rice with a mortar and pestle;

mbéndrong *or* **mbéndrongi** to produce pounding beats rhythmically; **béndrongan** pounding on an empty mortar with pestles rhythmically.

II object used as a kite-string reel;

mbéndrong *or* **mbéndrongi** to wind a kite string.

bendu *lit* angry;
  bebendu wrath of God.

bendung, mbendung to dam s.t. up;
  bendungan 1 dam; 2 dammed-up water.

bènèh *reg* 1 different; 2 strange.

benem, mbenem to roast (*esp* cassava) in a bed of hot coals and ash;
  beneman 1 a bed of hot coals and ash for roasting foods; 2 roasted foods.

bener *ng*, **leres** *kr* 1 right, true; 2 indeed, really; 3 straight; 4 real;
  mbeneri to coincide with;
  mbeneraké 1 to correct, rectify; 2 to justify;
  beneré the right thing would be;
  bener-beneran seriously;
  bebener *or* **bebeneran** 1 justice, rightness; 2 a decision (of justice);
  kabeneran 1 fortunately; 2 just right; 3 properly done;
  sabeneré *ng*, **saleresipun** *kr* actually, in fact;
  bener luputé the true facts;
  dudu sabeneré *or* **ora sabeneré** improper, wrong.

benèt low wooden chest.

bèng *adr* young man! (*shtf of* **jebèng**).

bengah, mbengah to low, moo.

bengagah, mbengangah bright and glowing.

bengangang *var of* **bengangah**. *Also* **bengèngèng**.

béngas-béngos having black streaky marks on the face.

béngat ceremonial appointment (of Islamic religious official).

bengawan *ng*, **benawi** *kr*, large river.

bengèk I asthma.
  II *reg* to shout, yell (*var of* **bengok**);
  mbebengèk to repeatedly disturb/irritate;
  bengèk-bengèk *or* **bengak-bengèk** to keep shouting, keep crying out;
  thèthèk-bengèk *see* **thèthèk**.

bengel (to have) a cold and headache.

bengengeng, mbengengeng to buzz, whine, hum.

bengèngèng *var of* **bengangang**.

bengep swollen in the face.

bengèr (of baby) to cry;
  mbengèr to cry;
  mbengèr-mbengèr to keep on crying.

bèngès substance used for reddening the lips;
  mbèngèsi to redden the lips with a certain substance;
  bèngèsan having reddened lips;
  bebèngèsan hypocritical (of men).

bènget bewildered (*reg kr for* **bingung**).

benggala a breed of large ox (originally from Bengal).

benggang distantly spaced, wide apart; with space(s) between;
  mbenggang to make a space between things;
  mbenggangaké to space s.t. at a distance.

benggèl *var of* **bendhol**.

benggol *var of* **bendhol**.

bénggol 1 *or* **bénggolan** gang leader; 2 *or* **bénggolan** coin worth 2½ cents during the colonial period.

bengi *ng*, **dalu** *kr*, evening, night;
  benginé on the evening of the same day;
  kebengèn to be overtaken by night;
  bengi-bengi in the middle of the night;
  bengi-benginan *or* **bengèn-bengènan** 1 rather late in the evening; 2 to see who can stay awake the latest. *See also* **wengi**.

bengingèh whinny;
  mbengingèh to neigh, whinny.

bengis stern, fierce-looking. *See also* **wengis**.

bengka (of stomach) hard, bloated.

bengkah (having) a crack or cleft.

bengkak I a tied bundle of long thin objects;
 mbengkaki to tie (things) into a bundle.
 II swollen.
 III mbengkak to shout.

bengkalahi *reg* to quarrel, argue.

bengkarokan big, old and repulsive-looking (of ape, *cr* of man).

béngkas, mbéngkas to complete, finish off;
 pambéngkas deliverer, messiah.

béngkat a game played by children with certain fruits (**béndha**).

bengkek a tied bundle (*var of* **bengkak I**).

bengkeleng throughout; **sedina (m)-** all day long.

bengkélot, mbengkélot tough, hard to chew.

bengkeluk, mbengkeluk bent at the end;
 mbengkelukaké to bend s.t. at the end.

bengkelung *var of* **bengkeluk**.

bengkeng I stiff, hard, sore.
 II bamboo fish trap with a swinging gate.

bengkerengan to argue heatedly.

bengkerok, mbengkerok (of skin) speckled and dirty.

bengket a bundle of small things;
 mbengket *or* **mbengketi** to bundle s.t. in handful-sized bunches;
 bengketan (tied) in such bunches.

bengkiyeng, mbengkiyeng 1 solid, firm, strong, muscular; **2** heavy to carry.

bengkok ricefield assigned to the village head or officials as recompense for their services.

béngkok *reg var of* **béngkong**.

béngkong *or* **mbéngkong** curved, crooked, bent;
 mbéngkongaké to cause s.t. to be curved.

béngkot, mbéngkot 1 to turn the face aside,

e.g. in disapproval; **2** to disregard s.o.'s wishes.

bengkowang a certain edible juicy tuber.

bengkoyok a skin disease characterised by running sores;
 bengkoyoken to suffer from such a skin disease.

bengkrèh *or* **bengkrèhan** to dispute, quarrel, squabble.

bengkrès, mbengkrès *reg* to look smart; finely dressed.

bengkrik *var of* **bengkrèk**.

bengkring thin and sickly;
 bengkringen to suffer from a certain wasting disease, consumptive.

bengkrung *or* **mbengkrung** bent, curved (of the human back), (*var of* **bang-krung**).

bengkuk *or* **mbengkuk** bent, crooked, curved;
 mbengkukaké to cause s.t. to bend.

bengkung I long cotton band worn around the abdomen by women after childbirth, to hold the muscles firm;
 mbengkungi to put a long cotton band on s.o. after childbirth;
 bengkungan wearing a band around the body after childbirth.
 II (*or* **mbengkung**) bent, curved, twisted (*var of* **bengkuk**);
 mbengkungaké to shape into an arc.

benglé a medicinal root of the ginger family;
 mbenglé resembling such a herb; -**kéris** (of skin) resembling the colour of the cut root, pale yellow.

bengok a shout, shouting, yelling;
 bengok-bengok *or* **bengak-bengok** to shout repeatedly;
 mbengok to shout, yell;
 mbengoki to shout at, call to;
 mbengokaké to shout s.t.;
 pating brengok *pl* to shout, keep cheering and screaming.

bengong 1 dazed, stupefied; **2** become

stunned (with open mouth).

béngor, béngoren (of lips) sore from too much lime in the betel quid.

béngos, béngas-béngos (of face) streaked with dirt.

bèngsèng *reg* gangster, crook, thief.

benguk a certain variety of bean; **témpé -** bean-cake made from a certain bean (*see* témpé).

bengung, mbengung to produce a shrill buzzing or humming sound.

bengus, mbengus to snort.

benik button; **- thik** *or* **- cethèt** *or* **- ceplès** press-stud;
   mbeniki to sew buttons on (clothing);
   mbenikaké to button (clothing);
   benikan 1 buttoning; **2** (clothing) with buttons.

bening 1 clear, transparent, pure; **2** weak (of liquids);
   mbeningaké to make s.t. clear;
   bening banyu leri very turbid; even rice-washing water is clearer.

bénjang 1 *lit* future, next; **2** *subst var of* **bénjing**.

benjèt, mbenjèt to pull s.t. to right and left.

benji *reg* to feel enervated; lacking strength.

bénjing future, next (*kr for* **bésuk**, **suk**).

bénjis *reg* can, to be able, capable.

bénjit *reg* piglet.

bénjo oval, elliptical.

bénjoh *var of* **bénjuh**.

bénjol 1 lump, bump; **2** (*or* **mbénjol**) bruised, swollen, misshapen;
   bénjolan swelling, lump;
   bénjal-bénjol bumpy, lumpy.

bènjrèt, mbènjrèt to have diarrhoea.

bénjuh *reg* can, to be able, capable.

benjut 1 lump on the head resulting from a blow; **2** squashy (of fruits).

bentar *lit* split in two; to crack open.

bentayang, bentayangan 1 to go every-where in quest of a livelihood; **2** to writhe in pain.

bentèl bundle of rice seedlings ready for planting.

bènten different (*kr for* **béda**).

bèntèng *reg var of* **bètèng**.

bentèr hot (*kr for* **panas**);
   bentèran a hot drink (*kr for* **wédang**).

bentet 1 the exact amount; **2** completely filled.

benthèt cracked but not broken through;
   benthètan a cracked part of something.

benthik 1 a children's game played by batting away a short stick with a long stick; **2** knocking each other; **3** *fig* to clash;
   mbenthik to knock, hit against;
   kebenthik to get knocked against;
   benthikan 1 knocking each other (of two hard items); **2** to clash.

benthot sturdy, muscular.

benthuk *or* **benthukan** to collide;
   mbenthuk to collide against;
   mbenthukaké to collide head on;
   kebenthuk to get tossed against.

benthung I strong, muscular.
   II ape with long black hair.

benthut sturdy, muscular (*var of* **benthot**).

bentil dedicated, devoted; **tani -** dedicated farmer (*see* **tani II**).

benting *reg* woman's sash;
   mbentingi to put a sash on s.o.;
   bentingan to wear a sash.

bentis a certain fruit, often made into a drink for stomachache (*reg var of* **pacé I**).

bentoyong, mbentoyong 1 (of burdens) many and heavy to carry; **2** to be a heavy burden or extra responsibility.

bentrok to clash;
   bentrokan 1 clash, confrontation; **2** to clash with each other.

bentul a variety of tuber.

bentur I severe, rigorous (*var of* **gentur**);
   mbentur to do s.t. rigorously.

II **mbentur** to hit;
mbenturi 1 to hit s.t. repeatedly; 2 to throw stones at;
mbenturaké to strike s.t. (against);
kebentur to get hit.
bentus, mbentus to bump;
mbentusi to bump repeatedly against;
mbentusaké to bump s.t. (against);
kebentus to get a bump on the head.
bènyèk (of wounds) watery and infected.
benyènyèh (of wounds) watery and infected;
benyènyèhen or **pating benyènyèh** (of skin) covered with small infected sores.
benyinyih *var of* **benyènyèh**.
benyunyuk, benyunyukan or **benyunyak-benyunyuk** ill-mannered, boorish.
ber or **mak ber** *repr* flight through the air;
bar-ber *repr* repeated flights.
bèr, bèrbudi generous.
bera fallow, unproductive land;
mbera empty (of one of the hollows where seeds should be, in the game of **dhakon**);
mberakaké to allow (land) to lie fallow;
bebera to cultivate fallow land;
(be)beran fallow land.
berah I labour(er) (*kr for* **buruh**).
II **mberah** *reg* plentiful, in abundance.
bérang large knife.
beras *ng*, **wos** *kr*, uncooked rice; - **kencur** mixture of powdered raw rice and medicinal roots used for massaging; - **kuning** rice coloured yellow with tumeric, *usu* served as ritual meal; - **wutah** 1 a certain design of batik or decoration on a kris blade; 2 (of bullets) raining down; 3 (of modern furniture) having a multicoloured pebbled effect; - **panganen** feeling bloated from eating half-cooked rice; - **tuton** hand-husked rice;

beras wutah arang mulih marang takeré *expr* it's no use crying over spilt milk;
dudu berasé ditempuraké *expr* to interrupt conversation in a wrong way.
bérat *see* **birat**.
bèrbudi generous. *See* **bèr**.
bercak pockmarked.
berci 1 a certain fine gauzy fabric; 2 spangle;
bercèn clothing made of the above fabric.
bercoh or **bercuh** 1 obscene (of speech); 2 confused.
berdondi dispute (*var of* **perdondi**).
berduli to care, heed (*var of* **perduli**).
bereg, mbereg 1 to chase off, shoo; 2 to let (cattle) out to graze.
bèrèk, mbèrèk 1 to slaughter, butcher; 2 to cut and rip open.
berem soft and squashy (of fallen fruits).
bèrem I light blue (of dyed indigo).
II edge of a road.
bèrèng I skin disease with red specks;
bèrèngen to suffer from such a skin disease.
bèrès settled, in good order;
mbèrèsi or **mbèrèsaké** to put in good order.
berèt scratched;
mberèt to scratch;
mberèti to cause s.t. to be scratched;
mberètaké to have s.t. to be scratched;
keberèt to get scratched.
bergada brigade, group (of soldiers). *See also* **bregada**.
bergagah, mbergagah to stand with the legs wide apart (*var of* **begagah**). *Also* **bregagah**.
bergajul playboy, wolf (*var of* **begajul**). *Also* **bregajul**.
bergas or **bregas** having a fresh attractive appearance.
bergasi or **begasi** 1 car boot; 2 freight transported by rail; 3 railway freight

office; 4 goods van.

bergedèl rissole. *Also* **bregedèl**.

bergegeg, mbergegeg to remain motion-less (*var of* **begegeg**). *Also* **bregegeg**.

bergègèh, mbergègèh to stand with the legs slightly apart. *Also* **bregègèh**.

bergigih, mbergigih 1 adamant in one's refusal to help; 2 *var of* **bergègèh**. *Also* **bregigih**.

bergodog I mbergodog (of skin) covered with rash. *Also* **bregodog**.

II mbergodog to massage the whole body.

bergogok *var of* **begogok**. *Also* **bregogok**.

berguguk *var of* **beguguk**. *Also* **breguguk**.

bergundung, mbergundung obstinate, headstrong. *Also* **bregundung**.

beri I eagle.

II mberi 1 to join in a card game; 2 to toss in one's hand (in a card game).

bèri 1 a gong without knobs; 2 serving-tray.

bèri-bèri disease characterised by swollen limbs.

berik *or* **berikan** (of goat, buffalo) to fight by locking horns; (of goat) to butt with the horns.

bering disagreeable odour (of a certain fruit (**jéngkol**).

béring 1 unbalanced, lopsided; 2 *fig* mentally unbalanced; 3 cross-eyed; 4 unfair.

berit a variety of mouse which produces a bad smell when disturbed (**clurut**).

beritan *or* **buritan** a small backyard planted with fruits and vegetables.

bèrji silver leaf-shaped ornament sewn on a lady's dress.

berkah blessings; - **pangèstu** blessing from the elders;

mberkahi to give one's blessings.

berkakas equipment, necessities (*var of* **bekakas**).

berkas, berkasan *reg* bundle, package.

berkasakan jungle demon, jungle robber

(*var of* **bekasakan**).

berkat 1 food, blessed by a religious offi-cial, taken home from a ritual meal by the guests after they have eaten a por-tion of it; 2 blessing (*reg var of* **berkah**). **mberkat** to take home (food) from a ceremony;

berkatan the food taken home from a ritual meal.

berkecek, mberkecek to chatter (*var of* **mbekecek**). *Also* **brekecek**.

berkèngkèng, mberkèngkèng having the legs spread wide apart (*var of* **bekèngkèng**). *Also* **brekèngèng**.

bèrko electric bicycle lamp.

berkongkong, mberkongkong to sit idly loafing (*var of* **mbekongkong**). *See also* **brekongkong**.

berkuh, berkah-berkuh to keep com-plaining (*var of* **bekah-bekuh**, *see* **bekuh**).

berkutut the barred ground-dove (*var of* **perkutut**).

bèrlin 'Berlin-silver', white metal (*var of* **barlèn**).

berliyan I diamond (*var of* **barléyan**).

II a variety of wood good for carving.

berngangang, mberngangang glowing, radiant (*var of* **mbengangang**).

berngangas, mberngangas to laugh in a jeering tone (*var of* **merngangas**).

berngèngèng I, mberngèngèng glowing, radiant (*var of* **berngangang**).

II to keep crying softly.

See also **brengengeng**.

berok, mberok to shout;

berak-berok to keep shouting.

bérok *see* **wedhus**.

bérong dirty streak on face;

bérongen (of lips) sore from too much lime in the betel quid (*var of* **béngoren**).

berot, mberot to attempt to free o.s. from restraint.

bersat *or* **bresat, pating bersat** spread

about untidily. *See also* **bresat**.

berselo, mberselo stubborn, unwilling to listen to others.

bersih clean, cleansed, cleared; - **désa** traditional annual village event with ritual meal and performances, held after the harvest season;
mbersihi to cleanse s.t. ritually;
bebersih to clean graves and place offerings of flowers on them; cleanse o.s. ritually;
bersihan beauty-case.

bersot, mbersot to disregard others' wishes, advice or warnings.

beruk coconut half-shell used as a measure for rice.

berung, mberung obstinate, to disobey;
pamberung obstinacy, disobedience.

berut a scratch, scratched (*var of* **barut**).

bérut *see* **entut**.

besalèn a smithy, blacksmith's forge.

bésan parent(s)-in-law of one's child;
(**be**)**bésanan** to be in the mutual relationship of parents of a married couple.

besaos *reg kr for* **baé** only, just.

besar 12th month of the Islamic calendar;
besaran feast-day occurring during the above month.

besaran mulberry fruit.

besasih, mbesasih *or* **pating besasih** messy, in disorder.

besasik messy (*var of* **besasih**).

besat, mbesat to fly away, take off suddenly.

bèsèk small covered box of plaited bamboo.

besel *or* **beselan** a bribe;
mbeseli to bribe s.o.

besélat a certain system of self-defence. *See also* **silat**.

besem 1 gloomy, droopy; 2 withered, faded, wilted; 3 *root form: subst kr for* **obong**.

besèn a variety of grass.

besengèk a certain dish made of vegetables and soy sauce.

besengut, mbesengut to frown, scowl;
besengat-besengut to keep frowning.

bèsèr 1 to have to urinate frequently; 2 *cr* to urinate.

beseseg, mbeseseg bloated from overeating.

besèt peeled, scraped (of skin);
mbesèt to peel the rind (from), to skin, graze.

bèsi bowl (*var of* **basi**).

besik clean (of yard, garden);
mbesiki to weed.

besilat a certain system of self-defence (*var of* **besélat**). *See also* **silat**.

besisik, mbesisik dried out and scaly (of skin).

besiwit, mbesiwit to cheat at cards.

besiyar out (walking, riding) for pleasure.

beskal a certain colonial administrative rank.

beskap short double-breasted jacket, worn by men.

beskuwit Dutch rusk.

beslah seizure, confiscation;
mbeslah to seize, confiscate;
beslahan booty, confiscated goods.

beslit 1 decree, letter of appointment; 2 official document of notification.

besmi to burn (*root form: kr for* **obong**).

besolé a certain tree.

besono, besona-besono *or* **mbesono** ill-mannered, boorish, rude.

besoso, mbesoso ill-mannered, crude.

besot, mbesot to clean (metal) by blowing flame on it.

besta I *reg* rope for handcuffing (*kr for* **banda**);
mbesta to tie s.o.'s hands.
II to bake cake in a pan with sugar.

bestèl to order by mail;
bestèlan merchandise sent by mail or railway;
mbestèlaké to send by mail or railway.

bestik 1 steak; 2 any Western-style dish with meat and vegetables, *e.g.* **bestik ayam** chicken and vegetables.

bestrong I blunderbuss.
II wide-sleeved shirt.

bestru a creeper with cucumber-like edible fruits.

bestu realisation;
mbestu to realise a plan.

besturu slackness, carelessness;
kabesturon slack, careless.

besuk *reg* a field covered by volcanic ash, sand and stones carried down by water.

bésuk *ng*, bénjing *kr*, 1 in future; 2 next, coming;
bésuk-bésuk at some indefinite future time;
bésuk manèh next time, *see* suk I.

besur, mbesur to do as one pleases without regard for others.

besus 1 neat and fine (dress, home); 2 to be fond of dressing well.

besusu the yam-bean, its tuberous root used medicinally.

besut, mbesut 1 to refine, smooth out; 2 to press clothing; 3 to edit an article.

besuwel *repr* a quick tucking-in motion;
mbesuwelaké to tuck s.t. hastily.

bet *repr* a swift motion/action.

beta *kr inf var of* bekta.

betah I 1 to feel comfortable; 2 to endure;
mbetahi to cause to be endurable;
mbetah-mbetahaké to persist in, persevere at;
betah-betahan to compete in endurance.
II need (*kr for* butuh).

betamal evidence, indication, sign.

betatung black maggot.

bètèh exchange of pleas in a court case;
mbètèhaké *or* ngadu bètèh to present arguments and counter-arguments in court.

betèk I s.t. that has been used for some purpose.

II because of.

bètèng 1 fort(ification), bastion, rampart; 2 rook, castle (in chess); 3 brick walls surrounding a palace; jeron - the whole complex surrounded by a high brick wall (*esp* in Yogyakarta);
mbètèngi to fortify, function as a fort for;
bètèng-bètèngan imitation or toy fort.

bèter *var of* blèter.

bethak to boil rice (*root form: kr for* liwet).

bethara male deity (*var of* bathara).

bethari female deity (*var of* bathari).

bethat, mbethat to break loose suddenly from one's group.

bethèk I bamboo fence;
mbethèki to build a fence around s.t.; to fence s.t. in.
II *var of* bedhèk.

bèthèk baskets hanging at either end of a shoulder pole (pikulan) for carrying things.

bethem I seed of the kluwih fruit.
II mbethem having a round fat face.

bèthem, mbèthem to puff checks and clasp the lips tightly.

betheng, kebetheng *or* kebethengen to be stranded, *esp* by rain.

bèther, mbèther (of nose) large, broad; (of chin) fat, multiple.

bèthèt I a green parakeet;
mbèthèt (of nose) hooked.
II mbèthèti to clean a slaughtered animal by removing the insides.

bethèthèr, mbethèthèr *or* pating bethèthèr scattered about in disorder.

bethethet I, mbethethet tight.
II the whole time; sedina - the whole day.

bethèthèt *var of* bethethet.

bethik a certain edible freshwater fish.

bethithing, mbethithing narrow-waisted.

bethithit, mbethithit 1 tight-fitting; 2 all dressed up.

bétho, **mbétho** to whistle by blowing on the slit between the two palms pressed together.

bethok I 1 a certain fish; 2 a certain shape of a kris.
II **mbethok** to take out; - **cèlèngan** to take one's savings out of the piggy bank.

béthong, **béthongan** shirt resembling a short jacket.

bethot, **mbethot** to pull s.t. off, remove forcibly;
mbethoti to pull s.t. off repeatedly;
bethotan 1 pulling; 2 the act of pulling;
bethot-bethotan to pull back and forth;
kebethot accidentally snatched.

bethu, **mbethu** round and fat face.

bethur, **mbethur** (of girls, women) lazy, unwilling to work at one's tasks.

bethuthut, **mbethuthut** gloomy, clouded (of face).

beton I the pit of the jackfruit.
II concrete; **témbok beton** concrete wall.

betotong, **mbetotong** to have a large bowel movement.

bewah to support or contribute food materials to s.o. who holds a feast (*kr for* **buwuh**).

bèwèh a certain fruit (**jéngkol**) which is prepared for eating or cooking by burying it for a period of time.

bèwèl, **mbèwèl** numerous, profuse (of scabies).

bèwès, **mbèwès** 1 to drool, slobber; 2 *cr* to give birth again and again; 3 over-abundant (of debt).

béwok long sideburn hair (*var of* **bréwok**).

béya 1 cost, charge; 2 customs, duty, tax, toll, excise;
mbéyani to tax;
pabéyan customs office. *See also* **prabéya**.

bèyès small river crab (young of the **yuyu**).

béyo mynah bird;
mbéyo to mimic.

béyong 1 tadpole (*see also* **cébong**); 2 *or* **béyongan** the young of a certain freshwater fish (**kutuk**).

bi 1 *adr* aunt; 2 *reg* mother. *See also* **bibi**.

bibal *reg* to peel off.

bibar (*kr for* **bubar**) to disperse; finished, over; after.

bibas free (*var of* **bébas**).

bibèk aunt (*var of* **bibi**).

bibi 1 aunt (parent's younger sibling); 2 *adr* mother (term used at court by children of a concubine). *See also* **bi**.

bibis 1 water beetle; 2 **bibisan** a certain plant.

bibit 1 origin, beginning, seed; - **kawit** origin, motivation; 2 (*or* **bibitan**) plant or animal used for breeding;
mbibitaké 1 to use for breeding; 2 to provide with s.t. for breeding;
bibit bobot bèbèt heredity, worldly wealth and moral character (the criteria for evaluating a prospective son-in-law).

biblak (to have) an open wound;
biblakan skinned place.

biblèk *var of* **biblak**.

bibrah out of order, in disrepair (*kr for* **bubrah**).

bibrik, **bibrik-bibrik** to start (a job, a business);
mbibrik to trespass on s.o.'s land.

bicanten to speak (*rg var of* **wicanten**).

bicara to speak (*reg var of* **wicara**).

bidhag pawn (in chess).

bidhal to leave (*kr for* **budhal**).

bidhar dugout canoe.

bidho a variety of hawk.

bidhug *reg* stupid, ignorant.

bidhung, **mbidhung** *or* **mbebidhung** to bother;

ambidhung api rowang harmful intention in disguise.

bidhur itching, skin rash;
　bidhuren to suffer from such a rash.

bigar frisky, frolicsome, glad.

bihal mule.

bihalal see halal.

bijaksana endowed with wisdom (var of wicaksana).

biji mark, grade;
　mbiji or mbijèni to mark, grade, judge;
　bijèn pertaining to marks.

bijig, mbijig to butt;
　mbijigi to butt s.t. repeatedly;
　bijig-bijigan to butt each other.

bijil (of eyes) burst and with bulging pupils.

bikak open (kr for bukak).

bikal or bikal-bikal having an itchy skin condition.

bikang or carabikang a pancake made from sticky rice flour, sugar and coconut milk.

bikin, dibikin to be tricked, victimised.

bikir coconut-shell spinning-top.

biku ascetic, priest.

bikut busy, bustling.

bil ½-cent coin, used during the colonial period (shtf of bribil).

bilahi see bilai.

bilai disaster, calamity, bad luck;
　mbilaèni 1 to endanger, imperil; 2 dangerous, perilous. See also blai.

bilal muezzin.

bilas to rinse with clean water after washing; to bathe with fresh water after swimming at the beach or river;
　mbilasi to rinse s.o. or s.t. with clear water after bathing or washing.

bilih when(ever), if (opt kr for yèn, menawa). See also bok II.

bilik a small inner room;
　bilik-bilik separated into groups.

bilis rake.

bilo with poor vision.

bilug, mbilug-mbilug big and fat.

biluk, mbiluk to turn, veer, return.

bilulung, bilulungan, pl pating bilulung to turn around in panic.

bilur(-bilur) with weals from lashing.

bima 1 lit frightening, awesome; 2 way name of one of the Pandhawa; - sekti the Milky Way;
　Bima akutha saksi to have strong character and personality;
　bima para sama to play favourites in presiding over the case.

bimbang or kebimbang infatuated.

bimbing, mbimbing to guide, lead;
　bimbingan guidance.

bin son of.

binantang lit animal, beast (pejorative term).

bincih, kebincih castrated, spayed (kr for kebiri).

bincil, mbincili to calculate a propitious time for an event;
　bincilan time-calculation for holding rituals.

bindhel a bound volume (var of bèndhel).

bindheng nasal (of speech).

bindhiwala lit spear.

bindi or bindhi cudgel, bludgeon, club.

bing, mbing I reg only (var of mung).
　II reg in, at, on (var of ing).

bingah happy (kr for bungah).

bingar bright (of face);
　mbingaraké to make one's face appear happy.

bingbing, mbing-mbing, ari-ari lit placenta, afterbirth.

binggel ankle bracelet;
　mbinggeli to put s.t. around s.o.'s ankle;
　binggelan to wear a bracelet on the ankle.

bingkar, mbingkar to unload (reg kr for bungkar).

bingkas, mbingkas to straighten out (var of béngkas).

bingkem to keep the mouth closed (*reg kr for* **bungkem**).

bingkil workshop, repair shop.

bingkrak, **bingkrak-bingkrakan** *or* **bebingkrakan** wasteful, extravagant.

bingleng in a quandary.

bingung confused, bewildered;
  mbingungi to act in a confused way; suffering from disorientation;
  mbingungaké to bewilder, fluster, confuse;
  mbebingung *lit* to cause s.o. bewilderment;
  bingungan easily bewildered.

bintal, **kebintal** to get lost, disappear.

bintang I (star-shaped) award medal.
  II star.
  III *reg* a brass teapot-tray.

bintangur a certain large tree.

binté, **mbinté** to kick s.o. in the calf of the leg with one's shin;
  bintèn a kicking contest (children's game).

binteng *or* **binteng-jahé** ginger chewing-candy.

bintit red and swollen (of eyes, from disease or crying).

bintu a certain blue chemical used in processing batik;
  mbintoni to dye (fabric) the basic blue by dipping it in a solution of this substance.

bintul (having) a small itchy swelling from insect bites;
  mbintul having such a swelling.

bintur *reg* pincers for catching crabs;
  mbintur to catch crabs with such an implement;
  kebintur to get trapped; *fig* to be led astray.

bioskup cinema.

bipèt buffet, refreshment bar. *Also* **bupèt**.

bir beer.

birahi *see* **brahi**.

birama *lit* attractive, pleasing, beautiful.

birat away, gone, disappeared;
  mbirat to do away with, remove, banish.

biri *or* **birèn** *ng*, **bincih** *kr*, castrated, spayed;
  mbiri to castrate, spay. *See also* **kebiri**.

biring long spear with straight head.

biru blue; **abang** - *or* - **èrem** (to be) black-and-blue; - **kecu** deep blue; - **maya-maya**, pure clear light blue;
  mbiru to make s.t. blue;
  mbironi to cover (the dyed portion of batik) with wax to protect it from reddish-brown colour of the next dyeing;
  mbirokaké to have s.t. dyed blue.

bis I bus;
  ngebis to go by bus;
  ngebisi to bus s.o.; to buy a bus ticket for s.o.;
  ngebisaké to send by bus;
  ngebisan bus station, bus terminal;
  bis-bisan 1 bus station; 2 toy bus; 3 to go everywhere by bus.
  II letterbox;
  ngebisaké to post a letter.
  III concrete water pipe.

bisa *ng*, **saged** *kr* 1 can, able; 2 to manage to do, succeed in (do)ing; 3 to be good at (doing); - **uga** perhaps, possibly; **ora** - **ora** definitely, certainly (*see also* **isa** I);
  bisané what one is capable of; what one is able to;
  kabisan ability, capability;
  sabisané according to one's capacity;
  dibisak-bisakaké to make s.t. possible;
  bisa-bisané how is it possible!;
  sabisa-bisa if possible;
  sabisa-bisané to the best of one's ability;
  masa bisaa it is inconceivable, impossible. *See also* **masa**.

biséka king's name given at consecration. *See* **abiséka**.

bisik I *or* bisikan a whisper;
  mbisiki to whisper to;
  mbisikaké to whisper s.t. to s.o.;
  bisik-bisik *or* bisak-bisik *or* bebisik
  to whisper;
  bisik-bisikan to whisper to each other.
  II bebisik king's name.
biskop I Roman Catholic bishop.
  II movie, cinema (*var of* bioskup).
biskucing a certain medicinal shrub,
  touch-me-not (*var of* piskucing).
biskup *var of* bioskup.
biskuit *var of* beskuwit.
bismillah in the name of God.
bisu dumb, mute;
  mbisu to refuse to say a word; to act
  dumb; to keep quiet.
bithet scar from a wound.
bithi fist;
  mbithi to punch.
bithu, bithu-bithu having a round, full
  face.
biting I coconut leaf rib sharpened to a
  point for pinning wrapping leaf;
  mbitingi to fasten a wrapping leaf
  with such a pin;
  bitingan pinned with a leaf rib pin.
  II *reg var of* bètèng.
  III *lit* unit of 400.
  sabiting 400.
biwada *lit* honour, esteem;
  ambiwada *lit* to esteem, revere, hold in
  awe.
biwara *lit* announcement, publication;
  mbiwarakaké to publish, announce.
biya, biya-biya *excl of amazement.*
biyada 1 female court servant; 2 girls in
  service at ceremonies.
biyah *excl of disparagement.*
biyak, mbiyak to unveil, expose, open.
biyang 1 *reg* mother; 2 woman of low
  status;
  biyangané *term of abuse.*
biyantu help, aid, assistance;
  mbiyantu to help, assist;

mbiyantoni to support and help s.o.;
  pambiyantu help, aid, assistance;
  sabiyantu in cooperation with,
  supporting.
biyas to turn pale suddenly from surprise
  or shame.
biyasa 1 usual, ordinary; 2 accustomed
  to, familiar with.
biyayak, biyayakan *or* byayakan to keep
  moving around restlessly.
biyèk in the past (*var of* biyèn).
biyèn *ng*, rumiyin *kr*, once, formerly,
  previously; - mula from the very
  beginning.
biyet, mbiyet abundant (of fruit on the
  tree).
biyuh *or* biyuh-biyuh *excl of astonish-*
  ment.
biyung 1 *reg* mother; 2 *adr: reg* woman of
  low status; 3 *or* biyung-biyung *excl of*
  pain, astonishment, compassion.
blaba generous.
blabag I board, blackboard;
  mblabag 1 boardlike; 2 hard as a
  board.
  II one who is responsible for s.t.;
  keblabag to be given a responsibility.
blabar I strong cord used as a boundary
  marker; - kawat arena for combat;
  mblabari 1 to sketch, delineate; 2 to
  draw up a sketch or outline (of);
  blabaran sketch, outline.
  II mblabar to overflow, spill over;
  blabaran to overflow, spilling everywhere.
blabuk, mblabuk *or* mblabukaké to sell
  fake articles as genuine.
blabur I 1 *reg* flood; 2 abundant (of foods).
  II hazy, blurred (*var of* blawur).
blacan a certain wild cat.
blaco unbleached cotton, raw shirting.
blacu *var of* blaco.
blad pattern transferred to another paper
  underneath by drawing heavily over the
  lines;

ngeblad to trace a drawing in this way.

blader, mblader 1 cluttered, cluttering; 2 plenty.

bladhak, mbladhak 1 to run out of the path of; 2 to swerve from the right direction, *fig* badly behaved (of women).

bladheg, mbladheg to happen continuously;

bladhegan continuous successive occurrences.

bladho a certain star. *See* lintang.

bladhog I *reg* gluttonous.

II mbladhog to split (wood).

bladhu muddy, mucky;

mbladhu muddy;

kebladhu to get trampled into the mud.

blaèr *or* blaèran to salivate freely when about to vomit.

blaès *reg var of* blai.

blai *excl of unlucky feeling*: damn it! darn it! *excl expressing fear or alarm*.

blajar to learn, study;

mblajari to teach;

blajaran at the learning stage.

blak I *or* mak blak *repr* opening;

ngeblak wide open;

ngeblakaké to uncover the reality;

blak-blakan 1 wide open; 2 frankly speaking; 3 roofless spot/place.

II paper pattern.

ngeblak to use s.t. as a pattern;

ngeblakaké to make s.t. by using a pattern for s.o.;

blak-blakan s.t. produced by using s.t. as a pattern.

blaka 1 frank, candid; 2 to tell the truth, admit frankly; - suta frankly speaking;

mblakani to tell the truth to s.o.;

mblakakaké to tell the truth about;

blakan-blakanan to tell each other frankly.

blaki *subst kr of* blaka.

blakin *or* blaking *reg* tar.

blalak, mblalak (of eyes) wide open and clear;

mblalakaké to open the eyes widely;

blalak-blalak (of eyes) wide open and clear.

blanak a certain edible fish.

blandar I 1 roof frame; 2 main section of a roof frame.

II blandaran *reg* a race; to race.

blandhang, mblandhang to run fast; at high speed (*var of* bandhang II);

mblandhangaké to make s.t. go fast; to cause to run fast.

blandhit, pating blandhit 1 scattered around, piled up any way; 2 inconsistent, shifty, unreliable.

blandhong woodcutter;

mblandhong to cut wood for a living;

blandhongan 1 lumber or timber business; 2 felling of trees; 3 *or* blandhungan a big tree trunk used for making a canoe.

blandrang, mblandrang to keep on running;

keblandrangen passing by too far from the destination.

blandreng *reg var of* blandrang.

blang, blang-blangan always out visiting; running errands; roaming.

blang-bleng to enter continuously. *See also* bleng I.

blanggem cassava cake.

blanggrèng I blossom of the coffee plant.

II fried cassava.

III mblanggrèng courageous and good-looking.

blangkem, blangkemen 1 stunned, speechless; 2 hard to talk or eat (from feeling stiff in one's jaw).

blangko 1 form to be filled in; 2 to abstain from voting;

tukang blangko headdress (blangkon) maker. *See* tukang.

blangkok half-and-half (colour).

blangkon male batik headdress, sewn into shape;

blangkonan to wear such headgear.

blangkrèh, pating blangkrèh in disorder (*var of* bléngkrah).

blangsi *reg* sugar-bag.

blanja 1 to shop, to go shopping; 2 housekeeping money;
mblanja to hire, employ; to pay s.o. regularly;
mblanjakaké 1 to spend (money); 2 to buy things on s.o.'s behalf.
blanjan 1 payday; 2 items purchased;
beblanjan to go shopping.

blanjèt, mblanjèt *reg* good-looking, handsome.

blanthong, blanthongan an ant-like insect.

blantik broker, middleman in livestock.

blarah, mblarah *or* blarahan 1 scattered about; 2 pervasive (of a disagreeable odour).

blarak dry coconut leaves.

blarat, mblarat *reg* to leave with no intention of returning; to run away.

blarong, blarongan to smell foul, reek.

blarud, blarudan stricken by disaster (epidemic, flood *etc*).

blarut *or* blarutan a scratch;
mblarut scratched, cut; to scratch;
keblarut scratched;
pating blarut having many scratches.

blas 1 *repr* a swift motion; 2 all, totally;
waras - fully recovered (*see* waras);
blas-blasan to go everywhere; wander around in haste.

blasah, mblasah *or* pating blasah scattered about on the ground, to spread, strew.

blasak, mblasak *or* mblasak-mblasak 1 to wander here and there; 2 astray, on the wrong road (*var of* blasuk);
blasakan to stray.

blasar, mblasar astray, on the wrong road.

blaster crossbred bird; - lumut crossbreed with a male grey-green dove;
mblaster, mblasteraké to crossbreed (of animals);
blasteran 1 crossbred (of animals); 2 of mixed blood.

blasuk, mblasuk to stray, wander on the wrong road;
mblasukaké to cause s.o. to go wrong;
keblasuk astray, on the wrong road.

blasur, pating blasur disorderly.

blatèr popular, friendly, outgoing.

blathi dagger, knife.

blathok a type of axe.

blatung maggot, in wounds.

blau laundry blue.

blaur 1 *var of* blawur; 2 stubborn, headstrong.

blawah, mblawah 1 wide, gaping; 2 to overflow; 3 very wealthy;
blawahan to overflow here and there.

blawan I mblawan *reg* a match for, the equal of;
mblawani to contradict;
blawanan 1 contradictive; 2 to talk coarsely.
II mblawani to cooperate with.

blawong long and big around.

blawu cement in powdered form. *See also* semèn.

blawur blurred, not clearly visible.

blawus 1 faded (of coloured clothing); 2 ragged and dirty.

blayang, mblayang to go somewhere for pleasure;
blayangan to saunter everywhere for pleasure.

blebah (of rain) heavy, hard, pouring; - panènan harvest time, when rice is plentiful and cheap.

blebed bandage; protective covering/ wrapping;
mblebed to wrap;
mblebedaké to apply a wrapping;
blebedan in a wrapped condition.

blebeg *or* mak blebeg *repr* sudden submergence;
mblebeg to submerge s.t.;
mblebegaké 1 to cause to be submerged; 2 to hold s.t. under water to fill it;

keblebeg 1 to get submerged; 2 to get drowned.

blèbèk, mblèbèk 1 to flow outward in all directions; 2 to come open; opened out; blèbèkan thick flat piece; sablèbèk (of metal) one sheet.

bleber or mak bleber *repr taking a flying leap*; pating - *pl* to fly, jump; blebar-bleber to jump or fly back and forth.

blèbèr *var of* blabar II.

blebes I or mak blebes 1 *repr sudden submergence*.

II long ruler used as an aligning tool, *e.g.* by carpenters, fabric sellers *etc*.

III mblebes 1 downward; apes - *see* apes; 2 too wet to burn.

blecat *var of* plecat.

bleder *var of* blader.

bledhag, mbledhag to blow up, shoot out; bulging (of stomach), cracked.

bledheg, mbledheg (of baked brick) underdone.

bledhèg lightning. *See also* samber.

bledhèh, mbledhèh partly opened up, coming open; mbledhèhaké to leave (the shirt) partly open.

bledheng or mak bledheng *repr entering*.

bledhes or mak bledhes *repr sudden submergence or diving*; mbledhesaké to submerge s.t., *fig* to press s.o.

bledhog, mbledhog to explode noisily; bledhogan 1 large loud firecracker; 2 loud explosion.

bledhos, mbledhos to explode, erupt; mbledhosi to explode at/in s.t.; mbledhosaké to cause to explode; kebledhosan to be affected adversely by an explosion; pambledhos the act of exploding.

bledhu dust (*reg var of* bledug).

bledhug I mud.

II *var of* bledhog.

bledig, mbledig to chase, *fig* to drive s.o. into a corner with questions.

blèdru *reg* different, varying from.

bledug I dust, *esp in the air*; mbledug 1 dusty; 2 totally destroyed like dust; mbledugi to get dust onto.

II earnings apart from salary (tips, commission *etc*).

III baby elephant (young of the gajah).

bleg 1 or mak bleg *repr falling*; - seg *repr dropping off to sleep*; 2 altogether; ireng - all black; 3 closely similar (*var of* plek); geblegi 1 to fall on s.t. heavily; 2 to resemble closely (*var of* ngepleki); ngeblegaké 1 to drop s.t. heavy; 2 *fig* to ruin one's reputation; keblegan to be hit by a falling heavy object; blag-bleg *repr falling repeatedly*; *repr repeated impacts*.

blèg metal can; metal of which cans are made; ngeblègi to can (foods *etc*); blèk-blègan in cans; in tins. *See also* blèk.

blegag, mblegag to crack widely; to split.

blegedheg, mblegedheg to boil with a plopping noise (*e.g.* thick porridge); blegedhegan real, pure, true; santri - a strict Islamic adherent (*see also* santri).

blegenek, mblegenek short and fat-looking.

bleger figure, shape.

blegidhig, mblegidhig disgusting; mblegidhigi to arouse feelings of disgust.

blegong, mblegong (of soil, road) having a hole; mblegongi to cause to fall into a hole; keblegong to fall into a hole by accident; *fig* to get conned; blegongan a hole.

blegug, mblegug excessively fat, bulging.

blejed *or* mblejed 1 stark naked; 2 altogether, completely; **wuda** - stark naked (*see* **wuda**);
blejad-blejed to keep appearing stark naked.

blèjèd, mblèjèdi 1 to strip, remove the outer layer or clothing from; 2 to rob s.o.

blejog, mblejog to (do) on an impulse;
blejogan on an impulse, on the spur of the moment.

blekecek muddy, dirty, not clear.

blekenek, mblekenek mushy and disgusting.

bleketépé woven coconut leaves (for roofs, walls, fences).

blekethek, mblekethek *or* mblekathek muddy, unwashed.

blekètrèk, mblekètrèk thin and watery, oozing disagreeably.

bleketupuk a variety of owl.

blekik, keblekik to get trapped, discovered.

blekok a certain heron.

blèkrèk, mblèkrèk to cut off;
mblèkrèki to cut off many objects.

blekuk, mblekuk 1 bent, curved; 2 *or* mblekuki *or* mblekukaké to bend, curve; blekukan a curved place;
blekak-blekuk 1 halting, hesitant; 2 rumpled. *See also* blengkuk.

blekuthak I a certain fish.
II blekuthak-blekuthuk *see* blekuthuk.

blekuthuk, mblekuthuk 1 to boil, bubble; 2 to tell lies;
blekuthak-blekuthuk *or* pating blekuthuk 1 bubbling; 2 telling lies.

bléla, mbléla to rebel (*var of* baléla).

blèlu untrained, lacking in knowledge (*reg var of* blilu).

bleman brazier for roasting foods over coals (*var of* beleman).

blemben a certain tall stiff grass.

blembeng, mblembeng *reg* thick and short in shape.

blembong, mblembong big and ungainly.

blembung, mblembung 1 large and round-shaped; 2 inflated, puffed.

blencat, blencatan *or* pating blencat at random rather than in consecutive order.

bléncong lamp used in shadow-play performances for throwing the puppet's shadows on a screen.

blencung, mblencung *reg* to walk purposefully without turning the head to either side.

blèndèr, mblèndèr 1 to slide, slip; 2 to slip out of position; 3 to engage in banter or word play; 4 unreliable about keeping one's word; 5 (of women) promiscuous;
mblèndèri to cause to slide easily;
mblèndèraké 1 to joke by playing on words; 2 to delegate one's authority to s.o. else;
keblèndèr to slide accidently;
blèndèran 1 joking, punning; 2 a slippery place. *See also* bléndré.

blendhang, mblendhang 1 bloated, 2 *cr* pregnant.

blèndher I food blender;
mblèndher to blend (food).
II ball-pitcher;
mblèndheri to pitch to (players).
III mblèndher fat, roly-poly.

blendhing, mblendhing 1 distended, bloated; 2 *cr* pregnant.

blendhuk, mblendhuk 1 bulging; 2 round in shape; 3 *cr* pregnant;
mblendhukaké to inflate, swell s.t. up.

blendhung I boiled corn kernels.
II mblendhung inflated, swollen; to swell up.

blendok sticky and reddish tree resin;
mblendok 1 (of tree) to produce sticky resin; 2 (of resin) to harden.

bléndrang a tasty soup cooked more than a day before it is consumed (*var of* béndrang).

bléndré, mbléndré 1 to slip, slide; 2 untrustworthy, slippery.

blèndrèng *reg var of* blèndèr.

blenek I mblenek *or* blenek-blenek short and fat, roly-poly.

II fed up, sated (from greasy food).

blenet *var of* plenet. *See also* plènèt.

blénja, mblénjani reluctant; to fail to keep one's word.

blenjat, blenjat-blenjat *or* pating blenjat not in consecutive order.

blenjog *var of* blejog.

bleng I *or* mak bleng *repr entering; repr exploding*;
ngeblengaké to enter s.t. in; to enter a goal (of soccer);
blang-bleng 1 to go in and out easily; to get in repeatedly; 2 to keep booming. *See also* blang.

II throughout; sesasi - the whole month;
ngebleng to stay awake for 24 hours (as ascetic practice).

III saltwater spring.

bléngah, mbléngah *or* bléngah-bléngah (of face) light-skinned and friendly-looking.

blenger, mblenger *or* blenger-blenger repelled by disagreeable odour; eating too much fatty food.

blèngèr, mblèngèr (of lips, face) rosy and healthy-looking.

blenggi golden thread edging;
blenggèn cloth edged with golden thread.

blenggu handcuffs;
mblenggu to handcuff s.o.

blengker 1 an iron tyre of wheel, hoop of barrel *etc*; 2 frame of a picture, bamboo basket *etc*;
mblengkeri to equip with a frame or edging material.

blèngkèt close (of friendship or other relationships);
mblèngkètaké to cling together.

blengkik, pating blengkik 1 devious, roundabout; 2 *var of* blengkuk.

bléngkrah, mbléngkrah *or* mbléngkrahi to put into disorder, disarrange;
pating bléngkrah in disarray, messy.

blengkuk, mblengkuk 1 bent at the end or at the top; 2 *or* mblengkukaké to bend s.t.

blengur gosling (young of the banyak).

blentèng I blentèng-blentèng spotted, covered with dots of another colour.

II (to remember) vaguely.

blenthot (of body) firm and compact.

blentong spot, blemish;
blentong-blentong *or* pating blentong spotted, covered with blemishes.

blenyak, blenyak-blenyak in random rather than consecutive order.

blenyèk, mblenyèk soft and mushy.

blenyik small fish (teri) salted and rolled up ready to fry.

blépot *or* blépotan muddy, messy, greasy (*var of* glépot).

blérah, mblérah (of eyes) to become red;
blérah-blérah (of eyes) bright, shining.

blérang *reg* striped.

bléré to have a ready laugh.

blerek *reg var of* bleret.

blèrèk *var of* blèkrèk.

blereng, blereng-blereng 1 (of eyes) hazy, blurred; 2 blindingly glary;
mblereng *or* keblerengen blinded by glaring light, dazzled;
mblerengi to dazzle with glaring light; to bedazzle.

blèrèng I *reg var of* lèrèng.

II *var of* bèrèng.

bleret, mbleret to dim, become gloomy;
mbleretaké to make s.t. dim/gloomy.

bléro 1 out of tune, inharmonious, dissonant; 2 interfered (of vision); 3 to waver between alternatives.

bles *or* mak bles *repr entering, stabbing*;
ngeblesaké to stick/stab s.t. into;
blas-bles stabbing repeatedly.

blesar, pating blesar scattered about.

blesat, pating blesat unbound and coming apart.

bleseg, *or* mak bleseg *repr entering, inserting*; mbleseg 1 wedged/pressed into; 2 made lopsided by pressing; mblesegaké to wedge s.t. into; to press down s.t.

blèter inflatable bladder of a leather ball; bal - soccer ball.

blethok mud; mblethok muddy; blethokan muddy place.

bléwah I a variety of melon. II mbléwah to open up wide (*var of* blèwèh).

blèwèh, mblèwèh to open up wide, come open; blèwèhan 1 a ditch; 2 an opening with the edges turned back.

blèwèk *var of* blèwèh.

blibar fruit bud of the mangosteen; blibaran s.t. shaped like a mangosteen bud.

blidhuk *var of* blithuk.

bligo wax-gourd; bligon egg-shaped.

bligon crossbred cow.

bligung, mbligung *or* bligang-bligung undressed, shirtless.

blila rebellion (*var of* baléla).

blilu untrained, lacking in knowledge or skill; mblilu 1 to act ignorantly; 2 to cheat, swindle; mblilu tau pinter durung nglakoni *expr* good experience is better than unapplied knowledge.

blimbing star fruit, carambola, six- or eight-sided; - wuluh a small sour carambola for cooking; blimbingan s.t. shaped like a carambola, six- or eight-sided.

blindhis *or* mblindhis 1 bare, naked; 2 bald; 3 bankrupt, broke.

blindrik, mblindrik *reg* very pretty.

blinger, keblinger 1 to come to think the wrong way about s.t.; 2 to get cheated; 3 to be taken unawares.

blingkrah *var of* bléngkrah.

blinjo *reg var of* mlinjo.

blirik *reg* blirik-blirik speckled, flecked with colour (of feathers or fur).

blithuk deceit, swindle; mblithuk *or* mblithuki to swindle, cheat; keblithuk to get swindled.

bliwur 1 (of vision) blurred, hazy; 2 *or* kebliwur bewildered, confused.

bliyar, bliyar-bliyar *var of* bliyar-bliyur.

bliyur, mbliyur *or* bliyar-bliyur drowsy, sleepy.

bliyut *var of* bliyur.

blobok sleep (dirt in eye); mblobok to have sleep in/around the eye.

blobor, mblobor 1 absorbent; 2 to get absorbed; mblobori to soak into; bloboran liquid absorbed; kebloboran having been absorbed, soaked.

blobos *reg var of* brobos.

blocok *or* blocokan (of batik product) fuzzily or indistinctly patterned.

blodhog a certain freshwater fish.

blodro, mblodro to smear s.t. (onto).

blog I *repr* a thud, slap. II 1 roll, bolt (of fabric); blog-blogan 1 (fabric) in rolls/bolts (*see also* emblog); 2 block or plot of land.

blojod, mblojodi 1 to remove the clothing from s.o.; 2 to rob, hold up, clean out.

blokang stem of a coconut palm leaf.

blokèk, mblokèk to vomit, retch; blokèken to suffer from nausea and vomiting.

blokèng *reg var of* blokang.

blolok, mbloloki blindingly glary;

bl**loken** blinded by glaring light.

katonjok blolok to talk about s.o.'s badness with them sitting close by.

blondrong, mblondrong (of vehicle) to roll by accident;

mblondrongaké to cheat or mislead s.o.;

keblondrong 1 to get cheated, *esp* over-charged; **2** to be misled.

blong 1 *repr sudden relief from strain or tension;* **2** empty; **3** (of car brake) not working.

blongkèng *reg var of* **blongkang.**

blongsong 1 case, cover (for weapon); **2** woven bamboo covering to protect fruit on the tree;

mblongsong *or* **mblongsongi** to encase, cover;

blongsongan protective casing, covering.

blonthang *or* **blonthang-blonthang** with large patches of colour (animal).

blonthèng *var of* **blonthang.**

blonyo *var of* **blonyoh.**

blonyoh, s.t. to rub with;

mblonyoh *or* **mblonyohi** to rub;

mblonyohaké to rub s.t. onto.

blorok (of chicken) motley; spotted;

jago blorok speckled cock.

blorong I black and white striped.

II glaring light (*var of* **blereng**).

III a certain viper.

blorot 1 *reg var of* **plorot; 2** *reg var of* **blondrong.**

blos *or* **mak blos** *repr* piercing.

blosok, mblosok to go through; to slip into;

mblosokaké to thrust s.t. down into;

keblosok slipped into, fallen down into.

blosong *var of* **blongsong.**

blothong I remains of peanuts after the oil has been extracted.

II mblothong mushy from overcooking.

blotrong sagging in the abdomen.

blowok, mblowok to step into a hole;

blowokan a hole in the ground;

keblowok 1 to step into a hole accidentally; **2** to get overcharged for merchandise.

blubud, mblubud inconsiderate; brazen.

blubuk fine and powdery;

blubukan fine ash for cooking in.

blubur, mblubur soft and crumbly.

blubus *var of* **blubud.**

bludag, mbludag 1 to overflow, spill out/over; **2** boastful; **3** generous to others;

bludagan overflow, spillage.

bluder a certain (Dutch) cake.

bludhuk, mbludhuk soft and crumbly;

bludhukan 1 soft crumbly substance, *esp* soil; **2** *var of* **blubukan.**

bludhus, mbludhus to gatecrash.

bludir, mbludir to embroider;

bludiran embroidery, embroidered silk.

bludru velvet.

blug *or* **mak blug** *repr* a thud;

blag-blug *repr* repeated thudding falls or beats.

bluju, mbluju 1 having clean simple lines without ornamentation (of kris); **2** symmetrically shaped cylindrical object.

bluk *or* **mak bluk** *repr* bursting into flame.

blukang *var of* **blokang.**

blukèk *var of* **blokèk.**

blukèr *var of* **bluwèr.**

bluluk coconut in its first stage of development on the tree.

blulung, blulungan *or* **pating blulung** panic-stricken.

blumbang pond, pool;

blumbangan 1 bed of a pond; **- siwakan** fishpond; **2** batik-bordered fabric used for headdress, brassières.

bluncat, mbluncat to jump, leap;

mbluncat-mbluncat to do out of sequence rather than in consecutive order, to jump around.

blundhus, mblundhus stark naked.

blundrah *reg* spotted, stained.

blundrèh *var of* blundrah.

blung *or* mak blung 1 *repr a sudden submerging*; 2 *intsfr* empty; - blung completely empty.

blungka (over)ripe cucumber.

blungker, mblungker 1 to cower, quake; 2 to hug the knees to the chest;
pating blungker quaking, cowering (from cold, fear).

blungkak melon.

blungkang *var of* blongkang.

blungon *reg* chameleon (*var of* bunglon).

bluru, blura-bluru *or* pating bluru to spread in all directions.

blurut, mblurut to commit a burglary in broad daylight.

blus *or* mak blus *repr* stabbing;
blas-blus stabbing repeatedly.

blusuk *or* mak blusuk, *repr* entering, falling into a hole accidentally;
mblusuk to enter;
mblusukaké 1 to push s.t. into; 2 to persuade s.o. to do wrong;
blusukan to wander about squeezing into;
keblusuk 1 to enter by mistake; 2 to be cheated;
blusak-blusuk to keep entering (places where one does not belong).

bluthak a certain fish.

bluthèh slushy, oozy; partially melted.

bluwek *or* mak bluwek *repr entering into a hole*; *repr slipping easily into s.t.*;
mbluwek (of place) hidden deep;
bluwekan a hole in the ground;
kebluwek to slip into a hole by accident;
bluwak-bluwek to keep going into a hole.

bluwer I mbluwer curved, coiled up.
II 1 (of road) muddy; 2 to play in mud.

bluwèr, mbluwèr *or* bluwèran nauseated.

bluwi *reg* prison (*var of* buwi).

bluwus (of clothing) old and faded;
mbluwus to wear faded old clothing.

bobat horsehair (*var of* bubat).

bobok I medicinal ointment or liquid to rub on body;
mboboki to rub s.o. with such an ointment;
mbobokaké to apply (a powder-and-water mixture) to s.t.;
bobokan applying a healing ointment to the body.
II *chld* to sleep (*var of* bubuk).
III mbobok to break through.

bobol collapsed, broken through;
mbobol to break through;
mbobolaké to break s.t. through;
bobolan a pierced hole;
kebobolan pierced, hit (by theft).

bobor 1 (of eggs) infertile; 2 a soup of spinach and coconut milk.

bobot I *ng*, wawrat *kr*, 1 weight; a weight; 2 importance, significance; - timbang consideration of the alternatives;
mboboti to weigh s.t. down;
saboboté 1 in proportion; 2 despite the fact that.
II mbobot pregnant (*k.i. for* meteng).
III bobotan to defecate (*k.i. for* ngising).

bobrak *reg* badly damaged, broken apart;
mbobrak to break, damage.

bobrok 1 ramshackle, dilapidated; 2 rotten, *fig* immoral.

bocah *ng*, laré *kr*, child, young person; - lanang boy; - wadon girl; - wingi soré a very young child, *fig* inexperienced young person;
mbocahi to act childishly;
mbocahaké to regard s.o. as a child;
kebocahen 1 excessively young; 2 childish;
ninggal bocah ing bandhulan 'to leave a child behind on a swing', irresponsible;

ora mambu bocah (of a child) having a mature attitude.

bocèl chipped.

bocok var of bonyok.

bocong buttocks (k.i. for bokong, var of pocong).

bocor 1 to leak out, leaky; 2 (of birds) to sing habitually;
mbocori to leak on(to) s.t.;
mbocoraké to let s.t. leak out, fig to disclose (secrets);
kebocoran to get wet from leaking;
bocoran leakage.

bod paid in full;
ngebodi to pay off a debt; to complete payment on a debt;
ngebodaké 1 to use s.t. to pay off a debt; 2 to pay s.o.'s debt for them;
bod-bodan 1 money or a substitute for paying a debt; 2 to pay off a debt by giving s.t. of the same value.

bodhag broad shallow woven-bamboo basket in which rice is kept.

bodhèh I wild betel vine.
II reg crude, rough.

bodhèng busy and pressed for time.

bodhik long sickle, scythe.

bodhing var of bodhik.

bodho stupid, ignorant;
mbodho or mbodhoni to pretend to be ignorant;
mbodhokaké 1 to consider s.o. stupid; 2 to cause s.t. to be undeveloped;
mbebodho to make a fool of s.o.; to cheat s.o.;
bodhon taking a simple view, making an uninformed guess;
bodho-bodhonan to compete in stupidity;
bodhon-bodhonan to (do) in a simple way.

bodhol 1 to come out (of hair, feathers etc); come off; 2 worn out (mattress, pillow); 3 departure (var of budhal);
mbodhol to come out easily (of hair);

mbodholi 1 to moult; 2 to pull s.t. out;
mbodholaké 1 to cause to come out; to remove the feathers from; 2 to order (troops) to depart; to send s.o. off;
bodholan 1 removed hair, feathers etc; 2 departure of troops.

bodhor reg comedian, joker;
mbodhor to joke;
bodhoran joking.

bodong I (of navel) protuding.
II stupid, ignorant.

bog I or mak bog repr a dull plop.
II ngebog to buy up the entire stock; to buy the crop of a fruit tree before the fruit is harvested;
ngebogaké 1 to let s.t. fall with a plop; 2 to sell the crop of a fruit tree;
bog-bogan contracted for on a job basis.

boga 1 lit food; 2 reg maize.

bogang (of corn, rice) damaged by crop disease.

bogèl (cut) short;
kebogèlan too short, esp of a shadow-play performance which improperly ends before dawn.

bogem I a certain fruit; - mentah fig blow with the fist.
II box in which jewelry is kept.

boging 1 missing a lot of teeth; 2 very old.

bogoh a variety of tree.

bogor reg sugar-palm tree;
mbogor to tap the sap of that tree.

boja lit food; bojakrama a reception, banquet.

bojana lit feast, banquet; - andrawina large dinner party;
pambojanan dining room.

bojlèng boastful, excl used by wayang ogres;
bojlèng-bojlèng iblis lanat excl of astonishment: for goodness' sake! blow me down!

bojo ng, sémah kr, garwa k.i., spouse; -

jaka lara one's original wife whom one has never divorced;

bebojoan to be married.

bojod (of woven bamboo basket) broken through, damaged.

bojog a small woven bamboo basket used for measuring rice.

bok I (*pron as:* **mbok**) mother; **- enom** second wife; **-mas** *adr* woman of lower class; **-ajeng** *or* **-ngantèn** *adr* young woman of middle class; **-ayu** *or* **mbakayu** *adr* elder sister.

II (*pron as:* **mbok**) *or* **bokan** *or* **bok ya** (coaxing) please;

bok-bok *excl of astonishment*;

bok bèn let it happen;

bokbilih if, when(ever) (*kr for* yèn);

bok iya please do!;

bokmenawa perhaps, possibly, probably;

bok wis (**ta**) that's enough now.

III (*pron as:* **mbok**) *reg var of* kok (*2nd person passive prefix*).

bokong 1 *ng*, **bocong** *or* **pocong** *k.i.*, buttocks; **2** bottom or back part of s.t.; **- kukusan** to keep moving from place to place;

mbokong 1 to push s.t. with the buttocks; **2** to attack from the rear; **3** to support financially;

mbokongi 1 to support s.o. financially; **2** to turn one's back on s.o.;

bokongan 1 the back (part, *esp* of a vehicle); **2** bottom (of a container); **3** a small ricefield located among fields belonging to others; **4** flattened top part of a river dyke; **5** puppet figure with round back part;

nyangga bokong to take care of s.o.'s reputation for the sake of their safety.

bokor large bowl, *usu* of brass.

bol rectum; **- jaran** a variety of snack.

bolah (sewing) thread.

bolèd *reg* cassava; sweet potato;

mbolèd 1 tall and thin; **2** (moving)

with wriggling snake-like motions.

bolèg *var of* **bolèd**.

bolèng *or* **bolèngen** (of sugarcane, tuberous roots) with cavities and hardening from plant disease.

bolèr small fruit worm;

bolèren (of fruits) infested with worms.

bolong 1 hollow; **2** perforated; **3** having a hole in it;

mbolong *or* **mbolongi** to make a hole in s.t. deliberately;

mbolongaké to make a hole in s.t. accidentally;

bolongan a hole, orifice; **- irung** nostril(s). *See also* **sundel**.

bolor respiratory disease of horses.

bolos, mbolos to slip away from one's obligation, play truant.

bolot dirt on the human skin;

boloten having dirty skin.

bolu I soft baked cake; **- kukus** a kind of sponge cake.

II a certain creeping plant and its fruits;

bolu rambatan lemah *expr* a complicated interminable problem.

bom 1 bomb; **2** fart;

ngebom to bomb (a target);

ngebomi to bomb repeatedly;

bom-boman to bomb each other; bombing-raid.

boma I *lit* dry grass.

II *or* **boman** inner room in a traditional house.

bomantara *lit* heaven, sky.

bombang, kebombang to get neglected because no help is available.

bombong optimistic, confident;

mbombong to encourage, impart confidence;

kebombong encouraged, bolstered;

bombongan 1 act or way of encouraging; **2** (of one's nature) pleased to be praised.

bombrong a variety of vegetable soup with coconut milk;

mbombrong 1 to make soup as above; 2 (of woman or girl) not neatly combed and dressed.

bon I 1 account, bill; 2 voucher for payment, an IOU;

ngebon to buy on credit.

II 1 a team of players chosen to represent a certain city or area in competition; 2 alliance, league;

ngebon to recruit a player from another team;

bon-bonan recruited player from another team.

bonang gamelan instrument consisting of row of tuned inverted bronze bowls;

mbonang to play the bonang;

mbonangi to join the gamelan orchestra by playing the bonang;

bonangan act or style of playing the bonang.

boncèng, mboncèng 1 to ride on the back of a bicycle or motorcycle; 2 *fig* to ride along on s.o.'s successes;

mboncèngi to get a ride from;

mboncèngaké to give s.o. a ride.

boncis *see* **buncis**.

bondhan a classical dance, performed by a female, depicting a mother caring for her child;

mbondhan to perform this dance.

bondhol a certain bird.

bonékah doll.

bong I (*or* **bong supit**) person other than a doctor who performs a circumcision.

II (*or* **bong Cina**) Chinese cemetery.

III to lie down, go to bed (children's word).

bongbong *var of* **bombong**.

bonggol the part of a tree trunk or plant stalk where it emerges from the soil.

bongkang a certain insect; **kebo** - a cockroach-like insect that walks backwards (*see also* **kebo**).

bongkar *var of* **bungkar**.

bongkèng (of sugarcane, tuberous roots)

with cavities and hardening from plant disease. *See also* **bolèng**.

bonjor *reg* a long bamboo cylinder.

bonjrot, mbonjrot *cr* to shit, have diarrhoea.

bongko rice-accompanying dish, made from beans and grated young coconut steamed in banana-leaf wrapping.

bongkok I stem of coconut-palm leaf.

II *or* **bongkokan** a tied bundle;

mbongkok *or* **mbongkoki** to make into a bundle.

bongkor I *or* **bongkoran** *reg* lying fallow;

mbongkoraké to allow (land) to remain fallow.

II 1 *reg cr* dead; to die; 2 down with! death to…! *See also* **bangka**.

bongkot 1 base of a stem/stalk, tree stump; 2 *or* **bongkotan** the end; - **pucuk** lower and upper ends; beginning and end; *fig* the facts/circumstances of.

bongkrah in disrepair, out of order (*var of* **bungkrah**).

bongkrèk residue of peanuts after extracting oil; **témpé** - fermented beancake made with peanut residue;

bongkrèkan waste from sugarcane.

bonglot *var of* **bolot**.

bongoh (of decoration, physique) pleasing.

bongsor to grow tall fast.

bontèng *reg* cucumber.

bonto *cr* dumb, stupid.

bonyèh running sores;

bonyèhen suffering from running sores.

bonyok 1 overripe, beginning to spoil; 2 severely wounded;

bonyoken to have/get a certain scalp affliction.

bopati *var of* **bupati**.

bopong I (of horses) having a light-coloured body and dark legs.

II mbopong to pick up or hold and carry s.t. against the chest;

bopongan 1 position for carrying or holding s.t. against the chest; **2** a cock carried as gift to the village head when he holds a wedding party *etc.*

bor (black)board.

bora(k), **mbora(k)** *excl of indifference*; I don't care; to hell with it!

borah-barèh *see* **barèh**.

boral *reg* generous, extravagant.

boran *or* **mboran** *reg* possibly, probably.

borang booby trap of sharpened bamboo points stuck in the ground.

bordhès balustrade, platform at the ends of a railway carriage.

bordhir embroidery;
mbordhir to embroider.

boreg I guarantee, security, warranty; an asset used to secure a loan;
mboregi to secure a loan; to put up security for;
mboregaké to use an asset to secure a loan.
II mboregi *reg* to buy a treat for.

borèh *ng*, *kr* **konyoh** *k.i.* a mixture of pounded pandanus and yellow leaves and flowers, used as a cosmetic application applied to the body;
mborèhi to apply this mixture to the body;
borèhan 1 mixture as above; **2** applied with such a mixture.

borok sores on the scalp;
mborok to be ulcerous, fester;
boroken to have/get sores on the scalp; to have an ulcer;
borok ilang rasané *prov* to be accustomed to suffering pain.

borong I mborong 1 to buy up the entire stock, take all of s.t.; **2** to do an entire job; **3** to hold various positions;
mborongaké 1 to sell wholesale; **2** to give the entire contract; **3** to have (a job) contracted for;
borongan 1 total sale; (by the) whole-sale (lot); **2** work contracted for as a job;
pamborong 1 wholesale supplier, purveyor; **2** contractor.
II *or* **mangsa borong** to disclaim responsibility (*var of* **mangsa bodhoa**).

boros I extravagant, wasteful;
mborosi *or* **mbeboros(i)** causing high expenditures, wasteful;
mborosaké to waste, squander.
II sprout of a certain root (**kunci**).

borot leak, to have a leak.

bos I carton (of cigarettes);
bos-bosan in cartons; by the carton.
II *or* **mak bos** *repr* deflating, a rush of escaping air (*see also* **gembos**).
III axle.

bosah-basih *or* **bosah-basèh** in disarray, messy.

bosen bored (with); tired of;
mboseni 1 boring, tiresome; **2** to bore s.o.;
mbosenaké to make s.o. bored;
bosenan easily bored.

bosin (of hunting) unlucky.

boso a certain freshwater fish.

bosok rotten, decayed;
mbosoki decaying;
mbosokaké to cause to rot;
bosokan in a rotted or decayed state.

bot I *ng*, **wrat** *kr*, weight; - **rèpot** troubles, burdens; - **sèlèh** difficult, burdensome; **-sih** biased, partial;
ngeboti *or* **ngebotaké** to consider s.t. more important;
ngebot-boti to make s.t. heavier or more difficult;
saboboté however hard;
bot-boté for the sake of.
II paid in full (*var of* **bod**).

boten (*pron as:* **mboten**) no; not (*kr for* **ora**).

bothèk, **bothèkan** medicine chest with small drawers.

bothi large woven grass bag.

bothok rice-accompanying dish, made of salt fish *etc*, grated young coconut, chili, wrapped in banana leaf and steamed;
   mbothok to make (ingredients) into the above.

botoh 1 croupier, gambling-chief, gambler;
   - jago cock-fight addict; **2** (*or* **bebotoh**) one who bets on s.o.'s case;
   mbotohi to bet on;
   botohan *or* **bebotohan** *or* **ngabotohan** to gamble;
   pambotohan gambling place/association.

botol I bottle.
   II having a hole in the bottom; having no bottom.

botor seed of a certain leguminous plant (**kecipir**). *See also* **lonjong**.

botrawi *lit* ornamental pond, small lake.

boya *reg* (*irregular pronoun*) no; not.

boyong, mboyong, 1 to take (wife and children) to a new home; **2** to take a bride off to her new home (bridegroom);
   boyongan to move with all one's possessions from one location to another.

bowèk having a hole torn in it;
   mbowèk to tear a hole in s.t.

bowol having a hole in it, so that the contents can run out.

bowong *lit* tiger.

B.P.H. *see* **bendara**.

B.R.A. *see* **bendara**.

bra *lit* light, radiance, shining.

brabad, brabadan cooking spices and other kitchen needs; to sell such items in the market.

brabah to speak raucously, having a loud speaking voice.

brabak, mbrabak 1 to flush with anger; **2** having tears of emotion in the eyes.

brabas, mbrabas 1 to seep out; **2** porous.

brabat *or* **mak brabat** *repr* a sudden dash;
   mbrabat to dash, sprint.

brabèh 1 *reg* to have problems; **2** *or*
   kebrabèhan too talkative.

brabon clothing dyed with the bark of a certain tree (**kudhu**).

bracok rope on a horse's mouth used as a halter.

bradhat *or* **mak bradhat** *repr* a sudden dash;
   mbradhat 1 *var of* **mbrabat**; **2** to steal livestock; **3** to seize;
   kebradhat seized.

bradhil, mbradhil *or* **pating bradhil** *or* **brodhal-bradhil** frayed, fraying.

brag-breg *see* **breg**.

brag-brèg *see* **brèg**.

bragalba *lit* tiger. *See also* **pragalba**.

bragedhir brigadier.

brah *reg* scattered, spread about untidily.

brahak-brahok *see* **brahok**.

brahala 1 giant; **2** idol, idolatry.

brahat traditional ritual during the month of Ruwah; **malem** - the night before holding this traditional ritual (*see also* **malem**).

brah-brèh *see* **brèh**.

brahi *or* **brai 1** adolescent, to have reached one's teens; **2** to feel passionate; **3** attracted, keen on (dressing, make up).

brahmacari student of a priest.

brahmana Hindu priest (*var of* **bramana**).

brahmani Hindu priestess (*var of* **bramani**).

brahok *var of* **braok**.

brai *see* **brahi**.

braja *lit* **1** weapon; **2** windstorm;
   sumengka pangawak braja *lit* overbold, to act bravely.

brajag I 1 leader, person in charge.
   II trap of sharpened bamboo points stuck in the ground.
   III mbrajag 1 to sing habitually (*esp* birds); **2** to gush out (of water).
   IV robber; pirate (*var of* **bajag I**);
   mbrajag to rob.
   V mbrajagi to intersperse (plants).

brak *or* **mak brak 1** *repr* a ripping action;

2 *repr* splitting wood; 3 *repr* a slapping sound.

brak-bruk *see* **bruk**.

brakithi *lit* ant (*var of* **blekithi**);
brakithi angkara madu to suffer disaster because of too much ambition to gain wealth.

brakot, mbrakot to bite;
mbrakoti to gnaw on;
kebrakot to get bitten (*esp* by a dog);
brakotan gnawing, biting.

bral, ngebral *or* **ngebralaké** 1 to sell out; 2 to spend recklessly, squander.

bral-brol *see* **brol**.

brama *reg, kr* fire. *See also* **grama**.

bramacorah 1 criminal, felon, bandit; 2 the accused, defendant.

bramakarsa *or* **bramakroso** floral procession.

bramana *var of* **brahmana**.

bramani *var of* **brahmani**.

bramantya *lit* furiously angry. *Also* **bremantya**.

bramara *lit* bee.

bramastra *lit* fire-arrow, rocket.

brambang I red onion;
mbrambang *or* **mbrambangi** (of eyes) to water from irritation, to start trickling (of tears).
II a rice plant disease.

brambet red onion (*reg, kr for* **brambang**).

bran *reg* every day. *See also* **bera**.

brana I *or* **rajabrana** jewelry, riches, treasure. *See also* **raja**.
II *lit* a wound;
kebranan wounded.
III **mbrana** (Yogya slang) *var of* **mrana**.

branah, mbranah *or* **bebranahan** 1 to breed rapidly; 2 to multiply, flourish.

branang, mbranang 1 bright red; 2 to get scorched;
kebranang 1 furious; 2 to get scorched.

brancah of free-and-easy morals, unable to say no.

brandang, mbrandang to need urgently;
brandangan urgent need.

brandhal gangster, rascal, scoundrel;
mbrandhal 1 to be a gangster; 2 to commit an act of banditry;
brandhalan to behave like a felon, ill-mannered.

brandhèng *or* **brandhing** band(s) of thin bamboo.

brandon, *or* **brandonan** to pool capital for a business enterprise; to buy a share in an enterprise.

brang I on the other side (*shtf of* **sabrang** I);
brang kulon the western side of the river.
II **brang-brangan** to drum.

brangas, mbrangas 1 to scorch; 2 to make s.o. angry;
brangasan 1 quick-tempered; 2 bestial, brutal;
kebrangas 1 to get overcooked, to get burnt; 2 furious; 3 growing old too fast.

branggah spreading widely (of horns, branches, antlers); **keris** - kris with a widely spreading crosspiece (*see also* **keris**); **tani** - farmer who owns cattle (*see also* **tani**).

brangkal rubble;
mbrangkal to cover or fill with rubble;
mbrangkalaké to have s.t. covered with rubble;
brangkalan rocky road, rubbly path.

brangkang, mbrangkang to creep, crawl;
brangkangan to crawl around on all fours.

brangkar stretcher (for carrying patients).

brangsang *or* **mbrangsang** to feel uncomfortably warm.

brangta *lit* in love with, enchanted by. *Also* **branta**.

brangti *var of* **brangta**.

brangus muzzle (of dogs);
mbrangus 1 to muzzle an animal, *esp* a dog; 2 *fig* to prevent freedom of speech;

brangusan in a muzzled condition;
pambrangus act of muzzling.

brani magnet; **wesi** - magnetic iron (*see also* **wesi**).

branjang I clay mixed with sand.

II a certain square net; - **kawat** wire netting;
mbranjang 1 wide apart (of woven bamboo *etc*); **2** to enclose with a wire netting.

branta *see* **brangta**.

brantas, mbrantas to wipe out, remove, fight (against); - **wutasastra** to eliminate illiteracy; ~ **pageblug** to combat an epidemic;
pambrantas 1 act of abolishing; **2** exterminator; s.o. or s.t which abolishes.

branwir fire brigade; fire extinguisher, fire engine.

branyak, mbranyak 1 dashing; **2** with one's nose in the air.

braok, mbraok *or* **broak-braok** loud, shrill;
braokan a shrill-voiced person.

brasak 1 coarse sand; **2** *reg* coarse, crude, boorish.

brasat, mbrasat to run away;
mbrasataké to run off with s.t. belonging to s.o. else;
kebrasat to be routed, driven from (the battlefield).

brasta, mbrasta *lit* to wipe out; - **wutasastra** to eliminate illiteracy.

brastha *var of* **brasta**.

brata to undertake an ascetic exercise (a fast *etc*); - **semadi** the practice of religious concentration and meditation; -**yuda** *way* war of Pandawa against Kurawa; **tapa** - *see* **tapa**;
mbratani to fast for (a special goal);
pabratan 1 place where an act of asceticism is performed; **2** *or* **pabaratan** battlefield.

bratawali bitter-tasting leaves used in traditional medicines.

brati I a crossbred duck.

II one who isolates himself and lives ascetically to achieve his aim.

bratos *reg kr for* **bratu**.

bratu advanced money loan, credit.

brawala *lit* struggle, quarrel, dispute, brawl.

brawasa *var of* **brawala**.

brawuk, mbrawuk to claim (ownership of).

brayan *or* **bebrayan 1** society; one's fellow men; **2** to get along well together.

brayat nuclear family, parents with children;
bebrayatan to live together as a family group.

brayut parents with many children;
mbrayut 1 to carry more than one child at a time; **2** to tie together in a bundle.

bré, ngebré to knit.

brebah *subst kr for* **brubuh**.

brébah to change (from its former condition), (*kr for* **brubah**). *Also* **bribah**.

brebeg, mbrebegi to disturb with noise; - **kuping** deafeningly loud;
kebrebegen to suffer from too much noise.

brebek mouldered; to weather, deteriorate;
brebekan mould, decayed wood.

brebel *or* **mak brebel** *repr* welling up, flowing out (of tears);
mbrebel to flow (of tears).

brèbèl, kebrèbèlan to be given a share;
mbrèbèli to hand out bit by bit.

brebes, mbrebes 1 to soak gradually into; **2** to flow freely;
mbrebes mili to shed tears.

brèbès, mbrèbès (of tears) to flow, trickle.

brebet *or* **mak brebet 1** *repr* the sound of ripping; **2** *repr* a fleeting sound or sensation; **3** *repr* whisking past;
brebet-brebet *or* **brebat-brebat** to whisk past frequently.

brèbèt *repr* a ripping sound.
    sabrèbètan at a quick glance.
brécok, pating brécok *pl* (of tree trunks)
    badly scarred with cuts.
bredhel, mbredhel to crack or snap
    easily (*var of* mbedhel).
brèdhel ban, prohibition;
    mbrèdhel to ban.
breg *or* mak breg *repr* s.t. heavy dropping;
    breg-bregan to keep coming one after
    the other;
    kebregan to be felled.
brèg *repr* a thump;
    brag-brèg *repr* repeated thumps.
bregada brigade *var of* bergada.
bregadag, mbregadag 1 yellowish red; 2
    a certain skin rash (*var of* bergadag).
bregagah, mbregagah to stand with the
    legs wide apart (*var of* mbegagah); *fig*
    to commit o.s. to.
bregajag, mbregajag *or* bergajagan ill-
    mannered, discourteous.
bregajul playboy, wolf.
bregandang, mbregandang to drag s.o.
    (*var of* bergandhang).
breganjok, mbreganjok hard to get along
    with (*var of* berganjok).
bregas having a fresh attractive appear-
    ance (*var of* bergas).
bregedeg, mbregedeg in large quantities
    (*var of* bergedeg).
bregedèl *see* begedèl, bergedèl.
bregedud, mbregedud obstinate, deaf to
    advice, headstrong.
bregegeg *see* bergegeg.
bregègèh *see* bergègèh.
bregejeg, bregejegan to quarrel, have a
    dispute *or* difference of opinion. *See
    also* regejeg.
bregènggèng, mbregènggèng 1 to be
    getting better; 2 to start being wealthy.
bregodog *see* bergodog.
bregogok *see* bergogok.
breguguk *see* berguguk.
bregundung, mbregundung obstinate,

wilful, headstrong (*var of* ber-
    gundung).
brèh, brah-brèh *or* ngebrèh wasteful,
    extravagant; - wèh overgenerous.
brejel *or* mak brejel *cr repr* a birth;
    mbrejel *repr* emerging, *esp* from a hole.
brèjèl 1 *var of* brojol; 2 mbrèjèl to come
    out; 3 kebrèjèl to come out uninten-
    tionally.
brek 1 *or* mak brek *repr* ; 2 *repr* feet
    marching in unison;
    brek-brekan plenty, in a great column.
brèk *or* mak brèk 1 *repr* ripping; 2 *repr* a
    slamming sound;
    brak-brèk to make slamming, banging
    sounds.
brekat *see* berkat.
brekecak, mbrekecak *or* mbrekecek to
    splutter; *fig* to talk copiously (*var of*
    bekecek).
brekeneng, brekenengan to argue
    heatedly (*var of* bekeneng).
breketépé *var of* bleketépé.
brekik (*pron as:* breki:k), pating brekik
    pl to shriek. *See also* bekik.
brem I 1 an alcoholic liquor of fermented
    rice; 2 cakes made with this liquor.
    II a small beetle.
bremana *var of* brahmana.
bremani *var of* brahmani.
bremantya *see* bramantya.
brendhèl, mbrendhèl *or* pating brendhèl
    1 full of knots or tangles; 2 having
    many small things to carry. *Also*
    brendhil.
brèndhèl to drop, fall off/out, moult. *See
    also* brindhil).
brèndhi brandy.
brendhil *var of* brendhèl.
brendhol *pl of* bendhol.
brendhul, mbrendhul *or* pating brendhul
    pl having many things to carry.
bréné, mbréné (Yogya slang) *var of* mréné.
breng, *or* mak breng 1 *repr* perceiving an
    odour; 2 *repr* a concerted departure;

3 syllable chanted in making a concerted effort.

brèng or **mak brèng** repr a metallic clang;
brang-brèng to keep clanging.

brengangah, mbrengangah flushed with emotion.

brengangang, mbrengangang 1 to buzz, whine, hum; fig to complain; **2** redfaced with emotion.

brengengeng, mbrengengeng to buzz, whine, hum.

brengganu a variety of citrus fruit (var of **trengganu**). See also **jeruk I**.

brènggèh 1 branched out, ramified; **2** false, perfidious.

brenggèl, mbrenggèl bumpy, uneven.

brenginging high-pitched whining, e.g. of a mosquito;
mbrenginging to whine.

brèngkal, mbrèngkal 1 to raise (s.t. heavy) on one side/edge; **2** inf to wake s.o. up.

brèngkèl, mbrèngkèl to contradict, oppose;
brèngkèlan disputatious.

brengkélé, mbrengkélé selfish, self-centred.

brengkelo, mbrengkelo stubborn, obstinate, opinionated.

brèngkès or **brèngkèsan** fish or meat baked in a banana-leaf wrapping;
mbrèngkès or **mbrèngkèsi** to make (ingredients) into this dish.

brengkiyeng var of **bengkiyeng**.

brengkolang, mbrengkolang to throw a missile.

brengkowang, mbrengkowang or **brengkowangan** to talk loudly.

brengkunung, mbrengkunung stubborn, headstrong.

brengkut, mbrengkut 1 to be carrying a number of things all at once; **2** to start on a task in a brisk businesslike way.

brengkutis a kind of dung beetle.

brengok, pating brengok pl to shout (see also **bengok**).

brengos ng, kr, **rawis** k.i. moustache; -**kèplèh** drooping moustache; - **lèmèt** slim moustache;
- **sumpel** small close-cropped moustache; - **wulu lutung** false moustache made of long black ape hair;
mbrengosi to apply a false moustache on s.o.'s face;
brengosan to wear a moustache.

bréngos var of **brengos**.

brengungung a deep, far-off roaring or rumbling;
mbrengungung to produce such a sound.

brenjèh, brenjèhen covered with skin infections.

brenjih var of **brenjèh**.

brenjul a bump on a surface;
mbrenjul bumpy, uneven;
brenjulan a bumpy part;
pating brenjul pl bumpy, knobbly.

bres 1 repr sudden heavy rain; **2** repr the sound of s.t. colliding.

bresat, mbresat to go away in the face of advice to the contrary. See also **brisat**.

brèsèt 1 unfair (cockfighting tactics); **2** excessively fond of the opposite sex.

bresot, mbresot 1 to go away; **2** var of **bresat**.

bret or **mak bret 1** repr perceiving an odour; **2** repr cloth tearing.

brèt or **mak brèt 1** repr cloth tearing; **2** repr farting; **3** repr blowing the horn.

bréwo, bréwa-bréwo poorly groomed.

bréwok whiskers, long sideburn hair;
bréwoken to be whiskered, bearded.

brèwu or **mbrèwu** very wealthy.

bréyo, bréya-bréyo poorly groomed, sloppy in personal appearance.

bréyot, mbréyot heavy and unwieldy to carry.

bribah var of **brébah**.

bribi, mbribèni to wake s.o. up by

making too much noise;

kebribènan to be awakened by noise;

bribin *lit* disturbed by sounds;

bribin-bribin *reg* to keep telling s.t. to s.o.

bribik I woodworm.

II bribik-bribik just starting out on a job/career.

bribil ½-cent coin used during the colonial period. *See also* bil.

bribuk, mbribuk 1 to grease; 2 to persuade.

brigi, briga-brigi to scowl.

brigih, brigah-brigih to feel uncertain.

brikut *var of* brukut.

bril *reg var of* bribil.

brindhil 1 denuded; 2 to fall off/out; mbrindhili 1 to denude s.t.; 2 to drop off (of leaves).

bringas hot-tempered, wild; bringasan furious, jumpy, restless (rather than calm and serene).

bringkal *var of* bréngkal.

bringkil small lump, *reg var of* pringkil; mbringkil forming a lump.

bringkung, bringkang-bringkung *or* pating bringkung to feel aversion to s.o. *esp* because of their undesirable behaviour.

bringkut *reg var of* brengkut.

bringsang unbearably hot; hot and sweaty.

brintik curly hair; kinky.

bris hair on the chest.

brisat, mbrisat to go away in the face of warnings to the contrary (*var of* bresat).

brisik, noisy, boisterous, tumultuous, uproarious; mbrisiki to produce an irritating rasping noise.

britan backyard (*var of* buritan).

briyeng, mbriyeng (to have) sick headaches.

briyut I *var of* biyet.

II *var of* bliyut.

brobah *var of* brubah.

brobol, mbrobol to come out of a hole.

brobos, mbrobos to creep under or through; brobosan (s.t. which is) crawled under/through.

brocèl scarred; pating brocèl scarred in many places. *See also* bocèl.

brodhol 1 to drop off/out; 2 threadbare; mbrodhol *or* mbrodholi to lose hair/feathers.

brog *repr* a soft thud.

brojol lower on one side than the other; mbrojol to slip out of a hole; kebrojol to come out accidently; kebrojolan 1 to give birth unexpectedly; 2 to come out accidently.

brok *repr* a sudden fall, *esp* s.o. falling on their rear; ngebrok 1 to stay s.w.; 2 to settle in; 3 (of kites) to fail to get off the ground; 4 to dirty one's pants; ngebroki to take up occupancy of; to occupy a place.

brokat brocade(d fabric).

brokoh a basket that stands on four short legs; brokohan 1 ceremony held for a child at birth, when the umbilical cord drops off, and in connection with the naming ceremony; 2 voluntary help offered to the village head by his people; mbrokohi to hold the above ceremonies for (an infant).

brokok *reg var of* brokoh.

brol *or* mak brol *repr* copiously or effortlessly coming forth; brol-brolan to emerge in large quantities; to come out profusely; bral-brol to come out easily; sabrolan emerging copiously and simultaneously.

brom bronze metal paint;

ngebrom to paint s.t. with bronze paint;

brom-broman painted with bronze paint. *Also* **bron**.

brombong water pipe (*var of* **brumbung**).

bron *var of* **brom**.

brondhol sparse (of hair, feathers);

mbrondhol to cut or wear one's hair short;

brondholan stump of a cut sugarcane plant.

brondong I popcorn.

II **mbrondong** to fire missiles at;

brondongan spray of bullets;

bebrondongan volley of gunfire, to keep firing.

broneng (browning-) revolver.

brongkal, mbrongkal to raise (s.t. heavy) on one side/edge;

brongkalan (forming) a heap, a pile of stones.

brongkos a vegetable dish seasoned with a certain fruit (**kluwak**);

mbrongkos 1 to make (ingredients) into the above dish; 2 to wrap, make into a bundle.

brongos, mbrongos to touch with a burning object; to singe, scorch;

kebrongos to get scorched/singed.

brongot *var of* **brongos**.

brongsong *var of* **blongsong**.

bronjong cylindrical basket for transporting large bulky objects.

brono, mbrono (Yogya slang) *var of* **mrono**.

brontak a rebellion;

mbrontak to rebel; to carry out a coup;

pambrontak 1 a rebel; 2 rebellion.

brontok (of skin) rash or acne;

mbrontok having skin rash or acne.

brosot, mbrosot 1 to leave without explanations; 2 to drop, fall; to become low(er), (*var of* **mrosot**);

kebrosot to be given the slip.

brotol the part of a bird below the cloacal opening.

brubah to change s.t. from its former condition;

brubahan a change; changed (of rules).

brubuh destroyed, wiped out; **perang** - fierce war that causes total destruction (*see* **perang**); - **Ngalengka** the destruction of the kingdom of Ngalengka;

mbrubuh *or* **mbrubuhi** to destroy, wipe out.

brubul, mbrubul *or* **pating brubul** to pour out in large numbers. *See also* **gumrubul**.

brubus *repr* smoke puffing out;

mbrubus to escape by hissing;

mbrubusi to boil s.t. to get rid of its bad taste.

brubut *or* **mak brubut** *repr* fast running;

pating brubut *pl* running swiftly;

mbrubut to break into a fast run.

brucèl *var of* **brocèl**.

bruder Roman Catholic brother.

brudhul *var of* **brubul**.

brug I *repr* a plopping sound.

II soil-tamping metal plate attached to a handle.

II *reg* bridge.

brugul rough skin, pimples on a face.

bruju *reg* youngest child in a family. *See also* **waruju**.

brujul I a small plough without mould board;

mbrujul to work (soil) with such a plough.

II *var of* **brubul**.

bruk I *or* **mak bruk** *repr* s.t. dropping down;

ngebruk 1 to stay s.w. (*see* **brok**); 2 to embrace suddenly, in a rush of emotion;

ngebruki to fall onto;

ngebrukaké 1 to drop s.t.; 2 to drop things here and there;

kebrukan to get fallen on;

brak-bruk 1 *repr* repeated dropping sounds or actions; **2** to drop s.t. (clothing *etc*) as one pleases. *See also* **ambruk**. **II** *reg* trousers.

brukuh, mbrukuh to chop off, lop (branches).

brukut 1 tightly wrapped/bundled; **2** well enclosed; tightly constructed.

brul *or* **mak brul** *repr* emerging copiously; **brul-brulan** to come out in swarms.

brumbun (of chicks) covered with down.

brumbung *or* **brumbungan** water pipe (*var of* **brombong**);

mbrumbung to get pregnant again after giving birth with no intervening menstrual period.

bruncah, mbruncah to hand out (food) to those partaking of a meal.

brundhul sparse (of feathers). *See also* **brondhol, brindhil**.

brung *or* **mak brung 1** *repr* throwing s.t. light (wrapping leaves *etc*); **2** *intsfr* empty; **suwung -** completely empty; **3** *repr* a sudden concerted departure.

brungkah I a cut-off stump complete with roots.

II mbrungkah to cease one's fasting or avoidance of certain foods.

brungkut *var of* **brukut**.

brungut *reg* suddenly appearing.

brunjung main roof of a traditional Javanese house;

mbrunjung shaped like this roof.

brus *or* **mak brus** *repr* a collision.

brusut *or* **mak brusut** *repr* a smooth easy exit.

brutu coccyx (of a bird, chicken); tailbone.

bruwah fast-breaking meal at the end of a fasting period;

mbruwah to eat one's fill after a fasting period;

mbruwahi to eat (certain foods) at the close of the fast.

bruwang bear (animal);

bruwang-bruwangan toy bear, teddy bear.

bruwès hairy, shaggy (beard *etc*).

bruwet 1 not clearly visible; obscure, hazy; **2** depressed, gloomy.

bruwun I (of hair) fluffy, fuzzy; bushy.

II mbruwun to gather vegetables from garden or field.

III mbruwun *or* **mbebruwun** to use s.o. else's money for one's own interest.

bu 1 mother (*shtf of* **ibu**); **2** *adr* mother; wife; older and/or higher-status woman;

budhé aunt (*shtf of* **ibu gedhé**);

bulik aunt (*shft of* **ibu cilik**).

bubak marriage ceremony held for the first daughter of a family;

mbubak to open up (virgin soil) for cultivation; **- kawah** traditional ceremony performed when bride and groom first meet during the wedding;

bubakan opened up for cultivation (of land).

bubar *ng*, **bibar** *kr* **1** to disperse; **2** finished; to be over; **3** after;

mbubaraké to disperse (a group);

bubaran to disperse; to break up;

sabubaré 1 after; **2** until finished.

bubat horsehair.

bubrah *ng*, **bibrah** *kr* out of order, in disrepair;

mbubrah *or* **mbubrahaké** to damage, wreck, disrupt;

mbubrahi to keep wrecking; to break through.

bubrak, mbubrak 1 to open s.t. (up) for use; **2** to demolish (a building).

bubruk 1 unsuccessful (trade); **2** (girl) not in demand.

bubu fish trap with bamboo bars (*reg var of* **wuwu**).

bubuh *ng*, **bebah** *kr*, **mbubuhi** to assign a responsibility to s.o.;

bubuhan a task assigned to s.o.;
kebubuhan 1 to be assigned or saddled with a responsibility; 2 to get s.t. in it by accident.

bubuk I 1 powder; **2** pounded coffee; **wédang** - hot coffee; **3** termite-like insect;
mbubuk to crush to a powder;
bubukan in powdered form;
bubuken 1 eaten away by wood insects; **2** *fig* (of girl) unmarriageable; on the shelf.
II *chld* to sleep;
mbubuki to sleep on s.t.;
mbubukaké to put (a child) to bed;
bubukan to lie down; to lie around;
bubuk olèh elèng *prov* to work out a scheme for doing s.t. harmful.

bubul I 1 yaws; **2** durian fruit sprout;
bubul wuta an unburst swelling;
mbubul to form a swelling;
bubulen to have yaws.
II mbubul to keep pouring out.

bubur porridge; - **sungsum** a ceremonial porridge made from rice flour and palm sugar. *See also* **jenang**;
mbubur 1 to make porridge; **2** to eat porridge instead of rice; **3** to become mush.

bubus rice-accompanying dish prepared from certain leaves (**lumbu**).

bubut I a kind of owl.
II lathe;
mbubut to operate a lathe; to turn s.t. on a lathe;
bubutan shaped on a lathe.
III mbubut to pull s.t. out by the roots;
mbubuti to keep pulling s.t. out; to pluck (a chicken);
mbubutaké to pull s.t. out for s.o.;
bubut-bubut to keep pulling out; to uproot (grass).

bucal *root form: kr for* **buwang**.

bucek cracked or broken but still holding together, *e.g.* an eggshell.

bucèl detached, chipped, skinned (*var of* **bocèl**).

buceng a cone of rice for ritual meal.

bucik 1 *var of* **bucèl**; **2** *var of* **bucek**.

bucu hump, hunch (on the back).

buda I Buddha; **agama** - Buddhism; **jaman** - pertaining to the pre-Islamic era, **sastra** - pre-Islamic literature; **kabudan** pertaining to Buddhism.
II *lit* Wednesday; - **cemengan** ritual name of the day **Rebo Wagé**.

budaya culture, civilisation;
mbudaya to be entrenched; to be part and parcel of (a society);
kabudayan culture, civilisation.

budhak slave; **mbudhak** to be, act like a slave.

budhal *ng*, **bidhal** *kr*, **jengkar** *k.i.*, to leave, set out (as a group);
mbudhalaké to send out (a group); to despatch troops;
budhalan 1 *pl* act of moving elsewhere; **2** the movement of troops.

budhé *see* **bu**.

budheg 1 deaf; **2** stupid; **3** counterfeit, fake; **layang** - anonymous letter, unsigned letter;
mbudheg *or* **mbudhegi** to act as though one were deaf;
mbudhegaké 1 to deafen; **2** to treat s.o. as a deaf person;
mbudheg-mbudegaké to abusively call s.o. deaf.

budheng 1 dull(-sounding); dull(-witted); **2** black monkey.

budhug leprosy;
budhugen to have/get leprosy.

budhur *reg* nectar from a coconut bud.

budi I 1 character, temperament; **2** mind, intelligence, mental power; - **rahayu** virtue, virtuousness;
bebudèn character, temperament;
pambudi effort, attempt.
II (to exert) power;

mbudi to make an effort, attempt;
sabudiné with all one's strength.
III the Bodhi tree, the sacred fig.

budiarda lit ambition, greed, desire.

budidaya a strong effort;
mbudidaya to exert o.s.;
pambudidaya a strong effort.
kabudidayan agricultural enterprise, estate, plantation.

budidarma 1 generosity; noble-mindedness; 2 good deeds.

budiman lit intelligent; skilled (in).

budin var of bodin.

bug or mak bug repr a plop or thud;
bag-bug repr repeated thuds.

buga lit food (var of boga).

bugel 1 short piece of firewood; 2 stupid person; 3 cut off short (var of pugel).

buger see seger.

buh I reg feeble with old age.
II mbuh I don't know; I doubt it. See also embuh.
mbuh-mbuhan nobody knows.
III bow, curve, arc;
ngebuh to bow, bend, curve.
IV buh-buhan a task assigned to s.o. See also bubuh.

bui var sp of buwi.

buja lit arm, hand.

bujad var of bejad.

bujaga lit serpent, dragon (var of bujangga).

bujana feast, banquet. See also bojana.

bujang or bujangan 1 bachelor; 2 reg labourer.

bujangga var of pujangga.

bujel having a rounded tip.

bujeng, mbujeng to hunt, chase (kr for buru).

bujid, bujiden reg stunted in growth.

bujil a runt, dwarf.

bujug, bujug-bujug or bujug-besèt excl of astonishment or incredulity.

bujul var of brujul.

bujuk persuasive talk;
mbujuk or mbujuki 1 to mislead s.o. with talk; 2 reg to cheat s.o.;
mbebujuk to talk s.o. into s.t.; to persuade s.o.;
bujukan blandishment, enticement.

bujung I sugarcane leaf (kr for godhong tebu).
II bujung, mbujung lit to chase. See also bujeng.

buk I 1 all even; without profit or loss; 2 paid in full;
ngebuki to pay up.
II a small bridge over a stream.
III or mak bluk repr a soft thud.
IV kabuk to get nothing (disappointed).

buka 1 opening, beginning; 2 (to eat) a meal that breaks one's fast;
mbuka to open (up, out), disclose;
mbukani to begin, start (music);
bebuka 1 introduction, preface, fore-word; salutation of a letter; 2 opening, beginning;
pambuka opening, beginning. See also bukak.

bukak ng, bikak kr open(ed), uncovered;
- kunci wages paid to s.o. for looking after graves; - topi 1 hatless; 2 to respect, admire;
mbukak 1 to open, uncover, disclose; opened, uncovered, disclosed; 2 to remove, take off;
mbukaki to open (many objects);
mbukakaké to open s.t. (for s.o.);
bukakan 1 open; uncovered; 2 opener;
bukak-bukakan to be open to all. See also buka.

buket thick (of liquids).

bukèt bouquet.

buki 1 (of cassava, potato etc) too old; 2 old mlinjo fruit.

bukti I proof, evidence;
mbuktèkaké to prove, establish, show; to give evidence of;
kabuktèn proven, shown.

II *lit* food; to eat;
abukti *lit* to eat.
buku book;
mbukoni to codify.
bukuh, mbukuh cross-legged;
mabukuh *lit* to sit (cross-legged) in a respectful posture.
bukung 1 (of birds) tailless; **2** cut short;
mbukung to cut off; to cut short;
bukungan (of hair) cut short.
bukur I a variety of clam.
II *lit* heaven's gate; - **pangarip-arip** *lit* a gate of the realm of the deities.
bul I large bowl-shaped earthenware container.
II *or* **mak bul** *repr* puffing upward;
bal-bul *repr* repeated puffings.
bulak *or* **bebulak** a broad treeless field.
bulan *or* **mbulan** *ng,* **wulan** *kr,* moon. *See also* **rembulan**.
bulé 1 albino; **2** white person.
bulek 1 misty smoke; **2** to feel suffocated by misty smoke;
mbuleki suffocating; to get smoke/steam on s.t.;
bulekan smoke, steam.
bules *var of* **bulek**.
bulet I 1 solid, firm; **2** oval, elliptical.
II **mbulet 1** tangled, snarled; **2** evasive;
mbuletaké to twist or snarl s.t.
bebuletan to wind around, encircle.
buli *or* **buli-buli** *reg* small earthenware container.
bulik *see* **bu**.
bulsak mattress.
bulu I a certain tree.
II **bulu-bulu 1** feather duster; **2** decorative feathers on female headdresses.
bulubekti tribute paid to a sovereign power.
bulud (to the) exact (measure).
bulug 1 short and thick (of cylindrical shapes); **2** dusty; **3** *or* **bulugen** mildewed.
buluk *see* **bulug**.

bulus large freshwater tortoise.
bum I wagon shaft.
II tollhouse.
bumbu 1 cooking spices, seasonings; **2** flavour;
mbumboni 1 to season, flavour; **2** to add spice to the conversation;
mbumbokaké to use as seasoning;
bumbon seasoning in general;
bumbonan way of seasoning;
bumbon-crakèn dried seasoning; medical herbs.
bumbung I bamboo pipe; - **wungwang 1** hollow bamboo section; **2** cone-shaped bamboo utensil used above a steaming pan (**kukusan**).
II **mbumbung** to get pregnant again immediately after having a child, *i.e.* with no intervening menstrual period. *See also* **brumbung**.
bumi earth; - **pinendhem** *prov* very humble; - **pulihan** soil consisting of river sediment; **bumèn** *reg* communally owned ricefield; **wong** - a native (*see* **wong**);
malik bumi to change one's mind completely.
buminata *lit* king.
bumipala *var of* **buminata**.
bumipati *var of* **buminata**.
bumitala *lit* the surface of the earth.
bumpet closed, stopped at one end; clogged, blocked;
mbumpet to clog, stop up, block;
mbumpeti to stop up, close off, block s.t.;
kebumpetan to be stopped up, closed off, clogged.
bun dew;
ngebunaké to let dew get on s.t.;
ngebun-bun 1 to put s.t. out in the dew; **2** to take (a baby) for an early morning walk;
ngebun-bun ésuk ngudan-udan soré *prov* to approach in a roundabout way,

viz the subject of a girl's marriage, to her parents.

buncang, mbuncang to blow away;
kebuncang to get blown.

bunci a certain card in the game of **pèi**.

buncik flesh wound;
bunciken wounded.

buncis green beans (*also* **boncis**).

buncit 1 youngest member of the family; **2** the last to be eliminated, *e.g.* in a competition.

buncrit *or* **buncriten** stunted in growth; emaciated.

buncur lump on the head caused by a blow.

bunder 1 round; spherical; **2** firm(ly determined); - **kepleng** *or* - **memet** perfectly round;
mbunderi 1 to make s.t. round; to shape into rounds; **2** to circle;
bunderan 1 circle; **2** roundabout.

bundhas *or* **babak bundhas** black and blue. *See also* **babak**.

bundhat to clear up (problems, debt *etc*). *See also* **pundhat**.

bundhel 1 *or* **mbundhel** having a knot in it (string, rope, cat's tail *etc*); **2** linked in mating position in mid-air (of dragonflies *etc*); **3** *or* **bebundhel** revered village elder; **4** close, intimate; **5** *reg* a batch of 1,000 (*e.g.* corn ears, tobacco cuttings);
mbundheli 1 to tie a knot in s.t.; **2** to bear in mind; **3** to knot (valuables) into the corner of a handkerchief;
bundhelan *or* **bebundhelan 1** a tied knot; **2** money, valuables, wisdom *etc* kept safe; **3** appointment, promise.

bundhet *or* **mbundhet** *or* **mbundheti** tangled, snarled.

bundhu stupid, narrow-minded.

bunek 1 to feel cramped, claustrophobic; **2** to feel oppressed.

bunel depressed, bewildered, at a loss.

bunèn place in a ricefield for sun-drying rice plants.

bung stalk, shoot, tall blade;
ngebung 1 resembling a tall stalk; **2** to put out a shoot.

bungah *ng*, **bingah** *kr*, **rena** *k.i.*, happy, glad;
mbungahi to gloat; to rejoice unjustifiably;
mbungahaké *or* **mbebungah** to make happy; to cheer s.o. up;
mbungah-mbungahaké to force o.s. to be happy.

bungas last part, end.

bungbang *var of* **wungwang**.

bungeng I *reg* hollow; having a hollow place in it.
II *reg* in a quandary.

bungis pig or boar's snout;
mbungis to cut the lips off (punishment for lying).

bungkah I base, lowest part; foot (of a mountain).
II a cut-off stump plus its roots. (*var of* **brungkah**).
III mbungkah to cease one's fasting or avoidance of a certain food (*var of* **brungkah**).

bungkak I roof peak of a traditional Javanese house (**joglo**).
II happy, glad (*var of* **bungah**).
III (of voice) not clear.

bungkang a cockroach-like insect that walks backwards (*var of* **bongkang**).

bungkar, mbungkar 1 to unload (things) from a vehicle or ship; **2** to dismantle, pull apart (engine, house) *Also* **bongkar**.

bungkem to remain silent, keep the mouth closed;
mbungkem to gag, silence; to prevent s.o. from speaking (by bribery).

bungker 1 not quite right in the head; **2** to shrivel; to remain stunted.

bungkik stunted in growth.

bungkil 1 remains of peanuts or copra after the oil has been pressed out;

2 lower end of a bamboo stalk or banana-tree trunk.

bungkrah *reg* pulled down (building); pulled up (plants).

bungkrèk I *var of* **bungkil**.
II sort of skin disease.

bungkuk crooked, bent (over), humped;
mbungkuk to bend;
mbungkukaké to bend the back; to bow.

bungkul knob, knob-like object;
bawang sebungkul a clump of garlic (*see also* **bawang**);
bungkulan knobby shape, knobby part.

bungkus 1 wrapped packet; wrapping material; 2 (born) with a caul covering the head;
mbungkus to wrap;
mbungkusi to wrap up repeatedly;
mbungkusaké to wrap s.t. for s.o.;
bungkusan 1 a wrapped packet; 2 (food) cooked in a leaf wrapping;
pambungkus act or way of wrapping. *See also* **wungkus**.

bunglon 1 chameleon; 2 vacillator; 3 *fig* opportunist;
mbunglon changeable, opportunistic; to vacillate, shilly-shally.

bungsu last-born, youngest child in a family.

bungur 1 a certain timber tree, also its flower; 2 (of livestock) part of the nose through which the ring is passed.

buntak a certain fish.

buntal floral decoration worn by bridegrooms;
mbuntal to make (flowers, leaves) into decorative pieces.

buntar 1 lower end of a spear handle; 2 far end of an irrigation ditch;
mbuntar to prod with a spear handle.

buntas I 1 last part, end; 2 finished (of study).
II loud (*var of* **bantas**).

buntek short and thick (of cylindrical objects).

buntel wrapping (paper, cloth *etc*);
mbuntel *or* **mbunteli** to wrap s.t.;
mbuntelaké to wrap for s.o.;
buntelan s.t. wrapped; parcel, package;
buntel kadut ora nginang ora udut *prov* very poor and miserable.

buntet closed at one end;
mbunteti to close, clog;
kebuntetan clogged with s.t.

buntil dish of roasted taro leaves wrapped around spices.

bunting I youngest in a family.
II **mbunting** slender-waisted.

buntu 1 stopped at one end; clogged; blocked, dead end; 2 deadlocked; 3 stumped, stymied;
mbuntu *or* **mbuntoni** to clog, stop up.

buntul *reg* youngest in a family.

buntung 1 lopped off or amputated (arm, leg, tail *etc*); 2 bad luck, misfortune.

buntut 1 tail; 2 rear end, latter part; 3 aftermath, consequence; - **colok** white tip on a black tail; **lotré** - illegal lottery tied to the last (three) numbers of the official sponsored lottery (*see also* **lotré**); - **urang** hair on the back of the neck;
mbuntut to follow s.o.'s example;
mbuntuti to follow s.o. secretly;
buntutan *or* **pambuntut** lastborn child;
nggéndholi buntuté macan to hold a tiger's tail; to keep tagging along with a criminal.

bunuh *or* **bunoh** *reg* confused, bewildered.

bunyak scraped, skinned, wounded. *See also* **babak**.

bupati regent, top administrative officer of a regency;
kabupatèn district, regency.

bupatos *reg kr for* **bupati**.

bupèt *var of* **bipèt**.

bur I *or* **mak bur** *repr* flight through the air; - **manuk** to depart in haste with only the clothes on one's back;

ngeburaké to have/let (a bird *etc*) fly;

bur-buran birds of the air. *See also* **abur**.

II a drill; **sumur** - drilled well.

III 1 gone, wasted; **2** lost, not to be found; **3** lapsed, unredeemed;

ngeburaké 1 to relinquish possession of; **2** to let (a pawned item) go unredeemed. *See also* **kabur**.

burak I out of order; in disrepair;

mburak to damage, wreck.

II the winged horse on which Muhammad visited Heaven.

burakrakan *reg* in disarray, disorganised.

buras eczema-like skin disease; white spots on the skin;

burasen to suffer from this skin disease.

burat mixture used as a liniment on skin; **- sari** *or* **- wangi** flower sachet.

burcèt a snipe-like bird.

burdir *var of* **bordir**. *See also* **bludir**.

burek unclear (*var of* **bureng**).

burem (of the moon) clouded over, hazy. *See also* **surem**.

bureng 1 vague, unclear; **2** (of the moon) hazy.

buri *ng*, **wingking** *kr*, **1** back, rear, behind; **2** later, after a while; **3** last, past;

mburi in/at the back part of the house.

burik pock-marked, scarred, blemished.

burit, buritan 1 back yard; **2** hind part.

buru I *ng*, **bujeng** *kr*, **mburu, mbeburu 1** to hunt; **2** to pursue; **3** to strive for;

keburu-buru always pushed, pressed for time;

buron, beburon 1 game (animal hunted); **2** fugitive;

paburonan, pamburonan area where hunting is done;

mburu cukup *expr* to make a long story short; **mburu kalahé** *expr* to try to make up a loss.

II *reg* only, just (recent past).

burus flawless, unblemished.

bus *or* **mak bus** *repr* the hissing of air escaping.

busana 1 garment, raiment (*k.i. for* **penganggo**); **2** to get/be dressed (*k.i. for* **dandan**);

mbusanani to decorate; to dress s.o. up; to deck out.

busak, mbusak to erase;

mbusakaké to erase for s.o.;

busakan eraser.

busek I *var of* **busak**.

II busekan *lit* crowding each other.

busèt 1 *reg* ape; **2** *excl of surprise*.

busik 1 (of skin) dry and flaking; **2** hurt, vulnerable.

busuk 1 ignorant, stupid; **2** (of firecrackers) no good, a dud.

busung 1 pregnant (of animals; *cr* of people); **2** disease that causes bloating;

busung kèkèt swelling of the legs.

but *or* **mak but** *repr* a whisking motion;

bat-but *repr* a series of deft movements;

ngebut 1 to drive fast; **2** to work quickly.

buta ogre, giant.

butajeng jealous (*root form: kr for* **butarep**).

butarep, butarepan *ng*, **butajengan** *kr* excessively jealous of one's spouse;

mbutarepaké to suspect (one's spouse) of infidelity.

buteng short-tempered.

buthak bald, bare.

buthek (of water) not clear, turbid;

mbuthekaké to cause s.t. to be turbid.

butuh *ng*, **betah** *kr* **1** to need; **2** need, necessity, thing needed;

mbutuhaké to need, require;

kabutuhan need, a necessity; needed article.

buthuk (of fish or egg) beginning to spoil.

buthung animal's haunch(es).

butun a certain citrus fruit.

butul through to the other side;

mbutul to pierce;

butulan doorway or entrance to a house or yard.

buwak *reg var of* **buwang**.

buwal, mbuwal to bubble forth copiously, *e.g.* water from a spring.

buwana I 1 continent; 2 *lit* world; 3 universe.
II **buwananen** (of vision, view) blurred, hazy.

buwang, mbuwang *ng*, **mbucal** *kr* 1 to throw out; 2 to exile s.o.; 3 to put s.t. in an inappropriate place; 5 to place (a child) in an adoptive or foster home;
mbuwang tilas to alibi o.s.; to hide the traces of one's guilty act;
pambuwangan (place of) exile; banishment;
mbuwang rasé olèh kuwuk *prov* to discard s.t. worthless (in one's greed for s.t. better) and get s.t. even worse;
buwangan 1 outlet, drain (of irrigated field); 2 s.t. cast off, discarded object; exile, outcast.
See also **guwak, guwang**.

buwara, mbuwara *reg* to find a livelihood far from one's place of origin.

buwel to billow upward in clouds.

buwi *or* **buwèn** jail, prison;
mbuwi to put s.o. in jail.

buwuh, mbuwuh *reg* 1 to add one's own share; 2 to make a contribution in money toward a customary ceremony;
buwuhan contribution.

buya, kabuya-buya *lit* chased, pursued.

buyar 1 to disperse in all directions; 2 scatterbrained, unable to concentrate;
mbuyaraké to cause to disperse, scatter.

buyuk a variety of palm tree.

buyun2g big-bellied earthenware jar.

buyut 1 (*or* **mbah buyut**) great-grandparent; 2 great-grandchild;
buyuten 1 senile; 2 unsteady with old age;

bebuyutan for generations; long-standing (of enemies);
kabuyutan 1 place where a priest lives and works; 2 sacred ancestral worship-place; 3 ancestral and sacred (of places such as cemeteries).

bwat *see* **bot** I, **byat**.

byah *or* **mak byah** *repr* suddenly breaking apart;
ngebyah 1 to generalise; 2 common, general.

byak *or* **mak byak** *repr* suddenly opening;
ngebyakaké to open s.t. (out) wide;
byak-byakan acting hurriedly, looking for s.t. in a hurry.

byantara, *lit* presence;
ngabyantara to make a formal appearance (before a king);
ngabyantarakaké to present s.o. (before a king).

byar I 1 on (of lights); 2 a flash; to flash; 3 suddenly open (of eyes); 4 (*or* - **padhang** *or* - **rahina**) daybreak; **mak** - *repr* suddenly lighting up; daybreak; - **pet** to go on and off (of light);
ngebyar to stay awake all night;
byar-byaran to have activity all night; to stay awake all night.
II **byar-byur** *repr* bathing by using a ladle.

byat *lit* heavy, weight (*var of* **bwat**);
nempuh byat *see* **tempuh**;
kabyatan *lit* to find s.t. too heavy; excessively heavy.

byor shining, sparkling. *See also* **abyor**.

byuh *var of* **biyuh**.

byuk, *or* **mak byuk** *repr* coming in large numbers; *repr* mass movement;
ngebyuk to flock around;
ngebyuki to heap s.t. onto; to flock together; to pour s.t. copiously;
kebyukan to have s.t. swarming all over it;
byuk-byukan to come in large numbers; to cluster around;

ngebyukaké to pour out the whole thing.

byung, *or* **mak byung** *repr* a swarming movement;

ngebyung to move as a group;

byung-byungan to flock out; to move in large numbers.

byur I *or* **mak byur** *repr* splash; *repr* scurrying off together;

byar-byur *repr* bathing by using a ladle;

ngebyuri to splash s.t. with;

ngebyuraké to plunge s.t. into water;

byur-byuran to jump into water (for fun).

II monochromatic; **prada** - plain gold varnish (*see also* **prada**);

ngebyur to apply plain colour to s.t.

III **ngebyuri** to scatter for (*e.g.* feed for chickens);

ngebyuraké to scatter, spread s.t.

C

ca *adr* friend! mate! (*shtf of* **kanca**).

cabak I slate for school (*reg var of* **sabak**).

II *var of* **tebak** II.

III a swallow-like nocturnal bird (*var of* **cebak**).

cabang 1 branch, arm (of an organisation); to branch off, split; 2 weapon used for self-defence training (*see also* **cawang**, **pang**);

nyabang to branch off, split.

cabar 1 ineffectual; 2 failed.

cabé a certain vine, also its fruit (used in traditional medicines); - **lempuyang** a traditional medicine brewed from the vine fruits above; - **rawit** 1 chili pepper; 2 *fig* a person who is physically small but very capable; **ula** - a certain small harmless snake;

nyabé covered with goose-pimples (of skin when one is cold);

cabéan a certain small bird that feeds on caterpillars and insects.

cablaka straightforward, direct, honest (*var of* **blaka**).

cablèk a slap;

nyablèk to slap s.o.;

nyablèki to slap repeatedly;

cablèk-cablèk to keep slapping; - **pupu** to slap one's thigh (as an emotional reaction);

cablèk-cablèkan to slap each other in a friendly way.

cabol 1 short legs of wooden bench; 2 *var of* **cébol**.

cabud *see* **cabut**.

cabuk 1 food made from extracted sesame seeds; 2 sesame seeds from which the oil has been extracted.

cabul obscene; engaging in obscene activity.

cabut, **nyabut** 1 to pull out, (with)draw; 2 to revoke, suspend;

nyabutaké to have s.t. (with)drawn.

caca 1 break, crack; 2 defect, flaw; - **upa** any act that can cause a relationship to be weakened.

cacab I 1 to become gradually immersed; 2 to sink below the surface;

nyacabi to wade across a flooded area;

kacababan to get inundated.

II 1 efficacious; 2 poisonous liquid;

nyacab to apply a poisonous liquid to sharp weapons.

III shampoo made from aloe leaves;

nyacab to wash one's hair with such a shampoo.

cacad defect, flaw, mutation, trouble;
nyacad or **nyacad** to find fault; to criticise;
cacadan object of criticism;
panyacad or **panacad** 1 criticism; 2 object of s.o.'s criticism.

cacah I 1 number, amount; - **jiwa** population; 2 census; - **eri** counting unit for fish; - **molo** house count; - **pecahan** fraction; - **sirah** a headcount of people or animals; - **camboran** mixed fraction, compound fraction; - **wutuh** integer; - **wuwung** 1 number of roofs or roofed sections to a house; 2 counting unit for households in a village;
nyacah or **nacah** to count;
nyacahaké or **nacahaké** to count up, make a count of;
kecacah to be counted;
panyacah or **panacah** calculation, count.
II **nyacah** to reduce to small pieces;
cacahan 1 s.t. ground; 2 s.t. used for grinding;
panyacah or **panacah** the act of grinding.

cacah-cucah 1 insignificant, unimportant; 2 unworthy, not lucrative.

cacak I **nyacak** reg to try, make an effort;
cacak-cacak to give s.t. a try;
kalah cacak menang cacak to try to do s.t. by trial and error.
II a tool for slicing tobacco leaves;
nyacak to shred tobacco with such a tool.
III **aja cacak** let alone…, to say nothing of…

cacal chipped, marred;
nyacal to peel or flake off a small bit (from); to cut into small pieces.

cacap see **cacab**.

cacar 1 smallpox; - **banyu** chickenpox; **mantri** - official who vaccinates for smallpox (see also **mantri**); 2 pustular skin eruption, pock-mark;
nyacar to vaccinate for smallpox;
nyacaraké to have s.o. vaccinated;
cacaran vaccination, vaccinating.

cacaya lit facial expression. See also **caya**, **cecaya**.

caci 1 wooden tripod; supporting stand; 2 belt, buckle of a belt.

cacing worm, intestinal worms; - **kermi** threadworm; - **pita** tapeworm; - **tambang** noodle-like intestinal worms;
nyacing resembling a worm, vermiform;
nyacingi to treat for worms;
cacingen to suffer from worms.

cadhang, **nyadhang** or **nyenyadhang** to hold out the hands to receive s.t.;
nyadhangi 1 to hold out the hands as though preparing to catch s.t.; 2 to retard, check; to catch (livestock thief);
nyadhangaké to hold in reserve;
cumadhang available, set aside;
cadhangan reserve, back up, spare.
See also **cadhong** I, **candhang**.

cadhok nearsighted, myopic; having defective vision.

cadhong I one's share or portion;
nyadhong 1 to ask for s.t.; 2 var of **nyadhang**;
nyadhongaké to ask for s.t. on s.o.'s behalf;
cumadhong to ask for (orders);
cadhongan share, portion.
II (of chicken quill or horns) backwards.

cadhuk reg ladle;
nyadhuk reg to take, ladle, scoop (liquid).

caé-caé reg very clear.

caèk, **caèk-caèk** reg to shout, speak to in greeting.

caèng, **sacaèng** 200 bundles of (rice).

cag, **cag-cagan** to enjoy working;

cag-ceg to keep touching or handling. *See also* **ceg**.

cagak 1 pole, post; **2** support, mainstay; - **elèk** a means of staying awake; - **palang** barrier;
nyagak *or* **nyagaki** to support with a pole;
cagakan s.t. used as a supporting post.

cagar preservation; - **alam** nature reserve.

cager *or* **cageran** pilework, palisade.

cagir, nyagir to stand up, immobile. *See also* **agir**.

cagluk, nyagluk *reg* to take.

cah *adr* child! (*shtf of* **bocah**); - **bagus** boy! (affectionate); - **ayu** girl! (affectionate).

cahak, nyahak 1 to trespass on the rights of another; **2** to violate s.o.'s authority; **3** to seize s.t. illegally.

cahya 1 beam, ray; **2** appearance, aspect.

cai *var of* **kucai**.

caing unit of quantity of newly harvested rice (*ca* 200 bundles).

caya facial expression.

cak I act or way of doing, application;
ngecaki to do, accomplish;
ngecakaké to do, carry out, practise;
kacakan to get accomplished;
cak-cakan application, act of applying or practising.
II *reg, adr* fellow! brother!

cakadhong, nyakadhong to open (the hand) so wide that it bends back in an arc.

cakah, nyakahi 1 to push (against, off, away); **2** to resist, defy, stand up to.

cakal I nyakal to pervert (words, facts).
II - **bakal** first inhabitant of a settlement (later revered as protective spirit).

cakar (animal's) paw, claw; (bird's) foot, *cr* human foot;
nyakar 1 to scratch with claws; **2** *cr* to eat meal with hand; **3** to play soccer without wearing shoes;

nyakari 1 to claw repeatedly; **2** (of chickens) to scrape in search of food;
kecakar scratched;
cakar-cakar to keep scratching in search of food. *See also* **cèkèr**.

cakarwa *reg* blacksmith's forked poker.

cakep, nyakep all-embracing, all-encompassing;
nyakepi to reach all the way around s.t.;
cakepan 1 act of embracing or encompassing; **2** words or text of a traditional song (**tembang, suluk** *etc*).

caket near, close (to);
nyaket to get near(er);
nyaketi to approach s.t.;
nyaketaké to bring s.t. closer;
caketan *or* **cecaketan** to associate with, become acquainted with;
kecaket loved (by).

cakil I bamboo peg used to hold bamboo wall sections in place;
nyakili to fasten (bamboo sections) with pins.
II *way* an ogre who has an extended lower jaw with long sharp fangs;
nyakil 1 to perform as this figure; **2** resembling this figure.
III cakilen to have insomnia.

cakma a certain plant.

cakodhong *var of* **cakadhong**.

cakot a bite;
nyakot 1 to bite; **2** to involve s.o. in a lawsuit by accusing them; **3** to become habituated or addicted (to); **4** to join, get attached;
nyakoti to bite repeatedly;
nyakotaké to bite for s.o.;
kecakot 1 to get bitten; **2** to get drawn into a legal entanglement;
cakotan a bite; act of biting. *Also* **cokot**.

cakra 1 a round frame; **2** a mythical powerful arrow having a toothed round frame as a head; **3** a diacritic mark indicating *R* in Javanese script; -

manggilingan the cycle of life through reincarnations; the wheel of fortune;
nyakra to shoot with such a weapon;
- **manggilingan** to proceed through cycles; to change cyclically.

cakrabawa suspicion;
nyakrabawa to suspect s.o.;
panyakrabawa suspicion;
kacakrabawa suspected.

cakrak *or* **cakrak-cèkrèk** handsome, fine-looking.

cakrawala 1 horizon; 2 sky.

cakrawa(r)ti, nyakrawa(r)ti 1 to rule the world; 2 highly esteemed as a supreme king.

cakrik 1 appearance, facial aspect; 2 pattern, design.

cakruk a hut used as a base by night watchmen or as a shelter when guarding crops against birds.

caksana wise, endowed with wisdom (*shtf of* **wicaksana**).

cakub *see* **cakup**.

cakul a freshwater fish.

cakup, nyakup 1 to grasp between the palms; 2 to cover (in a speech, discussion *etc*).
kacakup 1 to get hold of, grasp; 2 contained, included, covered;
cakupan handful of loose things (coins, grains *etc*).

cakur I medicine-horn, powder-flask.
II **cakur-cakur** (of horses) to paw the ground with the forelegs;
nyakur to paw, claw at;
nyakuri to claw repeatedly;
kecakur to get pawed accidentally.
See also **thakur**.

cakut 1 in preparation for hard work; 2 to start working hard.

cal shawl.

cala I *or* **cecala** 1 a messenger or a message sent around to invite guests to a celebration; 2 opening words; to begin talking.

II *lit* mountain (*shtf of* **acala, ancala**).
III *lit* defect, flaw.
IV *lit* cunning, shrewdness.

calabéka *lit* to change into bad thing; to destroy s.t. valuable intentionally.

cala-culu *repr* bursting in.

calaina partially or totally blind.

calak I a man who performs traditional circumcisions.
II, **calakan** person of many talents, one who learns easily.
III flippant;
calak cangkol kendhali cemethi tai to interrupt the conversation with s.t. trivial.

calang *or* **cecalang** to prepare; to be ready for carrying out;
nyalangi to prepare before s.t. happens;
panyalang advance guard, scout.

calapita I *lit* a sudden rapid movement.
II 1 a certain gamelan melody; 2 bamboo whistle that produces fine sounds.
III a certain grasshopper.

calathu *ng*, **wicanten** *kr*, **ngendika** *k.i.* to say, to talk, speak;
pacalathon speech, talking, what s.o. says. *See also* **celathu, clathu**.

calawenthah immorality, profligacy.

calek 1 *reg* near, close; 2 *reg* short. *See also* **cedhak, cendhak**.

calik I 1 (to make) a one-day excursion; 2 to come and then go straight away.
II **nyalik(aké)** to turn over; to turn the other way around.

calo I a small edible ocean fish.
II *var of* **calok**.

calok 1 ticket scalper; 2 passenger recruiter for public vehicles;
nyalok to work as a ticket scalper.

calon *or* **calonan** 1 candidate, prospective; 2 applicant;
nyaloni to nominate, designate;
nyalonaké to appoint s.o. as a candidate.

caluk I *reg* a cutting knife, chopper.

II young tamarind fruit.

calung I a certain bamboo music instrument.

II shank of a horse's leg.

cam I appearance;

ngecamaké to consider advisable; to bear in mind;

cam-camé it appears, it seems.

II **ngecam** reg to calculate, estimate.

camah not respected, in disrepute;

nyamah to show disrespect (for);

nyenyamah to treat with a lack of disrespect;

nyamahaké (act of) showing disrespect;

kecamah to get a lack of respect;

panyamah (act of) showing disrespect.

camat head of a subdistrict, i.e. an administrative officer having authority over village heads;

kecamatan subdistrict, territory under the above official.

cambah bean sprout (shtf of **kecambah**).

cambang 1 (of sideburns) long and wide; **2** side whiskers.

camben reg kr for **candu**.

cambeng or **cecambeng** advance preparations, arrangements, provisions;

nyambengi to prepare;

nyambengaké to provide, prepare s.t. for.

cambil reg coconut. See also **kambil I**.

cambor, nyambor to mix;

camboran 1 a mixture; **2** compound; **3** gram compound word.

cambuk reg var of **sambuk**.

cambur var of **cambor, campur**.

camcao a certain vine, the leaves of which are used for cool drinks and gelatin-like foods.

camèh, nyamèh (of the lower lip) drooping; fig talkative.

camik, camikan or **nyamikan** snacks, refreshments.

campah I reg insipid, tasteless.

II or **cecampah** criticism, ridicule;

nyampah or **nyampahi** to criticise, ridicule.

III (of roof) not aslant enough, almost level.

campaka frangipani.

campleng reg to break instantly.

camplong a crude ladder consisting of a notched board.

camprèng, comprang-camprèng chronically short of money.

campuh 1 to link up; **2** to fight, duel; **3** to gather.

campur to mix (with); mixed; - **adhuk** all mixed in together; - **bawur 1** mixed up; **2** a mixture of flower fragrances for perfume; **3** medley; **4** confused; - **sari** to menstruate;

nyampur to mix;

nyampuri 1 to mix s.t. in; **2** to meddle in, interfere;

nyampuraké to mix s.t. (up) with (s.t. else);

kacampuran mixed (with), mingled with;

campuran 1 (a) mixture (of); **2** meddling, interference.

camu unit of ten billion;

sacamu ten billion.

camuk, camuk-camuk or **nyamuk-nyamuk** or **nyomak-nyamuk** (to eat) with the mouth stuffed.

canang a certain variety of yellow betel leaf.

cancala I 1 lit to shake violently; to unsettle; **2** lit lightning.

II reg to have troubles, filled with obstacles; disturbance.

cancalan reg a scapegoat. See also **sangsalan**.

cancang, nyancang 1 to tie up, tether; **2** to give a down payment; to pay (as) a deposit;

panyancang act or way of tethering;

cancangan 1 tethered; **2** pole or s.t. used for tethering an animal.

cancing *or* cancingan 1 handy and quick; 2 to wear practical clothes.

cancao *var of* camcao.

cancut with sleeves rolled up or cloth tucked up, in preparation for hard work; - tali-wanda *lit* to gird up one's loins, to get set for some hard work; nyancutaké to tuck up one's sleeves or clothes before starting to work; to gird o.self for work.

candhak the next, continuation, sequel; - cekel to take possession of s.o.'s property as a payment on a debt; - kulak credit system for small investors; nyandhak 1 to take, catch, grasp, seize; 2 to understand; 3 to reach; nyandhakaké to continue, resume; kecandhak 1 to get caught, seized; 2 to be found; can be picked up; candhakan 1 to understand things easily; 2 solution; candhaké the next one; sacandhaké *or* sakecandhaké whatever one can grasp/attain.

candhang, nyandhangi to retard, check; to catch. *See also* cadhang.

candhèn *see* candhi.

candhet, nyandhet to restrain, check, hold; panyandhet restraint, control, prevention.

candhi 1 ancient Hindu or Buddhist temple or shrine; 2 stone floor-tile; - bentar temple gates with the appearance of a single facade split in the middle; nyandhi 1 to enshrine in a temple; to bury s.o. in such a temple; 2 *fig* to cherish, take scrupulous care of; to hold in esteem; candhèn having the appearance of such a temple.

candhik I counting unit for the leaves used in betel quid; nyandhiki to make betel leaves into a betel-chewing packet; sacandhik one betel-chewing packet. II candhik-ala (-kala) twilight, dusk; the spirits that emerge at dusk.

candhuk I a liquid measure. *See also* canthuk I. II nyandhuk *reg* to drain blood. III candhuk to meet each other; meeting; - lawung to come into contact with. *See also* canthuk.

candhung *reg* a certain type of sickle or scythe.

candra I 1 *lit* moon 2 *lit* month. II a description couched in figurative terms; - sengkala chronogram used as a cryptic way of expressing dates, *esp* the year a building was constructed; - sengkala memet complex chronogramatic representation of the year; nyandra to describe s.t. figuratively; cinandra *lit* described; panyandra a description couched in beautiful figures of speech; candra kalamukan buda 'the moon covered by a star'; the wrong finding of a court.

candramawa a cat with a certain coat and eye colouring, said to have the magical power of stopping a mouse in its tracks by merely staring at it.

candrasa *lit* sword.

candu opium; - gelap black market opium; nyandu 1 to have become addicted to; 2 (of smoking tobacco) to produce tars.

canéla sandals, slippers. *See also* cenéla.

canès *reg var of* sanès.

canik, nyanik (of face) small and cute.

cangak a heron-like bird.

cangap 1 a wide opening; 2 *reg* waterchannel into a ricefield; 3 *var of* cangar; nyangap to force open the mouth of (*e.g.* a child, an animal);

nyangapaké to open s.o.'s mouth.

cangar, nyangar *var of* nyangap;

cangaran act of opening s.o.'s mouth.

cangcalan pretext, subterfuge, excuse.

cangcang *var of* cancang.

cangcing handy, skilful, adroit.

canggah I 1 forked stick or branch; 2 having a forked shape.

II great-great-grandchild; 2 great-great-grandparent.

canggal a dead tree or stump.

canggèh 1 apt to tease or pester; 2 prone to steal.

Cangik *way* name of a tall and thin female clown-servant;

nyangik resembling this wayang figure;

cangik-cangik tall, thin and long of neck.

cangkah a forked branch (*var of*) canggah.

cangkang 1 eggshell, nutshell; 2 seashell.

cangkèl stubborn, headstrong.

cangkélak to return with a quick motion. *See also* cengkélak.

cangkem *ng, kr,* tutuk *k.i.* 1 mouth; 2 *cr* talk, chat; bad words;

nyangkemi *cr* to speak to angrily or accusingly;

cangkeman 1 resembling a mouth; 2 with a mouth, oral;

nyangkem kodhok to have/get a three-cornered tear in fabric;

cangkem rusak, godhong jati krasa énak *prov* to eat indiscriminately; gluttonous.

cangkerem *var of* cengkerem.

cangket *reg* pretty, pleasing.

cangking, nyangking to take or carry in the hand or arm;

nyangkingaké to carry for s.o.;

nyangking-nyangking to involve; to drag s.o.'s name into;

kecangking to get picked up or carried off inadvertently;

cangkingan 1 handle; 2 s.t. used to carry things; 3 s.t. carried in the hand.

cangkir cup (for tea or coffee).

cangklak, nyangklak 1 to feel sore in the armpit area; 2 rebellious, disobedient; cangklakan armpit.

cangklek, nyangklek (of distance) very close.

cangklèk, nyangklèk to carry on the waist or hip;

cangklèkan a wooden sickle-holder tied to the waist or hip.

cangklèt *var of* cangklèk.

cangklong I a long wide band, worn over the shoulder, with pockets at either end for carrying small things;

nyangklong to carry s.t by hanging it over (the shoulder or arm);

nyangklongaké to hang s.t. over the shoulder.

II pipe;

nyangklong to smoke a pipe.

cangklung one's reach; one's stride;

cangklung-cangklung long-armed, long-legged.

cangkok 1 outer shell, *esp* of molluscs; 2 tray of a balance scale; 3 landowner, as contrasted with sharecropper (indhung); 4 basic, fundamental, original;

nyangkok to transplant, graft; to take a cutting from a living plant;

cangkokan 1 a transplant, a graft; transplantation, transplanting; 2 grown from a cutting.

cangkol 1 hook; benik - hook-and-eye fastener (*see also* benik); 2 *var of* cangkul;

nyangkol to catch on;

nyangkoli to hang s.t. on;

nyangkolaké to hang up (clothing);

cangkolan hook, hanger. *See also* canthèl, canthol.

cangkrak 1 *repr* a sudden swift movement; 2 *or* cangkrakan to act impulsively or irresponsibly.

cangkrama *lit* to relax and enjoy o.s.;
 nyangkramani to make love to (a woman).

cangkrang chickenpox;
 cangkrangen to have or get chickenpox.

cangkreg, cangkreg-cangkreg to keep sticky.

cangkrim, cangkriman a riddle, an enigma, a conundrum; to say a riddle;
 nyangkrimi to ask s.o. a riddle.

cangkring a certain thorny-trunked tree; bamboo branch;
 cangkringan thorny underbrush.

cangkul I a hoe-like farm tool for loosening soil;
 nyangkul to use or work with this tool;
 nyangkuli to keep hoeing a soil;
 nyangkulaké to hoe a soil for s.o.;
 cangkulan work done with this tool. *See also* cangkol, pacul.
 II nyangkul to accept responsibility (for).

canglung *var of* cangklung.

canguk 1 person at a lookout assigned to observe enemy movements from a distance; 2 head herdsmen.

cangungong peacock's cry;
 nyangungong (of peacock) to cry. *See also* cengungong.

canthaka *lit* conceit;
 cumanthaka conceited, boastful, arrogant.

canthang I nyanthang to touch with a burning object.
 II pustule, rash;
 canthangen to have/get pustules.
 III canthang balung chief of the female court dancers;
 canthang balungan brothel.

canthas intelligent and energetic; dynamic.

canthèl I 1 hook, clasp; 2 belt with a clasp fastener; - atur to pass along a request to s.o. higher up; - batin to have a secret understanding (with); - rembug to come to an agreement through discussion;
 nyanthèl 1 to be(come) fastened or stuck; 2 *fig* (of money) spent on s.t. worthy;
 nyanthèli to put a hook on;
 nyanthèlaké 1 to hang s.t. on a hook; 2 to buy s.t. worthy;
 kecanthèl 1 to get caught; 2 to acquire, latch onto;
 cumanthèl 1 hooked (onto); 2 hanging (from); 3 *fig* memorised; 4 *fig* (of money) spent on s.t. worthwhile;
 canthèlan 1 hook, clasp; 2 *fig* s.t. to hold onto, *e.g.* an ideal, a memory;
 pacanthèlan 1 a small village; 2 head of a neighbourhood organisation;
 pating cranthèl (*pl*) hanging (in disorder);
 gumantung tanpa canthèlan *fig* homeless, not belonging anywhere.
 II (*or* jagung canthèl) a corn-like grain (*see also* jagung).

canten *subst kr* talk, discussion; to talk. *See also* catur, wicanten.

cantheng whitlow (skin infection);
 canthengen to have/get whitlow.

canthik I stem or beak of a ship.
 II a curved sharp-pointed knife;
 nyanthik (of sharp-pointed object) curved.

canthing 1 a small dipper used to apply wax in the batik process; - jemblokan a large wax applying ladle (as above); 2 comb with a curved tapering handle (*var of* centhing II);
 nyanthing resembling a dipper (as above).

canthoka *lit* frog. *See also* canthuka.

canthol, nyanthol to catch on a branch;
 nyantholi to cause to catch on it; to hang s.t. on;

nyantholaké to hang s.t.;

kecanthol to get caught (on).

canthuk I 1 a liquid measure: *ca* ½ pint = 1.2 litres; 2 curved sharp-pointed object; 3 equipment for cupping, *i.e.* bringing blood to the surface by creating a partial vacuum over the skin; nyanthuk curved at the tips.

II to contact;

canthuk lawung to have the slightest acquaintance with.

canthuka *lit* frog (*var of* canthoka).

canthula ill-mannered, rude;

nyanthulani to be rude to s.o.

cantrik pupil who lives in the home of a Hindu or Buddhist teacher and does service to him while learning from him.

canuk, canuk-canuk to grope; to walk slowly and feel around (like a blind man).

cao drink made from the leaves of a certain vine. *See* camcao.

caos 1 to give (*root form: k.i. for* wènèh); 2 to serve as a court guard; - dhahar to set out food as offering for the spirits.

cap 1 brand, trademark; 2 stamp (mark), seal (mark); - jempol *or* - dumuk thumb print; bathik - batik with the design stamped on (rather than being hand-worked) (*see also* bathik);

ngecap 1 to place a stamp or mark on; 2 to brand, label, stigmatise;

ngecapi to affix seal or label to s.t.;

ngecapaké to have s.t. printed/stamped;

cap-capan printing, impression;

pangecapan printer, publisher.

capaga a variety of tree.

capang (of moustaches) long and extending sideways.

capé I tired, exhausted, weak, weary.

II nyapé to guess (the answer to);

capéan (to play) a guessing-game.

capeng to stretch the arms before fighting.

capet, capet-capet vague, dim; vaguely remembered.

capil *reg var of* caping.

caping a broad hat made from woven bamboo or palm leaves, worn as a sunshade or umbrella;

capingan to put on or wear such a hat.

capit (*or* capitan) pincers, tweezers;

nyapit to pinch, squeeze.

capjaé a Chinese meat and vegetable dish.

caplak 1 wart; 2 tick (bloodsucking insect).

caplang (of ears) sticking out.

caplek just like, coinciding with. *See also* plek II.

caplok, nyaplok 1 to snatch and swallow; to gulp down; 2 to seize, annex (a country); 3 (in games) to capture;

nyaploki to snap at s.t. repeatedly.

capluk *or* mak capluk *repr* a quick snapping;

coplak-capluk to keep putting food in the mouth.

caprang (of moustache) spreading and pointed (*var of* crapang).

capret *or* mak capret *repr* throwing too short;

nyapret 1 too small, too narrow, cramped; 2 (of clothing) tight fitting (*var of* ngapret).

caprèt, nyaprèt to splatter onto (*var of* cèprèt);

coprat-caprèt splattered around; messily marked, stained;

nyoprat-nyaprèt spattered all over everything.

capu *reg* round (of head).

cara manner, way, custom, style, language; done in a certain way; - Jawa Javanese (language, custom *etc*);

nyara to do s.t. in a certain way;

sacarané according to the custom;

désa mawa cara, negara mawa tata *prov* each region has its own ways.

carabikang a rice flour and sugar pan-cake.

carak a hollow buffalo horn used for rinsing horses' mouths out;
nyarak to rinse a horse's mouth with the above.

caraka *lit* messenger, courier.

carakan Javanese alphabet, *i.e.* sequence of script characters for teaching purposes.

carang I 1 bamboo branch; **2** cylindrical bamboo section; - **buntala** fringes on saddle or on a sash; - **gantung** a name of gamelan melody; - **landhep** a sharp weapon.
II carangan an invented composition; **lakon** - *way* an invented play that departs from the events depicted in epic or mythology.

carat I the pointed tip of a batik-making instrument (**canthing**).
II reef, sandbank, shoal.
III *reg* cracked, chapped.
IV - **taun** *or* - **warsa** rain and wind storm. *See also* **clèrèt**.

carek *reg* near, close (to) (*var of* **cerak**, **cedhak**).

carem I (of newlyweds) compatible.
II careman *reg kr* durian fruit.

carik 1 secretary, clerk (village adminis-trative position); **2** hand-worked batik;
nyarik 1 to become a clerk, **2** to do a batik design by hand.

caring *reg* clear, bright, lucid, serene.

carita *ng*, **cariyos** *kr* story, narration;
nyaritani to tell s.o. (a story; about s.t.);
nyaritakaké to tell (about);
kacarita *lit* it is told;
cinarita *var of* **kacarita**. *See also* **crita**.

cariwis *var of* **criwis**;
cariwis cawis to protest against a superior but ready for any decision.

cariyos to tell (*kr for* **carita**). *See also* **criyos**.

carma *lit* teaching(s).

carmin *lit* mirror.

caru *lit* ritual offering.

carub mixed together;
nyarub to mix together;
nyarubi to mix s.t. in; to meddle (in);
kecarub mixed together accidently;
caruban a mixture.

carubuk I a certain kris blade design.
II a certain freshwater fish. *See also* **crubuk**.

caruk I 1 *reg var of* **carub**.
II nyaruk *reg* to scratch with the nails or claws.
III nyaruk 1 to scoop up s.t. with hands; **2** to round up people (in a raid);
carukan 1 s.t. scooped up with hands; **2** *reg* raiding.
IV *or* **carukan** *reg* fight, conflict.

cas I *or* **mak cas** *repr* the stroke of a cutting tool;
cas-casan 1 act of cutting; **2** the result of cutting.
II 1 ngecasi (of prices) to decide (on); to make a rule (about); **2** to cover the fact precisely.
cas-casan ruling, decision (of prices).

cat now (one thing), now (another);
cat murub, cat mati (of light) off and on.

cathak 1 a certain fly that swarms around livestock; **2** dog flea;
nyathak to behave disrespectfully.

cathek I nyathek (of dogs) to bite.
II cathèk gawèl *or* **cathèk cawèl** gossip.

cathèk (of dogs) *var of* **cathek I**.

cathem 1 a small clamp; **2** *reg var of* **cathut**;
nyathem (of mouth) clamped shut;
nyathemaké to close the mouth tightly.

cathet, nyathet *or* **nyatheti** to take notes (on); to note down;
nyathetaké to note on for s.o.;
kecathet recorded; registered;

cathetan notes, memoranda.

cathil I nyathil to snatch away a part of s.t.

II **nyathil** (of small things) extending outward.

cathis, nyathis (of chin) prominent, protruding.

catho, catho-catho having defective vision.

cathok 1 belt; 2 buckle of a belt used with men's lower garment; -**cawèl** or -**gawèl** 1 walking hand-in-hand; 2 to meddle with, interfere with (what's not one's business); - **rembug** to come to an agreement through discussion (var of **canthèl rembug**);

nyathok 1 to attach a rope or metal binding to secure a joint where two sections of wood meet; 2 to catch (flying insects) with the bare hand;

cathokan 1 metal band or rope for binding wood; 2 to put on or wear a belt.

cathuk, cathuken (of teeth) chattering because of the cold.

cathut pliers, pincers; **tukang** - middleman who jacks up prices for retailers;

nyathut to extract money from (retail customers);

cathutan 1 to pluck the beard with tweezers; 2 profits from reselling goods at a higher price; 3 goods sold in this way.

catu 1 a ration(ed amount); 2 a share in (the harvest of) a communal ricefield; 3 the privilege of raising a crop on s.o.'s ricefield as repayment on a loan;

nyatu 1 to ration s.t. out; 2 (or **nyatoni**) to heal by faith or magic spells;

panyaton 1 (the practice of) rationing; 2 a ricefield loaned out as above.

catur I talk, discussion, what s.o. says; **nyatur** to talk about;

cinatur lit 1 it is said; 2 to be talked about; - **luput** - it goes without saying (see also **luput**);

caturan or **cecaturan** to talk, converse, chat;

panyatur 1 act of discussing; 2 one who talks or gossips about people;

ana catur mungkur to disregard whisperings.

II lit four; - **pada** four-legged.

III chess, chess set, a chess game.

cawad negligence, omission; to neglect, omit; nervous habit that causes blemishes;

nyawadi to nag, criticise, find fault with.

cawak to be a habitually loud talker.

cawan small saucer; small bowl.

cawang 1 forked stick or branch; 2 having a forked shape; 3 fig hesitant, uncertain;

nyawang to split, bifurcate.

cawar reg ineffectual (var of **cabar**).

cawé, cawé-cawé to join in what others are doing or talking;

cowa-cawé to join in excitedly or frenziedly.

cawèl, nyawèl 1 (of animals) to bite; 2 fig to drag s.o. into court, involve s.o. in litigation.

cawengah reg 1 awkward, ill at ease; 2 unwilling, dead set against.

caweni a kind of white muslin.

cawet 1 men's brief; 2 loincloth; 3 cloth worn by women as a sanitary napkin;

nyawet (of garment) too tight like a loincloth; resembling a loincloth;

nyaweti to put loincloth on s.o.;

nyawetaké to wear (a long garment) pulled up between the legs, e.g. for wading across a stream;

cawetan to wear a loincloth.

cawi a small brush for painting fine lines on a leather puppet;

nyawi to paint with this brush;

cawèn finely painted with this brush.

cawik to clean o.s. after going to the toilet (k.i. for **céwok**).

cawis to prepare; prepared;
   nyawisi to provide s.o. with; to prepare for s.o.;
   nyawisaké to prepare s.t.;
   cumawis or cemawis ready to be used/consumed;
   cawisan stock, supply, preparations.

cawuh mixed, blended; not sharply distinct.

cawuk (of water) the amount one can hold in the cupped palm;
   nyawuk to scoop s.t., e.g. water;
   sacawuk one palmful.

caya facial expression.

ceb repr stabbing, piercing. See also anceb, enceb, tanceb.

cebak a swallow-like nocturnal bird.

cebèk, nyebèk to curl one's lips in scorn.

cebelèh var of ceblèh.

cebilak reg sallow; fig drab.

ceblaka straightforward, direct, honest. See also blaka, cablaka.

ceblèh pallid, wan.

ceblèk var of cablèk.

cèblek repr a stab into s.t. soft;
   nyèblekaké to stick s.t. into (s.t. soft).

ceblok to fall, drop;
   nyebloki to drop s.t. onto;
   nyeblokaké to drop s.t.;
   ceblokan (having) fallen, dropping, falling or fallen (fruit).

céblok var of ceblok.

céblong tadpole (young of the kodhok). See also cébong.

ceblung or mak ceblung repr splashing;
   nyeblung to plunge into the water;
   nyeblungaké to plunge s.t. into (water);
   ceblang-ceblung to plunge (s.t.) into (water) repeatedly.

cébol 1 dwarf, midget; 2 unfruitful;
   cébolan to walk like a dwarf;
   cébol kepalang (of stature) one who looks short when standing, and looks tall when sitting;

cébol nggayuh lintang one who attempts things far beyond his ability.

cébong tadpole (var of céblong).

cebrik damp and messy, dirty and muddy;
   nyebriki to mess s.t. up with mud or dirty water.

cebuk I a certain crop pest that attacks peanut plants.
   II cebuk-cebuk or cebak-cebuk repr splashing sounds. See also kecebuk.

cebur or mak cebur repr s.t. splashing into deep water;
   nyebur to dive into;
   nyeburaké to throw s.t. into (water);
   kecebur to fall into (water).

cecak I small lizard commonly found on house walls.
   II 1 dot, point (see also cecek); 2 a diacritic mark indicating NG in Javanese script;
   nyecak to put such a diacritic mark above a Javanese letter.

cecaya lit facial expression. See also caya.

cécé, cécébucé having many chipped or scratched places (var of cècèl bucèl).

ceced lit flaw, defect. See also cacad.

ceceg see cecek.

cècèg 1 to agree (with); 2 to match, suit; 3 confirmed var of cocog.

cecek I dot, point;
   nyeceki to apply dots to (fabric);
   cecekan dots on a batik cloth.
   II nyecek (of cigarettes) to tamp, tap.

cècèk var of cècèg, cocog.

cecel compact, tightly compressed;
   nyecel 1 to crowd in(to); 2 or nyeceli to push in.

cècèl, - bucèl detached, chipped, damaged.

cécému s.t. trivial, insignificant, worth nothing.

cécémuwé var of cécému.

cecep, nyecep 1 to sip, suck; 2 fig to absorb knowledge.

cecer, nyecer 1 to drill efficiently; 2 to ask uninterruptedly.

cècèr missing, lacking; dropped off/out; pating kecècèr to drop out little by little everywhere.

cécok to quarrel, squabble, bicker. *See also* cèkcok.

cècrèk, nyècrèki to chip; to slash (dry branches) from a tree; cècrèkan chip of wood; slivers of bark.

céda *lit* flaw, defect, blemish.

cedhak near, close (to); nyedhak to draw near; nyedhaki to approach s.o. or s.t.; nyedhakaké to bring s.t. close(r); kecedhaken too close; cedhakan a short distance; cedhak-cedhakan 1 a place close by; 2 to compete in closeness; sacedhaké close to; nearby

cédhak *reg var of* cedhak.

cédhal (speech defect) inability to pronounce the Javanese rolled R (*var of* célad); nyédhalaké to fail to roll the R's of words.

cedhek *var of* cedhak.

cèdhek *reg var of* cedhak.

cedhil, ora nyedhil to be ineffectual, not much help, no use.

cedhis I bad, wicked, evil, immoral. II *var of* cedhil.

cedhit, nyedhit having small pointed buttocks. *See also* bokong.

cédhok scoop. *See also* cidhuk.

cedhot broken, interrupted (*reg var of* pedhot).

cedhut *repr* a sudden jerk or tug.

ceg *or* mak ceg *repr* snatching; cag-ceg 1 to keep touching or handling; 2 to handle (a number of things) deftly.

cègcog *see* cèkcok.

cegah *or* nyegah to restrain;

panyegah prevention; cegah dhahar lawan guling *lit* to restrain the desire to eat and sleep.

cegat, nyegat 1 to hail, flag down; 2 to hold up; 3 to wait for (s.t. to come along); nyegati 1 to hold up, waylay; 2 to block, impede, ambush; cegatan interception, checkpoint (police, army *etc*).

cegèg *or* mak cegèg *repr* falling into shallow water.

cegèh stuffy, tight in the chest, oppressed.

cegèk *reg* too short; scratched.

cegélé, nyegélé to withdraw, seclude o.s.

cegemek *or* mak cegemek *repr* a sudden snatching; nyegemek to catch immediately.

cegemok, cegemak-cegemok to keep touching or handling things.

cegemol, dicegemol to be accused of s.t. embarrassing. *See also* cogemol.

cèger *or* mak cèger *repr* an arrow or spear finding its mark; nyèger to stick, stab, pierce; cèger-cèger *or* cégar-cèger (of arrows, spears) to keep hitting target.

cegil, nyegil to sit alone, in a prominent place.

ceglik, ceglak-ceglik *repr* 1 to stick out all alone; 2 to stay awake all alone when in attendance on a sick person; nyeglik *var of* nyegil.

ceglug *or* mak ceglug *repr* joints cracking.

ceglung *or* mak ceglung *repr* s.t. falling into deep water.

cégoh *or* cégoh-régoh *reg* infirm (through age); faulty (language).

cegok *or* mak cegok *repr* swallowing water; sacegokan at a draught. *See also* cegug.

cegot *reg* broken, interrupted (*var of* cedhot).

cégrok *or* mak cégrok *repr* alighting, perching.

cegu a belch, hiccup; to belch, hiccup (*var of* segu);
cegunen to hiccup; to swallow the wrong way (*kr for* cekiken).

cegug *or* mak cegug *repr* swallowing water;
cegug-cegug *or* cegag-cegug *repr* swallowing repeatedly.

ceguk, ceguken a hiccup; to have the hiccups.

cegur *or* mak cegur *repr* a splash;
nyegur to jump into water;
nyeguri to plunge s.t. into water;
nyeguraké to plunge s.t. into water;
kecegur to fall into water.

cèh, ngecèh-ngecèh to squander, waste (money).

cek *see* ceg.

cèk *or* mak cèk *repr* the sound effect produced by tapping a metal object.

cekak short, brief; - budiné short tempered; - napasé short of breath; breathless; crita - a short story (*see also* crita);
nyekak to shorten;
nyekaki to make s.t. (so that it is) small;
nyekakaké to make s.t. shorter (than it was);
cekakan 1 an abbreviation; abbreviated, cut; 2 in brief, briefly;
cekak cukupé 1 in short, in brief; 2 short but to the point;
cekaking rembug to make a long story short.

cekakah, nyekakah having the legs spread wide apart;
cekakahan (of legs) spread wide apart.

cekakak I a variety of bird.
II nyekakak to laugh loudly;
cekakakan laughing one's head off.

cekakar, nyekakar *or* cekakaran lying down with the legs sticking up.

cekakik 1 (of coffee) lees, dregs; 2 nicotine.

cekaklak *var of* cekakak.

cekangkang *or* mak cekangkang *repr* falling down on the back stiffly;
nyekangkang to lie on the back stiffly;
cekangkangan *or* pating cekangkang *pl* to lie or fall on the back stiffly.

cekap 1 sufficient (*kr for* cukup); 2 adequate (*kr for* sedheng).

cékas *reg* message; to give a message. *See also* wekas II.

cekanthuk, nyekanthuk curled at the tips. *See also* cekathuk, clekathuk;
pating cekanthuk *pl* curled at the tips.

cekathak I *or* cekathakan a wooden saddle covered with velvet.
II cekathakan ill-mannered; to keep moving around aimlessly in such a way as to disturb others.

cekathuk *var of* cekanthuk.

cekathung, nyekathung to raise a hand with a cupped palm.

cèkcok to quarrel, argue.

cekédhong, nyekédhong *or* nyekédhongaké to cup the hand.

cekedhung *var of* cekédhong.

cekèh, cekèh-cekèh to keep coughing.

cèkèh to stand or walk with the feet apart. *See also* cèngkèh.

cekèk I *cr excl of swearing.*
II pure, true; Jawa - a true Javanese.
III nyekèk *cr* to eat.

cekékal *or* mak cekékal *repr* getting right up again.

cekékar *or* mak cekékar *repr* lying down with the legs sticking up.

cekèkèh, nyekèkèh with legs apart below the knees;
nyekèkèhaké to place the lower legs apart.

cekeker, cekekeran, cekekar-cekeker to crawl slowly; to inch slowly.

cekèkèr, cekèkèran lying down with the

139

legs moving in different directions, *e.g.* after a sprawling fall.

cekekrek, nyekekrek dejected, dispirited, out of sorts;

pating cekekrek *pl* dejected, dispirited.

cekel *ng*, **cepeng** *kr* to hold; - **gawé** *ng*, - **damel** *kr* to have or take up a job; to hold office.

nyekel to hold, take hold of, grasp; to catch;

nyekeli to hold on to;

nyekelaké 1 to hold for s.o.; to grasp on s.o.'s behalf; **2** to give s.t. as security for a loan;

kecekel to get caught/seized;

cemekel (to look) tempting to handle;

panyekel way of holding/handling; technique of grasping;

cekelan 1 to hold, grasp, catch hold of; **2** a handle, holder; **3** security held for indebtedness; **4** money alloted for s.o.'s use.

cèkèl pupil, disciple of a priest.

cekeneng, pating cekeneng (of skin, muscles) feeling taut or stretched.

cekéngkang, nyekéngkang to fall down with the legs sticking up.

cekengkeng *or* **mak cekengkeng** *repr* stiffening;

nyekengkeng to stiffen; seized with a cramp, convulsed.

cekenik *or* **mak cekenik** *repr* a sudden appearance (of a small thing);

nyekenik small, tiny;

pating cekenik many (of small things).

cekenthang, nyekenthang to pop up, curl up.

cekenthik, nyekenthik curled at the tip (of small thing);

pating cekenthik *pl of* **nyekenthik**.

cekenthing *var of* **cekenthik**.

cekenthit *var of* **cekenthik**.

cekénthong *var of* **cekédhong**.

cekenthung *var of* **cekenthing**.

cekenuk *var of* **cekenthung**.

cekep enough, sufficient, adequate (*reg var of* **cukup**).

cèkèr 1 chicken's leg; **2** *cr* hand;

nyèkèr 1 walking without wearing shoes; **2** to scratch;

nyèkèri (of chicken) to scratch for food;

cèkèr-cèkèr (of chicken) to scratch for food; (of people) to scratch a living.

cekèt *or* **mak cekèt** *repr* biting, pinching; *repr* a small bite or sting. *See also* **cekit**.

cèket quick (*reg var of* **rikat 1**);

cékat-cèket to move quickly, hurry up.

cekethek I cekethak-cekethek to strive to withdraw in an underhand way from (work).

II pating cekethek *pl* messy, dirty, untidy.

cekèthèk, nyekèthèk very easy to find.

cekethem, nyekethem to grasp, hold tight, clutch.

cekethik, cekethak-cekethik engaged in s.t. intricate;

pating cekethik having an intricate structure.

cekéthok, nyekéthokaké to cup the hand.

cekénthong small shallow banana-leaf container, *esp* for rice boiled in coconut milk.

cekethut, nyekethut to fold up, crease.

ceki a game played with the Chinese cards (*kertu cilik*).

cekidhing *var of* **cekithing**.

cekigrèk the crowing of a wild cock.

cekik *or* **mak cekik** *repr* hiccuping;

nyekik to strangle or choke s.o.

cekikèr the crowing of a wild cock (*var of* **cekigrèk**).

cekikik, cekikikan to giggle, chuckle, laugh lightly;

pating cekikik *pl* to giggle, chuckle.

ceking 1 thin, slender; **2** emaciated.

cekit *or* mak cekit *repr* biting, pinching; *repr* a small bite or sting. *See also* cekèt, clekit.

cekithat, nyekithat 1 tapering to a point at the tip; 2 (of dress, grooming) neat, meticulous (*var of* jekithat, jlekithat).

cekithing, nyekithing to carry or hold things with a thumb and index finger; cekithang-cekithing holding things without having a tight grip on them.

cekithong *var of* cekéthok.

cekiwing *see* cengkiwing.

ceklèk broken; nyeklèk to break (a dry branch), snap; ceklèkan 1 broken fragment; the way to break; 2 *fig* short-tempered.

cèkli small, attractive, cute (of houses).

ceklik *or* mak ceklik *repr* sound of clicking; nyeklik to click; to switch on (the light *etc*).

cekluk *or* mak cekluk *repr* joints cracking; nyekluki to crack one's joints by pulling or bending them.

céko having an arm permanently bent at the elbow; cékon walking with a bent arm.

cekodhok, nyekodhokaké to cup the hand.

cekodhong *var of* cekodhok, cekédhong.

cekoh to cough (*k.i. for* watuk).

cekok I the hollow in the neck below the Adam's apple.
II *or* cekokan a traditional medicine forcibly given to children; nyekoki 1 to give such a medicine to a child forcefully; 2 *fig* to indoctrinate; nyekokaké to put s.t. in s.o.'s mouth forcefully; to ram s.t. down.

cékor (of feet) deformed.

cekot *or* mak cekot *repr* a stab of pain; cekot-cekot to throb with pain. *See also* clekot.

cékot *var of* céko.

cekothèh *or* pating cekothèh to be smeared with a dirty substance.

cekothok *var of* cekuthung.

cekothong *var of* cekuthung.

cekowak, nyekowak having a hole/dent in it; pating cekowak full of holes or dents.

cekowèk *var of* cekowak.

cekowok, nyekowok having a large hollowed or indented shape; pating cekowok full of good-sized holes or dents.

cekrak *or* mak cekrak *repr* a pricking sensation; nyekrak to prick (skin) and cause pain.

cékré stunted, unable to achieve normal growth.

cekrèh, cekrah-cekrèh to cough repeatedly.

cekrèk *or* mak cekrèk *repr* snapping shut; punching s.t.; cekrak-cekrèk making repeated clicks.

cèkrèk, nyèkrèk to appear handsome. *See also* cakrak.

cekrik (*pron as:* cekri:k) *or* mak cekrik *repr* a small pricking sensation; nyekrik to prick (skin) and cause pain; *fig* to hurt one's feelings; cekrak-cekrik *repr* pricking skin repeatedly.

cekroh, cekrah-cekroh to keep coughing.

cekrok *var of* cekrak.

cekukruk, nyekukruk (of chicken) to droop with neck drawn in; cekukrak-cekukruk having a sickly appearance.

cekung curving, bent.

cekuntheng, nyekuntheng curly. *See also* clekuntheng.

cekut *var of* cekot.

cekuthik *var of* clekuthik.

cekuthis *var of* clekuthis.

cekuthu, nyekuthu to make a fist.

cekuthuk I a rounded woven bamboo hat.

II **cekuthuk-cekuthuk** to trudge on; to walk slowly.

cela defect, flaw, blemish;

nyela to criticise, disapprove of, find fault with.

célad inability to pronounce the Javanese rolled R (speech defect);

nyéladaké to fail to roll the R's of words (*var of* **cédhal**).

celak I 1 near, close (to) (*kr for* **cedhak**); **2** short (*kr for* **cendhak**).

II eye shadow;

nyelaki *or* **celakan** to apply eye shadow.

celaka *var of* **cilaka**.

celathu *ng*, **wicanten** *kr*, **ngendika** *k.i.* to say, speak, talk;

nyelathu to scold;

pacelathon conversation, talk. *See also* **clathu**.

celeb *see* **celep**.

célé-célé *or* **cèlèn** *reg excl of surprise*: good heavens!

celèk, nyelèkaké to retract (skin); to roll back (eyelid).

célémèndhé a small oval short-legged cockroach with white spots. *See also* **cérémèndhé**.

celeng black, dark;

celengan indigo dye (*subst kr for* **nila**).

cèlèng 1 wild pig, boar; **2** *term of abuse*;

nyèlèng resembling a wild pig;

nyèlèngi to save up (money);

nyèlèngaké to save money for s.o.;

cèlèngan 1 piggy bank; **2** savings; **3** a bamboo or wooden support; **4** wild boar made from plaitwork with which a man dances himself into a trance.

celep 1 indigo dye (*kr for* **wedel**); **2** *var of* **celup**.

celer, nyeler to snatch away. *See also* **seler**.

celet, nyelet to go back on (a bargain), back out of; to hold back, withhold;

celetan secretiveness, reticence, closeness.

celik *or* **kecelik 1** mistaken in an identification or interpretation; **2** disappointed in a hope or expectation.

célik *var of* **celik**.

celom (of face) wan and pinched-looking (after suffering from illness).

celong *var of* **celom**.

celor adulterous;

nyelor to engage in illicit sex;

celoran, anak celoran an illegitimate child.

cèlu, kecèlu *reg* strongly attracted. *See also* **kacèlu**.

celub *see* **celup**.

celuk, nyeluk to call;

nyeluki to call s.o. repeatedly;

nyelukaké to call on behalf of s.o.;

celuk-celuk *or* **celak-celak** to keep calling.

célung the blossom of the **dhadhap** tree.

celup, nyelup to soak;

nyelupaké to dip s.t. in liquid;

kecelup to get dipped/soaked inadvertently;

celupan liquid for soaking s.t.;

celap-celup to go in and out of (liquid).

celus 1 a certain leech (in a cow's nose); **2** penis.

cem, cem-ceman coconut oil hair preparation.

cèm *excl* mine! (word by which children lay claim to s.t.);

ngecèmi to claim s.t. by calling **cèm**!

cemak, nyemak to touch, feel.

cemani 1 dark in skin colour; **2** *intsfr* dark, black; **ireng** - jet black; pitch black.

cemara I a certain evergreen tree, casuarina.

II **1** false hair worn by ladies in a knot; **2** a horsehair brush for sweeping.

cèmbèng a special day of cemetery-cleaning and prayer held by the Chinese. *See also* **cèngbèng**.

cembring *reg* desolate, deathly still.

cembuk *reg* a big boar.

cembung curved; dome-shaped; chubby (of cheeks).

cemburu jealous; envious;
cemburuan 1 having a jealous nature; 2 excessively jealous of one's spouse.

cémé I a game played with the Chinese cards (*kertu cilik*). *See also* jèmèh I.
II *or* kecémé a certain edible fruit.

cemedhing *reg* a cooked vegetable salad with hot spiced peanut dressing. *See also* pecel.

cèmèh *see* cémé.

cemek, nyemek with a fair amount of water, fairly wet.

cemèk *reg* lamb; kid (young of the wedhus). *See also* cempé.

cememek, nyememek dirty and watery;
pating cememek *pl* as above.

cemèmèk *cr* female genitals.

cememet, nyememet *or* cememetan to chase after girls.

cemèmrèng, nyemèmrèng threadbare.

cemendhil pellet-shaped animal droppings. *See also* temendhil.

cemeng black (*kr for* ireng I);
cemengan 1 opium (*kr for* candu); 2 *kr for* Wagé.

cemèng kitten (young of the kucing).

cemer soggy, messy, muddy;
nyemeri *or* nyemer-nyemeri to cause to be soggy.

cemera *reg* dog.

cèmèt, nyèmèt to drag (boat) with a rope.

cemethi *ng, kr* tembung *k.i.* whip, riding crop;
nyemethi, nyemethèni to whip with a riding crop.

cemil I nyemil to eat snacks;
cemilan snacks.
II sacemil a little bit.

cemimi, cemima-cemimi speaking softly but distinctly;

pating cemimi *pl* as above.

cemimik *cr* female genitals (*var of* cemèmèk).

cemiming, cemimingan to walk carefully from fear.

cemindrikan (to hold a party) on a small scale.

cemirik *reg* puppy (young of the asu).

cemit, sacemit a tiny bit.

cemlèk, nyemlèk damp, moist.

cemlik *var of* cemit.

cemo-é a sweet hot drink made from coconut milk, sugar, bread and slices of coconut.

cemok, nyemok to touch with the hand. *See also* demok.

cemol, nyemol to grasp with the fingers.

cemomong *var of* cremomong.

cemot *repr* snatching.

cémot I *or* mak cémot *repr* drawing s.o. into one's arms against the chest;
nyémot *repr* to carry tightly against the chest.
II cémot-cémot (of face) smeared from eating.

Cempa Champa, a former kingdom in Indo-China; - rowa a children's game; pari - the plant that produces short-grained rice.

cempad decision, judgment; opinion;
nyempad *reg* to decide that s.t. is bad, reject.

cempaka frangipani (var of campaka).

cémpal leaf for picking up s.t. dirty. *See also* timpal.

cempala wooden mallet used for producing sound effect and music signals during shadow-play performances;
nyempala to rap with the above on the wooden puppet chest;
nyempalani to hit.

cempaluk young tamarind fruit.

cempé lamb; kid (young of the wedhus);
cempéning Allah Lamb of God;
nyempé kèri to bleat like a lamb/kid.

cempèd *see* cempèt.

cempedhak a certain variety of jackfruit.

cèmpèh a small round woven bamboo basket. *See also* cèpèh.

cempelak, nyempelak to reply angrily; to snarl at, snap at, snub. *Also* cemplak.

cempélo *or* mak cempélo *repr* a leap into the saddle. *Also* cémplo.

cempirut, pating cempirut full of wrinkles.

cemplak *var of* cempelak.

cémplak, nyémplak to jump onto; to hop on (a bike). *See also* céngklak.

cemplang 1 insipid, tasteless; 2 pointless, dull;
cemplang-cemplang to talk pointless nonsense.

cemplek, nyemplek plump, chubby.

cempli, nyempli (of stomach) rounded, chubby.

cémplo *var of* cempélo.

cemplon 1 sweet fried cassava balls; 2 a small earthenware pot; 3 a small canoe-like boat.

cemplong, nyemplong to make a wide deep hole;
cemplongan holes (of sugarcane *etc*).

cemplu, nyemplu 1 round(ed) in shape; 2 bulging in the middle.

cempluk 1 a small earthenware pot; 2 *var of* cemplu.

cemplung *or* mak cemplung *repr* a splash;
nyemplung to fall (into), plunge into; nyemplungi *or* nyemplungaké to plunge s.t. into;
kecemplung to fall in accidentally;
cemplang-cemplang to dump things into; to plunge s.t. repeatedly into.

cempol short fibres covering the 'eyes' of a coconut.

cempolèh *reg* shortcoming, failing, deficiency; demerit, imperfection;
nyempolèhi to reprimand s.o.; to scold s.o.

cempor oil lamp.

cemprèng (of voice) high-pitched and dissonant.

cèmprèng 1 useless, trivial; 2 (*or* cèmprèngan) (to hold a party) on a small scale.

cempulek *reg* it's obvious that.

cempuling a hooked fishing spear;
nyempuling to catch fish with the above.

cempuri *see* cepuri.

cempurit I 1 the puppet stick, *usu* made from horn, for manipulating the puppet and its arms to which it is attached;
nyempurit to hold a puppet on its stick.
II the pulp cavity of teeth, horns, antlers.
III plant disease;
cempuriten (of plants) sickly.

cempurung woven bamboo or rattan canopy for a bier (pendhosa) on which a body is borne to the cemetery.

cemukir, cemukiran a certain batik pattern. *See also* semukirang.

cemumuk, cemumukan *or* cemumak-cemumuk to grope or feel one's way. *See also* cenunuk.

cemuru *lit* deer, roe deer, antelope.

cemung bowl.

cémut *var of* cémot I.

cenanal, cenanalan to gesture habitually with the hands and arms (rather than preserving the desirable attitude of repose).

cenanang, cenanangan to look around wildly as one walks along.

cenanil *var of* cenanal.

cenanuk, pating cenanuk *pl* with heads frozen into motionlessness through amazement, surprise, shock.

cenanul *var of* cenanal.

cencang, nyencang to tether (animals);
cencangan a tethering rope;

kecencang bound, fastened, attached.

cencem coconut oil mixed with flowers and fragrant leaves;

nyencem to soak s.t.;

cenceman liquid in which s.t. is soaked.

cendhak *ng*, **celak** *kr* short;

nyendhaki to make s.t. shorter;

nyendhakaké to shorten s.t.;

kecendhaken excessively short;

cendhak-cendhakan 1 brief(ly); **2** even though short; **3** to compare or compete for shortest.

cendhala contemptible, shameful.

cendhana sandalwood.

cendhani slender Chinese bamboo; - **raras** couch.

cendhek *var of* **cendhak**.

cendhèk *ng*, **andhap** *kr* **1** short in stature; **2** low;

nyendhèk to descend;

nyendhèki to make s.t. lower (than s.t. else);

nyendhèkaké to lower s.t.;

cendhèk-cendhèkan 1 to compare or compete for lowest; **2** to do s.t. at a low level.

cendhéla window. *See also* **jendhéla**.

cendheng relatives.

cendhèp *reg var of* **cendhèk**.

cèndhèp *reg var of* **cendhèk**.

céndhok *reg var of* **séndhok**.

céndhol 1 small, doughy rice flour droplets used in cold drinks; **2** a beverage made with such droplets.

cené defect, flaw;

nyené to criticise, find fault;

kecenèn to get caught doing s.t. wrong.

cènel *or* **mak cènel** *repr* springy, trembling.

cenéla sandals, slippers (*var of* **canéla**).

cenèng a bowl used for measuring rice.

cènèng, **nyènèng** to pull s.t. toward o.s.;

kecènèng to get pulled.

cenès different (*reg var of* **sanès**).

ceng a pin used to put opium in an opium pipe.

cèng I 1 sugarcane sap; **2** molasses.

II ngecèngi to step over (in a children's game).

III *repr* to pay cash.

cenganglung, **pating cenganglung** *pl* to stand with the heads weighed down.

cenganguk *or* **mak cenganguk** *repr* looking out at s.t. and showing disappointment;

nyenganguk to look out (the window).

cengap, **nyengap** to yell out;

cengap-cengap 1 to open the mouth again and again, as when gasping for air; **2** having trouble doing s.t.

cèngbèng special day of cemetery-cleaning and prayer held by the Chinese during April (*var of* **cèmbèng**).

cengèh, **nyengèh-nyengèhaké** to show s.t. off which is not worth showing off.

cèngèh *reg var of* **cèngèk**.

cengèk, **nyengèk** to wail, sound shrilly;

nyenyengèk to torment s.o. to make them cry or moan.

cèngèk a small, very pungent kind of chili.

cengel nape of the neck.

cengèl, **nyengèl** conspicuous, eye-catching.

cèngèl, **nyèngèl 1** to appear; **2** to lift the head while lying; to crane the neck;

nyèngèlaké to crane (the neck); to stick (the head) up high;

nyèngèl-nyèngèlaké to keep sticking s.t. up high. *See also* **crèngèl**.

cengeng to feel stiff in the neck.

cèngèng to cry easily.

cengèngès to laugh jeeringly, showing the teeth;

nyengèngès to grin shyly;

cengèngèsan to keep jeering, sneering;

pating cengèngès *pl* to keep jeering, sneering.

cengèr *or* mak cengèr *repr* the sudden cry (of a baby);
    nyengèr to cry loudly;
    cengar-cengèr to cry loudly again and again.

cèngèr *reg var of* cangar.

cengès, nyengès to tease, ridicule.

cenggama *reg* worried, apprehensive.

cenggami *var of* cenggama.

cenggé Chinese ceremonial procession.

cènggèr comb of a cock. *See also* jènggèr.

cenggèrèng fried mixture of small peanut slices with spiced rice flour. *See also* rempèyèk.

cenggèrètnong a certain flying insect that makes a loud 'rèt-nong' sound.

cengging, nyengging *reg* to seize s.o. by the nape of the neck.

cenggir *var of* cengging.

cenggring, nyenggring to insult s.o., hurt s.o.'s feelings.

cengil wicked, evil;
    nyengil *or* nyengili to do harm to s.o.

cengingak, cengingakan *or* pating cengingak *pl* to gaze (at) in astonishment or wonder. *See also* cingak.

cengingis *or* mak cengingis *repr* a jeering grin;
    nyengingis to bare the teeth when laughing jeeringly or flirtatiously;
    cengingisan *or* cengingas-cengingis to keep sneering at; to keep ridiculing.

cengir, nyengir to gesture with the face, grinning foolishly;
    cengar-cengir to keep grinning foolishly or screwing up the face;
    nyengar-nyengir to keep grimacing or grinning foolishly; *fig* helpless, ineffectual; unable to do anything.

cengis I *reg* a certain variety of very hot chili.
    II, nyengis to show (the teeth) (in pain; when jeering, sneering);
    cecengisan to keep jeering, sneering.

See also cengingis.

cengkah a clash, a conflict; to clash, conflict;
    nyengkah 1 to push against s.t., *e.g.* to support it; 2 to engage in a contest of strength by pushing against each other, sometimes at either end of a pole;
    cecengkahan to conflict with each other.

cengkal I a kind of hook to hold up the clothing of a newly circumcised boy; 2 (s.t. used as) a doorstop;
    nyengkal 1 awkward, ungrammatical, meaningless (of the sentence arrangement); 2 to prop s.t. (with a piece of wood).
    II a unit of length: 3.75 metres;
    nyengkali to measure in units of length as above.

cengkalak a crossbeam or a piece of wood/bamboo used for tying hands at the back;
    nyengkalak to tie hands at the back with the above.

cengkalang, cengkalangan wooden frame of a wheel.

cengkang a unit of length: the distance between the tips of thumb and index finger when stretched wide apart;
    nyengkangi to measure s.t. in the above unit of length;
    sacengkang one hand-span, approx. 18 cm.

cengkanuk, nyengkanuk close by, right under one's nose.

cengkao Chinese broker, middleman.

cengkar (of soil) unproductive;
    nyengkaraké to let (land) lie fallow.

cengkaruk I the flower of the jambu.
    II dried cooked rice fried without oil.

cengkeg a prop, support;
    nyengkeg to prop s.t. up;
    nyengkegi to prop s.t. up with.

cèngkèg *var of* cengkeg.

cengkèh 1 clove (tree; fruit); 2 clubs (playing-card suit).

cèngkèh I a bunch or hand of bananas.
II (to stand) with the feet apart.
III 1 *reg* forked stick; 2 tripod.

cengkélak *repr* a sudden turning back.

cengkelang, nyengkelangaké to stick (a sickle *etc*) into the back of the belt.

cengkelek, cengkelekan to try swallowing a big piece of food with difficulty.

cengkèng I the sound of a barking dog.
II *reg* capable. *See also* cengkong.

cengkenik *var of* cekenik.

cengkenuk *var of* cekenuk.

cèngkèr contentious, disputatious, quarrelsome.

cengkèrèk, pating cengkèrèk (of plants) sickly; (of writing) streaky.

cengkerem, nyengkerem 1 to grasp with claws; to grip with the nails; 2 *fig* to hold firmly.

cengkerung, pating cengkerung (of skin) wrinkled.

cengkèwèk *var of* cengkiwing.

cengkèwèng *var of* cengkiwing.

cengkidhing *var of* cekithing.

cengkig, nyengkig to catch, detect; to tread (upon).

cengkiling apt to hit when angered.

cengkir a very young coconut (not yet edible); - gadhing a small yellow decorative coconut;
nyengkir gadhing ivory-coloured (of beautiful breasts);
cengkir ketindhihan kiring to have trouble getting married as one's older sibling is not yet married.

cengkirig, nyengkirig (of hair, fur, feathers) standing on end.

cengkiwing to hold or carry s.t. by holding it at the outer edge with one or two fingers; to hold (a child or an animal) by the middle.

céngklak, nyéngklak to hop on; to jump onto.

cengklé, nyengklé to sit idly staring into space. *See also* jengglé.

cengklèng I (*or* mak cengklèng) *repr* a metallic clang;
nyengklèng *or* cumengklèng to clang.
II, nyengklèng 1 to contrast (with the surroundings); 2 far from the destination.

cèngkleng *or* mak cèngkleng *repr* jumping on a bike.

cengkli a small bottle.

cengklik, nyengklik to sit alone on a high place.

cengkling *or* mak cengkling *repr* metallic tinkle;
cumengkling to ring, tinkle.

cengklong, nyengklong to deduct, withdraw (money).

cengkluk, nyengkluk to sit with bowed head.

cengklung I, cengklungen to hanker for s.o.'s coming.
II, cumengklung *repr* the sound of gamelan music heard from afar.

céngkok 1 singing or speaking style; 2 regional variety of a language; 3 variation in pitch or key in singing a classical song.

cengkolak wooden reinforcement in the middle of a bow.

cengkolong, nyengkolong to catch out with trick questions.

cengkong *var of* cengkèng.

cengkorèk, nyengkorèk to open and spread around the contents of; *fig* to reveal and spread (a secret).

cengkorog *var of* cengkirig.

cengkorong, nyengkorongi to draw up a sketch or outline (of);
cengkorongan sketch, outline.

cengkowak, pating cengkowak *pl* full of holes or dents;
nyengkowak having a hole/dent on it.

cengkowèk *var of* cengkowak.

cengkowok *var of* cengkowak;

cengkowokan a large hole; a hollow.

cengkrang *or* **mak cengkrang** *repr* a pricking sensation;
cumengkrang to feel a pricking sensation.

céngkrang *var of* **théngkrang**.

céngkré fond of teasing; a teaser.

cengkrèk, nyengkrèk rising steeply.

cengkring *var of* **cengkrang**;
cengkrang-cengkring to keep feeling a pricking sensation.

céngkrong 1 (of arms, legs) curved, bent; 2 a certain kind of sickle or knife (*see also* **cingkrong**).

cengkruk, nyengkruk engrossed, bent over in concentration.

cengkung *repr* the tones of a certain gamelan instrument (**kempul**);
cumengkung noted for being able to speak in ringing tones.

cengkurek, pating cengkurek scrawled, messy (of handwriting).

cengkuwèh *var of* **tengkuwèh**.

cengkuwer curved or bent into a hooked shape.

cengkuwik, nyengkuwik to form a hole, having a hole in it;
pating cengkuwik *pl* full of small holes, dents, hollows.

cengoh, nyengoh in plain view; right there in sight;
nyengohaké to allow s.t. to be seen.

cengol, nyengolaké to raise s.t. above the surface.

cengonglong *or* **mak cengonglong** *repr* a sudden coming into view.

cengongoh, cengongah-cengongoh to keep showing o.s.

cengongok, pating cengongok *pl* extending the neck forward.

céngos, céngosan (of face) streaked with dirt;
pating créngos *pl as above. See also* **créngos**.

cenguk baby monkey (young of the **kethèk** I);
nyenguk flabbergasted, dumbfounded;
nyenguki (of babies) just learning to talk.

cengungong *repr* the cry of the peacock;
nyenyungong (of peacock) to cry.

cengunguk *repr* showing up suddenly;
nyengunguk to pop up suddenly.

cenil I 1 any small round springy-textured object; 2 small round cakes made from sticky rice flour, sugar and grated coconut.
II *or* **mak cenil** *repr* pinching, pecking;
cenal-cenil 1 having a rubbery texture; 2 lively, vivacious.

céning *reg* a certain cake (var of **cining**).

cenining, ceniningan defiant, inconsiderate, cocksure.

cénol *or* **mak cénol** *repr* the elastic movement of s.t. springy being released suddenly.

centhak, nyenthak (of horses) to start; frightened.

centhang I small platter of vegetables or stew.
II a kind of hook to hold up the clothing of a newly circumcised boy;
nyenthang to bend/curve upward; with the tip turned up, sticking out;
centhangan to use curved wood as above.

cénthang, nyénthangi to tick off; place a mark (against);
cénthangan a mark, note.

centhé I a small metallophone (*var of* **peking** II).
II, **nyenthé-nyenthé** (of speaking voice) grating, strident.

cènthèl *var of* **canthèl**.

centhèng I guard, watchman.
II, **nyenthèng** to speak loudly;
nyenthèng-nyenthèng to keep speaking loudly and angrily;

centhang-centhèng (of speaking voice) loud, harsh.

cèntheng *or* mak cèntheng *repr* a sharp object striking s.t.

centhèt, kecenthèt sickly; stunted in growth.

centhing I a small sash-like garment;
nyenthingi to put such a sash on s.o.;
centhingan to wear such a sash.
II any long thin object with a pointed tip;
nyenthing to extend outward.

centhok, nyenthok to anger or hurt s.o.;
kecenthok to sulk.

cénthong 1 rice ladle; 2 shoulder blade spoon;
nyénthong to ladle out (rice).

centhuka *var of* canthoka.

centhul 1 term of abuse; 2 *cr* penis.

centhula *var of* canthola.

centhung curled hair on the forehead;
nyenthung (hair on the forehead) curled;
nyenthungaké to curl hair on the forehead.

cenuk, nyenuk to remain sitting motionless; to fix one's eye upon s.t.;
nyenukaké to keep s.t. handy.

cenunuk, cenunukan *or* cenunak-cenunuk to grope one's way;
pating cenunuk *pl* groping. *See also* nunuk.

cenunut, cenunutan acting in a hurried or restless way; ill-mannered.

céok, nyéoki to gather up/in with the hands.

céos, nyéos to pour water on the fire.

cep 1 *repr* a sudden silence as s.o. stops talking or singing; 2 hush! (to a crying child); - klakep total silence.

cèp *var of* cèm, cim.

cepak 1 close to, almost at; 2 apt, prone;
cepak-cepak to make preparations; ready and waiting;
nyepak *or* cumepak in readiness;

nyepaki to prepare s.t. for s.o.;
nyepakaké to make s.t. ready for use;
cepakan s.t. which is in readiness.

cepaka frangipani (*var of* cempaka).

cepaplak, cepaplakan *or* pating cepaplak to sprawl.

cepaplang, nyepeplang to stick out, protrude sideways (horns, arms).

cepaplem, nyepaplem to keep quiet without talking or eating.

cepedhak *var of* cempedhak.

cèpèh *reg* small saucer. *See also* lèpèk.

cepel sticky.

cepeng to grasp, hold (*kr for* cekel).

cepèpèh, nyepèpèh I to sit and bow the head (before s.o.).
II nyepèpèh spread flat on the floor, not curved upwards.

cepèr shallow; saucer-shaped.

cèpèr *var of* cepèr.

cepet quick, fast; with a swift motion;
nyepetaké to speed up, to accelerate;
kecepeten too fast;
cepet-cepetan in a hurry, hastily.

cepèt a gripping instrument;
nyepèt 1 to pinch or grip with a tool; 2 to press s.t. between two things.

cepéthé, cepéthé-cepéthé trivial, of little worth, insignificant.

cepit, nyepit to pinch, squeeze, press s.t.;
nyepiti to clip many objects;
nyepitaké to press s.t between two things;
kecepit to get squeezed/pressed;
cepitan clips, tweezers, clamps.

cepithing *reg var of* kepithing.

céplak, céplak-céplak to smack.

ceplé to speak Javanese with a Banyumas accent.

céplé, nyéplé to sit close to s.o. *See also* dhéplé.

ceplèk *or* mak ceplèk *repr* slapping.

ceplès *or* mak ceplès *var of* ceplèk;
nyeplèsi to slap (a naughty child).

cèples just right, exact, on the knocker;

nyèplesi to resemble closely, be just the same as. *See also* jèbles, jiblès.

ceplik stud of a Javanese earring, with stone.

cepling *or* mak cepling *repr* becoming detached.

ceplis *or* mak ceplis *repr* s.t. small being crushed.

ceplok I 1 a circle-shaped mark; 2 fried egg;
nyeplok to fry an egg;
nyeploki to decorate s.t. with the circle-shaped marks.
II *or* mak ceplok *repr* stamping sound;
ceplak-ceplok to produce a stamping sound repeatedly.

ceplong *repr* a sudden opening;
nyeplong to make a hole all the way through s.t.;
cumeplong relieved.

ceplos 1 straight out (describing direct, unadorned speech); 2 *repr* bursting apart;
nyeplos to burst a hole in s.t.;
nyeplosaké to explain forthrightly;
keceplos to let words slip out inadvertently;
cumeplos plainly stated;
ceplas-ceplos to speak one's mind forthrightly.

cepluk I (*pron as:* ceplu:k) *or* mak cepluk *repr* a small burst.
II (throughout) the morning;
sakésuk - all the morning. *See also* jepluk II.

cèpluk, cèplukan 1 a certain bird; 2 a certain wild shrub; also its edible grape-like fruit.

ceplus *or* mak ceplus *repr* squirting with a small burst;
nyeplus to bite or press (chilis) into the mouth;
keceplus to bite (chilis) unexpectedly;
ceplas-ceplus to bite (chilis) again and again.

cepol to become detached; to come off.

cepon a kind of bamboo basket.

cepong *reg* dung, muck.

cépor, nyépor (of lips) thick and spread wide.

cepot *reg var of* copot.

cèprès, nyèprès (of moustaches) long and limp.

ceprèt 1 (*or* mak ceprèt) *repr* the click (of a camera shutter); 2 *repr* s.t. soft getting squashed.

cèpret *repr* sticking of a knife or a pointed weapon;
céprat-cèpret to stab with a pointed weapon repeatedly.

cèprèt *or* nyèprèt to splatter;
nyèprèti to splatter onto;
kecèprètan splattered with.

ceprok, nyeprok broad, spreading.

ceprol *or* mak ceprol *repr* a sudden easy detachment.

ceprot *or* mak ceprot 1 *repr* s.t. bursting out; 2 *repr* s.t. sharp stabbing;
nyeprot to burst out.

cepuk *or* cepukan a small covered round container;
nyepuk having the shape of the above container.

cepuri 1 masonry wall around a house or garden; 2 a court metal betel-box; 3 *lit* a hole in the side of a grave for laying the corpse;
nyepuri to enclose (an area) with a masonry wall.

cepurung canopy covering a howdah or sampan cabin.

cer I full (sibling relationship).
II *or* mak cer *repr* s.t. pouring out.

cèr *or* mak cèr 1 *repr* metal vibrating; 2 *repr* an engine starting up.

cerah *see* crah.

cerak near, close (to) (*var of* cedhak).

cérak *reg var of* cedhak.

ceramah lecture, speech, talk.

cerbak *reg* to eat everything;

cerbakan (of foods) nothing avoided.

cerbek *see* cerbak.

cerceb, pating cerceb sore or sensitive from many injuries; (to feel) prickly (all over the body). *Also* terceb.

cercel, nyrecel *or* pating cercel (of children) too many and born too close together. *See also* tercel.

cercèt *reg* handkerchief.

ceré I pure, unmixed.

II a variety of long-grained rice.

III to divorce; no longer married; nyeré to divorce one's spouse.

céré *or* cérémédhé a small cockroach with white spots.

cerek 1 dash, hyphen; 2 a certain diacritic mark in Javanese script; nyerek to write the above character (on).

cerèk, cerèk-cerèk to keep shouting.

cèrek *reg var of* cedhak.

cèrèm trivial, of little worth, insignificant.

cérémédhé *see* céré.

ceret a tiny amount of liquid poured out; saceret a splash of liquid.

cèrèt kettle.

ceri, I nyeri-nyeri to avoid strictly; cumeri-ceri to dislike; very annoying.

II, pacerèn ditch and cesspit for household water disposal.

cerik, cerik-cerik to utter shriek after shriek; to keep screaming.

cérit, kecérit to discharge a small amount of loose faeces by accident (var of cirit).

ceriyos story (*var of* cariyos, *kr for* crita).

cerkakah, nyerkakah to spread, open out; pating cerkakah *pl* to spread, open out.

cerkèkèh *var of* cerkakah.

cerkot, pating cerkot throbbing with pain.

cèrles *var of* cèples.

cerma *lit* leather, hide.

cermé a certain small sour edible fruit.

cermed, nyermed *or* cermedan to tell dirty stories; to talk obscenely or coarsely. *See also* cremed.

cermèmèh, cermèmèh-cermèmèh (of face) depressed, dejected.

cermin mirror, looking-glass.

cermomong, nyermomong (of fires) glowing.

cermumuh, nyermumuh (of sores) reddish and infected-looking.

cerngèngèh *var of* cengèngèh.

cerngèngès *var of* cengèngès.

cerngingis *var of* cengingis.

cerngungus *var of* cengungus.

cérok *var of* sérok.

cérong *var of* clérong. *See also* corèng.

cerpèpèh, nyerpèpèh bowed low, crawling humbly.

certhil, pating certhil throbbing with pain.

cerung (of ravine, gorge) deep and with steep sides.

ces *or* mak ces *repr* sudden cooling/chilling; *fig* an emotional cooling off.

cès *or* mak cès *repr* dripping; ngecès to drool; cas-cès to drip steadily.

cespleng just right; having the desired result; to cure instantly, provide instant relief.

cèt I paint; ngecèt to paint; ngecètakè to have s.t painted; to paint for s.o.; cèt-cètan act or way of painting; painted.

II *repr* monkey chatter.

cetha clear, obvious; - wéla-wéla very clear; nyethakaké to explain, clarify, show; kacetha to be shown; to be explained; cethané explicitly, in other words.

cethak palate; roof of the mouth; swara - gram palatal sounds (*see also* swara).

céthak pertaining to printing; **mesin** - printing press; **tukang** - printer; **salah** - misprint;

  nyéthak or **nyéthaki** to print;

  nyéthakaké to have s.t. printed;

  céthakan act or way of printing; edition;

  panyéthak act of printing.

  See also **cithak**.

cethanthang, **nyethanthang** *or* **cethanthangan** standing in a defiant pose with the legs wide apart.

cethantheng, **cethanthengan** clumsy.

cethathel, **cethathel-cethathel** to trudge along with difficulty.

cethèk shallow; superficial;

  nyethèkaké to cause to be shallow.

cèthèk *reg var of* **cethèk**.

cethèn whip, riding crop.

cethentheng *or* **mak cethentheng** *repr* stiffening suddenly.

cethèr, **cethar-cethèr** (of whips) to keep cracking. *Also* **clethèr**.

cethèt 1 *or* **mak cethèt** *repr* turning an electric switch or pressing a stud;

  cethèt-cethèt *or* **cethat-cethèt** to keep snapping the thumb against the middle finger;

  nyethèti to make a soft sound (to a bird) by snapping as above, to encourage it to sing;

  cethètan 1 a bird that sings only when stimulated as described above; **2** an electric switch.

cèthèt *repr* bursting open;

  nyèthèt to cause to burst open by squeezing or pressing. *See also* **mecèthèt**.

cethethek, **nyethethek** silent and huddled up with cold;

  pating cethethek *pl* as above.

cethetheng, **nyethetheng** standing around doing nothing rather than working at a job; **pating cethetheng** *pl* as above.

cethèthès, **nyethèthès** speaking fluently.

cethèthèt a small bird of the wagtail family, flycatcher.

cethéthol, **cethétholen** to stutter, stammer.

cèthi a female servant at court, handmaiden.

cethik **I** hip, pelvic bone.

  II to ignite; - **geni** to light a fire;

  nyethikaké to get a fire blazing; *fig* to stir up s.t. that had quietened down.

cethil **I** stingy, tightfisted.

  II (*pron as:* cethi:l) *or* **mak cethil** *repr* a tug, jerk;

  nyethil to pull s.t. out with a sudden jerk.

cething a small bowl-shaped basket for serving rice;

  nyethingi to hold a ceremony for a woman seven months pregnant with her first child;

  cethingan (rice placed) in a serving basket.

cethit *or* **mak cethit** *repr* a pinch; a snap; a click;

  kecethit 1 out of joint, sprained; **2** to make a slip of the tongue. *See also* **cethèt**.

cethithèt *reg* pickle, brine, salt water.

cethithis, **nyethithis** crouching shivering with cold, *esp* when wet;

  pating cethithis *pl* as above.

cétho **I** blind.

  II a certain small freshwater fish.

céthok a bricklayer's trowel;

  nyéthok to dip and apply (mortar) with a trowel.

cethol *or* **mak cethol** *repr* a bird pecking.

céthong *reg* rice ladle (*var of* **cénthong**). *See also* **énthong**.

cethor *var of* **cethèr**.

cethot a pinch;

  nyethot to pinch and twist flesh;

  nyethoti to pinch and twist flesh repeatedly;

cethotan act of pinching; a pinch.

cethuk I (*pron as:* cethu:k) *or* mak cethuk *repr* a knock; bal - *reg* tennis ball (*see also* bal I).

II *or* kecethuk *coll* to meet s.o. *See also* pethuk II.

cethunthung, cethunthungan unhandy.

cethus, capable; ora - incapable.

cethut *or* mak cethut *repr* a cracking of joints;

nyethuti to crack one's joints by pulling the fingers.

cethuthuk, cethuthukan *or* cethuthak-cethuthuk lackadaisical, without energy;

nyethuthuk bumbling, fumbling.

cethuthur, nyethuthur to remain silent and motionless;

pating cethuthur *pl* remaining silent and motionless.

cethuthut, nyethuthut *or* cethuthat-cethuthut having a morose expression.

cèwèh, cèwèhan gutter, gully, water drainage.

cèwèk *reg* a whiner, weeper; to cry easily; - gambrèng cry-baby.

cèwèng I, nyèwèng to pull s.t. toward o.s. (*var of* cènèng).

II a card game played with the Chinese cards (*kertu cilik*).

cewèni a kind of white muslin (*var of* caweni).

cèwèr *reg var of* cuwèr.

cèwèt incomplete, lacking or missing s.t.

cewèwèk *see* cuwèwèk.

cewiwi *reg* wing (*var of* suwiwi).

céwok *ng, kr,* cawik *k.i.* to clean o.s. with the left hand and water after urinating or defecating;

nyéwoki to clean s.o. as above.

céwol *or* mak céwol *repr* getting a firm grip on s.t.;

nyéwol to grasp in the fingers. *See also* cuwol.

céyos, nyéyos to pour water onto. *See* cèos.

ci 1 10 cents (during the colonial period); 2 a measure of opium (= one catty).

ciblèk a certain small bird.

ciblok *var of* ceblok.

ciblon *or* ceciblon to make 'music' by slapping the surface of water rhythmically in unison (children playing).

ciblung, ciblungan *var of* ciblon.

cibuk *reg* object used for ladling or scooping. *See also* cidhuk.

cibur *see* cebur.

cicig *see* cicik.

cicik to have a small appetite.

cicil, nyicil *or* nicil 1 to pay in installments; to buy on credit; 2 to do bit by bit in advance;

nyicilaké 1 to buy on credit on behalf of s.o.; 2 to spend the money for buying s.t. in installments;

cicilan loan repaid in installments; installment paid on a debt;

panyicil paying out in installments.

cicip, nyicipi *ng, kr,* ngedhapi *k.i.* 1 to taste; 2 *fig* to try out;

cicip-cicip to taste food during its preparation to check the spices. *See also* icip.

cicir missing, lacking.

cicrik, nyicrik to examine one by one.

cicut almond-eyed. *See also* cithut.

cidhal *var of* cédhal, célad.

cidhuk object used for ladling or scooping;

nyidhuk to ladle or scoop (water); *fig* to arrest for criminal or political causes;

nyidhuki to keep scooping;

nyidhukaké 1 to use s.t. for scooping (water); 2 to scoop (water) for s.o.

cidra *lit* untrue, deceitful, disloyal;

nyidra to kill for revenge; - asmara to commit adultery with s.o.;

nyidrani 1 to betray, be disloyal to; 2 to murder treacherously, assassinate; cinidra *lit* betrayed, deceived.

cig *excl* quiet! down, dog!

ciglog *see* ciglok.

ciglok *reg var of* ceblok.

ciha-ciha *see* ciya-ciya.

cihna *lit* sign, indication, evidence; kacihna it's obvious that; shown, made clear or evident. *See also* pracihna.

cik *reg var of* cikbèn.

cikal 1 sprouting coconut (for planting); 2 - bakal founder of a village or settlement (*var of* cakal-bakal); cikalan small pieces of coconut left after grating a large piece; cikalen *reg* stiff(ened) as a result of an ailment.

cikar an open cart pulled by a draught animal; - kasur *or* - pir two-wheeled horse-drawn cart.

cikasi *reg var of* cikbèn.

cikat quick, nimble, agile. *See also* cukat.

cikbèk *reg var of* cikbèn.

cikbèn *ng*, kajengipun *kr* 1 so that (s.t.) will; 2 to let (s.t. happen), leave alone, let go. *See also* bèn, karebèn.

ciker bent fingers.

ciking Chinese sealing-wax.

ciklah *reg var of* cikbèn.

ciklu bent (from old age).

cikluk, ciklukan *or* cikrukan *var of* ciblungan.

cikmaraha *reg var of* cikbèn.

cikmasi *reg var of* cikbèn.

cikmèk *reg var of* cikbèn.

cikmèn *var of* cikbèn

cikné *reg var of* cikbèn.

ciknèk *reg var of* cikbèn.

ciknèn *reg var of* cikbèn.

cikngèk *reg var of* cikbèn.

cikntah *reg var of* cikbèn.

cikpèk *reg var of* cikbèn.

cikpèn *reg var of* cikbèn.

cikrak I wastebasket.

II, cikrak-cikrak to romp, frisk.

cikruk *see* cikluk.

cilaka 1 misfortune; 2 bad luck, unlucky; at odds with one's environment; 3 *excl* dammit! darn it!

nyilakani dangerous;

nyilakakaké to bring misfortune on, ruin;

kacilakan 1 bad luck, misfortune; 2 accident, mishap.

cilakak *excl* damn it! darn it! I'm out of luck now! what a thing to do!

cilèkèk *coll, var of* cilakak.

cilékik *coll, var of* cilakak.

cilékin *coll, var of* cilakak.

cilèmèt *coll, var of* cilakak.

cilénthing *coll, var of* cilakak.

cili *reg* small (*var of* cilik).

cilik *ng*, alit *kr* small, little; - ati 1 discouraged; 2 timid; - menthik tiny; - mula ever since childhood;

nyiliki to make s.t. smaller (than s.t. else);

nyilikaké to make s.t. smaller;

nyilik-nyilikaké to consider trivial;

keciliken too small;

cilikan 1 childhood; 2 small coins, small change;

cilik-cilikan 1 on a small scale; 2 to compare or compete for smallest.

cilili *see* clili.

cilim *reg* small, little (*var of* cilik); ciliman on a small scale. *See also* climèn.

ciloh *reg* sleep, dirt in the corner of the eye.

cilon *reg* to do one's business, relieve o.s.

cilong, cilong-cilong to gaze, stare.

cilu(k)ba(h) peekaboo; a game played by hiding the face from a child and then suddenly popping into view with an exclamation.

cilum *or* mak cilum *repr* diving; cilam-cilum (of duck) diving repeatedly.

cim that's mine!

ngecim *or* ngecimi to lay undisputed claim to s.t.; to bag.

cimak *see* simak.

cimcao *var of* camcao.

cimik, cimik-cimik *or* nyimik-nyimik to pick at one's food.

cimit 1 *var of* cimik; 2, sacimit a small amount, a pinch.

cimplek *var of* cémplo, céngklak.

cimpli *reg* a small oil lamp.

cimplik *var of* cimpli.

cimpling *var of* cimpli.

Cina Chinese; - mindring Chinese moneylender; - craki miserly, stingy; pacinan Chinese area, Chinatown; Cina diedoli dom *prov* to carry coals to Newcastle; Cina lélé abang buntuté miserly; klebon Cina gundhulan to get cheated.

cincal, kecincalan to (do) laboriously or against obstacles.

cincim *see* cincin.

cincin 1 ring for the finger; 2 thimble.

cincing (worn) too high on the body; nyincingaké to raise, hitch up one's garment at the bottom, *e.g.* when walking.

cincug, kecincugan *or* kecincag-kecincug to have trouble walking.

cindhé a fine silken material; cindhèn 1 to wear the above fabric; 2 imitation cindhé material.

cindhek short *reg var of* cendhak.

cindhil small mouse/rat (young of the tikus).

cing, ngecing to oppress s.o.; cing-cingan to oppress each other.

cingak to gaze (at) in astonishment or wonder.

cingar-cingir *see* cingir.

cingbing *var of* cèngbèng.

cingcinggoling a black wagtail with a scissor-shaped tail.

cingcong unnecessary talk or comments.

cingèng to cry easily (*var of* cèngèng).

cinggoling *see* cingcinggoling.

cinging *var of* cingèng, cèngèng.

cingir animal's snout, *var of* cingur; nyingir *or* nyingiraké to move or raise the nose or upper lip; cingir-cingir *or* cingar-cingir (of nose) to twitch.

cingkir cup (for tea or coffee) (*reg var of* cangkir).

cingklak *var of* céngklak.

cingklok the back (hollow) of the knee.

cingkluk to beg charity; to ask alms.

cingkrak, cingkrak-cingkrak to jump with joy. *See also* jingklak, jingkrak.

cingkrang (of clothing) too short; kecingkrangan to live in poverty.

cingkreng *reg* having the arm permanently bent at the elbow.

cingkrik *or* mak cingkrik *repr* a sudden upward motion. *See also* clingkrik.

cingkrong a certain kind of sickle (*var of* céngkrong).

cingkup a bud (of flower).

cinguk, cingak-cinguk astonished, amazed, dumbfounded. *See also* cingak.

cingur snout, *cr* nose.

cining a kind of cake made from glutinous cassava flour rubbed with grated coconut.

cinta, cininta *lit* to think about s.o. (lover); to keep thinking about s.o.

cintaka *lit* idea, thought.

cintantya *lit* beautiful, pretty.

cinten Chinese (*kr for* Cina).

cinthung I a kind of veil. II a small ladle; nyinthung to scoop (liquid) with a small ladle. III, nyinthung to lead down; to distract.

cintra *lit* defect, flaw.

cintraka destitute, poverty-stricken. *See also* papa.

cintya *lit* beautiful, pretty.

cip, ngecipi to taste (food). *See also* icip.

cipir a leguminous plant that bears a peapod-like vegetable; also the fruit of the pods (*shtf of* kecipir).

ciplèk (a)like, similar (to). *See also* jiblès.

ciples, nyiples to press (s.t. small) with the thumbnail.

cipling *reg* tiny.

ciplok *reg* small fire-pump.

ciplong *cr* blind.

ciplos *cr* eye.

cipluk, cipluk-cipluk short and thick. *See also* thipluk.

cipo *reg* manure.

cipok a big, smacking kiss;
cemipok (the quality of s.o.) as if you would like to give (her/him) such a kiss.

cipowa(h) abacus.

ciprat, ciprat-ciprat to keep splattering;
nyiprat 1 to spatter, splatter, splash;
nyiprati to splatter onto; to spray on;
nyiprataké to spatter s.t. onto; to cause to spray;
kecipratan to be splashed, get spattered; *fig* to get involved, to get a share of the profit;
cipratan a splash; *fig* a share.

cipta 1 ideas, aspirations; 2 creation, conception;
nyipta to think about, aspire to; 2 to create, conceive;
kacipta conceived in the mind, dreamed of;
cinipta *lit* to be created; to be thought;
panyipta thought; result of one's thinking.

cipuh, kacipuhan under a strain, feeling uncomfortable or awkward.

cipwah *var of* cipowa.

cir, car-cir bit by bit over a long period of time.

cirak a children's game played with fruit seeds.

ciri sign, identifying mark, scar;
nyirèni to mark s.t.;
kecirèn to have a bad reputation;
ciri wanci (lelahi ginawa mati) *prov* an incurable defect of character.

cirit, kecirit to release a small amount of loose faeces by accident;
cirat-cirit emerging little by little. *See also* icrit.

ciruk ladle (*reg var of* cidhuk).

cis a short spear for guiding elephants;
ngecis to lead (elephants) with the above.

cit, ngecit to squeak.

cita 1 patterned fabric; 2 *lit var of* cipta.

cithak I, nyithak *or* nyithaki to form (*e.g.* mud bricks); to mould;
cithakan mould.
II var of céthak.

cithes, nyithes to press s.t. against the thumbnail.

cithing, cithing-cithing to hold s.t. at its tip.

citho blind (*var of* cétho).

cithut almond-eyed.

citra 1 form, figure; 2 a prose or musical composition; depiction in story or song.

ciwèk *reg* whiner, weeper (*var of* cèwèk).

ciwel, nyiwel to pinch between thumb and index finger.

ciwik *reg* small saucer.

ciwing *var of* cèwèng I.

ciwit *var of* jiwit.

ciya, ciya-ciya glad, joyful.

ciyak to eat.

ciyèt, ciyèt-ciyèt *repr* squeaking;
nyiyèt to catch (a thief).

ciyit cheep! peep! (baby bird's cry).

ciyu Chinese brandy.

ciyum *reg* to kiss. *See also* ambung.

ciyung a wild béyo (talking mynah bird) (*var of* siyung, tiyung).

ciyut small, narrow;
   nyiyuti *or* nyiyutaké to make s.t. narrower.

clab *see* clap.

clacap I meaning, intention, purpose;
   clacapé it seems that's the purpose.
   II gilt ornament in the shape of stars;
   clacapan adorned with gilt stars.

clamit *reg* to have the appetite aroused, to desire.

clana trousers, long pants.

clandhak, clandhakan always handling or touching things annoyingly.

clangap a wide aperture.

clangkrak, nylangkrak to sit (impolitely) in a higher position than others;
   clangkrakan sitting as above.

clangkrang, clangkrangan crass, having no regard for proper social conventions.

clangob, clangoban to keep yawning.

clap 1 *describing a sudden departure*;
   2 panic-stricken.

clapèt, clapètan *or* clopat-clapèt to have the tongue hanging out and moving from side to side.

claprèt, nylaprèt streaked with dirt.

clarat winged lizard. *See also* clèrèt.

clarèng, clorang-clarèng messy, streaked with marks. *See also* clorèng.

clarik, pating clarik covered with scratches or streaks.

claring *var of* claring.

clathu *ng*, wicanten *kr*, ngendika *k.i.*, matur *k.a.* to say; to talk, speak.

cleb *see* clep.

clebek *reg* ground coffee.

clebèk marked-off square in a ricefield.

clebung *or* mak clebung *repr* plunging into water;
   pating clebung *or* clebang-clebung (of talk) random, aimless; impulsive, heedless.

clècèk *reg var* tlècèk.

cledhik *reg* punctilious, precise; cautious, prudent.

cleg *or* mak cleg *repr* flopping right down. *Also* clek.

clégrok *var of* cégrok.

cleguk *or* mak cleguk *repr* gulping;
   clegak-cleguk to keep drinking.

clek *see* cleg.

clekanthang, nylekanthang (of long things) sticking out;
   pating clekanthang *pl* as above.

clekanthuk, nylekanthuk curled at the tips;
   pating clekanthuk *pl* as above.

clekathak, clekathakan wooden saddle (*var of* cekathak).

clekathem, nylekathem to shut the mouth tightly.

clekathuk, clekathuken to rattle, clatter.

clekedhok, pating clekedhok full of shallow holes.

clekenik *var of* cekenik.

clekenthang, nylekenthang to protrude way out.

clekenthik, nylekenthik curled, turned.

clekenthing *var of* cekenthing.

clekénthong, nylekénthong distorted, disfigured.

clekenthung *var of* cekenthung.

clèkèr, pating clèkèr disorderly; (of handwriting) to be all higgledy-piggledy.

clekethut, pating clekethut rumpled, full of creases.

clekik, clekiken to have hiccups.

clekit *or* mak clekit *describing the sting or bite of an insect*;
   nylekit (of words) to cause a lot of hurt feelings;
   pating clekit covered with insect bites or stings.

clekop, nylekop *cr* to speak, say.

clékor *var of* clèkèr.

clekot, nylekot throbbing with pain;
   clekot-clekot *or* pating clekot throbbing with pain. *See also* cekot.

clekuntheng, nylekuntheng curly;

nylekunthengaké to curl s.t.

clekut or mak clekut repr a stab of pain (var of clekot).

clekuthak, nylekuthak to slap s.o. in the face.

clekuthik intricacy, complication;
pating clekuthik complicated.

clekuthis, nylekuthis 1 to desire indiscriminately; 2 looking thin and sour;
pating clekuthis or clekuthis-clekuthis (of faces) sour-looking.

clèlèk, nylèlèk ugly, shocking, repellent (in appearance, nature, behaviour);
clèlèkan or clélak-clèlèk dumbfounded with astonishment or shock.

cleleng simple-minded;
nyleleng 1 to act as if one is simple-minded; 2 to look around with a vacant expression;
clelengan or clelang-cleleng to look around vacantly as though dazed.

cleler prone to steal;
nyleler stealthy;
clelar-cleler to steal habitually. See also clemer.

clembring, pating clembring pl to go away one by one without permission.

clemed var of cremed.

clemèk, clemèkan to grope, feel around.

clemer prone to steal (var of cleler);
nylemer to steal (deliberately or compulsively).

clèmèt var of cilèmèt.

clemik, nylemik talking in quick low voices;
clemikan or pating clemik pl talking as above.

clemong, nylemong to make an unfortunate remark impulsively;
clemongan or pating clemong or clemang-clemong to blurt things out repeatedly or habitually.

clémot see cémot II.

clempung a zither-like gamelan instrument played by plucking;
nylempung to play the above instrument;
clempungan 1 manner of playing the above instrument; 2 music played on it.

clemut repr snatching.

clèncèng, clèncèngan to misrepresent; slanting; obscene.

cleng or mak cleng repr a stab of severe pain.

clèng repr metallic clanking.

clengep or mak clengep repr covering s.t. with a quick movement;
nylengep to cover s.t. as above.

clengker, nylengker curled, crumpled;
pating clengker pl as above.

clengkrang, clengkrang-clengkrang or pating clengkrang throbbing wih mild pain.

clèngkrèk repr a sudden leap up onto s.t.

clengkring var of clengkrang.

clengor, pating clengor pl to remain utterly motionless (e.g. loafing).

clènthing, clènthingané excl darn it! I'm out of luck!

clèntrèng, nylèntrèng (to use, give etc) just a little bit, only a small amount;
saclèntrèngan a little bit, a small amount; a short while.

clénthot var of clènthut.

clénthut, clénthutan to engage in word play (puns, double meanings etc);
keclénthut to say the wrong word by mistake.

clep or mak clep repr piercing (of arrow, spear, knife).

clèpèr pl completely flat.

clépot var of clémot.

clèprèt or nylèprèt splattered, spread about;
keclèprètan splattered by;
pating clèprèt full of splatters.

clepuk a long-eared owl.

cleput repr snatching.

cléram *repr* a flash of light (*var of* tléram);
  sacléraman instantaneous, momentary.
clereng, pating clereng *pl* staring fixedly.
clerèng *reg* (of water) clear and clean.
cleret *or* **mak cleret** *repr* a sudden light dimming.
clèrèt *or* **mak clèrèt** 1 *repr* a flash of light(ning); 2 *repr* a dotted line; 3 *repr* a gliding lizard; 4 *repr* a swooping, gliding motion; - **gombèl** a variety of gliding lizard; - **taun** rain and wind storm; **saclèrètan** a moment, flash.
clerik, pating clerik *pl* to keep screaming (in a high-pitched voice).
clering *var of* **clerik**.
clérong, nylérongi to put dirty streaks on (the face);
  clérongan to have dirty streaks on the face. See **cérong, clorèng**.
cles *or* **mak cles** *repr* sudden cooling/ chilling (*var of* **ces**).
clethèr *pl form of* **cethèr**.
clècèk *var of* **tlècèk**.
cléthong animal dung, manure (*reg var of* tléthong).
clethor *var of* **clethèr**.
cléthot, pating cléthot (of speech, talk) confused.
cléthut *var of* **cléthot**.
clèwèh, nylèwèh slit, opened;
  clèwèhan a long opening, a slit.
clèwèk *var of* **clèwèh**.
clèwèr *var of* **clèwèh**.
cléwo, pating cléwo *pl* speaking one's mind, saying anything that comes into one's head;
  cléwa-cléwo to talk baby talk.
clikrak, clikrak-clikrak *or* **pating clikrak** (of children) skipping about merrily.
clileng, clilang-clileng to look around searchingly.
clili I *or* **mak clili** *repr* embarrassing, flustering;
  clila-clili embarrassed, flustered.

II a trap for catching **gemak** birds.
cliling, clilingan to look around.
climèn on a small scale; with little fanfare. See also **cilim**.
climit *reg* to have the appetite aroused (*var of* **clamit**).
climprit *lit* a dart used as a weapon.
climut prone to steal.
cling *repr* metallic ring.
clingker *or* **mak clingker** *repr* slipping into concealment;
  nylingker to keep under cover; to crouch down behind.
clingkrik *or* **mak clingkrik** *repr* a sudden upward motion;
  clingkrak-clingkrik up and up; to rise steadily.
clinguk, clingukan *or* **clingak-clinguk** bewildered, puzzled;
  pating clinguk *pl* as above.
clingup, nylingup narrow, cramped.
clingus I bashful about being seen;
  clingusan shy by nature. See also **cliyus**.
II hairs growing in the nose.
clinthis, clinthisan ill-mannered, not well brought up.
clinthut, nylinthut to do secretly; to act furtive; to sneak around;
  nylinthutaké to conceal s.t.;
  clinthutan secretive, furtive.
clirit *or* **mak clirit** *repr* a streak of light;
  nylirit forming a thin line;
  clirat-clirit (of small things) to streak repeatedly.
clithut *var of* **clinthut**.
cliyus, cliyusan shy by nature (*var of* **clingus**).
clob *var of* **club**.
clobèk, clobèkan a dent or hollow place in a surface (*var of* **clowèk**).
clolo, clola-clolo distraught.
clolong, clolang-clolong to move the head slowly from side to side as though in a daze.

clomor prone to steal (*reg var of* **clemer**).

clomot, **clomotané** *slang* what bad luck!

clonas *reg* a dealer in livestock.

cloncong, **cloncongan** *or* **cloncang-cloncong** going one's own way. *See also* **tloncong**.

clonèh, **nylonèh** 1 varicoloured; 2 *var of* **nylenèh**;
nylonèhi to streak s.t.;
pating clonèh multicoloured.

clonèng *var of* **clonèh**.

clong, **clang-clong** to waver between alternatives;
clong-clongan (to walk) with a quick striding gait.

clongob, **nylongob** to keep the mouth wide open;
clongoban to keep yawning;
clongab-clongob to have the mouth hanging open (*e.g.* confused);
pating clongob *pl* (of mouths) wide open.
Also **clongop**, **clungup**.

clongop *var of* **clongob**.

clonthang *reg* badly behaved, ill-mannered (*var of* **clunthang**).

clop *see* **clup**.

clor *see* **celor**.

clorèk, **nylorèki** to make scribbled marks on s.t.;
pating clorèk covered with scribble.

clorèng, **nylorèngi** to make messy streaks on (*var of* **corèng**).

clorèt *var of* **clorèk**.

clorong ray, beam;
cumlorong to emit beams. *See also* **corong I**.

clorot I *or* **mak clorot** *repr* swooping, streaking;
nylorot to swoop, glide, dart;
cumlorot to dart, shoot, swoop;
clorotan to keep swooping.
II a certain horn-shaped cake, made from sticky rice flour, palm sugar, coconut milk, wrapped in young palm-leaves.

clowèk *see* **clowok**.

clowok, **clowokan** a dent or hollow place in a surface.

club *see* **clup**.

clulu *repr* bursting in;
clula-clulu *or* **pating clulu** *pl* as above.

cluluk to say; to give information; to point out.

clumed *var of* **clumik**.

clumik, **pating clumik** *pl* speaking low but distinctly;
clumak-clumik (to speak) as above.

clumpring 1 leaf-sheath growing out from a bamboo stalk joint; 2 a certain style of ancient earring;
clumpringan a certain style of bracelet.

clunas, **clunasan** badly behaved, ill-mannered, cheeky.

clungup *var of* **clongop**.

clunthang, **clunthangan** badly behaved, ill-mannered.

clup *or* **mak clup** *repr* a plunge into s.t.;
2 *repr* blurting out a shocking utterance;
ngeclupaké to plunge s.t. (into);
keclup to get plunged into s.t.;
clap-clup *repr* repeated actions as above.

clupak earthenware oil lamp.

cluring I a rare gamelan instrument consisting of small bronze cups nailed to a frame.
II, **nyluring** (of face) thin, pinched-looking.

clurit a small sickle.

clurut I *or* **mak clurut** *repr* swishing.
II a species of rat that emits a strong disagreeable odour (*see* **curut**).

clus *or* **mak clus** *repr* stabbing, piercing.

cluthak 1 (of pets) always thieving food; 2 (of man) willing to make love with any woman; 3 thievish, disobedient, greedy.

cluwed *reg* to peddle one's wares from place to place.

cluwek, nyluweki to dig into;
cluwekan small hole, burrow. *See also* cuwek.

cluweng, nyluweng to form a deep dent (in the ground);
cluwengan a deep dent.

cluwik, cluwikan a small hole in a hard surface;
cluwak-cluwik having holes here and there.

cluwok, cluwokan a large hole in a hard surface.

coba *ng*, cobi *kr* 1 look!; 2 to have a go at; to do and see what happens;
nyoba to try (out), test;
coban a testing-ground; a guinea pig;
coban-coban an experiment; to try s.t.;
panyoban a trial, try-out, test run; a means of testing.

cobak *reg var of* coba.

cobèk *var of* cowèk.

cobi *kr for* coba.

coblok *reg* open oil lamp. *See* coblong I.

coblong I 1 *reg* short round earthenware jar; 2 *var of* coblok.
II solar or lunar eclipse.

coblos, nyoblos to stab, prick, pierce;
kecoblos to get pierced;
coblosan pierced, stabbed.

cobolo stupid, ignorant.

cocak a thrush-like bird; - gunung, - rawa varieties of this thrush.

cocing *reg* small cup.

cocog I 1 to agree (with); 2 to match, suit; 3 congenial;
nyocogi to suit;
nyocogaké 1 to check with; 2 to make conform;
cocog-cocogan to conform each other.
II, nyocog to stick s.t. sharp (into);
kecocog to get pierced or poked.

cocoh a pencil-sized metal rod used for crushing or grinding betel nuts for chewing.

cocok see cocog.

cocol, nyocol *or* nyocoli 1 (of birds) to peck fruits; 2 to put bundles of rice on a pointed bamboo pole and carry them;
cocolan pointed bamboo carrying-pole.

cocoméyo unrespectable. *See also* cotoméyo.

cocor 1 beak, bill; 2 roof-tip point at the end of the ridgepole; 3 bottom part of a kris sheath;
nyocori to peck.

cocot *cr* mouth.

cocrop, nyocrop to sip noisily from the container.

codhot a certain bat that feeds on fruits;
codhotan fruits that have been nibbled by bats.

cogemol, ngecogemol to accuse s.o. of s.t. embarrassing.

coglèk joined in such a way that the parts can move, *e.g.* a hinged piece of wood.

cogmol see cogemol.

cogo (of child) stupid.

cohung 1 peacock; 2 *repr* a peacock's cry.

cojog *reg var of* cocog.

cojoh *var of* jojoh.

cok *or* mak cok *repr* alighting.

cokak vinegar. *See also* cukak.

cokèh *reg* only.

cokèk, cokèkan to perform gamelan music in the street.

cokèr, nyokèr to mess up, scratch around in (sand *etc*).

cokik *cr* dead.

coklak *or* coklakan *reg* a hole for planting s.t.

coklat *var of* soklat.

coklèh *reg var of* coklèk.

coklèk broken; to break, snap;
nyoklèk 1 to break s.t.; 2 to lose patience;

coklèkan (atèn) short-tempered.

cokoh, nyokoh *reg* to insult, humiliate.

cokol I *reg* sugarcane or corn foliage used as a fodder.

II, nyokol to force s.o. to eat.

cokor *cr* foot, leg.

cokot *var of* **cakot**.

cokoteng a hot ginger-flavoured drink (*var of* **sekoteng**).

cokrèk, nyokrèk to prod at (soil *etc*).

col *reg* (of distribution, share) unequal.

colèd a kitchen implement. *See* **solèd**.

colèk *var of* **colèd**.

colèt *var of* **colèd**.

colik to go and return on the same day (*var of* **calik**).

colok I 1 torch; light used as a torch; **2** message; messenger;

nyoloki to light s.t. up in order to search.

II a stick;

nyolok to stick s.t. into; - **mata** to hit in the eye;

nyolokaké to stick s.t. into (an eye);

kecolok to get stuck in the eye.

colong (*root form*) to steal; - **jupuk 1** thievery; **2** to steal habitually; - **laku** in secret; - **playu** to sneak away, run off;

nyolong to steal; - **ulat** to steal a glance (at); - **pethèk** to have a deceptive appearance;

nyenyolong to steal habitually;

nyolongi to steal again and again;

nyolongaké to steal for s.o.;

colongan stolen (goods);

kecolongan to be stolen from; to experience a theft.

colot, nyolot to jump, leap;

colot-colot *or* **colat-colot** *or* **nyolot-nyolot** *or* **nyolat-nyolot** to keep leaping, keep bounding;

nyoloti to jump onto.

combang, ngecombang filled with water, *esp* rainwater.

combèr, combèran *or* **kacombèran** *or* **pacombèran** open sewage ditch or basin for household waste water.

comblang matchmaker, go-between.

combor, nyombor to feed a horse;

comboran horse-feed: grass, rice bran, and rice husks mixed with water.

combrang *see* **kecombrang**.

comong *reg* dark, black.

comot, nyomot to take up, pick up.

complong hole, opening, gap;

nyomplong (of hole) open; to make a hole in s.t.;

nyomplongi to make a hole in s.t.; to make an opening in;

pating cromplong riddled with holes.

comprèng I *or* **kecomprèngan** short of money.

II a type of boat.

comris 1 *cr* female genitals; **2** *cr* worthless.

concong, noncong (of s.t. long and spiky) extending outward;

concongan that which is offered to s.o. (*var of* **cong-congan**).

condhok I to agree. *See also* **condhong**.

II, cumondhok *lit* to stay s.w. temporarily.

condhong in agreement (with) (*var of* **condhok**);

nyondhongi to concur (with); to agree (with).

condré dagger, dirk. *See also* **cundrik**.

cong with wholehearted consent;

ngecong *or* **ngecongi** to offer s.t. to s.o.;

ngecongaké to offer s.t. by holding it out;

cong-congan that which is offered to s.o.

congah, nyongah *or* **nyenyongah** to tantalise s.o.

congat, nyongat *or* **mencongat** to extend outward/upward;

congat-congat extending outward/upward (of s.t. long and spiky);

nyongataké to hold s.t. extending outward/upward;
pating crongat *pl* sticking out.
conggah, keconggah capable of doing s.t. difficult; able to carry out s.t.
congkèl *reg var of* **songkèl**.
congklang I galloping pace;
nyongklang to gallop;
nyongklangaké to run (a horse) at a gallop;
kecongklangan to run with difficulty to chase s.o.
II (of a garment) too short. *See also* **cingkrang**.
congklok, nyongklok to catch s.o. with trick questions.
congkog *see* **congkok**.
congkok I 1 a support, prop; **2** intermediary in arranging a marriage;
nyongkok to support, prop up;
nyongkoki to hold a ceremony.
II procurer, pimp.
congkrah in disagreement, disputing;
cecongkrahan to quarrel.
congkrang too short, too small (*var of* **cingkrang**).
conglong, nyonglong to lean over, stick the head out.
congo, nyongo to gape open-mouthed, do nothing.
congok, nyongok to pierce an ox's nose for a bridle.
congol *var of* **cungul**.
congor 1 animal's snout; **2** (of people) *cr* mouth, nose and lips;
nyongor 1 having the lips thrust forward; **2** to press s.o.'s cheeks with the fingers so that the lips thrust forward.
congot *var of* **congat**.
cono a big pustule or swelling on the head.
conthal, nyonthal-nyonthal to walk with great difficulty;
keconthalan *or* **keconthal-conthal** in

frantic pursuit; following with great difficulty.
conthang *var of* **cunthang**.
conthèng *var of* **corèng**.
conthok, keconthokan to get caught in the act.
conthong banana leaf or paper twisted into a cone-shaped container;
nyonthong to put s.t. into such a cone; to form s.t. into a cone;
conthongan served in such a cone-shaped container.
conti, nyonti to retard, hinder.
conto example, model;
nyonto to imitate, copy; to use as an example;
nyontoni to give an example of; to set an example (for).
cop I a hole occupied by eels.
II *reg* a certain small oil lamp.
III *or* **mak cop** *repr* piercing;
ngecopi to pierce repeatedly.
copèt a pickpocket;
nyopèt to make one's living by picking pockets; to empty pockets;
kecopètan to be the victim of a pickpocket.
coplok to come loose;
nyoplok 1 to detach s.t.; to take s.t. off; **2** to fire s.o.
copot 1 to come loose; to come off/out; **2** to remove (clothing);
nyopot 1 to remove, take apart; **2** to discharge, dismiss;
copotan to come apart easily; detachable.
cor, ngecor to pour from one container into another;
ngecori 1 to pour onto; **2** to water s.t.;
ngecoraké to pour s.t. into another container;
cor-coran 1 molten substance; **2** that which is poured.
corah 1 thief, bandit; **2** bad person.
corak *see* **corèk**.

corèk I 1 batik design; 2 or corèkan a drawing or written line;
nyorèk to draw a line on (under, through) s.t.;
nyorèki to draw lines repeatedly;
corak-corèk to draw lines aimlessly, doodle.
II, nyorèk reg to show off one's appearance.

corèng var of clorèng.

corèt var of corèk.

coro I 1 cockroach; 2 a lowly person.
II, nyoro pursed (lips).

corok stick used for prodding;
kecorok 1 to get prodded; 2 to be engaged for another purpose;
corok jero to make love to s.o.'s wife.

corong I ray, beam.
II 1 microphone; 2 loudspeaker.

cos or mak cos repr sizzling;
ngecos to touch with a hot iron; to brand.

cothé, nyothé to stick a kris on the side of the belt with the handle extending forward;
cothèn (of kris) stuck as above.

cotho lacking s.t. necessary to one's work; missing s.t. essential.

cothom reg a broad woven bamboo hat (var of caping).

cothot, nyothotaké to press s.t. to eject the contents. See also pecothot.

cotoméyo unrespectable (var of cocoméyo).

cotung reg broken, to break (var of putung).

cowèk 1 small saucer-shaped stone bowl for grinding spices in; 2 saucer-like earthen platter.

cowok reduced;
nyowok to decrease (a larger amount); to dock;
kecowok reduced inadvertently.

cowong (of face) wan and pinched-looking.

crabak, pacrabakan lit place for learning under the guidance of a holy hermit.

cracas, cracasan to drip copiously (of tears, raindrops). See also crècès.

cracèt handkerchief. See also crècèt.

crah divided, cracked, split up;
ngecrahaké to split up (friendship/relationship).

crak or mak crak repr slashing/jabbing a hard object.

craki, crakèn container in which herbs and drugs are stored;
kaya Cina craki prov miserly, close-fisted.

cramuk, pating cramuk pl to eat with the mouth stuffed full.

crang or mak crang repr a dull metallic clang.

crangap, nyrangap cr to talk loudly;
pating crangap pl (of mouth) wide open.

cranthèl, pating cranthèl hanging in disorder; hanging everywhere.

crapang spreading and pointed;
nyrapang (of moustache) to spread outward to either side.

cras or mak cras repr a slash with a sharp blade.

cratho, pating cratho halting, broken (of language).

crawak having a disagreeable loud speaking voice.

creblung, pating creblung pl chattering, jabbering.

creceb see crecep.

crecel, nrecel to have many children.

crecep, pating crecep to feel sticky all over the body.

creces, pating creces to feel cold all over the body.

crècès, pating crècès running down everywhere (tears, raindrops).

crecèt handkerchief.

crècèt var of crecèt.

cremed, nyremed or cremedan to tell

dirty stories; to talk obscenely or coarsely.

cremimi(h), nyremimi(h) sad-looking;
　pating cremimi(h) pl sad, melancholy.

cremomong, nyremomong glowing, burning red (fires);
　pating cremomong pl as above.

crémot, crémotan or pating crémot all messed up; (of face) streaked with dirt.

cremumuh, nyremumuh reddish and infected-looking (sores);
　pating cremumuh pl as above.

crèncèng gleaming, glimmering; dawn.

crèng 1 cash (as opposed to credit); 2 or mak crèng repr a metallic clang.

crengèk, pating crengèk pl (of children) to keep wailing loudly.

crèngèl, pating crèngèl pl to keep craning the neck; pl to keep sticking the head up high.

crèngès, nyrèngès to show the teeth (smiling; making a face);
　pating crèngès pl as above.

crènggèh, pating crènggèh pl sticking out/up.

crèngkèh var of crènggèh.

crengkèng, pating crengkèng pl to keep yelping/whining.

crèngkèng fish spear.

crengkling, pating crengkling pl repr repeated metallic clanking sounds, e.g. metal being pounded.

crengklung, pating crengklung pl repr repeated deep metallic sounds, e.g. from thumping a steel drum.

créngos, créngosan or pating créngos (of face) streaked with dirt.

crenthé, pating crenthé repr heavy metallic sounds, e.g. of steel girders banging together.

crenthèng var of crenthé.

crep or mak crep repr piercing, stabbing.

crepèpèh, nyrepèpèh to plead, beg.

cres or mak cres repr a sharp point spearing s.t.

cret or mak cret repr a sudden dripping;
　ngecreti to spatter s.t. with drops of liquid;
　sacret, sacretan a small amount, a mere drop.

crèt or mak crèt repr a sudden squirting/spurting;
　ngecrèti to spatter onto;
　crat-crèt squirting repeatedly; to have the runs.

crethil, pating crethil repr the stinging sensation of an open cut.

crèwèk, crèwèkan (of fruit) a hole eaten by a bat.

crèwèng, pating crèwèng pointing in various directions, divided. Also criwing.

crèwèt 1 cr to talk too much; 2 cr to complain constantly.

cricis, nricis 1 to talk a lot; 2 to speak fluently.

criga lit kris (var of curiga).

crigis talkative by nature.

crik or mak crik repr (of metallic things) loud jingling.

cring or mak cring repr (of coins) loud jingling.

cringih, nyringih pointed and sharp;
　cringih-cringih or pating cringih pl as above.

cringis, nyringis to show the teeth (smiling, grimacing etc);
　pating cringis pl as above.

criping fried chips made from thin slices of cassava (banana etc).

cripu thong sandals, slippers.

crit or mak crit repr water squirting;
　crat-crit repr repeated squirts.

crita ng, cariyos kr story, narration;
　nyritani to tell s.o. (a story; about s.t.);
　nyritakaké to tell about.
　See also carita.

criwing var of crèwèng.

criwis talkative; to jabber, prattle.

criyèt, **pating criyèt** *pl* squeaking.

criyos to say, tell (*kr for* **kandha, crita**).

crobo careless, untidy; sloppy, grubby.

crobong chimney.

crocoh 1 (of ceilings, roofs) to leak; 2 delighting in yelling abusively. *See also* **trocoh**.

crocok, **crocokan** gluttonous, greedy.

crocop, **nyrocop** to slurp (bad table manners).

crocos, **nrocos** 1 (of tears) to flow; to drool; 2 *cr* nonstop speaking.

crog *see* **crok**.

crok *or* **mak crok** *repr* cutting/chopping/ striking;
  crok-crok *repr* the sloshing of wet fabric against a board or stone when being washed;
  crak-crok *repr* chopping repeatedly;
  ngecrok-crok to launder clothes by pounding them against s.t.

crolot, **pating crolot** *pl repr* to keep jumping/bounding.

cromplong, **pating cromplong** riddled with holes.

crondhol *reg* water rat.

crondholo *see* **trondholo**.

crongat, **nyrongat** to stick out;
  pating crongat *pl* sticking out. *See also* **congat**.

crongoh not fussy about one's choice (of women).

crongol, **pating crongol** *pl* to come to the surface. *See also* **congol, cungul**.

crongos, **pating crongos** *pl* voracious, gluttonous; **2** to show the teeth (greedily).

crongot, **nyrongot** (of teeth) sticking outward;
  pating crongot *pl* as above. *See also* **congot**.

crop *repr* sipping loudly.

crot *or* **mak crot** *repr* liquid spurting, squirting;

ngecroti to spurt onto s.t.;
  ngecrotaké to squirt s.t.;
  kecrotan to get squirted accidentally.

crowal, **pating crowal** full of dents or chipped places.

crowèt *see* **cruwèt**.

crowok, **crowokan** *reg* gutter, gully, drain.

crubuk I 1 a certain sea fish; 2 salted eggs of sea fish.

II a certain shape of kris.

crucuk *reg* pilework, palisade *var of* **trucuk**.

crucup, **nyrucup** to sip by putting the lips on the pouring spout (of earthen carafe/pitcher).

crucus, 1 n(y)rucus nonstop talking (*var of* **crocos**); 2 crucusan sizzling.

cruk *or* **mak cruk** *repr* striking earth;
  crak-cruk *repr* hoeing repeatedly.

crumpleng, **pating crumpleng** riddled with cavities/burrows.

crumpung *lit* a kind of sedan chair. *Also* **crupung**.

crungul, **pating crungul** *pl* coming into view, popping up.

crungus, **nyrungus** (of face) thin, narrow.

crupung *var of* **crumpung**.

crut *or* **mak crut** *repr* a small squirt of liquid;
  ngecruti to squirt s.t. onto;
  ngecrutaké to squirt s.t.;
  crat-crut squirting repeatedly.

cruthak thievish (*var of* **cluthak**).

cruwek *reg* dirty (woman); messy.

cruwèk *var of* **cruwèt**.

cruwèt, **cruwat-cruwèt** *or* **pating cruwèt** *pl repr* squealing of children, birds, monkeys.

cruwil, **pating cruwil** in tatters, badly torn.

cruwit, **pating cruwit** *pl* twittering, squeaking.

cu I name of boy's game.

II a unit of width (of fist plus outstretched thumb).

cubak 1 to agree exactly (quantity); **2** to break even, sell without profit or loss. *Also* **jubak**.

cuban *reg* needle for mending fishing nets.

cublak 1 small perfume container; **2** hollowed out;
　nyublak to hollow s.t. out;
　cublak-cublak suweng (to play) hunt the earring (children's game).

cublek hollowed out (*var of* **cublak**).

cubles, nyubles to pierce with a sharp-pointed object;
　kecubles to get pierced.

cublik I small oil lamp.
　II, nyublik to vaccinate for small-pox.
　III, nyublik to remove from s.t.;
　cublikan portion removed from s.t.;
　sacublik a small piece taken from s.t.; an excerpt.

cublok to fall down (*reg var of* **ceblok**).

cubluk I ignorant, stupid.
　II 1 a pit for trapping animals; **2** jail, prison.

cubrik *reg* damp, mushy, gooey.

cubung a certain poisonous plant, narcotic, drug (*shtf of* **kecubung I**);
　nyubung to poison s.t. (*e.g.* to make crickets fight).

cucah I *excl* boring!
　II *see* **cacah**.

cucak *var of* **cocak**.

cucal leather (*kr for* **lulang**) (*shtf of* **wacucal**).

cuci, nyuci to wash, launder;
　cucian laundry to be washed.

cucud pleasant to listen to, witty.

cucuk I 1 beak, bill; **2** pouring spout.
　II or **cuk** house fee, *i.e.* a percentage of one's gambling winnings for the host.
　III reasonable, commensurate (with); worth the trouble, worthwhile. *See also* **kurup**, **sumbut**.
　IV decorative hairpin (*var of* **tusuk**).

V change (*var of* **susuk II**).

cucul 1 lukar *k.i.* to take off (clothing); to get undressed; **2** to pay out.

cucup, n(y)ucup to sip by attaching the lips to the spout when drinking from an earthen flask;
　cucupan spout of a pitcher.

cucur a fried sweet made from rice flour and brown sugar; **- bawuk** name of a Javanese melody.

cucut shark; **- gandhèn** hammerfish; **- pedhang** swordfish.

cudaka *lit* emissary, spy (*var of* **cundaka**).

cudhing, nyudhing *or* **nyudhingi** *reg* to point out. *See also* **tuding**.

cugag to come to an end, ended; short(ened);
　nyugag to cut off (a narration) in the middle; to break off;

cuget, cugetan quick to take offence; easily put in a bad mood.

cuh *or* **mak cuh** *repr* spitting.

cuk *reg adr* little boy!

cukak vinegar (*var of* **cokak**).

cukakak *see* **cekakak**.

cukat quick, agile.

cukèh (of talking) finished, at an end.

cukeng obstinate, hard to convince;
　nyukengi to maintain s.t. obstinately.

cuki, nyuki to stitch all the way through from top to bottom;
　cukèn stitched as above; **kasur -** a stitched-through mattress.

cukil I 1 descendant of an original settler; **2** possessions or customs handed down from the original settlers.
　II a pick;
　nyukil *or* **nyukili** to extract s.t. (from);
　cukilan picked/pried from.

cukit 1 chopsticks; **2** bamboo sticks used (in pairs) for mixing tobacco and opium for smoking;
　nyukit to use the above sticks.

cukul to grow, come up (plants) (*var of* **thukul**).

cukup *ng*, cekap *kr* 1 enough, sufficient, adequate; 2 well-to-do;
　nyukupi to fulfil (requirements; a need); to supply enough of;
　nyukupaké to make s.t. suffice; to be adequate for;
　nyukup-nyukupaké to try to make s.t. suffice;
　kacukupan well off;
　cukupan good enough, mediocre;
　sacukupé (to an) adequate (degree) for the purpose.
cukur *ng*, *kr*, paras *k.i.* (to have/get) a haircut; - bathok (to have) the hair cut at the sides and bottom, leaving the hair on the crown in a coconut-shell shape; - gundhul (to have) the hair cut completely; (*fig* to beat badly in a game; - poni (for girls) (to have) the hair cut in a fringe;
　nyukur 1 to cut s.o.'s hair; 2 to beat s.o. in a game with a one-sided score;
　nyukuri to cut s.o.'s hair;
　nyukuraké to have s.o.'s hair cut;
　cukuran 1 a haircut; 2 the act of cutting hair or having one's hair cut; 3 instrument for shaving;
　cukur-cukuran to cut each other's hair;
　panyukur 1 a haircut; 2 a blade (razor) for cutting hair; 3 a measure of sharpness.
cukurukuk cock-a-doodle-doo!
cul *or* mak cul *repr* breaking loose;
　ngeculi to loosen (restraints);
　ngeculaké to release;
　cul-culan 1 running loose; 2 outspoken;
　cal-cul to pour forth, gush out.
cula horn of a rhinoceros.
culat, culat-culat to jump, leap, bound.
culek, nyulek to poke s.o. in the eye;
　keculek to get jabbed in the eye.
culeng (of eyes) deep and sharp;

　nyuleng to gaze angrily at.
cules finished.
culik I female nocturnal cuckoo.
　II, nyulik(i) 1 to test (s.o.'s knowledge); 2 to try out (rice).
　III bogeyman who pries people's eyes out.
culika untrustworthy, dishonest;
　nyulikani to steal s.t.
culu, cula-culu to burst in noisily.
culuh, nyuluh *lit* to seduce.
cumah *reg* only, just.
cumbana *lit* (to have) sexual intercourse.
cumbu to feel at home s.w.; to visit frequently;
　nyumbu *or* nyenyumbu to make s.o. feel at home;
　nyumbokaké to tame, domesticate (animal);
　cumbon a domesticated animal;
　cumbu laler 1 to change homes frequently; 2 fickle, unpredictable.
cumengklung *repr* the sound of gamelan music heard from afar.
cuming *reg* only, just.
cumleng 1 to be assaulted; 2 to get a headache.
cumles overpowering; cloyingly sweet.
cumlik, nyumlik small, tiny;
　cumlikan a small bit;
　sacumlik a tiny amount.
cumpi, nyumpi *or* nyumpèni to ration s.t. out; to restrict an allotment/distribution;
　cumpèn (of stock, supply) limited;
cumpleng *or* cumplengan hole, cavity, burrow;
　nyumpleng to form a hole.
cumplik *var of* cumlik.
cumplung 1 skull (human or animal); 2 head of a dead person; 3 hollowed-out coconut the flesh of which has been eaten by squirrels.
cumpu 1 *reg* perfect fit; just exactly; 2 satisfied, well-done;

nyumponi to supply enough of; to fulfil one's wishes;

kecumpon to have (one's wishes) fulfilled.

cumur soggy, messy, muddy (*var of* cemer).

cundaka *lit* espionage, spying;

nyundaka to spy out, scout.

cundhamanik *lit* flaming arrow.

cundhang, kecundhang defeated.

cundhit a fishing net on a frame.

cundhuk I in agreement, in harmony; -laris to lower prices to stimulate sales;

nyundhukaké to be harmonious (with);

cumundhuk in harmony (with);

durung cundhuk acandhak *prov* to enter a conversation without knowing what it is about.

II 1 hair ornament; 2 having a sharp hairform on top of the forehead;

nyundhuki to decorate (the hair) with;

nyundhukaké to use as a hair ornament.

cundrik a short dagger.

cunéya *reg* a certain small boat.

cung errand boy! (*adr; shtf of* kacung).

cungap *reg* voracious, gluttonous; indiscreet, immodest.

cungih *reg* weak, tender.

cungir, nyungir to turn the nose up;

cungir-cungir *or* cungar-cungir to turn the nose up in reaction to a bad odour.

nyungar-nyungir to keep sniffing.

cungkag to come to an end, ended; short(ened).

cungkil *var of* cukil.

cungkir *reg* long-handled shovel of wood or bamboo;

nyungkir to shovel s.t. with the above.

cungkrik *reg* prow, beak.

cungkub a roofed shelter erected over a grave;

nyungkub to build a shelter as above.

cungkup (of flower) bud.

cungul *or* mak cungul *repr* coming into view;

nyungul to appear; to stick the head out;

nyungulaké to cause s.t. to come into view.

cungur *cr* nose and mouth (*var of* congor).

cuniya *var of* cunéya.

cunthang bamboo container for rice as purchased in the market.

cunthel the end (*var of* cuthel).

cuntheng, nyuntheng *reg* to look (at) coyly while scowling.

cup I *or* cup embil mine!;

ngecupi to claim s.t.

II *excl* hush! (to quieten a crying child).

cupak 1 head of opium pipe; 2 earthenware lamp (*var of* clupak).

cupar 1 distrustful, suspicious (of one's wife in managing housekeeping money); 2 jealous of one's wife.

cupet short, inadequate;

nyupet to cut off, cut short;

kacupetan shortage of; short of, running out of;

kecupeten excessively short.

cuplak I a skin disease characterised by a small hard blister.

II to come loose (*var of* coplok);

nyuplak to detach s.t.; to pry out;

cuplak andheng-andheng yèn ora prenah panggonané *prov* a relative who is unwelcome because he makes trouble.

cuplik, nyuplik to quote;

nyuplikaké to quote s.t. from;

cuplikan a quotation;

sacuplik a bit.

cupu I a small box or pot for perfume or cosmetic cream;

nyupu 1 to put/keep s.t. in a cosmetic

cup; **2** to use a cup to staunch the flow of blood;

cupumanik astagina an octagonal cup-shaped jewelry box.

II kneecap of large domesticated animals.

cur *or* **mak cur** *repr* flowing, outpouring;

ngecuri to pour onto;

ngecuraké to pour s.t.;

kecuran to get poured on;

cur-curan to pour out;

car-cur continuous outpouring.

curab mixed together (*var of* **carub**);

nyurabi to mix (with).

curah I *reg* ravine, gully, gorge, chasm.

II, **nyurahaké** to pour out.

curak ear wax. *See* **curek**.

curang *reg* to cheat at cards or other games.

curat, **nyurati** to cause s.t. to spring or bound.

curek ear wax (*var of* **curak**).

cureng, **nyureng** to scowl;

nyurengi to scowl at.

cures 1 wiped out to the last man; **2** to be last in a genealogical line, *i.e.* to be an unmarried only child;

kecuresan to be without descendants.

curet (of plant) unable to grow.

curi jagged cliff.

curiga *lit* kris, dagger.

curing I 1 jagged cliff (*var of* **curi**); **2** (of gorges) deep and with steep sides.

II a rare gamelan instrument (*var of* **cluring**).

curna *lit* broken to pieces, smashed, wrecked, crushed.

curug *reg* waterfall.

curung banana stalk with bunches of fruit growing on either side;

curungan the bunches on a stalk;

sacurung a stalk of bananas.

See also **tundhun**.

curut a species of rat that emits a strong disagreeable odour (*also* **clurut**).

cus *or* **mak cus** *repr* sizzling, piercing, stabbing.

cut *or* **cutan** *reg* and then (*shtf form of* **bacut**).

cutak *reg* district head.

cuthak 1 *var of* **cutak**; **2** passing (one) over.

cuthat, **nyuthat 1** to flick away; **2** to fire s.o.; to dismiss summarily.

cuthel to come to an end; ended;

nyuthel to finish; bring to an end (story).

cuthes *var of* **cures**.

cuthik a stick for prodding;

nyuthik to poke with a stick;

nyuthiki to poke s.t. repeatedly.

cuti leave, furlough, (time) off.

cuwa disappointed; regretful;

nyuwani or **nyuwakaké** to disappoint.

cuwak a prop, a support (*var of* **tuwak**).

cuwawak, **nyuwawak** *or* **cuwawakan** talking and laughing too loudly;

pating cuwawak *pl* as above.

cuwan *reg excl* be careful! think about it!

cuwawuk, **nyuwawuk** to slap s.o.'s mouth.

cuwek, **nyuwek** to dig the nails into s.t.

cuwèk earthen platter (*var of* **cowèk**).

cuwengah awkward, ill at ease; averse, reluctant.

cuwèr (of liquid) thin, weak, watery; (of coffee) weak, thin;

nyuwèri to make (coffee, tea *etc*) thin/weak;

nyuwèraké to cause (liquid) thinner;

kecuwèren (of coffee, tea *etc*) too thin/weak.

cuwèt, **cuwèt-cuwèt** (of baby birds) to keep cheeping/squeaking.

cuwèwèk, **nyuwèwèk** to have the mouth with the corners drawn down;

nyuwèwèkaké to draw down the corners of the mouth;

cuwèwak-cuwèwèk crying or whining with the mouth in the above position.

cuwik, nyuwik to pry s.t. up/off with the nails;

cuwikan a mark left where s.t. was peeled with a fingernail.

cuwil chipped, torn off;

nyuwil *or* **nyuwili** to tear a piece off; to tear to pieces;

nyuwilaké to tear off for s.o. else;

cemuwil such that you feel as if you would like to tear a bit off it;

cuwilan a broken-off piece (of); taken from (a larger piece);

sacuwil a little bit; a torn-off or chipped-off fragment.

cuwir excessively thin (*intsfr of* **cuwèr**).

cuwiri a certain batik design character-ised by many curls which may be worn at court.

cuwit, nyuwiti to twitter; to squeak;

cuwit-cuwit *or* **cuwat-cuwit** to keep twittering, squeaking;

cumuwit to let out a peep.

cuwo a broad shallow earthenware bowl.

cuwol, nyuwol to grab in the fingers.

cuwowo, nyuwowo to press s.o.'s mouth with thumb and forefinger.

cuwowol *var of* **cuwol**.

cuwut I *reg* squirrel.

II, nyuwut *reg* to take/snatch away.

cuyu *reg* a crab (*var of* **yuyu**).

D

dabag I 1 rough-woven bamboo used for wall or fence panel; **2** sharp-pointed bamboo poles used for fence;

ndabag resembling bamboo spears.

II measles (*var of* **gabag**);

ndabag *or* **dabagen** to have/get measles.

III, ndabag crowded (of people).

dablag *var of* **dabag**.

dableg, ndableg stubborn, obstinate.

dadah, ng, kr, ginda *k.i.* massage; to be massaged;

ndadah 1 to massage (a baby); **2** to treat (a helpless victim) harshly;

dadahan massage;

pandadah act of massaging.

dadak *or* **ndadak 1** suddenly, without warning; **2** unexpectedly and/or undesirably; **3** to (do) right away, (do) ahead of time; all at once; **- apa** now what?; **- mangsa** to speed up the normal pace; to try to force s.t. before its time;

kedadak 1 sudden; **2** to be caused to happen suddenly;

dadakan suddenly, immediately;

dumadakan all of a sudden, suddenly; all at once.

dadar I omelette, egg pancake; **- gulung** rolled egg pancake; **- lèlèr** reward for services;

ndadar to make (egg) into omelette.

II, ndadar to examine, test, try out;

pandadar *or* **pandadaran** examination, test;

dadaran product of training.

III, ndadari (of the moon) to rise.

dadi *ng*, **dados** *kr*, **1** to be, become, assume the role of; **2** as, in(to), so as to become; **3** done, ready, successfully completed; **4** (in games) to be 'it', to be a defender; **5** so, therefore, thus; **- ati** to take s.t. to heart; **- gawé** to be dangerous; **- lan** to be the cause of; **- wong** to be(come) important/influential;

ndadi 1 to grow rapidly; **2** to increase in intensity; **3** to go into trance; **4** to let o.s. get caught and become 'in' in a game; **5**

to set (fruits, on a tree);

ndadèkaké 1 to cause s.t. to be/become;
2 to consider s.t. (as);

dumadi *ng*, **dumados** *kr*, **1** to come into
existence; **2** (to be) made from; **3** consist
of;

kedadian *or* **kedadéyan 1** result, consequence; **2** occurrence, eventuality;
3 brought to a (successful) conclusion;
4 (to be) made up of;

ora dadi apa it doesn't matter.

dados *kr for* **dadi**.

dadra, ndadra to worsen (of illness, vices
etc); to increase.

dadu light red.

dadya *lit var of* **dadi**.

daga I, dagan the bottom or foot end (of
s.o. in a lying position);

ndagan *or* **ndedagan** to sit in meditation
at the foot of a buried person;

ndaganaké to place s.t. (kris, flower *etc*)
at the foot of (buried person).

II, ndaga to disregard (orders).

dagang I to engage in business; **- gawé** (*or*
ndagang gawé) to consistently take
longer to do one's work in order to
get more wages; **- laku** (*or* **ndagang
laku**) to keep walking while offering the
price of a merchandise in order to get
a higher price from the purchaser;
- layar to do business by sailing from
place to place;

dagangan 1 business, trading; **2**
merchandise;

dedagangan (to have) business/
commercial dealings with;

merdagang to deal in merchandise; to
buy and sell in the marketplace;

padagang businessman;

padagangan trade;

dagang tuna andum bathi to do good
for/to others.

II, ndagangi (of calf) at the stage of
learning to walk.

dagel, ndagel (of fruit) to remain hard (*var*

of **dhagel II**).

daging meat, flesh;

ndaging (of animals, fruits) fleshy,
meaty;

daging-dagingan 1 meats; **2** resembling
meat;

kulit daging *see* **kulit**.

dah *excl* boo!

dahana *lit* fire.

dahat *lit* very.

dahuru turmoil, chaotic situation. *Also*
dauru.

dahwèn a busybody, nosey, inquisitive;

dahwèn pati opèn to be fond of being
nosey.

dajal evil spirit.

dak I *prefix; var of* **tak**.

II (*or* **ndak**) *inf var of* **andak**.

dakar male genitals.

dakdir *var of* **takdir**.

dakik, ndakik *or* **ndakik-ndakik**
sophisticated, detailed, intricate,
elaborate.

dakmenang to behave in an overbearing or
domineering way.

daknang *inf var of* **dakmenang**.

daksa *lit* wise, smart.

daksina *lit* **1** south; **2** right (opposite of
left).

dakwa accusation, charge, indictment;

ndakwa to accuse, charge;

pandakwa accusation.

dakwenang *var of* **dakmenang**.

dal I name of the 5th year in the **windu**
cycle.

II out (*shtf of* **wedal**, *kr for* **wetu**).

dalah and (also), together with.

dalan *ng*, **margi** *kr* **1** road, path, street,
passage; **2** way, route; **3** means, way;
- butulan access road; **- buntu** dead end;
- simpangan side road;

ndalanaké to handle (merchandise) in
the capacity of middleman;

didalani *or* **kedalanan** to have a road,
passage *etc* on/through it;

dalanan pathway, street areas, roadways; **sadalan-dalan** all along the road; in every road;
 dedalan lit var of **dalan**.
dalas, dalasan var of **dalah**.
dalem 1 in(side), within; 2 the inner room of a house, i.e. the main family section; 3 house, home (k.i. for **omah**); 4 walled-in residence compound of an aristocratic family; 5 your; he, his (referring to s.o. exalted); 6 k.a. I, me; my (also a response when called);
 dedalem to live in (a place) (k.i. for **manggon**).
dalir stripe(s) on an animal's coat;
 ndalir striped; stripe-shaped, in long rows.
dalit, dalitan a patched place.
dalon reg kr boar.
dalu I evening, night (kr for **bengi**, **wengi**);
 kedalon overtaken by night.
 II fully ripe (fruit);
 kedalon overripe;
 kadalu mangsa or **kadalu warsa** to have lapsed/expired.
daludag see **dludag** I.
dama, daman precious because of its scarcity;
 dinama-dama (of child) spoiled;
 dedaman money or things kept carefully as the last reserve.
damar 1 hardened tree resin; 2 lamp, lantern.
damel job, task; celebration; to make, do, cause (kr for **gawé**).
dami 1 dried rice straw; a field of dried rice stalks; 2 inner peel of a ripe breadfruit or jackfruit section;
 damèn 1 dried rice stalk; 2 whistle or bubble pipe made from such a stalk;
 damènan field of dried rice straw;
 ndamèn bosok resembling decaying straw;
 ndamèn teles reddish yellow.
damu, ndamu or ndamoni to blow (on, out).

dan, ndan lit 1 then, afterwards; 2 quickly.
dana 1 charitable gift, funds; 2 district head (inf var of **wedana**).
danar, danar-danar (of female complexions) light, fair.
danas reg var of **nanas**.
dandan ng, dandos kr, to get/be dressed;
 ndandani 1 to repair; 2 to dress s.o.;
 ndandakaké 1 to have s.t. repaired; 2 to have (clothing) made;
 dandan-dandan 1 to fix things up; 2 to keep repairing s.t.;
 dandanan 1 apparel, way of dressing; 2 accessories; embellishments; 3 a place to dress; 4 a foregone conclusion.
dandang bottom part of a rice steamer; a copper pot for water, over which a woven bamboo cone (**kukusan**) containing the rice is placed.
dandos kr for **dandan**.
dang I, ngedang to cook (esp rice) by steaming;
 ngedangaké to steam rice for s.o.;
 padang 1 person who steams rice; 2 the time required to steam rice;
 padangan kitchen;
 kayu dang firewood;
 sapadang sapanginang a moment, a short while;
 dang-dangan 1 cooked by steaming; 2 the way to steam rice.
 II, ndang quickly, promptly.
dangak reg var of **dhangak**.
dangan or danganan holder, handle.
dangdanan reg var of **dandanan**.
dangu I (a) long time (kr for **suwé**).
 II to ask (a question) (k.i. for **takon**).
 III stem of the sugar-palm blossom.
dangur cassava.
dangus harsh, stern, gruff, easily angered.
daning reg var of **andèkna**.
danten pigeon (reg kr for **dara** I).
danu lit wild buffalo.
daoké boss, a Chinese foreman; term for addressing a Chinese foreman.

dapak I *reg* if, when.

II *reg* moreover, beyond that, even.

III *reg* maybe.

daptar list.

dara I pigeon, dove; - **bandhangan** *or* - **kaplakan** male pigeon being trained by use of a tame female; - **gambir** brown pigeon; - **giring** homing pigeon; pigeon in the mating season; - **kucir** crested pigeon; - **pos** carrier pigeon; - **topong** black pigeon with a white head.

II, **ndara** 1 master, mistress (*shtf of* **bendara**); 2 Sir, madam (*term for addressing one's master or mistress*); - **ajeng** daughter of the master; - **kakung** the master of the house; - **mas** son of the master; - **putri** wife of the master.

daradasih *or* **ndaradasihi** to materialise, come about.

daragepak a certain style of Javanese house with verandahs on all sides.

darah *see* **dharah**.

daraka *lit* solid, strong, resistant.

daran, ndarani 1 to name/call s.t. (*var of* **ngarani**); 2 to accuse.

darana *lit* steadfast, able to bear s.t., patient.

darani *lit* earth.

darapon *lit* in order to, so that.

darbé *lit* to have, own, possess;

ndarbèni to have possession of. *See also* **darbèk**.

darbèk the possession of, belonging to.

darès a variety of owl.

dari, ndari to rise (moon) (*var of* **ndadari**).

daridra *lit* needy, indigent, destitute.

daring, daringan 1 container for storing rice; 2 large flat bamboo surface where husked rice is spread out to dry before storing;

padaringan *same as* **daringan**.

darma I *lit* father.

II 1 (**darmi** *kr*) duty, obligation; 2 donation, contribution; to donate, contribute; 3 service, good deed;

ndarmani to contribute to;

ndarmakaké to contribute s.t. for;

sadarma *or* **saderma** (to do) from a sense of duty or as an obligation;

darmabakti volunteer work, service of value to the state;

darmawisata excursion, outing, field trip, a group study trip;

darmawan donor, philanthropist, generous person; contributor.

III close, intimate; **mitra** - a best friend.

darmaja *lit* child, son.

darmi duty, obligation (*kr for* **darma**).

darpa *lit* 1 eager; 2 desirous; 3 impulse, instinct.

darpaya *var of* **darpa**.

darsana *lit* example, model, instance.

daru falling star that gives off bright blue light; an omen of great good fortune. *Also* **andaru**.

darubeksi misfortune brought about by black magic.

daruna *lit* cause, reason.

darung, ndarung to do repeatedly or habitually;

kedarung-darung to go astray;

darungan and then, after that.

darus, ndarus to recite from the Quran.

darwya *lit* to have, own, possess (*var of* **darbé**).

das zero.

dasa the 10 digit (*kr for* **puluh**).

dasanama synonym; synonymous words.

dasih *lit* servant.

dat 1 essence; essential nature; 2 substance; chemical substance. *Also* **zat**.

datan *lit* no, not.

datapitana *lit* so it happened; as the story goes.

datar *lit* no, not (*var of* **datan**).

datatita *var of* **datapitana**.

datuk, ndatuk to form an addiction; to become addicted.

datullah the supreme essence (God).

daugan a young coconut (*reg var of* **degan**).

daulat blessing bestowed by a dignitary; - **becik** a good omen.

dauru turmoil, chaotic situation.

daut *or* **dhaut 1** (*k.i. for* **ompong**) to be toothless; **2** to fall out (teeth), get new teeth (child) (*see* **pupak**); **3** to fall off (umbilical cord, after birth) (*see* **puput puser**);
kedaut *lit* attracted, swept away.

dawa *ng*, **panjang** *kr* long; - **ambané** the dimensions/area (of); - **cendhaké** the length (of); - **ilaté** to tattle; - **tangané** light-fingered;
ndawani to make s.t. longer (in relation to s.t. else);
ndawakaké to make s.t. longer;
ndedawa to lengthen;
kedawan excessively long;
kedawa-dawa long-drawn-out; (dragged) on and on.

dawala white silk scarf worn by a dancer around the neck to hold the batik in place.

daweg I 1 *var of* **saweg**; **2** *subst kr for* **ayo**. **II** *reg var of* **degan**.

dawèr, **ndawèr** careless(ly), negligent(ly), unheeding(ly). *See also* **dlawèr**.

dawi extremely long (*intsfr of* **dawa**).

dawir torn, ragged (of human ears).

dawu extremely long (*intsfr of* **dawa**).

daya 1 power, energy, capacity, strength, force; **2** influence;
ndayani to give energy to; to influence;
kedayan strengthened by; influenced by;
daya-daya to exert force.

dayinta *lit* princess, queen, noblewoman.

dayita *var of* **dayinta**.

dé *lit* with regard to. *See also* **déné**.

débag, **débagan** *or* **gedébagan** to roll around in one's sleep.

debal, **ndebal** to prick out turf;
debalan turf, sod. *See also* **gebal**.

dèbès (of dressing) neat.

déblag, **ndéblag 1** broad and thick; **2** to slap s.o. on the back; **3** to repair an eroded dyke separating a ricefield;
sadéblag (of cake) a big piece.

dèbleg, **ndèbleg** *var of* **ndéblag**.

dèblèg, **ndèblèg 1** forming big and thick sheets; **2** cluttered; having many objects adhering to it.

déblo *var of* **dèblèg**.

debog banana tree log (*shtf of* **gedebog**).

dedah *var of* **tedah**.

dédé no; not (*subst kr/md for* **dudu**).

dedeg height, stature; - **pangadeg** *or* - **piadeg** height, stature;
ndedegi to attend (a party); to be present at;
sadedeg the same height (as);
sadedeg pangadeg as high as a standing person;
sadedeg sapangawé as tall as a person can reach upward.

dedel, **ndedel 1** to ascend quickly; to come up; **2** to push, press.

deder, **ndeder** steep(ly graded).

dedreg to remain adamant.

deg, **ngedegi 1** to build, set up; **2** to be present at (a party); **ngedegi sayembara** to take part in a contest;
ngedegaké 1 to build, set up; **2** to raise s.o. to the position of; **ngedegaké sayembara** to hold a contest. *See also* **adeg**.

degan young coconut with sweet juice and soft flesh;
dumegan (of coconuts) to be at the above stage of development.

degèg, **ndegèg** to thrust the chest forward.

degsura conceited, obstinate, inconsiderate.

dekep, **ndekep 1** to grasp firmly; **2** to trap (*e.g.* an insect), esp with the downturned palm.

dèkèk, **ndèkèk** *or* **ndèkèki** *or* **ndèkèkaké** to place/put/lay s.t. on;
pandèkèk the way of placing s.t.

dèkèng oneself, *see* **dhéwé**.

dèkna *see* andèk.

dèkpuna *see* andèk.

deksina *see* daksina.

deksiya sadistic; cruel.

deksura *see* degsura.

dekung crooked, curved, bent;
ndekung to bow, bend, curve.

del *or* mak del *repr* a sudden upward motion.

delahan 1 the future; 2 the hereafter, the next life.

delalah, ndelalah by God's will, by chance; as luck would have it.

délan *reg* a condiment made from pounded and fermented shrimp or fish, usually used as ingredient for peppery sauce.

delap covetous;
delap-delapé what a cheek! (as a comment on s.o.'s greed).

delapon *lit* in order to; so that (*var of* darapon).

delas and also (*var of* dalah). *See also* dalasan.

delasan *var of* dalasan.

délé, délé-délé *excl of surprise.*

deleg I a pike-like fish.
II the facts of the matter.
III cross-section of a tree trunk.
IV *or* delegan rolled-up tobacco leaf.

dèlèh, ndèlèh to lay/place/put s.t. on.

dèlèk *reg var of* dèlèh.

delem hollowed-out coconut shell, for holding water.

deleng *ng*, tingal *kr*, ndeleng to look at; to see;
ndeleng-ndeleng to depend (on), be up (to);
ndedeleng to look around, browse, observe; to see things;
ndelengi let me see!;
ndelengaké to see, observe;
pandeleng 1 the way of observing; 2 vision, eyesight.

dèlèng to have squinty eyes;
ndèlèngaké to squint the eyes.

delep, ndelep to enter a hole,
ndelepaké to conceal; to hide from view. *See also* mendelep.

delèp, ndelèp 1 stubborn; 2 (of animals) difficult to kill; 3 to keep everything to o.s.

dèlèp, ndèlèp *reg* 1 to persist with what one decided to do; 2 able to endure pain and sorrow; 3 to have s.t. all to o.s.

delèr I the title of a member of the Council of the Indies.
II, ndelèr to stream in, pour in; copious, abundant.

dèlèr, ndèlèr to flow, ooze; to trickle out; to run down.

deles I 1 pure-bred; 2 unmixed blood.
II black.
III a cloth strip serving as a wick in an oil lamp.

delik *see* pendelik.

deling I bamboo (*kr for* pring).
II, dumeling (of sound) clearly audible.

delir *var of* delèr.

deloh, ndeloh to put s.t. s.w (*reg var of* dèlèh).

delok *inf var of* deleng.

delul, ndelul headstrong, strong-willed.

demak, ndemak *reg* 1 to touch with the hand; 2 to catch (chicken, insect *etc*) with the hands.

demang 1 village head; 2 a title of a court official; 3 customary law expert;
kademangan 1 the position of demang; 2 the area of a demang; 3 the residence of a demang;
demang ngiras tangkilan *prov* self-service (of guest).

demari, demarinen (of baby that is not yet weaned) sickly and fussy.

dembaga *var of* tembaga.

démblo, ndémblo forming thick sheets/layers.

demblok, ndemblok smudged, smeared, messy.

demek *see* demak.

demèk, ndemèk to touch/feel with the hand;

ndemèki to keep touching;

kedemèk to touch accidentally;

demak-demèk to touch s.t. repeatedly;

demèkan the feel of s.t.

demèmèl *var of* dermimil.

demenak, ndemenakaké 1 pleasant, agreeable, causing delight; 2 appetising, delicious-looking.

demimil *var of* dremimil.

demok, ndemok to touch with the hand (*var of* demèk).

demumung, ndemumung *reg* to mutter, grumble.

demung a large bronze gamelan instrument;

ndemung to play this instrument.

den, ngeden 1 to strain, *esp* for defecating, giving birth; 2 to concentrate one's strength toward a goal.

dèn I *adr* high-status male (*shtf of* radèn).
II 1 *lit, 3rd person passive verbal prefix*; 2 *lit* in a certain manner (*var of* sing, ingkang).

denang, ndenangi to see s.o. doing s.t. furtively; to observe s.t. what has gone unnoticed to others;

kadenangan to get caught doing s.t. one does not want noticed.

denawa *see* danawa.

déné 1 that (*introductory clause*); 2 while, whereas; 3 regarding, as for.

dènèng *reg var of* déné.

dengak *reg var of* dhengak.

dengang, ndengangi *reg var of* ngonangi.

dengangak, ndengangak facing upward. *See also* dhangak.

dengangap, ndengangap to keep wanting to eat.

dengap, dengap-dengap to breathe laboriously; *fig* to find life overwhelmingly difficult.

dengarèn how strange! it's unusual that… *See also* dingarèn, kadingarèn.

dengèngèk, ndengèngèk to lift the head suddenly.

dengguk, ndengguk to gain weight; thick and ungainly.

dengingak, ndengingak to stare upward.

dengkèk, ndengkèk *or* ndengkèkaké to bend s.t. into an arch; to flex s.t.;

kedengkèk 1 to get bent or arched; 2 *fig* to be the victim of misfortune.

dèngkèk 1 (having) a bent or hunched back; 2 name of one of the small playing-cards (*kertu cilik*).

dengkèng, ndengkèng arc-shaped, curved, swaybacked.

dengki to bear a grudge; to wish s.o. ill. *See also* drengki.

dengok, ndengok *reg* to look at, observe.

dengongok *var of* dengèngèk

déning 1 (done) by; 2 because of.

dènira *lit* by you; by him/her.

denta *lit* ivory; white as ivory.

dènta *var of* dènira.

dentawyanjana *gram* order of Javanese characters.

dènten *md for* déné.

dènya *var of* dènira.

depara nonsense, impossible (*var of* dupara).

depok, ndepok *reg* to touch *var of* demok). *See also* gepok.

derana *see* darana.

derap, nderap to gallop; to run at a gallop.

derapon *see* darapon.

derbala, nderbala to become richer and richer.

derbé *see* darbé.

derbis a certain type of cannon.

derbombok a dark grey long-necked, long-legged water bird (*var of* sribombok).

derbus a certain type of cannon (*var of* derbis).

derdah a quarrel, dispute.

dereng wish, desire;

kadereng eager.

dèrèng not yet (*kr for* durung).

derep 1 to harvest rice; 2 to offer one's services at the rice harvest;
    nderepaké to have (workers) harvest rice;
    derepan the harvested crop.

deres I hard, heavy (of a downpour);
    kaderesan to get saturated by rain.
    II, **nderes** to read aloud from the Quran until finished (*var of* **darus**).

dèrès, ndèrès 1 to tap a tree for sap; 2 to strip the bark from (a tree, to process it);
    dèrèsan a coconut palm used only for tapping.

dergil, ndergil enterprising, resourceful, industrious.

dering I *reg* no; not.
    II sharp projecting edge.

derkuku a variety of dove.

derma *var of* darma.

dermaga *ng*, dermagi *kr* 1 main road, thoroughfare; 2 pier, harbour.

derman (of woman) having many children; to be a mother many times over.

dermèmèl *var of* dermimil.

dermemeng, ndermemeng to grumble, mutter to o.s.

dermèn *or* dermènan child's whistle made from a rice stalk.

dermi *var of* darmi.

dermimil, ndermimil 1 to recite a prayer continuously; 2 to mutter, talk constantly under one's breath.

dermimis *var of* dermis.

dermis, ndermis to ask things all the time without shame.

dersana a variety of roseapple (jambu).

deruk a certain variety of dove which is tamed as a pet or used for hunting.

derwis dervish.

derwolo, nderwolo headstrong, stubborn, self-willed.

désa *ng*, dhusun *kr* village, rural settlement; - ngadésa all over the villages;
    ndésani to act/be like a rustic, countrified;

padésan 1 rural area; 2 rural, pertaining to villages;
    désa mawa cara, negara mawa tata *prov* each region has its own ways.

destun 1 it's supposed to be better if…; 2 but on the contrary.

dètèng, ndètèng (to stand or to walk) with chest high and shoulders back.

détiya *or* détya *lit* ogre, giant. *See also* ditya.

déwa male deity, god;
    kadéwan 1 realm of the deities; 2 having a deity-like nature.

déwadaru *or* déwandaru 1 a certain mythological tree with magical properties, wishing-tree; 2 one of two banyan trees in front of the palace in north square, Yogyakarta.

déwaji *lit adr* king; **kanjeng** - Your Majesty.

déwalaya *lit* realm of the deities.

déwanggana *lit* fairy. *See also* diwangkara.

déwangkara *lit* sun.

déwaresi mythological being, divine sage.

déwasa adult, of age.

déwata deity, god.

dèwi female deity; goddess; - **Sri** the Goddess of Rice.

déyos *see* dhéyos.

dhablang *var of* dhaplang.

dhabreg a large quantity;
    sadhabreg a large amount, a lot.

dhabyang, ndhabyang(-dhabyang) to support (a weak person) and help him walk.

dhacin unit of weight: *ca* 61.76 kg;
    dhacinan 1 balance scale for weighing by *dhacin*'s; 2 in *dhacin*'s, by the *dhacin*.

dhadha I *ng*, *kr*, **jaja** *or* **pranaja** *k.i.* chest, breast; - **manuk** barrel-chest;
    - **menthok** breast of poultry; the white chicken meat;
    ndhadha 1 to let s.t. bounce off one's chest; 2 to admit one's mistakes; 3 to accept with courage;
    pandhadha third child in the family.

II certain note of gamelan scales.

dhadhah I a hedge.

II *see* **dhah**.

dhadhak a sap that causes skin itch;

dhadhakan 1 occasion, inducement; 2 an irritant to a personal relationship.

dhadhal 1 to fall down or burst apart (as of dyke or dam); 2 disarranged, out of order; 3 finished, all gone (of money, capital *etc*);

ndhadhal to repossess one's ricefield because the lessee failed in his obligations;

ndhadhali to trim, prune;

ndhadhalaké to break (through) s.t.

dhadhali a swallow-like bird.

dhadhap 1 a certain shade tree; 2 shield; - **ayam** *or* - **bong** common varieties of **dhadhap** tree; - **srep** tree the leaves of which are used in traditional medicines;

ndhadhap to strike with a shield;

si Dhadhap si Waru hypothetical people; A or B.

dhadhar, **ndhadhari** (of the moon) to rise (*var of* **ndadari**).

dhadhat, **ndhadhat** to tear/break through s.t.

dhadhil, **dhodhal-dhadhil** badly torn.

dhadho steel and flint device for lighting fires.

dhadhu dice; **main** - gambling by using a dice;

ndhadhu cube-shaped.

dhadhuk dried-out vegetation.

dhadhung heavy rope; - **tapuk** rope halter;

didhadhunga medhot, dipalangana mlumpat *prov* to resist restraint, not want to be fenced in.

dhadhut chubby.

dhaèng title of rank in Buginese society.

dhag *reg* absent, out;

ngedhag *or* **ngedhag-edhag** uncovered, unprotected, out in the open;

ngedhagaké to leave open/uncovered.

dhaga, **ndhaga-ndhaga** to have an appetite (for).

dhagé *reg* a variety of fermented sticky rice (**tapé**).

dhagel I, **ndhagel** to joke, clown around;

dhagelan 1 clown; 2 joking, clowning; 3 short humorous skit.

II still hard (fruit).

dhagi *inf var of* **undhagi**.

dhaglig, **dhoglag-dhaglig** shaky, wobbly.

dhaglo, **ndhaglo** *reg* sitting and doing nothing.

dhagrèg *reg* old and useless.

dhagu *reg* chin.

dhah word of farewell: 'bye!';

ngedhahi to say/wave goodbye to;

dhadhah-dhadhah to say bye-bye.

dhahar to eat (*k.i. for* **mangan**); - **kembul** to eat together; to share a meal from a common plate;

ndhahar 1 to eat; 2 to believe (in), follow (*k.i. for* **nggugu**); - **atur** to heed, follow advice.

dhahas (of soil) dry, dried out.

dhahat *lit* very (*var of* **dahat**).

dhahwèn *see* **dahwèn**.

dhahyang *var of* **dhanyang**.

dhajeng *var of* **dhiajeng**.

dhak I to descend; unload (*root form: kr for* **dhun**).

II, **ndhak** or else (*inf var of* **mundhak**).

III, **ndhak** every (*inf var of* **pendhak**).

dhakah 1 greedy; 2 great, big, large.

dhakal, **kedhakalan** to climb with difficulty.

dhaken *subst kr for* **dhaku**.

dhakik *see* **dakik**.

dhakir, **dhakir-dhakir** to dig a hole with the hands or forefeet (of animals).

dhakom, **ndhakom** to sit with knees drawn up; to lie protectively over s.t. *See also* **dhekem**.

dhakon (to play) a certain game consisting of a shallow oval-shaped wooden board containing rows of round hollowed-out places into which fruit pits (**kecik**) are placed according to certain rules.

dhaku, ndhaku to claim (ownership of); to acknowledge as one's own.

dhakur *var of* **dhakir**.

dhakwa *or* **ndhakwa** of different/disparate lengths (*shtc from* **cendhak dawa**).

dhal, dhal-dhalan to wander, leave home frequently; one who wanders.

dhali a swallow-like bird (*shtf of* **dhadhali**).

dhalang 1 narrator and puppeteer of traditional shadow-plays; **2** mastermind, power behind the scenes;
ndhalang to conduct a shadow-play performance, act as **dhalang**;
ndhalangi to mastermind, be a power behind the scenes;
ndhalangaké to depict in a shadow-play;
padhalangan 1 shadow-play lore, including knowledge of the tales, the language used and the art of manipulating the puppets; **2** shadow-play performance;
dhalang ora kurang lakon *prov* a smart person can always find a way.

dhalung a large kettle for cooking rice.

dham I dam.
II *reg* a turn at night watch in the village watchman's base.
III checked (design);
ngedham to draw based on a certain pattern.
IV dham-dhaman to play draughts.

dhamang 1 to understand; **2** easily done;
ndhamangaké to clarify, make comprehensible.

dhambul a game played by tossing small balls or pebbles in the hands.

dhami *inf var of* **bedhami**.

dhamis 1 to fit together; **2** aesthetically harmonious.

dhampa skin disease characterised by a red rash.

dhampak barrel-chested.

dhampar 1 throne; **2** low (round) table

where people sit cross-legged to eat, play cards *etc.*

dhampèng, ndhampèng 1 to hide by crouching behind s.t.; **2** *lit* to plead for sympathy.

dhamping steep wall of a ravine.

dhamplak *or* **dhamplak-dhamplak** big around (of banana, horns or long roughly cylindrical objects).

dhamplèng *reg* form, shape, face.

dhampit boy-girl twins.

dhampyak, dhampyak-dhampyak 1 in throngs, in great numbers; **2** (of people) spreading out and marching abreast, blocking the road.

dhana, ndhana to go there (*Yogya slang, var of* **mrana**).

dhana-dhini boy-girl sibling combination (*shtf of* **kedhana-kedhini**).

dhancang fast (*var of* **bancang**).

dhandha *lit* club, bludgeon.

dhandhan I handle of an umbrella.
II *reg* **1** wire cord; **2** big cord made from young bamboo.

dhandhang I carrion crow;
ndhandhang resembling a carrion crow;
dhandhang diunèkaké kuntul *prov* a bad man made out to be good.
II *or* **cucuk dhandhang** pickaxe. *See also* **cucuk**.
III, dhandhang-gula a certain classical verse form;
dhandhang-gendhis *kr for* **dhandhang-gula**.

dhandheng, ndhandheng to wander, roam.

dhandher *reg* cassava.

dhandhing, ndhandhing slender and graceful.

dhang I *honorific title applied to a priest*.
II, ngedhang to wait for, lie in wait for;
ngedhang-dhangi to block s.o.'s way; to put s.t. in the way of.
See also **adhang**.

dhangah, dhangah-dhangah (to walk) briskly, to stride.

dhangak, ndhangak facing upward; craning the neck (var of ndangak); ndhangakaké to face s.t. upward.

dhangan 1 well (k.i. for waras); 2 to recover from (k.i. for mari); 3 willing (to help); 4 pleased, to like (k.i. for seneng); 5 comfortable (k.i. for kepénak).

dhangdhang lit crow (bird) (var of dhandhang).

dhangdheng var of dhandheng.

dhangdher var of dhandher.

dhangdhing see dhing.

dhangdhong reg sometimes (var of dhongdhong).

dhanget to hear (shtf of midhanget, k.i. for krungu).

dhangglong, dhangglongan reg 1 inconstant; 2 idiotic, witless.

dhanghyang honorific title applied to a priest.

dhangir, weeding and loosening of surface soil with a hoe; ndhangir to weed and loosen (soil); -alis to shave and shape eyebrows.

dhangka 1 place, location; 2 cr habitation of an ogre or evil spirit; 3 cave where a corpse is kept.

dhangkak reg having a short neck and bulging chest.

dhangkal I reg self-willed, obstinate (var of wangkal).
II reg (of fruits) hard.
III reg dirt on the skin; ndhangkal or dhangkalen (of skin) dirty.

dhangkèl main root of a tree; ndhangkèl 1 to remove a tree by the roots; 2 to practise asceticism by eating several kinds of roots only; dhangkèlan 1 main root of a tree; 2 fig gang leader.

dhangklèh, dhangklèh-dhangklèh broken and hanging (from). See also dhènglèh.

dhangkrok, ndhangkrok 1 climbing by pressing the chest against a tree; 2 to sit with the knees drawn up and the back bent.

dhangkruk var of dhangkrok.

dhangleng reg idiotic, eccentric, deranged.

dhangling var of dhangleng.

dhangsah Western-style dancing; to perform this.

dhangsul shtf of kedhangsul soybean (subst kr for dhelé, kedhelé).

dhangsur, ndhangsur reg to sleep everywhere.

dhanu lit lake. See also ranu.

dhanyang a spirit who guards a particular locality.

dhaon reg a plant leaf.

dhaos reg kr for dhacin.

dhapa, ndhapa shtf of pendhapa.

dhaplang, ndhaplang to stretch the arms out to the sides.

dhaplok very old. See also gerang.

dhapuk assigned a role to; ndhapuk 1 to arrange, set up; 2 to assign a role to; dhapukan 1 arrangement(s), formation; 2 role assigned; pandhapuk the way to set up.

dhapur or dhapuran 1 shape, form, design; 2 clump, cluster; adhapur in the form of, resembling; dhapurmu excl, cr stupid!; dhapur kebeneran lucky for us.

dhara 1 having reached the reproductive age (poultry); 2 medium-sized, not too large.

dharah 1 descendant, esp of an aristocrat; 2 lineage, descent; 3 blood.

dharak, dharak-dharak 1 in neat rows; 2 too long (garments).

dharang, kedharang-dharang in desperate straits, at the end of one's tether.

dharat 1 land (as contrasted to water, air); laku or mlaku - to walk; to go overland (walking or by vehicles); ndharat 1 to go overland; 2 to land; 3 to come ashore, reach the shore;

ndharataké to bring to land; to land s.t.;
dharatan land;

dhedharatan *lit* to go walking or riding
a horse overland.

II heavy rope. *See also* kendharat.

dharik, dharik-dharik in orderly rows. *See
also* tharik.

dhasar 1 bottom; 2 basis, foundation, principle; 3 basically, by nature; 4 background; 5 to arrange or display
merchandise;

ndhasar at/on the bottom;

ndhasari 1 to use as a foundation; 2 to
base s.t. on;

ndhasaraké 1 to place on display; 2 to
base s.t.;

adhedhasar based on;

pandhasaran 1 a place where merchandise is displayed; 2 a display of
merchandise.

dhat now (one thing) now (another); -
nyeng fickle, changeable;

dhat-dhatan fitful (of sleep). *See also*
cat.

dhateng 1 to come, arrive (*kr for* teka); 2
(to go) to, toward (*kr for* marang); 3
concerning (*kr for* marang); - sendika
k.a. yes; as you order!

dhumateng *lit var kr for* marang.

dhatu *lit* king;

kedhaton palace; court.

dhauk *var of* dhawuk.

dhaulu I snake with two heads.

II confused speaking by mixing *ngoko*
and *krama* words.

dhaun *reg* plant leaf.

dhaup to marry;

ndhaupaké to hold a wedding ceremony
for, marry off.

dhaut *lit* to set out (troops);

ndhaut to pull up (young rice plants
from the nursery bed, for transplanting
into the field). *See also* daut.

dhawah 1 to fall, drop (*kr for* tiba); 2 *lit* to
order, command (*var of* dhawuh); 3 to

say, speak (*reg k.i. for* celathu, tutur);

ndhawah to sow seeds (*reg kr for*
nyebar);

dhawahan dam (*kr for* bendungan).

dhawak *coll* oneself (*var of* dhéwé).

dhawet a drink prepared from coconut
milk, rice flour and palm sugar.

dhawoh *reg var of* dhawah.

dhawuh 1 an order, command (*k.i. for*
pakon); to tell s.o. to do s.t. (*k.i. for*
kon); 2 to say, speak (*k.i. for* celathu); 3
to advise (*k.i. for* tutur);

ndhawuhaké to hand down, issue
(order).

dhawuk 1 dappled, grey with coloured
dots; 2 faded from repeated washing,
very old (of clothing).

dhawul, dhawul-dhawul untidy, in
disarray.

dhaya *inf var of* bedhaya.

dhayoh guest, visitor;

ndhayohi to pay s.o. a visit;

merdhayoh to come on a visit;

kedhayohan 1 to have a visitor; 2 *fig* to
receive an unwelcome visit, *esp* to be
burgled;

padhayohan 1 place where one visits; 2
place where one receives a guest;

dhayoh-dhayohan to play at going
visiting (*children's pastime*).

dhayum (of soil) loosened and aerated
preparatory to planting.

dhayung I oar, paddle.

II *var of* dhayum.

dhé *shtf of* gedhé; pak- a parent's elder
brother; bu- a parent's elder sister.

dhebat *see* dhébat.

dhébat a debate;

ndhébat to criticise, argue about,
debate;

dhébat-dhébatan to exchange opinions,
debate with each other.

dhèbleng *see* dhénok.

dhèblèng, ndhèblèng (of horn) turning
back, upward and outward;

dhèblèngan the tied ends of a headdress (iket).

dhebus I, *or* **lenga dhebus** kerosene, petroleum.

II ritual display of invulnerability in West Java.

dhècèh, ndhècèh to expose s.t. as much as possible.

dhécol a bump of irregular shape.

dhedhak rice chaff.

dhedhali a variety of swallow (bird).

dhédhé to sun o.s., bask.

dhedheg I rice chaff (*var of* **dhedhak**).

II, **ndhedheg** *or* **ndhedhegi** 1 to hammer softly; 2 to play (a gamelan percussion instrument) with gentle beats.

dhèdhèh, ndhèdhèh I 1 to lie around outside; 2 to sun o.s.

II to unpack.

dhedhek *var of* **dhedhak**.

dhèdhèk, ndhèdhèki to set aside for later use; to have an eye on.

dhedhel 1 sluggish; 2 *or* **kedhedhelen** constipated.

dhèdhèl to rip;

ndhèdhèl *or* **ndhèdhèli** to rip s.t. open; **ndhèdhèlaké** to cause s.t. to be ripped.

dhedhem an attention-getting cough, clearing the throat; to cough or clear the throat for attention.

dhedhep I quiet; - **tidhem** deathly quiet.

II, **ndhedhepi** to watch from a concealed place.

dhedhepa, ndhedhepa to plead for mercy or sympathy.

dhedher, ndhedher 1 to sow seeds; 2 *fig* to train, indoctrinate, forge;

dhedheran 1 seedling; seedbed; 2 trained fellow;

pandhedheran 1 seedbed; plot where seeds are sown; 2 training centre.

dhèdhèr, kedhèdhèran loose and ill-fitting (of clothing); to bustle.

dhedhes, ndhedhes to plague s.o. with questions about what they have been up to;

pandhedhes the way of investigating.

dhèdhès civet, excreted by the civet cat, used in perfumes.

dhedhet I, **ndhedhet** dark; **peteng - lelimengan** pitch dark.

II, **ndhedhet** to tug (at) with jerking motions;

ndhedheti to tighten when jerked.

III, **ndhedheti** to trample on (soil *etc*) to firm it.

dhèdhèt I tendril of a vine.

II lightning storm; - **érawati** thunderstorm.

dheg 1 *or* **mak dheg** *repr* a sudden heartbeat; 2 *repr* a beat; 3 throughout, whole; **sedina** - all the day, the whole day;

ngedheg-dhegi to give s.o. a scare;

dheg-dhegan startled, frightened; with heart pounding;

sadhegan at one time.

dhèg I ship's deck.

II blanket.

dhéga, ndhéga ship's crew (*shtf of* **bendhéga**).

dhegel, ndhegel resentful, mortified.

dhegèl, ndhegèl stiff and bulging.

dheglag, ndheglag to sit leaning back so far that one falls;

ndheglagaké to tip the chair back;

kedheglag to fall by leaning back too far.

dhegleg simple-minded; crazy (*var of* **dhèglèng**).

dhèglèg, ndhèglèg to sit leaning back.

dhegleng *see* **degleg, dhèglèng**.

dhèglèng I simple-minded, ignorant, stupid; crazy.

II, **ndhèglèng** to sit leaning back (*var of* **ndhèglèg**).

dheglig *or* **mak dheglig** *repr* a sudden bending;

ndheglig (of knee) slightly bent and forward; to bend s.o.'s knee from behind;

dheglag-dheglig crippled, (of legs) unstable, wobbly.

dhegling, **ndhegling** to prod s.o.'s knee from behind to bend it. *See also* **dhengkling**.

dheglo simple-minded, ignorant, stupid (*var of* **dhegleg, dhèglèng**).

dhéglog to limp because of an injured leg or because one leg is shorter;
dhéglogan *or* **kedhéglogan** to walk with a limp.

dheglug, **dheglag-dheglug** crippled; (of legs) wobbly (*var of* **dhéglog**).

dhegol (of arms, leg joints) enlarged, knobbly.

dhégol *var of* **dhegol**.

dhegrès *reg* idiotic, crazy.

dhegros, **ndhegros** to remain seated and to do nothing.

dhegrus *var of* **dhegros**.

dhégus tall and handsome (*shtc from* **gedhé bagus**).

dhèh, **dhèhé** s.o.'s act of (do)ing (*reg var of* **olèhé**).

dhèhèh, **ndhèhèh** to remain seated in the wrong place.

dhèhèm to cough, clear the throat (*esp to* attract attention).

dhèk I when (past); last, past; - **mau** just now, a short while ago; - **wingi** yesterday; - **biyèn** formerly, a long time ago, in the past.
II belonging, possession;
dhèkmu yours (*inf var of* **duwèkmu**);
ngedhèki 1 to claim s.t. as one's own; 2 to set aside for future use (*var of* **dhèdhèk**).
III *see* **dhèg** I, II.
IV *title of or adr to younger person* (*reg var of* **dhi** *or* **dhik**).

dhekah small village, hamlet (*kr for* **dhukuh**).

dhèké he, him; she, her (*3rd person pronoun*) (*var of* **dhèwèké**).

dhekeh *reg var of* **dhekah**.

dhekek having a neck so short it seems to be growing out of the shoulders;
ndhekekaké to retract the head into the shoulders.

dhekekel, **ndhekekel** huddled up with cold.

dhekem, **ndhekem** 1 (of birds, animals) to sit/lie with legs folded under the body; 2 (of people: *cr*) to sit with knees drawn up; to lie with knees folded under the body;
ndhekemi 1 to sit/lie protectively over s.t.; 2 *cr* to refuse to share.

dhekeman I soybean (*subst kr for* **dhelé**).
II *reg* stone-filled basket for reinforcing a dam.

dhèken, **ndhèken** to mark (an opponent, *e.g.* in soccer).

dheker, **ndheker** *cr* to lie curled up (asleep).

dhèk-éré *var of* **dhèk-èri**.

dhèk-èri *reg* maybe, perhaps.

dhekes, **ndhekes** to sit cross-legged. *See also* **kedhekes**.

dheket closely spaced. *See also* **dhengket, rengked**.

dhekik small indentation; dimple.

dhekis, **ndhekis** to hide. *See also* **dhelik**.

dheklak, **dheklak-dhekluk** to keep nodding sleepily.

dhekluk *or* **mak dhekluk** *repr* nodding sleepily.

dhèkman *reg* of course, indeed.

dhèkné he, him (*reg var of* **dhèwèké**).

dhèknèn *var of* **dhèkné**.

dhekok I 1 (to have) a dent, hollow; 2 deep-set (eyes);
ndhekoki *or* **ndhekokaké** to dent s.t.;
dhekak-dhekok full of dents.
II, **ndhekok** *cr* to sleep.

dhekong *var of* **dhekok**.

dhékong with big buttocks (*shtc of* **gedhé bokong**).

dhekos, **ndhekos** to take room and board;
ndhekosi to board at s.o.'s house;
ndhekosaké to allow s.o. to board;
dhekosan, kos-kosan room and board; boarding house. *Also* **indhekos**.

dhékor I, ndhékor to sit on the bare floor.
II decor.

dheku, ndheku to sit cross-legged before an exalted person in a humble and deferential attitude.

dhekukul, ndhekukul with head bowed.

dhel 1 (or mak dhel) repr a sudden motion, usually upward; 2 repr a breaking sound; 3 repr an explosion.

dhéla a moment shtf of sadhéla.

dhelak, I ndhelak 1 facing upward and opening the mouth widely because of thirst; 2 to have an appetite (for).
II, dhelak-dhelik to stay alone and feel lonely. See also dhelik.

dhelé soybean. See also kedhelé.

dheleg, dheleg-dheleg stunned with grief.

dhèlèk, ndhèlèki to set aside for later use (var of ndhèdhèki).

dheleleg, ndheleleg downcast, gloomy.

dheles, ndheles reg to leave without saying goodbye.

dhèlet coll a moment (var of dhéla).

dhelik, ndhelik 1 to hide; 2 isolated, hidden away;
ndhelikaké to hide s.t.;
dhelikan 1 in secret; 2 hide-and-seek; 3 (or pandhelikan) hiding-place.

dhélik relative size (shtc of gedhé cilik).

dhelog, I dhelog-dhelog stunned with shock and grief.
II earthenware crock.

dheluk reg var of dhéla.

dhèlut coll a moment (var of dhéla).

dhem, ngedhem to cool o.s. or s.t.;
ngedhemaké 1 to cool s.t., make cold(er) or cool(er); 2 to make comfortable/ secure; to calm s.o. down. See also adhem.

dhèm, ngedhèmi 1 to claim s.t. as one's own; 2 to set aside for later use (var of dhèk).

dhembel (of unwashed hair) sticky, greasy.

dhembèl var of dhembel.

dhèmbèl var of dhembel.

dhemblé I firmly attached, stuck together, adhering to one another.
II a certain children's game.

dhemblèk var of dhemblé.

dhemek, dhemek-dhemek (to walk) slowly with short steps. See also kedhemek.

dhemel wet and sticky.

dhemèl var of dhemel.

dhèmèl var of dhemel.

dhemen ng, remen kr to like, take pleasure in; - nyar to acquire and tire of new things quickly;
ndhemeni 1 to like, have a fondness for; 2 to love illicitly;
ndhemenaké pleasing, appealing;
dhemenan 1 cr girl/boy friend; 2 to have an extramarital affair; 3 activity (usu improper);
kedhemenen to take great pleasure in.

dhèmes with a distinguished manner, refined attitude (woman).

dhemit spirit that inhabits a particular place;
dhedhemit spirit;
dhedhemitan furtive, secretive;
dhemit ora ndulit, sétan ora doyan freed from ghosts and spirits.

dhémo three-wheeled motorcycle.

dhempak 1 (of nose shape) large and thick with a bump at the end; 2 low and flat; 3 stocky.

dhempal physically strong.

dhempel I 1 to stick together; 2 close, intimate.
II door or window frame.

dhempèl reg 1 helper; 2 branch office, branch shop.

dhèmpèl, ndhèmpèl to stick to, stay close to.

dhempèng, ndhempèng 1 to take shelter under a tree; 2 to be under the protection of.

dhempès empty of its normal contents. See also kempès.

dhempèt, ndhempèt to press;
kedhempèt to get pressed, jammed.

dhèmpèt growing as one, stuck together, jammed together (two things).

dhempil to sit or stay close to s.o. else on a small spot.

dhemping *var of* **dhempèng**.

dhempipit, ndhempipit to remain unobtrusive.

dhempit, ndhempit *var of* **dhempèt**.

dhèmplèk, dhèmplèk-dhèmplèk side by side spreading over a wide area. *See also* **dhampyak**.

dhemplo, dhemplo-dhemplo chubby, plump.

dhempo ball of earth or clay.

dhempok (of nose shape) large and thick with a bump at the end (*var of* **dhempak**).

dhémpok, ndhémpok *reg* to sit down wearily.

dhémpol, ndhémpol *reg* to live in a part of another's home with the permission of the owner.

dhempul glazier's putty, boat caulking;
  ndhempul to apply putty or caulking;
  dhempulan 1 applied with putty; **2** s.t. used as putty.

dhèmpyèk *var of* **dhampyak**.

dhèmpyèng *var of* **dhampyak**.

dhemraga *var of* **dermaga**.

dhèncèng, dhedhèncèngan *or* **dhèncèng-dhèncèngan 1** in rows (with joined hands); **2** lined up.

dhendha I a fine;
  ndhendha to fine, assess;
  dhendhan fining.
  II *lit* club, cudgel.
  See also **bau, sapu**.

dhéndhang I a variety of beetle.
  II a certain poison.

dhèndhèk (to walk) with a limp because one leg is shorter than the other.

dhendhem 1 grudge, resentment; **2** revenge, vengeance; **3** to bear a grudge, resent.

dhendheng I, ndhendheng obstinate, headstrong, stubborn.
  II, ndhendheng to stretch, trail, extend on and on.

dhèndhèng sliced seasoned dried meat, ready for cooking; - **gepuk** fried meat pounded and seasoned with pepper; - **kenting** meat (prepared as above) with red pepper; - **ragi** the above meat with seasoned grated coconut;
  ndhèndhèng to prepare meat as above.

dhendhes, ndhendhes fine, good, tasty.

dhèndhi, ndhèndhi with fresh attractive dress (man).

dhendhong, dhendhongan to hum.

dhéné, ndhéné *Yogya slang: var of* **mréné**.

dhènèh, ndhènèh *or* **dhènèh-dhènèh** with the chest and belly thrust forward.

dheng 1 *repr* loud sound of a big drum; **2** noon, the noon mosque drum; **3** whole, throughout; **bakda** - the end moment of the fasting period and the beginning of the holiday, signalled by the mosque drum; **sedina** - the whole day.

dhèng I *repr* a sound produced by knocking a metallic object.
  II, ngedhèng to let s.t. show;
  ngedhèngaké to reveal, expose.

dhénga whoever.

dhéngah, sadhéngah of any kind, no particular one; anyone, anything.

dhengak *var of* **dhangak**.

dhengal, ndhengal to emerge (upward) from a flat surface.

dhéngan a certain bird.

dhengat, ndhengat in an upright position.

dhèngdhèng *see* **dhèndhèng**.

dhengèk *var of* **dhangak**.

dhèngèk *var of* **dhangak**.

dhengèl *var of* **dhengal**.

dhengèngèk *see* **dengèngèk**.

dhengen a spirit that causes disease; - **balung** a kind of rheumatism; - **panas** fever with stiffness of joints.

dhèngèn *reg* light, easy.

dhènger *reg* to hear, to know.

dhèngèr, ndhèngèr to lift the head suddenly.

dhenggar roomy, spacious;
ndhenggaraké to give s.t. plenty of room.

dhenggel cr human head;
dhenggelmu term of abuse: bother you!

dhenggleng simple-minded, idiotic, foolish.

dhengglong var of dhenggleng.

dhenggul var of dhenggung.

dhenggung I 1 leader or most prominent member of a group; 2 major stone in a certain game played with stones.
II one's turn (at s.t.); ketiban - to get one's turn; to get the blame for s.t.

dhenggruk to sit concentrating. See also jenggruk.

dhengil, ndhengil alone, by oneself;
dhengal-dhengil to keep emerging above a surface.

dhengis var of dhengus.

dhengit, ndhengit in an upright position. See also jengit.

dhengkak 1 with neck too short and chest too high (crippled); 2 reg cr old duffer (useless for anything).

dhengkek reg deaf.

dhengkèk, ndhengkèk to have a neck too short and chest too high.

dhèngkèk var of dhengkèk.

dhèngkèl inability to move the legs;
dhèngkèlen unable to move the legs, rooted to the spot.

dhengket to adhere (to), be right next (to), close;
ndhengketaké to bring things nearer to each other;
kedhengketen too close.

dhèngkèt var of dhengket.

dhèngkèt var of dhengket.

dhengklak, ndhengklak to bend (the neck) back;
kedhengklak to get bent backwards (neck).

dhengklang lame, limping.

dhèngklang crippled, limping.

dhengklèh or dhengklèh-dhengklèh broken and hanging (from).

dhèngklèh var of dhengklèh.

dhengklèk var of dhengklak.

dhèngklèk, ndhèngklèk to hop on one foot.

dhengklik, dhengklik-dhengklik repr the bone-knocking gait of a very thin person.

dhengkling var of dhengklang.

dhengklok, ndhengklok to flex the knee;
kedhengklok to bend the knee inadvertently.

dhengklong (var of dhengklang).

dhengkluk, ndhengkluk to lower, nod the head (var of ndhingkluk);
dhengklak-dhengkluk to keep nodding (when drowsy).

dhengklung name of a folksong.

dhéngkok, ndhéngkok to sit with bowed head.

dhéngkol grown crooked and stiff, misformed (foot).

dhengkul ng, kr, jengku k.i. knee; - paron strong-kneed;
ndhengkul to hit s.o. with a knee;
kedhengkul to be hit by s.o.'s knee inadvertently;
sadhengkul knee-high, knee-deep.

dhengkuk, ndhengkuk to bow the head deeply;
dhengkak-dhengkuk to keep nodding with downturned face.

dhengleng simple-minded, idiotic, foolish.

dhengor, dhengor-dhengor to remain utterly motionless and speechless.

dhèngsèl, ndhèngsèl reg knotty, knobbly, lumpy.

dhèngsèr, ndhèngsèr reg to slide down.

dhengul var of dhengus.

dhengus or mak dhengus repr a sudden appearance (var of bedhengus).

dhénok 1 young girl; 2 (or dhénok-

dhénok) pleasantly plump, chubby; dhénok dhèbleng pretty plump.

dhéos *see* dhéyos.

dhep, ngedhepi to have s.t. in front of it; ngedhepaké to face s.t. in a certain direction; dhep-dhepan 1 that which is placed in front (of); 2 face to face. *See also* adhep.

dhèp, ngedhèp 1 to withhold (a document) so that it cannot be acted upon; 2 to claim as one's own; dhèp-dhèpan s.t. claimed as one's own.

dhepa fathom (measure of length, *i.e.* the distance between the fingertips of the outstretched arms); ndhepani to measure in fathoms; -lemah to lie face down with arms outstretched; *fig* fainted, dead.

dhépah physically short but wiry.

dhepaplang *var of* jepaplang.

dhépara, ndhépara *reg* unbelievable, nonsensical, absurd. *See also* dupara.

dhépé, 1 dhépé-dhépé 1 to sit huddled close to s.o.; 2 *fig* to attach o.s. to s.o. with an ulterior motive; 3 to flatter s.o. humbly with a certain hope.

dhèpèl, ndhèpèl to attach to; dhèpèl-dhèpèl to attach o.s. to s.o. with an ulterior motive.

dhepèpèl *var of* dhèpèl.

dhepèpès *var of* dhepis.

dhepès *var of* dhepis.

dhepipil, ndhepipil to sit lost in thought.

dhepipis *var of* dhepis.

dhepipit *var of* dhepis.

dhepis, ndhepis to sit huddled up; dhepas-dhepis to keep huddling up.

dhéplé *var of* dhèpèl.

dhèplèk *var of* dhèpèl.

dheplok, ndheplok to pound fine; dheplokan 1 s.t. pounded; 2 pestle.

dhepok, ndhepok *reg* to touch. *See also* gepok.

dhépok *or* padhépokan 1 camp, holy man's settlement; 2 a complex of communal housing; dhedhépok 1 to live in a camp; 2 to reside.

dhépor, ndhépor to sit on the bare floor (*var of* dhékor I).

dhéprok, ndhéprok to sit down wearily.

dhepus *or* lenga depus *reg* petroleum, kerosene (*var of* dhebus I).

dhèr boom! bang! dhar-dhèr *repr* repeated bangs or boomings.

dheradhog *var of* dherodhog.

dherak, ndherak *reg* to crowd around.

dherdheg, ndherdheg to shake, tremble.

dhéré young female chicken that has reached the age for reproducing (*var of* dhara).

dherek *see* dherak.

dhèrèk I, ndhèrèk 1 to accompany (*k.a. for* mèlu); 2 to obey, follow (*k.a. for* nurut, manut); ndhèrèkaké 1 to take s.o. (to), accompany, escort; 2 to have (a person) go to live with and be supported by s.o.; pandhèrèk follower, attendant, retainer. *See also* sadhèrèk. II, dhèrèk-dhèrèk in rows/ranks. III, dhèrèkan *reg* candlenut (*kr for* kemiri).

dherik a treeless mountain area.

dherodhog *repr* a triple knocking on the wooden puppet chest with a rapping hammer/mallet to give signals to the gamelan musicians. *See also* dhrodhog.

dherodhug *var of* dherodhog.

dherok, ndherok *reg* to sit doing nothing.

dherum, ndherum *reg* lying at ease (of cattle, *e.g.* while chewing the cud). *See also* jerum.

dhes *or* mak dhes *repr* punching, beating.

dhesak *var of* dhesek.

dheseg *see* dhesek.

dhesek, ndhesek 1 to push, shove; 2 to urge, insist;

ndhesekaké 1 to help s.o. push; 2 to urge on s.o.'s behalf;
kedhesek to get pushed;
dhesekan 1 a push, shove; 2 pressure, request;
dhesek-dhesekan to push each other, crowd each other aside.

dhesel, ndhesel to push (into);
ndheseli to push repeatedly (into);
ndheselaké to push s.t. (into);
dhesel-dheselan pushing each other, crowded.

dhèsèl *reg* limestone;
ndhèsèl lumpy, knobbly.

dhèsi *reg* tie (clothing).

dhesok dented.

dhestha 11th month of the Javanese agricultural calendar.

dhesthar headcloth (*k.i. for* iket, blangkon).

dhesthi *or* guna dhesthi a magic spell for doing harm to another (*see* guna II).

dhestrik administrative district.

dhesuk *var of* dhesak.

dhet *or* mak dhet *repr* pulling a fishing rod;
dhet-dhet *repr* normal heartbeats.

dhèthèng, ndhèthèng to walk with chest high and shoulders back.

dhéwé *ng*, piyambak *kr*, 1 oneself; 2 by oneself, alone; 3 the most (*superlative*);
ndhéwé by oneself;
ndhèwèki 1 to have s.t. all to oneself; 2 to go it alone;
ndhèwèkaké to isolate, keep apart;
dhèwèkan alone, by oneself;
dhéwé-dhéwé separately, (by) oneself, (each) his own.

dhèwèké *ng*, piyambakipun *kr*, panjenenganipun *k.i.* he, him; she, her (*3rd person pronoun*).

dhéwot *var of* dhiwut.

dhéwut, dhéwutan a certain grass.

dhéyal, kedhéyalan to stumble off.

dhéyé a certain locust-like insect.

dhèyèk, dhèyèk-dhèyèk hunched over, greatly burdened.

dhéyog (to walk) with a limp because one leg is shorter than the other.

dhéyos a small (Chinese) image of a deity (porcelain or soapstone).

dhéyot pimples or boils on the face.

dhi *adr* 1 younger sibling; 2 person younger than o.s. (*shtf of* adhi); - ajeng *adr* 1 younger sister; 2 younger female friend; 3 *adr* (one's) wife; -mas *adr* younger brother; younger male friend.

dhidhal to become detached, lose the outer layer, be peeled off.

dhidhèh *see* dhidhih.

dhidhih congealed animal blood (used as a food).

dhidhik, ndhidhik to educate, train;
dhidhikan that which has been learned;
pandhidhikan (formal) education.

dhidhil reduced (debt).

dhidhis to remove lice from the hair;
ndhidhisi to delouse s.o.

dhidhong, Dutchman. *See* Landa.

dhigul, ndhigulaké to banish s.o. to Digul (in West Irian).

dhihik 1 *reg* formerly; 2 (at) first (*var of* dhisik).

dhihin *lit* (at) first.

dhik I *var of* dhi.
   II *or* dhikan, dhiké really, indeed (*var of* dhing); iya -; yes indeed; ora - not at all!
   III, ndhik in, at, on.
   IV when (past) *var of* dhèk.
   V *or* ndhik possession, belonging; -ku mine; -mu yours.

dhikné *var of* dhèwèké.

dhikep *var of* dekep.

dhiker, ndhiker firm, steady.

dhikih small and weak.

dhikik *reg var of* dhisik.

dhikir (to recite) a certain Islamic chant repeatedly;
ndhikiri to chant for a religious service;
dhikiran to hold a ceremony at which the above is chanted.

dhikté dictation;
  ndhikté to dictate.
dhikut in haste.
dhil I *or* **mak dhil** *repr* jerking s.t. loose.
  II, ndhil ½-cent coin (*var of* **bil**).
  III volume;
  dhil-dhilan in volumes (books).
dhileng to have an eye ailment or defect.
dhilit, sedhilit a very short moment.
dhilman two-wheeled horse-drawn passenger
  carriage.
dhiluk, sedhiluk a moment, a short while
  (*reg var of* **sedhéla**).
dhilut *var of* **dhiluk**.
dhimas *see* **dhi**.
dhimik I *reg var of* **dhisik**.
  II, dhimik-dhimik (to walk) slowly and
  silently, to tiptoe. *See also* **kethemek**,
  kethimik.
dhimin *reg var of* **dhisik**.
dhimpil I chipped at the edge.
  II name of one of the small playing-
  cards (*kertu cilik*).
dhin *or* **mak dhin** *repr* a horn honking.
dhindhal, ndhindhal *reg* to sell s.t. to raise
  money for repaying a debt.
dhindhing partition, wall.
dhines 1 employed, working in a certain
  office; **2** official; **3** according to the
  regulations.
dhing I *or* **dhingan** *particle emphasising
  preceding word:* it is so (in contrast to
  what was asserted) (*also* **dhik II**).
  II *reg var of* **sing**;
  dhang-dhing whoever, anybody;
  sadhing-dhingé anyone (at all).
dhinga *var of* **dhéngah**.
dhingan *see* **dhing**.
dhingdhing *reg* partition, wall (*var of*
  dhindhing).
dhingdhong *repr* the sound of a bell ringing.
dhingik *reg var of* **dhisik**.
dhingin *lit* first, formerly.
dhingkal, dhingkal-dhingkul to keep
  bowing the head.

dhingkel I a certain fatal chicken disease.
  II, kedhingkelan to exert o.s. to the
  utmost.
  III fireplace made from stones placed
  together, hearth.
  IV, ndhingkel to hang around the house
  all the time.
dhingklang crippled;
  kedhingklangan (to walk) with a limp.
dhingklik a low wooden stool or bench;
  dhingklikan 1 to use s.t. as a stool; **2** s.t.
  used as a stool.
dhingkluk, ndhingkluk to bow the head;
  kendhingkluken (to bow the head) too
  much.
dhingkruk, ndhingkruk with head bowed
  and shoulders drooping.
dhingkrung, ndhingkrung to lie curled up,
  lie with the knees drawn up to the chest.
dhingkul to bow the head;
  dhingkal-dhingkul to keep bowing the
  head.
dhipan wooden bedstead.
dhipet tightly closed (eyes); **merem** - to
  have the eyes closed tight;
  ndhipet 1 to close the eyes; **2** to sleep.
dhipik *coll* first; ahead (*var of* **dhisik**).
dhir a marble;
  dhir-dhiran to play marbles.
dhiri oneself; - **pribadi** one's identity.
dhis I military service; **mlebu** - enlisted.
  II, dhisé in spite of the fact that.
dhisik *ng*, **rumiyin** *kr*, **1** formerly,
  previously; **2** first (before doing s.t.
  else); **3** before, prior; **4** for the time
  being; **mengko** - wait a moment;
  ndhisiki to go ahead of, precede, pre-
  decease;
  ndhisikaké to give precedence or
  priority to;
  dhisik-dhisikan to race one another;
  kedhisikan to be preceded by;
  dhisiké at first, the first thing.
dhisin *reg* corpse, cadaver (*var of* **jisim**).
dhisit *reg var of* **dhisik**.

dhistrik administrative district. *See also* dhestrik.

dhit *coll* money (*var of* dhuwit).

dhithing, ndhithing finely dressed, carefully groomed.

dhiwut *or* dhiwut-dhiwut covered with hair, smooth and long fur.

dhiyem *reg* quiet, silent.

dho *or* ndho two.

dhobel double(d), duplicated.

dhobis 1 percussion cap; 2 caps (for toy guns).

dhoblé gold plating.

dhocang grated coconut mixed with soybean.

dhoceng (to walk) with unequal speed (*shtc of* kendho kenceng).

dhocèng uneven (work, mood).

dhodhèl, dhodhèl-dhodhèl badly torn.

dhodhèt, ndhodhèt to tear s.t. open and remove its insides. *See also* dhudhèt.

dhodhog, ndhodhog to knock on s.t.; ndhodhogi to knock repeatedly; dhodhogan *way* knocking sounds produced by a puppeteer with a rapping instrument (cempala) in various rhythms for various effects.

dhodhok, ndhodhok to squat, crouch; ndhodhoki to squat on; ndhodhokaké to have s.o. squat; dhodhok acung-acung to point out a house marked for burglary; dhodhok mungkur to squat with the back toward an exalted person (a former practice of servants as the King passed by). *See also* laku.

dhodhokérok a large green dragonfly.

dhodhos, ndhodhos to make a hole in the ground; ndhodhosi to put a hole through s.t.; dhodhosan hole, depression.

dhodhot, ndhodhot to watch from a concealed place.

dhog *or* mak dhog 1 *repr* a knock; 2 *repr* a recent arrival;

dhag-dhog *repr* pounding sounds.

dhogdhèng magically invulnerable. *See also* dhugdhèng.

dhogèr a street dance performed to music by one or more females.

dhogjèr to start up instantly (car engine). *Also* thokcèr.

dhogjur to come irregularly.

dhoglèg, dhoglèg-dhoglèg *repr* the sound of lumbering metal wheels.

dhoglèng eccentric, queer.

dhoglig *var of* dhaglig.

dhogling *var of* dhoglèng.

dhoglong *var of* dhoglèng; dhoglong-dhoglong physically thick and large, awkwardly built (woman's body).

dhogol I 1 young and hairless (bird, animal); 2 unclothed, undressed. II *cr* genitals.

dhograg wobbly, infirm, unstable, unsteady.

dhogrèg *var of* dhograg.

dhohan *see* tawon.

dhok *coll* 1 place where s.t. is usually to be found; 2 on, at, in; - kéné here, at this place; kadhokan to be included, get a place.

dhokar two-wheeled horse-drawn carriage.

dhokèr any tool used for scratching soil; ndhokèr *or* ndhokèri to scratch, claw at; dhokèr-dhokèr to claw earth.

dhokkur to squat with the back toward s.o. (*shtc from* dhodhok mungkur).

dhoklonyo eau-de-cologne.

dhoko, ndhoko to collapse.

dhokoh 1 greedy, voracious; 2 resolute, diligent.

dhokot *var of* dhokoh.

dhokur high, tall (*reg var of* dhuwur).

dhol worn out, damaged because of overuse.

dholar dollar.

dholog spar, log.

dhom 1 domino; 2 to play dominoes.

dhoman, dhoman-dhoman sitting and chatting together.

dhomas 800.

dhompèl *var of* dhomplèng.

dhompèt wallet, purse.

dhomplèng, ndhomplèng to content o.s. with a little space alongside s.o. else, double up. *See also* dhompèl.

dhompo wrong, mistaken (of wicker or basketwork; rhythmical dance movements *etc*).

dhompol bunch, cluster;
  ndhompol to form a cluster;
  (dhe)dhompolan in clusters (fruits);
  sadhompol a bunch (fruits).

dhompyok *var of* dhompol.

dhondhang container for transporting foods to be distributed.

dhong I 1 time when s.t. happens; 2 while (s.t. happens); 3 to be s.o.'s turn.
  II to understand.
  III *repr* tapping, pounding.
  IV in fact;
  dhongé the fact is.

dhongdhang *see* dhondhang.

dhongdhing 1 the fact about s.t.; 2 to matter; 3 vowel scheme of a classical verse form.

dhongdhong *reg* sometimes.

dhongglèng *repr* metal clanging.

dhongkah torn open;
  ndhongkah to tear open.

dhongkal *reg* torn out by the roots.

dhongkèl, ndhongkèl 1 to uproot, pry up/out; 2 *fig* to oust.

dhongkèr *var of* dhungkar.

dhongklak *var of* dhungklak.

dhongklèh broken off, cast down.

dhongkloh, dhongklok-dhongklok nearly severed.

dhongkok, ndhongkok *reg* to sit stooping.

dhongkol I *or* dhongkolan retired, resigned, ex-, former; lurah - former village head;
  ndhongkol to resign.
  II, ndhongkol to feel resentful.

dhongkrah, ndhongkrah *or* ndhongkrahi to pry s.t. out.

dhongkrak jack;
  ndhongkrak to jack s.t. up.

dhongkroh turning back and downward (buffalo horns).

dhongkrok, ndhongkrok to sit idle, remain motionless.

dhongkrong *var of* dhongkrok.

dhongoh thick and compact.

dhongok, ndhongok to lean forward;
  ndhongokaké to crane the neck to see.

dhongol, ndhongol to stick the head out, appear.

dhongsok, ndhongsok to push (against) s.t. (*var of* dhosok I);
  ndhongsokaké to push s.t. in a certain direction.

dhono, ndhono (*Yogya slang: var of* mrono).

dhop 1 top, cap; 2 hub-cap.

dhopèt wallet, purse (*reg var of* dhompèt).

dhopok, ndhopok *reg* to boast, tell tall tales.

dhoprok *var of* dhéprok.

dhor 1 *repr* sound of gunshot; 2 *repr* sound of drum; jaran - *reg* folk dance using a hobby-horse;
  ngedhor to shoot s.t.;
  dhor-dhoran gunfire.

dhorèng *or* dhorèng-dhorèng streaked, striped.

dhorit *reg* a certain sickle.

dhorong, ndhorong *or* ndhorongaké to push forward.

dhos *reg* finishing-line.

dhosin dozen.

dhoso, ndhoso angry.

dhosok I, ndhosok to push (against) s.t. *See also* dhongsok.
  II *see* jarwa.

dhosot, *reg var of* dhesek.

dhot I nipple, dummy;
  ngedhot to suck a nipple;
  ngedhoti to give (a baby) a nipple.
  II beep! toot!
  ngedhoti to toot the horn (at).

dhothong, ndhothong-ndhothong to carry a heavy object by hand together with many people.

dhothor, ndhothor to sit idle.

dhowah I, **ndhowah** *cr* to cry.
II **dhowah-dhowah** open wide.

dhowak *var of* **dhowah**.

dhowal, dhowal-dhowal 1 badly torn; 2 scattered about untidily.

dhowan *see* **tawon**.

dhowang *reg* only, no more than, nothing but.

dhowèk *var of* **dhowah**.

dhowèl *var of* **dhowal**.

dhoyok I a clown who wears a black mask.
II, **ndhoyok** to lean, list;
dhoyok-dhoyok to stagger, have difficulty walking.

dhoyong 1 slanting; 2 deviant, not standard;
ndhoyong to lean to, slant to.

dhradhag, ndhradhag to split open widely (walls).

dhradhas, dhradhasan to slink away secretly.

dhradhat, dhradhatan to receive a shock.

dhradhil, ndhradhil *or* **pating dhradhil** in shreds, ripped to pieces.

dhrakalan hastily, in great haste.

dhrandhang, ndhrandhang *intsfr* bright, clear, hot.

dhrawul, pating dhrawul disarranged, untidy. *See also* **dhawul**.

dhredheg, ndhredheg to shake, tremble (*var of* **dherdheg**).

dhredhet, ndhredhet to move with a jerk;
dhredhet-dhredhet *or* **dhredhat-dhredhet** to keep moving jerkily.

dhrèdhèt, ndhrèdhèt to shoot with a machine gun.

dhrèkèl, dhrèkèl-dhrèkèl *or* **dhrèkèlan** to have a hard time climbing s.t.

dhremplah, pating dhremplah 1 (of tree branches) broken and hanging; 2 (of clothing) tattered, in rags.

dhrèndhèng, ndhrèndhèng thundering (drums).

dhrèng *repr* drumbeats.

dhréngkol, pating dhréngkol drooping, bending downward (tree branches).

dhresel, ndhresel to attempt to intrude between. *See also* **dhesel**.

dhridhil *var of* **dhrindhil**.

dhridhis, ndhridhis to ask for things all the time without shame.

dhridhit *var of* **dhridhil**.

dhrindhil, ndhrindhil 1 to pour forth; 2 to talk continuously; 3 to have many children.

dhrodhog, ndhrodhog to shiver, tremble.

dhrodhos, ndhrodhos *or* **dhrodhosan** to push one's way through an overgrown area.

dhrudhul, ndhrudhul to pour forth.

dhrudhus *var of* **dhrodhos**.

dhrudhut, ndhrudhut 1 to shoot s.t. with a machine-gun; 2 to produce beeping sounds repeatedly.

dhrusul *var of* **dhresel**.

dhucung *see* **rebut**.

dhudha widower; - **bantat** childless widower; - **kawuk** elderly widower or divorcé; - **kembang** young widower or divorcé;
ndhudha to be left without a wife.

dhudhah, ndhudhah *or* **ndhudhahi** to open s.t. with the intention of removing the contents; to remove, withdraw;
dhudhah-dhudhah to keep opening things or removing the contents of things;
dhudhahan opened up and/or taken out;
pandhudhah (act of) opening/removing.

dhudhak a certain venomous snake (*shtf of* **bedhudhak**).

dhudhat *var of* **dhudhèt**.

dhudhèt, ndhudhèt to tear s.t. open and remove its insides.

dhudhuh, ndhudhuh to clean up the

193

ricefield after a harvest for planting another crop.

dhudhuk I, ndhudhuk to dig (up, out *etc*);
ndhudhuki to dig s.t. up/out;
dhudhukan 1 a dug hole; **2** act of digging;
pandhudhuk act of digging;
dhudhuk apus kependhem *prov* to dig into the forgotten past;
ndhudhuk perkara to rake up a past matter.

II, *reg* to sit; **angin** - internal 'wind' that can be fatal (*see also* **angin**); **dhudhuk bojo** legally married; **dhudhuk prèi** to live together out of matrimony; **lampu** - table lamp (*see also* **lampu I**).

dhudhul, ndhudhul to pour out in large numbers.

dhug *or* **mak dhug** *repr* knocking, pounding;
dhag-dhug *repr* knockings, poundings;
ngedhugaké to pound s.t. (against).

dhugal I bloating of the stomach.
II, ndhugal ill-mannered, badly behaved.

dhugdhag *var of* **dhugdhèng**.

dhugdhèng magically invulnerable.

dhugdhèr a certain folk festival.

dhugdhug *repr* repeating pounding;
ngedhugdhugaké to pound s.t. repeatedly (against).

dhugel charred firewood.

dhugul, dhugulan *reg* not dressed properly, not wearing a kris.

dhuh *excl* ouch! ow! (*shtf of* **adhuh**).

dhuhur *var of* **dhuwur**.

dhuk to descend (*root form: var of* **dhun**).

dhukir, ndhukir *or* **ndhukiri** to dig (around in).

dhuku a certain small round yellowish fruit.

dhukuh *ng*, **dhekah** *kr* small village, hamlet, cluster of houses;
dhedhukuh to found a new settlement;
padhukuhan area where a hamlet is located.

dhukun indigenous medical practitioner, healer, black magic practitioner; - **bayi** midwife; - **klenik** shaman who goes into a trance; - **mantèn** person who oversees marriage procedures; - **paès** one who makes up a bride; - **patah** chiropractor; - **pijet** masseur; - **sunat** man who performs circumcisions;
ndhukuni 1 to deliver (a baby); **2** to act as a healer for curing s.o.'s problem;
ndhukunaké to take s.o. to a shaman to get his problem cured; to undergo treatment by a healer;
me(r)dhukun to undergo treatment by a healer;
padhukunan indigenous medical knowledge.

dhukur *reg* tall, high (*var of* **dhuwur**).

dhul *or* **mak dhul** *repr* pushing the ball with the head.

dhulang round wooden tray.

dhumateng *see* **dhateng**.

dhumpak *var of* **dhupak**.

dhumpal wooden block used as a pillow or Quran reading-desk.

dhumpil, ndhumpil to live with others (free), live off;
ndhedhumpil to sit in a narrow space and crowding each other;
dhumpilan a narrow space where one can sit.

dhumpyuk indistinguishable.

dhun, ngedhuni 1 to descend from, get off; **2** to go lower than (price);
ngedhunaké 1 to lower, cause to descend; **2** unload, bring down;
sadhunan one load;
dhun-dhunan 1 things unloaded; **2** unloading-place; **3** a way down.

dhung *or* **mak dhung 1** *repr* striking a small gong or wooden drum; **2** *repr* an explosion.

dhungdhungprong *repr* pounding sound from a wooden trough (**lesung**).

dhungkah torn open;

ndhungkah to tear open.

dhungkar, ndhungkar to dig down to the roots (of).

dhungkèl var of dhongkèl.

dhungkir var of dhungkar.

dhungklak stump, esp of a cut bamboo stalk.

dhungklèh reg broken, hanging loose (branch).

dhungkrah, ndhungkrahi to pull out and scatter.

dhungkruk, ndhungkruk stooping, with bowed head and shoulders.

dhungkul curving low and downward to the rear (buffalo horns).

dhungsak, ndhungsak to make/push one's way through s.t.;
kedhungsakan or kedhungsak-dhungsak to experience great difficulties.

dhungsal, ndhungsal to stumble.

dhungsang var of dhungsak.

dhungsir, ndhungsiri to dig, root around in (soil).

dhunuk, dhunuk-dhunuk bent, esp with age;
dhunak-dhunuk unable to see clearly (because of poor vision or poor light).

dhupak a kick;
ndhupak to kick;
ndhupaki to kick repeatedly;
kedhupak to be kicked inadvertently;
dhupakan 1 a kick; 2 object kicked;
dhupak-dhupakan to kick each other.

dhur I continuing, going on through;
dhur-dhuran to continue on through.
II repr a heavy explosion;
dhar-dhur repeated explosions.

dhurlup a long passageway connecting the main part of a house with the annex.

dhurit a variety of sickle.

dhus carton, cardboard box.

dhusuk, ndhusuk reg nearly the same.

dhusun village, rural settlement (kr for désa).

dhuwak var of dhowak.

dhuwel I a certain small poisonous snake.
II, ndhuwel to stay at home all the time, remain indoors.

dhuwet a tree with dark blue fruit.

dhuwik reg money (var of dhuwit).

dhuwit ng, arta or yatra kr, money; - cring coins; - kertas paper money, bill; - pecah coins, small change; - putih coins, silver money; - rècèh or - cilik coins, small change;
ndhuwiti to pay for s.t.;
dhuwit-dhuwitan toy money, play money;
ora ndhuwit free of charge;
mata-dhuwiten overfond of money.

dhuwok reg a certain small earthenware platter.

dhuwung kris (kr for keris).

dhuwur ng, inggil kr, high, tall;
ndhuwur at the top, above;
ndhuwuri to make s.t. higher (with regard to s.t. else);
ndhuwuraké to make s.t. higher;
dhuwur-dhuwuran 1 to compare or compete for height; 2 comparative height;
kedhuwuren too high/tall, excessively high/tall;
pandhuwuran or dhedhuwuran people of high status;
sadhuwur-dhuwuré 1 no matter how high; 2 the highest possible;
dhuwur kukusé famous.

dhuyung dugong, sea-cow.

dibleg stubborn, obstinate (var of dableg).

dibya having supernatural power; magically empowered;
kadibyan invulnerability, supernatural power.

digdaya supernaturally powerful, magically invulnerable;
kadigdayan supernatural invulnerability, magical power.

digsura ill-mannered, badly behaved.

dika I, ndika you md.

II, **ndikakaké** *k.i. (pass)* to have received orders to. *See also* **andika, ngendika.**

dikara *lit* rank, position, status.

dikep *var of* **dekep.**

dikir *var of* **dhikir.**

dikné, ndikné if, in case.

diktya *lit* ogre, giant.

dilah lamp, lantern;
　dumilah bright, light.

dilalah, ndilalah by God's will, by chance.

dilat a lick;
　ndilat to lick;
　ndilati to lick s.t.;
　ndilat iduné dhéwé *prov* to go back on one's word.

dilem a certain plant with aromatic leaves.

dilep, ndilep to stay by o.s., not join in.

dilik, ndilik to see, look at, watch. *See also* **tilik.**

dilir, ndilir copious, abundant, non-stop (food offered to a guest).

dim a thumb, measure of length, = *ca* 1 inch or 2.5 cm.

diman *var of* **dimèn.**

dimar lamp, lantern.

dimek, ndimek to touch (*var of* **demek**).

dimèk *var of* **dimèn.**

dimèn in order to, so that.

dimer, ndimer *reg* headstrong, obstinate, stubborn.

dimik I 1 sulfur-tipped stick for kindling a fire with flame from another fire; **2** *reg* matches.
　II, **dimik-dimik** (to walk) slowly and silently, tiptoe. *See also* **dhimik.**

dimok *reg var of* **dimèn.**

dimon *reg var of* **dimèn.**

dina *ng*, **dinten** *kr*, day;
　sadina-dina day after day, every single day;
　padinan daily.

dinakara *lit* sun.

dinar golden coin.

dindang *reg* tree frog.

dingarèn it's unusual that…; how strange!

See also **kadingarèn.**

dingaryan *lit var of* **dingarèn.**

dingkik, ndingkik to keep watch secretly, lie in wait.

dinten day (*kr for* **dina**).

dipa *lit* **I** lamp.
　II island. *See also* **dwipa I.**

dipak *reg var of* **dimèn.**

dipaka *lit* elephant. *See also* **dwipaka.**

dipaké *see* **dipak.**

dipangga *lit* elephant. *See also* **dwipangga.**

dipara, ndipara impossible, out of the question (*var of* **dupara**).

dipati regent, ruler, sovereign (*shtf of* **adipati**).

dipatya *lit var of* **dipati.**

dipta *lit* beam, ray.

diptya *var of* **dipta.**

dir, ngedir-diraké to boast about.

dira *lit* courageous, bold.

dirada *lit* elephant. *See also* **dwirada.**

dirèn *reg* envious, jealous of each other.

dirga *lit* long.

dirgahayu long live! good fortune!

dirgama *lit* trouble, difficulty.

dirganca *lit* to quarrel, debate.

dirgantara *lit* the sky;
　ndirgantara to fly into the sky, up in the air.

dirham golden coin with Arabic script.

dité *lit* Sunday.

ditya *lit* ogre, giant.

diwangkara *lit* sun.

diwasa adult.

diwayah old (of age).

diweg *reg kr subst var of* **daweg I.**

diya, diya-diniya to quarrel.

diyan lamp, lantern.

diyat fine imposed for failure in one's religious duties.

diyer, ndiyer to keep doing bad things.

diyon vying for a job.

diyu *lit* (small) demon (*esp* female).

dladag, ndladag to flow swiftly.

dlajah, ndlajahi 1 to explore; **2** to wander

aimlessly in a place.

dlajat foreboding, presentiment, omen, indication;
ndlajati to indicate, foretell.

dlajeg, pating dlajeg (of people) to stand up rudely.

dlajid *var of* **dlajig**.

dlajig, dlajigan *or* **pating dlajig** to move about restlessly, fidget, lack repose.

dlalah *var of* **dilalah**.

dlamak, ndlamak to step barefooted;
dlamakan sole (of the foot).

dlamé, ndlamé raving, delirious.

dlamong, ndlamong to speak thoughtlessly or irresponsibly.

dlampu *reg* preferable, better than.

dlancang paper (*kr for* **dluwang**).

dlanggu *var of* **dlanggung**.

dlanggung road, street.

dlangkup *reg* cage-like tiger trap.

dlapak *reg var of* **dlamak**.

dlarèh, pating dlarèh streaked with red, *e.g.* scraped skin.

dlarung, ndlarung to get (too) far from, exceed the limits;
kedlarung(-dlarung) 1 to stray; **2** (when speaking) to get off the subject.

dlawèr, ndlawèr 1 to hang down too far; **2** to wander aimlessly.

dledeg, ndledeg to come together in great numbers.

dlèdèk, ndlèdèk to ooze, flow slowly.

dlèdèr, ndlèdèr *or* **dlèdèran** to swagger, show off (fine clothes, of a young man).

dlejeg *var of* **dlajeg**.

dlejer *var of* **dlajeg**.

dlélah, ndlélah 1 listless, disinclined to work; **2** inattentive, not keep one's attention focused.

dleleg, ndleleg to sit deep in thought.

dleles, ndleles used up before long.

dlélo *var of* **dlélah**.

dlemèk, pating dlemèk *or* **dlemèk-dlemèk** covered with spots of dirt.

dleming, ndleming raving, delirious.

dlemok *or* **dlemokan** spot, blemish, mark;
pating dlemok full with spots;
ndlemok to have/make a spot or stain;
ndlemoki to stain s.t.;
dlemok-cung shared out unequally.

dlemong *var of* **dlemok**.

dlendeng, ndlendeng to drip out continuously.

dlèndèng, ndlèndèng constantly pouring/flowing.

dlenjeg *var of* **dlejeg**.

dlenjet, ndlenjet to look for everywhere.

dlèngèr, ndlèngèr careless, inattentive.

dlepak *reg var of* **jlupak**.

dléré, dléra-dléré to throw avid glances at a man (woman).

dlèrèd, sadlèrèdan (at) a glance.

dlèrèng, I ndlèrèng *or* **dlèrèng-dlèrèng** marked with reddish streaks.
II sadlèrèngan a brief glimpse, a glance.
III ndlèrèng careless, inattentive.

dlèsèr, ndlèsèr 1 (moving) at a low altitude; **2** to stray, not keep one's attention focused.

dlèwèr *or* **mak dlèwèr** *repr* flowing;
ndlèwèr to ooze, drip, flow;
dlèwèran trickling out;
kedlèwèran to get dripped on.

dléya, ndléya to allow one's thoughts to stray from the matter at hand.

dléyor, dléyar-dléyor to walk unsteadily.

dlidir, ndlidir (of food served to a guest) copious, abundant; (of traffic) bumper-to-bumper.

dlijig, ndlijig smooth and good to drive on (road).

dligung, dligang-dligung undressed, shirtless (*var of* **bligung**).

dlika cross-beam (of bed, bridge).

dlima pomegranate.

dlinding, ndlinding *cr* to keep on shitting.

dlinges, kedlinges *reg* to get run over.

dlingo a medicinal plant, sweet flag or calamus.

dliring sugar-palm leaf (used for cigarettes).

dlodog, ndlodog I to have a fun-loving temperament.
II, **ndlodog** to pour out;
kedlodogen pouring too much.

dlodok *var of* **dlodog** II.

dlodor, ndlodor stubborn and ill-mannered.

dlohok, dlohak-dlohok to talk boorishly.

dlojor, ndlojor to slide down (long objects).

dlolé, ndlolé to hang down.

dlolèr, ndlolèr to protrude outward/downward.

dlolo, ndlolo (of eyes) wide open, bulging, boggling.

dlomok, ndlomok exaggerated;
ora ndlomok *excl* surprising.

dlondèng, ndlondèng lank, weedy, tall and slender (physique).

dlondong I *cr* child, offspring;
ndlondong *cr* to give birth.
II *cr* faeces.

dlondor, ndlondor insolent(ly), impudent(ly).

dlongèh, dlongah-dlongèh pleasing and having a good character (woman).

dlongop, ndlongop to hang open (mouth);
dlongap-dlongop to keep gaping.

dlonjor, ndlonjor to slide down (long objects).

dlonyok, dlonyak-dlonyok to behave in a crude way.

dlosor, ndlosor 1 to sprawl on the ground, flop down; 2 to humble o.s. excessively.

dludag I a kind of Javanese flag, a bamboo pole with narrow strip of cloth attached, without pennant. *Also* **daludag**. *See also* **umbul-umbul**.
II, **ndludag** to overflow.

dludug, ndludug 1 to resolve without fear; 2 to be resolute in one's attempt.

dludus, ndludus to keep asking impudently.

dlujur I 1 a straight path or track; 2 trunk, main stem;
ndlujur 1 straight; 2 to keep straight on

going; 3 rigid, unyielding.
II, **ndlujuri** 1 to stitch; 2 baste (a seam).

dlundèng *see* **dlondèng**.

dlupak *var of* **clupak**.

dlurek, ndlurek grim-faced, angry-looking.

dlurung *var of* **dlarung**.

dlusup, ndlusup to slip into concealment.

dlusur, ndlusur to slide along a surface;
pating dlusur swishing.

dluwang *ng*, **dlancang** *kr*, paper; -**kemplong** indigenous bark paper.

dluwèk, dluwak-dluwèk to grin, grimace, make wry faces (while speaking).

dluya *var of* **dléya**.

doblé, ndoblé (of the lower lip) thick and hanging down.

doblog, ndoblog to keep one's mouth shut.

doblong, ndoblong to boast, swank, brag.

dobol 1 bulging, worn out (so that the contents emerge); 2 prolapse of the rectum;
ndobol *cr* to shit.

doblèh *var of* **doblé**.

dobong I a large woven bamboo basket.
II a kiln for processing earthenware, bricks, lime.

dobos, ndobos to boast, brag, tell tall tales.

dodod *see* **dodot**.

dodok informer.

dodol I *ng*, **sadé** *kr*, to sell; - **bokong** to accept payment for occupying s.o.'s seat in order to hold it;
dodolan 1 act or way of selling; 2 to sell as a livelihood; to trade, sell merchandise. *See also* **adol**, **dol**.
II a confection made of sticky rice, coconut milk and palm sugar.

dodor, ndodor *or* **ndodoraké** to poke/prod (at), jab.

dodot *ng*, *kr*, **kampuh** *k.i.*, ceremonial batik garment with a train;
dodotan to put on or wear the above.

doh *ng*, **tebih** *kr*, far-off;
ngedoh to move far(ther) away from;
ngedohi to keep at a distance (from);
ngedohaké to keep s.t. at a distance.

doki *reg* let me see! (*shtf of* ndeloki).

dokok *var of* dèkèk.

dol *ng*, sadé *kr*, ngedol to sell;
ngedoli 1 to sell (many objects); 2 to sell (food) and serve it to the buyer;
ngedolaké to sell for s.o. (as middleman);
pangedol trade, selling;
pangedolan place where s.t. is sold;
dol-tinuku to buy and sell, do business.

dolan to relax;
ndolani to give s.o. s.t. to play with;
ndolanaké to give s.o. a good time;
dolan-dolan to go out to enjoy o.s.;
dolanan 1 to play a game; 2 game, pastime, source of amusement;
dolanan ula mandi *prov* 'to play with a venomous snake', to court danger, play with fire.

dolèk *reg var of* golèk.

doloh, *reg var of* dèlèh.

dolop detective;
ndolopi to spy on.

dom needle; - bundhel pin (with head);
ngedomi to insert a needle/pin into;
dom sumurup ing banyu *prov* stealthy, in secret; in disguise for the purpose of getting information.

domba I 1 a boss, the biggest in a group; 2 big, large;
ndombani 1 to keep an eye on; 2 to lead, be in charge of.
II sheep.

dombang *see* angin.

domblé *var of* doblé.

domblèh *var of* doblé.

domblo, ndomblo chubby-cheeked.

domblong, ndomblong open-mouthed in wonder, confusion, surprise.

dombong *see* apem.

domèl, ndomèl to whine and complain.

don *lit* 1 place; 2 aim, goal; tekan ing don to arrive at the place intended, to reach the end.

dondom sewing, stitching;

ndondomi to sew, stitch;
dondoman 1 sewn items, sewing to be done; 2 seam, stitch; suture.

dondon, ndondon *reg* to go and do s.t. somewhere regularly;
dondonan used regularly, daily.

donga a prayer (in Arabic);
ndonga to to recite a prayer;
ndongani to recite a prayer over (food, at ritual meal);
ndongakaké to pray for s.o.;
ndedonga to keep praying;
donga-dinonga to pray for each other;
pandonga prayer, act of praying.

dongèng fairy tale, legend;
ndongèng 1 to tell a tale; 2 to tell a falsehood;
ndongèngi to tell stories to;
ndongèngaké to narrate (stories *etc*);
dongèngan 1 myth, false story; 2 (various kind of) stories.

dongong, ndongong to stare open-mouthed.

dongos *or* ndongos (of upper teeth, upper lip) protruding.

donok, ndonok it's impossible!

donya the world;
kadonyan worldly things.

dopok, ndopok to boast.

dora (to tell) a lie; - cara *or* - sembada a cover-up lie.

doradasih *var of* daradasih.

doran handle of a certain agricultural tool (pacul).

dorès, ndorès *reg* to sit chatting.

dorèsa *reg* 1 sad; 2 it's a pity!

dos *kr, shtf of* dados.

dosa 1 sin; 2 sinful, guilty;
wong dedosan sinner;
pidosa *lit* sin.

dosok, ndosok *reg* to lie down.

dospundi how? (*kr, shtf of* kadospundi).

dowa *reg* prayer. *See also* donga.

dowèh, ndowèh hanging open (lower lip).

dowèr, ndowèr 1 *var of* dowèh; 2 to chat,

slander, speak ill.

doyan *ng, kr,* **kersa** *k.i.* to like, have a taste for;

ndoyani to want s.o. sexually;

doyanan 1 favourite food; **2** one who will eat anything.

drad the thread of a screw;

ngedradi to thread a screw, screw on.

drah a certain grass with fine leaves.

drajad 1 status, position; **2** degree of temperature;

kedrajadan to be raised, elevated, reach a high rank.

drajag, drajagan to behave impolitely, *esp* to enter s.o.'s house without first announcing one's presence.

drajak a fence of stakes.

drajat *see* **drajad**.

dragem chestnut, brown (colour of horse). *See also* **jragem**.

drana *lit* patient, calm, strong.

drap trot (horse);

ngedrap to trot.

drapon *lit* in order to; so that (*var of* **darapon**).

drawa *lit* **1** to melt; **2** melted, fluid.

drawalan excited, agitated.

drawas, ndrawasi 1 dangerous, harmful; **2** to endanger, threaten;

kedrawasan to have a misfortune or accident.

drawaya *var of* **drawa**.

drawili, ndrawili to talk constantly.

drawina *lit* feast, banquet (*shtf of* **andrawina**).

drawya *lit* to have, own.

drebya *var of* **drawya**.

dredah 1 to quarrel, dispute; **2** a quarrel.

drèdès, ndrèdès to water, well up (in the eyes).

drejeg, pating drejeg extending upward (s.t. long and spiky).

drèjès, ndrèjès to hiss, sputter, splutter (oil on fire).

drejet *var of* **drejeg**.

dreg *see* **udreg**.

drèg I two-wheeled horse-drawn cart.

II, drèg-drègan to behave boisterously.

dregil, ndregil enterprising, industrious, resourceful (*var of* **dergil**).

drèi screwdriver.

drèl military salute, salvo;

ngedrèl 1 to fire a salute (for); **2** *or* **ngedrèli** to fire many shots (at).

drema *var of* **derma**.

dreman *var of* **derman**.

dremba greedy.

drembombok *var of* **derbombok**.

dremi *var of* **dermi**.

dremimil *var of* **dermimil**.

dremis *var of* **dermis**.

dremolen merry-go-round.

dremunuh to covet others' belongings.

drèndès, ndrèndès messy, unable to manage.

drenjet, ndrenjet to look for s.t. everywhere (*var of* **dlenjet**).

dreng *var of* **dereng**.

dréngas, dréngas-drèngès to grin, grimace, make wry faces.

drènges, *see* **drèngas**.

drengki to wish s.o. ill, bear a grudge.

drereg, pating drereg *pl* to press, shove, jostle.

dres *lit, var of* **deres**.

dresel, ndresel 1 to sneak into; **2** to push one's way in near the front of a line.

drèwès, ndrèwès to drip, flow. *See also* **drèdès**.

drewya *var of* **drawya**.

dri *lit* mountain. *See also* **adri**.

dridhis, ndridhis to ask for things all the time without shame.

drig I, drig-drigan printed matter;

ngedrig to print (books *etc*);

ngedrigaké to have s.t. printed.

II, drig-drigan to behave boisterously.

drigama 1 danger; **2** dangerous hindrance or obstacle.

drigul a variety of bird.

driji, *ng, kr,* **racikan** *k.i.* finger, toe.

drijis, ndrijis *reg* 1 to covet others' belongings; 2 stingy, close-fisted.

dril drill (heavy cotton fabric).

drimolen *var of* dremolen.

dringin textile interwoven with gold threads for man's cummerbund.

dringo *var of* dlingo.

dringsem a certain very high tree.

driwili *see* drewili.

driya *lit* heart, feelings.

driyah charitable gift; dana - to give generously to help others;
ndriyahi to give charity to;
ndriyahaké to donate s.t.

drodos, ndrodos to pour forth, flow continuously.

drojog, ndrojog 1 steep(ly pitched); 2 to pour forth copiously.

drojos *see* drodos.

drohaka *see* druwaka.

drohi pleased with another's misfortune.

drohun *way, term of abuse*.

drokong, ndrokong to speak rudely.

drom, drom-droman (in the form of) a noisy mob.

dromblong, pating dromblong *pl* open-mouthed in wonder, confusion, surprise.

dromos, ndromos *reg* to beg charity all the time without shame.

dronjong, ndronjong steep;
dronjongan steeply sloping.

drop delivery, supply;
ngedrop 1 to deliver, drop off, unload; 2 to provide aid outside ordinary budget;
ngedropi to supply (a place) with s.t. essential;
drop-dropan dropping (of supplies *etc*).

drub trump (in card-playing).

drubiksa *lit* giant, ogre.

drudhul, ndrudhul to pour forth (*var of* dhrudhul).

drudhus, ndrudhus to push one's way through an overgrown area (*var of* dhrudhus).

drug, ngedrugaké to stamp (the foot).

druhaka *see* druwaka.

druju a shrub with white flowers, the branches used to ward off evil spirits.

drum I metal barrel, drum.
II, compatible.

druni *reg* frugal, thrifty.

druwaka 1 a sinful or treasonable act; 2 to sin, commit treason.

druweng, ndruweng obstinate, self-willed.

druwis, ndruwis to ask for things all the time without shame.

du *ng*, ben *kr*, ngedu to pit against each other.

dubang saliva reddened by chewing betel (*shtc from* idu abang).

dubilah *excl of surprise*.

dublag, ndublag to force-feed.

dubleg I, ndubleg steep, precipitous.
II, ndubleg silent and motionless.

dublong excrement;
ndublong *cr* to shit.

dubug swollen (of legs) because of leprosy.

dubur anus.

duding pointing-stick (*var of* tuding);
nduding to point out;
ndudingi to point at.

dudu I *ng*, sanès *kr*, 1 not, other than, different; 2 wrong, not as it should be; 3 no (*as an equative reply*).
II, kedudu-dudu incredible, extraordinary.

duduh I 1 juice, sap; 2 sauce, gravy.
II *var of* tuduh.

duduk I, nduduk to launch (an arrow).
II, nduduk to commute from (home), go back and forth in one day.
III, nduduki (of a singing bird) to have a good time for singing.
IV, duduken to suffer from a carbuncle.

dudul, ndudul to push s.t. into or out of.

dudur a wooden or bamboo pole used for supporting roof frame.

dudut, ndudut 1 to pull, pull out/away; 2 - ati to attract, appeal to;

nduduti to get taller (growing child);
dudutan 1 a pull, tug; **2** cord *etc* that is pulled; **3** conclusion.

duga *ng*, **dugi** *kr* - **prayoga** good judgement; - **rumeksa** to look after s.o.; - **watara** common sense;
duga-duga *or* **deduga** judgement, common sense;
nduga to guess;
nduga-nduga to try guessing;
keduga capable of (do)ing;
panduga assumption, guess;
ora duwé duga to act thoughtlessly.

dugang, ndugang *or* **ndugangi** to kick;
dugangan 1 act of kicking; **2** thing kicked; **bala** - unimportant team-mate (*see also* **bala**).

dugi I guess, estimate (*kr for* **duga**).
II to come (*md for* **teka**).

duging small locust (young of the **walang**).

duhkita *lit* **1** sad; **2** grief, sorrow, pain.

duk I black fibre from the trunk of the sugar-palm, used for rope, brooms *etc*.
II *lit* past; when (in the past).

duka 1 to be(come) angry (*k.i. for* **nesu, srengen**); **2** *or* **duka-dalem** I don't know (*k.a. for* **embuh**).

dukacipta *lit* grieving, sorrowful.

duksina *lit* south. *See also* **daksina**.

dukut *reg* grass.

dulang, ndulang to feed s.o.;
ndulangaké to put rice into s.o.'s mouth;
dulang-dulangan to feed each other (in a wedding ceremony);
dulangan the part of a wedding ceremony where the bride and the groom feed each other.

duleg, nduleg 1 to insert a finger into (s.t. soft, an opening); **2** overpowering (of tastes, odours).

duli *coll* to care, be concerned (*shtf of* **perduli**).

dulin *reg var of* **dolan**.

dulit amount taken on the fingertip;
ndulit to take on the fingertip;

sadulit a fingertipfull of s.t. soft.

dulkangidah 11th month of the Islamic calendar.

dulkijah 12th month of the Islamic calendar.

dulu looking;
ndulu *or* **andulu** *lit* to see, look at;
kadulu *or* **dinulu** to be seen;
pandulu sight, view;
sapandulu *or* **sapandulon** (at) a brief glimpse;
ala duluné inappropriate, unsuitable.

dulur *ng*, **dhèrèk** *kr*, relative of the same generation. *See also* **sedulur**.

dum, ngedum to share, distribute, apportion;
ngedumi to distribute (to, among);
ngedumaké to distribute s.t. to;
dum-duman portion, one's share;
keduman to be apportioned;
pandum 1 one's share; **2** one's lot in life;
panduman share.

dumadakan suddenly, unexpectedly. *See also* **dadak**.

dumadi *lit* to come into existence;
kang dumadi creation, living creatures, nature. *See also* **dadi**.

dumara *lit* deity;
kang dumara the deity, God.

dumbul *reg* the same, indistinguishable.

dumèh *var of* **dupèh**.

dumel, kedumelan to grumble with dissatisfaction within earshot of the offender.

dumeling clear and sweet (sounds).

dumil, sadumil a tiny bit, very few.

dumilah shining, bright. *See also* **dilah**.

dumlundung to give birth again and again.

dumugi (up) to, as far as, until (*kr for* **tekan, tutug**); to the end (*kr for* **tutug**);
kadumugèn to be brought about (*kr for* **ketekan**);
ndumugèkaken to accomplish, bring about (*kr for* **nekakaké**).

dumuh *reg* blind.

dumuk a mark or touch of the finger;
ndumuk to touch with the finger(s);

- irung 1 very close to, almost on top of; 2 pitch dark;

sadumuk bathuk sanyari bumi *prov* willing to lay down one's life for a woman or piece of land.

dumung a certain black snake.

duna dungkap *var of* tuna dungkap.

dundum to distribute.

dunga *see* donga.

dungik *lit* female servant of a priest.

dungis, ndungis too short on one side.

dungkap, ndungkap 1 (almost) to reach the point (that); 2 to be able to understand; sadungkapan menèh just a little bit more (to get there).

dunung 1 location, where s.t. is; 2 the fact of the matter; ora - *or* durung - to not understand/agree;

dedunung 1 located, situated; 2 to reside s.w.;

ndunungi to live s.w.;

ndunungaké 1 to put s.t. s.w.; 2 to explain, describe;

dumunung situated in, at;

kadunungan to be the repository of (an emotion, trait *etc*);

padunungan dwelling-place, place where s.t. is/belongs.

dupa incense;

ndupani to burn incense over s.t./s.o.;

padupan censer, thurible.

dupak *reg* earthenware lamp.

dupara *reg*, ndupara impossible, absurd. *See also* wayang.

dupèh, pèh just because (of the wrong reason); dupèh apa why on earth? *Also* dumèh.

dupi *lit* when (s.t. happened).

dur *lit* bad, evil.

dura *see* dora.

duracara ill-mannered, false.

duradasih *var of* daradasih.

duraka a sinful or treasonable act.

duratma *var of* duratmaka.

duratmaka 1 *lit* abductor; 2 thief.

durbiksa *var of* drubiksa.

durbus a certain cannon.

durcara bad-mannered.

durdah *excl* shoo!

duré *reg var of* dumèh.

durèk, ndurèk *reg* grim-faced, angry-looking.

durèn durian (tree and fruit).

durgama *lit* 1 danger; 2 dangerous obstacle.

durjana *lit* 1 thief; 2 evildoer.

durlaba *lit* difficult.

durlaksana *lit* ill-mannered.

durma a certain classical Javanese verse-form.

durmala *lit* ill-tempered.

durna cross stick in basketwork.

durnadur governor.

durniti *lit* 1 ill-mannered; 2 enemy.

dursila 1 criminal; 2 criminality.

durung *ng*, dèrèng *kr*, not yet; - sepiraa not so much; - suwé not long ago; - tau never; not yet ever;

durung-durung still not finished;

sadurungé before.

durus, kedurusan to come true, be fulfilled.

duryat good luck, fortune.

dus, ngedus 1 to clean s.t. ritually; 2 to gild (a metal object);

ngedusi to give s.o. a bath. *See also* adus.

duta *lit* messenger, courier; - pamungkas messenger with full mandate; - pang-lawung messenger bringing word of a death;

nduta to send s.o. as a messenger.

duwa, nduwa 1 to push (against, off, away); 2 to resist, defy, stand up to.

duwaja *var of* dwaja.

duwara *var of* dwara.

duwé *or* nduwé *ng*, gadhah *kr*, kagungan *k.i.* to have, own; - gawé to hold a celebration, *esp* a marriage or circumcision; - perlu to have a problem to be solved; - rembug to bring s.t. up for discussion; sing - the owner;

nduwèni to have, get possession of;

demuwé *or* dumuwé to take good care of one's possessions;

duwèn-duwèn to own things;

sing duwé omah the host, hostess;

wong ora duwé a poor person, a have-not.

duwèk *ng*, gadhahan *kr*, kagungan *k.i.* 1 the possession (of); 2 belonging (to); duwèkku mine;

duwèkmu yours.

duwung I rather than, it would be better if (*var of* luwung).

II, keduwung remorseful.

dwaja *lit* flag, emblem.

dwara *lit* door, gate.

dwi *lit* two; - lingga *gram* doubled root; - lingga salin swara *gram* doubled root with vowel variation; -purwa *gram* reduplication; - tunggal inseparable; two in one; - warna the Indonesian flag, the Red and White; -wasana *gram* reduplication of final syllable.

dwija *lit* spiritual teacher, holy man.

dwijawara *lit* greatly revered holy man.

dwipa I *lit* island; Jawa- the island of Java. II *lit* elephant.

dwipangga *lit* elephant.

dwipantara Indonesia(n Archipelago).

dwirada *lit* elephant.

dyah *lit* noble lady, princess.

dyaksa *lit* 1 skilled, intelligent; 2 a judge.

dyan *title applied to male royal descendants. See also* radèn.

dyatmika *var of* jatmika.

E

é *emphatic particle*; bingung é aku I didn't know *what* to do! See also jé II and jaré.

éba 1 *lit* fine, beautiful, good; 2 how... (*see also* iba, méndah).

ebab *see* bab.

ébah to move (*kr for* obah).

ebak *see* bak II, kebak.

eban *see* ban.

ebang *see* bang III.

ébar, ngébaraké to make a display of, to show s.t. publicly. *See also* kébar.

ébat, marvellous, excellent;

ngébat-ébati wonderful, miraculous. *See also* hébat, édab.

èbèg 1 decorative saddle lining; 2 a village dance using a woven bamboo hobby-horse.

ebek *see* kebek.

èbek 1 full; 2 full of cares;

ngèbeki to fill;

kèbekan full of.

ebèng *see* bèng.

èbèr, ngèbèr *or* ngèbèraké to sell goods taken from the supplier;

èbèran merchandise which the seller has taken on credit from the supplier.

èbi tiny shrimp dried and salted.

eblad *see* blad.

eblak *see* blak I, II.

ebleg *see* bleg.

èblèg a folk dance (*var of* èbèg).

ebleng *see* bleng.

ebles *see* bles.

éblis devil, evil spirit. *See also* iblis.

ebod *see* bod.

ébor long-handled scoop;

ngébori to irrigate with water by using long-handled scoop;

ngébor-ébori to hold a ceremony for (a woman in the third month of pregnancy).

ébra, ngébrakaké 1 to allow s.t. to expire; 2 to fail to carry s.t. out; to cancel.

ébrah *reg* looking good, well-dressed.

èbrèk, ngèbrèk to rip to pieces.

ebuh *see* buh III.

ebuk *see* buk.

ebun *see* bun.

ebut *see* but.

ebyar *see* byar.

èbyèk *or* èbyèk-èbyèk 1 noisy (talk); talkative; 2 very busy, tied up. *See also* èpyèk.

éca tasty, delicious; pleasing to the senses (*kr for* énak).

écak *reg var of* icak, idak.

écé I 10-cent coin (used formerly).

II, ngécé to make fun of, tease.

ecèh *see* cèh.

ècèk, ngècèk to challenge, threaten with words.

ècèr I, ngècèr to buy/sell in small amounts; ngècèraké to sell (merchandise) retail; ècèran retail, price of single item.

II, ngècèri to give a small amount to; ngècèraké to cause s.t. to be scattered; ngècèr-ècèr to scatter, strew, spatter; kècèr 1 scattered; 2 to get left behind; kècèran 1 s.t. left behind in a small amount; 2 to get s.t. left behind in a small amount.

ecu I measure of length: a distance between the tip of the stretched thumb and the edge of the fist.

II a certain children's game.

édab, ngédab-édabi wonderful, miraculous.

édah *var of* idah.

édan 1 mad, crazy; 2 wild, inspiring strong emotion; - taun to feign madness habitually;

- kewarisan in a crazy manner habitually;

ngédan to feign madness;

ngédani to cause to be madly in love;

ngédanaké to call or consider s.o. crazy;

kédanan crazy (about);

édan-édanan 1 in a crazy manner; 2 the clowns at a royal wedding.

édang-édong to have difficulty walking prior to giving birth.

édé, ngédé-édé to mock, deride, jeer at.

edhag, ngedhag-edhag to lie exposed, in the open;

ngedhag-edhagaké to leave s.t. out in the open.

édhang each, apiece; siji - one (for) each. *Also* édhing.

édhar, ngédhari to circularise;

ngédharaké to circulate (a written message);

édharan circular.

édhar-édhor 1 loose and ill-fitting (of clothing); 2 flabby. *See also* édhor.

èdhèg shaking legs while sitting;

èdhèg-èdhèg to clatter, chatter, clack.

èdhèl to rip, to be torn;

ngèdhèl to rip s.t. open.

édhelèr member of the Council of the Indies.

èdhèng, ngèdhèng to display;

ngèdhèngaké to show s.t. to everyone.

èdhèr, ngèdhèr-èdhèr to leave s.t. lying around conspicuously.

édhing *var of* édhang.

édhor, édhor-édhor *or* édhar-édhor 1 flabby, loose, without stiffness; 2 (of clothing) too large.

édhos *reg* nice, delicious; pleasurable, comfortable.

édhul *reg var of* èdhos.

édhum shady; sheltered;

ngédhum to take shelter from sun, rain.

èdi beautiful (*var of* adi); - pèni beautiful and valuable.

egah averse (to);

egah-egahan leisurely, unhurried. *See also* wegah.

ègal-égol shaky, wobbly, unsteady, unstable. *See also* égol.

egas *see* gas I.

ègèng, ngègèng to walk with difficulty;

égang-ègèng to have difficulty walking.

égik *reg* still, (even) now; remaining (in a certain condition); to be or keep on (do)ing.

égla, ngégla in plain sight, clearly visible.

églé *var of* **égla**.

èglèh *var of* **égla**.

èglèng *var of* **égla**.

égol, égal-égol shaky, wobbly, unsteady, unstable;

ngégolaké to move s.t. from side to side; sway s.t.;

mégal-mégol to walk and moving the hips from side to side;

égolan (to walk) swaying the hips.

égos, mégos to one side; askew; slantwise (rather than straight across);

ngégosaké to avoid s.t by turning aside.

égot I *reg* chief of a group.

II, *var of* **égol**.

égrah-égroh not very particular about dressing.

égrang stilts;

égrang-égrangan to use stilts, walk on stilts.

ègrèk flimsy (*var of* **èkrèk**).

égroh *see* **égrah**.

éguh *or* **pangiguh** instigation, effort, exertion;

ngéguhaké to exert one's efforts toward s.t. *See also* **iguh**.

égung, mégung placed randomly this way and that;

ngégungaké to place (things) in a disorderly or uneven line.

èh *excl of disgust, rejection.*

éhé 2nd year in the **windu** cycle.

ehem 1 ahem (*self-conscious cough*); 2 *excl of criticism, ridicule.*

eja, ngeja to wish, want to be.

éja *or* **éjan** spelling;

ngéja to spell.

éjawantah, (ma)ngéjawantah *lit* (of deities) to take form, become visible.

èjèg 1 to jog, run with small steps; 2 to keep saying/asking s.t.;

ngèjèg 1 to jog; 2 to keep dropping in;

èjèg-èlèr to say/ask again and again.

èjèk *reg var of* **ajak**.

èjèt *reg* nice, delicious, pleasant.

ejib, ngejibaké to rely (only) on; to put too much faith in.

èjlèg, ngèjlèg to keep moving along without paying attention to distractions;

èjlèg-èwèr to keep going back and forth (in and out, up and down).

éjrah I *reg* 1 consideration, calculation; 2 plan, intention, aim;

ngéjrah(-éjrah) to consider, calculate.

II Islamic era (*var of* **hijrah**).

èjrèt *reg* nice, delicious.

èk-èk *chld* to do a pooh.

éka I *lit* one;

ékan the units digit in a number.

II, ngéka-éka to think over, plan in advance.

ékadasa planning;

ngékadasa to plan.

ékah, ékah-èkèh (to walk) with the legs far apart.

ékakapti agreement;

saékakapti *or* **saékacipta** *or* **saékaprana** in agreement; a joint effort.

ékapada to sit with the legs close together (in meditation).

ékapraya cooperation;

saékapraya in cooperation for a common goal; a joint effort.

ékar (of legs) crooked, lopsided; (to walk) with a limp.

èkèg, ngèkèg-èkèg to cut (meat) with a blunt knife; to saw away at.

èkèh *see* **ékah**.

èkèk *var of* **èkèg**.

èkèl, èkèl-èkèl short and stocky (of physique).

èkèr I 1 restless; 2 **èkèr-èkèran** to altercate, argue, quarrel.

II, ngèkèr to scratch or claw at;

èkèr-èkèran scratch marks.

èket, èketan by 50s; 50 at a time. *See also* **sèket**.

éklas accepting, unaffected by loss;
  ngéklasaké 1 to accept s.t. with resignation; **2** to give up s.t. freely, to sacrifice s.t. for a cause. *See also* **iklas**.

èklèk sent by s.o. to and fro without rest.

ékoh, ékah-ékoh *or* **mékah-mékoh** (to walk) with legs far apart.

ékrak 1 bamboo dust pan (*also* **ikrak**); **2** bamboo stretcher.

ékral *var of* **ékrar**.

ékrar statement of guiding principles; to draw up a platform;
  ngékraraké to draw up a statement of guiding principles. *Also* **ikrar**.

èkrèk, èkrèk-èkrèk flimsy, poorly constructed.

ekrok, mekrok spread out, unfolded; (of flower) in bloom;
  ngekrokaké to spread s.t. open; to ruffle out.

ékrok, ékrak-ékrok unsteady, loose in the joints.

èksi *lit* eye;
  ngèksi to see, look at;
  k(a)èksi visible, in sight;
  pangèksi vision, sight;
  Ngèksiganda *lit* a name of the kingdom of Mataram.

ela-ela, ngela-ela to care about.

éla-èlu to do what others are doing, go along with the crowd.

elak *see* **lak**.

élar, élar-élur to march in a long procession.

eleb *see* **leb II**.

elèb *see* **lèb**.

èlèd, sticking out the tongue;
  ngèlèdaké to stick the tongue out;
  mèlèd (of tongue) sticking out;
  mèlèd-mèlèd to keep sticking the tongue out.

eleg *see* **leg**.

èlèk bad, ugly (*inf var of* **ala**);
  ngèlèk-èlèk to talk badly about s.o. behind their back;

ngèlèk-èlèki to make s.t. bad looking;
  èlèk-èlèkan of inferior quality.

èlèng, mèlèng to deviate from the straight-and-narrow;
  mèlèngan to have a tendency to break the rules.

elèp *see* **lèp**.

èlèr *see* **lèr II**.

èles *see* **iles II**.

èlèt *see* **èlèd**.

elho *see* **lo I, lho**.

elik *see* **ngelik**.

élik, ngélikaké 1 to warn; **2** to forbid;
  élik-élik to warn s.o.

éling *ng*, **ènget** *or* **émut** *kr*, **1** to remember, bear in mind; **élinga marang pati** remember Death; **2** to regain consciousness; **ora éling** unconscious; to lose consciousness;
  éling-éling in the light of;
  ngélingi considering, in the light of;
  ngélingaké 1 to remind, make s.o. think about s.t.; **2** to warn, admonish;
  ngéling-éling to remember, keep in mind;
  kèlingan to recall, think back to;
  élingan to have a good memory;
  éling-élingan to remember only vaguely;
  pangéling-éling 1 a reminder; **2** s.t. that should be kept in mind;
  saélingé all that one remembers; as far as one can remember.
  See also **péling**.

èlmi *kr for* **èlmu**.

èlmu *ng*, **èlmi** *kr*, knowledge, science. *See also* **ngèlmu**.

elo *see* **lo II**.

élo ell (measure of length: *ca* 0.688 metres = *ca* 45 inches);
  élon by the ell;
  ngéloni to measure (fabric) in ells.

élok out of the ordinary, marvellous, miraculous;
  ngélok-éloki strange; to act strangely;
  kaélokan a miracle, a wonder.

èlu to accompany (*childish var of* mèlu);

ngéloni to go along with s.o. as a companion;

ngélokaké 1 to have s.o. live with and be supported by (s.o.); 2 to include s.o. in the company, allow s.o. to join in;

mèlu *ng*, tumut *kr*, ndhèrèk *k.i.* to accompany, follow;

mèlu-mèlu to follow, go along with;

kèlu to be carried along (with);

éla-èlu to do what others are doing, go along with the crowd;

élon-élonen 1 to tag along with people habitually; 2 to side with s.o. in an argument. *See also* ilu II.

elur *var of* élur.

élur earthworm;

ngélur resembling a worm.

émah, émah-émah to marry, have one's own home (*kr for* omah-omah).

emak 1 mother, mum (*var of* embok); 2 maidservant who takes care of the children.

éman 1 (*or* éman-éman) unfortunate, regrettable; to regret; 2 to care about;

ngéman 1 to care about, have concern for; to cherish, care for deeply; 2 to respect, spare;

émané unfortunately; what a pity.

emas *see* mas.

émba, ngémba to do an imitation of;

ngémba-émba to do one's best to mimic;

mémba like, resembling;

mémba-mémba to pretend (to be).

embag *see* embeg.

embah *ng, kr* éyang *k.i.* 1 grandparent; 2 *adr* old man; old woman; - kakung grandfather; - putri grandmother; - buyut great grandparent;

ngembah to call s.o., or regard s.o., as one's own grandparent.

émbal *or* émbalan compensation of services.

emban nursemaid; mbok - an old nursemaid; - cindhé a child-carrying shawl of fine soft material;

ngemban 1 to carry a child in a shawl on one's chest; 2 to carry out (a task), execute, perform;

ngembani 1 to serve as a nursemaid to/for; 2 to serve as s.o.'s supervisor;

ngembanaké to carry a child for s.o.;

embanan *or* emban-emban batik shawl for carrying a child slung from the shoulder;

emban-embanan *or* embanan child or s.t. being carried in a shawl;

emban cindhé emban siladan *prov* to play favourites; biased, partial.

embang *reg* side, direction; - kidul to the south.

embat 1 timberwork on a bridge, dam; 2 bouncing;

ngembat 1 to bounce; 2 to align (a spear, arrow) with the target before releasing it; 3 to heft (a carrying-pole load) to test whether it is too heavy; 4 to mull s.t. over, consider s.t.; 5 to manipulate;

membat springy; to bounce;

embatan carrying-pole;

embat-embatan *or* mbat-mbatan balancing, consideration.

embeg *or* embeg-embeg swampy land, marshland.

embek, ngembek to have plenty, piles of s.t.

embèk 1 goat or sheep's bleat; 2 *excl conceding defeat in a contest*;

ngembèk 1 to bleat; 2 to call 'chicken!'; 3 to follow like sheep;

embak-embèk to keep bleating;

embèk-embèkan to wrestle with the rule that one cedes by saying embèk.

embel *or* embel-embel swamp, marsh;

ngembel to be(come) swampy;

kembel to get stuck in a muddy place.

èmbèl, èmbèl-èmbèl a small addition, postscript;

ngèmbèl-èmbèli to add a little something to.

embèn the day after tomorrow;

embèn buri later on; at some future time.

èmbèr pail, bucket.

embes, ngembes 1 to ooze, seep; 2 covered with condensed moisture; 3 soggy, sodden;

embes-embesan 1 water that has soaked into soil; 2 extra earning from an unrevealed source.

èmbèt, ngèmbèt or ngèmbèt-èmbèt to involve/incriminate s.o.;

kèmbèt to get involved or incriminated.

embil *expression with which children lay claim to s.t.*;

ngembil to pick, choose.

embing I side, direction.

II, embing-embing or mbing-mbing placenta.

emblèg chunk, wad, mass;

ngemblèg-emblèg to form into wads; to heap into mounds;

emblèg-emblègan in the form of chunks or lumps; swollen and lumpy.

èmblèg see emblèg.

emblog roll, bolt (of fabric);

ngemblog to apply thickly;

emblog-emblogan 1 in large quantities; extensive; 2 in rolls; by the roll.

embok mother, mum;

ngembok to call s.o., or regard s.o. as one's mother. *Also* bok, mbok.

embong *reg var of* embok.

émbong *reg* road, street.

émbrat *reg* 1 watering-can; 2 roadworker.

èmbrèh 1 sweeping the ground (of excessively long clothing); 2 having a clean or neat appearance; 3 having enough for one's needs; not poor and not rich;

ngèmbrèh sweeping the ground (of long clothing).

embrèt *see* èmbrèt.

èmbrèt *reg* worker who is paid by the day;

ngèmbrèt to travel at low cost in a carriage hired by a group;

ngèmbrètaké to hire work done by the day.

embuh *or* mbuh *ng*, kilap *kr*, duka *k.a.* I don't know; I'm not sure;

ngembuhi to say 'I don't know' to;

mbuh-mbuhan dubious;

embah-embuh to keep saying 'I don't know'.

embun I dew. *See* bun.

II, ngembun 1 to have (s.t) on top of the head or at the very top; 2 to accept respectfully;

embun-embunan *ng, kr,* pasundhulan *k.i.* fontanel, crown of the head, highest part of s.t.;

pangembun that which is respectfully accepted.

embur, embur-embur *or* ngembur-ngembur soft and spongy. *See also* gembur.

embut, membut soft, mushy;

ngembut-embut to soften (fruit) by pounding to release the juices inside;

embut-embutan (fruits) softened by pounding as above.

embyah, ngembyah *or* ngembyah-embyah 1 plentiful, abundant, generous; 2 to try first one then another.

embyang dry grass used as kindling material (*var of* ambyang).

èmèm *reg* in order to, so that (*var of* mèn).

emen, ngemen-emenaké to consider urgent, take seriously.

emèn *see* mèn, bèn.

èmèn, ngèmèn *reg* to give.

emèng *see* mèng.

èmeng 1 bewildered; 2 sad (*k.i. for* susah).

emi, ngemi-emi to take solicitous care of.

emin *see* min.

émod *reg* soft under the skin (fruit).

emoh unwilling, to not want to;

ngemohi 1 to be such that one gets sick of it; 2 to have enough of s.t.; 3 to say 'emoh!' to, refuse.

emok, ngemok-mok to keep fingering s.t.

See also **demok**, **demèk**.

émor *reg* soft, mushy (of fruits).

empak, **ngempakaké** 1 to ignite, inflame; 2 to apply s.t. to.

empal slices of spiced meat fried in coconut oil;

empal-empalan in heaps (swarming ants).

empan 1 place, function; **- papan** the appropriate circumstances, the right time and place; 2 s.t. used for igniting; 3 effective for its purpose;

ngempani to feed (*reg var of* **makani**);

ngempanaké to light (a smoke);

mempan effective;

empan-empanan wick or tinder for igniting.

émpang *reg* garden pond with fish.

èmpèd *reg* a variety of small crab.

èmpèh *reg* 1 not too expensive; 2 not too steep.

empèk, **ngempèk** to ask if one may share;

ngempèk-empèk to plead (for).

empel *see* **ampel**.

empèng, **ngempèng** 1 to suck; 2 to have one's baby suckled by s.o. else;

ngempèngi to suckle s.o. else's baby.

èmpèng light (not heavy) (*var of* **ampang**).

èmper resemblance;

ngèmperi to resemble s.t.;

ngèmperaké to cause to resemble;

ngèmper-èmper to compare for resemblances;

mèmper 1 to resemble; 2 to be expected, appropriate, not surprising;

èmper-èmperan to resemble each other;

èmperé it seems (as if).

èmpèr *or* **èmpèran** 1 verandah, porch; 2 overhang, awning.

empet *see* **ampet**.

empèt, **empèt-empètan** crowded, jammed.

èmpèt *see* **èmpèd**.

emping chips made from **mlinjo** fruits, pounded, dried and fried;

ngemping 1 to make chips as above; 2 to

lease (farm land); 3 to request payment before the job is completed;

ngempingi to pay land rental to (s.o.);

kumemping nearly ripe, *i.e.* just at the right stage for making chips;

ngemping lara nggénjah pati *prov* looking for danger or trouble.

émplag, **émplag-émplag** to have difficulty walking because of obesity.

emplah, **ngemplah-emplah** 1 (to have) a large torn place; 2 a broad treeless plain.

emplak, **ngemplak-emplak** (of plain) large and treeless with soil too poor to cultivate.

emplang, **ngemplang** 1 to fail to pay one's debts; 2 to open s.t. wide.

émplas trivial, insignificant.

emplèk sheet, layer;

emplèk-emplèkan forming sheets/layers;

emplèk-emplèk ketepu a children's hand-clapping and singing game.

emplèng *var of* **emplèk**.

emplep, **ngemplep** to gain or retain possession of s.t. selfishly or dishonestly.

emplok, **ngemplok** *or* **ngemploki** to put (food) into the mouth;

saemplokan one mouthful.

émplok *var of* **amplok**.

emplong *var of* **emplang**.

èmplop *var of* **amplop**.

empluk covered earthenware food container.

empok, **ngempok** *or* **ngempoki** 1 to release wind; 2 to get a whiff of s.t.; 3 to play a joke on s.o.

émpok *reg var of* **ampok**.

empot, **ngempot** to draw on (a cigarette);

empot-empotan *reg* sensation of rapid heartbeat (caused by fear, anxiety *etc*).

emprah, **ngemprah** (to do) in a careless or slipshod fashion;

emprah-emprahan dropped or scattered in disarray.

émprak certain Arabian style of dance accompanied by music.

emprèt trumpeting of an elephant;
ngemprèt (of elephant) to trumpet.

emprit a certain small honeyeater; - gantil a variety of the above bird; *fig* roof embellishment; - kaji a white-headed variety of the above bird.

emprok, ngemprok-emprok to launder (clothing) by pounding it against s.t.

empu I title of outstanding artist, poet, kris-maker.
II tuberous root used in medicines;
empon-empon, mpon-mpon medicinal tubers (in general).

empuk 1 soft (mattress *etc*); 2 tender, well-done (of food); 3 easy to defeat or cheat; 4 soft and pleasant (of voice, sounds); 5 *fig* unable to say no; to promise easily.

empun 1 don't (*md for* aja); 2 finished; already (*md for* wis).

empur, mempur pleasantly mealy in the centre (of cooked cassava, sweet potato).

empus, ngempus to blow on;
empusan bamboo section used for blowing on fire to make it burn hotter.

emput var of amput.

empyak 1 roof frame; 2 sheltering roof for young plants; - gajah central portion of a roof frame.

émyah var of èmyèh.

èmyèh insignificant, trivial;
ngèmyèhaké to consider inconsequential.

èmrèh *reg* insignificant, of little worth, trivial.

èmu soft, mushy from being handled (of fruits).

émut to remember (*kr for* éling).

enak, ngenak-enik to take care of all the necessary details. *See also* nak-nik.

énak *ng*, éca *kr*, tasty, delicious (of foods); comfortable (of senses); agreeable (of smell); pleasing, pleasant (of voice, sounds, seat);
ngénaki to give pleasure/comfort to;
ngénakaké 1 to make s.o. comfortable; 2 to make s.t. taste good/better;

ngénak-énak to take things easy; to be comfortable.

énang *subst kr for* onang I.

encak-enci to hesitate with indecision.

enceb, ngencebi *or* ngencebaké 1 to stick s.t. into; 2 to cling fast to.
See also tanceb.

encèh glass tube.

èncèk, ngèncèk-èncèk to carry s.t. heavy together.

èncèng diagonal direction;
ngèncèngaké to place diagonally opposite;
èncèng-èncèngan facing diagonally. *See also* pèncèng.

èncep *see* enceb.

èncèr 1 (of liquids) thin, weak; 2 mentally active;
ngèncèri to make (a liquid) much thinner (than it was);
ngèncèraké to make (a liquid) thin.

èncès, ngèncès to cut s.t. aslant;
ngèncèsaké to lay s.t. aslant.

encik I, ngenciki to stand on s.t.;
kencikan 1 to get stood (up) on; 2 to lengthen one's reach.
II, 1 *title of a full-blooded Arab*; 2 *adr* Chinese woman.

encim (Chinese) sister; *adr* Chinese woman.

encit, ngencit to suck;
encit-encitan 1 dummy; 2 squeaky rubber doll.

énclok, ngéncloki to alight on s.t.;
ngénclokaké to have/let (a creature) alight on s.t.;
kénclokan alighted on.

énco tasty, comfortable, pleasant (*reg var of* énak).

encod up-and-down movement of the feet;
ngencod to move the feet up and down on s.t.;
encod-encodan to keep moving the feet up and down.

éncok I rheumatism.
II var of énclok.

éncon team-mate, partner.

éncong, ngéncongaké to cause s.t. to be off-centre. *See also* péncong.

éncos, méncos 1 slantwise, crooked, lop-sided; 2 to twist the lips;
méncas-méncos to keep twisting the lips.

èncrèt *var of* incrit.

encrit *var of* incrit.

encung *reg* eggplant.

encup, ngencup 1 to catch with thumb and finger; 2 to guess (the answer to);
ngencupaké to catch as above for s.o. else.

éncup *var of* encup.

éndah beautiful, fine;
kaéndahan beauty, loveliness.

éndahané *or* édahanéya how strange it is!

endang *ng*, énggal *kr*, quick, soon; immediate.

endat, ngendat-endat bouncy, resilient;
mendat to rebound, bounce; spring;
mendat-mendat *or* mendat-mentul to bounce; springy.

endel *var of* andel.

èndel 1 act of stopping (*kr for* endheg *or* andheg); 2 quietness (*kr for* eneng).

endem *ng, kr,* wuru *k.i.* stupor caused by liquor or drugs;
ngendemi to get s.o. drunk/drugged;
mendem drunk, drugged;
mendemi intoxicating;
endem-endeman 1 intoxicating drinks; 2 to get drunk together.

endha, ngendhakaké to cause s.t. to subside;
mendha to subside.

éndha I to elude, dodge;
ngéndhani 1 to pull to one side avoid s.t.; 2 to avoid s.t.
II, méndha to imitate, look like.

éndhag *reg* clever, capable, skilful, fit.

endhak, mendhak to subside; to stoop;
ngendhakaké to cause to subside; to calm s.o. down;
mendhak-mendhak to stoop, duck;
mendhak mendhukul full of ups and downs; bumpy (of road).

éndhang I (grand)daughter of a holy man.
II *or* ngéndhangi to visit, call on s.o.

endhas 1 head (of an animal); 2 *cr* head (of human) (*see also* sirah);
ngendhasi-endhasi to make (a cricket) afraid to go out; *fig* to make s.o. ashamed to appear;
endhas-endhasan 1 locomotive; 2 the upper or front part of s.t.;
endhas gundhul dikepeti *prov* to make s.o. even more comfortable.

endhé, ngendhé-endhé to wait for a long time; to delay, put off, procrastinate (of paying debts).

endheg I *ng*, èndel *kr* stop;
ngendheg to stop;
ngendhegi to stop in (at);
ngendhegaké to stop;
endheg-endhegan place to stop, a pause.
II, endheg-endheg residue.

endhèg *var of* emblèg.

endhek short (*var of* cendhek, cendhak).

endhèk 1 low, close to the ground; 2 short in stature;
ngendhèki to lower o.s.;
ngendhèkaké to lower s.t.;
endhèk-endhèkan to do s.t. on a low scale;
endhèk èrèk-èrèk extremely short/low.

èndhèk *var of* endhèk.

endhem, ngendhem to conceal, keep hidden;
endhem-endheman 1 thing concealed; 2 mutual ill feelings.

endheng, ngendheng (people) in large numbers.

endhèp *see* èndhèp.

èndhèp *var of* andhap.

èndhèr, ngèndhèraké 1 to explain (*var of* andhar); 2 to reveal, disclose.

endhet, ngendhet 1 to keep s.t. to o.s.; 2 to take s.t. for o.s.

endhih, ngendhih 1 to beat, overcome; 2 to take over, preempt; 3 to take s.o.'s seat by pushing them;

kendhih to lose, get overpowered; pushed off the seat.

endhik in, at, on (*reg var of* **ing**).

endhog *ng,* **tigan** *kr,* egg; **- amun-amun** fog; **- ceplok** fried egg; **- dadar** omelette; **- kamal** salted duck egg; **- pindhang** egg salted (in the shell) with spices;

ngendhog to lay egg(s);

endhog-endhogan (to play) a children's game by piling fists on one child's back and then withdrawing them by turns;

endhogé si blorok 1 speckled hen's egg; **2** *fig* uncertain what to expect.

endhok *reg* in, at, on;

ngendhok to be in or to stay in. *See also* **andhok.**

éndhol, éndhol-éndhol a waddling gait; **méndhol-méndhol 1** to move with a waddling gait; **2** (of a chicken's crop) stuffed with feed; **3** (of bag or pocket) full of contents.

endhon, ngendhon to be/stay s.w.;

endhong, ngendhongi to apply (water) to; **ngendhongaké** to allow (land) to lie fallow.

éndhong I 1 a small container; **2** a quiver (for arrows).

II, ngéndhong to go visiting; **ngéndhongi** to visit s.o. (*var of* **ngéndhangi,** *see* **éndhang II**).

endhut mud, sediment;

ngendhut (to become) muddy; covered with sediment.

endi *ng,* **pundi** *kr,* **1** where? **2** which (one)?;

ngendi-endi everywhere, (in) every place; anywhere;

ngendi ana how could it be? impossible!

endika *see* **andika, ngendika.**

endip, endip-endip frail, sickly, nearing death.

endon end, goal. *See also* **don.**

éndra *lit* **1** king; **2** Indra, king of the gods; **kaéndran** the realm of the gods, heaven.

éndracapa *lit* rainbow.

éndrajala *lit* a trick, stratagem;

mangéndrajala to practise trickery.

éndrak a gum disease.

éndralaya *lit* the realm of the gods.

éndrasara *lit* a ruse, trickery.

éndrawila *lit* blue diamond.

endut, endut-endut *or* **mendut-mendut** *or* **mendat-mendut** bouncy, springy;

ngendut-endutaké to make s.t. springy.

ènèh *var of* **wènèh.**

enek, nek sick, nauseated; **ngenek-eneki** sickening, nauseating.

ènek *var of* **ana.**

ènèk *inf var of* **ana.**

ènèl, ngènèl to hurry along;

ènèl-ènèl in a hurry.

eneng, neng stillness, inner calm;

meneng 1 to say nothing, be silent; **2** to do nothing, be motionless;

ngenengaké 1 to ignore, disregard; **2** to keep quiet about, hush s.t. up;

ngeneng-enengi to comfort, hush (crying child);

neng-nengan to ignore each other, not be on speaking terms.

ènèng *var of* **ana.**

ener, ner direction (straight to the goal);

ngener to head straight for;

ngeneraké to direct s.t. straight in the direction of. *See also* **pener.**

enes, nes deep sorrow;

ngenes deeply grieved;

ngenes-enesi to cause deep sorrow.

enet, ngenet to press, compress, squeeze. *See also* **penet.**

ènèt *var of* **nyèt.**

eng *excl* er... um!

enga, ngengakaké to open (*e.g.* door, window). *See also* **wenga.**

èngèh, èngèh-èngèh to distribute, give away;

ngèngèhi to leave food;

ngèngèhaké to leave food for s.o. else;

ngèngèhan remains, food left.

èngèk, èngèk-èngèk *repr* playing a stringed instrument;

ngèngèk-èngèk 1 to saw away at (a stringed instrument); 2 to cut with difficulty with a blunt knife.

èngès, ngèngès to cut off at an angle, obliquely;

mèngès to cast an oblique glance;

mèngès-lèngès to turn the face away in disgust.

ènget to remember; to regain consciousness (*kr for* éling).

engga *md* please (help yourself); here you are (*giving s.t.*). *See also* mangga.

éngga *or* saéngga up to, until.

enggak no; not (*reg var of* ora).

énggak to tread water.

énggal 1 new (*kr for* anyar); 2 quick (*kr for* gelis).

énggar, ngénggar-énggar to relax, take it easy.

enggé to use, wear (*root form: kr for* enggo).

enggèh *reg var of* inggih.

enggèk in, at, on (*reg var of* ing, nèng).

enggel main (essential, central) part.

enggèn place (*kr for* enggon).

enggeng, ngenggeng to leave s.t. where it is.

enggèr *var of* anggèr.

engget, engget-engget *or* engget-enggetan line of demarcation, dividing-point;

ngengget-enggeti to mark with a dividing-line.

enggih yes (*md for* iya).

enggik, menggik narrow at the centre, hourglass-shaped;

ngenggik-enggik very slim;

ngenggikaké to make s.t. thin;

enggik-enggikan a narrowing in the middle of s.t. long;

enggik-enggiken sickly, prone to illness.

enggo *see* anggo.

enggok in, at, on (*reg var of* ing, nèng).

énggok, ménggok to turn (in, off, aside);

ménggak-ménggok to turn this way and that, keep zigzagging;

ngénggokaké to turn s.t., swerve (the car);

ngénggak-ngénggokaké to turn this way and that; to manoeuvre;

énggokan pretext, excuse;

énggok-énggokan a turn in a road; a branch road.

enggon *ng*, enggèn *kr*, I place;

ngenggoni to occupy (a place);

enggon-enggonan 1 here and there; 2 regional.

II, enggoné *ng*, enggènipun *kr*, s.o.'s act of (do)ing.

enggos, enggos-enggosan *or* menggos-menggos out of breath.

enggreg, ngenggreg-enggregi to slow s.o. down, interfere with one's pace.

enggrik, enggrik-enggriken thin and sickly.

enggrog, enggrog-enggrog *repr* a wild boar snorting.

enggrok, ngenggroki to stay at, stop (over) s.w.;

saenggrokan (to stay s.w.) for a while. *See also* anggrok.

engguh, ngengguh to consider, think of as, imagine. *See also* sengguh.

engis, ngengis-engis to hurt s.o.'s feelings, offend s.o.

engkap, mengkap-mengkap to peel off, break off.

engkas next, yet to come.

engké later or presently; in the future (*md for* mengko).

èngkèl I, ngèngkèl to argue and remain unconvinced;

èngkèl-èngkèlan to argue.

II, ngèngkèl immovable; to have difficulty moving;

èngkèl-èngkèlan immobile.

engkèt, engkèt-engkèt *repr* creaking sound made by a shoulder carrying-pole (pikulan).

èngkèt *see* engkèt.

engklèk, ngengklèk-engklèk to carry (*esp a* baby) against the breast and rock it.

èngklèk 1 to hop on one foot; 2 (to play) hopscotch;

ngèngklèk to go by foot;
ngèngklèk-èngklèk to carry s.t. while hopping.

engko *coll* later on, in the future (*var of* **mengko**).

éngko to plot, scheme.

engkod, engkod-engkod *repr* wood creaking.

éngkog, éngkog-éngkog *or* **éngkag-éngkog** to waddle.

éngkok I, ngéngkoki to lead, guide (a discussion);
éngkokan act or way of guiding (a discussion).
   II, éngkok-éngkok rippled, wavy.

éngkol 1 wrench; curved wrench handle; 2 strange; roundabout; 3 unit of measurement: the distance from elbow to fingertips;
ngéngkol 1 twisting and turning; 2 to measure s.t. in units as above (3);
ngéngkolaké to turn or bend s.t.;
éngkol-éngkol *or* **éngkal-éngkol** zigzag.

éngkong, ngéngkongaké to bend (a straight object);

éngkrah, saéngkrah-éngkrahé whatever s.o. does.

éngkrang I *var of* **éngkrah**.
   II, ngéngkrang (to sit) in a casual pose (with the feet on the table);
ngéngkrangaké to lay one's legs on the table.

èngkrèg, èngkrèg-èngkrèg I *repr* creaking sounds.
   II (too) weak (to).

engkreng, ngengkrengi *or* **ngengkrengaké** to place s.t. on a burner; to put s.t. on the stove.

engkuk I a certain barbet-like bird.
   II, ngengkuk to curve, bend;
ngengkuk-engkuk to keep massaging s.o. *esp* in the neck; *fig* to overwork s.o.

engkup, ngengkupaké to close (up).

ènglèng, mènglèng to tilt/turn a head to one side;
ngènglèngaké to tilt/turn s.o.'s head.

éngos, méngos *or* **ngéngosi** to avert the head so as to avoid s.o.;
ngéngosaké to turn away (the face).

èngsèl hinge: - **dir** door hinge; - **kenir** folding hinge; - **kupu** flat hinge on a box lid.

èngsem *var of* **èsem**.

engu *reg var of* **ingu**.

enguk I, enguk-enguk to sniff.
   II, ngenguk *reg* to go and visit s.o. to see how they are.

eni *var of* **ani**.

èni *var of* **ani**.

ening *lit* clear (of the mind, thoughts);
ngeningaké to make clear, purify. *See also* **wening**.

enir, enar-enir *or* **enir-eniran** afraid, fearful.

enjah, ngenjah-enjah to want to have everything available.

enjak *var of* **idak**.

énjang *reg var of* **énjing**.

ènjep, mènjep with lower lip thrust forward as a gesture of disliking or disparagement. *Also* **èncep**.

ènjèr (of dance movement) to run around on the stage.

enjet *ng*, **apu** *kr*, slaked lime (to be mixed with betel nut, for chewing).

enjih yes, indeed (*Yogya var of* **inggih**).

énjing morning (*kr for* **ésuk**).

enjlog, ngenjlogi to jump down onto;
ngenjlogaké to cause or assist s.o. to jump down;
enjlog-enjlogan to keep jumping; to trample.

énjoh *reg* can, to be able.

énjor, énjor-énjor swollen.

enjot a pedal;
ngenjot to operate s.t. by a pedal;
enjot-enjotan to pedal, pump.

énjuh *see* **énjoh**.

éntar 1 metaphoric(al use of words); 2 (of knowledge) vast, far-reaching.

entara *see* **antara**.

entas, ngentas 1 *or* **ngentasi** to bring in

(out of rain, water); 2 (*or* ngentasaké) to marry off (one's child).

entawis *see* **antawis**.

enteb, ngenteb *or* **ngentebaké** to place on the stove.

èntèh early in the evening. *See also* **enthé**.

entèk *ng*, **telas** *kr*, 1 all gone; used up; 2 to consume, require;
  ngentèk at the outer limit;
  ngentèkaké to finish, use up completely;
  kentèkan short of, low on; to run out of;
  saentèké at the end of; after s.t. is over;
  entèk-entèkan 1 to the last one; 2 to an extreme degree; 3 finally; the end;
  entèk atiné 1 frightened; 2 dispirited;
  entèk jaraké 1 out of money; 2 at the end of one's creative powers;
  entèk-enting all used up, completely gone.

entèn, entèn-entèn peanuts coated in brown sugar.

ènten to exist (*md for* **ana**).

éntha, ngéntha *or* **ngéntha-éntha** to create an image (of); to depict;
  pangéntha-éntha image created.

enthak, ngenthak-enthak vast and barren, void of vegetation.

enthang, ngenthang-enthang vast and barren; void of vegetation.

enthar, ngenthar to run away;
  ngentharaké to abandon, leave s.t. unprotected or unattended.

enthé *or* **soré enthé** early in the evening (*var of* **èntèh**).

enthek full;
  menthek *or* **menthek-menthek** filled out (of women's breasts).

ènthèng light (not heavy; not difficult; not serious);
  ngènthèngi *or* **ngènthèng-ènthèngi** 1 (of baby) to start to learn walking; 2 to recover;
  ngènthèngaké to lighten, alleviate;
  ènthèngan quick to help, generous;
  ènthèng-ènthèngan doing things lightly/ easily.

enthil I, **ngenthil-enthil** to save, put away bit by bit.

  II, **ngenthil** to keep wanting to suck its mother's nipple (small child), be attached to its mother. *See also* **penthil**.

énthog manila duck (*reg var of* **ménthog**).

enthok, enthok-enthing having a large head and a small body; having a small head and a large body.

énthong rice ladle of coconut shell or wood; - **palwa** *lit* paddle, oar;
  énthong-énthong(an) shoulder blade(s);
  ngénthong to ladle out (rice).

énthos *reg* can, to be able.

enthung cocoon;
  ngenthung in the cocoon stage.

enthu, ngenthu *or* **ngenthu-enthu** to make one's way s.w. in the face of difficulties.

enti *ng*, **entos** *kr*, **ngentèni** 1 to wait; 2 to wait for, await. *See also* **anti I**.

enting *intsfr* all gone, used up. *See also* **entèk**.

entol, ngentol 1 to make a show of standing firm on an offer; 2 to jack s.t. up; 3 to pry;
  entol-entolan to bargain strenuously with a market-seller.

entos to wait (*root form: kr for* **enti**).

éntos able; capable (*var of* **énthos**).

éntra mark, symbol;
  éntra-éntra plan, scheme;
  ngéntra *or* **ngéntra-éntra** to imitate; do in the same way (as);
  éntran imitation; imagination.

entrah, entrah-entrahan plan, intention.

éntrah, saéntrah-éntrahé whatever one does.

èntré entry-fee.

èntrès I *reg* orderly, well-regulated.

  II, **ngèntrèsi** to give daily interest (on debt);
  ngèntrèsaké to have s.o. act as substitute with compensation.

entrig, entrig-entrigan to jump up and down; to proceed by small prancing paces.

entrog, ngentrog *or* **ngentrogaké** to shake

s.t.; to trample on s.t.;

ngentrog-entrog to shake (up);

entrog-entrogan to keep trampling.

éntrok camisole, underbodice.

éntuk *ng*, **pikantuk** *kr*, 1 to get, obtain; 2 to receive permission; 3 to receive as spouse;

ngéntukaké to allow, let;

éntuk-éntukan things obtained (*e.g.* profits from sales; stolen loot; gifts from a generous person).

entul, ngentul-entul to bounce up and down (on);

mentul-mentul bouncing.

entung all gone (*var of* **enting**).

entup stinger;

ngentup *or* **ngentupi** to sting;

entup-entupan stinging creatures.

entut 1 (*sarib k.i.*) fart; 2 *slang* baloney!;

ngentut (*sarib k.i.*) to break wind;

ngentutan to have a tendency to fart;

kepentut to break wind inadvertently;

entut bérut stomach gas, wind. *See also* **kentut**.

énuk *reg* extremely delicious (*intsfr form of* **énak**).

enung, ngenung-enung to take care of; to look after.

enya *see* **nya**.

enyak *var of* **idak**.

enyang *see* **nyang** I, II.

enyeng *see* **nyeng**.

ènyèng *reg* mentally defective.

enyet, ngenyet to crush fine;

ngenyet-enyeti to pinch, squeeze (in massage). *See also* **penyet**.

enyong *reg* I, me.

ényong *var of* **enyong**.

enyot *var of* **enyut**.

enyuk *see* **nyunyuk**.

enyut *see* **nyut**.

épah loan (*kr for* **opah**).

èpèk I 1 leather or velvet belt; 2 bunch of bananas coming from a single bud; 3 share of stock.

II, **èpèk-èpèk** palm of the hand.

èpi, ngèpi-èpi to dream about;

kèpi to dream constantly about s.t. *See also* **impi**.

epik, ngepik-epik to handle, touch.

èplèg, èplèg-èplèg to flap, flop together.

epoh *see* **poh** II.

épok betel box.

épor *reg* having no strength in one's legs.

èpyèk 1 very busy, tied up; 2 *or* **èpyèk-èpyèk** noisy (talk); talkative.

èr *lit* water.

éra (of eyes) not functioning together, out of focus with each other; **mata-** cross-eyed. *See also* **kéra**.

erak hoarse.

érak *var of* **erak**.

éram awesome; awed;

ngéram-érami *or* **ngéram-éramaké** awe-inspiring;

pangéram-éram 1 that which inspires awe; 2 a miracle, magic.

érang, ngérang-érang to get angry at; raise one's voice at.

érawati *lit* loud sounds of thunder.

ereb, ngereb *or* **ngerebi** to cut, slice.

èrèd, ngèrèd *or* **ngèrèd-èrèd** to drag s.o. along, involve s.o. else in (nefarious activity).

èrèg I **èrèg-èrèg** 1 signature; 2 to sign.

II, **ngèrèg-èrèg** to persuade, talk s.o. into.

erèh *see* **rèh**.

èrek hoarse (of voice) (*var of* **érak, erak**).

èrèk I, **ngèrèki** to court (of chickens; *cr of* people);

èrèk-èrèkan to circle (*e.g.* an opponent) warily.

II, **èrèk-èrèk** *intsfr* short, low; **cendhèk** - extremely short, low.

èrem (to get) black-and-blue mark; **biru** - black-and-blue.

ereng, ngereng-ereng 1 to keep roaring; 2 to keep moaning with pain.

èrèng *or* **èrèng-èrèng** sloping valley wall or hillside. *See also* **pèrèng**.

èrep estate, property.

eres *see* res.

erès *see* rès I, II.

èrès I bluffing, bluster.

II *reg var of* iris.

èrèt *see* èrèd.

èrgelèk liquor bottle.

èrgeni variety of semiprecious stone.

èrgulo rose (flower).

eri *see* ri.

erih *see* rih.

erik *see* rik.

éring to respect;

ngéringi to hold in respect;

ngéringaké to inspire awe/respect in;

ngéring-éringi *or* ngéring-éringaké inspiring awe/respect;

kéringan held in respect.

erit *see* rit II.

èrkembang a variety of semiprecious stone.

èrlaut a variety of semiprecious stone.

èrloji watch.

èrmawar rose water.

èrmoni harmonica, accordion.

èrnawa *lit* sea, ocean.

erog *see* rog.

éroh in uncertainty. *See also* éruh.

érok *or* érok-érok 1 skimmer (kitchen implement); 2 bricklayer's trowel; dhodhok-érok large green dragonfly (*see also* dhodhok).

erong *see* rong I.

eros *see* ros.

èrtali brooklet, rill, runnel; stream (of water).

erti *see* ngerti.

èrtambang *var of* èrtali.

eru *see* ru I, II.

èru, éra-èru tumult, violent disorder.

éruh in uncertainty (*var of* éroh).

erut *see* rut.

érut arrowroot. *See also* gaérut.

es psst!

ès ice.

esab *see* sab II.

esah *see* sah I.

esak *see* sak I.

ésak *lit* good, beautiful, fine, pleasing.

èseg hoarse.

èsèk, èsèk-èsèk *repr* rustling, rubbing; ngèsèk-èsèk to rub, scrub, brush.

èsèl 1 railway points; 2 *var of* èngsèl.

èsem a smile;

ngèsemi to smile at;

mèsem to smile;

mésam-mèsem to keep smiling; to grin.

èsi, ngèsi-èsi to torment, torture; kaèsi-èsi to get treated cruelly; to be ridiculed.

ésih *reg var of* isih.

eslup *see* slup.

èsmu *lit* appearance, aspect; it seems, judging by appearances.

ésok *reg var of* ésuk.

èsprès express.

èsrèg *see* srèg.

èstha *var of* istha.

èsthi, ngèsthi to think about, reflect on; to fix, set (of will).

èstri I female (*kr for* wadon, wédok).

II, ngèstrèni to attend, be present at.

èstu *or* saèstu really, actually (*kr for* nyata, temen(an));

ngèstokaken to obey;

ngèstu pada to do homage to, show esteem for;

pangèstu blessing, good wishes, prayers.

ésuk *ng*, énjing *kr*, 1 morning; 2 *or* ésuk-ésuk early in the morning;

ésuké the next day;

sakésuk *ng*, sakénjing *kr* 1 the whole morning; 2 a day's work, as much as can be ploughed in a morning.

étak *reg var of* idak.

étan east;

ngétan *or* mangétan (to go) eastward;

saétan(é) to the east (of).

See also wétan.

étang arithmetic; calculation (*kr for* étung).

etas *see* tas.

été, ngètèk-ètèkaké to show one's bare tummy.

etèg reg, ngetèg to incite.

ètèg var of etèg.

ètel reg 1 solid, firm; 2 calm, courageous.

eter see ter, ater.

etes forceful, significant.

èthèh, ngèthèh-èthèh to lie sprawled face up.

èthèk I, èthèk-èthèk repr the rattling of a loose object;
ngèthèk-èthèk to rattle.
II, ngèthèk to push one's own will.
III reg shallow, superficial.

èthèng 1 male classical spear dance; 2 obstinate, self-willed;
ngèthèng unwilling to yield.
II, ngèthèng-èthèng to carry around.

èthèr, ngèthèr-èthèr to scatter, strew.

èthès 1 talkative; 2 flirtatious, coquettish.

éthok, éthok-éthok to pretend;
éthok-éthokan make-believe, faked, imitation, artificial.

éthol var of étol.

éthor var of éthos.

éthos reg can, to be able.

étikèt I etiquette, manners.
II label, ticket, tag.

étung ng, étang kr, arithmetic; calculation;
- awangan mental arithmetic;
ngétung or ngétungi 1 to count s.t., calculate; 2 to consider, regard;
ngétungaké to count on s.o.'s behalf;
étung-étung 1 to count; 2 considered as;
ngétung-étung to calculate;
kepétung to be calculated;
pangétung enumeration, calculation;
étung-étungan 1 to calculate; 2 calculation;
ora étung to pay no attention, not stop to think. See also kétang.

étol, étol-étol to waddle, walk with difficulty because of big buttocks.

éwa jealous;
ngéwani to be jealous (toward);
ngéwak-éwakaké to act superciliously (toward), treat with disdain.

éwadéné even so, nevertheless, in spite of (the foregoing).

éwah 1 to change (kr for owah); 2 crazy (kr for édan).

éwan see éwa.

éwang I reg each; separo éwang half each (see also sowang).
II, ngéwangi to help s.o., help with s.t.;
éwang-éwang to help, lend a hand.

èwed (kr for éwuh) 1 busy (at); 2 (to feel) uncomfortable, ill at ease; 3 slang to have a menstrual period.

èweg uneasy, uncomfortable;
ngèweg-èweg to disturb, trouble.

èwèg, ngèwèg-èwèg to carry around.

èwèh reg var of wènèh.

èwèng, ngèwèng-èwèng or ngéwang-èwèng 1 to carry around; 2 to keep shoving.

èwèr, ngèwèr-èwèr to pull s.t. out.

éwoh reg var of éwuh.

èwu thousand;
sèwu 1,000;
éwon 1 (or éwonan) a currency note with the value of 1,000; 2 in thousands, by the thousand; 3 a digit occupying the thousands' place;
éwon-éwon in thousands, by the thousand.

éwuh ng, èwed kr, 1 busy (at); 2 uneasiness, reluctance; 3 (to feel) uncomfortable, ill at ease;
ngéwuhaké troublesome, disturbing;
ngéwuh-éwuhi to cause difficulties for s.o.;
kéwuhan at a loss, troubled;
éwuh aya (ing pambudi) in a dilemma, torn between alternatives. See also pakéwuh.

éyang grandparent (k.i. for embah);
ngéyang 1 to call s.o. grandfather/grandmother; 2 to regard s.o. as grandparent.

èyèg restless;
ngèyèg to move about restlessly;

éyag-èyèg to keep fidgeting restlessly.

èyèl, ngèyèl stubborn, unwilling to yield; èyèl-èyèlan to argue with each sticking to their own view.

èyèng var of èyèl.

éyong meowing;

ngéyong or méyong to meow;

ngéyang-ngéyong to keep meowing.

éyub 1 shady; sheltered; 2 dusk;

éyub-éyub shelter from sun, rain; ngéyub to take shelter; éyuban shady place; kéyuban protected, sheltered (by); kéyuben overprotected; pangéyuban 1 protection, shelter; 2 protector.

éyung, éyang-éyung shifty, unreliable.

F

faédah use(fulness), benefit. See also paédah.

faham 1 to understand; knowledgeable; 2 body of knowledge or thought; doctrine, -ism. See also paham.

fajar dawn.

fakir indigent holy man who begs and performs magic for a living; - miskin the poor.

falak, ilmu - astronomy.

fasèh fluent (in speaking language).

fasih var of fasèh.

fatwa pronouncement (by a jurist).

filem film, cinema.

firman saying, decree (divine or royal); - Allah commandment of God.

fitnah slander, calumny. See also pitenah.

fitrah tithe in rice or cash paid at end of the Fasting Month. See also pitrah.

fitri see idul.

G

ga I also (*shtf of* **uga**).

II, **ngga** come on!; here you are!; go ahead! (*shtf of* **mangga**; *md for* **ayo**, **enya**).

III *coll* to bring, carry, take (*var of* **gawa**).

gabag I measles;

gabagen to suffer from measles.

II, **nggabag** sticking out (lances).

gabah I rice (loose from ear, unmilled);

- **sinawur** a certain batik design;

nggabah 1 to feed rice to; 2 shaped like a grain of rice (eyes);

gabahan *way* a type of the wayang puppet characterised by its grain-like eyes.

II, **gegabah** hasty, rash, ill-mannered;

nggegabah to treat irresponsibly;

kaya gabah diinteri in a state of confusion or chaos.

gabar 1 no longer effective; 2 to evaporate. *See also* **abar**, **aber**.

gaben planted during the dry season (*reg kr for* **gadhu**).

gabeng dried up/out (cane).

gaber, **nggaber** to snort (horse);

gaber-gaber to eject (air, food) forcibly through the lips.

gabes I *or* **nggabes** *or* **gabes-gabes** dry and tasteless (fruits).

II, **nggabes** to keep nibbling.

gabig, **gobag-gabig** 1 to keep shaking the head; 2 to wobble, shake.

gablag, **nggablag** *cr* to keep talking.

gableg to have (*cr var of* **duwé**).

gablog I a hit on s.o.'s back with the palm of the hand;

nggablog to hit as above.

II, a certain dish made with mashed glutinous rice.

gablug I *or* **mak gablug** 1 *repr* a thud.

II *reg* blunt, dull.

gabrès I, **nggabrès** to pay attention.

II messy, smeared.

gabro, **nggabro** to acquire dishonestly. *See also* **gabrul**.

gabrol *var of* **gabrol**.

gabrug (*pron as:* **gabru:g**) *or* **mak gabrug** *repr* a heavy thud;

gabrugan to get s.t. without exertion.

gabrul, **nggabrul** to acquire dishonestly.

gabrus (*pron as:* **gabru:s**) *or* **mak gabrus** *repr* a collision;

gabrusan 1 a collision; 2 to collide.

gabrut smeared with s.t dirty.

gabu *reg* a large whitish banana.

gabug 1 empty (rice ears); 2 sterile, childless (people);

nggabugi unable to produce milk (nursing mother).

gabul I smeared with s.t. dirty.

II *var of* **gabrul**.

gabung, **nggabung** to join forces with;

nggabungaké to join (two things);

gabungan joint, cooperative.

gabus I 1 cork, the tree the bark of which produces cork; 2 pith of the cassava plant.

II an eel-like river fish.

III, **nggabus** to sharpen, whet.

IV, **nggabus** 1 to bet on (a fighting cock); 2 to hold s.o.'s cards for them while they leave the game temporarily.

gabyeg, **nggabyeg** to nag constantly.

gabyes *var of* **gabyeg**.

gacar, **nggacar** to chase.

gacé, **nggacé** small but early ripe, precocious.

gacleng I, **nggacleng** *intsfr* black (*var of* **gancleng**).

II *or* **mak gacleng** *repr* a chopping knife slashing.

gaclok *or* **mak gaclok** *repr* an axe chopping.

gaco 1 object (marble, picture *etc*) used in children's games for winning the opponent's similar object; 2 *cr* girl/boy friend; 3 companion.

gacos *or* **mak gacos** *repr* a sharp implement striking s.t.

gacrok *repr* a sharp implement piercing s.t.

gacruk *var of* **gacrok**.

gacuk *var of* **gaco**.

gada club, bludgeon.

gadag, **nggadag** pervasive (odour).

gadan *see* **gada**.

gadaréna 1 help; 2 a precaution(ary measure).

gadhag thick rope.

gadhah to have, own (*kr for* **duwé**);
gadhahan the possession/belonging (of) (*kr for* **duwèk**).

gadhang, **nggadhang** to want, wish for;
nggadhang-gadhang to expect, look forward to.

gadhé *ng*, **gantos** *kr*, pawning; - **peteng** unlicensed pawnshop/pawnbroker;
tukang - pawnbroker (*see also* **tukang**);
nggadhé to lend money on articles;
nggadhèkaké 1 to pawn s.t.; 2 to lease out (a ricefield);
gadhèn (**gantosan** *kr*) 1 pawnshop; 2 (an article) in pawn or to be pawned;
pagadhèn *or* **pagadhéan** *or* **nggadhéan** pawnshop; pawnbroker.

gadheh to have, own (*reg var of* **gadhah**).

gadhel I a certain poisonous root; 2 tartar that collects on teeth;
nggadhel 1 to stick to the throat; 2 coated with tartar.

gadhil boar's tusk.

gadhing 1 elephant tusk; 2 ivory; 3 nasal mucus (*k.i. for* **umbel**);

gumadhing resembling ivory, *esp* in colour.

gadho, **gadho-gadho** vegetable salad with peanut sauce;
nggadho to eat accompanying dishes without the rice;
gadhon 1 accompanying dish to be consumed without the rice; 2 steamed beef-and-egg roll; 3 a music programme consisting of a variety of pieces.

gadhog 1 *repr* a bumping sound; 2 not (going) through.

gadhu *or* **gadhon** rice plant planted during the dry season; - **walikan** rice plant that can be planted in either dry or rainy season;
nggadhu to plant during the dry season.

gadhug 1 a bump, thump; 2 (*or* **mak gadhug**) *repr* the sound of a bump;
nggadhug to bump;
kegadhug to knock against s.t.

gadhuh, **nggadhuh** to have the use of s.t.;
nggadhuhi *or* **nggadhuhaké** to give s.t. to s.o. to use but not to own;
gadhuhan what is given to s.o. on the above basis.

gadhul tartar *var of* **gadhel**.

gadhung I a variety of creeping edible tuber which is toxic if not cooked properly;
nggadhung 1 to plant the above tuber in (a plot); 2 to get s.o. stupefied by having them eat the above tuber.
II, **gadhungan** not real, **macan** - human being in the form of a tiger;
nggadhung to cheat at games.
III light green;
nggadhung to dye s.t. pale green.

gadri section of a Javanese-style house behind the front part where guests are received; gallery surrounding the central part of the Javanese-style house.

gadrug, **gadrug-gadrug** corpulent.

gaduk *see* **gaduk**.

gaduk within reach;
  nggaduk-gadukaké to do one's best to reach/attain s.t.;
  sagaduk-gaduké whatever one can attain.

gadul *or* **mak gadul** *repr* a rebound;
  godal-gadul to bounce back and forth.

gadur, nggadur to prattle on and on, talk nonsense.

gaé *inf var of* **gawé.**

gaèk *reg* old;
  nggaèk to nag.

gaèl, nggaèl-gaèl 1 to snarl (at); 2 to gnaw.

gaèng, nggaèng to cry, whine.

gaérut arrowroot. *See also* **érut, garut.**

gaga *or* **pagagan** non-irrigated land on which rice is planted; - **rancah** rice planted in a dry field;
  nggaga rancah to plant directly in the field (not in a nursery bed).

gagah 1 manly, courageous; 2 strong, muscular;
  nggagahi to face up to (danger, difficulty);
  gumagah having an inflated opinion of one's own manliness;
  gagahan rough type of male classical dance;
  gagah-gagahan to show off one's possessions or strength.

gagak crow (bird); **lincak** - to keep moving from place to place (*see also* **lincak**);
  nggagak *or* **nggagaki** to take away and eat (a sacrificial offering left for the spirits).

gagal to fail; **perang** - *way* battle scene that customarily closes the first section of a shadow-play (*see also* **perang**);
  nggagalaké to cause s.t. to fail.

gagan, gagan-gagan a certain edible plant.

gagana *lit* sky. *See also* **gegana.**

gagang 1 central stalk, stem; 2 handle;
  nggagang stalk-like; - **aking** very thin.

gagap I stammer, stutter
  nggagap to stammer, stutter.
  II, **nggagapi** 1 to grope in search of s.t.; 2 to probe, sound out;
  gagap-gagap 1 groping, grasping; 2 sounding out;
  nggagap tuna nggayuh luput to fall far short of one's aspirations.

gagar 1 to fail to complete the normal cycle; - **mayang** bouquet used traditionally at the funeral of an unmarried person;
  nggagar resembling a funeral bouquet.
  II **gagaran** 1 handle; 2 guide, manual.

gagas, nggagas to think about, think over;
  gagasan idea, thought.

gagat, nggagat addicted to;
  gagat ésuk *or* **raina** daybreak, sunrise.

gagé quick, immediate;
  gagé-gagé immediately, instantly, in a rush.

gagi I *reg var of* **gagé.**
  II *reg* non-irrigated field (*kr for* **gaga**).

gaglag, nggaglag *cr* to eat, devour.

gagrag I style, fashion; - **anyar** new style/fashion, modern;
  nggagrag to create, invent.
  II damaged, spoiled.

gagrak, nggagrak 1 dashing, splendid; 2 to laugh happily from time to time.

gagu 1 speech defect; 2 mute, dumb.

gaguk 1 *repr* tooting sound; 2 *reg* bicycle.

gagut, nggagut to eat with gusto.

gah 1 unwilling; 2 no! I don't want to! (*shtf of* **wegah**).

gaib 1 secret, esoteric; **daya** - magical powers (*see also* **daya**); 2 (of a child) intelligent and mature beyond its years;
  gumaib 1 haughty, arrogant; 2 knowledgeable beyond one's years;

ginaib to have mystical powers.

gaing *cr*, *excl* of surprise, disbelief.

gajah *ng*, **liman** *kr*, elephant; - **meta** furious, enraged;
  nggajah resembling an elephant;
  pagajahan *or* **nggajahan** elephant-stable.

gajeg, gajegé 1 I think; **2** (in questions) do you think?
  gojag-gajeg hesitant, undecided.

gajig, gojag-gajig shaky, unsteady.

gajih I fat (of meat, as opposed to the lean);
  nggajih fatty (meat);
  nggajihi to oil or grease s.t.
  II salary, wages.
  nggajih to pay s.o. a salary or wages;
  gajihan 1 payday; **2** to receive one's salary at a fixed time.
  III, **pagajih** dry riverbed (which gets inundated during the rainy season) used as a ricefield.

gajul I a kick;
  nggajul to kick with the tip of the foot.
  II a substitute for the real thing;
  nggajuli to act as a substitute for.

gak *reg* no, not (*var of* **ora**).

gak-pat a small poor house supported by four poles (*shtc of* **cagak papat**).

gakug 1 *repr* tooting sound; **2** *reg* bicycle (*var of* **gaguk**).

gal *or* **nggal** *reg* every. *See also* **unggal**.

gala filling of resin;
  gala-gala *or* **gegala** *lit* commander;
  galan candlenut filled with tin pellets used for children's game;
  nggala-gala *or* **nggegala** to strengthen (the spirit).

galah a long pole.

galak wild, untamed, dangerous, fierce, vicious;
  nggalaki to treat s.o. viciously;
  sagalak-galaké however cruel s.o. is.

galan *see* **gala**.

galang I *reg* wooden framework, slipway, dock (for boats);
  nggalang to set up (house), put in dock (boat);
  galangan building, construction.
  II *reg* **nggalang** to impound (wandering stock).

galap, galap-gangsul fault, shortcoming.

galar a mat made from bamboo split open and laid flat.

galat out of the rules.

galé *reg* (look) over there!

galèg to know s.t. well.

galeng I line, stripe, welt.
  II, galengan dyke, bank of earth dividing ricefields;
  nggalengi to provide with dykes.

galer 1 a line; **2** lines on the palms of the hands;
  nggaler to have the appearance of a line;
  galer-galeran lines, paths.

gales, nggales deep, intense (colour).

galib, galibé as a rule.

galih I hard core in wood.
  II heart, mind (*k.i. for* **ati**).

galik, nggalik *or* **galik-galik** high-pitched and melodious.

galing a certain vine;
  golang-galing a certain batik design.

galiyeng, nggaliyeng to feel dizzy. *See also* **gliyeng**.

galiyung galleon.

galnisir, nggalnisir to galvanise.

galo *ng*, **punika lo** *kr*, (look) over there!

galok, nggalok-galok to howl/yowl continuously.

galon 1 gallon; **2** gold lace; **3** *reg* clay.

galong *reg* clay, loam.

galuga 1 a variety of plant with red leaves; **2** red colouring cosmetics;
  nggaluga bright red.

galuh *lit* **1** diamond, jewel; **2** girl.

galung, galungan name of the 11th **wuku**.

galur, nggalur interminable, lengthy.

gama, gama-dirgama *lit* danger, misfortune.

gamam to waver, vacillate, hesitate.

gaman *or* gegaman *ng*, dedamel *kr*, weapon.

gamar *reg* 1 afraid; 2 to fear that... *See also* samar.

gambak *var of* gambèk.

gambang a gamelan instrument with wooden keys;
nggambang 1 to play this instrument; 2 resembling this instrument;
nggambangi to accompany the melody with a gambang;
gambangan act or manner of playing the gambang.

gambar picture, drawing, illustration;
- idhup moving picture;
nggambar to make a picture of;
nggambari to make a picture on;
nggambaraké 1 to make a picture for s.o.; 2 to depict, imagine, create a picture of;
gambaran *or* gegambaran 1 illustration, picture of s.t.; 2 image.

gambas 1 a certain fruit which when young is edible if cooked; 2 dried pod of the above fruit when mature: for household uses.

gambèk *reg* until, to the point that.

gambèn *or* gegambèn 1 courageous gang leader; 2 *reg* spoiled, overindulged.

gambèr, nggambèr hanging limp.

gambir 1 a climbing shrub, the gambir plant; 2 a decoction of the leaves used in betel-chewing; also used in tanning and medicines; 3 reddish-brown colour (of doves); - sawit 1 a certain gamelan melody; 2 a certain batik pattern;
gambira *lit* 1 glad, happy; 2 cheerful, gay.

gambiralaya *lit* ocean.

gamblang clear, understandable.

gamblèh, nggamblèh 1 (of the lower lip) drooping; 2 *fig* talkative; 3 *cr* to cry, weep.

gamblèng *reg var of* gamblèh.

gambli *excl* expressing disbelief.

gamblik, nggamblik in a precarious position near the edge of s.t.

gamblis *var of* gambli.

gamblok, nggamblok to cling to;
nggambloki to cling to s.o.;
nggamblokaké to cause s.t. to cling;
gamblokan 1 bunch, bundle, sheaf; 2 to join together.

gamblong cheap sort of coconut oil.

gambos soft, spongy in texture (cassava).

gambreng I, nggambreng 1 thick, bushy; 2 to smell disagreeable; 3 to grumble with dissatisfaction.
II dung beetle.

gambrèng apt to cry over nothing.

gambrès, nggambrès to harvest (rice) by cutting each stalk individually close to the ear.

gambret I flirtatious.
II, nggambret very fragrant.

gambuh a certain classical verse form;
nggambuh to sing this form of verse.

gambul, nggambul to rub the horns/antlers against s.t.

gambus an Arabian six-stringed lute;
gambusan song-and-dance performance with tambourines and gambus.

gambyok, nggambyok to join; to cling to (*var of* gamblok).

gambyong a certain classical dance performed by females;
nggambyong to perform such a dance;
gambyongan to engage in social (rather than classical) dancing.

gambyung *var of* gambyok.

gamel I, nggameli to accompany with classical music;
gamelan *ng*, gangsa *kr*, 1 classical Javanese musical instrument; 2 an ensemble of such instruments.

II groom (for horses);

nggamel to act as groom;

gamelan the quarter where grooms live.

gameng, nggameng clearly visible from afar (clouds).

games, nggames to eat all one can get of (a favourite food).

gamil, nggamil to talk incessantly.

gamoh soft, tender (meat).

gamol thick and tender (meat).

gampang *ng*, **gampil** *kr*, 1 easy; 2 (*or* **gampangan**) easy-going, not demanding;

nggampangaké 1 to make s.t. easier; 2 to facilitate, smoothe (the way);

nggegampang to treat lightly rather than seriously;

gampang-gampangan taking things easy, easy-going;

gumampang irresponsible, apt to take things too lightly;

gampang-gampang angèl unpredictable, *i.e.* sometimes easy to please and sometimes not.

gampar, nggampar to kick;

gamparan 1 wooden sandals; 2 a game in which a stone is kicked around.

gampèng 1 hollow place under an overhanging bank; 2 *fig* unseen danger, a lurking threat;

nggampèng to conceal o.s. under an overhang.

gampil easy (*kr for* **gampang**).

gamping I lime, limestone.

II (*intsfr, pron as:* **gampi:ng**) extremely easy.

gampleng *repr* the sound of a punch landing.

gamplong a cheap sort of coconut oil (*var of* **gamblong**). *See also* **lenga**.

gampung rare, scarce;

nggampung *reg* 1 to break; 2 to glean (the rest of rice in a ricefield after harvest);

nggampungi to cut rice with harvesting knife, harvest rice plants.

gana I the man's share (of property, divided after divorce); - **gini** property acquired jointly during marriage and which is thus divided in the event of divorce.

II in the form of; - **dhuwit** in the form of money;

ngganani to make a payment.

III 1 foetus; 2 small bee, larva, pupa (young of the **tawon**);

gumana in a state of an embryo.

IV *lit* cloud.

V figurine of a person or animal;

ngganani made into a certain shape.

VI name of a deity with an elephant's head.

ganal 1 strong, robust; 2 (*or* **ganalan**) crude, boorish.

ganan *see* **gana**.

ganas 1 savage, ferocious, vicious; 2 malignant (of tumor); 3 lavish.

gancam, nggancam *reg* to talk nonsense.

gancang fast, speedy, quick;

nggancangaké to speed up, accelerate;

gancanging carita to make a long story short;

gegancangan to make haste.

gancar fluent, smooth, fast.

ganceng, ngganceng to stretch between two points (*e.g.* rope).

gancèt to mate (of dogs; *cr* of people).

gancleng 1 *repr* an axe swinging through its arc; 2 (*or* **nggancleng**) *intsfr of* black; pitch black.

ganco pickaxe.

ganda odour, scent, smell, aroma; -**kusuma** a certain classical verse form; -**maru** a right-angled wooden board; -**pura** a tree with fragrant leaves used medicinally; -**riya** a certain tree, also its fruit; -**rukem** a certain plant resin used in batik-making and soldering; - **rusa** a certain tree the wood of which is often used for fences; -**suli** a certain classical batik pattern; **-wida** a mixture used as a cosmetic application for brides *etc*;

ngganda 1 to have an odour; **2** to smell, perceive an odour;

pangganda 1 olfactory sense; **2** the way s.t. smells.

gandar 1 lower part of a wooden kris sheath; **2** wooden arrow shaft; **3** a squared length of wood used in furniture-making; **4** mortal remains; **5** having slender graceful lines; **- iras** kris handle and cover made from separate pieces of wood.

gandarwa *lit* a mythological, semidivine being.

gandarwi *lit* a female of the above.

gandarwo *var of* **gandarwa**. *See also* **gendruwo**.

gandèk *reg* knowledgeable, able, competent.

gandem good to eat.

gandes gracious, charming. *See also* **gandhes**.

gandhang loud;

nggandhang *reg* to sing loudly.

gandhèk a certain palace official whose function is to pass on the monarch's orders.

gandhèn a big wooden hammer. *See* **gandhi**.

gandhèng 1 connected, related; **2** side by side, arm in arm, coupled; **- kunca** *lit* to plot with;

nggandhèng 1 to connect; **2** to hold hands;

nggandhèngi to accompany, go hand-in-hand with;

nggandhèngaké 1 to link, hook together, join; **2** to couple;

gandhèngan 1 *or* **gegandhèngan** connected, with joined hands; **2** connection, linking;

panggandhèng 1 act or way of joining or coupling; **2** *gram* conjunction.

gandhes gracious, charming.

gandhéwa bow.

gandhi *lit* hammer;

gandhèn a wooden mallet;

nggandhèni to hit with a mallet;

gandhèn cucut swordfish with a hammer-shaped head.

gandhik I cylindrical mortar for rolling or grinding up herbs, spices *etc* on a square stone pestle (**pipis** *or* **pipisan**);

II *or* **nggandhik** to mate (cats).

gandhil ear lobe.

gandhok I bunch, bundle.

II front verandah.

gandhol, nggandhol (*or* **gandholan**) to have a firm grip (on);

gandholan s.t. used to grip on.

gandhon 1 a children's game using dark brown hard-shelled fruit (**gandhu**); **2** a certain shape of kris sheath.

gandhong, nggandhong *or* **nggandhongi** to tie into a bunch.

gandhor softened and hollowed by disease (bamboo).

gandhos rice flour and coconut cake; **- wingka** one variety of such a cake.

gandhowara a certain ear ornament.

gandhul I *or* **mak gandhul** *repr* hanging;

nggandhul *or* **gandhulan 1** to hang onto s.t.; **2** dependent on; **3** to hold onto, cling to;

nggandhuli 1 to hang s.t. on(to); **2** to stick to;

nggandhulaké to hang s.t.;

gondhal-gandhul to dangle.

II *reg* papaya.

gandhung, gondhang-gandhung *reg* bicycle.

gandi *reg* skilled, clever, well-versed.

gandis *var of* **gandi**.

gandra power, strength;

nggandra strong;

ora nggandra sepira negligible, insignificant.

gandri *var of* **gadri**.

gandrik *excl* heavens! my god!

gandrung I dragonfly.

II passionately devoted to;

nggandrungi to be in love with;

gandrungan love scene in traditional drama;

gandrung-gandrung kapirangu love-sick.

gandum 1 wheat; **2** maize (*md for* **jagung**).

ganèng, ganèngan *reg* therefore, that is why.

ganep 1 complete(d); (in) full; **2** even (not odd);

ngganepi to make s.t. complete;

ngganepaké to round off, complete s.t.;

ganepan that which makes s.t. complete;

ora ganep mentally defective.

ganès, gonas-ganès attractive, flirtatious.

ganéya *lit* south-east.

gang I alley(way), passage.

II gap, compartment, partition.

III *lit* strong.

IV *shrt of* **wegang**.

gangga *lit* river, water.

ganggam *or* **ngganggam** hesitant, reluctant.

ganggang I 1 to have a space or gap between; **2** separated by (a certain distance);

ngganggang 1 to separate, part; **2** to crack, split.

See also **ginggang, gonggang**.

II *var of* **ganggeng**.

ganggas *reg* **1** strong, dashing, healthy-looking; **2** in good physical condition.

ganggeng a certain water weed.

ganggrang, ganggrangan (*or* **ganggarangan**) *reg* mongoose. *See also* **garangan**.

ganggu, ngganggu to bother, disturb, interfere with;

gangguan *reg* interference, hindrance, nuisance, bother.

gangsa I 1 classical Javanese musical instrument or ensemble of instruments (*kr for* **gamelan**); **2** bronze; **3** gamelan gong.

II goose (*reg kr for* **banyak**).

III, nggangsa 1 to dry-fry; **2** to gag s.o. to prevent them from speaking.

gangsal I five (*kr for* **lima**).

II *reg* pomegranate (*kr for* **dlima**).

gangsar to go along smoothly, go without a hitch.

gangsing, gangsingan spinning-top.

gangsir mole-cricket;

nggangsir 1 resembling a mole-cricket; **2** to tunnel under a wall;

gangsiran 1 hole through which a thief tunnels under a wall; **2** *reg* a snack of fried **mlinjo** skin; **3** a dish of fried seasoned beef.

gangsrut, nggangsrut to glide on;

nggangsrutaké to glide s.t. over.

gangsul 1 improperly grouped, out of order; **2** curt; **3** odd (not even); **4** *var of* **gingsul**.

gangsur, nggangsur 1 to creep, wriggle (on the stomach); **2** to rub, massage.

ganita *lit* count (of syllables in poetry).

ganitrikundha *lit* rosary.

ganja 1 upper part of a kris, forged to the blade; **2** top part of a decorative pillar; **- iras** top part of a kris that matches the bottom; **- wulung** top part of a kris that does not match the bottom.

ganjah *reg* easily bored. *See also* **gènjèh**.

ganjak *reg* till, until, so that.

ganjar, ngganjar to reward s.o.; to give a prize to;

ginanjar received from God's hand;

ganjaran 1 reward, prize; **2** punishment, retribution.

ganjèk *var of* **ganji**.

ganjel *or* **ganjelan 1** a wedge; **2** a prop, support;

ngganjel 1 to wedge in, wedge tight; 2 to prop s.t. up; 3 to have s.t. wrong with the eye or stomach; 4 to weigh on one's mind.

ganji *reg* till, until, so that.

ganjil odd (not even);

ganjilan remainder after an odd number is divided by 2.

ganjing, gonjang-ganjing to shake, tremble.

ganjit, gonjat-ganjit unsteady.

ganjling *reg* easy, good (way).

ganjras exquisite, well-dressed,

ganjret, ngganjret to rotate rapidly.

ganjur *lit* spear;

ngganjur to attack with a spear.

ganol *reg* cassava flower;

ngganol to sit around idly.

ganong *var of* **ganung**.

gantal I a betel leaf rolled and thrown down by both bride and groom to each other at the the moment they meet at the wedding ceremony. II, **gantalan** lapse of time; **ora gantalan**... within a... (period of time).

gantang measure of rice equivalent to 3.125 kg, around one quart; **nggantang** to pound (rice) to remove the husks (*kr for* **tutu**); **gantangan** a large wooden mortar for pounding rice (*kr for* **lesung**).

gantar long bamboo pole, *esp* for reaching things high up. *See also* **gèntèr**.

gantas I loud *var of* **bantas**. II, **nggantasi** to cut off/down (trees, plants). *See also* **rantas**.

gantèn betel quid (*kr for* **kinang**).

ganter, ngganter 1 to produce loud steady sounds; 2 to do s.t. ascetic (fast, remain awake for a long period of time *etc*) rigorously in order to fulfil a wish.

gantha idea, notion, concept; **nggantha** *or* **nggantha-gantha** to picture, imagine;

ganthan *or* **geganthan** visualisation, imaginings.

ganthang, ngganthang to dry s.t. in the sun; **ganthangan** equipment for hanging s.t in the sun and air.

gantheng, nggantheng 1 handsome, dashing; 2 straight and strong (*esp* of rope).

ganthèt clinging together, connected; **ngganthètaké** to fasten things together, *e.g.* by stringing things on a line.

ganthol hook, barb-shaped piece of wood; **ngganthol** *or* **nggantholi** to hook; to catch s.t. with a hook; **gantholan** 1 large hook to seize with; 2 hanger, a hook to hang s.t. on.

ganti *ng*, **gantos** *kr*, 1 substitute, replacement; 2 (to make) a change (name, address, clothes *etc*); 3 in turn; **ngganti** to change, replace, substitute for, make up for; **ngantèni** 1 to substitute, replace; 2 to continue as a replacement; **gonta-ganti** 1 to take turns, by turns; 2 to keep changing back and forth. *See also* **genti**.

gantil *or* **gantilan** object from which s.t. hangs (stalk, hook, ring *etc*); **nggantil** hanging (from).

ganting *var of* **gantil**.

gantos I to pawn (*root form: kr for* **gadhé**). II (to make) a change, replacement (*kr for* **ganti**).

gantung, hanging, suspended; - **siwur** seventh-generation ancestor or descendant; **nggantung** 1 to hang o.s.; 2 to hang s.t.; - **kepuh** to wear the same clothing day after day; - **laku** ready to be sent as a messenger; **nggantungi** 1 to hang up (clothing); 2 to hang objects on;

nggantungaké 1 to hang s.t. on; 2 to depend on;

gantungan hanger for clothing;

gumantung 1 to hang (down); 2 to depend;

panggantungan gallows, hangman's noose.

gantya *lit* changing. *See also* **ganti**.

gantyan *lit* betel quid. *See also* **gantèn**.

ganu *reg* formerly.

ganung inedible hard core of pineapple or breadfruit.

ganyang, ngganyang 1 to eat (foods) raw; 2 to crush, stamp out;

ganyangan snack food.

ganyong a variety of arrowroot.

ganyuk, ngganyuk to get too close (to);

gonyak-ganyuk improper, unseemly.

gaocèh, nggaocèh to chat, talk mindlessly.

gaok 1 *reg* crow; 2 the cawing of a crow.

gaol, nggaol-gaol to gnaw s.t. with difficulty.

gaong a hollowing out, erosion.

gaota, nggaota to work, earn one's living;

panggaota occupation, livelihood.

gap, gap-gapan to grope around, fumble.

gapah, nggapah to look down on, consider of no importance.

gapé, nggapé to pay attention to.

gapèt *var of* **gapit**.

gapit 1 tongs; 2 stick by which a shadow-play puppet is held; 3 bamboo handle; 4 pincers, tweezers;

nggapit 1 to pick up with tweezers; 2 to equip s.t. with a stick or handle; 3 partial, unjust, biased;

gapitan 1 s.t. held with tongs; 2 s.t. used as tweezers;

ilang gapité *fig* to lose one's power or authority.

gaplah *reg* in vain, vainly.

gaplèk I dried cassava root slices;

nggaplèk to make (cassava root) into dried slices.

II a spank;

nggaplèk to spank.

gaplik, nggaplik 1 teetering on the edge of s.t.; 2 in small numbers/quantities.

gaplok 1 a worn-out bamboo pole; 2 *or* **mak gaplok** *repr* the sound or action of spanking;

nggaplok to spank;

gaplokan 1 act of spanking; 2 a person who is worn out but experienced;

goplak-gaplok (to deliver) repeated blows.

gapluk *var of* **gaplok**.

gaprek crumbling, decayed, rotting.

gapruk *or* **mak gapruk** *repr* bodies colliding;

nggaprukaké to bump into, collide with (another person);

gaprukan act of colliding.

gaprus (*pron as:* **gapru:s**) *or* **mak gaprus** *repr* breaking, shattering.

gaprut smeared, spattered.

gapuk 1 rotting, decayed, crumbling; 2 *cr* old (of people).

gapunten *subst kr for* **gapura**.

gapura gate, gateway, portal.

gapyak I wooden sandals (*var of* **bakyak**).

II friendly (*var of* **grapyak**).

gapyuk *or* **mak gapyuk** *repr* an embrace;

nggapyuk to embrace, throw the arms around s.o.;

nggapyukaké to acquaint s. o. (with).

gar, ngegaraké to open s.t. out, develop;

megar to open out, expand, bloom;

megar-mingkup 1 to open and close by turns; 2 (of breathing) constricted.

gara, gara-gara 1 tumult, disturbance in nature; 2 commotion; 3 *coll* cause, instigation.

garad, nggarad *reg* to take wood from the forest.

garagaji a saw (*reg var of* **graji**).

garagati a small shade tree, the edible pods of this tree.

garah, nggarah to chat irresponsibly.

garaita variety of banana.

garakasih, nggarakasih or **anggarakasih** alternative name for **Selasa Kliwon** (an auspicious day).

garami (to engage in) business (*subst kr for* **dagang**). *See also* **grami II**.

garan handle, *esp* of a tool;
gegaran instruction book.

garang I fierce, cruel, ferocious.
II roasted; - **asem** rice-accompanying dish of steamed meat, chili and tamarind, wrapped in banana leaves;
nggarang 1 to roast (food) over coals; **2** to dry s.t. near a fire;
garangan 1 roaster; **2** roasted (food).

garangan mongoose.

garanggati *var of* **garagati**.

garap way of working, process of making;
nggarap to work (at, on), do;
nggarapi to tease s.o.;
nggarapaké to work on for s.o.;
garapan 1 work (to be) done; **2** homework.

garasi garage.

garba I *lit* **1** womb; **2** innermost part. *See also* **guwa**.
II, nggarba 1 to join (words) by vowel assimilation; **2** to summarise the contents (of); to interpret by selecting the essential parts;
garban assimilation of vowel sounds on word boundaries.

garbini, nggarbini *lit* pregnant.

garbis *reg* a variety of melon.

gardhèn 1 window curtain; **2** folding screen.

gardhu sentry box, guard's hut.

garebeg Muslim religious celebration; - **Mulud** festival commemorating the Prophet's birth. *See also* **grebeg**.

garèk *reg* left over. *See also* **kari**.

garem salt.

Garèng *way* clown-servant, the slow-witted eldest son of Semar.

garènggati *var of* **garagati**.

garèngpung a variety of cicada.

garep to want (*reg var of* **arep**).

gares I shin bone;
nggares to kick s.o. in the shins.
II hard, stony (soil);
nggares to hurt s.o.'s feelings.

garès shin bone (*var of* **gares**).

garet groove, furrow, trench;
nggaret or **nggareti** to make scratch marks (on);
garetan or **garet-garet 1** grooved, furrowed; **2** marked with scratches.
Also **geret**.

garèt scratched mark (*var of* **garit**).

garéyan *reg* coconut stalk.

gari left (over) (*reg var of* **kari**).

garing *ng*, **aking** *kr*, dry, dried up/out; - **kemlingking** or - **mekingking** bone dry;
nggaringaké to dry out;
garingan 1 dishes that are fried (as contrasted with soups or sauced foods); **2** to dance without musical accompaniment.

garini *lit* wife, queen.

garis 1 line separating one thing from another; **2** fate, lot;
nggaris or **nggarisi** to make a line;
ginaris predestined, preordained;
garisan ruler.

garit scratch mark;
nggarit to scratch with s.t. sharp.

garjita, nggarjita *lit* swept with a strong emotion;
panggarjita idea, awareness.

garningson or **garnisun** garrison, fort.

garoh I *reg* waterless, dry (coconut).
II *reg* illegal, contraband.

garok, nggarok *reg* to scratch.

garon rake. *See also* **garu**.

garong I robber, plunderer, looter;
nggarong to rob;
garongan plunder, stolen goods.
II, garong-garong or **gorang-garong**

loud and long (weeping);
 nggarong to weep.
garot, nggarot to gnaw on/at.
garpu fork.
garu I 1 harrow; 2 *reg* comb;
 nggaru 1 to harrow; 2 *reg* to comb.
 II aloe wood.
garudha a mythological bird; - yaksa
 mythological bird with a giant's face.
garuh *reg* tasteless, insipid.
garuk, nggaruk 1 to scratch (head, arm
 etc), curry (horse), scrape (pan *etc*),
 rake; 2 to round up people (in a raid);
 3 to rob, clean out;
 garukan 1 scratches; 2 scratching; 3 a
 round-up.
garung *reg* no longer fertile (ricefield).
garut I arrowroot.
 II *var of* garuk.
garwa spouse (*k.i. for* bojo).
garwita *lit* rough, defiant.
gas I 1 petrol; 2 gas;
 ngegas to speed up.
 II gauze.
 III, gas-gasan in a great hurry.
gasah, nggasah I to hone, polish.
 II, nggasah *or* nggegasah to stir up,
 provoke, incite.
gasak hit;
 nggasak 1 to attack, assault (by hitting or kicking); 2 to rub hard; 3 to
 take by force; 4 to steal, pilfer; 5 to
 thrash; 6 to devour;
 gasakan *or* gasak-gasakan to fight, hit
 or drub each other.
gasang I, nggasang *reg* 1 to set in place;
 2 to set fire to, ignite s.t.; 3 to trap;
 gasangan 1 s.t. kept ready, a spare; 2 a
 trap.
 II, gasangan *reg* 1 engagement,
 betrothal; 2 fiancé(e). *See also* pasang.
gasèk *reg* till, until.
gasik I early; (*pron as:* gasi:k) very early.
 II cleaned up, drained out (a garden
 area).

gasir *reg var of* gangsir.
gasruh *reg* to lose track, get things out of
 order.
gatal *var of* gantal.
gatel 1 itch; 2 eager for s.t.;
 nggateli to cause itching;
 nggatelaké 1 to irritate s.o.'s feelings;
 2 to cause to itch;
 gumatel to begin to sting (the morning sun at about 10 o'clock);
 gatelen 1 to suffer from itching; 2 to
 have the urge, be very keen to do s.t.
 (*e.g.* make love).
gatèn *see* gati.
gateng a certain freshwater fish.
gates boundary, limit (*reg var of* wates).
gatha *lit* (water)jar.
gathak I bamboo stalks used as a living
 fence or separation between areas;
 nggathaki to use s.t. as a border for.
 II, nggathaki to cheat s.o. out of
 (money, property).
gathèk, gathèkan intelligent, bright,
 quick to catch on.
gathèl *cr* penis; glans penis.
gatheng *var of* gathèng.
gathèng a children's game resembling
 jacks, played with pebbles.
gathèt odd (not even).
gathik 1 (of glasses *etc*) to tick against,
 make a tinkling or chinking sound;
 2 to squabble with each other, fall out.
gathil *var of* gathèl.
gatho *reg cr* penis.
gathok, I gathok-gathok to cut wood.
 II, nggathok to be addicted to.
 III, nggathok 1 to fix; 2 *reg* to press;
 gumathok fixed, stable, firm;
 gathokan *reg* s.t. that has been fixed
 (*see also* pathok).
gathot sliced dried cassava boiled in
 coconut milk.
gathuk 1 to meet, match, coincide;
 2 (*pron as:* gathu:k) *or* mak gathuk
 repr an unexpected coming together;

nggathukaké to match (things) up; gathukan 1 to be matched, joined, in harmony; 2 a harmonious match.

gathul *var of* gathèl.

gathung fierce, vicious.

gati I *lit* way (of doing).

II *ng*, gatos *kr*, serious, important; nggatèkaké 1 to take seriously; 2 to pay close attention to; gumati affectionately attentive; nggematèni to heap affection on.

gatos *kr for* gati. *See also* wigati.

gatra 1 form(ed), shap(ed); 2 in the formative stage; 3 *gram* clause; 4 in poetry, a group of lines forming a sense-unit; nggatra to fashion, shape.

gau long drawn-out wailing sound; nggau to wail.

gauk *var of* gau.

gaul, gaul-gaul to chew with difficulty from lack of teeth.

gaung echo, reverberation; nggaung to echo, reverberate.

gaup, nggaup to gather up/in with the hands.

gauta *see* gaota.

gawa *ng*, bekta *kr*, nggawa to bring, carry, take; nggawani 1 to take away; 2 to give s.t. to be taken away; 3 to give (a wedding gift) to a bride; nggawakaké to carry s.t. on s.o.'s behalf; nggawa-gawa *or* nggegawa to bring in, involve, drag into; gawan 1 that which is carried, s.t. to carry; 2 that which goes along with; 3 nature, character, temperament.

gawang I 1 two wooden uprights joined by a horizontal piece across the top; 2 goalposts; goalkeeper (in soccer); 3 measuring unit for firewood; gawangan wooden frame shaped as above (1) for making batik.

II, gawang-gawang *or* gumawang 1 clear; 2 to remember clearly.

gawar cord strung to mark off a forbidden area; - kentheng palm-fibre cord used for marking s.t. off; nggawari to mark off (an area), furnish (an area) with a boundary marker.

gawat serious, tense, critical, risky, fraught with danger.

gawé *ng*, damel *kr*, 1 job, task; 2 celebration; 3 trouble, problem, burden; 4 *or* agawé to cause, make; dadi - dangerous, risky; duwé - to hold a celebration; - pari- things to be done; gawé-gawé to invent tall tales; nggawé to make, construct, do; nggawèkaké to make for s.o.; digawé (saka) made of; me(r)gawé to work a field, plough using draught animals; gawéné one's habit or practice; gegawéan, gawéan 1 work; 2 a product of, made in; 3 manufactured (not natural); pagawé employee, official; pagawéan *or* panggawéan task, job, work; digawé-gawé *pass* done in an artificial manner; panggawé 1 deed, action; 2 act or way of making; 3 (evil) action, sorcery.

gawèl, nggawèl to bite (dog).

gaweng, nggaweng 1 to become dark, cloudy; 2 thick, bushy (moustache).

gawer I *var of* gawar.

II, nggawer strong; ora nggawer sepiraa negligible, insignificant.

gawil, nggawil *or* gowal-gawil loose, coming off.

gawing, nggawing at the edge, in a precarious position.

gawok astonished, surprised, amazed; gawok-gawok *or* gawokan *reg* very astonishing;

nggawokaké 1 to cause astonishment; **2** to be astonishing.

gawuk *see* **bawuk II**.

gayahan bamboo handle of a coconut-shell dipper.

gayam a certain tree with fragrant flowers and edible fruits;

gayaman a certain style of kris sheath.

gayar, nggayar *reg* to hire labour.

gayas, nggayas *reg* **1** to guess; **2** random, arbitrary.

gayat *reg* a long time.

gayel, nggayel to nibble, eat constantly.

gayem, nggayemi 1 to chew the cud; **2** (of people) *cr* very old;

gayeman 1 cud; **2** favourite dish.

gayeng I pleasant, warm, cordial.

II (*or* **nggayeng**) in rotation.

gayer, nggayer to go on and on without stopping.

gayes, nggayes to eat constantly.

gayol *reg* a trowel-like tool for weeding.

gayong *reg* dipper used for scooping water when bathing (*var of* **gayung**).

gayor I a hook on which a **gong** is hung.

II (of jaw, chin) prominent, jutting forward.

III deer tusk (*also* **gayur**).

gayuh, nggayuh to reach, attain, aspire (to);

gegayuhan aspiration, objective, ideal;

panggayuh act of achieving or aspiring to s.t.

gayuk within reach;

nggayuk to reach (*var of* **gayuh**).

gayung dipper used for scooping water when bathing. *Also* **gayong**.

gayur deer tusk (*var of* **gayor III**).

gayut, nggayutaké to connect, take in connection with;

gegayutan a connection, in connection with.

gé I *coll* to be made into s.t. (*var of* **gawé**).

II *coll* quick(ly) (*var of* **agé, gagé**).

III a day of the five-day market week (*shtf of* **wagé**).

gebag I at the same age level.

II 1 stick, club (*kr for* **gebug**); **2, nggebag** to win (a lottery); **3** to choose a winner in a game of chance;

gebagan a batch, group.

gebal, gebalan turf, sod; **nggebal** to cut sods.

gebambèr, nggebambèr hanging down, dangling loosely.

gebang I a certain palm tree the bark and leaf fibres of which are made into sacking material.

II, nggebang 1 to fight against each other, engage in battle; **2** to stab with a dagger;

gebang-gebangan to strike each other.

gébang, nggébang 1 to make fun of, tease, do in fun; **2** *way* to court, make love to.

gebeg, nggebeg to polish, scour;

gebegan 1 act of scouring; **2** the result of polishing.

gèbèg, gèbèg-gèbèg *or* **gébag-gèbèg** to shake one's head.

gèbèl *var of* **gèmbèl**.

gebeng, nggebeng to hold deep feelings;

gegebengan 1 innermost feelings; **2** guiding principle; **3** classification, category.

gebentus *var of* **kebentus**. *See* **bentus**.

geber a screen;

nggeberi to screen off (an area), furnish (a place) with a screen.

gèbèr *var of* **gèmbèl**.

gèbès to shake one's head as a dance movement;

gèbès-gèbès 1 to shake one's head in disagreement; **2** to refuse, turn down.

gebetheng *var of* **kebetheng**. *See* **betheng**.

gebibir, nggebibir wet and cold.

gebimbir *var of* **gebibir**.

gebincih *subst kr for* **kebiri**.

gebing *or* gebingan (in) slices, sliced;
nggebing *or* nggebingi to slice.

gebiri *var of* kebiri.

geblag 1 the day s.o. dies; 2 to lean backward too far (in a standing position);
nggeblag to fall on one's back;
nggeblagi to fall backwards on;
nggeblagaké to cause s.o. to lie or fall on their back;
kegeblag to fall over backwards.

geblas, nggeblas to depart suddenly without a word;
nggeblasaké to cause to go (away, off) suddenly.

gebleg 1 stupid, ignorant; 2 certain fabric of inferior quality.

geblèg 1 mat or mattress beater; 2 a snack made from scraped cassava;
nggeblèg to spank;
nggeblègi to clean (a mat, mattress) by beating it, beat s.t. with a wide implement.

geblog 1 palm's-breadth as a measure of width; 2 roll/bolt of fabric;
nggeblogi to beat s.t. with a wide implement.

geblug 1 (*pron as:* geblu:g) *or* mak geblug *repr* a thud; 2 dull, blunt;
nggeblugi 1 to hit, land a blow (on); 2 to tread on (soil) to tamp it firm.

gebog 1 a large wooden container; 2 banana tree log (*var of* debog, gedebog); 3 roll/bolt of fabric.

gébog, nggébog to tie (up) securely.

gebos *cr* to fart.

gebrag *or* mak gebrag *repr* s.t. striking a wooden surface;
nggebrag 1 to hit (s.t. wooden); 2 to frighten.

gebral *or* mak gebral *repr* a bursting sound.

gebras *var of* geblas, kepras.

gebrès 1 *repr* a sneeze; 2 to sneeze;
gebrès-gebrès 1 to keep sneezing; 2 to eject forcibly from the mouth.

gebrug (*pron as:* gebru:g) *repr* a heavy thud;
nggebrug to drop s.t. heavily;
gumebrug to fall heavily.

gebug *ng*, gebag *kr*, 1 club, cudgel; 2 to club;
gebugan 1 act of striking with a club; 2 (*or* gebug-gebugan) to beat each other;
nggebug to strike, beat; - racak to generalise;
nggebugi to beat repeatedly;
ngebugaké to strike with a stick.

gebuk *var of* kebuk.

gebung roll, bolt;
nggebung *or* nggebungi to roll, make into a roll;
gebungan in rolls.

gebyag I, nggebyag to fall off/down.
II, nggebyagaké to perform;
gebyagan a performance.

gebyah, nggebyah 1 to generalise; 2 to work (soil) fine with a hoe-like tool;
nggebyah-uyah to generalise, make no distinction.

gebyar 1 to glitter, sparkle, shine; 2 glance, sight; 3 superficially attractive;
gumebyar *or* gebyar-gebyar sparkling;
sagebyaran a glance.

gebyas flask, vial.

gebyog wooden exterior house wall;
gebyogan coast, shoreline (*var of* gebyugan).

gebyug similar, almost the same;
nggebyug 1 (of water, waves) to hit, pound, beat; 2 to go along with the crowd, do as others do;
gebyugan 1 coast, shoreline; 2 to guess at random.

gebyur 1 (*pron as:* gebyu:r) *repr* splashing; 2 to take a splash bath;
nggebyur 1 to plunge into; 2 to splash water on one's body; 3 to make (coffee, tea) with sugar in it;

gebyuran coffee or tea with sugar dissolved in it;

gebyar-gebyur to take a bath by scooping and pouring water on one's body repeatedly.

gecak, nggecak 1 to beat, pound, soften up; **2** to attack (the enemy).

gecas, gecas-gecos (to make) repeated axe strokes.

gecek *see* **gecak**.

gècèk *var of* **gocèk**.

gecel, nggecel to massage the neck and head.

gècèl *reg* **1** uneven; **2** a bump or swelling of irregular shape.

gecem, nggecem *cr reg* to sleep with s.o.

gecèt *reg* inconstantly, fickle.

geci, nggeci (of child) crafty like an adult.

gecil *reg* (of nut) having one seed.

gecing, nggecing I small at the centre, hourglass-shaped.

II accustomed to.

III 1 cured, reformed; **2** wary, chary.

gecit, nggecit to run fast.

gecok a dish prepared from minced meat;
nggecok to tenderise (meat) by pounding;

gecok gunem word of mouth;

gecok mentah raw minced meat.

gécol *var of* **gècèl**.

gecos *or* **mak gecos** *repr* a sharp blade striking;

gecas-gecos *see* **gecas**.

gécot *reg* slanting, sloping.

gecrak, gecrak-gecrèk *see* **gecrèk**;
gecrak-gecrok *see* **gecrok**.

gecrèk, gecrak-gecrèk to chop (at) with a sharp blade.

gecrok, gecrak-gecrok (to make) repeated axe strokes. *See also* **gecas**.

gecul roguish, arch;

nggecul to do roguishly, archly.

gecut *reg* to fade away.

gedabag woven bamboo wall panel of inferior quality. *See also* **dabag**.

gedabig (*pron as:* **gedabi:g**) *or* **mak gedabig** *repr* falling down after slipping;

gedabigan 1 to keep moving around, twist, writhe; **2** to keep tossing and turning. *See also* **gedébag**.

gedabrul, nggedabrul to play around, fool around.

gedabul, nggedabul 1 dirty, muddy; **2** *var of* **nggedabrul**.

gedabur *var of* **gedabrul**.

gedandap *or* **mak gedandap** *repr* a disagreeable surprise;

gedandapan taken aback, unsettled, disagreeably surprised.

gedebag-gedebug to stamp repeatedly. *See also* **gedebug**.

gedébag, nggedébag 1 to roll in one's sleep; **2** broad, expansive;

gedébagan to roll around in one's sleep, sleep restlessly.

gedebeg, gedebag-gedebeg *or* **pating gedebeg** making the sound of stamping feet.

gedéblag *var of* **gedébag**.

gedebog banana tree log. *See also* **debog**.

gedebug *or* **mak gedebug** *repr* a heavy thudding *or* stamping.

gedebus, nggedebus to babble, talk a lot of nonsense.

gedhabrah, nggedhabrah baggy, messy (clothes).

gedhabyah, gedhabyah-gedhabyah *repr* the visual impact of s.o. walking in loose floppy clothing;

nggedhabyah 1 overlarge clothing; **2** too much clothing;

pating gedhabyah dressed in loose, sagging garments.

gedhag I, nggedhag to snap at, to speak to s.o. angrily.

II gedhagan, sagedhagan *coll* (at) this time (as contrasted with other).

gedhag-gedhig 1 boastful; **2** to boast about o.s.

gedhag-gedhog to produce rapping sounds repeatedly. *See also* dhog.

gedhagrah, nggedhagrah big, lumbering and ugly.

gedhah 1 thick green window-glass; 2 green porcelain.

gedhah-gedhih *var of* kedhah-kedhih.

gedhakal, gedhakalan *var of* kedhakalan. *See* dhakal.

gedhana-gedhini boy-girl sibling combination (*var of* kedhana-kedhini).

gedhandho *reg* hesitant, undecided (*var of* bedhandho).

gedhandhul *or* mak gedhandhul *repr* a sudden drop into a hanging position when knocked off balance;
nggedhandhul to drop into a position as above.

gedhang *ng*, pisang *kr*, banana; - selirang 1 a bunch of bananas; 2 a certain roof type of a traditional house.

gedhangklik fitting loosely (a dove-tailed joint);
nggedhangklik to fit too loosely into its matching part;
pating gedhangklik *or* gedhongklak-gedhangklik (loose-fitting joints) to wobble.

gedhangkrang *var of* kedhangkrang.

gedhangsang, gedhangsangan 1 to try to catch up with, overtake; 2 to do with great difficulty or in the face of obstacles.

gedhapal, gedhapalan to trudge on.

gedhawa, nggedhawa *reg* to regard s.t. as the wrong one.

gedhé *ng*, agéng *kr*, big, great, large; - cilik all sizes, everyone in every age group; wong - an important person;
nggedhèni to make s.t. larger;
nggedhèkaké 1 to make larger; 2 to do to a large extent; 3 to increase; 4 to raise (children);
nggedhèk-nggedhèkaké to exaggerate, magnify out of proportion, over-

state s.t.;
manggedhèni to preside over, be in charge of;
kegedhèn too big, excessively large;
- sirah obstinate, conceited;
- rumangsan having a feeling of pride or superiority;
gedhèn on a large scale;
gedhèn-gedhènan 1 to compete for size; 2 on a large scale;
gumedhé conceited, arrogant;
panggedhé 1 an official, authority, functionary; 2 a high-ranking official, very important person, big shot;
gedhé-gedhéné at the very most, at the outside;
gedhé-ciliké the (comparative) size;
gedhé atiné encouraged, proud and happy;
kegedhèn empyak, kurang cagak *prov* to live beyond what one's station in life entitles one to.

gedhébyah, nggedhébyah 1 (of hair) long and unkempt; 2 hanging in loose folds (of overlarge clothing). *See also* kedhébyah.

gedhèdhèr *var of* kedhèdhèr.

gedheg I, gedheg-gedheg to shake the head in disbelief (*var of* gèdhèg).
II, nggedheg to dress elegantly.

gedhèg a panel of woven bamboo; rai - *idiom* thick-skinned, insensitive;
nggedhèg *or* nggedhègi 1 to provide (a house) with bamboo panel walls; 2 to enclose (a house) with a bamboo panel fence.

gèdhèg to shake the head; - anthuk *idiom* 1 to merely nod or shake the head rather than contributing opinions; 2 to collaborate in a scheme;
gèdhèg-gèdhèg *or* gédhag-gèdhèg to keep shaking the head;
nggèdhègaké to shake the head.

gedhegel *var of* bedhegel.

gedhelé *var of* kedhelé.

gedhem huge, enormous.

gèdhèng a measuring unit for rice plants: the amount that can be encircled by the thumbs and index fingers of the two hands;
nggèdhèngi to bundle (rice plants) as above;
gèdhèngan a bundle of rice plants formed according to the above measure; act of forming such bundles.

gedhempal *var of* gedhampal.

gedhengkreng *var of* kedhèngkrèng.

gedhepek *var of* kedhepek.

gedhepes *var of* kedhepes.

gedhi very big, enormous (*var of* gedhem).

gedhig 1 back part of a sickle (for beating); 2 (*or* gedhigan) flail;
nggedhig 1 to beat with the back part of a sickle; 2 to thresh (*e.g.* soybeans).

gedhingkring, nggedhingkring (to sit) in a high position, higher than s.o. else (a breach of etiquette).

gedhini *see* gedhana.

gedhobrah *var of* gedhobroh.

gedhobroh, gedhobrohan too large, loose, ill-fitting (clothes).

gedhobyah *var of* gedhabyah.

gedhobyah-gedhobyoh loose, ill-fitting.

gedhodhor, nggedhodhor loose, dragging on the ground (clothes).

gedhog I heavy thumping sound;
wayang - *see* wayang;
nggedhog (to make) repeated thumping sounds.
II, gedhogan horse stable.

gedhoh, gedhohan 1 dregs; 2 *cr* behaviour, actions.

gedhok *reg* ricefield (*var of* kedhok II).

gedhong I building of brick or stone (as contrasted with wood, bamboo); - kiwa royal court official who is in charge of the left building; - komidhi theatre; - tengen royal court official who is in charge of the right building;

- mayangarum residence of a king's wives; - peteng jail, prison;
nggedhong to build a brick house;
gedhongan 1 a complex of brick houses; 2 sleeping room at the back of a Javanese house; 3 palace outbuilding where food is stored and prepared;
digedhongana dikuncènana *idiom* no matter how well protected s.o. is.
II a cloth used for wrapping a baby's body, arms and legs to keep it warm;
nggedhong to wrap a baby in such a way.

gedhongklak-gedhangklik *see* gedhangklik.

gedhug I, nggedhugaké to knock s.t. (against s.t.);
kegedhug to get knocked inadvertently;
gedhag-gedhug to keep pounding, produce knocking sounds repeatedly.
II, gegedhug heroic leader in battle.

gedhut *var of* kedhut.

gedhungsangan *var of* kedhungsangan. *See* dhungsang.

gedibag *see* gedébag.

gedibal 1 dirt adhering to the feet; 2 *cr* a subordinate, servant;
nggedibal (of dirt) to adhere to the feet.

gedibel, nggedibel to feel heavy and clumsy to the wearer or user.

gedibig, gedibigan to keep moving restlessly.

gedobrol, nggedobrol to boast, tell tall tales.

gedobros *var of* gedobrol.

gedrah *or* nggedrah usual, commonplace, normal.

gedrig 1 printing (as contrasted with handwriting); 2 printed (by hand, rather than written in cursive style).

gedrug I young laos plant.
II *or* nggedrug to stamp the foot (on);
nggedrugaké to stamp (the foot);

gedrug-gedrug *or* gedrag-gedrug to keep stamping the feet.

gedubang saliva reddened by chewing betel (*var of* dubang).

gedublong, nggedublong 1 to defecate; 2 to prattle, talk nonsense.

gedug *var of* gadug.

geduga *see* keduga.

géduk *var of* gaduk.

geduwung *see* keduwung.

gega to believe; to act according to (*root form: kr for* gugu).

gegana *lit* sky (*var of* gagana).

gégé I speeding-up process; banyu - water for bathing a baby to make it grow faster;

nggégé *or* nggégé mangsa to speed up the normal pace, try to force s.t. before its time. *See also* gé II.

II *var of* gaga.

gègèk, nggègèk 1 to laugh persistently; 2 to keep asking.

gegel a joint;

gegelan a jointed place, *esp* of puppets; kéwan - insect with jointed legs.

gegem a clenched fist;

nggegem 1 to grip; 2 - watu *fig* to secretly plot revenge;

nggegemaké 1 to make a fist; 2 to hold s.t. for s.o.;

gegeman 1 s.t. held in the clutched hand; 2 a fist;

sagegem a fistful.

geger *ng, kr,* pengkeran *k.i.* the upper back;

nggeger sapi (of roads) high in the middle and sloping off at the sides.

gègèr *or* gègèran turbulence, tumult, chaos; jaman - time of war, tumultuous period;

nggègèraké to cause panic or tumult.

geges, nggeges 1 *intsfr* cold; 2 sorrowful.

gègès, nggègès 1 to cough persistently; 2 to make merry; 3 *cr* to say, talk.

geget, nggeget to clench (the teeth) in anger;

geget-geget suruh exasperated, fuming with anger.

gegleg, nggegleg to sit silent and sorrowful.

gégoh to keep moving around restlessly *or* noisily;

nggégohi to disturb, bother s.o.

gègrèg (of hair, feathers) to fall *or* drop out;

nggègrègi to moult, shed;

nggègrègaké to pluck (out).

gèh *or* nggèh *reg var of* inggih.

gejojor, nggejojor to sit with the legs sticking out (impolite position).

gek *or* mak gek *repr* swallowing;

gek-gek *repr* drinking.

gèk I 1 (and) then, after that; 2 *urging* come on! quick!; 3 *expression of doubt* I wonder, could it be...; gèk iya gèk ora indecisive, undecided; 4 (at the time) when (*var of* dhèk); 5 *coll var of* lagi in the process of.

II, nggèk in, at, on.

gekeng, nggekeng 1 with concentrated effort; 2 firm, fast.

gela disappointed, let down;

nggelani disappointing, irritating;

nggelakaké to disappoint, irritate s.o.;

kegelan disappointed, hurt.

gelah, gelah-gelah the dregs;

gelah-gelahing jagad the dregs of society.

gelak, nggelak to (do) quickly, quicken one's pace;

gelakan quickly finished.

gelang *ng, kr,* binggel *k.i.,* bracelet;

nggelangi to provide s.o. with a bracelet;

gelangan 1 ring, hoop; 2 watch bracelet; 3 gymnastic rings; 4 wrist, ankle; 5 to wear a bracelet;

gegelang 1 *lit* to wear a bracelet; 2 (various kinds of) bracelets.

gelap I dark, undercover, illicit;

nggelap to flee;

nggelapi to break through (a roof), to repair or replace it;

nggelapaké 1 to embezzle; 2 to break through (a roof) on s.o.'s behalf.

II lightning; - ngampar lightning that strikes s.t.

gelar I array, layout, deployment;

nggelar or nggelari to reveal, spread, disseminate;

nggelari to spread onto;

nggelaraké to spread, unfold, reveal (on s.o.'s behalf);

gelaran mat (kr for klasa);

pagelaran 1 an open hall where a monarch holds audience; 2 (of wayang, theatre etc) performance.

II title, academic degree;

nggelari to confer a title/degree on.

gelas 1 drinking glass; 2 glassful; 3 reg glass (the substance);

nggelas to coat (a kite string) with glue containing sharp glass fragments;

nggelasaké to glass s.o.'s kite strings;

gelasan 1 (of kite strings) coated with bits of ground glass; 2 ground glass for kite strings. 3 using glasses for drink.

gelek reg frequently.

gelem ng, purun kr, kersa k.i., to be willing, accept willingly;

nggelemi to agree (to), express willingness;

geleman 1 willing, obedient; 2 promiscuous; 3 covetous, apt to steal;

sagelem-gelemé to do as much as one likes;

gelem-gelem ora hesitant, undecided;

gelem ora gelem compulsory; to have to, must.

geleng quite certain;

nggeleng or gumeleng to make up one's mind.

gèlèng, gèlèng-gèlèng or gélang-gèlèng to keep shaking the head.

geli 1 annoyed; 2 to have a compulsion to laugh.

gelik, gelik-gelik alone in a deserted place.

gelis ng, énggal kr, speedy, quick;

nggelisaké to speed up;

gelis-gelisan 1 to compete; 2 to do hastily.

gélo I reg rupiah.

II, géla-gélo to move the head to left and right.

geluk reg smoke.

gelung ng, kr, ukel k.i. traditional Javanese ladies' hairstyle; - bokor ladies' hairstyle for a special occasion; - kondhé everyday ladies' hairstyle; - kadhal-mènèk male hairstyle worn beneath a headdress: long hair wound on top of head; - supit urang ladies' hairdo with the hair wound on both sides in a bun; - tekuk ladies' hairstyles for special occasions;

nggelung 1 (or gelungan) to arrange (the hair) as above; 2 to tie into a bundle.

gelut or gelutan to fight, struggle, wrestle.

gemah prosperous (of a country); - ripah prosperous and abundant in wealth and population.

gemak a small female quail, formerly used for fighting;

gemakan 1 Indian wrestling with thumbs rather than forearms; 2 a striped locust-like insect.

gemang unwilling.

gembak large woven bamboo container.

gembala beard (k.i. for jénggot).

gembaya red material for kerchiefs.

gembel a short iron-headed club;

nggembel productive, fruitful.

gèmbèl 1 dewlap (of cattle); 2 wattles (of rooster); 3 unkempt, tangled, unruly (of hair).

gembèlèng, nggembèlèng haughty;

gembèlèngan or gembélang-gembèlèng 1 conceited; 2 (to walk, conduct o.s.) with a superior air.

gembélo, nggembélo 1 large (of the head); 2 *fig* vain, conceited.

gembèng to cry easily; - krèwèng *or* - cèngèng/cingèng apt to cry at the slightest provocation.

gembes *reg var of* ngembes.

gembès I flat(tened), deflated;
  nggembès to go flat;
  nggembèsi to deflate (tyres);
  nggembèsaké to deflate, let the air out of;
  nggembèsan prone to go flat;
  gembèsan flat and wide (teapot).
  II 1 small leather bag; 2 *reg* pocket.
  III, nggembès *reg* to heed, give one's attention to.

gembil fat, plump (of cheeks).

gembili a plant which produces an oval turnip-like tuber with a potato-like flavour.

gembira overjoyed (*var of* gambira).

gembiralaya a deep ocean (*var of* gambiralaya).

gemblak I brass-smith;
  gemblakan quarter of the brass-smiths.
  II small bottle.
  III *or* gemblakan male performer of classical songs and dances;
  nggemblaki to have homosexual relations with.

gemblang, nggemblang *or* gumemblang clear and bright (sky, weather).

gembleb chubby-cheeked.

gèmblèh, nggèmblèh *or* gèmblèh-gèmblèh *or* gémblah-gèmblèh hanging down limply (of fleshy parts).

gembleng 1 to be firm in a desire or intention; 2 totally;
  nggemblengaké to total up, consolidate, to concentrate;
  gemblengé roughly totalling, approximately.

gemblèng, nggemblèng 1 to forge (iron);

2 to train rigorously;
  gemblèngan 1 forged iron (bars); 2 blacksmith's hammer used in forging; 3 rigorously trained.

gémblok, nggémblok to cling to.

gemblong a snack made of mashed glutinous rice or cassava.

gemblung crazy, maddened;
  nggemblung 1 to feign madness; 2 to root out (wild tubers); 3 to plunge or roll into.

gembok padlock;
  nggembok to padlock.

gémbol, nggémbol to carry s.t. concealed;
  gémbolan 1 s.t. carried concealed on one's person; 2 a secret talent.

gembolo a certain edible tuber.

gémbong leader, head.

gembor I watering-can;
  nggembor to water plants with a watering-can.
  II, nggembor to cry noisily;
  gembor-gembor *or* gembar-gembor to do a lot of loud talking or shouting.

gembos *or* nggembos to become deflated suddenly.

gembrang *repr* a metallic clatter.

gembrèk, gembrèk-gembrèk to keep shouting from pain.

gembrèng 1 tin can used as a noisemaker; 2 oil can.

gembrèt, nggembrèt 1 out of tune, off key; 2 to scamper, scurry.

gembring 1 filmy, gauzy; 2 *reg* fake, counterfeit.

gembro lazy, lackadaisical.

gembrong, (ge)gembrongan *reg* to make a lot of noise.

gembrot I bulky, ponderous (physique).
  II a dish made with shredded coconut with boiled vegetables.

gembur, gembur-gembur soft and spongy. *See also* embur.

gemes irritated, provoked;

nggemesaké irritating, provocative.

gemet all gone, completely finished.

gemi frugal, thrifty; - **nastiti** thrifty and careful;

nggemèni to use frugally.

gemiyèn formerly (*reg var of* **biyèn**).

gemladhag flowing swiftly. *See* **gladhag III**.

gemledheg producing a heavy rumbling. *See* **gledheg I**.

gemlèdhèg to flow swiftly. *See* **glèdhèg**.

gemlidhig to flow freely, smoothly. *See* **glidhig II**.

gemlindhing to roll. *See* **glindhing**.

gemludhug producing a thunder-like noise. *See* **gludhug**.

gemlupak *reg* startled, flustered.

gemluwèh careless, frivolous, inattentive. *See* **gluwèh**.

gempal eroded, dilapidated (crumbling in ruins);

nggempalaké to damage s.t. accidentally.

gempang done away with, eliminated, cleaned out.

gémpar, nggémpar to kick.

gempi soft, requiring little or no chewing.

gempil chipped, damaged;

nggempilaké to chip a piece from;

gempilan a chip, something chipped.

gemplang I, nggemplang *reg* to throw.

II, nggemplang to dry s.t. in the sun;

gumemplang excessively hot (sunshine).

gempleng total, whole, at all (*var of* **gembleng**);

nggemplengaké to total up.

gemplung *intsfr* empty; **suwung** - completely empty.

gempol 1 a certain fruit, also its tree; 2 rice balls used in a certain porridge.

gémpor, nggémpor to kick (*var of* **gémpar**).

gemprong scolding, verbal abuse;

nggemprong to scold, abuse.

gemprongan 1 scolding; 2 sounds produced by beating a wooden pounder rhythmically against a wooden trough (**lesung**).

gempung 1 annoyed, vexed; 2 *var of* **gempang**.

gemrayah 1 prolific; 2 itchy all over. *See* **grayah**.

gemrining *intsfr* clear, pure. *See also* **grining**.

gemuh big and fat.

gemuk lubricating grease;

nggemuk to grease s.t.

gemuruh (to make) loud thundering sounds. *See* **guruh**.

genah 1 well-behaved, conforming to normal standards, polite; 2 clear, plain; **ora** - improper; abnormal;

nggenah (of one's behaviour) normal, within proper limits;

nggenahaké to make clear;

panggenah act of clarifying.

genau to learn, study (*reg var of* **sinau**).

gencer 1 continuous, right on, unswerving; 2 incessant;

nggencer to interrogate incessantly.

gencèr *var of* **gencer**.

gendam a charm, magic spell;

nggendam 1 to cast a spell (on); 2 to meditate in order to bring about a miracle; 3 to catch fish by using poisoned bait.

gendani a tiny bamboo-like plant.

gendèr instrument with bronze keys suspended over bamboo sounding-tubes;

nggendèr to play such an instrument;

nggendèri to accompany a melody with such an instrument;

gendèran act of playing the above instrument;

panggendèr 1 player of the above instrument; 2 act of playing the above instrument.

gendéra flag.

gendhak I, nggendhak *or* gendhakan to

interfere with; - **sikara** *lit* to disturb.

II gendhakan concubine, mistress, lover.

gendhalungan to talk impolitely or misuse the speech levels, *e.g.* to use Krama improperly.

gendharah-gendhèrèh *see* **gendhèrèh**.

gendhek short and thick (neck).

gèndhel a bound volume (*var of* **bèndhel**).

gèndhèl 1 bunch, bundle; **2** small packet of coconut sugar;
nggèndhèl to hang s.t.;
gèndhèlen hanging down and swollen (*e.g.* newly pierced ears);
gèndhèl-gèndhèl to hang down.

gendheleng, nggendheleng *or* **gendhelang-gendheleng** to have a stupid look.

gendheng crazy, idiotic;
nggendheng to behave witlessly.

gendhèng I 1 roofing tile; **2** tiled roof.
II, nggendhèng *or* **gendhèngan** *reg* to sing to the accompaniment of gamelan music.

gèndhèng, (*root form*) to pull (at), drag;
- **cènèng** relation, cooperation;
nggèndhèng to pull (at), drag;
- **cènèng** to cooperate, pull together;
gèndhèng-gèndhèngan *or* **gèndhèng-ginèndhèng** to pull back and forth;
kegèndhèng to get pulled/dragged;
panggèndhèng act of pulling.

gendhèrèh, gendharah-gendhèrèh to hang untidily, sloppily, loosely (of overlarge clothing).

gendhéwa bow (for shooting arrows);
nggendhéwa bow-shaped.

gendhi *reg* earthenware water carafe with a spout (*var of* **kendhi**).

gendhil, nggendhil *reg* **1** (of child) to keep suckling on the breast; **2** to keep being carried in a **sléndang**.

gendhila *or* **nggendhila** *reg* crude, rude.

gendhing I gamelan melody;

nggendhing to play a melody;
gendhingan to sing a song.
II gamelan instrument-maker;
gendhingan quarter of the gamelan makers.

gendhis sugar (*kr for* **gula**).

gendhok half of a pair of sugar cakes;
sagendhok one such piece. *See also* **tangkep II**.

géndhol, nggéndholi 1 to hang onto, cling to; **2** to hold back;
nggéndholaké to hang, suspend;
géndhol-géndhol to keep bouncing;
pating gréndhol *pl* hanging down.

gendhon I rattan or **arèn** worm (grilled and eaten).
II queen (flying) termite.
III, gendhon rukon *prov* (of marriage partners) to get along well together, to be compatible.
IV earthen balls for supporting a corpse in the grave.

géndhong 1 piggyback ride; **2** carrying in a sling;
nggéndhong 1 to carry on the back; **2** to carry in a sling; **3** to carry (*esp* a child) astraddle;
géndhongan 1 thing carried on the back; **2** to ride on s.o.'s back; **3** carrying cloth;
géndhong-géndhongan to take turns carrying on the back;
nggéndhong lali *idiom* single-minded, oblivious to everything else;
nggéndhong-mikul overburdened.

géndhor, géndhor-géndhor soggy, squashy.

géndhot, nggéndhoti to hang s.t. onto.

gendhuk lass, girl.

gendhung, gendhungan *or* **gumendhung** to boast;
adol gendhung to boast (*see also* **adol**).

gendhut fat, paunchy.

gendir, nggendir to shoot (a marble);
gendiran 1 to play marbles; **2** *way* a

certain puppet arm movement in a shadow-play.

gendug *see* **genduk.**

genduk I, **genduk-genduk** very soft, tender.

II, **nggenduki** (of crickets) near at hand, within touching distance.

gendul bottle;

gendulan by the bottle(ful), in bottles.

gendut 1 *repr* bouncing, springing; **2** fat, paunchy (*var of* **gendhut**).

gendra turbulent.

gendrèh 1 fine, pretty; **2** beauty, prettiness.

gendring, **nggendring** to flee, speed off, run fast.

gendruk plump, chubby.

gendruwo a kind of ghost inhabiting lonely places (trees, woods).

genem, **nggenem** to cook (leaf-wrapped foods) by steaming in hot ash;

geneman 1 steamed leaf-wrapped food; **2** piled up hot ash for steaming foods.

See also **benem.**

geneng in a high location; **ledhok** - hilly (*see also* **ledhok**);

genengan high ground, high location.

genep 1 complete(d), (in) full; **2** even (not odd) (*inf var of* **ganep**).

genet flour.

généya why? how come? *Also* **yagéné.**

geng large, big, great (*var of* **ageng**).

genggeng, **nggenggeng** to look splendid/majestic.

geni *ng*, **latu** *kr*, fire;

nggenèni to warm s.t. up, put s.t. on the stove to heat;

gegeni *or* **gegenèn** to stay near a fire, *esp* to warm o.s.;

ora ana geni tanpa kukus *prov* the truth will out.

genitri a certain seed, often used for necklaces and other trinkets (*also* **jenitri**).

geniwara to deny o.s. cooked foods as a self-sacrificial act in order to be granted one's desire.

geniyara *var of* **geniwara.**

genjé cannabis.

gènjèh easily bored, fickle, unreliable.

gentayang, **nggentayang** to stagger, sway from side to side;

gentayangan 1 staggering; **2** wandering, roaming about.

gentéyong, **nggentéyong** to hang down;

gentéyongan *or* **gentéyang-gentéyong** to keep hanging down;

pating gentéyong *pl* hanging everywhere.

genter, **nggenter** to keep making loud noises.

gèntèr long bamboo pole, *esp* for reaching things high up;

nggèntèr to get s.t. down from a high place with a pole.

gentéwang *or* **mak gentéwang** *repr* a downward swoop or unexpected fall.

gentha 1 large metal bell with a clapper; **2** cow-bell;

genthan bell-shaped.

genthana, **nggenthana** *reg* **1** to (do) s.t. recklessly; **2** to work assiduously. *See also* **gethini.**

genthélo, **nggenthélo** (of child) to sit comfortably on s.o.'s lap.

genthèng 1 roofing tile; **2** tiled roof (*var of* **gendhèng**).

genthileng, **nggenthileng** black and shining (eyes).

genthiyeng, **nggenthiyeng** strong, robust.

gentho robber, bandit.

genthong large earthen pitcher for keeping a supply of water handy;

nggenthong resembling an earthen pitcher; - **umos** *idiom* unable to keep a secret.

genthot *reg* female singer or dancer.

genti *ng*, **gentos** *kr* **1** a change, replacement; **2** to change, shift; **3** in (one's) turn; - **tapak** to follow in s.o.'s foot-steps;

nggenti to replace;

nggentèni 1 to take the place of, fill the position of, substitute; **2** to receive (goods) through other than normal retail channels;

nggentèkaké to sell s.t. newly bought to s.o. else;

gentènan *or* **genti-gentèn** to take turns.

genting *or* **nggenting** frayed, nearly broken through;

gentingan in a frayed or nearly broken condition.

gentos a change; by turns (*kr for* **genti**).

gentoyong, nggentoyong 1 (top) heavy; **2** (of gait) unsteady, lopsided.

gentur with complete devotion;

nggentur to meditate rigorously.

gentus, nggentus *reg* to bump. *See also* **bentus**.

gentya *lit, var of* **genti**.

genuk small clay container for rice.

genurasa *lit* to hold a discussion.

genyal *or* **gumenyal** soft and yielding (*var of* **kenyal**).

genyang (of speaking) in a deliberately attractive way.

genyèng *var of* **genyang**.

genyol *var of* **genyal**.

gepah in a hurry (*md for* **gupuh**).

gepak flat (as contrasted with convex or pointed).

gepang *reg* destroyed, exterminated.

gepèng *var of* **gèpèng**.

gèpèng flat, two-dimensional;

nggèpèngaké to make s.t. flat;

gèpèngan flattened.

gepit, nggepit to squeeze. *See also* **jepit**.

gepok a touch; - **sénggol** to have a connection with;

nggepok 1 to touch; **2** to come into contact with; to concern; **3** to repri-

mand lightly;

gepokan to be in contact with;

magepokan concerned/connected (with).

geprak 1 noisemaker for scaring birds or squirrels away from a crop (*see also* **goprak**); **2** *reg* small wooden box tapped for a castanet-like beat.

gepruk, nggepruk to beat, smash, crack, break (*var of* **kepruk**).

gepyah, nggepyah to generalise (*var of* **gebyah**).

gepyok a bundle of palm-leaf ribs used for killing flies or mosquitoes;

nggepyok *or* **nggepyoki** to hit, whack;

gepyokan a variety of traditional tonic or medicine *esp* for a woman after giving birth.

ger 1 *or* **mak ger** *repr* laughing; **2** funny;

gar-ger *repr* laughing together repeatedly;

ger-geran *pl* to laugh constantly.

gerah 1 sick, ill (*k.i. for* **lara**); - **uyang 1** feverish; **2** bewildered; **3** having a compulsive appetite.

II *lit* thunder; - **kapat** thunder in the fourth month or beginning of the rainy season.

gerak to move; - **badan** sports, athletics.

gerang 1 worn out, of no further use; **2** old enough to know better; - **dhap-lok/gaplok** an old hand, one who is sophisticated, worldly-wise.

gerap *reg var of* **geras**.

geras 1 absorbent; **2** generous with one's money.

gerat *reg* **1** feverish; **2** (of weather) very hot.

gerba assimilation (*var of* **garba**);

nggerba 1 to summarise the contents (of); **2** to join (words) by vowel assimilation;

gerban 1 assimilation of vowel sounds at word boundaries; **2** word formed by assimilation.

gerbong railway carriage.

gerdim *var of* gerdin.

gerdin *reg* bed with mosquito net.

geré not productive (ricefield).

gerèh a small flat round dried salt fish.

gereng, nggereng 1 to growl; 2 to moan, groan.

geret *see* garet.

gerih *reg var of* gerèh.

gering 1 languishing, sickly; 2 thin, emaciated; 3 sick (of animals, *cr* of people);
geringan prone to illness;
geringen sickly, frail;
gegering *or* pagering epidemic.

gerit *repr* a squeaking sound;
nggerit to squeak;
gumerit to make a squeaking sound;
pating glerit *pl* to make squeaking sounds everywhere.

germa 1 hunter; 2 brothel-keeper; 3 pimp, procurer, panderer.

gero, nggero to roar;
gero-gero 1 to utter a cry/snarl/growl; 2 to cry with loud wailing;
panggero act of roaring.

gerok hoarse.

gerong *or* nggerong hollow, sunken (eyes).

gerot *or* mak gerot *repr* a scraping sound, nggerot *or* gumerot *or* gerot-gerot to make scraping sounds.

gerpu *reg var of* garpu.

gertak, nggertak to shout down, bluff;
gertakan (act of) bluffing.

geru, geru-geru *reg* in haste.

gerung, nggerung 1 to make a roaring noise; 2 to cry loudly.

gerus I, nggerus 1 to grind; 2 to press, polish (textile).
II, nggerus to suffer pain.

gerut I (*pron as:* geru:t) *or* mak gerut *repr* a scraping sound. *See* gerot.
II, gerut-gerut (of skin) wrinkled, creased, furrowed.

gesah *var of* gusah.

gesang 1 life; 2 to live; 3 functioning, operating, active (*kr for* urip).

gesau to learn, study (*reg var of* sinau).

geseng 1 burned, scorched; 2 bruised, black-and-blue;
nggesengaké to let s.t. get burned, scorched.

geses *lit* all gone, finished.

gesik 1 sand, ground brick; 2 toothpaste made from powdered red brick;
nggesik to brush with this powder.

gesil, nggesil to munch.

gesuh, nggesuh *reg* to fade away.

getak snarl, snapping; - gajah a plant the leaves of which are used in medicines;
nggetak 1 to shout, snarl at; 2 *reg* (of highly spiced foods) bitingly hot.

getap, getapan 1 easily shocked; 2 easily annoyed, quick tempered.

getèh blood (*reg var of* getih).

getem, getem-getem to experience pent-up anger, be angry but not let it show;
nggetem untu to show or clench the teeth in anger.

getèn hardworking, industrious.

geter 1 to shake, tremble; 2 *way* continuous taps on puppet chest producing sound effects; 3 rapid beating of the heart under emotional stress; - pater turbulence in nature, *esp* wind and lightning;
nggeteri *or* nggegeteri to cause trembling;
nggeteraké to cause the heart to quiver;
gumeter to shake, tremble.

gethek I *or* gethekan a mark scratched on a bamboo stalk before cutting it.
II, gethekan chin (*k.i. for* janggut, *var of* kethekan II).

gethèk I 1 the morning half of a day.
II bamboo fence. *See also* bethèk.

gèthèk I 1 raft (of wood or bamboo); 2 stick, pole for reaching s.t.
II scar.

getheng, nggetheng 1 to hold tightly; 2 to work assiduously (at); 3 to (do) seriously.

gethet indignant.

gethik I a dish made from birdmeat.
II, **nggethik** to knock the knee. *See also* **gethok**.

gethil, nggethil *reg* 1 to eat s.t. little by little; 2 to nibble at.

gething to have an aversion (to);
nggething to hate, have an aversion to, be unable to bear the sight of;
nggethingaké irritating.

gethini, nggethini *reg* to work assiduously.

gethok, nggethok to knock the knee (*var of* gethik II).

géthok, nggéthoki *reg* to deceive, kid s.o.;
géthokan *or* **géthok-géthokan** in fun, in pretense.

gethu, nggethu 1 to work with full concentration; 2 to (do) assiduously, have one's attention devoted wholly to the task at hand.

gethuk 1 mashed food, *esp* cassava; 2 cassava cake; - **lindri** mashed cassava pressed through a grinder.

gethunu *var of* **gethu**.

geti cake made from palm sugar and sesame seed.

getih *ng*, **rah** *kr*, **ludira** *k.i./lit* blood;
getihen bleeding, bloodstained.

getir sour, tart.

getol, nggetol eager, anxious.

getul *reg* through to the other side.

getun remorseful;
nggetuni to regret, feel remorseful (about).

géwar, nggéwar to swerve, veer, move out of the path of.

gèwel *or* **mak gèwel** *repr* biting.

géwol poor quality, inferior.

géyang-géyong hanging, dangling, swinging. *See also* **géyong**.

gèyèt *reg* a pole for picking fruit high up on a tree.

géyol I tough, rubbery (of **salak** fruit);
géyol-géyol *or* **géyal-géyol** to chew s.t. rubbery.
II to sway;
géyolan *or* **géyal-géyol** swaying with the hips.

géyong to swing;
géyongan *or* **gegéyongan** *or* **géyang-géyong** hanging, swinging.

géyot, nggéyot heavy to lift or carry.

géyuk *reg* within reach (*reg var of* **gaduk**).

gibas I fat-tailed sheep. *See also* **wedhus**.
II fat.

giber, giber-giber *intsfr* fat, flabby.

giblah, giblah-giblah *intsfr* fat, obese.

gibrah, gibrah-gibrah to dance around with joy. *See also* **gidrah**.

gicel, nggicel *reg* to massage the neck and head (*var of* **gecel**).

gicèng *reg* one-eyed, blind in one eye.

gidhal tartar that collects on teeth.

gidhang, nggidhang *reg* to call, invite.

gidher, gidher-gidher to quiver, shake (*e.g.* jelly, frog eggs). *See also* **kither**.

gidhuh confused, distracted;
nggidhuhi to confuse, distract.

gidra-gidro *or* **gidro-gidro** 1 to struggle (with arms and legs); 2 to keep stamping the feet. *Also* **gidro**.

gidrah *or* **gidrah-gidrah** to dance around with joy.

gidrang, gidrang-gidrang to run around frantically, dash about frenziedly.

gidro, gidro-gidro *var of* **gidra-gidro**.

gigah, nggigah to wake s.o. up (*kr for* **gugah**).

gigal to drop (off, out).

gigat to accuse (*root form: kr for* **gugat**).

gigih steamed glutinous rice.

gigik I cog, gear.
II, **nggigik** to giggle.

gigil, nggigil 1 to keep on (persistent cough); 2 to shiver;

gigilen to shiver with cold.

gigir 1 *lit* the upper back (*var of* **geger**);
2 (mountain) range.

gigis eroded, worn in spots.

gigit, nggigit to bite (on), bite (down)
on, clench the teeth (*var of* **geget**).

giglag, nggiglag *reg* open (of area).

giglok *reg* to fall, drop.

gigol *reg* to fall, drop.

gigrig I frightened.
II to fall, drop out (*var of* **gogrog**).

gigrik, nggigrik to keep laughing.

gigu 1 revolted, disgusted; 2 to be horrified, shocked;
nggigoni 1 revolting; 2 horrifying,
horrible.

gih, nggih *md* yes, indeed. *See also* **inggih**.

giha *or* **giya** *lit* cave, cavern, grotto. *See
also* **guwa**.

gik *or* **nggik** *reg* in, at, on (*var of* **ing I**).

gil, gil-gilan unsteady, restless, fidgety.

gila I to be revolted, find loathsome;
nggilani *or* **nggegilani** causing loathing or revulsion;
kamigilan easily revolted, repelled.
II, **kagila-gila** extreme, extremely.

gilang, gilang-gilang I lying in the open
uncovered (corpse).
II bright, glittering, shiny.

gilap shiny, gleaming;
nggilapaké to cause to shine/gleam,
polish.

gilar, gilar-gilar 1 shining, glowing;
2 broad, vast; 3 immaculate, spick-
and-span.

gilé (see) here! (*subst kr for* **iki lo**).

giles, nggiles to mash, flatten.

gili I *reg* road, street.
II rocky islet.

gilig 1 cylindrical; 2 well developed, well
formulated;
nggiligi to form (things) into cylindrical shapes;
nggiligaké 1 to form into a cylinder;

2 *fig* to round out; 3 to stiffen (the
determination);
giligan 1 formed into a cylinder; 2 to
have reached a decision.

giling, nggiling to grind, mill;
gilingan 1 mill, millstone; 2 ground,
milled;
sagilingan a handful of cooked rice,
used as a measuring unit.

gilir, - gumanti by turns, periodically, off
and on;
nggilir to take turn;
giliran 1 one's turn; 2 by turns.

gilis, nggilis to mash, flatten (*var of*
giles).

gilo *coll* here you are! (*var of* **iki lo**)

gilok, gilok-gilok *reg* sometimes, from
time to time.

gilut, nggilut to exert o.s., exercise.

gim I golden thread or braid in decorative applications to clothing.
II 1 (end of the) game, result of the
game (*esp* tennis); 2 *cr* dead.

gimbal 1 unkempt (hair); 2 loose skin
folds hanging from the neck of certain
animals; 3 a dish made with fried rice
flour chips containing peanuts or
fish.

gimblah, gimblah-gimblah *intsfr* fat.

gimbleg *var of* **gimblah**.

gimer a certain game of chance;
nggimer 1 (of dice) to throw; 2 to
turn, spin.

gimi, gimi-gimi *reg* in a hurry.

gimik *reg var of* **dhisik**.

gimin *reg var of* **dhisik**.

gimir, kegimir touched (feelings).

gina use(fulness), benefit, (*kr for* **guna I**).

ginak-ginuk very fat. *See also* **ginuk**.

ginau *reg* to learn, exercise (*var of* **sinau**).

gincu Chinese red paint, vermilion,
rouge;
nggincu to redden the cheeks or lips
with cosmetics.

ginda massage (*k.i. for* **urut, pijet**).

gindhal *reg* 1 to come loose, come off/out; 2 *reg* divorce.

gindhala *lit* a signal given by pounding a wooden mortar. *See also* gundhala.

ginem 1 talk (*kr for* gunem); 2 dialogue.

gini *see* gana.

ginjal, ginjal-ginjal 1 to jump up and down (from walking barefoot in hot places); 2 to struggle, resist.

ginjel kidney.

ginjlong *var of* kinclong.

ginggam *var of* ginggang.

ginggang distantly spaced, wide apart; ngginggang to be apart, spaced; ngginggangaké to space s.t. at a distance. *See also* gonggang.

ginggung unstable, shaky, worried.

gingsir to move from its place, move aside, shift; - élingané not right in the head.

gingsul uneven (teeth).

ginonjing *see* gonjing.

gintel, nggintel to pinch with thumb and forefinger.

ginten *md* for giri.

ginteng *reg* ironwood tree.

gintes *var of* gites.

gintung a certain tree.

ginuk, ginuk-ginuk very fat.

ginyer, ngginyer to press and fondle (in massage).

gipih *lit* in a hurry, quick. *See also* gupuh.

gipit *reg var of* dhisik.

gir gear, cogwheel (of car, bicycle *etc*).

girah I, nggirah *or* nggirahi to rinse, launder; girah-girah to do the washing; nggirahaké to launder for s.o. II to drive away, shoo off (*kr for* gurah II).

girang I a variety of tree. II *or* girang-girang jubilant, triumphant, exultant.

girap, girap-girap to feel intense loathing.

giras wild, untamed, afraid of human beings.

giri I *lit* mountain; -laya *lit* mountain range. II, *lit* giri-giri to rush into action. III, *lit* kagiri-giri frightful, terrifying.

girik note (as proof), chit.

giring (*root form*) to drive; - ésuk the time (in the morning) when livestock are driven to the river for bathing and watering; - soré the time (in the evening) when livestock are returned to the stall; nggiring 1 to herd (livestock); 2 to drive (the ball toward goal); 3 to escort a criminal (to prison, court *etc*).

giris frightened; nggegirisi frightening, terrifying.

girisa a certain classical verse form.

giro, giro-giro to leap up screaming (in fright); nggegiro to give s.o. a terrible fright (by appearing suddenly). *See also* gero.

gisang *reg* banana (*var of* pisang).

gisau *reg* to learn, exercise.

gisik beach, shore.

gisit *reg var of* dhisik.

gistha *lit* words, talk, topic of discussion; nggistha to speak about, discuss.

gisus bustle, commotion, tumult.

gita I song, chant. II *or* gita-gita (*or* magita-gita *lit*) in great haste.

gitar guitar; nggitar 1 to play the guitar; 2 resembling a guitar (woman's waistline); nggitari to accompany (s.o.'s singing) with guitar.

gitaya *lit* song, poetry, narrative to be sung.

gitel *var of* gintel.

gites, nggites to kill (lice) by pressing with the thumbnail.

githang *var of* gothang.

githes *var of* gites.

githet scar from a wound;
  nggithet to sew up a torn place.
githi, githi-githi in haste.
githing, nggithing *reg* **1** to grip, clasp;
  2 to flank.
githir (*pron as:* **githi:r**) fast (running
  pace).
githok *ng, kr,* **griwa** *k.i.* nape of the neck.
gitik stick, club;
  nggitik 1 to beat with a stick; **2** (of
  fighting cocks) to beat with the wings
  and legs; **3** to draw the winning lottery number;
  nggitiki to beat with a stick repeatedly;
  nggitikaké to use a stick for beating
  s.o.;
  gitikan a beating.
giwang I earring set with a large jewel.
  II, ora giwang unshakable, unwaver-
  ing;
  gumiwang 1 *lit* (of sun) to sink in the
  west; **2** to incline, be favourable to.
giwangkara *lit* sun.
giwar, nggiwar to swerve, veer;
  nggiwari to move out of the path of.
giyak I command to a span of buffaloes
  so that the one on the right goes faster
  and the pair turn left. *See also* **her.**
  II enthusiastic, energetic;
  giyak-giyak clattering, noisy.
giyanti I a certain small tree with purplish flowers.
  II site of the 1755 treaty which resulted
  in the kingdom of Mataram being
  divided into Yogyakarta and Surakarta.
giyar, nggiyaraké to announce, broadcast;
  giyaran a radio broadcast (*var of* **siyar**);
  panggiyar announcer.
giyat vigorous, energetic;
  nggiyataké to stimulate, encourage,
  press for activity.
giyao *reg* flustered, bewildered.
giyer, nggiyer to go on and on without
  stopping (*var of* **gayer**).

giyota *lit* ship, boat.
giyu I repeated coil shapes used as a
  batik design.
  II, nggiyu *reg* to pry, exert leverage.
giyuh *or* **magiyuh** *or* **margiyuh** *lit* sad,
  sorrowful, grieving.
giyung I turbulence, tumult.
  II fed up, sated.
  III, giyungan swinging, dangling. *See
  also* **géyong.**
glabad membrane (fruits), skin (milk).
glabèg *reg* stubborn and lazy.
glabèt, globat-glabèt to have the tongue
  hanging out, to lick the lips (with
  hunger).
gladhag I 1 split-bamboo fence support;
  2 bamboo floor of rice storage (**lumbung**); **omah -** a house with bamboo
  or wooden floor;
  gladhagan bamboo rack, drying-rack.
  II, short lance used for hunting;
  nggladhag to hunt with a short lance;
  gladhagan place for keeping this
  weapon.
  III, nggladhag 1 (of stream/current of
  a river) running rapidly, fast; **2** (*or*
  gumladhag) *reg* (of road) smooth, free
  of holes.
  IV, gladhagan 1 vagrant; **2** *cr* prostitute.
gladhé *var of* **gladhi.**
gladhi 1 drill, training, rehearsal; **2** to
  practise, rehearse; **- resik** dress/final
  rehearsal; general rehearsal;
  nggladhi to exercise, train, drill;
  gladhèn (to engage in) drill, training;
  panggladhi act of practising/drilling.
gladrah, nggladrah 1 spreading everywhere; **2** (of act or speech) uncontrolled;
gladri gallery.
glaèng, ngglaèng *reg* to be self-willed, go
  one's own way.
glagah 1 a kind of high, thick reed-grass;
  2 stalk of the sugarcane flower.

glagar lengths of bamboo *or* wood fastened together for fence sections.

glagat outward indication;
glagaté it looks like.

glagep, glagepan 1 to gasp for air; 2 to be lost for words;
glagep-glagep *or* **glogap-glagep** 1 to keep gasping for breath; 2 (*or* **glagepan**) to be lost for words.

glagut, ngglagut *reg* to work assiduously (at).

glajes, ngglajes to talk lightly rather than seriously. *See also* **glajis**.

glajis, ngglajis *reg* to take things (too) lightly.

glaler, ngglaler showing lines;
pating glaler full of lines.

glali lollipop, any hard lolly.

glambèr dewlap;
ngglambèr *or* **glombar-glambèr** to hang down untidily.

glambir *var of* **glambèr**.

glambrèh, ngglambrèh *or* **pating glambrèh** hanging about in disorder.

glamèh, glomah-glamèh *or* **glamèhan** *reg* to have a big appetite (for food).

glamit a fine woven edging for mats;
ngglamit to edge a mat.

glana *lit* sad, sorrowful.

glandhang I, ngglandhang to pull, drag;
glandhangan vagrant, homeless drifter.
II, gumlandhang loud and clear.

glandhang-glandhung *see* **glandhung**.

glandhung, ngglandhung *or* **glandhang-glandhung** *reg* unemployed and drifting; idle.

glang, glang-glangan to be out and about (women).

glanggang 1 arena for combat; 2 *fig* field, area.

glangsar *or* **mak glangsar** *repr* a person or animal falling;
ngglangsar to fall to the ground;
glangsaran to lie on the ground taking it easy.

glangsi *reg* rough woven bag used for sugar.

glangsur I, ngglangsur *or* **glangsuran** to inch forward on the stomach (baby).
II, ngglangsur to anoint, rub.

glanthang, ngglanthang 1 to dry s.t. in the sun (*see also* **klanthang**); 2 *intsfr* hot (of sun).

glantong, ngglantong hanging around;
glantongan to keep hanging around;
pating glantong *pl* hanging around.

glanuk, ngglanuk to get engrossed, be deeply absorbed (in the enjoyment of). *See also* **glathuk**.

glanyong, glanyongan to converse nonsensically *or* inconsequentially.

glapé to pay attention to (*var of* **gapé**).

glaput covered with s.t. dirty.

glarang, glarangan *reg* wandering far afield, without fixed abode.

glarap, glarapan *reg* startled, caught unawares.

glasah, ngglasah *or* **glasahan** lying strewn about untidily.

glasar *var of* **glangsar**.

glathak I, ngglathak having an all-consuming appetite for both normal and bizarre food items.
II *reg* bamboo fence.

glathé, ngglathé *or* **glotha-glathé** aimless, without purpose.

glathi knife used as a weapon.

glathik a small bird that frequents ricefields; **- bélong** black-headed whitecheeked **glathik** bird;
ngglathik resembling this bird;
- mungup (of fingernails) reddened at the tips; **- sakurungan** cooperative, harmonious.

glathuk, ngglathuk *reg* to get engrossed, be deeply absorbed (*var of* **glanuk**).

glawat, ngglawat 1 to stand suffering, hold out; 2 to struggle against superior forces.

glayar, ngglayar *or* glayaran 1 to wander from place to place; 2 (*or* glayar-glayar) to reel, stagger.

glayem, ngglayem *or* gloyam-glayem to flatter, speak hypocritically, tell the listener what he wants to hear.

glayung one sheaf (two bundles) of newly harvested rice (about twelve catties).

glebag-glebeg to be restless, keep tossing and turning. *See also* glebeg II.

glébag *or* mak glébag *repr* a turning motion;
ngglébag to turn (over, around);
glébagan to keep tossing and turning.

glebeg I 1 *reg* a large wooden wheel; 2 a cart with two wooden wheels drawn by a man;
ngglebeg to transport (a load) in such a cart.
II, glebegan *or* glebag-glebeg restless, to keep tossing and turning.
III, ngglebeg 1 (to do s.t.) continuous(ly); 2 tightly woven.

glèbèg I, ngglèbèg *or* glébag-glèbèg to shake the head.
II, ngglèbèg to miss the target.

glèbès, ngglèbès to shake the head;
glèbèsan to keep shaking the head.

glebyar 1 glance, sight; 2 glittering, sparkling, shining;
glebyar-glebyar to glitter, sparkle. *See also* gebyar.

glebyur, pating glebyur *pl* sparkling.

gléca, gléca-glécé *see* glécé.

glécé, gléca-glécé *or* nggléce to shirk, lie down on the job.

glédhag *or* keglédhag to fall on one's back;
ngglédhag to lie down and relax.

glédhah, ngglédhah to search s.t., search through;
glédhahan act of searching.

gledheg I *repr* a heavy rumbling;
gumledheg producing a heavy rumbling.
II a small wooden cabinet for storing food.
III, gledhegan to flare up or spread rapidly (fire).

glèdhèg 1 *repr* the sound of rolling; 2 swiftly flowing;
gumlèdhèg 1 to roll; 2 to flow swiftly;
glèdhègan 1 on wheels, rolling (door); 2 wagon; 3 *reg* driveway leading up to the porch of a residence.

glédrah *see* glidrah.

gledrug, pating gledrug *pl* stamping the feet. *See also* gedrug.

glega trunk of a coconut palm (*subst kr for* glugu).

glegag-glegeg *see* glegeg.

glégak-glègèk *see* glègèk.

glegar-gleger *see* gleger.

glegeg *or* mak glegeg *repr* gurgling;
glegag-glegeg *repr* gulping (drink), repeated gurgles.

glegek *see* glegeg.

glègèk 1 a belch; 2 to belch;
ngglègèki to cause burping (fizzy drink);
glègèken to have the burps;
glégak-glègèk to keep burping.

gleger *repr* a sudden heavy sound;
gumleger to boom, crash;
glegar-gleger to keep booming.

gleges I, nggleges to laugh softly;
glegas-gleges to keep laughing to o.s.
II sugarcane flower.

glègès *var of* gleges I.

glégot, ngglégot *reg* to keep hanging around, not go away.

glegut, ngglegut to work seriously.

glélang-glèlèng *see* glèlèng.

gleleng I, nggleleng *or* glelang-gleleng to keep gazing at.
II, nggleleng *reg* to engage in wayward behaviour.

glèlèng, ngglèlèng *or* glélang-glèlèng *or* glèlèngan (to walk) with a swaggering or arrogant gait.

gleler, nggleler to leave without saying goodbye, sneak away/out.

gleles *var of* **gleler**.

glélo, ngglélo to nod drowsily.

glémang-glèmèng, *see* **glèmèng**.

glémboh *or* **glémboh-glémboh** fat, obese.

glémbong *var of* **glémboh**.

glembor, pating glembor *pl* 1 to do a lot of loud talking or shouting; 2 to cry noisily. *See also* **gembor**.

glembos large and spongy.

glémbos *var of* **glembos**.

glembug *see* **glembuk**.

glembuk, ngglembuk to try to convince or persuade s.o.;
glembukan *or* **pangglembuk** an attempt at persuasion.

glembus, ngglembus bloated and pale from illness.

glémbyor, glémbyor-glémbyor hanging about in disorder.

glèmèng, glémang-glèmèng to keep changing, doing s.t. new.

glémpang, ngglémpang to fall down, tip over;
ngglémpangaké to cause s.t. to fall down, tip s.t. over;
glémpangan *or* **pating glémpang** *pl* to lie sprawled everywhere.

glempeng, ngglempeng *reg* to work assiduously (at).

glémpo *reg* a large handkerchief.

glendam-glendem *see* **glendem**.

glendar-glender *see* **glender**.

glendem, ngglendem 1 (*or* **glendam-glendem**) to behave quietly; 2 to sneak off with other people's property.

glender *or* **mak glender** *repr* swallowing s.t. at once;
glendar-glender to drink s.t. repeatedly.

glèndèr I stick of wood or bamboo used as prop.
II, **ngglèndèr** to slope.

glendhah-glendhèh *see* **glendhèh**.

gléndhang, nggléndhang 1 empty (*see also* **glondhang**); 2 to go travelling without money or provisions.

glendhèh, glendhèh-glendhèh *or* **glendhah-glendhèh** (of walking gait) slow-paced and with arms swinging.

glendheng, glendhengan (of bamboo or wood) in the form of long uncut stalks.

glèndhèng, ngglèndhèng 1 to drag s.t.; 2 speedy.

glenèh, ngglenèh *reg* peculiar, out of the ordinary.

gleneng, nggleneng to flow smoothly and placidly.

glenes, ngglenes *or* **glenas-glenes** to leave without saying goodbye, sneak away/out.

glenggem *var of* **glendem**.

glenggeng *or* **mak glenggeng** *repr* gulping (down);
glenggang-glenggeng to gulp repeatedly;
saglenggengan at a gulp.

glènggèng, ngglènggèng to sing loudly for one's own pleasure.

gléngsor, nggléngsor to sit on the ground;
gléngsoran sitting around on the ground.

glenik, ngglenik *or* **glenikan** *or* **glenak-glenik** to talk in a low voice.

glénjor, glénjor-glénjor flabby, slack.

glénoh, glénoh-glénoh to walk in a stately way.

glenteng, ngglenteng *reg* to work continuously without stopping.

glèntèr, ngglèntèr to play alone and not cry (child).

glenyèh I, **nginang ngglenyèh** to chew betel constantly.
II *var of* **glènyèh**.

glènyèh, ngglènyèh *or* **glènyèhan** repellent.

glepang flour (*subst kr for* **glepung**).

glépat-glèpèt *see* **glèpèt**.

glèpèt, glépat-glèpèt *reg* to work at a comfortable pace.

glépot soiled, stained.

glepuk, ngglepuk to hit, *esp* with a stone.

glepung flour, powdered substance; ngglepung to make into flour.

glerek, glerek-glerek husky (voice, caused by throat infection).

glereng, pating glereng *pl* growling everywhere. *See also* gereng.

glerit *repr* sound of scratching.

glèsèh *var of* glasah.

glèsèk, ngglèsèk *or* glèsèk-glèsèk to try to find leftovers, glean. *See also* grèsèk.

gleser *repr* crawling motions; nggleser *or* gleser-gleser 1 (of snake) to wriggle off; 2 to move along the seat. *See also* tleser.

glésor, glésoran to roll around on the ground.

gléthak, ngglèthak lying scattered or sprawled; ngglèthakaké to put down in a sprawling position; gumléthak sprawled, laid out.

glethek *or* mak glethek 1 *repr* the sound of s.t. falling; 2 *repr* an unexpected piece of good luck; 3 *repr* a joint twisting.

glèthèk, ngglèthèk ubiquitous; glèthèk pethèl obvious, plain.

gléthot, pating gléthot *reg pl* crooked, not straight enough.

gléwang, nggléwang 1 to tip over; 2 to pass the zenith (sun, moon).

glèwèng, ngglèwèng *reg* 1 to stray, wander; 2 to commit adultery; glèwèngan to wander here and there.

gléwo, gléwo-gléwo chubby, plump (baby).

gléyah, gléyah-gléyah (to walk) at a comfortable pace.

gléyang *repr* swinging.

glèyèh, ngglèyèh to rest, *esp* lying down. *See also* lèyèh.

gléyong *var of* gléyang.

gléyor I string bean.
II, nggléyor *or* gléyar-gléyor to walk unsteadily.

glibed to pass by, go past; mak - *repr* passing by; ngglibed 1 to hang around; 2 to twist/distort s.o.'s words; glibedan *or* glibad-glibed to keep going past.

glibrah, pating glibrah moving or dancing ponderously. *See also* glidrah.

glidhah, ngglidhah to search through s.t. (*var of* glédhah).

glidhig I 1 to work as a day labourer; 2 one who helps at a ceremony.
II, *reg* ngglidhig smooth, in good condition (road).

glidrah moving or dancing ponderously (*var of* glibrah).

gligap, gligapan *reg* to be startled, look startled.

gligat-gligut *see* gligut.

gligèn *see* gligi.

gligi cylindrical; gligèn 1 forming a cylinder; 2 to reach an agreement or understanding.

gligik, gligik-gligik *or* gligak-gligik to chuckle.

gligir, nggligir to form a hexagon; gligiran hexagonal.

gligut, gligat-gligut *or* to hang around, mill around; pating gligut *pl* as above.

glijab, ngglijab *reg* to sit nicely and enjoy a meal.

glijad, ngglijad *reg* clean and smooth.

glimbang, glimbang-glimbang *see* glimbung.

glimbung, glimbang-glimbung to lie around taking it easy.

glimpang *var of* glémpang.

glimpung *or* mak glimpung *repr* a sudden fall; ngglimpung to lie curled up snugly; pating glimpung lying strewn about.

glindhang-glindhung *see* **glindhung**.

glindhing 1 *repr* rolling; 2 ox-cart with solid wheels; 3 small round pellets; 4 name of one of the small playing-cards (*kertu cilik*).

glindhung, **glindhang-glindhung** to be unemployed and drifting, drift aimlessly.

gling, **gling-gling** *reg* somewhat deficient mentally.

glinggang *reg* dead tree/wood.

glingseng, **ngglingseng** pitch black, deeply suntanned.

glintheng, **ngglintheng** intensely dark/black.

glinting *or* **mak glinting** *repr* sprawling;
ngglinting to lie sprawled;
glintingan to roll around on the ground.

glintir 1 small round object, pellet; 2 counter used with small pellet-like objects: grain;
ngglintiri to form into pellets or balls.

glinuk, **glinuk-glinuk** *or* **glinak-glinuk** awkwardly fat.

gliput covered with s.t. dirty (*var of* **glaput**).

glirih, **ngglirih** to moan, groan, weep in pain.

glis *lit* quick(ly), fast.

glisik, **ngglisiki** *reg* to whisper to s.o. *See also* **bisik**.

glithak *see* **gléthak**.

glithik, **ngglithik** 1 (*or* **ngglithiki**) to tickle s.o.;
pating glithik a tickling sensation all over.

glitho, **ngglitho** to flick the thumb against s.o.'s head as a reprimand;
ngglithoni to reprimand s.o. as above.

glithu *reg* a small wooden pestle used in the kitchen for grinding spices.

gliwang *see* **gléwang**.

gliyak, **gliyak-gliyak** (to walk) at a comfortable pace.

gliyek, **nggliyek** *or* **gliyek-gliyek** *or* **gliyekan** to stroll, saunter.

gliyeng, **nggliyeng** to feel faint, dizzy.

gliyer *or* **mak gliyer** 1 *repr* falling asleep; 2 *repr* a dizzy feeling; 3 *repr* a bobbing movement;
nggliyer to feel dizzy;
gliyeran feeling dizzy.

globag, **globagan** 1 to keep turning; 2 (of horses) to roll repeatedly on the ground.

globat, **globat-glabèt** *see* **glabèt**.

globod, **ngglobod** to wear worn out clothing.

globroh too large (clothing).

gloco *reg* hangman, executioner.

glodhag 1 *or* **mak glodhag** *repr* a thrown object hitting a hard surface; 2 roomy, spacious;
ngglodhag empty of passengers.

glodhog I wooden beehive.
II *or* **glodhog-glodhog** *repr* a deep rumbling.
III, **ngglodhog** *or* **ngglodhogi** to peel off (skin).
IV, **glodhogan** a hole, hollow.

glodro *or* **mak glodro** *repr* sliding down suddenly.

glogog *or* **mak glogog** *repr* liquid gurgling;
ngglogog to gurgle.

glogok *or* **mak glolok** *repr* pouring all at once;
ngglogok to pour water from a bottle or a water pitcher into the mouth;
glogak-glogok to pour repeatedly.

glogor I wooden or bamboo flooring material.
II, **glogor-glogor** *repr* the croak of a hoarse voice.

glolo, **ngglolo** to wail loud and long;
pating glolo *pl* to wail loud and long everywhere.

glomah-glamèh *see* **glamèh**.

glombor too large (clothing).

glombyar-glombyor *see* glombyor.

glombyor, ngglombyor *or* glombyar-glombyor flabby, loose, without body or stiffness.

glompong fat, overweight (children). *See also* glumpang.

glondhang *or* mak glondhang *repr* a hollow thud;
ngglondhang empty of passengers;
glondhangan to make a resounding sound, *e.g.* an empty can.

glondhong I leader of a council of village heads.
II log, unsawn timber.

glondor 1, ngglondor to slide down, slip and fall; 2 *var of* glontor.

glong *or* mak glong *repr* feeling a surge of relief.

glonggong I 1 stem of the papaya leaf; 2 a certain thick reed.
II, ngglonggong to sing/chant loudly;
ngglonggongaké to sing s.t loudly;
gumlonggong (to sing, chant) loudly, strongly.

glongsor *or* mak glongsor flopping down;
ngglongsor *or* glongsoran to flop down anywhere.

glontar-glontor *see* glontor.

glontor, ngglontor 1 to wash down (food); 2 to flush (the toilet);
glontar-glontor to keep making washing (pouring, flushing) sounds.

glopot stained, messy, covered with s.t. dirty. *See also* gluprut.

glorok, glorok-glorok 1 to snore; 2 to clear the throat hoarsely.

gloso *or* mak gloso *repr* flopping down, sprawling;
nggloso to flop, sprawl.

glosod *var of* gloso.

glosor *var of* gloso.

glotha *reg* barely passable (path).

glothak *or* mak glothak *repr* an impact;
glothakan *or* glothak-glothak to keep making impact sounds.

gloyam, gloyam-glayem *see* glayem.

gloyor *or* mak gloyor *repr* suddenly staggering;
nggloyor *or* gloyoran (to walk) staggering.

glubud, ngglubud *reg* impudent, barefaced, brazen (*var of* blubud).

gludhug 1 thunder, deep far-off thunder; 2 (*pron as:* gludhu:g) (*or* mak gludhug) *repr* a deep thunder-like sound;
gumludhug producing a thunder-like noise.

gluga red colouring matter extracted from a fruit (pacar).

glugu trunk of a coconut palm.

glugur *reg* wooden or bamboo flooring material (*var of* glogor);
ngglugur lying stretched out.

glugut 1 tiny hairs on the bamboo leaf-sheath that cause itching; 2 particle, bit;
ngglugut 1 to have such particles; 2 *fig* irritable.

glumpang fat, overweight (children) (*reg var of* glompong).

glumut *reg* stained, messy, covered with mud. *See also* gluput.

glundheng *or* mak glundheng *repr* slipping or rolling right into a hole.

glundhung 1 a roll, rolled-up object; 2 counting unit for coconuts; 3 (*or* mak glundhung) *repr* plunging into a deep depression; - semprong 1 (of women) to marry without a dowry; 2 to turn s.t. over to s.o. in unaltered condition; - suling (of men) to marry without giving a bride-price;
ngglundhung to roll;
ngglundhungi to roll onto;
ngglundhungaké to roll s.t.;
gumlundhung to roll;
keglundhung to get rolled, roll accidentally;
glundhang-glundhung to keep rolling;
glundhungan forming a roll.

glunek 1 a complaint; 2 a grudge. *See also* grunek.

glungsar *var of* glongsor.

glungsur *var of* glongsor.

gluntung *or* mak gluntung *repr* falling and rolling;
nggluntung to fall and roll;
pating gluntung *pl* to roll, writhe;
gluntungan 1 to keep rolling; 2 a roll.

glupak, glupak-glupuk *see* glupuk.

gluprut stained, messy, covered with mud.

glupuk, glupak-glupuk apprehensive, nervous.

gluput *var of* gluprut.

glura 1 uncertain(ty); 2 rebellion, insurrection.

gluruh, nggluruh to moan softly.

glusur, ngglusur to glide down, slide, slip.

gluthèh slushy, oozy, partially melted (*var of* bluthèh).

gluthek *repr* light clattering sounds;
nggluthek to clatter around;
pating gluthek *repr* clattering sounds;
gluthekan to keep clattering around.
See also kluthek.

gluthik, nggluthik to devote one's attention to s.t. intricate;
pating gluthik patiently absorbed in a complex task.

gluthuk *var of* gluthek.

gluwah-gluwèh *see* gluwèh.

gluwèh, gluwah-gluwèh *or* gumluwèh frivolous, careless, inattentive;
gluwèhan to fool around.

gluwer *var of* kluwer.

gluyur *var of* gloyor.

go, nggo for, for the benefit/purpose of (*shtf of* kanggo).

gobab *reg* to lie, cheat, deceive.

gobag a children's game in which the players try to reach the enemy goal; - bunder (to play) this game with a round goal; - sodor (to play) this game with an oblong-shaped goal.

gobag-gabig to shake the head repeatedly.

gobang I large bladed knife.
II obsolete coin worth 2½ cents.

gobèd I 1 slicing knife with a serrated blade; 2 knife for chopping tobacco leaves;
nggobèd to slice s.t. very thin, grate.
II, gobèdan folds in a batik garment finger-pressed into place and held with a pin or clip.

gobèr 1 flapping loosely; 2 false-sounding, *e.g.* a voice over a loudspeaker.

gobig, nggobig *or* gobig-gobig 1 to shake from side to side; 2 *fig* to refuse to acknowledge s.t.

gobis cabbage (*reg var of* kobis).

goblah, goblah-goblah *reg* too large (clothing).

gobleg I *reg* too roomy.
II *reg* to have severe headache.

goblog *cr* stupid, idiotic.

gobog I *cr* ear.
II 1 former Chinese coin with a hole in the middle; 2 *reg* 5-cent coin during the colonial period.

gobrah *or* gobrah-gobrah smeared, messy, covered with s.t. *See also* gubrah.

gobrès *var of* gubris.

gobyag, nggobyag to shake s.t.

gobyog (of a party, gamelan melody *etc*) merry and lively.

gobyos *or* nggobyos to sweat profusely.

gocèk, nggocèki to take hold of;
nggocèkaké to hold for s.o.;
gocèkan 1 to cling to; 2 s.t. to hold onto.

gocèl *var of* gocèk.

goci glazed Chinese jar.

goco a punch;
nggoco to punch s.o.

godag *cr* able, capable.

godha 1 temptation, a testing of the character; 2 disturbance; - rencana temptation;

nggodha 1 to test s.o.'s character, subject s.o. to temptation or torment; 2 to seduce, bother; - rencana to plague, torment;
kegodha subjected to temptation;
panggodha temptation.

godhag I space, interstice;
nggodhagi to divide into separate spaces.
II, nggodhag to chase.

godhang var of gudhang I.

godheg to shake the head (var of gèdhèg).

godhèg 1 hair worn at the side of the face, side-levers (men), combed-back part at the temple (ladies); 2 copper decorations for a horse bridle.

godhem reg obsolete coin worth 2½ cents.

godhen var of godhem.

godhi cloth strip for wrapping or tying.

godhog boiled;
nggodhog 1 to boil; 2 fig to train rigorously;
godhogan 1 boiled; 2 equipment for boiling.

godhong ng, ron kr, 1 leaf; 2 leaf of a double door or window; 3 the broad part of an oar; 4 spades (playing-card suit);
gegodhongan (ron-ronan kr) 1 foliage; 2 (edible, medicinal) leaves.

godog I reg torch made from strung castor fruits.
II a wooden sledgehammer with a long handle;
nggodog to strike with that hammer.

godor bar, material shaped into a bar.

godrag restless, unable to settle down (girls).

godrah stained, smeared.

godrèg var of godrag.

godrès var of godrah.

gog, gog-gog petok repr the cackle of a hen.

gogèt to fight with the teeth (animals).

gogik I reg dried cassava root slices.
II a hornbill-like bird.

goglog, nggoglog cr to eat (var of gaglag).

gogo or gogo-gogo to grope in the water with the hand;
nggogoni to grope for s.t., e.g. fish.

gogoh, gogoh-gogoh to feel around with the hand;
nggogohi to grope around in s.t.

gogok spoutless earthen pitcher;
nggogok to drink straight from a pitcher or bucket.

gogol reg 1 a heavy wooden boom; 2 householder, paying tax and entitled to own fields;
nggogol reg 1 to till (a field); 2 to try to induce s.o. to do s.t.

gogor tiger cub (young of the macan).

gogos cave in a riverbank, cliffside etc.
nggogosi to dig roots with the snout (boar).

gogot var of gogèt.

gograg damaged from being shaken up.

gogrog 1 to fall off, drop off prematurely (fruits, buds); 2 to have a miscarriage;
nggogrogi 1 to drop off, shed; 2 to fall onto;
nggogrogaké to cause to be detached prematurely;
gogrogan s.t. fallen off;
kegogrogan to get fallen on by light objects (e.g. fruits, leaves, flowers).

goh lit ox.

gojag, nggojagi to wash out (a bottle etc) by shaking water in it.

gojag-gajeg hesitant, undecided. See also gajeg.

gojèg or (ge)gojègan to fool around, laugh and joke.

gojèh reg with a sensitive stomach.

gojog var of gojag.

gojrèt smeared, stained.

gol wedge used as a lever with a certain prying tool;
ngegoli to pry with that wedge.

golang *see* goling.

golé *reg var of* olèhé.

golèk I *ng*, pados *kr*, to seek, get;
nggolèk to get, obtain;
nggolèki to look for, try to get, find;
nggolèkaké to get or seek on s.o.'s behalf;
golèkan thing obtained or sought;
golèk-golèk to make an effort to get;
nggolèk-golèkaké to make an effort to get or find;
golèk-golèkan 1 to look for each other; 2 thing obtained or sought;
golèk menangé dhéwé *idiom* unwilling to accept defeat.
II *or* golèkan doll, wooden puppet.

golèng, golèng-golèng *reg* pretty, pleasurable.

golèt to seek, get (*reg var of* golèk).

goli *reg var of* olèhé.

goling *or* nggoling to tip over;
golang-goling shaky, unsteady.

golok dagger.

golong unanimous;
nggolong 1 to form a group, come together in a group; 2 to be unanimous;
nggolongaké 1 to classify, group; 2 to make a decision together;
gumolong 1 (grouped) together; 2 unanimously;
kagolong 1 to belong to, be a member of; 2 grouped with, considered as;
golongan 1 group, organisation; 2 class, subgroup; 3 a Kraton department.

golor leaf stalk, central stalk of a leaf.

gom I sprue, oral ulceration;
gomen to have an ulcer in the mouth.
II (vegetable) gum.

goman *reg* gift.

gombak children's hairstyle: head shaved everywhere except on the crown.

gombal *or* gombalan rag, scrap, ragged clothing;
nggombal 1 to wear ragged clothing; 2 *fig* poor.

gombèl rooster's neck wattles. *See also* clèrèt.

gombèng I heavier on one side than the other.
II, nggombèng to cut a tree trunk roughly into a square beam.
III, nggombèng to fill in ditches.
IV, nggombèng to make a space between things.

gombing *var of* gombèng.

gomblah-gamblèh *see* gamblèh.

gombloh with a guileless or dull-witted look;
nggomblohi to assume such a look.

gombol undergrowth, thicket;
nggombol to flock together, gather. *See also* grombol.

gombong I hollow; 2 pumice.
II, nggombong to soak s.t. in water.

gombrang 1 *or* nggombrang to cut off, lop of; 2 too loose (clothing).

gombrèk *reg* very poor.

gombrik *var of* gombrèk.

gombyak, nggombyaki to join together in enjoying fun;
gegombyakan enjoying fun together.

gombyok 1 fringe, tassel; 2 floral design on a kris;
nggombyok to resemble a fringe, form a fringe;
nggombyoki to decorate (a kris) with a floral design;
gombyokan 1 fringed, tasselled; 2 forming a cluster.

gombyong *reg var of* gombyok.

gompèl chipped (*var of* gopèl).

gon *see* enggon.

gonah conforming to a normal standard (*reg var of* genah).

gonas-ganès lovable, sweet, amiable.

gondar-gandir soft, slimy and sticky (*e.g.* jelly, frogs' eggs).

gondhal-gandhul *see* gandhul.

gondhang I 1 a certain large tree (many varieties).

II esophagus; - **kasih** similar things of disparate appearance, *esp* siblings with different skin colouring.

III, **nggondhang** to butt with the horns.

IV a variety of snail.

V, **nggondhang** empty (*var of* ngglondhang).

gondhèl I earrings.

II, **nggondhèli** 1 to hold onto firmly; 2 to dissuade;

gondhèlan to have a firm grip (on).

gondhil *reg* hairless. *See also* gundhil.

gondho, nggondho *reg* to throw.

gondhok 1 goiter; 2 short and thick; **nggondhok** to be angry in a suppressed way; gondhoken to have a goiter.

gondhol, nggondhol 1 to carry in the mouth (of dog *etc*); 2 walk away with or win (a championship); 3 to pilfer, to steal, swipe.

gondhong I shuttle (part of weaving loom).

II goiter; gondhongen to have a goiter.

gondem *reg* millet grain.

gondrong 1 long-haired (*esp* men); 2 long and unkempt (hair).

gonès 1 flirtatious, coquettish; 2 talkative.

gong gong; ngegong to strike a gong; ngegongi 1 to supply with a gong beat, play the gong to; 2 to agree with, not contradict; gongan 1 the playing of the gong; 2 section of a gamelan composition punctuated by a gong-beat; gong-gongan 1 to play gamelan; 2 resembling a gong; pagongan (*or* gong-gongan) place occupied by the gamelan instruments, *esp* the gongs.

gonggang separated by (a certain distance).

gonggo a certain large spider.

gonggong I (to play) a certain card game played with Chinese cards (*kertu cilik*).

II, **nggonggong** to bark (dogs).

III, **nggonggong** restless and never satisfied.

gonggos, nggonggos *or* nggonggosi *reg* (pig, boar) to dig soil with the snout. *See also* gogos.

gonggrong, nggonggrong not tightly closed, opened a mere crack (*var of* gronggong); nggonggrongaké to heap s.t. up loosely.

gongsèng I belled anklets (worn by children).

II, **nggongsèng** to dry-fry. *See also* gangsa III.

gongsor to slide down (earth); nggongsori to slide onto; gongsoran soil erosion.

goni 1 jute; 2 gunnysack.

gonjak, nggonjak 1 to take too lightly, make fun of; 2 (*or* nggegonjak) to attempt to seduce s.o.; gegonjakan to exchange pleasantries, erotic banter.

gonjang-ganjing to slope, tilt, be unsteady.

gonjèh *var of* génjah.

gonjèng, nggonjèng 1 to drag, pull; 2 to keep asking for s.t.; 3 to stir (up), agitate.

gonjing 1 to slope, tilt, tip up; 2 unsteady; nggonjingaké to unsettle, disrupt; ginonjing 1 to feel inclined to; 2 agitated, shaken.

gonjit *var of* ganjit.

gonjol calluses on shoulders or neck.

gonjong 1 main roof of a Javanese house; 2 cylindrical basket for transporting large bulky objects.

gonor tangled, confused.

gontèng 1 a certain large-headed termite; **2** *reg* cucumber.

gontok, nggontok to punch; **gontok-gontokan** to punch each other.

gonyak-ganyuk *see* **ganyuk**.

gonyèh 1 sensitive, tender; **2** (*or* **nggonyèh**) (of undercooked or over-ripe tubers) disagreeably crumbly or mealy.

gop, gop-gopan to eat or drink noisily and greedily.

gopa *lit* herdsman, shepherd.

gopala *lit, var of* **gopa**.

gopé, wédang - stale weak tea.

gopèk *reg* to seek, look for (*var of* **golèk**).

gopèl chipped; **gopèlan** chip, broken-off piece.

gopès chipped at the edge.

gopok 1 (of golden object) with too many substances mixed into it; **2** *reg* weak; **3** *reg* stupid; **gopokan** weak, sickly.

goprak 1 noisemaker for scaring birds and squirrels away from a crop; **2** of inferior quality.

goprèk, goprèkan inferior (*var of* **goprak**).

goprok inferior (*var of* **goprak**).

gopura *lit* gateway, portal (*var of* **gapura**).

gor, gor-goran neglected, left uncared for; **ngegoraké** to neglect.

gora *lit* horrible, frightful, terrible, dreadful; **-godha** *lit* to intimidate, to alarm; alarming, intimidating.

goraya *lit, var of* **gora**.

gordhel leather belt.

gordhèn 1 window curtain; **2** folding screen.

goreg, nggoregaké to shake, jolt. *See also* **oreg**.

gorèh erratic, uncontrolled; **nggorèhaké** to upset, agitate.

gorèk, nggorèki *reg* to look around (for); **gorèkan 1** useless or unworthy things; **2** *fig* (of people) lower rank; **3** obscene, smutty.

gorèng deep-fried; **nggorèng** to deep fry; **nggorèngi** to fry s.t. repeatedly; **nggorèngaké** to fry for s.o.; **gorèngan 1** deep-fried (foods); **2** (*or* **panggorèngan**) pan for deep-frying.

gori jackfruit in its unripe state, used in cooking.

goring (*reg var of* **gorèng**).

goroh (to tell) a lie; **nggorohi 1** to lie to s.o.; **2** to cause trouble to s.o. by lying; **3** to say s.t. untruthful as a joke; **nggorohaké** to lie about s.t.; **gorohan 1** untruthful by nature; **2** just as a joke, not serious.

gorok claw-shaped rake; **graji** - handsaw; **nggorok 1** to cut (an animal's) throat; **2** to overcharge customers; **gorokan** throat.

gorong, gorongan *var of* **gurungan**.

gos, gos-gosan in a great hurry (*var of* **gas-gasan**).

gosang *reg* burnt, scorched (*var of* **gosong**).

gosèk, nggosèk to cut trees in the forest, clear forest land.

gosok rubbing, polishing; **nggosok 1** to rub, polish; **2** to incite, goad, egg on; **nggosokaké 1** to rub s.t. (into, onto); **2** to have s.t. rubbed; **gosok-ginosok 1** to rub each other; **2** to incite each other; **gosokan** *or* **panggosok 1** act of rubbing, polishing; **2** provocation, goading.

gosong burnt, scorched.

gosthi 1 deliberation; **2** discussion; **nggosthi** to confer about.

got gutter, ditch.

gotèk saying, telling, report;
nggotèki *reg* 1 to say to s.o.; 2 to ask for (s.o.'s) hand in marriage;
gotèké it is said;
gotèkan to tell each other.

gothak-gathuk *see* gathuk.

gothang 1 incomplete, imperfect; 2 *reg* empty, unoccupied.

gothèk I pole for getting fruit from a tree.
II possession (*reg var of* duwèk).

gothil 1 *reg* trickery; 2 incomplete, missing a part (*var of* gothang);
nggothili *reg* to deceive s.o.

gotho I a variety of dung beetle.
II *reg* locomotive.

gothok *reg* in fun, in pretense.

gothol *var of* gothok.

gothot strong, robust.

gotong, - mayit to travel a dangerous route with two companions; - royong *or* - royom 1 community self-help, mutual cooperation; 2 to cooperate, share work;
nggotong to carry cooperatively;
gotongan heavy burden, shared load.

gotra *lit*, 1 blood relative(s); 2 social group;
sagotra *lit* all. *Also* gotrah.

gotrah 1 blood relative(s); 2 social group.

gotram *reg* to converse noisily.

gotri buckshot, pellet.

gotrok *reg* small railway truck.

gowah a certain long-eared owl. *See also* guwek I.

gowak-gowèk *see* gowèk.

gowal-gawèl 1 to keep biting; 2 to keep criticising.

gowang (of blades, hoe *etc*) nicked, notched.

gowèh sprue, oral ulceration.

gowèk 1 to retch; 2 to clear one's throat; 3 *repr* the sound of vomiting;
gowèk-gowèk *or* gowak-gowèk 1 to feel nauseated; 2 to keep vomiting.

gowèng chipped at the edge.

gowok I 1 a purplish berry, the plant it grows on; 2 hollow (in the rock);
gowokan a certain children's game.
II *reg* a woman who is socially assigned to examine a man's virility before he is married;
gowokan traditional examination of man as above.

gowong I royal carpenters.
II, pagowong a total eclipse.

goyang 1 unsteady, wobbly; 2 to shake or swing;
nggoyang to swing/shake s.t.

goyor lightweight (fabric).

gra *lit* top, peak, point.

grabad *or* grabadan spices, ingredients for cooking;
nggrabad to deal in the above items in the market.

grabag I harrow-like farm implement;
nggrabag to loosen soil with a harrow;
grabagan harrowed land.
II, nggrabagi to make s.t in the first stages.
III to generalise.

grabah crockery, earthenware.

grabyag, nggrabyag *or* grabyag-grabyag to come on strongly and suddenly;
grabyagan 1 flash flood, flooding wave; 2 sloppy, careless.

grabyas I slices of meat.
II, gumrabyas going out quickly (fire);
sagrabyasan instantaneous, (happening) in a flash.

grad grade, rank, degree.

gradag *or* mak gradag *repr* clatter or tumult caused by people swarming into a place;
nggradag to pull forcibly;
gradagan (to do s.t.) brainlessly.

grag-greg *see* greg.

gragal gravel, pebbles.

gragap *or* **mak gragap** *repr* a sudden start, *esp* from sleep;
    nggragap to act as if flustered or startled;
    gragapan startled, caught unawares, flustered.

gragas, nggragas to eat indiscriminately, *esp* things that are not good for one.

gragèh, gragèh-gragèh to grope around.

grago I a small prawn.
    II uncertain, unsteady.

grah *see* **gerah**.

graha eclipse (*var of* **grahana**).

graham molar.

grahana eclipse.

grahita *see* **graita**.

graita *lit* mental grasp, comprehension;
    nggraita to realise, understand, comprehend;
    panggraita idea, awareness.

grajag, grajag-grajag *repr* water falling;
    nggrajag to flow rapidly, pour (down);
    gumrajag to keep pouring down heavily.

grajèn *see* **graji**.

graji saw;
    nggraji to saw;
    grajèn 1 sawdust; 2 sawmill.

gram gram (unit of weight).

grama *reg* fire (*kr for* **geni**).

gramang, nggramang to creep, crawl (insect).

gramblèh, pating gramblèh hanging about in disorder.

grambyang, nggrambyang *or* **grambyangan** to stray, wander (thoughts).

gramèh I a freshwater fish often kept as a pet.
    II, **nggramèh** 1 discourteous; 2 to prattle inconsequentially.

grami I *reg* fire (*subst kr for* **geni**).
    II (*or* **gegrami** *or* **gegramèn**) to engage in business (*subst kr for* **dagang**).

gramopun gramophone.

gramyang *var of* **grambyang**.

grana nose (*k.i. for* **irung**).

granat grenade.

granceng, nggranceng *or* **pating granceng** *pl* suspended between two points, strung between two poles. *See also* **ganceng**.

grandhah, nggrandhah *or* **grandhahan** to have too much (baggage *etc*) to carry.

grandhèl a certain long-stemmed papaya;
    nggrandhèl to cling to;
    pating grandhèl *pl* hanging on(to);
    grondhal-grandhèl to dangle.

grandhul, pating grandhul *pl* hanging. *See also* **gandhul**.

granggam *var of* **ganggam**.

granggang bamboo spear.

grangsang, nggrangsang wanting to eat everything one sees, eat compulsively.

grantang a gamelan instrument, now obsolete;
    nggrantang 1 to play this instrument; 2 resembling the sound of this instrument.

grantes, nggrantes in despair.

grantos saw (*subst kr for* **graji**).

grantil, nggrantil hanging on;
    pating grantil *pl* hanging everywhere.

granting *pl form of* **ganting**.

granyah I, **nggranyah** fond of eating snacks.
    II, **nggranyahi** to reprimand, scold.

graok, pating graok *pl* noisy, boisterous. *See also* **gaok**.

graong, nggraong to yelp, howl.

graos saw (*subst kr for* **graji**).

graot, nggraot *or* **nggraoti** to bite (into), gnaw (on).

grapyak friendly and outgoing.

grasak coarse sand.

grasi pardon, amnesty.

grat *see* **grad**.

gratak, nggratak *reg* unquiet, restless, turbulent.

grates, nggrates sorrowful (*var of* grantes).

grathil, nggrathil destructive.

grathul, nggrathul *or* grathul-grathul *or* grothal-grathul (of speaking) halting, awkward.

grati a variety of duck.

gratis free of charge.

graul *var of* graut.

graung, pating graung howling or wailing sounds everywhere. *See also* gaung.

graut, nggraut to scratch with the nails or claws;
nggrauti to keep scratching s.o. with the nails;
grautan a scratch.

grawah, grawah-grawah *repr* the sound of swiftly flowing water, *esp* in a deep gorge;
gumrawah to flow swiftly.

grawal, grawalan in haste.

grawil *pl form of* gawil.

grawul, pating grawul in coarse grains;
growal-grawul rickety, unsteady.

grawut *var of* graut.

grayah, nggrayah *or* to grope, feel with the hands;
nggrayahi *or* grayah-grayah to feel around in;
grayahan to keep groping, feel around;
gumrayah prolific.

grayak hold-up man;
nggrayak to rob;
grayakan stolen.

grayang a touch;
nggrayang to touch;
nggrayangi 1 to touch s.t.; 2 to grope, feel around;
grayang-grayang to feel around;
panggrayang 1 act of touching/feeling; 2 sense of touch.

grayeng *intsfr* dark: pitch dark.

gréba, nggréba to conjure up in the imagination.

grebeg traditional religious festival held three times annually, featuring a procession and offerings of rice 'mountains';
nggrebeg to surround and escort s.o.;
ginarebeg escorted in procession (king, dignitary, bride).

grébyag 1 thin flat copper, a sheet of copper; 2 copperware.

grècèh, nggrècèh incessant, continuous (rain).

grècèk, nggrècèk talkative.

grecih *var of* grècèh.

grecok, nggrecoki to keep calling s.o.'s attention to their shortcomings.

grécok *see* grecok.

gredèb, gredèb-gredèb to have a tic affecting the eye.

gredeg *or* mak gredeg a rush of people arriving simultaneously.

gredhu *see* gerdhu.

greg *or* mak greg *repr* a jolt, *esp* a sudden stop;
grag-greg to stop and start by turns;
nggrag-nggreg hoarse (voice).

gregel *or* mak gregel 1 *repr* feeling s.t. poking one; 2 to feel affected;
nggregel 1 to feel; 2 affected, moved in sympathy.

gregelèk liquor bottle.

greges I, greges-greges *or* gregas-greges to have chills (when one is feverish). II pebbly soil, earth mixed with gravel.

greget a strong urge, intensity of feeling;
- saut agile and assiduous conduct or behaviour;
nggregetaké irritating, exasperating;
gregeten exasperated.

gregèt *or* mak gregèt *repr* a squeaking door.

grègèt, nggrègèt to take the trouble to.

gregut, nggreguti *or* gumregut assiduous, energetic.

gréja I church.

II *or* manuk gréja sparrow.

gréjah, nggréjah 1 to count, enumerate; 2 to consider, think about/over.

grejeg, nggrejeg to force, compel; grejegan to quarrel.

grejèh *var of* grecèh.

grèk *or* mak grèk *repr* rasping.

grema *see* germa.

grembel, nggrembel 1 thick; 2 to flock to, gather in.

grembul *var of* grembel.

grémbyang *or* mak grémbyang *repr* a sudden about-face.

grembyeng, grembyeng-grembyeng 1 buzzing; 2 *repr* soft conversation.

gremeng, nggremeng *or* gremeng-gremeng *or* gremang-gremeng 1 to converse softly, talk in murmurs; 2 to loom up in the dark; gremengan to talk to o.s. in murmurs; gumremeng to talk in murmurs.

grèmèng, nggrèmèng *or* grèmèngan to rave deliriously.

gremet, gremet-gremet *or* gremat-gremet to move by creeping, proceed at a crawl; nggremet to creep, move at a crawling pace; nggremeti to creep on s.t.; gremetan characterised by crawling; gegremetan (the class of) crawling creatures (*i.e.* insects).

gremis light rain (*see* grimis).

gremus, nggremus 1 to bite s.t. crunchy; 2 to devour.

grénda I revolving grindstone; nggrénda to sharpen with such a grindstone.

II, nggrénda to massage (*k.i. for* pijet, urut). *See also* grinda.

grendhèl, nggrendhèl to lag behind.

grèndhèl door or window bolt.

grendheng, nggrendheng *reg* to grumble; nggrendhengi to grumble to/over;

grendhengan to mutter, grumble.

grendim, nggrendim to coax, persuade s.o. repeatedly.

grénjal, nggrénjal to beat with arms and legs.

grenjel *or* mak grenjel *repr* the feel of s.t. hard; grenjel-grenjel *or* grenjal-grenjal to keep feeling s.t. pressing against one; nggrenjel to feel s.t. hard or uncomfortable pressing against one.

grènjèng (gold, silver, tin) leaf.

grenjet impulse, urge.

greneng a complaint; greneng-greneng *or* grenang-greneng to mutter, grumble; nggreneng to grumble; nggrenengi to grumble to/about; grenengan to keep grumbling.

grènèng (of kris) a small crooked ornament.

greng I *or* mak greng *repr* a jerk, jolt, caused by an electric shock.

II thicket of thorny bamboo.

III the whole appearance. *See also* jenggereng.

grengseng enthusiasm, urge, desire; nggrengseng *or* gumrengseng (to behave) with enthusiasm.

grèngsèng a large open frying pan; nggrèngsèng to fry (a fatty food) without additional oil.

grenyang, grenyangan to engage in disgraceful behaviour.

grenuk, pating grenuk *pl* sitting around talking.

grèpès chipped, broken (teeth).

gres *repr* cutting, slashing.

grès I 1 *repr* a knife slashing, *esp* when performing a circumcision; 2 to perform a circumcision.

II brand new.

gresah, nggresah to bemoan one's fate; panggresah a complaint.

grèsèk, nggrèsèk *or* grèsèk-grèsèk to look around (for), try to find a leftover; grèsèkan leftover.

grèthèl a pole used for getting fruit down from high on a tree.

gréwal *or* mak gréwal *repr* rock breaking;
nggréwal to crack rock.

grèwèng, pating grèwèng having too much to carry.

gribig woven bamboo panel used as a screen.

gridig, gridig-gridig *or* gumridig (walking) grouped, bunched.

grija *var of* gréja.

grig *or* mak grig *repr* a stab of fear.

grigis *reg* 1 to drizzle; 2 drizzling rain.

griguh, grigah-griguh to walk unsteadily with age.

grik-griken feeble, sickly.

grim I a certain black coloured fabric.
II gravel ballast on a railway track.

grimah *reg* backyard.

griming, griming-griming *or* pating griming *or* gumriming 1 to feel chilly; 2 to feel itchy or irritated.

grimis, udan - light rain, rain (to rain) in little drops.

grinda, nggrinda 1 to massage (a baby); 2 *var of* grénda.

gringging, gringgingen to have pins-and-needles, be asleep (leg, arm);
gringging-gringging 1 to tingle with a pins-and-needles feeling; 2 to hesitate timidly.

gringsang oppressively hot.

grining, gumrining *intsfr* clear, pure.

grinting a variety of grass.

grip slate pencil.

gripir clerk in a law court.

gripis chipped, broken (teeth).

grita *see* gurita.

griwa nape of the neck (*k.i. for* githok).

griya house (*kr for* omah).

griyeng I *or* mak griyeng *repr* a quick

upward motion.
II, nggriyeng *or* griyeng-griyeng to wail.

griyèt *or* mak griyèt *repr* creaking, squeaking (door).

griyul *or* mak griyul *repr* chewing on something lumpy;
griyal-griyul (to chew) laboriously;
kegriyul to hit s.t. hard (when chewing, stepping on s.t.).

grobag 1 two-wheeled roofed ox-cart; 2 railway truck; - cèlèng one-wheeled pushcart, wheelbarrow; - wong ox-cart drawn by manpower;
nggrobag to drive an ox-cart as one's trade;
nggrobagaké to load s.t. into an ox-cart;
grobagan cartload.

grobog 1 large storage box; 2 food cupboard.

groboh I rough, crude.
II, nggroboh to search through s.t.

grobyag *or* mak grobyag *repr* a heavy thump;
grobyagan 1 to make thumping sounds; 2 to bustle, stir; very busy and noisy.

grobyos *or* gumrobyos (to sweat) profusely.

groda banyan tree (*var of* gurda).

groden *reg* coin worth 2½ cents during the colonial period.

grog, grag-grog *repr* snorting, coughing.

grogol 1 strong bamboo or wooden fence; 2 animal trap;
nggrogol 1 to put a strong fence around; 2 to trap wild animals;
pagrogolan an area fenced for trapping wild animals.

grojog, grojog-grojog *repr* water falling;
nggrojog *or* gumrojog to fall continuously (water);
nggrojogaké to cause (water) to fall;
grojogan waterfall.

grok *repr* seating o.s.

gromah-gramèh *reg* rather impolite.

grombol 1 group, gathering; 2 grove of trees;

nggrombol to gather, form a crowd;

grombolan 1 group; 2 gang of bandits.

grombyang *or* mak grombyang *repr* metallic clatter;

grombyangan to produce a clattering sound.

grompol cluster, bunch;

nggrompol to form a group, gather, assemble. *See also* krompol.

grong *lit* hollow, excavated. *See also* gerong.

gronggang *var of* gronggong.

gronggong, nggronggong not tightly closed, opened a mere crack.

gronjal, nggronjal 1 to jump up and down, flail the arms and legs; 2 bumpy;

pating gronjal characterised by ups and downs, bumpy.

gronong spoiled, overindulged.

grontol cooked corn mixed with salted shredded coconut.

gropak I fried cassava chip.

II *repr* a branch snapping; - sénthé ancestor, or descendant, in the 8th generation.

gropyak, pating gropyak to keep banging, thumping.

gropyok (to engage in) a hunt, chase;

nggropyok to chase together, hunt down;

panggropyok a hunting down, a concerted closing-in action.

grosok coarse in texture (sand).

grothal, grothal-grathul halting, lacking fluency (speech).

growah 1 caved in; 2 lacking support; 3 eclipse.

growak 1 with a hole torn into it; 2 cave, hole in the ground.

growal, growal-growal *or* pating growal rough, uneven, with stones on it.

growong 1 hollow; 2 *reg* eclipse;

nggrowongi to hollow out, make holes in.

groyok brusque.

grubug, grubug-grubug *repr* roaring sound, *esp* fire, wind;

gumrubug (to make) a roaring sound.

grubyug 1 (to do) as others are doing (*see also* anut); 2 *or* mak grubyug *repr* coming together in a group; 3 *repr* a thudding fall;

nggrubyug to move in a group, do as others are doing, flock together;

grubyugan (to do things) with others;

gumrubyug flocking together.

grudag, grudag-grudug to follow the crowd. *See also* grudug.

grudug *or* mak grudug *repr* a sudden rush as people converge;

nggrudug to move in a group;

nggrudugi to go s.w. in swarms;

grudugan (act of) going along as one of a group;

gumrudug *pl* (to come) swarming;

grudag-grudug to follow the crowd.

grujug to pour (water);

nggrujug *or* nggrujugi to pour (water) onto;

nggrujugaké to pour water (onto);

gumrujug to keep flowing, running, pouring (water).

grugah, grugah-gruguh. *See also* gruguh.

grugak, nggrugak very thin.

gruguh, nggruguh to groan, moan;

panggruguh groaning, moaning.

grugus, pating grugus *pl* mouldered.

grumah, grumah-grumuh to walk slowly and carefully (from age).

grumbul undergrowth, thicket;

grumbulan *or* gegrumbulan area of undergrowth or thickets.

grumbyung, grumbyungan to gather for company.

grumpung (of nose) deformed (flat, tipless).

grumuh sturdy, physically sound.

grumut, **nggrumut** to sneak along, sneak up on s.o.;
  nggrumuti to approach furtively, sneak up to;
  grumat-grumut *or* **grumut-grumut** *or* **grumutan** to lurk, hang around.

grumyung boisterous, loud.

grunak, **grunak-grunek** to complain, grumble. *See also* **grunek**.

grundaya *lit* a variety of swallow. *See also* **gurundaya**.

grundel, **nggrundel** *or* **grundelan** to grumble with dissatisfaction;
  nggrundeli to grumble at, complain to.

grunek a complaint, grudge;
  grunekan *or* **grunak-grunek** to complain, grumble.

gruneng, **nggruneng** to grumble, complain.

grunggung a buzzing, humming, murmuring;
  gumrunggung to produce such a sound.

grup group, gathering.

grusa, **grusa-grusu** to act impetuously. *See also* **grusu**.

grusah, **nggrusah** to bemoan one's fate (*var of* **gresah**).

grusu, **grusa-grusu** to act impetuously.

gruteni full dress (uniform);
  grutnèn in full dress.

gruwak *var of* **gruwek**.

gruwek, **nggruwek** to wound by piercing with nails or claws.

gruwel *or* **mak gruwel** *repr* crumpling, embracing;
  nggruwel 1 crumpled, curled; 2 to embrace.

gruwung 1 hollow; 2 (of nose) flat or tipless (*var of* **grumpung**).

gruyah, **gruyah-gruyuh** very poor.

gruyuh, **nggruyuh** *or* **gruyah-gruyuh** to live in poverty, be very poor.

gubab *reg* to lie.

gubah I movable screen for creating privacy as desired;
  nggubahi to conceal s.t. with a movable screen;
  gubahan bed concealed by a movable screen.
  II, **nggubah** to make an artistic creation;
  ginubah created (composed, drawn *etc*);
  gubahan an artistic creation.

gubar a certain type of gamelan gong without knob.

gubed, **nggubed** to wind around, encircle;
  nggubedaké to wind s.t. around;
  nggubed-gubed to wrap round and round;
  gubedan act or way of encircling s.t.

gubeg *or* **gubegan** to bandage, bind up.

gubel I, **nggubel** to keep on at, pester.
  II *var of* **gubed**.

gubet *see* **gubed**.

gubis *reg* cabbage.

gublug *reg* stupid.

gubrah *var of* **gubras**.

gubras spattered, smeared.

gubrat *var of* **gubras**.

gubres *reg* to quarrel.

gubris, **ora nggubris** to take no notice of.

gubug 1 hut, shack; 2 shelter in ricefield.

gudag, **nggudag** to chase.

gudèl buffalo calf (young of the **kebo**);
  nggudèl resembling a buffalo calf;
  - **bingung** to behave erratically or frenziedly.

guder, **guderan** (to make) loud bustle.

gudhal dirt on the penis.

gudhang I warehouse, storehouse.
  II *or* **gudhangan** vegetables mixed with grated coconut and chilis;
  nggudhang to make (ingredients) into the above dish.

gudhas *reg* very tasty.

gudhé a tree that produces a bean eaten as a vegetable.

gudheg a dish consisting of young jackfruit cooked in coconut milk with spices;

nggudheg to make (jackfruit) into the above dish.

gudher *see* **sepur**.

gudhig scabies;

gudhigen to suffer from scabies.

gudhis *reg* very tasty (*var of* **gudhas**).

gudir jelly produced from seaweed.

gudrah messy, stained, smeared (with).

gudras *var of* **gudrah**.

gudu *reg* not (s.t. other than). *See also* **dudu**.

gugah *ng*, **gigah** *kr*, **wungu** *k.i.*, to (try to) wake s.o. up;

nggugah to wake s.o. up;

nggugahi to wake up (several people);

nggugahaké to wake s.o. up on behalf of s.o. else;

panggugah motivating force, instigation.

gugat, **nggugat** to accuse, sue, indict;

nggugataké to bring a charge or suit against;

gugatan accusation, indictment.

gugrag *see* **gograg**.

gugrug to slide down(ward).

gugu *ng*, **gega** *kr*, **nggugu** to believe, trust, obey, act according to;

nggugoni to follow, live up to, obey;

gugon tuhon superstition;

gugonan credulous;

nggugu karepé dhéwé obstinate.

guguh very old, toothless.

guguk, **ngguguk** 1 to cry with gasping; 2 unrestrained, uncontrolled, *esp* weeping.

gugup nervous, startled;

gugupan nervous by nature.

gugur 1 to fall, drop; 2 *fig* to die; 3 to collapse, cave in; - **gunung** (to do) communal work on a project in time of disaster (unpaid);

ngguguraké 1 to disturb, interfere with (faith, religious observance); 2 to abort.

gugus chipped.

gugut I protruding chin.

II toothless (*k.i. for* **ompong**).

III, **nggugut** to kill (lice) by pressing them against the front teeth.

gujeg, **nggujeg** 1 to hold s.o. tight; 2 to nag.

gujeng I laugh (*kr for* **guyu**);

nggujeng to laugh (*kr for* **ngguyu**).

II, **nggujengi** *or* **gujengan** to hold onto;

nggujengaké to hold for s.o.

gujer, **nggujer** to hold s.t. tight (*var of* **gujeg**).

gujig *reg* inquisitive.

gujih *reg* scanty, scraggy.

gul a goal; -**pal** goal post;

ngegulaké 1 to score a goal; 2 to allow (the ball) to enter the goal; 3 to push through until accepted;

gul-gulan to take turns being goalkeeper while the other kicks;

kegulan to get scored against.

gula *ng*, **gendhis** *kr* sugar; - **arèn** sugar from the areca palm; - **batu** lump sugar; - **jawa** palm sugar; - **klapa** 1 sugar made from coconut palm sap; 2 striped red and white; - **pasir** granulated or refined sugar;

nggulani to sweeten s.t. with sugar.

gulaganti a children's game played with pebbles.

gulak, **gulak-gulak** *reg* to boil, bubble up.

gulali lollipop, any hard sweet (*see* **glali**).

gulan seedbed consisting of heaped-up soil.

gulang, **nggulang** *or* **nggegulang** to teach, train.

gulat, **nggulati** *reg* to look for, seek.

gulawenthah education;

nggulawenthah to educate.

guldhen guilder.

gulé a curry-like dish.

gulèk *reg* and then, afterward (*var of* **guli**).

gulet 1 intimate, chummy with; 2 wrestling;

nggulet to tag along, hang around.

guli *reg* and then, afterward.

guling I bolster, 'Dutch wife'.

II dam-reinforcing material of woven bamboo.

III 1 *lit* to sleep; 2 *or* **ngguling** to roll;

nggulingaké to roll s.t.;

gumuling to roll (away, around);

pagulingan a bed.

gulma billion.

gulo that's it, there it is!, there you are!; (*var of* **iku lo**).

gulu *ng*, *kr*, **jangga** *k.i.* neck; - **ancak** 1 lower part of the neck of poultry (prepared as food); 2 tapering end of a knife blade; - **banyak** 1 swan-like neck; 2 long thin object formed like a goose neck;

gulon collar or neck of a garment;

panggulu the second child.

gulud, **nggulud** to make a seedbed by heaping up soil;

guludan seedbed in a ricefield.

guluh dirt on the skin;

guluhen to have/get dirt on the skin.

gulung 1 a roll; 2 rolled (up).

gumagus (of males) proud of one's looks (whether justified or not). *See* **bagus**.

gumampleng *repr* splashing (against s.t.).

Gumarang name of a mythological ox.

gumati *ng*, **gumatos** *kr*, affectionately attentive;

nggumatèni to heap affection on, pamper. *See* **gati**.

gumatos *kr for* **gumati**.

gumbala *lit* 1 moustache; 2 beard (*k.i* for **jénggot**).

gumbeng I *reg* opium pipe.

II a certain gamelan instrument made from a bamboo stem.

gumblis *excl* you don't say!

gumbreg the 6th **wuku** of the Javanese calendar.

gumbreng, **nggumbreng** *reg* angry with grumbling.

gumedheg 1 very exasperated; 2 excessively joyful.

guméla seen clearly from afar.

gumemplang burning hot (sunshine).

gumisa *ng*, **sumaged** *kr*, to act as if competent or capable. *See* **bisa**.

gumoh to spit up while being fed (babies).

gumpes flat.

gumping a precipitous mountainside.

gumrah I usual, normal, ordinary (*reg var of* **lumrah**).

II *lit* (to make) loud thundering sounds.

gumrebeg deafening, ear-shattering. *See also* **brebeg**.

gumredeg *repr* a rush of people arriving simultaneously.

gumreg loud, boisterous.

gumreng, **nggumreng** to reprimand s.o. by grumbling.

gumrèwèl 1 easy to move, unsteady; 2 helpful; 3 easy to persuade.

gumridig (walking) grouped, bunched.

gumrubul to move in a swarm. *See also* **brubul**.

gumuk small hill, knoll.

gumul to wrestle.

gumulak *reg* boiling, bubbling up.

gumun astonished, surprised;

nggumuni 1 to admire, be amazed by; 2 astonishing;

nggumunaké to be astonishing, cause amazement;

gumunan easily surprised.

gumunggung I conceited, fond of adulation.

II added up. *See* **gunggung**.

gumyah 1 *var of* **gumyak**; **2** known publicly.

gumyak noisy.

gumyek talkative, fluent.

gumyur bewildered, in shock.

gun I comb (part of loom).

II *reg cr* sweetheart.

guna I *ng*, **gina** *kr*, use(fulness), benefit;
nggunakaké to use, make use of;
kagunan 1 art, artistic skill, craftsmanship; **2** art object/form.

II, **guna-guna** *or* - **piranti** *or* - **sarana** *or* - **sekti** a magic spell for doing harm to another;
nggunani to cast, or have s.o. cast, a spell on another;
guna ing aguna *lit* any kind of magic spell.

gunah *reg* known precisely.

gunakaya money for support, given to a wife.

gunawan *lit* **1** virtuous, noble; **2** useful (person).

guncang shaky, swaying, unstable. *See* **goncang**.

gundam, gundam-gundam to cry out in fear or disgust.

gundem *reg* a corn-like grain.

gundha a certain plant that grows in the ricefield;
gumundha lemara rice plants before the leaves become greenish.

gundhal 1 *reg* groom (for horses); **2** sycophant, yes-man. *See also* **begundhal**.

gundhala I *or* **gundhala titir** alarm signal.

II earring (*var of* **kundhala**).

gundhik I mistress, concubine;
nggundhik to take as one's mistress.

II **1** female (flying) termite (**laron**); **2** queen ant.

gundhil I (of rice plants, coconuts) with no hair or fibres.

II (Javanese which is) written in Arabic characters without vowel diacritics.

gundhul 1 devoid of hair or vegetation; **2** *cr* the part of the head where the hair grows; **3** one of the Chinese playing-cards (*kertu cilik*).

gunem *ng*, **ginem** *kr*, talking, speech;
nggunem to discuss, talk about;
nggunemi to (try to) persuade;
guneman talking, conversation.

gung I 1 large, great; **2** high, full (water-level);
ngegungaké 1 to assign too great a value to; **2** to increase the supply of (water).

II not yet (*reg var of* **durung**).

III *repr* the sound of the gamelan gong.

gunggung I sum total; - **kepruk** *or* - **kumpul** the sum total, all told;
nggunggung to total up;
gunggungan 1 sum, total; **2** numbers (to be) totalled; **3** addition.

II, **nggunggung** to encourage, impart confidence; - **dhiri** *lit* to boast, be conceited;
gumunggung conceited, fond of adulation.

gunggrung *reg* esophagus, windpipe.

gungsir, nggungsir *or* **nggungsiri** to dig (in).

guni jute, gunny sack (*var of* **goni**).

gunita *lit* ability, artistic skill.

guntang I *reg* bamboo cylinder used as container.

II, **ngguntang** to pound (rice) to remove the husks (*reg var of* **gentang**).

gunten I *reg* ingenuity.

II *reg* village labourer, villager.

gunting scissors, shears;
ngubunting to cut with scissors;
ngguntingi to cut s.t. with scissors;
ngguntingaké to cut s.t. on behalf of s.o. else;

guntingan 1 clipping (from newspaper *etc*); 2 cut, style of cutting (a pattern *etc*).

guntur thunder.

gunung 1 *ng*, **redi** *kr*, mountain; 2 head of an administrative or police district; 3 name of one of the Chinese playing-cards (*kertu cilik*); - **anakan** hill; - **geni** volcano; - **sepikul** a small earring with a diamond on each side;

nggunungi mountain-bred, boorish, crude;

gunungan 1 *way* symbolic puppet used in wayang performances, with various functions (*also* **kayon**); 2 *or* **gegunungan** village administrative head;

pagunungan mountain range.

gunyer, nggunyer to press and fondle (in massage) (*var of* **ginyer**).

gupak messy, smeared.

gupala a giant statue that guards a gate or portal.

gupé *lit* sad, sorrowful. *See also* **gupya**.

gupermèn government.

gupernur governor; - **jéndral** governor-general;

gupernuran governor's official residence.

gupis chipped (teeth).

gupit *or* **gupitan** alley(way); - **mandragini** royal sleeping-apartment.

gupita *lit* a poetic narration, composition, expression (words);

ginupita composed, arranged.

gupoh quick, in a hurry (*reg var of* **gupuh**).

gupon dovecote. *See* **gupu**.

gupruk *var of* **gupyuk**.

gupu a shelter for people or animals;

pagupon *or* **gupon** dovecote.

gupuh quick, in a hurry.

gupur *lit* fear, afraid, scared, shocked.

gupya *lit* sad, sorrowful (*var of* **gupé**).

gupyuk lively, animated.

gur I *or* **nggur** *reg* only.

II (*pron as:* gu:r) *repr* a gong beat.

guragada *lit* badly-behaved.

gurah I to rinse out the mouth and gargle.

II, **nggurah** to drive away, shoo off. *Also* **gurak**.

gurak *var of* **gurah**.

gurawa *see* **gorawa**.

gurawal *see* **grawal**.

gurda *lit* banyan tree.

gurdi tool for drilling holes.

gurem 1 chicken flea; 2 trivial, insignificant, of little consequence; - **thèthèl** a common person with grandiose ambitions.

guri back, rear (*reg var of* **buri**).

gurih pleasantly rich-tasting, *esp* suggesting the flavour of coconut milk.

gurinda grindstone (*var of* **grénda**).

guris, ngguris 1 to scratch; 2 to scrape s.t. left behind, scoop out.

gurit I, **guritan** backyard (*var of* **buritan**).

II, **nggurit** to scratch;

guritan a scratch.

III, **nggurit** to compose a song or poem;

geguritan 1 song (in simple metre, with rhyme); 2 poem in modern style;

juru gurit poet.

gurita I octopus.

II a band with strings at either end put on newborn babies (*var of* **grita**).

guritan *see* **gurit**.

gurma hunter (*var of* **germa**).

gurnadur governor.

gurnan *reg* willing; **ora** - dead set against.

gurnat a variety of bomb.

gurnita *lit* loud, boisterous.

gurtak snarl, snappping;

nggurtak to snap at.

guru teacher; - **aleman** fond of praise; - **bakal** raw material; - **dadi** objects for offerings or dowries; - **lagu** poetic metre; - **laki** husband; - **nadi** instructor in metaphysical matters; - **sastra** having the same consonants in the same order (complex alliterative device); - **sejati** teacher who instructs in the perfect truth; - **swara** having same vowels in the same order; - **wilangan** syllabic scheme, metric scheme;

ngguroni 1 to instruct, *esp* in religious or mystical matters; 2 to learn under the guidance of a teacher;

nggurokaké to put s.o. in the hands of an instructor;

nggeguru *or* **maguru** to acquire knowledge from a teacher.

guruh thunder;

gumuruh (to make) loud thundering sounds.

gurung esophagus, windpipe;

gurungan water channel.

gus polite term of address by adults to boys or youths.

gusah, nggusah to chase away.

gusak *var of* **gusah**.

gusali blacksmith.

gusar I, **gusaran** to have the teeth filed.

II *reg* furious.

gusek eraser (*reg var of* **busek I**).

gusi *ng*, *kr*, **wingkisan** *k.i.* gums (in the mouth); - **papak** the obsolete custom of filing the teeth level;

gusèn gum-shaped, gum-like.

gusis finished, all gone, completely destroyed.

gusthi, nggusthi *lit* to consider, deliberate on.

gusti lord, master; - **Allah** God; **kanjeng** - your majesty.

gut, gut-gutan very exasperated.

guthaka *lit* cave, well.

guthang incomplete, imperfect (*var of* **gothang**).

guthek, ngguthek-guthek to divide into small rooms;

guthekan a room created by partitioning.

gutheng *intsfr* black.

guthet *var of* **guthek**.

guthi small, low, inferior; **cili** - teeny-weeny (*see also* **cili**).

guthik, guthikan *reg* to butt each other with the horns (buffaloes).

guthil stingy, close-fisted.

guthit bad to walk on (paths).

guthul *cr* glans (of the penis).

gutuk I a stick for throwing;

nggutuk to throw a stick;

nggutuk lor kena kidul *prov* to criticise obliquely by directing one's comments to B in A's hearing.

II commensurate (with), balanced (by).

III *or* **gutuk waja** toothless (*reg k.i. for* **ompong**).

gutul *reg* to reach; **ora** - out of reach.

guwa cave, cavern, grotto; - **garba** uterus, womb;

ngguwa to burrow through or under, undermine;

guwan resembling a cave.

guwab to lie, cheat, deceive (*reg var of* **gobab**).

guwak *var of* **guwang, buwang**.

guwan *see* **guwa**.

guwang *var of* **buwang**.

guwaya complexion, healthy glow (face).

guwèh, guwèhen to have/get sores in the mouth.

guwek I a certain long-eared owl.

II, **ngguwek** to pierce with claws or nails.

guwing harelipped.

guwul *reg* a certain tool for catching fish.

guyang, ngguyang to bathe livestock (in waterhole, river, stall);

pangguyangan place where livestock are bathed.

guyeng *reg* pleasant, warm, cordial (*var of* gayeng I).

guyer, ngguyer to pet, fondle.

guyu *ng*, gujeng *kr*, a laugh;
ngguyu to laugh;
ngguyoni to keep s.o. amused;
ngguyokaké 1 funny, amusing; 2 to make s.o. laugh;
nggeguyu to laugh at;
guyon *or* geguyon to joke, banter;
guyonan 1 laughing-stock; 2 mockery.

guyub friendly, mutually helpful;
ngguyubi to take a personal interest in;
paguyuban a social relationship *or* association based on mutual interests.

guyur, ngguyur to splash or pour water (onto).

H

ha 1 *excl, irregular pronoun* so! aha!; - iya yes indeed!; 2 what about…?

habib Arab descendant of the prophet Muhammad.

hacing atchoo!

haco *var of* hacing.

hacu *var of* hacing.

hadé *lit* wrong, impossible.

hadiningrat 'first, best in the world', a designation of the cities of Surakarta and Yogyakarta.

hadipati title for bupati.

hadiyah 1 prize; 2 gift; 3 reward.

hadhang, kahadhang *lit* ambushed, blocked.

hadyan *lit, male nobility title: shtf of* rahadyan.

hah *excl* see! well!

ha-hak *repr* laugher.

hailolah *excl of dismay, despair.*

hajat a celebration with communal meal (*var of* kajat).

hajeng safe and sound (*md for* hayu, rahayu) (*shtf of* rahajeng).

haji I 1 one who has made the pilgrimage to Mecca; 2 title and term of address

for such a pilgrim.
II atchoo!

hak I 1 right; 2 rightful authority; 3 privilege.
II *excl* open mouth!
III hook (and eye).
IV (high) heel.

hakékat 1 truth, reality; 2 essence; 3 basically, actually, truly.

hakiki true, real, authentic, essential.

halah *excl* well!

halal permitted, allowed, permissible.

halal-bihalal 1 to ask and give forgiveness at the end of the Fasting Month; 2 the gathering of social group for such a purpose.

halat heaven-sent retribution (*var of* walat).

haliman *lit* elephant.

halo *excl* hello!

halpbèk halfback (in soccer).

halte stopping-place for public vehicles.

hambok 1 please; why don't you…?; 2 if, when(ever). *See also* bok, mbok.

hanacaraka the Javanese alphabet.

hancinco Chinese-style jacket without

274

collar.

handhuk towel (*var of* **andhuk**).

hangabèhi an official rank at court (*var of* **ngabèhi**).

hara 1 *excl* there! see!; **2** *excl of impatient amazement.*

harak *excl inviting agreement or confirmation. See* **rak**.

haram forbidden, sinful.

harharan *reg* to splurge, waste money.

harsaya *lit* glad, happy.

harsuka *lit*, *var of* **harsaya**.

harta wealth, money.

hartaka 1 treasurer; **2** *lit* money.

hartati *lit* **1** sugar; **2** sweet.

haruhara 1 disturbance; **2** riot.

harya *a title of male nobility.*

hasti *lit* elephant.

hatmaja *lit* son, child (*var of* **atmaja**).

hatmaka *lit* son, child (*see also* **atmaka**).

haung 1 *chld* dog; **2** *repr* a dog's growl or snarl.

hawa 1 air; **2** weather.

hawa-napsu *lit* passions, desire.

hawan *lit* way;
    mahawan to go, pass through.

hawani *lit* earth.

hayat life.

hayo *excl* for shooing away animals *etc.*

hayuningrat *lit* salvation of the world.

hé *excl* hey!

hébat splendid.

he-eh *coll* yes; *excl* uh huh.

heh *excl of surprise, dismay.*

hèh 1 *repr* indrawn breath; **2** *excl* hey!

hek *repr* a grunt (of exertion, of disgust).

hèk fence.

helang *lit* hawk.

hèlep assistant.

hem *excl of pleasure, admiration.*

hèm man's shirt.

hening *lit* clear, pure. *See also* **ening**.

her *command to a span of buffaloes to turn right. See also* **giyak**.

hèrdher German shepherd dog.

hes *excl* shoo! sh! (*var of* **hus**).

hi 1 *excl of revulsion or fear*; **2** jeering sound.

hih *var of* **hi**.

hijrah 1 the Prophet Muhammad's Separation from Mecca to Medina in A.D. 622; **2** the Islamic era.

hikmat 1 wisdom, philosophy; **2** supernatural power.

hima *lit* cloud, mist.

himalaya *lit* mountain.

himantaka *lit* mist rising from water.

himawan *lit* mountain.

Hindhu pertaining to Hinduism.

hing *syllable chanted in making a concerted effort.*

his 1 *excl of scorn*; **2** *command to a farm or draught animal to stop.*

hla *excl* (*var of* **la, lha**).

hlo *excl* (*var of* **lo, lho**).

hohah huge object, enormous.

holopis to work together cooperatively;
    holobis kuntul baris *words chanted by a group of workers to keep their concerted motions rhythmic.*

homa *lit* sacrifice, victim;
    pahoman 1 place where sacrifices are offered; **2** place for solitary meditation.

hop *excl* stop!

horé *excl* hurray!

horeg to shake from a mighty force. *See also* **oreg**.

horoh *excl* oh-oh!

hos *excl of deep breath.*

hosé *excl* hurray!

hoyag to shake violently. *See also* **oyag**.

hredaya *lit* heart, feeling (*see also* **wardaya**).

hret *repr* stopping.

hru *lit* arrow.

hu 1 *excl of scorn*; **2** *repr* mild laughter used as a conventional device rather than to express amusement.

huh *excl* (*var of* **hu**).

huhah huge object, enormous (*var of* **hohah**).

huk (*pron as:* **hu:k**) huk-huk bow-wow!

hulu head, leader (*var of* **ulu** I).

hulun *lit* I, me (*var of* **ulun**).

hun unit of weight for opium.

huncuwé tobacco pipe.

hunkwé gelatinous pudding made from green bean flour.

hunur *lit* hill.

hup I *excl* stop!

　II head, chief.

hur *excl* gee up!

hurdah 1 *excl* shoo!; 2 who goes there?

huré *excl* hurray! (*var of* **horé**).

hus 1 *excl* shoo!; 2 sh!; 3 *excl of disapproval*.

husé *excl* hurray!

Hutipati another name of Bathara Guru.

hwang *var of* **hyang**. *Also* **ywang**.

hyang title of a native or Hindu deity.

hyas *lit* ornamentation, finery;

　mahyas to make up, array o.s. in finery.

hyun *lit* to want, wish (*see also* **ayun** II).

I

i *excl* oh!

iba *or* **saiba** how…!

ibadah 1 religious practices; 2 act of devotion;

　ngibadah 1 to be devout, pious; 2 to perform one's religious obligations.

i *excl* oh!

iba *or* **saiba** how…!

ibadah 1 religious practices; 2 act of devotion;

　ngibadah 1 to be devout, pious; 2 to perform one's religious obligations.

ibadat *var of* **ibadah**.

ibah *or* **ibahan** grant, donation, bequest;

　ngibahi to give grant, donate, bequeath.

ibarat *or* **ngibarat** 1 like, in the matter of; 2 simile, metaphor;

　ngibarataké 1 to compare s.t. to; 2 to make a comparison.

ibat *or* **ngibat-ibati** admirable, amazing, astonishing.

ibek *lit* full (of).

iben 1 saliva; 2 to salivate (*reg kr for* **idu**).

ibeng, ibengan rotation, time around (*reg kr for* **ubeng**).

iber flight (of a bird);

　miber to fly;

　ngiberi to fly over/around s.t.;

　ngiberaké 1 to let s.t. fly; 2 to release (bird, butterfly *etc*) to fly;

　iber-iberan flying creatures.

ibing I *reg* dance;

　ngibing to dance;

　ibingan a dance.

　II to know, see (*reg k.i. for* **idhep**).

iblis devil, Satan, evil spirit.

ibnu son of (in name).

ibu 1 mother; 2 *term for addressing or referring to one's wife, or a woman of higher age or social standing*;

　ngibu to call s.o. mother, regard s.o. as one's own mother;

　ngiboni to behave as a mother (girl, young woman);

　ibuné *adr* term for addressing one's wife; - **gendhuk** *or* - **tholé** *idiom* my wife. *See also* **bu**.

ibug *reg* to pay attention, care about;

　ora ibug to not care.

ibur I *reg var of* **iber**.

II *reg* uproarious, stormy.

ibut busy (at), involved (in).

ica pleasing to the senses (*reg var of* **éca**).

icak, ngicak to (take a) step (*var of* **idak**);
ngicak-icak to trample.

ical gone; lost (*kr for* **ilang**).

icer, ngicer 1 to aim (gun, arrow *etc*);
2 to have an eye on s.o. or s.t. (*var of* **incer**).

icik (*pron as:* ici:k), **ngicik-icik** to make (coins) jingle;
icak-icik to play around in the water;
icik-iwir housekeeping money.

icip, ngicipi 1 to taste, sample (food);
2 to prove, test, try out;
icip-icip **1** food sample; **2** to taste, sample (*esp* while cooking food, to test the taste);
icip-icipan a taste, a sample.

icir I a certain type of fish trap with barred doors.
II, ngicir to sell retail.
III, ngicir-icir to scatter untidily.

icis breezy, cool, refreshing (*reg var of* **isis**).

icrit, icrat-icrit to take or give s.t. bit by bit;
saicrit a small amount, a small squirt (*var of* **crit, incrit**).

icul 1 loose, astray; **2** to get loose (*reg var of* **ucul**).

idab, ngidab-idabi astonishing, amazing, admirable (*var of* **édab**).

idah *or* **ngidah** the period during which a widow or divorced woman may not remarry, lasting three full menstrual cycles or 100 days; should the woman be pregnant the idah is extended to 40 days after childbirth.

idak, ngidak to (take a) step;
ngidaki to step on;
ngidak-idak to trample.

idayat (God's) guidance.

idep eyelash(es);
idep-idep the doors on certain fish traps (**icir, wuwu**).

ider to peddle wares from place to place;
ngideri **1** to go all around s.w.; **2** to pass around; **3** to plough around the edges of (a ricefield); **4** to burn incense s.w. to ward off evil spirits;
ngideraké **1** to peddle (wares) from place to place; **2** to circulate, distribute; **3** to take up a collection;
mider-mider to wander, go from place to place, circulate;
ideran **1** peddler who travels about; **2** peddler's wares; **3** passed around; **4** circuit of a ricefield being ploughed; **5** community owned and worked ricefield.

idham, ngidham to yearn for certain foods during pregnancy; - **kaworan** to look pregnant;
ngidham-idham to wish, dream, desire;
idham-idhaman a wish, dream, desire.

idhem same, as above, as cited.

idhep I 1 to know, see; **2** *lit* thought(s), knowledge.
II *lit* obedient.
III, idhep-idhep oh well! (expressing resigned acceptance).

idhi *or* **idhi-idhi** *excl of disgust, revulsion.*

idhop, idhop-idhopan *reg* to exchange with each other.

idhum shady, sheltered (*var of* **édhum**).

idhun, midhun 1 to descend; **2** to get off (*var of* **dhun, udhun**).

idhup 1 life; **2** to live; **gambar** - moving picture (*see also* **gambar**);
ngidhupi to bring to life.

idi permission;
ngidèni to give permission to;
kaidènan to receive permission.

idid, midid *or* **ngidid** to blow steadily.

idin permission (*var of* **idi**).

idu *ng, kr,* **kecoh** *k.i.* **1** saliva; **2** to salivate; - **geni** to have everything one says come to pass; - **wilut** sacred spit

(used by healer in treatment);
ngidoni to spit on s.o.;
ngidokaké to spit s.t. out;
kidonan to get spat on;
idu didilat manèh *idiom* to eat one's words.
idul I, **idul-idul** *or* **idal-idul** to go round naked.

II, **idul-adha** *or* **idul-kurban** Feast of the Sacrifice, the day that commemorates the sacrifice of Ismail by Ibrahim, a holy day associated with the pilgrimage to Mecca;
idul-fitri feast celebrating the end of the Fasting Month, Lebaran.
iga rib; **-** **landhung** longest rib; **-** **wekas** shortest rib;
iga-iga split bamboo crosspieces used as a reinforcing framework for fences.
igah-iguh effort, exertion. *See* **iguh**.
igar, **saigar** a half;
igaran obsolete coin worth ½ **dhuwit**.
igèh (*reg var of* **isih**).
igel, **ngigel** *or* **igelan** 1 (of peacocks) to spread the tail; 2 to dance; 3 to bend the hand (a classical dance movement);
ngigelaké to open out (the tail);
pangigel act of spreading the tail or making the above dance movement.
igih *reg var of* **isih**.
igik *reg var of* **isih**.
igin *reg var of* **isih**.
igir, **igir-igir** *reg* mountain ridge.
igit, **ngigit-igit** to be exasperated with;
pangigit exasperation, resentment.
iglag in plain sight, clearly visible (*reg var of* **égla**).
iglag-iglig unstable, wobbly.
iguh effort, exertion; **-** **pretikel** advice;
igah-iguh efforts, exertions;
ngiguhaké to exert one's efforts toward s.t.;
kéguh, **ora -** unmoved, unchanged;
pangiguh way of exerting, making efforts.

igul, **igul-igul** *describing a feminine hip-swaying walk.*
ih *excl of disgust or fear.*
ihi 1 *excl of disgust*; 2 *excl of anger.*
ihnil dead.
ihtiyar (to make) effort. *See also* **istiyar**.
ijab, **- kabul** marriage contract (offering of the bride by her **wali** and acceptance by the bridegroom);
ngijabi to enter into marriage with (one's bride);
ngijabaké to join in marriage.
ijabah granting, hearing (a prayer);
ngijabahi to grant a prayer.
ijajah *var of* **ijasah**.
ijak *var of* **idak**.
ijasah 1 diploma; 2 certificate of course completion.
ijèh *reg var of* **isih**.
ijèk *reg var of* **isih**.
ijem green (*kr for* **ijo**).
ijemak consensus of opinion among Muslim scholars, the third basis of **fikh**.
ijèn *see* **iji**.
ijengandika *lit* you; your (*var of* **jengandika**).
ijep eyelash(es) (*k.i. for* **idep**).
iji, I unit, item, piece;
ijèn unit, digit occupying the unit position.

II, **ijèn** *ng*, **piyambak** *kr* 1 alone, by o.s.; 2 single (not married);
ngijèni 1 to do by o.s.; 2 in a class by itself, unique; 3 unmatched, without equal;
kijènan 1 lonely; 2 to get left by o.s.;
ijèn-ijèn 1 separated; 2 one by one;
ijèn-ijènan all alone;
ijèn padha ijèn one against one.
ijig, **ijig-ijig** *reg* suddenly, unexpectedly. *See also* **ujug-ujug**.
ijih *reg var of* **isih**.
ijik *reg var of* **isih**.
ijir 1 a bit at a time; 2 stingy, mean;

ngijir 1 to deal with (things) little by little or one at a time; 2 to calculate.

ijlag-ijlig to go back and forth repeatedly.

ijmak *see* **ijemak**.

ijo *ng*, **ijem** *kr*, green; - **royo-royo** *or* - **riyo-riyo** pure clear green;
  ngijo to colour s.t. green;
  ngijon to buy (a rice crop) while it is still growing;
  ngijoni 1 to make s.t. green; 2 to make s.t. greener (than before);
  ngijokaké 1 to make s.t. green; 2 to sell the crop while growing in the field;
  ijon *or* **ijonan** 1 rice that is sold while still growing in the field; 2 money paid for such a crop;
  ijon-ijon vegetables.

ijoan 1 oral (message); 2 content (of letter); **ijoané** that is to say...

ijol *ng*, **lintu** *kr*, exchange item; replacement;
  ngijoli to exchange (one thing) for (another);
  ngijolaké to exchange, replace;
  ijolan *or* **ijol-ijolan** to exchange with each other;
  ijol anggon to swap temporarily.

ijot *reg var of* **ijol**.

ijrah *var of* **hijrah**.

ika that (*see also* **kaé**).

ikal spool, reel, object used as a reel;
  ngikal 1 to wind or thread s.t. around or through s.t.; 2 - **basa** to twist words in order to win an argument; 3 - **gada** to swing a club;
  pangikal act of reeling s.t.

iker, **iker-iker** border decoration;
  ngiker-iker to decorate the edge (of).

iket *ng*, **udheng** *kr*, **dhesthar** *k.i.* a batik headcloth which the wearer dons by winding it around his head;
  ngiket 1 to tie together; 2 to compose, construct;
  ngiket-iketi to put a headcloth on s.o.;

iketan *or* **iket-iketan** to wear a headcloth;
  pangiket 1 composition; 2 act of composing.

iki *ng*, **punika** *kr* 1 this; this thing; 2 *general perspective indicator: e.g.* **aku iki** I for my part;
  ika-iki to hem and haw.

ikih *reg* after all, it is a fact that..., for a fact.

ikin *reg var of* **isih**.

iklas accepting, unaffected by loss;
  ngiklasaké 1 to accept with resignation, acquiesce in; 2 to give s.t. up freely.

iklik *reg* to keep o.s. busy.

iklim climate.

ikluk absorbed, engrossed.

ikmat *var of* **hikmat**.

ikrak *var of* **ékrak**.

ikral *var of* **ikrar**.

ikram the state of ritual purity and dedication assumed by a pilgrim to Mecca, involving abstinence from wearing sewn clothes or shoes and from using perfumes.

ikrar statement of guiding principles; to draw up a platform;
  ngikraraké to draw up a statement of guiding principles.

ikrik choosy, hard to please, finicky. *See also* **kikrik**.

iksak exact.

iksamen (to take) a test/examination;
  ngiksamen to give s.o. a test.

ikstra extra.

iksu *lit* sugarcane.

iktidal the standing or balanced position in Islamic prayer.

iktikad determination, intention.

iku *ng*, **punika** *kr*, 1 that; 2 that thing.

ikut I foreskin.
  II, **ngikut** *or* **ngikuti** to pick up/out, choose.

ila, **ila-ila** 1 taboo; 2 ancestral prohibition; 3 curse.

ila-ilu to do what others are doing (*var of* **éla-èlu**). *See also* **ilu** II.

ilab, ilab-ilaban 1 in layers; **2** (coming or leaving) in succession.

iladuni occult sciences;
  ngiladuni to practise the occult sciences.

ilafat symbol;
  ngilafat to symbolise, be an omen (of).

ilag, ilag-ilag *reg* certain leaves planted by the inlet of a ricefield as magical protection;
  ngilag-ilagi to provide with such a sign.

ilahi the Lord.

ilak I, ilak-ilak *var of* **ilag-ilag**.
  II, **ngilak-ilak 1** spreading out broad and level; **2** *intsfr* clear, light, bright.

ilam the neckbone, which joins the skull and the backbone.

ilang *ng*, **ical** *kr*, lost, gone;
  ngilang to disappear;
  ngilangi to remove, take away, reduce;
  ngilangaké 1 to cause s.t. to go away, make s.t. disappear; **2** to lose s.t.;
  ngilang-ilangaké to ignore, disregard, take no account of;
  kélangan 1 to lose (possession of) inadvertently; **2** to suffer from a loss;
  ilang-ilangan likely to cause a permanent rift, running the risk of losing s.o.;
  ilang gapité to have lost what one relies on for effectiveness/strength.

ilapat *var of* **ilafat**.

ilar I, ngilar-ilar broad, vast.
  II, **ngilari** to look for.
  III, **ngilari** to shun, avoid.

ilas, ilas-ilas *reg* **1** external appearance, facial expression; **2** (to say) for the sake of politeness.

ilat 1 (**lidhah** *k.i.*) tongue; **2** wooden peg used to regulate the flow of water in a pipe;

ilat-ilat 1 a certain shrub the leaves of which are used medicinally; **2** bamboo bridge; **3** sole (sea fish);
  ilat-ilatan 1 tongue-shaped object; **2** leather shoulder holster for a kris or sabre; **3** prong of a buckle or clasp.

ilé *reg* fussy.

ileb, ngilebi to flood, inundate;
  kileban to get flooded/inundated. *See also* **leb** II.

ilèn *see* **ili**.

ilep, ngilepaké to put under water, soak.

iler drooling saliva;
  ngiler 1 to drool; **2** to drool over s.t., have the mouth water (for); **3** (of food) spoiled;
  ngileri to drool on;
  kileran to get drooled on.

ilèr a certain plant the leaves of which are used in traditional medicines.

iles I, iles-iles a variety of tuberous root.
  II, **ngiles 1** to step on; **2** to remove rice grains from the straw by treading;
  ngiles-iles to oppress, suppress;
  kèles to get stepped on.

ilet flow (*reg kr for* **ili**).

ilham 1 divine inspiration; **2** inspiration, brainstorm.

ili I flow, current;
  ngili 1 to drift away; **2** to flee from approaching danger;
  ngilèni to irrigate a field;
  ngilèkaké 1 to cause s.t. to flow; **2** to remove (people) from (a threatened area);
  mili to flow, run;
  kèli to get carried along on the current;
  ilèn a river-irrigated ricefield;
  ilènan stream, flow;
  ilèn-ilèn stream, flow;
  kilènan to get irrigated by flowing water;
  pangilèn 1 act of fleeing people; **2** place evacuated by fleeing people.

II money or item given to replace what s.o. lost;

ngilèni 1 to buy in small quantities, *usu* fruits while still on the tree; **2** to replace lost money or articles for s.o.; **ilèn-ilèn** replacement.

ilik, ngilik-ilik to tease (with tickling).

iling I, ngiling to pour s.t.;

ngilingi *or* **ngilingaké** to pour s.t. into.

II, ngiling-ilingi to keep looking for/at;

miling-miling *or* **milang-miling** to look this way and that, look around.

ilir I large woven bamboo fan;

ngiliri to fan s.t.

II, milir to drift with the current;

ngiliraké to allow (a boat) to drift.

III, ngilir to select (an ear) from which to raise new rice plants.

ilis act of putting the finger on the edge of the measurer in order to get a bit more content when buying rice.

ilmi knowledge, science (*kr for* **ilmu**).

ilmiah scientific.

ilmu (body of) knowledge, science; a science. *See also* **ngèlmu**.

ilo, ngilo, ngilo-ilo 1 to look at o.s. in the mirror; **2** to look closely at; **3** to ponder, reflect;

ngiloni to hold a mirror for s.o. to look at themselves;

pangilon looking-glass;

ora ngilo githoké dhéwé *prov* to not look at o.s., *i.e.* blame others for s.t. in which one falls short o.s.

ilok I suitable, proper, acceptable;

ngiloki *or* **ngilokaké** to warn against;

ora ilok unsuitable, not acceptable;

ora ilok-ilok extreme, out of the ordinary.

II, ilok-ilok *reg* sometimes, occasionally.

ilu I mucus, phlegm, discharge from sores;

ngilu to discharge foul matter.

II to accompany (*chdl, var of* **mèlu**);

ilon 1 to go along with others characteristically; **2** team-mate;

ngiloni to go along with s.o. as companion or team-mate;

ngilokaké 1 to have s.o. accompany a person; **2** to have s.o. go to live with and be supported by (a relative);

ilu-ilu kapiluyu to tag along with others, join s.o. in an activity;

ilon-ilonen to do what others are doing. *See also* **èlu**.

III, ilu-ilu evil spirit.

ima *see* **hima**.

imah *var of* **émah**.

imalaya *see* **himalaya**.

imam person who leads the prayer in Islamic rituals;

ngimami to lead (prayers).

iman 1 1 belief, faith; **2** to believe (in), trust; **2** integrity.

imantaka *lit* cloud.

imat *reg kr for* **umat**.

imawan *see* **himawan**.

imba I 1 eyebrow(s) (*k.i. for* **alis**); **2** a certain plant with slim shapely leaves.

II *var of* **émba**.

imbah to launder (*root form: subst kr for* **umbah**).

imbal I 1 to repeat a musical theme; **2** repetition of a theme; - **pangandika** *or* - **wacana** to have a conversation/discussion.

II *or* **imbalan** wages, compensation.

III, ngimbalaké to convey a message.

imbang 1 weight; **2** side.

imbar *reg kr for* **umbar**.

imbasara *lit* messenger.

imbet I to ripen fruits (*root form: kr for* **imbu**).

II supplement, add (*kr for* **imbuh**).

imbu, ngimbu 1 to allow (fruits) to ripen in a warm, covered place; **2** *fig* to keep s.t. concealed;

imbon fruits set aside to ripen;
imbon-imbon s.t. concealed.

imbuh *ng,* imbet *kr,* tanduk *k.i.* 1 to add;
2 s.t. in addition, a supplement, addition;
ngimbuhi to give s.t. as a supplement or as a second addition;
imbuhan s.t. to be given as a second addition;
imbuh-imbuh s.t. regarded as a second helping.

imel, ngimel to keep nibbling;
imel-imelan snacks; s.t. to nibble on.

imet, saimet *reg* a tiny bit, a very few. *See also* imit.

iming, iming-iming temptation;
ngiming-iming to tantalise;
ngiming-imingi to tantalise with s.t. attractive;
pangiming-iming 1 s.t. to tantalise with; 2 act of tantalising.

imit, ngimit-imit to use or consume s.t. bit by bit;
saimit a tiny bit, a very few.

impeng I 1 person in charge of the village irrigation system; 2 (*or* impeng-impeng) water channel. *See also* impleng I.
II, ngimpeng *reg* to peek.

imper *lit* resemblance.

impes I 1 bladder; 2 cow's bladder used for holding oil.
II, mimpes 1 to go flat (of s.t. that was inflated); 2 to go down (swellings).

impi, ngimpi *ng, kr,* supena *or* nyupena *k.i.* to dream;
ngimpèkaké to dream of/about;
ngimpi-impi to dream of, long for;
impèn a dream;
impèn-impènen to keep seeing in one's dreams, dream constantly of;
pangimpèn a dream.

impleng I *var of* impeng.
II, ngimpleng to peep at/through.

implik (*pron as:* impli:k), ngimplik *or*

implik-implik (to walk) with quick short steps.

impling tiny, small; lombok - *reg* 1 a certain small chili; 2 very small firecrackers (*see also* mercon).

impor an import;
ngimpor to import.

imprah-imprih to move back and forth.

impun, ngimpun to collect, compile;
impunan collection, compilation.

ina lowly; - papa inferior, lowly;
ngina to insult, humiliate;
pangina an insult;
kainan remiss, deficient.

inah time allotment;
nginahi to allow (a time period);
nginahaké to allow s.o. (a certain time).

inalilahi *excl uttered upon hearing of a death.*

incak *reg var of* idak.

incat to make one's escape (*subst kr for* oncat).

inceng, nginceng 1 to peek at/through; 2 to take aim, take sight, aim (at) (*var of* incer);
ngincengaké to peek for s.o.;
inceng-inceng to peek at/through, keep peeking;
inceng-incengan to peek at each other.

incer compass needle;
ngincer 1 to take aim, take sight; 2 to go after, try for; 3 to have one's eye on s.o. or s.t.; to set one's sights on s.o.;
nginceraké to take aim with;
inceran 1 target; 2 aim, thing aimed at;
pangincer act of aiming at s.t *or* trying for.

inci inch.

incih, ngincih to try to get, covet, go after;
incih-incihan to covet each other's possessions.

incim, ngincim-incim to threaten, intimidate;

incim-inciman to threaten each other.

incip *var of* icip.

incon *var of* éncon.

incrit, ngincrit-incrit 1 to give out in small amounts; 2 to pay little by little; 3 to use s.t. sparingly.

incup, ngincup to catch (a flying creature) between thumb and forefinger.

indel I, ngindel *reg* to boil s.t.

II, ngindelaké *reg* to leave s.t. as it is.

indeng I, saindenging all over, everywhere in, throughout.

II, ngindengaké to perpetuate, preserve, conserve.

indhak rise, increase (*kr for* undhak).

indhekos to take room and board;
ngindhekosi to board s.w.;
ngindhekosaké to board s.o., have s.o. board;
indhekosan 1 room and board; 2 boarding house. *Also* dhekos.

indhèn to order and pay a deposit on (a piece of merchandise).

indhet, ngindhet to keep, hold back (*var of* endhet).

indhik, ngindhik to sneak up on;
ngindhik-indhiki to eye covetously, inch toward;
mindhik-mindhik to go quietly on tiptoe (in order to sneak up).

indhil, indhil-indhil 1 newly born (baby); 2 not fully grown.

indhing cloth used as a sanitary napkin.

indhit, ngindhit to carry at the waist or hip;
kéndhit to get carried along.

indho a Eurasian.

Indhu *var of* Hindhu.

indhul, indhul-indhul 1 chubby; 2 *repr* the motions of a plump person walking.

indhung people who reside in a village but lack the rights of ownership because they are not members of the communal group (according to customary law); - gandhok an inhabitant who has rights of ownership; - tlosor one who lives in another's home;
ngindhung 1 to occupy (without owning) a house one has erected; 2 to live in s.o. else's house;
pangindhung one who lives in another's home or on another's property;
ngindhung cangkok to live on s.o.'s property and have the rights of ownership;
ngindhung tèmpèl to live in s.o. else's house, or on another's land in a house one has built there, but lack the rights of ownership.

Indra the god Indra, king of the gods;
indraloka the abode of Indra, heaven.

indrak thrush (gum disease);
indraken to suffer from thrush.

indriya 1 the senses; 2 *lit* heart; 3 *lit* wish, desire.

indu *lit* moon;
indupati *lit* moon.

indung *lit* mother.

ineb, mineb closed, to get closed;
nginebaké to close;
kineban locked in or out;
ineb-ineban window shutters.

inep, nginep *ng*, nyipeng *kr*, nyaré *k.i.* to spend the night, stay overnight (or longer);
nginepi to stay s.w. overnight;
nginepaké to put s.o. up overnight;
panginepan 1 lodging for the night; 2 inn.

ing I at, on, in.

II -ing/-ning *gram, possessive suffix.*

ingah (to keep) domestic animals (*root form: kr for* ingu).

ingah-ingih incongruous.

ingak *subst kr for* ungak.

ingaluhur a high official.

ingas a certain tree with poisonous sap.

ingatasé *see* atas II.

ingel, ngingel-ingel 1 to massage the neck at the base of the skull to relieve headache; **2** to tease;

kèngel to have a sprained neck.

inger direction;

ngingeri 1 to renounce, turn one's back on; **2** to have s.t. at one's back or behind one;

ngingeraké to turn s.t. in a different direction;

ngingar-nginger to keep turning s.t.;

minger to turn, be turned (in a certain direction);

minger-minger or **mingar-minger 1** to turn this way and that; **2** to talk evasively or off the subject.

inget, ngingeti or **ngingetaké** to look intently at;

inget-ingetan to watch, stare at each other.

ingga var of **éngga**.

inggah rise (*kr for* **unggah**).

inggar var of **énggar**.

inggat, nginggati to avoid;

nginggataké to abscond with;

minggat to run away, flee, escape.

inggih 1 yes, indeed; **2** also, too (*kr for* iya).

inggil high, tall (*kr for* **dhuwur**).

inggit var of **igit**.

inggita *lit* behaviour, conduct.

Inggris English.

inggu a certain plant the disagreeable-smelling sap of which is used for cough medicines.

ingi *inf var of* **wingi**.

ingih, ingih-ingih inspiring pity because of poorness.

ingip, ingip-ingip or **mingip-mingip** to stick out a little at the tip or head;

ngingipi or **ngingip-ingipi** to show the tip of s.t. to;

ngingipaké or **ngingip-ingipaké** to show the tip of.

ingkang (one) who; (that) which (*kr for*

kang, sing); - **rayi** your wife; - **sin-uwun** your/his majesty.

ingkar, ngingkari to deny, not honour (*e.g.* promise);

mingkar to evade, sidestep;

mingkar-mingkur to dodge, be evasive.

ingked, mingked to move;

mingkad-mingked to keep moving. *See also* **ingsed**.

ingkel, ngingkel-ingkel 1 to tease, pester; **2** to wrestle s.o.;

ingkel-ingkelan to playfully wrestle each other.

ingkem, ngingkemaké to close (the mouth);

mingkem 1 to close one's mouth; **2** *fig* to refrain from speaking.

ingklig, ngingklig to walk fast without heed for one's surroundings;

ingklag-ingklig to move back and forth.

ingklik I flower of the cassava plant;

ngingklik resembling this flower.

II, mingklik-mingklik in a high precarious position, balanced in a high place.

ingkling I to hop on one foot;

ngingkling *reg* to carry on the shoulder.

II ingkling-ingkling *repr* tinkling;

ngingkling-ingkling *reg* to tinkle.

ingko var of **éngko**.

ingkrang, ngingkrangaké to raise (the feet).

ingkug, ingkug-ingkug or **ingkag-ingkug** to waddle.

ingkul *reg* **1** to (do) fast; **2** to walk fast with the head bowing.

ingkung chicken cooked whole;

ngingkung to cook a chicken whole.

ingkup, ngingkupaké to close by folding;

mingkup closed up, folded.

ingkus, ngingkusaké to make narrower, draw in;

mingkus draw in(ward), (of the chest)

sunken.

inglar, nginglari 1 to deny, disavow; 2 to avoid s.t.;

minglar to swerve, veer, to avoid s.t.

inglep *var of* **ingslep**.

ingong *lit* I, me.

ingsed, ngingsed to shift;

ngingsedaké to move or shift s.t.;

mingsed to move, shift position;

mingsad-mingsed to keep moving/shifting;

ingsedan act of moving/shifting.

ingseg, mingseg-mingseg to sob, cry uncontrollably.

ingsep, ngingsep 1 to suck (at); 2 to absorb. *See also* **isep**.

ingser, ngingser to move, shift the position of;

ngingseraké to move or shift s.t.;

kèngser 1 to have been moved/shifted; 2 sprained (joints);

mingser to move, change one's position;

mingsar-mingser to keep moving, move this way and that.

ingslep, mingslep 1 to slip into, enter; 2 (of sun) to set;

ngingslepaké to slip s.t. s.w.

ingsun *lit* I, me.

ingu *ng*, **ingah** *kr*, **ngingu** 1 to keep (a domestic animal); 2 to groom;

ngingoni to provide meals for (workers);

ngingokaké 1 to have s.o. keep an animal for one, look after s.o.'s pet; 2 to serve a meal to neighbours who are lending a hand;

ingon-ingon domestic animal, pet;

panginonan a place where domestic animals are kept.

inguk, nginguk to look in at s.o.;

inguk-inguk *or* **ingak-inguk** to keep peeping in;

minguk-minguk *or* **mingak-minguk** to look around here and there.

ingwang *lit* I, me.

inis, nginis *reg* to rest in a cool place. *See also* **ninis**.

injak *var of* **idak**.

injen, nginjen to peek, peer at;

injen-injen *or* **injan-injen** to keep peeking;

injen-injenan to peek each other.

injih *reg var of* **inggih**.

injil the Gospels; the New Testament.

injoh capable, able.

injuh *var of* **injoh**.

innalilahi *see* **inalilahi**.

insaf *var of* **insap**.

insan man, human being.

insap 1 to be aware (of), realise; 2 to become reformed after acknowledging one's mistaken ways.

insya'llah by God's will.

intar *lit* metaphor(ic) (*var of* **éntar**).

inten diamond, precious jewel; - **barléyan** jewelry.

inter, nginteri 1 to whirl (rice grains) on a woven bamboo tray to separate out the unhusked grains; 2 *fig* to whirl briskly;

kaya gabah diinteri *idiom* in a state of confusion, chaos.

internat dormitory.

interpiu interview.

intha *var of* **éntha**.

inthar, nginthar 1 to run fast; 2 to run away.

inthik, inthak-inthik to move back and forth constantly.

inthil I sheep/goat dung;

nginthil (of sheep, goat) to drop dung. II steamed cassava flour and brown sugar dish served with shredded coconut.

III, **inthil-inthil** 1 poultry liver; 2 uvula.

inti essence.

intip I scorched rice at the bottom of the pan;

ngintip to form a scorched layer of rice at the bottom of the pan.
II, ngintip to peep (at);
mintip-mintip to be just in sight at the top.

intir I 1 to keep burning low (fire); **2** *or* **ngintiri** to give small amount regularly.
II, ngintir-intir *intsfr* very hungry, famished.

inum, minum *or* **nginum** to drink, *esp* liquor;
nginumi to offer/give an alcoholic drink to;
inuman intoxicating drink;
inum-inuman 1 to drink liquor habitually; **2** intoxicating drink.

inyong *reg* I, me.

ipah I earnings (*reg kr for* **opah**).
II grated coconut mixed into coconut sap during coconut-sugar processing.

ipak, ngipak-ipak *lit* to move in rolling wave-like motions.

ipat, ipat-ipat curse, malediction;
ngipat-ipati to forbid s.o. to do s.t. on pain of invoking a dreadful curse.

ipé brother- or sister-in-law.

ipel, ipel-ipel short and fat.

ipeng *var of* **impeng**.

ipet *var of* **ipit**.

ipi *var of* **impi**.

ipik, ngipik-ipik stingy with one's possessions.

ipil, ipil-ipil to gather bit by bit;
saipil a tiny bit.

ipit, saipit a tiny bit, very small amount;
saipit-ipita even the smallest bit.

iplik, ngiplik *or* **iplik-iplik** (to walk) with quick short steps.

ipret, saipret a tiny bit (*var of* **ipet**).

iprik, iprik-iprik to gather firewood.

ipuk, ngipuk to urge, persuade;
ipukan place where s.t. in sown;
ipuk-ipuk dealer in second-hand articles, junk man;

ngipuk-ipuk 1 to sow, cultivate; **2** to collect, gather.

iradat *var of* **wiradat**.

irah, irah-irahan 1 theme, basic idea; **2** clarification, analysis; **3** a certain type of male dancer's headdress;
ngirah-irahi to take as a theme.

irama 1 measure, tempo (in Javanese music); **2** (changeable) custom, habit;
ngiramani 1 to create rhythm (in), give a rhythm (to); **2** to be in rhythm (with). *See also* **wirama**.

iras I two things combined into one;
ngiras *or* **ngiras-ngirus** to combine two things;
irasan (of a kris) having a top part that matches the bottom (*see also* **ganja**).
II, ngiras to eat from the utensil the food was cooked in or at the place where the food was bought.

irat, ngirat *or* **ngirati** to split into thin strips;
iratan *or* **irat-iratan** split piece.

irèh *var of* **irih**.

ireng I *ng*, **cemeng** *kr*, **1** black; **2** dark in colour;
ngireng *or* **ngirengaké** to blacken;
ngirengi 1 to blacken; **2** to make dark(er);
irengan 1 *slang* opium; **2** indigo dye.
II, irengan 1 fallow land; **2** village-owned land.

iri envious, jealous;
irèn 1 to argue about who will do what; **2** envious by nature;
irèn-irènan to envy or be jealous of each other.

irib form, appearance;
ngiribi to resemble, give an impression of, be reminiscent of;
mirib to have the appearance of, resemble;
sairib 1 having the same appearance; **2** appropriate (to), harmonising (with).

irid I, **ngirid** to escort, accompany, lead; **irid-iridan** to go one after another.
II *see* **irit**.

irig large bamboo sieve for sifting sand or catching fish.

irih I, **irih-irih** slowly, cautiously.
II, **ngirih** *or* **ngirihi 1** to clean s.t.; **2** to divert the flow of (a watercourse).

irik I, **ngirik-iriki** to have a covetous eye on s.t.
II, **irik-irik** *intsfr* short, low.
III, **irik-irik** *imit* writing.

irim, **irim-irim** a certain plant.

iring I 1 side, flank; **2** fallow land; **3** land measure: not quite half an acre;
ngiringaké to slant or slope s.t.;
miring slanting, at an angle;
iringan side, flank;
iring-iringan side by side.
II, **ngiring** to escort, accompany;
ngiringi to accompany;
ngiringaké to accompany s.o.;
pangiring person or thing which accompanies;
iring-iringan a procession.

iris *or* **irisan** slice, cut piece;
ngiris to cut;
ngirisi *or* **ngiris-iris** to cut up;
ngirisaké to cut for s.o.;
pangiris act of cutting.

irit economical, frugal;
ngirit to economise, save;
ngirit-irit to use as sparingly as possible.

irsaya *lit* **1** jealous; **2** to wish s.o. ill, bear a grudge.

iruh *reg var of* **weruh**.

irung *ng, kr,* **grana** *k.i.* nose;
irung-irungan nose-shaped latch on a folding door;
ngirung-irungi to equip (a folding door) with such a latch;
saben irung everybody.

irup, **ngirup 1** to take up, draw in; to suck; **2** to rabble-rouse.

irus soup ladle of coconut shell or wood;
ngirusi to scoop with a ladle;
ngiras-ngirus to combine two things.
See also **iras**.

isa I capable, to be able (*inf var of* **bisa**).
II the time (about 7:30 p.m.) at which the evening prayer is performed.

isab, **ngisab-isabi** embarrassing, humiliating;
ngisab-isabaké to subject s.o. to embarrassment.

isah, **ngisahi** *or* **isah-isah** to wash (dishes);
isah-isahan 1 dishes to be washed; **2** washing-place. *See also* **asah**.

isan I (in) all; altogether; at once (*reg var of* **sisan**, **pisan**).
II after work (*reg var of* **wisan**).

isarah *var of* **isarat**.

isarat signal, sign.

isbat parable;
ngisbataké to illustrate with a parable.

isèh *var of* **isih**.

isek *var of* **isih**.

isel fleshy, plump.

iseng *or* **iseng-iseng** to do s.t. for fun, do s.t. without any serious purpose, just to kill time.

isep 1 to smoke (*kr for* **udud**); **2** blotting-paper;
ngisep 1 to suck (at); **2** to smoke (*kr for* **udud**); **3** to absorb; **4** *fig* to learn s.t. by hearing it from others rather than by studying it for o.s.;
pangisepan *lit* spy.

isi 1 contents, insides; **2** filled (with), full (of); **3** to have contents;
ngisi to put s.t. into;
ngisèni to fill, put s.t. into;
ngisèkaké 1 to put s.t. into, fill s.t. in as contents; **2** to fill on behalf of s.o.;
isèn-isèn the contents;
saisiné (together with) the contents.

isih *ng,* **taksih** *kr,* still, yet, (even) now,

remaining (in a certain condition);
ngisihaké 1 to keep s.t. in effect; 2 to
have leftovers.

isik *reg var of* isih.

isim a written Arabic text used for warding off danger or illness.

isin *ng, kr,* lingsem *k.i.* embarrassed, shy,
ashamed;
isin-isin *or* isan-isin acutely embarrassed or self-conscious;
ngisin-isin to humiliate, make fun of;
ngisin-isini embarrassing, humiliating;
ngisin-isinaké to subject s.o. to
embarrassment;
kisinan overcome with embarrassment;
isinan shy by nature;
isin ora isi *idiom* timidity doesn't get
you anywhere.

ising, ngising (bebucal *or* wawratan *kr,*
bobotan *k.i.*) to defecate, relieve o.s.;
ngisingi to do, get excrement on;
ngisingaké to relieve o.s. of (excrement);
kepésing 1 to defecate inadvertently;
2 to need to go to the toilet;
ising-isingen to have diarrhoea.

isis refreshing, cool, breezy;
ngisis 1 to go out for some fresh air;
2 to air, aerate, expose to the air;
késisan *lit* 1 blown by the wind;
2 bared, exposed, deprived of.

Islam Islam, the religion of Muslims;
ngislamaké 1 to convert s.o. to Islam;
2 to circumcise;
islaman circumcision ceremony.

ismu *var of* èsmu.

iso sinuous portion of animal intestine
(used as food).

isoh *reg var of* isuh.

isor *ng,* andhap *kr,* ngisor under, below,
at the bottom; - ndhuwur above and
below, top and bottom;
ngisoran a subordinate;
sangisoré under, below.

istha *lit* appearance, aspect;
ngistha to resemble.

istidrat idol, image.

istijab 1 effective, efficacious; 2 (of a
wish, prayer) granted.

istijrat *var of* istidrat.

istika, salat - *lit* communal prayer for
rain.

istingangkah without doubt, to be sure.

istingarah *var of* istingangkah.

istipar prayer asking for forgiveness.

istiyar (to exert) effort;
ngistiyaraké to (do one's best to)
obtain.

istri *reg var of* èstri.

isuh *var of* wisuh.

isuk *var of* ésuk.

isun *var of* ingsun.

itang *var of* étang.

item black; watu - hard black rock (*see
also* watu).

ithar *var of* inthar.

itheng very black.

ithi, ngithi-ithi to take scrupulous care
of.

ithik I a little bit (*inf var of* thithik).
II, ithak-ithik to keep coming and
going.
III, ngithik-ithik to tickle.

ithing, ngithing to take good care of.

ithir, ngithir to trickle out;
ithir-ithir *or* ithar-ithir 1 *repr* pouring
little by little; 2 to do bit by bit rather
than all at once;
ithiran to trickle in a thin stream.

ithu *reg* busy.

ithuk *var of* ithu.

itik I 1 tame(d); 2 in the habit (of).
II hair louse (*k.i.* for tuma);
ngitiki to hunt lice from s.o.'s hair.
III, ngitiki *or* ngitik-itiki to make but-
tonholes in (a garment);
itik-itik buttonhole.
IV, ngitik-itik 1 to bring up (a child);
2 to raise (an animal) as a pet.

itikad *var of* iktikad.

itil *ng*, klentit *kr*, prana *k.i.* clitoris.

itip, ngitip *reg* to peek (at).

itung *var of* étung.

iwak *ng*, ulam *kr*, 1 fish; 2 meat for the table; - loh live freshwater fish;
iwak-iwakan toy fish, imitation fish;
iwak klebu ing wuwu *idiom* caught in an ambush.

iwel, iwel-iwel a cake made of glutinous rice flour, shredded coconut and brown sugar.

iwèn birds, fowl, poultry.

iwi, ngiwi-iwi to grimace (at).

iwir, ngiwir-iwir to stretch s.t. (bit by bit);
miwir to stretch, become elongated.

iwit frugal, thrifty.

iwud I with hasty motions;
ngiwud with quick hurried motions;
ngiwad-ngiwud to keep making frenzied motions.
II, iwud-iwud a certain hawk.

iwuh *lit* difficult. *See also* éwuh.

iwut *var of* ibut.

iya *ng*, inggih *kr*, 1 yes, indeed; 2 also; 3 *excl inviting agreement*; 4 *particle with syntactic function*;
ngiyani to agree to s.t., answer s.t. in the affirmative;
kaya iya-iyaa it looks good, but basically it isn't.

iyag, iyag-iyag *or* ngiyag-iyag to rush about helter-skelter;
ngiyag-iyagaké to hurry s.o., try to speed s.t. up.

iyak *excl of disbelief*.

iyan large square tray for spreading rice and cooling it by fanning;
ngiyan to spread and cool rice as above.

iyat, ngiyat to deal (cards);
iyatan a deal, *i.e.* a hand of dealt cards.

iyeg I in agreement;
saiyeg unanimous.
II, ngiyeg-iyeg 1 to move in a ponderous *or* unwieldy manner; 2 to knead, squeeze.
III, saiyeg-iyeg heavy, cumbersome.

iyem, ngiyem to humidify (tobacco).

iyer, ngiyer to blink, wink;
ngiyeraké to blink (the eyes).

iyik , iyik-iyik 1 *repr* a baby bird's cheeping; 2 tiny;
ngiyik-iyik to make fun of.

iyo I 1 *excl* hurray!; 2 *excl* oh my!; 3 come on! (*var of* ayo).
II a certain group of playing-cards (*kertu cilik*).

iyok *var of* iya.

iyom *reg var of* ayom.

iyong *reg var of* iyung.

iyub *var of* éyub.

iyuh *excl* oh dear!

iyung *excl of pain or strong emotion*.

iyuran dues, contribution.

J

ja don't! (*shtf of* aja).

jab *reg* what a...! wow!; - gedhéné wow, look how big it is!

jaba *ng*, jawi *kr*, 1 outside; 2 outside of, except for (*inf var of* kejaba);
jaban 1 outlying territory; 2 superficial, on the exterior only;
jaban-jabanan on the exterior only, on a superficial level;
sajabané (on the) outside (of);
jaba jero in(side) and out(side);
njabakaké to exclude.

jabah I *reg* a certain large earthenware container.
II granting (of prayer) (*var of* ijabah).

jabal *lit* mountain.

jaban *see* jaba.

jabang *or* jabang bayi newborn baby.

Jabarail the Archangel Gabriel, who brought the Quran to the Prophet.

jabat, njabat 1 to take hold of; 2 to occupy an office;
jabatan 1 function, position; 2 office held temporarily; 3 *or* - tangan to shake hands.

jabeg, njabeg 1 unable to cope; 2 *reg* clogged, choked, stopped up.

jabel, njabel 1 to pull s.t. loose from its moorings; 2 to take back, retract; 3 to withdraw;
jabelan 1 s.t. retracted; 2 revocation.

jabing, njabingi *reg* to encircle.

jablas gone, vanished.

jablog, njablog *reg cr* to eat.

Jabrail name of an angel (*var of* Jabarail, Jibrail).

jabris I, njabris to give s.o. a dirty look.
II, njabris sticking out untidily (moustache).
III, jabrisan small catfish (young of the lélé).

jabrut, njabrut having a disagreeable facial expression.

jabud, njabud 1 to pull out, draw, extract; 2 to dismiss (from office);
njabud nyawa to kill, murder;
njabudi to keep pulling.

jabung a certain resinous substance used as glue, joiner's glue;
njabung to join, connect;
jabungan extension connected with such glue.

jabur, njaburi to serve (refreshments) at a collective prayer-gathering during the evening in the Fasting Month.

jadah a snack made from sticky rice.

jadham resin, used as glue, produced by a certain broad-leafed aloe plant.

jadhé, njadhé *reg* to guess (at), answer a riddle (*var of* bedhèk, pethèk, badhé).

jadhel *reg var of* jabel.

jadhem I *see* jadham.
II, jadhem-parem iodoform.

jadhi large copper cauldron with a rounded bottom, used *esp* for processing sugarcane (*var of* jèdhi).

jadhir, njadhir thick, swollen (lips).

jadhor *var of* jadhir, jédhor.

jadhug I *reg* strong and robust.
II *reg* leading to, coming out at (*var of* jedhug).

jadhul, njadhul scowling, gloomy-looking.

jadhum, jadhuman *reg* to sit around and talk in a relaxed atmosphere.

jadwal schedule, timetable.

jaé ginger (root).

jaétun olive, olive tree. *Also* jétun, zaétun.

jag I, jag-jagan 1 to walk around in a carefree, inconsiderate manner; 2 to

intrude where one does not belong.
II, **njag iya** it's true; it is so.

jaga *ng*, **jagi** *kr*, **1** guard, watch; **2** to guard, keep watch; **3** provisions; **-baya** village policeman; **- satru** half-open front gallery or porch;
  njaga to guard, look after, watch over;
  njagani to prevent, provide (against);
  njagakaké to count on;
  jagan a precaution(ary measure);
  jaga-jaga 1 (to act as) a precautionary measure; **2** to be on the safe side, be careful;
  njagakaké endhogé si blorok *prov* to await an uncertain outcome.

jagad 1 world, earth; **2** the universe, the cosmos; **- gedhé** *or* **- raya** the cosmos, the universe, macrocosm; **- cilik** microcosm.

jagal butcher;
  njagal to butcher, slaughter;
  jagalan 1 place where animals are slaughtered; **2** area where butchers live.

jagan *see* **jaga**.

jagang I 1 tripod; **2** prop, supporting pole; **- gunting** bamboo stems crossed scissorwise as a supporting prop;
  njagangi to support s.t. that may fall.
II moat surrounding a palace.

jagat *see* **jagad**.

jager, **njager** to stand straight up;
  jageran sawhorse.

jagi guard, watch (*kr for* **jaga**).

jagir, **njagir** to stand and stare openmouthed.

jago *ng*, **sawung** *kr*, **1** rooster, cock; **2** champion; **3** candidate, contestant; **- adon** gamecock; **- kapuk** older person who keeps active in his former field(s) of interest; **- katé** a coward; **- kawakan** former champion gamecock; **- kepruk** brawler; **- mlilé** rooster that is afraid of hens; *fig* man who is shy with women;
  njagoni 1 to back; **2** to pit against;

  njagokaké 1 to put s.o. up as a candidate; **2** to sponsor, back, champion s.o.;
  jagoan 1 young rooster that has reached the reproductive stage; **2** candidate, contestant;
  jago-jagoan *reg* ceremony held as part of the wedding procedures for a bride who has not yet begun to menstruate;
  jago wiring galih 1 fighting cock that always wins; **2** *fig* outstanding person.

jagong *or* **njagong** to attend a party or ceremony, *esp* a wedding;
  jagongan 1 to sit around in a relaxed atmosphere; **2** *or* **pajagongan** a place where people sit around at a ceremony.

jagrag 1 tripod; **2** supporting stand.

jagul 1 a substitute for the real thing (*var of* **gajul**); **2** supporting pole.

jagung corn, maize;
  jagung-jagung a certain classical gamelan melody.

jagur 1 fist; **2** bamboo instrument for driving away birds;
  njagur to pound with a fist.

jah *adr* elephant (*shtf of* **gajah**).

jahanam 1 hell; **2** *excl* damn!

jahat a flaw, crack (wood, earthenware).

jahé *see* **jaé**.

jahil *see* **jail**.

jahit *see* **jait**.

jaib *reg* awe-inspiring (*see also* **ajaib**).

jaid, **njaid** almond-shaped (eyes).

jail (to have) ill feelings toward s.o.; **- mekathil** malicious, spiteful; **- mringkil** person with a grudge;
  njaili to wish s.o. ill.

jais fate, destiny;
  kejais (pre)destined.

jait 1 line; **2** pertaining to sewing;
  njait to sew, stitch, suture;
  menjait to make clothing;
  penjait *or* **tukang jait** tailor, seamstress.

jaja I chest, breast (*k.i. for* **dhadha**);

jaja bang mawinga-winga *lit* furiously angry.
II itinerant peddler; - **rumat** to pass along rumours.

jajag, njajagi 1 to measure, estimate, judge; **2** to fathom;
jajag-jajag to size up.

jajah 1 having a lot of experience in travelling to many places; **2** familiar with the environment;
njajah 1 to colonise, take over (a country); **2** to travel to many places; **3** to get to know, become familiar with, explore;
jajahan a colony;
panjajah colonialist, subjugator;
panjajahan colonialism, colonisation;
njajah désa milang kori *idiom* to travel to many places.

jajal *or* **jajalé** have a try! let's see!;
njajal 1 to try, attempt; **2** to test;
njajali 1 to try on; **2** to put to the test;
jajal-jajal to try, make an effort.

jajan 1 snacks, sweets; **2** to buy and eat snacks; **3** *or* **njajan** to eat out; - **pasar** sweets, flowers *etc* bought in the market serving to complete the dishes/offerings in ceremonies;
njajan 1 to eat out; **2** to have intercourse with a prostitute;
njajani to buy and eat snacks regularly;
njajakaké to buy s.o. a snack or a meal out;
jajanan various kind of snacks.

jajang *reg* bamboo. *See also* **janjang**.

jajap *reg* can, to be able.

jajar I lowest rank among the court administrative officials.
II 1 near, next to; **2** having equal rank or position; **3** lined up in a row;
njajari to walk side by side in ranks;
jajaran 1 in rows, side by side; **2** *reg* net yield of a harvest.

jak I, ngejak to ask s.o. to do s.t. with one (*var of* **ajak**).
II *command to a draught animal when ploughing a field.*
III, jaké *reg* have a try (*var of* **jajal**); come on, try! (*var of* **ndang**).

jaka 1 young unmarried man; **2** *or* **jejaka** young adult male; - **bèlèk** Mars (planet); - **blaro** a variety of bird; - **bolot** a certain variety of rice; - **kumala-kala** male teenager; -**lara** *or* - **rara** one's first spouse; -**lodra** wild man in a street show; - **thing-thing** virgin male; -**tuwa** cockatoo (*var of* **kakaktuwak**).

jakat annual tithe on income and possessions for distribution to the poor; - **pitrah** tithe in rice or money paid on the last day of the Fasting Month;
njakati to pay tithes to. *Also* **zakat**.

jakèt jacket.

jaké *see* **jak III**.

jaksa public prosecutor;
njaksani to prosecute (a criminal, a case);
kajaksan *or* **pajaksan** prosecutor's office.

jal *or* **jalé** have a try! come on, try! *See* **jajal**.

jala net for catching fish;
njala to net (fish).

jaladara *lit* cloud.

jaladi *var of* **jaladri**.

jaladri *lit* sea, ocean.

jalak starling, a variety of bird kept as a pet; - **ampir** to stop off at places frequently when on the way s.w.; one who does this habitually; - **dhindhing** characteristically feminine way of walking; - **jamang** talking mynah bird; - **mempan** to work a bit at a time; - **ngoré** a certain shape for kris blades; - **orèn** *or* - **urèt** black and white mynah bird;
njalaki (of unweaned babies) to have diarrhoea.

jalal (of God) Almighty, most holy, supreme.

jalang I *reg* stalk (of rice).

II 1 of easy virtue; **2** prostitute, prostitution.

jalanidhi *lit* sea, ocean.

jalantara *reg* aqueduct, gutter over a ditch or path.

jalar I, njalar 1 to spread, become prevalent; **2** (of disease) to infect.

II njalari to cause;

jalaran 1 because; **2** cause, reason.

jalé *see* **jal**.

jalèn *see* **jali**.

jaler male; manly (*kr for* **lanang**).

jali a kind of grass, millet or 'Job's tears'; **- ketan**, **- watu** varieties of the jali.

jalidri a variety of vegetable (**kangkung**) that grows on land.

jaliger a variety of fish.

jaling the portion of the skull above the ears;

njaling *or* **njalingi 1** to hit above the ear; **2** to say a word that causes s.o. to be embarrased;

kejalingan 1 injured above the ear; **2** to be embarrassed by s.o.'s words.

jalir *reg cr* a secret lover.

jalirih *reg* sprout of a certain medicinal herb (**lempuyang**).

jalisu a variety of tree.

jalma 1 *lit* human being; **2** reincarnation; **- manungsa** human being;

njalma *or* **manjalma** *lit* to be incarnated, take on human form.

jalmi *kr for* **jalma**.

jalon bamboo lengths used to hold a straw roof in place.

jalu 1 spur on a cock's foot; **2** *lit* male, manly; **- lèpèk** a blunt spur; **- mampang** a certain parasitic plant;

njalu to strike with the spur;

kejalu injured by a cock's spur.

jaluk *ng*, **tedha** *kr*, **pundhut** *k.i.*, **suwun** *k.a.*, **njaluk** to ask for, request, beg;

njaluk-jaluk to beg (beggars);

njejaluk to ask, pray (for);

njalukaké to ask for on s.o.'s behalf;

njalukan to have a tendency to ask for things;

jalukan *or* **panjaluk 1** a request, s.t. asked for; **2** demand;

njaluk lawang to request admittance.

jalwèstri *lit* male and female (*var of* **jaluèstri**).

jam 1 watch, clock; **2** o'clock; **3** hour;

ngejami to time s.t. in hours;

jam-jaman 1 for hours (on end); **2** by the hour.

Jamajuja name of a giant who will be released from his shackles at the end of the world.

jamah, njamah 1 to touch, handle s.t.; **2** to have illicit intercourse with.

jamak usual, ordinary; **- lumrah** customarily, normally;

ora jamak out of the ordinary.

jamal *lit* beauty.

jaman period, epoch, time span; **- édan** time of turmoil; **- kalanggengan** the hereafter;

njamani to be current, up-to-date.

jamang 1 ornamental head-piece worn in the classical dance, diadem; **2** a ring put on the end of a bamboo flute;

jamangan to put on or wear a diadem.

jamas to wash one's hair (*k.i. for* **kramas**).

jambak, njambak to pull s.o.'s hair.

jambal I 1 a certain edible freshwater fish; **2** meat together with its fat.

II a certain dye used in batik-making.

jamban bathroom (and toilet combined).

jambang, jambangan large earthenware pot used for water or as a flowerpot. *Also* **jembangan**.

jambé betel nut; **- suruh** betel nut prepared for chewing;

kaya - sinigar as alike as two peas in a pod.

jambet I roseapple (*kr for* jambu).

II medicine (*subst kr for* jamu).

III cock's spur (*subst kr for* jalu).

IV net for trapping fish (*subst kr for* jala)

V web, net for trapping birds (*subst kr for* jaring).

VI castor oil plant and its fruit (*subst kr for* jarak).

VII drill (*subst kr for* jara).

VIII harrow (*subst kr for* garu).

IX bamboo fence (*subst kr for* jaro).

X joiner's glue (*subst kr for* jabung).

jambèt, kejambèt involved, associated.

jambéyah *var of* jambiyah.

jambiyah curved Indian double-edged dagger.

jamblang *reg* blueberry. *See also* dhuwet.

jamblik, njamblik close together, not far apart.

jambon I pink. *See also* jambu I.

II homosexual. *See also* jambu III.

jambor, njambor to mix, compound;

jamboran 1 a mixture; 2 a compound. *See also* cambor.

jambu I *ng*, jambet *kr*, roseapple, pink in colour (many varieties).

II hearts (playing-card suit).

III, njambu to have homosexual relation (with other males);

jambon homosexual.

jambul 1 crest, tuft (hair, feather); 2 a feather *etc* put on a hat as a decoration;

njambul to form (hair) into a crest;

jambul wanen grey-headed, very old.

jamin I, njamin to guarantee;

jaminan a guarantee.

II njamin to serve food to, entertain (visitor);

jaminan food *etc* served to visitors.

jamirah *lit* basin, bowl.

jamjam, banyu - holy water drawn from a sacred well in Mecca; sumur - sacred well in Mecca.

jampang I a certain swamp grass.

II, njampang *or* njampangi to watch from a distance.

jampel 1 knee-stocking; 2 pot holder.

jampeng 1 *cr* deaf, stone deaf; 2 (of silver coin) false.

jampès hornet, gadfly.

jampi medicine, treatment (*kr for* jamu, tamba).

jamprah long and luxuriant (tail hair).

jamprak *var of* jamprah.

jamprit handsome and jaunty-looking.

jamprok *var of* jamprah.

jamprong *var of* jamprit.

jamprut *var of* jamprit.

jamrut emerald.

jamu *ng*, jampi *kr*, loloh *or* usada *k.i.* medicine, treatment;

njamoni to treat (a malady) with medicine;

njamokaké to give medicine to;

jejamu to take health potions continuously.

jamur 1 mushroom, toadstool; 2 fungus (of any kind);

njamur 1 to mushroom; 2 mouldy;

jamuren mouldy, to be covered with mould;

jamuran 1 mushroom-shaped; 2 a children's singing game.

jamus *lit* pure black.

jan real; jané *or* jan-jané *or* sajané really, actually;

ngejani *or* ngejanaké to set a price on (one's merchandise).

jana I *lit* human being.

II *shtc from* aja ana.

janah I 1 clear, plain; 2 well-behaved (*var of* genah).

II 1 heaven; 2 deceased (*see also* jenat).

janak a short stick used in a certain children's game (benthik).

jandhom, jandhoman to sit around in a relaxed atmosphere.

jandhon, jandhonan *reg* 1 to come to

chat around; **2** (of gamecock) defeated but still holding out.

jandhuk *reg* to be on good terms again.

jandhum *var of* **jandhom**.

jandika *lit* you (*var of* **jengandika**).

jané *see* **jan**.

jangan vegetable soup;
njangan to make vegetable soup;
janganan vegetables prepared for cooking soup.

janges, njanges pitch black.

janget rawhide rope;
njanget 1 to make rawhide rope; **2** to tie with rawhide rope; **3** to plough a ricefield starting from the centre and revolving outwards;
kaya janget kinatelon *prov* very strong, sturdy.

jangga *lit* neck, *also k.i. for* **gulu**.

janggal awkward, discordant, improper.

janggan *or* **jejanggan** pupil of a holy man.

janggar I rice plants that have sprouted.
II *reg* a young cock.

janggel I 1 a cob, young corn on the cob; **2** the bones of a horse's tail.
II, janggelan on probation, tentative, provisional, awaiting a final decision;
njanggelaké to sell s.t. on approval.

janggèl, janggèlan 1 a certain grass; **2** a certain gelatin used in cool drinks.

janggereng physical appearance.

jangget, njangget *reg* to adhere to firmly.

janggir male calf or young buffalo.

janggit, janggitan devil, imp.

janggleng I fruit of the teak tree;
jangglengan young teak tree ready for planting.
II, njanggleng to stare motionless and absorbed.

janggol I *reg* village worker with a special task.
II, njanggol to sit or stand and keep waiting for s.o. or s.t.;
janggolan a ship or vehicle which is waiting for passengers.

janggreng, njanggreng to look big, loom up.

janggrung I (*or* **janggrung-janggrung**) tall and well-built (of physique). *See also* **jlanggrung**.
II *or* **janggrungan** a Javanese social dance in which a professional female dancer asks spectators to dance with her after giving money;
njanggrung to dance with a female dancer in the above manner.

janggut I 1 (**kethekan** *k.i.*) chin;
njanggut 1 to press s.t. with the chin; **2** to stroke the chin in self admiration;
teken janggut suku jaja to go to any lengths to achieve s.t.
II, njanggut close by, on hand.

jangji promise, agreement (*var of* **janji**).

jangka I 1 goal, objective; **2** prediction, prophecy; **3** what is predestined;
njangka 1 to have an objective for s.o.; **2** to predict, foresee;
panjangka goal, objective.
II compass for drawing circles;
njangka to use a compass.
III tool for shredding tobacco leaves;
njangka to use a tobacco shredder.

jangkah 1 step, stride; **2** goal;
njangkah 1 to step forward; **2** to set as a goal;
njangkahaké to advance (the foot);
jumangkah to step;
jangkahan *way* large leather puppets with wide foot stance.

jangkang a certain nut the shell of which is used for making shampoo.

jangkar I 1 anchor; **2** anchor-shaped hook on a rope, for retrieving a bucket from the bottom of a well;
njangkar to retrieve (a bucket) with the above.
II, njangkar to address s.o. improperly by name only (omitting title);
jangkar-jangkaran to address each other by name only (omitting title).

jangkep 1 complete, in full; 2 even (not odd);
njangkepi to make s.t. complete;
jangkepan what makes s.t. complete.

jangkrak, njangkrak *reg* to address s.o. improperly by name (*var of* **jangkar**).

jangkrik 1 house cricket (often used for fighting); 2 *term of abuse*: shut your face!
jangkrik génggong name of a classical melody;
kaya jangkrik mambu kili *idiom* infuriated.

jangkung I tall and slender, long-legged (person).
II, **njangkung** to guard from afar, watch from a distance.
III a certain design of kris blade.

jangla 1 fickle, inconstant; 2 undiscriminating.

janglar 1 cracked but not broken through; 2 (of friendship) broken off.

jangleng, njangleng to stand and stare (*var of* **janggleng** II).

janglot a certain tree the wood of which is used for making lance handles.

janguk, njanguk *reg* to sit around idly.

jangur I *var of* **janguk**.
II, **njangur** to assemble a wooden frame before building a house.

jani *reg* money paid for services to a healer. *See also* **ujani, wejani**.

janjam *var of* **jamjam**.

janjan dun-coloured (horses).

janjang I a cluster of coconuts or **salak**.
II 1 long and slender; 2 long (neck).

janjèn *see* **janji**.

janjéyan *see* **janji**.

janji 1 one's appointed time (to die); 2 to make a promise, have an agreement;
janjiné 1 if, any time that; 2 providing, on condition that;
njanji to hold s.o. to their promise;
njanjèni to promise s.o.;
njanjèkaké to promise s.t.;

janjèn to make an appointment;
janjèn-janjènan to promise each other;
prajanjèn 1 promise, agreement; 2 to have/make a promise or agreement;
prajanjéan 1 promissory note; 2 condition, provision; 3 agreement, understanding;
Prajanjian Lawas/Anyar the Old/New Testament.

janjras *reg* good-looking.

janma *var of* **jalma**.

jantar *reg* cracked but not broken through (*var of* **janglar**).

janten a bamboo fence (*reg kr for* **jaro**).

jantèn *or* **jantènan** young corn on the cob.

janthok, njanthok *reg* to sit huddled up.

janti a certain tree (*see* **giyanti** I).

janton *see* **jantu**.

jantra 1 wheel, cog, moving part; 2 spinning-wheel; 3 wheel in a machine or device; 4 cycle, pattern of behaviour or events.

jantrung, njantrung cast down, dejected, low-spirited.

jantu *or* **janton** spices or herbs used as ingredients, *esp* in traditional medicines;
njantoni to add such ingredients to.

jantung 1 heart; 2 banana flower; 3 hearts (playing-card suit);
jejantung *lit* heart;
njantung resembling a banana flower.

jantur I magic tricks, sleight-of-hand, conjuring;
njantur to conjure up;
mbarang jantur to perform tricks.
II, **njantur** *way* to declaim a certain part of the wayang performance, describing a character's appearance, accompanied by the gamelan;
janturan *way* narration declaimed as above.
III, **njantur** to hang s.t. upside down;
janturan poles from which tobacco leaves are suspended in sheds.

janur young pale green coconut leaf, often used for decorations;
  njanur gunung *excl of surprise at an unusual event:* how extraordinary!

japa magical incantation; - **mantra** a magical incantation uttered to cure illness; - **yoga** *or* **japa semadi** a magical incantation in the practice of yoga;
  njapani to utter an incantation over s.o.

japah *reg* pus, matter from a wound.

japan *see* **kenong**.

japana a certain leaf used for treating insect bites.

japi *subst kr for* **japa**.

japit *or* **japitan** gripping tool, pincers, squeezer;
  njapit to squeeze, pinch, grip. *See also* **jepit**.

japlak I, njaplak to fake, copy, duplicate;
  japlakan a fake, a copy of the original. *See also* **jiplak**.
  II, njaplak (of head cloth, moustache) sticking out and pointed.
  III, njaplak to press s.o.'s head down by holding the neck.
  IV, njaplak close by.

japlèk, njaplèk close by (*var of* **njaplak IV**).

japrèt, njaprèt (of hair, grass) sticking out.

japrit *var of* **japrit**.

japrut, njaprut to scowl, frown, have a severe expression.

japu, jopa-japu *magic words uttered by a healer before he begins his procedure, or by s.o. trying to console an ill or injured person.*

jar, ngejaraké 1 to let, allow; **2** to leave s.o. alone;
  jarna leave it alone!

jara I drill, brace and bit;
  njara to drill, bore;
  njara angin *or* **njara langit 1** to do the impossible; **2** to have divine power.
  II *lit* old.

jarag, njarag 1 to do intentionally; **2** *reg* to bother, disturb;
  kejarag done on purpose;
  jaragan intended, destined;
  jinaragan done intentionally.

jarah I, njarah to seize, snatch;
  njarah rayah to seize violently;
  jarahan (what is) obtained by looting.
  II to seclude o.s. in a cave, go s.w. for solitary meditation (*var of* **jiarah**).
  III nimble, hard to catch.

jarak 1 castor oil plant; **2** *fig* material or spiritual benefits;
  njaraki 1 to calculate using castor oil beans as counters; **2** to tell s.o.'s fortune.

jaran *ng*, **kapal** *kr*, **titihan** *k.i.* **1** horse; **2** chess knight; - **dhawuk 1** grey horse; **2** a certain star; **3** a certain *lurik* fabric pattern; - **èbèg-èbègan** *or* - **képang** woven bamboo hobby-horse used in a folk dance; - **guyang** magic power for gaining a woman's love; - **koré** a small horse with long hair and tail; - **momotan** packhorse; - **rakitan** a team of horses; - **sembrani** legendary flying horse; - **panolèh** magic power for gaining wealth;
  njaran on horseback;
  njarani to act like a horse;
  jaranan an imitation (toy) horse;
  jaran-jaranan to play horses.

jarang I hot or boiling water;
  njarangi to pour boiling water on.
  II *reg* **1** scarce, rare; **2** seldom.

jarapah giraffe.

jarat *reg* grave; **jaratan** *or* **pajaratan** cemetery.

jaré (*or* **jaréné**) *ng*, **criyosipun** *kr*, **ngendikanipun** *k.i.*, **1** it is said; **2** 'you know' (*stressing a statement*). *See also* **é, jé**.

jarem, njarem bruised, black and blue.

jari *lit* finger.

jarik *ng*, **sinjang** *kr*, **nyamping** *k.i.*,

1 batik garment; 2 rag; ragged clothing; 3 *reg var of* **sléndhang**.

jaring, 1 net for trapping fish, birds; 2 *fig* trick for snaring an unwary person; 3 spider web;

njaring to trap in a net;

jaringan 1 intestine; 2 internal organ(s); 3 *fig* nature, character(istic).

jarit *var of* **jarik**.

jarna *see* **jar**.

jaro bamboo fence.

jaroh *var of* **jaruh**.

jarong a variety of tree.

jarot 1 fibres of certain fruits (*e.g.* tamarind, mango); 2 tough and wiry;

jejarotan brawn, vigour.

jaruh I casual (friendship).

II to lose track, get things out of order, get mixed up;

njaruhi to disturb.

III found out by the public.

jarum *reg* needle;

njarumi to sew;

jaruman 1 hands (of clock); 2 needle (of compass); 3 go-between (in romantic affairs).

jarwa 1 meaning, explanation; 2 the modern Javanese equivalent of a literary or archaic expression; - **suta** to tell the truth, admit frankly (*see also* **blaka**);

njarwani *or* **njarwakaké** to explain, give the meaning of;

jarwa dhosok 1 modern Javanese equivalent of an archaic saying; 2 (*in folk etymology*) a search for underlying or original phrases from which words are derived.

jarwi *lit, var of* **jarwa**.

jas coat, jacket; - **bukak** open jacket with lapels; - **tutup** jacket that buttons up to the neck and has a high collar;

jas-jasan to put on or wear a jacket.

jasa 1 merit; 2 service, service rendered.

jasad body, substance, organism.

jasem wild tamarind tree.

jasirah peninsula.

jas-jis to be impatient, stick at s.t. impatiently.

jas-jus *var of* **jas-jis**.

jasmani physical;

jasmaniyah bodily.

jat substance, essence (*var of* **dat**, **zat**).

jatah 1 allotment, allocation; 2 quota; 3 ration(ed amount);

njatahi to ration, set quotas (for).

jatha I *lit* tooth, canine tooth, fang, tusk.

II *lit* hair, bunch of hair.

III sub-stalk of rice (from which the ear grows).

jathak, **njathak** *reg* near, close by.

jathek *var of* **jathak**.

jathèk *var of* **jathak**.

jathil I, **njathil** (of front lower-tooth) extending outward.

II, **jathilan** a trance dance performed while riding a woven bamboo hobby-horse accompanied by music;

njathil to perform such a dance.

jathok *var of* **jathak**.

jathos *var of* **jathak**.

jathuk *var of* **jathak**.

jathur *var of* **jathak**.

jathus *var of* **jathak**.

jati I, *ng*, **jatos** *kr*, teak;

jatèn *or* **pejatèn** a place where teak trees grow, teak forest.

II *or* **sejati** true, pure, genuine;

njatèni to tell the truth;

kajatèn truth;

jati ketlusuban wuyung *prov* good blemished by bad.

jatmika *lit* modest, demure.

jatos *kr for* **jati**.

jatuh (to go) bankrupt.

jatukrama *lit* spouse, partner for life.

jauh *reg* far, far-off.

jauk, **njauk** *reg* to ask for, beg (*var of* **jaluk**).

jaul, **njaul** to make a certain profit;

njauli to make a profit on (a transaction);

kejaul to get overcharged.

Jawa ng, Jawi kr, 1 Java, Javanese, pertaining to Java; 2 native, of local origin rather than the imported or foreign kind; 3 well-bred; 4 plain language, gist;

njawani to have Javanese characteristics, behave like a real Javanese;

njawakaké to translate into Javanese;

ngejawa to go to Java;

kejawan or kejawèn 1 Javanism, Javanese philosophy; 2 pertaining to Java; 3 land that is not to be leased to outsiders.

jawab I reg, njawab to approach with a request, ask for (a girl).

II, njawab 1 to reply; 2 to answer back (rudely).

jawah rain (kr for udan).

jawal reg half-mad, unmanageable.

jawat, njawat or njejawat to approach, make advances to; njawat tangan, jawatan to shake hands.

jawata lit god, mythological deity.

jawèl, njawèl reg to stare open-mouthed in wonder.

jawès hair that grows under the lower lip.

Jawi I Java, Javanese (kr for Jawa).

II or njawi outside (kr for jaba).

III or jejawi wild ox, wild bull.

jawil a touch, a prod;

njawil 1 to touch s.o. in order to get attention; 2 fig to invite s.o. informally; jawilan 1 touching; 2 fig informal invitation.

jawoh var of jawuh.

jawuh rain (subst kr for udan).

jé I name of the 4th year in the windu cycle.

II it's said, they say, you know (shtf of jaré; see also é).

jebabah, njebabah extending outward at the sides;

njebabahaké to place s.t. with the parts extending outward.

jebad 1 damaged (var of bejad); 2 (of bamboo) coming unwoven.

jebag I reg flat stone or clay bowl used for preparing spices with a pestle. See also jobag, layah.

II reg window of a bird trap.

III reg too old to get married. See also jubag.

jebamblang, jebamblangan abundant, plentiful.

jebebeg, njebebeg 1 feeling bloated; 2 fig resentful, irked, vexed.

jebèbèh, njebèbèh spread wide;

njebèbèhaké to spread s.t. wide.

jebeber, njebeber soaking wet.

jebèbèr, njebèbèr to have a broad flaring rim.

jèbèh, njèbèh to have the headdress tied with the wide ends extending outward; jèbèhan wide ends of a headdress extending outwards.

jeben to be absorbed in doing s.t.; -bebed a boy who is at the age (8–9 years old) when he enjoys wearing batik garments.

jebeng 1 fringe; 2 tassel;

jumebeng 1 (of hair) in the form of fringe; 2 forming a tassel.

jebèng adr young man!

jeber, njeber thick and wide (lower lip); njeberaké to curl the lower lip down (to tease).

jèber, njèbèr to spread out;

njèbèraké 1 to spread, open out, display; 2 to explain.

jèbèt, jèbètan borderland between forest and arable land.

jebibir, njebibir blue with cold (lips).

jebimblik, njebimblik with face screwed up ready to cry caused by disappointment.

jeblag, njeblag open widely;

njeblagaké to open s.t. widely;

jeblagan in a wide open condition;

kejeblag open widely by accident (door).

jeblas-jeblès see **jeblès**.

jeblèg, njeblèg to slam s.t. shut. See also **jeglèg**.

jèblèk, jèblèkan in (the form of) sheets.

jeblès, njeblèsaké to bump (the head) against a hard object;

kejeblès (of head) to get struck accidentally;

jeblas-jeblès (to make) repeated sounds of s.t. knocking against a hard object.

jèbles just like, coinciding with, just the same as. Also **cèples, jiblès**.

jebling or **mak jebling** repr a quick detaching motion. See also **cepling**.

jeblis or **mak jeblis** repr the sound of drawing on an opium pipe.

jeblog 1 muddy; **2** unlucky at cards; **3** of inferior quality; **4** or **mak jeblog** repr a muffled thud;

njeblog to get muddy;

njeblogaké 1 to cause s.t. to be muddy; **2** to cheat s.o.; **3** to cause to get stuck in s.t.; fig to give s.o. incorrect directions;

kejeblog 1 to fall into or get stuck in s.t.; **2** to get cheated;

jeblogan 1 mudhole; **2** cr female genitals; **3** prostitute.

jeblong, njeblong to cave in (var of **jemblong**).

jeblos or **mak jeblos** repr a bursting or explosion;

njeblos 1 to explode, burst; **2** to fail to get an expected result;

njeblosaké 1 to throw s.o. into; **2** fig to throw into jail;

kejeblos 1 to step into a hole or ditch; **2** to fall into or get stuck in s.t.; **3** to be cheated, fooled, tricked;

jeblosan 1 explosion, bursting; **2** a way out, back (side) door.

jeblug, njeblug 1 to burst, explode, detonate; **2** to break out, erupt.

jebluk var of **jepluk**.

jeblus var of **jebus**.

jebobog, njebobog 1 to ruffle (of feathers); **2** to stand on end (of hair).

jebod reg **1** damaged (var of **jebad**); **2** to fall apart.

jebol 1 broken down, broken through at the bottom; **2** penetrated;

njebol or **njeboli 1** to uproot; **2** to make s.t. break down or through;

njebolaké to cause s.t. to be broken down or through;

jebolan 1 dropout or graduate; **2** ex-, former; **3** s.t. uprooted.

jebomblog var of **jebombrot**.

jebombrot, njebombrot or **pating jebombrot** untidy in personal appearance.

jébor long-handled dipper.

jebos var of **jebus**.

jébot reg impoverished, suffering from troubles and difficulties.

jebrag, njebrag (of hair, feathers) to stand on end (var of **jegrag**).

jebrèd I, or **mak jebrèd** repr slamming the door;

njebrèd or **jumebrèd** slamming.

II, njebrèd flaring outward at the edges (lips, wound etc).

jèbrèng var of **jèmbrèng**.

jèbrès, njèbrès messy, unwiped (the mouth, after eating).

jebrèt see **jebrèd**.

jebrig, njebrig or **pating jebrig** stiffly upright. See also **jegrig**.

jebrod, njebrod 1 to break out (off); **2** cr to be born.

jebrol, njebrol 1 to be born easily; **2** to uproot (var of **jebol**).

jebrot see **jebrod**.

jebrul var of **jebrol**.

jebubug, njebubug bunched up.

jebug I mature betel nut.

II powder(ed substance).

jebul 1 but, instead; jebulé as it turned out; 2 or njebul to lead to (of passageway).

jebumbung var of jebubug.

jébung, jébungan reg to be friends, to associate with friends.

jebur var of jegur.

jebus to meet up with, join with (road); jebusan a connecting way.

jedeng var of jèdèng.

jèdèng cr dead.

jedhag I cr can, to be able (to), capable.
II, njedhag to lie face up motionless.
III, scarce, lacking;
kajedhagan shortage, scarcity of.

jedhar-jedhir see jedhir.

jedhar-jedhèr see jedhèr.

jedhar-jedhor see jedhor.

jedhé, njedhé to guess (the answer to) (var of bedhé).

jedhèd or mak jedhèd var of jebrèd.

jedheg able to go no further;
njedhegaké to take s.t. as far as possible;
kejedheg to get stuck with the job of;
kejedhegan to run out of ideas as to what to do. See also judheg.

jedhèk var of jedhé.

jèdhèng reg very young.

jedhèr or mak jedhèr repr sound of a firearm or a slamming door;
njedhèr to slam, bang;
njedhèraké 1 to slam (a door); 2 to fire (a gun);
jedhar-jedhèr (of door) to slam or fire (a gun) repeatedly.

jèdhi large cauldron with a rounded bottom;
njèdhi to boil s.t in a large cauldron.

jedhidhig, njedhidhig (of hair) in need of cutting.

jedhig, njedhig fluttering in all directions, messy (hair).

jedhil, njedhil to pull s.t from its moorings, extract s.t.

jedhindhil, njedhindhil soaking wet.

jedhing reg bathroom, tank for storing water for bathing.

jedhir, njedhir thick-lipped;
jedhar-jedhir to thrust forward the lips to signal disgust, disbelief.

jedhit, njedhit all dressed up, usually in a tight-fitting garment.

jedhodhog, njedhodhog cr to sit (down).

jedhodhot, njedhodhot var of jedhodhog.

jedhok, njedhok reg to be located s.w., be or to stay s.w.

jedhor or mak jedhor repr banging, booming;
jedhar-jedhor repr repeated sound of a firearm.

jédhor I a large drum used as a musical instrument for accompanying a performance;
jédhoran to play such an instrument.
II, njédhor thick, swollen (lips).

jedhot or mak jedhot repr bumping, explosion;
njedhot 1 to bump; 2 to explode;
kejedhot to get hurt by bumping against s.t.

jedhudhug var of bedhudhug, jebubug.

jedhug to lead to, come out at, arrive at (road).

jedhul or mak jedhul repr a sudden appearance;
njedhul 1 or jumedhul to emerge into view, surface; 2 to join, meet up with (var of jedhug).

jedhung a certain green hairless caterpillar.

jedhur var of jedhor.

jédok female (reg var of wédok).

jeg, I sajeg throughout (a lifetime), in (my) whole life.
II, jegé I think; (in questions) do you think? (shtf of gajeg).

jèg I, ngejègi to occupy by force, take over a place;
kejègan occupied by force.

II, jèg-jègan to walk around in a care-free, inconsiderate manner (*var of* jag-jagan).

jegé *see* jeg.

jegadhul, njegadhul with an unsatisfied expression, with a disappointed face.

jegadul *var of* jegadhul.

jegagig *or* **mak jegagig** *repr* a sudden face-to-face meeting.

jégal, njégal 1 to trip, intercept s.o.; **2** to keep an opponent from succeeding; **njégali** to interfere with, interrupt; **kejégal** to be intercepted; **jégalan** interfering, intercepting.

jégang to sit improperly, *e.g.* with one knee drawn up (*also* jigang).

jegedhag *see* jegedheg.

jegedheg, njegedheg 1 to be motionless, come to a standstill; **2** magnificent, dashing.

jegèg, njegèg to thrust the chest forward (*var of* degèg).

jègèg *reg* in a quandary, unable to cope.

jegegeg, njegegeg to remain motionless (*var of* begegeg).

jegègeg *or* **mak jegègeg** *rep* a sudden stop, a sudden standstill; **njegègeg** to come to a standstill.

jegègèng *see* jegènggèng.

jegènggèng, njegènggèng *reg* to recover (from illness).

jegègès, njegègès *cr* to laugh; **jegègèsan** to keep laughing.

jègèn, njègèn *reg* to share, give a portion.

jegèr very young.

jegereg *var of* jegreg.

jegidheg, njegidheg not willing to speak or act.

jegigig *see* jegigik.

jegigik, njegigik to laugh lightly.

jegigis, njegigis to laugh constantly.

jeginggat *or* **mak jeginggat** *repr* startling; **njeginggat** to startle, give a start.

jeginggis, njeginggis 1 scrawny and pale looking; **2** ragged (ragged).

jegir, njegir to stand up straight.

jeglag I, njeglag to lean back (*var of* dheglag).

II, njeglag to open widely (*var of* jeblag).

III, jeglag-jeglèg *repr* repeated slamming sounds. *See also* jeglèg.

jeglèg I, njeglèg to become locked by slamming; **njeglègaké** to shut s.t. by slamming.

II, jeglag-jeglèg to make a clicking sound repeatedly; **jeglègan** stapler.

jeglig *or* **mak jeglig** *repr* an arm or leg suddenly bending or twisting; **njeglig** to be stuck; **kejeglig** suddenly twisting accidentally; **jegligan** *reg* sliding-door.

jeglog I, njeglog *reg* to sit and relax.

II, njeglog to shape s.t. in a mould; **jeglogan** *reg* button-mould made from cow's horn.

jeglong 1 a certain downward movement in the classical dance; **2** concave; **njeglong** having a hole in it; **njeglongi** to make holes in s.t.; **njeglongaké 1** to cause s.o. to fall into a hole; **2** *fig* to lead s.o. to fall into a trap; **kejeglong 1** to fall into a hole; **2** *fig* to be trapped; **jeglong-jeglong** bumpy (of road), full of holes; **jeglongan** pothole.

jeglug *or* **mak jeglug** *repr* bumping; **njeglug** to bump (the head) deliberately; **kejeglug** to bump (the head) inadvertently.

jéglug *or* **njéglug** crippled, lame.

jegnèn I think (*var of* gajegé).

jegodhag, njegodhag spacious and empty (room).

jegodhah, njegodhah wide (of holes), broad (*var of* jegodhag).

jegog 1 a dog's bark; **2** (*or* **njegog**) to bark;

njegogi to bark at;

jegog-jegog to bark repeatedly.

jegogos, njegogos to sit motionless.

jegogrog, njegogrog *var of* **jegogos.**

jegong deep, concave;

jegongan a depression in the ground, hole.

jégong, njégong *reg* to sit.

jegos, njegos *var of* **jegogos.**

jégos 1 can, to be able; **2** to know how (to).

jegot, njegot to sulk, be unwilling to do things.

jegrag, njegrag (of hair, feathers) to stand on end.

jégrang (to have become) too short, outgrown (clothing).

jegreg, njegreg 1 to sit or stand motionless, stock-still; **2** to stop in one's tracks.

jegrèg *or* **mak jegrèg** *repr* a slam; slam!;

njegrèg *or* **njegrègaké** to slam.

jègreg *or* **mak jègreg** *repr* a sudden stop.

jègrèg, njègrèg to stand (up) straight.

jegrig, njegrig *or* **pating jegrig** stiffly upright.

jegros *var of* **jegos.**

jegudru, njegudru depressed, drooping.

jegug *var of* **jegog.**

jégung, njégung to twist, entangle s.t.;

kejégung to get twisted *or* entangled.

jegunggut, njegunggut *or* **jegunggat-jegunggut** to move around or back and forth in the same place.

jegur *or* **mak jegur** *repr* a splash;

njegur to plunge;

njeguri to plunge into;

njeguraké to plunge s.t. into water;

jumegur 1 to produce a splashing sound; **2** to produce a booming sound.

jèh I *reg* still, (even) now (*var of* **isih**).

II of easy virtue (*shtf of* **lènjèh**).

III *reg* as you well know (*var of* **jenèh**).

jèhèh, njèhèh to keep staying at s.o.'s place without any right to it.

jejak a kick;

njejak to kick, move (the legs) in a stiff-kneed kicking motion;

njejaki to kick or push with the leg;

kejejak to get kicked inadvertently;

jejakan act of kicking.

jejeg I 1 straight, upright; **2** regular, standard, not deviating from the standard; **3** with wholehearted consent;

njejegaké 1 to make s.t. straight/upright; **2** to make a correction.

II *var of* **jejak.**

jèjèg I, njèjèg at a trot (horse).

II, njèjèg *or* **jèjègan** *reg* skilled, experienced.

jèjèh, njèjèh to sit higher up than others (breach of manners).

jejel to crowd in(to);

njejeli to force-feed;

jejel riyel jam-packed.

jejep, njejep 1 to wait expectantly or apprehensively; **2** *intsfr* cold, *intsfr* insipid (*see* **njejet**).

jejer 1 basic principle; **2** plot (of story); **3** scene (in drama); **4** *gram* sentence subject;

jejeran 1 *way* opening (audience) scene at court; **2** standing (*i.e.* growing) riceplants; **3** pole, staff; **4** capital, investment money; **5** spear handle (*k.i. for* **landhéyan**); **6** carved kris handle (*k.i. for* **ukiran**);

njejer to stand upright;

njejeri 1 to dry rice plants by standing them in the sun; **2** to apply carvings to (a wall).

jèjèr next to, near;

njèjèr to put next to each other;

njèjèri to be beside, sit or stand next to;

njèjèraké to place next to each other;

jèjèr-jèjèr *pl* side by side;

jèjèr wayang *idiom* side by side like puppets in a row.

jejet, njejet 1 *intsfr* cold; 2 *intsfr* insipid, lacking salt (*var of* jejep).

jèk I *or* mak jèk *repr* the sound effect produced by tapping metal bars.
II *var of* jèg.
III *reg var of* jak, ajak.

jekangkang, njekangkang to lie or fall on the back with the legs up.

jekat *inf var of* jakat.

jekèk genuine, pure, (like the) original.

jekékal *or* mak jekékal *repr* suddenly getting up;
njekékal to get up and remain upright.

jekèkèl *var of* jekékal.

jekéngkang *var of* jekangkang.

jekengkeng, njekengkeng to lie with stiffened body.

jekening, njekening neat and clean.

jekenong, njekenong curled up (cloth).

jekèthèk, njekèthèk commonplace, prevalent. *See also* jlekèthèk.

jekethet, njekethet tight, too small (clothing).

jekèthèt, njekèthèt (of moustache) thick and heavy, curving upward. *See also* jlekèthèt.

jekethut, njekethut wrinkled (skin or clothing). *See also* jlekethut.

jekithat, njekithat small and slim with pointed ends. *See also* jlekithat.

jekithing *var of* cekithing.

jekithit *var of* jekithat.

jekithut *var of* jekethut.

jeklèk *or* mak jeklèk *repr* breaking, snapping;
njeklèk to break, snap s.t.;
njeklèkaké to turn on/off (the lamp) by turning the switch;
jeklèkan trigger, light switch, stapler (things that make a clicking sound).

jekluk *or* mak jekluk *repr* a cracking sound;

njekluki to crack s.o.'s joints by flexing the fingers or toes.

jèkman *reg* certainly, really, for a fact.

jèkmula *var of* jèkman.

jekrèk *or* mak jekrèk *repr* s.t. snapping shut;
njekrèk to snap shut;
njekrèki to punch (a hole in) *e.g.* a ticket;
jekrèkan 1 punch; 2 mousetrap.

jeksa public prosecutor (*var of* jaksa).

jekut, njekut *intsfr* cold: intensely cold.

jekutrut, njekutrut downcast, out of sorts.

jelag, njelag 1 *reg* to eat up; 2 *fig* to swindle, cheat.

jelah, jelah-jelih to keep shouting. *See* jelih.

jelak *reg* on the verge of, a condition necessitating urgent action (*var of* selak).

jèlèdèng *cr* dead.

jéléding *var of* jèlèdèng.

jelèh I bored (with), tired of;
njelèhi boring;
jelèhan easily bored.
II, njelèh *reg* to shout (*var of* jelih);
jelèh-jelèh to keep shouting.

jèlèh *reg* infected and watering (eyes).

jelèk *reg cr* female, woman.

jèlès *var of* jèlèh.

jelih, njelih to shout;
jelih-jelih *or* jelah-jelih to keep shouting.

jelir, njeliraké *or* njelir-jeliraké 1 to tell the truth about; 2 to explain and bring s.o.'s wrongdoing home to them;
kejelir to have o's wrongdoing discovered and censured.

jelit, njelit to economise, use as sparingly as possible.

jelma *var of* jalma.

jélok *reg* a certain bean eaten raw as a rice-accompanying dish. *See also* jéngkol.

jelu, njelu irritated, annoyed;

njela-njelu to keep feeling exasperated (at, about).

jeluk *reg var of* **celuk**.

jélung, jélungan (to play) hide-and-seek.

Jemahat Friday (*var of* **Jemuwah**).

jemak *var of* **jamak**.

jemala *lit* stick, club;
  njemalani to beat with a stick.

jemampleng intensely hot (sun).

jemamut, njemamut *reg* to appear, be present.

jembak a certain vegetable grown in a swampy area.

jembangan large earthenware container used for water or as a flowerpot.

jembar I broad, spacious;
  njembaraké to make s.t. broad(er), broaden;
  jembar atiné compassionate;
  jembar dhadhané patient;
  jembara kuburé may you go to heaven! (*said to a dead person*);
  jembar segarané always pleased to give forgiveness to others.
  II, **jembaran** a narrow earthenware tank.

jembat *reg var of* **jembar**.

jembeg mucky, muddy, damp and messy.

jèmbèl shabby, squalid, poor.

jembélit to take a break (game-player).

jembèng, njembèng to open up or widen (an opening) with the fingers.

jember muddy, mucky;
  njemberi 1 muddy; 2 nauseating; 3 to make s.t. muddy.

jèmbèt, njèmbèt *reg cr* to have intercourse with.

jémbit *var of* **jembélit**.

jembèwèk, njembèwèk with lips drawn apart and turned down.

jembimblik, njembimblik to have the face screwed up to cry.

jemblang, njemblang bloated (the belly).

jemblèk 1 spotted with absorbed liquid; 2 *fig* spotty in performance, not up to standard; 3 to absorb (stains);
  kejemblèkan to get spotted.

jèmblèk 1 discharged matter from the eye; 2 mushy and revolting; 3 *reg* to be at the end of one's wits; 4 failed.

jèmblem a fried snack made from mashed cassava filled with palm sugar;
  njèmblem 1 chubby in the face; 2 to remain silent, contribute nothing to the conversation.

jembleng, njembleng speechless, struck dumb.

jembling, njembling bloated (the belly).

jemblok, njemblok smudged, smeared.

jemblong, njemblong 1 to subside, cave in; 2 vacant, unoccupied (land, position);
  jemblongan subsidence.

jembluk, njembluk bulging, puffed up.

jemblung a wayang performance which is performed orally without puppets;
  jemblungan 1 to perform such a show; 2 *reg* small variety of water melon.

jembombrong, njembombrong untidy, not neatly groomed (women).

jémbrak thick, long and hanging down (horse's mane).

jémbrang *var of* **jémbrak**.

jembreg muddy and dirty.

jembrèng, njèmbrèng to spread or lay out s.t.

jembrèt *reg* small shrimps or fish (pounded and fermented in the process of making paste condiment).

jembrung, njembrung messy, unkempt, littered.

jembul decorative plume stuck in a hat (*var of* **jambul**).

jembut pubic hair.

jembuwal, njembuwal (of live freshwater fish) to swirl together.

jèmèh I a game played with the Chinese cards (*kertu cilik*).
  II *reg* dead, defeated.

jemèk soft and damp.

jèmèk *reg var of* jemèk.

jemika modest (*var of* jatmika).

jeminul, njeminul to be unsteady, shake, wobble.

jemok, njemok to take (*reg var of* jupuk).

jemot *var of* jemok.

jempalik, njempalik to turn upside down;
jempalikan topsy-turvy.

jempana royal palanquin.

jemparing arrow (*kr for* panah).

jèmpèr exhausted. *See also* jempor.

jempérok, njempérok 1 too heavily made up with cosmetics; 2 nicely groomed.

jempina 1 a certain tuberous root; 2 prematurely born child.

jempling I, njempling 1 to emit a high-pitched sound; 2 to squeal. *See also* jemprit.
II *reg* variety of small but very hot chili.

jempo feeble with old age (*var of* jompo).

jempol 1 thumb; 2 the best; 3 *excl* great!

jempor exhausted.

jémpor *var of* jempor.

jemprit I, njemprit to squeal (*var of* jempling I).
II *reg* a variety of small but very hot chili (*var of* jempling II).

jemput, njemput to take a bit (of powder) with the fingers (*var of* jumput).

jemrut emerald.

jemu tired of, bored.

jemuk, njemuk to take (*reg var of* jupuk).

jemumut, njemumut *or* pating jemumut all dirty, covered with dirt.

jemunten *subst kr for* jemuwah.

jemurut emerald (*var of* jemrut).

jemut, njemut to take (*reg var of* jupuk).

Jemuwah Friday.

jèn *reg* really, indeed, certainly (*reg var of* pancèn).

jenak 1 to feel at home; 2 deeply absorbed (in the enjoyment of).

jenang a certain porridge or soft pudding; - abang a sweet red-coloured porridge served at various ceremonies; - baro-baro porridge with grated sugared coconut;
njenang to make (ingredients) into porridge; - abang to hold a ritual ceremony serving red porridge;
njenangaké to hold a ritual ceremony for s.o. by serving porridge to signal a significant event.

jenar 1 *lit* yellow; 2 a variety of tree with small fragrant blossoms and yellow wood.

jenat 1 *ng, kr,* swargi *k.i.,* the late, the deceased one; 2 heaven (*see also* janah).

jendhel, njendhel 1 to become thick/solid; 2 to remain stuck s.w.; 3 to coagulate, curdle, clot (of blood);
njendhelaké to thicken, to make s.t. congeal;

jendhéla window.

jendhil, njendhil having a small knob or bump on it;
jendhal-jendhil to keep bobbing up and down.

jendhol, njendhol swollen, having a knob or bump on it;
jendholan a knob, bump.

jéndhol *var of* jendhol.

jéndral general (military rank);
jéndralan reception held for generals.

jendhul *var of* jendhol.

jené 1 yellow (*kr for* kuning); 2 gold (*kr for* emas);
jenéan brass (*kr for* kuningan).

jènèd, njènèd harmonious, well built (physique).

jenèh 1 as you well know; it is plain that…; 2 (just) because.

jenek *var of* jenak.

jeneng I *ng,* nama *or* nami *kr,* asma *k.i.* 1 name; 2 to be called, known *or* regarded as; - cilik childhood name; - pancer family name; - tuwa adult name;
njenengi *or* njenengaké to name s.o.

II, **njenengi** to be present at (*k.i. for* nekani);

panjenengan you; your, yours (*k.i. for* kowé, -mu); **panjenengané** he, she (*k.i. for* dhèwèké);

jumeneng 1 to stand (*k.i. for* ngadeg); 2 to become (*k.i. for* dadi).

jenes damp and dirty.

jenès, njenès to ridicule, jeer at. *See also* **jengès**.

jenèwer gin.

jeng I *term of adr* younger sister, younger female.

II 1 *lit* foot, leg; 2 *nobility title* (*shtf of* kangjeng).

jengal, jengal-jengil 1 lone, alone; 2 loose, coming off. *See also* **jengil**.

jengandika *lit* you; your, yours.

jengat, njengat in an upright position.

jengèk, njengèk to produce a sudden scream, squeal.

jèngèk, njèngèk to crane the neck.

jengen name (*reg var of* **jeneng**).

jengèngèk, njengèngèk to lift the head suddenly.

jenger, njenger stunned, shocked, taken aback.

jèngèr, njèngèr to lift the head, with nose in the air (conceited).

jengès, njengès to tease, ridicule. *See also* **cengès**.

jenggama *lit* trouble, difficulty.

jenggami *var of* **jenggama**.

jenggan pupil of a holy man (*var of* **janggan, jejanggan**).

jenggar roomy, spacious;

njenggaraké to give s.t. plenty of room.

jenggarang, njenggarang tall, sizeable (buildings).

jenggé I to sit idly staring into space. *See also* **jengglé**.

II a monster in the procession of a Chinese festival. *See also* **jenggi**.

jènggèl, njènggèl to lift the head up;

golèk jènggèl a variety of doll that can lift its head up when the string is pulled. *See also* **golèk**.

jenggeleg *or* **mak jenggeleg** *repr* a sudden appearing;

njenggeleg to stand steadily;

pating jenggeleg to loom up, to stand out (of separate objects in a group).

jenggèlèk, njenggèlèk *repr* 1 a sudden awakening and arising; 2 recovered (from illness).

jenggeneg *var of* **jenggeleg**.

jengger, njengger magnificent, splendid.

jènggèr comb (of cock); - **sumpel** small comb; - **wilah** large billowing comb.

jenggereng, njenggereng 1 (of houses) magnificent; 2 (of people) to make a splendid appearance.

jenggèrèng, njenggèrèng in dashing (gallant) style, fine-looking.

jenggèrètnong a certain cicada that makes a loud buzzing sound (*var of* **cenggèrètnong**).

jènggès a certain kind of black magic.

jenggi I a monster in the procession of a Chinese festival.

II, **njenggi** to carry on the shoulder.

jenggileng wide and staring (eyes);

njenggileng to stare (at), wide-eyed and steadily.

jengginggat *var of* **jenggirat**.

jengginggis *var of* **jeginggis**.

jenggirat *or* **mak jenggirat** *repr* a sudden start;

njenggirat to give a start, spring out (of).

jenggiri mythological tiger with horns.

jenggit, njenggit to pull hairs from s.o.'s scalp by the roots.

jengglé, njengglé to sit idly staring into space (*var of* **jenggé**).

jènggglèh, njènggglèh clearly visible, in plain sight.

jengglèng *or* **mak jengglèng** *repr* the clash of metal against metal, clanging loudly;

njengglèng *or* **njengglèngaké** to smash s.t. against a metal object.

jengglik, njengglik to sit separated from others.

jenggluk, njenggluk to sit concentrating. *Also* **jenggruk**.

jengglung *repr* the sound of a gong; **jumengglung**; **lesung** - title of a modern gamelan melody.

jénggo, njénggo *reg* to keep the mouth closed.

jenggodhag *var of* **jegodhag**.

jenggonggos *var of* **jegogos**.

jenggorong large shape; **njenggorong** excessively big and tall.

jénggot *ng, kr,* **gumbala** *k.i.* beard; - **wesi** a certain plant the bark of which inhibits fermentation of sugar-palm sap; **jénggotan** to wear a beard; **jénggoten** *fig* suffering from old age.

jenggreng *var of* **jenggereng**.

jenggrik, njenggrik 1 to teeter, threaten to topple; 2 *intsfr* thin: thin as a rake.

jenggruk *var of* **jenggluk**.

jenggul *or* **jejenggul** the leader, the top man.

jengguleng, njengguleng to churn, tumble (waves, clouds).

jenggung *repr* a stroke of a gamelan gong.

jenggunuk, njenggunuk to loom, stick up.

jenggureng, njenggureng stern-faced, grim-looking.

jenggut, njenggut to graze (on). *See also* **senggut**.

jengil, njengil lone, alone (tooth, only one left); **jengal-jengil** loose, coming off.

jengit, njengit in an upright position; **jengat-jengit** to keep assuming an upright position.

jengkang, njengkangaké to put s.o. over backwards;

kejengkang to fall over backwards, fall on one's back.

jengkang-jengking *see* **jengking**.

jengkar 1 to depart, set out (*k.i. for* **budhal, mangkat**); 2 to move, change residence (*k.i. for* **ngalih, pindhah**).

jèngkèl irritated, frustrated, exasperated; **njèngkèlaké** to cause to be irritated; **jèngkèlan** easily irritated.

jengkélang, njengkélang 1 to fall down from a high place; 2 to fall out of a vehicle.

jengkelit, njengkelit 1 to fall head over heels; 2 to get thrown head over heels; 3 to do a handspring, tumble; **jengkelitan** to turn somersaults for one's amusement.

jengkénang *var of* **jengkélang**.

jèngkèng to kneel (on one knee).

jengkengker, njengkengker stiff, rigid (in death) (*var of* **jekengker**).

jengker big and strong.

jèngkèr *reg* to say, tell, explain; **njèngkèraké** to explain s.t.

jengkerung, njengkerung curled up, rolled into a ball.

jengkerut 1 furrow, wrinkle; 2 curl (fabric); **njengkerut** 1 to frown, fold into creases, be furrowed, wrinkled; 2 curled; **pating jengkerut** full of creases.

jengking, njengking to lie prostrate with head down and bottom up; **jengkang-jengking** to keep moving in the above position repeatedly; 2 *joking cr* to pray repeatedly (the Islamic praying attitude).

jéngklak, jéngklak-jèngklèk to jump with joy. *See* **jèngklèk**.

jengklèk, kejengklèk to get twisted, get turned (ankle).

jèngklèk to keep leaping on one leg; **jéngklak-jèngklèk** *see* **jéngklak**.

jengklok *var of* **jengklèk**.

jengkok *reg* short-legged bench or table.

jéngkol a variety of edible bean eaten as a dish.

jengku knee (*k.i. for* dhengkul);
njengku to push with the knee or elbow;
kejengku to be pushed with the knee or elbow inadvertently.

jengok *var of* jenguk.

jengongok *var of* dengongok.

jengor *var of* jenguk.

jenguk, njenguk to sit idly staring into space.

jengur *var of* jenguk.

jeni *kr* deep golden (*intensified form of* jené).

jenis kind, class, (sub)group (*var of* jinis).

jenitri a certain seed, often used for necklaces and other trinkets.

jènjèk *reg* to lose, be defeated.

jenjem secure, at peace, untroubled.

jènjèt I corn chaff.
II, njènjèt wide open (eyes).

jenten *var of* jinten.

jenthar, njenthar pointing straight up (*esp* of long tails).

jenthara, njenthara handsome and elegant (young man).

jenthat *var of* jenthar;
jenthat-jenthit *see* jenthit.

jenthik little finger; - manis ring finger, fourth finger.

jenthir, njenthir pointing straight up (small short tails).

jenthit, njenthit to move with the rear end higher than the front;
jenthat-jenthit to keep moving as above.

jenthok, njenthoki to encounter s.t.;
kejenthok to encounter by chance.

jentol, njentol to become swollen (from insect bites/stings).

jéntol *var of* jentol.

jenthot, njenthot to shoot a marble by holding it in the crook of the index finger and snapping it with the thumb.

jenthu thick and muscular (physique).

jèntrèh, njèntrèh to explain, set out clearly. *See also* jlèntrèh.

jèntrèk *or* jèntrèk-jèntrèk lined up;
njèntrèk *or* njèntrèki to put in a line.

jentrung *var of* jentung.

jentul *var of* jentol.

jentung, njentung to remain sitting disconsolately.

jentus, njentus to bang one's head (on);
kejentus to get knocked against s.t.

jenu a certain plant that is poisonous to fish;
njenu to catch fish by poisoning them with the ground-up root of this plant.

jepapang *see* jepaplang.

jepaplang, njepaplang to extend the arms out to the sides;
jepaplangan to keep the arms stretched out, extend the arms repeatedly.

jepat, njepat to emerge suddenly, spring out;
jepatan act of springing out;
kejepatan to get hit by s.t. springing out.

jepèplèk, njepèplèk (to sit huddled) close (to s.o.).

jepèt clip, clamp; - rambut hair clip.

jepiping, njepiping to cock the ears.

jepit (*or* jepitan) pincers, gripping tool, tongs;
njepit to pinch, grip, use a pinching tool;
kejepit 1 to get pinched; 2 *fig* situated in an unobtrusive *or* out-of-the-way place, in a difficult or undesirable position;
jepitan 1 *var of* jepit; 2 place to squeeze into for concealment or to be unobtrusive.

jeplak, njeplak 1 to open up/out; 2 *cr* to speak, blurt out;
jeplakan 1 mouth of a trap; 2 top-hinged window or door that opens outward;

njeplakaké to open (a hinged-panel door, window).

jéplé, njéplé obvious.

jèplèk *var of* jéplé.

jeplih, njeplih not pure white.

jepluh *intsfr* intact; wutuh - completely intact.

jepluk, njepluk I 1 to explode; 2 to fade, become drab; 3 to fail.

II, njepluk throughout; sakésuk - the whole morning.

jepot, njepot to go away at once to avoid conversation.

jeprah, njeprah ubiquitous, present everywhere.

jeprak, njeprak to open up/out, to spread.

jeprèt *or* mak jeprèt *repr* a zipping, clicking or snapping;

njeprèt 1 (*or* njeprèti) to shoot with a catapult; 2 to take a snapshot of;

njeprètaké to snap (a photograph) for s.o. else;

jeprètan 1 stapler; 2 catapult.

jeprik, njeprik *or* pating jeprik standing up/out (hair, feathers).

jeprot *repr* stabbing.

jepruk, njepruk 1 piled high, puffed up; 2 throughout (*var of* jepluk II).

jeprut *or* mak jeprut *repr* s.t. breaking with a snap.

Jepun Japan.

jepupung, njepupung lying face down humped up and stiff.

jeput throughout (the morning) (*var of* jepluk).

jer after all (*see also* pijer).

jèr I, ngejèr *or* ngejèri to melt/dissolve s.t.;

ngejèraké to melt for s.o.; to have s.t. melted;

jèr-jèran in a molten *or* dissolved state;

pangejèran 1 act of melting; 2 melting-place.

II a certain diacritical mark in Arabic script.

jeram citrus fruit (*kr for* jeruk).

jerbabah *var of* jebabah.

jerbabak, njerbabak to flush with anger.

jerbèbèh *var of* jebèbèh.

jerbèbès, njerbèbès to keep dripping (damp, moisture).

jéré it is said (*reg var of* jaré).

jerèh *reg* afraid, faint-hearted, cowardly (*var of* jirih).

jèrèké *reg var of* jaré.

jèrèn *reg var of* jaré.

jèrèng, njèrèng 1 to spread (out), extend, lay out; 2 to disclose in detail, unfold fully;

njèrèngi to spread out constantly.

jèrigèn jerrycan.

jerih *var of* jirih.

jering a certain bean eaten raw as a rice-accompanying dish.

jerit a scream;

njerit to scream;

jerit-jerit *or* jerat-jerit to keep screaming.

jerkangkang *var of* jekangkang.

jermunuh, njermumuh having an infected swollen sore.

jernèh 1 as you well know; it is plain that...; 2 (just) because (*var of* jenèh).

jernih clean, clear, pure.

jero *ng*, lebet *kr*, 1 deep; 2 the interior; 3 the court, the palace;

(me)njero (mlebet *kr*) 1 (farther) to the inside; 2 to enter, go in the house;

njeroni to make s.t. deeper (than s.t. else);

njerokaké to deepen;

kejeron too deep;

jeroan entrails as food;

kejeron tampa (panampa) misunderstood;

jeroné *or* jero cethèké the depths;

jeron inside, within (*var of* jero);

sajeroné 1 during, while; 2 inside.

jerpupung *var of* jepupung.

jerthek messy and dirty;

pating jerthek messy everywhere.

jerthot, pating jerthot repeated knuckle-cracks.

jerthut *var of* jerthot.

jerug a certain tiny mouse. *See* tikus.

jeruk I *ng*, jeram *kr*, citrus fruit; - bali pomelo; - nipis, pecel sour lime-like fruit; - purut a small fragrant lemon-like fruit;

njeruk purut deeply wrinkled (human skin).

II, njeruk *reg* homosexual.

jerum, njerum lying at ease (of cattle, *e.g.* while chewing the cud).

jes *or* mak jes *repr* a piercing, stabbing.

jès 1 *repr* a locomotive puffing; 2 *repr* a match striking (*var of* jrès).

jesa *var of* jeksa.

jèsbèn jazz band.

jesmani *var of* jasmani.

jet *or* mak jet *repr* a jerk, jolt.

jethathus, njethathus undershot, jutting forward (jaw).

jethathut, njethathut gloomy, depressed.

jèthek dirty, nasty.

jethèt *or* mak jethèt *repr* the switching of an appliance (off or on);

njethèt to switch with a snapping sound;

njethètaké to turn a lamp on (by switching the appliance).

jethit *or* mak jethit *repr* joints clicking when flexed.

jethot *var of* jethut.

jethothor, njethothor to remain motionless.

jethothot *var of* jethuthut.

jethung, njethung depressed, stunned with grief.

jéthung home, on base (children's games);

jéthungan 1 to play tag; 2 base, home, free place (in games).

jethut *or* mak jethut *repr* knuckles cracking;

njethut to pull one's fingers or toes to crack the joints;

njethuti to crack s.o.'s joints;

pating jethut *or* pating jrethut repeated knuckle-cracks.

jethuthut, njethuthut 1 feeling chilly; 2 scowling in anger.

jetmika *see* jatmika.

jétun *var of* jaétun.

jetung *var of* jethung.

jèwèr a tweak (ear);

njèwèr to tweak (s.o.'s ear).

ji one (*counting form, shtf of* siji); jiro 2 against 1; jitus 100 against 1.

jiarah *see* jiyarah.

jib, ngejibaké to rely on s.o. or s.t.

jibah, njibahaké to assign (a responsibility) to;

kejibah entrusted (with), assigned (to);

jejibahan responsibility to be entrusted.

jibar-jibur *see* jibur.

jibeg weighed down with sorrow or care.

jibeng *var of* jibeg.

jibil to fail; incompetent.

jibir pig's snout;

njibir 1 to have a broad flaring rim; 2 (of people) to have fleshy lips (*var of* jebèr).

jibleg, njibleg silent and motionless.

jibleng *cr* 1 to lose, be defeated; 2 less, inferior.

jiblèng *reg var of* jiblès.

jiblès (a)like, similar (to), exactly alike, just the same.

jiblok *reg* to fall, drop.

Jibrail, Jibril *var of* Jabarail.

jibris, njibris 1 to have thick lips; 2 *fig* talkative.

jibung, jibungan chatting together.

jibur, jibar-jibur to make a splashing

sound, to splash while bathing (*var of* jebar-jebur).

jibus, njibus *cr* (of a man) to have intercourse with.

jicing nicotine.

jidar *var of* jidhar.

jideng *cr* dead.

jidhar line;

njidhari to make lines;

jidharan 1 straight line; 2 ruler.

jidheg in a quandary (*var of* judheg).

jidhèt *cr* dead.

jidhor care; ora - to not care about, not pay any attention.

jidhul I *cr* penis;

njidhul *cr* to mate.

II *reg var of* jedhul.

jidhur *var of* jédhor.

jidik, jidikan *cr* homosexual partner.

jidun, njidun to pinch with the knuckles of the fingers.

jigal, jigalan *reg cr* servant.

jigang *var of* jégang.

jiglog to limp because one leg is shorter or because of an injured leg (*var of* dhéglog).

jiglok *reg* to fall, drop.

jiglug *var of* jiglog.

jigol *reg* to fall, drop.

jigrang too short (clothing).

jiguh *reg* in a difficult position, awkward, uncomfortable.

jigung I *reg* straight, straightforward.

II, njigung *reg* able to move easily due to having enough space.

jigur residue of coffee, dregs;

njigur to pour hot water into a cup which contains coffee dregs.

jih *coll* still, (even) now (*var of* isih).

jihad holy war.

jiit 'twenty-one', a game played with Chinese cards (*kertu cilik*).

jijal *reg var of* jajal.

jijik revolted, disgusted;

njijiki disgusting, sickening.

jik *coll* still, (even) now (*var of* isih).

jikik, njikik *reg* to take (*var of* jupuk).

jikuk *var of* jikik.

jikot *var of* jikik.

jikut *var of* jikik.

jil, njil limited to one.

jilak *or* njilak *reg* to deny. *See also* sélak.

jilat, njilat to lick (*var of* dilat).

jilep *intsfr of* 1 cold, excessively cold; 2 bland, insipid.

jilid volume;

njilid to bind;

jilidan 1 in volumes; 2 by the volume.

jilih, njilih to borrow (*reg var of* silih).

jiling the portion of the skull above the ears (*var of* jaling);

njiling to hit s.o. on the head;

kejilingan to get hit on the head.

jilma *var of* jalma.

jim I evil spirit, devil;

kajiman 1 realm of the evil spirits; 2 possessed by devils.

II time out! (in games: requested by extending the arm with a thumb up).

jimak sexual intercourse.

Jimakir name of the 8th (final) year in the windu cycle.

jimat charm, talisman, amulet.

Jimawal name of the 3rd year in the windu cycle.

jimbit *see* jémbit.

jimbrang, njimbrang *intsfr* bright, intensely light.

jimbun 1 very old; 2 dull-witted in one's old age.

jimleng *intsfr* very quiet.

jimpé exhausted, weak, powerless (arms, legs).

jimpit a small acount, a pinch;

njimpit *or* 1 to move a small thing with the tips of the fingers; 2 to take a pinch (of).

jimpo *reg* handkerchief.

jimprak, jimprak-jimprak to keep jumping with joy.

jimprek, njimprek enervated, without strength, depressed.

jimrah *reg* usual, ordinary.

jimuk, njimuk *coll* to take, put (*var of* **jupuk**).

jimur a venomous snake.

jin evil spirit, devil (*see also* **jim**).

jina *see* **jinah II**, **zina**.

jinada *lit* mouse.

jinah I ten (market term); **rong** - twenty.
II 1 adultery; 2 to commit adultery.

jinajah corpse, body (*var of* **jenasah**).

jinak *reg* tamed, domesticated (animals).

jinantra (large) machine-wheel, water-wheel.

jinasah *var of* **jenasah**.

jinasat *var of* **jenasah**.

jinawi *see* **loh**.

jindhel *var of* **jendhel**.

jindhul *reg* a small itchy swelling;
njindhul to get a slight bump, *e.g.* from insect bite. *See also* **bintul, jintul**.

jindik, njindik *cr* to perform a homosexual act (*var of* **jidik**).

jinem 1 quiet and withdrawn; 2 - **mrik** *lit* bedchamber;
jineman, kajineman 1 secret police; 2 watchman.

jing I (*or* **njing**) future, next (*inf kr for* **suk, bésuk**).
II *reg* (Yogya slang) (the one) which (*var of* **sing**).

jingga 1 colours ranging from orange to bright red; 2 red essence used for colouring foods.

jingglang I a certain shrub with sweetish leaves, which can be used as tea.
II, **njingglang** *intsfr* very bright.

jinggleng, njinggleng 1 concentrated; 2 to gaze, fix the eyes (on).

jinggrang *var of* **jingglang**.

jinggring, njinggring 1 long-stemmed (glass), high-heeled (shoes); 2 spindly, thin-looking.

jinggruk, njinggruk (to sit) motionless with knees drawn up and head lowered.

jingkat, njingkat 1 to be startled, to start from one's sleep; 2 to jump with surprise.

jingkeng painfully stiff (arms, legs, back);
jingkengan to wear a stiff-pointed headdress.

jingklak, jingklak-jingklak to keep jumping with joy.

jingklong *reg* a species of large mosquito.

jingkol *var of* **jéngkol**.

jingkrak *var of* **jingklak**.

jingkruk *var of* **jinggruk**.

jingkrung, njingkrung to lie curled up with the knees drawn up to the chest.

jinguk, njinguk to put, take away, *reg var of* **jupuk**.

jinis kind, sort, species.

jinja to get over s.t., learn one's lesson, never do it again.

jinjang unsteady, unstable;
jinjang api goyang *prov* pretending to trust.

jinjing, njinjing to carry (s.t. small);
njinjingaké to have s.t. carried for s.o.;
jinjingan 1 act of carrying s.t. small; 2 s.t. to be carried.

jinjit to stand on tiptoes; **sepatu** - high-heeled shoes.

jintel, njintel 1 (to sleep) curled up; 2 to shut o.s. up in one's room.

jinten cumin seed, caraway seed (various kinds).

jintul a small itchy swelling (*var of* **bintul**).

jipang I a prickly-skinned gourd-like vegetable used for soup.
II a variety of snack made from sticky rice (*var of* **bipang**).

jipik, njipik *reg* to take (*var of* **jupuk**).

jiplak, njiplak to copy, duplicate;

jiplakan a fake, a copy of the original.

jipuk *coll* to take (*var of* jupuk).

jipun a variety of tree.

jiput *reg var of* jupuk.

jirab, njirab to swarm (teem) with (flies, people *etc*).

jirak a children's game played with candlenuts.

jirap *see* jirab.

jirat, njirat *reg* to count.

jirèh *reg var of* jirih.

jirek *var of* jirak.

jiret snare, lasso;

njiret 1 to snare, rope (an animal); 2 to kill by strangulation;

kejiret 1 to get choked, strangled; 2 snared, tangled.

jirigèn jerrycan (*var of* jèrigèn).

jirih afraid, faint-hearted, cowardly.

jirim *reg* portion;

njirim-jirim to share, distribute, divide into separate parts.

jiring I *reg* with a sharp edge standing up.

II jiring section, segment (of fruit, *e.g.* durian). *See also* juring.

jirit *var of* jlirit.

jiro one (against) two (*shtc of* siji loro);

njiro (to fight) two against one.

jis *excl of revulsion.*

jisim corpse, cadaver.

jisin *var of* jisim.

jit I don't do that!; no!

II, jat-jit to wobble, move unsteadily.

jitah pus, fester, purulent discharge.

jithek dirty, greasy, messy.

jithet scar, cicatrice;

njithet to sew up a torn place.

jithok *reg* neck (*var of* githok).

jitu excellent, accurate, precise.

jitun, njitun to hurt s.o. by pinching.

jitus one (against) a hundred (*shtc of* siji satus); rate of equation 1:100;

njitus to fight a hundred against one.

jiwa 1 soul, spirit, life; 2 person (as a sta-

tistic); 3 state of mind; - raga *or* -ngga (*shtc of* jiwa angga) body and soul;

njiwani 1 to pervade, imbue s.t. with a certain spirit; 2 to inspire, be the soul of;

kajiwan pertaining to the mind, inner life;

sajiwa in the spirit of;

nganyut jiwa to commit suicide;

suduk jiwa *or* suduk salira to commit suicide by stabbing o.s.

jiwagra *lit* (tip of the) tongue.

jiwandana name of a classical verse.

jiwaretna name of a classical verse.

jiwatma *lit* soul, spirit.

jiwang one (for) each (*shtc of* siji éwang).

jiwel a pinch;

njiwel to pinch (*var of* ciwel).

jiwir *var of* jèwèr.

jiwit a pinch;

njiwit to pinch between the thumb and index finger;

jiniwit katut *prov* to share in a relative's sorrow or disgrace.

jiwo, njiwo *reg* to put, take away (*var of* jupuk).

jiwut *var of* dhiwut.

jiyad, njiyad to force, compel.

jiyarah pilgrimage, visit (*esp* to a holy grave);

njiyarah to make a pilgrimage, visit a holy grave.

jiyot *reg var of* jupuk.

jiyut *reg var of* jupuk.

jlabur, jlaburan *reg* dainty bit, titbit, refreshment.

jladrèn *see* jladri.

jladri I *reg* section of a Javanese-style house behind the front part. *See also* gadri.

II, jladrèn dough, batter.

jlag, jlag-jlig to come up frequently.

jlag-jlog to jump repeatedly.

jlager, pating jlager *pl* to stand upright (big and tall objects).

jlagur *var of* jlager.

jlagra I phlegm (*k.i. for* riyak).
II a stoneworker.

jlajah, njlajah *or* njlajahi 1 to travel around (to); 2 to try to use all things one by one.

jlajat a bad omen;
njlalati to signify a bad omen.

jlalat *repr* a quick glance;
njlalat beautifully wide and clear (eyes);
jlalatan *or* jlalat-jlalat to glance about.

jlamprah, njlamprah scattered over a wide area.

jlamprang I *reg var of* jlamprah.
II a wild gardenia tree.

jlamprong *var of* jamprong.

jlamun *reg* empty, vacant (market).

jlanah, njlanah *reg* spread everywhere.

jlang, jlang-jlangan to wander around, go aimlessly here and there.

jlanggrung, jlanggrung-jlanggrung tall and well-built (physique).

jlantah used cooking-oil (for reuse);
kejlantah to have a bad reputation.

jlanthir, njlanthir handsome, good-looking (young man).

jlaprat, njlaprat thick and curving upward at the ends (moustache).

jlarang a certain large squirrel.

jlarat, njlarat *reg* handsome, good-looking.

jlarèh streak, stripe;
njlarèh having or forming a streak;
jlorah-jlarèh striped, full of streaks.

jlarèt *var of* jlarèh.

jlarit thin line, narrow strip;
njlarit forming a slim line, slender crescent.

jlathek, njlathek dirty.

jlèbèk, njlèbèk *reg* dented and opened out.

jlèbèr, njlèbèr large and broad.

jlébrah, njlébrah large, broad.

jlebud, njlebud unkempt.

jlebuk *reg* a certain large but narrow woven bamboo basket.

jledhor bang! boom!;
pating jledhor *or* jledhar-jledhor *repr* repeated explosions.

jlèdeng *cr reg* dead.

jlèding *var of* jlèdeng.

jleg *or* mak jleg 1 *repr* a quick downward motion; 2 *repr* a quick change;
ngejlegi to drop onto s.t., jump on s.t.

jlèg *or* mak jlèg *repr* slamming.

jlegabid, njlegabid pleasant, deeply enjoyable.

jlegedhag, njlegedhag to have a fresh attractive appearance (*var of* jegedhag).

jlegédhag, njlegédhag 1 to fall on one's back; 2 to lean backward too far.

jlegedheg *var of* jlegedhag.

jlegid, njlegid exceedingly pleasurable.

jlegidheg, njlegidheg not willing to speak or to act (*var of* jegidheg).

jlegodhah, njlegodhah big, bulky, taking up lots of space.

jlegong *var of* jegong.

jlégor the (edible) leaves of the sweet potato plant.

jlégrang, jlégrang-jlégrang thin and tall.

jlegur *or* mak jlegur *repr* a splash;
jumlegur 1 to splash; 2 to boom.

jlegut, njlegut absorbed in activity.

jlekèthèk, njlekèthèk commonplace, prevalent.

jlekèthèt, njlekèthèt thick and heavy, curving upward (moustache, eyebrows).

jlekethut, njlekethut *or* pating jlekethut wrinkled (skin, cloth *etc*).

jlekithat, njlekithat small and slim with pointed ends.

jlekithit *var of* jlekithat.

jlémbrak, pating jlémbrak hanging down untidily (hair, overlong clothing).

jlempah, pating jlempah messy, in disorder.

315

jlemprah *var of* jlempah.

jlémprak, pating jlémprak scattered about untidily.

jlèng *or* mak jlèng *repr* metal clanking.

jlenggur *var of* jlegur.

jlenggut *var of* jlegut.

jlengut *reg var of* jlegut.

jlèntèh, *var of* jlèntrèh.

jlenter, njlenter languid, faint.

jlenthar, njlenthar pointing upward (long object) (*var of* jenthar).

jlenthir, njlenthir to stick up/out (short object) (*var of* jenthir).

jlenthot, njlenthot large, compact and muscular.

jlèntrèh clear, comprehensible; njlèntrèhaké to explain clearly.

jleprak, njleprak *or* pating jleprak 1 to point stiffly upward; 2 to spread (fan) out (of peacock's feathers).

jleprik, njleprik *or* pating jleprik to point stiffly upward (small objects) (*var of* jeprik).

jlèrèt *var of* jlarèh.

jlerit *pl form of* jerit.

jléthok, njléthoki to smear with mud or s.t. soft.

jlèwèh, jlèwèhan 1 an opening with the edges turned back; 2 a ditch.

jlèwèr, njlèwèr *or* jlèwèran *reg* to flow, drip.

jlig *or* mak jlig quick motion; jlag-jlig to move back and forth (*see also* ijlig).

jliger, pating jliger to hang around, mill around.

jligur *reg* residue (of coffee), dregs (*var of* jigur).

jligut *var of* jiger.

jlimet I, njlimet intricate, detailed. II, njlimet *intsfr* very dark.

jlimprak, pating jlimprak moving or dancing ponderously.

jling I *or* mak jling *repr* metal clanking (*var of* jlèng).

II *intsfr* all gone; entèk - completely finished.

jlinggring, njlinggring 1 to have a long and thin stem (glass); 2 short, showing the legs (clothing).

jliring *reg* areca palm leaf, used for smoking (*var of* dliring).

jlirit, njlirit forming a thin line.

jlitheng black, dark (skin).

jlithet *pl form of* jithet.

jlog *or* mak jlog a sudden descent; jlag-jlog to keep going up and down, jump repeatedly.

jlomprong, njlomprongaké to mislead, misdirect, misrepresent; kejlomprong to get lost, be misled.

jlonèt, njlonèt handsome, good-looking (young man).

jlong *or* mak jlong *repr* a long stride; jlang-jlong (to walk) with long strides.

jlonggrong, jlonggrong-jlonggrong tall and well-built (physique).

jlorah, jlorah-jlarèh striped, full of stripes. *See also* jlarèh.

jlujur I, njlujur to glide sinuously, straight (*var of* dlujur I); II, njlujuri to baste (a seam) (*var of* dlujur II); jlujuran 1 a basted seam; 2 (act of) basting.

jlug *or* mak jlug *repr* a thudding.

jlugur, njlugur to sit idle and motionless.

jlumat, njlumat *or* njlumati to mend with fine stitching.

jlumprit, pating jlumprit *pl* to cry out, shriek; jlumpritan to play game of tag.

jlungup, njlungupaké to cause s.o. to fall by pushing them from behind; kejlungup to fall forward, fall face down.

jlupak a small earthenware oil lamp.

jlurung *var of* dlurung.

jluwag, pating jluwag full of depressions.

jluweg *var of* jluwag.

jluwog *var of* jluwag.

jluwok *var of* jluwag.

jo green (*shtf of* ijo); **bang-jo** traffic lights.

joan meaning (*inf var of* ijoan).

jobag a variety of mortar made from a flat stone or clay, grinding-stone (*var of* jebag I).

jobar, njobari *reg* to dig out/up.

jobin 1 floor tile, tiled floor; 2 diamonds (playing-card suit);
jobinan 1 with a tiled floor; 2 forming a diagonal or diamond shape. *Also* jubin.

jobleg, njobleg *reg* silent and motionless.

joblig *cr reg* rogue, rascal.

joblog *var of* jobleg.

joblos stabbed, pierced, pricked;
njoblos to stab, pierce, prick;
joblosan stabbing, piercing, pricking.

jobong I *reg* a variety of woven bamboo basket.
II *reg cr* prostitute.
III *or* jobongan *reg* a small hollow in an inner room for storing s.t.

jodhang a litter for transporting foods to be distributed.

jodhas *var of* judhas.

jodhèh careless in keeping secrets;
njodhèhi 1 to disclose; 2 to catch s.o. in a secretive act.

jodhèr, kejodhèran to get caught in the act, be revealed/exposed.

jodhi, kajodhi *lit* to be defeated, killed by the enemy.

jodho 1 marriage partner; 2 the union of a mated pair; 3 the right match (for); to be a match, be a mate (to); 4 to come to an agreement about the price;
njodhoni to mate (two things);
njodhokaké 1 to match (people); 2 to give in marriage;
jejodhoan 1 to be paired; 2 to be married; 3 act of marrying;

jodhon the right match for;
sajodho 1 a pair; 2 twosome, couple.

jodhog *reg* 1 a small bench; 2 pedestal for an oil lamp.

jodhong 1 *reg* a variety of small woven bamboo basket; 2 a small storage shed *esp* for rice.

jojo a certain climbing vine;
jojo-jojo itinerant peddler.

jojog, njojog to trot.

jojoh, njojoh to pierce with a sharp object, stab;
njojohi to stab s.t. repeatedly;
njojohaké to stab with a sharp object;
kejojoh to get stabbed.

jog I *or* mak jog *repr* a sudden arrival.
II (to add) an additional amount;
ngejog *or* ngejogi to add s.t. into;
ngejogaké to pour s.t. into;
kejogan 1 to get s.t. added to it; 2 *fig* to be invaded or descended upon;
jog-jogan hot drink in a teapot kept for adding refreshment.

jogah a variety of hide-and-seek.

jogan floor.

jogang, njogangi to dig a hole in the ground (*var of* jugang);
jogangan a hole in the ground.

jogèd *ng*, *kr*, beksa *k.i.* the classical Javanese dance (an art form accompanied by gamelan music);
njogèd to dance, to perform a dance;
njogèdi to dance to gamelan accompaniment;
njogèdaké to dance a certain kind of dance;
jogèdan *or* jejogèdan to dance up and down, jump with joy.

joglo a type of roof construction (high, resting on four pillars) covering the pendapa of a house, especially belonging to a man of high position.

joglog, njoglog to sit idly.

jogol, njogol to wrestle by holding each other's hands.

jogrog *var of* joglog.

jogros *var of* joglog.

joh *coll* don't (*var of* aja).

johan a variety of dove which is tamed as a pet. *Also* jowan.

johar I a certain shade tree with tiny luxuriant leaves.

II the planet Venus.

jok *var of* joh.

joki jockey. *Also* jongki.

jol *or* mak jol *repr* a sudden appearing.

jola, njola to jump with surprise, give a start.

joli palanquin.

jolok within reach, close by.

jolor, njolor to sway, move sinuously.

joluk *reg var of* juluk I.

jomblah *var of* jumlah.

jomblak, njomblak to jerk, be startled;
jomblak-jomblak to keep jumping with joy.

jomblang matchmaker.

jomblo 1 tainted, unsound, spoiled; 2 stupid, mentally defective.

jomblong *var of* domblong.

jombok low and often covered in water, swampy (field).

jombor *var of* jombok.

jombrèt *var of* jombrit.

jombrit to take a break during a game.

jombros, njombros dirty and unkempt (hair, moustache).

jombrot 1 *reg* ramshackle, dilapidated; 2 bankrupt.

jomplak *var of* jomblak.

jomplang, njomplang to tip over, turn over, capsize.

jompo feeble with old age.

jompong I *reg* young leaf of the teak-tree.

II *reg* tuft of hair from the crown to the forehead.

III *reg* toothless and with sunken cheeks.

IV *reg* a bulging bone near a horse's ears.

jondhang *var of* jodhang.

jondhil, njondhil to jerk, jump;
njondhil-njondhil *or* njondhal-njondhil to keep jerking up and down.

jondhol *reg* the nightwatch in the village.

jonjang I punishment by cutting arms and legs;
njonjang to cut arms (as a punishment).

II crippled, lame, one leg shorter than the other;
njonjang *or* jonjangan 1 to walk with a limp; 2 (to walk) with a lopsided gait because the legs are of different lengths.

jonjit to limp (*var of* jonjang).

jonjong I oval, egg-shaped, disproportionately long.

II tall but inharmonious.

III, njonjong to spoil (a child).

jong I *lit* umbrella.

II a variety of boat;
ngejong to ride in a boat.

jonggla, njonggla *reg* to jump with surprise, start.

jonggol I, njonggol lumpy(-looking).

II collateral, guarantee;
njonggolaké to make s.t. collateral, use s.t. as collateral.

jonggrang, njonggrang *or* jonggrang-jonggrang tall and lean.

jonggring, jonggringsalaka realm of the deities.

jonggrok, njonggrok *cr* to sit (down).

jonggrong, jonggrong-jonggrong big, tall and well-built (physique).

jongkang, njongkang to tip over;
njongkangaké to tip s.t. over;
kejongkang overturned accidentally.

jongkèng, njongkèng 1 to raise s.t. with a lever; 2 *fig* to remove, unseat s.o. by force.

jongkèt *var of* jongkèng.

jongki *var of* joki.

jongkit, njongkit to skip, whip up (*var of* jungkit);

jongkat-jongkit to skip repeatedly.

jongkla, njongkla *reg* unsteady, restless, fidgety.

jongkok I, njongkok to squat.

II, njongkokaké to push s.o. forward so that they fall;

kejongkok to fall forward;

jongkok-jongkokan to push forward each other.

jongkong I soft sweet cake made from rice flour and coconut milk.

II *var of* jongkok.

jongkot, njongkot to sit doing nothing.

jongla, njongla to jump with surprise, start (*var of* jola).

jonglok *reg var of* jongla.

jongok I, njongok to lean forward, crane the neck to see.

II, njongokaké to push s.o. forward so that they fall (*var of* jongkok II).

jongor 1 *cr* mouth, snout; 2 *var of* jongok;

njongor *cr* thick and protruding (lips);

kejongor to fall forward on one's face.

jongos 1 restaurant waiter; 2 houseboy, servant in a foreign household.

jonthit, njonthit *reg* to raise the hind legs (horse).

jonthok, njonthok *reg* close by.

jontong, njontong to long, yearn.

jontrot a decoy;

njontrot to capture by decoying.

jor, ngejor to let s.o. have their own way;

ngejori to top s.t.;

ngejoraké to outdo on s.o.'s behalf;

kejoran to be topped;

jor-joran to vie with each other.

jorak, jorak-jarikan *reg* 1 scrap, rag; 2 patch, mend.

jorang, I jorang-jaringan *reg* peritoneum.

II, jejorangan *reg* insufficiently

respectful, reckless.

joré *reg* bad, ugly.

jorèt, jorètan *reg* (to play) hide-and-seek.

jori a medicinal plant.

jorna *reg* to let s.t. happen.

jorog I *reg* a gift to a prospective bride;

njorogi 1 to give s.t. to a prospective bride; 2 to give s.t. to s.o. before asking them for help;

II, njorogaké to push s.o. from behind;

jorog-jorogan to keep pushing each other from behind.

jorong I *var of* jongor, jorog.

II, jorongen *reg* to feel light in the head, about to collapse.

III, njorongi *reg* to pour into (cup, bowl);

jorongan *reg* gutter, canal;

jorong pancur *reg* bleeding profusely.

jos *or* mak jos *repr* hissing, sizzling.

jot *or* mak jot *repr* a start of surprise;

kejot startled, taken aback (*k.i. for* kagèt).

jothak, njothak to sever friendly relations;

jothakan not on speaking terms.

jothok *reg* to stay fast.

joto, menjoto to be swollen, swell up.

jotos a punch;

njotos to punch, hit;

njotosi to punch repeatedly;

jotos-jotosan to punch each other, box.

jowal, jowal-jawil to keep prodding at s.o. with the finger. *See* jawil.

jowan *var of* johan.

jowar *see* johar.

jrabang reddish (the colour of a certain cricket).

jrabing, pating jrabing swarming around/over.

jraga *reg* opium pipe.

jragan *reg* businessman, owner of a business (*shtf of* juragan).

jragem chestnut brown (colour of horse). *See also* **dragem**.

jrak settled. *See also* **anjrak**.

jrakah a variety of banyan tree with edible fruits.

jrambah 1 low wooden platform used as a seat; **2** floor.

jranggol, **njranggol** *or* **pating jranggol** *pl* standing and just watching.

jrangking *reg* dry, dried up/out;
   njrangking 1 to dry out in the sun; **2** to cut down on food in order to become thin; **3** to lessen s.o.'s portion.

jrangkong skeleton;
   jejrangkongan (animals) having a backbone.

jranthal *or* **mak jranthal** *repr* quick running;
   njranthal *or* **jumranthal** to scurry.

jras *or* **mak jras** *repr* cutting, slashing.

jrawil, **pating jrawil** *pl* to prod with fingers to get attention.

jrèjès, **njrèjès 1** to well up (in the eyes), to water; **2** to produce a puffing sound repeatedly.

jreg *var of* **jleg**.

jrèg *var of* **jèg**.

jrendhol, **pating jrendhol** full of lumps or swellings (*pl of* **jendhol**).

jréndhol *var of* **jrendhol**.

jrèng *or* **mak jrèng** *repr* coins clinking.

jréngkang *var of* **jengkang**.

jrengki *reg* to wish s.o. ill, bear a grudge. *See also* **drengki**.

jrengking, **pating jrengking** *pl* to lie prostrate with head down and bottom up.

jrep *or* **mak jrep** *repr* a sudden piercing, stabbing.

jrès *or* **mak jrès** *repr* a match striking;
   ngejrèsaké to strike a match.

jrèt *or* **mak jrèt 1** *repr* a whizzing sound; **2** *repr* emission of faeces in diarrhoea.

jrethot, **pating jrethot** repeated knuckle-cracks.

jrethut *var of* **jrethot**.

jrèwès, **jrèwèsan** *or* **pating jrèwès** to flow, ooze, trickle out.

jrih *lit* fear, afraid.

jriji *reg var of* **driji**.

jrijis, **njrijis** *reg* stingy, mean.

jrimet *var of* **jlimet**.

jrinjing *reg* slender, slim.

jring *reg* a variety of edible bean that can be eaten as a rice-accompanying dish. *See also* **jéngkol**.

jrithet *var of* **jlithet**.

jro *var of* **jero**.

jrobong *reg* a kiln for processing bricks, lime (*var of* **dobong II**).

jrog *or* **mak jrog** *repr* a heavy thud.

jrojog, **njrojog 1** to show up unexpectedly; **2** to pour forth copiously; **3** steep(ly pitched);
   jrojogan waterfall (*var of* **grojogan**).

jrojos, **njrojos** *or* **jrojosan** to pour forth, flow continuously (*var of* **drojos**).

jromah inside the house (*shtc of* **jero omah**).

jromblong *pl form of* **jomblong**.

jrong *reg* epidemic.

jrongan *reg* ravine, gorge.

jrongkong *var of* **jengkang**.

jronthol, **njronthol** to run, scurry (*var of* **jranthal**).

jros *or* **mak jros** *repr* chopping.

jrot *or* **mak jrot** *repr* a spurting sound.

jrowan *var of* **jeroan**. *See* **jero**.

jru *coll* person who performs a certain job (*var of* **juru**).

jrug *var of* **jrog**.

jrum *lit* slander;
   anjrum to slander s.o.

jrumat *var of* **jlumat**.

jrunjung, **njrunjung** to slide down, to plunge (into);
   kejrunjung to plunge accidentally.

jrungjung *var of* **jrunjung**.

jrungup *var of* **jlungup**.

jrunthul, **njrunthul** to scamper, scurry;
   jrunthal-jrunthul to scurry repeatedly.

jrus *var of* jros.

jrut *var of* jrot.

ju forward (march)! (*shtf of* maju).

jubad to fall apart, be damaged (*var of* bujad, bejad).

jubag *reg* feeble with old age.

jubah cassock.

jubak *reg* to come out exactly (profit and loss) (*var of* cubak).

jubar *reg var of* jugar.

jubeg *var of* judheg.

jubel crowded, jammed.

jubin *var of* jobin.

jublang, jublangan *reg* a pond dug for getting drinking water.

jubleg I, njubleg sloping steeply (*var of* juleg).

II *reg* square wooden pounding-block.

III, njubleg obstinate, stubborn.

jublig *reg* rogue, knave, rascal.

jublus, njublus to pierce, stab.

jubris, njubris (face) dirty(-looking).

jubriya haughty, arrogant. *See also* ujubriya.

jubung small cup;
njubung *or* njubungi 1 to wrap money and roll it up; 2 to put a sheet of woven bamboo on the edge of a basket to enlarge the container;
jubungan 1 money wrapped and rolled up; 2 a sheet of woven bamboo used as above.

jubur anus (*var of* dubur).

judhag deep ravine;
njudhag 1 to push s.o. off a cliff; 2 *fig* to bring harm to s.o.; 3 to evict; to ask s.o. to leave.

judhas irresolute, easily led, treacherous.

judheg in a quandary;
njudhegaké to cause s.o. to be in a quandary;
kejudhegan unable to cope.

judhel 1 (to have reached) the end (*see also* cuthel); 2 *var of* judheg.

judhi *reg* 1 to gamble; 2 gambling.

judhir, njudhir to have an overhanging upper lip (*var of* jedhir).

judhul title (of book *etc*).

jug *or* mak jug *repr* a sudden coming up;
jug lap *or* jug plencing to drop in briefly and go away.

juga, sajuga *lit* the only one.

jugag 1 short(ened), abbreviated; 2 *way* a song with shortened lyrics;
njugag to shorten, to break off, terminate.

jugah a term in the game played by children with certain fruits (béndha).

jugang, njugangi to dig a hole in the ground;
jugangan a hole dug in the ground.

jugar I to fail to materialise;
njugaraké to call off, forestall, prevent.

II to slide down, collapse;
njugar *or* njugari to collapse.

jugil iron crowbar, lever;
njugili to pry out with this tool.

jugrog, njugrog to sit motionless (*var of* jogrog).

jugrug to slide down, collapse;
njugrugi to bury s.t. under sliding earth;
kejugrugan to get buried;
jugrugan 1 earth that has slid; 2 (act of) earth sliding.

jugug 1 a dog's bark; 2 to bark (*var of* jegog).

jugul I a substitute, representative, stand-in;
njuguli to substitute, represent, act in place of or on behalf of. *See also* jagul.
II stupid.

jugur, njugur to sit idle and motionless.

juh, njuh *reg* able, capable.

jujag, jujagan I (to do) right away, (do) ahead of time.

II, jujagan not according to proper custom, simplified (*e.g.* celebration). *See also* bejujag.

III, **njujag** to go and stay at s.o. else's place;

jujagan a place to stay while away from home.

juju, njuju to have the mouth full of food.

jujug, njujug to go toward, head for;

njujugi to go s.w. frequently;

njujugaké to take s.o. s.w.;

jujugan 1 place frequently visited; **2** destination.

jujul I too short for the purpose.

II change (from payment).

III unable to stand for fear.

IV, njujul to (try to) overtake.

jujur 1 honest; **2** direct, straight (not crooked);

njujur (to go) straight across/through, take a direct route by way of.

jujut, njujut 1 to pull, jerk; **2** to attract, appeal to;

jujutan 1 a pull, tug; **2** that which is pulled.

jug or **mak jug** repr a sudden arriving.

juk I, njuk reg and then, after that (var of **banjur**).

II, njuk coll to ask for (var of **njaluk**).

jukok reg var of **jupuk**.

juku reg I think, I guess.

jukuk reg var of **jupuk**.

jukung canoe.

jukur reg swollen.

jukut I reg var of **jupuk**.

II lit **1** grass; **2** vegetables.

jul change (from payment) (shtf of **jujul**).

julalat, julalatan to glance about (var of **jlalat**).

juleg, njuleg sloping steeply.

julig cunning, sly.

juluk I or **jejuluk 1** official title; **2** bearing the title (of);

julukan nickname;

njuluki to apply a nickname to s.o.

II or **julukan** lit the hollow at the nape of the neck (also k.i. of **githok**).

III, njulukaké to move s.t. up higher. See also **penjuluk**.

julung destined for unnatural death.

jum, ngejum or **ngejumi 1** to put in good order; **2** to do one's hair; **3** to patch up a quarrel.

Jumadilakir 6th month of the Islamic calendar.

Jumadilawal 5th month of the Islamic calendar.

jumagar tiny and very young (of pig etc).

Jumahat Friday (var of **Jumuwah**).

jumantara lit sky.

jumanten emerald (subst kr for **jumerut**, **jamrut**).

jumara lit emerald.

jumblah total amount (var of **jumlah**).

jumblang, jumblang-jumbleng full of holes in the ground.

jumbleg, njumbleg to sit motionless;

sajeg jumbleg throughout (a lifetime).

jumbleng buried toilet tank.

jumblo var of **jomblo**.

jumbuh 1 similar, along the same lines; **2** in the category (of);

njumbuhaké to accord with;

jumbuhan similar to each other.

jumbul, njumbul to jerk, jump, start.

jumed, njumed reg to light, ignite (var of **sumed**).

jumeneng 1 to stand erect (k.i. for **ngadeg**); **2** to ascend the throne, be in power, rule (as king); (k.i. for **madeg**);

njumenengaké to appoint, raise to office;

jumenengan accession, installation.

jumerut emerald.

jumlah sum, amount, total.

jumleg var of **jumbleg**.

jumot reg var of **jupuk**.

jumpalik var of **jempalik**.

jumput 1 small pincers, tweezers; **2** a pinch of s.t. (var of **jimpit**);

njumput 1 to get a pinch of; **2** to pick up with thumb and forefinger;

jumputan 1 a scarf with white floral decoration processed by tying knots in it; 2 act of tying knots.

jumrojog *see* **jrojog**.

jumrunuh to keep asking without shame (*var of* **jermunuh**).

jumrut *var of* **jemrut**.

jumuk *coll* to take, put (*var of* **jupuk**).

Jumunten *subst kr for* **Jumuwah**.

Jumungah *var of* **Jumuwah**.

jumurung *see* **jurung**.

jumut *reg var of* **jupuk**.

Jumuwah Friday.

jun large earthenware water crock.

juné luckily (*shtf of* **tujuné**).

junjang *var of* **jonjang**.

junjung, njunjung 1 to lift, raise; 2 *fig* to exalt;
junjungan 1 a burden; 2 lifting, raising.

jung I land measure for ricefield (*ca* 7 acres).
II junk (Chinese boat).

junggel *reg var of* **jungkel**.

junggla *reg var of* **jola**.

junggring, junggringsalaka realm of the deities. *See also* **jonggring**.

jungjung *var of* **junjung**.

jungkang, njungkang *or* **njungkangaké** to lift and tilt s.t.

jungkar, jungkar-jungkir to keep turning upside down. *See also* **jungkir**.

jungkas *var of* **jungkat**.

jungkat *ng*, **serat** *kr*, **pethat** *k.i.*, comb;
njungkati to comb s.o.'s hair;
jungkatan to comb one's hair.

jungkel, njungkel to turn upside down, turn a somersault;
njungkelaké to cause s.t. to turn over;
kejungkel to fall head first.

jungkir, njungkir 1 upside down, bottom up; 2 to turn a somersault.

jungkit, njungkit to rise slightly;
njungkitaké to raise s.t. a bit.

jungklang I, **njungklang** to gallop (*reg var of* **congklang**);

njungklangaké to run (a horse) at a gallop.
II, **njungklang** sloping steeply.

jungkrah *var of* **dhungkrah**.

jungkrug *var of* **jugrug**.

jungkruk *var of* **dhungkluk**.

jungkung *var of* **jukung**.

jungkur, njungkur to slide down, collapse.

jungla *var of* **jola**.

jungok *reg var of* **jupuk**.

junguk *reg var of* **jupuk**.

jungut *or* **pajungutan** *lit* bedchamber, with bathing-place.

junthit, njunthit (of animals) to stand on the forelegs, raise the hind legs (*var of* **jonthit**).

juntrung 1 proper order; 2 aim, purpose;
ora ana juntrungé heading nowhere (discussion);
njuntrung to have a clear line, aim, purpose;
njuntrungaké to arrange clearly, clarify the purpose.

junub in a state of major ritual impurity (after sexual intercourse, childbirth *etc*), requiring major ablution.

junun free of troubles, leisurely.

jupot *var of* **jupuk**.

jupuk *ng*, **pendhet** *kr*, **pundhut** *k.i.*,
njupuk to take (away), fetch, pick up, go and get;
njupuki to take s.t. repeatedly;
njupukaké to take on behalf of s.o.;
jupukan *or* **panjupuk** act of taking.

jur I, **njur** and then, after that.
II, **ngejur** 1 to melt, liquefy; 2 to digest, reduce to fragments;
jur-juran (that which is) crushed, melted, dissolved.

jurag, njurag *reg* to chase, hunt.

juragan businessman, owner of a business, master.

jurak *var of* **jurag**.

juran *or* **ujuran** a share of one's profits. *See also* **ujur** II.

jurang ravine, gorge.

juré, njuré *reg* to repair a fishnet.

juri 1 jury; **2** umpire, referee;
njurèni to judge (a competition). *See also* **yuri**.

juring a section, segment of fruit (*e.g.* durian, pomelo);
njuring to separate into segments. *See also* **jiring**.

juris *reg* monkey.

jurit *lit* war, battle.

juru I person who performs a certain job; **- dang** person who cooks the rice; **- basa** interpreter; **- gambar** painter; **- gedhong** administrator of the possessions of high officials; **- kunci** cemetery caretaker; **- ladi** waiter; **- lélang** auctioner; **- ma(ng)sak** professional cook; **- mudhi** ship's helmsman; **- nujum** soothsayer, fortune-teller; **- pamisah** referee, arbiter; **- rawat** nurse; **- sabda** orator; **- sita** process server, bailiff; **- slamet** Saviour (Christian); **- tambang** ferry operator; **- tik** typist; **- tulis** secretary; **- warta** reporter; **- wicara** announcer, spokesman.
II, sajuru-juru *lit* to be in groups.

jurug mound;
njurug *or* **njurugi** to fill s.t in with earth, bury. *See also* **urug**.

juruh sweet thick syrup or sauce, made from coconut sugar.

jurung, njurungi *or* **njurungaké** *or* **jumurung** to agree (to s.t.), give one's consent to s.t.;
panjurung 1 financial contribution to a bereaved family to help with the expenses; **2** instigation, stimulus.

jurus 1 movements in martial arts; **2** certain hand movements in traditional self-defence (**pencak**).

jus section of the Quran.

justak *reg* (to tell) a lie, be untruthful.

jut I, *or* **mak jut 1** *repr* a jerking stop; **2** *repr* air flowing under pressure.

II, njut and then (*inf var of* **banjut, banjur**).

juthil, njuthil to steal, pick pockets. *See also* **util**.

juti *lit* bad, evil, harm.

jutu, menjutu lumpy, swollen.

juwadah glutinous rice snack (*var of* **jadah**).

juwa *reg* fried **mlinjo** eaten as a snack.

juwal, njuwal *reg* to sell.

juwara champion, number one, the best known;
kajuwara famed, renowned.

juwarèh, njuwarèhi boring to listen to.

juwas, juwas-juwas *reg* not willing to lead on.

juwata *var of* **jawata**.

juwawah, njuwawah wide open, badly torn.

juwawul, njuwawul *or* **pating juwawul** messy, unkempt.

juwawut millet.

juwèh 1 nosey, inquisitive; **2** garrulous, to keep on talking;
njuwèhi to keep after s.o., keep saying the same thing to.

juwet I blueberry (*var of* **dhuwet**).
II, kejuwetan always fidgeting, continually fussing with one's clothes or hair.

juwèwèh *var of* **juwèh**.

juwèwèk, njuwèwèk to have the lips drawn outward and downward (*var of* **cuwèwèk**).

juwi squid.

juwing, njuwing-juwing *or* **njejuwing** to mutilate, dismember.

juwis, njuwis thin-lipped.

juwit, njuwiti to mumble, mutter.

juwita *lit* girl, lady.

juwiwig, njuwiwig thin, fine (hair).

juwiwis *var of* **juwiwig**.

juwog *or* **juwog-juwog** fluttering loosely, waving.

juwot *reg var of* **jupuk**.

juwowog, njuwowog tangled, messy, unkempt.

juwowol, njuwowol *or* pating juwowol *pl* untidy, scattered, disarranged.

juwowos *var of* juwowog.

juwut *reg var of* jupuk.

jwalita *lit* shining, sparkling.

jwawut *var of* juwawut.

K

ka from (*shtf of* saka).

kaba-kaba *lit* 1 worried, uneasy; 2 not seriously.

kabar news, report, information;
kabar-kabar to send news about o.s.;
ngabari to inform, let s.o. know;
ngabaraké to report s.t., give news of;
pakabaran the news, the press.

kabat *or* kabatullah the Kaabah, the holiest building in Mecca.

kabayan a village official in charge of security.

kabèh *ng*, sedaya *kr*, (in) all, all (of them), every one, everything.

kabel cable.

kabélan keen on, crazy about (*esp* a certain food).

kabir mighty (of God); ngalam - macrocosm, the universe.

kabla *reg* 1 before (the time of); 2 (of a girl) married but not having intercourse.

kablak, ngablakaké to ruffle, flap the wings;
kekablak to ruffle the feathers, fluff out.

kabluk *reg* cassava flour.

kabogan *reg* to be obliged.

kabong fed up (with), sick and tired (of).

kabor gamelan melody *usu* played at the beginning of a shadow-play.

kabruk *or* mak kabruk 1 *repr* beating with the wings (of cockfighting); 2 *repr* falling;

ngabruki to attack (of birds);
kabrukan to beat each other with the wings. *See also* bruk.

kabul 1 1 acceptance (of bride by bridegroom, part of the marriage ceremony); 2 donga - prayer of dedication of food during ritual meal; 3 answered, granted (prayer, request);
ngabuli to cause to come true;
ngabulaké 1 to grant (a wish), fulfil a request; 2 to answer a prayer.
II *reg* spoiled (of raw rice that has been stored too long).

kabuli cooked rice served with mutton or goat curry.

kabur 1 to get blown away; 2 gone, vanished. *See* abur, bur.

kaburi 1 left behind; 2 last, past. *See also* buri.

kabut, kalang-kabut in a state of panic; panicky, chaotic, confused. *See* kalang II.

kabyak, kekabyak to dart about hurriedly and nervously.

kabyuk, ngabyukaké *reg* to throw s.t. in s.o.'s face. *See also* kapyuk.

kaca 1 1 glass; 2 mirror; - benggala large decorative wall mirror; *fig* model, an example held up to s.o.; - mata *or* - mripat glasses; - paèsan large decorative mirror; - praksana binoculars; microscope; -puri *lit* brick wall (*var of* cepuri); - suryakantha magnifying glass;
kaca-kaca to be glistened with tears;

ngaca to look in the mirror; *fig* to conduct self correction through introspection;

ngacani to hold the mirror in front of s.t.; to look at s.t. by holding a mirror in front of it;

kekaca to look at o.s. in the mirror.

II page;

ngacani to paginate.

kacak *or* **kacakan** to get one's turn.

kacang bean; peanut; - **brol** peanut; - **cina** peanut; - **lanjaran** climbing-beans; - **pendhem** peanut; - **polong** kidney bean; - **tanah** peanut;

ngacang to plant (a field) with beans/peanuts;

kacangan 1 a variety of goat with a puffed neck; 2 neck meat, *esp* of cattle; **pakacangan** land planted with beans/peanuts;

kacang mangsa ninggala lanjarané *prov* like father like son, a chip off the old block.

kacap *var of* **kacak**.

kacapa *lit* tortoise.

kacapi *see* **kecapi**.

kacapuri *lit* brick wall. *See also* **capuri**.

kacaryan spellbound, enchanted.

kaceb stuck (into). *See* **ceb**.

kacèk 1 different, dissimilar; 2 better, superior;

ngacèki to make s.t. different from s.t. else, stand out above others;

kinacèk regarded as an exception.

kacel cassava that does not become tender (as it should) when cooked.

kacèlu 1 attraction, appeal; 2 attracted; to long/yearn for;

kumacèlu *lit* to long deeply.

kacélung *reg* flower of the **dhadhap** tree.

kacer a thrush-like bird.

kaci I (*or* **mori kaci**) a fine white cotton fabric.

II *var of* **kacèk**.

III to be the first turn (of game).

kacik, kocak-kacik spilling out/over. *See also* **kocak**.

kacip shears for slicing betel nut;

ngacip to slice with this tool.

kacir I, **ngacir** to stick up (s.t. thin, spindly).

II, kocar-kacir 1 in a mess, in disorder/confusion; 2 scattered in little pieces.

kacor a whip;

ngacori to whip.

kacu handkerchief;

kacon square cloth.

kacubung I datura, a variety of poisonous plant with large trumpet-shaped flowers. *Also* **kecubung**.

II amethyst.

kacuk 1 *adr* young boy; 2 penis (of a boy).

kacung 1 lad, boy; 2 errand boy, houseboy.

kacur a variety of climbing plant with gourd-like fruit.

kacus, kacus-kacus (to walk) in an unseemly way.

kad limitation, restriction;

ngekad to limit, restrict.

kadang 1 relative; 2 sibling; - **kadéyan** relatives; - **katut** a relative by marriage only; - **konang** relatives who are acknowledged because they are rich or successful.

kadar 1 whatever is available; 2 fate, destiny;

kekadar to sleep out in the open;

sakadaré whatever one wishes.

kadas a state of ritual impurity, in which one cannot perform the **salat**.

kadé like, as (*reg var of* **kaya**).

kadèk I naturally, of course; that is why;

kadèkna so that's the reason!

II like (*reg var of* **kaya**).

III from (*reg var of* **saka**).

kadèn a piece of white cotton material used as a carrying cloth.

kader *var of* kadar.

kadéyan *see* kadang.

kadga *lit* kris.

kadgada *lit* quickly, before long.

kadhak, malangkadhak in a boastful or defiant attitude with hands on hips.

kadhal 1 garden lizard; 2 copper ornament on a riding horse;
kadhal mènèk a certain hairstyle;
ngadhal resembling a lizard's crawl;
kadhalan 1 a certain fish; 2 a certain bird; 3 a weed with edible roots; 4 lizard-like, in a squatting position.

kadhang now and then, sometimes, occasionally;
kadhang-kadheng *or* kadhang-kadhing *or* kadhang-kala sometimes, occasionally;
kadhang-kawis *kr for* kadhang-kala.

kadhar *var of* kadar.

kadhas a certain skin rash;
kadhasen to suffer from this rash;
kadhas kudhis ringworm. *See also* kudhis.

kadhaton royal palace.

kadhatun *var of* kadhaton.

kadhatwan *lit* royal palace (*var of* kedhaton).

kadhatyan *var of* kadhatwan.

kadhawa a green dove-like bird.

kadhelé *see* kedhelé.

kadheng *see* kadhang.

kadhèt cadet.

kadhi from (*reg var of* saka).

kadhil *reg* tusk of wild boar.

kadhing *or* kadhing-kala *reg var of* kadhang, kadhang-kala.

kadhingnaha *reg* anyone at all, whoever.

kadho-kadho *reg* hesitant, undecided, worried.

kadhung too late (of s.t. already past and irreversible);
wis kadhung it can't be helped.

kadi *lit* like, as;
kadi paran *or* kadi pundi *lit* how?

kadim eternal.

kadingalem to seek out compliments.

kadingarèn strange, surprising, out of the ordinary.

kadiparan *see* kadi.

kadipatèn *see* adipati.

kadipundi *see* kadi.

kadiran *reg* to boast of one's excellence or one's possessions.

kadis traditions relating words and deeds of the prophet Muhammad.

kados like, as (*kr for* kaya).

kadospatèn *subst kr for* kadipatèn.

kadospundi how? (*kr for* kepriyé).

kadud gunny sack, burlap sack.

kadug *var of* gadug.

kaduhung *lit* remorseful (*var of* keduwung).

kaduk to overdo;
kaduk ati béla tampa misunderstood;
kaduk wani kurang deduga foolhardy.

kadung not sufficient.

kadut *see* kadud.

kaduwung remorseful. *See also* keduwung.

kadya *lit* like, as.

kadyangga *lit* like, as.

kaé *ng*, punika *kr*, 1 that, that (remote) thing/place/time; 2 (with subjunctive) though it be…

kaèk-kaèk *or* koak-kaèk (to speak) loudly, aggressively, boastfully.

kaèt connection, link (*reg var of* kait).

kafir unbeliever, unbelieving.

kaga *lit* bird.

kagak *reg* no; not.

kagèt 1 startled, taken aback;
ngagètaké surprising, startling;
ngagèt-agèti (*or* ngegèt-gèti) to cause to startle;
kagètan jumpy, nervous; easy startled;
jambu kagèt common variety of rose-apple. *See* jambu.

kagok 1 (to feel) awkward, disagreeable; 2 (of speech) aberrant, accented, dialectal; 3 strange, extraordinary.

kagol to feel frustrated;
ngagolaké to frustrate, cause s.o. to feel helpless.

kagum I to awake screaming from a horrible dream.
II amazed, impressed;
ngagumi to find s.t. amazing;
ngagumaké 1 amazing, awe-inspiring; 2 to astound or impress s.o.

kagyat *lit* startled; taken aback.

kah *reg* that (*var of* **kaé**).

kahar *reg* two-wheeled horse-drawn cab.

kahwa *reg* coffee.

kaim *subst kr for* **kaum**.

kain 1 garment worn by ladies; 2 fabric, cloth.

kaing, kaing-kaing *repr* a dog yelping in pain.

kait connection, link;
ngait to catch on;
ngaitaké to form a connection (with, between); to have a verbal understanding (with).

kajang 1 roof of dried palm leaves; 2 (*or* **kajangsirah**) pillow (*k.i. for* **bantal**);
ngajang to make a roof of dried palm leaves.

kajar the white tuberous edible roots of a certain plant with itchy leaves.

kajat (to hold) a ceremonial event;
kajatan 1 to hold a celebration; 2 food provided for a celebration.

kajeng I wood, tree (*kr for* **kayu**).
II intention; wish (*kr for* **karep**).

kaji a person who has made the pilgrimage to Mecca; title used before the name of such a person.

kajo *reg* surprising, amazing.

kajog displeased with the turn of events.

kaju *see* **kajo**.

kak I *reg* older brother (*var of* **kang**).
II 1 *lit* true, real; 2 rights.

kaka *lit* older brother.

kakag (of meat) tough, hard to chew.

Also **kakal**.

kakah, ngakahi to take things as one's own possession.

kakaktuwak 1 cockatoo; 2 pincers, pliers with pincer shape (like the beak of cockatoo).

kakal *reg var of* **kakag**.

kakang *ng*, **kangmas**, **raka** *k.i.* 1 older brother; 2 *adr* husband; 3 'big brother', larger size of s.t.;
ngakang to treat or regard s.o. as one's own older brother;
kakangmas *lit* older brother.

kakap an edible sea fish.

kakas hard (*var of* **akas**).

kakbah the Kaabah (in Mecca).

kakèk grandfather;
kakèk-kakèk (having become) very old.

kakékat 1 truth, reality; 2 essence.

kaken stiff; awkward (*kr for* **kaku**).

kaki 1 old man; 2 grandfather; 3 *adr: affectionate, respectful for young man*;
kumaki cocky, overwise, insolent;
kaki-kaki very old;
kaki among good male spirit that protects human beings. *See also* **nini**.

kakiki true, real, authentic.

kakim judge, religious official who officiates at weddings.

kakkong having a long trunk and short legs (*contracted from* **tungkak cedhak bokong**).

kakrak torn (off);
ngakrakaké to tear (off).

kakrèk, kakrèkané damn it!

kakrok *var of* **kakrèk**.

kaksiyat *see* **kasiyat**.

kaku stiff, awkward;
ngaku to stiffen, become rigid;
ngakokaké 1 to stiffen s.t.; 2 to offend or irritate s.o.;
kakon atèn easily offended, unforgiving.

kakung male (*k.i. for* **lanang**).

kakus toilet.

kal I moment;

  sa-kal that very instant.

  II, kalé *reg* whereas, but actually the case is.

kala I 1 time, season; **2** last, past (*kr for* dhèk); **kalané** at the time of; **kala-kala** from time to time. *See also* **rikala**, **tatkala**.

  II bird-trapping noose on a long handle.

  III stinging animal; **-jengking** scorpion.

  IV (in names of demons) - **bancuring**, **-luwang**, - **pracik** *etc* names of ogres in the wayang stories; **Bathara** - *way* the God of Death, who is exorcised using **ruwatan** rituals.

kalabendhu a natural disaster sent as retribution.

kalacakra I *lit* sun.

  II certain lines on the palm of the hand. *See also* **rajah**.

kalah *ng*, **kawon** *kr*, **1** to lose, be defeated; **2** less, inferior to;

  ngalah to give in/up, yield;

  ngalahi to accommodate o.self or s.o. else;

  ngalahaké 1 to defeat, overcome; **2** to let/have s.o. win;

  ngalahan 1 to have the tendency to give up; **2** to put others first;

  kalahan 1 accommodating by nature; **2** likely to lose;

  kalah-menang whether one wins or loses.

kalak a certain flower, the wild **kenanga** (several varieties).

kalal legal, rightful; allowed, permitted.

kalam I *lit* word; **kalamullah** Word of God.

  II 1 reed pen; **2** penis (*k.i. for* **palanangan**).

kalamangga spider. *Also* **kemangga**.

kalamenjing Adam's apple.

kalamenta a certain kind of grass.

kalamentasan a kind of rust on a kris.

kalamtara *see* **kemlandhingan**.

kalamudheng number value of days used by thieves before stealing in order to be successful.

kalamun *see* **lamun**.

kalana *see* **klana**.

kalanjana an alfalfa-like grass used as cattle fodder.

kalang I a social group of unknown origin formerly specialising in woodworking in the service of royalty.

  II, kalangan 1 arena, circle; **2** realm; **ngalang 1** to surround, encircle; **2** to detour around s.t.;

  kalang-kabut confused, chaotic, panicky. *See also* **kabut**.

kalantara *var of* **kalamtara**.

kalap 1 carried off by an evil spirit; **2** to be beside o.s. with anger. *See also* **alap**.

kalar, ngalar to let out, pay out (rope *etc*).

kalas, kalas-kalas 1 indistinct, hazy; **2** spidery (handwriting).

kalasangka a couch trumpet.

kalawija *var of* **palawija**.

kalayan *lit* and, with.

kalbu *lit* heart, mind.

kaldhu broth, bouillon.

kalèk condition or limitation on a promise;

  ngalèk *or* **ngalèki** to set a time limit (on, for).

kalem calm.

kalèng tin;

  kalèngan tinned; in tins.

kalengka I *lit* stain, impurity.

  II *lit* renowned, famous.

kalèt *var of* **kelèt**.

kali *ng*, **lèpèn** *kr*, river;

  ngalèni to furnish with a channel;

  kalèn *or* **kalènan** ditch, small canal.

kalih 1 two (*kr for* **loro**); **2** and, with (*md for* **karo**);

ngalih or ngalih-ngalih two each;
kalihan or kaliyan and, with;
sekalihan or sekaliyan (together) as a couple; together with one's spouse.
kalika I lit tree bark. Also klika.
II reg (at a past time) when (var of nalika).
kalimah 1 utterance, statement; 2 the two parts of the Profession of Faith. See also klimah.
kalimasada way magical book having the power to resurrect a hero who has died before his time.
kaling I nosering for cattle.
II, kalingané it turned out that…
III, kolang-kaling the edible insides of the fruit of the areca palm.
kalinggamurda lit revered, received with respect.
kalinggawarsa 1 superannuated; 2 expired.
kalipah or kalipatullah 1 caliph; 2 caliphate.
kalir, sabarang kalir anything one wants;
sakaliré all, everything; of every kind.
kaliren to starve.
kalis 1 impervious, unreceptive; 2 immune, free from (misfortune).
kaliyan and, with (kr for karo).
kalkir, ngalkir to trace s.t. onto transparent paper placed over the original.
kalkul var of kalkun.
kalkun turkey.
kalo bamboo sieve.
kalok fame, renowned.
kaloka var of kalok.
kalong a certain large bat. See also long II.
kaloren shaking (with age, weakness, nerves).
kalpika lit ring (for finger).
kalung ng, kr, sangsangan k.i. necklace, garland;
ngalungi to place around the neck of;
ngalungaké to place around s.o.'s neck;

kalung usus expr to look attractive in anything one wears.
kalwat (niche in the wall of) a grave for a corpse.
kama 1 love, sexual passion; 2 semen.
kamajaya the God of Love.
kamal I salted duck eggs;
ngamal to salt (eggs).
II tamarind.
kamalagi lit tamarind.
kamandaka lit misleading, deceitful.
kamandalu waterpot.
kamandhalu see kamandalu.
kamangkara lit 1 impossible; 2 improbable, unlikely, uncommon.
kamantyan lit very, extremely.
kamar room; - bolah club rooms;
ngamar 1 to confine in a room; 2 to take a room and board, rent a room.
kamas older brother; respected male of equal status. See also mas, kangmas.
kamat exhortation to prayer (following the call).
kambala clothing material from goat hair.
kambang 1 to float; 2 fishing-rod float;
ngambang 1 to float; 2 to come to the surface;
ngambangaké to cause s.t. to float;
kumambang floating;
kambangan duck (kr for bèbèk).
kambé var of kambi.
kambèk var of kambi.
kambeng, kambengan I arena (kr for kalangan).
II, kambengan jungle grass (kr for alang-alang).
III a male classical dance movement.
kambi and, with.
kambil I coconut (var of krambil).
II saddle (k.i. for lapak, abah-abah II);
ngambili to saddle up (a horse).
kambing goat.
kamblok var of gamblok.
kambong a certain ocean fish.
kambu swarm (of bees).

kambuh (to have) relapse or recurrence of illness;
  ngambuhi to cause a worsening of (an illness that was on the mend);
  kambuhan prone to recurrent illness.

kambul, I ngambul *or* **ngambuli** to butt the ground with the horns.
  II, ngambul *or* **kambulan** to gather (*reg var of* **kumpul**).

kamdulilah thank God!

kami *lit* we, us.

kamijara *reg* citronella grass.

kamil perfect; **insan kamil** the perfect man.

kamisepuh *kr for* **kamituwa**. *See also* **sepuh** I.

kamituwa village elder, village official. *See also* **tuwa**.

kamla *lit* sour.

kamli kind of woollen fabric.

kampah *reg* to take a rest along the way.

kampak I band of robbers;
  ngampak to rob as a gang.
  II large axe;
  ngampak to chop with this axe.

kampanye campaign.

kampèh *var of* **kampah**.

kampèk I *reg* small rice barn.
  II *reg* pillow;
kampèkan cloth bag (for clothes).

kampemèn army encampment.

kamper mothballs.

kampi champion (*inf var of* **kampiyun**).

kampil, kampilan 1 a small purse woven from dried grass; **2** *reg kr* pillow.

kampita *lit* shaking; heavy disturbance.

kampiyun champion.

kamplèh *or* **kamplèh-kamplèh** loose and nearly detached.

kampleng a hit;
  ngampleng to hit s.o. in the face or on the head.

kamplèng, ngamplèng way of wearing a kris stuck in the belt at the side of the waist.

kamplong *reg* papaya.

kamplung 1 to fall into (water); **2** all used up.

kampo to take a rest along the way.

kampong *var of* **kampung**.

kampot measure for harvested rice plants: *ca* 37 kg.

kampreng, kampreng-kampreng to go visiting friends and relatives.

kampret, ngampret (of clothing) too small, tight-fitting.

kamprèt I 1 a certain small bat (flying animal); **2** *term of abuse*.
  II *var of* **kampret**.

kampuh I beaten, worsted.
  II ceremonial batik garment (*k.i. for* **dodot**).

kampul, kampul-kampul *or* **kompal-kampul** to keep drifting or floating;
  ngampul *or* **kumampul** to float.

kampung 1 village; **2** urban quarter; **3** *or* **pakampungan** residential area for lower classes in town or city;
  ngampungi to behave in a crude boorish way;
  kampungan countrified, boorish.

kamsol camisole.

kamud, kamud-kamud (to eat) with the mouth stuffed.

kamus 1 soft leather; **2** belt (of satin, leather, with buckle).

kan 1 porcelain teapot; **2** covered enamel pitcher for cool boiled drinking water.

kana *ng*, **ngrika** *kr*, **1** (over) there, that (remote) place; **2** he, she, they; **3** go ahead, go on;
  (ing)kanané 1 (in) another world; **2** (in) a dream;
  kana kéné (**ngrika ngriki** *kr*) here and there.

kanak *see* **anak**.

kanaka I *lit* gold.
  II nail, claw (*k.i. for* **kuku**).

kanal 1 canal; **2** channel.

kanan *lit* right (as opposed to left); starboard;

kanan-kéring *lit* left and right; all around.

kanang *lit* (one) who, (that) which.

kanas *reg* pineapple.

kanca friend; - **buri** (- **wingking** *kr*) wife; - **jaler** (*kr*) my husband; - **èstri** (*kr*) my wife;

nganca to make friends with;

ngancani to accompany s.o., keep s.o. company;

kekancan to associate (with).

kancana *lit* gold, golden.

kancil mouse deer; hero of many folk tales and expert in outwitting other animals; *fig* a clever individual.

kancing 1 lock, door lock; 2 button;

ngancing *or* **ngancingi** to lock s.t. (up);

ngancingaké to button (up);

kancingan closed/locked up;

kekancingan 1 to get locked out; 2 official resolution, order (of government);

kumancing locked (up);

kancing gelung a piece of sparkling jewelry worn in the hair.

kancit *lit* after a while.

kancuh *or* **kancuhan** friend, mate.

kandel thick, heavy;

ngandeli to make s.t. thicker;

ngandelaké to make s.t. thick (for s.o.);

kandel tipis thick and thin; the thickness (of).

kandha 1 *ng*, **criyos** *or* **sanjang** *kr*, **ngendika** *k.i.*, **matur** *k.a.* to say, tell, talk (to); 2 script of a wayang play;

ngandhani 1 to tell s.o. s.t.; 2 to give s.o. a talking-to, serious advice;

ngandhakaké to tell (about), report;

kandha-kandha to keep telling s.t. to s.o.;

kekandhan to talk; to converse.

kandhah *reg var of* **kandha**.

kandhang stable, stall, animal pen;

ngandhang to return to the stable;

ngandhangi to fence in a yard, pasture;

ngandhangaké to put (animals) into a pen.

kandhas 1 to reach the bottom (well, grave); 2 to run aground; 3 to the deepest point;

kandhasan a shallow place, shoal.

kandhat *reg* string used for lashing things together. *See also* **sandhat**.

kandheh *lit* overcome.

kandhèh cured of a bad habit.

kandhèk *reg var of* **kandhi**.

kandhi gunny sack, jute sack.

kandhil lamp, candle, lantern.

kandhidhat candidate.

kandhung *var of* **kandhut**.

kandhut, **ngandhut** 1 pregnant; 2 to contain, have within it;

kandhutan 1 womb, uterus; 2 what s.o. carries concealed (*e.g.* in the pocket, in the heart).

kandil *see* **kandhil**.

kang I 1 *ng*, **ingkang** *kr* one (who); that (which); 2 your/his/her/(relation).

II *adr* elder brother (*shtf of* **kakang**).

kangjeng title for royalty/highest nobility; - **gusti** his/your highness the prince; - **ratu** *adr* queen.

kangèh, **kongah-kangèhan** to moan in deep distress.

kangen to yearn for, miss, keep thinking of (absent loved ones);

ngangeni to cause yearning/longing;

kangen-kangenan to enjoy meeting again after a long absence.

kanggé for (*kr for* **kanggo**).

kanggeg to be interrupted, discontinued.

kanggek *see* **kanggeg**.

kanggo *ng*, **kanggé** *kr*, **kagem** *k.i.* 1 for; for the benefit/purpose of; 2 usable; in use; used.

kangih *var of* kangèh.

kangkam *lit* sword.

kangkang I a certain large crab.

II, ngangkang to sit or lie with the legs spread apart;

ngangkangi to claim or take things as one's own possession. *See also* pekangkang.

III *see* angkang.

kangkrang large red tree ant.

kangkung I a certain vegetable growing in swampy places.

II large frog or toad.

kangmas 1 older brother; 2 husband.

kangrang *var of* kangkrang.

kangsèk until, up to, as far as (*reg var of* kongsi).

kangsi I to collect, gather, unite;

kangsèn to have/make an agreement, appointment, date;

makangsi *lit* to band together.

II until, up to, as far as (*reg var of* kongsi).

kangsrah to touch *or* drag on the ground;

ngangsrahaké to drag s.t. on the ground.

kangwong 1 familiar, well known; 2 to feel at home;

kangwongan to have taken on certain characteristics. *See also* kawong.

kani *reg var of* kanil.

kaniganten *subst kr for* kanigara.

kanigara *see* kuluk.

kanil coconut cream, *i.e.* the thickened part of pressed coconut milk;

nganil to become s.t. like coconut cream.

kanin *lit* a wound; wounded.

kaning *var of* kanil.

kanjar *lit* knife used as a weapon.

kanjat not too bad, better than nothing.

kanjeng *see* kangjeng.

kanji I powdered starch (for cooking or laundry);

nganji *or* nganjèni to starch (fabric);

kanjèn starched.

II scared off, not going to do s.t. again.

kanjo left unfinished.

kantaka *lit* to faint.

kantar, kantar-kantar to blaze up;

makantar-kantar *lit* to blaze up.

kanté *reg* thread, yarn.

kanteb 1 to fall to a seated position heavily; 2 to have a piece of bad luck.

kantèk until, up to (*reg var of* nganti).

kanten, kantenan 1 that's why; 2 certain, definite (*kr for* karuhan, karuwan).

kantha I shape, form appearance; image, conception.

II *lit* companion (*var of* kanthi);

tanpa kantha tanpa kanthi *lit* alone in the world.

kantheng, ngantheng *or* kantheng-kantheng to keep waiting impatiently, for a long time.

kanthèt I small but smart.

II fastened together.

kanthi 1 companion; 2 with, accompanied by; in a certain manner;

nganthi 1 to take by the hand, lead; 2 to take along as a companion;

nganthèni 1 to accompany; 2 to give s.t. to be taken along;

nganthèkaké to have s.o. take s.t. along;

kekanthèn 1 to cooperate; 2 hand-in-hand;

panganthi companion, colleague.

kanthil I to hang (from), stick (to);

nganthili to hang s.t. on;

nganthilaké 1 to hang s.t.; 2 to have s.o. go along with (s.o.);

kanthil-kanthil *or* konthal-kanthil to dangle loosely;

kanthilan place to hang s.t.

II, nganthil to hold back dishonestly.

III a variety of flower (magnolia-like).

IV bench, bedstead, bier.

kanthing a certain type of small boat.

kanthong 1 bag, cloth sack; 2 *or* kanthongan pocket;

nganthong resembling a sack; **nganthongi** to put s.t. in the pocket.

kanti *ng*, **kantos** *kr*, (to wait) patiently.

kantil *var of* **kanthil**.

kantos *kr for* **kanti**.

kantra *lit* known far and wide.

kantrak to wilt (crops).

kantring, **kontrang-kantring** distracted, shattered.

kantrog shaken up, bounced around. *See also* **entrog**.

kantru, **kantru-kantru** to mope in sorrow.

kantu I to be filled too late, run out; **ngantu-antu** to wait for a long time. **II** *var of* **kantru**.

kantug *reg* within reach.

kantuk to get (*md for* **olèh**). *See also* **pikantuk**.

kantun left over; (left) behind (*kr for* **kari**).

kanya *lit* an unmarried girl. *See also* **kenya**.

kanyaka *var of* **kanya**.

kanyel (of cassava) when it does not become tender (as it should) when cooked.

kanyil, **konyal-kanyil** 1 restless, jittery; 2 flirtatious.

kanyut to get carried along/away. *See also* **anyut**.

kao *var of* **kau**.

kaol *var of* **kaul**.

kaop, to pay attention, care about; **ora -** indifferently, carelessly, insouciantly.

kaos I 1 stocking, sock; 2 singlet; **- oblong** T-shirt; 3 pressure lamp mantle. **II** *subst kr for* **kaji**.

kaot different (*var of* **béda**, **kacèk**).

kaoyah a sourish cake made from tart fruits. *Also* **koyah**.

kap hood (of carriage, **becak**).

kapa *or* **kekapa** saddle; **ngapani** to saddle (up) (a horse).

kapah I, **ngapah** *reg* to peel (coffee berries). **II**, **kapah-kapah** soaking wet, soggy, damp. *See also* **kopoh**.

kapak axe without a handle (carpenter's tool); **ngapak** to use such a tool.

kapal I ship. **II** horse (*kr for* **jaran**); **kapalan** *way* a scene with cavalry. **III** callus; calloused skin; **ngapal** *or* **kapalen** 1 suffering from calluses; 2 *coll* to have done s.t. so often you don't need to be told (pun on **apal**).

kapala chief, head, supervisor. *See also* **kepala**.

kapan I when; **dhèk -** (**kala punapa** *kr*) when? (past); **suk -** (**bénjing punapa** *kr*) when? (future); **kapan-kapan** any time, some time. **II** white cotton cloth, shroud; **ngapani** to wrap (a body) in a shroud.

kapang I to long, yearn (for) (*var of* **kangen**). **II**, **kapang-kapang** formal walking step with which female dancers enter the performing area (at court).

kapas cotton; cotton plant; **ngapas** 1 to apply cotton to; 2 to plant cotton.

kapcao Chinese teapot.

kapénak *see* **kepénak**.

kapénakan nephew, niece (*kr for* **keponakan**).

kaper a certain small butterfly.

kapes, **kapes-kapes** spongy, soft in texture.

kapi *lit* monkey.

kapila light red.

kapilah merchant who travels with a desert caravan.

kapindra *lit* king of the monkeys.

kaping 1 (number of) times (*kr for* **ping**); 2 *ordinal marker*.

kapinta *lit, var of* **kapita**.

kapinten neglected, abandoned (*kr for* **kapiran**).

kapir unbeliever, unbelieving.

kapiran neglected, abandoned.

kapita troubled, disturbed.

kaplak I very old;
  ngaplak to become very old.
  II, ngaplaki to train (a male pigeon) to come to one's hand by using a female pigeon;
  kaplakan a male pigeon being trained as above.

kapling parcel of land, land divided into lots.

kapluk, ngapluk to have lots of grey hair.

kapodhang golden oriole.

kapok to have learned one's lesson, be cured;
  ngapoki to cause to be cured;
  ngapokaké to teach s.o. a lesson;
  kapok lombok *expr* to never, ever do it again (from painful experience).

kaponakan nephew, niece (child of elder/ younger brother or sister). *See also* **ponakan, prunan, pulunan**.

kaprah usual, ordinary;
  ngaprahaké 1 to become usual; **2** to make s.t. ordinary. *See also* **salah**.

kaprès having the remains of food around one's mouth after eating. *See also* **gabrès**.

kapret *see* **kampret**.

kapri edible peapod.

kapsao *var of* **kapcao**.

kapsel non-Javanese ladies' hairstyle;
  kapselan to wear the hair in such a style.

kaptèn captain.

kapti *lit* a wish, desire;
  saiyeg saéka kapti *expr* working together with a common purpose.

kapuk kapok.

kapul *reg* fibre rope.

kapulaga cardamom.

kapung *reg* while one has the opportunity. *See also* **pumpung**.

kapur I udder.
  II 1 slaked lime; **2** chalk;
  ngapur to whitewash.
  III - Barus camphor.

kapurancang sharpened bamboo sticks arranged in a row on top of a wall. *See also* **apurancang**.

kapuranta, abang kapuranta orange (-coloured).

kaput rundown, unkempt-looking.

kapwa *lit* all, one and all.

kapya *var of* **kapwa**.

kapyuk *or* **mak kapyuk** splash!;
  ngapyuk to sprinkle s.t. with (a liquid);
  ngapyukaké to spatter (liquid) onto.

kar map. *Also* **kart**.

kara I a certain climbing vine that produces flat oval nuts; the peanut-like product of this vine (many varieties).
  II, kara-kara hindrance, obstacle.

karabèn carbine rifle.

karabin *see* **karabèn**.

karag rice scraped from the bottom of the cooking pan, sun-dried, and fried as chips.

karah metal band, ring by which a blade is fixed to a handle.

karam forbidden, proscribed (*var of* **haram**).

karana *lit* reason, cause; because.

karandhang a variety of edible root.

karang I, - melok decorative flower headdress worn by a bride;
  ngarang 1 to weave together; **2** to compose, write (literature);
  ngarangaké to write s.t. for s.o.;
  karangan 1 - kembang garland; **2** article, piece of writing.
  II place, settled area, home; **- abang** devastated area; **- kitri** fruit-producing trees in a yard; **- kopèk** village that has no ricefields; **- ulu** pillow;

pekarangan dwelling, house and yard, compound;

ngarangulu to marry the widow of one's deceased brother.

III 1 coral, coral reef; **2** rock; **3** vein (of ore);

ngarang to become a rock.

IV *reg* why...! well...! it is to be expected that... **ngarang** to estimate, guess. *See also* **arang**.

karantèn quarantine;

ngarantèn to quarantine.

kararap *lit* a small gliding lizard. *See also* **klarap**.

karas I *reg* yard surrounding a house.

II niche in the wall of a grave for the corpse.

karat I carat.

II stain, rust;

ngarat *or* **karaten 1** rusty, corroded; **2** rusty and old; **3** bad, disgraced, blemished (of reputation).

karatala *lit* palm of the hand.

karaton royal palace, court. *See also* **kraton, ratu**.

karawistha ornamental border.

karbon carbon paper.

karcis 1 ticket; **2** visiting-card.

kardi *lit* work.

kardos *subst kr for* **kardi**.

kardhin curtain.

karé a dish of meat cooked in a spicy sauce, curry.

karebèn *ng*, **kajengipun** *kr*, **1** so that; **2** to let s.t. happen/go. *See also* **bèn**.

karèk left (over); (left) behind (*reg var of* **kari**).

karem 1 to take special pleasure in; **2** addicted to, to abandon o.s. to (a vice);

ngaremi to have a special fondness for;

kareman *or* **kekareman 1** s.t. one especially likes; **2** pleasure, enjoyment;

pakareman excessive fondness for s.t.

karep *ng*, **kajeng** *kr*, **karsa** *k.i.* wish, intention, purport;

ngarepi 1 to make an offer for, be willing to buy; **2** to be willing to do s.t., agree to;

ngarepaké 1 to want s.t.; **2** to want (a girl) as one's wife; **3** to convey (a meaning);

kekarepan wish; thing wanted/intended;

sakarepé whatever s.o. wants;

dudu karepé dhéwé *expr* not in command of o.s. *See also* **arep**.

karèt 1 rubber, rubber tree; **2** elastic.

karga I *lit* leather bag.

II *lit* kris.

kari *ng*, **kantun** *kr*, **1** left (over); **2** left (behind); **3** later, last;

ngari to walk at the back;

ngarèni to be at the end, to be the last one;

ngarèkaké to leave s.t. behind;

karèn *or* **kekarèn** what is left; leftovers;

karèn-karèn the very last one;

kari aran *or* **kari jeneng** *expr* dead (*i.e.* only the name remains);

karia slamet goodbye (to one staying behind). *Also* **kèri**.

karib close, intimate.

karing, kekaring to go out for some fresh air in the cool of the evening.

karit, korat-karit 1 in disorder, scattered, dislocated; **2** disorganised (financially);

ngorat-arit to scatter.

karmenaji chop, cutlet.

karna *lit* ear.

karni *var of* **karna**.

karo *ng*, **kaliyan** *kr*, **1** and; with; **2** compared with; **3** by (a person); **4** (to say/speak) to; **5** to, as, of, from *etc* (in certain expressions); **6** two; **7** 2nd period of the Javanese agricultural calendar;

karon asmara/jiwa/lulut/sih to make love with;

karo-karoné (**kalih-kalihipun** *kr*) both of them;

karo déné *or* **karo manèh** moreover, furthermore;

karo belah 150;

karo tengah 1½.

karoh *reg var of* **karuh**.

karongron *var of* **karongrong**.

karongrong *lit* to divert o.s. together, take pleasure together.

karsa 1 to want; to intend, be going to (do) (*k.i. for* **arep**); 2 will, be going to (do) (*k.i. for* **bakal**); 3 to be willing to; would like to (*k.i. for* **gelem**); 4 intention (*k.i. for* **karep**); 5 celebration (*k.i. for* **gawé**).

karsèt jewelry chain.

kart map.

karta *lit* welfare, well-being.

karti *var of* **karta**.

kartipraja *lit* service to the nation.

kartisampéka *lit* military strategy.

kartiyasa *lit* 1 famous; 2 skilful, superior.

kartika *lit* star.

karton cardboard.

kartu card, playing-cards (*var of* **kertu**).

karu, **ngaru** to cook (rice) by steaming it half done, removing it to a large bowl and pouring boiling water over it, then returning it to the steamer to finish cooking;

karon rice cooked as above;

pangaron wooden or earthen container used when cooking rice as above;

ngaru napung to have a lot of things to do.

karuh I, **mitra -**, **kekaruh** an acquaintance;

ngaruh to become acquainted with;

ngaruhaké 1 to introduce s.o.; 2 to restore to good terms.

II, **karuhan** (*pron as:* **karuwan**) 1 clear, plain; 2 certain, fixed;

ngaruhaké to seek clarity regarding s.t.;

ora karuh-karuhan unimaginable, beyond belief.

karuhun *lit* formerly; first.

karuk I various kinds of flower bud (**kapok** *etc*).

II *reg* dried rice, fried.

karun hidden treasure.

karuna *lit* sad, sorrow; to weep.

karung jute sack, gunny sack;

ngarungi to put into a sack;

karungan by the sack.

karuni *var of* **karuna**.

karunya *var of* **karuna**.

karut *reg* young corn.

karuwan *see* **karuh**.

karya *lit* 1 work, job, opus;

ngaryakaké 1 to rent out, use a possession as a means of earning money; 2 assign s.o. to;

kinarya *lit* to be used (for, as);

makarya (*lit*) to do (work);

pakaryan a job, work, trade.

kas I 1 money supply; 2 cashier's window; 3 treasury.

II wooden case.

III strengthening.

kasa 7th period of the Javanese agricultural calendar (22 June–2 August).

kasab I rough(-surfaced).

II a living, a job; 2 merchandise.

kasah fine woven mat.

kasak, **ngasak** *reg* to rub smoothly.

kasang pouch, kitbag.

kasapah I cassava.

II *lit* glans penis.

kasar coarse, rough, unrefined; **- alus** coarse and refined;

ngasari to treat roughly or harshly;

ngasaraké to roughen, coarsen s.t.;

kasaran of rough quality;

kasar-kasaran a coarse way or act.

kasat, **kasat mata** visible, in (plain) sight.

kascaryan *lit* amazed, astonished. *See also* **ascarya**.

kasdik to know in advance. *See also* sidik.

kasdu *lit* willing; to want.

kasèk until, up to (*reg var of* kongsi I).

kasèp too late;

ngasèpaké to cause to be late;

kasèp lalu wong meteng sesuwengan *prov* much too late (for s.t.).

kasèr *reg var of* kasèp.

kasi until, up to. *See also* kongsi I.

kasih compassion, sympathy;

ngasihi 1 to love; 2 to show favouritism to;

kasihan *or* kinasih beloved.

kasil to succeed; to produce results;

ngasilaké to produce s.t. as a result. *See also* asil.

kasingi a certain plant.

kasiyat 1 special quality or virtue, merit; 2 (power of) good; 3 peculiar property.

kaskarat poor, destitute.

kaskaya *lit* strong, powerful.

kasmala *lit* dirt, filth, impurity.

kaspa *var of* kaspé.

kaspé cassava.

kaspundi how? (*inf of* kadospundi).

kasrah to touch or drag on the ground (*var of* kangsrah).

kastawa *lit* gift or honour bestowed on one.

kastéla *reg* sweet potato.

kasti (to play) a certain game resembling baseball or softball.

kastil castle.

kastroli castor oil.

kasturi 1 musk, civet (used in perfumes); 2 a certain shrub, the seeds of which are pounded to produce a fragrant oil.

kasub *lit* renowned, widely known, famous.

kasud *see* kasut I and II.

kasuh *reg* unable to bear s.t. any longer. *See also* kesuh.

kasur mattress;

ngasuri to equip (a bed) with a mattress;

kasuran 1 seat cushion; 2 equipped with a mattress; 3 (to sleep) on a mattress.

kasut I sandal, slipper, shoe.

II, ngasut to shuffle (cards).

kasuwari cassowary.

kaswara *lit* famous.

kaswari *var of* kasuwari.

kaswasih *lit* inspiring pity.

kasyasih *var of* kaswasih.

kat *reg* from; - ngendi from where?

kata *lit* words, talking, speech.

katak I fruit of the gembili.

II beard of a wild pig.

katalika *lit* direct, immediate.

katam to have finished one's reading of the Quran;

ngatamaké to finish the reading of the Quran;

kataman a ceremony upon completion of reading of the Quran for the first time.

katang, katang-katang *or* kekatang a variety of grass.

katar, katar-katar to blaze up, burn brightly (*var of* kantar).

katawurag *lit* to disperse in all directions.

katbuta *lit* very angry.

katé 1 midget, dwarf, pygmy; 2 bantam chicken.

kateg *var of* katog.

katek *reg var of* katog.

katèl I a kind of kettle (*var of* kètèl).

II a certain large spider.

III 1 thick sole (of chicken, horse); 2 a bulging root at the top of an edible turnip.

IV, ngatèl *or* katèlen *reg* to keep staying s.w. (in the enjoyment of).

katéla *var of* ketéla, téla.

katelah *see* telah.

katelu 3rd period of the Javanese agricultural calendar. *See also* katiga.

katen like this/that (*shtf of* **mekaten**, *kr for* **mengkéné/mengkono**).

katèngong *lit* I, me, my.

katès papaya.

katga *see* **kadga**.

katgada *see* **kadgada**.

kathah much, many (*kr for* **akèh**).

kathak fish glue, isinglass;
kathaken *reg* dirty, greasy, filthy.

kathèk a shoot growing from the stem (bamboo, reed).

kathel, kathel-kathel too short (to be used).

kather, ngather soft, limp;
kather-kather to hang soft and limp.

kathik I an edible green pigeon-like bird.
II moreover; and at the same time.
III *excl of surprise, esp at s.t. contrary to one's expectations or wishes.*
IV intimate, trusted;
ngathik 1 to consider, or regard s.o. as a trusted friend; **2** to look after horses;
pakathik *or* **juru kathik** one who looks after horses.

kathil bench, bedstead, bier (*var of* **kanthil** IV).

kathing, kathing-kathing to carry in the outstretched hand.

kathir, kathir-kathir to squirm, wriggle (of long thin objects).

kathok *ng*, *kr*, **lancingan** *k.i.* shorts, underpants; - **monyèt** children's play-suit;
ngathok 1 to wear shorts/underpants only; **2** *fig* to flatter, fawn on;
ngathoki to put shorts/underpants on s.o.;
kathokan to wear shorts/underpants.

kathung I 1 to be lacking in, be deficient in; **2** without notion, stupid.
II 1, **ngathung** to stretch the hand out (*see also* **athung**); **2** empty-handed;
kathung-kathung to raise the hand.

kati *ng*, **katos** *kr*, catty: unit of weight equivalent to *ca* 617 grams;

ngatèni to weigh s.t. in catties;
katèn in catties;
katènan 1 in catties; **2** way of weighing in catties.

katib 1 a preacher at the mosque; **2** a mosque official.

katiba a certain tree.

katibabal *reg* a very young jackfruit.

katiga the 3rd period of the Javanese agricultural calendar; the dry season.

katigen *subst kr for* **katiga**.

katilampa a variety of tree.

katilayu a variety of tree.

katimaha a certain beautifully grained wood, used for making kris sheaths and walking sticks. *See also* **timaha**.

katimbel a variety of tree.

katimumul I maybug, may beetle.
II a skin disease that attacks the nails.

katimun cucumber. *See also* **timun**.

katir I unequal;
ngatir to do s.t. in an unbalanced way.
II outrigger; a boat with outriggers.
III leaf that grows on a fruit stalk.
IV *or* **katiran** a small stream leading to the ricefield.
V piece of honeycomb.

katirah, ngatirah *lit* to become red (of eyes).

katiyon *reg* indeed.

katog 1 (to) the utmost; (to) the limit *or* end; **2** to have one's fill (*see also* **kateg**);
ngatogaké 1 to exert o.s. to the limit; **2** to (do) to the fullest;
sakatogé as much as one wants;
katogna sabudimu do it with all your strength!
See also **tog**.

katok *reg* to appear, seem; to be seen, visible, in sight (*var of* **katon**).

Katolik Catholic.

katon *ng*, **katingal** *kr*, to appear, be seen, visible;
ngaton to appear; to put in an appearance;

ngatoni to appear as an apparition;
ngatonaké *or* ngatokaké to show, make a display of;
katoné it looks as if;
katonen *or* katon-katonen to see in the mind's eye.
See also ton.

katong *lit* king.

katoran, ngelak katoran perishing of thirst.

katos catty (*kr for* kati).

katrak *reg* to languish, wither.

katrek *see* katrak.

katrem to feel very much at home (s.w. or with s.o.).

katrol pulley;
ngatrol 1 to hoist by pulley; 2 to raise the level, help s.o. up;
katrolan s.t. hoisted by a pulley.

katu a certain shrub with edible leaves (used as a vegetable) and berries.

katub I *lit* blown by the wind.
II (of fruits on a tree) abundant.

katul very fine rice chaff mixed with small broken grains.

katulistiwa the equator.

katun cotton (fabric).

katut to get carried along/away, get included; - angin swept away by the wind, *fig* to do what others are doing;
ngatut to go along with;
ngatutaké to cause s.t. to go along;
katutan 1 to carry s.t. along; 2 to take s.t. unintentionally;
swarga nunut neraka katut *prov, see* swarga.

kau 1 dowdy, slovenly; 2 quick-tempered.

kauk, kauk-kauk to shout repeatedly.

kaul (punagi *k.i.*) a vow, promise to do a certain act if one's hope is fulfilled;
ngauli to do s.t. in fulfilment of one's vow;
kaulan 1 celebration held in fulfilment of a vow; 2 to eat (delicious foods) with great enjoyment;
pakaulan place where a vow fulfilment celebration is held.

kaula *reg* I, me; we, us (*var of* kawula).

kaum 1 group, class, category (of people); 2 religious official who is in charge of the mosque;
kauman the area around the main mosque inhabited by strict Muslims.

kaur *reg* to have (enough) time (for doing s.t.).

Kawa Eve (first woman).

kawaca *lit* cuirass, coat of chain mail.

kawadaka *lit* to become known, get about (of secret).

kawagang able. *See also* kuwagang.

kawah I volcanic crater.
II amniotic fluid.

kawak old, antiquated;
kawakan 1 past its prime; 2 experienced, veteran.

kawal I, ngawal to guard, escort.
II *lit* blanket;
ngawali to cover s.o with a blanket.
III, ngawali to make s.t. in excess. *See also* awal.

kawalat 1 accursed, damned; 2 struck down by a calamity. *Also* kewalat, kuwalat; *see also* walat.

kawan *or* sekawan four (*kr for* papat).

kawanaring *reg* inside wall.

kawanda *lit* body. *See also* kuwanda.

kawasa powerful; in authority (*var of* kuwasa).

kawastara *var of* kawistara.

kawat 1 wire, cable; 2 telegram;
ngawat 1 to equip s.t. with wire; 2 to send a cable.

kawatgata *lit* accident, disaster; stricken by misfortune.

kawatir apprehensive, fearful (*var of* kuwatir).

kawatos *kr for* kawatir.

kawawa able (to), capable (of), strong enough (to) (*var of* kuwawa).

kawedaka *see* kawadaka.

kawèh *reg* strange.

kawekèn to feel inconvenience, at a loss, to have trouble.

kawel *reg* wild pig, boar.

kaweng *reg* handkerchief placed around s.o.'s neck;
ngawengi *or* ngawengaké to put s.t. around the neck.

kawèr, ngawèr to hang (down) loosely;
kawèr-kawèr hanging down, dangling.

kawès a certain freshwater fish.

kawestara *see* kawistara.

kawet 1 perineum; 2 a metal band or ring around s.t. that is cracked;
ngawet 1 to bite the lower lip in fury; 2 to put between the legs (*e.g.* tail).

kawi 1 a literary or archaic form of Javanese, used in classical poetry; 2 *lit* author, writer;
ngawi to compose classical verse;
kakawin (*or* kekawin) poetic epic written in Old Javanese;
kumawi-kawi to pretend that one is skilled in classical literature.

kawil, ngawil to prod s.o. with the fingers to get attention. *See also* jawil.

kawin to get married; - gantung marriage by proxy while apart;
ngawin *or* ngawini to marry s.o.;
ngawinaké 1 to marry s.o. off; 2 to mate an animal;
kawinan 1 wedding, marriage; 2 mating, breeding of animals.

kawindra *lit* a great court poet.

kawir, ngawir *or* kawir-kawir, kowar-kawir attached only loosely, nearly severed.

kawiraja *var of* kawindra.

kawis I name of a certain tree and its sour fruit.
II, kawis-kawis obstacle (*kr for* karakara).
III, pakawisan yard (*kr for* pakarangan).

kawistara *lit* obvious, plain to see.

kawiswara *var of* kawindra.

kawit 1 since, beginning from; 2 because;
ngawiti to begin s.t. *See also* awit, wiwit.

kawo *reg* coffee.

kawogan entrusted, assigned (to).

kawok, kowak-kawok to speak loudly and/or boastfully.

kawolu the 8th period of the Javanese agricultural calendar (4 February–1 March).

kawon (*kr for* kalah).

kawong 1 familiar, well known; 2 to feel at home;
kawongan having taken on certain characteristics. *See also* wong.

kawruh knowledge; lore;
ngawruhi to know; to see;
kawruhan to be seen. *See also* weruh.

kawud *lit* dispersed, blindly; scattered, strewn. *See also* awud.

kawuk I old, decrepit. *See also* kawak.
II a kind of iguana;
kawuk ora weruh slirané *prov* the pot calls the kettle black.

kawul sugar-palm fibres used for igniting fires; - kayu wood shavings used as kindling.

kawula 1 servant; 2 I, me (*formal var of* kula); 3 subject (of a monarch);
ngawula to serve, be in service (in a high status household);
ngawulani to be a servant to (a high status household);
pangawula service, being in service (as above);
kawula-Gusti servant-Lord relation (in Javanese mysticism);
kawula-warga family (*var of* kulawarga);
kawula-wisudha *lit* promotion of a servant to a higher rank.

kawung 1 sugar-palm leaf, used for cigarette wappers; 2 a certain batik pattern.

kawur I *reg* 1 lime; 2 calcium. *See also* kapur.

II *lit* dispersed, scattered.

kawuryan to appear, be seen. *See also* wuryan.

kawus, kapok - *reg* to be cured, learn one's lesson.

kawut-awut scattered, dispersed.

kaya I *ng*, kados *kr*, like, as; as if, as though;

kaya-kaya (it seems) as if;

dikaya to be treated as;

kaya déné (it seems) as though;

kaya ta such as;

kaya apa how... it is!

II 1 *reg* rich; 2 earnings; 3 support (given by husband to wife);

ngayani *or* kekaya to give money regularly (to one's wife) for household expenses.

kayah, ngayah to (do) arbitrarily, (do) as one likes.

kayal, kayalan 1 to work with difficulty; 2 to gather food (fruits) in a forest.

kayang I, *or* ngayang to do a back bend.

II, ngayang to throw/hurl at.

III, ngayang to do with all one's might, as much as possible;

sakayangé with all one's might.

kayas a kind of poison (containing bronze filings).

kayat life.

kayéka *lit* like that.

kayèki *lit* like this.

kayèku *lit* like that.

kayim religious official who is in charge of the mosque. *See also* kaum.

kaying, koyang-kayingan to scatter in panic. *See also* paying.

kayol *reg* chopper, cleaver.

kayon *see* kayu.

kayong *reg* like, as; as if, as though.

kayu *ng*, kajeng *kr*, 1 wood; 2 tree; - agaran firewood; - apu a certain floating plant; - cendhana sandalwood; - dang firewood; - daya wood used for construction; - glinggang dead wood, dead tree; - legi *or* - manis cinnamon; - obong firewood; - putih myrtle tree; - taun ironwood;

ngayu 1 resembling wood; 2 to grow into a tree;

kayon symbolic puppet used in wayang performances, with various functions (*also* gunungan);

kekayon trees, wooded area;

nggugat kayu aking *prov* to claim s.t. from s.o. who is already dead;

sèndhèn kayu aking *prov* to lean on a poor family;

wastra bedhah kayu pokah *idiom* seriously injured.

kayuh I unit of length for measuring fabric.

II, ngayuh to sell (merchandise) on commission;

kayuhan merchandise sold on commission.

III, ngayuh to reach for s.t. high above one's head.

IV, ngayuh to embrace.

V, ngayuh to paddle (a boat).

kayul *var of* kayol.

kayun *lit* a wish.

kayut, ngayutaké to connect, take in connection with;

kayutan 1 a connection; 2 in connection with.

kaywan *lit* trees, wooded area.

ké *reg* you (*shtf of* kowé).

keba woven straw material.

kebak full (of), filled (with); - menceb completely full;

ngebaki to fill.

kebar counting unit for flat things: sheet, leaf.

kébar to show off one's ability.

kebas, ngebasi to clean with a duster.

kebat quick; - kliwat hasty and careless.

kebaut *reg* to spend inadvertently. *See also* **baut**.

kebayak woman's blouse the front of which is pinned together, *usu* worn with a sarong.

kebayan messenger, errand-runner. *See also* **baya**.

kebek *reg* completely full;
ngebeki to fill completely.

keben a certain tree the wood of which used for construction.

kebes wet;
ngebes to get soaked.

kebet I, **ngebet** to have an urgent need to do s.t.
II, **kebet-kebet** to wave, flutter, flap.

kebèt leaf, sheet (of paper);
kebètan (in the form of) sheets.

kebiri *or* **kebirèn** castrated, spayed;
ngebiri to castrate, spay.

kebit, **kebat-kebit** worried, apprehensive, jittery.

keblak a kind of ghost in the form of a bat, detected from the flapping of its wings.

keblas *repr* a swift motion.

kéblat 1 the direction of Mecca (for prayer); 2 niche in mosque; 3 point of the compass;
ngéblat oriented toward.

kéblong *reg* to lose, be defeated.

kebluk I lazy, good-for-nothing;
ngebluk lazy, shiftless.
II, **ngebluk** to beat, whip;
keblukan (of eggs) beaten, scrambled.

kebo *ng*, **maésa** *kr* water buffalo; - **sapi** cattle, livestock;
keboan 1 to give rides to children on the back while crawling on hands and knees; 2 to play buffalo; a toy buffalo;
ngebo resembling a buffalo (referring to sluggish actions and constant eating);
ngebokaké to treat like an animal;
kebo kabotan sungu *prov* unable to care for one's many children;

kebo nusu gudèl *prov* parents learn from their children.

kebon 1 garden for vegetables or fruit trees (around, behind house); 2 area planted with a single crop; 3 plantation;
ngebonaké to oust (a wife) without divorcing her;
kebonan planted area.

kebos, **ngebosi** to blow fumes at/on;
kebosan to get blown on.

kébos *reg* to lose, be defeated (playing cards).

kebu *reg* deep basket of woven bamboo (*var of* **kembu**).

kebuk I lung.
II, **ngebuk** *or* **ngebuki** to slap, beat with the flat of the hand (s.t. soft, *e.g.* pillows).

kebul smoke, steam;
ngebuli to get smoke/steam on s.t.;
kumebul to give off smoke/steam;
kebul-kebul 1 steaming (hot food); 2 to have a smoke.

kebuli rice served with mutton or goat curry; rice prepared with spices.

kebur, **ngebur** to stir, mix thoroughly (food, cooking).

kébur *reg* to get blown away (*var of* **kabur**). *See also* **bur**, **abur**.

kebus wet, soaking wet (*var of* **kebes**). *See also* **klebus**.

kebut I 1 duster; 2 referee's signal flag; 3 s.t. for shooing insects;
ngebuti 1 to wave, shake (a cloth) at/on; 2 to swish away (insects); 3 to dust (furniture *etc*);
kebut-kebut *or* **kekebut** 1 to do the dusting; 2 to wave s.t. to keep insects away;
ngebutaké to wave s.t.
II complete(d); altogether.
III, **ngebut** to speed, drive too fast.

kebuya, **kebuya-buya** to be treated with contempt/scorn.

kebuyak *var of* kebuya.

kebyok a wet cloth for getting rid of insects;
ngebyok to wash by dipping;
ngebyoki 1 to dip repeatedly; 2 to wave a wet cloth at (*e.g.* mosquitoes);
ngebyokaké to wave s.t. at/on;
kebyokan the act or way of waving a cloth.

kecai a certain vegetable.

kecak *reg* smeared, messy.

kecam, ngecam to criticise, condemn;
kecaman criticism.

kecambah bean sprout;
ngecambah 1 to plant bean sprouts; 2 resembling bean sprouts.

kecambil *reg* coconut.

kecap 1 to say s.t.; 2 to smack the lips;
kumecap to utter a single word;
sakecap (to utter) a single word.

kécap soy sauce; dish prepared with soy sauce;
ngécap 1 to engage in empty talk; 2 to boast, brag about o.s.;
ngécapi 1 to put soy sauce on; 2 to stir, lay it on, kid.

kecapah *reg* cassava.

kecapi a stringed instrument.

kecas *see* kecos.

kécé I an oyster- or scallop-like shellfish.
II *reg* one-eyed; blind in one eye. *See also* pécé.

kecebuk, kecebuk-kecebuk, kecebak-kecebuk *repr* splashing through water.

kececeng, ngececeng to stiff, rigid;
pating kececeng *pl* stiffened, rigid (*usu* in death).

kecèh to splash around in water with one's bare feet;
kekecèh *or* kecah-kecèh to keep splashing;
kecèh dhuwit swimming in money, very rich.

kecèi *var of* kecai.

kecek cricket's sound; chirp;

ngecek (of cricket) to chirp.

kècèk I a certain dice game.
II, ngècèk to cook (herbs) in coconut oil: a preparation for treating skin rashes.

kecèl *reg* 1 a left-handed person; 2 awkward, inept.

kecémé a cucumber-like fruit. *See also* cémé.

kecemut, ngecemut to smile slightly/ secretly.

keceneng stiff and sore;
pating keceneng to have sore muscles.

kècèng *reg* (of fruit) stunted in growth.

keceput throughout; sedina - all day long.

kecer, ngeceri to squeeze juice over s.t. (*e.g.* from lemon);
kumecer to salivate (in anticipation of s.t. tasty).

kecèr I gamelan instrument resembling cymbals;
ngecèr to play the gamelan cymbals.
II (*or* kecèran) round flat sheath at the base of a growing coconut on the tree.

kècèr to fall and be scattered. *See also* ècèr.

kecet *reg* frequent; (to do) again and again.

kecèt Achilles tendon (*var of* kencèt).

kèci I mori - a variety of white cotton fabric.
II a variety of small ship.

kecik sawo-pit, used in children's games.

kecing I a sharp disagreeable odour.
II coward.

kecipak *var of* kecepak.

kecipik *var of* kecepik.

kecipir a leguminous plant that bears a peapod-like vegetable; also, the fruit of the pods. *See also* cipir.

kecit, ngecit to suck a nipple.

keclap *or* mak keclap *repr* a glimpse;
sakeclapan for a brief moment;
kumeclap to flash past.

kecoh 1 to spit; 2 spittle, saliva (*k.i. for* idu);
 kecohan *or* pakecohan cuspidor (*k.i. for* paidon).

kecombang a plant of the ginger family, used in some foods.

kecopak *repr* a splash;
 ngecopak to splash;
 kecopakan to splash around in water.

kecos, kecas-kecos *or* kecos-kecos to blurt out, pour forth, gush out.

kecowak *reg* 1 small saucer-shaped stone bowl for grinding spices; 2 saucer-like earthen platter (*var of* cowèk).

kecrak *repr* a slash with an axe.

kecras *repr* a slash with a sharp implement.

kecrèk 1 handcuffs; 2 a brass sounding instrument on which the puppet-master raps;
 ngecrèk 1 to handcuff s.o.; 2 to rap with the above instrument.

kecrès *or* mak kecrès *repr* a quick slash with a cutting instrument.

kècrèt *or* kècrèt-kècrèt to spill out bit by bit from a container.

kecrik *or* mak kecrik *repr* metal striking.

kecrit *repr* ejecting a small amount of liquid.

kecrok *or* mak kecrok *repr* a hoe striking the soil;
 ngecrok to work the surface of soil with a hoe;
 ngecroki to dig out with a hoe.

kecros *or* mak kecros *repr* a hard slash with a cutting implement.

kecruk *var of* kecrok.

kecu, biru kecu deep blue. *See also* biru.

kècu robber gang, band of thieves or bandits;
 ngècu (of a gang) to rob.

kecubuk, kecubak-kecubuk to make splashing sounds.

kecubung I a certain poisonous plant

with large trumpet-shaped flowers; thorn-apple.
 II amethyst.

kecuh, kecah-kecuh to keep spitting.

kecupuk, kecupak-kecupuk to splash around in water.

kecut sour;
 ngecutaké to make s.t. sour.

keda a large porcelain bowl or cup with lid.

kedabig *var of* gedabig.

kedabul *var of* gedabul.

kedad *reg* (of legs) stiff and sore from weariness.

kedah ought to, have to (*kr for* kudu).

kédah *reg* intention, plan;
 sakédah-kérah anything, any way at all.

kedal way of speaking, enunciation;
 ngedalaké to utter, pronounce (words).

kedarung-darung to go astray. *See also* darung.

kedebeg *var of* gedebeg.

kededer *reg* to tremble (with fear).

kedèkèng-dèkèng in constant difficulty or trouble.

kedèndèng, kedèndèng-kedèndèng affectedly (walking).

kedeng, kedengan *reg* to lie down, lie back.

keder stiff and strict.

kèder 1 to lose one's way; 2 squinting, cross-eyed. *See also* kèdher.

kedhabyak, kedhabyak-kedhabyak *or* pating kedhabyak loose, floppy (of an overlarge garment).

kedhah-kedhèh *var of* kedhah-kedhih.

kedhah-kedhih, ora kedhah-kedhih *reg* plain, not special, not fancy.

kedhakal, kedhakalan to move awkwardly or laboriously. *See also* kedhampal.

kedhali a swallow-like bird.

kedhampal, kedhampalan *or* kedhampal-kedhampal 1 to move awkwardly or laboriously; 2 to scramble, move hastily.

kedhana-kedhini boy-girl sibling combination.

kedhangkal *var of* kedhakal.

kedhang-kedhing *var of* kedhah-kedhih.

kedhangklik, pating kedhangklik hanging down, dangling;
kedhongklak-kedhangklik hanging down and swaying.

kedhangkrang, ngedhangkrang *or* kedhangkrangan to sit improperly in a place which elevates one above others.

kedhangsang *var of* gedhangsang.

kedhangsul soybean (*subst kr for* kedhelé).

kedhap I short interval of time (*root form: kr for* dhéla);
sekedhap a moment.
II, ngedhap apprehensive, afraid;
kumedhap frightened;
kedhapan timid, easily frightened.
III (*root form: k.i. for* icip), ngedhapi to take a taste of;
kedhapan food sampled.
IV, ngedhap (of kites) to take a dive, drop suddenly.
V to wink (*var of* kedhèp); - kilat *or* - liring a wink; to wink;
kumedhap to wink; (of stars) to sparkle, glitter.

kedhaplang, ngedhaplang to stretch the arms out to the sides;
pating kedhaplang *pl* with outstretched arms.

kedhar, kekedhar to go out for some fresh air.

kedharang-dharang in desperate straits, at the end of one's tether. *See* dharang.

kedhasih a cuckoo-like bird;
ngedhasih to produce the cry of such a bird.

kédhé left-handed;

ngédhé to use the left hand (on, for).

kedhébyah, kedhébyah-kedhébyah hanging in loose folds (of overlarge clothing).

kedhédhar-kedhèdhèr *see* kedhèdhèr.

kedhèdhèr, kedhèdhèran *or* kedhedhar-kedhèdhèr to sweep on the ground (of a garment that is too long).

kedhekes to assume a cross-legged sitting position;
ngedhekes to sit cross-legged before an exalted person, showing respect and humility.

kedhelé soybean;
ngedhelé soybean-shaped.

kedhemek, kedhemek-kedhemek to tiptoe, to walk slowly with short steps.

kedheng I *var of* kedeng.
II, kedhengé *reg* sometimes.

kèdheng *reg* cross-eyed.

kedhengklak to bend backward;
kedhengklèk *var of* kedhengklak.

kedhèngkrèng, ngedhèngkrèng to sit in a more elevated place than others (breach of etiquette).

kedhèp *ng, kr,* kejep *k.i.* a wink, a blink;
ngedhèp to wink/blink as a signal;
ngedhèpi to wink/blink at s.o. as a signal;
sakedhèp nétra a moment, the twinkling of an eye;
sakedhèpan (in) one wink/blink.

kèdhep, kèdhep-mantep steadfast, loyal.

kedhepek *or* mak kedhepek *repr* sitting in a slumped position;
ngedhepek to slump into a seat.

kedhepes seated cross-legged (*see also* kedhekes);
ngedhepes to seat o.s. in a cross-legged position.

kedheprek *var of* kedhepek.

kedher to vibrate;
ngedheraké to cause to vibrate.

kedhèr-kedhèr scattered about in disorder.

kèdher 1 to lose one's way; 2 cross-eyed (*var of* kèder).

kèdhèr, kekèdhèr to take a stroll, take a pleasure trip.

kedhésé to be snowed under, to lose, be defeated.

kedhi 1 an unfeminine woman; 2 an asexual person.

kedhih, kedhih-kedhih *var of* kedhah-kedhih.

kedhik a little, a few (*kr for* thithik).

kedhimik, kedhimik-kedhimik to walk with little, slow steps.

kedhindhing I a variety of bird.
II name of a certain tree and also its wood.

kedhingaha *reg* any… (at all), every…

kedhingkring, ngedhingkring (to sit) in a high position; (to sit) higher than s.o. else. *See also* gedhingkring.

kedhini *see* kedhana.

Kedhinten *subst kr for* Kedhiri.

kedhodhor, kedhodhor-kedhodhor to hang loosely and messily, drag on the ground (woman's kain).

kedhogan *var of* gedhogan.

kedhok I 1 mask, front; 2 pretense.
II, kedhokan compartment, plot (of ricefield).

kédhol *reg* to lose, be defeated.

kedhomblo chubby-cheeked.

kedhondhong a certain tree; its edible fruit.

kedhongdhong *see* kedondhong.

kedhongklak-kedhangklik *see* kedhangklik.

kedhongkrong to assume a hunched-over sitting position;
ngedhongkrong to sit hunched over.

kedhot *reg* tough (of leather).
kedhotan invulnerable (to bullets *etc*).

kédhot *reg* to lose, be defeated (*var of* kédhol).

kedhuk, ngedhuk to scoop (out);
ngedhuki to dig (into, up);

kedhukan a hole dug in the ground;
pangedhuk act of digging/scooping.

kedhul *reg* blunt, dull (blades, wits).

kedhung 1 eddy; 2 deep pool in a river;
ngedhung to form a deep pool.

kedhut thick and tough (of leather, fabric).

kedhuwel, ngedhuwel *or* kedhuwelan 1 to flow round and round, *e.g.* water running out of a bathtub; 2 to linger, dawdle, hang back;
kedhuwal-kedhuwel 1 to keep fussing with one's hair or clothing; 2 to express displeasure, grumble with dissatisfaction (*var of* keduwel).

kedhuweng *or* mak kedhuweng *repr* a sudden swerve;
ngedhuwengaké to turn toward s.t.

kedhuwet *var of* kedhuwel.

kedibal *var of* gedibal.

kediki *reg* like this.

kediku *reg* like that.

kedomblo *see* kedhomblo.

kedubang saliva redden by chewing betel. *See also* dubang.

kedug *reg* up to, as far as, having arrived at.

keduga *ng*, kedugi *kr* 1 ready, prepared (to do s.t.); 2 happy, pleased;
ngedugani to please.

keduk *reg* sugar-palm fibre. *See also* duk.

kédul *reg* south (*var of* kidul).

kedumel, ngedumel *or* kedumelan to grumble with dissatisfaction.

kedumplag *repr* drumbeats.

kedut muscular twitch (the location on the body predicts one's luck);
keduten to have a twitch.

keduwel, ngeduwel *or* keduwelan to grumble;
keduwal-keduwel 1 to keep fussing with one's hair or clothing; 2 to express displeasure, grumble with dissatisfaction.
See also kedhuwel.

keduwul *var of* keduwel.

keduwung remorseful;
  ngeduwungi to regret s.t.;
  keduwung nguntal wedhung *prov* to cry over spilt milk.

kègès to get slashed. *See also* gès.

kègi *reg* jealous.

kégok *var of* kagok.

kéguh, ora - *lit* unmoved, unchanged. *See also* iguh, kéngguh.

kégut *var of* kéguh.

kèh the number, amount (of);
  kèh-kèhé at the most;
  ngekèh-kèhi 1 to increase the number or amount of; 2 to cause to be too much;
  sakèhé all of;
  sakèh-kèhé 1 no matter how much/many; 2 as much/many as possible;
  kèh-thithiké *ng*, kathah kedhikipun *kr* a quantity, amount.
  See also akèh.

kejaba *ng*, kejawi *kr*, except (for), apart (from), besides (*see also* jaba);
  ngejabakaké to exclude.

kejalèr *reg* to meet, run into.

kejambar *lit* to get revealed, be disclosed.

kejanjur *reg* (having gone) too far; too late (now).

kèjèk, kekèjèk to writhe, squirm.

kejèl, kejèl-kejèl 1 to have spasms/convulsions; 2 to twitch in death throes (*var of* kejèt-kejèt).

kejem cruel, pitiless.

kejèn I ploughshare.
  II triangular roof area;
  ngejèn resembling the above.

kejeng (of arm, leg) stiffened because of damage to the joint.

kejep a wink, a blink; to blink (*k.i. for* kedhèp);
  kejepan eyelashes (*k.i. for* idep).

kejèp *var of* kedhèp.

kejer 1 (*or* kejer-kejer) hard (of crying); 2 *or* kekejer to flutter; 3 to hover in midair;

ngejeri to flutter around *or* hover over s.t.

kejèr, kejèr-kejèr to wink, blink (*var of* kejèp).

kejèt, kejèt-kejèt to twitch in death throes. *See also* kejèl, kojèl.

kejojor *var of* gejojor.

kejot startled, shocked (*reg k.i. for* kagèt).

keju stiff (from weariness of hands, legs).

kek *or* mak kek *repr* choking.

kèk I *var of* kek.
  II, ngekèki *coll* 1 to give; 2 to put s.t. into (*var of* wènèh);
  ngekèkaké to give s.t. to;
  kèk-kèkan 1 to give to each other; 2 a gift.
  III *reg* possession (*var of* duwèk).

kekah solid, strong (*kr for* kukuh).

kékah *or* kékahan offering for a child on the occasion of the first head shaving;
  ngékahi to hold the above ceremony for (a baby).

kekeb 1 rice cooker lid; 2 (metal, porcelain) shade (on lamp);
  ngekebi to put the lid on (a rice-cooking pot).

keked *see* keket.

kekel I (of laughing, coughing) hard, convulsive;
  ngekel to laugh hard;
  ngekelaké uproarious;
  kumekelen to keep laughing hard;
  kamikekelen to have a fit of laughing.
  II (of rice) well-done and sticky;
  ngekelaké to cook (rice) to the well-done, sticky stage.

kekep, ngekep *or* ngekepi to hug, embrace, clasp;
  kekep-kekepan to clasp each other;
  pangekep act of clasping.

keker firm, tightly bound, strongly built, muscular;
  ngeker to fence off, enclose, keep secret;
  kekeran s.t. kept hidden or secret;

pakekeran a place where s.t. is kept hidden, fenced off on all sides.

kèker binoculars; telescope;
ngèker to look through binoculars or a telescope.

kekes I chilly; chilled with emotion, *esp* fear; - miris shivering with fear.
II, ngekes to hide s.t.; to store.

keket 1 strict (rule, regulation); 2 firm, binding (contract *etc*);
ngeketi to tighten.

kèkèt I a soft green hairless caterpillar.
II firmly attached;
ngèkèt to stick tight, hold together firmly.

kékéyan *reg* peg-top.

kéklak to come off, become detached or separated.

kèklèk (of eyes) stinging from staying awake too long.

kèkrèk, ngèkrèk 1 to make a rasping sound; 2 to cut or tear s.t. apart/off;
ngèkrèki to cut (dry coconut leaves) off;
kèkrèkan s.t. cut off.

kèksi *lit* visible, in sight. *See also* èksi.

kékuk clumsy, inept (*var of* kikuk).

kèl *ng, kr,* tarab *k.i.* to menstruate.

kela, ngela to boil in water (vegetables);
kelan *or* ngelan (to make) vegetable soup.

kelab, kelab-kelab *or* kumelab to move in wave-like motions.

kelad *see* kelat.

kelag, kelagan *reg* and, with.

kelah I 1 complaint, a charge; to complain; 2 *or* ngelahaké to bring (a civil case) to court.
II, kelah-kelih, ora kelah-kelih nothing special, ordinary.

kelam metal clamp (*var of* kelèm).

kelamun *lit* if, when(ever). *See also* lamun.

kélan a variety of Chinese vegetable.

kelang (of wood) to become hard.

kélang *var of* kilang.

kelap, kelap-kelap to glisten, sparkle;
kumelap 1 to glitter; 2 to quake in panic.

kelap-kelip *see* kelip II.

kelar I *ng*, kuwawi *kr*, able, strong enough.
II finished, ready;
ngelaraké to finish s.t.

kelas class, grade, rank;
kelas-kelasan stratified; with many consecutive levels.

kelat I, kelatan a large rope for pulling a tree down;
ngelat to pull with such a rope.
II tight fitting, firmly attached (*var of* kelèt).
III, kelat-bau bracelet worn on the upper arm, as part of classical dance costume.

kelayan *lit* and, with. *Also* kalayan.

kelayatan, ora - *lit* without delay. *See also* layat.

kelé, kelé-kelé out of use, lying idle.

kélé I *reg* a small bamboo tube.
II *reg* a loss;
kélé-kélé limp and hopeless.

kelèd *reg* lazy, sluggish.

kèlèh *reg* to lose (*var of* kalah).

kelèk, kelèk-kelèk to keep chirping/squeaking.

kèlèk 1 armpit; 2 *or* kèlèkan underarm of a garment;
ngèlèki to force s.o. to smell one's armpit.

kelem I *or* ngelem to sink, to submerge, founder;
ngelemaké to immerse, sink.
II, keleman 1 steamed sweet cakes, of various types, made from rice flour, sugar, and coconut milk; 2 sweet potato (*subst kr for* ketéla); 3 crocodile (*subst kr for* baya).
III dull, lusterless.

kèlem to submerge, founder (*var of* kelemi).

kelèm a metal clamp; **ngelèm** to clamp.

keleng black;

keleng-keleng glossy black;

ngeleng *or* **ngelengi** to blacken the batik fabric;

kelengan batik fabric dyed with black colour.

kelèng *cr* ear;

ngelèngi *cr* to tell, advise;

kekelèng *see* **gentha**.

kelèp valve (in engine), key (in musical instrument).

kelèr, **kelèr-kelèr** dispersed, spread around.

kèlèr crate, used for measuring a quantity of sand.

kèles all gone; finished up. *See also* **iles**.

kelèt 1 tight-fitting; 2 emaciated; 3 firmly attached;

ngelèti 1 to skin, peel (*esp* a deer skin); 2 to paste s.t.

keli *var of* **kelik**.

kèli to get carried along on a current;

ngèli to allow o.s. to be carried on a current;

ngèlèkaké to set s.t. adrift on a current. *See also* **ili**.

kelik *adr* little boy.

kelim *or* **keliman** a hem;

ngelim to hem s.t.

kelimput 1 *lit* hidden from view; 2 clouded by passion. *See also* **limput**.

kelin *var of* **kelim**.

keling I pertaining to South India.

II a rivet;

ngeling to rivet s.t.;

kelingan s.t. riveted.

kelip I 5-cent coin (used during the colonial period).

II, **kelip-kelip** *or* **kelap-kelip** 1 to glitter, flicker, gleam; 2 to flutter;

kumelip 1 to flutter, flicker; 2 *fig* everything in the world, creatures.

kelir I 1 white screen used for shadow-play or cinema; 2 screen wall behind a gateway; **nganggo** - not straightforward;

ngeliraké to play puppets on a screen;

pakeliran outline of plot, scenario (in **wayang wong**).

II colour; **ngelir** to colour.

kelit I firmly attached (*var of* **kelèt**).

II *lit* to deceive.

kéloh, **kéloh-kéloh** *or* **kélah-kéloh** unsteady, weak and wobbly, without strength.

kelok famous, renowned (*var of* **kalok**).

kelon *or* **kelonan** lying next to each other (mother and child);

ngeloni to take (a baby, child) to bed with one to sleep.

kélong reduced (*reg var of* **kalong**). *See also* **long II**.

kelop I, **kelop-kelop** (of eyes) wide open and shining.

II to tally, match, fit; just right (*var of* **klop**).

III a round red signal at a railway gate.

kélor a certain tree the leaves of which are used in medicines;

kéloren *var of* **kaloren**.

kelos spool, reel; **benang** - thread wound on a spool;

ngelos to roll, reel s.t.;

kelosan (of thread) in spools.

kelot hard to defeat (of gamecock).

kélot, **kélat-kélot** to hang back, drag one's feet.

kelu I dumb, mute, speechless (from fright).

II slightly overripe, overdue for harvesting (rice).

III *see* **kelon**.

kèlu to be carried along (with). *See also* **èlu**.

kelud duster, whisk;

ngeludi to clean with the above.

keluh I bridle with nosering for cattle;

ngeluh *or* **ngeluhi** 1 to equip (cattle) with a bridle; 2 to lead (cattle).

II, **ngeluh** to complain;
ngeluhaké to complain about s.t.;
ngeluhan to have a tendency to complain.

keluk I 1 smoke, steam; **2** *reg* dust.
II *reg, var of* **kelok**.

kelun I a rolling, billowing motion;
ngelun 1 to roll on (like a wave); **2** to roll up, together; **3** to gather men (for battle); **4** to drag off everything for o.s.;
kumelun to billow upwards (smoke *etc*).
II **kelun alané** notorious.

keluron *ng, kr,* **terag** *k.i.* to have a miscarriage. *See also* **kluron**.

keluwarga *var of* **kulawarga**.

keluwas *reg* miscarriage.

kemadha a certain batik pattern used for edging a headcloth or breastcloth.

kemadhèh a certain parasitic plant.

kemadhéyan *var of* **kemadhèh**.

kemadhiyan *var of* **kemadhèh**.

kemadhuh a certain tree the leaves of which cause itching.

kemaga I *or* **kemagan** disappointed, let down.
II, **kemagan** a kind of small gamelan orchestra.

kemah, ngemah-emah to keep chewing on s.t. without swallowing it.

kémah tent.

kemaha *reg* to (do) intentionally.

kemalan *or* **kemalan cangkem** to talk big.

kemalo a resin used for lacquering kris sheaths.

kemamang a fire-drooling demon.

kemampo nearly ripe.

kemanak a brass percussion instrument in the shape of a banana used for accompanying a classical court dance performed by females (**bedhaya**).

kemandèn to suffer from a dangerous internal illness (such as inflammation of the abdomen, also puerperal fever). *See also* **mandi**.

kemandhah tour of duty (of soldier or employee);
ngemandhakaké to move (a soldier or an employee) to a new post.

kemandhang an echo (*var of* **kumandhang**);
ngemandhang to echo.

kemangga spider.

kemanggang suitable for roasting (chicken). *See* **panggang**.

kemangi a certain plant the leaves of which are usually eaten with rice and chili paste.

kemangrang (of coconuts) in the mature state when the fibres are reddish-brown like the red ant (**angrang**).

kemanjon disturbed and unable to get to sleep again.

kemantèn bride and/or bridegroom (*var of* **mantèn**).

kemaos *reg kr for* **kemadha**.

kémar donkey.

kemara *lit, var of* **kumara**.

kemarang I *reg* bee.
II container made from woven palm ribs.

kemaron I large earthenware pot (*reg var of* **pengaron**).
II *see* **maru**.

kemaruk happy with and proud of a new acquisition;
ngemaruki to have a voracious appetite after recovering from illness; *fig* to have an appetite for s.t.

kemarung thorn of a certain edible tuber.

kemat evil spell, black magic;
ngemat to put an evil spell (on).

kematal (of maize) nearly dry.

kematus *or* **kematus getih** tuberculosis.

kémawon just, only (*kr for* **baé**).

kemba insipid; without spirit.

kembang *ng,* **sekar** *kr,* flower, blossom;
(*or* **ngembang**) to bloom, blossom;

- **api** fireworks; - **asem** orange-yellow (colour of ginger cat); - **borèh** a certain flower for religious offerings; - **gula** lollipop; hard sweet; - **karang** a certain plant growing in a rock; - **lambé** a common topic of conversation; - **mimi** a variety of linen; - **paès** flower that produces no subsequent fruit (*e.g.* on a fruit tree in its first blooming); - **pala** mace (the spice); - **setaman** a bouquet of mixed varicoloured flowers for ceremonial use; - **telon** 1 grave offering of three kinds of flower (**kenanga, mawar** and **kanthil**); 2 tortoiseshell (colour of cat); - **waru** final glowing ember of an extinguished oil lamp;

ngembang 1 to be in bloom, blossom; 2 resembling a flower, having a flower design; 3 to develop, rise, expand;

ngembangi to decorate; to put a flower on;

ngembangaké to develop, expand;

kembangan 1 ornament; 2 floral decoration;

kekembangan flowers (of various kinds);

kembang-kembangan 1 various kinds of flowers; 2 flowers used decoratively: *fig* 1 embellishments, flourishes; 2 resembling a flower, toy flower.

kembar 1 twin; 2 in duplicate; 3 of similar or identical appearance; 4 match;

ngembari 1 to make s.t. like (s.t. else); 2 to stand up to; to match; 3 to challenge; to equal.

kembel *see* **embel**.

kemben *ng, kr,* (ka)**semekan** *k.i.* breastcloth (wrapped around the upper part of a woman's body).

kembeng I to rinse out the mouth (*k.i. for* **kemu**).

II *reg* chewing tobacco (*var for* **susur**).

III, **ngembeng** (water) filling a place and not flowing;

kembeng-kembeng (of eyes) to fill with tears.

kèmbèt *see* **èmbèt**.

kembeti *reg* wickerwork, basketwork.

kembik, kembik-kembik on the verge of tears.

kembong, ngembong *or* **kembong-kembong** filled with standing water.

kembroh soaking wet.

kembu *reg* basket with a lid. *See also* **sekembu**.

kembul *or* **kembulan** 1 (to eat) together; 2 (*or* **kembul ajang**) (to eat) from the same plate;

ngembuli 1 to join s.o. at a meal; to eat from s.o.'s plate; 2 to join battle.

kembung I a mackerel.

II to feel bloated; (of stomach) suffering from wind.

keméja shirt;

keméjan to wear a shirt.

kemel sticky, clammy.

kemèn *reg* let (it go).

kemendhak jewelled band encircling a kris just below the handle. *See also* **mendhak I**.

keméndho not yet properly ripe (coconut).

kemendir command;

ngemendir to command.

kemeng I stiff and sore from overexertion;

sakemengé with all one's strength.

II, **ngemeng** *reg* to withhold.

kemèng high-pitched (of voice).

kemèntèng a tree with edible sour fruit. *See also* **mèntèng**.

kemenyan incense. *See also* **menyan**.

kemerki chicken flea. *See also* **merki**.

keméron *var of* **kemaron**, *see* **maru**.

kemidhi 1 comedy; 2 theatre, stage play (Western style). *See also* **kumidhi**.

kemil I a propitious day according to traditional numerological calculation.

II, **ngemil** to hold (food) in the mouth for a long time;

ngemili to nibble at;

kemilan 1 food held in the mouth but not swallowed; 2 snacks; food, things to eat;

kemal-kemil to keep nibbling, eat all the time.

kemilon *reg* mirror (*var of* pangilon).

kemini to act wise (girl). *See also* nini.

kemiri 1 candlenut; candlenut tree; 2 ankle bone.

Kemis Thursday;

ngemis 1 to beg on a Thursday evening; 2 to beg;

ngemisi to beg from s.o.;

ngemisaké to beg for s.t.;

Kemisan weekly administrative reports made on a Thursday.

kemit I nightwatch; - bumi servants who take turns to keep watch in the Kraton and perform other duties;

ngemiti to guard s.w. at night;

kemitan 1 nightwatch; 2 to perform nightwatch duties.

II, kemitan *lit* protective amulet.

kemitir supervisor, foreman. *See also* kometir, kumetir.

kemladhéyan a certain parasitic plant, mistletoe.

kemlanda *or* kemlanda-landa European-minded; to act like a Dutchman/European. *See also* Landa.

kemlandhingan I a small shade tree; the edible pods of this tree.

II a large tree spider. *Also* mlandhingan.

kemlingking *intsfr* dry.

kemlondho 1 (of young cricket) not to have wings yet; 2 *fig* young and inexperienced. *See also* tlondho.

kemluhung *lit var of* kemluwung.

kemlungkung to act superior, be arrogant, enjoy praise.

kemluwung rather, preferable. *See also* luwung.

kemodhong I a certain type of black magic.

II gamelan instrument consisting of two metal bars over a sounding box, producing a gong-like sound when struck.

kemong a gamelan instrument (small gong).

kempal to gather (*kr for* kumpul).

kempang *reg* to have no appetite any more.

kempar I a certain edible ocean fish.

II, kempar-kempor to keep shouting everywhere (*var of* gembar-gembor).

kempas, I kempas-kempis *see* kempis.

II, kempas-kempos *see* kempos.

III, kempas-kempus *see* kempus.

kempèk *reg* rice barn.

kempel concentrated; adhering to one another.

kèmper *lit* to be blown by the wind.

kempès 1 deflated, flat (tyre *etc*); 2 sunken (of chest *etc*);

ngempès 1 to be(come) deflated; 2 to exhale forcibly, as when winded.

kempis, kempis-kempis *or* kempas-kempis to pant, to breathe heavily.

kempit, ngempit 1 to hold or carry under the arm or between the thighs; *fig* to protect, look after solicitously; 2 to sell (clothes, garments) on commission;

kempitan 1 (that which is) carried under the arm; 2 (that which is) sold on commission.

kemplang I a cake made from sticky rice flour and sugar.

II, ngemplang *or* ngemplangi to not pay for s.t., fail to pay what one owes.

III a hit (*var of* kampleng);

ngemplang to hit s.o. in the face or on the head.

IV, ngemplang to put s.t. in the sun to air or dry.

kemplé, kemplé-kemplé all alone.

kempleng 1 *reg* round cake; 2 *intsfr* round (*var of* kepleng).

kemplèng I *reg* flank;

ngemplèng to flank.

II a twanging sound.

III, kemplèngan (to wear) a headband part of which is stretched out and stiff.

IV var of kempling.

kemplès var of kempès.

kempling reg skilled, expert.

kemplong mallet for softening batik cloth;

ngemplong or ngemplongi to pound (fabric) to make it soft.

kemplung, kemplung-kemplung (of stomach) containing too much water.

kémpol ng, kr, wengkelan k.i. calf of the leg (also kéntol).

kempong I, or kempongan baby's dummy;

ngempong to suck a dummy.

II having sunken cheeks from old age;

kempong pérot (of people) very old.

kempor, ngempor 1 to talk much louder than necessary; 2 to chain-smoke;

kempar-kempor 1 to keep talking loudly; 2 to smoke continuously (var of kempas-kempus).

kempos to be(come) deflated;

ngempos (of cattle) to snort; to exhale forcibly;

kempos-kempos or kempas-kempos 1 to snuffle, snort; 2 to exhale forcibly, as when winded; 3 to smoke continuously (var of kempas-kempus).

kempot having sunken cheeks, from excessive thinness or from the toothlessness of old age.

kemprang or mak kemprang repr the sound of s.t. smashing of bits.

kemproh slovenly, dirty, untidy, unfastidious.

kemprong var of kemprung.

kempros boasting, big talk, bragging;

ngemprosi to brag to s.o.

kemprung I, ngemprung to run away.

II, kemprungan reg tapping bamboo tubes together rhythmically.

kempu reg round covered box for betel nut quid.

kempul small gong;

ngempul to play the above instrument.

kempung, kempung-kempung (of stomach) repr full of water.

kempus I big talk (var of kempros).

II, ngempus to blow on;

kempas-kempus 1 to keep blowing; 2 to smoke continuously.

kemput complete, from one end to the other, on all sides;

ngemputi to cover completely;

ngemputaké 1 to completely enclose; 2 to go all the way, work hard to finish the job;

sakemputé one's fill; to the limit or end.

kempyang I gamelan instrument consisting of the single inverted bronze bowl; 2 loud, noisy;

ngempyang to play the above instrument.

II, ngempyangi to join in (an activity).

kempyung harmonious sound effect produced by playing two tunes on a gamelan music instrument (gendèr) together;

ngempyung to produce a sound effect as above.

kemropok irritated, fed up. See also kropok II.

kemu I, ng, kr, kembeng k.i. to rinse out the mouth;

ngemoni to rinse out (the mouth);

ngemokaké to use s.t. as a mouthwash.

II, ngemu filled (with), containing (liquid); - waspa lit brimming with tears.

kemucing chicken-feather duster.

kemuda 1 lotus flower; 2 a certain leaf used in traditional medicines. Also kumuda.

kemudhi 1 rudder, helm; 2 steering wheel;

ngemudhèni to steer, guide, pilot.

kemukus I comet. *See* **lintang**.

II a variety of pepper, **cubeb**.

kemul *ng*, *kr*, **singeb** *k.i.* blanket; s.t. used as a blanket;

ngemuli to cover s.o. with a blanket;

ngemulaké to use s.t. for covering s.o. as a blanket;

kemulan to cover o.s. with a blanket.

kemumu 1 a variety of tree the leaves and roots of which are eaten; **2** a variety of seaweed.

kemunah medium, tool, means; planning to reach s.t.;

ngemunah to make a plan for materialising s.t.

kemuning a variety of tree the blossoms of which are yellowish and fragrant. *See also* **kuning**.

kemunjilan *reg* the youngest child.

kèn I to tell s.o. to do s.t (*rootform: kr for* **kon**).

II ancient title for male or female nobility.

kena *ng*, **kénging** *kr*, **1** hit, struck, affected by; **2** to hit the mark, succeed; **3** able (to be done); **4** can, allowed;

ngenani 1 about, connected with; **2** to hit, touch, reach;

ngenakaké 1 to permit, allow; **2** to subject to;

kakenan to be subjected to s.t. unpleasant;

kenan-kenanan to hit home, score a bull's-eye;

sakenané whatever is possible;

kena apa why?;

ora kena ora it must, will definitely…; obliged (to).

kenaka nail (*k.i. for* **kuku**).

kenal to know, be acquainted with;

ngenal to become acquainted with;

ngenali to get acquainted with; to know s.o.;

ngenalaké to introduce s.o.;

kenalan an acquaintance, a friend;

kenal-kenalan to get to know each other.

kenang, kenang apa I *coll* why? (*var of* **kena apa**).

II *reg* boy, little boy.

kenanga a certain flower used in grave offerings.

kenap a small table.

kenapa why? (*var of* **kena apa**).

kenari I a certain tree, also its almond-like nuts.

II canary.

III, **kenarèn** scent box.

kenas I *lit* monkey.

II *lit* deer.

kénas *lit* to go away.

kenca I 1 string for making a straight line; **2** outline.

II, **kencan** appointment; (*or* **kencanan**) to make an appointment or date.

kénca syrup, made from palm sugar and coconut milk (*var of* **kinca**).

kencana *lit* gold, golden;

kencanan resembling gold;

kencana wingka *expr* child whose parents regard him as superior.

kencang, ngencang to stretch and tie (rope *etc*) between two points.

kencar, kencar-kencar (of light) bright, intense.

kenceng 1 tight, without slack; **2** straight, direct; **3** strong;

ngenceng to go straight;

ngencengi *or* **ngencengaké** to tighten, to make tight;

pangenceng, pakenceng down payment, deposit.

kencèng cash (as opposed to credit).

kèncèng a large copper cooking pot for steaming foods.

kencès *reg* (of fruit) seedless.

kencèt I Achilles tendon.

II **1** askew, awry; **2** lame.

kenci name of one of the small playing-cards (*kertu cilik*).

kencing 1 urine; 2 to urinate; - **manis** diabetes.

kenclèng *or* **mak kenclèng** *repr* a metallic clink;
kumenclèng to clink.

kencling I *var of* **kenclèng**.
II *or* **kencling-kencling** clear, sparkling, gleaming (*var of* **kincling**).

kenclong *repr* a deep metallic clanking.

kenclung *var of* **kenclong**.

kencong, ngencong to pound.

kéncong, ngéncong to wear a garment with the bottom of the fold tucked into the sash.

kencot *reg* hungry.

kencrang *repr* metal clanking;
kumencrang to clank.

kencrèng cash (as opposed to credit) (*var of* **kencèng**).

kencring *repr* coins jingling;
ngencring 1 to clink (metal objects) (together); 2 to buy for cash;
kumencring to produce clinking sounds;
kencrang-kencring to keep clinking.

kencrung, ngencrung to play the guitar;
kencrung-kencrung *repr* playing the guitar.

kencur I greater galingale, a root crop resembling ginger, used as spice and medicine.
II *or* **kumencur** (of girl) still a virgin, still young and inexperienced, physically immature.

kendap-kendip shaky.

kendel courageous, bold;
ngendeli to defy;
ngendelaké to rely on;
ngendel-endelaké to steel o.s.;
kekendelan courage, bravery;
kekendelen overbold.

kèndel 1 to stop, halt (*kr for* **mandheg**); 2 to stop, discontinue (*kr for* **lèrèn**);

3 to become or remain quiet (*kr for* **meneng**).

kendhaga 1 cowries, shell money; 2 an oblong box for keeping valuables.

kendhagi *kr for* **kendhaga**.

kendhak 1 to give up, surrender; 2 to lose heart, get discouraged. *See also* **endhak**.

kendhal thick fat, grease;
ngendhal 1 to become thick; 2 covered with thick fat (soup).

kendhali horse's bit, bridle;
ngendhalèni 1 to equip (a horse) with a bit or bridle; 2 to restrain (one's desire *etc*); 3 to manage, lead (firm *etc*).

kendhang small gamelan drum covered with leather at each end and beaten with the palms of the hands and fingers;
ngendhang to play a drum;
ngendhangi to accompany gamelan orchestra by playing a drum;
kendhangan 1 playing the gamelan drum; 2 drumbeat; 3 to drum idly, for one's own amusement; - **dhengkul** to sit around taking it easy; - **kuping** ear drum;
pangendhang 1 gamelan drummer; 2 act or way of drumming.

kéndhang 1 to float (away); 2 driven away, chased off;
ngéndhangaké 1 to send s.o. into exile; 2 to set s.t. floating on the current.

kendangsul *subst kr for* **kendhali**.

kendharah, ngendharah *or* **pating kendharah** (of clothing) untidy, sloppy, too large and dragging on the ground.

kendharak, kendharakan a certain small heron.

kendharat a rope for tying up or leading cattle;
ngendharat to drag, pull;
ngendharati to tie up or lead (cattle) with a rope.
See also **pandharat**.

kendhat I a break, interruption; an end;

ora - ceaseless, incessant;

ngendhati to space, thin out.

II, ngendhat to commit suicide by hanging o.s.

kendhèh *reg var of* kendhih.

kendhek *var of* kendhak.

kendhela a certain large dragonfly.

kendhelang, kendhelang-kendhelong to move loosely. *See also* kendhelong.

kendhelong, ngendhelong loose, slack, sagging; *fig* low, dispirited.

kendheng I bowstring.

II a mountain range;

ngendheng resembling a mountain range, having a mountainous appearance;

kumendheng (of smoke, clouds) streaming, stretching.

kendherak-kendherek *see* kendherek.

kendhèrèh *var of* kendharah.

kendherek, ngendherek *or* kendherak-kendherek washed out, off-colour.

kendhèrèk, ngendhèrèkaké to spread the wings to court (of chicken);

pating kendhèrèk spread (of chicken wings).

kendhi *ng*, lantingan *kr*, earthenware water carafe with a spout.

kendhih to lose, get overpowered. *See also* endhih.

kendhil earthenware or copper utensil for cooking rice;

ngendhil resembling such a utensil.

kendhit cloth belt, sash;

ngendhit to carry in one's sash;

ngendhiti to put a sash on s.o.;

kendhitan to wear a sash;

kendhit mimang kadang déwa *expr* a person who escapes danger.

kendho I loose, slack;

ngendho to become loose/slack;

ngendhoni *or* ngendhokaké to make s.t. loose/slack;

kendho tapihé of loose morals (woman).

II *reg* flying squirrel.

kéndho a dish made with shredded coconut;

ngéndho to prepare such a dish.

kendhon (of villager) having a house and yard but no ricefield.

kendhor *var of* kendho.

kendhukur, ngendhukur 1 piled up; 2 *fig* boastful; to talk too much;

pating kendhukur *pl* in heaps, piles.

kendhurak a certain sea snail.

kendhurak-kendhuruk *see* kendhuruk.

kendhuri a ritual meal given for a special purpose;

kendhurèn *or* kendhurènan to hold such a meal.

kendhuruk, ngendhuruk 1 hanging in loose folds; 2 large, looming;

kendhurak-kendhuruk to keep looming.

kendip, kendap-kendip shaky.

kéndran I *reg* to get lost.

II realm of the deities. *See also* éndra, indra.

kéné *ng*, ngriki *kr*, 1 here, this place; 2 I, me; we, us;

ngéné like this;

ngènèkaké to treat s.t. in this way.

kenèh, kenèh-kenèh *reg* strange, very much out of the ordinary.

kenèk I an assistant to a driver. *See also* kenèt.

II *coll var of* kena.

kenèker marbles;

kenèkeran to play marbles. *Also* nèker.

kènel, kènel-kènel soft and springy (*e.g* like a marshmallow).

kènèn this, like this (*reg var of* ngéné).

kenèng *coll var of* kena;

kenèng apa *or* kenèng géné why?

kenep *var of* kenap.

kenèper clothes-peg.

kenès 1 flirtatious, coquettish; 2 talkative.

kenèt assistant to a driver (*var of* kenèk).

keng *coll* (one) who, (that) which (*var of* **ingkang**).

kéngang *reg* able, strong enough. *See also* **kongang**.

kengangrang large red tree ant (*var of* **ngangrang**).

kènges buzzing, soughing.

kèngès to get cut, gashed. *See also* **ènges I**.

kéngguh, ora - unmoved, unchanged.

kénging can, may; to touch, hit (*kr for* **kena**).

kéngis *lit* just visible, showing a little.

kèngkèn to have s.o. to do s.t. (*root form: kr for* **kongkon**).

kengkeng sturdy; stiff, rigid;
  ngengkengi to have/take a firm grasp on;
  me(r)kengkeng having a tight grip.

kèngkèng, kèngkèngan (of dog) howling. *See also* **klèngkèng II**.

kèngser I 1 a certain gamelan melody; **2** a certain movement in a female classical dance, to move sideways.
  II moved, shifted, pushed from its place, driven away; **wedhi -** sandbank, shifting sands;
  ngèngseraké 1 to shift, displace; **2** to dislocate; **3** *lit* to put to flight. *See also* **ingser**.

kèngsi until, up to (the point that) (*var of* **kongsi I**).

kèngsrèh to touch or drag on the ground;
  ngèngsrèhaké to drag s.t. on the ground.

kengulu *reg* pillow. *See also* **karangulu**.

keni I *lit, var of* **kena**.
  II, ngeni-eni to treat with much care.

kèni, kèni-kèni fine things (*var of* **pèni-pèni**).

kenikir I a certain plant the leaves of which are eaten as a vegetable.
  II the African marigold (smells of dogshit).

kenil *reg* to lose; defeated.

kening *reg* clear, pure; transparent.

kenini *var of* **kinine**.

kenir *reg* hinge.

kenit *reg* white arrack.

kènjek *lit* (easily) persuaded.

kènjèr *or* **kekènjèr 1** to walk around; **2** a certain classical dance movement *e.g.* to move around and form a circle.

kènji *reg* powdered starch (*var of* **kanji**).

kénjik, ora kénjik-kénjik not seen appearing for a long time.

kénjing *see* **ésuk**.

kenol tuber, root-crop.

kénol, kénol-kénol soft and springy.

kenong I gamelan instrument consisting of inverted bronze bowls; **- Japan** a type of large **kenong**;
  ngenong to play the above instrument;
  kenongan way of playing the above instrument.
  II a helping of rice;
  ngenongi to dish out rice;
  kenongan a helping of rice.

kenop switch, button.

kenot a rubber blackjack.

kéntar *lit* to get carried along by the current, to float away.

kentara *var of* **ketara**.

kéntas 1 (of ship) to reach the shore; **2** to fly away, get chased away. *See also* **entas**.

kéntasa *kr, reg* just, only (*var of* **kémawon**).

kéntarsa *var of* **kéntasa**.

kentawis *var of* **ketawis**.

kentèl a punch;
  ngentèl to punch, sock;
  kentèlan act of giving s.o. a knockout blow.

kènten left (*reg kr for* **kèri, kiri**).

kenthang I potato; **kenthang kimpulé** *expr* the facts of the matter.
  II, kenthang-kenthang, kenthangan to lie neglected in the open;

ngenthang-enthang *or* ngenthangaké to leave s.t. lying around outdoors, in the sun.

kekenthang to stand, lie in the open.

kenthel 1 thick, strong, solidified; 2 (of friendship) close, intimate; 3 - rembugé to have reached a decision;
ngentheli to make s.t. thicker *etc*;
ngenthelaké to thicken (strengthen *etc*) s.t.;
kenthelan thick part;
kekenthelan that which has been made thick *etc*.

kentheng 1 strong cord; 2 accurate, exact; 3 serious, earnest;
ngentheng to set plants in a straight line using a cord;
ngenthengi to mark into sections with cord;
kenthengan act of marking lines with cord.

kenthèng I container for catching the blood of slaughtered animals.
II, ngenthèng *or* ngenthèngi to hammer (dented metal) back into shape with a wooden mallet;
ngenthèngaké to have (dents) fixed as above;
kenthèngan 1 tools used for repairing dented metal; 2 dented metal to be fixed into shape.

kenthès cudgel;
ngenthès to hit s.o. with a cudgel.

kenthi a variety of pumpkin.

kenthil *see* enthil.

kenthing *repr* the sound of metallic objects striking each other.

kenthiwiri to keep going back and forth.

kenthiwul *reg var of* thiwul.

kenthong, kenthongan drum made of wood which is struck to sound an alarm;
ngenthongi to signal s.t. with the above.

See also penthong.

kenthos 1 a lump of hardened (edible) flesh inside an old coconut; 2 a salak pit;
ngenthos 1 to form such a lump; 2 to be about to sprout.

kenthug I *reg* firm, muscular, strong (*var of* kenthut).
II *reg* idiotic, foolish.

kenthul, ngenthul *or* kenthul-kenthul definite, certain.

kenthung, kenthung-kenthung *repr* drumbeats.

kenthut muscular, strong.

kenting *see* dhèndhèng.

kèntir to get carried along on a stream.

kéntol *ng, kr,* wengkelan *k.i.* calf of the leg (*var of* kémpol).

kentrung 1 tambourine-like musical instrument; 2 a recitation by wandering storytellers to the accompaniment of this instrument;
ngentrung *or* kentrungan to perform kentrung.

kéntun left (over); (left) behind (*subst kr for* kari).

kentut a fart; to fart (*var of* entut).

kenul *or* mak kenul *repr* a gentle plop.

kenup 1 collar button; 2 *var of* kenot.

kenur cord, string, fishing line.

kenut *var of* kenot.

kenya an unmarried virgin girl; Sang Ibu Kenya the Virgin Mother;
kenyapuri palace quarters for the princesses.

kenyak *reg* to step on s.t. muddy accidentally.

kenyal 1 (*or* kenyal-kenyal) tough, rubbery (of meat *etc*); 2 elastic (of fibres *etc*). See also kenyil.

kenyam a taste, impression;
ngenyam 1 to take a taste (of); 2 to have a taste (of) *i.e.* to experience;
kenyaman s.t. (foods) to be tasted.

kenyang *reg* full, sated.

kenyar ray, beam, light.

kenyas *or* mak kenyas *repr* a sudden touching of s.t. hot.

kenyèh, ngenyèh to chew;
kenyèh-kenyèh to chew on (s.t. tough);
sakenyèh *or* sakenyèhan a quid. *See also* kenyoh.

kenyer, kenyer-kenyer *or* kekenyer real (relatives); dear (friend).

kènyès, kènyès-kènyès brand new.

kenyil, kenyil-kenyil tough, rubbery in texture (*var of* kenyal).

kenyit, ngenyit to suck.

kenyoh *var of* kenyèh;
sakenyoh-kenyohé (to scold) to the utmost, to the bitter end.

kényok *reg* to lose, be defeated.

kenyol, kenyol-kenyol bouncy, soft and springy.

kenyos *reg* fermented cassava.

kenyul *var of* kenyol.

kenyung baby monkey (young of the kethèk).

kenyus *or* mak kenyus *repr* a burning sensation.

kenyut a sucking motion (as baby when sucking);
ngenyut to suck (a nipple);
kumenyut nice to suck, as if you would like to suck it; - atiné to be touched.

kepah, ngepah to chew and suck, then spit out the remains, *esp* sugarcane;
kepahan a chewed piece (of sugarcane).

kepala 1 chief, head, supervisor; 2 *lit* head;
ngepalani to have charge of.

kepalang *lit* only half, in-between.

kepama well-off, well cared for.

kepang surrounded; to surround (*root form: kr for* kepung).

képang 1 woven bamboo; 2 woven coconut leaves (for roofs, fences); 3 *reg* hair-plait;
ngépang to weave bamboo as one's livelihood;
ngépangi to furnish s.t. with woven bamboo work.

kepara somewhat, rather.

keparat 1 (you) villain!, (you) scoundrel! 2 damn it!

kepareng 1 to have permission; 2 to ask permission to leave;
ngeparengaké to give permission. *See also* pareng.

kepati 1 *or* kapati-pati exceedingly, greatly; 2 (of sleep) deep, sound. *See also* pati.

kepaung to stray from the straight and narrow.

kepaya *reg* papaya.

kepé *reg* let it be done!

kepéca *reg* comfortable, pleasant (*reg kr for* kepénak).

kepedhak I (*or* kepedhakan) *reg* to meet.
II a group of low-ranking court servants.

kepèh, ngepèh to chew on;
kepèhan s.t. to chew on.

kèpèh, kèpèh-kèpèh soaking wet.

kepèk 1 notes for cheating at an examination; 2 a small flat bag;
ngepèk to cheat at an examination;
ngepèki *or* ngepèkaké to copy from s.o.'s exam notes.

kèpèk I a young kemlandhingan fruit.
II 1 not yet filled (fruit); 2 flat-chested (girl).

kepel I 1 fist; 2 the amount of food taken in the cupped hands when eating;
ngepel 1 to make (the hand into) a fist; 2 (*or* ngepeli) to take (food) in the cupped hands.

kèpèl horse (*subst kr for* jaran).

kepénak *ng*, sekéca *kr*, dhangan *k.i.* pleasant, comfortable;

ngepénaki to make s.o. feel good;
sakepénaké as one pleases;
kepénaken to make too comfortable/pleasant.

kepénakan nephew, niece (*kr for* **keponakan**).

kèpèng ½-cent coin.

kepep covered with an airtight cover. *See also* **pep**.

keper I receipt, docket (of tax).
II door hinge.

kèper I twilled cloth.
II a certain freshwater fish.

kepès empty of its normal contents (*var of* **kempès**).

kepesa *var of* **kepeksa**. *See* **peksa**.

kepet a hand fan;
ngepeti to fan;
kepetan 1 fan-shaped; **2** to fan o.s.;
kekepet to use a fan.

kepèt *reg* thin, empty.

kèpèt I caudal fin; tail fin; **2** serrated ridges on a crocodile's tail;
kèpèt-kèpèt to wag (the tail).
II *see* **kopèt**.

kèpi to dream about s.t. or s.o.

kepik I a small basket.
II a certain malodorous flying beetle.

keping thin.

kepis fishing basket.

kepithing edible saltwater crab.

kepiyé how? (*var of* **kepriyé**).

keplak a slap on the head;
ngeplak *or* **ngeplaki** to slap s.o.'s head;
kumeplak naughty, deserving a slap.

keplas *repr* a swift motion;
sakeplasan at a glance.

képlé 1 unworthy; **2** prostitute; **3** drooping (*var of* **kèplèh**);
ngéplé to engage in prostitution.

keplèh soaking wet.

kèplèh drooping, hanging down limply.

keplek stupid.

keplèk 1 a card game played for money;
2 (*or* **mak keplèk**) *repr* a slashing;
ngeplèkaké to slash, smash.

kèplèk old and worthless.

kepleng *intsfr* round, full.

keplik, keplak-keplik pale, faded-looking.

keploh soaking wet (*var of* **keplèh**).

keplok 1 applause; to clap; **2** in harmony (with); **- bokong** to laugh at s.o. who is in trouble;
ngeplok to beat (clothing) while washing it;
ngeploki to clap for s.o. (in applause; to summon them);
keplok ora tombok 1 to disparage, belittle; **2** to take part in the fun without sharing the cost.

kepluk I, ngepluk to lie around in bed instead of getting up.
II a slap, *esp* in the face.
III, **ngepluki** to crumble (lumpy soil) fine.

kepodhang golden oriole (*var of* **podhang**).

kepoh *var of* **kepuh**.

kepok I a variety of banana.
II *reg* to clap (*var of* **keplok**).
III, **ngepok** at the very end. *See also* **pok**.

keponakan nephew, niece.

kepong muck, dung (of cow).

kepoyuh *see* **uyuh**.

keprak 1 a small wooden box tapped with a mallet to produce castanet-like beats for sound effects; **2** metal sound effect bars (*var of* **kepyak**);
ngeprak to produce sounds with the above.

kepras, ngepras *or* **ngeprasi** to trim, prune, cut back (shrubs or other growth).

keprèh *var of* **keplèh**.

keprèhé *reg var of* **kepriyé**.

keprèhpun *reg var of* **kepripun**.

keprèk, keprèkan *reg* worthless.

keprèmèn *reg var of* kepriyé.

keprépun *see* kepripun.

kèprès messy, smeared (with).

kepret I to run away.

II, ngepreti to belittle, look down on, to consider s.t. useless.

kèprèt *var of* kèprès.

kepréwé *reg var of* kepriyé.

keprèwèn *reg var of* kepriyé.

kepribèn *reg var of* kepriyé.

keprigèn *reg var of* kepriyé.

keprijèn *reg var of* kepriyé.

keprimèn *reg var of* kepriyé.

kepripun *md for* kepriyé.

kepriwé *reg var of* kepriyé.

kepriwèn *reg var of* kepriyé.

kepriyé *ng,* kadospundi *kr,* how? - manèh what else?; what can one do?; - waé any way (at all).

keproh soaking wet (*var of* keploh).

keprok, jeruk keprok a little mandarin, kind of citrus fruit. *See also* jeruk.

kepruk, ngepruk to smash, break open; ngepruki to break s.t. open frequently; ngeprukaké to smash s.t. against; keprukan 1 act or result of breaking s.t. open; 2 (*or* kepruk-keprukan) to smash each other; kumepruk to break, smash.

kepu *or* kepu-kepu chubby-cheeked.

kepuh I pommel.

II a bunch of folds at the back of the dodot.

III a variety of tree producing soft, cheap wood and striking flowers.

kepundhung a variety of tree with sour fruit.

kepung *ng,* kepang *kr,* ngepung 1 to surround, encircle; 2 to be (sit, stand) around s.t.; 3 to attend a ceremony, *i.e.* sit around at a communal meal; kepungan 1 surrounded, encircled; 2 the partaking of a communal meal;

pakepung seige, encirclement; pangepung the act of encircling.

kepus, ngepus to blow (on); to exhale strongly.

képwan *lit* bewildered, in a quandary.

kepyak I set of bronze (or other metal) bars with which a puppet-master produces rapping sound effects.

II, ngepyakaké 1 to announce s.t.; 2 to organise a reception for s.o.; sakepyakan quick as a wink.

képyan *var of* képwan.

kepyar loose, not sticky (cooked rice); kepyar-kepyar *or* kumepyar 1 coming apart, not sticking together; 2 to feel refreshed; pating klepyar *pl* to come apart.

kepyek *reg* noisy, busy.

kepyèk *var of* kepyak.

kepyok *var of* gepyok, kepyuk.

kepyuk, ngepyukaké to splash (onto).

kepyur in little drops; ngepyuri 1 to sprinkle lightly on; 2 to scatter, strew small objects (*e.g.* rice, for chickens); kumepyur 1 to fall, scatter in little drops; 2 to have a throbbing headache, see stars; - atiné fearful, worried.

kera thin, undernourished (*kr for* kuru).

kéra 1 cross-eyed; 2 name of one of the small playing-cards (*kertu cilik*); ngéra 1 to cross the eyes; 2 to look at s.t. cross-eyed or with one non-focusing eye.

kerab, ngerab *or* kumerab to crowd together and push against each other.

kerah a fight (between animals); to fight; ngerah (of animals) to bite, attack; kerahan fighting.

kérah, sakérah-kérah *reg* some, any (at all); not serious enough to (do).

kerak 1 old and dried up; 2 dry crust(y part) at bottom of the pan; ngerak crusty, very dry; ketiga ngerak the height of the dry season.

keram (to be seized with) a cramp. *Also* kram.

keramik ceramic ware.

keran *see* kran.

kéran *reg* awesome; awed.

kerana *reg* because.

kerang a certain mussel, also its shell.

keranten *reg kr for* kerana.

kerap, ngerap to run;
  ngerapaké to make s.t. go fast;
  kerapan 1 a race; 2 to race (*esp* bulls, in Madura).

keras hard, harsh, strong;
  ngerasi 1 to make fast, tighten; 2 to use force on; 3 to confine, restrain.

kéras, ngéras to speak symbolically or figuratively;
  kérasan figure of speech, verbal symbol.

kérat *inf var of* akérat.

kérata *lit* hunter;
  kératabasa folk etymology.

kerbek, ngerbekaké to submerge a pot to fill it.

kerbèn *var of* karebèn.

kerbil I example.
  II roof-frame supporter.

kerbin small rifle.

kercap *pl form of* kecap.

kercip, pating kercip making sucking noises.

kerdhap *var of* kerlap.

kerdhu a large leather bag.

kerdhus carton, cardboard box.

kerdim 1 curtain, folding screen; 2 fringe;
  ngerdim 1 to put a curtain on; 2 to decorate with a fringe.

kerdut, pating kerdut twitching everywhere.

kerdyat *lit* frightened, startled.

keré roll-up bamboo blind; - waja bulletproof vest;
  ngeré to equip with a bamboo blind.

kéré beggar;

ngéré 1 to be(come) a beggar; 2 to resemble *or* act like a beggar;

ngèrèkaké to consider s.o. a beggar;

kéré menangi mulud to take advantage of an opportunity to enjoy the most of s.t.;

kéré munggah balé from rags to riches.

kèrèg cross-hook for cleaning cotton (kapok).

kerèh, kerèh-kerèh to shout.

kerek, ngerek to clench, grasp, hold on and not let go (angrily, protecting one's possession).

kerèk *var of* kerik.

kèrèk *or* kèrèkan a pulley;
  ngèrèk to hoist with a pulley.

kerem, ngerem 1 to put in a cage; 2 to keep locked up at home;
  kereman 1 confinement; 2 chicken coop.

kèrem to become submerged;
  ngèremaké to cause to submerge. *See also* kèlem.

keren bottomless earthen brazier.

kèrèn *see* kèri.

kereng harsh, stern, gruff, easily angered;
  ngerengi to be harsh with, treat sternly;
  kerengan to come to blows.

kerèng, kerèngan crust, hard layer of s.t. (in a pot, pan).

kerep *ng*, asring *kr*, frequent, often, over and over;
  ngerepi *or* ngerepaké 1 to place (things) at closer intervals; 2 to do s.t. (more) often;
  kekerepen too often *or* close together.

keret I (cut-off) section, joint (of bamboo, sugarcane);
  ngereti to cut (sugarcane, bamboo) into sections with a knife, using a circular motion around the stalk;
  keretan a section of sugarcane (bamboo) cut with a knife;

pangeret act of cutting (as above).
II carat.
III a diacritic mark in Javanese script indicating *r*.

kerèt, ngerèt 1 to pull off with a twisting motion; **2** to cheat, rip off.

kerga a leather bag with a strap (for letters *etc*).

keri to feel a tickling sensation;
kerèn ticklish;
kerèn ora pinecut *idiom* to have a chip on the shoulder.

kèri I 1 left (over); **2** left (behind); **3** later, last;
ngèrèkaké to leave behind, out;
kèrèn remnant; **kèrèn-kèrèn** to be last. *See also* **kari**.
II *var of* **kéring**.

kerig to turn up in a group to do a job;
ngerigaké to summon or mobilise (a group) to do a job.

kerik I shaving and shaping of the hair on a bride's forehead;
ngerik to shave and shape (hair, eyebrows);
kerikan act or way of shaving and shaping.
II, **ngerik** to chirp.
III *var of* **kerok I**.

kering I dry, dried up;
keringan 1 dry bread, cracker, biscuit; **2** dry sugarcane leaves.
II *reg* hoe.

kéring *lit* left.

keris *ng*, **dhuwung** *kr*, **wangkingan** *k.i.*, kris, ceremonial dagger;
ngerisi to provide with a kris;
kerisan to wear a kris.

kerja to have a job, be employed;
ngerjakaké to do a job for.

kerjik precise (attention to detail), difficult to satisfy.

kerjut, pating kerjut to twitch everywhere.

kerkas pistol case, holster.

kerkat drive, energy (to undertake s.t.).

kerket *var of* **kerkat**.

kerkèt, kerkèt-kerkèt *repr* creaking, *esp* of bamboo or trees rubbing against each other.

kerkit *repr* creaking, *esp* of bed springs.

kèrkop cemetery for the burial of Christians.

kerkot *repr* heavy creaking, *e.g.* of bamboo poles swaying against each other.

kerkuh, kerkah-kerkuh unwilling, disinclined, reluctant.

kerkut, kerkut-kerkut *repr* grinding one's teeth.

kerlap, kerlap-kerlap *or* **pating kerlap** to glitter, sparkle everywhere.

kerlèp *var of* **kerlap**.

kerlip I *var of* **kerlap**.
II to fall in love;
kerlip-kerlipan to be in love with each other.

kerlop, kerlop-kerlop *or* **pating kerlop** to glitter, flash.

kermi worms, intestinal parasites;
kerminen to suffer from worms.

kermun drizzle;
kermun-kermun to drizzle, rain lightly.

kermus, ngermus to munch, crunch;
kermus-kermus *or* **kermas-kermus 1** to make crunching sounds; **2** to eat s.t. crunchy.

kernèt assistant to a driver (*var of* **kenèk**).

kernik, kakèhan - too much fuss and bother.

kernuk, pating kernuk *pl* to sit around outdoors doing nothing much.

kérod, ngérodi to scrape, rub, clean s.t. off; **anak kérodan** last, youngest child.

kérog, kérogen to itch (all over the body).

kerok I scrubbing tool for cleaning a horse, curry comb;
ngerok to scrape, rub;
ngeroki 1 to scrub; **2** to massage s.o. with a coin and oil;

kerokan 1 to have a warming massage by having the body rubbed with oil and scraped with a coin; **2** coin used for scraping.
II name of one of the Chinese playing-cards (*kertu cilik*).

keron *reg* scorched rice at the bottom of the pan.

kéron *reg* hesitant, undecided.

kerot, ngerotaké to gnash, grind (the teeth) in anger;
kerot-kerot to gnash, grind the teeth;
kumerot to make a grinding sound.

kerpana *lit* inspiring pity.

kerpèk I a small flat bag. *See also* **kepèk**.
II notes for cheating (at an examination). *See also* **kepèk**.

kerpis *reg* porcelain teapot.

kerpu sparkling crystal.

kerpus I 1 peaked cap worn by children, *esp* babies; **2** roof-ridge.
II cell for incarcerating soldiers;
ngerpus to lock up (a soldier) as a disciplinary measure.

kersa *inf var of* **karsa**.

kersil (too) small to hold.

kèrsmis Christmas.

kerta prosperity and welfare; **- aji** value, worth; **- kerti** prosperity and peace; **- wadana** leader;
tata tentrem kerta raharja orderly, peaceful, and prosperous (of the condition of a country).

kertan *reg* to hear (the news).

kertap, kertap-kertap glittering.

kertarta *lit* thoroughly imbued (with knowledge).

kertas paper.

kertep jewelled belt buckle.

kertèp, kertèp-kertèp to glitter, sparkle.

kerthap, pating kerthap to glitter, twinkle, sparkle, with tiny spots of light.

kerthip *var of* **kerthap**.

kerti *lit* work (*var of* **kirti**).

kertiyasa *lit* expert, superior.

kertos playing-cards (*kr for* **kertu**).

kertu playing-cards; **- cilik** *or* **- Cina** small playing cards of Chinese origin; **- Landa** playing-cards, bridge cards; **- lima** name of a card game; **- pos** postcard.

kérud to get swept away;
ngérudaké to sweep/carry s.t. off (of current).

keruh *reg* dirty, troubled, turbid.

keruk a tool for scooping; **kapal -** dredge;
ngeruk to scoop/scrape out; *fig* to get one's hands on s.o.'s belongings;
ngeruki to keep scooping/scraping out;
kumeruk buntut (of coconut) very young and tender.

keruron *see* **kluron**.

kerus *reg* to be subjected to s.t. unpleasant.

kerut furrow, wrinkle;
kerut-kerut furrowed, wrinkled.

késah to go (*kr for* **lunga**).

kesambi a tree yielding wood used for charcoal.

kesar, kesar-kesar *or* **kumesar** dismayed, alarmed, shocked, confused.

kesat dry, dry to the touch.

kesdik clairvoyant.

kesdu *lit* to want, desire.

kesed 1 firm (flesh); **2** well done, not soft (cooked rice).

kesèd lazy;
ngesèd to act in a lazy way;
kesèd-kesèdan 1 to loaf, take it easy; **2** to try to outloaf each other.

kèsèd 1 door mat; **2** (*or* **kekèsèd**) to wipe the feet on a doormat;
ngèsèdi to provide with a doormat.

kesel tired;
ngeseli *or* **ngeselaké** to tire s.o. out;
keselan to tire easily.

keseng *reg* industrious, diligent.

kèser defeated, routed.

kèsèr, ngèsèr to transport (a load) in a two-wheeled cart drawn by manpower;

ngèsèraké to have s.t. transported as above;

kèsèran two-wheeled cart pulled by men;

kèsèr-kèsèr to drag (a heavy load).

keses, ngeses to make a hissing sound;

kesas-keses various hissing sounds;

ngesas-ngeses to keep making hissing sounds;

pating kreses pl producing the above sound. See also ses.

kesesa in a hurry (kr for kesusu).

keset see kesed.

kesik, ngesik to rub, polish, whiten (the teeth with a powdered substance).

kesit wild, shy, timid.

keskil reg attentive to detail, meticulous.

keskul pouch, bag for foodstuffs.

késod, ngésod, késodan to slide sideways over the floor using the hands (e.g. a cripple, child unable to walk).

kespur spurs (on riding boots).

kesrèk or mak kesrèk repr scratching, scraping.

kèsrèk 1 to scratch, scrape against; 2 violin bow;

ngèsrèk to bow (the rebab);

ngèsrèkaké to bow (the bow) against;

kèsrèkan way of playing (the rebab or violin); sound produced by bowing the rebab.

kesrik, ngesrik to chip up (e.g. weeds).

késruh to lose track, get things out of order (reg var of kisruh).

kestabel gunner, artillerist.

kestal, kestalan stalls (for horses), stabling.

kestèl 1 a matching set; 2 to go well (with).

kestèn reg marble(s).

kestin var of kestèn.

kesting var of kestèn.

kestiwel boot. See also setiwel.

kestop European material for dresses.

kestroli var of kastroli.

kestul pistol.

kesud cloth for wiping;

ngesud to wipe (up) or sponge with a cloth.

kesuh reg 1 downcast, sad; 2 unable to bear it.

késuk see ésuk.

kesumba safflower.

kesusu ng, kesesa kr, in a hurry.

késwa lit hair.

ketab, ngetab to urge on a horse by kicking its belly;

ngetabaké to knock s.t., against s.t. (to get the dirt out);

ketab-ketab to knock dirt etc from s.t. by hitting it against s.t.

ketak-ketèk see ketèk.

ketampul or mak ketampul repr swinging downward, falling gently;

ketumpal-ketampul to keep swinging.

ketan ng, ketos kr sticky rice;

ngetan 1 to steam sticky rice; 2 to become glutinous like sticky rice.

kétang, ora - at least; even if.

ketar-ketir see ketir.

ketara ng, ketawis kr, obvious, showing plainly;

ngetarani 1 to show, display a sign of, allow to be seen; 2 to be obvious.

ketas-ketis see ketis.

ketat 1 tight, constricting; 2 stiff and a bit sticky.

ketawang 1 a certain group of Javanese musical compositions played by gamelan instruments; 2 bedhaya - a certain court dance performed by nine girls (see also bedhaya);

ketawangan annual performance of the above dance.

ketawis kr for ketara.

kété-kété difficult to account for.

keteb in a dense mass. See also ketep.

ketébang-ketébang repr (to be seen) approaching in the distance.

keteblug, pating keteblug repr repeated thuds.

keteg *or* **keketeg** heartbeats.

ketel thick, luxuriant, dense.

kètèl 1 steam boiler; 2 large rice kettle with a handle.

ketéla *var of* **téla**.

ketèn *reg* agile.

kèten like this, in this way (*subst kr for* **mengkéné**).

ketengklang-ketengkling *see* **ketengkling**.

ketengkling, ketengklang-ketengkling to stumble along.

ketep I 1 edge, fringe; 2 fringe worn on girl's forehead;
ngetepi 1 to provide with neat edge; 2 to cut hair in a fringe.
II *or* **keketep** troops which bring up the rear;
ngetepi to form a rear line.

ketèp I sequins (*usu* silver, gold) for clothing ornamentation.
II, kumetèp hot to the taste (in temperature or in spiciness).

kètèp *reg* dirt in the corner of the eye. *See also* **kèthèp**.

ketepas-ketepus *see* **ketepus**.

ketepèl catapult;
ngetepèl to shoot s.t. with a catapult.

ketepil *see* **ketepèl**.

ketepu very small grains of broken rice (smaller than **menir**).

ketepus, ngetepus to boast about o.s.;
ketepas-ketepus to keep boasting about o.s.

keter to tremble, shake.

ketès *repr* a slap.

kètès I to drip;
kètès-kètès to keep dripping.
II brand new.

ketèwèl *var of* **tèwèl**.

kethak I a knock on the head;
ngethak to knock s.o. on the head;
kumethak irritatingly boastful (as if you would like to knock him on the head).

II a cake made from peanuts or coconut.

kethaklik, kethaklik-kethaklik *repr* the weak motion of a thin body running, as though the bones were knocking against each other;
pating kethaklik *pl* to walk slowly with knocking sounds.

kethamul, ngethamul to eat with good appetite (*pl* **pating kethamul**).

kethap, kethap-kethap just showing, a speck in the distance.

kethapel, ngethapel to hold on with the arms and legs;
ngethapelaké to wind (the arms and legs) around s.t. to hold on.

kethathar, ngethathar to lie sprawled (*pl* **pating kethathar**).

kethathel *or* **mak kethathel** *repr* (cloth) getting caught or stuck on s.t.

kethawé, ngethawé to wave the hand;
pating kethawé with outstretched hands;
kethawéan to reach out the hand.

kethawèl, pating kethawèl (of arms, legs) flailing about, thrashing the air.

kethawil *var of* **kethawèl**.

kethawit, pating kethawit thick with little objects (*e.g.* fruit).

kethek I, ngethek to make a tongue-clicking sound;
ngetheki to express disapproval by making a tongue-clicking sound.
II, kethekan chin (*k.i. for* **janggut**).

kethèk I monkey;
ngethèk resembling a monkey.
II *repr* a light brittle thud.
III, kethèkan abacus.

kèthèk *reg var of* **kèthèp**.

ketheker flower of the **salak**.

kethèkèr, kethèkèran to struggle on with difficulty.

ketheklik sprained;
ketheklik-ketheklik *repr* the footsteps of s.o. wearing wooden sandals;

ketheklak-ketheklik 1 to make repeated clippity-clop sounds; 2 (of walking gait) slow.

kethekluk to nod drowsily;
ketheklak-kethekluk to keep nodding.

kethekrek, kethekrek-kethekrek clippity-clop; to clatter along.

kethekur I repr the cooing of a turtledove.
II, ngethekur to loaf, idle, unemployed.

kethèl mixture of lye and castor oil for preparing cloth to be dyed.

kethem, ngethem to clutch. See also cekethem.

kethemek, kethemek-kethemek to walk slowly with short steps.

kethemil, ngethemil to nibble constantly;
kethemil-kethemil (to eat) little by little.

kethemul var of kethamul.

kèthèng ½-cent coin.

ketheng-ketheng var of kentheng-kentheng.

kethéngkrang, ngethéngkrang to sit (impolitely) in a more elevated position than others; fig to consider o.s. above pitching in and helping;
kethéngkrangan to lumber along, move ponderously.

kethèngkrèng var of kethéngkrang.

kethéngkrong var of kethéngkrang.

kèthèp dirt in the corner of the eye;
kèthèpen to have dirt in the eye.

kethepek var of kethemek.

kethèpèl, ngethèpèl or kethèpèlan to struggle (upward, onward).

katheplèk-katheplèk to clatter;
pating katheplèk repr clip-clop sounds when walking in sandals.

ketheplok, ketheplok-ketheplok (of horses' hoofs) to clatter.

kethèprèh, pating kethèprèh to hang untidily, sloppily.

ketheprek, ngetheprek to trot along clattering the hoofs;
ketheprek-ketheprek repr the clatter of horses' hoofs.

kether var of geter.

kèthèr 1 neglected, in a mess; 2 slow, late.

kethether, ngethether 1 to sit idle; 2 to suffer from cold;
kethetheren suffering from cold.

kethèthèr, kethèthèran in disorder, in a mess;
ngethèthèr to lie in a messy heap;
pating kethèthèr spread in disorder.

kethèwèr, kethèwèran or pating kethèwèr scattered around.

kethi hundred thousand;
kethèn (numbering in the) hundreds of thousands.

kethik I, ngethik to privately talk s.o. into (or out of) doing s.t.;
kethikan secret persuasion.
II tooth-file; (of teeth) filed even (k.i. for pasah).

kethiklèk wooden sandal.

kethilang var of kuthilang.

kethimik, kethimik-kethimik to walk carefully with little steps.

kething, kethingan reg a ceremony held for a child to mark touching the ground for the first time.

kethingkrang var of kethéngkrang.

kethinthal, kethinthalan to plod laboriously.

kethip I 10-cent coin.
II, 1 kethip-kethip far in the distance; 2 or kethap-kethip to keep blinking the eyes.

kethipel, ngethipel to walk slowly and ponderously.
kethipel-kethipel or kethipal-kethipel repr a clumsy walking gait.

kethiplak I cr subordinate, servant.
II see kethiplek.

kethiplek, kethiplek-kethiplek or

kethiplak-kethiplek *repr* sandals clopping.

kethiplik, ngethiplik to toddle; to walk with short quick steps;

pating kethiplik *pl* sluggish, listless.

kethiwul *var of* thiwul.

kethoh *reg* slovenly, unwashed.

kethok, ngethok 1 to cut off; 2 (of arms, legs) exhausted;

ngethoki to cut into pieces;

ngethokaké to cut for s.o.;

kethokan 1 a cut-off piece; a cut place; 2 act or way of cutting.

kethop, kethop-kethop (of eyes) wide open and shining (*var of* kelop).

kethoprak I a Javanese popular drama depicting historical or pseudo-historical events;

ngethoprak to be a player of the above drama;

kethoprakan to perform the above drama.

II, kethoprakan *or* pating kethoprak *repr* to make knocking sounds.

kethoproh, ngethoproh *or* pating kethoproh sloppy, slovenly.

kéthor *reg* wart, mole, skin blemish.

kethot *reg* 1 tough, hard to chew; *fig* hard to handle; 2 (of horse) slow.

kethothor, ngethothor to hang down loose or limp;

pating kethothor *or* kethothoran to hang down untidily.

kethu a kind of cap, worn with a turban wound around the outside;

kethon to put on *or* wear the above.

kethuh *var of* kethoh.

kethuk 1 gamelan instrument consisting of a single inverted bronze bowl; 2 *repr* a beat of the above instrument; 3 *repr* a knocking sound;

ngethuk to play the above instrument;

ngethuki to agree with.

kethul dull, blunt (of blade; of wits);

ngethulaké to dull s.t.

kethumuk, ngethumuk *or* kethumuk-kethumuk *or* kethumukan to walk carefully and unsteadily.

kethuplak, kethuplak-kethuplak *repr* the clatter of hoofs.

kethuthur, pating kethuthur (of birds) shivering with cold or dampness.

kethuwak-kethuwik *see* kethuwik.

kethuwal-kethuwel *see* kethuwel.

kethuwel *or* mak kethuwel *repr* crumpling;

kethuwelan *or* kethuwal-kethuwel to turn the hands (when learning to dance);

pating kethuwel to keep turning the hands.

kethuweng *repr* a turn or twist of the body. *See also* thuweng.

kethuwik, kethuwak-kethuwik (of fingers) to keep moving.

kethuwil, kethuwal-kethuwil (of fingers, hands) in constant motion;

pating kethuwil with constant motion of hands, fingers.

kethuyuk, kethuyuk-kethuyuk bent and bowed with age. *See also* thuyuk.

ketib assistant to a religious official.

ketiga dry season (*also* katiga).

ketik *repr* sound of ticking or clicking;

ketak-ketik to make a ticking sound repeatedly;

ngetik to typewrite;

ngetikaké to type for s.o.; to have s.t. typed;

ketikan 1 act or way of typing; 2 typing, s.t. typed;

pengetik typist.

ketimaha *var of* timaha.

ketimang *var of* timang.

ketimun cucumber. *Also* timun.

keting a small sea fish.

ketinggi *var of* tinggi.

ketiplak *see* kethiplak.

ketiplèk *see* kethiplek.

ketiplik *see* kethiplik.

ketipung small gamelan drum;
  ngetipung to produce sounds by beating this drum.

ketir, ketir-ketir *or* ketar-ketir fearful, apprehensive;
  ngetir-ngetiri to cause apprehension/anxiety.

ketis, ketis-ketis (of voice) sweet and clear.

ketiwang, ketiwang-tiwang to go farther than one had intended.

ketiwar *var of* ketiwang.

ketiyon *reg* to be proved true; to come true.

ketog I, ngetog to (do) to the utmost; to exert o.s. to the limit;
  II, ketogan (of moustache) short and neat.

kétok to appear, show, seem (*inf var of* katon).

kétol, kétol-kétol to lumber (big buttocks, walking with difficulty).

ketomah to be accustomed to.

ketombé *var of* tombé.

keton 2½ guilders (during the colonial period).

ketonggèng a kind of scorpion;
  ngetonggèng to rise like a scorpion's tail.

ketopros, ngethopros to boast about s.t., to brag to each other.

ketos sticky rice (*kr for* ketan).

ketriwal lost, mislaid.

ketug up to, as far as, arrived at.

ketul baby tortoise (young of the bulus).

ketumbar coriander;
  ngetumbar nicely round(ed) (Javanese script). *Also* tumbar.

ketumpal-ketampul *see* ketampul.

ketunggèng *see* ketonggèng.

kéwak, ngéwak to form a sharp corner, angle.

kéwal, ngéwal to give a twist to, turn.

kéwala *lit* only, nothing but, simply.

kewalat *see* walat.

kéwan animal (including all sub-human forms);
  kéwani pertaining to animals.

kéwat having a good opinion of o.s.

kéwé *reg* left.

kèwèh *reg var of* pakéwuh.

kèwèk flirtatious, coquettish.

kewelèh *lit* discovered, revealed, exposed. *See also* welèh.

kèwèr, kèwèr-kèwèr to dangle.

kèwes smooth, sophisticated; gracious, elegant, poised.

kéyang name of one of the small playing-cards (*kertu cilik*).

kéyok 1 the screaming (squawking) of a chicken when it is seized, attacked or loses a fight; 2 defeated (of people) in a fight or game;
  ngéyoki 1 to scream (as above); 2 to give up, admit defeat.

kéyong a water snail;
  kéyongen to suffer from a fatty tumour (animals).

ki I *male title of respect: shtf of* kyai, kaki.
  II this (*inf var of* iki).

kibik cubic.

kibir (sinful) presumption, confidence in o.s.

kicah-kicih to splash around in water with one's bare feet.

kicak a cake made from sticky rice, coconut and sugar.

kicat to hop (a classical dance movement);
  kicat-kicat uncomfortable feeling in the feet from walking barefoot in hot places.

kicé *reg* blind. *See also* pécé.

kicel, ngicel 1 to massage, rub; 2 to pinch.

kicèng *var of* kicé.

kicer having one eye closed;
  ngicer to close one eye;
  kicer-kicer to keep blinking one eye.

kicih, **kicah-kicih** to play around in water.

kicik I (*or* **kicikan**) meat or fish mixed with coconut milk and cooked until the liquid is absorbed;
ngicik to prepare (meat, fish) as above.
II *var of* **kicih**.

kicir a certain type of fish trap with barred doors (*var of* **icir**).

kidam uncreated; God's uncreated nature.

kidang small antelope; roe deer;
ngidang resembling a deer.

kidhal left-handed.

kidhik *reg* a little, a few (*var of* **kedhik**).

kidhung awkward, inept.

kidib (to tell) a lie; untruthful.

kidih, **kidih-kidih** to have s.t. of a dislike, feel uncomfortable;
kidihan reserved by nature.

kidul south; - **wétan** southeast; - **kulon** southwest;
ngidul southward, to go south;
ngidulaké (*pass* **dingidulaké**) to move s.t. to the south;
mangidul *lit* southward;
kidulan *or* **kidul-kidulan** the southern part.

kidung song, poem; (*or* **kidungan**) sung poem in classical metres;
ngidung 1 to sing Javanese songs, *esp* as a means of warding off danger; 2 to compose poetry to be sung;
kekidungan to sing Javanese songs.

kijab screen, before God's face.

kijat *reg* (to tell) a lie; to deny the fact.

kijing I gravestone;
ngijing *or* **ngijingi** to place a gravestone on;
kijingan provided with a gravestone.
II a certain freshwater mussel.

kik *or* **mak kik** (*pron as:* **ki:k**) 1 *repr* a hiccup; 2 *repr* a brief laugh behind the hand.

kikib, **ngikib** *or* **ngikibi** to keep s.t. concealed, not tell the whole truth about s.t.

kikid *reg* stingy, mean.

kikik I, **ngikik** to giggle.
II a small long-haired dog. *See also* **asu**.

kikil I leg of lamb, calf *etc*, as food.
II, **ngikil** persistent, constant (coughing).

kikip *see* **kikib**.

kikir a file (for smoothing);
ngikir to file;
kikiran filings.

kikis I border, boundary, edge (of land);
ngikis 1 to border, go to the border; 2 to travel along the edge of s.t.
II a measure of rice.

kiklak (to have) an open wound *or* skinned place.

kikrik choosy, fussy, finicky.

kikuk clumsy, inept.

kilah, **kilah-kilah** sparkling clean.

kilak to buy (up) for resale (*kr for* **kulak**).

kilan measure of length; the distance between the tip of the thumb and little finger;
ngilani 1 to measure s.t. in handspans; 2 to consider trivial; 3 to challenge, dare;
kilanan a measure in spans.

kilang liquid produced by boiling sugarcane;
ngilang to boil sugarcane.

kilap I *reg* lightning (*var of* **kilat**).
II *or* **kekilapan** to forget, overlook; unaware, oblivious.

kilat 1 (flash of) lightning; 2 lightning-like, swift; - **thathit** lightning followed by thunder;
kebat kaya kilat *expr* quick as a flash of lightning.

kilem *reg* to sleep.

kilèn west (*kr for* **kulon**).

kileng, **kileng-kileng** having an oily, shiny appearance.

kili I object (feather, blade of grass *etc*) used as a goad to fighting crickets, or to scratch an itch;
ngilèni to use s.t. to goad a cricket or scratch an itch.
II *lit* nun, female hermit.

kiling bundle of rice(plant).

kilo 1 kilogram; 2 kilometre;
ngiloni to weight s.t. out;
kilon by the kilogram.

kilong, kilong-kilong wide-eyed and innocent-looking.

kilung *reg* to pretend to be ignorant.

kilusuh *lit* withered, drooping, power-less; to slump down.

kilwak sentry.

kilyan *lit* west.

kima a large shell and the mollusc that lives in it.

kimat to have a relapse (*kr for* kumat).

kimawon *var of* kémawon.

kimbah to launder, wash (*kr for* kum-bah).

kimlo a variety of soup.

kimpès *var of* kempès.

kimplah, kimplah-kimplah 1 filled to the edge, brimming; 2 rippling with fat.

kimplang *var of* kileng.

kimplek, kimplek-kimplek 1 chubby, cute; 2 thick, coagulated, not flowing.

kimpleng *var of* kileng.

kimpling, kimpling-kimpling (of water) sparkling clear and pure.

kimpul I a plant that produces edible tuberous roots.
II *reg* purse, money-bag.

kimput *reg* embarrassed, mortified.

kina I old-fashioned (*kr for* kuna).
II *var of* kinah.

kinah quinine; cinchona tree.

kinang *ng*, gantèn *kr*, betel quid (betel nut mixed with leaves and lime);
nginang to chew betel;
kinangan *or* pakinangan *or* pangina-ngan container for betel;

panginang the act of chewing betel;
sapanginang a brief time, *i.e.* as long as it takes to chew betel.

kinanthi a certain classical verse form;
nginanthi to compose *or* sing such a verse.

kinca syrup made from palm sugar and coconut milk.

kincang I outrigger.
II village worker.

kincer, ngincer 1 to aim; 2 to keep one's eye on s.t. one wants;
kinceran taking aim with one eye closed.

kincih, kincih-kincih appealing, tempt-ing.

kincip 1 bud (of flower); 2 closed (of flowers).

kinclap, kinclap-kinclap sparkling clear.

kincling, kincling-kincling 1 brand new; 2 sparkling clear.

kinclong, kinclong-kinclong (of water) sparkling clear.

kinel, kinel-kinel soft and jelly-like in texture.

kiner *var of* kinel.

king *kr* from (*shtf of* saking).

kinging *see* kénging.

kingkin *lit* sad, sorrowful, grieving, lovesick.

kingking *var of* kingkin.

kingsèp (of swellings) to be reduced, go down.

kinine quinine.

kinjeng dragonfly (various species);
kinjeng tangis tanpa soca *prov* to go out without having any clear destina-tion.

kinjik, ora kinjik-kinjik to not turn up, not show o.s.

kinjiri *lit* wild boar.

kintaka *lit* letter, document.

kintèki *var of* kintaka.

kintel I a certain frog that can inflate itself like a balloon;

ngintel resembling a frog.
II carpenter's plane;
ngintel to plane s.t.

kinten thought, guess, opinion (*kr for* **kira**).

kinthil (*or* **kekinthil**) to follow along;
nginthil to follow, keep on the trail of.

kintun to send (*kr for* **kirim**).

kinyih, kinyih-kinyih 1 looking tasty, juicy; 2 tempting (pretty woman); 2 oily-looking, greasy.

kinyis, anyar kinyis-kinyis 1 brand new, straight from the shop; 2 virgin (females).

kipa, kipa-kipa to reject in disgust, refuse to accept s.t.

kiparat expiation, reconciliation, atonement.

kipas a fan;
ngipasi 1 to fan s.t.; 2 to instigate, stir up;
ngipasaké to fan s.t. for s.o.;
kipasan to fan o.s.

kipat, kipat-kipat to shake the hand or arm to get rid of s.t.;
ngipataké to shake s.t. off.

kipé *var of* **ipé**.

kiper I goalkeeper.
II twill.

kiping 1 edge, side; 2 (of an army) wing.

kipit, kipit-kipit *or* **kipat-kipit** to wag the tail.

kiprah 1 *or* **kiprahan** (in classical dance) a series of iconic movements depicting grooming and dressing; 2 merriment, gaiety; merry; 3 to engage in social activities.

kipsao a Chinese teapot.

kipsau *see* **kipsao**.

kipu *or* **kekipu** to take a dust-bath;
pakipon a place where birds take dust-baths.

kipyah, kipyah-kipyah to dance around with joy, wild, excited.

kir 1 test, examination; 2 motor vehicle inspection; 3 to get o.s. examined, get s.t. inspected;
ngekir to examine s.o. for ailments, examine s.t. for defects;
ngekiraké to have s.t. examined;
kir-kiran 1 act of examining; 2 s.t. that has been examined.

kira *ng*, **kinten** *kr*, thought, guess, opinion;
ngira 1 to think, guess, have an opinion; 2 to suppose, assume; 3 to estimate, calculate s.t.;
ngira-ira to estimate approximately;
pangira *or* **pangira-ira** thought, guess;
kira-kira 1 probably; 2 approximately; 3 reasonable, within reason;
ora kira-kira unbelievable;
sekirané in case, if perhaps.

kirab to move about in the course of an activity.

kirana *lit* beam, ray.

kirang inadequate, short, lacking; less (*kr for* **kurang**);
kirangan I don't know (*subst kr for* **embuh**).

kirata *lit* hunter (*var of* **kérata**).

kirda *var of* **kridha**.

kiri *reg* left.

kirig *or* **kirig-kirig** to shudder; to shake o.s.

kirih *or* **kekirih** to clean out (irrigation ditch);
ngirihi 1 to clean a ditch; 2 to bring s.o. to see reason.

kirik puppy.

kirim *ng*, **kintun** *kr*, to send; - **donga** to pray; - **slamet** to send one's greetings;
ngirim 1 to send; 2 to take food to workers in the field; 3 to place flower offerings on a grave;
ngirimi to send to s.o.;
ngirimaké to send s.t.;
kiriman that which is sent; **udan** - heaven-sent rain (in the dry season);
kiram-kirim to send frequently;

pangirim sender;

pangiriman thing sent.

kiring (of coconut) old and dried up.

kirna trillion;

kirnan in trillions, countless.

kirpus *reg var of* **kerpus**.

kirta *var of* **kirti**.

kirti *lit* work, task.

kirtya *var of* **kirti**.

kisa a small temporary cage or carrying case for a fighting cock, of woven young coconut leaves.

kisang banana (*subst kr for* **gedhang**; *reg var of* **pisang**).

kisas, ukum - a sentence of death;

ngisas to sentence to death.

kisat *var of* **kesat**.

kisi bobbin, spool, reel (in spinning).

kisik I coast, shore, beach (*var of* **gisik**).

II, ngisik to stroke smoothly;

kisikan act or way of stroking.

kisma *lit* earth, ground.

kismis raisin.

kisruh to lose track, get things out of order;

ngisruhi *or* **ngisruhaké** to disturb, disrupt, interfere with; to make lose count of.

kisut I wrinkled, shrivelled;

ngisut to become wrinkled/shrivelled.

II name of one of the small playing-cards (*kertu cilik*).

kit a place to sell opium.

kita we, (all of) us; our.

kitab book; religious book; **- suci** holy Quran, Bible.

kiter spin, rotate (*var of* **kitir**);

ngiteri to revolve around;

kekiter to keep revolving around.

kitha town, city (*kr for* **kutha**).

kithal awkward, ill at ease, clumsy.

kither, kither-kither slimy and sticky (*e.g.* jelly, frog's eggs).

kithik *reg* hair louse (*k.i. for* **tuma**).

kithing (of fingers, toes) crooked, deformed;

ngithing to hold the fingers in a clawing position.

kithung awkward, inept, clumsy (*var of* **kidhung**).

kiting, ngiting *reg* to chase.

kitir I 1 note, brief letter; **2** marker, emblem; **3** small leaf attached to a fruit stem; **4** last leaf remaining on a banana tree;

ngitiri to send a letter to;

ngitiraké to send a letter.

II, kitiran 1 propeller; **2** windmill;

kumitir *or* **kekitir** to flutter, quake.

III, kitiran kind of turtle-dove.

kitrah, jaman kitrah age of no prophet.

kitrang, kitrang-kitrang *or* **kekitrang** to run around frantically.

kitri I (*or* **karang kitri**) fruit-producing trees in a yard. *See also* **karang**.

II *reg* marks in a clearing.

III hereditary personal possession.

kiwa left; **- tengen** left and right; both sides;

ngiwa 1 to turn left; **2** *fig* to engage in immoral acts;

ngiwakaké 1 to move s.t. to the left; **2** *fig* to treat with contempt, consider of no importance;

pakiwan privy, toilet, latrine.

kiwat *see* **kéwat**.

kiwé *reg var of* **kiwa**.

kiwi, kekiwi *lit* to lodge s.w.

kiwih-kiwih, anyar - brand new.

kiwil 1 tangled (hair); **2** difficult to get on with; **3** *var of* **kiwir**.

kiwir, kiwir-kiwir nearly cut off, hanging by a thread.

kiwul *or* **kekiwul** *lit* **1** to take revenge on, to attack; **2** to defend o.s.

kiya-kiya *var of* **kiyah-kiyah**.

kiyah-kiyah to take a relaxed stroll.

kiyai *var of* **kyai**.

kiyak *see* **kiyuk**.

kiyal tough, hard to chew.

kiyam, ngiyam *reg* **1** to prove; **2** to elect;

kiyaman election (of village head).

kiyamat the end of the world, Judgement Day.

kiyambak *md* 1 alone (*md for* **ijèn**); 2 (by) o.s. (*md for* **dhéwé**). *See also* **piyambak**.

kiyambek *reg var of* **kiyambak**.

kiyanat 1 disloyal; 2 treachery, betrayal; **ngiyanati** to betray s.o.

kiyangkaban *see* **kyangkaban**.

kiyas analogy, comparison; **ngiyas** to compare, make an analogy with.

kiyat strong (*kr for* **kuwat**).

kiyé *reg* this (*var of* **iki**).

kiyèk, kiyèk-kiyèk *repr* the cheeping of baby chicks.

kiyen *reg* this (*var of* **iki**).

kiyeng firm, muscular, tough; **ngiyeng** persistent (loud crying).

kiyer, ngiyer *or* **kiyer-kiyer** to half-close the eyes (with pleasure or delight, in response to a feeling or taste).

kiyi *reg* this (*var of* **iki**).

kiyih, kiyih-kiyih dripping with sweat.

kiyik *var of* **piyik**.

kiyip *var of* **kriyip**.

kiyok I *var of* **kéyok**.

II, kiyokan *reg* to play cards.

kiyong I water snail (*var of* **kéyong**).

II *or* **kekiyong** *reg* ankle.

kiyu weary, stiff, cramped (arms, legs).

kiyuk, ngiyak-ngiyuk to struggle to make do with very little; **kiyukan** to make up a loss.

klabak, klabak-klabak *or* **klabakan** 1 to flounder, thrash about, rush to and fro; 2 panic-stricken; **nglabaki** to cause panic.

klabang a certain small poisonous centipede; - **ayam** a variety of playing dice; - **nyander** (of shape of the house) long and narrow; **nglabang** 1 to resemble a centipede; 2 to plait the hair;

klabangan pigtail, braid; to wear the hair plaited.

klabar sandbank, shoal.

klabet grey, ash-coloured (*reg kr for* **klawu**).

klabèt *var of* **klèbèt**.

klabut *see* **klebut**.

klacap, nglacapi to peel a thin inner layer of skin from s.t., *esp* peanuts; **klacapan** s.t. peeled; a peeled-off inner skin.

klacèn a groove, ditch.

klacir, pating klacir *pl* sticking up spindly and thin; **nglacir** to stick up as above.

klacup *repr* closing (of flower *etc*).

kladuk to overdo (*var of* **kaduk**).

klafer clubs (playing-card suit).

klagan *reg* and, with.

klak-klek *see* **klek**.

klak-kluk *see* **kluk**.

klakah a split section of bamboo.

klakep, mak klakep *repr* falling silent suddenly; **nglakep** 1 to close the mouth; 2 to open the mouth wide and then close it again; **klakepan** 1 to be silenced suddenly; 2 to keep yawning.

klakson car horn.

klalar I dirt on the human skin; **nglalar** to rub dirt off the skin. **II pating klalar** to crawl everywhere (*e.g.* big caterpillars).

klaleng *var of* **kleleng**.

klalun *see* **lalun**.

klamad 1 spider web; 2 thin inner membrane (*e.g.* of a **salak**).

klamar I rope marking a boundary that is not to be crossed. **II** *see* **klamad**.

klamat *see* **klamad**.

klambi *ng*, **rasukan** *kr*, shirt, jacket; - **kurung** woman's long tunic; pullover shirt;

nglambèni to dress s.o.;
klambèn to put on or wear clothing;
kumlambi (of rain) light, drizzling (no need for an umbrella, a klambi is enough).

klambrang, nglambrang to wander around;
klambrangan wandering far afield.

klambrèh var of klèmbrèh.

klambu mosquito net;
nglamboni to equip (a bed) with a mosquito net;
klambon equipped with a mosquito net.

klamed, nglamedi to chew s.t. as below;
klamedan or klamed-klamed or klomad-klamed to move the lips and tongue in order to swallow without chewing (e.g. eating ice cream);
saklamedan 1 a mere taste of s.t.; 2 a poor meal.

klamèh, klomah-klamèh lingering, drawling (affected speech).

klamit reg excuse me; I ask permission to leave (contracted form of kula amit).

klampet, mak - to disappear totally.

klampok a variety of jambu.

klampra, nglampra to roam everywhere.

klamprah, nglamprah or klamprahan 1 to lie around unattended; 2 (of over-long garments) to drag on the ground.

klamud, nglamudi to suck (lolly, fruit);
klamud-klamud or klomad-klamud to keep sucking.

klamuk hazy, obscure.

klamun see klamuk.

klamut see klamuk.

klana 1 a fierce character, originally a prince from overseas; 2 the classical dance performed by a male masked dancer;
nglana to depict Klana in the above dance.

klanang, klanangan reg scrotum, penis. See also lanang, planangan.

klanceng the small bee that produces wax (var of lanceng).

klancopan reg too much, excessive.

klandhing fruit of the gebag palm.

klandhung, klandhungan reg testicles.

klangkèt thin, emaciated.

klangkling reg to walk back and forth.

klangkrang reg large red tree ant.

klangla reg not wearing a shirt, bare.

klangleng var of klaleng.

klangso reg over time.

klangsrah or nglangsrah to touch or drag on the ground (var of klèngsrèh).

klanjer 1 a painful swelling of the glands in the armpit, neck or groin as a result of infection; 2 gland. See also planjer.

klanthang, nglanthang to lay out in the direct sun to dry completely;
klanthangan s.t. dried as above.

klanthé joining-cord between two collar-buttons at the neck of a Javanese jacket.

klanthung, nglanthung to walk along with nothing to carry;
klonthang-klanthung unemployed and drifting, idle;
panji klanthung unemployed person.

klantih to miss a meal and feel sick with hunger.

klantur see lantur.

klanyum or mak klanyum repr suddenly disappearing/finished.

klapa coconut (kr for krambil).

klaper var of klafer.

klapes var of kapes, gabes.

klaprut, nglaprut or pating klaprut having a messy mouth.

klaput, klaput-klaput only thinly, meagerly.

klarah, klarahan 1 spread out carelessly; 2 neglected, abandoned.

klarang large red tree ant.

klarap a small gliding lizard.

klaras 1 dry banana leaf, used for wrapping; 2 reg corn bract used as a cigarette wrapper.

klari *reg* dry coconut leaves.

klas class; classroom; - **kambing** lowest-price class.

klasa *ng*, **gelaran** *kr*, woven mat; - **bang-ka** cheap poorly made mat; - **pasir** fine thick mat; - **pacar** patterned mat.

klasi sailor.

klasik classic(al).

klasud, **klasud-klasud** to wiggle about on the floor (baby, animal).

klasut, **klasutan** thin membranous covering.

klathak I fried **mlinjo** seeds eaten as a snack.

II *or* **mak klathak** *repr* a clattering thud;
kumlathak 1 to make a cracking or clattering sound; 2 hardened, caked.

klaung, **klaungan** *reg* (of dog) to keep howling, whining.

klawan *lit* and, with.

klawé, **klawéan** to wave (hands);
pating klawé *pl* to keep waving;
kumlawé to move in undulating motions.

klawer, **klawer-klawer** strands of slime floating about in water.

klawèr, **nglawèr** to dangle;
pating klawèr *pl* dangling.

klawu grey, ash-coloured.

klawung, **klowang-klawung** idle, with nothing to do;
kumlawung feeling empty and useless.

klayab, **nglayab** *or* **klayaban** to wander about without purpose.

klayar *var of* **klayab**.

klayu I 1 to follow after s.o. (out of attachment); 2 strongly attracted;
nglayoni 1 to follow s.o., want to be with them; 2 to redeem a pledge.
II a certain tree with edible fruit.

klebak-klebek *see* **klebek**.

klebak-klebik now and then, here and there.

klébat *or* **mak klébat** *repr* a fleeting glimpse;
nglébat to put in a brief appearance, be visible for only a moment.

klebek, **klebek-klebek** *or* **klebak-klebek** *or* **klebekan** to put up a struggle;
pating klebek *pl* as above.

klèbèk *var of* **klebek**.

klebes soaking wet (*var of* **kebes**).

klèbèt, **klèbèt-klèbèt** fluttering, flapping (flag);
nglèbètaké to wave (flag);
kumlèbèt to flutter, flap.

klebus soaking wet (*var of* **kebus**).

klebut wooden head-shaped stand on which wrapped headdresses are folded into shape (*var of* **klabut**).

kléca a certain tree and its fruit.

klécam-klècem *see* **klècem**.

klécan *reg kr* forgotten, to slip one's mind.

klécap *var of* **klècèp**.

klècèk *var of* **klècèp**.

klècem *or* **mak klècem** *repr* a sudden happy smile;
nglècem to smile;
klécam-klècem to keep smiling happily.

klècèp, **nglècèp** to peel off, come off;
nglècèpi to remove the outer layer from;
klècèpan a peeled-off outer layer.

klècèt peeled off;
nglècèt *or* **nglècèti** to peel off;
klècètan s.t. peeled off.

kleci a kind of potato.

klecing *reg* a sharp disagreeable odour.

klecir, **pating klecir** in little heaps, divided into separate groups, spread out.

klecis, **nglecis** to smoke habitually, nonstop;
pating klecis to be chatting energetically everywhere.

kledhak, **pating kledhak** in a mess, in disorder.

klédhang, klédhang-klédhang to come out for a walk, turn up;
nglédhangi to look up (a girl), turn up at s.o.'s place.

kledhek var of kledhak.

klèdhèk reg var of tlèdhèk.

klèdheng, klèdhengan tangled, in a tangle; confused, in confusion.

kledhar var of kledhèr.

kledhèr, pating kledhèr scattered about in disorder.

kledhing var of klejing.

klédhok var of klédhon.

klédhon to make a mistake when counting, speaking;
nglédhoni, nglédhokaké to throw into confusion.

klédhong name of a fruit, also its tree.

klédhung a climbing shrub with edible fruit.

klégok var of klégon.

klegon to have an obligation to return a kindness.

klégon var of klédhon.

klèhèn reg why, how?

kléja var of kléjo.

klejang-klejing see klejing.

klèjem, klèjemé (he) looks as if (he is going to…).

kléjo name of one of the Chinese cards (*kertu cilik*).

kléjok var of klédhon.

klejing, klejingan to come (go) empty-handed;
klejang-klejing to leave shamefaced.

klek or mak klek repr breaking with a snap;
klak-klek pl to break, snap.

klèk or mak klèk repr cracking, snapping;
klak-klèk pl to break again and again, keep snapping.

klekab-klekeb to close s.t. repeatedly.

klékab see klékap.

klékap, nglékap to peel, come off (*e.g.* skin);

nglékapi to peel, take the skin off.

klékar or mak klékar repr a body falling face up;
nglékar, lékaran to lie down, drop on the floor.

klekeb or mak klekeb repr covering or closing s.t. tightly. See also krekeb.

klèkèh var of klèkèk.

klekek or mak klekek repr choking, s.o. being choked.

klèkèk or mak klèkèk repr a knife stroke;
nglèkèk to slaughter.

klekep see klekeb.

klèkèp, nglèkèp to peel/come off;
nglèkèpi to peel s.t., take the skin off;
klèkèpan peelings, parings.
See also klokop.

kleker I or mak kleker repr lying curled up; kleker-kleker, pating kleker lying curled up everywhere;
ngleker to curl up and sleep.
II hoarse, croaking (of the voice).

kleket impulse; drive, enthusiasm, spirit. See also kerkat.

klélad-klèlèd see klèlèd.

klelang-kleleng see kleleng.

klelar-kleler see kleler.

klèlèd I, klélat-klèlèd to tarry, linger (be slow to move, take too long);
nglèlèd to be listless, move sluggishly, unwillingly.
II klélad-klèlèd to keep poking the tongue out.

kleled, kleledan to have s.t. stuck in the throat.

kleleg, klelegen to swallow s.t. by accident;
nglelegi likely to get swallowed (*e.g.* a sweet).

klelek see kleleg.

kleleng or mak kleleng repr sneaking away/out;
ngleleng to leave without a word.

klelep to sink below the surface. See also lelep.

kleler I mak - *repr* a shudder of revulsion; kleler-kleler, kleleran to crawl, poke along;
klelar-kleler to dawdle, hang back.
II, ngleler 1 to calm down, almost doze off; 2 to leave unobtrusively, creep off;
ngleleri to soothe.

klèlèr, nglèlèr to loaf, take it easy;
klèlèran neglected, abandoned.

klelet *see* kleled.

klèlèt nicotine.

klemad-klemed *see* klemed.

klemah-klemèh slow, disinterested, without spirit.

klemak-klemèk *see* klemèk.

klémas a variety of banana.

klémat, klématé judging from appearances...

klembak a variety of rhubarb, the fragrant root of which is used medicinally and for flavouring cigarettes.

klémbar, klémbar-klémbar *reg* to appear, be visible now and then.

klembeng, klembengan to get together (to chat, eat).

klembrèh, nglembrèh to hang down loosely;
pating klembrèh *pl* to hang untidily.

klèmbrèh *var of* klembrèh.

klembret, nglembret *or* pating klembret (of clothing) ragged;
klembretan rag, scrap; ragged clothing.

klembung, klembungan *reg* balloon.

klemed, klemedan *or* klemad-klemed *see* klamed.

klemek, nglemek not dry enough, not crisp, soggy (food).

klemèk, nglemèk *or* klemak-klemèk (to speak) slowly, deliberately, hesitantly; (to do) sluggishly.

klèmèn *reg* why, how?

klemeng, nglemeng *or* klemeng-klemeng stifling, sweltering (overcast weather).

klèmeng, klèmengan *reg* to forget, to have s.t. slip one's mind.

klemer, nglemer *or* klemer-klemer to loiter, linger, dawdle.

klemèr (of child) very weak, sickly.

klemet *see* klemed.

klemir, nglemir *or* klemir-klemir to feel very thin and soft (fabric).

klemis *reg* sleek (*var of* klimis).

klempak altogether; as a group (*kr for* klumpuk).

klempas-klempus *see* klempus.

klemper *reg* to faint.

klemperek *var of* klemprek.

klempis, nglempis to pant, breathe heavily.

klempon *reg* to drop off to sleep accidentally, doze off.

klempor, pating klempor aglow, twinkling with many small points of light.

klemprak-klemprek *see* klemprek.

klémprak, nglémprak *or* klémprakan to sit around casually (on the floor);
pating klémprak *pl* as above.

klemprang-klempreng *see* klempreng.

klemprek *or* mak klemprek *repr* a flop, crumpling and falling;
nglemprek to lie weakly;
klemprak-klemprek to keep falling weakly.

klempreng, nglempreng to walk slowly, sedately, sunk in thought; to stride purposefully;
klemprang-klempreng to pace back and forth.

klempuruk, nglempuruk *or* pating klempuruk to form piles, lie in heaps.

klempus, nglempus to sleep soundly, without stirring;
klempas-klempus to breathe noisily (asleep);
pating klempus *pl* to sleep soundly.
See also klepus.

klemuk a large covered earthenware container for oil *etc.*

klemun, klemun-klemun 1 dim, hazy; 2 dizzy, light headed.

klencar, pating klencar *pl* gleaming, glowing, shining.

klencèr *var of* klencar.

klèncèr, nglèncèr *or* klèncèran to go out s.w. for pleasure;
nglèncèri to go out to meet s.o. (with romantic intentions);
nglèncèraké to take s.o. out for pleasure.

klencrang, pating klencrang to produce loud jingling sounds.

klencring, pating klencring to produce light tinkling sounds.

klendhah-klendhèh *see* klendhèh.

klendhak *reg* earthenware water jug.

klendhang, klendhang-klendhang *or* pating klendhang slimy, running (*e.g.* eyes); standing in dirty puddles.

klendhang-klendhong *see* klendhong.

klendhèh, nglendhèh 1 to slouch, sag; 2 to become weak (of spirit); 3 slow down (work);
klendhèh-klendhèh *or* klendhah-klendhèh (of walking gait) slow-paced.

klendheng *var of* klendhang.

klendhet I *reg* slow; behind. *See also* rendhet.
II *reg* deep feeling, great longing. *See also* krenteg.

kléndho *reg* remains of coconut from which oil has been extracted.

klendhok *reg* earthen cooking pot.

klendhong, nglendhong loose, slack, sagging;
klendhang-klendhong *or* pating klendhong *pl* to move loosely.

klendi *reg* how?

kleneng, ngleneng to flow smoothly, to keep going steadily.

klenèng, klenèngan programme of gamelan music.

klenger 1 to lose consciousness; 2 to be 'knocked out' (by an emotion);

nglengeri, nglengeraké to render unconscious.

klengkang-klengkeng *see* klengkeng.

klengkeng *or* mak klengkeng *repr* twitching death throes;
klengkang-klengkeng (of animals) to die one after the other.

klèngkèng I a certain small fruit, similar to lychee but smaller with smooth brown skin.
II, nglèngkèng *or* klèngkèngan 1 to howl (dogs); 2 *cr* to sing in a loud, carrying voice; 3 (of an empty stomach) to growl, rumble.

klèngsrèh *var of* kèngsrèh.

klenguk, pating klenguk *pl* sitting around idly, thinking of nothing much.

klenik I magic; dhukun - practitioner of black magic; ngèlmu - the black arts; nglenik to practise black magic.
II, nglenik, *or* klenik-klenik *or* klenikan to talk privately.
III, pating klenik laid out, set in place (little items, trinkets).

klening, kleningan *reg* informal gamelan concert. *See also* klenèng.

klenis *var of* klethis.

klenjar gland.

klènjèr *var of* klenjar.

klénthang name of fruit of a certain plant (kélor).

klenthar 1 hanging loose; 2 neglected, not finished; pating - lying about in disorder;
nglenthar 1 to hang loose, come loose (*e.g.* rope); 2 to be left neglected, unfinished;
nglentharaké 1 to leave undone, in disorder; 2 to neglect, break (promise), let s.o. down.

klenthé, nglenthé *or* klenthé-klenthé 1 to walk slowly without anything to carry; 2 broke.

klènthèk, nglènthèk to come off, come unstuck;

nglènthèki to peel s.t. off, unstick s.t.; klènthèkan peeled off.

klentheng kapok-seed.

klenthèng Chinese temple.

klènthèng, pating klènthèng or kumlènthèng pl to clang.

klenthing earthenware water jug.

klenthung I, nglenthung 1 to go, come empty-handed, unsuccessful; 2 to loiter, lounge, loaf.
II, nglenthung to roll up. See also lunthung.

klenthus, klenthusen reg suffering from swollen limbs, beriberi.

klentik coconut oil;
nglentik 1 to extract the oil from (coconuts); 2 fig to try to get money out of s.o.;
klentikan oil produced from extracting coconuts.

klentit clitoris (kr for itil) .

klentreng, nglentreng, klentreng-klentreng or klentrang-klentreng to walk slowly, saunter.

klèntrèng, klèntrèngan to walk about busily (e.g. searching).

klèntu wrong, mistaken (kr for klèru).

klenyam-klenyem see klenyem.

klényam or mak klényam repr peeling off;
nglényam 1 to come/peel off; 2 to peel s.t.

klenyem I fried cassava cake.
II, nglenyem or klenyam-klenyem (to eat) with great enjoyment.

klènyèm var of klényam.

klenyeng, nglenyeng 1 to feel dizzy, have a headache; 2 a bit crazy;
klenyeng-klenyeng feeling dizzy.

klenyer or mak klenyer repr a sudden thrill of pleasure;
nglenyer, kumlenyer delightful, refreshing (of a physical feeling);
klenyer-klenyer repr the feel of s.t. soft and slippery.

klenyir, gurih - reg very rich-tasting, esp suggesting the flavour of coconut milk.

klenyis var of klenyir.

klenyit 1 a more or less sharp smell; 2 a bit crazy; pating - mixed, hard to distinguish (unpleasant tastes or smells);
klenyitan 1 soft, gentle (gamelan); 2 bold, suggestive (jokes).

klèp valve.

klépak (var of klèpèk).

klépak-klèpèk see klèpèk.

klepar-kleper see kleper.

klepas-klepus see klepus.

klépat or mak klépat repr a quick turn, swerve;
nglépat, kumlépat to turn suddenly and depart.

klepèh reg soaking wet.

klepek I 1 or mak klepek repr sudden choking; 2 to die suddenly.
II pating - , klepek-klepek to flap the wings (chickens, restlessly).

klèpèk or mak klèpèk repr a flapping, turning motion;
klèpèkan 1 to keep flapping (fish out of water); 2 fig to struggle to do s.t.
klépak-klèpèk to keep wriggling.

klèpèn reg why, how?

kleper, ngleper to flutter;
kleper-kleper or klepar-kleper to keep flying about, back and forth.

klèpèt messy (eating);
klèpètan to be affected by association (esp bad reputation). See also lèpèt.

klepis, nglepis to smoke heavily, chainsmoke;
pating klepis pl same as above.

klepoh var of klepèh.

klepon I a glutinuous rice flour cake filled with coconut sugar.
II ovaries and uterus of slaughtered animals.

klépos, pating - lying about fast asleep.

kleprèh soaking wet. See also keprèh, keproh.

klepruk, pating klepruk broken, smashed to bits.

klépun *reg kr* why, how?

klepus, nglepus *or* klepas-klepus 1 to smoke continuously, blow a lot of smoke; 2 to brag, talk big, sound off.

klépyan *reg* forgotten; to slip one's mind.

klepyar *pl form of* kepyar.

klepyur *pl form of* kepyur.

klérap, pating klérap to sparkle, glitter (reflected light).

klerek, klerek-klerek sore (of the throat); hoarse (of the voice).

klèrek clerk;
nglèrek to work as a clerk.

klèru *ng*, klèntu *kr*, 1 mistaken, confused; 2 wrong; 3 to make a mistake;
kléra-klèru to keep making mistakes;
nglérokaké confusing (causing you to get the wrong idea).

klésa *lit* impurity.

klesak-klesik *see* klesik.

klesed *repr* a sudden slight movement;
nglesed to shift, budge, move slightly;
klesed-klesed *or* klesad-klesed to keep shifting, making small movements.

klèsèd, nglèsèd to sit/lie helplessly on the floor;
klèsèdan to sit/lie around listlessly or wearily.

klesik, klesik-klesik *or* klesak-klesik (to talk) in whispers.

klésod, nglésod to sit on the floor/ground without caring where;
klésodan to keep moving around in a crouching position.

klethak *or* mak klethak *repr* cracking with the teeth;
nglethak to crack with the teeth;
kumlethak to make a cracking sound;
klethak-klethuk *see* klethuk.

klethar-klethir *see* klethir.

klethek *or* mak klethek *repr* a dull rattling;

klethek-klethek to keep on rattling;
nglethek *or* klethekan to make a rattling sound while doing s.t.

klèthèk I *var of* klènthèk.
II *or* mak klèthèk *repr* clatter;
kléthak-klèthèk to keep clattering;
kumlèthèk to clatter.

klethes *or* mak klethes *repr* pressing, squashing, crushing.

klèthi *reg* iron club, cudgel.

klethik *repr* the sound of eating s.t. crisp (*e.g.* a chip), crunch;
nglethik to bite into, chew s.t. crisp;
kumlethik to produce the above sound;
klethikan crisp snack.

klethir, klethar-klethir *or* pating klethir to (do) little by little rather than all at once.

klethis *repr* the sound of biting s.t. that is hard (*e.g.* little fruits, uncooked rice grains);
nglethis 1 to bite a small hard object; 2 (of steamed rice) not cooked through.

kléthot *reg* mistaken, wrong.

klethuk *or* mak klethuk *repr* teeth biting down on s.t. hard;
nglethuk to crack s.t. hard with the teeth.

klethus *or* mak klethus *repr* teeth cracking s.t. hard;
nglethus to bite s.t. hard.

kletik *reg var of* klentik.

kleting I a spool of thread for weaving.
II, ngleting to force s.o. to drink medicine.

kléyak-kléyok to wobble unsteadily, rock.

kléwa, kléwa-kléwa to act coolly, be unwilling to converse;
ngléwani to treat s.o. coolly.

kléwah *or* mak kléwah *repr* splitting, slashing;
ngléwah to break open;

kumléwah split wide open.

kléwang sword with a broad curved blade; **ngléwang** to strike or cut with the above.

kléwas, **ngléwas** to avert the face, turn away (as a sign of dislike).

klèwèr, **nglèwèr** 1 to hang limp/loose; 2 to hang around; 3 to let hang; **klèwèran** hang down limp; **pating klèwèr** *pl* to wave, flutter, hang down limp.

klèwès, **nglèwès** *or* **kléwas-klèwès** to turn aside the head.

kléyang, **pating -** to flutter downwards (*e.g.* falling leaves); **ngléyang** *or* **kléyang-kléyang** to flutter down, tumble (*e.g.* kite).

klèyèg, **klèyègan** to wander around aimlessly.

klèyèk *var of* **klèyèg**.

kléyos *reg* to disappear, run away.

klicat, **klicatan** to shift uneasily, move restlessly.

klicèt *reg* to take off (clothes).

klici, **nglici** to polish up, give a shine.

klicir, **klicir-klicir** *or* **pating klicir** to be spread in little bits here and there.

klicit (of hair) smooth and oily.

klicut, **klicutan** embarrassed and shy, to not dare look s.o. in the eye.

klidheng, **klidhengan** confused, to make a mistake, forget

kliga, **kligané** *reg* luckily, by good luck.

klik *or* **mak klik** *repr* cracking, snapping, breaking with a snap.

klika bark of a tree.

klikat, **klikaten** *reg* to have a muscular spasm, cramp.

kliki *reg* castor oil plant.

klikik, **klikikan** *or* **klikak-klikik** (of empty stomach) to rumble softly; **nglikik** to giggle, titter; **pating klikik** to keep giggling.

klikip, **klikipan** a covered partition in a large storage box.

klilab, **klilaban** 1 passed by; 2 overlooked; 3 unaware, oblivious of.

klilan *see* **lila**.

klilap *see* **klilab**.

klilin *reg var of* **kliling**.

kliling to go around, make rounds; **klilingan** a circular; **saklilingé** around, surrounding.

klilip 1 a speck in the eye; 2 *fig* nuisance, pest; **klilipen** to have/get s.t. in the eye.

klimah utterance, statement. *See also* **kalimah**.

klimeng, **klimengan** *reg* to grope about in the dark. *See also* **limeng**.

klimis glossy, sleek; (of hair) smooth and oily.

klimpé *see* **limpé**.

klimput *see* **limput**.

klimun *var of* **klimeng**.

klincir *reg* soaking wet.

klincur *var of* **klincut**.

klincut *var of* **klicut**.

klindhen driving-cord of a spinning-wheel.

klingking I little finger.
   II, **klingkingan** to yelp in pain. *See also* **klèngkèng** II.
   III, **kumlingking** *intsfr* dry, bone dry.

klingkung mistaken.

klingsi tamarind pit. *See also* **klungsu**.

klinik clinic, hospital.

klintang-klinting *see* **klinting**.

klintar-klinter *see* **klinter**.

klinter, **nglinter** to circle around (awaiting the moment to approach and seize s.t.); **nglinteri** to circle around s.t.; **klinteran** *or* **klintar-klinter** to keep circling.

klinthang-klinthing *see* **klinthing**.

klinthing I the sound of a little bell; **klinthang-klinthing** to keep ringing; **klinthingan** a little bell (*e.g.* cat's).
   II, **nglinthing** *or* **kumlinthing** wrinkled, shrivelled, dried up.

klinthung, klinthungan *or* **klinthang-klinthung** to wander about aimlessly.

klinting I, klintingan to lie untidily on the ground.

II, klintang-klinting to wander around, pass the time aimlessly.

klintong, klintong-klintong to take a stroll.

klintrek, klintrek-klintrek to look too soggy, watery.

klinyem *var of* **klényam**.

klinyit shiny and oily.

klipcan *reg* to have s.t. slip one's mind. *See also* **klépyan**.

klipyan *var of* **klépyan**.

klirak *see* **lirik**.

klirik, klirak-klirik to look around furtively. *See also* **lirik**.

kliru *var of* **klèru**.

klisa the edible root of the **kacipir**, a climbing plant.

klisé 1 cliché; **2** photographic negative; **3** plate for making engravings.

klisik, nglisik *or* **klisikan** to toss restlessly, not be able to sleep.

klithah-klithih *see* **klithih**.

klithak-klithik *see* **klithik**.

klithih, nglithih *or* **klithihan** to pace back and forth restlessly; **klithah-klithih** to keep moving and looking after s.t. lost.

klithik *or* **mak klithik** *repr* clinking; **nglithik** (*or* **klithikan**) **1** to make clinking sounds while doing s.t.; **2** small second hand; **klithikan** small second-hand articles sold by peddlers in the market.

kliwat *see* **liwat**.

kliwed, kliwed-kliwed to show up s.w., to put in a brief appearance; **kumliwet** to pass by swiftly.

kliweng *var of* **kliyeng**.

kliwer, ngliwer *or* **kumliwer** to appear briefly; **kliweran** *or* **kliwar-kliwer** to keep darting about;

pating kliwer moving about in large numbers.

kliwon 1 a day of the five-day week; **2** an administrative official of low rank.

kliyang *var of* **kléyang**.

kliyek, ngliyek *or* **kliyekan** to stroll, saunter back and forth.

kliyeng, ngliyeng *or* **kliyengan** *or* **kliyeng-kliyeng** dizzy, light-headed.

klobak, klobakan *or* **klobak-klobak** to wash, slop back and forth (waves).

klobot (**wiru** *subst kr*) dried covering of a corn cob, used as cigarette wrapper; **nglobot** to smoke such cigarettes.

klocok *var of* **klocop**.

klocop, nglocop to peel, skin, remove the outer covering from s.t. hard.

klocut soaking wet; **nglocut** to get o.s. wet, *esp* by going out in the rain.

kloko *or* **mak kloko** *repr* a sudden release from a grasp, a sudden becoming slack; **ngloko** loose, slack.

klokop, nglokop to come/peel off; **nglokopi** to peel s.t.; **klokopan** peelings, parings; **pating klolop** *pl* to come/peel off.

klokor I, nglokor (of the voice) hoarse, husky.

II, nglokor to become loose or slack.

klokro *or* **mak klokro** *repr* a sudden giving up; **nglokro** to lose hope, give up.

klolar-klolor *see* **klolor**.

klolod, kloloden to choke from getting s.t. stuck in the throat; **nglolodi** to cause choking, get stuck in the throat.

klolor, nglolor 1 to to crawl, creep over the ground, make twisting movements; **2** clumsy, indolent; **klolar-klolor** to work clumsily; **kloloran** *or* **pating klolor** *or* **klolor-klolor** *repr* twisting, crawling, creeping about.

klomah-klamèh *see* klamèh.

klombèr, klombèran *reg* sewer, drain, gutter, gully.

klombot *reg var of* klobot.

klombroh I loose and ill-fitting; nglombroh *or* klombrohan sloppy-looking. II soaking wet.

klombrot, nglombrot too big, sloppy (clothes).

klombyar-klombyor *see* klombyor.

klombyor, nglombyor *or* klombyor-klombyor *or* klombyar-klombyor 1 watery, thin; 2 flabby, limp.

klomod *reg var of* klomoh.

klomoh covered, thick with oil, grease; nglomohi 1 to grease, rub with oil; 2 to cheat or deceive s.o.

klomprot, nglomprot *or* pating klomprot to dress sloppily.

kloncèr *var of* koncèr.

klongkang-klongkong *see* klongkong.

klongkong, nglongkong 1 to howl in pain (dogs); 2 *cr* to sing loudly; klongkongan *or* klongkang-klongkong 1 to keep howling in pain; 2 to keep singing loudly.

klonthang-klanthung *see* klanthung.

klonthok, nglonthok to peel off; klonthokan peeled off. *Also* klèthèk, klothok.

klonthong I 1 a small drum-like implement which one shakes to produce light rat-a-tat sounds; also the sounds produced in this way; 2 an itinerant peddler who deals *esp* in clothing fabrics and daily goods, and who attracts customers with the above implement; also goods peddled in this way; nglonthong 1 to rat-a-tat with the above noisemaker; 2 to sell goods as above; klonthongan noisemaker as above. II, klonthongan 1 hollow, cavity; 2 anything that is empty, empty shell, box *etc.*

klontrong, nglontrong to walk off in anger; pating klontrong *pl* slipping and sliding everywhere.

klonyo eau-de-cologne.

klonyom *or* mak klonyom *repr* peeling off in big strips; nglonyom to peel s.t. that peels easily. *Also* klunyum.

klop 1 to agree, tally; 2 to match, fit.

klopak, nglopak *or* klopakan *or* pating klopak (of fish) to splash around in the water.

klopod smeared with dirt.

klopok *var of* kropok II.

kloprah abundant, lots and lots (of s.t.); kumloprah to make a display of one's generosity.

kloprot dirty, messy; ngloproti to get s.t. messy.

klorèh, klorèhan too long-winded (explanation).

klosod, nglosod *or* klosodan 1 to move along the ground; 2 to sit/lie on the floor/ground.

klothak *or* mak klothak *repr* a thud; klothakan *or* pating klothak to thud everywhere.

klothèk *var of* klothak.

klothak-klothèk to keep thudding.

klothok I *var of* klonthok. II pure, unmixed, genuine.

klotor *reg* a variety of four-wheeled cart.

klowang-klawung *see* klawung.

klowoh an earthen spittoon; nglowoh to gape open-mouthed.

klowong I 1 *repr* going slack, loosening. II, nglowongi to outline a batik pattern on fabric; klowongan outlined pattern on fabric.

klowos, nglowos empty-handed.

kloyong, ngloyong to take a stroll, wander about; kloyongan *or* kloyong-kloyong to stagger, reel, roll.

kloyor, ngloyor *or* kloyoran *or* kloyor-kloyor to walk with a stagger.

kluban *see* kulub.

klubuk, nglubuk *or* klubukan *or* klubuk-klubuk 1 to flutter, flap the wings (trying to escape); 2 to rush about in distress.

klucèh, klucèh-klucèh pallid, wan.

klucup *or* mak klucup *repr* a sudden smooth, slippery emergence.

klucut *see* klocut.

kludhag-kludheg *see* kludheg.

kludheg, kludhegan *or* kludhag-kludheg to produce bumping, knocking sounds.

klugur, pating klugur *pl* all lengthwise, stretched out.

kluk *or* mak kluk *repr* joint cracking; klak-kluk *repr* snapping sounds.

klukak-klukuk *see* klukuk.

kluku, ngluku to soak a magically powerful object in water to make medicine; klukon medicine produced by soaking such an object.

klukuk, nglukuk *or* klukak-klukuk (of empty stomach) to rumble.

klulik *reg* young leaf of the nipah palm (for wrapping cigarettes).

klulur, nglulur *or* klulur-klulur *or* klular-klulur (to move) slowly, crawl (worm, caterpillar).

klulut *lit* beloved, loved one. *See also* lulut.

klumah *see* lumah.

klumbruk, nglumbruk forming a heap; nglumbrukaké to pile things in disorderly heaps; klumbrukan *or* pating klumbruk *pl* heaped about in disorder.

klumpeng, klumpengan in a quandary, unable to think of a way out.

klumpruk, nglumpruk to collapse in a heap; nglumprukaké to drop, throw in an untidy heap; pating klumpruk *pl* flopping down in a heap;

klumprak-klumpruk lying about in an untidy heap.

klumpuk *ng*, klempak *kr*, as a group, together; klumpuk-klumpuk *or* keklumpuk to accumulate bit by bit; nglumpuk to gather together, forming a group; nglumpukaké to gather, collect; klumpukan 1 to come together; 2 group, collection.

klumud soiled, dirty.

klumur, klumur-klumur to loiter, dawdle, move at a snail's pace.

klumus *reg* soaking wet.

kluncing *reg* dripping (wet). *See also* klunyut.

kluncur *var of* kluncing.

klungsu tamarind pit.

klungsur sagging, hanging (cheek).

klunthang, klunthangan ill-mannered, impudent, insolent.

klunthuh, nglunthuh *or* klunthuh-klunthuh (to walk) with stooped shoulders and bowed head.

klunthung I, nglunthung to roll up; kumlunthung forming a roll. II, klunthung-klunthung *repr* a clatter, rattle (wooden cow-bell).

kluntrung, ngluntrung *or* kluntrung-kluntrung to walk off in disappointment; kluntrang-kluntrung to walk back and forth aimlessly.

klunyat, klunyatan boorish, churlish.

klunyum *var of* klonyom.

klunyut *reg* dripping (wet).

kluron *ng, kr*, terag *k.i.* to have a miscarriage.

kluruk 1 rooster's crow; *fig* boastfulness; 2 (of stomach) to rumble with hunger.

klusad-klusud *see* klusud.

klusud *or* mak klusud *repr* a quick slip or slide;

klusudan *or* **klusad-klusud** to keep slipping, sliding about.

kluthak-kluthek *see* **kluthek**.

kluthek, ngluthek to clatter around;
kluthekan *or* **kluthak-kluthek** 1 to making little rattling sounds; 2 to clatter around busily.

kluthuk I pure, unmixed, genuine, real.
II *or* **mak kluthuk** *repr* a small hard object rattling;
kluthuk-kluthuk *or* **kluthak-kluthuk** *or* **kumluthuk** to keep making rattling sounds.
III 1 a wooden cow-bell; 2 a small wooden box; 3 a kind of beehive; 4 a kind of box lantern.
IV a variety of **jambu**.

kluwa candied fruits, sugared preserves;
ngluwa to make candied fruits.

kluwak mature seeds of the **pucung** tree, used as a food.

kluwar-kluwer *see* **kluwer**.

kluwas *reg* miscarriage.

kluwat grave, burial pit.

kluwek *var of* **kluwak**.

kluweng *or* **mak kluweng** *repr* a sudden swerve;
ngluwengaké to turn to(ward) s.t.;
kluwengan 1 to keep coiling up, turning around; 2 circle, coil.

kluwer *or* **mak kluwer** *repr* turning, swirling, eddying;
ngluwer 1 to turn, curve, curl; 2 to turn off, take a side road;
ngluweri to go around s.t., surround;
ngluweraké to turn s.t.; to put s.t. around;
kluwar-kluwer *or* **pating kluwer** all in curls.

kluwuk *var of* **klawus**.

kluwus *var of* **klawus**.

kluyu, ngluyu (of batik) to renew the blue colour;
kluyon renewed batik colour.

kluyug, kluyugan *reg* to wander about aimlessly.

kluyur, mak - *repr* a leaving abruptly;
ngluyur *or* **kluyuran** to wander about aimlessly;
kluyur-kluyur to stroll, amble about.

ko *coll* later on (*shtf of* **mengko**).

koak-kaèk 1 to shout, call out loudly; 2 to boast, talk nonsense.

kobak *reg* famous, renowned.

kobar flaming, in flames. *See also* **obar** I.

kobèk *var of* **kobik**.

kober to have (enough) time, the opportunity;
ngoberaké to make time for s.t.

kobèt to have plenty of room (for), plenty of supply or stock;
ngobètaké to take care of, run s.t.

kobik, kobik-kobik to be in great difficulties.

kobis cabbage.

koblok *reg* stupid (*var of* **goblog**).

kobok, kobok-kobok, ngobok to put the hands (or feet) in a container of water and splash them about;
kobokan *ng*, *kr*, **wijikan** *k.i.* fingerbowl.

kobol to be in deficit;
kobol-kobol to lose a lot of money.

kobong, kobongan I 1 screened-off room, bedroom; 2 central, innermost room in a traditional house where the bridal bed stands.
II *see* **obong**.

kobot *reg var of* **klobot**.

kobra great; **kiyamat** - the great Day of Resurrection.

kocak 1 to slosh about (liquid in a container); 2 to wash to and fro (sea); 3 expressive, lively (eyes);
ngocak *or* **ngocak-ocak** to shake s.t. up.

kocap *see* **ucap**.

kocar-kacir scattered (in little bits);
ngocar-acir to scatter s.t. in confusion.

kocèh 1 to splash about in water; 2 to splurge money;

ngocèh to chatter meaninglessly, babble.

kocèk, ngocèki *reg* to peel off. *See also* **oncèk**.

koci sloop (*var of* **sekoci**).

kocing cat (*reg var of* **kucing**).

kociwa *reg var of* **kuciwa**.

koclak *var of* **kocak**.

koclok *var of* **kocok**.

kocoh, ngocoh to tease, ridicule s.o.

kocok, ngocok 1 shake up up and down; 2 to shuffle;

ngocok-ocok to masturbate (males).

kocol, kocolan 1 baby fish (young of an **iwak**); 2 the young of a certain freshwater fish (**kutuk**).

kocor, ngocor to pour water;

ngocori to pour water on;

kumocor to drool.

kocrat-kacrit to spill out, a bit here and there.

kocrok, ngocrok to shake, mix, stir, shuffle (cards). *See also* **kocok**.

kocrot, kocrotan to get an unexpected benefit from s.o. else's good luck.

kodag *cr* able; capable. *See also* **godag**.

kodal, ora - to have no effect.

kodhak camera.

kodhé, ngodhé *reg* to work for wages;

kodhéan 1 wages, salary; 2 job, work to get wages.

kodhèk flat wooden kitchen tool resembling a pancake turner;

ngodhèki 1 to pick at (the remainders of a meal); 2 to scrape clean with the above tool.

kodheng 1 bewildered, confused; 2 (of eyeballs) turning outward;

ngodhengaké confusing.

kodhi a score (counting term used in the marketplace);

sakodhi (of cotton material) 20 pieces;

kodhèn 1 by the score; 2 of inferior quality.

kodhik *reg* narrow, tight.

kodhok frog, toad; **- ijo** a certain edible green frog; **- ngorèk** an archaic three-toned gamelan kept in the Kratons of Yogyakarta and Surakarta, played only on solemn occasions; **- ula** gambling game played with dice on a revolving board; **mobil -** beetle (VW);

ngodhok 1 to pick (betel leaves) from a tree while standing on the ground; 2 (to ride a bicycle) standing on the pedals, sitting on the cross-bar, or with feet up;

kodhokan 1 resembling a frog; 2 *fig* (of glassware, lamps) having no base/foot;

kodhok-kodhokan 1 toy frog, imitation frog; 2 to play frogs;

kodhok ngemuli lèngé *prov* a highly improbable event;

kodhok nguntal gajah *prov* to attempt the impossible;

kodhok sajroning bathok *prov* narrow-minded.

kodhol, kekodhol, ngodhol to follow at a distance to stay on s.o.'s track.

kodhor *reg* a house with dried palm leaf roof.

kodo 1 boorish, gauche; 2 stupid.

kodrat 1 the almighty power of God; 2 disposition, nature; 3 by nature, inborn.

ko'en *reg* you.

kogel to feel sorry for s.o.

kogèl, ngogèl *or* **kogèl-kogèl** to wriggle, writhe. *See also* **ogèl**.

kogug to have a strong aversion to, feel revulsion for.

kogung *see* **ugung** I.

koh *reg* why? how come? (*var of* **kok**).

kohen *reg* you.

kohir 1 (tax) assessment register; 2 assessment number; 3 extract from register.

koho *reg* shortly, soon.

kohong *reg* lonely.

koja merchant (usually Muslim Indian); **pakojan** the Indian merchants' quarter.

kojah 1 exposition, account, argument; 2 to tell;
ngojahi to instruct;
ngojahaké to give an account of.

kojar *see* **ujar**.

kojat *lit* famous, renowned.

kojèk, kojèk-kojèk to have difficulties.

kojèl, kojèl-kojèl to have death throes, twitch spasmodically.

kojong mosquito net for a baby's cot;
ngojongi to equip (a cot) with a mosquito net.

kojor I *reg* stick, long piece of wood.
II **kekojor** fortified camp.

kojrat *var of* **kodrat**.

kojur I to have bad luck; **ngojuraké** unlucky, to bring bad luck.
II *see* **sakojur**.

kojut, **ngojutaké** *reg* to hold a ritual gathering involving a meal on behalf of s.o.;
kojutan ritual meal;
sakojuté to the best of one's ability, as much as there is.

kok I 1 (in initial position) a particle expressing surprise, sometimes wondering what the reason is; 2 (in final position) particle lending emphasis, reminding the hearer of s.t. they should know.
II *2nd person passive prefix:* done by you.

kokap *lit* 1 cloud; 2 incense.

kokar cockade, rosette.

koki cook.

kokila *lit* bird (*also* **kukila**).

kokis a variety of pancake.

koklok damaged, broken down, not functioning.

koko I *coll* shortly, soon (*shtf of* **mengkomengko**).
II, **ngoko** 1 the speech style used

when addressing a social equal or inferior, *i.e.* s.o. addressed as **kowé** 'you'; 2 to speak Ngoko (to). *See also* **ngoko**.

kokoh I rice mixed into soup at mealtime (rather than eating each separately);
ngokoh to eat one's meal by mixing the rice into the soup;
kokohan rice-soup mixture.
II *see* **kukuh**.

kokok I muscular, sturdy.
II - **petok** *repr* a hen's cackle;
ngokok to cackle, cluck.
III **kokokbeluk** a variety of owl. *See also* **kukuk**.

kokol *reg* a wooden drum which is stuck to sound an alarm.

kokop, **ngokop** to slurp up, drink like an animal.

kokos, **kokosan** a certain small round yellowish fruit (*var of* **duku**).

kokot 1 firmly attached (*var of* **kèkèt**); 2 clasp; - **bisu** speechless with rage; - **bolot** dirt on the human body; **kokoten** to have dirt adhering to the skin.

kokrok *var of* **koklok**.

kol I cabbage.
II *or* **slametan kol** annual ceremony commemorating a death anniversary. *See also* **slamet**.

kolah tank (in bathroom). *Also* **kulah**.

kolak sweet dish made from cassava or banana stewed in coconut milk and sugar;
ngolak to make (ingredients) into the above.

kolam pond, pool.

kolang-kaling palm fruit.

kolé *var of* **kolèr**.

koled *reg* tardy, slow, indolent.

kolèd, **ngolèd** to wriggle, writhe;
kolèd-kolèd to writhe in snakelike motions.

koleg, koleg-koleg *reg* to have eaten more than enough.

kolèhé *see* **kulèhé.**

kolek *reg var of* **kolak.**

kolèk I (*or* **kolèkan**) small sailing vessel.
II, **ngolèk** to work for one's living.

kolèktur tax collector.

kolem column.

kolèr, ngolèr *or* **kolèr-kolèr** unwound, lying lose, not coiled (*e.g.* rope).

kolérah cholera.

koli piece, bag, bale.

kolik I female nocturnal cuckoo whose melancholy cry is said to presage thievery.
II, **ngolik 1** to eye covetously; **2** to work for one's living.

kolir 1 lose; **2** to suffer misfortune.

kolmak authorised, empowered.

kolog defective, unsatisfactory. *See also* **kolug.**

koloh I, ngoloh to soak s.t. in liquid (kris in arsenic, batik in dye);
kolohan liquid in which s.t. has been soaked.
II, *reg var of* **loloh.**

kolok, kolokan spoiled, overindulged.

kolonèl colonel.

kolong I 1 a measure: the amount that can be grasped in the circle formed by ⁻thumb and forefinger with tips touching; **2** a rope bird-trapping noose; **3** (*or* **kolongan**) ring-shaped object; metal ring for holding things together; **ngolong** *or* **ngolongi 1** to encircle/ enclose s.t. with a ring; **2** to catch in a noose.
II, **kolongan** the space under a bed, bench or house.

kolontara *var of* **lamtara.**

kolor cord used as a belt for trousers, pyjamas;
ngolor *fig* to bootlick;
ngolori to equip (trousers *etc*) with a cord.

kolot conservative.

kolu *see* **ulu II.**

kolug defective, unsatisfactory.

koma-koma, ora nganggo - to have no consideration (for subordinates).

komak variety of bean.

komala *lit* jewel, diamond (*var of* **kumala**).

komar, komaran to offer (flowers and food) for invisible spirits.

kombak-kombul to bob, rock on the waves (ship).

kombang a large black buzzing bee; **ngombang-ombang** to grumble.

kombar, kombar-kombar with too much juice (food).

komboh, ngombohaké to submerge or immerse s.t.

kombong, kombongan pen, coop.

kombor I long and wide-legged (pants).
II, **ngombor** (of horses) to eat bran and grass feed from a bucket;
ngombori 1 to feed (a horse) with bran and grass from a bucket; **2** (of people) *cr* to drink;
komboran 1 horse feed: bran mixed with grass; **2** cold weak tea or coffee.

kombot *reg* dried corn husk, used as cigarette wrappers.

kombul *see* **umbul I.**

komet *see* **umet.**

kometir *var of* **kumetir.**

komidhi circus; operatic, theatrical performance (Western style).

komindhi *var of* **komidhi.**

koming I 1 to roll on the ground (horse); **2** to turn this way and that, trying to find a way out of great difficulty.
II stunted; to remain small, not grow big.

komis clerk.

komisi 1 commission, board of investigators; **2** commission, *i.e.* percentage for selling; **3** bonus, reward.

komité committee.

komod *var of* **komoh.**

komoh *or* **komoh-komoh** soggy, sloppy, wet.

kompa a pump;
  ngompa to pump air (into);
  ngompakaké to have s.t. pumped.
kompèk a certain travel basket with a lid.
komper stove (*var of* **kompor**).
kompèren not up to much, unable to keep up.
komplah, komplah-komplah gaping, wide open (tear, wound).
komplang I vacant, unoccupied;
  ngomplangi *or* **ngomplangaké** to vacate, leave unoccupied.
  II, **komplang-komplang** filled to the brim, to lap the edge.
komplèh (of dog's ears) drooping, hanging down limply.
komplèk *reg* complete (*var of* **komplit**);
  komplèkan a set (of clothing, dinnerware *etc*).
komplèt *see* **komplit**.
komplit complete;
  ngompliti *or* **ngomplitaké** to complete;
  komplitan a set (of clothing, dinnerware *etc*).
komplo stupid, ignorant.
komplong, ngomplong to stand and stare, gape.
komplot, ngomplot to conspire;
  komplotan gang, a group of troublemakers.
kompol *reg* gunny sack.
kompor kerosene stove.
kompra low-class, common.
komprang, komprangan cut in a loose, baggy style (coat or shorts, worn by farmers).
komprèng I *var of* **komprang**.
  II, **ngomprèng** to give s.o. a ride but make them pay for it. *See also* **omprèng**.
  III fawn (a young of the **kidang** *or* **menjangan**).
komprèngsi a conference.

komprès cold compress, ice pack;
  ngomprès to apply an ice bag to.
komuk famous, renowned. *See also* **umuk**.
Komuni Holy Communion.
kon *ng*, **kèn** *kr*, **ngekon** (**dhawuh** *k.i.*, **ngaturi** *k.a.*) to order, tell s.o. to do s.t.;
  pakon 1 an order, command; 2 *gram* imperative.
  See also **akon, kongkon**.
konang I firefly;
  konangen (to see) stars/spots before the eyes; to feel the head reeling or throbbing.
  II, **ngonangi** to catch s.o. in the act;
  konangan to get caught doing s.t.
  See also **onang**.
konca train of a ceremonial kain (**dodot**). *See also* **kunca**.
koncar-kancir *reg* to walk back and forth.
koncé plaited (with flowers, horse's mane);
  ngoncé to plait the mane as above;
  koncèn plaited and decorated with flowers.
koncèr 1 a hanging decorative object (tassel, ribbon); 2 pendant, ear-drop. *Also* **kloncèr**.
konclak *var of* **konclang**.
konclang to get tossed away. *See also* **onclang**.
koncong *var of* **kojong**.
koncrat *reg* shaken, rattled.
kondhang famous, renowned.
kondhé hair wound into a smooth bun at the back of the head, chignon.
kondhèktur train conductor; ticket collector on a bus or train.
kondhisi to drink a toast.
kondhong *reg* a small inner room; a room created by partitioning.
kondhor 1 stretched, flabby (*e.g.* a worn-out rubber band); 2 rupture, hernia;
  kondhoren to have a rupture, hernia.
kondul *reg* to bring up (s.t. just swallowed).

kondur to return home, return to one's original place (*k.i. for* ulih); konduran to have left for home.

kongah-kangèh *or* kongah-kangih to feel restless, under increasing pressure.

kongak *lit* seen, caught sight of (in the distance). *See also* ungak.

kongang *lit* able, strong enough (to do s.t.).

kongas *lit* 1 to pervade (fragrance), spread; 2 well-known. *See also* ungas.

kongkal, kongkalan overwhelmed (*e.g.* by a mass of work).

kongkang a certain large frog.

kongkih *see* ungkih.

kongkil *see* ungkil.

kongkilèn *var of* konkirèn.

kongkirèn competitor, rival; kongkirènan to compete.

kongkon *ng*, kèngkèn *kr*, utus *k.i.*, ngongkon *or* kongkonan to order s.o. to do s.t.; to send s.o. on an errand; ngongkoni to send s.o. on an errand repeatedly; ngongkonaké to give orders to do s.t. for s.o. else; kongkonan 1 messenger, person sent on an errand; 2 an errand, message.

kongkrus, kongkurs a competition between singers or singing birds.

kongseb *see* ungseb.

kongsèng, ngongsèng to turn (food being fried).

kongsi I *ng*, ngantos *kr*, until, up to, as far as.
II company, firm, association, group; kongsèn 1 to enter into a commercial partnership; 2 merchant's association; shared ownership of a business.

kongsulèn *var of* konsulèn.

konjem *see* unjem.

konjuk *see* unjuk.

kono *ng*, ngriku *kr* 1 there, that place; 2 go ahead!; 3 you; ngonokaké to treat/handle in that way.

konok I *reg* I don't know.
II konokan that sort of thing; konok onggrok *cr* a person like that.

konsulèn consultant.

konta *lit* a short lance, spear (*var of* kunta).

kontab famous, renowned.

kontak to come into contact with; ngontak 1 to switch/turn on (a light, engine); 2 to contact (s.o.); kontakan electric switch.

kontal to get hurled, flung.

kontan 1 cash (as contrasted with credit); 2 at that very moment, on the spot; ngontani to pay cash for.

kontang-kanting swung back and forth.

kontap *see* kontab.

kontelir inspector, supervisor (*var of* kontrolir).

konten door (*md, kr for* lawang).

konthal-kanthil *see* kanthil I.

konthèng, konthèngan *reg* courageous, bold.

konthèt stunted, unable to achieve normal growth (*var of* kunthèt).

konthing *reg* a small boat.

konthol 1 scrotum; 2 penis; kontholan padlock.

konthong *reg* a small inner room (*var of* kondhong).

kontit defeated, to be no match for.

konto a Chinese system of self-defence.

kontrag to shake violently (*e.g.* the earth); ngontragaké to to shake s.t.

kontrak contract; agreement; ngontrak to lease s.t. with a contract; ngontrakaké to contract s.t. out; kontrakan s.t. leased (out).

kontrang-kantring *or* kontrang-kantringan bewildered, desperate, in deep trouble.

kontribisi a contribution, *usu* of money.

kontrolir inspector, supervisor.

kontul a certain white heron (*var of* kuntul);

nggolèki tapaking kontul nglayang *fig* to attempt the impossible;

kontul diunèkaké dhandhang *prov* to call white black, distort facts, twist the truth.

kontung 1 hardship, loss; 2 to suffer a setback.

konus *see* **unus**.

konyal-kanyil lively, coquettish.

konyar-kanyir unreliable, to give nothing to hold onto.

konyas-kanyis (to speak) sweetly and pleasantly.

konyoh cosmetic cream (*k.i. for* **borèh**).

konyol inviting bad luck, silly.

konyor I, **konyor-konyor** 1 smooth, easy to swallow; 2 (of meat) tender, soft.

II spanking new.

kop I, **ngekop** to head (a soccer ball);

kop-kopan act or way of hitting (a ball) with the head.

II, **ngekop** to treat a headache by pressing a hollow hemispherical object against the forehead;

kop-kopan mark on the skin resulting from treating as above.

kopah, kopah-kopah wet with blood.

kopak *reg* section, part, group (belonging to s.t.).

kopang *lit* 100 (*var of* **kupang**).

kopar unbelieving, godless (*var of* **kapir**).

kopat-kapit to wag (the tail).

kopèk floppy, pendulous (breasts);

ngopèk 1 to become floppy; 2 to hang onto the breast (child).

kopèn *see* **opèn**.

koper bag, suitcase.

kopès, ngopès to peel.

kopèt 1 to fail to wash o.s. properly after going to the toilet; 2 dirty, unwashed.

kopi coffee (tree, bean, drink); - **luwak** coffee made from beans that have been digested by a **luwak**;

ngopi to drink coffee;

pakopèn coffee plantation.

kopik I *reg* ora - to have lost nothing, not be reduced.

II (to play) a certain game with the Chinese cards (*kertu cilik*).

koplak I to rattle around inside a container (*e.g.* seed inside fruit); to slosh about (water in coconut);

ngoplakaké endhasé *cr* to make the head pound (with thinking).

II, **koplakan** stopping-place, waiting-place (for carts, waggoners, merchants).

kopling 1 clutch (part of car); 2 coupling (railway carriage).

koplo idiotic;

koplo-koplo (of cheeks) fat and sagging.

koploh hanging loose, flapping.

koplok I old, worn-out, ragged.

II clapper, made of a bamboo section split lengthwise, for scaring off birds.

III, **ngoplok** to shudder, shiver.

IV, **ngoplok** to beat, whisk (*e.g.* eggs).

koplos *reg var of* **koploh**.

kopo *reg* butterfly (*var of* **kupu**).

kopoh, kopoh-kopoh soaking wet, soggy, sopping.

kopok pus, matter discharged from an infected ear;

kopoken 1 having infected ears; 2 *cr* deaf.

kopong 1 empty, without content (fruit); 2 *fig* empty-headed, ignorant.

kopos *var of* **kopong**.

koprah copra.

koprak 1 noisemaker for scaring birds and squirrels away from a crop (*var of* **goprak**); 2 sickle sheath.

kopral corporal.

koprat-kaprèt *repr* to talk noisily together (women).

koprèk *var of* **koprak**.

koproh slovenly, messy (clothes).

kopros *reg* (of moustaches) thick and unkempt.

koprot *or* **koprot-koprot 1** to lose a lot of blood; **2** to suffer a serious loss or setback (*var of* **kobol**).

kopyah a cap of cloth worn by Muslims.

kopyok, ngopyok 1 to shuffle (cards *etc*); **2** to beat (eggs *etc*); **3** to shake up; **ngopyokaké** to shuffle or shake for s.o.; **kopyokan 1** a beating tool, beater, blender; **2** s.t. which is shaken up.

kopyor 1 a coconut that has developed differently from the others in the bunch and has soft tasty flesh; **2** (of eggs) rotten; **3** *fig* to get a headache from thinking hard about an unsolved problem.

kor I small louse (young of the **tuma**). **II** choir.

korad-korèd *see* **korèd**.

korak I *reg* noise; **korakan 1** sickle sheath; **2** wooden bell hung around a cow's neck. **II** *lit* renowned.

koran newspaper.

Kor'an the holy Quran (*var of* **Kur'an**).

korang-karèng completely dried up, all gone.

kordhèn curtain.

korèd, ngorèdi *or* **korèd-korèd** to scrape out the last remnants of food; **korèdan 1** the scrapings; **2** the last child.

korèh *reg* (of chickens) to scratch for food.

korèk I 1 cigarette lighter; **- api** a match; **2** a trowel; **ngorèk 1** to scrape clean; **2** to clean the ears with an earpick; **3** to dig up (secrets); **ngorèkaké** to light (s.o.'s cigarette) with a match. **II, ngorèk-orèk 1** to scribble; **2** to cross out. **III, ngorèk** to croak loudly (frogs, at rain).

korèksi correction of an error; corrected material;

ngorèksi to correct s.t.

korèng a sore, ulcer, festering wound; **ngorèng** to get infected, fester (*also fig*); **korèngen** to suffer from open sores.

korep I corrupt. **II** military corps.

korèp ringworm; **korèpen** to have/get ringworm.

kori (*kr for* **lawang**) **1** door; **2** outer door, gate; **3** bailiff (of court); **4** *ng, kr* secretariat (one of the Kraton departments).

kornèt corned beef.

korog I *reg* angles of a grass roof. **II, ngorog** to shake up. *See also* **orog**.

korok long-handled swab for cleaning s.t. from the inside (bottle *etc*); **- kuping** earpick. **ngoroki** to clean with the above.

koros a variety of small snake.

korud I *lit* very thin. **II, kamané** to have an involuntary emission of semen.

korup worthwhile, worth the trouble. *See also* **urup**.

kos *see* **dhekos**.

kosala *see* **kusala**.

kosèk I, ngosèk 1 to whet, rub; **2** to scrub, rub (with water); **kosèkan 1** act or way of rubbing; **2** a certain method of playing the drum (**kendhang**). **II** to toss, move about while asleep.

kosèr I, ngosèr *or* **kosèr-kosèr** to propel o.s. along the ground, glide along. **II, kosèran** poorest quality of a product, *e.g.* the lowest leaf on a tobacco plant.

kosi *var of* **kongsi**, **nganti**.

kosik *coll* just a minute! (*shtc of* **mengko dhisik**).

kosod to rub/brush against s.t. (an animal); **ngosodi** *or* **ngosodaké** to rub the body against s.t.; **kosod-kosod** *or* **kekosod** to keep rubbing the body against s.t.;

kosodan 1 rubbing-post; 2 to rub together, *i.e.* compare ideas.

kosok 1 scrubber; 2 (of **rebab**) bow;
   ngosok 1 to scrub; 2 to play (the rebab);
   ngosoki to scrub s.t.;
   ngosokaké to scrub s.t. against;
   kosokan 1 to scrub o.s. while taking a bath; 2 act or way of playing (the rebab).

kosok-bali *ng*, **kosok-wangsul** *kr* opposite; **kosok-balèn** opposite from.

kosong 1 empty (*var of* **kothong**); 2 unoccupied, without passengers.

kosot *see* **kosod**.

koswa, bala - *lit* host, army.

kosya *var of* **kuswa**.

kotang 1 camisole, a woman's armless vest; 2 brassiere;
   kotangan to wear a brassiere.

kotbah sermon delivered in a mosque.

kotbuta *lit* furious.

koten like that, in that way (*md for* **ngono**).

kotèng-kotèng unable to keep it up, not up to it.

kotès I, **ngotès** to babble, chatter.
   II **kotès, kotèsan** the young of the **perkutut**.

kothak box, chest, box-shaped object; wooden chest for storing puppets.

kothèh *or* **kothèh-kothèh** *or* **kekothèh** dirtied, soiled.

kothèk, ngothèki *or* **kothèkan** to produce rhythmic sounds by tapping with sticks or pounding on mortars.

kothok I a variety of vegetable soup;
   ngothok 1 to cook up and thicken; 2 to melt on the fire; 3 to boil **kothok**.
   II, **kothok-onggrok** *var of* **konok-onggrok**.
   III, **ngothokaké** *reg* to handle/treat in that way (*var of* **ngonokaké**).

kothong 1 empty, without content; 2 *fig* dull-witted; - **blong** *or* - **plong** completely empty;

ngothongi *or* **ngothongaké** to empty s.t.;
   kothongan (in an) empty (condition).

kothor I *reg var of* **kèthèr**.
   II 1 dirty; 2 to have a menstrual period; 3 immoral; 4 gross (not net);
   kothoran 1 dirt (in general); 2 excrement; 3 *reg kr* dirty washing.

kothos, kothosen *reg* dirty, unwashed.

kothot 1 gristle; 2 (of meat) tough, hard to chew;
   ngothot-othot to chew and tear s.t. tough.

kothung *reg* severed (of hand, arm); broken. *See also* **kuthung, putung**.

kotis dung beetle (*reg var of* **kutis, brengkutis**).

kotlèt cutlet.

kotok-ayam weak-eyed.

kotos *or* **kotos-kotos** *or* **kumotos** to keep dripping, fall in a steady stream.

kotrèk I corkscrew;
   ngotrèk to pull (a cork) with a corkscrew.
   II *reg var of* **potrèk**.

kowah *reg* a large washbasin.

kowak I gaping, with a big tear in it;
   kowak-kowak gaping open;
   ngowaki to make a big hole in.
   II **kowak-kowak** *reg* to protest loudly.

kowal, ngowali to chop into smaller pieces.

kowan *reg* to have no results for one's efforts.

kowang I **kari kowang-kowang** left all alone.
   II **kowang-kowang** *reg* to howl (dogs).
   III **kowangan** a kind of large water beetle.

kowar 1 vague, hazy, without clear indication; 2 of unclear paternity.

kowar-kawir *see* **kawir**.

kowé I *ng*, **sampéyan** *kr*, **panjenengan** *or* **nandalem** *k.i.*, you.
   II small monkey (young of the **lutung**).

kowen you (*reg var of* **kowé**).

kowèn 1 washtub; **2** trough for mixing cement; **3** pit for disposing of rubbish, manure.

kowèng, ngowèng *or* **kowèng-kowèng** to yelp in pain.

kowi melting-pot, crucible.

kowok a certain card game.

kowung concave (*reg var of* **kuwung**).

koyah a kind of Chinese cake.

koyal-kayil to wobble.

koyan 1 steelyard; **2** unit of weight: 27–30 **pikuls**.

koyang-kayingan to move this way and that in confusion or uncertainty (*var of* **poyang-payingan**).

koyar-kayir *reg* hanging loosely.

koyèk I *reg* monkey.
II insignificant, trivial.

koyok I bandit;
ngoyok to rob.
II *var of* **koyuk**.
III *coll* as, like (*var of* **kaya**).

koyong (*reg var of* **kaya**).

koyor tough (meat).

koyuk a kind of Chinese plaster for wounds.

krabah a variety of dolphin.

krabang, pating krabang to have reddish patches (*e.g.* skin).

krabat relatives.

krabu *reg* an earring.

krabyak, krabyakan in great haste, in a rush.

kracak I hoof (*reg var of* **tracak**).
II, kracak-kracak *repr* water splashing;
kumracak to splash down (stream of water).

kraèk, pating kraèk to yell noisily, make a racket everywhere.

kraèng *title applied to a Bugis or Makassarese noble*.

krah shirt collar.

krahang *reg* greedy, covetous; excessively ambitious.

krai a variety of cucumber.

krajan the main settlement of a Javanese village (where the Lurah resides).

krak *or* **mak krak** *repr* a rasping sound.

kraka *reg* fallen dry leaves.

krakab *var of* **krukub**

krakad a large dragnet;
ngrakad to catch in a dragnet.

krakah *reg* house and courtyard.

krakal stones, rocks;
ngrakal to cover (a road) with stones;
krakalan rocky road, stony path.

krakas, krakas-krakas (of sand *etc*) coarse, rough.

kraket firmly attached. *See also* **raket I**.

krakot, ngrakot to bite a piece of food and eat it;
ngrakoti to keep on biting pieces;
krakotan 1 s.t. bitten off; **2** s.t. from which a piece has been bitten off.

krakup, ngrakup to rake together with the arms. *See also* **rakup**.

kral *lit* strong; able, strong enough (to carry).

kram I (to be seized with) a cramp.
II *lit* to shine.

krama I 1 the speech level of Javanese used to superiors and strangers or on formal occasions, also called Basa; **2** to say in Krama; **- andhap** humble Krama; **- inggil** 'high Krama', honorific vocabulary; **- désa** rural Krama; **-ntara** ordinary Krama;
ngramani to speak in Krama to s.o.;
ngramakaké to put sentences into Krama.
II 1 to marry; **2** married (*kr for* **rabi**).

kraman rebellion, uprising;
ngraman to rise up, revolt.

kramaniti *lit* etiquette, good manners.

kramas *ng, kr,* **jamas** *k.i.,* to wash one's hair;
ngramasi to wash s.o.'s hair.

kramat 1 holy, able to work wonders (saint, tomb); **2** (*or* **kramatan**) tomb of a holy person.

krambang, pating krambang *pl* to float about everywhere. *See also* kambang.

krambil *ng*, klapa *kr*, coconut.

krambyang, ngrambyang, krambyangan 1 to wander, roam; 2 to be confused, talk nonsense.

krami *subst var of* krama.

krampo *var of* krampyang.

krampul, pating krampul *or* krampul-krampul *or* krompal-krampul *pl* to float, drift about everywhere.

krampyang, ngrampyang to yell at, speak angrily to.

kramun, grimis kramun-kramun drizzling (rain). *See also* kremun.

kramyang, kramyang-kramyang dim, obscure, hazy.

kramyas, kramyas-kramyas *or* kumramyas 1 (to taste) hot, biting; 2 (to feel) stinging, burning.

kran tap.

krana *lit* 1 reason; 2 because of; - becik willingly, of one's own free will.

krandhah *reg* family, relatives.

kranjang rattan or bamboo woven basket; ngranjangi to put s.t. into a basket; kranjangan by the basket(ful), in baskets.

kranji chicken coop.

kranjingan *see* anjing.

krang *reg* a certain mussel, also its shell. *Also* kerang.

krangan tap (*var of* kran)

kranggèh *see* ranggèh.

krangkat to suddenly recur (illness).

krangkèng cage for wild animals; ngrangkèng to cage.

krangla *reg* to live in poverty, have a hard life. *See also* klangla.

kranglah *var of* krangla.

krangrang *var of* rangrang.

krangsang, krangsang-krangsang *or* krangsangan to sing, hiss (water about to boil). *See also* krengseng.

kranten *subst kr for* krana.

krantheng, pating krantheng 1 stretched in all directions; 2 to sit around waiting. *See also* kantheng.

kranthil, ngranthil to hang, dangle; pating kranthil *pl same as above*.

kranthuk, pating - nodding on all sides. *See also* anthuk.

kranthul *var of* kranthil.

kranyas, kranyas-kranyas *or* kumranyas 1 (to taste) hot, biting; 2 (to feel) stinging, burning; pating kranyas (to feel) stinging everywhere.

kranyuk, pating kranyuk *pl* to sit idly or lethargically.

kraos 1 to feel (*kr for* krasa); 2 to feel at home (*kr for* krasan). *See also* rasa, raos.

krapa *reg* a fisherman's boy, servant.

krapak (dry) bark, kindling (for fire); ngrapak to become hard and brittle with dryness; krapaken dried out (*e.g.* leaves in the wind).

krapes, krapes-krapes spongy, soft. *See also* kapes.

krapu I a certain sea fish. II the flower of the rice plant.

krapyak I a clatter, rattle; kumrapyak to clatter, rattle. II a fenced-in game preserve; ngrapyak to fence in (land) for a game preserve. III pebbles (gathered from riverbed, for paving).

kraras *var of* klaras.

kras strong, firm, hard, harsh (*var of* keras).

krasa *see* rasa.

krasak, krasak-krasak *repr* rustling, swishing sounds; kumrasak to rustle, swish.

krasan *ng*, kraos *kr*, to feel at home, feel comfortable; ngrasanaké comfortable, homely;

ngrasan-rasanaké to make efforts to feel comfortable in a place. *See also* rasa.

krastala *lit* supernaturally powerful.

krastin satin.

kratak, I kratak-kratak *repr* crackling, rattling sounds, *e.g.* fire, wheels on a stony road.

II, kratakan *reg* to look around anxiously for a place to lay an egg.

kratok a variety of bean.

kraton 1 kingship, reign; 2 residence of a king, palace complex. *See also* ratu.

krawak, krawak-krawak *repr* water rushing;
kumrawak to make a rushing sound (*e.g.* waterfall).

krawang, ngrawang *or* krawangan (of basket, fabric *etc*) open-worked. *See also* trawang.

krawat, ngrawat to bind with wire;
krawatan bound with wire.

krawu, ngrawu to mix s.t. with grated coconut;
ngrawokaké to mix (grated coconut) into;
krawon mixed with grated coconut.

krawus, ngrawus 1 to claw; 2 to attack verbally.

kré rolled-up bamboo blind (*reg var of* keré).

krebak, ngrebakaké to fill (a bottle) by submerging it in water.

krebek *var of* krebak.

krebet rustling sound of a garment;
krebet-krebet *or* krebat-krebet *or* pating krebet to keep rustling.

krèbèt *var of* krebet.

krebul *pl form of* kebul.

krebut *var of* krebet.

krecèh, ngrecèh to drizzle steadily.

krecek, krecek-krecek, ngrecek, kumrecek *or* kemrecek 1 to clatter, rattle (water pouring out); 2 to jabber, gabble.

krècèk I crisp beef rind (used in cooking);
ngrècèk to make (hide) into the above.

II 1 skeleton (of people); 2 frame.

III, ngrècèk to calculate in detail;
rècèkan detailed calculation.

IV, krècèk-krècèk rattling, jingling (metal).

krecih, ngrecih (of rain) incessant (*var of* grecih).

krecik *var of* krecek.

kredan *reg* neck (of carcase).

kredhah-kredhih, ora - to not care about.

kredhak, pating kredhak lying about not put away.

kredhek, rembulan - late rising moon, past the full.

kredhuh, pating kredhuh *pl* yelling in pain.

krega *see* kerga.

kregeng *reg* worn out, dead tired.

krejet a slight movement, little spasm, twitch; krejeting ati a feeling that arises in the heart;
pating krejet to have the twitches.

krejèt, pating krejèt to jerk, quiver everywhere (the body).

krejot *var of* krejèt.

krékal, krékalan to struggle to one's feet after a fall.

krekas-krekes *see* krekes.

krekeb *or* mak krekeb *repr* covering or closing s.t. tightly;
ngrekebi to put the lid on s.t.

krekek, pating - stiff and sore everywhere (from exertion).

krekel, pating krekel winding, meandering about.

krèkèl, krèkèl-krèkèl to climb or descend laboriously, clamber.

krekep *see* krekeb.

krekes 1, ngrekes (*or* krekes-krekes *or* krekas-krekes) to have chills; 2 (*or* krekes-krekes) shivery, shivering.

krèkès, ngrèkès to cadge, badger, pester (for money).

kreket var of krekut.

krekuh, krekah-krekuh or pating krekuh to sigh, moan everywhere.

krekut, krekut-krekut or krekat-krekut to keep nibbling.

krelap var of kerlap.

krelun, pating krelun to billow everywhere. See also kelun.

kremah I a certain herb.

II, ngremah to chew on s.t. without swallowing it. See also kemah.

krembah a species of small grey tiger.

krembeng reg large basket.

krembès, pating krembès to give off smoke/steam.

krembik, pating krembik brimming with tears.

krembos var of krembès.

krembyah, krembyah-krembyah or pating krembyah to flutter, wave loosely (e.g. hair).

krembyang var of krembyah.

kremes I a cassava and brown sugar dish.

II, kremes-kremes or kumremes crisp; kremas-kremes repr chewing s.t. crisp. See also remes.

kremi see kermi.

kremin, kremin-kremin (to hear) vaguely, indistinctly.

krempel, ngrempel to stick together, form a cluster, lump;

pating krempel all clustered together.

krempis, pating krempis pl out of breath, panting. See also kempis.

krempyag, pating krempyag with too much (to carry, deal with).

krémpyang I or mak krémpyang repr a metallic clang.

II ngrémpyang to have far too many bits and pieces attached.

krempyeng, krempyeng-krempyeng to hum with activity, but only for a short time.

kremun I see kermun.

II reg stretcher-like conveyance, carried by two bearers.

kremus see kermus.

kremya, kremya-kremya sparse, scanty, widely spaced.

krénah deception;

ngrénah to deceive or cheat s.o.

krenca, ngrenca to measure with a string.

krencal var of kroncal.

krencang var of krenceng.

krenceng, pating krenceng pl firm, tight, taut.

krèncèng, krèncèng-krèncèng clattering, rattling (metal on metal).

krencil, pating krencil bit by bit, in little groups (not together).

krendha I coffin, bier.

II a species of duck.

krèndhèt to get a scratch (see rèndhèt).

krendhi lit a deer with speckled coat.

kreneng rough basket of woven bamboo, used for carrying fruit, also for protecting fruit on the tree;

ngrenengi to put s.t. into this basket;

krenengan in baskets.

krengeng, pating krengeng buzzing, humming, whizzing, swishing.

krenges, krenges-krenges or pating krenges to grind, grate between the teeth.

kréngga 1 to fall from the tree before ripening (e.g. mango); 2 to fail to come to completion.

krénggak, pating krénggak pl treading water (swimmers).

krénggok, pating krénggok to turn this way and that.

krenggos, krenggosan or krenggas-krenggos panting, out of breath;

pating krenggos pl out of breath.

krengkab, pating krengkab pl standing open everywhere.

kréngkang, kréngkangan, kréngkang-kréngkang or kumréngkang to fall in an awkward position for getting up again.

krengkeng stiff, finding it hard to move.

krengkèt *repr* squeaking, creaking;
krengkèt-krengkèt *or* **krengkat-krengkèt** *or* **pating krengkèt** to keep creaking.

krengkit *repr* a high-pitched squeak/creak;
krengkit-krengkit *or* **pating krengkit** to keep making squeaking sounds.

krengkot *repr* a heavy creaking sound;
krengkot-krengkot *or* **pating krengkot** to keep making such sounds.

krengseng, krengseng-krengseng, kumrengseng 1 to fizz, hiss (*e.g.* water about to boil); 2 to give the first signs of; 3 to feel the first signs of labour pains.

krèngsèng, ngrèngsèng to fry (a fatty food) without additional oil.

krengus *var of* **kremus**.

krenis, pating krenis *pl* having a nice time chatting, socialising.

krenteg 1 a moving of the spirit, prompting; 2 an arising thought, idea, desire.

krentès, pating krentès to drip everywhere.

krentheng *var of* **krantheng**.

krenthil, pating krenthil (of things being carried) numerous, small, and varied.

krenuk, pating krenuk *pl* sitting around aimlessly.

krenyah, pating krenyah *or* **krenyah-krenyoh** *pl* chewing s.t. crisp, crunchy.

krenyap, pating krenyap *pl*, glinting, glistening (*e.g.* fish in the water).

krenyep, pating krenyep to feel chilly all over (the body).

krenyes *or* **mak krenyes** *repr* crumbling;
krenyes-krenyes *or* **kumrenyes** 1 to melt in the mouth; 2 (of carbonated drinks) to give the tongue a pricking sensation.

krepek *var of* **krepyek**.

krepèk cheating notes (*var of* **kepèk**).

krepes *or* **mak krepes** *repr* cracking, crunching;

krepes-krepes *or* **kumrepes** 1 crisp; 2 to make a rustling sound.

krèpès flattened, pressed flat; **krèpès-krèpès** thin and frail.

krepluk, pating krepluk *repr* repeated slapping sounds.

krépo weak, feeble, lame.

krepu *see* **kerpu**.

krepyak-krepyek *see* **krepyek**.

krépyak-krèpyèk *see* **krèpyèk**.

krepyek, krepyek-krepyek *or* **krepyak-krepyek** to rain down, clatter, patter.

krèpyèk *or* **mak krèpyèk** *repr* a crashing fall;
krèpyèk-krèpyèk *or* **krèpyak-krèpyèk** rattling, clattering.

kres *or* **mak kres** *repr* cutting, slashing;
kras-kres *repr* repeated cutting;
ngekres to cut with scissors.

kresa *see* **kersa**.

krésé small dried edible freshwater fish.

kresek, kresek-kresek *or* **kumresek** to produce rustling sounds.

krèsèk *var of* **kresek**;
kakèhan krèsèk too much fuss.

kreses, pating kreses *repr* hissing sounds.

kresna *lit* black.

krestin satin.

kreta *see* **kerta**.

kréta 1 cart, carriage; 2 train;
ngréta to go by cart;
krétan 1 to ride in a cart; 2 s.t. which serves as a cart.

kretanjali *lit* respectful greeting, made with palms together.

krété baby crocodile (young of the **baya**).

kreteg I bridge.

II *or* **mak kreteg** *repr* splintering and about to break;
kumreteg to make repeated splintering sounds.

krètèg 1 bare, sparse (*e.g.* leaves, fruit); 2 to diminish, be used up (*e.g.* possessions);
ngrètègi to get poorer and poorer.

kretek I the sound of s.t. falling in small

quantities (*e.g.* raindrops on the roof);
kumretek to patter, clatter.

II appearance, sign of good or bad.

krètèk I cigarette containing chopped cloves;

ngrètèk to smoke such a cigarette. *See also* rokok.

II **kumrètèk** *or* **krètèk-krètèk** *repr* rustling sounds.

III *reg* two-wheeled horse-drawn cab.

kretep decorative buckle on a men's belt (kamus).

kretes, mak - 1 the sound of squashing (*e.g.* a louse); 2 biting s.t. crisp.

krétol, pating krétol (to walk with) trouser pockets stuffed full.

kretu *see* kertu.

kréwali, pating - full of bumps and holes;

ngréwal to break (crack, chip) rock;

kréwalan a lump of rock;

II, **kréwalan** *or* **pating kréwal** to have difficulty holding or carrying s.t.

krèwèd, krèwèdan 1 meat which is left behind attached to the bone; 2 a small leftover, small profit.

krèwèk, ngrèwèk to make small hole in s.t.;

krèwèkan pierced by a hole.

krèwèng 1 sherd, fragment of broken tile, pot; 2 *fig* something useless.

krewes *var of* kruwes.

krewik 1 *var of* kriwik; 2, **krewikan** *reg* a small piece (of food).

kréyab, kréyab-kréyab *or* **pating kréyab** *pl* (of hair) hanging down loose. *See also* réyab.

krèyèng *reg* 1 wastebasket; 2 prostitute, whore.

kréyok, pating kréyok to squawk everywhere.

kribit, kumribit to blow gently and coolly (breeze).

kricak-kricik *see* kricik.

kricik, ngricik to trickle, drip;

kumricik 1 to trickle, drip; 2 to make a clinking sound (metal);

kricikan act of trickling;

kricikan dadi grojogan *expr* a trickle becomes a waterfall, *i.e.* to make a mountain out of a molehill.

kricik-kricik *repr* trickling or tinkling. *See also* kriwik.

kridha *lit* 1 pleasure, amusement; 2 practice, training.

krigan *reg* compulsory labour, service (in the village). *See also* kerig.

krikil (small) gravel, pebbles;

ngrikil resembling pebbles;

ngrikili to apply gravel or pebbles to;

krikilan gravelled, pebble-covered.

krikit, ngrikiti to nibble s.t.;

krikitan crumbs made by nibbling.

krimpying, ngrimpying *or* **krimpying-krimpying** to jingle, tinkle.

krinan *see* rina.

krincing *or* **mak krincing** *repr* jingling;

krincing-krincing *or* **kumrincing** to jingle.

krincung, krincungan to walk and keep turning the head from fear or doubt.

krinjang basket (*reg var of* kranjang).

kring I *or* **mak kring** *repr* ringing;

ngekring to ring a bell;

krang-kring repeatedly ringing.

II circle, group of Catholics below parish level.

kringet *ng*, *kr*, riwé *k.i.*, sweat;
- **buntet** heat rash;

ngringet *or* **kringeten** *or* **kumringet** to sweat.

kringgek, pating kringgek *pl* to keep winding, making twisting movements.

kringik (*pron as:* kringi:k), **ngringik** to weep softly;

pating kringik *pl* weeping softly. *See also* ringik.

kringkel, ngringkel to curl up (in a lying position);

kringkelan 1 in a curled-up lying position; 2 children.

kringsing, kringsing-kringsing, kumringsing thoroughly dry.

krinyis, krinyis-krinyis or kumrinyis to sizzle.

kripik fried slices of various fruits or roots (*e.g.* banana, cassava);
ngripik to make kripik;
kumripik dry and crisp.

kris *see* keris.

krisik I *var of* klisik.
II, kumrisik to rustle, make a dry rustling sound;
krisik-krisik *repr* rustling sounds.

krisis 1 a crisis; 2 short of money.

kristal crystal.

Kristen Protestant.

kritig, pating kritig *repr* the crackling sound of s.t. on fire.
II kumritig, kritig-kritig to expand in great numbers, swell.

kritik 1 a critic; 2 (*or* kritikan) a critique, criticism;
ngritik to criticise.

kriting tightly curled, kinky.

kriwed, pating kriwed *pl* moving to and fro, milling around.

kriwid, kriwidan small expenses.

kriwik, kriwikan a trickle of water;
kriwikan dadi grojogan *expr* a trickle becomes a waterfall, *i.e.* to make a mountain out of a molehill;
ngriwik *or* kriwik-kriwik *or* kumriwik to trickle.

kriwil I 1 kinky, tightly curled; 2 difficult or complicated to handle (*var of* riwil, rèwèl).
II freewheel (bicycle).

kriwis, kriwis-kriwis thin, sparse.

kriya 1 skill, craft; 2 craftsman; tembung - gram verb; seni - artistic skill.

kriyak, kriyak-kriyak 1 *repr* chewing s.t. fresh and crisp; 2 (*or* kumriyak) crisp.

kriyak-kriyuk *see* kriyuk.

kriyeg *see* kriyek.

kriyek *or* mak kriyek *repr* crushing, cracking.

kriyes *var of* kriyek.

kriyèk, *var of* kriyik.

kriyik, kriyik-kriyik *or* pating kriyik *repr* (of young chickens, birds) cheeping.

kriyin 1 formerly (*md for* biyèn); 2 first, ahead (*subst kr, md for* dhisik).

kriyip, ngriyip, kriyip-kriyip to narrow the eyes.

kriyuk I, kriyuk-kriyuk *or* kriyak-kriyuk *repr* chewing s.t. crisp.
II a kind of earthenware coffee pot.

kriyung, ngriyung to collect the whole pot (in gambling).

krobok *var of* kobok.

krobong *or* krobongan inner room, divided with a curtain;
ngrobongi to divide with a curtain.

krobyok, ngrobyok to make splashing sounds when walking through water;
krobyok-krobyok *repr* walking through water.

kroco 1 a small river snail; 2 worthless, having little or no value; 3 lowest-ranking soldier.

krocok I, ngrocok 1 to attack together with sharp weapons; 2 to attack verbally;
krocokan a bawling out.
II, krocok-krocok *or* kumrocok to run, pour (water).

krodha *lit* fury, anger; furious, angry.

krodhèn curtain, cloth screen (*var of* kordhèn).

krodhong a cloth covering; - bayi mosquito net; - lampu lampshade;
ngrodhongi to equip with such a cover;
krodhongan covered with cloth.

krog, krog-krog *or* krag-krog *repr* cutting strokes.

krogèl, krogèl-krogèl *or* krogal-krogèl *or* pating krogèl to writhe, move spasmodically. *See also* ogèl.

krojèl, kojèl-kojèl in death throes.

krojong, ngrojongi 1 to agree (upon, to);

2 to join (the party) for company.

krokèt croquette.

krokos I, ngrokos to snarl, threaten, intimidate.

II *var of* **kropos**.

krokot I, ngrokoti to chew on, gnaw at;
krokotan a hole made by biting (*e.g.* in fruit by bats). *See also* **krakot**.

II a green vegetable resembling purslane.

kromoh, kromohan *reg* useless leftovers, rags.

kromong *reg* a bronze bowl-shaped gamelan instrument.

kromos *reg* roasted;
ngromos to roast.

krompal, pating krompal (of clothing) all worn out, in rags.

krompang, krompang-krompang *or* **pating krompang** damaged, not working properly.

krompol, ngrompol to form a group; to gather, assemble;
krompol-krompol *or* **krompolan** *or* **pating krompol** forming a group, getting together.

krompyang *or* **mak krompyang** *repr* crashing, breaking, shattering;
krompyang-krompyang *or* **krompyangan** shattering, crashing;
kumrompyang to shatter, crash.

krompyong *var of* **krompyang**.

kromyos, ngromyos to touch with a burning object;
kumromyos to feel burning, stinging.

kroncal, kroncalan *or* **kroncal-kroncal** *or* **pating kroncal** to struggle to get free, keep sprawling, floundering.

kroncong I a type of popular Indonesian music (originating from Portuguese music);
ngroncong to perform such music, hold a performance of **kroncong**;
kroncongan to play **kroncong**.

II metallic bracelet or ankle-ring.

III, **kroncongan** (of an empty stomach) to rumble.

krondhah, krondhahan *or* **pating krondhah** (of long objects) difficult to carry, awkward to manage.

krondho a variety of large rough basket.

kronèh, kronèhan too troublesome, too much hassle.

krongkong, krongkongan throat, gullet.

krongsi chair (*reg var of* **krosi**).

kronjo *var of* **krondho**.

kronjot *var of* **krondho**.

kronong *reg* 1 wrist or ankle bracelets (consisting of several rings) (*var of* **kroncong II**); 2 cow-bell.

kronyos *or* **mak kronyos** *repr* the sputtering or sizzling of food frying.

kropak 1 palm leaf used to write on; 2 a palm-leaf book.

kropèk *reg, see* **kropok**.

kropok I 1 withered, hollow (crop); 2 brittle, with empty bumps (plaster);
kumropok 1 dry and crumbly; 2 very cross, annoyed;
kumropokan hot-tempered;
kropokan a plant, ring-in.

II, **ngropok** to roast in hot coals;
kropokan s.t. roasted in hot coals.

kropos rotten, porous, hollow;
ngropos to have a hollow space inside.

kropyak *or* **mak kropyak** *repr* the sound of wooden or bamboo objects clattering;
kumropyak to make such a sound.

kropyok, dibayar - paid in cash;
kropyok-kropyok *or* **kumropyok** *or* **pating kropyok** (of coins) to jingle.

krorèhan *see* **kronèhan**.

krosak *or* **mak krosak** *repr* rustling;
kumrosak to rustle, swish.

krosi chair (*var of* **kursi**).

kroso small basket of woven bamboo. *See also* **kreneng**.

krosok I 1 dried tobacco leaves; 2 coarse (sand).

II **krosok-krosok** *or* **kumrosok** to make

crunching sounds.

kroto I the egg of the red ant.

II young **mlinjo** blossom.

III a large four-wheeled cart.

krotog *repr* a thudding fall;

krotog-krotog to make many thudding falls.

krowak having a hole torn (broken, eaten *etc*) into it;

ngrowaki to tear a hole in s.t.;

krowakan a part that has a hole torn.

krowal, krowal-krowal *or* **pating krowal** rough, in big chunks.

krowèk *var of* **krowak**.

krowod, krowodan (general term for) field crops (except rice);

ngrowod to subsist on a diet of roots *etc* (no rice) as an ascetic exercise.

krowok I with a cavity, hole;

ngrowoki to make a hole in/through.

II, krowok-krowok *or* **kumrowok** (of a waterfall) to gurgle, roar.

kroya *reg* a banyan tree.

kroyag, kroyag-kroyag rickety, wobbly.

kroyak *see* **kroyag**.

kroyok, ngroyok to attack s.o. together, to outnumber;

kumroyok to act as a group;

kroyokan to fight together as a gang. *See also* **kruyuk**.

krubeng *var of* **ubeng**.

krubut, ngrubut to outnumber;

kumrubut to crowd in/out/around; to come/go with a great rush;

krubutan act of mobbing or overwhelming;

krubut-krubut *or* **pating krubut** *repr* noisy and/or confused rushing.

krubyuk *or* **mak krubyuk** *repr* splashing;

ngrubyuk to splash through water;

krubyukan *or* **krubyuk-krubyuk** *or* **kumrubyuk 1** to splash; **2** to converge on, mob.

krucil small, undersized;

krucilan small *or* undersized (things);

pating **krucil** in little pieces;

wayang krucil *see* **wayang**.

krucuk I lowest-ranking private (*var of* **kroco**).

II krucuk-krucuk *or* **kumrucuk** (producing) a rushing sound of water.

krudhak *see* **krudhek**.

krudhek able to move only with great difficulty.

krudhug, krudhug-krudhug *or* **krudhugan** to stumble, stump about.

krudhuk *var of* **krudhung**.

krudhung 1 cloth worn wound around the head; **2** cover(ing), lid;

krudhungan to put a cover on one's head;

ngrudhungi 1 to cover s.o.'s head; **2** to conceal s.t. with a cover;

ngrudhungaké to put a cover on s.o.'s head;

krudhung-krudhung to move about while covered with s.t. *See also* **kudhung**.

krugat-kruget *see* **kruget**.

kruget, kruget-kruget *or* **krugat-kruget** *or* **krugetan** to wriggle, squirm, make worm-like movements.

kruhun *lit* in the past; formerly.

krukub 1 cloth (kain *etc*) used to cover o.s.; **2** to use/wear a cloth to cover o.s.;

ngrukub *or* **ngrukubi** to cover tightly with cloth;

ngrukubaké to put a cover cloth on s.t.;

krukuban lying covered with cloth.

krukud I, ngrukud to pack away (all one's wares).

II, krukudan to set to work early in the morning.

kruma a kind of minute worm under the skin, causing itching eruptions.

krumpul, ngrumpul to gather, assemble;

krumpul-krumpul a gathering, group; to gather;

pating krumpul forming in groups.

krumpyang *var of* **krompyang**.

krumpyung, **ngrumpyung**, **krumpyung-krumpyung** to come together as a crowd.

krun 1 crown; 2 ceremonial arch.

kruncil *var of* **krencil**.

kruncung, **pating kruncung** always together, inseparable, one after the other.

krungkeb *see* **rungkeb**.

krungsung, **krungsung-krungsung**, **kumrungsung** 1 about to come to the boil, producing a hissing sound; 2 to become agitated.
See also **krengseng**.

krungu to hear. *See also* **rungu**.

krunteg, - **atiné** to feel unsettled;
kruntegan *or* **pating krunteg** forming a wriggling mass, a wriggling heap.

kruntel, **kruntelan** *or* **pating kruntel** curled up, huddled together.

krunyus, **krunyus-krunyus** (of fatty meat) sizzling when it is fried.

krupuk crisp fried chips;
ngrupuk 1 to have **krupuk** with the meal; 2 to make **krupuk**.

krupyuk *or* **mak krupyuk** *repr* dull or muffled jingling;
ngrupyuk to brush, sweep away (coins, jingling);
kumrupyuk to clatter, like a big pile of coins.

krura *lit* wild, fierce, fearsome.

krus carbonated drink. *See also* **oranye**.

krusak-krusek *see* **krusek**.

krusek, **krusekan** *or* **krusek-krusek** *or* **krusak-krusek** *or* **pating krusek** to rustle.

krustin chimney.

krusuh, **krusuhan** bewildered, confused. *See also* **rusuh**.

krusuk, **ngrusuk** *or* **kumrusuk** *or* **krusuk-krusuk** *or* **pating krusuk** to make a rustling sound.

krutil trivial, insignificant, useless.

krutug *or* **mak krutug** *repr* a sudden dropping (of many objects, more or less at the same time);
krutug-krutug to make the above sound;
ngrutug *or* **ngrutugi** to rain (missiles) on, bombard;
kumrutug to make the sound of the above.

krutuk *see* **krutug**.

kruwad-kruwed *see* **kruwed**.

kruwed, **pating kruwed** *or* **kruwad-kruwed** to wriggle, squirm everywhere.

kruwek, **ngruwek** to scratch with the nails, claws.

kruwel, **ngruwel** 1 to curl up; 2 to twist, tangle;
pating kruwel 1 curled up together; 2 twisted, tangled.

kruwes *or* **mak kruwes** *repr* scratching, clawing;
ngruwes 1 to crumple in the hand; 2 to scratch, crumple.

kruwik, **ngruwik** to scratch s.t. lightly. *See also* **kuwik**.

kruwil I, **ngruwil** *or* **pating kruwil** broken into little bits.
II, **ngruwil** hard, mean.

kruwing I a kind of pitch or putty for caulking ships;
ngruwing to caulk.
II, **kruwingan** a certain technique of chiselled metallic work;
ngruwing to apply such a technique.

kruwis, **kruwis-kruwis** *or* **pating kruwis** thin, meagre, sparse.

kruwit *var of* **kruwis**.

kruwuk, **kruwuk-kruwuk** *or* **kruwak-kruwuk** 1 (of stomach) to rumble; 2 (*or* **kumruwuk** *or* **pating kruwuk**) to make a loud, disturbing noise.

kruwun, **kruwun-kruwun** thin, meagre, sparse.

kruwung *or* **mak kruwung** *repr* ladling or scooping water;
ngruwungaké to use an object for ladling or scooping.

kruwut *var of* kruwun.

kruyel, ngruyel *or* kruyelan *or* pating kruyel to mill around in a tight space.

kruyuk, kruyukan *or* kumruyuk *or* pating kruyuk to crowd around, mob; ngruyuk to mob, rush s.o.

kubang *reg* garden pond.

kubeng surroundings, circle, circumference. *See also* ubeng.

kubleg *reg* a square wooden pestle.

kubluk, ngubluk to blend; kublukan blender.

kubra, kiyamat - the great Day of Resurrection.

kubuk I 1 cubic (*var of* kubik); 2 cube; 3 *reg* handkerchief; ngubukaké to form a cube; kubukan a variety of game of chance. II commensurate (with), worth the trouble; ngubukaké to make s.t. worth the trouble. *See also* kurup.

kubur grave; kuburan *or* pakuburan *ng, kr,* pasaréan *k.i.* graveyard, cemetery; ngubur, nyarèkaké *or* metak *k.i.*, to bury; pangubur act or way of burying.

kucah *or* kekucah, kucahan 1 leftovers from a meal; 2 gift (from superior to inferior).

kucai leek, green onion.

kucak *see* kocak.

kucek *reg var of* ucek.

kucem pallid, pale due to shame; ngucemaké 1 to rob of lustre; 2 *fig* to bring shame on, sully one's name.

kucing I 1 cat; - bundel cat with a knot in the end of its tail; 2 name of one of the Chinese playing-cards (*kertu cilik*); kucing-kucingan 1 to play hide-and-seek; 2 to play cat and mouse with each other; kemucing feather duster shaped like a cat's tail;

kucing endhasé ireng thief.

II biceps; ngucing to flex the biceps; kucingen 1 to get goose pimples; 2 to strain the biceps.

kucir bunch, tuft of hair (gathered on top, at the side or back of the head); kuciran to wear one's hair in bunches.

kucira *lit* inferior.

kuciwa 1 to be inferior, fall short; 2 to display a shortcoming, be disappointing; kuciwané unfortunately, to one's disappointment; nguciwani to fail to live up to expectations, disappointing.

kucu 1 protruding knob of a gamelan gong (*see also* pencu); 2 a fist with protruding middle finger; nguconi to rub (a stained portion of) a garment between the hands.

kucumbi *lit* wife.

kucup, ngucupaké to hold (the hand) with upturned palms, in a gesture of praying or begging.

kucur I 1 a sweet fried snack of rice flour, brown sugar and coconut milk (*var of* cucur); 2 knotted corner of a handkerchief. II water spout; ngucur *or* kumucur to pour out in profusion (*var of* kocor); kekucur to wash o.s. under a water spout; kacar-kucur to pour out various seeds during a wedding ceremony as a symbol of the husband's responsibility to fulfil his duty.

kuda *lit* horse; kuda-kuda 1 trestle; 2 supporting roof beam.

kudang, ngudang 1 to hold out the prospect of s.t.; 2 to sing to (a child), praising and expressing hopes for a shining future; kudangan, kekudangan 1 words of praise, hope for the future; 2 promise, undertaking; **3** *lit* pet-name.

kudhampel, **ngudhampel** to hold on with the arms and legs, wind (the arms and legs) around s.t. to hold on.

kudhar *reg* loose, loosened. *See also* **udhar**.

kudhas-kudhis a skin disease, scabies.

kudhek *reg var of* **udhek**.

kudhi grass-cutting knife with a curved blade and a bulge in it near the handle; **kudhi pacul singa landhepa** *prov* may the best man (of an evenly-matched pair) win!

kudhis a skin disease, scabies; **kudhisen** to suffer from scabies.

kudhu 1 a tree, *Morinda tinctoria*; **2** a red or dark brown dye made from its bark or root; **ngudhu** to dye s.t. red with the above.

kudhung 1 cloth worn around the head; **2** cover(ing), lid; **ngudhungi 1** to cover s.o.'s head; **2** to conceal, cover s.t.; **ngudhungaké** to use as a head covering; **kudhungan** to wear on the head; **kudhung indhing (tapih)** to be under the wife's thumb (of a henpecked husband); **kudhung lulang macan** *fig* to use s.o. important's name without permission, in order to get favours. *See also* **tudhung**.

kudhup 1 flower bud; **2** sheath or covering of a flower bud; **3** in the bud, budding; **4** (of the eyes) slanted; **ngudhup 1** to put forth a bud; **2** resembling a flower bud; **ngudhup turi** shaped like the **turi** bud.

kudrat *see* **kodrat**.

kudu *ng*, **kedah** *kr*, **1** to really have to (do s.t.); **2** to feel an inner compulsion to (do s.t.); **ngudokaké** to make s.t. compulsory, make s.o. do; **kuduné** ought to; **kumudu-kudu** to feel a strong compulsion or longing to;

kudon (by nature) stubborn, to have to have s.t. now, insist on having one's way.

kudur *or* **kuduran** obligatory assistance, *esp* with work in fields for village head.

kudus *lit* holy.

kujang *reg var of* **kudhi**.

kukama *lit* jurist, scholar of Islamic law.

kukang *reg* a variety of ape, sloth.

kukila *lit* bird.

kuku (**kenaka** *k.i.*) **1** fingernail, toenail; **2** claw; **nguku** to scratch, claw (at), press with the nail; **kukon** a scratch, scratch mark, claw mark; **sakuku ireng** tiny, very small.

kukub I, **ngukub**, **ngukubi** to cover up, place s.t. over; **kukuban** domain, territory; **sakukuban** the whole family. **II ngukub** to perfume, burn incense under s.t. *See also* **ukub**.

kukud to close up shop, go bankrupt; **ngukud** to cause s.t. to close up, put s.o. out of business; **ngukudi** to pack away (one's wares) and close up.

kukuh *ng*, **kekah** *kr*, solid, strong, unmovable; **ngukuhi** to adhere to, defend; **ngukuhaké** to strengthen, reinforce; **pangukuh** betrothal gift; **pangukuhan** confirmation, acknowledgement; **pikukuh** written confirmation, letter of appointment.

kukuk *or* **kukukbeluk** owl; **ngukuk** (of laughter) loud and jeering; to hoot.

kukukluruk cock-a-doodle-doo!

kukul pimples on the face, acne; **kukulen** to suffer from pimples.

kukum *var of* **ukum**.

kukup, **ngukup 1** to pick up in (two)

cupped hands; **2** to take care of, take pity on, befriend;

ora ngukup past saving, a hopeless case; **tanpa kukupan** a total loss.

kukur, ngukur to scratch with the nails; **ngukuraké** to scratch an itch on s.o.'s body;

kukur-kukur to scratch o.s.;

kukuran 1 a scratch(ed place); **2** scraper.

kukus I 1 smoke; **2** steam; - **gantung** cobwebby dust in ceiling corners;

ngukus to steam, to cook by steaming;

ngukusi 1 to get smoke/steam on; **2** to smoke/steam;

kumukus to give off smoke/steam; **lintang - kumukus** comet, shooting star;

kukusan cone-shaped utensil of woven bamboo in which rice is steamed over boiling water;

dhuwur kukusé to have a great name. **II kumukus** cubeb, the small spicy berry of *Piper cubeba*, used medicinally.

kul I a variety of snail.

II cabbage.

III, ngekul to disparage; to treat with contempt.

kula 1 I, me (*kr for* **aku**); **2** (done) by me (*kr for* **tak-**); **3** my, our (*kr for* **-ku**; **4** yes? what? (in response when called);

kula aturi please (do…);

kula nuwun may I come in? (*phrase for announcing one's presence as a visitor at the door of s.o.'s house*);

kula nuwun inggih *lit* yes I do; yes it is.

kulagotra *lit* family.

kulamitra *lit* family and friends.

kulasentana *lit* family and relatives of aristocrats.

kulawanda(wa) *lit* family, relatives; relation, kinsman.

kulawangsa *lit* **1** kinsmen, family, relatives; **2** descendant; **3** people, race, nation.

kulawarga 1 family, family members; **2** members of a specific group;

kinulawarga regarded as a member of the family.

kulawisudha, ngulawisudha 1 to appoint; **2** to inaugurate.

kulah I tank (of masonry) for bathing (*var of* **kolah**).

II stained, messy (with).

III, ngulah *reg* to mix, knead together (in cooking).

kulak *ng*, **kilak** *kr*, **ngulak** *or* **kekulak** to buy (up) at wholesale for resale;

kulakan, rega - wholesale price;

kulak warta, adol prungon to go out and hear the latest news.

kulakuli familiar (with), used (to). *See also* **kulina**.

kulandara, nglandara to be a vagabond, have no fixed abode or occupation.

kulanthé name of a classical verse form.

kular *reg* thread attached to a needle.

kulawu grey. *See also* **klawu**.

kuldi donkey.

kuled *reg, lit*, slow, tardy, sluggish.

kulègèn why, how (come)? *reg var of* **kepriyé**.

kulèhé *reg var of* **kepriyé**.

kulèhen *reg var of* **kepriyé**.

kulèhèn *reg var of* **kepriyé**.

kulem *lit* **1** night; **2** (*or* **kulé**) *reg* to sleep.

kulhu name of the 112th **Sura** of the Quran, used as an introduction to prayer.

kuli 1 common villager; **2** wage labourer; **3** porter, carrier; - **baku, kenceng, ngarep** *or* **pokok** village member with full rights (share in common fields); - **buri, gamblok, gandhok** *or* **kendho** village menber with partial rights;

nguli to work as a labourer;

ngulèkaké to have work done by paid labourers;

kulèn a share in the fields in common possession.

kulihi *reg* why?

kulik *var of* **kolik I**.

kuliling *see* kliling.

kulina 1 accustomed to; 2 well acquainted with; 3 usual, ordinary;
ngulinani to become accustomed to;
ngulinakaké to accustom s.o. to;
pakulinan habit, what one is accustomed to.

kulinten *md for* kulina.

kulit 1 outer layer, skin; 2 leather; 3 bark; - ayam epidermis; film, membrane; - daging flesh-and-blood relative; - waja strong, tough;
kulitan 1 outer skin, peel; 2 unpeeled;
pakulitan skin colour; complexion;
kinulit daging *expr* as close as one's one family.

kuliyah lecture;
nguliyahi to lecture s.o.

kuliyen *reg var of* kepriyé.

kulkul *reg* wooden drum which is struck to sound alarm.

kulmak s.o. authorised to act on behalf of the host at a ceremony.

kulnèl colonel.

kulon *ng*, kilèn *kr*, west;
ngulon to(ward) the west, to go west;
ngulonaké (*pass* dingulonaké) to move s.t. to the west;
kulonan Western, Occidental;
kulon-kulonan the western part;
sakuloné to the west (of).

kulu I a certain freshwater fish.
II, kulu-kulu (of body, clothing) dirty and dusty.

kulub, ngulub to boil (green vegetables) briefly;
kuluban briefly boiled green vegetables.

kuluh *var of* kulu.

kuluk I, makutha, panunggul *k.i.* fez-like headdress (various colours) worn by officials at court; - kanigara high black gold-trimmed headdress worn by monarchs and also by bridegrooms;
kulukan to put on or wear the above headdress.

II a type of divorce (temporary, to allow marriage to another).

kulung I conduit pipe, gutter, drain; - ati 1 the portion of the body below the heart and ribs; 2 *fig* the heart as the seat of emotions. *See also* pulung.
II handle of harvesting knive.
III leg of meat.

kulup *lit* 1 with foreskin intact; 2 *adr* young boy, son.

kulwan *lit* west.

kum, ngekum to soak s.t. in water;
kum-kuman 1 what is soaked; 2 act of soaking.
See also kungkum.

kumajaya *var of* kamajaya.

kumala *lit* jewel, diamond;
ngumala jewel-like; resembling a diamond;
jaka kumala-kala pubescent boy (14–16 years).

kumalancang *see* lancang.

kumandhang an echo;
ngumandhang to echo.

kumara I *lit* young man.
II *lit* soul, spirit.
III *lit* jewel, diamond (*var of* kumala).

kumaruk *var of* kemaruk.

kumat *ng*, kimat *kr*, to have a relapse, recurrence (of illness, *fig* of a vice);
kumat-kumatan to keep recurring, recurrent.

kumatus *var of* kematus.

kumba *lit* 1 waterpot; 2 head;
ngedu kumba to knock two people's heads together.

kumbah, ngumbah to wash, launder;
ngumbahaké to have s.t. washed;
kumbahan laundry, clothes to be washed.
See also umbah.

kumbala 1 tassel; 2 moustache (*k.i. or lit for* brengos).

kumbang *var of* kombang.

kumbaya red material for kerchiefs (*var of* **gembaya**).

kumbi to deny, keep s.t. back, not own up; **ngumbèni** to deny s.t., keep silent about s.t.

kumbu a certain sweet filled cake.

kumed miserly, stingy.

kumel worn-out, ragged, rumpled.

kumendhan commander.

kumendhir commander.

kumendhur *var of* **kumendhir**.

kumendir *see* **kumendhir**.

kumetir 1 person delegated, authorised; 2 supervisor, foreman.

kumidhi *var of* **komidhi**.

kumis moustache.

kumisaris commissioner.

kumisi *var of* **komisi**.

kumis-kucing a medicinal plant (*var of* **piskucing**).

kumpa *var of* **kompa**.

kumpé *reg* cold weak tea.

kumpeni 1 the Dutch East India Company, VOC; 2 (a company of) soldiers.

kumplang, kumplang-kumplang brimming with water.

kumplit *var of* **komplit**.

kumprung asinine, very stupid.

kumpul *ng*, **kempal** *kr*, 1 to come together, gather; 2 to have sexual intercourse; - **kebo** to live together unmarried; **ngumpul** to gather, form a group; **ngumpuli** 1 to be or associate with; 2 to have sexual intercourse with; **ngumpulaké** to gather, bring together, to collect; **kumpulan** 1 an associate; 2 to associate with; 3 meeting, gathering; **kumpul-kumpul** to hang around as a group; **pakumpulan** association, organisation, club.

kumram *lit* shining, clear, bright.

kumucing *var of* **kemucing**.

kumud I coconut cream *i.e.* the thickened part of pressed coconut milk which rises to the top when the liquid is boiled or allowed to stand.
II, **kumud-kumud** messy and dirty.

kumuda 1 *lit* lotus (white); 2 the leaf of the **kemladhéyan** when used for making medicine.

kumur, ajur kumur-kumur crushed, utterly destroyed.

kumukus *see* **kukus** II.

kumyus streaming (sweat, blood).

kun *reg* excuse me! (*shtc of* **kula nuwun**).

kuna *ng*, **kina** *kr*, 1 from ancient times; 2 old-fashioned; **kuna-makuna** in *or* since ancient times.

kunang *lit* now as for…, furthermore… (continuing the narrative).

kunapa *lit* corpse.

kunarpa *see* **kunapa**.

kunca train of a ceremonial batik garment (**dodot**); **kuncan** having a train.

kuncang *lit* **nguncang** *or* **manguncang** to throw away; **kinuncang** to be blown away.

kuncara *lit* famous, renowned.

kuncèh *reg* long Chinese pipe.

kunci I 1 key; 2 lock; - **Inggris** stillson wrench, monkey wrench; **ngunci** (*or* **nguncèni**) to lock; **kuncèn** 1 in locked condition; 2 (*or* **pakuncèn**) cemetery keeper's lodge.
II a certain root used in cooking and in traditional medicines.

kuncir *var of* **kucir**.

kuncit *var of* **kucir**.

kuncung 1 children's hairstyle: head left unshaved only from crown to forehead; 2 covered portico of a Javanese-style house connecting the front verandah with the inner hall or else extending out from the front verandah to the street; 3 object worn at the forehead; 4 tuft, tassel (of a plant); **nguncung** *or* **kuncungan** to wear

the hair in children's hairstyle as above;
nguncungi to give s.o. the above hair-style;
wiwit kuncung nganti gelung *prov* from childhood till adulthood.

kuncup I 1 in bud, budding, not yet open; **2** flower bud.
II *var of* **kucup**.

kundha I *lit* ritual brazier.
II *reg* (of sea) high tide but calm.

kundhah *or* **makundhah** *lit* to lie (fall) flat on the ground.

kundhang I *lit* companion, follower.
II *reg* irrigation canal.

kundhi 1 potter, earthenware maker; **2** *var of* **kendhi**;
pakundhen potter's workshop.

kundhisi (to drink a) toast (*var of* **kondhisi**).

kundhuh fruit of a certain palm tree (**gebang**).

kundhur the wax gourd.

kundur, mati kunduran to die in childbirth.

kuneng *lit* furthermore, and then (introducing next part of story).

kung I *lit* **1** heartache; **2** deep longing, lovesickness.
II 1 imitation of the call of the **perkutut**; **2** to have a mature singing voice (**perkutut**).

kungkang large frog.

kungkong *repr* frogs croaking.

kungkum to bathe by submerging o.s. in the water; *also* as a form of ascetic practice.

kungkung I, ngungkung 1 to confine, incarcerate; to shackle, restrain; **2** (in children's games) to make s.o. be in, or a defender, for a long time.
II, ngungkung (of gamelan music) to reverberate.

kuning I *ng*, **jené** *kr*, **1** yellow; **2** (of skin) light, fair; **3** ripe(ned, of rice growing in the field); **4** egg yolk; **5** (of vision)

blurred, hazy; **sakit -** jaundice;
kemuning a certain tree and its beautiful yellow-veined wood;
kuningan brass;
kuning gumrining pure clear yellow;
kuning nemugiring 1 fresh clear yellow; **2** (having skin) as fair as the **temu** root.
II kuningan the 12th **wuku**.
III *see* **uninga**.

kunir turmeric: used in cooking, also in traditional medicines;
ngunir resembling turmeric.

kunjana *lit* (to have) heartache, cares.

kunjara jail, prison;
ngunjara to imprison, put in jail;
kunjaran *or* **pakunjaran** jail, prison.

kunjeng *reg* stunted.

kunjur *reg* with legs extended;
ngunjuraké to stretch (the legs) out.

kunta *lit* spear, lance.

kuntan *var of* **kontan**.

kuntek, nguntek *reg* to pour out completely.

kunten labourer (*subst kr for* **kuli**)

kunthèt *var of* **kunthing**.

kunthing stunted, unable to achieve normal growth.

kunthiwiri *reg* to keep coming back.

kuntul a certain white heron;
kuntulan a dancing game;
kuntul diunèkaké dhandhang *prov* to call white black; to distort facts, twist the truth.

kunu there, that place (*reg var of* **kono**).

kunun *reg* excuse me! (*shtf of* **kula nuwun**).

kunut a formula recited on special occasions in the context of ritual prayer.

kunyik the loser, the last one (*reg var of* **unyik**).

kunyit *reg* turmeric.

kunyuk 1 *reg* little monkey; **2** a crook.

kunyur, kunyur-kunyur soft, tender (meat).

kupang 1 *reg* 4-duit coin (during the colonial period); **2** *lit* 100.

kupat rice steamed in a palm-leaf wrapping;
ngupat 1 to cook such a food; **2** resembling the above food;
kupatan to cook such a food as celebration for Lebaran.

kupeng, ngupeng to circle, surround, sit around s.t.

kuper (of ear) small and malformed;
kuperan without earstuds.

kuping, talingan *k.i.*, ear;
nguping to listen in, eavesdrop;
kupingan handle (of pot, cup);
kuping gajah 1 a certain plant with large decorative dark-green leaves; **2** a sweet chip.

kupiya 1 copy (for publication); **2** model, example; **3** copy, transcript;
ngupiya to make a copy/imitation of.

kupling *var of* **kopling**.

kupluk I a kind of cap; **- porong tèh** teacosy.
II, ngupluk to beat (eggs *etc*).

kupu butterfly; **- tarung** a set of double doors opening outward and inward;
kupon resembling a butterfly;
kupu-kupu prostitute.

kupur I unbelieving (in God) (*var of* **kapir**).
II *reg* broken off (at the end).

kupyah *var of* **kopyah**.

kur I *reg* only.
II *syllable to call chickens to be fed*;
ngekuri to call chickens at feeding time.
III, kur-kuran in the twenties (*shtf of* **likur-likuran**).

kura a species of land tortoise.

kurah to rinse out the mouth and gargle (*var of* **gurah**).

Kur'an the holy Quran.

kurang *ng*, **kirang** *kr*, **1** not enough, lacking; **2** not very; **3** less than, minus; **- ajar** ill-mannered;

ngurangi to lessen, reduce;
ngurang-ngurangi 1 to cause s.t. to be lacking; **2** to reduce food and sleep in order to get some result;
kekurangan 1 to suffer a lack of s.t.; **2** poor, underprivileged;

kuranti, *lit* **ngurantèni** to restrain.

kurantil name of the 4th **wuku**.

kurap a severe skin affliction;
kurapen to suffer from this.

kuras, nguras 1 to clean by scrubbing and rinsing (tank, drain); **2** to clean out (money).

Kurawa *way* family name of the 99 brothers and one sister (descendants of Kuru) who are the first cousins and enemies of the Pandhawas.

kurban 1 sacrifice, offering (to God); **2** a victim;
ngurbanaké to sacrifice; to offer as a sacrifice;
pangurbanan a sacrifice.

kurda *lit* fury; furious.

kureb hollow underside;
ngurebi to lie on s.t. face down;
ngurebaké to place s.t. face down *or* underside down;
kumureb lying face down *or* with the concave *or* underside down;
kumureb ing abahan to submit utterly, yield up one's life;
sakurebing langit *expr* the whole world, everything under the sun.

kuren I 1 *lit* husband; **2** *reg* adult, married man.
II, nguren *reg* to serve to a guest.

kurès *see* **barès**.

kurih, ngurih to wipe clean.

kurim, kurimen *reg* (of chicken) sickly, frail.

kurir messenger.

kuris, ngurisi to shave and shape the hair on a bride's forehead.

kurma I *lit* turtle.
II date (fruit).

kurmat 1 honour, respect, esteem; 2 to honour, respect;
ngurmati 1 to show honour or esteem to/for; 2 to salute;
pakurmatan honour, token of esteem. *See also* **urmat**.

kursi 1 chair; 2 seat, position;
kursèn seated on a chair.

kursus 1 course; 2 to follow a course.

kuru *ng*, **kera** *kr*, 1 thin, emaciated; 2 sickly; 3 meagre, scanty (crops);
nguroni 1 to become thin; 2 to emaciate, make thin.

kurulut *see* **kuruwelut**.

kurung *ng*, **sengker** *k.i.*, **nyengker** 1 to enclose, pen up; 2 to put in brackets;
kurungan 1 cage, enclosure; 2 caged, confined.

kurup I worth something, worth the trouble;
ngurupaké to make s.t. worth the trouble.
II *lit* 1 Arabic letter; 2 year-letter in almanacs.

kuruwelut name of the 17th **wuku**.

kusala *lit* 1 good, righteous; 2 skilled, expert; 3 well, safe.

kusan *reg var of* **kukusan**.

kusi (of skin) grimy, dirty and dry.

kusik I, *lit* **kusikan** restless, nervous, agitated.
II, a certain knife used for hollowing out the kris sheath.

kusika *lit* skin, hide.

kusir driver of a horse-drawn carriage;
ngusir to drive a carriage (as livelihood);
ngusiri to drive a carriage;
kusiran driver's seat.

kusta *lit* leprosy.

kustim *reg* full, formal dress.

kusuk devout, devoted, humble before God.

kusuma *lit* 1 flower; 2 the 'flower', most beautiful (woman); 3 nobility;
trahing kusuma of noble descent.

kusung, **kusung-kusung** to do one's best, try one's hardest to.

kusur, *lit* **tanpa kusur** without comprehension, understanding.

kusus 1 accepted as right and fair, settled; 2 specific, particular.

kusut 1 sad, gloomy; 2 bewildered, confused; 3 put to shame; 4 crumpled (clothes);
ngusutaké 1 to put to shame; 2 to throw into confusion, make depressed.

kuswa, **nguswa** *lit* to kiss.

kutah to spill out (*reg var of* **wutah**).

kutang *var of* **kotang**.

kutbah sermon delivered in a mosque.

kutha *ng*, **kitha** *kr*, 1 surrounding wall, fort; 2 town, city;
ngutha 1 resembling a city wall; 2 *or* **nguthani** to behave like a city person;
kekutha to found a city;
mbeguguk ngutha waton *prov* stubborn as a brick wall.

kuthagara *lit* city gate.

kuthah *or* **kekuthah** messy, smeared (with).

kuthèh *reg var of* **kuthah**.

kuthèt *var of* **kunthèt**.

kuthilang a black-headed grey and yellow songbird. *Also* **thilang**.

kuthip *lit* very contemptible.

kuthong empty (*reg var of* **kothong**).

kuthubaru a chest-piece attached to a woman's traditional jacket (**kebaya**).

kuthuk I a young chicken.
II tame; *fig* to feel at home, not want to leave.

kuthumbi *lit* wife.

kuthung severed (of hand, arm).

kutil I wart;
kutilen to suffer from warts.
II, **ngutil** to pick s.o.'s pocket;
ngutilaké to pick pockets on s.o.'s behalf. *See also* **util**.

kutis dung beetle (*shtf of* **brengkutis**)

kutkutan *reg* greedy, gluttonous, covetous.

kutu I, kutu-kutu *or* kekutu the class of small insects;
kutu-kutu walang antaga all living creatures.
II, ngutu determined, to go forward with a goal in view.

kutub (north, south) pole.

kutug 1 incense; 2 (*or* kekutug) to burn incense;
ngutugi to burn incense over;
kumutug (to produce) billowing smoke.

kutuk a certain edible freshwater fish;
kutuk nggéndhong kemiri to go into a thief-infested area conspicuously decked out in valuables;
kutuk marani sunduk *prov* to walk deliberately into danger.

kutut turtle-dove (*inf var of* perkutut).

kuwadhé *reg* dais on which the bridal couple sit.

kuwaga having a crooked arm.

kuwagang able (to), capable (of), strong enough (to).

kuwah soup, sauce, gravy.

kuwal sapwood.

kuwalat *see* walat.

kuwali earthen or metal cooking pot.

kuwalon step(-relation); adopted (relative); bapak - stepfather.

kuwanda *lit* 1 body; 2 dead body, corpse.

kuwangsul cooking pot (*subst kr for* kuwali).

kuwangwung coconut beetle.

kuwaos powerful (*kr for* kuwasa).

kuwara *lit* famous, renowned.

kuwas I 1 paintbrush; 2 tassel.
II a lemon or orange drink, squash.

kuwasa *ng*, kuwaos *kr*, 1 powerful, mighty; 2 power, authority; 3 to have power, authority, be authorised;
para - those in power;
nguwasani to have authority over;
nguwasakaké to empower, give authority to;

panguwasa 1 power, authority; 2 one in authority.

kuwat *ng*, kiyat *kr*, 1 strong (physically); 2 strong enough to;
nguwati to strengthen, reinforce;
nguwataké to make stronger;
nguwat-uwataké to make an effort, summon up one's strength;
kakuwatan strength;
panguwat reinforcement, supporting strength;
pikuwat a support, a strengthening device;
sakuwaté with all one's might.

kuwatir *ng*, kuwatos *kr*, anxious, fear-ful;
nguwatiri causing worry/anxiety, worrying;
nguwatiraké to worry about;
kuwatiran easily worried.

kuwatos apprehensive (*kr for* kuwatir).

kuwawa able (to), capable (of), strong enough (for).

kuwawi *kr for* kuwawa.

kuwawung *var of* kuwangwung.

kuwaya gall, bile.

kuwé cake, sweet snack (*var of* kuwih).

kuwek, nguwek 1 to paw, scratch (the ground); 2 to pinch and twist (s.o.'s flesh);
nguweki to keep scratching.

kuwel a wad, lump;
nguwel crumpled, curled. *See also* uwel.

kuwen *reg* you.

kuwènen *reg* to suffer from sores under the nails.

kuwéwung *reg var of* kuwangwung.

kuwi *ng*, punika *kr*, 1 that (near the hearer); 2 the aforementioned (one); 3 the (referring to a general class); manungsa - human beings (in general); 4 *general perspective indicator, e.g.*
kowé kuwi you for your part. *See also* iku.

kuwih *var of* kuwé.

kuwik, nguwik to scratch s.t. lightly.

kuwil, nguwil to clean o.s. after defecating by rubbing with a finger (while washing).

kuwir, kuwiran *reg* share of the harvest kept for o.s. (by owner of field).

kuwu I *reg* **1** village head; **2** village messenger.

  II *or* **kekuwu** to camp, set up camp, reside temporarily;

  pakuwon camp, temporary dwelling.

kuwuk I wildcat.

  II, kuwukan a children's game.

  III a certain variety of large seashell;

  nguwuk to glaze (fabric) by rubbing it with the above shell.

  IV rotten (egg);

  kuwukan rotten egg.

kuwung I 1 concave; **2** hollow, nestbox (for birds).

  II, kuwung-kuwung rainbow;

  nguwung to shine, radiate light;

  kekuwung aura.

  III *lit* peacock.

kuwur confused, headachy.

kuya-kuya, nguya-nguya to torment, provoke, tease.

kuyu, kuyu-kuyu streaming with sweat.

kuyus *var of* **kuyu-kuyu**.

kwaci salted melon seeds, eaten as snacks.

kwagang *see* **kuwagang**.

kwartal quarter, three-month period;

  kwartalan 1 quarterly, by the quarter; **2** to complete a (school) quarter; **3** to issue reports at the completion of a quarter.

kwasa *see* **kuwasa**.

kwatir *see* **kuwatir**.

kwatos *see* **kuwatos**.

kwawa *see* **kuwawa**.

kwaya *see* **kuwaya**.

kwèh *lit* many, much. *See also* **akèh**.

kwèni a variety of mango.

kwintal unit of weight: 100 kg.

kwitangsi a receipt.

kwolu *see* **kawolu**.

kyai 1 *title applied to highly respected (educated, eminent) males*; **2** *title applied to a revered heirloom*;

  kyainé 1 tiger; **2** boss, big boss.

kyambak *var of* **kiyambak**.

kyanapatih *lit* **1** assistant to a regent; **2** prime minister, king's chief counsellor. *See also* **patih**.

kyangkaban to go around intruding, touching things, without caring about others' feelings.

kyangkangan *reg* to walk slowly, thoughtfully.

kyati *lit* well-known, famous.

kyayaban *var of* **kyangkaban**.

kyengkengan *var of* **kyangkangan**.

kyèyèt, ngyèyèt thin and weak;

  kyèyèt-kyèyèt weak, too listless to work.

kyuyus, pating kyuyus *pl* rained on and soaked.

L

la I (*irregular pronoun, also spelled* hla *or* lha) *indicating a minor transition in topic*: well; well then; now…;
- iya yes, certainly!; - wong 1 no wonder that; 2 *excl of surprise*; 3 *excl of disgust*.
II (*shft* kula) (*answering a call*) yes! here! at your service!

laba *lit* gain, benefit.

labah beginning of the rainy season (*reg var of* labuh III).

laban *reg* sluice in fishponds.

labas *reg* (suddenly) all finished up.

labda *lit* skilful. *See also* lebda.

labeh *reg var of* labuh.

labet I devoted service (*kr for* labuh II).
II 1 trace left behind; 2 wound; 3 - sangka because of.
III *reg* jawah - a rain of ash (from a volcano) (*kr for* lebu, awu).

lab-lub *repr* dipping frequently.

labrag, nglabrag 1 to thrash, beat severely; 2 to attack verbally, tongue-lash.

labu a kind of white gourd.

labuh I to anchor, drop anchor;
nglabuh to cast s.t. into the sea as appeasement to the spirits;
labuhan the ceremony of casting offerings to the spirits into the sea;
pelabuhan harbour, port.
II ng, labet kr, devoted service, good deeds; - pati to sacrifice one's life;
nglabuhi to serve unselfishly, dedicate o.s. (or one's time, energy, resources) to; to defend;
lelabuhan devotion, dedicated service, defence;
labuh sabaya pati *idiom* together through thick and thin.
III labuh 1 the season when the first rains come, the change from dry to wet season; 2 to begin working the fields. *See also* mangsa.

labur whitewash;
nglabur *or* nglaburi to whitewash s.t.;
nglaburaké 1 to apply (whitewash) to; 2 to whitewash for s.o. else;
laburan 1 act or way of whitewashing; 2 s.t. which has been whitewashed.

laca-lucu 1 jokes, joking around; 2 to joke with each other. *See also* lucu.

lacak trace, track, trail;
nglacak to trace, track down, follow the trail of;
kelacak to get tracked down;
lacakan tracing, reconstruction (of a route).

laci drawer in a table or desk;
lacèn (of desk) equipped with drawer.

lacur I 1 to cheat; 2 *reg* unlucky.
II, nglacur to perform prostitution;
palacuran prostitution.

lacut exceeding proper limits;
kelacut having gone too far.

ladak 1 boastful; 2 harsh; overbearing;
- ririh *lit* conceited in a soft way;
ngladaki to tease/torment (a child) to make it cry.

ladalah *excl of surprise*; my goodness!

ladan *reg* especially.

ladat *lit* 1 enjoyment, pleasure; 2 enjoyable, pleasant.

ladhang *reg* having space or time to spare. *See also* lodhang.

ladhat *or* ladhatan (as a) result, consequence.

ladheg *reg* very muddy, filthy;
ladhegan filth, dirt (on the floor *etc*).

ladhu I 1 volcanic mudflow (down river bed); 2 flood;
keladhon flooded with volcanic mud;

ladhon field covered with volcanic sand;
pladhu or **paladhu** a time of floods.
II to win abundantly (playing cards).
III *reg* village official in charge of irrigation.
IV pockmark after vaccination.

ladhug I *reg* (of ricefield) deep and muddy.
II, **diladhug 1** *cr* to get fucked; **2** (or **dladhug**) *used as a term of abuse*; damn it!

ladi *ng*, **lados** *kr*, to serve, be of service, to wait on;
ngladèni 1 to serve, take care of (customers), be of service to; **2** to return blow for blow (in a fight);
ngladèkaké 1 to serve s.t.; **2** to bring a person before (s.o. higher);
leladi or **leladèn** to serve;
lumadi 1 to be served up; **2** to be of service to;
ladèn or **ladènan 1** person served or waited on; **2** act or way of serving, servicing;
pladèn one who serves or waits on people.

lading I *ng*, **marisan** *kr*, sharp-bladed knife; - **gapit** clasp-knife; - **tunggul** big butcher's knife.

ladrag, **ngladrag** to loiter aimlessly (considered as improper for a woman).

ladrang I (or **ladrangan**) a certain style of the head of a kris sheath, shaped like a leaf.
II a certain class of gamelan melodies.

ladreg, **ngladreg** *reg* littered with rubbish.

laduk, **keladuk** excessive, too much.

ladya to serve, to dedicate o.s. to (*lit var of* **ladi**).

laé, **dhuh laé** (or **laé-laé**) oh dear! my goodness!

laèn *reg* different, other, another.

laga I, **lelaga** way of behaving.

II *lit* war, battle;
palagan battlefield;
ingalaga in battle.

lagag, **lagag-lagag** (to laugh) uproariously, boisterously. *See also* **lakak**.

lagak, **lagaké kaya** to appear as if, act like.

lagan I *reg* kitchen utensils.
II *reg* and, with;
nglagani *reg* **1** serve; **2** to help, join in with;
lagan-lagan *reg* server; serving.

lagang (of child) growing fast, shooting up. *See also* **wlagang**.

laganu *reg* at that (remote past) time.

lagar I, **nglagar** to burn off (grass, forest, to make fields);
lagaran slashed and burned area.
II, **nglagar** or **lagaran** to ride a horse without a saddle.

lagéhan *var of* **lagéyan**.

lagèk *reg var of* **lagi**. *See also* **gèk**.

lagep *reg* will, about to (*shtc of* **lagi arep**).

lagéyan (or **kelagéyan**) mannerism, idiosyncrasy, peculiarity.

lagi *ng*, **saweg**, **nembé** *kr*, **1** to be (do)ing...; to be in the process of; **2** (*also* **lagiyan**) just, only; - **baé** to have just done, no sooner...; - **iki** only now; - **apa** to be doing what; - **sedhéla** after a short time.

lagis without anything extra, without a bonus (when purchasing).

lagu melody, tune, song; - **dolanan** songs which are sung while playing games;
nglagokaké to sing a song; to carry the melody of s.t.;
lelagon to sing along; songs.

lagur *reg* joist, supporting beam.

lagya *lit, var of* **lagi**.

lah well then!

laha I *reg* **1** window blind; **2** *reg* bamboo fence used for fish trap;
nglaha to build a fence for catching fish in the sea.

II, **nglaha** empty, quiet (no activity); empty-handed while walking;
mlaha uncovered;
lahan unplanted area, plain;
lahanan *or* **lelahanan** 1 gratis, free of charge; 2 empty-handed;
lalahan (of newly cleared area) ready to be planted.

lahan *see* **laha**.

lahang *reg* sugar-palm sap;
lahang karoban manis *prov* good-looking and well-behaved.

lahar I a flow of hot mud and lava (*see also* **wlahar**).
II *reg* **wis** - usual, natural.

lahru *lit* dry season;
kelahron drought-stricken.

lai *or* **lelai** 1 a bad habit; 2 (of horses) wild behaviour, untamed.

lailahailallah Good God! My word! (*excl uttered when under extreme emotional stress*).

lailatulkadar the 'Night of Power', a night during the last 11 days of the Fasting Month which brings great blessing if observed with prayer and Quran recitation.

lain *var of* **laèn**.

laip 1 weak, sickly; 2 poor;
kelaip *or* **kelaipan** miserable, poverty-stricken.

lair I 1 to be born, come into being; 2 birth; - **mula** ever since s.o.'s birth;
nglairaké to give birth to, bear (a child);
lairan *ng*, *kr*, **wiyosan** *k.i.* birth;
kelairan pertaining to birth, sprung from.
II outward, external; - **batin** of body and soul;
lairé on the outside, externally;
nglairaké 1 to utter s.t., express (openly); 2 to think out (an idea);
kelair to be uttered.

lais a variety of magical street performance.

laja *reg* galingale root (*var of* **laos**).

lajar I, **mlajar** *or* **lumajar** (*subst kr for* **mlayu**) 1 to run; 2 to run away, bolt.
II *reg* plough;
nglajar to plough.

lajeng I and then, after that (*kr for* **banjur**).
II *see* **payu** I.

lajer 1 main root of a plant; 2 main issue, central topic; 3 leader, one who presides.

lajim normal, usual;
lajimé normally, usually.

lajo, nglajo 1 to commute from (home); 2 (*or* **lajon**) to go s.w. and return on the same day;
lajon 1 *var of* **nglajo**; 2 place usually visited;
lelajon custom, habit.

laju I 1 *lit* straight (on), forward, continuous; 2 and then, after that.
II, **nglaju** to commute from (home); to go back and forth (*var of* **lajo**).

lajuk *var of* **laduk**.

lajur row, line, lane;
nglajur to form a row;
lajuran in a row;
salajur a row of s.t.

lak I, outlet (of irrigated ricefield). *See also* **tulak** IV.
II, **lak-lakan** the soft palate. *See also* **telak**.
III raw, sore (in the mouth).
IV sealing wax;
ngelak to seal with wax;
lak-lakan 1 sealed with wax; 2 the way to seal.

laka *reg* uncommon, unlikely. *See also* **langka**.

lakak, lakak-lakak (to laugh) uproariously, boisterously.

lakang (*or* **wlakang**) groin, inner part of the thigh;
kelakang to be struck in the groin;
lakangan *or* **palakangan** groin.

lakar I *reg* certainly, really, for a fact; it is true, indeed.

II *reg* raw material; element;

nglakari to sketch; to set in;

lakaran a sketch; provisionally worked up.

laken fine woollen cloth, broadcloth.

laket *reg var of* raket.

laki 1 sexual intercourse; 2 husband; - rabi to get married;

alaki to marry;

nglakèni (of animals, *cr* of people) to copulate with;

nglakèkaké to mate or breed (animals);

lakèn 1 to mate (animals); 2 *cr* sexual intercourse; 3 *cr* to have lots of men;

salaki rabi married couple.

lakon *see* laku.

laknat 1 a curse, malediction; 2 devil, demon;

laknatullah God's curse.

laksa unit of 10,000 (*formal var of* leksa);

laksan (numbering in the) tens of thousands.

laksana *lit* I mark, sign, attribute.

II *lit* action, doing, performing;

nglaksanani *or* nglaksanakaké to put into action, carry out;

lumaksana *lit* to act, take action, proceed.

laksita *lit* 1 behaviour; 2 rule of life.

laksmi *lit* beautiful (woman).

laku *ng*, lampah *kr*, tindak *k.i.*, 1 walk, gait; forward motion, progress; 2 behaviour, conduct, attitude; to act, conduct o.s.; 3 *reg* to sell well; 4 technique, manner, way; 5 ascetic (religious) regimen; - bokong *or* - dhodhok to walk in a squatting position when approaching a high-ranking personage, to show humility and esteem; - cidra (to engage in) untrustworthy conduct; - dagang to trade; - gawé to fulfil an obligation to the government by doing public work without pay; - jantra cycle of events; pattern of behaviour; - ngiwa (to engage in) bad conduct; - sandi to act secretively;

laku-laku *ng*, lampah-lampah *kr*, manners and customs;

nglakoni 1 to endure difficulties voluntarily; 2 to undergo, endure;

nglakokaké 1 to put s.t. in motion; to make s.t. move/function; 2 to depict; to perform (the role of);

mlaku to walk;

mlaku-mlaku to go for a walk;

mloka-mlaku to keep walking back and forth;

lakon 1 plot or scenario of a drama; 2 leading player; 3 (*or* lelakon) fate, destiny;

lelaku in death throes;

lelakon biography, story of one's life; fate, destiny;

kelakon 1 to happen, come about; 2 to be accomplished;

kelakuan conduct, behaviour;

lumaku *lit* to walk. *See also* palaku I, II.

lala, nglala to be kind to, care for. *See also* ela.

lalab I *or* lalaban raw vegetables.

II, lalaban a wooden wedge for splitting wood;

nglalabi to use a wedge as the above.

lalad, laladan territory, jurisdiction.

lalahan *see* laha.

lalana *var of* lelana.

lalalucu joking around; jokes.

lalaluya light-hearted.

lalar dirt on the human skin;

nglalar to remove dirt from the body by rubbing.

lalawa *lit* a certain small bat (flying animal).

lalawora 1 nonsense; 2 (to talk) stuff and nonsense.

laler fly (insect); - méncok the 'perching fly', a type of small moustache on the upper lip;
nglaler to behave like a fly, i.e. fly here and there, never stay still.

lali ng, supé or kesupèn kr, 1 to forget; 2 to no longer think of, neglect, be indifferent to; 3 to be absorbed, lost in thought, unconscious; - jiwa a variety of mango;
lali-lali 1 lit to try to forget; 2 (or lola-lali) to keep forgetting;
nglali to forget intentionally;
nglali-lali to try to forget;
nglalèkaké to forget about, put s.t. out of one's mind;
kelalèn to have s.t. escape one, slip one's mind;
lalèn or lalènan forgetful.

lalilah reg my God!

lalim lit cruel.

lalis lit 1 to go away, disappear; 2 to die, pass away.

lalos to forget (subst kr for lali).

lalu I, nglalu to commit suicide.
II, nglalu or milalu to subject o.s. to; to prefer to do s.t.
III to pass; - mangsa 1 (- yuswa k.i.) past the time, old; 2 behind the times.

lalun, kalalun lit carried off by the waves.

lalya lit var of lali.

lam, lam-lam admiration, awe;
lam-lamen lost in admiration;
ngelam-lami causing admiration or wonderment.

lama long (time) (subst kr for lawas).

lamad 1 spider web; 2 gauze (bandage). See also lamat.

lamak I a protective mat;
nglamaki to furnish with a protective mat.
II, nglamak reg to act rudely;
nglamakaké to look down on, treat with contempt.

lamar, nglamar 1 to ask for the hand of (girl); 2 to apply for a job;
nglamaraké to apply for a job or another's hand in marriage on behalf of s.o. else;
lamaran or panglamar 1 (marriage) proposal; 2 application for admission; 3 process of applying.

lamat I, lamat-lamat 1 vague, indistinct, barely visible/audible; 2 (or lela-matan) thinly coated, lightly powdered.
II sign, symbol (var of alamat).

lamba I 1 single, not double; 2 simple, guileless;
lamban single, unmarried.
II lit counting unit for small and flat things, sheet (leaf, hair etc);
salamba one sheet.

lambah, lambah-lambah to form puddles (water).

lambak reg var of lémbak.

lamban I slow, sluggish, languid, indolent;
lamban-lamban slowly, clumsily;
nglambanaké to slow down, make s.t. slow.
II reg fabric which is already cut for a skirt but not sewn yet.
III see lamba I.

lambang I sign, symbol, emblem;
nglambangi to provide a sign, signify;
nglambangaké to symbolise, represent.
II (or lambang gantung) a crosspiece in the rafters of a Javanese house;
lambangan cross-beam used to support a ship's mast.
III, nglambangi to exchange, replace.

lambangsari or lambangsekar lit to make love, enjoy intimacy.

lambar (or lambaran) 1 an underlayer, object for s.t. to rest on, e.g. saucer; 2 basis, support;
nglambari to furnish with an under-layer, put a base under.

lambat *reg* old, long ago.

lambau large, red Chinese temple candle.

lambé *ng, kr,* **lathi** *k.i.* **1** lip; **2** edge, rim; - **gajah 1** decorative notch where a kris handle joins the blade; **2** a certain style of kris sheath; - **dang** having a flared rim (*see also* **bédang**);
lambé satumang kari samerang *prov* hard to advise.

lambèh *var of* **lèmbèh**.

lambir, lambiran a low riverbank, shoreline.

lambok *see* **bok, mbok**.

lambu, nglamboni to mix with.

lambung side, flank; - **lengis** waistline;
nglambung 1 to wear at one's side; **2** to attack at the side/flank.

lambut *reg var of* **lembut**.

lamèh, lomah-lamèh 1 slow, easy-going; **2** pleasant, outgoing, friendly.

lamèn *var of* **damèn**. *See* **dami**.

lameng a short broad sword.

lami old; (a) long (time) (*kr for* **lawas**).

lamis (*or* **lelamisan**) **1** fine words; **2** insincere, feigned, sham;
nglamisi tembungé to use fine words.

lamit *reg* excuse me! (*shtc of* **kula amit**).

lamlam *see* **lam**.

lamon *lit, var of* **lamun** I.

lamong *lit* rather crazy, deranged;
nglamong delirious, raving.

lampad, lampadan *reg* a laid-out meal (*var of* **rampadan**).

lampah walk; behaviour (*kr for* **laku**).

lampeg *reg* to rise (of water level, *e.g.* during a flood, when the tide comes in).

lampèng *reg* hollow place under an overhanging riverbank.

lampes a certain plant, holy basil.

lampet, nglampet *reg* to plug, stop, block (dam, dyke).

lampi *reg var of* **lampin**.

lampin cloth for holding hot objects;
nglampini to provide with such a cloth.

lamping *var of* **lampin**.

lampir *or* **lampiran** enclosure, attachment;
nglampiri to enclose, attach, append to s.t.;
nglampiraké to append s.t.;
lampiran 1 enclosure; **2** appendix, annex.

lampit mat made of woven rattan or bamboo strips.

lampor roaring, howling sound heard on rivers at sunset, believed to be followers of Ratu Kidul riding through the air in search of little children.

lampu I lamp, light; - **abang** red light (traffic signal), *fig* warning; - **dhudhuk** table lamp; - **gantung** hanging lamp; - **robyong** chandelier; decorative lamp; - **sènter** torch, flashlight; - **téplok** kerosene lamp hung on wall or pillar.
II, nglampu to undergo, to subject o.s. to.

lampus *lit* dead, to die;
nglampus to kill;
nglampus dhiri to commit suicide.

lamuk I *reg* mosquito.
II, lamuk-lamuk 1 haze, hazy; **2** dim with soot (lamp);
nglamuki 1 to make hazy; **2** to blacken with soot.

lamun I *lit* if, when, when(ever);
kalamun if, provided that.
II, nglamun to muse, daydream;
nglamunaké to daydream about;
lamunan daydream, fantasy.

lamur I to have defective vision, not able to see clearly;
lamuren to suffer from weak eyes.
II nglamuri to become interested in the opposite sex (adolescent boy).

lamus I bellows made from goatskin;
nglamus to blow with such bellows.
II grey (buffalo-skin colour).

lamut, nglamuti to put or hold s.t. in the mouth. *See also* **klamut**.

lan 1 and; **2** with; **3** plus;
  ngelanaké to add (arithmetical process);
  lan-lanan addition (arithmetical process).
lana *lit* always, lasting, unchanged; **ora -** unreliable (character).
lanang *ng*, **jaler** *kr*, **kakung** *k.i.* **1** male; **anak -** son; **bocah -** boy; **wong -** man, husband; **- kemangi** *idiom* coward; **sing -** her husband; **- wadon/wédok 1** male and female; **2** husband and wife; **2** manly, brave;
  nglanangi masculine, man-like (complimentary, of men; derogatory, of women);
  lanangan 1 stud, male breeding animal; **2** *cr* husband;
  lelananging jagad *idiom* the bravest man in the world;
  planangan male parts, penis.
lanas I withered, drooping (because of heat).
  II quick-tempered, explosive (woman). *See also* **ganas**.
lanat evil, cursed (*var of* **laknat**).
lanbau agricultural adviser.
lancang I 1 ahead of time; premature; **2** impetuous; **3** to dare to do s.t. without proper permission, insolent;
  nglancangi 1 to overtake and pass; to get in front of; **2** to do s.t. one doesn't have the right to do;
  lancang-lancangan to compete for the lead; to get ahead of each other;
  kumalancang rash, hasty, importunate.
  II a boat-shaped container for betel quid;
  lancangan *reg* salver, tray for serving betel quid.
lancap (of face shape) oval, narrow.
lancar I smooth, fluent, flowing;
  nglancaraké to cause s.t. to be smooth/fluent;

lancaran a basic rhythm of gamelan melody;
  lelancaran moving quickly and smoothly.
  II (of tail feathers) long and slender.
  III, lancaran *reg* plate (*kr for* **piring**).
lanceng a small black stingless bee that produces wax.
lancing I, lancingan pants, trousers (*k.i. for* **kathok**, **sruwal**).
  II, loncang-lancing not yet married, free.
lancip sharp, pointed;
  nglancipi *or* **nglancipaké** to sharpen s.t.;
  nglancipi eri *fig* to infuriate an angry person still further.
lancung *reg* false, counterfeit.
lancur 1 rooster's tail feather; **2** (*or* **lancuran**) young rooster reaching maturity;
  lelancur a young man who wants to be in front, top man;
  lumancur starting to grow tail feathers (young rooster).
Landa *ng*, **Landi** *kr*, **1** Dutch; **2** European, Western (*var of* **Wlanda**, **Walanda**).
landang I *reg* friend, servant;
  palandang one who serves, waits on.
  II, mlandang *reg* to achieve, be successful, get rich.
landeng, nglandeng 1 to extend, stretch far (cloud, smoke); **2** to spread, pervade the air (smell);
  nglandengaké to take a long time at, stretch, prolong (work).
landep I a shrub sometimes grown in hedges, the leaves used for hair tonic, stomachache *etc*.
  II name of the 2nd **wuku**.
landha lye; water in which burnt rice stalks have soaked: used as shampoo and spot remover; **- awu** burnt rice stalks to be soaked in water;

nglandha to wash (hair) or remove spots from (clothing) with the above;
nglandhani to apply lye.

landhak porcupine;
nglandhak 1 resembling a porcupine; 2 to dig a tunnel;
landhakan tunnel, shaft (*esp* for irrigation).

landhep 1 sharp, pointed; 2 clever, shrewd;
lelandhep sharp weapons;
nglandhepi 1 to make sharper than it was, sharpen; 2 to make biting remarks about;
nglandhepaké to sharpen;
landhepan sharp, clever.

landhes 1 block (for chopping, cutting, hammering); 2 base, foundation; 3 next younger brother or sister;
landhesan 1 base, underlayer: *fig* basis, foundation; 2 one who gets blamed; 3 to be based on s.t.;
nglandhesi to base s.t. on;
nglandhesaké to rest s.t. on s.t.

landhéyan *ng*, **jejeran** *kr, k.i.* 1 spear shaft; 2 kris handle.

landhung 1 protracted, drawn-out; 2 (of growth) luxuriant;
nglandhungi to make longer (garment);
landhungan 1 *or* **landhungan atèn** *or* **landhungan usus** tolerant and patient; 2 *cr* female genitals. *See also* **plandhungan**.

Landi Dutch (*kr for* **Landa**).

landrat court of law;
nglandrat to try (a court case);
nglandrataké to bring s.o. to court, *esp* in a civil case.

langak (puppet with an) upturned gaze;
nglangak to crane the neck, stretch the head back;
langakan *or* **langak-langak** to hold the head in a stretched-back position.

langar 1 harsh, overbearing; 2 quick-tempered.

langen pleasure, enjoyment; **-arjan** a coat-like garment worn by men for ceremonial occasions; **- asmara** to be in love with each other; **- beksa** to practise dancing; **- jiwa** *or* **- gita** certain classical verse forms; **- mandrawanara** a Yogyakarta court drama in which the performers kneel and sing as they dance, relating Rama stories; **- swara** to practise singing; **- driya** *lit* to devote o.s. to pleasure; **- driyan** a Mangkunagaran court drama in which the performers sing as they dance, relating the Damarwulan;
lelangen *lit* to devote o.s. to pleasure;
kelangenan 1 concubine; 2 a pet kept for enjoyment; 3 pleasure.

langenarjan *see* **langen**.

langenastra, panakawan - a particular group of retainers at the Yogyakarta court.

langendriyan *see* **langen**.

langes lampblack, soot from the smoke of an oil lamp;
nglanges to give off sooty smoke.

langga, nglangga to drink by pouring into the mouth.

langgan, nglanggani to purchase at the same shop habitually, become a regular customer at (a shop, restaurant *etc*);
langganan 1 client, regular subscriber; 2 to be a customer/consumer, subscriber.

langgana *lit* disobedient, to disobey.

langgar I a small prayer house.
II, **nglanggar** 1 to disobey, violate, break (the law); 2 to collide with, run into; 3 to overtake, catch up with;
palanggaran violation of law/regulations.

langgat I, **nglanggati** 1 to serve as partner for; 2 to respond or react (to); 3 to converse with;

lelanggatan to keep each other company.

II, **palanggatan** place for meditation or teaching mystical knowledge. *See also* **sanggar**.

langgen, langgenan 1 support, prop; 2 chopping-board.

langgeng eternal, everlasting;

nglanggengaké to perpetuate;

kalanggengan eternity;

jaman kalanggengan *idiom* the other world, life after death.

langgi rice served with dry foods.

langguk *reg* haughty, proud.

langgung *reg* eternal, everlasting. *See also* **langgeng**.

langgur, nglanggur to select (good seed, from harvest).

langi, nglangi to swim;

nglangèni 1 to swim across; 2 to swim approaching s.t.;

langèn 1 swimming; 2 to go swimming;

nglangèni tai baya *prov* to go to a lot of trouble without any repayment.

langip *reg* needy, indigent.

langit 1 sky; 2 mood, state of mind; 3 skin (on milk *etc*);

nglangit to form a skin (on milk *etc*);

langitan 1 ceiling; 2 canopy; 3 *reg* palate;

lelangiten to suffer from vertigo looking down from a height.

langka 1 most unlikely; 2 uncommon, scarce, rare.

langkah 1 step, stride; 2 too far, beyond the objective, wide of the mark;

nglangkahi 1 to step over s.t., stride by; 2 to skip, bypass; 3 to disregard (instruction *etc*); 4 to pass over (of a younger sister marrying before an older);

nglangkahaké to stride out;

mlangkah to step over, step forward;

langkahan a part of a wedding ceremony held when a younger sibling is marrying before an older one;

kalangkahan 1 to get stepped over, bypassed; 2 to be transgressed;

palangkah *or* **plangkah** a gift (a complete outfit of clothing) given to an older sibling by a younger one when marrying before the older one.

langkak *reg* scarce, rare. *See also* **langka**.

langkap *lit* bow (for shooting arrows).

langkas swift-moving, agile, deft.

langkep *reg* full. *See also* **jangkep**.

langkèt, nglangkèt emaciated.

langkib, nglangkib to make a fold in, turn down;

kelangkib to get folded unintentionally;

langkiban a fold; s.t. folded, pleated.

langking *lit* black, dark.

langkir name of the 13th **wuku**.

langkung I unit of 25 (*kr for* **lawé**).

II 1 to go past; to go (by way of) (*kr for* **liwat**); 2 more; exceeding (*kr for* **luwih**);

sakalangkung exceedingly.

III, **nglangkung** tall and crooked.

langlang (*or* **nglanglang**) to travel (wander, fly) around, do the rounds of (*also* **nganglang**).

langsam slow (car, train);

nglangsamaké to slow s.t. down.

langsang tray, under-frame.

langsar, nglangsar 1 slide over the floor; 2 to drag s.t. over the ground;

langsaran (of clothing) worn daily.

langsé (*or* **langsèn**) curtain (around bed, grave).

langseb a sweet yellow fruit that grows in clusters on a stalk.

langseng steaming basket;

nglangseng to (re)heat by steaming.

langsep *see* **langseb**;

nglangsep (of skin) resembling the

colour of the **langseb** fruit.

langsing slim, slender, svelte;
nglangsingaké to make s.t. slim, streamline (the body).

langsir 1 to shunt into position; **2** *fig* to shift (of the eyes, *usu* to look girls over);
nglangsir to shunt railway carriages/trucks from one track to another;
langsiran shunting yard.

langsung straight, direct, undeviating.

langsur I, nglangsur 1 to rub with oil after bathing.
II, nglangsur (of baby) to inch forward on the stomach (*var of* **glangsur**).

langu (of odour, taste) unpleasant, disagreeable.

langun *lit* pleasure, enjoyment (*var of* **langen**).

langut, nglangut far-off, remote, desolate.

lanja *or* **lelanja** often out of doors; to go visiting;
nglanja to pay a visit.

lanjah *reg* fickle, inconstant (*var of* **lènjèh**).

lanjak I, nglanjak 1 to jump, reach upwards, go further; **2** to jump over (fire);
nglanjakaké to increase s.t., raise.
II, nglanjakaké to rent land out.

lanjam ploughshare.

lanjang *reg* virgin, unmarried girl.

lanjar I young childless widow or divorcée (*see also* **wulanjar**).
II additional merchandise thrown in free;
nglanjari to throw in (additional merchandise) free.
III, lanjaran 1 supporting pole for climbing plant; **2** a child adopted in the hope of having one of one's own.

lanji I *reg* a wooden crowbar;
nglanji to dig with the above.

II 1 changeable, to keep moving about; **2** *cr* prostitute;
nglanji to fit, test whether s.t. fits.

lanjo *var of* **lajo**.

lanjrat *var of* **landrat**.

lanjuk I, nglanjuk *reg* to reach for s.t. high (over one's head).
II, kelanjuk *reg* excessive. *See also* **laduk**.

lanjung 1 *reg* small and slender (of sugarcane *etc*); **2** *reg* weak, soft.

lanjut I *reg* **1** long, protracted; **2** to go on; **3** carrying far (sound);
nglanjut to go s.w. and return on the same day (*see also* **lanjo, lajo**);
nglanjutaké to continue (up to the end).

lantak ramrod; **lantakan 1** bar (gold *etc*); **2** plunger (of pump).

lantap quick-tempered, touchy.

lantar, lantaran 1 a means of reaching s.t.: pole, well-hook *etc*; **2** mediator, intermediary; **3** spoon (*k.i. for* **séndhok**); **4** banana leaf used as a spoon (*k.i. for* **suru**); **5** walking stick (*k.i. for* **teken**) **6** bamboo railing of a bridge; **7** cause, reason;
nglantari to cause s.t. to occur;
nglantaraké 1 to convey, transport; **2** to act as mediator or middleman;
lumantar through, (conveyed) by way of.

lantas 1 smooth, even, without bumps; **2** straight to the point; **3** penetrating (sound).

lanté 1 floor; **2** (*k.i. for* **lampit**) mat.

lantèh *var of* **lantih**.

lantéra *var of* **lentéra**.

lanthang, lanthang-lanthang to walk fast without turning the head, stride out.

lantih practised, skilled, thoroughly familiar;
nglelantih to train, make o.s. familiar with.

lanting, nglantingi 1 to take/hold s.t. at

arm's length; 2 to give s.o. a helping hand;

lantingan earthenware carafe (*kr for* **kendhi**).

lantip mentally quick/agile, intelligent, clever.

lantrah, lantrah-lantrah long and slow;

nglantrah to drag on and on (*e.g.* speech, story);

nglantrahaké to explain in detail, at length.

lantrang I, **lantrang-lantrang** overlong (of garments).

II **lantrang-lantrang** to walk proudly, head in the air.

lantun I line, row of plants (*subst kr for* **larik**).

II track, footsteps (*subst kr for* **lari**);

nglantun to follow, try to find the track.

lantur, nglantur 1 to keep on going with s.t., persist, not cease; 2 to stray, get off the track;

nglanturaké to let s.t. go on;

kelantur 1 (*or* **kelantur-lantur**) to keep on going, go too far (in the wrong direction); 2 to become established (wrong use of a word).

lanyah 1 experienced, practised, at home in; 2 accustomed to, familiar with; 3 skilful, fluent at doing s.t.;

nglanyahaké to master by constant practice;

palanyahan, planyahan a woman of easy virtue.

lanyak, nglanyak *or* **lanyak-lanyak** to barge in, push in rudely.

lanyap, lanyapan with an upturned gaze (puppet).

lanyo, lanyo-lanyo impudent, ill-mannered.

laop, laop-laop *or* **loap-laop** to keep yawning.

laos galingale root, used medicinally and in cooking.

lap I dishcloth, cleaning rag;

ngelap *or* **ngelapi** to wipe clean;

ngelapaké to wipe (a dishcloth) on s.t.

II *or* **mak lap** *repr* whisking, fluttering;

lap-lapan worried, jumpy.

lapa *lit* hungry;

nglapani to fast for (a certain objective);

nglapakaké to fast on s.o.'s behalf as a means of achieving s.t. for them.

lapak I, *ng*, **kambil** *k.i.* saddle;

nglapaki to saddle (up) (a horse).

II *or* **lapak-lapak** metal box with a hinged lid in which tobacco or betel leaves are kept. *Also* **lapak-lapak**.

III **lapaké** and so; after that, consequently.

lapal (Arabic) text (of prayer, formula, spell);

nglapali to pronounce, recite such a text for/over.

lapan 35-day period;

selapan one **lapan**, *i.e.* the cycle when a day of the five-day week coincides with a day of the seven-day week;

selapanan a ceremony held on the 35th day after the birth of a child.

lapang broad, spacious, roomy;

lapangan plain, field.

lapat *var of* **ilapat**.

lapis 1 layer; outer layer; 2 rice flour layer cake;

nglapis 1 to arrange in layers; 2 (*or* **nglapisi**) to furnish with a(n outer) layer;

lapisan 1 layer; 2 in layers.

lap-lip inserted here and there. *See also* **selip**.

lapor *see* **lapur**.

lapur to report, make a report;

lapuran a report;

nglapuri to report (to s.o.);

palapuran a report;

nglapuraké to report s.t.

lar I 1 wing(s); **2** feather; **3** spoke (of small wheel);
manglar (of mature insects) to have grown wings;
lar-laran resembling feathers or wings (of batik motif).
II, ngelar *or* **ngelaraké** to expand, broaden, lengthen;
melar *or* **melaraké** to expand.

lara I *ng*, **sakit** *kr*, **gerah** *k.i.* **1** to hurt, be painful (part of the body); **2** to be sick; **3** pain; **4** sickness; - **ati** offended, hurt, insulted; - **brangta** lovesick; - **dhadha** tuberculosis; - **ayu** smallpox; - **ireng** addicted to opium; - **kuning** yellow fever; jaundice; - **panas** fever; - **tuwa** old age as a pathological condition; - (*or* **gerah**) **uyang** *ng* feverish;
lara-lara *or* **lora-lara** sickly; easily getting sick;
lelara an illness;
nglara to feign illness, just pretend to be sick;
nglarani 1 to inflict pain or suffering on s.o.; **2** to hurt s.o.'s feelings; **3** unhealthy; **4** to have labour pains;
nglarakaké to cause s.o.'s feelings to be hurt;
kelaran in pain; to suffer pain;
laranen *or* **lelaranen** sickly, in poor health;
kelara-lara sorrowful, grieving, broken-hearted;
lara laraning lara *idiom* **1** the ultimate in illness/suffering; **2** physical illness brought on by mental anguish.
II 1 virgin girl; **2** young girl of noble birth;
palara-lara 1 serving girls at court; **2** a man's mistress.

larab sheet, layer, covering;
nglarabi to place a cover over s.t.;
nglarabaké to place in layers. *See also* **larap**.

larad 1 to recede, diminish, be carried away; **2** pallid (complexion); **3** to come loose.

larag, nglarag to attack, advance in large numbers.

larah I 1 trace (of s.t. lost); **2** course of events;
nglarah to trace, check, investigate.
II, nglarahi to litter;
larahan litter, rubbish spread about.

larak, nglarak to drag forcibly.

larang I *ng*, **awis** *kr*, **1** scarce, hard to find; **2** expensive, high in cost;
nglarangi *or* **nglarangaké** to make s.t. (more) expensive.
II *ng*, **awis** *kr*, **nglarang** *or* **nglarangi** to forbid, prohibit;
larangan forbidden (thing), prohibition.

larap I 1 a flashing past, swooping movement; **2** intention, meaning; **larapé** it seems, looks as if (he) is going to…
II, nglarapaké 1 to direct in a particular direction; **2** to announce, present (a guest);
tanpa larapan *lit* without being announced.
III, nglarap to avoid, keep out of s.o.'s way.
IV, larapan 1 kinds of metal plate as forehead ornament; **2** slicing-board (for tobacco); **3** a kind of bench with holes for standing wayang puppets; **4** (*or* **palarapan**) forehead (*k.i.* *for* **bathuk**).

laras I *lit* bow.
II 1 *lit* beautiful, charming; **2** musical scale; **3** in tune (gamelan); **4** harmonious, fitting, appropriate;
nglaras 1 to tune (gamelan); **2** to harmonise, bring into agreement; **3** to sing for one's own enjoyment; **4** to relax, take it easy;
nglaras-laras to think over, consider (the harmoniousness, appropriateness of s.t.).

laré child, young person (*kr for* **bocah**); -
angon 1 herdsboy; 2 a kind of harmless snake.

larèk *reg var of* laré.

larèn, larènan ditch, small stream;
nglarèni to furnish with a channel.

lari I fluid (molten metal).
II trace, remains; **tanpa** - (gone) without a trace;
nglari to trace, track down, investigate.
III to run away, abscond.

larih, **nglarih** *or* **nglarihaké** to pour
liquor into a glass and serve it to s.o.;
nglarihi 1 to serve liquor; 2 *lit* to stab
with (a weapon);
larihan serving guests, one by one.

larik I 1 line, stripe; 2 row (crop, seats
etc); 3 furrow; 4 line of poetry;
larikan in rows.
II (**sigitan** *k.i.*) ointment for rubbing
on the forehead (treatment for
headache).

laris quick-selling;
nglarisi *or* **nglarisaké** to make s.t. sell
quickly;
kelarisan to be all sold out;
palarisan *or* **panglaris** magic formula
to make things sell fast;
panglarisan act or technique of selling
fast;
lumaris *lit* to go on one's way.

laron flying termite.

laru I additive to palm sap, to prevent it
from going sour.
II, **nglaru** to make charcoal.

larub, **nglarub** to grab.

larud 1 carried away (*e.g.* by river); 2 to
withdraw, disperse;
nglarudaké 1 to wash/sweep s.t. away;
2 to dissolve s.t.;
larudan a chemical solution.

larug 1 to slip, slide (of embankment,
hills *etc*); 2 advance (of troops); 3 trail
of s.t. dragged on the ground;

nglarug 1 to drag the feet; 2 to do s.t.
roughly, reluctantly.

laruh, **nglaruhi** *reg* to tell s.o. to (do).

larung *lit* bier, container for a dead body;
nglarung to consign (a body) to the
water (river).

las I 1 grain of unhusked rice; 2 a grain-
like object; 3 s.t. which stands out
from its group; 4 the 'black sheep', a
modest term for one's own child;
las-lasan loose, not set (precious
stones).
II weld, join;
ngelas to weld;
ngelasaké to have s.t. welded;
pangelasan welding-place;
las-lasan 1 welded; 2 act or way of
welding.
III teens; **telu-** thirteen.
IV **watu las** a kind of emery, used for
polishing. *See also* **welas**.

lasah, **nglasah** to try to trace, track
down.

lasak *reg* **wedhi** - shell grit.

lasar *reg* indeed, really. *See also* **dhasar**.

lasem 1 a variety of batik pattern; 2 name
of a gamelan melody.

lasir, **nglasir** to classify (fields, for taxa-
tion).

laskar soldier, infantryman.

lastari *see* **lestari**.

lastri *lit* night. *Also* **ratri**.

lasun *reg* 1 empty-handed; 2 blank,
vacant.

lat late, delayed. *See also* **telat**.

lata *lit* climbing vine, creeper, tendril.

latah a neurotic behaviour found in older
women, triggered by surprise or
shock, featuring involuntary obscene
language or conduct, often mimetic.

latak sediment in indigo batik dye, lees.

latar 1 (*or* **palataran**) yard or grounds
around a building; 2 background
colour, field.

latek 1 mud, bog; 2 *var of* **latak**.

lateng stinging nettle.

latha-lithi *see* lithi.

lathek oil dregs.

lathi I lip(s) (*k.i. for* lambé).
II, (*or* lelathi) to have blackened teeth (*k.i. for* sisig).

latin Latin, Roman;
nglatinaké to romanise (script *etc*).

latip *lit* weak.

latra *reg* flat, level.

latri *lit* night (*var of* ratri).

latu 1 spark; 2 fire (*kr for* geni).

latung, lenga - kerosene; petroleum.

laun *reg* leaves of the peanut plant, as fodder.

laup, laup-laup to shout repeatedly;
nglaup to shout or sing boisterously.

laur, lauran *reg* to open up a fallow field for cultivation.

laut I *reg* sea.
II to knock off work (for lunch, for the day; of blue-collar workers).

lawa I a certain small bat (flying animal);
payung - large, black umbrella.
II, lawa-lawa long-handled feather duster for cleaning high places;
nglawa-lawa to clean high walls and ceilings with such a duster.

lawad, nglawad *reg* to pay a visit (out of sympathy).

lawak ship's hull;
lelawak 1 howdah; 2 covered chest carried on poles, for carrying food at the palace.

lawan 1 *lit* opponent, adversary, rival; *lit* and, together with;
nglawan to fight;
lumawan 1 to fight, oppose; 2 opposed, fought against;
lawanan to resist, oppose;
lelawanan to compete with each other.

lawang *ng*, kori *kr*, konten *md*, door, gate, entrance;
lawangan 1 doorway; 2 small door.
See also plawangan.

lawar, lawaran *or* lelawaran 1 pure, unmixed; 2 unarmed; 3 (to eat) meat without rice.

lawas *ng*, lami *kr*, 1 old, from long ago, previous, former; 2 (dangu *kr*) (a) long (time); ora - before long;
lawas-lawas at last, eventually;
kelawasen 1 (kelamèn *kr*) excessively old; 2 (kedangon) an excessively long time;
salawasé as long as, during, in the time that;
salawas-lawasé for the whole time that, forever.

lawat *see* lawad.

lawé I, *ng*, langkung *kr*, unit of 25;
lawéan *or* lawén *or* lawénan (langkungan *kr*) 1 25-rupiah note; 2 in 25s;
selawé 25;
nyelawé 25 each.
II thread, yarn;
nglawé to strangle;
plawéyan 1 a seller of yarn; 2 market where yarn is sold.

lawed, nglawed 1 *reg* to plough for the second time; 2 to knead together (with water);
lawedan 1 *reg* a field that has been ploughed twice; 2 s.t. that has been kneaded.

lawèh a prop placed at the edge of a brazier;
nglawèhi 1 to prop s.t. up; 2 to be of assistance to, lend a hand to.

lawer *reg* late-bearing (fruit, children).

lawèt a variety of swallow (bird).

lawéyan 1 dimples on the cheeks, shoulders or buttocks; 2 a kind of evil spirit.

lawih *var of* lawèh.

lawis *see* wis.

lawon white cotton fabric, for shrouds.

lawong I, lelawongan (of sound) to keep resounding, reverberating.
II *see* wong.

lawuh side dish, eaten with rice;
  nglawuhi 1 to prepare or provide (dishes) for; **2** appropriate to be served as a side dish; **3** to add fresh dye to a bath;
  lawuhan *or* **lelawuhan 1** (the array of) dishes for a meal; **2** to have a meal complete with side dishes.

lawun, lawun-lawun mountain mist, fog.

lawung I 1 spear; **2** classical spear dance;
  nglawung 1 to pierce with a spear; **2** to perform a spear dance;
  palawungan a rack for keeping spears, krises.
  II, nglawungaké to permit (stock) to go loose.

laya I *lit* **1** ruined, destroyed; **2** dead.
  II lelaya to roam about.
  III *lit* (*in compounds*) the abode of.

layab, nglayab *cr* to be out for a walk.

layad *or* **nglayad** to visit s.o. out of sympathy (after a death or accident); to go and pay condolences;
  layadan, dadi - to be an object of morbid curiosity;
  palayadan place where a death has occurred, a bereaved home.

layah stone or clay mortar used for preparing spices with a pestle.

layak 1 proper, right, fitting; **2** quite natural, understandable, no wonder.

layan I *reg* and;
  kalayan *lit* and;
  nglayani 1 to respond to; **2** to pay attention to, take proper care of;
  lelayanan mate, partner.
  II small additional cooking stove.

layang I *ng*, **serat** *kr*, **1** (**nawala** *k.i.*) letter; **2** written document; **3** book, literary work; **- budheg** anonymous letter; **- kabar** newspaper;
  nglayangi to send a letter to;
  layang-layangan to correspond;
  palayangan postman.
  II, nglayang to glide in the air;

layangan a kite;
  layang-layangan, lelayangan to fly kites.
  III, layangan shadow; **ora kena kepidak layangané** *expr* hot-tempered, hypersensitive.

layap the condition of seeing dimly when about to fall asleep;
  layap-layap half-asleep, sleeping but still able to preceive;
  nglayap to go wandering; **salayapan** 40 winks, the time of a nap.

layar I 1 sail; to sail; **2** projection screen; **3** diacritical mark in Javanese script denoting *r* after a vowel;
  lelayaran to set sail, go sailing;
  palayaran pertaining to sailing.
  II, nglayari to go looking for s.t. elsewhere (*e.g.* work, trade).

layat I *see* **layad**.
  II lumayat *lit* to run away, leave;
  kelayatan 1 left behind; **2** late, to take too long, tarry.

layeg, nglayeg 1 to keep on doing s.t., stick at s.t. patiently; **2** to keep busy, be always on the go.

layon 1 withered, faded flower; **2** corpse (*k.i for* **jisim, mayit**); **dadi -** to die. *See also* **layu**.

layos *reg* a (temporary) roof affixed to a house to provide additional space.

layu I to wither, fade;
  lelayu 1 death; **2** news about s.o.'s death.
  II *ng*, **lajeng** *kr*, running pace;
  lumayu *lit*, **mlayu 1** to run; **2** to run away, flee. *See also* **klayu, playu**.
  III lelayu 1 a lance with pennant attached; **2** runner, courier.

layub, nglayub to look dim, dull (eyes).

layung I a yellow glow in the sky at sunset (thought to cause conjunctivitis if looked at);
  II, nglayung to fade away, languish, from sadness or illness.

III *lit* nangis layung-layung to weep bitterly, brokenheartedly.

layup, layup-layup faint (*describing the sound of a voice heard from afar*).

layur a small, thin sea fish.

lé I s.o.'s act of (do)ing (*contracted form of* olèhé); *gram*: nominalising function, transposing verb or adjective to substantival phrase.

II *affectionate adr* little boy (*shtf of* tholé).

leb I, lab-leb to eat avidly, with a good appetite.

II, ngelebi to flood, inundate;
keleban to get flooded/inundated.

III, nglebi *reg* to close the doors, be all closed up.

lèb *var of* leb II.

lebak a plain, valley, lowland; flat terrain in a lowland;
lebak ilining banyu *prov* subordinates are always blamed for any problem.

lebar 1 to leave, retire; 2 finished with (work); 3 over, completed (time, season); 4 after;
nglebaraké to bring to a close;
salebaré after;
Lebaran 1 holiday, celebrated at the close of the Fasting Month; 2 to celebrate Lebaran ; - haji festival celebrated on the 10th day of the 12th Islamic month; - kupat festival celebrated on the 8th day of the 10th Islamic month by providing a meal characterised with rice boiled in a coconut leaf wrapping (kupat).

lebda *lit* experienced, skilled.

lebé vilage mosque official.

lebek (of road) often trodden.

lebeng, nglebeng to care for, feed well;
lebengan *reg* unirrigated ricefield on the bank of a river.

lèbèr, nglèbèri to pour out onto;
lèbèran outpouring. *See also* lubèr.

lebet 1 deep; inside (*kr for* jero); 2 to enter (*root form: kr for* lebu).

lebih *reg* more, more than, plus.

leboh *var of* lebuh.

lébot, nglébotaké *reg* to shift one's work over to a co-worker;
lébotan an exchange item, a job that has been shifted over.

lébrag, nglébrag 1 spacious, roomy; 2 empty of passengers.

lebu I dust (on ground, road).

II, *ng*, lebet *kr*, act of entering;
mlebu 1 to enter; 2 to attend (school, office);
ngleboni 1 to enter s.t.; 2 to insert s.t. into;
nglebokaké to insert s.t. into; to enter s.o. in;
lebon 1 what has to be delivered at a fixed time; 2 periodic payment on debt; 3 costs to be paid or materials needed to get s.t. done; 4 intake (pupils, soldiers);
klebu 1 contained (in), classified as, included (in the category of); 2 to get accepted;
klebon 1 to be entered, *esp* by s.t. detrimental; 2 possessed (by); 3 (of football) to get scored against;
mleba-mlebu to enter again and again;
mlebu-metu to keep going in and out;
lumebu *lit* to enter;
lebu-wetu (of breath, money *etc*) in and out.

lebuh 1 uncultivated land; 2 road; 3 *reg* rubbish dump.

lebuk, lebuk-lebuk *reg*, *excl of* astonishment.

lebur 1 melted; 2 completely destroyed; 3 lost, irredeemable (pawned article); 4 forgiven, wiped out (sin, error); 5 paid off (debt);
nglebur 1 to destroy, wipe out; 2 to melt, fuse;
ngleburaké 1 to cause to be destroyed; 2 to cause to be melted down;

panglebur destroyer;

pangleburan process of breaking down.

lebus covered in dust.

lècèk 1 loose in its setting, not tightly fitting; **2** loose, careless (words); **3** unreliable, untrustworthy.

leceng *reg* fast, quick.

lecet *reg* quick-moving, hard to catch.

lècèt grazed.

lecit *reg* **1** foul-smelling; **2** dirt on teeth.

lécok, **nglécok** to crush or grind finely (betel) for chewing.

lécun, **I salécun** *reg* very much.

 II, **nglécun** to cheat, deceive.

led, **ngeled** to swallow up (*var of* **leg**); **- pait** bitter aftertaste;

 led-led throat;

 led-ledan s.t. to make (a tablet) easier to swallow.

léda indifferent, not serious;

 leléda whim, vagary.

ledeg muddy.

lèdèng soft, half-melted (wax, metal);

 nglèdèngi to dissolve, melt (down);

 lèdèngan 1 melted, dissolved; **2** act of melting/dissolving.

lèdèr 1 mushy, gooey; **2** melted (*var of* **lèdèng**).

lédhang I, **lelédhang** to go (out) for a stroll.

 II annoyance, irritation;

 nglelédhang to annoy, pester.

ledheg *reg* muddy.

lèdhèk I a female dancer and singer;

 nglèdhèk to perform a dance while singing.

 II, **nglelèdhèk** to tease, needle, bait.

lèdheng 1 water pipe; **banyu** - piped water; **2** irrigation ditch.

lèdhès 1 bare, eroded (ground); **2** sore, inflamed (eyes); **3** rubbed, grazed.

ledhis I to smell unwashed.

 II 1 finished, all gone; **2** destitute, to have lost everything.

lédhog *reg* muddy.

ledhok 1 level part along a riverbank at the foot of a steep slope; **2** (*or* **ledhokan**) a depression in the ground.

ledhung, **ledhung-ledhung** (of plant leaves) luxuriant.

lédré a waffle-like wafer made of rice flour and sometimes filled with mashed banana.

lèdrèg *or* **nglèdrèg** damp, decaying, mouldy.

lèdrèk 1 mushy; **2** *var of* **lèdrèg**.

lédrok mushy (*var of* **lèdrèk**).

leg *or* **mak leg** *repr* swallowing;

 ngeleg to swallow;

 keleg to get swallowed.

lega 1 free, not occupied; to have time; **2** easy (not constipated); **3** relieved; **4** satisfied, pleased; **5 - lila** to have no objection, to do with pleasure;

 nglegani to fulfil (wish);

 nglegakaké 1 satisfying; **2** to give relief;

 legan 1 free, at leisure; **2** single, unmarried.

 kelegan content(ed), relieved;

 legan golèk momongan *idiom* a well-off person seeking hardship.

legak-legok *see* **legok**.

legandha variety of snack, made from sticky rice flour, wrapped with young palm leaves.

légang *reg* unburdened, empty-handed.

legarang, **nglegarang** to lie across s.t., in an improper position.

legawa generous, magnanimous, kind-hearted.

leged, **legedan** character, inclinations.

legeg *or* **legeg-legeg** nonplussed, at a loss, speechless.

lègeg, **lègeg-lègeg** to rock to and fro.

lègèg, **lègèg-lègèg** *or* **nglègèg** to sit up proud and high.

legèh empty, with no cargo, empty-handed.

legen I original, initial capital.

II *reg* 1 ordinary, regular; 2 original, free of outside influence (*kr for* lugu).

legèn sap tapped from the flower stalk of the coconut or sugar-palm. *See also* legi.

legena (of Javanese script characters) bare, *i.e.* without vowel-indicating diacritics;

nglegena nude; bare; without additions.

legendar rice flour cake.

legender *or* mak legender *repr* sudden swallowing, gulp.

legenjong to walk with long steps.

leger, ngleger *reg* stunned with grief.

lèger I hogshead, large vat.

II register, logbook.

lègèr, nglègèr *reg* naked, bare.

legeser *or* mak legeser *repr* sneaking away/out.

legeses, nglegeses *reg* to be sound asleep.

leget *see* leged.

legéwa, nglegéwa to pay attention to, care about.

legéyah, legéyah-legéyah to stagger step by step.

legèyèh, nglegèyèh to let o.s. drop, lean back (against).

legi I sweet(-tasting); - bratawali intensely bitter;

nglegèni to make s.t. sweeter (than s.t. else);

nglegèkaké to make s.t. sweet;

legèn sap tapped from the flower-stalk of the coconut or sugar-palm;

lelegèn sweets.

II a day of the five-day market week.

légo *slang*, nglégo to sell up (one's belongings) to raise cash.

legog *var of* legeg.

légoh (of arms, legs) limp, lacking strength (*see also* régoh).

legojo executioner.

legok to have/get a shallow hole in it, concave;

nglegoki to make shallow holes in s.t.;

nglegokaké to make a depression/hole in s.t.;

legokan dent, hollow, depression.

légok, légok-légok to turn this way and that, meander (road, river);

légokan 1 bend ; 2 inlet.

legon a sprout of kélor or dhadhap used as a medicine.

légong, légongan a bend in the road, river (*reg var of* légokan).

legorong *var of* legarang.

legoso *or* mak legoso *repr* flopping, sprawling;

nglegoso to flop, sprawl.

legoyor, nglegoyor *or* legoyoran (of walking gait) unsteady; to stagger, sway.

legunder dragoon, cavalry.

legundhi a certain shrub.

légung *or* légungan place for tethering buffaloes at night. *See also* plégung.

leguta, ngleguta to have become accustomed to;

legutan habit, custom.

legutak attached, addicted.

leguyur *var of* legoyor.

lèh I s.o.'s act of (do)ing (*inf var of* olèh).

II, ngelèhaké to confront s.o. with their misdeed, reproach. *See also* welèh.

léha, léha-léha to be at leisure, have nothing to do.

léhah *see* léha.

lèhèh, lèhèh-lèhèh to lean back comfortably. *See also* lèyèh.

leheng *reg* preferable. *Also* luwung.

lèhèr *reg* neck.

lèi *reg* school slate.

lejar happy, contented, to have cheered up;

nglejaraké to cheer s.o. up.

lèjèg 1 muddy from many feet (path); 2 to be a frequent visitor;

lèjègan *reg* prostitute, whore.

lèjem *or* lelèjem *lit* intention, meaning; lèjemé to judge from appearances, he looks as if he is going to…;

nglèjemi to give a sign of, let it be seen that;

kléjam-klèjem to give a hint with a smile.

lejer form, shape, physique.

lèk I 1 (of moon) visible; 2 date (after new moon); 3 *lit* month; 4 month of pregnancy; 5 moment when the birth is expected; lèkné when, at the time, if; wis lèké (of baby) it's time to be born; jer padha déné lèk sanga *idiom* after all we are all human.

II to stay awake; cagak - a means of staying awake;

ngelèki to stay awake for a certain purpose;

ngelèkaké to open or keep open (the eyes);

melèk 1 to open the eyes; 2 to stay awake;

lèk-lèkan (wungon *k.i.*) to remain awake during the night for ritual purposes.

III, lèké *or* lèkné *reg* perhaps, possibly.

IV *reg* possession, property.

V *reg excl of doubt, apprehension* (*var of* gèk) *e.g.* lèk kepriyé what are we to do?

VI *particle of urging, e.g.* - wis, - énggal hurry up, get on with it!

leka scale in a teapot (*var of* weka).

lekak biting (taste).

lekak-lekik *see* lekik.

lékak-lékok *see* lékok.

lekas 1 to make a start, to begin; 2 *lit* manner, way of behaving; 3 *reg* quick; nglekasi to start the job;

nglekasaké to carry out, make s.t. happen;

lekasan 1 act of getting started; 2 the early stages of pregnancy.

lekek I (of neck) short and thick.

II *var of* lekak.

lèkèk, guyu lèkèk-lèkèk to laugh happily, uproariously.

leken *reg* steady, reliable.

leker circumference;

ngleker 1 curled up, coiled; 2 *cr* to sleep;

nglekeri to coil around s.t.;

lekeran coil, circle;

lekering wadana *lit* facial line, profile.

lèker *reg* 1 delicious; 2 pleasant, enjoyable;

lèkeran s.t. enjoyable.

lèkerkos *reg* delicious and gratis.

leket 1 to adhere, stick firmly to; 2 to be very close, intimate;

lumeket to be closely connected with.

leketep *or* mak leketep *repr* a sudden entering.

lekètèr *var of* lekétré.

lekétré *or* mak lekétré *repr* sliding down.

lekètrèk *var of* lekétré.

lekik a little hollow, dimple;

lekak-lekik full of dimples.

lekoh muddy.

lékoh 1 all mixed up (food); 2 dirty, smutty (talk).

lekok (to have) a dent, hollow, hole (*var of* dhekok).

lékok, lékak-lékok full of curves, bends.

lekotro *or* mak lekotro *repr* suddenly sliding, slipping off (*e.g.* clothing).

lekotrok *see* lekotro.

lèkrèk to come loose, fall apart.

leksa I unit of 10,000;

leksan (numbering in the) tens of thousands.

II 1 thin noodles similar to vermicelli; 2 a kind of dish prepared with such noodles.

leksana to make s.t. come true; to grant (a wish); bawa - to fulfil a promise (*see also* bawa);

kaleksanan 1 to have (one's wishes,

hopes) fulfilled; **2** carried out, done, happened;

ngleksanani to fulfil (s.o.'s wishes). *See also* **laksana**.

leksara *reg* letter of an alphabet (*var of* **aksara**).

léla I, **ngléla** clearly visible, uncovered, bare.

II, **léla-léla** *syllables of chanting lullabies*;

ngléla-léla 1 to sing a lullaby to; **2** to praise, compliment (sarcastically);

pangléla-léla praise, affection.

III swivel-gun, small cannon.

lélah, **nglélah** weak, limp (body). *See also* **léloh**.

lelana *lit* to wander, go on a journey.

lélang an auction; to sell at auction;

nglélang to hold an auction;

nglélangaké to auction s.t. off;

lélangan 1 bought at auction; **2** auction price; **3** place where an auction is held.

lélar-lélur *see* **lélur**.

lélé a certain freshwater fish, catfish.

leleb *see* **lelep**.

leled 1 slow, sluggish (speech); **2** to start late;

ngleled to act or move sluggishly.

lèlèh I 1 to get soft, about to melt; **2** to yield, agree;

nglèlèh *or* **nglèlèhaké** to melt s.t.

II, **nglèlèh** *or* **lèlèh-lèlèh** *reg* to lie back and have a rest, relax.

lelep, **nglelepaké** to hold/push s.t. below the surface;

klelep 1 to sink below the surface; **2** to get drowned out, overwhelmed; **3** to stay away a long time and still not come back;

klelepan to get filled with water and sink.

leler, **ngleler** to creep forward slowly, crawl. *See also* **kleler**.

lèlèr I, **nglèlèr** to spread;

nglèlèraké to leave s.t. lying spread out;

klèlèran to get left out, abandoned, neglected.

II, **nglèlèr** to put the quality (of gold) to the test;

nglèlèraké to have (a piece of gold) put to the test.

III reward, prize;

nglèlèr to reward s.o., give a prize to.

IV *reg* **nglèlèr**, **lèlèran** to harrow, prepare soil for planting.

leles *or* **lelesan** crossed sticks used for twirling coconut fibre;

ngleles to spin with such an implement.

lèlès I *or* **nglèlès 1** to try to find what is left, glean; **2** to beg.

II 1 to step aside; **2** *reg* no, you don't! (on discovering an attempt to trick).

lelet, **nglelet** to wind, twist, roll (cigarette).

lèlèt, **nglèlèti 1** to smear with a finger; **2** **dilèlèti** to get a touch of (some bad quality);

nglèlètaké to smear s.t. soft with a finger onto;

salèlètan a fingertipful of s.t. soft.

lèli *coll* to forget (*see also* **lali**).

léloh *or* **lélah-léloh** limp, weak, not firm.

lélur, **nglélur** *or* **lélar-lélur** enervated, listless.

lem I praise, a compliment;

ngelem to praise, compliment;

lem-leman a public commendation. *See also* **alem**.

II *reg term of address for calling old people*.

lema fat (*kr for* **lemu**).

lemah I *ng*, **siti** *kr*, soil, land, ground, earth; - **teles** reddish-brown, *i.e.* the colour of wet earth;

lemahen *or* **lelemahen** to be attached to one's home ground;

palemahan 1 land, area; a parcel of

land; 2 the bottom line of a white screen (for shadow-play).

II *reg kr* (*see* **lumuh**) to be disinclined.

lemak fat, grease.

lemantun cupboard (*kr for* **lemari**).

lemar an offering set as a requirement by a **dhukun** (traditional healer).

lemarèng *reg* brief interval between the close of the rainy season and the onset of the dry season. *Also* **marèng**.

lemari *ng*, **lemantun** *kr*, cupboard, cabinet; - **wesi** safe, strongbox.

lembah I valley.

II *or* **lembah-manah** calm, patient, tolerant in nature.

lembak *reg var of* **lebak**.

lémbak, **lémbak-lémbak** *or* **nglémbak** *or* **lumémbak** (of water) forming waves, swelling.

lembana praise, a compliment;
nglembana to praise, compliment.

lémbang *var of* **lémbar**.

lembar sheet (of s.t. thin like paper, cloth, fabric *etc*);
lembaran 1 sheet; flat object; 2 (*or* **lelembaran**) in sheets, consisting of sheets.

lémbar, **mlémbar** *or* **lumémbar** 1 to spread from one place to another (plants); 2 to be spread, be passed from one to another (illness).

lembara, **nglembara** to wander, roam (looking for s.t.).

lembat fine, thin, very small, smooth (*kr for* **lembut**).

lémbat, **nglémbataké** to move s.t. along, pass s.t. on (*var of* **lémbar**);
lémbatan one to whom s.o. else's work is passed on;
lumémbat *var of* **lumémbar**.

lembayung peanut leaves eaten as vegetable.

lèmbèh, **nglèmbèhaké** to swing (the arms);
lèmbèhan (*pron as:* **lémbéyan**) to swing

the arms as one walks.

lembèk weak, soft, spiritless.

lèmbèr *reg* flirtatious, coquettish.

lembèrèh, **nglembèrèh** to hang down loosely touching the ground. *See also* **klèmbrèh**.

lemberek, **nglemberek** to lie weakly, collapse in a heap.

lembing I a kind of short lance.

II a kind of small beetle with a strong smell; **ama** - a disease of rice plants.

lémbon to sleep deeply;
nglémboni 1 (of convalescent) fond of sleeping; 2 at the time of life when one sleeps a lot.

lémbong a tuberous plant with large edible leaves and stalk. *See also* **lumbu**.

lembrèh, **lèmbrèh** *var of* **lembèrèh**.

lembu cow (*kr for* **sapi**).

lembur work done outside normal working hours;
nglembur to work overtime;
lemburan overtime work.

lemburah, **nglemburah** to flop, sprawl.

lemburuk *var of* **lempuruk**.

lembut 1 fine, thin; 2 gentle;
lelembut ghosts, invisible beings;
nglembutaké to make finer.

lemek, **nglemek** 1 damp, limp from dampness; 2 to fade, lose colour.

lèmèk lining, protective underlayer;
nglèmèki to line s.t., furnish s.t. with an underlayer;
lelèmèk *or* **lèmèkan** to use a lining.

lemèn *see* **lemi**.

lemeng 1 a bamboo tube used for cooking food, *esp* sticky rice; 2 a bamboo tube used for curing tobacco;
nglemeng 1 to cook food as above; 2 to cure tobacco as above;
lemengan *reg* rice steamer.

lèmeng, **kelèmengan** to have s.t. slip one's mind.

lèmèr, **lèmèren** fickle, flighty, changeable;
lèmèran fickle by nature.

lemes 1 pliant, supple; 2 weak, soft; 3 refined, smooth (manners, language); 4 yielding;
  nglemesi 1 to soften; 2 to treat in a gentle way; 3 to cause weakness (illness);
  nglemesaké to cause s.t. to be flexible *etc*, to stretch (the muscles);
  lemesan 1 s.t. soft, smooth; 2 silk materials.
lemèt I a dessert of shredded cassava and coconut with brown sugar, steamed in a banana leaf.
  II, **nglemèt** (of the belly) flat, concave (*var of* **lempèt**);
  nglemètaké to flatten or pull in (the stomach).
lèmèt thin and flat.
lemi decaying vegetable matter;
  lemèn compost, humus, rich soil;
  nglemèni to apply compost to (soil).
lemir, nglemir thin and soft (fabric).
lempaung a tree with sour edible fruit.
lempé, lempé-lempé exhausted, ready to drop.
lempeng 1 dead straight, true; 2 fair (judgement); 3 in tune;
  nglempeng to go in a straight line.
lempèng I 1 a hollow in a riverbank; 2 the portion of the side between hip and ribs; 3 flank.
  II *reg* rectangular basket.
lèmpèng I a thin flat object; counting unit for such objects;
  nglèmpèng to become thin and flat;
  lèmpèngan a sheet of metal; (of flat broad metal) in sheets.
  II sweet pancake with sliced banana;
  nglèmpèng 1 to make such a pancake; 2 resembling a pancake.
lemper I to calm down, get less, lose strength (*e.g.* illness, anger, heat).
  II snack made from steamed glutinous rice filled with meat and wrapped in a banana leaf.

lèmpèr I large flat bowl for cooking.
  II unable to walk because of weak legs (child).
lempérak, nglempérak to sit sprawled, in a sloppy attitude.
lemperek *see* **lemprek**.
lempèt, nglempèt (of the belly) flat; concave;
  nglempètaké to flatten or pull in (the stomach).
lempir leaf, sheet (of paper); classifier for paper *etc* (*var of* **lembar**);
  nglempir thin and soft (*see also* **lemir**);
  lempiran in loose leaves, in sheets.
lempit, lempit-lempit to do the folding (clothes);
  nglempit *or* **nglempiti** to fold s.t.;
  nglempitaké to fold for s.o.; to have s.t. folded;
  lempitan 1 a fold; 2 folded; 3 way of folding;
  kelempit 1 to get folded inadvertently; 2 to get overlooked.
lempog I short and fat.
  II a method of cooking rice by steaming between layers of leaves.
lémpoh 1 crippled; 2 too tired to walk; 3 unable to achieve anything;
  lémpoh ngideri jagat *idiom* 'a cripple tours the world', *i.e.* impossible.
lempong I valley, lowland.
  II *reg* mattress.
lémpong *reg* mattress (*var of* **lempong**).
lemprèh, nglemprèh (to walk) straight ahead without looking to either side.
lèmprèh, nglèmprèh to glide slowly downwards (bird).
lemprek, nglemprek to flop, drop, fall weakly to the ground.
lempreng *var of* **lemprèh**.
lempuk an edible freshwater fish.
lempung 1 clay; 2 constipation;
  lempungen to suffer from constipation.

lempuruk, nglempuruk to lie in a mess, collapse in a heap.

lempuyang a medicinal herb of the ginger family (several varieties); durung ilang pupuk lempuyangé *idiom* still in infancy;

lempuyangan a lempuyang garden.

lemu *ng*, lema *kr*, 1 fat, fleshy, sleek; 2 luxuriant, flourishing;

lemon manure;

nglemoni (of babies, during their first year) to begin to put on weight;

nglemokaké to make fat; to put on weight;

nglelemu to fatten s.t. (up).

lemud I *see* lemut.

II, nglemud misty, feeble, weak (eyes).

lemuk *reg*, *see* lemut.

lemungsir shoulder (of beef *etc*).

lemut mosquito.

lèn *lit* other, different.

léna I inattentive, careless of danger;

ngléna to sneak up, do secretly;

kelénan to be off guard;

léna marga layu *lit* if you are careless you will be killed.

II deceased, dead.

lénah linen.

lénang *reg* male (*var of* lanang).

lencèg a certain implement for farming, spade.

lenceng straight, direct, without bends.

lencer *var of* lenceng.

lèncèr soft, watery, runny; - otaké smart, clever.

lencir 1 tall and straight; 2 attractively slim and tall (woman).

léncok, ngléncokaké *reg* to shift one's work to s.o. else.

léncung soft chicken droppings.

léndhang *var of* sléndhang.

léndhé, ngléndhé *or* léndhéan to lean, rest one's back against;

nglèndhèni to lean against s.t.;

léndhéan chair back, back rest;

léndhé-léndhé to lean (against).

lèndhèh *var of* léndhé.

lendhèh, nglendhèh to slow down; lendhèh-lendhèh (to walk) slowly.

lèndhek *reg* sluggish, slow.

lèndhèt *reg var of* léndhé.

lendhi a certain freshwater fish.

léndho *reg* rich, fertile (fields).

lendhong a certain freshwater fish.

léndhot, ngléndhot *or* léndhotan to lean (on), to hang (on) (*var of* léndhé, lèndhèt).

lendhut mud, slime, ooze.

leneng *see* kleneng.

leng I *or* mak leng *repr* a sudden departure.

II *lit* rather, preferably.

III lenging cipta the centre of one's thoughts/desires;

ngeleng *or* ngelengaké to concentrate on, focus the attention on. *See also* peleng.

lèng I 1 a (small) hole, burrow (*esp of* insect);

ngelèng 1 to live in a hole, enter a hole; 2 to make a hole; 3 to form a hole;

ngelèngi to make a hole in;

lèng-lèngan 1 nostril; 2 ear-opening; 3 eye of a needle; 4 having hole(s).

II *or* lènglèng the ins and outs, the tricks of the game.

lenga *ng*, lisah *kr* oil; - cèlèng residue of oil in an earthenware lamp; - gas *or* - mambu *or* - patra kerosene; - wangi perfume;

nglenga oily;

nglengani to apply oil or grease to;

lengan *or* lelengan to apply oil to the hair.

léngah-lèngèh I to keep smiling happily (babies). *See also* plèngèh.

II *reg* careless, negligent.

léngah-léngoh pleasant, friendly-looking (woman).

lengak, nglengak to crane the neck, turn the head to have a look, look in.

lengang-lengong to stand and stare in amazement.

lengar (of forehead) broad.

lengé, lengé-lengé 1 half-dead, paralysed; 2 unable to move (because of full stomach); 3 stricken with longing.

léngé *var of* **lengé.**

lenged, lengedan to have diarrhoea with cramps (child).

lengeg, nglengeg to be silent, having got s.t. one has no right to.

lèngèk, nglèngèk *or* **lèngèk-lèngèk** to swing the head, bend the neck (*e.g.* in swimming).

lengen arm (including the hand);
lengenan 1 sleeve; 2 mechanical arm;
lelengan trusted, indispensable person, one's 'right hand'.

lengeng *lit* charmed, enchanted.

lèngèng, dilèngèng! *cr* damn it!

lenger, lenger-lenger motionless, speechless, stunned, stupified. *See also* **klenger.**

lenggah 1 to sit (*k.i. for* **linggih**); 2 place where one lives or usually to be found (*k.i. for* **enggon**);
kalenggahan 1 dignity, position, office; 2 (only *k.i.*) possessed by a spirit.

lenggak, lenggak-lenggak, lenggak-lengguk 1 to turn the face up and down (in annoyance); 2 to sit relaxed doing nothing;
k(e)lenggak 1 to fall face up; 2 to have a stiff neck from looking up and down.

lénggak-lénggok *see* **lénggok.**

lenggan *var of* **langgan.**

lenggana *lit* to resist, oppose.

lenggang long, slender, tapering.

lénggang swaying, swinging the arms (walking gait).

lenggarak, nglenggarak *reg cr* to eat, hog.

lenggarang, nglenggarang to stand tall, stand out, be visible at a distance.

lénggat-lénggot *see* **lénggot.**

lenggèk, lenggèk-lenggèk 1 to let the head hang loosely (with exhaustion); 2 destitute.

lengger, nglengger 1 *cr* to be sound (of sleep); 2 to stay lying down, suffering from serious illness; 3 to sit motionless as if dazed, stunned.

lenggerek, nglenggerek large and looming in appearance.

lenggirik, nglenggirik bumpy and repulsive-looking (*e.g.* pock-marked face).

lénggok, lénggok-lénggok *or* **lénggak-lénggok** to twist and turn.

lénggot, lénggotan *or* **lénggat-lénggot** to sway the hips provocatively.

lenggotro, nglenggotro drooping, depressed.

lengguk I to keep silent, showing one's displeasure.
II *var of* **lenggut.**

lengguruk, nglengguruk to lie weakly (*esp* of chickens in death throes).

lenggurung, lenggurungan *reg* throat. *See also* **gurung.**

lenggut, lenggut-lenggut 1 to keep nodding while dozing; 2 (*or* **lenggat-lenggut**) (of head) to sway rhythmically.

lengis I smooth, slippery.
II properly spaced out, with a gap (*e.g.* plants).
III **waru** - a variety of hibiscus tree, the wood used for various purposes.

lengit *lit* 1 vaguely visible in the distance; 2 to disappear from sight.

lengka I *reg* very bitter.
II, *see* **kalengka.**

lengkad-lengkèd *see* **lengkèd.**

léngkak-léngkok *see* **léngkok.**

lengkang *reg* with a wide space between.

lengkap complete, full;
nglengkapi to complete, fill in;

nglengkapaké to complete for s.o.

lengkara, nglengkara impossible, improbable.

lengkèd see **lèngkèt**.

lengkèh 1 hillside, a slope, incline; **2** a range of sloping hills.

lengkep var of **lengkap**.

lengker reg a curl, winding.

lèngkèt to stick together, be firmly attached; **lumèngkèt** to adhere.

léngkok bend, curve;
léngkok-léngkok or **léngkak-léngkok** **1** to twist and turn; **2** to turn this way and that to show discontentment.

lengkong, lengkongan reg **1** bend, recess (of a river); **2** partition (off a room).

léngkot var of **lénggot**.

lengkung, lengkung-lengkung tall and slim, bending gracefully at the top (e.g. bamboo). See also **plengkung**.

lengkur, nglengkur 1 to wind around, tie to; **2** to lie curled up.

lengleng, lenglengan I 1 bewildered, perplexed; **2** infatuated, enchanted;
nglenglengi enchanting.
II to keep going out.
III lenglengan a certain edible plant, with medicinal use.

lengong, lengang-lengong to gaze vacantly, look on in a daze.

lèngsèr I 1 round tray for serving; **2 watu** - hard flat stone.
II 1 (or **lumèngsèr**) to slide, shift (earth from slope); **2** to withdraw, retreat, retire.

lenguk, lenguk-lenguk (to sit) by o.s. as if not thinking of anything much.

lengur, lengur-lengur tall and spindly (child).

lengus easily annoyed, touchy, testy.

lengut, lengut-lengut grumpy, in a bad mood, discontented.

lenjang reg slender, slim.

lènjèh or **lènjèhan 1** worn from much use; **2** changeable, fickle.

lenjer stem, stalk (var of **lonjor**).

lenjing a short wooden pestle for pounding things in a mortar.

léno or **mak léno** repr slapping, daubing. See also **létho, léthok**.

lénong a form of folk theatre found in the Jakarta area.

léntab reg to spread out.

lentéra lantern, lamp.

lentéré, nglentéré weak, fading away from lack of food.

lénthang, lénthang-lénthang empty-handed. See also **lènthèng, lonthang**.

lenthar, nglenthar to leave suddenly (in anger);
nglentharaké to leave in the lurch, disappoint, ignore, neglect.

lenthé, nglénthé, lenthé-lenthé to walk slowly, wearily.

lèntheng or **mak lèntheng** repr throwing and hitting the mark.

lènthèng, lènthèng-lènthèng empty-handed (var of **lénthang**).

lenthu, nglenthu to cheat, swindle.

lenthuk, nglenthuk, lenthuk-lenthuk to keep drooping the head (with sleepiness).
See also **lentuk**.

lenthung, nglenthung, lenthung-lenthung to return home without bringing anything.

léntor queen of the termites.

léntrah-léntroh weak, drooping.

lentreng, lentreng-lentreng, nglentreng to walk with heavy steps, drag the feet (in sadness, deep thought).

lèntrèng, nglèntrèng to stretch in a long, thin line.

lentrih, nglentrih, lentrih-lentrih (to walk) with a plodding, laboured gait.

lentring I a variety of small dagger.
II a variety of small freshwater fish.

lentruk, nglentruk or **lentrak-lentruk** weary, listless, apathetic, reluctant.

lentuk var of **lentruk**.

lényam-lényom shifty, unreliable.

lenyed *reg* careless, negligent.

lènyèd 1 squashed, flattened, bruised; 2 damp, clammy, sticky;
nglènyèd *or* **nglènyèdi** to flatten, squash.

lènyèh *or* **mlènyèh** soft and watery, squashy (fruit).

lenyir fine and soft to the feel.

lenyu 1 to have shooting pain all over the body; 2 exhausted.

lep *or* **mak leb** *repr* submerging. *See also* **leb II**.

lèp, lèp-lèpan flickering, twinkling.

lépa 1 plaster (lime and sand mixture); 2 mud smeared on a ricefield dyke;
nglépa to apply plaster;
lépan plastered.

lépak *or* **lépak-lépak** metal box for storing tobacco or betel.

lepas I 1 detached, loose(ned); 2 temporary, casual; 3 set free, discharged; 4 divorced; 5 exempt (of tax); 6 finished, settled, concluded; 7 - **makan** (of workers) to get a wage only, without meals;
nglepasaké to let loose, release, let fly;
lumepas *lit* to fly away, move away swiftly;
kalepasan mystical knowledge about release from this world.
II 1 to go far, carry (sound); 2 far-reaching (ideas).

lepat 1 wrong, mistaken; 2 to miss (*kr for* **salah, luput**).

lèpca *reg* ploughshare.

lepèh, nglepèh 1 to spit out (s.t. one has chewed); 2 *fig* to reject (advice);
lepèhan 1 food that has been chewed and then spat out; 2 s.t. rejected, no longer of any use.

lèpèk 1 flat; 2 small saucer;
lèpèkan s.t. used as a small saucer.

lèpèn I river (*kr for* **kali**).
II *reg* ring (*kr for* **ali-ali**).

lepet I a snack made of glutinous rice wrapped in a young coconut leaf;
nglepet to make such a snack.
II, lepetan a certain children's game accompanied with a song.

lèpèt sticky dirt;
lèpèt-lèpèt smeared slightly;
nglèpèti to incriminate s.o.;
kalèpètan to get involved or incriminated.

lepiyan 1 draft, original; 2 s.t. that has been used but is still kept; 3 *lit* example (of good conduct).

lépos, nglépos (to sleep) soundly.

lépra leprosy;
lépranen to suffer from leprosy.

leprèh *var of* **lemprèh**.

lepus *var of* **lépos**.

lépya *or* **lépyan** to forget (*kr for* **lali**);
kelépyan 1 to have s.t. slip one's mind; 2 to get overlooked/forgotten.

ler 1 strand, piece; counting word for long, thin objects;
ngeler 1 to pull a thread *etc* out of a bunch (*see also* **seler**); 2 to steal;
ler-leran in the form of strands.
II 1 a slipping down motion; 2 (*or* **mak ler**) *repr* dozing off;
ler-leran to keep nodding off, unable to stay awake;
saleran a nap.

lèr I north (*kr for* **lor**).
II, ngelèr to expose, leave out/uncovered;
anglèr *lit* 1 to expose, to leave uncovered; 2 left exposed;
ngelèraké to spread s.t. out for s.o.;
lèr-lèran 1 left exposed or untended; 2 spread, laid out flat; 3 ready for planting (field);
kelèr-kelèr to get left exposed;
palèran 1 a spread-out layer; 2 a ricefield ready for planting.
See also **lèlèr**.

léra-léré *see* **léré**.

léra-léro *var of* léra-léré.

lérab, nglérab *or* lérab-lérab to sparkle, glitter;
  saléraban (at) a quick glance. *See also* klérab.

lerag-lereg *see* lereg.

lérag-lèrèg *see* lèrèg.

lérah, lérah-lérah red, gory.

lerak 'soap-berry', a small hard round fruit used to produce suds for washing batik;
  nglerak to wash batik cloth with such suds.

léram *reg* to forget, fail to recognise.

léran-lèrèn *see* lèrèn.

lérang-lérong covered in streaks, marks.

lérap *see* lérab.

léré *or* mak léré *repr* slipping, skidding;
  léra-léré sliding back and forth, to keep sliding, slipping;
  léré-léré name of a certain gamelan melody.

lereb 1 to subside, calm down, diminish; 2 to stay overnight (*k.i. for* nginep);
  nglerebaké to cause to subside;
  lereban *or* palereban place to rest, spend the night (*k.i. for* panginepan).

lereg, lereg-lereg *or* lerag-lereg to have chills (when one is feverish).

lèrèg 1 sloping, leaning (toward); 2 turning in the direction of; 3 tendency;
  nglèrèg *or* nglèrègaké 1 to turn (toward); 2 to shift, slide in a certain direction;
  lèrègan 1 a drawer; 2 sliding (door);
  lérag-lèrèg to keep sliding.

lèrèh I 1 slow, calm, patient; 2 to wait, pause, rest; 3 to not be in service, give up a position;
  nglèrèhi 1 to calm s.o. down; 2 to discharge s.o.
  II, lèrèh-lèrèh streaked with blood.
  III, lèrèhan *or* kalèrèhan subordinate. *See also* rèh.

lèrèk I, lèrèk-lèrèk stripe, streaked (*var of* lorèng, lorèk);

nglèrèkaké to make stripes/streaks on s.t.
  II, nglèrèk to make a slit.

lerem to have calmed down (*var of* lerep);
  ngleremaké to calm s.o. down; to settle s.t.;
  palereman place to rest. *See also* rerem.

lèrèn ng, kèndel kr, lereb k.i. to stop, take a rest, discontinue an activity;
  nglèrèni 1 to stop s.t.; 2 to stop at/for; 3 to discharge or suspend s.o.;
  nglèrènaké 1 to bring to a stop(pingplace); 2 to cause s.t. to stop or rest;
  léran-lèrèn to stop and rest a lot (too much);
  palèrènan stopping-place, place to rest.

lèrèng (fabric which is) patterned with diagonal stripes.

lèrèp I a band on a belt to push the end through.
  II small earthenware saucer.

leres 1 right, correct (*kr for* bener); 2 direction, aim (*kr for* arah, ner); 3 right at (a place) (*kr for* pener).

lèrès, nglèrès to cut, slice.

leret to dim, become gloomy;
  ngleretaké to make s.t. gloomy/darker. *See also* bleret, pleret.

lèrèt I, *or* lèrètan row, line.
  II, salèrètan (at) a brief glance.

leri water in which rice has been washed before cooking (various uses).

lèri small railway truck, *usu* used for carrying sugarcane from a field to the factory. *Also* lori.

léring *reg* bicycle.

lérob, nglérobi to skim s.t. from the surface (of).

lérod, nglérodi to scrape the leftovers.

lérok I 1 *reg* a dance which is performed by a female dancer publicly.
  II *var of* plérok.

lérong, ngléróngi to streak s.t.;
   lérang-lérong streaky, varicoloured.
lérut *reg* a variety of arrowroot.
lèrwèh slovenly, sloppy.
les *or* **mak les** *repr* falling asleep;
   las-les to go to sleep easily;
   les-lesan to feel o.s. losing consciousness, through sleep or faintness.
lès I (to take) a training course; extra-
   curricular tutorial lesson;
   ngelèsi to give s.t. as extra-curricular
   lesson; to train s.o.;
   ngelèsaké to send s.o. for such a
   course.
   II reins, bridle;
   ngelèsi to hold the reins, drive.
   See also **lis**.
   III, ngelès to aim at, try to hit;
   lésan *or* **lès-lèsan 1** target; **2** *fig* scapegoat; **3** *gram* object.
lesah enervated, weak, tired.
lésan I 1 tongue, speech; **2** oral; orally;
   nglésanaké to pronounce (words).
   II foetus.
leseh *var of* **lesah**.
lèsèh flattened, lying on the ground;
   nglèsèh to spread out on the ground;
   lèsèhan to sit on the floor/ground/
   mat.
lèsèng *reg* hardened soil.
leser I *reg kr*, right, correct (*var of* **leres**).
   II, ngleser (of snake) to creep/crawl
   on the ground. *See also* **kleser, tleser**.
lèsèr I, nglèsèr *reg* to polish, burnish.
   II, nglèsèr *reg* to drag.
leses, ngleses to take one's ease, relax.
lésiyun 1 legion; **2** association.
lesmèn *var of* **losmèn**.
lesmi *lit* beauty.
lèsnar reading desk, lectern.
lesning 1 without any extra; **2** without
   any profit; **3** flawless, clean.
lésoh *reg* enervated, tired, weak.
leson *see* **lesu**.
lespangan *reg* colic in the stomach.

lesta *lit* **1** earth, land; **2** to go on foot.
lestantun *kr for* **lestari**.
lestari *ng*, **lestantun** *kr*, to continue on
   without impediment or misfortune,
   fortunate;
   nglestarèni providing lasting good
   fortune;
   nglestarèkaké to continue, perpetuate, keep in effect, preserve.
lestha *lit* finished, completed.
lestrèn *reg* ricefield on a riverbank.
lestrèng *reg* trace (part of harness). *See
   also* **setrèng**.
lèstrik electric.
lestrung (venereal) sore on the nose;
   lestrungen ulcerated, festering.
lesu 1 listless; **2** *reg* hungry;
   nglesoni to feel weak during convales-
   cence;
   leson *or* **leleson** to lie down to rest;
   kaleson starved, starving;
   paleson a place to lie down and rest.
lesung a large wooden mortar or trough
   (for pounding rice to separate the
   husks from the grain).
lésus whirlwind, squall.
let 1 interval of time or space; **2** after (an
   interval of);
   let-let *or* **let-letan** divider;
   ngeleti *or* **ngelet-leti** to put an interval
   between;
   ngeletaké to space s.t. at a short distance;
   keletan *or* **kelet-letan** to get divided/
   separated (by).
lèt *or* **mak lèt** *repr* a smear;
   ngelèti *or* **ngelèt-lèti** to smear with s.t.
   soft;
   lat-lèt (to make) repeated smears. *See
   also* **lèlèt**.
leta *reg* level part at the foot of a valley.
letak *var of* **leta**.
lètèh *reg var of* **letih**.
leteng stale, rancid.
leter, ngleter absorbed, engrossed.

443

lèter I 1 letter of the alphabet; 2 large let-
tered writing;
  nglèteri to put letters on s.t. (mark s.t.).
  II *reg* litre (*var of* liter).
lètèr, flat, level, smooth;
  nglètèr 1 to make level/smooth; 2
  smooth, graceful (dance movements);
  lètèran *or* plètèran a flat spot.
léthak, ngléthak thin as a rake, skinny,
  boney.
lèthèh wet and dirty, messy, muddy.
lethek dirty;
  ngletheki to cause s.t. to be dirty;
  lethekan dirty place; s.t. dirty;
  lelethek dirt, filth; *fig* scum, dregs.
letheng stinking (of s.t. dead).
létho *or* mak létho *repr* daubing s.t. soft.
léthok a daub of s.t. soft;
  ngléthok *or* ngléthoki 1 to daub with
  s.t. soft; 2 to take s.t. soft in the hand;
  léthokan s.t. soft that has been
  daubed.
léthong animal dung, manure. *See also*
  tléthong.
léthop, léthop-léthop *or* léthap-léthop to
  keep eating with big mouthfuls.
lethus, nglethus to crack with the teeth.
  See also klethus.
letih, asin letih as salty as brine. *See also*
  asin.
létré, nglétré to spread thin, press flat;
  nglètrèkaké to make s.t. (soft) flat.
lètrèk *var of* létré.
letuh *reg* 1 dirty, muddy (*see also* tlutuh);
  2 dirty, obscene, pornographic.
léwa, leléwa affectations, airs, precious
  manners;
  kakèhan léwa of many whims, capri-
  cious, to put on airs.
lewar *reg* free, released. *See also* luwar.
léwar *var of* liwar.
lèweg *or* mak lèweg *repr* scooping up s.t.
  soft;
  léwag-lèweg to scoop s.t. soft repeatedly.

lèwèh, lèwèhan ditch, gully.
leweng *reg* 1 deep hole, pit, cave; 2 earth-
  en oven. *See also* luweng.
lèwèr loose in its fitting; sembèr - of
  loose morals. *See also* sembèr II.
lèyèh, nglèyèh, lèyèh-lèyèh, lèyèhan to
  lean back, sit (lie) back (in chair).
léyo lion.
léyong Chinese dragon. *See also* liyong.
lha *excl of surprise* (*var of* la).
lho *excl of surprise* (*var of* lo).
li *reg* now!
libar *reg* 1 (of the moon) to rise; 2 full
  moon.
libur (to have) a holiday, time off;
  ngliburaké to let s.o. go on vacation;
  liburan 1 (to take) a vacation; to go
  on vacation; 2 free, having time off;
  libar-libur to take a vacation many
  times (too often).
licik cowardly, faint-hearted.
licin *reg* slippery, worn smooth;
  nglicin *reg* to iron.
licit *var of* klicit.
licut *var of* lincut.
lid I 1 meaning (of a proverb); 2 moral
  (of a story);
  ngelidaké to explain (the meaning of).
  II member (of council, committee,
  panel).
lidhah 1 tongue (*k.i. for* ilat); 2 beef
  tongue; 3 (*or* lelidhah) lightning;
  lidhah sinambung *idiom* to spread by
  word of mouth.
lidhas (of tongue, lips) rough, coarse,
  chapped.
lidhi coconut leaf rib. *See also* sapu.
lidhig *reg* worn, trodden by many feet
  (path). *See also* lijig.
lidhis *reg var of* ledhis.
lidok (to tell) an untruth; ora - really and
  truly!
liga, ngliga 1 not wearing a shirt; 2 to
  unsheathe (weapons);
  ligan unsheathed.

ligas, ligasan *reg* (to ride a horse) unsaddled.

ligeng, ligengan *reg* whirlpool.

liger, ngliger to seize, take possession of (*var of* **liyer**);

ngligeraké 1 to pass along (a task); **2** to shift one's work to s.o. else, delegate;

ligeran to exchange.

ligung, ligungan *reg* a curve, a bend.

ligur, ngligur *reg* to flop down, sprawling.

lih, ngelih to move s.t. from one place to another, transfer;

lih-lihan 1 *or* **lihan** to change places; **2** s.t. which has been moved.

See also **alih.**

lijig *reg* worn, trodden by many feet (path) (*var of* **lidhig**).

lijok *reg* to tell an untruth (*var of* **lidok**).

lik 1 little (*shtf of* **cilik**); **2** uncle, aunt (younger sibling of either parent).

lika-liku *see* **liku.**

likak-likuk *see* **likuk.**

likas, nglikas to wind (thread);

likasan reel, spool of thread.

likat, likaten to have/get a muscular cramp.

likem *lit* naked.

liker *var of* **leker.**

likir liqueur.

likrik *reg* choosy, hard to please, finicky. *See also* **kikrik.**

liku, liku-liku, lika-liku twists and turns.

likuk, likak-likuk winding, full of curves.

likung, likungan a curve, a bend.

likur twenty- (*as a digit in numbers*); **pitu-** 27;

likuran *or* **likur-likuran** number between 21 and 29;

selikur 21;

selikuran 1 to hold a celebration on the 21st of the Fasting Month; **2** a certain game with playing-cards.

lila I 1 consent, permission; **2** to agree, be ready and willing; **3 suka -** to be content with, accept gladly; **- legawa** willing acceptance;

nglilani to allow, permit, approve;

nglilakaké to accept with resignation;

kalilan *or* **klilan** to be allowed; to have permission;

kalilana allow me; may I have your permission?

II lilac, light purple.

lilab, lilab-lilaban *reg* a match;

dudu lilabané it has nothing to do with, no connection with.

lilah *or* **palilah** permission, approval;

nglilahi to give permission to.

lilahi for (or to) God; divine.

lilèh *reg var of* **lilih.**

lili, nglili to treat kindly.

lilih calmed down;

nglilihaké to calm s.o.

lilin 1 (*kr for* **malam**) wax; **2** (*kr for* **damar**) candle; **ès -** ice block;

nglilin to polish with wax.

liling, ngliling to look closely, in the face (playing with a baby).

lilir, nglilir to wake up (at night);

ngliliran to have a tendency to wake up (when you need the sleep).

lilis neatly groomed (hair).

lilit, nglilit to twist, wind around.

lim glue, paste;

ngelim to glue or paste s.t.;

lim-liman 1 glued, pasted; **2** with glue.

lima *ng*, **gangsal** *kr*, five; **-las** fifteen;

nglima *or* **lima-lima** five each;

nglimani 1 to form a group of five; **2** to hold a ceremony for (a woman in the fifth month of pregnancy);

nglimakaké to make s.t. five in number;

lelima *or* **lima-limané** all five of them;

kalima 1 fifth; **2** the 5th period (**mangsa**) of the Javanese agricultural calendar (12 October–9 November);

limang five (*as modifier*); *e.g.* - dina five days.

liman elephant (*kr for* gajah).

limar a fine silk fabric.

limas *or* limasan a type of Javanese house, with a roof of a certain design.

limbak *var of* lémbak.

limbang, nglimbang 1 to pour from one container to another (to measure it); 2 to bathe (eyes); 3 to weigh up, compare two things with each other, consider.

limbuk fat and ungainly (woman).

limbung unbalanced, unsteady, unstable, uneven.

limbrah I *reg var of* limrah.
II dark; - limengan pitch dark.

limeng, limengan *or* lelimengan *intsfr* dark, pitch dark;
kelimengan to forget (*k.i. for* lali);
palimengan dark place;
peteng ndhedhet lelimengan *lit* wrapped in darkness.

limit worn smooth (path).

limpa 1 spleen; 2 beef spleen (as food).

limpad wise, consummate (in knowledge).

limpah *reg* affluent, fortunate;
nglimpahi *reg* to bestow (good fortune) on;
kalimpahan blessed with good fortune.

limpang-limpung *see* limpung II.

limpé, nglimpé to sneak up on, take by surprise;
nglimpèkaké to do s.t. to s.o. stealthily;
kelimpé, klimpé caught off guard.

limpeng *reg* in a quandary, unable to find a way out.

limprah *var of* limrah.

limprek *var of* lemprek.

limpung I a short javelin or spear.
II (*or* limpang-limpung) a snack of fried sweet potato.

limput, nglimputi 1 to cover, envelop s.t.; 2 to include, comprise; 3 to pervade;
kelimput 1 withdrawn from view; 2 clouded, blinded (*e.g.* by passion);
kelimputan *or* klimputan to get encompassed or surrounded.

limrah usual, normal, ordinary (*kr for* lumrah).

limun I lemonade; a citrus-flavoured carbonated soft drink.
II fog, mist, haze;
limunan hazy, blurred, misty; aji - magic formula to render one invisible;
peteng alimunan pitch dark;
lelimunan invisibility;
kalimunan 1 darkness; 2 to have s.t. slip one's mind.

limur, nglelimur *lit* to comfort, soothe. *See also* lipur.

limut 1 mist, clouds covering a mountain; 2 dimmed, covered by mist;
kelimutan to have s.t. slip one's mind.

lin tape, ribbon;
lin-linan to wear a ribbon.

lina *lit* dead, to die (*see also* léna II).

lincad I (of soil) dried up and cracked.
II 1 to slip out, give way (support); 2 disloyal, deceitful.

linca-linci to keep coming back, to come again and again.

lincak I low bamboo bench.
II, lincak-lincak to jump for joy;
lincak gagak 1 a step in classical dance; 2 (in children's games) to take a short walk.

lincat, nglincati to fail to keep one's word, break a promise. *See also* lincad II.

lincek *var of* lincak II.

lincing *reg* pointed, sharp. *See also* lancip.

lincip *var of* lancip.

lincis loop of cord (around button, to close clothing).

lincung soft chicken droppings (*var of* léncung).

lincut, kelincutan *or* **klincutan** to suffer from embarrassment.

lindhek *reg* tardy, sluggish.

lindhih heavy object used to weigh s.t. down (*var of* **tindhih**);
   nglindhihi to be on top of, weigh s.t. down with;
   kelindhih 1 *lit* defeated; 2 weighed down, oppressed;
   kelindhihan to get s.t. put on it;
   lindhihen *reg* to be disturbed in one's sleep by having cut off the circulation s.w. *See also* **tindhih**.

lindhik *var of* **lindhek**.

lindi *var of* **lindri**.

lindhu earthquake.

lindhuk deserted, lonely;
   palindhukan a lonely or spooky place.

lindhung, nglindhung to seek shelter;
   - pura *reg* to wander;
   nglindhungi to protect, cover, shelter;
   nglindhungaké to have s.t. protected;
   palindhungan shelter, protection.

lindri I *see* **gethuk**.
   II, lindri beautiful, sweet (eyes).

lindur, nglindur to talk in one's sleep;
   nglinduran to have a tendency to talk in one's sleep.

lined *reg* silt, sediment.

ling *lit* words, what s.o. says;
   ngling to say, speak. *See also* **angling**.

lingak-linguk *see* **linguk**.

lingga I *gram* root, unaffixed form; **dwi-**reduplication, doubled root (*see also* **dwi**); **- andhahan** affixed form.
   II, nglingga to pile up (in the process of producing bricks);
   linggan pile of bricks.

linggamurda, kalinggamurda *way* highly esteemed.

linggar *lit* to go away, leave, depart;
   nglinggari to avoid, escape s.t.

lingged unit of ten bunches (of fruit).

linggi curved pointed prow and stern of a sailing boat.

linggih to sit (*ng, kr, var of* **lungguh**).

linggis sharp-bladed iron crowbar, used for digging;
   nglinggis to dig with the above.

lingguh to sit (*ng, kr, var of* **lungguh**).

lingi (*or* **wlingi**) a certain grass.

lingir I sharp angle, corner, side (*e.g. of* square pillar, table);
   lingiran s.t. with a sharp side or sides.
   II sculpted figure, image;
   nglingir to sculpt, carve.

lingkab, nglingkab to open, unfold, uncover;
   kelingkab 1 accidentally opened, uncovered; 2 discovered, revealed.

lingkis, nglingkis to roll up (sleeves).

lingkung, lingkungan a curve, bend.

linglap, kelinglap to get lost/mislaid.

lingling *var of* **liling**.

linglung 1 mentally disturbed, confused; 2 intoxicated (with love), doting.

lingsa I nit, louse egg.
   II *see* **pada**.

lingsang *or* **wlingsang** a marten-like animal.

lingsem ashamed, embarrassed (*kr, k.i. for* **isin**).

lingsèn a pretext.

lingseng a small (horse) leech.

lingsing *reg* slim, slender.

lingsir 1 (*or* **lingsir kulon**) the period around 3 p.m. when the sun is about halfway through its western descent; **- wétan** the period around 9 a.m.; **- wengi** (*or* **- bengi**) the period from midnight to pre-dawn; 2 approaching old age.

linguk, lingak-linguk to look this way and that (in confusion).

lining, nglininging to cut into thin pieces (*e.g.* fruit, bamboo);
   liningan cut into thin slices;

salining one thin slice.

linjak, linjak-linjak to move up and down, bounce.

linjek, linjek-linjek to walk with heavily pounding footsteps.

linjik *reg* a variety of edible tuberous root.

lintah leech; - dharat moneylender.

lintang I star; - alihan *or* - ngalih falling star, meteor, comet; - Bimasekti the Milky Way; - gubug pèncèng the Southern Cross; - kemukus comet; - wluku Orion; - wuluh the Pleiades; palintangan the zodiac; ngèlmu - astrology.

II to go past, exceed; kelintang(-lintang) exceedingly.

linthing, nglinthing to form a roll; kelinthing to get rolled up.

linting, nglinting to roll (tobacco, cigarette *etc*);

lintingan rolled up, in the form of a roll; kalintingan *or* klintingan 1 to roll around, writhe; 2 bewildered.

lintir, nglintir 1 to flow down(ward); 2 to receive a transferred position, *e.g.* through inheritance;

nglintiraké to transfer (a position); lumintir to flow ceaselessly.

lintreg, lintreg-lintreg quivery, wobbly.

lintrik name of one of the small playing-cards (*kertu cilik*).

lintring ring set with stones in a row.

lintu 1 (ex)change (*kr for* ijol); 2 exchange item (*kr for* liru, ijol).

linu (to have) shooting pains.

linyap *lit* disappeared.

linyok not true; a lie.

lipca *reg* to forget (*kr for* lali);

kelipcan 1 to have s.t. slip one's mind; 2 to get overlooked, get forgotten. *See also* lépya.

lipenstip lipstick.

lipet 1, nglipet to fold; 2 multiple; nglipetaké to multiply; lipetan folded.

lipur comforted, soothed, calmed, cheered;

nglipur *or* nglelipur to comfort, soothe, cheer;

panglipur a means of comforting, entertainment.

lipus *var of* lepus.

lipya *reg* to forget, have s.t. slip one's mind (*var of* lépya, lipca).

lir I (*or* lir péndah) *lit* like, as.

II essence, meaning;

liré in other words; the essential thing is...;

III, saliré all, everything.

lira in a loom, the bar used to press the weft down. *See also* wlira.

lira-liru *see* liru.

lirang I sulphur. *See also* welirang.

II one half of a paired set;

lirangan in bunches;

gedhang salirang a bunch of bananas (which matches with a similar one opposite it on the stalk); a certain type of traditional roof (*see also* gedhang).

lirap *var of* lérap.

lirèh *reg var of* lirih.

lirèn *reg var of* lèrèn.

lirig, nglirig *reg* to drive (livestock) home in the evening.

lirih (of sound) soft, low, gentle;

nglirihaké to cause to be soft;

lirih-lirih softly, gently;

lirih-lirihan in a soft manner, keeping the sound low.

lirik I, nglirik to cast a meaningful side-long glance at;

lirak-lirik to look sideways repeatedly. II, lirik-lirik striped.

liring *lit* a sidelong glance, look, gaze;

ngliring *or* lumiring to look sideways, steal a glance.

lirip I 1 worn down, blunt; 2 to weaken, diminish; ngliripi to fade out.

II, ngliripi to select carefully.

liris *lit* rain; drizzling rain. *See also* riris.

lirna it is quite understandable that…

lirning *var of* lirna.

liru *ng*, lintu *kr*, 1 an exchange item; 2 to change, exchange; - pernah to change places;

ngliru *or* nglironi to give s.t. in exchange for;

nglirokaké to give in exchange for;

nglira-ngliru to interchange;

keliru, kliru to get exchanged inadvertently;

lira-liru to (ex)change repeatedly;

liron 1 what is exchanged; 2 - sih, sari *lit* to make love. *See also* klèru.

lirwa *lit* negligent;

nglirwakaké to disregard, neglect.

lis I reins;

ngelisi 1 to equip with reins; 2 to guide (a horse) with reins.

II list.

III frame, edge;

ngelisi to frame.

lisa *var of* lingsa.

lisah oil (*kr for* lenga).

lisig *reg* neatly arranged, well laid out. *See also* risig.

lisir *var of* lingsir.

listya *lit* beautiful; handsome.

lisuh weak, weary.

lisus *var of* lésus.

liteng *see* litheng.

litha-lithi to keep coming and going; to move back and forth.

litheng 1 dark-coloured, ripe (fruit); 2 black (skin).

lithing, nglelithing to care for lovingly.

liwang-liwung, alas gung - *lit* a deep and lonely forest.

liwar 1 to miss (a target), not right on (a certain line/spot); 2 half-mad; 3 going the wrong way.

liwar-liwer *see* liwer.

liwat *ng*, langkung *kr*, 1 to go past; 2 to go (by way of) (miyos *k.i.*);

ngliwati 1 to pass; 2 go by way of; 3 to exceed;

kliwat past;

kliwatan to get bypassed;

keliwat-liwat exceedingly;

ora liwat the only thing left is…

liwer, leliweran *or* liwar-liwer to mill around, swarm about in crowds. *See also* kliwer.

liwet *ng*, bethak *kr*, ngliwet to boil rice;

ngliwetaké to boil rice for s.o.;

liwetan (rice) boiled;

sega liwet 1 rice boiled till all the water has been absorbed; 2 rice boiled in coconut milk.

liwung 1 to stagger (kites); 2 *lit* furious, raging, senseless, crazed.

liya *ng*, sanès *kr*, other, different; ora - none other than, nothing (else) but;

ngliya 1 (of woman) to have someone else; 2 to have changed one's attitude, *esp* to have become indifferent or hostile;

ngliyakaké to give, sell s.t. to another person;

keliya 1 to fall into the possession of…; 2 treated as an outsider;

liya saka iku besides that, moreover;

liyan another, others;

lan liya-liyané *etc*, and so forth;

saliyané besides, other than;

wong liya other people (non-family);

- dina some other day;

wong liyan kebrayan a stranger.

liyak *reg* to get hit by accident.

liyan *see* liya.

liyang, ngliyangi to lean on/against, support o.s. on;

liyangan 1 leaning on/against; 2 s.t. for leaning against, support; 3 to use s.o. else's name.

liyar *reg* widely spaced;

ngliyaraké to transplant, plant out at a distance.

liyep, ngliyep to close the eyes in sleep;

liyepan (of refined puppet's eye-shape) long and gracefully narrow;
saliyepan (to take) a brief nap;
liyep-liyep heavy-lidded, to drop off to sleep.

liyer, **ngliyer** to seize, take possession of;
ngliyeraké to pass along (the task); to shift one's work over to;
liyeran a taken over job; to take over jobs with each other.

liyong Chinese dragon.

liyu tired, exhausted.

liyun kerosene.

liyur I, **liyur-liyur** to move (bend, sway) flexibly (*e.g.* branch).
II, **liyuran** *reg* to help each other.

liyut *var of* **liyur**.

lo I *excl of surprise, warning, disapproval.*
II a certain kind of banyan tree with large fruits, said to harbour malevolent spirits;
cocak nguntal lo *expr* 'the cocak (a little bird) swallowing the lo', *i.e.* s.t. unlikely to happen, unbelievable, impossible (*see also* **cocak**).
Also **elo**.

loap-laop *or* **loap-laup** to keep yawning.

lobak Chinese radish.

lobar with plenty of space.

lobis *reg* cabbage.

lobo *reg* loose-fitting. *Also* **lobok**.

lobok loose-fitting.

lobong I blossom of the **cémé** plant.
II name of a gamelan melody.

locan silk crepe.

locana *lit* eye.

locita *or* **panglocita** thoughts, musings.

loco, **ngloco 1** to hold in the hand (cricket, to tame it); **2** to shuffle (cards); **3** to masturbate.

locok, **nglocok** to pound fine, soften up (betel quid);
locokan betel quid pounder.

locut, **nglocut** to go out in the rain unprotected.

lodan whale.

lodhag, **isih** - to still have plenty of space (vehicle).

lodhang having space or time to spare;
kalodhangan elbow-room, leeway, extra time.

lodhèg *var of* **lojèg**.

lodhèh, **sayur** - vegetables cooked in coconut milk till soft, spiced with chilis, and with **témpé**.

lodhen 2$\frac{1}{2}$-cent coin.

lodhoh (root) rot (plant disease).

lodhok *reg* loose-fitting (*var of* **lobok**).

lodhong 1 a bamboo tube for holding liquids; **2** a covered glass jar.

lodok I spinal marrow (as food).
II, **nglodok** to stick the finger in a hole.

lodong 1 (of fruits) overripe; **2** (of food) overcooked; **3** diarrhoea; **4** *reg* dead.

lodrog *see* **lodrok**.

lodrok rotten, mushy, decaying.

log, **ngelog** to swallow up, gobble, gulp down (*var of* **leg**).

loga-lagi *reg* single, alone.

logat 1 precise meaning; **2** sound (of words), accent; **3** word list, vocabulary;
nglogati to explain, interpret (the meaning).

logok s.t. used for prodding;
nglogok to prod.

logor *reg* to fall off; to drop off (the tree).

logrèg loose, shaky, rattly.

logro loose, not too tight.

logrog *var of* **logrèg**.

logur *reg* to fall off (*var of* **logor**).

loh fertile and well irrigated; - **jinawi** *lit* fertile and prosperous, 'flowing with milk and honey'; **iwak** - freshwater fish.

lohat *var of* **logat**.

lohor one of the five daily prayer times, shortly after midday (*var of* **luhur II**).

lojèg loose, shaky.

lojèh, nglojèh to stab, pierce.

loji 1 trading establishment; 2 European quarter; 3 fort; 4 large brick building; lojèn built in the European style.

lojok *var of* lonjok.

lok I *lit* fame, report;
kalok famed, renowned;
ngelokaké 1 to call, brand s.o. openly as; 2 to make uncomplimentary remarks about s.o.; 3 to cry (fire, thief);
lok-lokan to call each other things. *See also* alok.

loka I *lit* world, realm.
II *lit* kaloka famed, praised by many.

lokak 1 not completely full; 2 half-witted. *Also* lukak I.

lokananta *lit* (gamelan) music from heaven.

lokapala *lit* lord of the world.

lokcan silk crepe.

loklak *var of* lokak.

lokèt window, booking office.

loko *reg var of* lokro.

lokomontip locomotive.

lokro loose, slack;
nglokro despondent, without hope.

lokrok *reg* wrecked, dilapidated, ruined.

lola 1 alone in the world; orphaned; 2 lone, solitary (*e.g.* fruit, flower).

lolèk *reg* young nipah palm leaf (used for cigarettes).

loling Chinese lantern.

loloh (*k.i. for* jamu) 1 medicine; 2 to take medicine;
ngloloh 1 to feed (a baby bird, of mother bird); 2 to spoonfeed (students, of parent or teacher);
nglolohi to put s.t. in s.o.'s mouth forcibly;
lolohan 1 still needing to be fed; 2 still dependent on parents;
loloh-lolohan to put food into each other's mouth (lovers);
keloloh duped, misled.

lolopis kuntul baris words chanted to accompany heavy work.

lolor, nglolor to pull out, extract from a bunch.

lolos 1 to come loose, undone (of s.t. that was bound); 2 to run away, flee;
nglolos *or* nglolosi to pull s.t. out/off;
lolosan loose.

lom *reg* hungry.

loma generous; loman goodhearted;
kaloman generosity.

lomah-lamèh tardy, sluggish, indecisive.

lomban *reg var of* lumban, *see* lumba II.

lombo foolish;
nglomboni to cheat, deceive s.o.

lombok chili (many varieties).

lomoh *reg var of* lumuh.

lompat *see* lumpat.

lompiyah *see* lumpiyah.

lompong (hollow) stalk (of various plants, eaten as a vegetable).

lon, lon-lonan slowly;
ngelon-loni to slow s.t. down. *See also* alon.

loncang-lancing to lead a bachelor's life, without wife and children.

loncèng 1 bell; 2 clock.

loncok *var of* lonjok.

loncom *var of* oncom.

loncong *var of* lonjok.

londèr, nglondèr to project (of s.t. long), to stand out (tall, thin people).

londhah *reg* sluggish, slow.

londhèt *see* londhot II.

londho, londho-londho exhausted, fatigued.

londhog *reg* slow to move.

londhok *see* londhog.

londhot I worn, stripped (screw).
II wet rot (plant disease).

long I large cracker.
II, ngelong *or* ngelongi to decrease s.t.; to reduce;
long-longan things removed;
kalong reduced;

kalongan to suffer a loss.

longa-longo *see* **longo.**

longak-longok to peep in, have a look surreptitiously.

longan space under a bed or other furniture.

longgang *reg var of* **longkang.**

longgar having (enough) room, having leeway;

nglonggari to give room, provide leeway;

nglonggaraké to increase the space or time for s.t.;

kalonggaran latitude, leeway, opportunities for doing s.t.

longgor to grow up fast (child).

longkang to have open space;

longkangan 1 exterior passageway; open space between two separately-built sections of a house; **2** space between two objects; **3** time between.

longkrang *reg* space under a bed or other furniture.

longlang, longlang-longlang too long, to project too far.

longo, longo-longo to stare vacantly into space with open mouth;

longa-longo empty-headed, dull-witted.

longok, nglongok to stretch out the neck;
  longok-longok to look up, hold up the head, stretch the neck.

longong *var of* **longo.**

longop, nglongop to gape, stand wide open;

longopan 1 a gaping opening; **2** opening in a wall, alley.

longsong *see* **blongsong.**

longsor to shift, slide, settle;

nglongsor to sit with the legs stretched out;

nglongsori (of earth) to slide onto.

lonjok, nglonjok 1 to advance too far; **2** to be more than it should be;

kelonjok excessive.

lonjong oval, egg-shaped;

lonjong botor *or* **lonjong mimis** *describing the visual effect of s.o. running very fast.*

lonjor counting word for stalks/stems.

lontar 1 a palm leaf on which may be written; **2** manuscript of such palm leaves.

lonthang I with large patches of colour (animal). *See also* **plonthang.**

II, nglonthang *or* **lonthang-lonthang** empty-handed.

lonthé prostitute;

nglonthé 1 to be(come) a prostitute; **2** to go to a prostitute;

nglonthèkaké to prostitute;

palonthèn *or* **plonthèn** house of prostitution.

lonthèng, lonthèng-lonthèng speckled, dappled. *See also* **lothèng.**

lonthong I steamed rice wrapped in a banana leaf, formed into a roll.

II a broad cloth sash worn by men.

lontop sword-stick.

lontor, nglontor *cr* to eat, drink.

lontra-lontro *see* **lontro.**

lontro, lontro-lontro *or* **lontra-lontro** to walk out (off) in anger.

lontrong I *reg* path, lane.

II, lontrong-lontrong *var of* **lontro-lontro.**

lonyo cangkemé unable to hold one's tongue, to talk thoughtlessly.

lonyoh 1 *or* **mlonyoh** damaged by burning or scalding; **2** soft, tender.

lonyok I soggy, overripe.

II *reg* funny.

lonyot foul-mouthed.

lopa, nglopa to bribe.

lopak, lopak-lopak metal box for keeping betel or tobacco.

loper messenger; delivery-man.

lopis a sweet cake of glutinous rice, grated coconut, and sweet thick syrup.

lor *ng*, **lèr** *kr*, north;

ngalor, **mangalor** northward, to go northward;

ngaloraké (*pass* **dingaloraké**) to move s.t. to the north;

ngalor ngidul *idiom* 1 here and there, everywhere; 2 to be contrary to, on opposite sides;

saloré to the north of;

lor-loran the northern part;

kaloran located to the north.

lorèk *or* **lorèk-lorèk** striped.

lorèng *var of* **lorèk**.

lori I small railway truck used for carrying sugarcane from a field.

II small wooden club used as a weapon.

lornyèt pince-nez.

loro *ng*, **kalih** *kr*, two; **loro-loro** in two's, two together;

ngloro to have two of s.t.;

ngloroni to set upon (two persons);

kaloron *or* **sakaloron** (**sekaliyan** *kr*) man and wife, as a married couple;

loro-loroné both of them.

See also **rong II**.

lorod, nglorod 1 to demote; 2 to give away (to a social inferior); 3 to remove s.o.'s leftovers; 4 to remove wax from;

nglorodaké 1 to have (food) left on one's plate taken away; 2 to give away, hand down (to a social inferior); 4 to remove wax from (fabric) between dyeings, in batik-making;

lorodan 1 food left on s.o.'s plate; 2 a hand-me-down; 3 batik from which the wax has been removed.

lorog, nglorog *or* **nglorogaké** to push forward;

lorogan drawer;

lumorog to agree, concur. *See also* **lèrèg**.

loroh, nglorohi to speak to in greeting, address. *See also* **luruh II**.

lorok, lorok-lorok striped with large lines.

lorop, ngloropaké 1 to trick into doing s.t. wrong; 2 to lure into a trap;

kelorop 1 tricked, trapped; 2 to get into difficulties through thoughtlessness.

los I 1 shed, store.

II 1 off, away, (on the) loose; 2 out loud (voice); 3 home! (in children's games);

ngelosi 1 to let s.t. go; 2 to square (a debt).

III spool, reel (*shtf of* **kelos**).

losin dozen;

losinan by the dozen.

losmèn lodgings, a place to stay.

losoh completely rotten.

losor *var of* **longsor**.

lot plummet, plumb;

ngelot to use a plummet;

lot-lotan s.t. used as a plummet.

lotèk a dish made from mixed vegetables with a hot peanut sauce.

lotèng attic, loft, upper storey;

lotèngan with an attic (style of house).

lothèk *repr* a scooping action;

nglothèk *or* **nglothèki** 1 to feed (a baby) with the finger; 2 to smear with s.t. soft.

lothèng, nglothèng *or* **nglothèngi** to speckle, dapple;

lothèng-lothèng speckled, dappled (*var of* **lonthèng**).

lotis a snack consisting of fruits to be dipped in hot sauce;

nglotis to make (ingredients) into the above dish.

lothung *reg* better than nothing (*var of* **lowung**).

lotré 1 lottery, raffle, pool; 2 lottery ticket; 3 lottery prize; 4 by lottery, drawing lots;

nglotré 1 to raffle off; 2 to take part in a lottery;

nglotrèkaké 1 to raffle s.t. off; 2 to supply a lottery prize.

lowah 1 gap, space between; 2 having (enough) space;
    nglowahi to provide room;
    lowahan room, space.
lowak, **tukang** - seller of second-hand goods;
    nglowakaké to sell second-hand;
    lowakan 1 second-hand goods, junk item; 2 flea market.
lowar *see* **lowèr**.
lowèh, **nglowèh** to leave an opening, gap; (of wounds) open, opened up.
lowèk *var of* **luwèk**.
lowèr worn, loose, too big.
lowok I *var of* **lowong**.
    II **lowokan** dent, small shallow hole.
lowong 1 vacant, blank, unfilled; 2 absent, empty;
    nglowong to fast, *e.g.* every second day;
    nglowongi to make empty, vacate (a room);
    nglowongaké to leave unfilled;
    lowongan 1 a space, vacancy, (job) opening; 2 gap, vacuum, void.
lowuk *reg var of* **lowung**, **luwung**.
lowung 1 rather than, better than; 2 acceptable, reasonable.
loyan *var of* **loyang**.
loyang 1 brass (alloy of copper and zinc); 2 baking pan; **sega** - cooked rice dried in the sun, then cooked again with coconut milk.
loyo weak, limp.
loyop 1 leaning down low, about to fall over; 2 hanging down limply; 3 *or* **ngloyop** (of sleepy eyes) nearly closing, hard to keep open.
loyor, **ngloyor** to treat (fabric) by dipping in a lye solution prior to batik process.
loyos, **ngloyos** to go out and get wet in the rain.
lu three (*shtf of* **telu**).
luamah 1 greed, desire; 2 ungodly passions (in mysticism).
luar *see* **luwar**.

lubar *reg* (all) over, done, finished; after (*var of* **lebar**).
lubèr to overflow;
    nglubèri to pour out onto, inundate with;
    nglubèraké to pour out (*e.g.* one's blessing);
    lubèran overflow; bubbling over;
    nglubèraken pangaksama *idiom kr* to excuse.
lucu 1 funny, amusing; 2 peculiar;
    nglucu to joke; to be amusing;
    ngluconi 1 to act funny; 2 to do funny things to s.t.;
    lelucon jokes, humour, jest.
lud I, **ngelud** *or* **anglud** *lit* to follow, pursue.
    II, **lud-ludan** to play cards without betting money and the loser has to shuffle.
ludhang *var of* **lodhang**.
ludhes all gone; finished up;
    ngludhesi to use all of s.t., finish s.t. up.
ludira *lit* blood.
ludrug I folk drama dealing with contemporary subjects, acted by males and wearing modern dress;
    ngludrug to perform such a drama as a player;
    ludrugan to hire a **ludrug** performance.
    II *reg* muddy.
lugas simple, unadorned;
    nglugas *or* **lugasan** to wear simple, plain clothes (not formal dress).
lugèk *reg* long stick;
    nglugèk to prod (s.t. in a hole) with a long stick.
lugu 1 ordinary, normal; 2 natural, original, free of outside influence;
    nglugoni to (do) in a natural/unaffected way;
    nglugokaké to make s.t. natural/original;
    luguné as a matter of fact; originally;
    saluguné in fact, normally.
lugut itchy hairs clinging to a bamboo stem (*var of* **glugut**).

luh I *ng, kr,* **waspa** *k.i.* tears;
  ngeluh to produce tears;
  kamiluh moved to tears.
  II *see* **keluh**.
luhung (*or* **linuhung**) noble, supreme, exquisite, superb.
luhur I 1 noble, aristocratic; **2** high, exalted; **bangsa** - *or* **para** - noblemen;
  ngluhuri 1 to overcome; **2** to consider o.s. superior;
  ngluhuraké to revere, hold in high esteem;
  linuhur *lit* revered, esteemed, hallowed;
  ngaluhur noble, aristocratic;
  kaluhuran nobleness, nobility;
  leluhur revered ancestor(s).
  II 1 the midday prayer in Islam; **2** midday, noon.
lujeng I safe, well (*md for* **slamet**; *inf var of* **wilujeng**).
  II (*or* **wlujeng**) plough (*subst kr for* **wluku**).
luju a form for shaping kris sheaths.
luk curve of a kris blade;
  ngeluk to bend, curve.
lukak I *reg* **1** not completely full; **2** dull-witted;
  lukak apapak *idiom* to pretend to be clever.
  II *reg* wounded, injured.
lukak-lukik (of road) to have many curves.
lukar 1 to undress (*k.i. for* **cucul**); **2** to come loose (*k.i. for* **ucul, udhar**); **3** naked (*k.i. for* **wuda**).
lukat *reg* freed from evil, exorcised;
  nglukat to deliver from evil, exorcise.
lukat-lukit the secrets, inner workings of s.t.
luké *reg* a variety of chopper.
luket close, intimate. *See also* **ruket**.
lukik, lukikan curve, bend; winding, crinkling, coil;
  lukak-lukik to curve; to turn this way and that.
lukis, nglukis to draw, paint;

lukisan picture, painting.
lukita *lit* words, composition, depiction;
  nglukita to depict, describe.
luku plough (*var of* **wluku**);
  ngluku to plough;
  nglukokaké 1 to plough, **2** *fig* to assign s.o. to.
lulang *ng,* **cucal** *kr,* leather, hide;
  nglulangi to skin, remove the hide from. *See also* **walulang, wacucal**.
lulmat *lit* darkness.
lulu, nglulu to let s.o. have their way, give them what they want and more (sarcastically, even though one does not agree).
lulub fibre from the bark of the **waru**, twined to make string.
luluh I 1 to melt, become dissolved; **2** calmed down; **3** *gram* phonetically assimilated;
  ngluluh to melt or dissolve;
  ngluluhaké 1 to melt or dissolve s.t.; **2** to calm s.o. down;
  luluhan 1 melted, dissolved; **2** mixture.
  II *reg* centipede.
lulur I a yellow cream used as stage make-up for dancers;
  nglulur to apply this cream;
  ngluluri to apply this cream to;
  luluran to wear this cream.
  II meat adhering to beef backbone.
lulus to pass (a test);
  nglulusi to give permission;
  nglulusaké 1 to pass or graduate s.o.; **2** to grant (a request, permission);
  lulusan 1 a graduate; **2** permission, permit.
lulut devoted, deeply attached;
  ngluluti to love deeply.
lum, ngelum-lumi to droop, fade, wither. *See also* **alum**.
lumah surface, upper side;
  lumah-lumah 1 to keep lying on one's back, relax in a bed; **2** to lie face up;
  mlumah 1 to lie on the back; **2** with surface or upper side up;

nglumahaké 1 to put s.t. in a face-up or surface-up position;
kelumah *or* **klumah** to be face up unintentionally, to fall over backwards;
salumahé all over (the surface of);
salumahing bumi, sakurebing langit *idiom* everywhere.

lumayan pretty good, not bad, reasonable, better than nothing.

lumba I, **nglumba** to buck, shy;
mlumba-mlumba to jump, spring up.
II, **lumban** *or* **lelumban** 1 to splash, play in the water; 2 to be deeply involved in s.t.

lumbrah *reg var of* **lumrah**.

lumbu a tuberous plant with large leaves and stalk. *See also* **lompong**.

lumbung I 1 rice barn; 2 good fortune; - **désa** communal village supply of stored rice for emergencies;
II, **lelumbungan** to get together for a social meeting, discussion.

lumèng *lit* moist, soft, melted.

lumer soft, fine, smooth, even.

lumèr molten; to melt, become melted;
nglumèraké to melt s.t.

lumintu uninterrupted, one after the other.

lumoh *reg var of* **lumuh**.

lumong *reg* rotten (of egg).

lumpang I mortar, in which things are pounded fine with a pestle.
II **lumpangen** to suffer from mouth ulcers.

lumpat, mlumpat to jump (over);
nglumpati to jump over s.t.;
nglumpataké to cause *or* help to jump;
lumpatan a leap, jump, jumping.

lumpiyah large spring roll filled with beansprouts.

lumping *reg* leather.

lumpuh lame, disabled, paralysed;
nglumpuhaké 1 to paralyse; 2 to incapacitate, disable; 3 to deactivate.

lumpuk *see* **klumpuk**.

lumpur I *reg* mud.

II a variety of cake.

lumrah *ng*, **limrah** *kr*, 1 to spread everywhere; 2 usual, normal, customary; 3 generous, liberal;
nglumrahi to be nothing special, act normally;
nglumrahaké to make s.t. customary;
salumrahé (according to what is) usual, normally;
kalumrah *or* **klumrah** (to have become) normal, ordinary;
kalumrahan customary practice.

lumuh unwilling, not to want to bother o.s. with;
nglumuhi to give in to s.o. (for the sake of peace).

lumur to dry up, begin to heal over (wound).

lumut 1 moss; 2 water weeds;
nglumut mossy; **lumuten** 1 mossy; 2 *cr* old and decrepit.

lun *see* **kelun**.

lunas I paid in full;
nglunasi to pay up, pay in full.
II ship's keel.

luncup sharp, pyramid-shaped (*var of* **lincip**, *see also* **lancip**).

luncur, ngluncur to launch, slide into/ against.

lundhu, lundhu-lundhu childish, foolish.

lung I tendril, shoot, stem or tender young growth of a creeper of vine;
ngelung resembling a curled stem;
lumung *lit* gracefully bent;
lung-lungan curling tendril motif used in ornamental designs for batik, furniture, woodwork.
II, **ngelungi** to give, hand over (s.t.);
ngelungaké to hand over s.t. to;
lung-lungan to give to each other.
See also **ulung II**.

lunga *ng*, **késah** *kr*, **tindak** *k.i.*, 1 to go (away, out); 2 to be out, to have gone;
nglungani to avoid; to steer clear of;
nglungakaké to remove, send away;

lungan *or* lelungan to travel.

lungayan *lit* I neck.

II hand, arm.

lunggé *reg* late, over the time;
lunggèn 1 extra; 2 reserve, spare;
nglunggèni 1 to add more to s.t.; 2 to give more time to s.o. to pay off a debt.

lungguh *ng,* linggih *ng, kr,* lenggah *k.i.* to sit;
lunggah-lungguh to keep standing and sitting again;
nglungguhi to sit on;
nglungguhaké to seat s.o.;
kalungguhan position, situation, office;
lungguhan 1 seat, place to sit; 2 to be in a seated position; 3 (*or* lelungguhan) to sit around;
nglungguhi klasa gumelar *prov* to inherit valuables;
nglungguhi klasa pengulu *prov* to marry the husband of one's deceased sister;
palungguhan 1 seat, place to sit; 2 position, office.

lungid I *lit* 1 sharp; 2 *or* nglungid *lit* (of mystical knowledge) subtle, fine;
lelungidan subtle (mystical) matters.

lungka clod, lump of clay;
nglungka full of lumps (of clay).

lungkrah 1 decomposing; 2 feeling really miserable.

lunglit skin and bones, emaciated (*shtc from* balung kulit).

lungsé past the right time, late.

lungsèn 1 hair used for tying a bun; 2 warp (threads in weaving).

lungsed 1 used, no longer in good condition; 2 rumpled, messy; 3 gloomy, sad.

lungsi *see* pada I.

lungsung, nglungsungi 1 to shed the old skin and grow a new one; 2 to provide s.o. with a change of clothing;
lungsungan old skin (of snake).
See also wlungsung.

lungsur, nglungsur to demote s.o.;
nglungsuri 1 to give s.o. (a used arti-cle); 2 to receive s.t. second-hand;
nglungsuraké to give, hand down (a used article);
lungsuran 1 used article passed down to s.o.; 2 former (formerly occupying a higher rank);
lumungsur (of a rank or position) to pass to s.o. lower.

lungur *or* lelungur *reg* mountain ridge.

lunjak, nglunjak 1 to jump up to reach s.t.; 2 to act with lack of respect;
lunjak-lunjak to jump up and down (with joy);
lunjakan the act or way of jumping.

lunta, kelunta-lunta to get deeper and deeper into difficulty, go from bad to worse;
lumunta-lunta to pass along from one to another.

luntah rubbish, garbage.

luntak 1 to spill out; 2 to vomit (*kr, k.i. for* mutah);
luntak-luntak to vomit repeatedly;
luntakan vomit.

luntas a shrub sometimes grown as a hedge (the edible leaves have various uses).

lunthung, nglunthung to roll (up), make into a roll;
lunthungan in the form of a roll.

luntur 1 to run, wash out (colours); 2 to fade; 3 - sih to show sympathy;
nglunturi to come off, run onto s.t.;
nglunturaké to bestow s.t. on s.o.;
lumuntur passed down to;
kalunturan to have s.t. bestowed on one;
lunturan 1 fading quickly; 2 s.t. bestowed on one.

lunyu 1 slippery; 2 *fig* evasive, unreliable;
nglunyoni to make slippery.

lup I barrel (gun).

II magnifying glass.

lupa I *reg* 1 weary; 2 to fall (*esp* young coconuts).

II *reg* to forget, be negligent.

III *reg* exempt from service or work assignment in the village.

lupai a kind of Chinese brooch, pin.

lupiya *lit* example, model.

luput *ng*, **lepat** *kr*, **1** to miss, escape; **2** wrong, at fault; **- pecing** to beg shamelessly;

luput-luput 1 by bad luck; **2** (*or* **lupat-luput**) to keep making mistakes or missing;

ngluputaké 1 to put the blame on s.o.; **2** to err intentionally;

kaluputan 1 mistake, fault; **2** to get blamed;

luputé at least;

luput-tembiré *idiom* lest (*var of* **sisip-sembiré**);

luput cinatur *idiom* no need to say more;

luput pisan, kena pisan *idiom* to put all one's eggs in one basket.

lur I earthworm.

II (*pron as:* **lur**) *or* **mak lur** *repr* s.t. long and thin being extended (*e.g.* rope).

lurah 1 head, chief (appointed over others); **2** village head;

nglurahi 1 to be leader of a group; **2** to have charge of (a village) as head;

lelurah a leader of a group;

kalurahan *or* **klurahan 1** domain of the village head; **2** residence of the village head;

Ki Lurah Semar *way* clown-servant figure, father of Nala-Garèng, Pétruk and Bagong, also a manifestation of the highest divinity.

lurak, lurak-lurak *reg* roaring (of the sea).

luri *or* **leluri** predecessor, forerunner, ancestor;

ngluri *or* **ngleluri** to preserve, maintain, honour;

nglurèkaké to pass down (ancestral custom).

lurik 1 speckled (chickens); **2** striped (woven cotton fabrics, many kinds);

lurikan *or* **lurik-lurikan** material worked in stripes.

luring *reg* striped. *See also* **lorèng**.

luru I **luru-luru** *or* **ngluru** *or* **ngluroni** to go in search of, try to find.

II 1 faded, no longer fresh (leaves); **2** soft enough to beat (gold, silver).

III *lit* to fall (leaves).

lurub 1 cloth used as a covering (*e.g.* to keep the dust off); **2** pall, shroud;

nglurubi to cover s.t.;

kaluruban covered with;

luruban to cover o.s. with a cloth.

lurug, nglurug to go forth to battle; to go s.w. as a group;

nglurugi to go forth against (an opponent);

nglurugaké to send (combatants) forth;

lumurug to march, go forth;

lurugan 1 going forth to battle; **2** a group sent out for a purpose, *esp* to fight.

luruh I 1 peaceable, gentle, calm; **2** having a refined, modest mien (wayang puppets); **3** to subside.

II ngluruh, ngluruhi 1 to address, ask s.o. about s.t.; **2** to seek out, go and look for (s.o. who has gone away). *See also* **aruh**.

lurung narrow street, alley.

lurus 1 straight, direct; **2** unswerving, honest.

lus, ngelus to rub s.t. smooth;

ngelusi to treat s.o. gently;

ngelusaké to make s.t. smooth, fine;

ngelus dhadha to express grief, pity by drawing the hands downward over the chest.

lusah, lusah-lusah (of grass) trodden down.

lusi *var of* **lungsi**.

lusmèn *var of* **losmen**.

lusuh no longer in use; old and faded; worn-out (of clothing).

lusut, mlusut to slip away/out.

lut *see* lud.

lutak *var of* luntak.

lutèh pale (*var of* lutih).

lutheng, lutheng-lutheng *intsfr* dark, black; pitch dark.

luthik *var of* lothèk.

luthu dirty-looking.

luthuk *var of* luthu.

luthung *reg var of* lowung.

lutih *reg* pale.

lutung a species of black long-haired monkey.

luwah *var of* lowah.

luwak I stone marten.
II, luwakan *reg* district, area of.

luwang, ngluwangi to dig a hole in;
luwangan 1 hole, pit (to bury s.t. in); 2 trap, pitfall.

luwar I freed, released from;
ngluwari 1 to release s.o.; 2 to fulfil (a pledge);
ngluwaraké to bring about release, free s.o. (from).
II *reg* outside.

luwas old, worn out (clothing); - getih past the menopause.

luwat grave, burial pit (*var of* kluwat).

luwé I hungry;
keluwèn excessively hungry, half-starved.
II *reg* centipede. See also luwing.

luwèh *reg* I don't care!

luwèk, luwèkan depression, small hole.

luweng 1 (or luwengan) deep hole, pit, cave; 2 earthen oven;
ngluweng to meditate in a deep hole for a special goal;
ngluwengi to dig a hole in the ground.

luwer, ngluwer to swerve; to curl up;
ngluweri to swerve around s.t.;
ngluweraké to swerve (a vehicle).
See also kluwer.

luwes I (*also* - dhèmes) 1 graceful, smooth, fluent; 2 flexible, adaptable to many purposes;

ngluwesaké to smooth out.
II *reg* lamp wick.

luwih *ng*, langkung *kr*, 1 more (than); 2 (*after number*) more; more than; 3 exceptional, extraordinary; 4 (*in clock time*) plus, and; - dhisik before, more in advance; - manèh especially, even more; luwih-luwih especially, all the more;
ngluwihi 1 to exceed, go beyond; 2 to increase by adding to;
ngluwihaké 1 to increase s.t.; 2 to cause s.t. to be excessive;
keluwihen surplus, excess, too much;
kaluwihan superiority;
linuwih *ng*, linangkung *kr*, 1 esteemed, revered, distinguished; 2 having powers beyond the normal;
luwih rupa, kurang candra indescribably beautiful.

luwing I a species of fat dark-brown harmless centipede.
II a certain fig tree that produces large fruits.
III hungry (*reg var of* luwé).

luwuk I a variety of sword.
II preferable (*reg var of* luwung).
III a kind of snake, boa.

luwung *or* aluwung preferable, it would be better to…

luwur I *var of* luhur.
II, luwur batang a bamboo scaffolding covered with a cloth, set up over a grave.

luwus old, worn-out, dirty-looking.

luyu powerless, weak.

luyung wood, trunk of the sugar-palm.

luyup *lit* sleepy, drowsy. See also loyop.

luyut *lit* dimming, fading (of consciousness).

lwah *lit* river, water.

lwir *lit* like, as.
lwirnya 1 like, as; 2 that is to say.
See also lir.

lyan *lit* other, different; another, others.

M

ma I 1 father (*shtf of* **rama** *k.i.*); **2** *adr* father.
II five (*shtf of* **lima**); - **lima** the five sins (opium-smoking, gambling, drinking, pursuing women, stealing).

ma'ap sorry! (*word of apology*).

maben honey (*subst kr for* **madu**).

mabluk whitish, like tapioca powder (**kabluk**).

mabok *see* **mabuk**.

mabrut, mabrut-mabrut *or* **mobrat-mabrut** snarled, tangled.

mabuk 1 intoxicated; **2** to suffer from motion sickness;
mabukaké 1 intoxicating; **2** to get s.o. drunk;
mabuk-mabukan to run around drunk.

mabur to fly. *See* **abur**.

mabyor sparkling, shining. *See also* **abyor, byor**.

macan *ng*, **sima** *kr*, tiger; - **gémbong** Indian tiger; - **gadhungan** were-tiger; - **kombang** panther - **luwé** (of walking gait) graceful and sinuous; - **malihan** human being disguised as a tiger; - **tutul** spotted leopard;
macanan 1 (to play) a certain game resembling Chinese checkers; **2** (*or* **macan-macanan**) resembling a tiger; toy tiger.

macapat I a category of classical verse of various forms based on syllable-count and final vowel per line;
macapatan a gathering for singing verse of this type.
II, other villages (around one's village). *See also* **mancapat**.

macé *reg* completely finished, nothing left.

macem *reg* kind, sort, variety.

mada *reg* somewhat, quite; a little (*var of* **rada**).

madahab one of the four schools ('directions') of Islamic law.

madak *reg* **1** unexpectedly and/or undesirable (*var of* **dadak**); **2** *reg* how come!

madapléra *reg* to criticise by teasing.

madat opium;
madati *or* **madatan** to smoke opium.

madé I *lit* middle. *See also* **madya**.
II 1 hall; **2** front hall of residence used for entertaining; **3** *reg* bed; -**rengga** royal pavilion.

mader *reg* **1** as you well know; **2** (just) because.

madharan 1 *reg* stomach (*kr for* **weteng**); **2** cook (of prominent person). *Also* **padharan**.

madhèh, madhèhi boring, irritating. *See also* **wadhèh**.

madhek *see* **padhek**.

madhèng *see* **marèng**.

madhug (of soil) well-worked, loose.

madhuk *var of* **madhug**.

madon I underdone (of boiled eggs).
II *see* **wadon**.

madu *ng*, *kr*, **maben** *subst kr*, honey; - **mangsa** a sweet snack made from black glutinous rice.

Madunten *subst kr for* **Madura**.

madya 1 *lit* middle; -**ntara** *or* -**pada** the world; **2** *lit* waist; **3** *lit* of medium size; **4** the speech level between Ngoko and Krama.

madyama *var of* **madya**; - **purusa** *gram* 2nd person.

maéjan *var of* **maésan**.

maem to eat (*children's word*).

maèn I *reg* to play (*var of* **main**).
II *reg* beautiful.

maénda *reg* goat (*kr for* wedhus).

maeng *reg coll* just now (*var of* mau).

maésa water buffalo (*kr for* kebo).

maésan grave-marker.

maétala *lit* earth (*var of* mahitala).

magag *lit* reluctant, hesitant.

magak *reg* 1 fixed; 2 to stay at home; 3 not growing up well.

magang candidate for a position in the Javanese bureaucracy, apprentice official;
   magangan street of the apprentice officials.

magé *reg* come on! hurry up!

magèk *var of* magé.

magel *reg* half-ripe; *fig* dotty, half-witted.

magelang stubborn.

mageleng *var of* magelang.

magèn *var of* magé.

magéné *reg* even so; but still; in spite of (the foregoing). *See also* éwadéné.

magep, magep-magep to keep sobbing.

magersari one who occupies (by permission) a house on the premises of a wealthy or aristocratic person, retainer. *See also* pager.

magersantun *kr for* magersari.

magesin store.

magih *reg var of* taksih.

magir 1 mountain ridge; 2 to rise like a mountain ridge.

magleg *reg* very tasty, spicy.

maglik *reg* conspicuously high.

mag-meg *see* meg.

magol *var of* mégol.

magreg, mograg-magreg 1 to stop frequently; 2 undecided, vacillating.

magrib *see* mahrib.

magro *see* magru.

magrong, magrong-magrong (of buildings) looming large and tall, of impressive size.

magru *reg* unfinished, unable to come to a decision.

magung *lit* large, great. *See also* agung.

mah I *reg, adr* mother (*shtf of* mamah).
   II *reg* almost, nearly (*var of* mèh).

maha high, superior, extreme; - agung the great (one), God; - guru university professor; - Kuwasa the Almighty; - muni *or* -resi great ascetic, holy man ; - prana capital letter (in Javanese script); -raja emperor, sovereign; - siswa university student; - suci most holy; - wikan the Omniscient.

mahal *reg* 1 expensive; 2 scarce, hard to get.

mahambara *lit* extraordinary, exceptional.

mahar bride-price, settlement by bridegroom on bride.

mahardika *lit* sage, wise.

maharja *lit* prosperous, fortunate.

maharsi a great ascetic holy man.

mahas *lit* to wander;
   mahas ing asepi *or* mahas ing asamun *idiom* to withdraw to a secluded place for meditation.

mahitala *lit* earth.

mahrib 1 *lit* west; 2 time of the sunset prayer; 3 sunset.

mail talisman.

main 1 to play, to perform in, put on (entertainment); 2 to gamble; 3 to behave badly (in a particular way);
   mainan 1 plaything, s.t. not to be taken seriously; 2 (*or* main-main) to play around/along with;
   main-main (doing s.t.) not seriously, just for amusement.

mair skilled, capable.

maisa *var of* maésa.

maisi *lit* queen.

maja I a certain tree, also its fruits; the wood used for kris hilts.
   II, maja-maja *var of* paja-paja.

majad in proportion, proper, suitable, appropriate.

majak, majak-majak *reg* plenty of time.

majakan gall-nut.

Majalengka *var of* Majapait.

majan blue dying.

Majapait, Majapahit Hindu-Buddhist kingdom in East Java (1293–1478).

majar a gambling game; heads or tails.

majas I figuratively expressed, not real, apparent.

II very sharp and of good steel (weapon, tool).

majeg to have a standing order for meals.

majelis council.

majemuk, majemukan to hold a ceremonial meal together.

majeng 1 *kr for* **maju** (*see also* **aju**); 2 *kr for* **madhep** (*see also* **adhep**); 3 *kr for* **maju** (*see also* **paju**).

majenun 1 insane; 2 frenzied (with love of God).

majer sterile, unable to reproduce.

maji *reg* I don't believe it! *See also* mangsa II.

majik *reg* to lodge in s.o.'s home.

majikan master, boss, employer.

majir *reg* sterile, unable to reproduce (*var of* majer).

majoh *var of* majuh.

maju *ng,* majeng *kr,* 1 to move forward, come forward (*see also* aju); 2 to do well at; 3 to face, confront (*see also* adhep); 4 side; -pat four-sided (*see also* paju);

kemajon *or* kemajunen 1 too far forward; 2 *fig* too Westernised, brash, pushy;

maju mundur 1 to go back and forth; 2 to vacillate;

kemajuwan progress.

majuh *reg* to eat.

majusi *lit* magician, wizard.

mak I *gram: a particle which in combination with the following word represents a sudden or unexpected sound or action, imitative in nature;* - **dhèr** smash!; - **lap** swish!

II a gum used medicinally, also for violin bow rosin.

III mother (*see also* emak).

IV father (*shtf of* ramak).

V, mak-makan *reg* egocentric, selfish.

makadi *lit* and especially, and in addition.

makam tomb, grave.

makan effective (brakes).

makandhah *see* makandheh.

makandheh *lit* chapter, scene of a play.

makaten like this/that, in this/that way (*kr for* mengkéné, mengkono, mengkana). *See also* mekaten.

makbud worship, reverence for God.

makdum 1 member(s) of the Islamic clergy; 2 man of religious learning.

makelar agent, broker, middleman.

makena *see* mekena.

makidhupuh to sit silent with bowed head, showing respect and humility.

makikikan *lit* (of snake) to blow and spit.

makluk creature, part of God's creation.

maklum 1 understandable, to be expected; 2 pardon, forgiveness;

maklumé excuse me! (for not giving money to a beggar);

makluman to forgive to each other.

maklumat proclamation, announcement, declaration.

mak-mek *see* mek.

mak-mok unevenly spread.

makmum 1 led by the Imam at prayer; 2 to follow the Imam at prayer; 3 to follow, join in.

makna meaning conveyed, significance;

maknani to explain the meaning of a term.

makrak *lit* to scream, rage (*var of* mangkrak).

makramah *see* makromah.

makripat sight, seeing God (in Islamic mysticism).

makromah Islamic women's veil.

makruh undesirable, to be avoided (according to Islamic law).

makrup *lit* 1 known; 2 good (of deeds).

maksih *reg var of* taksih.

maksiyat sin, wickedness;
maksiyatan sinful; to engage in immoral acts.

maksud intention, purpose, meaning;
maksudi to explain the meaning.

maktal I name of the 21st **wuku**.
II (of corn in a field) nearly dried. *See also* **matal**.

makutha 1 crown; 2 fez-like headdress worn on formal occasions, also by bridegrooms.

mal model, pattern, mould;
ngemal to use s.t. as a pattern;
mal-malan model used for making a dress.

mala blemish, flaw;
malanen to have blemishes/flaws;
memala skin flaw or laceration.

maladi *lit* striving, desiring deeply;
semadi maladi hening *idiom* deeply absorbed in meditation.

malad kung *or* mamalad kung *lit* to court, bid for love.

malad sih *var of* malad kung.

malaékat angel.

malah *or* malahan 1 contrary to expectation, instead; 2 even, moreover, beyond that.

malak *or* malaki striving to get the biggest portion for o.s., greedy.

malam wax.

malandhi *reg* ready (to do s.t.).

malangkerik with arms akimbo.

malangkadhak to stand defiantly.

malanji *var of* malandhi.

malar I *var of* malah.
II, malar-malar *reg* let's hope, may it happen that... *See also* muga.

malaya *lit* mountain.

malbèng *lit* to enter.

malèh *reg var of* malih.

malek *var of* malak.

malékat *var of* malaékat.

maléla black iron.

malem I 1 night, evening (*in certain compounds*); 2 eve, night before; - jagal the last night of the Fasting Month; - lowong (at night) on the 21st, 23rd, 25th, 27th and 29th of the Fasting Month;
maleman ceremony or fair held on the eve of Lebaran.
II still damp.

males *reg* lazy; korsi - easy chair (*see also* korsi).

maligé *lit* throne.

malih I again; more (*kr for* manèh).
II to change in appearance, shape;
malihan in disguise;
molah-malih to keep changing. *See also* alih.

malikat *var of* malaékat.

malim *var of* mualim.

malimirma *lit* pity, mercy. *See also* palimirma.

maling *ng*, pandung *kr*, 1 thief; 2 to steal (*esp* at night);
malingi to rob;
memaling *lit* to steal;
malingan 1 to steal habitually; 2 stolen;
maling-malingan stolen goods, loot;
kemalingan to get robbed;
maling dhèndhèng *fig* to seduce, abduct.

mal-mil to keep nibbling. *See also* mil II.

mal-mol to eat greedily.

mamah I *ng*, *kr*, kenyoh *k.i.* 1 to chew; 2 to do without difficulty; 3 to berate, be angry with;
kemamah defeated;
mamahan 1 s.t. chewed; 2 s.t. easy to do, a walkover.
II mother.

mamak, I mamak-mumuk to behave senselessly, incoherently.
II *reg* mother; father.

mamang I uncertain, unable to decide.
II *reg* uncle (younger than father or mother).

mamar dim, dusky, obscure.

mamas nickel.

mambak, mambak-mambak *reg* lying scattered about.

mambang a kind of supernatural being.

mambeg clogged, choked, not flowing.

mambek conceited, snobbish. *See also* **ambek**.

mambrah, mambrah-mambrah lying scattered about.

mambu *see* **ambu**.

mami *lit* I, me, my.

mampang, mampang-mampang to burst out in anger.

mampèh *reg* calmed down; to resign o.s. to.

mamprah to spread, extend out(ward) (trade).

mamprang *var of* **mampang**.

mamprat *reg* to go off, leave in anger.

mamprung to dash/fly off swiftly. *See also* **maprung**.

mampu *reg* well-off; **ora -** unable to afford.

mampul, mampul-mampul to keep drifting or floating. *See also* **kampul**.

mampus 1 *cr* dead; **2** *reg* to go away.

mamring, sepi - very quiet, nobody around.

man *adr* uncle (*shtf of* **paman**).

mana 1 unit of 'that' scope; **2** *emphatic particle with sarcastic or ironic effect, suggesting s.t. contrary to the fact;* **semana** one such unit, so much, as much as that.

manah 1 heart, feelings (*kr for* **ati**); **2** liver (*kr for* **ati**); **3** mind, thought, idea (*kr for* **pikir**); **4** (*also* **manahi**) to think of, about; **kamanah** to come to one's mind; to be thought about; **manah-manah** to keep thinking.

manail name of the 23rd **wuku**.

manang, abang manang-manang gorily, bright red.

manasuka *reg* voluntary, of one's own free will.

manawa *ng*, **manawi** *kr*, **1** if, when(ever); **2** (to say *etc*) that...; **3** (**mbok -**) probably, possibly; **4** as for, regarding.

manca foreign, alien; **-kaki** *reg* the old people in a village; **-negara 1** the outer provinces of the Javanese kingdom in West and East Java; **2** overseas; **-rawat** *or* **-udrasa** *lit* to cry; **-warna** various kinds (or colours); **ngamanca** (in, from) a foreign country; **mancapat mancalima** other villages (around one's own village).

mancak to pair, couple (animals).

mancala, mancala putra mancala putri *idiom* to be able to change one's shape/ appearance magically; **- warna** to be able to assume any form magically.

manci enamel cooking pot, pan (*var of* **panci**).

manco *reg* rice cake.

mancuh *reg* to rise, flood.

mancrut to splash, spurt; **mancrut-mancrut** to keep splashing, spurting.

mancung 1 coconut blossom sheath; **2** a cluster; **mancungan** *or* **adu mancung** the way to fold a batik headcloth with its sharp point on the forehead.

manda I, manda-manda a little, a few; somewhat.

II, manda-manda soft, vague, faint, weak.

mandamaruta *lit* a gentle breeze.

mandaswara *gram* semi-vowel.

mandah *var of* **méndah**.

mandang *inf var of* **tumandang**, *see* **tandang**.

mandar even, moreover, contrary to expectations (*reg var of* **malah**).

mandaraka *lit* very beautiful.

mandaya *lit* (surface of the) sea.

mandhèkné and yet, even so. *See also* **andhé**.

mandéné *reg var of* **méndah**.

mandha *lit* sad, sorrowful.

mandhah to move to a different place temporarily, be stationed;
mandhahaké to move s.o. to another post temporarily.

mandhak 1 *reg* even; **2** mere(ly); trivial;
mandhakaké to consider trivial, underestimate.

mandhakiya a pavilion used for meditation.

mandhasiya name of the 14th **wuku**.

mandhèng to diminish, improve (illness).

mandho to hold out the hand(s) to receive s.t.

mandhor foreman, work supervisor.

mandi I 1 powerful, strong, efficacious (medicine, poison, magic); **2** sharp, poisonous.
II 1 similar to; **2** comparable to.

mandos *subst kr for* **mandi**.

mandra I *lit* to travel (*var of* **méndra**).
II extraordinary, great.
III mandra-mandra *lit* gentle, soft.

mandraguna *lit* supernaturally powerful.

mandrawa, *lit* **saking** - from afar.

mandul, mandul-mandul springy, bouncy (breasts).

manèh *ng*, **malih** *kr*, **1** again; more; **2** even... (in a disparaging sense);
manèhé (and) besides; in addition to that;
manèh-manèh 1 one more time; **2** again; (**aja**) **manèh-manèh** (never) again.

manèng, manèngan so, therefore.

mang *md* you (*inf var of* **samang**).

manga *reg* to open one's mouth; gape.

mangah, mangah-mangah to glow, blaze, burn brightly. *See also* **mongah**.

mangang *lit* (of mouth) wide open.

mangar, mangar-mangar *intsfr* red, flushed, burning (face).

mangas *reg* greedy, covetous.

mangga 1 as you please; **2** please (inviting s.o.: come in, go ahead *etc*). *See also* **sumangga**.

manggala, manggalaning prang *lit* commander, commanding general;
manggalani to lead one's troops in war.

manggar flower of the coconut-palm.

manggis mangosteen.

manggrok-manggrok 1 to alight, perch (birds); **2** to settle down s.w.

manggu, manggu-manggu *or* **monggamanggu** to waver, vacillate.

manggung I serving-girls who attend the king on ceremonial occasions and carry the regalia.
II to keep cooing (doves). *See also* **anggung II**.
III *see* **panggung**.

manggut-manggut to nod the head (in agreement).

mangka 1 whereas; **2** even though, in spite of the fact that.

mangkah, mangkah-mangkah big and full of milk (breasts).

mangkak drab, dull, faded.

mangkana *ng*, **makaten** *kr* like that, in that way, thus. *See also* **mengkana**.

mangkara *lit* lobster.

mangké shortly, soon, in the future (*kr for* **mengko**);
samangké now, at the moment.

mangkel resentful, annoyed;
mangkeli annoying;
mangkelaké to cause to be annoyed.

mangkéné *ng*, **makaten** *kr*, **1** like this, in this way; **2** as follows. *See also* **mengkéné**.

mangkir 1 to fail to appear, not turn up for work; **2** to miss a payment.

mangkok 1 a small bowl used for eating soup; **2** basin used for carrying liquid foods.

mangkono *ng*, **makaten** *kr*, **1** like that, in

that way, so; **2** as above, before. *See also* **mengkono**.

mangkrak *lit* to scream, rage.

mangkruk, mangkruk-mangkruk to sit, perch in a high perch.

mangli a variety of sugarcane.

mangmang *reg* uncertain; unable to decide (*var of* **mamang I**).

mangsa I 1 time, season; **2** period according to the Javanese agricultural calendar; - **ketiga** dry season, about August–September; **mangsané** when, as soon as;
- **paceklik** period of food shortage;
- **rendheng** rainy season;
mangsan seasonal.
II *excl of disbelief*; - **bisaa** I don't believe you can, of course you can't!;
mangsa borong(a), - **bodhoa** it's up to you, I don't care.
III to feed on; animal's food, prey.

mangsah I to advance, go forward bravely (*see also* **angsah**).
II ora - to be no match for, have no effect on.

mangsak to cook (*var of* **masak**).

mangsi I (black) ink;
mangsèni to write or draw with ink;
mangsèn 1 written in ink; **2** inkpot.
II *excl of disbelief* (*subst kr of* **mangsa**).

mangsuk 1 to enter; **2** suitable, becoming; - **angin** to catch a cold. *See also* **masuk**.

mangsur *or* **mangsur-mangsur 1** to flow out in a stream; **2** to have diarrhoea.

mangu, mangu-mangu *or* **monga-mangu** to waver, vacillate.

mangunah the power to achieve s.t. (through possessing true belief).

mani I sperm.
II, mani-mani 1 coral; **2** coral beads (*var of* **manik**).

manih *lit* again; more. *See also* **manèh**.

manik I *or* **manik-manik** coral beads, precious stone, jewel.

II pupil of the eye.
III Adam's apple.

manikem 1 jewel; **2** *lit* germ of life.

maning *reg* again (*var of* **manèh**).

manira I, me (Basa Kadhaton: used by royalty to subordinates). *See also* **pak-enira**.

manis I 1 *reg* sweet; **2** appealing, sweet, lovely, nice (face, sound, colour); **driji** - ring-finger;
manisi to sweeten s.t.;
manisan fruit in sugar;
memanis 1 ingratiating behaviour; **2** s.t. to be added as an ornament.
II *lit* a day of the five-day week. *See also* **legi**.

manjul, manjul-manjul to walk with a springy step.

manjung, manjung-manjung piled high with s.t.; heaped full. *See also* **unjung**.

manjur efficacious, effective (medicine).

manjut *reg* and then (*var of* **banjur**).

manobawa *lit* to display authority, majesty.

manohara *lit* pleasant to hear, captivating, appealing.

manol coolie, carrier.

manon *lit* to watch, look (at);
Hyang Manon God (the All-Seeing);
manoni 1 to appear (to s.o., in dream or vision); **2** to give the appearance that... *See also* **ton**.

manpangat use, benefit.

mantah, mantahané *reg* it could be that..., possibly.

mantak, mantak aji to utter, recite a magic spell. *Also* **matak**.

mantan *reg* how...! what (a)...! *See also* **méndah**.

mantel raincoat.

manten unit of this/that scope (*kr for* **méné, mono, mana**).
semanten this/that such.

mantèn 1 bride; groom; **2** wedding; - **anyar** newlyweds; - **pangkon** a bride who has not yet menstruated, so that the bridegroom may not have intercourse with her;

mantènan to play weddings, have a pretend wedding. *See also* **pangantèn**.

manthal, manthal-manthal (of woman) not properly dressed (uncovered breasts while walking).

manthang, manthang-manthang glowing red hot.

manthuk *see* **anthuk**.

mantol *var of* **mantel**.

mantos *reg excl of disbelief* (*kr for* **mangsa**).

mantra I a magically powerful formula of words, transmitted only to the initiated, and used by specialists (*e.g.* **dhalang, dhukun**);

mantrani to use a **mantra** on s.o.;

mantrakaké to utter (a **mantra**);

mantran a formula for producing magical effects.

II, mantra-mantra, ora mantra-mantra not the slightest chance.

mantri 1 palace official; 2 government official in charge of a certain office or activity; 3 rural medical orderly; 4 king (in chess); - **alas** (*or* - **blandhong**) official in charge of forestry; - **anom** ; - **aris** assistant district chief; - **cacar** official who vaccinates for smallpox; - **dhudhuk** official in charge of census; -**gudhang** warehouse keeper; - **guru** school superintendent; -**jero** name of a troop of palace soldiers; - **kéwan** official in charge of livestock; - **lanbau** official in charge of agriculture; - **lumbung** village official who supervises the rice supply; -**mukya** *or* -**wisésa** king's chief minister; - **pulisi** chief of police; - **ukur** land registrar; **kamantrèn** office or residence of the above official.

mantrus sailor, ship's crewman.

mantu 1 son- or daughter-in-law; 2 (to hold) a wedding;

mantokaké to hold a wedding for (one's child);

manton (to hold) a wedding.

mantuk to return to one's own place, go home (*kr for*).

mantun to recover (from), (*kr for* **mari**).

mantyanta *lit* exceedingly.

manuk *ng*, **peksi** *kr*, 1 bird; 2 *chld* penis; **manukan** 1 place for birds; 2 *or* **manuk-manukan** imitation bird, toy bird;

manuki *or* **memanuki** to keep an eye on from a distance.

manungsa human being;

kamanungsan 1 humanity, human nature; 2 pertaining to human beings; 3 to appear human; 4 *lit* to be caught doing wrong in secret.

manyak I, manyaki to start working; to carry out, perform.

II, manyak-manyak to barge in uninvited or unexpectedly.

manyar weaverbird.

manyer *reg* to stand (up), stand in a disrespectful attitude near s.o. else.

manyuk *or* **manyuk-manyuk** 1 to dash in for a moment; 2 (*or* **monyak-manyuk**) to wander around s.o.'s place without announcing one's presence.

manyul bulging, protruding (forehead).

manyura I *lit* peacock.

II a certain key or mode (**pathet**) in which Javanese music is played.

Maospait *var of* **Majapait**.

maot *lit* 1 dead, to die; 2 death.

mapan I *lit* 1 for; 2 meanwhile.

II *see* **papan**.

mapatih *lit* prime minister, king's chief councillor. *See also* **patih**.

maphum *reg* understandable, to be expected.

maprah *or* **maprah-maprah** all over the place, spread wide.

maprung to dash/fly off swiftly (*var of* **mamprung**).

mar to have one's heart in one's mouth (seeing the danger of another); ngemar-mari hair-raising.

mara *lit* come on! (*var of* ayo).

marahi *ng* (*pass* dimarahi), murugaken *kr* (*pass* dipunpurugaken), to cause, bring s.t. about.

marakata *lit* emerald. *See also* markata.

marakèh name of the 18th wuku.

marang *ng*, dhateng *or* dhumateng to, toward; concerning.

maras I chicken lung (fried and eaten as a rice-accompanying dish).
II fearful, apprehensive.

maratuwa *ng*, marasepuh *kr* parent-in-law; bapak - father-in-law; ibu - mother-in-law.

marcapada *lit* earth; place of human habitation.

mardawa *lit* pleasing, pleasant.

mardika 1 free, independent; 2 not subject to tax; 3 private, not employed as an official;
kamardikan freedom, liberty, independence.

marem satisfied, content;
maremi satisfying, pleasing.
maremaké to cause to be satisfied;
kamareman satisfaction.
See also arem.

marèng the period between the close of the rainy season and the onset of the dry season (about March, April and May).

mares a march, marching music.

marga I *ng*, margi *kr*, because.
II *lit* road, way; - catur *lit* crossroads, intersection.

margana *lit* arrow.

margiyuh *lit* sad, sorrowful.

margupé *lit* tired, exhausted.

marhum deceased, late.

mari *ng*, mantun *kr*, 1 (dhangan *k.i.*) to get over, recover (from); 2 to stop, subside; 3 after; 4 *reg* finished;

marèni 1 to get over s.t.; 2 to cure o.s.;
marèkaké to cure;
mari(-mari) mati *idiom* unchanging.

marik, marik-marik *or* morak-marik untidy, in disorder.

marikelu *lit* to sit silently with bowed head, as a sign of esteem and humility.

maring *reg* (to go) to (*var of* marang, menyang).

marinyu *reg* village messenger, policeman.

markata 1 emerald; 2 bright green; 3 bright.

markis I awning against sun, built onto the front of a house.
II *var of* markisah.
III kind of setting for gems.

markisah 1 passion-fruit; 2 syrup made from passion-fruit.

marlesu *lit* weary, exhausted.

marlupa *var of* marlesu.

marma I *lit* therefore; hence;
marmané the reason why...
II *lit* sympathy, concern.

marmer marble (stone, for floors).

marmut guinea pig.

maron earthenware pot, tank. *See also* pengaron.

marong *or* marong-marong to burn hotly, blaze, glow.

marsosé mounted police, constabulary.

marta *lit* gentleness.

martabak an omelette with meat and onion.

martabat degree (of mystical knowledge).

martani *lit* bringing comfort, blessing.

martèl *reg var of* martil.

martil hammer.

maru 1 any wife after the first in a polygamous household; 2 rival;
dimaru (*passive form*) to make s.o. a co-wife by marrying another;
kemaron pikiré distracted, with divided attention.

marug *see* maruk II.

maruk I, kemaruk *or* maruki *or* nge-maruki to have a big appetite after recovering from illness.

II *reg* (of soil) dry and loose (*var of* madhuk).

marung *reg* 1 dancing beggar; 2 to beg while dancing.

marus 1 *lit* blood; 2 congealed animal blood (used as a food).

maruta *lit* wind.

marjan *see* merjan.

mas I gold; - oré *or* - uré *or* - pasir gold nuggets, gold dust; iwak - goldfish (*see also* iwak);

mas-masan 1 jewelry (*esp* gold); 2 imitation gold.

II 1 brother, older brother (used to address or refer to contemporary males, including wife to husband) (*shtf of* kangmas); 2 *title for persons of lower status*; - agus *term used by servants to address the master's male children*; - ajeng , - ayu (*terms for addressing minor wives*); - lara *or* - rara *terms used by servants to address the master's female children*; - mirah *term of endearment for a girl*; 3 *title for men in minor official positions.*

masa *excl of disbelief* (*var of* mangsa II).

masak I *reg* tip given to a girl for acting as a man's dancing partner.

II to cook (*also* mangsak); masakan cooked food.

III, masakan *reg* packet for prepared betel.

masakèh *lit* scholar, pious person.

masalah problem, question; masalahaké to make a problem out of s.t.

masarakat society, the community.

masjid mosque.

Masèhi Christian.

maselat charm, magic means.

masem 1 sour, unripe; 2 (of clothing) old and faded but still nice-looking. *See also* asem.

masgul 1 sad, downhearted; 2 discontented, offended.

mashur well-known, famous.

masi I *excl of disbelief* (*var of* mangsa). II although.

masih *reg var of* isih.

masin 1 salty, briny; 2 salted fish.

masinis 1 person who operates a machine; 2 engine-driver.

masir I (of salak or other fruit) with a pleasant crumbly texture.

II to have a dust-bath (bird). *See also* pasir.

masiya although. *See also* masi II.

maskèt *reg* 1 precise, exact; 2 scrupulous.

maskumambang a certain classical verse form.

maslakat *lit* welfare, well-being, prosperity.

masmur 1 Book of Psalms; 2 kidung - psalm.

masnis *var of* masinis.

masra-masru *reg* very angry, raging.

masrik *lit* the orient.

masrut, sarat masrut 1 medicine; 2 payment given to a healer. *See also* sarat.

mastaka 1 (*or* mustaka) head (*k.i. for* endhas); 2 (royal) crown; 3 pinnacle of mosque roof.

masuk 1 to attend school; 2 to be at the office.

mat I 1 deeply enjoyable; 2 luxury, comfort;

ngemataké to give o.s. over to the enjoyment of s.t.;

mat-matan 1 to enjoy o.s. thoroughly; 2 to focus attention on enjoying s.t.

II exactly, just right.

III (check)mate.

mata 1 eye (of an animal; *cr* of a human being) (*see also* mripat); 2 eye-like part (*e.g.* knot in wood; centre of a pimple; precious stone in its setting); **3** spot, pip (on playing cards, dice); **4** kernel, grain; **5** a little extra paid to the village head with one's taxes; - **dheruk** small buttonhole for attaching a pin-on button; - **éra** (of wickerwork) loose, open; - **iwak 1** scar from a wound; **2** corn on the toe; **3** duckweed; - **kapèn 1** dimly visible; **2** it appears that...; - **kucing 1** dammar (resin used in batik work); **2** small light indicating that an electrical appliance has warmed up and is ready for use; - **lélé 1** the first leaf buds of tobacco plants; **2** whitish; light in colour; - **loro 1** one who tries to straddle conflicting alternatives; **2** double spy; - **pita 1** person entrusted with s.t.; **2** supervisor, person entrusted with care; **3** person who conducts guided tours; - **walik** a certain pattern in woven work; - **yuyu 1** tending to cry easily; **2** defect on an inflated balloon that might give way at any time;

matamu *cr term of abuse* you idiot!;

matani 1 to equip with eyes; **2** to impugn s.o.'s eyesight;

matak-matakaké *cr* to impugn s.o.'s eyesight;

kemata to be seen doing s.t. underhanded;

kematan 1 to have excessively large eyes; **2** *var of* **kemata**;

mata dhuwiten *idiom* overfond of money;

mata walangen *idiom* staring fixedly and unseeingly.

matak *see* **mantak**.

matal (of corn in a field *etc*) nearly dried (*var of* **maktal**).

matangga *lit* elephant.

matangnya *lit* the reason is...

Mataram 1 a district in Central Java around the present town of Kota Gede; **2** the kingdom and dynasty founded in this area.

mataya *lit* **1** dance; **2** to dance.

matèk *coll* dead (*var of* **mati**).

mateng 1 ripe, mature; **2** well done, cooked, ready to eat; **3** settled, decided; **4** curdled (milk), clotted (blood); **matengi** to cook until done;

matengaké to bring to readiness;

kematengen overripe;

mateng ati (of fruit) ripe only on the inside.

matengga *var of* **matangga**.

mathak a certain shining fabric for making a fez-like cap.

mathar *reg* orderly, neat.

mathem I to be crazy about.

II satisfied, calm and content.

mathi whorl in a horse's coat, indicating its temperament.

mathis 1 a perfect fit; **2** right, to the point.

mathuk 1 to agree; **2** to go well (with), to suit.

mati *ng*, **pejah** *kr*, **1** (**séda** *k.i.*, **murud** *or* **surud** *k.i. for king*) dead; to die; **2** not functioning; **3** gone out, extinguished (light, fire); **4** without feeling, numb; **5** fixed, unchangeable (price); **6** dried up (well, source of income); **7** abandoned, no longer frequented (path). *See also* **pati**.

matis *reg* to slaughter.

matra *lit* **1** a measure; **2** a little.

matrus sailor (*also* **mantrus**).

matswa *lit* fish.

mau *ng*, **wau** *kr*, **1** just now, a moment ago, earlier; **2** the (aforesaid); - **awan** this afternoon; - **bengi** last night; - **ésuk** this morning; - **soré** this (past) evening;

mau-mau earlier;

mauné *or* **mau-mauné** before (as contrasted with now), just before, as previously, formerly.

maulana the honorable (title of a Muslim scholar).

maulud birth and death day of the prophet Muhammad (*var of* mulud).

mawa I *ng*, mawi *kr*, with, having, making use of; - gawé to cause trouble; mawa-mawa depending, varying according to the circumstances. II glowing charcoal, ember.

mawak, mawak-mawak having a large tear in it.

mawar rose.

mawi with; having; making use of (*kr for* mawa).

mawon just, only (*md* baé) (*shtf of* kémawon).

mawur 1 scattered round about; 2 in grains.

maya I flower of the blimbing fruit tree. II, maya-maya 1 light (of colours). III hazy.

mayag, mayag-mayag having a potbelly.

mayak, mayak-mayak 1 heavy-burdened, unwieldy, heavy-looking. *See also* mèyèk. II *reg* 1 well-off, wealthy; 2 to have plenty of time.

mayang I blossom of the areca palm; disendhal mayang *idiom* to be separated, torn apart (by death). II neck muscles of a horse. III, mayangi to rage crazily; kemayangan, begja kemayangan great good luck. *See also* begja, beja. IV boat for fishing with purse seine. V *see* wayang.

mayar 1 to be lighter, easier, less of a burden; 2 to recover, get better (after illness); mayaraké to cause s.t. to be less burdensome; kemayaran 1 opportunity; 2 relief; 3 discount.

mayat slanting, sloping.

mayeg *var of* mayig.

mayeng, mayeng-mayeng *or* moyang-mayeng to go from place to place.

mayig, moyag-mayig unstable, wobbly.

mayit (layon *k.i.*) corpse.

mayo *reg var of* ayo.

mayor I major (military rank). II, mayoran *reg* to have a delicious meal.

mayug, mayug-mayug unstable, leaning (in a certain direction).

mayuk *var of* mayug.

mbah *see* bah III.

mbak *see* bak VI.

mbok *see* bok I.

mboten *see* boten.

mé, ngemé *or* amé to put s.t. outdoors to dry or air; méan *or* mém*éan* 1 things (to be) sundried or aired; 2 clothesline; paméan *or* pamém*éan or* pamép*éan* place for drying things. *See also* pé, pépé.

mèbel a piece of furniture.

mébilèr furniture.

mèbrèt *or* mèbrèt-mèbrèt *repr* the sound of tearing.

mecèthèt to burst open when squeezed. *See also* cèthèt.

médan *or* pamédan field, battlefield, arena.

médé, médé-médé (of fat flesh) to shake, wobble. *See also* mété, mèdèl, mètèng.

meded I 1 to rotate rapidly; 2 to look for s.t. everywhere. II well-dressed.

mèdèd to thrust the chest forward.

mededeng *var of* mbededeng. *See also* bededeng.

mèdèl *var of* mèdèng.

mèdèng, mèdèng-mèdèng 1 (of pants) worn low at the waist; 2 (of fat flesh) to shake, wobble.

medhak to go down, descend (*k.i. for* medhun). *See also* tedhak.

medhali medal, medallion.

médhang *reg* to go (out) for a stroll (*var of* midhang).

medhangkungan name of the 20th wuku.

medhedheg *var of* mbedhedheg. *See* bedhedheg.

medhèdhèh *var of* mbedhèdhèh. *See* bedhèdhèh.

medheng I 1 big enough; 2 just, in the process of (*var of* sedheng).

II *reg* 1 bewildered, confused; 2 to stand still, not be in demand (*var of* kodheng).

mèdhèng I *reg* coinciding with; to be (do)ing.

II, mèdhèng-mèdhèng clearly visible, on open display. *See also* èdhèng.

medhidhig to boast about o.s.; boastful.

medhing I *reg* to lift one's bottom while crawling on knees. *See also* pledhing.

II *reg* to ask one's share after fishing together.

medhit miserly.

medhok to swell, expand.

médhok, médhok-médhok (of face powder) applied thickly.

medhudhug *var of* mbedhudhug. *See also* bedhudhug.

medhuk I *var of* medhok.

II *reg* to descend, get off (*var of* medhun).

medhun *ng*, mandhap *kr*, medhak *k.i.* 1 to go down, descend; 2 to alight, get off; 3 to go down (price); 4 to come up with (help, present); medhun lemah (tedhak siti *kr*) the ceremony for a baby's first contact with the earth.

medi *or* memedi ghost. *See also* wedi.

mèdi *lit* anus.

medidang-mediding *see* mediding.

mediding *or* medidang-mediding to shudder, shiver (with cold or fear).

médol, médol-médol *or* médal-médol (to walk) with a lumbering gait.

médong, médong-médong *or* médang-médong (to walk) with a waddling gait.

meg, mag-meg to keep touching. *See also* mek.

méga *lit* cloud; - malang *lit* dark rain-clouds; - mendhung 1 clouds heavy with rain; 2 name of a batik pattern from Pekalongan; 3 name of a metre and a melody; 4 hot coffee mixed with coconut milk;

mégan 1 greyish-blue with black stripes on the wings (doves); 2 the clouds, cloudy heavens;

kamégan covered or obscured by clouds.

mégal-mégol *see* mégol, égol.

mégang-mégung zigzag.

mégantara dappled and blackish (horse's coat).

mégang-mégung 1 zigzag; 2 placed randomly this way and that (*var of* malang-mégung, *see* palang).

megap, megap-megap to pant, breathe in gasps.

megar to open out, expand. *See also* gar.

megari *reg* one who helps the host by serving at a party. *See also* pramugari.

mégat-mégot *see* mégot.

megatruh a certain classical verse form.

megawé *ng*, medamel *kr* to work (a field, with draught animals).

megeg, megeg-megeg (to sit, stand) stock-still, motionless.

mègèg *or* mègèg-mègèg to not change, take no notice, not move.

megegeg motionless, stock-still.

megegeh *var of* megegeg.

megègèh (of legs) spread wide apart.

mègèk *var of* mègèg.

megeng I 1 to hold (the breath); 2 to wean (*k.i. for* nyapih).

II dina - the 1st day of the Fasting Month (pasa);

megengan ritual meal held on the eve of the Fasting Month.

mègèng *or* mègèng-mègèng to begin to improve after illness, show signs of getting better (*var of* mbegènggèng). *See also* begènggèng.

megep *lit* settled, stately, grave. *See also* menggep.

meger, meger-meger 1 to stand erect (a large object); 2 still there, surviving.

megiglik *reg* too thrifty.

mégin *reg* still remaining, over.

mégla *see* égla.

méglang-mèglèng *see* mèglèng.

mèglèng *abusive term addressed to s.o.*; méglang-mèglèng to strut, swagger, show off.

meglik, meglik-meglik to sit in a high, prominent position.

megogok to sit utterly motionless.

mégol *or* mégol-mégol *or* mégal-mégol to sway the hips provocatively. *See also* égol.

mégos *see* égos.

mégot, mégot-mégot *or* mégat-mégot 1 to advance only slowly, with sidelong looks, twists and turns; 2 to be reluctant, refuse to go along.

megrak 1 to open (flower); 2 to stand straight up, stand on end (hair).

megrak-megrik *see* megrik.

megrok *var of* mekrok.

megruk *var of* mekrok.

meguguk *var of* mbeguguk. *See* beguguk.

megung to be high, full (water in pond, well) (*also* agung II).

mégung to deviate from a straight line.

mèh almost; - baé just about, very nearly; mèhan (*sentence final*) almost.

meheng *lit* only, just (*var of* muhung).

méja table, tabletop, counter.

mejaji *var of* mbejaji.

méjan *var of* maéjan.

mejana, mejanani to despise, humiliate, treat with contempt.

mejao uncertain, unable to decide between alternatives.

mejemuk *see* majemuk.

mejen 1 straining, associated with severe diarrhoea or piles, but producing little; 2 to fail to go off (firework, gun).

mejer *reg* to stand (up) straight.

mejing *see* wejing.

mejujag *var of* mbejujag.

mèk I *repr* a touch of the hand; ngemèk to touch; to feel; ngemèk-emèk to keep touching; to make messy by touching; mak-mèk to touch repeatedly; mèk-mèkan 1 to touch; 2 s.t. touched, groped; 3 to have a tendency to touch. II *reg* only, just (*var of* mung). III *or* mèké *reg var of* cikbèn.

mékah, mékah-mékah to waddle, walk like a duck. *See also* mèkèh.

mekak, pamekak a short strapless bodice worn by female dancers.

mekakah to stand with the legs wide apart.

mekakat, ora mekakat abnormal, out of the ordinary.

mekanjar a variety of war dance.

mekao I to shuffle cards (by one who is not taking part of the game). II rough undyed cotton fabric.

mekar 1 to open out, expand; 2 to bloom.

mekaten 1 like this, in this way (*kr for* mengkéné); 2 like that, in that way (*kr for* mengkono, mengkana).

mekeh, mekeh-mekeh to pant, struggle for breath.

mèkèh, mèkèh-mèkèh *or* mékah-mèkèh to walk with a waddle.

mekek *var of* mekak.

mekena white cloth, veil covering a woman's head.

mekèten *reg var of* mekaten.

mekoten *reg var of* mekaten.

mékrad ascension to heaven; mékradan 1 the day of Muhammad's ascension; **2** to celebrate this day (27 Rejeb).

mekrok 1 to open, come into flower; **2** to be open, raised (umbrella).

mekruh *var of* **makruh**.

mekruk *var of* **mekrok**.

meksih *reg var of* **taksih**.

mel, ngemel-mel 1 to mouthe constantly; **2** to nibble away.

mèl I magic incantation;
ngemèli to utter an incantation over;
ngemèlaké to utter an incantation on s.o.'s behalf.
II *reg* illegal highway toll, extortion;
ngemèli to pay s.o. (an illegal highway toll);
ngemèlaké to pay s.t. (as an illegal toll).

mela clear.

méla-méla *reg* clear, distinct (*var of* **wéla**).

mélai *reg* to begin (*kr for* **wiwit**).

melak *var of* **melok**.

melang, melang-melang uneasy, apprehensive, fearful.

melar to expand, open out.

mélar-mélor *see* **mélor**.

melathi jasmine (*var of* **mlathi**).

melaya *lit* to travel, wander around.

mélé, mélé-mélé hanging out of the mouth (tongue); to loll.

meled *reg* to be eager to (do), yearn for.

mèleg *reg* fed up (with), sick and tired (of).

melèh, melèh-melèh (of wound) skinned, raw.

melèk 1 (**wungu** *k.i.*) to stay awake; **2** (of the eyes) to open; **3** good-looking;
melèk-melèkan with open eyes, in broad daylight.
See also **lèk**.

mèlek condensed milk (from tin).

meleng I *reg* pupil (of the eye).
II, **meleng-meleng** dark, shiny and gleaming.

mèlèng careless, heedless.

mèlèr to run, drip (nose).

meles glossy (black).

melid *reg* mean, miserly.

melik I, 1 melik-melik to flash, sparkle; **2 merem-melik** to sleep badly, keep waking up.
II to wash, pan (for gold, precious stones). *See also* **sisik**.

mélik 1 possession, rightful property; **2** to desire to keep; **3** to want to obtain possession of; **4** so that, in order to;
mélik nggéndhong lali *prov* to have a desire to obtain s.t. by any means whatever; the end justifies the means.

melok 1 in plain sight; **2** conspicuous, striking.

melong I, melong-melong to shine brightly, gleam.
II wide-eyed.

mélor 1 rickety, wobbly; **2** weak, without inner strength;
mélar-mélor loose, wobbly.

mélot 1 to bend, yield; **2** reluctant;
mélat-mélot reluctant.

mèlu *see* **èlu, ilu II**.

mélung twisted, bent.

melung-melung to wail, howl, make a long drawn-out sound.

melur to bend easily, have too much give.

memak thick and soft (of hair on head).

mémang *reg* indeed, truly, really.

membak-membik *see* **membik**.

membès *reg var of* **membik**.

membik (*pron as:* **membi:k**), **membik-membik** *or* **membak-membik** with face screwed up ready to cry.

membis *var of* **membès**.

membleg, membleg-membleg 1 thick(ened), sticky; **2** flabby, blubbery.

mèmblèh, mèmblèh-mèmblèh having the lips drawn back ready to cry.

mèmblèk *var of* **mèmblèh**.

mémé *var of* **pépé**.

memedi ghost, something that frightens.

See also **wedi**.

memek very thick, luxuriant (black hair).

mèmèk *reg* to take away.

memel meaty without fat, having good firm flesh.

memela pitiful.

memeng *reg* to give s.t. up, forego an opportunity.

memes 1 soft, tender; 2 sweet-sounding.

memet I 1 intricate, complicated, difficult to grasp; 2 joined into one; mixed together from separate parts.
II (of clothing, fabric) in rags, worn out.

mèmèt 1 to fish with the bare hands; 2 to gather edible herbs;
mèmèti (of hens) to look around restlessly for a place to lay an egg.

mempan 1 to cut, go in deep (knife, weapon); 2 to be effective, to work; 3 able to grasp, to understand; 4 - **marang** to be applicable to.

mempen 1 to isolate o.s., stay inside; 2 to work hard with full concentration.

mempeng to work assiduously, with full strength and attention.

memping (of rice plant) nearly ripe (*shtf of* **kumemping**). *See also* **emping**.

mempis, mempis-mempis to be out of breath, breathe heavily.

memplak *intsfr* white, pure white.

mempuh puffy, swollen. *See also* **plempuh**.

mempur pleasantly soft and meaty (of fully ripened cassava).

mèmrèng I thin, threadbare.
II a ghostly animal resembling a tiger.

men I very, decidedly, really (*shtf of* **temen**);
ngemenaké to do s.t. seriously, to make every effort;
ngemen-men to do with great care.

II just, only (*shtf of* **mawon, kémawon**).

mèn *reg var of* **bèn**.

menag *var of* **menak**.

menak, menakan *or* **menaken** *reg* if, when(ever).

ménak I 1 obsolete title for a nobleman; 2 stories about the Islamic hero Amir Ambyah, depicted in **wayang golèk** performance.
II comfortable. *See also* **énak**.

menang I *ng*, **mimpang** *reg kr*, 1 to win; 2 to a greater degree;
menangaké to cause or allow to win;
menangan 1 to have the quality to win; 2 to put o.s. forward, self-centred;
menang-menangan to vie for top position;
menang akal karo okol *idiom* brains win over brawn.
See also **wenang**.
II, **menangi** (**meningi** *kr*), to experience, witness, know at first hand.

menapa *kr* what (*pronunciation form of* **punapa**). *See also* **apa**.

menara 1 tower; 2 lighthouse; 3 minaret, mosque tower, church steeple.

menatu *see* **penatu**.

menawa 1 if, when(ever); 2 probably, possibly.

menawi *kr for* **menawa**.

mencala *var of* **mancala**.

mencalang *reg* village policeman.

mencangah fresh, healthy (complexion).

mencangul mischievous, naughty, shameless.

méncas-méncos to keep twisting the lips. *See also* **méncos**.

mencening clean yellow, nice-looking (skin).

menceno clear, obvious, plain to see.

mencep *or* **mencep-mencep** *intsfr* full, jammed; filled to the brim.

mèncès slantwise, on the diagonal.

mencingkar *reg* to be aloof, isolate o.s.

mencir I *reg* to tap on the head.
II, mencir-mencir *or* menciri *reg* 1 to spread apart, spread out; 2 to be aloof.

mencira *var of* menjila.

mencit up to the top; cilaka - misfortune at its worst (*see also* cilaka).

méncla-ménclé shifty, unreliable.

ménco mynah bird.

mencono I swollen (pimple).
II impolite.

méncos 1 crooked, oblique; 2 wry (mouth).

mèncrèt 1 to have diarrhoea; 2 *fig* copious.

mencrit *var of* mencit.

mencul joker, wag, buffoon.

ménda goat, sheep (*kr for* wedhus).

méndah how…! what (a)…!
méndaha if only.

mendal *or* mendal-mendal to bounce, spring back.

mendang *see* mendhang.

mendap-mendip *see* mendip.

mendat *var of* mendal.

mendat-mendut *see* mendut II.

mendeking *var of* medeking.

mèndel 1 to refrain from speaking, be motionless (*kr for* meneng); 2 *reg* to stop, cease (*kr for* lèrèn).

mendelap-mendelip *see* mendlip.

mendelem *reg* water container made from coconut shell.

mendelep to enter a hole. *See also* delep.

mendèlès to stand one's ground stubbornly.

mendelo (of eyes) bulging, wide (*var of* mendolo). *See also* pendelo.

mendem 1 drunken, intoxicated; 2 drugged. *See* endem.

mèndès *reg* flirtatious, coquettish.

mendha to subside. *See* endha.

méndha to imitate, look like;
méndha-méndha to look exactly like.

mendhak I jewelled band encircling a kris just below the handle.
II to hold a ceremony one year after a death. *See also* pendhak.
III *see* endhak.

mendhalung, mendhalungan 1 of mixed blood; 2 confused (*esp* in applying the rules of speech level).

mendhang 1 broken-up discarded rice husks; 2 *fig* trivial, insignificant (*also* mendang).

mendhek *var of* mendhak III. *See* endhak.

mendhekel 1 to bulge with tendons/muscles; 2 irritated, provoked. *See also* pendhekel.

mendhèlès *see* mendèlès.

mendhelis to show as small round smooth surfaces. *See also* pendelis.

mendhelong loose, slack, sagging. *See also* pendhelong.

mendhelus to show as round glossy surfaces. *See also* pendhelus.

mèndhèng *reg* a variety of earthenware container.

mendhèsèl knobbly.

mendhikil bumpy, forming a small bump. *See also* pendhikil.

mendhil mouse droppings.

mendhing *reg* it would be better, preferable to.

mendhisil 1 headstrong, obstinate; 2 forming a small bulge. *See also* pendhisil.

mendho 1 stupid; 2 half-done.

mendhokol 1 swollen, bulging; 2 knobbly. *See also* pendhokol.

méndhol, méndhol-méndhol stuffed full.

méndhong I a rush-like grass used for weaving mats.
II a disease of rice plants.

mendhosol forming a large bulge. *See also* pendhosol.

mendhot full, abundant (fruit on a tree).

mendhuh, mendhuh-mendhuh *reg* (of fruits on the tree) abundant.

mendhulus to stick a shiny bald head out. *See also* pendhulus.

mendhung 1 dark rain cloud; 2 cloudy, about to rain.

mendhusul to bulge out, show as a hump. *See also* pendhusul.

mendi *reg* where? (*var of* endi).

mendlap-mendlip *see* mendlip.

mendlip, mendlip-mendlip *or* mendlap-mendlip 1 to waver, flutter, flicker; 2 to vacillate.

mendolo (of eyes) bulging, wide.

méndra *lit* to set out, go on a journey, travel.

mendrap-mendrip *see* mendrip.

mèndrès *var of* mèndès.

méndring *var of* mindring.

mendrip *var of* mendlip.

méndro, méndro-méndro pretty and flirtatious, seductively charming.

mendul *or* pendul (of eyes) swollen from crying.

mendut I a sweet cake made from glutinous rice flour with grated coconut and brown sugar in it, wrapped in banana leaf.

II, mendut-mendut *or* mendat-mendut springy, bouncy.

mené *lit, or* samené 1 now; 2 in the future; 3 *reg* tomorrow.

méné *ng*, manten *kr*, unit of this scope; seméné one such unit, as much as this.

menèh *inf var of* manèh.

menèk *reg* if, when(ever).

meneng *ng*, mèndel *or* kèndel *kr*, to be silent. *See also* eneng.

mènèng, mènèng-mènèng bright red (*var of* manang-manang).

meng I too lazy (to…), not feeling up to (do)ing.

II just now, a moment ago (*reg var of* mau).

III only (*reg var of* ming, mung).

mèng *reg* 1 don't!; 2 *reg* really?

menga 1 open; 2 to come open. *See* wenga.

ménga-méngo *see* méngo.

mengana *reg var of* mengkana.

mengangah (of fire) to glow red.

méngas *lit* to turn the head (*var of* méngos).

mèngèh, mèngèh-mèngèh 1 red, flushed (face); 2 brand-new. *See also* mangah.

mengéné *reg var of* mengkéné.

mengeng I *lit* 1 dazed, not knowing what to do; 2 difficult to work out.

II *lit* buzzing, whining, humming.

mèngèr, mèngèr-mèngèr *intsfr* red: very red (lips, from chewing betel, or bright lipstick).

menges *or* ireng menges-menges pitch black.

menggah I in the case of; in connection with (*kr for* mungguh).

II, menggah-menggah to pant, breathe heavily.

menggèh, menggèh-menggèh *var of* menggah-menggah.

menggep *lit* to look very proper, fully decked out.

mengger to stand out, rise (ground, hill).

mènggèr *reg* a kind of chickenpox.

menggik small at the centre; hourglass-shaped; - menthol thick and thin in turn.

menggos, menggos-menggos out of breath. *See also* enggos.

menggrik, menggrik-menggrik *or* menggrak-menggrik thin and sickly; (of plant) hard to grow. *See also* enggrik.

menggung *title of high ranking royal official* (*shtf of* tumenggung).

mengi I 1 asthma; 2 asthmatic, wheezy.

II an insect that makes a long 'ngi' sound.

mengkak I - atiné put out, disgruntled.

II kuna - ancient, very old-fashioned.

mengkakna *reg* whereas. *See also* mangka.

mengkana *ng*, mekaten *kr* like that, in that way.

mengkarag (of hair) to rise. *See also* pengkarag.

mengkarèk obstinate, difficult.

mengké in the future, later on (*md for* mengko).

mengkek, mengkek-mengkek uptight, unable to express pent-up feelings.

mengkelang 1 hard (faeces); 2 *lit* rebellious.

mengkéné *ng*, mekaten *kr*, 1 like this, in this way; 2 as follows;
mengkènèkaké to treat in this way, like this.

mengkeruk *reg* to scowl, glower.

mengkèten *var of* mekèten.

mengkik *var of* menggik.

mengkis, mengkis-mengkis to be out of breath, pant.

mengko *ng*, mangké *kr*, in the future, later on; - dhisik just a minute!
mengko-mengko by and by;
samengko *lit* now, at the moment.

méngkod, méngkod-méngkod *or* méngkad-méngkod unwilling, recalcitrant, reluctant.

méngkog, méngkog-méngkog *or* méngkag-méngkog to walk ponderously. *See also* mingkug.

méngkok, méngkok-méngkok *or* méngkak-méngkok 1 unwilling, ungracious; 2 to be recalcitrant.

mengkono *ng*, mekaten *kr*, 1 like that, in that way, so; 2 (*highlighting preceding word*) as for (in contrast to s.t. else); - uga likewise, and furthermore...;
mengkonokaké to treat in that way, like that.
See also mono, ngono.

mengkorog 1 horrified, scared stiff; 2 (of hair) standing on end. *See also* pengkorog.

mengkos, mengkos-mengkos out of breath (*var of* mengkis-mengkis).

méngkot *see* méngkod.

mengkurah I wooden fence around a grave. II simple coconut oil press.

mengkus *var of* mengkos.

méngo 1 to look aside; 2 to turn away, be averse;
ménga-méngo to keep looking from side to side.

méngol *reg* to get angry, be headstrong, obstinate.

mengono *reg* (to go) to that place.

mengsah 1 enemy, opponent; 2 against, up against (*kr for* mungsuh).

menika 1 this (*kr for* iki); 2 that (*kr for* iku, kuwi, kaé).

mening I, mening-mening spick-and-span.
II, meningi 1 to experience (*kr for* menangi); 2 to witness (*kr for* ngonangi).

meninga to know (*subst kr for* weruh). *See also* uninga.

menir I broken grains (rice);
meniran cake made from the above mixed with coconut milk.
II, jangan menir a certain soup made from young corn mixed with spinach.
III, meniren tingling (mouth, from too much talking).
IV meniran a certain plant the leaves of which are used in medicines.
V 1 schoolmaster; 2 boss.

menis, menis-menis small, round, smooth and attractive (face, breast). *Also* mlenis.

menit a minute;
meniti to time s.t. in minutes;
menitan by the minute;
samenit one minute, a moment.

menjalin rattan (*var of* penjalin).

menjait *or* penjait tailor.

menjangan (sangsam *kr*) large deer with pronged antlers.

ménjé unripe seeds of the pucung tree, young kluwak.

menjèng residue of sesame after extracting oil.

mènjèng I fried soybean ball.
II reg prostitute.

mènjep 1 to turn down the corners of the mouth; 2 to show dislike, disapproval. See ènjep.

menjila 1 solitary, isolated; 2 apart, in a class by itself, outstanding.

ménol with little round swellings on the skin.

mentah unripe, raw, uncooked;
mentahan in an uncooked/unprocessed state;
mentah-mentahan 1 plainly; 2 without forethought or consideration.

mentak reg probable.

méntak reg to ask, request, beg.

mental to bounce, rebound. See also pental.

mentala see wentala.

méntar lit to go away, leave.

mentas I just now, a moment ago. See also entas.
II see pentas.

mentéga reg butter (var of mertéga).

mentèh unripe, raw, uncooked (reg var of mentah).

mèntèng reg a certain tree with sour fruit (var of kepundhung).

menter, menter-menter (of women's breasts) round and filled (out).

mèntèr I 1 to burn well, catch fire easily; 2 to burn brightly; 3 cheerful, lively (mood);
mènter-mènter 1 blood, fiery red; 2 fresh, blushing colour.
II 1 tough, strong; 2 unmoved, unchanged;
mènteran tough, strong by nature.
III, mèntèr-mèntèr var of menter-menter.

mentèrèng 1 dressed up; 2 conspicuous, showy.

mentéring an outfit of official attire, presented to retainers.

mentes 1 well filled (out); 2 fig brainy.

ménthak-mènthèk to approach s.o. repeatedly with an ulterior motive.

mènthèh, mènthèh-mènthèh bulging, hanging out over the belt (fat stomach).

menthek 1 (or menthek-menthek) 1 plump, chubby; 2 content, happy.

menthèk 1 root-rot in rice plants (caused by spirits in the shape of little boys); 2 var of mènthèk.

mènthèk, mènthèk-mènthèk 1 intsfr short: extremely short; 2 describing a dwarf's gait.

menthel 1 to form a lump; 2 to form a tidy sum (money).

mènthèl coquettish, flirtatious.

menthélang mischievous, boyish.

menthélas (of head) clean-shaven.

menthélé var of menthèlès.

menthèlès 1 to stand one's ground, stand erect; 2 to care about nothing, defiant.

menthelos var of mentholos.

mentheng, mentheng-mentheng 1 swollen to bursting point; 2 serious, dedicated about one's work or responsibilities; 3 to desire strongly (to get s.t.); 4 hot and flushed with anger.

menthengel to pretend not to be concerned, give no sign of (e.g. pain).

menthengil 1 to just appear, come into view a little; 2 coll to pop in for a moment. See also penthengil.

menther var of menter.

menthèsèl var of mendhèsèl. See also pendhèsèl.

menthéyot to walk unsteadily under a heavy burden.

menthik I intsfr small, tiny.
II, menthikan (of rice plant) prematurely ripe.

menthilas (of head) clean-shaven.

menthing reg a small fishing boat.

menthiyèt to walk unsteadily from a heavy burden.

ménthog Manila duck.

mentholos (of head) round and bald. *See also* pentholos.

menthongol to show prominently, stick out. *See also* penthongol.

menthul 1 bumpy, knobbly; 2 to form a little mound; - atiné happy, content.

menthur, putih - clean, white (rice).

menthuyut *var of* menthéyot.

menuk (*pron as*: menu:k), menuk-menuk chubby, plump, nice and round.

menul, menul-menul soft and shaking, quivering (sweets).

menur 1 jasmine; 2 knob, ball, rosette (as ornament).

menus I, dudu - unbelievable, unreal.
II, menus-menus attractive, pretty.

menut a minute (*var of* menit).

menuwa custard-apple.

ményak *reg* oil (*var of* minyak).

menyambik monitor lizard (*also* nyambik).

menyan *ng*, séla *kr*, benzoin, gum-benjamin (used as incense).

menyang *ng*, dhateng *kr*, (to go) to, toward.

menyar-menyir *see* menyir.

ményar-ményor *see* menyor.

menyat 1 to get up from one's place, stand up; 2 to depart; 3 to set to work; 4 *coll* to nick off.

menyawak monitor lizard.

menyèr *var of* menyir.

menyes pleasant (of conduct, voice).

menyir, menyar-menyir 1 weak; 2 - atiné wishy-washy.

ményor, ményar-ményor 1 too limp to stand up; 2 without strength.

menyu 1 resembling tortoiseshell; 2 dull, dull-witted.

menyunyang impolite, impudent, insolent.

mérad I *coll* to buzz off. *See also* bérat, birat.
II 1 Muhammad's ascension to heaven; 2 celebration commemorating Muhammad's ascension to heaven.

merah-meruh *reg* dirty, unswept (of floor, yard *etc*).

mérah, ama mérah a variety of rice pest.

merak peacock;
merak kesimpir *lit* 1 as elegant as a peacock with large, sweeping tail; 2 a graceful, elegant walking gait (of a lady);
merakan a variety of long grass.

merang 1 dried rice straw; 2 *reg* rice chaff.

mérang *lit* embarrassed, ashamed. *See also* wirang.

mérat *see* mérad II.

mérat-mérot *see* pérot.

merbabak *lit* 1 to get tears of emotion in the eyes; 2 to flush with anger; 3 reddening of the sky during sunrise or sunset.

merbangbang reddening of the sky during sunrise.

merbebeng *lit* to flush with anger.

merbeng, merbeng-merbeng *var of* merbebeng.

merbes to seep through (*var of* mbrebes); - mili to shed tears.

merbot a certain low-ranking mosque official.

merbuk *lit* 1 fragrant; 2 to pervade (fragrance).

merbung *intsfr* old: exceedingly old; kuna - very ancient.

mercon fireworks, firecrackers; - bumbung bamboo cannon;
merconan 1 to set off fireworks; 2 resembling firecrackers.

merdagang to trade. *See* dagang.

merdamel to work (*kr for* mergawé). *See also* damel.

merdangga *lit* gamelan instrument. *See also* pradangga.

merdawa *lit* pleasing, pleasant (*var of* mardawa).

merdaya *lit* to use deceit, practise deception.

merdésa *ng*, merdhusun *kr*, to go into the country, to visit a rural area. *See also* désa.

merdhayoh to pay a visit. *See also* dhayoh.

merdhusun *kr for* merdésa.

merdi *see* perdi.

merdika *var of* mardika.

merdu *lit* (of voice) sweet, smooth, melodious. *See also* mredu.

merdud to not accept, to resist, rebel.

meré I to screech, cry (monkeys).
II to dive to the side (kite) (*var of* miré).

mèrèh, mèrèh-mèrèh blood-red (wound).

mèrek trademark, brand name.

mèrèl pretty, beautiful.

merem 1 closed (eyes); 2 to ignore one's obligations to others, be hardhearted; - dhipet tightly closed (eyes); - melik unable to get to sleep.

mèrèng *reg* to slope, slant. *See also* pèrèng.

mèrèt nice-looking.

merga *ng*, mergi *kr*, because (*var of* marga I).

mergag *reg* 1 to stop in one's tracks; 2 to hesitate, not dare to go on.

mergak *var of* mergag.

mergagah to stand with the legs wide apart (*var of* mbergagah). *See also* begagah.

mergawé *ng*, merdamel *kr*, to work, do a job;
mergawèkaké to cause to work.
See also gawé, megawé.

mergaya *reg* happily and unexpectedly.

mergedud obstinate, deaf to advice (*var of* mbregedud). *See also* begedud.

mergègèh to stand with the legs fairly wide apart (*var of* mbergègèh). *See also* begègèh.

mergegeg to remain motionless (*var of* mbergegeg). *See also* begegeg.

mergènggèng 1 in an arrogant pose; 2 recovered (from illness) (*var of* mbergènggèng).
See also begènggèng.

mergi 1 road, way (*kr for* dalan); 2 because (*kr for* merga) (*var of* margi).

mergil secluded, isolated.

mergogok *var of* mbergogok. *See* bergogok.

mergujug to rumble (stomach).

meri duckling (young of the bèbèk).

mèri envious, jealous;
mèrèn *or* mèrènan envious by nature;
mèrèni *or* mèrèkaké 1 to be the envy of (s.o.); 2 to covet (s.o.'s possessions); to envy (s.o.).

merit 1 tapering; 2 very high (note, voice).

merjan 1 red coral; 2 beads of a necklace or rosary.

merjao *reg* hesitant, in a dilemma, torn between alternatives.

merjauh *var of* merjao.

merkah to split open, crack.

merkakah to stand with the legs spread wide apart (*var of* mbergagah).

merkaki 1 aged, elderly; 2 the aged (no longer a full member of village community). *See also* kaki.

merkangkang to stand with the legs spread wide apart.

merkata *lit* emerald.

merkatak I with ears formed (stage in growth of rice plant). *Also* mratak.
II (producing) a cracking sound.

merkèkèh *var of* merkakah.

merkénco perverse, contrary, hard to get along with.

merkeneng heated and obstinate (*var of* mekeneng). *See also* pekeneng.

merkengkeng to lie stiff (*var of* mekengkeng). *See also* pekengkeng.

merkèngkèng to stand with the legs spread apart (*var of* mekèngkèng).

merkèngkèngaké to spread (the legs) apart.

See also pekèngkèng.

merkéngkong in a dilemma, torn between alternatives.

merkèngsèng *reg* conspicuous, eye-catching.

merketek (producing) a creaking, cracking sound.

merkètèk (of fire) crackling.

merkéwuh to cause difficulty. *See also* perkéwuh, pakéwuh.

merki 1 chicken flea; 2 *reg* dandruff.

merkinding to shudder (with fear) (*var of* mrinding). *See also* perkinding, prinding.

merkinting *var of* merkinding.

merkinyèh to have an oozing rash, small sores on the skin.

merkinyih *var of* merkinyèh.

merkitik 1 to crackle, sizzle (burning, cooking); 2 fuming, very angry.

merkiyu weary, stiff, cramped (arms, legs). *See also* kiyu.

merkongkong to sit with the legs wide apart (*var of* mekongkong, *see also* pekongkong).

merkungkung in a hunched or curled position, with bent back (*var of* mekungkung). *See also* pekungkung.

merkunung self-willed, wayward, wilful.

merkutuk I to have a severe skin rash. *See also* perkutuk.

II to force, constrain.

merlesu *lit* tired, exhausted. *See also* lesu.

merlupa *or* marlupa *var of* merlesu. *See also* lupa.

merlik to twinkle far off. *See* perlik.

mermomong to glow (fire) (*var of* nyer-momong). *See also* cermomong.

mermumuh (of skin) covered with infected sores and swollen. *See also* cermumuh.

mernèng, mernèng-mernèng beautifully dressed.

merngangah to glow red. *See also* per-ngangah.

merngangang thriving, prosperous, healthy.

merngangas to laugh a broad, jeering laugh.

merngèngès to laugh a light, jeering laugh.

merngingis to grin, show the teeth only a little.

merngongoh *cr* to open, expose a private part.

merngongos to grin broadly, showing the teeth.

méro *var of* mérok.

mérok, mérok-mérok (of face) thickly powdered.

mérong I *reg* to soil, daub.

II introductory movement (part of a gamelan melody).

merpèpèh. *See* repèpèh.

merpet *reg* dark, about to rain.

merpih *or* merpih-merpih to coax, plead (with).

mersobat *reg* friendly, on friendly terms with.

mersosé mounted police, constabulary.

mersul *reg* mischievous.

mersut *var of* mersul.

mertamu to pay a visit. *See also* tamu.

mertanggung halfway between, (only) partway to the goal, half-done. *See also* tanggung II.

mertami *reg kr for* mertamu.

mertandhu *see* tandhu II.

mertapa *see* tapa.

mertasami, mertasamèni 1 neatly, nicely; 2 to give satisfaction; 3 to make everything ready for.

mertéga butter;

mertégani to put butter on.

merti to care for; - désa traditional annual village event with feasting and the performance of a play after the harvest. *See also* perti.

mertingkah to perform silly antics; mertingkahan to be in the habit of performing silly antics. *See also* pertingkah, pratingkah.

mertinjo to pay a visit. *See also* tinjo.

mertobat to repent. *See* tobat.

mertonggong 1 to sit gaping blankly, vacantly; 2 to gape with surprise.

mertowin, ora - nothing special.

mertuwa parent-in-law (*var of* maratuwa).

mertuwi to pay a visit (*kr for* tilik). *See also* tuwi.

mertyu *lit* fire, flame.

mèru *lit* mountain; - pancaka funeral pyre.

mésa water buffalo (*var of* maésa).

mesah enemy (*kr for* mungsuh). *See also* mengsah.

mesail amulet, protective charm.

mesakaké *ng*, mesakaken *kr*, 1 to feel sorry for, have sympathy with; 2 to arouse sympathy or pity, pitiful.

mésan gravestone (*var of* maésan).

mesanak to treat as a relative or friend. *See also* sanak.

mesasa *reg* still, even so, in spite of the foregoing.

mesat *see* pesat.

Mesèhi *var of* Masèhi.

mèsem *see* èsem.

meses I to rush, sough (wind).
II finely dressed up.

mesgul sad, downhearted.

mesigit mosque (*var of* mesjid).

mesih still, (even) now (*md for* isih).

mésih *reg var of* mesih.

mesin 1 machine, engine; 2 sewing machine.

mesiya *reg* even though, even if it were so.

mèsiya *var of* mesiya.

mesjid mosque.

mesoyi masoi bark, a spongy and aromatic bark, used for medicinal and cosmetic purposes.

mespir imitation jewel in ring, earring.

mestagèn *reg var of* setagèn.

mestail inconceivable (*var of* mustail).

mestak 1 crotch (men's trousers); 2 fly-opening (men's trousers).

mestaka head (*k.i. for* sirah) (*var of* mastaka, mustaka).

mestèr 1 cement floor; 2 to cement; mestèran cement floor, concrete flooring, pavement.

mèster 1 lawyer, jurist; 2 former title of academic scholar in law.

mesthi inevitable, natural, predictable; mesthèkaké 1 to fix, set, determine; 2 to check, make sure of; mesthiné it should have been; samesthiné appropriate, as it should be.
See also pesthi.

mestri I, mestrèkaké to bring s.o. to the cemetery in order to be possessed by a spirit.
II *var of* mèstri II.

mèstri I a title (*var of* mèster).
II faith healer.

mesum 1 pale in the face; 2 depressed, gloomy.

met I soldier's cap.
II, met-metan to have bouts of dizziness. *See also* umet.
III exact, on the dot.

mèt *lit* to fetch, take away.

meta *lit* furious, crazed (elephant).

métal metal.

metamu to pay a visit (*var of* mertamu).

Metaram *see* Mataram.

Metawis *kr of* Metaram.

mété I cashew.
II, mété-mété (of fat flesh) to shake, quiver.

meteng *ng*, wawrat *or* ngandheg *kr*, mbobot *k.i.*, pregnant. *See also* weteng.

mèter 1 metre; 2 (*or* mèteran) instrument for measuring;

mèteri to measure with such an instrument;

mèteran by the metre.

metété to bulge somewhat (eyes).

metètèng 1 to act pompously; 2 cocksure, arrogant.

methakil 1 to wind the legs around s.t. (unseemly posture); 2 uncontrolled, noisy, boisterous. *See also* pethakil.

methakol to grasp s.t. by clasping it with the legs.

méthang-mèthèng *see* mèthèng.

methangkrèk to sit perched in a high place. *See also* pethangkrèk.

methangkrik *var of* methangkrèk.

methangkring *var of* methangkrèk.

methangkrok *var of* methangkrèk.

methangkrong *var of* methangkrèk.

methangkruk *var of* methangkrèk.

methangkrus high-handed.

methangkus *var of* methangkrus.

methathak to be seated with the legs spread (rudely);

methathakaké to spread (the legs) apart while sitting.

See also pethathak.

methathus to have an undershot jaw and jutting chin. *See also* pethathus.

mèthèh, mèthèh-mèthèh (to walk) with a waddle.

methekel muscular. *See also* pethekel.

methékol I *var of* methekel.

II 1 crooked, bent, twisted; 2 gnarled. *See also* pethéngkol.

methèklu absorbed, engrossed (in eating).

methekul *var of* methèklu.

methel to break easily (thread, rope).

metheng, metheng-metheng to be swollen to bursting point (*var of* mentheng).

mèthèng, mèthèng-mèthèng *or* méthang-mèthèng 1 in plain sight, disclosed, revealed; 2 to stick out (stomach). *See also* èthèng.

methéngkrak arrogant, proud.

methéngkrang to sit with the legs up on s.t.

methengkrus to sit motionless.

methet I tight.

II *reg var of* methel.

methéthah to sit with the knees apart.

methéthé (*var of* metètèng).

methèthèh to walk wide-legged with knees bent. *See also* pethèthèh.

methèthèk *var of* methéthé.

methethet too tight, uncomfortably full (*var of* mbethethet).

methétho *reg* glad, happy, gay.

methéthol, methétholen stunned, speechless.

methéthot *var of* methéthol.

methéthu *var of* methétho.

methingil to be in view (small things).

methinthing tight-fitting. *See also* pethinthing.

methisil small but strong (physique).

methit *see* pethit.

methithing small, slender, thin (bodypart).

methithit *var of* mbethithit.

méthok to show clearly, be in plain sight.

methokol *var of* methekel.

methongkrong sitting up high with the legs drawn up (improper posture).

methongsot *reg* to duck, stoop.

methonthong to protrude outward (long objects), (*also* metontong, metotong).

méthos *var of* méthot.

méthot curved, bent. *See also* péthot.

methotha *reg* well-situated.

methothok to squat on the haunches with the legs apart (in impolite position). *See also* pethothok.

methul *reg* dull, blunt. *See also* kethul.

methungkruk to sit with hunched back. *See also* pethungkruk.

methungkrung *var of* methungkruk.

methuntheng *intsfr* black: very black. *See also* thuntheng.

methunthang *reg* to engage in disgraceful behaviour.

methunthung swollen. *See also* pethunthung.

methuthuk to form a heap. *See also* pethuthuk.

metotong *var of* methonthong.

metri to take scrupulous care of, cherish. *See also* petri.

metu *ng*, medal *kr*, miyos *k.i.*, 1 to emerge, come forth; 2 to take (a certain route); 4 to quit, leave;
kemeton 1 emerging too far; 2 to have an emission of semen while asleep;
pametu product, yield;
metu mburi *idiom* to engage in a devious or underhand procedure.
See also wetu.

méwah surrounded by luxuries and extravagances.

mèwèh, mèwèh-mèwèh to have a large tear in it.

mèwèk 1 (*or* mèwèk-mèwèk) to cry long and loud (child); 2 *var of* mèwèh.

mi I noodle.
II, mi-mi-mi *syllable called for summoning goats, sheep.*

mibah to move (*reg kr for* mobah). *See also* obah.

miber to fly. *See also* iber.

mibur *reg* to fly. *See also* ibur I.

micik *reg* selfish, always thinking of one's own advantage.

mider *or* mider-mider to go around from place to place. *See also* ider.

midhang I 1 *reg* to go out for a stroll; 2 to go to perform an act in fulfilment of a promise.
II, midhangan *or* pamidhangan shoulder (*k.i. for* pundhak).

midhanget to hear (*k.i. for* krungu); midhangetaké (*k.i. for* ngrungokaké) to listen to.

midhet *cr* to sleep.

midid to blow strongly (breeze).

midhun *reg* to get off, down (*var of* medhun).

miduli to care about. *See also* perduli.

miduwung remorseful (*var of* keduwung).

migag-migeg *see* migeg.

migag-migug *see* migug.

migeg *lit* I to cover.
II migag-migeg to rock back and forth on the spot, unable to go on.

migug, migag-migug to move slowly and ponderously.

miguna *lit* skilful, clever. *See also* piguna.

migung *reg* to move aside, deviate from a straight line.

migut *var of* migug.

mihun rice flour noodle.

mijil I a certain classical verse form.
II *lit* to come forth. *See also* wijil.

mik I first, beforehand (*inf var of* dhisik).
II only (*inf var of* mung).
III *syllable called for summoning goats, sheep.*
IV (*pron as:* mi:k) 1 to drink (children's word); 2 (*or* ngemik) to suck, take milk from (the mother);
ngemiki to suckle (a baby).

miki *reg* just now (*shtc of* mau iki).

mikrab niche in a mosque indicating the direction of Mecca.

mikrad Muhammad's ascension to Heaven (celebrated on 27 Rejeb). *See also* mékrad.

mil I mile.
II, ngemil to nibble;
mal-mil to keep nibbling, eat constantly;
mil-milan snacks to nibble.

mila 1 originally; 2 therefore, that is why (*kr for* mula).

milag *lit* 1 to go away; 2 to give way.

milai *reg* to begin (*kr for* mulai).

milangoni *lit* lovely, delightful.

milang-miling *see* miling.

milar I to spring aside, avoid. *See also* ilar.

485

II to split lengthwise. *See also* **pilar**.

mileg, mileg-mileg to be able to take no more (food, drink), have had more than enough.

milep-milep 1 to keep going under (in water); 2 to almost go out, flicker (lamp).

milet I *reg kr for* **mèlu**.

II *reg kr for* **mili**.

III *reg kr for* **milih**.

mili I *shtf of* **milimèter**.

II *see* **ili**.

III *reg var of* **mélik**.

miling, miling-miling *or* **milang-miling** 1 to keep looking around; 2 to explore, investigate.

Milo *Dutch-language secondary school of colonial times. See also* **Mulo**.

milu to accompany, join in, go with (*var of* **mèlu**). *See also* **ilu** II, **èlu**.

milug, milug-milug big, beefy, muscular.

milulu *lit* exclusively.

milyar billion.

milyun million.

milyunèr millionaire.

mimang the (above ground) roots of the banyan tree, used to ward off danger.

mimbar pulpit.

mimbik, mimbik-mimbik 1 about to cry; 2 to start crying softly, whimper. *See also* **prembik**.

mimblik *var of* **mimbik**.

mimi I male sea crab which always stays clasped tightly to the female (**mintuna**); **lir mimi lan mintuna** *idiom* inseparable (lovers).

II, *var of* **emi-emi**.

mimik I a kind of gnat.

II (*pron as:* mimi:k) to drink (children's word). *See also* **mik**.

mimir I 1 soft and sheer (fabric); 2 fragile, frail.

II a variety of small crocodile.

III, **mimiren** to suffer from a red rash.

mimis I bullet;

lonjong mimis (to run) like a shot out of a gun.

II, **mimisen** to have a nosebleed.

mimpang to win (*reg kr for* **menang**).

mimpes *see* **impes** II.

mimrih *reg* in order to. *See also* **amrih**, **mrih**, **murih**.

mimring gauzy, filmy, transparent.

min, ngemin 1 to join in using s.t. together with s.o. else (*e.g.* reading the paper); 2 to call 'mine!' at an auction.

mina *lit* fish.

minak-minuk *see* **minuk**.

minal-minul *see* **minul**.

minangka (used) for, to serve as.

minangsraya *lit* to ask for help.

minanten *reg* if, when(ever) (*kr for* **menawa**).

mincak-mincek *see* **mincek**.

mincar-mincur *reg* (to walk) unsteadily.

mincek, mincek-mincek *or* **mincak-mincek** to walk, dance with little steps.

mincis, mincis-mincis *reg* very pretty-looking.

mincla-minclé *reg* shifty, unreliable.

minclo, mincla-minclo unreliable (*var of* **méncla-ménclé**).

mincrut *var of* **mincuk**.

mincuk, (*pron as:* mincu:k) **mincuk-mincuk** *describing the appearance of s.o., esp a woman, walking in a tight kain.*

minda *see* **ménda**.

mindah *see* **méndah**.

mindaka *or* **mindakani** *lit* to ruin, bring down treacherously.

mindel *reg* to refrain from speaking (*kr for* **meneng**, *var of* **mèndel**). *See also* **èndel**.

mindhak to increase, become greater (*kr for* **mundhak**). *See also* **indhak**, **undhak** I.

mindhik-mindhik to go quietly, on tiptoe (in order to creep up). *See also* **indhik**.

mindi I Persian lilac.

II *see* pindi.

mindring to buy on credit. *See also* Cina.

mindu disagreeably surprised, unbelieving.

ming 1 *coll* only (*var of* mung I); 2 *reg* but (*var of* nanging).

mingé *reg* to turn one's head, look aside (*var of* méngo).

minggrang-minggring *see* minggring.

minggring, minggring-minggring *or* minggrang-minggring to hesitate, waver, dilly-dally.

minggu 1 the seven-day week; 2 Sunday; minggon 1 weekly; 2 to spend Sunday; 3 to go on holiday.

mingip-mingip *see* ingip.

mingis-mingis razor-sharp.

mingit-mingit sharp-edged.

mingkar-mingkur *see* mingkur.

mingkeg, mingkeg-mingkeg (to walk) ponderously and laboriously.

mingklik (*pron as:* mingkli:k), mingklik-mingklik 1 (in a) high (place); 2 in a precarious position.

mingkrik *var of* mingklik.

mingkug *var of* mingkeg.

mingkuh to try to avoid, evade.

mingkung *lit* to resist, refuse (to do s.t.).

mingkur to dodge, be evasive; mingkar-mingkur to dodge frequently, be always evasive.

mingkus to shrink, shrivel (*var of* mringkus). *See also* pringkus.

minglar *var of* milar I.

minglep *var of* milep.

mingsa *reg* water buffalo (*kr for* kebo). *See also* maésa.

mingsel I (*or* mingsel-mingsel) fleshy, well-covered.

II, mingsel-mingsel to snuggle up to.

mingsil earnings, profit.

mingsra *see* misra.

mingsri I income (*var of* mingsil).

II residue of smoking, nicotine.

minguk-minguk to look around here and there. *See also* inguk.

mingut, mingut-mingut to scowl, wear an angry look.

mining, mining-mining deep-toned (red, pink).

mintar *var of* méntar.

mintasraya *lit* to ask for help.

minthak-minthik *see* minthik.

minthal-minthul *see* minthul.

minthel, minthel-minthel plump, well-covered.

minthi I Manila duckling (young of the ménthog).

II, minthi-minthi nice and round (child's tummy).

minthik (*pron as:* minthi:k), minthik-minthik to go on tiptoe; minthak-minthik to go back and forth or from one place to another on tiptoe.

minthing, minthing-minthing 1 tightly bound (woman's breastcloth); 2 *reg* well-dressed.

minthug (*pron as:* minthu:g), minthug-minthug 1 chubby; 2 (*or* minthag-minthug) to walk with a fat waddling gait (baby).

minthul, minthul-minthul *or* minthal-minthul to go around naked with dangly bits wobbling.

mintip-mintip to be just in sight at the top. *See also* intip II.

mintir-mintir 1 to keep burning low; 2 continuous, regular (but in small amounts). *See also* intir.

mintuhu *var of* mituhu.

mintuna a female sea crab which stays clasped tightly to the male. *See also* mimi.

minuk (*pron as:* minu:k), minuk-minuk *or* minak-minuk chubby, plump, cute-looking (babies).

minul *var of* minthul.

minum to drink liquor;

minum-minuman 1 to get intoxicated deliberately; 2 a party held for this purpose.

minus poverty-stricken, lacking in economic potential.

minyak perfume.

minyik (*pron as:* minyi:k), **minyik-minyik** 1 (*or* **minyak-minyik**) (to walk) slowly and carefully; 2 to take tentative steps.

minyuk *var of* **minyik**.

mipakat *reg kr for* **mupakat**.

mir, mir-miran worried, apprehensive, on edge.

mirah I cheap (*kr for* **murah**). II 1 ruby; 2 *lit* red.

miraos *kr for* **mirasa**.

mirasa *ng*, **miraos** *kr* tasty, delicious. *See also* **rasa**.

miré to move aside.

mireng to hear (*kr for* **krungu**).

miri *shtf of* **kemiri**.

mirib to resemble. *See also* **irib**.

mirid according to. *See* **pirid**.

miring slanting, at an angle. *See also* **iring** I.

miris fearful, anxious.

mirma 1 to feel solicitous toward; 2 (*or* **palimirma**) *lit* pity.

mirong 1 to wear a batik over the shoulder and around the body, denoting mourning or shame; 2 to cloak one's intentions, not come clean, dissemble. *See also* **rimong**.

mirowang to go to s.o.'s assistance. *See also* **rowang**.

mirunggan 1 extra, additional; 2 extra special; 3 fulfilling a particular need; **mirunggakaké** 1 to put aside, in a special place; 2 to treat s.t. as special.

mis I, **ngemis** to beg. *See* **kemis**. II the Mass.

misan related as a second cousin. *See also* **pisan**.

misbah (Christian) altar.

misi 1 mission; 2 Catholic mission.

misil *var of* **mingsil**.

mising *reg* to defecate (*var of* **ngising**, *see* **ising**).

miskin very poor.

misowa Chinese vermicelli.

misra, ora misra useless, not worth the trouble (*also* **mingsra**).

mistar ruler (for ruling lines).

mister *var of* **mèster**.

misuwur famous, widely known.

mit to ask permission (*shtf of* **amit**).

miterang to ask for information. *See also* **terang**.

mithi-mithi nice and round (child's tummy) (*var of* **minthi-minthi**).

mitra a close friend; **- darma** a proven friend; **- karuh** speaking acquaintance, superficial friend; **mitran** *or* **memitran** to be friends (with); **pamitran** friendship.

mituhu *see* **pituhu**.

miturut 1 according to; 2 in obedience to. *See also* **turut, piturut**.

miwah also, as well as (*kr for* **lan, karo**). *See also* **muwah**.

miyaga *reg* musicians of a gamelan orchestra (*var of* **niyaga, nayaga**).

miyang *reg var of* **menyang**.

miyangga *lit* 1 snake; 2 *reg* a kind of water spirit; 3 *reg* (*kr for* **baya** I) crocodile.

miyeg, miyeg-miyeg to struggle under a heavy burden.

miyos 1 to go out (*k.i. for* **metu**); 2 to be born (*k.i. for* **lair**); 3 to pass (*k.i. for* **liwat**).

miyud, miyud-miyud to sway, bend to and fro (branch of tree).

miyungyung to bind, tie up (hands and feet). *See also* **wayungyung**.

miyur, miyar-miyur indecisive, weak-willed.

mlagrang to tower, soar.

mlaha I clear, uncovered.

II empty, nothing there.

mlaku *ng*, mlampah *kr*, tindak *k.i.*, to walk. *See* laku.

mlalah preferable. *See also* plalah, pilalah.

mlalu to choose one alternative over another. *See also* pilalu.

mlampu *var of* mlalu.

mlana *reg* to go on a journey, travel about.

mlancong to go s.w. for enjoyment or sightseeing. *See also* plancong.

mlandhi *reg* in order, ready for use.

mlandhing, I mlandhingan (*or* kemlandhingan) a small shade tree; the edible pods of this tree.

II, mlandhingan a large tree spider. *Also* kemlandhingan.

mlangkring *see* plangkring.

mlangkrong *see* plangkrong.

mlangkruk *var of* mangkruk. *See also* plangkruk, angkruk.

mlanji *var of* mlandhi.

mlantar *reg* cracked but not broken through (earthenware).

mlanthing *var of* mlathing.

mlantrah 1 common, to be found everywhere; 2 to wander about, roam (animals).

mlantrang to go s.w. other than one's intended destination. *See also* plantrang.

mlapar to overflow (flood).

mlarat poor, needy;

kamlaratan 1 poverty; 2 impoverished, destitute.

mlas *lit* - asih *or* - arsa *or* - ayun pitiful, miserable. *See also* welas.

mlasah 1 scattered on the ground; 2 to spread, scatter, strew (*var of* mblasah). *See* blasah.

mlatah to become known everywhere.

mlatar *reg* outgoing, friendly, popular.

mlathi jasmine.

mlathing nicely arranged, neatly laid out.

mlatuk *see* platuk I.

mlawang wide open, revealed for all to see.

mlaya *lit* to travel.

mlayan *reg* reasonable, not bad (*var of* lumayan).

mlayu *ng*, mlajeng *or* mlajar *kr*, to run. *See* playu.

mlebeg *var of* mblebleg. *See also* blebeg.

mlèbèr *var of* mblèbèr.

mléca *lit* to break one's word.

mlècèh *var of* mlècèt.

mlècèt skinned, chafed, scratched. *See also* lècèt, plècèt.

mlecing *reg* thrifty, miserly.

mlecu I to pout, with lips thrust forward. *See* plecu.

II *intsfr* blue: very blue.

mledhag *var of* mbledhag. *See* bledhag.

mledhèh *var of* mbledhèh. *See* bledhèh.

mledhos *var of* mbledhos. *See* bledhos.

mledug *var of* mbledug. *See* bledug.

mlégrok to alight, settle, perch.

mlekèk *see* plekèk.

mlekenuk I cute, appealing (child).

II to sit with bowed head while working hard.

mlekok *var of* mlekèk. *See* plekèk.

mlekothar *see* mlekuthar.

mlekotho *var of* mlekothar.

mlekuthar to run away, to avoid doing one's duty.

mléla 1 clearly visible, obvious; 2 plain, common, ordinary.

mlélé (of eyes) wide open.

mlèlèk *var of* mlélé.

mlelet to wind, twist around. *See also* lelet.

mlempem 1 soggy, not properly dry and crisp; 2 lacking hardness, grown weak.

mlèmpèng to become thin and flat. *See also* lèmpèng.

mlempu puffed, swollen.

mlempuh *var of* mlempu.

mlénang *reg* 1 very beautiful; 2 bright red.

mlénas (of forehead) high, broad.

mlencung to jump out, break loose (from hold).

mlendhing *var of* mblendhing. *See* blendhing.

mléndho *reg* loose, slack.

mléndo 1 to not work any more (bad tools); 2 to turn out to be worthless (promise).

mlengah to look around happily, with a smiling face.

mléngak to turn the head to one side.

mlengèh, mlèngèh *see* mlengah.

mlengèk to look up in shock.

mlengkek *reg* to sulk.

mléngko *var of* mléngkong.

mléngkong bent, curving, not straight.

mlengok to look on in stunned surprise.

mlenguk ready (to hand).

mleni, tani - (to live) soberly (*esp a* man).

mlenis (*pron as:* mleni:s) small, smooth, round and attractive. *See also* menis.

mlenos *or* mlenos-mlenos smooth and shiny.

mlénthé of easy morals (woman).

mlenthi *see* plenthi.

mlenthing to have a little swelling (e.g. mosquito bite).

mlentho protruding, swollen.

mlenthos *var of* mlenthus.

mlenthus puffed up, swelling out. *See also* plenthus.

mlèntrèng *var of* mlantrang.

mlènyèh coming off, in a wet and slimy condition (skin).

mlenyèn *reg* neglected, left in an unfinished state.

mlenyok bruised, mushy (fruit).

mlépah, mlépah-mlépah to keep begging humbly, pitifully.

mlepes 1 sodden, water-logged; 2 limp,

dull, drained of one's strength; 3 to sit cross-legged with lowered head, *e.g.* when showing respect and humility before an older relative.

mlèpès *var of* mlepes.

mlepuh *see* plepuh.

mlérah, abang - blood-red.

mlèsdrèng *reg* beautiful, attractive.

mleseg *var of* mbleseg. *See* bleseg.

mlèsèh to lie flat on the ground.

mlété *reg var of* mloto.

mlethik to crack (glass).

mlethis 1 to crack; 2 to have a white fleck on the iris of the eye. *See also* plethis.

mletik 1 to emit sparks; 2 (of eye) *var of* mlethis. *See also* pletik.

mlewa-mlewu *reg* luxurious, extravagant.

mléwah *var of* mbléwah. *See* bléwah.

mlèwèd *var of* mlèwèr.

mlèwèh to open up wide (*var of* mblèwèh). *See* blèwèh, plèwèh.

mlèwèr *reg* to overflow, spill out/over.

mlicat *var of* mlicèt.

mlicèt to graze, rub (skin). *See also* plicèt.

mliding, kuning - fair, light, fresh clear yellow (skin).

mligi 1 pure, honest; 2 only, nothing but; mligèkaké to specialise.

mlikat *reg* angry, stern.

mliklik *reg* stingy, mean.

mlilé not much good.

mlincur 1 negligent, not punctual; 2 to stay away (from school, work).

mlingseng *intsfr* very dark (skin).

mlingsi hard, glossy.

mlinjo a certain tree the young leaves, flowers, and fruits of which are used in vegetable dishes; also, the hard-shelled nut-like fruit of this tree, fried as a snack or made into chips.

mlinthis bald and shiny.

mlintu uninterrupted, one after the other (*var of* lumintu).

mlinyah *var of* mlènyèh.

mlinyèh *var of* mlènyèh.

mlipis elegant, accomplished, refined. *See also* plipis.

mliring *reg* 1 to be off/aside (from); 2 to (move aside and) make way for.

mlithit 1 beautifully groomed; 2 well-dressed; 3 kept shiny and oily.

mliwé *var of* mlilé.

mliwis a species of wild duck.

mloco to slide down, slip off.

mlocoh *reg* 1 to peel (burned skin); 2 to fade (colour); 3 to fail to keep a promise.

mlodhok to peel (burned skin).

mlodong *reg* fair, light (skin) (*var of* mliding).

mlokèk *var of* mblokèk. *See* blokèk.

mlolé to gaze unblinking, stare in wide-eyed wonder.

mlolèk *var of* mlolé.

mlolèr *var of* mlolé.

mlolo to gaze wide-eyed.

mlondho young and inexperienced. *See also* kemlondho.

mlonyoh soft, mushy, squashed.

mlopor runny, gone soft.

mlosdrong *var of* mlèsdrèng.

mlosnong *reg* stark naked.

mlosoh rotten through and through, decomposing. *See also* losoh.

mlosok to collapse, fall down on the spot.

mloto to chatter and make jokes.

mlowa *reg var of* mulwa.

mlowèh gaping open, with nasty holes.

mlowoh *var of* mlowèh.

mlowok *var of* mlowèh.

mloyok tumbledown, decrepit. *See also* ployok.

mludag *var of* mbludag. *See* bludag.

mlukèk *reg* to feel nauseated, vomit.

mlukok *var of* mlukèk.

mlulèk to look longingly (at a woman).

mlulu *reg* only, nothing but.

mlunthuh *intsfr* complete, total.

mlunthus 1 bald; 2 having the hair combed very flat and close to the head; 3 without any make-up on.

mlunus big, round and bald.

mluwa vacant, not in use, uncultivated.

mluwèk gaping open. *See also* pluwèk.

moal *reg* impossible. *See also* mokal.

mobah to move;

   mobah-mosik to move slightly. *See also* obah.

moblah, moblah-moblah spacious, roomy. *See also* oblah.

moblong, moblong-moblong full, round and radiant (woman's face).

mobol, mobol-mobol to come out, spill out (contents of s.t.).

mobrol *var of* mobol.

mobrot, mobrot-mobrot in disorder, messy. *See also* obrot.

mobyar, mobyar-mobyar flaming, blazing.

mobyor, mobyor-mobyor brilliant, glowing, flourishing.

moco-moco to bulge, protrude (*var of* mucu-mucu).

mod, ngemod *reg* to hold or suck s.t. in the mouth (*var of* mut).

modang a plain panel in the centre of a batiked head or breastcloth.

modar 1 *cr* to die; 2 to hell with…!

modhal capital (to be) invested;

   modhali to provide s.o. with capital.

modhal-madhil pulled apart. *See* odhal-adhil.

modhal-madhul. *See also* adhul.

modhe 1 fashion; 2 to be in fashion.

modhèl 1 a model, example to be followed; 2 a small-scale representation of s.t.; 3 style, fashion; 4 strange, unaccustomed, new;

   modhèl to make s.t. in a certain fashion;

   modhèl-modhèl strange (of conduct, behaviour).

modhi kèngser a certain sideways shuffling step in a female classical dance.
See also wedhi kèngser.

modhol, modhol-modhol 1 in disorder,
in a terrible mess; 2 disembowelled.
See odhol IV.

modin 1 one who calls to prayers,
muezzin; 2 village religious functionary.

modir *var of* modar.

modo-modo to emerge, rise, grow higher
and higher.

moga I *reg* a new idea, discovery.
II a sash, band (part of ceremonial
costume).
III *reg* to fail, be useless.
IV *lit* 1 suddenly; 2 thereupon; 3 and
therefore.

mogak-magik unstable, wobbly. *See also*
ogak-agik.

mogal *reg* to get moving quickly.

mogat *reg* to have the intention to.

mogèl 1 to be able to move, be working;
2 ora - broke, with nothing more to
spend. *See also* ogèl.

moglé to protrude, stick out. *See also*
oglé, oglèng.

mogok 1 to stop, stall, fail to work; 2 to
disobey orders; 3 to refuse to work, go
on strike; 4 a strike;
mogok-mogok to just sit down doing
nothing, hang around;
mogokan apt to break down.

mogol 1 raw, uncooked; 2 only half done,
not finished; 3 to get stuck, unable to
think it through.

mograg-magreg to get stuck repeatedly.
See also greg.

moh unwilling, to not want to. *See also*
emoh.

mohèl *reg* ugly, bad.

mojah 1 sock; 2 glove.

mojèd *reg, cr* dead, to die.

mojèl in death throes.

mojid *var of* mojèd.

mok *repr* touching. *See also* emok.

mokah to break a fast by eating before
the time is up. *Also* mukah.

mokal impossible, out of the question;
mokalaké to regard as impossible.

mokcung not the same length, uneven.

mokla *reg* blood.

moklak-maklik in a wobbly, unsteady
condition. *See* oklak-aklik.

moklèk *reg* broken (*var of* coklèk).

moklis *see* muklis.

moksa *var of* muksa.

moksèl selfish, self-centred.

moksil *var of* moksèl.

mol *or* mak mol *repr* snatching by the
fistful;
mal-mol to keep snatching fistfuls.

molah-malih *see* malih II.

molai *var of* mulai.

molak-malik *see* walik.

molana *var of* maulana.

molang *reg* dealer in livestock.

molar-malir to glance back and forth.

molèk I *reg* to toss and turn in one's
sleep.
II 1 (of tobacco) good quality; 2 nice,
good.

molèr to hang down long.

molo I 1 ridge (of roof); 2 counting-word
for houses.
II, molo-molo to bulge with fullness
(mouth).

molog 1 fat and round; - atiné contented,
happy.

molor 1 to stretch, get longer and longer
in time or space; 2 to laze around; 3 *cr*
to sleep.

momah-momuh *reg* luxurious, extravagant.

momog, kemomogen, *see* wowog.

momoh, momohan worn out, ragged. *See
also* amoh.

momok I bogeyman (used to frighten
children).
II, momoki to apply, plaster s.t. on.

momol soft, tender (meat).

momong to take care of or bring up (children);

    momongan 1 a child to take care of; 2 a princess, girl of noble birth given as a wife;

    momong sarira 1 to care for one's appearance; 2 to be unmarried (girl, woman).

    See also among, mong II.

momor, - sambu spy, enemy who works from within;

    momoran 1 to mix with; 2 ingredient; 3 mixture;

    kamomoran mixed with, combined with.

    See also mor, wor.

momot I 1 to be able to hold, contain; 2 to carry, be loaded with; 3 to be able to understand, grasp;

    momoti to load s.t. into/onto;

    momotaké to load s.t.; to load for s.o.;

    momotan 1 having the function of carrying things; 2 a load;

    pamomotan 1 place where things are loaded, loading zone; 2 a load.

    See also amot, mot.

    II mushy from overcooking.

momplok, momplok-momplok (of clothing) old, worn-out, ragged.

momplong ragged and full of holes (clothing).

momprot, momprot-momprot messy.

mompyor to glitter, sparkle.

mon *lit* if, when (*var of* lamun I).

moncèr 1 clean, clear (liquid); 2 clear, detailed; 3 clever, intelligent; 4 to run, work well; 5 famous.

moncol *see* poncol.

moncong 1 snout; 2 (of people) *cr* mouth-rot; 3 to squirt/gush out.

moncrot to spurt out (any liquid). *See also* mèncrèt.

mondar-mandir to move back and forth aimlessly.

mondhah *reg* to nag. *See also* pothah.

mondhol, mondholan cloth knot at the back of a fabric headdress (blangkon, iket);

    mondhol-mondhol stuffed full (*var of* méndhol).

mondrèng *reg* female dancer.

mondring *var of* mondrèng.

moneng *see* oneng.

mong I *lit* tiger.

    II, ngemong to take care of (a child);

    ngemongaké to look after s.o.'s child for them;

    mong-kinemong to take care of each other.

    See also among, momong.

    III *reg* unwilling, to not want to (*var of* moh).

mongah, mongah-mongah red-hot, scorching, scalding.

monga-mangu *see* mangu.

mongal-mangil uncertain, wavering.

monggang *see* munggang.

monggat-manggut *see* manggut.

monggrak-manggrik 1 rickety; 2 sickly.

mongkak-mangkèk to change frequently, go from one thing to another.

mongkog proud. *See also* ongkog.

mongkrong I 1 to sit up high with the legs drawn up; 2 to sit around doing nothing. *See also* ongkrong.

    II *reg* wild boar hunter.

mongsok *excl of disbelief* (*var of* mangsa II).

mongsra-mangsru furious (*var of* mosra-masru).

monjo *reg* superior to one's fellows. *See also* onjo.

monmon s.t. one has a special desire for, specially selected and stored away to enjoy later.

mono *ng*, I (manten *kr*), unit of that scope; semono one such unit, so much, as much as that.

    II *shtf* mengkono (mekaten *kr*) (high-

lighting the preceding word) as for… (in contrast to s.t. else).

montang-manting *see* **ontang-anting, panting.**

monté bead (*var of* **moté**).

monten I cotton fabric (*kr for* **mori**).

II *md for* **mono**. *See also* **semonten.**

monthah *var of* **mothah.**

monthak-manthuk *see* **anthuk.**

monthol, montholan cloth knot at the back of a fabric headdress (**blangkon, iket**);

monthol-monthol stuffed full. *See also* **mondhol.**

montip locomotive.

montog *see* **ontog.**

montok I 1 big-bosomed; **2** plump and full (breast).

montong *see* **ontong.**

montor I 1 motor; **2** car; - **mabur** aeroplane; **pit** - motorcycle;

montor-montoran 1 toy car; **2** to go by car (or motorcycle).

II, montor-montor (*var of* **mèntèr-mèntèr**, *see* **mèntèr I**).

monyar-manyir untrustworthy.

monyèt 1 monkey; **2** *term of abuse*; **kathok** - child's overalls.

monyong 1 *cr* mouth; **2** *term of abuse*; **3** protruding (lips);

monyong-monyong to keep poking the lips out.

monyos, ora monyos *reg* unable, incapable.

mopo to rebel, resist, refuse (to do s.t.).

moprok to accumulate, get piled up. *See also* **oprok, poprok II.**

mor mixed;

ngemor *or* **ngemori** to mix s.t. with (s.t. else);

ngemoraké to make/let (things) mingle or mix;

mor-moran mixture.

See also **awor, amor, momor, wor.**

morah *reg* to nag (*var of* **mothah**).

morak-marik messed up, in disarray. *See also* **orak-arik.**

morat-marit *var of* **morak-marik.**

morèg to fidget, unable to sit still.

morèh streaked, *esp* with blood.

mori white cotton fabric, unbleached plain cloth (used for batik, shrouds *etc*).

mos *or* **mak mos** *repr* dripping out; **ngemos-mos** to waste, squander (s.o.'s property).

mosak-masik *see* **osak-asik.**

mosèl *var of* **moksil.**

mosik to move slightly.

mosil *var of* **moksil.**

moso, moso-moso *reg* to keep pressing s.o. angrily. *See also* **oso.**

mosok *excl of disbelief* (*var of* **mangsa**).

mosra-masru furious.

mot *ng*, **wrat** *kr*, **ngemot 1** to hold, contain; **2** (*or* **ngemoti**) to load s.t.; **ngemotaké** to load s.t. into/onto.

See also **amot, momot.**

moté bead (*also* **monté**).

motha 1 sail-cloth, canvas; **2** tent. *See also* **potha.**

mothah to nag. *See also* **pothah.**

mothal-mathil loose, coming off/apart.

mothar-mathir *var of* **mothal-mathil.**

mothik sickle (*var of* **muthik**).

mothuk *reg* **1** to agree; **2** to go well (with), suit (*var of* **mathuk**).

moto I monosodium glutamate, Aji-no-moto.

II *see* **poto.**

motol, motol-motol filled to bursting point, bulging (pocket).

motor *var of* **montor.**

mowak, mowak-mowak large (torn opening).

mowal, mowal-mowal torn, ragged, in shreds.

mowad-mawud *see* **mawud.**

mowol, mowol-mowol to fall apart, spill out.

mowot *reg* to cross a makeshift bridge. *See also* wot.

moyag-mayig wobbly, shaky. *See also* oyag.

moyag-mayug *var of* moyag-mayig.

moyang I to travel about; 2 restless, thinking of this and that; moyang-mayèng to move about, be unsettled. II nènèk - ancestors.

moyar confused (thoughts, feelings) (*var of* muyar).

mpu *see* empu.

mpun *see* pun, sampun.

mrabuk *lit* 1 fragrant; 2 to pervade (fragrance).

mracang to sell groceries.

mradeksa *lit* 1 to stand; 2 to rule, govern.

mraja *lit* king, monarch.

mrajak to flourish, grow vigorously (plants).

mragang, - gawé to set to work.

mrak-ati lovely, sweet.

mraman to spread (fire). *Also* mrèmèn.

mrambat *see* rambat.

mrambut rice chaff, outer husk of rice grain.

mramong to burn hotly, glow.

mramyong glorious, bright, splendid.

mrana *ng*, mrika *kr*, (to go) to that place; mranakaké to put s.t. (over) there (*pass* diranakaké); mrana-mrana (to go) to various places; mrana-mréné here and there.

mrancang to design, make a plan. *See also* rancang.

mranggi the maker of wooden sheaths for krises and pikes.

mranggo *var of* mranggu.

mranggu uncertain, hesitant.

mrangkang *var of* mbrangkang. *See* brangkang.

mrangsud to slide down.

mrantak I to spread out (over s.t.) (*also* mrèntèk). II poor.

mrantu, mrantu-mrantu to go from one place to another.

mrantun *var of* mrantu.

mrapit to close, join (ranks).

mrasa to feel. *See also* rasa.

mrasah to lie on the ground.

mrasuk to permeate completely. *See also* rasuk.

mratah to become known everywhere.

mratak 1 *var of* mrantak; 2 *var of* merkatak I.

mratanggung *see* mertanggung.

mrayang (of spirits) to roam. *See also* prayang.

mré *lit*, *var of* meré I.

mrebeng *see* merbeng.

mrebes *var of* mbrebes. *See also* brebes.

mrècèt to present o.s. nicely, be well dressed.

mrèdèh *reg* stubborn, intractable.

mregil isolated, secluded.

mreki *var of* merki.

mrelik *var of* merlik.

mrem I *lit* satisfied. *See also* marem. II *lit* to close the eyes. *See also* merem.

mrembeng 1 to go red in the face, *e.g.* when on the verge of crying; 2 *reg* to get flushed angrily. *See also* prembeng.

mrembes *see* rembes.

mrèmbèt *see* rèmbèt.

mrèmèn to spread.

mrempeng I to do in earnest. *See also* srempeng. II to flush in anger. *See also* prempeng.

mremyeng *or* mremyeng-mremyeng vague, obscure, hazy.

mrending nearly frayed through.

mréné *ng*, mriki *kr*, (to come) here/to this place; mrènèkaké to bring s.t. in this direction (*pass* dirènèkaké); mréna-mréné to keep coming here.

mrenèng *var of* mernèng.

mrenges, ireng - pitch black.

mrenget to become feverish.

mrenggik tapering hourglass-style in the middle.

mrengguk to grumble with dissatisfaction.

mréngkal to resist obstinately, be unwilling to cooperate.

mrengkang to resist, be recalcitrant (toward authorities).

mrèngkèl *var of* mréngkal.

mrengkeng stubborn, unwilling to move.

mrèntèk (*var of* mrantak).

mrènyèh *var of* mlènyèh.

mrenyen nicely, neatly dressed.

mrépal abundant, overflowing, plentiful.

mrepat (villages) surrounding one's village.

mrepeg *reg* to be pressed for time.

mrepèpèh *see* repèpèh.

mres *lit* to squeeze (out). *See also* pres I.

mresep to seep in. *See also* resep II.

mrecut, mrecuti beginning to ripen (rice).

mrica 1 pepper (white or black); 2 clubs (playing-card suit).

mricit *var of* mrècèt.

mrih *lit* in order to; so that.

mrik *lit* fragrant.

mrika (to go) to that place (*kr for* mrana);
　mrikakaken to move s.t. there (*pass* dipunrikakaken).

mriki (to come) to this place (*kr for* mréné);
　mrikèkaken to move s.t. here (*pass* dipunrikèkaken).

mrina to take to heart (insult or injury to s.o. else);
　mrinani 1 to be such that people want to defend you; 2 to stick up for, be concerned about s.o.
　Also murina.

mrinding to shudder, have the shudders, have the skin crawl, the creeps.

mring *lit* to, toward.

mringin (to sleep) with eyes slightly open.

mringkus shrunken. *See also* pringkus.

mrinyu village messenger, policeman (*var of* marinyu).

mripat *ng, kr* paningal *or* soca *k.i.* human eye (*see also* mata).

mriyang *see* priyang.

mriyangyang *lit* to rise up to the realm of the gods.

mriyem 1 a cannon, gun; 2 to fire on with cannon;
　mriyeman imitation cannon, toy cannon.

mriyi small and sickly (plants).

mriyos pepper (*subst kr for* mrica).

mrojok *reg* to flourish, grow vigorously (plants). *See also* mrajak.

mrokah 1 glowing; 2 merry, gay.

mrono *ng,* mriku *kr,* to that place;
　mronokaké to move s.t. in that direction (*pass* dironokaké).
　See also rono.

mrosot 1 to drop, fall; 2 to become low(er), decrease, decline;
　mrosotaké to cause to decline.

mrucah *reg* to cut into pieces. *See also* prutah.

mrucut to slip through the fingers. *See also* prucut.

mruga *var of* murga.

mrujuk *var of* mrajak, mrojok.

mrukah *var of* mrokah.

mrungsal *var of* mursal, mrusal.

mrupug dry and brittle.

mrusal *var of* mursal.

mrusuh I 1 soft, chubby, round (woman's body); 2 soft, well-cooked.
　II *see* prusuh.

mrusul bold, insolent, wild.

mrutu a kind of very small gnat (its bite causes itching).

mruwat *var of* murwat.

mruwun unkempt, tousled (hair).

mu 1 just now; 2 the aforesaid (*inf var of* mau).

mualap a convert to Islam.

mualim 1 guide, leader, teacher; 2 skipper, navigator.

mubadir to waste s.t.

mubah I permitted, *i.e.* neither recommended nor forbidden according to Islamic law.
II *reg* to come to nothing.

mubal to flare up, burst forth, pour over; **mubal-mubal** 1 to spread rapidly (fire); 2 *fig* very angry.
See also **ubal**.

mubalig preacher, religious propagator.

mubarang *or* **samubarang** *ng*, **mukawis** *or* **samukawis** *kr*, everything, anything at all; whatever.

mubilèr furniture.

mublak *or* **mublak-mublak** 1 evenly white, pale (complexion); 2 spacious, wide, open (land).

mubra-mubru to be well-off, able to afford anything, be living in luxury.

mubyar *or* **mubyar-mubyar** 1 bright, glowing, glary; 2 luxurious.

mucu, mucu-mucu 1 to bulge, protrude; 2 to pout mockingly.

mudal *see* **udal**.

mudalèh to confess, acknowledge one's mistake.

mudaris teacher of religion.

muded to rotate rapidly, spin.

mudha I *lit* 1 young; 2 the youth; **mudha tumaruna** (male) teenager.
II *lit* foolish, stupid.

mudhak *see* **budhak**.

mudhak-mudhek to walk to and fro, keep hanging around.

mudheng to understand; **mudhengaké** 1 to cause to understand; 2 comprehensible; **mudhengan** quick to understand.

mudhi I young (of females).
II *inf var of* **kemudhi**.

mudhik *see* **udhik** I.

mudhun 1 to descend; 2 to get off. *See also* **dhun, medhun, udhun**.

muga *ng*, **mugi** *kr*, (*or* **muga-muga**) may it happen that...; I hope, let's hope.

mugag-mugeg to get stuck, unable to go any further.

mugal to move aside agilely.

mugen 1 to stay calm; 2 to stay quietly at home to reflect; 3 to stick to one's guns, not budge.

muget, muget-muget *or* **mugat-muget** 1 to wriggle, squirm (on the spot); 2 to not shift, not get ahead. *See also* **uget**.

mugi may it happen that... (*kr for* **muga**).

mugut *var of* **munggut**.

muha *reg var of* **muwa**.

Muharam the 1st month of the Islamic calendar, **Sura**.

muhun *lit, var of* **muwun**.

muhung *lit* only, just. *See also* **mung** I.

mujadah to restrain carnal desires.

mujaèr *var of* **mujair**.

mujair an edible freshwater fish.

mujarab effective, efficacious.

mujisat *var of* **mukjijat**.

mujuh *reg* to accept, ask money (from a lover).

mujung to lie down covered with a blanket.

mujur I lucky. *See also* **ujur** II.
II in a lengthwise position. *See also* **ujur**.

muk I only, just (*coll var of* **mung**).
II, **muk-mukan** to grope about (like a blind person).
III 1 mug; 2 a large tin for **krupuk** *etc*.

muka *lit* face.

mukah to break a fasting period by eating before the time is up. *Also* **mokah**.

mukalid beloved by God.

mukarab close to God.

Mukaram *var of* **Muharam**.

mukaranah *reg* in the middle of (do)ing, coinciding with.

mukawis *or* **samukawis** everything, anything whatever (*kr for* **mubarang, samubarang**).

muket I *see* puket.

II 1 well mixed, so that the taste permeates; 2 tasty, delicious; 3 pleasing (story).

mukim 1 place of residence, location; 2 to live s.w.

mukir to deny (*var of* mungkir); mukar-mukir to keep denying.

mukitun all-embracing.

mukjijat 1 miracle; 2 the power to work miracles (of prophets).

muklis of a modest, retiring character.

mukmin the believers, the faithful.

mukok to throw up, to regurgitate (babies).

mukrim a female relative whom one is not allowed to marry but may associate with.

muksa 1 to be released from the body; 2 to vanish; 3 to die by the body vanishing; kamuksan release from the world.

muksil self-centred.

mukta *lit* dead; to die.

muktamar congress, conference.

muktamat authoritative (opinion, on Islamic religion).

mukti 1 to taste, enjoy; 2 comfortable, having a good life; - wibawa to devote o.s. to worldly pleasures, live a life of pleasure; muktèkaké provide s.o. with a good life; kamuktèn the good life, worldly comforts.

mukya *lit* foremost; mantri - chief minister (*see also* mantri).

mul, mul-mulan (to play) a game resembling checkers.

mula *ng*, mila *kr*, 1 originally; from the beginning; 2 (*or* mulané, mulakna *reg*) therefore, so, that is why; -buka origin, very beginning.

mulad, mulad-mulad to blaze, glow, burn brightly.

mulai *ng*, milai *kr*, to start, begin.

mulak, mulak-mulak to boil, bubble up, seethe.

mulana *var of* maulana.

mular to cry, weep (*reg kr for* nangis).

mulat *see* wulat.

mulé *or* memulé 1 to honour (deceased ones); 2 to preserve (old traditions).

mules to have stomach cramps. *See also* pules.

mulih *ng*, mantuk *kr*, kondur *k.i.* to go home. *See also* ulih.

mulku 1 palace; 2 king.

mulu I, *reg* mulu-mulu according to, depending on.

II somewhat rounded.

mulud 1 birth and death day of the Prophet Muhammad, on 12 Rabingul-awal; 2 the 3rd Islamic month; muludan 1 religious festival celebrated on the Prophet's birthday; 2 to recite Arabic texts with tambourine music to celebrate the Prophet's birthday.

mulung *see* ulung II.

mulur 1 to stretch, expand; 2 to exceed (a limit); 3 to become longer and longer. *See also* molor, ulur.

mulus pure, flawless, unadulterated.

mulut *reg* mouth.

mulwa 'bullock's heart' fruit, a variety of custard-apple.

mulya I restored to its former condition; mulyakaké to restore. *See also* pulih.

II 1 high, worthy; 2 to live in luxury, blessed with happiness and wealth; mulyakaké 1 to honour, hold in esteem; 2 to celebrate; minulya esteemed, honoured; kamulyan 1 prosperity; 2 honour, esteem.

mumah-mumuh *reg* luxurious, very wealthy.

mumblug *var of* mumbluk.

mumbluk foamy, frothy, sudsy.

mumbra-mumbru *reg* very wealthy.

mumbruk *or* mumbruk-mumbruk piled in a disorderly heap. *See also* umbruk.

mumbuk *var of* mumbruk.

mumet *see* umet.

mumpal, mumpal-mumpal boiled.

mumpang-mumpung *see* pumpung.

mumpangat use (*var of* munpangat).

mumpluk frothy, bubbly, sudsy.

mumpung *see* pumpung.

mumpuni 1 to have mastered; 2 skilled in all the sciences.

mumpyar *var of* mompyor.

mumuk *see* mamak-mumuk.

mumur pulverised. *See also* ajur.

mumut mushy from overcooking (*var of* momot II).

munajat to be in prayer with God.

munajim astrologer.

muna-muni *see* uni.

munapèk an unbeliever who pretends to be a Muslim, hypocrite.

munasabah in accordance with.

munasika to disturb, interfere with, plague.

muncang *reg kr for* kemiri, candlenut.

muncar sparkling, glittering.

muncèr *var of* moncèr.

munci *reg* housekeeper, concubine.

muncis 1 to fade, grow pale (colour); 2 emaciated.

muncla, muncla-muncla to get ruder and ruder.

munclup, munclap-munclup to keep popping in and out.

muncu *var of* mucu. *See also* puncu.

muncul to emerge, appear, turn up. *See also* uncul.

muncung animal's snout.

muncrat to spurt up/out, splash. *See also* uncrat.

mundhak 1 to increase, become greater; 2 to rise in rank; 3 or else, otherwise, lest. *See also* undhak I.

mundhing *reg* water buffalo.

mundhu a certain tree, also its fruit.

mundhuk, mundhuk-mundhuk (to walk) in a stooping or lowered position, as when passing esteemed persons who are seated, so as not to be too elevated.

mundhung (*or* kemundhung) a certain tree with sour fruit.

mundri I nipple (*k.i. for* penthil).
II golden tassel on a fez (kuluk).

mundur to move backward;
kemunduren too far back. *See also* undur.

muneg, muneg-muneg *or* munag-muneg queasy, nauseated.

mung I *ng*, namung *kr*, only, just;
ngemungaké to do only, think only of;
mung-mungan not more than, not much.
II a variety of small green bean.
III *repr* gong beats.

mungal protruding (*esp* the chest). *See also* ungal.

mungal-mangil hesitant, uncertain.

munger, munger-munger queasy, nauseated.

munggah *see* unggah.

munggang 1 Kyai - name of an archaic three-toned gamelan kept in the Kratons of Yogyakarta and Surakarta, played only on solemn occasions; 2 gendhing - the melody played on this gamelan. *Also* monggang.

munggèng *lit* (situated, located) in, on, at.

mungging *var of* munggèng.

mungguh *ng*, menggah *kr*, 1 (*also* mungguha) in case, in the event that; 2 about, as for, in connection with; 3 now (*as a narrational device*); 4 *ng, kr*, appropriate, fitting;
mungguhné *or* samungguhna supposing.

munggul superior, outstanding. *See also* unggul.

munggur **I** *reg* a certain large tree.
II 1 to stand out, rise (ground, hill); **2** to be placed in a high position (*var of* mengger).
III *reg* to top, poll (a tree). *See* punggur.

munggut to rise (fish);
munggut-munggut to get exasperated.

mungil to be in view (of small things).

mungkar *or* mungkar-mungkar to keep adding to one's possessions.

mungkag-mungkug *see* mungkug.

mungkir to deny, disavow (*also* mukir).

mungkok to throw up (*var of* mukok).

mungkred to shrink. *See* ungkred.

mungkug, mungkug-mungkug *or* mungkag-mungkug nauseated.

mungkul **1** to bow the head; **2** to concentrate on doing s.t. *See also* tungkul.

mungkur **1** past, overdue; **2** to turn one's back; **3** to refuse to cooperate; -gangsir not willing to intervene, to mind one's own business. *See also* pungkur.

mungsik *see* musik.

mungsing a variety of swordfish.

mungsra-mungsru furious (*var of* mosra-masru).

mungsuh *ng*, mengsah *kr*, enemy, opponent;
mungsuhi to be against, to attack;
mungsuhaké to set (one force) against (another);
mungsuhan *or* memungsuhan **1** in conflict with each other; **2** enmity, hostility.

mungur-mungur **1** red in the face; **2** furiously angry.

mungut, mungut-mungut to look stern.

muni **I** *lit* an ascetic, sage.
II 1 to emit sounds; **2** to say. *See* uni I.

munpangat use, benefit;
munpangati useful, beneficial;
munpangataké to put s.t. to use.

muntab to lose one's temper. *See* untab.

munté *var of* moté.

muntéring *see* mentéring.

muntha sailcloth, canvas (*var of* motha).

munthil *or* munthil-munthil small tight knot, *esp* in a Javanese-style hairdo.

munthu small wooden or stone tool used for grinding spices in a flat bowl (layah);
munthu katutan sambel *idiom* (of people) to be related only indirectly.

munthul *reg* cassava.

munting **1** with meagre fruits (tree); **2** very thin, spindly.

muntiyara *var of* mutiyara.

muntlap-muntlup to keep popping in and out.

muntup, muntup-muntup to peep out, show a little. *See* untup.

munyal, munyal-munyal to get ruder and ruder.

munyeng **1** to spin, rotate; **2** dizzy. *See* unyeng.

munyer **1** to spin, whirl; **2** to search high and low.

munyet to spin, whirl (thoughts).

munyik *reg* to smile.

munyuk **I** the young of the monkey.
II, munyuk-munyuk to approach slowly, come creeping in (in bowed posture, in humility or embarrassment);
munyak-munyak to keep on coming (unexpectedly, *e.g.* unwanted guests).

mupakat **1** to agree; **2** agreement;
mupakati to agree to/on/with;
mupakataké to bring into agreement;
mupakatan to reach an agreement with each other.

mupangat *var of* munpangat.

mupruk piled up, in big heaps, abundant.

mupung *var of* mumpung. *See* pumpung.

mur **I** nut for a bolt, screw.
II *lit* to disappear.
III watered silk, embroidered with gold or silver thread, for making kuluk.

IV myrrh.

mura *lit* to go away.

murad *lit* 1 intention; 2 meaning, significance.

murah *ng*, mirah *kr*, 1 cheap, low in price; 2 to be plentifully endowed with; 3 generous, gracious, merciful (God);
murahi to lower the price of (goods);
murahaké to make cheap;
murah-murahan at reduced rates;
murahan a cheap low-quality article;
kamurahan mercy, grace.

murakabi helpful, advantageous.

murang I to deviate from the normal way; - sarak *or* - tata contrary to good manners, rude.
II *reg* to lose its leaves (tree).

murat I completely finished, nothing left.
II pudenda.

murba to rule, have authority over. *See also* purba I.

murbé mulberry.

murbèng *contracted form of* murba ing (*see* murba);
kang Murbèng Dumadi 'He Who Rules Creation', God.

murca *lit* to faint, swoon.

murcat *lit* dead.

murcita *lit* to faint, swoon.

murda *lit* head; aksara - capital letter.

murga *or* murgan to make extra (in order to have enough).

murid 1 pupil, disciple; 2 schoolchild.

murih for the purpose of, in order to. *See* purih.

murina *lit*, *var of* mrina.

muring I *or* muring-muring (duka *k.i.*) to growl, grumble in dissatisfaction.
II a variety of small fly.

murit ring.

murka 1 selfish, greedy; 2 stupid, foolish; 3 furious;
kamurkan anger. *See also* angkara.

murni unmixed, pure, genuine; mas - solid gold.

murong *reg* to smoulder.

mursal badly-behaved, out of control.

mursid pious, God-fearing.

mursita *see* wursita.

murta *lit* to vanish, disappear.

murtad 1 apostate, renegade; 2 to renounce the Faith.

murti *lit* embodiment.

murud *lit* 1 to depart; 2 to pass away. *See also* surud.

murus to have diarrhoea. *See also* urus II.

murwakala a certain shadow-play story performed as a ritual to ward off calamities. *See also* purwakala.

murwat 1 in proportion; 2 to estimate, assess (value);
murwati to bring into proportion;
murwatan estimation, assessment;
samurwaté whatever is in proportion with.

musakat misery, distress.

musala *lit* club, cudgel.

musanip author, writer.

musapir traveller, wanderer, mendicant.

musarakat *var of* masarakat.

musawarat deliberation, negotiation;
musawarataké to discuss, deliberate over, negotiate;
musawaratan 1 deliberation; 2 to hold a meeting, engage in deliberations.

musi motion (passed by meeting).

musibat cursed, damned.

musik 1 music in Western style; 2 band.

musikan a musician, bandsman.

musikum religious address given by the pengulu containing advice to the bride and groom.

muslim a Muslim.

muslimah a female Muslim.

muslimin Muslims.

musna *lit* to vanish, disappear.

muspra in vain, for nothing.

musrik polytheist, heathen.

mustail impossible, inconceivable, out of the question.

mustajab potent, efficacious.

mustaka head (*k.i. for* sirah).

mustakil *var of* mustail.

mustapa beloved, the chosen (of God).

musthi *var of* mesthi.

musthika 1 bezoar; 2 the most excellent, a jewel.

mustijab *var of* mustajab.

mustika a fine jewel.

musuh *var of* mungsuh.

mut, ngemut to suck, hold in the mouth;
  ngemuti to put s.t. in the mouth and suck it;
  ngemutaké to put s.t. in s.o.'s mouth to hold or suck on;
  mut-mutan s.t. one holds in the mouth to suck, sweets.

mutabar known, well-known, spread.

mutajilah *lit* astray, in error, wrong.

mutah 1 to pour out; 2 to vomit, throw up; 3 (of colours) to run; - cècèk to vomit completely. *See* utah, wutah.

mutamat *var of* muktamat.

mutasawur interchangeable, unclear.

mutatuli *see* wutatuli.

mutawatir *ng*, mutawatos *kr*, fearful, apprehensive;
  mutawatiri provoking fear or apprehension, dangerous.

mutawatos *kr for* mutawatir.

muthakil full of tricks.

muthek to sit at home, not stir. *See* uthek I.

muthik sickle.

muthu *var of* munthu.

mutiyara pearl.

mutik *reg* offended, feeling angry toward s.o.

mutlak unconditional, absolute.

mutmainah at rest, at peace (soul).

mutra I *lit* urine.
  II mutrani *see* putra.

mutyara *see* mutiyara.

muwa *reg* to leave the nest (young bird).

muwah *lit ng*, miwah *kr* also, as well as.

muwak, muwak-muwak badly ripped.

muwal *reg* tender, soft (cooked food).

muwara rivermouth, estuary.

muwaril obstacle, prohibition.

muwat 1 to hold, have the capacity of; 2 to put s.t. in(to), load, carry.

muwel *see* uwel II.

muweng *var of* muwer.

muwer to spin, whirl.

muwun to weep, cry (*k.i. for* nangis).

muyar confused (thoughts, feelings).

muyeg *see* uyeg.

muyi, muyèn *reg* to remain awake during the night to watch over a newborn child.

mwang *lit* and, with.

myang *var of* mwang.

N

na I to exist, be (*shtf of* **ana**).
II Javanese letter; - **gandhul** *or* - **gond-hèl** a Javanese script character indicating *n* after a consonant.

naas unlucky, ill-omened (day, *e.g.* anniversary of a parent's death).

nabi I prophet;
kanabian *or* **kanabéan** 1 the office or position of prophet; 2 prophetic, pertaining to the prophets;
Nabi Isa Jesus;
nabi II (*k.i. for* **wudel**) navel.

nadar a vow (to do s.t. if prayer is granted; to make a promise of s.t.);
nadari to vow to present s.t.

nadi *lit* river.

nadhi pulse, artery.

nadyan even though, although (*shtf of* **sanadyan**).

najan *shtf of* **sanajan**, *see* **sanadyan**.

najis 1 filth, s.t. which causes pollution; 2 to have an abhorrence of;
najisaké to regard s.t. as unclean or abhorrent.

naèk *reg* to rise, be on the increase.

naga dragon, serpent; - **dina** serpent governing the propitiousness of directions taken in journey on a certain day; - **sasra** a kris blade with 13 curves.

nagara *lit* realm; city. *See also* **negara**.

nagari *kr for* **nagara**.

nagasari I a certain hardwood tree the fragrant flowers of which are used cosmetically.
II cake made from steamed rice flour and banana wrapped in banana leaf.
III a certain batik design.

nagri *see* **nagari**.

nagur I imitation, false (precious stone).
II to be halfway between, (only) partway to the goal.

nah I well, now!
II *adr* young lady (*shtf of* **nonah**).

nahan *var of lit* **nahen**.

nahen *lit* like this; well, then (often used to start a story).

nahas *var of* **naas**.

nahwu Arabic grammar, word formation.

nai *ng*, **ninja** *kr*, to have kittens. *See also* **tai**.

naib a local mosque official;
kenaiban residence of this official.

nain but (*reg var of* **nanging**).

naing *var of* **nain**.

nak 1 *adr* child (*shtf of* **anak**); -**dulur** (-**dhèrèk** *kr*) *or* -**sanak** first cousin;
nak-kumanak 1 to breed; 2 to flourish, multiply.

naka *lit* nail (*shtf of* **kenaka**).

nakal 1 naughty, mischievous; 2 ill-mannered, badly behaved; 3 promiscuous;
nakali to cheat s.o.;
nakal-nakalan 1 to try to get away with s.t.; 2 to compare or compete in bad behaviour.

nak-nik to keep handling s.t. with the fingers.

nakoda ship's captain.

nal, **nal-nalan** restless, fidgety.

nalangsa heartbroken, crushed with grief or hardship;
panalangsa feelings of grief or heartache.

nalar 1 mind, intellect, reason(ing power); 2 to think s.t. over; 3 reasonable, logical;
nalaraké to set out the reasons for.

naléndra *lit* king, monarch.

nalika (*or* **nalikané**) when (at a past time); - **kuwi** (- **punika** *kr*) *or* - **semana** (- **semantan** *kr*) at that time.

naluri I conscience, heart, instinct.

II 1 ancient customs; 2 ancestors, forefathers.

nam I, **ngenam** to weave (fibres); **ngenami** to make a woven article; **nam-naman** woven.

II, **nam-nam** (*or* **nam-naman** *reg*) a certain tree with fruit.

nama name (*kr for* **aran**, **jeneng**).

nambang *lit* thousand; **sanambang** one thousand.

nambong *var of* **nambung**.

nambung, - **laku** to keep on as if nothing has happened, act as if one knows nothing.

namèk *reg var of* **nanging**.

nami *kr* name (*var of* **nama**).

naming *reg var of* **nanging**.

nampéyan *reg* you, your (*var of* **sampéyan**).

namung only, just (*kr for* **mung**).

nanah pus; **nanahen** to have a pus-filled infection.

nanak-nunuk to grope one's way, go forward slowly.

nandalem *k.i.* you (when addressing a highly esteemed person).

nandhang to undergo, suffer, endure. *See also* **sandhang**.

nanjuk, **nanjuk-nanjuk** to keep knocking against, stumbling.

nanjung I *lit* to change (name). II *or* **sananjung** variety of basket (for rice).

nang I *adr* little boy. *See also* **kenang** II. II in, at, on. III (to go) to. IV to win (*shtf of* **menang**); **nang-nangan** to vie for top position.

nanging but, however.

nangka jackfruit; - **blonyo** sticky overripe jackfruit; - **sabrang** *or* - **Wlanda** soursop.

nangkoda ship's captain (*var of* **nakoda**).

nanthang-nanthang to act defiantly, throw one's weight about.

napa what (*md for* **apa**).

napas I breath; *fig* soul, life. II sorrel, bay (colour of horses).

napkah 1 income; 2 money given to one's wife for living expenses.

napi I what (*md for* **apa**, *var of* **napa**). II *reg* but, however.

napsi, **napsi-napsi** *reg* varying according to the circumstances.

napsu I *lit* anger. *See* **nepsu**, **nesu**. II *see* **hawa-napsu**.

naptu *var of* **neptu**.

nar, **nar-naran** *or* **nar-nir** in alarm and fright; **ngenari** alarming.

naraca I *lit* balance, scale. II *lit* arrow.

naradipa *lit* king, monarch.

naraka hell.

narakarya *lit* worker, labourer.

naranata *lit* king, monarch.

narapati *lit* king, monarch.

narapraja *lit* dignitary, official.

nararya *lit* king, monarch.

narawantah *lit* excellent.

narayana *lit* 1 young; 2 youth; **narayanani** to act as if young.

naréndra *lit* king, monarch.

naréswara *lit* king, monarch.

naréswari *lit* queen.

narmada *lit* river.

narpa *lit* king, monarch.

narpati *lit* king, monarch.

nas I *excl* calling attention in children's games: you're had your go, now it's my turn! II authoritative text or quotation (from the Quran), decisive dictum (to settle an issue).

naséhat advice, admonition.

nasib lot, destiny, fate.

Nasrani Christian; **agama** - Christianity.

nastapa *lit* 1 sad, sorrowing; 2 sadness, care.

nastijab efficacious, strong, powerful (medicine).

nastiti careful, scrupulous, precise;
  nastitèkaké to do carefully, take great
  care over s.t.

nata *lit* king, monarch.

naté ever (*kr for* tau).

Natal Christmas;
  natalan to celebrate Christmas.

natkala *lit* when, at the time. *See also*
  tatkala.

natos ever (*kr, subst var of* naté).

natya *lit* facial expression.

nawa *lit* nine;
  babahan - sanga the nine bodily openings.

nawala *lit* a letter ; - patra letter written
  on palm leaf.

nawi *shtf of* menawi.

nawin *reg var of* jer, rak.

naya I *lit* prudent conduct, prudence,
  wise policies.
  II *or* nayana countenance, facial
  expression.

nayadi *lit* friendly, smiling.

nayaga musician of a gamelan orchestra.
  See also niyaga.

nayaka 1 leader; 2 adviser to the king;
  3 minister.

nayung to fly in the air directly overhead
  (kite).

neb I, ngeneb *or* ngenebi to close (doors,
  windows);
  ngenebaké to close (doors, windows)
  for s.o.;
  neb-neban window shutters.
  See also ineb.
  II, meneb 1 to settle at the bottom of
  liquid; 2 calmed down after strong
  emotion;
  ngenebaké 1 to allow s.t. to settle at
  the bottom; 2 to calm s.o.

nebas-nebas *reg* to bump into things
  when fleeing; mlayu - to run away in
  fright.

nebok I *reg* to warn against.
  II *see* tebok.

neca *lit* facial expression.

nèces neat and orderly.

nècis *var of* nèces.

nedhas (of lips, tongue) rough, chapped.

nedheng *see* sedheng.

nèdhèng-nèdhèng to show o.s. openly.

nedya *see* sedya.

neg *see* nek.

negalé *reg* (look) over there!

negalo *reg, var of* negalé.

negara *ng*, negari *kr*, 1 capital (where the
  ruler resides); 2 main city (of a
  region); 3 realm; 4 country, state.

negari *kr for* negara.

nèger Negro.

negilé *reg* (look) here!

negilo *var of* negilé.

négin *reg* still, remaining (in a certain
  condition).

negulé *reg* (look) there!

negulo *var of* negulé.

nèh I 1 *excl* unbelieving; 2 after all.
  II more (*shtf of* manèh).

nek *see* enek.

nèk I *coll* if, when; that (*var of* yèn).
  II *coll* in, at, on (*var of* nèng, ana
  ing).
  III, nèké *or* nèk-nèké *coll* perhaps,
  probably.

néka, néka-néka various kinds (of
  things).

nekèk old for his age (boy).

nèkel nickel (metal); nickel-plated.

nèker marble(s);
  nèkeran to play marbles.

nèl, nèl-nèlan restless, fidgety.

nem six; -belas sixteen; -likur twenty-
  six;
  ngenemi to make six in number.

nèm young (*kr for* nom).

nembé 1 to be (do)ing (*kr for* lagi); 2 the
  future (*reg var of* tembé); 3 just (*kr for*
  mentas).

némbo *reg* to defecate on a large leaf and
  then throw it away.

némpol to be daubed, smeared (on s.t.).

néndra *lit* to sleep.

nènèk old woman, grandmother (*inf var of* nini).

nenem six (*var of* nem).

nenep *reg* to hide.

nenepi to withdraw to a quiet place for meditation. *See also* sepi.

nènèr baby milkfish (young of the bandeng).

nènès *lit* flirtatious, coquettish.

neng *lit, see* eneng.

nèng *coll* in, at, on (*shtc of* ana ing).

néngané *reg* well I never! (in amazement).

nenggala *lit* a kind of spear.

nenggih indeed, truly, in truth (stop-gap in verse).

nèngkès *reg* to persist with s.t. for a long time.

nènthèng, nènthèng-nènthèng to act defiantly. *See also* nanthang-nanthang.

nepdal *kr for* neptu.

néplé trivial, paltry, insignificant. *See also* séplé.

nepsu 1 impulse, urge; 2 angry;
kanepson anger. *See also* nesu.

neptu Javanese numerology, horoscope.

nepyu *reg* furious, raging.

ner *see* ener.

neraca *see* naraca I.

neraka *see* naraka.

nerpa, nerpati *lit* king, monarch.

nes *see* enes.

nesu *ng, kr,* duka *k.i.* angry, to become angry;
nesoni to be angry with, scold;
neson liable to get angry.

nestha I *var of* nistha.
II in the form of; - wolu eight-sided.

nesthil, nesthip *reg* contemptible, shameful (*var of* nistha).

nestiti *see* nastiti.

net *see* enet.

nèt I *var of* net.

II, ngenèt to copy out neatly, make a fair copy;
nèt-nètan fair copy of a draft.

nètèr slightly sloping.

nétra *lit* eye. *See also* tuna.

nétral non-denominational (education).

nétya *lit* shine, gleam, radiance.

nèwu *shtf of* panèwu. *See also* sèwu.

néyan *reg* how…! what…! (*stressing preceding word*). *See also* ané.

Ngaad Sunday.

ngabad *var of* abad.

ngabèhi, *or* angabèhi an official of middle rank in court hierarchy;
(pa)ngabéhan residence of the above official.

ngabèi *see* ngabèhi.

ngabekti to show deepest respect by kneeling and bowing before s.o.;
ngabektèn the action of showing one's respect as above;
kinabektèn esteemed, respected, honoured;
pangabekti one's respects.
See also bekti.

ngabid pious, devout.

ngabotohan to gamble. *See also* botoh.

ngabyantara in the presence (of the King).

ngadat *var of* adat.

ngadilaga battlefield (*var of* adilaga).

ngaèn *reg* certain, undoubted;
ngaènaké to confirm, ascertain, seek certainty.

ngagesang *lit, kr of* ngaurip life. *See also* urip.

ngah I *repr* to low (cattle).
II listless.
III, ngahi *reg* to give (*var of* ngèh). *See also* wèh.
IV, ngahi *reg* to leave (food *etc*) behind for s.o. (*var of* ngèh). *See also* ngèngèh.

Ngahad Sunday.

ngain *var of* ngaèn.

ngajeng in front (*kr for* ngarep). *See also* ajeng III.

ngak, ngak-ngak *repr* a goose honking; ngak-ngèk to keep crying. *See also* ngèk.

Ngakad *var of* Ngahad.

ngakak to roar with laughter. *See also* kakak.

ngakasa in, into the sky. *See* akasa, angkasa.

ngakèh *ng*, ngakathah *kr*, the public; many people. *See also* akèh.

ngakérat the hereafter (*var of* akérat).

ngakik I *reg* stunted in growth.
II *reg* cunning, sly.

ngalam world, universe (*var of* alam).

ngalamat 1 sign; 2 address;
ngalamati to be a sign of. *See also* alamat.

ngalek *reg* to hang in the air (aroma).

ngalik-alik high-pitched and shrill (voice). *See also* alik.

ngalim 1 learned; 2 religious scholar (*var of* alim);
ngaliman please forgive me (for not giving you anything: *usu* said to beggars).

ngalor *see* lor.

ngalualam fine needlework.

ngaluamah greedy, covetous.

ngaluhur noble. *See also* luhur.

ngamal good deed, charity (*var of* amal).

ngamanca a foreign country (*var of* manca).

ngana *ng*, ngaten *kr*, like that, in that way. *See also* mangkana, mangkono.

nganan oh, oh! what a pity! (*stress on preceding word*).

ngané *var of* nganan.

ngang *repr* flying.

ngangkrang a large red tree ant.

ngangrang I *var of* ngangkrang.
II, ngangrangan thin, gauzy (fabric).

ngangsi *reg* (*var of* nganti). *See also* kongsi.

ngantèk *var of* nganti.

ngantèn *var of* mantèn.

nganti *see* anti.

ngantos *kr for* nganti, *see* anti.

ngantya *lit var of* nganti.

ngaplak *see* kaplak, plak.

ngaprit to run fast.

Ngarab *var of* Arab.

ngaral hindrance, obstacle (*var of* aral).

ngaré 1 valley, lowland; 2 level, flat (terrain).

ngarep *ng*, ngajeng *kr*, ngarsa *k.i.* in front. *See also* arep.

ngaron earthenware pot. *Also* pangaron, *see* karu.

ngarot *reg* a ceremony held before tilling a ricefield.

ngarsa in front (*k.i. for* ngarep). *See also* arsa.

ngarti to understand, know (*var of* ngerti).

ngas, ngas-ngasan in a great hurry.

ngasèk *reg var of* nganti.

ngasi *reg var of* nganti.

ngasura religious feast held during the month of Sura. *See also* Sura.

ngaten 1 like this, in this way (*kr for* ngéné); 2 like that, in that way (*kr for* ngono).

ngathur 1 to spout upward; 2 to stand (up) straight. *See also* thur.

ngaurip *lit* life. *See also* urip.

ngayar I to catch a bird with the bare hands.
II *see* ayar.

ngayawara to talk nonsense.

ngayuwara *var of* ngayawara.

ngececeng stiffened, stiff, rigid. *See also* kececeng.

ngecemong to talk nonsense.

ngecenceng *var of* ngececeng.

ngecepoh soaking wet.

ngeceprèh *var of* ngecepoh.

ngecèprès to talk on and on.

ngeceproh *var of* ngecepoh.

ngecibris *var of* **ngecipris**.

ngecipir to run fast.

ngeciprèt *var of* **ngecipir**.

ngecipris to talk continuously.

ngeciput to scurry.

ngecit to suck (a nipple *etc*).

ngeciwis *var of* **ngecipris**.

ngecombar watery, mushy, with plenty of liquid.

ngecomé to talk foolishly, prattle.

ngecomèl to talk all the time, to grumble.

ngecoprès to talk on and on.

ngecriwis *var of* **ngecipris**.

ngecumut all covered (with s.t. messy).

ngecuprus to talk incessantly, to keep talking.

ngecut to suck (a nipple *etc*).

ngecucung *var of* **ngececeng**.

ngecuwèh *var of* **ngecuwis**.

ngecuwis to talk continuously.

ngecuwit *var of* **ngecuwis**.

ngedébag *var of* **nggedébag**. *See* **gedébag**.

ngedèndèng to walk with an affected air, a mincing gait.

ngedhabyah *var of* **nggedhabyah**. *See* **gedhabyah**.

ngedhag *see* **edhag**.

ngedhagrah *var of* **nggedhagrah**. *See* **gedhagrah**.

ngedhangkrang *var of* **nggedhangkrang**. *See* **gedhangkrang**.

ngedhap 1 to descend, not be able to stay up (kite); 2 afraid; to lose one's nerve. *See also* **kedhap IV**.

ngedhèbrèl *cr* to jabber.

ngedhebus to babble, talk nonsense.

ngedhèbyèh clumsy, awkward.

ngedhèdhèr *var of* **nggedhèdhèr**. *See* **gedhèdhèr**.

ngedhèng open, having nothing to hide. *See also* **èdhèng**, **nèdhèng-nèdhèng**.

ngèdhèng *var of* **ngedhèng**.

ngedhengkreng *var of* **nggedhengkreng**. *See* **gedhengkreng**.

ngedhingkring *var of* **nggedhingkring**.

See **gedhingkring**.

ngedhobyah *var of* **nggedhobyah**. *See* **gedhobyah**.

ngedhodhor *var of* **nggedhodhor**. *See* **gedhodhor**.

ngedhungkrung to sit with bowed head.

ngedobrol *var of* **nggedobrol**. *See* **gedobrol**.

ngedubleg to talk endlessly about inconsequential things.

ngeg *or* **mak ngeg** *repr* a grunt.

ngèh I *reg var of* **wènèh**.

II, **ngèhi** to leave behind for s.o. *See also* **èngèh**.

ngejawa *see* **Jawa**.

ngèjès *reg* nice, beautiful, fine.

ngejibris to talk at great length.

ngejojor *var of* **nggejojor**. *See* **gejojor**.

ngèk I *or* **mak ngèk** *repr* a baby's crying; **ngak-ngèk** to keep crying.

II, **ngèki** *reg* to give s.t. (*var of* **wènèh**).

ngèkèk to keep laughing loudly.

ngèkès to cough continuously.

ngèklèk *var of* **ngèkèk**.

ngèl, **ngengèl-engèl** *or* **ngengèl-engèli** to make s.t. difficult.

See also **angèl**.

ngelak *ng, kr,* **salit** *k.i.* thirsty.

ngelih hungry.

ngelik 1 high-pitched and penetrating (of voice quality, in singing a song); 2 to make a transition or change of mood in gamelan music.

ngèlmi *kr for* **ngèlmu**.

ngèlmu 1 knowledge; 2 esoteric knowledge; 3 wisdom.

ngelu *ng, kr,* **puyeng** *k.i.* to have a (physical) headache.

ngemasi *lit* to die (in battle).

ngembara *var of* **ngambara**, *see* **ambara**.

ngembek (to have or to exist) in abundance.

ngembeng *see* **kembeng III**.

ngember *var of* **ngembeng**.

ngembrah prevalent, widespread, commonplace, usual.

ngembreg overwhelming (quantity, supply). *See also* bebreg.

ngèmèl very fond of (*esp* food).

ngempet I to restrain; - ambegan to hold one's breath. *See also* ampet.
II mlayu - to run away fast, scurry off.

ngempret to run away fast, scurry off (*var of* ngempet).

ngemu *see* kemu II.

ngencrèt to dash, sprint, run (off) fast.

ngendhayah to hang down ponderously, *e.g.* a laden fruit tree branch.

ngendhanu dark, heavy (clouds).

ngendhayur *var of* ngendhayah.

ngendherek (of chickens) to sit in a hunched-over position.

ngendhuyuk bent low under a heavy burden.

ngendika *k.i.* to say, talk, tell, speak to (a social inferior) (*k.i. for* kandha, omong, celathu, tutur);
ngendikan to hold a conversation;
ngendikani to tell s.o. to;
ngendikakaké 1 to tell about, speak of, say; 2 to give orders to do s.t. *See also* andika.

ngéné *ng*, ngaten *kr*, like this, in this way, so; as follows;
ngènèkaké 1 to do this to; 2 to treat in this way;
ngéna-ngéné (ngétan-ngèten *kr*) like this, in this way.

ngènèh *reg var of* ngéné.

ngeng *or* ngeng-ngeng *repr* buzzing.

ngèngèr 1 to live in s.o.'s home as a servant; 2 (of a child) to live in the home of a relative, to serve them and to learn proper manners and become educated.

ngèngkèl *see* èngkèl I.

ngèngkèng 1 to keep crying/howling; 2 *var of* ngèngkèl.

ngengkrik to chirp.

ngengleng bewildered, dazed. *See also* lengleng I.

ngengreng stately, grand, dignified.

ngèngrèng 1 to draft (a document *etc*); 2 (*or* ngèngrèngi) to draw a pattern outline on fabric being worked in batik;
ngèngrèngan 1 a rough (first) draft; an outline; 2 s.t. drafted or outlined. *See also* rèngrèng.

ngentar *var of* ngenthar.

ngenthar, mlayu - to run (off) fast, dash off.

ngenthir I (of crickets) to chirp.
II *var of* ngenthar.

ngentiyeng, ngenthiyu 1 to bend and almost touch the ground (long, heavy object); 2 to wear o.s. out with hard work, work o.s. to the bone.

ngenthorang to run away fast.

ngenthorit *var of* ngenthorang.

ngenut to follow. *See also* nut I, tut.

ngènyèg to walk rapidly straight ahead, looking to neither right nor left.

ngènylèg *var of* ngènyèg.

ngenyos to douse a fire. *See also* nyos.

ngenyung *reg* to smoke too much.

ngèprèt to dash off, run away.

ngepipir to tremble, shiver.

ngerak *intsfr* dry (of season): exceptionally dry. *See also* kerak.

ngèrèng 1 (to make) a loud shrilling sound, *e.g.* crickets, cicadas; 2 to keep making a shrill sound, wail.

ngerik to chirp (crickets).

ngerti *ng*, ngertos *kr*, pirsa *or* priksa *or* uninga *k.i.*, to understand, know;
ngertèni to realise, appreciate the facts;
ngertèkaké to make s.o. understand, to explain;
ngertèn quick to understand;
ngerti-ngerti unexpectedly; (what s.o.) suddenly knows;
mangerti *lit* to understand, know;
pangertèn understanding;

sangertiné to the extent of one's knowledge.

ngertos to know, understand (*kr for* **ngerti**).

nges 1 exciting, nice; **2** touching, moving.

ngésuk *reg var of* **bésuk**.

nget I, ngenget *or* **ngengeti** to warm up (leftovers);

nget-ngetan warmed-up food.

See also **anget**.

II, ngeti *or* **ngetaké** to look intently at; **ngetana** take a look at that!;

nget-ngetan to watch each other.

See also **inget**.

ngétan *see* **wétan**.

ngetawang obvious, conspicuous.

ngetégé to stay quiet, not contribute to the conversation.

ngeteger *var of* **ngetégé**.

ngetègèr *var of* **ngetégé**.

ngetègès able to hold out for a long time, endure physical hardships.

ngèten like this, in this way (*md for* **ngéné**);

ngétan-ngèten this way or that.

ngetengi *see* **weteng**.

ngetépol covered with dirt, mud, grease.

ngetepus to babble, talk nonsense.

ngethakrah so abundant as to be worthless. *Also* **ngethokroh**.

ngethangkrong to sit (impolitely) in a higher position than others.

ngethaweng forming a fine sweeping curve.

ngethawit small and finely shaped, sharp.

ngèthèg I to zigzag, swerve from side to side (kite).

II to urge on (to work).

ngetheker 1 to stay put, stay in one place; **2** to remain off by o.s., sad and withdrawn, moping.

ngethèkèr 1 to struggle upwards; **2** to have difficulty achieving s.t.

ngethékor to bend low over the plate, eat with gusto.

ngethékrak to sit sloppily, loosely.

ngethekrek *var of* **ngetheker**.

ngethekul 1 to sit with the knees drawn up and the face buried in the arms; **2** to devote oneself wholly to the job.

ngethèl dirty, greasy.

ngethengkreng to sit stiffly, in a dignified way (*ironic*).

ngethengkruk *var of* **ngethengkreng**.

ngethengkrus *var of* **ngethengkreng**.

ngethepes to sit cross-legged in respectful silence.

ngethéprak to form a big pile (dung).

ngethèprès to keep up a steady stream of chatter.

ngethether to shiver from cold or dampness.

ngèthèti to clean (a slaughtered animal) by removing the insides. *See also* **bèthèt II**.

ngethikrak 1 to lounge; **2** to be scattered around in disarray, in a mess.

ngethingkrik 1 to sit on a high perch (chicken); **2** *fig* to consider o.s. too good to pitch in and work with the others.

ngethingkring *var of* **ngethingkrik**.

ngethipleng to run fast.

ngethiprat to run fast, dash.

ngethipret *var of* **ngethiprat**.

ngethiprèt *var of* **ngethiprat**.

ngethiyeng, ngethiyu *see* **ngenthiyeng**.

ngethokroh so abundant as to be worthless.

ngethongkrong to sit higher up than others (impolitely). *See also* **methongkrong**.

ngethopros to boast, tell tall tales.

ngethungkruk 1 to sit with bowed head, sit looking down; **2** to beetle (*e.g.* high building).

ngethungkrung *var of* **ngethungkruk**.

ngethupruk *var of* **ngethuprus**.

ngethuprus to talk non-stop, keep jabbering.

ngethuthur 1 to let the wings hang down (bird); 2 to shiver with wet and cold.

ngethuwik to pick at, fiddle with s.t.

ngetiging *reg* 1 to come to nothing; 2 to produce nothing. *See also* ngigling.

ngetol eager, anxious. *See also* getol.

ngetoprès *var of* ngecoprès.

ngetugur (to sit, lie) still, keep doing nothing.

ngéwas (to go, look) obliquely, aside.

ngèwèl to shudder, tremble. *See also* wèl.

ngèwès 1 to flow, pour out; 2 *fig* to keep talking.

nggon *see* enggon I, II.

ngi, ngengi to fan (rice) cool;
ngèn rice that has been cooled by fanning.
See also angi.

ngibadah 1 religious practices; 2 to be devout, pious; 3 to perform one's religious obligations. *See also* ibadah.

ngibarat *var of* ibarat.

ngidul *see* kidul.

ngigel to dance (animal, bird, *lit* humans).

ngiglig *var of* nginjlig.

ngigling *reg* 1 to come with nothing; 2 to produce nothing.

ngik *or* mak ngik *repr* the sound of squeaking (*e.g.* asthmatic wheezing, violin *etc*);
ngik-ngik 1 suffer from asthma; 2 (*or* ngak-ngik) to keep squeaking; suffer from asthma.

ngikik to giggle.

ngikil to have a persistent, dry cough.

ngiklik *var of* ngikik.

ngilmi *var of* ilmi.

ngilmu *var of* ilmu.

ngimel 1 to eat with much enjoyment; 2 to nibble constantly.

nging *inf var of* nanging.

nginggil above; at the top (*kr for* ndhuwur). *See also* inggil.

nginglang to auction s.t. off. *See also* lélang.

nginglung mentally disturbed, confused. *See also* linglung.

nginjig *var of* nginjlig.

nginjlig 1 to walk with little trotting steps; 2 to walk straight ahead looking to neither left nor right.

nginthar to run fast, scurry.

nginthik 1 to run fast; 2 to come along gladly (to do s.t., get s.t.). *See also* inthik.

ngis *see* engis.

Ngisa the evening prayer (about 7:30 p.m.). *See also* isa II.

ngithar *var of* nginthar.

ngiwas *var of* ngéwas.

ngiwung to rage, go berserk. *See also* liwung.

nglambrang *see* klambrang.

nglamprah *see* klamprah.

nglangkèt emaciated.

nglangsrah *see* klangsrah.

nglayub to look dim, dull (eyes).

nglecis *see* klecis.

nglemburuk *var of* nglempuruk.

nglempis *see* klempis.

nglempus *see* klempus.

nglèncèr to go out s.w. for pleasure. *See also* klèncèr.

nglepis *see* klepis.

nglethek to make a rattling sound while doing s.t. *See also* klethek.

ngok, ngengok to give a big kiss. *See also* nguk.

ngoko the basic speech style of Javanese used when addressing s.o. of lower social status, or of equal status with whom one has a close relationship; also when talking about o.s.

ngon *ng*, ngèn *kr*, ngengon *ng*, ngengèn *kr*, 1 to tend (livestock); 2 to keep an eye on;
ngengoni to keep a close eye on. *See also* angon.

ngong *lit* I, me; my.

ngono *ng*, ngaten *kr*, like that, in that way, so. *See also* mengkono, mono.

ngor *reg* to shriek, screech (cats).

ngot, ngot-ngotan 1 according to one's mood, when one feels like it; 2 recurrent, to keep recurring (illness, vice). *See also* angot.

ngoten in that way (*md for* ngaten).

ngrika (over) there (*kr for* kana).

ngriki here (*kr for* kéné).

ngriku there (*kr for* kono).

ngudubilah *excl* God preserve me! (uttered when one is shocked, stunned).

nguk (*pron as:* ngu:k) I, *or* mak nguk *repr* a kiss on a cheek;
   ngenguk to give s.o. a kiss;
   nguk-ngukan to kiss each other. *See also* ngok.
   II *reg* (it is) preferable.

ngulandara to wander, roam.

ngulon *see* kulon.

ngumbara *var of* ngambara, *see* ambara.

ngung (*pron as:* ngu:ng) *repr* the whine of an engine.

ngungun 1 amazed, astonished; 2 to wonder; pangungun astonishment.

nguni *see* uni II.

ngur *inf var of* angur.

ngwang *lit* I, me (*shtf of* ingwang).

ni female title of respect corresponding to the male title ki.

niaya *var of* aniaya.

nihan *lit* like that; as aforesaid.

nik, nak-nik the necessary details. *See also* enak.

nika that (thing, place, time) (*md for* kuwi, kaé).

nikah 1 formal marriage ceremony; 2 (*or* nikahan) to perform the marriage ceremony;
   nikahi to marry s.o.;
   nikahaké to marry s.o. off.

nikel I nickel (metal).

II *see* tikel.

nikèn lady (*title used before women's names*).

niki this (thing, place, time) (*md for* iki).

nikmat nice, enjoyable, comfortable.

niku that (thing, place, time) (*md for* kuwi).

nil I (*pron as:* ni:l) *or* mak nil *repr* a light accidental touch;
   sa-nil a mere touch, a tiny amount.
   II, nil-nilan restless, fidgety.

nila 1 sapphire; 2 *lit* blue, dark blue; 3 indigo dye.

nilakrama *lit* to greet in a polite manner.

nimas *respectful title applied to socially high ladies, usu by their husbands*;
   - ayu *respectful title applied to ladies of high standing*.

nimpuna *lit* highly accomplished, expert.

nindita *lit* irreproachable, excellent.

ninèk grandmother.

ning I but (*shtf of* nanging);
   nang-ning to keep saying 'but';
   ningan *var of* nanging.
   II *repr* the beat of a gamelan instrument.

ningkah *var of* nikah.

ningnang, ora - *reg* no different, exactly the same.

ningnong a bell of a horse-drawn cab, also its sound.

ningong *see* ngong.

ningrat an aristocrat, blueblood.

ningsun *see* ingsun.

nini 1 grandmother; 2 *affectionate term for addressing girls*.

ninis to go out and get some fresh air;
   paninisan a place in the house or yard where one can get some fresh air.

ninthing (of clothing) tight.

nipah swamp palm.

nipas *see* adus.

nipis *see* jeruk I.

nipkah *var of* napkah.

nipuna *var of* nimpuna.

nir I 1 *lit* lacking, without; 2 *lit* lost, gone.

II kidney.

III, **nir-niran** *or* **nar-nir** apprehensive, on edge. *See also* **nar**.

nirantara *lit* not long after that...

nirbaya *lit* without fear.

nirbita *lit var of* **nirbaya**.

nirdaya *lit* powerless.

nirdon *lit* fruitless, pointless.

nirmala *lit* clean, pure, spotless.

nirwana heaven.

nirwikara *lit* steadfast, stalwart.

nis *lit* lost, gone (*var of* **nir**).

nisab minimum level of income or possessions, for purposes of assessing liability to pay **zakat**.

nisbat 1 *lit* image, symbol; 2 **nisbaté** in the case of, with regard to.

niscaya *lit* certainly.

niskala *lit* I unharmed, safe.

II pure, holy; **hyang** - the Invisible (God); **ing** - in the hereafter; **pindha** - spiritual, invisible, immaterial.

niskara *see* **saniskara**.

nispu the half (of the month of Ruwah).

nistha 1 low, shameful, disgraceful; 2 to treat with contempt, despise;

nisthakaké to consider as contemptible;

kanisthan disgrace.

nisthip *lit, var of* **nistha**.

nit a certain gambling game.

niti *lit* wise conduct, good policy.

nitik I a batik pattern.

II *see* **titik** II.

nitya *or* **nityasa** *lit* constantly, always.

nlangsa *var of* **nalangsa**.

niya *reg* come here! (*var of* **rénéa**).

niyaga musician of a gamelan orchestra;

niyagani to act as a gamelan musician;

paniyagan place where the musicians are seated.

niyaka *var of* **nayaka**.

niyat 1 expression of one's purpose before performing a prayer; 2 intention;

niyati to determine, make up one's mind;

kaniyatan plan, intention.

niyaya *see* **niaya**.

no *inf var of* **ngono**.

nohan name of the 5th day of the nine-day week.

nok I *adr* young girl (*shtf of* **dhénok**).

II at, on, in (*reg var of* **ana**).

nokil I, **nokilan** extract, excerpt.

II *reg* false, untrustworthy.

nom *ng*, **nèm** *kr*, **timur** *k.i.* 1 young; 2 immature; 3 light (of colours);

ngenomi to look younger; to act like s.o. younger;

ngenomaké to make (a colour) lighter (than before);

nom-noman young person;

kanoman 1 youth; 2 young people; 3 pertaining to the state of the head of the younger generation (Crown Prince) as contrasted with the king's (**kasepuhan**).

nomer number in a series;

nomeri to assign a number to.

non *see* **ton**.

nonah an unmarried girl; Miss.

nong in, at, on (*inf var of* **ana ing**).

nongong to gape dumbly.

noni little (European) girl, Miss.

nonik (*pron as:* **noni:k**) *var of* **noni**.

nonob *reg* 1 to shelter from the midday heat; 2 to conceal o.s.;

nonoban 1 shelter, shade; 2 hiding-place.

nonok genitals of a little girl.

nonol a certain caterpillar that feeds on coffee.

nonoman *ng*, **nènèman** *kr* youthful, belonging to the youth. *See also* **nom**.

nonong (of forehead) protruding, bulging.

nonthong to keep silent, do nothing.

nonthor disinclined to work, do one's job.

nopal 1 a cactaceous plant from which the cochineal insect is collected; **2** the red dye prepared from this.

nor, - raga humble, modest (*shtf of* **anor-raga**; *see also* **sor II**).

nora no, not (*lit, var of* **ora**).

nori a parrot-like bird. *Also* **nuri**.

norong to stare wide-eyed

not 1 musical note; note of the scale; **2** note, memorandum.

notah *var of* **notisi**.

notaris notary public.

notes notebook.

notisi notes, jottings.

notulen minutes (of a meeting).

nraka hell (*var of* **neraka, naraka**).

nudur obstacle, hindrance.

nugraha favour, blessing or boon in the form of happiness, safety, security;
  nugrahani to grant a favour;
  kanugrahan to receive blessings;
  panganugraha *lit* mark of favour.

nujum the stars as agents of prophecy;
  juru - astrologer, soothsayer;
  ngèlmu panujuman astrology.

nuk, nuk-nukan to grope one's way. *See also* **nunuk**.

nuklun (to walk, sit) with an air of dejection, with bowed head.

nul I zero;
  ngenul-nul to form into round shapes.
  II (*pron as:* **nu:l**) *or* **mak nul** *repr* a light touch.

nuli and then, (right) after that. *See also* **tuli**.

nulya *lit, var of* **nuli**.

nun 1 - kula yes, sir (servant answering call); **2** if you please; **3** pardon? (what did you say?). *See also* **suwun**.

nung *repr* the sound of a note played by a gamelan instrument.

nungsung, - kabar *or* **- warta** to try to get news. *See also* **sungsung**.

nuninggih yes, indeed! (*inf var of* **nuwun inggih**).

nunuk, nunak-nunuk to grope one's way.

nunut 1 to go, ride along together (in s.o.'s vehicle); **2** to use s.t. together; **- turu** to go and sleep at s.o.'s place;
  nunuti to get a ride with s.o.;
  nunutaké to get space for s.o.;
  nunutan that which is carried along together.

nur 1 light; **2** the Divine Light; **- Muhammad** the light of divine revelation in the Prophet Muhammad.

nuraga *var of* **nor-raga**.

nurbuwah, cahya - divine prophetic light.

nuri *var of* **nori**.

nus, iwak - a kind of squid.

nusa *lit* island.

nusantara 1 the islands; **2** Indonesia.

nuswa *var of* **nusa**.

nuswantara *var of* **nusantara**.

nuswapada *lit* earth, world.

nusya *var of* **nusa**.

nusyantara *var of* **nusantara**.

nut I (to act) in accordance with. *See also* **tut**.
  II musical note (*var of* **not**).
  III (*pron as:* **nu:t**) *or* **mak nut** *repr* a stab of pain;
  nut-nut to throb with pain. *See also* **senut**.

nutpah germ of life, sperm.

nuwala *var of* **nawala**.

nuwun *see* **suwun**.

nya *coll* here, here you are! (when handing s.t.).

nyablik small, dainty (lips, mouth).

nyadham just about ripened (various fruits).

nyagir *var of* **ngagir**, *see* **agir**.

nyah *shtf of* **nyonyah**.

nyai *respectful term of address to older woman*.

nyak, nyak-nyakan 1 to barge in just like that; **2** thoughtless, inconsiderate, lacking manners.

nyal, nyal-nyalan to fidget, move about restlessly.

nyalawadi *ng*, nyalawados *kr*, mysterious, arousing suspicions.

nyalawados *kr for* nyalawadi.

nyam, nyam-nyamen 1 to keep savouring s.t. nice; 2 to have a longing for a certain delicious food. *See also* kenyam.

nyamat golden tassel on a fez worn by aristocrats on festive occasions.

nyambik monitor lizard (*reg var of* menyawak).

nyambut, nyambut gawé *ng*, nyambut damel *kr*, ngasta (*k.i.*) to work, do a job, be employed. *See also* sambut.

nyamikan light refreshments (*e.g.* biscuits, cakes) with tea, coffee.

nyamir, nyomar-nyamir to sneer, curl the lip.

nyamlang to boast, show off.

nyamleng very enjoyable (*esp* food).

nyamping batik garment (*k.i. for* jarit).

nyamplung I a section of ripe jackfruit, together with the pit.

II a certain tree from the seeds of which oil is extracted.

nyamu smell of burnt cloth.

nyamuk, nyamuk-nyamuk *or* nyomak-nyamuk (to eat) with the mouth stuffed. *See also* camuk.

nyamut, nyamut-nyamut far off, a long way away.

nyana to expect, think, imagine;

ora kanyana-nyana unexpected; ora nyana ora ndimpé *idiom* completely unexpected, out of the blue.

panyana what s.o. expects or anticipates.

nyang I *ng*, dhateng *kr*, (to go) to (*shtf of* menyang);

ngenyangi to go to.

II (awis *kr*), ngenyang to bargain, haggle;

ngenyangi to make a bid to (a seller);

ngenyangaké to bargain on behalf of s.o. else;

nyang-nyangan to haggle with each other.

See also anyang I.

nyangkin *reg* increasingly, all the more.

nyangklek located hard by.

nyangkleng for a very long time, for ages.

nyangkluk with head bowed and shoulders drooping.

nyangkrang *var of* nyangkreng.

nyangkreng to sit high up.

nyantheg *or* nyantheg-nyantheg (to speak) forcefully, loudly.

nyantug to be able to reach s.t.

nyantun a finger's breadth (*kr for* nyari).

nyanuk, nyanuk-nyanuk to grope, feel one's way forward.

nyanyah, nyanyah-nyunyah rough, coarse, common (talk).

nyanyak *reg* 1 to open the mouth, yawn; 2 to eat.

nyanyi to sing (Western-style);

nyanyèkaké to sing (a song) for s.o.;

nyanyian song, hymn.

nyaprang wide and stylish (moustache).

nyari *ng*, nyantun *kr*, a finger's breadth (as a unit of measurement: *ca* 1 centimetre).

nyarong *intsfr* crystal clear (water).

nyaros *reg kr for* nyari.

nyas *or* mak nyas *repr* touching s.t. hot. *Also* kenyas.

nyat *or* mak nyat *repr* getting up;

menyat to stand up from a sitting position;

nyat-nyatan always on the go.

nyata 1 true; 2 actually, in fact; nyatané the fact of the matter is;

nyatani to do s.t. seriously;

nyatakaké to check whether s.t. is true, confirm the facts;

kanyatan reality, the fact;

sanyata *lit* truly.

nyathis prominent, protruding (*esp* chin, jaw).

nyathus 1 to sit doing nothing, not join in the activity; 2 *var of* **nyathis**.

nyat-nyut *see* **nyut** I.

nyawa soul, spirit, life: (*fig*) *term of endearment for addressing one's beloved.*

nyek I, **nyek-nyek** *repr* a hushed sound or feel, such as when touching s.t. softly or walking softly on wet ground;
II, **nyek-nyekan** filled, crowded.

nyèk *or* **mak nyèk** *repr* the feel of stepping in s.t. soft and mushy;
ngenyèk 1 to squash s.t.; 2 *fig* to humiliate or offend s.o.;
ngenyèkan in the habit of teasing, putting people down.

nyel, nyel-nyelan jostling, crowding each other.

nyemek *or* **nyemek-nyemek** 1 neither too moist nor too dry (food); 2 rather wet (soil).

nyemèk *var of* **nyemek**.

nyèmèk *var of* **nyemek**.

nyeng *or* **mak nyeng** *repr* an effortless lifting motion;
nyang-nyeng *repr* lifting heavy objects easily.

nyèng *var of* **nyeng**.

nyenyeb *var of* **nyenyet**.

nyènyèh, menyènyèh *or* **nyènyèhen** to fester, suppurate.

nyènyèk *var of* **nyènyèh**.

nyenyep I very quiet, deathly still.
II the base of an arrow (where the cord is fitted).

nyenyes 1 chilly; 2 very quiet, lonely.

nyenyet *intsfr* very quiet, lonely.

nyep, ngenyep-nyep to cool s.t. with water. *See also* **anyep**.

nyes *or* **mak nyes** *repr* a chilly feeling;
nyenyes 1 chilly; 2 *intsfr* quiet, lonely.

nyet *or* **mak nyet** *repr* pressing, squeezing;

ngenyet-nyet to press, squeeze, massage.

nyèt *or* **mak nyèt** *repr* squeezing, crushing;
ngenyèt-nyèt to mash, squash.

nyi respectful *term of address to older woman* (*var of* **nyai**).

nyidham to long for certain foods during pregnancy;
nyidhamaké to long for (a food). *See also* **idham**.

nyik, sa-nyik a moment;
sa-nyikan for a moment.

nying *var of* **nyeng**.

nyinyih *var of* **nyènyèh**.

nyinyir 1 soft; 2 easy, a cinch.

nyir *or* **mak nyir** *repr* a pang of uneasiness.

nyiru piece of coconut shell placed at the bottom of a rice-steaming cone for the rice to rest on while it steams.

nylenèh peculiar, out of the ordinary.

nylenyer *var of* **nlenyer**.

nyles *repr* a chilly feeling (*var of* **nyes**).

nyo I a European boy, young master (*shtf of* **sinyo**).
II white porcelain teapot.

nyoh *coll* here you are! take it!

nyok I (*or* **nyok-nyok**) *reg* sometimes, on and off. *See also* **sok** I.
II *or* **mak nyok** *repr* the sound of s.t. plopping into mud.

nyong *reg* I, me.

nyonglong to bend forward, overhang.

nyongo to stand gaping, doing nothing.

nyonyah married woman, lady (European, Chinese).

nyonyo *reg* to talk rudely.

nyonyok to touch with a hot or sharp object;
kenyonyok to get burned by coming into contact with a hot or sharp object.

nyos *or* **mak nyos** *repr* sizzling;
ngenyos to touch s.t. with a hot iron, brand.

nyuh *lit* coconut.

nyuk (*pron as:* nyu:k) (*or* mak nyuk) *repr* a quick connection;
nyak-nyuk rough, careless.

nyung-nyang impudent, insolent, bad-mannered.

nyunyuk I *or* ngenyuk to touch with a burning object;
kenyunyuk to come into accidental contact with a burning object;
II, nyunyak-nyunyuk to act rudely.

nyunyur 1 soft and mushy (*esp* from overcooking).
II *cr* to talk constantly.
III very easy, a cinch.

nyus (*pron as:* nyus) (*or* mak nyus) *repr* a lunge with a sharp or hot object.

nyut I *repr* sucking;
ngenyut to suck.
II nyat-nyut fickle, to keep changing one's mind.

O

o *interjection expressing surprise*; oh!

obag I *reg* stone block used as the base of a pillar.
II *reg* a children's game in a yard in which the players try to reach the enemy goal.

obah *ng*, ébah *kr*, to move;
ngobahaké to move s.t.;
obah-obah to keep moving;
mobah-mosik to move.

obang-abing 1 to swing back and forth; 2 pendulum.

obar I, ngobar to burn;
kobar to get burned, be on fire.
II, obar-abir *lit* 1 a flash of light; 2 lightning (followed by thunder).

obat 1 medicine, potion; chemicals; drugs; 2 gunpowder; - cacing vermifuge; - kuwat a tonic; - nyamuk mosquito repellent;
ngobati to treat s.o. medically;
obat-obatan medicines.

obed whetted (knives); *fig* sharp, astute (*var of* ubed).

obèl, ngobèl to spin off-centre, to wobble;
ngobèlaké to spin, set spinning;
obèlan 1 screwdriver (*var of* obèng); 2 a pretext.

obèng I 1 screwdriver; 2 (*or* obèngan) cranking or winding tool, *e.g.* brace and bit, drill, engine crank;
ngobèng 1 to screw; 2 to crank up;
ngobèngaké to wobble.
II, ngobèng 1 to make batik for profit; 2 to work as a worker in a batik factory;
pengobèng worker in a batik factory.

obèt room, leeway, latitude;
ngobètaké to accommodate, take care of;
kobèt to have plenty of room (for).

obin I unit of land measurement, = 14.19 square metres;
ngobin to measure (land) in obin.
II floor tile;
ngobin to tile a floor. *See also* jobin, jubin.

oblag *reg* loose, detached;

ngoblag widely spaced.

oblah, ngoblah-oblah wide open, widely spaced.

oblang *reg cr* prostitute.

obli a variety of cake (biscuit).

oblo *var of* oblang.

oblog *var of* ublug.

oblok, oblok-oblok a dish consisting of leftovers or vegetables mixed with spices.

oblong *see* kaos.

obod, obodan *reg* rough (work).

obong *ng*, besmi *kr*, besem *md*, mati obong to immolate, set o.s. on fire;
obong-obong to burn rubbish; *fig* to rouse the rabble;
ngobong 1 to burn, set fire to; 2 to incite; 3 to do away with;
ngobongi to keep burning;
ngobongaké to ignite, to enflame;
kobong 1 on fire, to get burned; 2 *fig* smouldering with resentment;
kobongan 1 to get burnt, catch fire; 2 conflagration; 3 to suffer loss through fire;
pangobong act of burning;
pangobongan incinerator.

obor 1 torch; 2 *fig* enlightenment, guiding light; - giring *idiom* government;
ngobori 1 to illuminate; 2 to shed light on; 3 *reg* to cook by boiling; - pepeteng (*also fig*) to shed light in the darkness, to light the way;
gedhé oboré *idiom* (a place where) justice reigns;
kepatèn obor *fig* to lose track of the family connection, become strangers.

obos, ngobos 1 (of air) to rush out; 2 to break wind; 3 *reg cr* to chat, talk nonsense, make empty boasts;
obos-obosan *reg* to keep talking nonsense.

obrak-abrik, ngobrak-abrik to ransack, wreck;
mobrak-mabrik in utter disorder.

obral 1 clearance sale; 2 copious;
ngobral 1 to sell out, sell cheaply, put on sale, hold a sale; 2 to be quick to do s.t.;
ngobralaké to spend or dispose of s.t. freely;
ngobral-obral to give out copiously;
obralan 1 clearance sale; 2 sale items;
obral-obralan act of selling at bargain prices *or* giving things out lavishly.

obrog, ngobrog to wear everyday clothes;
obrogan 1 everyday clothes; 2 rough working.

obrok, ngobrok to dirty one's pants. *See also* brok.

obrol, ngobrol to chat, have a talk;
ngobrol-obrol to pull out the contents and spread them around;
ngobroli to boast to s.o. about s.t.; to repeatedly talk about, gossip about;
ngobrolaké to chat about, gossip about;
obrolan 1 a chat, a conversation; 2 tall talk.

obrot, ngobrot-obrot *reg* to tear apart, scatter;
mobrot *or* mobrot-mobrot 1 in disorder, messy; 2 disembowelled; 3 to keep farting.

obrus lieutenant colonel.

obyag in turmoil.

obyang *reg* generally known.

obyèk 1 object, thing; 2 middleman in a sale;
ngobyèk 1 to deal in lucrative side-jobs (not entirely legal), do outside work during or outside office hours; 2 to earn extra money by acting as intermediary in selling;
ngobyèkaké to use s.t. for one's own gain;
obyèkan 1 sideline business; 2 supplementary earnings, *usu* from moonlighting as a middleman.

obyog, obyog-obyog *reg* a social dance in which male members of the audience are invited to join female professional dancers.

obyok, ngobyok *or* ngobyok-obyok to shake s.t. and rinse in water.

obyong, ngobyongi 1 to support (an endeavour *etc*) by joining its proponents; 2 to decorate s.t. with leaves. *See also* ombyong.

obyor *reg* to glitter, sparkle, shine; sparkling light.

ocak, ngocak *or* ngocak-ocak to shake; to mix by shaking;
ngocakaké to spill s.t.;
kocak 1 to splash (inside coconut); 2 hilarious.

ocal to cook (*root form: subst kr for* olah). *See also* ucal I.

ocang-acung *see* acung.

ocar-acir *see* acir.

ocèh twitter, warble, chirp;
ngocèh 1 to warble, chirp, twitter; 2 to talk too much;
ocèh-ocèhan a talking bird.

ocèk *reg var of* oncèk.

ocèm, ngocèm *reg* to lay undisputed claim to s.t.; to want for o.s.

ocèn, ocèn-ocèn Javanese raspberry (*var of* oncèn-oncèn).

ocor, ngocor to pour out, gush forth;
ngocor-ocor to keep pouring liquid out;
ngocori to pour liquid on s.t.;
ngocoraké to pour s.t. out, make s.t. gush forth.

oder, ngoderaké *reg* to regulate, ordain.

odhag-adhig *var of* oglag-aglig.

odhak *reg* no, not (*var of* ora).

odhal-adhil, ngodhal-adhil 1 to unpack, pull apart; 2 to unravel (secret);
modhal-madhil pulled apart.

odhé, ngodhé to work for wages;
ngodhèkaké to hire s.o. for wages; to hire out (a job).

odheg loud, thunderous.

odhèg loose, unsteady, wobbly;
odhèg-odhèg loose and moving back and forth;
ngodhèg-odhèg to shake; to keep shaking (doors *etc*);
ngodhègaké to keep (one's legs) moving;
odhègan wobbling, waggling.

odhil, ora odhil *reg* to be of little use, benefit.

odhoklonyo eau-de-cologne.

odhèt, ngodhèt-odhèt to rip the guts out, disembowel.

odhog *var of* odhèg.

odhol I toothpaste.
II (of batik work) rough, crude.
III, ngodhol to shadow, tail.
IV, ngodhol-odhol to open and spread around the contents of;
modhol-modhol 1 in disorder, in a terrible mess; 2 (of stuffing, insides *etc*) disembowelled, spilling out.

odod, ngodod to let out, allow to stick out;
ngododaké to cause to emerge or rise;
modod to emerge, rise, grow higher or longer.

odok *reg* somewhat, quite; a little; (quite) a bit; rather (*var of* rada).

odor, ngodor to push ahead of (others) without waiting one's turn.

ogag *var of* ogak.

ogah averse (to); unwilling (to) (*reg var of* wegah).

ogak, ogak-agik loose in its socket;
ngogak-ogak to move s.t. back and forth to loosen it.

ogal-ogèl *see* ogèl.

ogèg *var of* ogak.

ogèk *var of* ogak.

ogel stirred up, in commotion.

ogèl, ogèl-ogèl *or* ogal-ogèl to keep moving back and forth;
ngogèl *or* mogèl to move back and forth, wobble;

ngogèlaké to move s.t. back and forth, making twisting movements with (*e.g.* hand).

oging *reg* unwilling, averse (to) (*var of* ogah).

oglag-aglig *see* aglig.

oglé *see* oglèng.

oglèng, ngoglèng *or* moglèng to protrude, stick out;
ngoglèngaké to cause s.t. to protrude, show s.t. off;
kethèk oglèng monkey show.

ogok, ngogok-ogok 1 to push (a stick) back and forth in a hole; 2 to irritate, disturb.

ograg, ngograg-ograg 1 to disturb, bother, irritate; 2 to poke *or* prod (at).

ogrèg *var of* ograg.

ogrèk *var of* ograg.

ogro, ngogro-ogro to disturb, bother, irritate.

ogrok, ngogrok-ogrok 1 to prod (with a long stick); 2 *var of* ogok.

ojar, ngojari *reg* to place an order (to buy).

ojat I *lit* a good talk;
dadi ojat to be much spoken of, famous.
II *reg* a ritual meal.

ojèh, ngojèh *reg* to tear to pieces, shred.

ojèl, ngojèlaké to open up old sore points;
kojèl to get pried up, opened up (secrets, problems *etc*).

ojit *reg* don't! (*var of* aja).

ojog, ojogan 1 carrier; 2 peddler, hawker.

ojok I *reg* don't (*var of* aja).
II, ngojoki *or* ngojok-ojoki to incite, urge to evil;
ojok-ojokan inciting to evil.

ojol *or* ojolan *reg* to exchange (*var of* ijol).

okèh *coll* much, many (*var of* akèh).

oker ochre.

okèr, ngokèr-okèr to scratch about in (sand, soil).

okih very much (*var of* okèh).

okit *var of* ojit.

oklak, ngoklak-oklak to shake, move s.t. back and forth to loosen it;
oklak-aklik wobbly, unsteady (as if it is about to fall off).

oklèk to walk one's legs off (walking a long way);
ngoklèk-oklèk to break in pieces. *See also* coklèk.

okol 1 physically sturdy, compactly built; 2 (*or* okol-okolan) to fight; to test each other's strength or endurance;
ngokoli to overpower (an opponent).

olah, ngolah 1 *lit* to practise; 2 to cultivate (a field); 3 to prepare (food);
ngolahaké to cook for s.o.;
olah-olah to do the cooking;
olah-olahan 1 things cooked; 2 cuisine;
pangolah act *or* way of cooking;
pangolahan cultivation.
See also ulah.

olak-alik *see* alik I, walik.

olan, olan-olan 1 a variety of caterpillar; 2 (*or* ngolan-olan) snakelike, *e.g.* a long graceful neck. *See also* ulan.

olang, olang-olang *reg* to look for, seek.

olang-aling, ngolang-aling to toss and turn in one's sleep.

olé I *var of* olèhé. *See* olèh.
II, olé-olé whirlwind.
III, ngolèkaké to stick out (the tongue);
molé to hang out. *See also* olér.

olèd, ngolèd *or* molèd 1 to stretch after sleeping; 2 flexible, elastic;
ngolèdaké to stretch (the body) after sleeping;
ngolad-ngolèd to wriggle, squirm, keep stretching;
kolèd-kolèd to writhe in snakelike motions.

olèh *ng*, angsal *kr*, 1 to get; 2 to accept; 3

to marry, take in marriage; 4 to receive permission; 5 to reach, attain; 6 s.o.'s act of (do)ing; - **angin** to get an opportunity; - **angin becik** to get a lucky break; - **ati** to get preferential treatment; - **gawé** to succeed in an effort;
olèh-olèh gifts brought home with one from a journey;
ngolèhi to grant permission;
ngolèh-olèhi to bring s.t. home as a gift;
ngolèhaké to marry s.o. off;
olèhan lucky in getting what one tries for;
olèhé s.o.'s act of (do)ing (*gram, function of nominalising*);
ngolèh-olèhaké 1 to bring (gifts) to those back home; 2 to do one's best to get/obtain;
olèh-olèhan what one receives for one's efforts;
saolèhé *or* **saolèh-olèhé** whatever one can manage. *See also* **pakolèh**.
olèk *reg var of* olèh.
olèng 1 shaky; 2 having a strong roll (of ship); 3 to writhe, move spasmodically;
ngolèng to shake, rock.
olèr, **ngolèr** *or* **molèr** to stick out;
ngolèraké to extend s.t., stick s.t. out.
olèt *see* olèd.
oli lubricating oil.
oliya a godly person (inspired, wonderworker).
olih *reg var of* olèh.
oling I *var of* olèng.
  II *reg* a variety of large eel.
olok, **ngolok-olok** to scoff, jeer, keep referring to s.o.'s faults;
olok-olokan scorn.
olor I, **ngolor** to pay out (rope *etc*);
ngolor-olor to extend s.t. repeatedly;
ngoloraké 1 to let out (rope *etc*); 2 to stretch (s.t. elastic); 3 to refer (a lawsuit) to a higher court;

molor 1 to hang down in droplets; 2 elastic.
See also **ulur**.
  II animal bone marrow.
  III channel for irrigating a ricefield.
  IV, **olor-olor** (*or* **kolor**) cord used as a belt for trousers, pyjamas;
ngolor *fig* to bootlick.
See also **kolor**.
  V, **ngolor** *reg* to smoke cigarettes.
omah *ng*, **griya** *kr*, 1 (**dalem** *k.i.*), house, home; 2 to live (in a house), make one's home (in); - **kampung** bamboo house with a saddle-shaped roof; - **kéyong** snail shell; **loji** large brick house (European style);
omah-omah 1 (**gegriya** *kr*, **dedalem** *k.i.*) to live in (a house), make one's home (in); 2 (**émah-émah** *kr*, **krama** *k.i.*); 2 to be married, set up house; to run one's home and household;
ngomahi 1 to provide for (one's family; 2 (**ndalemi** *k.i.*) to provide with a house; 3 to live in s.t.;
ngomahaké to tame, domesticate;
omahan 1 tame; 2 familiar to the household;
omah-omahan 1 tent; playhouse; 2 to play house;
saomah the whole family;
somah family, household;
pomah *ng*, **pémah** *kr*, tame, domesticated; to feel at home;
pomahan (**gegriyan** *kr*, **padaleman** *k.i.*) the area of a house, house and yard.
oman I *reg* rice stalk.
  II *var of* uman II.
omar-amèr *see* amèr.
ombak a wave; - **banyu** a certain classical male dance movement;
ngombak to resemble or move like waves;
kombak to get carried along (in the sea).

ombal *var of* umbal.

ombang, ngombang-ombangi *reg* to have s.t. against s.o.

ombé *ng, kr*, unjuk *k.i.*, ngombé to drink; ngombèni to offer s.t. for drinking; ngombèkaké 1 to have s.o. drink; 2 to offer s.t. for drinking; ombèn 1 a drink; 2 used for drinking; ombèn-ombèn a drink, beverage; ombèn-ombènan 1 s.t. to drink; 2 to get intoxicated deliberately; pangombèn drinking utensil.

ombèng *var of* ombang.

ombèr spacious; with plenty of room; ample; ngombèri to allow leeway; ngombèraké to give s.t. more space; saombèr-ombèré as broad/free as possible.

ombol, ngombol 1 to gather, form a crowd; 2 to be closely grouped; ombolan group, gathering.

ombrok *var of* umbruk.

ombyak trend, current; ombyakané *reg* to belong to.

ombyok bunch, cluster; ngombyoki to form s.t. into a bundle *or* cluster; ombyokan *or* ombyok-ombyokan 1 in bunches/clusters; 2 those belonging to a clique, party *etc*; 3 branch of a family (line descending from different siblings); saombyok 1 a bunch, bundle; 2 the whole group (of people); 3 commonplace.

ombyong, ombyong-ombyong leaves used as decorations; ngombyongi to support (an endeavour *etc*) by joining its proponents; ngombyong-ombyongi to decorate s.t. with leaves.

omèh talkative, loquacious, garrulous; ngomèhi *reg* to scold; omèhan scolding.

omèl, ngomèl to grumble at, nag; ngomèl-ngomèl to keep grumbling at, keep nagging; ngomèli to scold, complain to; ngomèlaké 1 to grumble about s.t.; 2 *cr* to talk about s.t.; omèlan grumbling, nagging.

omes *reg* careful; ora omes careless, not taking care.

omih *var of* omèh.

omong *ng*, cariyos *kr*, ngendika *k.i.*, to say, talk; - kosong 1 claptrap, nonsense; 2 chatter, gossip; omong-omong 1 to chat, talk about; 2 idle talk; 3 by the way…; ngomongi to tell s.o. about s.t.; ngomongaké to discuss, talk about; omongan gossip, food for conversation; omong-omongan to converse, chat together.

ompak *var of* umpak.

omplèh, ngomplèh (of lips) protruding and pendulous.

omplo, ngomplo to get nothing, go away empty-handed.

omplong, ngomplong 1 wide open (hole, crack, door); 2 *var of* omplo.

ompod *reg* industrious, diligent.

ompok *reg var of* ampok.

ompol urine released in bed or in one's pants; ngompol to wet the bed or one's pants; ngompolan to have a tendency to wet the bed; ngompoli to make s.t. wet by urinating on it.

ompong *ng, kr*, gugut *or* daut *k.i.*, toothless; missing teeth; - géyong toothless; very old.

ompot, ngompotaké *reg* to hide s.t.

omprèng, ngomprèng to transport passengers in a private car; omprèngan private car used for transporting passengers.

omprok *reg* ornamental leather headpiece worn by dancers.

omprong nest of containers for transporting food which is to be eaten elsewhere.

omprot, ngomprot-omprot *reg* to scatter around, spill.

ompyong *var of* **ombyong**.

on ounce (100 grams).

onang I, ngonangi 1 to see *or* catch (s.o.) in the act; 2 to disclose;

konangan 1 to get caught doing s.t.; 2 to get discovered;

kaonang-onang, konang-onang *lit* known everywhere, well-known.

II, onang-onang a certain gamelan melody.

onar trouble, disturbance, commotion; **gawé -** to cause a scandal, sensation.

oncat to make one's escape;

ngoncati to avoid, escape from;

koncatan 1 to avoid; 2 to have s.t. get away from one.

oncat-ancit, ngoncat-ancit *or* **ngoncat-ancitaké** 1 to cause s.t to move back and forth; 2 to cause s.o. to run helter-skelter, in any direction;

moncat-mancit 1 to sway; 2 to exert o.s.

oncé I, ngoncé to string, thread;

oncèn-oncèn 1 a string (of flowers); 2 the Javanese raspberry. *See also* **roncé**.

II pipe (for smoking);

ngoncé to smoke a pipe. *See also* **oncowé**.

oncèk, oncèk-oncèk to keep peeling, paring;

ngoncèk *or* **ngoncèki** 1 to peel, pare; 2 to reveal, disclose;

oncèkan 1 peeled, pared; 2 the way of peeling.

oncèng, ngoncèng-oncèng 1 to chase; 2 to pursue with demands.

oncèr I *reg* guinea corn, Indian millet.

II *see* **moncèr**.

oncèt *reg var of* **oncèk**.

oncit, ngoncit-oncit to chase.

onclang 1 variety of girls' game, played with pebbles; 2 to run away, get out;

ngonclang 1 to chase away, evict;

ngonclangaké to toss, flip, launch s.t. in midair;

ngonclang-onclangaké to keep tossing, launching. *See also* **uncang**.

onclong I, ngonclong *or* **onclong-onclongen** *reg* (to have) diarrhoea.

II 1 *reg* village messenger; 2 *reg* village watchman; 3 *cr* matchmaker; 4 *cr* prostitute.

oncog, ngoncog to walk on and on without stopping;

ngoncogi to go toward, head for.

oncom a certain cake made of fermented beans.

oncong *reg* torch flame.

oncor I oil-burning bamboo torch;

ngoncori to light with a torch.

II, ngoncori to supply water to a ricefield in turn;

oncoran water supply in a ricefield in turn.

III, ngoncori to compete with;

oncor-oncoran to try to outshine each other.

oncowé a long Chinese pipe.

onder subdistrict head or chief (*esp in* colonial era);

onderan subdistrict head's residence;

kaonderan subdistrict.

ondhal-andhil *reg var of* **ontang-anting**.

ondhé, ondhé-ondhé a round fried cake made from rice flour filled with sweetened ground mung beans sprinkled with sesame seeds.

ondhok, ngondhok-ondhok to have a lump in the throat.

ondhol I *reg* coarse, gross.

II, ngondhol 1 to chase girls; 2 *reg cr*

to go to a prostitute; to carry on or perform prostitution;

ngondholi to examine (poultry) to determine whether it can reproduce;

ondholan *reg cr* prostitute.

oneng *lit* longing, yearning, pining (for a loved one);

moneng to long, yearn, pine;

koneng-oneng to be yearning for, missing (a loved one);

oneng-onengan lovesick.

ongak *var of* **ungak**.

ongak-anguk *see* **anguk** II.

onggal *reg* every; - **dina** everyday. *See also* **unggal**.

onggèr, ngonggèr *reg* 1 to loosen; 2 to release, give vent to (*var of* **unggar**).

ong-ilahèng magic word used as opening of a narration.

onggloh, onggloh-onggloh to look a mess, be a real sight.

onggo, ngonggo-onggo to weep long and bitterly.

onggok I heart or pith of the sugar-palm, used for making sago.

II *var of* **onggrok**.

onggor, ngonggor *reg* thirsty.

onggrag-anggreg to proceed haltingly.

onggrok, ngonggrokaké *or* **ngonggrok-onggrokaké** to leave s.t. just as it is, not bother with it.

onggrong I, **ngonggrong** to allow space between things, pack loosely.

II, **ngonggrong** to flatter (with ulterior motives);

onggrongan to allow o.s. to be seduced by flattery;

pangonggrong act or way of flattering.

ongkak *reg* exhausted (arms).

ongkak-angkèk, ngongkak-angkèk to keep bending s.t; to overwork s.o.

ongkang, ongkang-ongkang 1 to sit with the feet dangling; 2 *fig* to loaf, take it easy;

ngongkang 1 to sit up high on the edge of s.t. with legs dangling; 2 *fig* to perch, be right on the edge (*e.g.* house); 3 - **atiné** anxious, concerned.

ongkeb *reg* hot and sweaty, sultry;

ngongkebi to make s.o. feel hot and sweaty;

ongkèk 1 object used as a lever; 2 shoulder-pole with racks attached to each end for carrying goods;

ngongkèk to lever.

ongkèl a kind of crowbar used for prying out;

ngongkèl to pry (out, up, open).

ongklak-angklek to walk with difficulty.

ongklang, ongklang-ongklang tall and thin.

ongklèng, ngongklèng-ongklèng to make s.t. difficult, make hard to get s.t.

ongkloh, ongkloh-ongkloh to walk weakly (from thirst and hunger);

ngongkloh to feel weak (*esp* with thirst and hunger);

ongklok, cooked potato shaken in a pan;

ngongklok to cook potato as above;

ngongklok-ongklok to shake hard.

ongklong *var of* **ongkloh**.

ongkog, ngongkog 1 to flatter s.o.; 2 (*or* **ongkog-ongkog**) to try to raise o.s. on all fours (of babies learning to crawl);

mongkog to feel rightfully proud with o.s.; **mongkogaké** to cause to be proud.

ongkok, ngongkok to stick to the price;

ongkok-ongkokan to bid against each other, not give up.

ongkong I *var of* **ongkog**.

II, **ngongkongaké** to push s.o. from behind. *See also* **jongkong** II, **jorog** II.

ongkos cost, fee, expense(s);

ngongkosi to pay the expenses of;

ngongkosaké to have s.t. done for payment.

ongkrag, ngongkrag-ongkrag to shake s.t.; to disturb.

ongkrag-angkreg to stop and start by

turns; to proceed haltingly. *See also* **anggreg**.

ongkrah, ngongkrah-ongkrah to mess things up, scatter things about.

ongkrèk object used as a lever;
ngongkrèk to pry with a lever.

ongkrong, ngongkrong to lie loosely on top of s.t. (*e.g.* lid on pot);
ngongkrongaké *or* **ngongkrong-ongkrongaké** to put s.t. up high. *See also* **mongkrong I**

onglang-angling *see* **angling**.

ongod, ongod-ongod *or* **ngongod-ongod** to cut, shape (wood, bamboo, with small knife);
ngongodi to sharpen s.t.;
ngongodaké to sharpen s.t. for s.o.;
ongodan sharpening tool, (pencil) sharpener;
pangod small knife.

ongol, ongol-ongol a gelatin-like food eaten with shredded coconut.

ongot *see* **ongod**.

ongseb *var of* **ungseb**.

ongslah, ngongslah to dismiss, sack.

ongsrong, ngongsrong to pant;
ngongsrongaké to make s.o. pant.

oni *reg var of* **uni I**.

onjèt *reg* a share of rice received for one's services during harvesting.

onjlog, ngonjlog to walk along in careless disregard of others.

onjo superior to one's fellows, outstanding;
ngonjoni 1 to raise the bid (when negotiating with a seller); **2** to overshadow (others of the same group);
onjo-onjonan 1 to compete in efforts to outshine each other; **2** to outbid each other.

onjog *var of* **onjlog**.

onjot time extension;
ngonjot *reg* **1** to extend (a contract, paying debt *etc*); **2** to continue carrying a heavy burden after taking a rest for a while;

ngonjoti to grant a time extension (to);
ngonjotaké to extend the time of (a contract *etc*);
onjotan 1 (*or* **pangonjot**) time extension; **2** period of time for carrying a heavy burden;
saonjotan 1 period of time, after a while; **2** throughout a period of time.

onta *var of* **unta**.

ontab *lit, var of* **untab**.

ontal, ngontalaké to knock s.t. to one side;
kontal to get flung aside.

ontal-antil, ngontal-antilaké to cause s.t. or s.o. to move back and forth.

ontang-anting I alone in the world, without relatives; an only child.
II *var of* **ontal-antil**.

ontang-ontang *reg* trusted person among the village people.

onté bunch, cluster;
onté-ontéan bunched together;
saonté a bunch.

ontèl flower of the **kluwih** (breadfruit) tree.

onten to exist; there is/are (*md for* **ana**).

onthal, onthal-onthalan *reg* to engage in wayward *or* disgraceful behaviour, play tricks.

onthèl (*or* **onthèl-onthèl**) crank(shaft);
ngonthèl 1 to crank (an old-style car, to start it); **2** to pedal, to operate a pedicab as one's livelihood.

ontho-ontho hot soybean ball.

onthoh, ngonthoh-onthoh to caress.

ontob *reg* brim (of basketwork).

ontog, ngontog-ontog, montog annoyed, irritated.

ontong 1 a half-open banana bud; **2** cob, counting unit for corn;
ngontong 1 (*or* **montong**) to bloom (of banana trees); **2** resembling a banana flower.

ontor I, **ngontor** to flush, pour water, wash down with water.

II, **ngontor-ontor** *reg* 1 furious, raging; 2 to rage (fire, flame).

ontrag shaking;

ngontragaké to cause s.t. to shake, agitate s.t.;

kontrag to shake, vibrate.

ontran, **ontran-ontran** commotion, tumult, rebellion.

ontung *reg var of* **untung**.

onya *reg* to go off, turn away somewhere else;

ngonyani to elude.

onyo, **ngonyo-onyo** to keep pressing s.o. angrily. *See also* **oso**.

onyok, **ngonyok-onyokaké** to push (merchandise on the customer), parade one's wares.

oom, **om** *term of address for older non-Indonesian male*, 'uncle'.

opah *ng*, **épah** *kr*, (*or* **opahan**) pay, wages, compensation for services;

ngopahi to pay s.o. for their services;

ngopahaké to have s.t. done for payment;

opahan 1 wages; 2 hired worker.

opak fried crisp chip made from a roll of steamed rice or cassava; - **angin** *or* - **gambir** wafer-like snack;

ngopak to make the above snack.

opas *var of* **upas** I.

opèl, **ngopèli** 1 to remove things adhering to s.t. and leave it smooth(er); 2 to pick (the kernels) off a cob of corn.

opèn 1 careful of one's (or s.o.'s) belongings; 2 acquisitive; 3 meddlesome;

ngopèni 1 to take good care of; 2 to acquire or take possession of (things, habitually);

kopèn well cared for, carefully tended;

pangopèn *or* **opènan** *or* **opèn-opènan** (good) care, maintenance, cultivation.

oper 1 transfer; 2 shifting (gears);

ngoper 1 to transfer, change the posi-

tion of; 2 to take s.t. over; 3 to hand over, pass s.t. to;

ngoperaké 1 to transfer to, pass down;

operan (act of) shifting, passing, transferring;

oper-operan to exchange, swap s.t.

oplèt a small urban bus.

oplok, **ngoplok** to shiver, tremble from fear;

oplok-oplok to flap.

opor meat or chicken dish cooked with coconut cream and various spices.

oprak, **ngoprak-oprak** 1 to keep after, drive, nag; 2 to drive out, scare off.

oprès, **ngoprès** *reg* to chatter, talk about s.t. trivial.

oprok, **ngoprok** 1 piled up; 2 exhausted; 3 to defecate in the wrong place, *e.g.* one's clothing;

oprokan a disorderly heap.

opsiner supervisor on plantations, school *etc* during the colonial period.

opsir officer.

opyak, **ngopyak-opyak** 1 (*or* **ngopyak-opyaki**) to demand loudly and persistently; 2 *var of* **oprak**.

opyan, **opyan-opyan** extravagant luxuries. *See also* **ropyan**.

opyok, **ngopyok** 1 to beat, whip (*e.g.* eggs, cream); 2 to dab with water;

ngopyok-opyok to prepare for use by moistening;

ngopyok-opyoki to apply moisture to.

ora *ng*, (*irregular pronoun*) **boten** *kr*, 1 not; 2 no; **apa** - ... or not?; **-(b)isa** cannot; - **kok** of course not!; **kok ora** why not?; **ya** - yes or no?, isn't that right?; **ora-ora**, **sing** - silly, improper; **ora-orané** (it is) out of the question (that...);

ngorani to say no (to);

ngorakaké to deny the truth of;

orané or not;

saora-orané at least;

oraa if not; even if it were not so;

ora wis-wis to keep on (do)ing endlessly.

orag *reg var of* **orog**.

orah *inf var of* **ora**.

orak I *inf var of* **ora**.

II s.o.'s turn (at) (*var of* **urak I**).

orak-arik *see* **arik**.

oran *reg* isn't it? doesn't it?

oranana *lit* there is not/are not; does not
exist (*var of* **ora ana**).

oranye orange(-coloured);

oranyekrus orange crush (drink).

oré, ngoré *or* **oré-oré** to allow (one's hair)
to hang down loosely;

oréan *or* **oré-oré** (of hair) hanging
loose.

oreg to shake with a mighty force;

ngoregaké to cause to shake violently;

oreg-oregan large-scale disturbance,
commotion, tumult.

orèh I a cosmetic flower mixture (*var of*
borèh);

ngorèh-orèh to apply the above flower
mixture to the skin.

II, ngorèhaké to explain, spell out;

orèhan 1 notes, sketches; **2** expression, account, narration; **3** *reg* inferior.
Also **oréyan**.

orèk I, ngorèk to croak (of frogs).

II, orèk-orèk 1 (to make) a sketch,
draft; **2** to scribble;

ngorèk-orèk *or* **ngorak-orèk 1** to
scribble, make marks (on); **2** to
scratch out, cross out;

orèk-orèkan 1 scribble; **2** sketched-in
drafts.

III, ngorèk to clean the ears with an
earpick (*see also* **korèk I**).

orem I *lit* to languish; grieving, anxious.

II, orem-orem *reg* a coconut milk
soup of fermented soybean cake and
green chili.

orèn *var of* **urèn**.

orèt I *var of* **orèk II**.

II, orèt-orèt *repr* rattling sound.

ori, pring - thorny bamboo;

orèn thicket of thorny bamboo.

ormat *var of* **urmat**.

orod I *reg* to ebb, recede;

ngorodaké to hand down, pass along
(*var of* **nglorodaké**, *see* **lorod**).

II, ngorod-orod to use wastefully.

orog, ngorog-orog to shake s.t.

orok I, orok-orok a plant that produces a
pea-like vegetable.

II, ngorok to snore.

orong, orong-orong mole-cricket;

kaya orong-orong kepidak *idiom* to
suddenly stop talking.

orot *see* **orod**.

osada *var of* **usada**.

osak-asik *see* **asik**.

osé I peeled peas or beans (*var of* **wosé**).

II hurray!

osèg to fidget.

osèng I a small fibre brush for cleaning
plates.

II, osèng-osèng 1 *repr* the sizzling
sound made by spreading cooking oil
around in a hot frying pan; **2** a meat
and vegetable dish cooked in a frying
pan prepared as above.

osèr, ngosèr-osèr to smear;

ngosèri to grease s.t.;

ngosèr-osèri to keep smearing;

ngosèraké to smear s.t. with;

ngosèr-osèraké to smear s.t. repeatedly (with).

osik 1 osiking ati intuition, idea; **2** (*or*
mosik) to move;

ngosikaké 1 to give s.o. the impetus to
(do); **2** to move s.o. to (do); to remind
s.o. of.

oso, ngoso to speak in a rough or angry
tone; to snarl;

ngoso-oso to keep pressing s.o. angrily.

osog I *repr* a rasping sound;

ngosog to rub, polish, scrape;

ngosog-osog to keep rasping.

II, **ngosog** *reg* to pick up s.t. with a cloth.

osok *see* **osog**.

osos, ngosos to hiss, sizzle;
ngososaké to let s.t. escape through an opening.

osrag-osrog to produce a grazing sound. *See also* **srog**.

ot *excl* expressing surprise, dismay, warning: 'look out, stop!'.

ota-oto 1 (to work) without artistry; 2 rough, crude.

otah *reg var of* **wutah**.

otak *var of* **utek**.

otang *var of* **utang**.

oté, oté-oté half-naked, not wearing a shirt.

otèk I a variety of grain used as birdseed.
II *reg* a small fishnet.

oter I *reg* to search everywhere.
II (*or* **oter-pater**) *lit* 1 loud sound of wind, thunder; 2 loud like thunder.

othak, I ngothaki 1 to pull s.t. apart; 2 to break (things) off.
II, **othak-othak** cane, walking stick;
ngothak-othak to prod at with a pole;
kaya othak-othak méga very thin and tall.

othé I, **othé-othé** *var of* **oté-oté**.
II, **othé-othé** a cricket-like insect.

othèh, ngothèh-othèh to scoop or stir up (*e.g.* the vegetables that have sunk to the bottom of the soup pot).

othèk I loose but still attached;
othèk-othèk *repr* the rattling of a loose object;
ngothèk-othèk to shake s.t. and produce rattling sounds.
II *coll reg* the possession (of);
othèkku mine.
III, **ngothèk** *reg* to purchase (daily needs) bit by bit.

othèng, othèng-othèngan to play cards without money *or* with small bets.

othik *var of* **uthik**.

othol *reg var of* **okol**.

othong I *var of* **otong**.
II, **ngothong-othong** *reg* to coddle, pamper.

othor, ngothor to trickle;
othor-othor *repr* pouring water.

othot, ngothot-othot to pull s.t. this way and that in an effort to overcome it *or* break it down;
kothot (of meat) very tough.

oto I auto(mobile).
II protective cloth placed on a baby's chest for warmth.

otong, ngotong-otong to bring, carry, take s.t. heavy back and forth.

otot 1 muscle; 2 blood vessel; - **bayu** tendon, sinew, muscle;
ngotot 1 obstinate, adamant; 2 to talk so loud that the tendons stand out on the neck;
otot kawat, balung wesi *idiom* marvellously strong.

otra *reg* disturbance, fuss.

owad-awud *see* **awud**.

owah *ng*, **éwah** *kr*, 1 to change; 2 (to go) insane; - **gingsir** to change constantly;
ora owah unchanging, permanent;
ngowahi to change s.t.;
ngowahaké 1 to cause to be changed; 2 to drive s.o. mad
owah-owahan a change.

owak, ngowak-owak wide open, gaping.

owal-awil *see* **awil**.

owat *reg* oh my! heavens!

owé *or* **owèn** *reg* (of tree) just bearing fruit.

owèh, ngowèh to slobber, drool.

owèk, owèk-owèk *repr* a baby's cry;
ngowèk *or* **ngowèk-owèk** 1 (of baby) to whimper; 2 to low (buffalo).

owel reluctant to be separated (from); regretful about an anticipated loss;
ngoweli *or* **ngowelaké** to feel unable to miss s.t.;

owelan *or* owel-owelan (by nature) unable to give up (possessions).

owok, ngowok (of eyes) sunken. *See also* wok I.

owol, ngowol-owol to mess up (things that were neatly arranged).

oyag to shake violently;
ngoyag-oyag to shake s.t. violently;
ngoyag-ayig to wobble, shake.

oyah, ngoyahaké to set a dog (on), incite (against).

oyak, ngoyak to chase;
ngoyak-oyak 1 to keep chasing; 2 to keep pushing s.o. to (do);
oyak-oyakan 1 to engage in a chase (one after the other); 2 to chase each other around;
ngoyak-oyak turus ijo *prov* 1 to chase young girls or married women; 2 to make trouble for an innocent bystander;
pangoyak act or way of chasing.

oyan Chinese black paint-powder.

oyang-oyong *see* oyong.

oyeg *var of* oreg.

oyèng *reg* restless, turbulent.

oyod root;
ngoyod 1 to take root; 2 *fig* to be settled in a certain place for many years;
oyod-oyodan various kinds of roots;
saoyod one growing period of a crop.

oyog, ngoyog *or* ngoyog-oyog to shake s.t. violently;
oyog-oyogan to shake each other.

oyok, ngoyok to take away by force, snatch away;
oyok-oyokan 1 to chase after, hunt down; 2 to struggle with each other to attain a goal.

oyol, I kind of small fish trap.
II ngoyol-oyol to fiddle with s.t.

oyong, oyong-oyong *or* oyang-oyong 1 to move (change residence) frequently; 2 to carry s.t. heavy back and forth;
ngoyong-oyong *or* ngoyang-oyong to move (s.t. large and unwieldy) often.
See also boyong.

oyos, ngoyos to go out and get wet in the rain (*e.g.* naughty boy). *See also* loyos.

oyot, ngoyoti *reg* to smooth, shave (wood, bamboo) with a knife.

P

pa what? (*shtf of* apa).

paben to quarrel (*kr for* padu I);

  pabenan *reg* to talk to each other.

pabrik factory.

paca *reg* to succeed in (do)ing.

pacak I an orderly arrangement; - baris in marching array or deployment; - gulu a certain neck movement in the classical dance;

  macak to dress up;

  macaki 1 to dress up s.o.; 2 to bedeck for a formal occasion; 3 well-dressed; 4 to trim a young coconut in order to make it ready for drinking;

  pacakan 1 formal dress; 2 formal decorations; 3 ready trimmed (of young coconut);

  pepacak regulations, rules.

  II, macak to set out (in a publication);

  kapacak set out (in a publication).

pacal I a variety of freshwater fish.

  II an adze (used by carpenters);

  macali to smooth s.t. with an adze.

pacalang *ng*, pacambeng *kr*, 1 a soldier who leads the march; 2 village police;

  macalang to be(come) one of the above.

pacambeng *kr for* pacalang.

pacang, macangi to take s.o. as one's betrothed;

  macangaké to arrange for s.o.'s engagement, affiance;

  pacangan 1 engaged, betrothed; 2 fiancé, fiancée.

pacar I a tree with fragrant flowers and small red fruits;

  macar to colour the fingernails red.

  II boyfriend or girlfriend; fiancé or fiancée;

  macari to make s.o. one's girlfriend;

  pacaran to go out with one's girl-friend/boyfriend.

pacara ceremony (*shtf of* upacara).

pacas *var of* pancas.

pacé I a certain fruit, often made into a drink as a folk medicine.

  II *reg* deception;

  macé to deceive.

pacek I *reg* stake, stick;

  pacekan short spear.

  II 1 main root of a plant; 2 line of descent.

  III, maceki (of animals) to mount for copulation;

  pamacek stud, male animal for breed-ing.

  IV, pepacek *reg* prohibition, regula-tion, rule;

  maceki to forbid, prohibit, interdict.

  V *reg* small leech (*var of* pacet I).

  VI, paceken *reg* to get a pain (stitch) in the stomach.

paceklak *var of* paceklik.

paceklik famine, time of scarcity before harvest.

pacel a large pin, peg;

  macel to fix, join (timbers) with such a peg.

pacenceng *see* pecenceng.

pacengès *see* pecengès.

pacengis *see* pecengis.

pacécé *see* pecécé.

pacèran *reg var of* pacerèn.

pacerèn gutter, ditch.

pacet I small kind of small leech.

  II, macet at an impasse, deadlocked, blocked.

pacèt I children's game played with can-dlenuts.

  II, pacètan snacks served with tea (*var of* pacitan).

pacical *see* pecical.

pacicil *see* **pecicil**.

pacima *lit* west(ern) (*also* **pracima**).

pacing a plant used to ward off evil influences (the root used medicinally).

pacira *reg* covered gallery attached to a house.

paciri identifying mark. *See also* **ciri**.

pacit, pacitan snacks served with tea.

pacok, macokaké to tease s.o. about liking the opposite sex;
pacok-pacokan to tease each other about s.o. of the opposite sex.

pacrabakan place for teaching at a holy man's shrine, school.

pacuca-pacucu *see* **pecuca-pecucu**.

pacuh, macuhi *or* **macuhaké** to ordain, decree;
pacuhan *or* **pepacuh** ordinance, rules.

pacuk *reg* go-between for arranging a marriage;
macuki to act as a go-between for arranging a marriage.

pacul a hoe, tool for loosening soil; - **bawak** a hoe with partly wooden blade; - **gowang** a style of Javanese house with a certain shape of roof; - **kolong** *or* - **slandhok** an iron hoe with a wooden handle; - **jejeg** *or* - **penet** spade;
macul to hoe;
maculi to work (soil) with a hoe;
maculaké to use s.t. as a hoe; to work (soil) for s.o. else.

pacumpleng property tax.

pacung, macungaké to give directions to s.o.

pacuri *reg* masonry wall around a house or garden (*var of* **cepuri**).

pacuwan *see* **pacuh**.

pada I Javanese script punctuation mark; 2 stanza; - **lingsa** comma; - **lungsi** full stop, point; -**jantra** *lit* bicycle; **purwa-** a Javanese script character used as an opening of the text; **madya-** 1 a Javanese script character used in the middle of the text; 2 earth, place of human habitation (*see also* **madya**); **wasana** - a Javanese script character used at the end of the text;
mada to punctuate.
II *lit* foot.
III clearly understood; **durung** - not yet clear (explanation, appointment).

padal, madal 1 to press against; 2 to resist;
madalaké to press s.t. against/to.

padasan a large earthen vessel with a tap, containing water for ritual cleaning of the face, hands and feet before prayer.

padha *ng*, **sami** *kr* 1 same, equal; alike; 2 *gram, plural marker*; - **déné** equally, as ... as; - **karo** 1 the same as, similar to; 2 equals (in arithmetic); - **siji** a hand-to-hand fight; one each; - **uga** (just) as, (just) like; - **waé** just the same;
padha-padha 1 likewise, alike; 2 among, out of the total; 3 likewise, in the same manner; **sami-sami** (the) same to you! (as a response to 'thank-you');
madha 1 to resemble; 2 to make (a)like;
madhani 1 to equal, be the same as;
madhakaké to compare, make equal;
pepadhané *or* **sapepadhané** 1 one's equals, one's fellows; 2 and the like;
sapadha-padha in the same or similar circumstances.

padhak I *reg* saltpan, place where salt is produced.
II near, close (*var of* **pedhak II**).

padhang 1 bright, light; 2 clear; 3 to become light; - **atiné** ; cheered up; - **bulan** moonlight; - **ndhrandhang** *or* - **njingglang** very bright; brightly lit;
madhangi to light, illuminate s.t.;
madhangaké 1 to illuminate, make s.t. light/bright; 2 to clarify, light up;
padhangan light place;

pepadhang light, brightness;
padhangan atèn cheerful by nature, good-humoured;
weruh padhang hawa *idiom* to see the light of day, to be born.

padhar, padharan stomach, belly (*k.i. for* weteng).

padhas (various kinds of) hard ground (not rock);
madhas hard, resembling padhas;
padhasan an area of hard ground.

padhati ox-cart (*var of* pedhati).

padhatos *kr for* padhati.

padhek *reg* near, close (to) (*var of* pedhak).

padhem extinguished; *reg* dead;
madhemi *reg* to kill.

padhet 1 solid, compact; 2 dense;
madhet tightly compressed;
madheti *or* madhetaké to compress tightly.

padhola *lit* earthquake.

padhung *reg* wooden bench.

padhidhing chilly, chilled; mangsa - cold weather, a nighttime chill in the dry season (*var of* bedhidhing).

padma *lit* lotus.

padmi, garwa - queen, a king's wife of equal rank.

pados to look for, seek (*kr for* golèk).

padpinder boy or girl scout (during the colonial period).

padu I *ng*, paben *kr*, to quarrel;
madoni to talk back, contradict;
madokaké to dispute on s.o.'s behalf;
padon *or* pepadon 1 (to have) a dispute or difference of opinion; 2 negotiator.
II, padon corner, angle;
madoni to plough the corners of (a field).
III, paduné the fact is…, actually.

padudon quarrelling. *See also* dudu.

paduka *lit* you, your.

paduraksa, padureksa *reg* the outside corners of a wall.

paé *lit* different; ora (tan) paé it makes no difference.

paédah use, usefulness, benefit, profit;
maédahi useful, beneficial;
maédahaké to put s.t. to use, turn s.t. to a useful purpose.

paéka *or* paékan a piece of deceit;
maéka *or* maékani to cheat or deceive s.o.

paélan *reg* 1 famine; 2 time of scarcity before harvest.

paèlu, maèlu to do as s.o. asks; to listen to s.o.'s advice.

paèran *lit* bathing-place, bathroom.

paès 1 bridal make-up and ornamentation; 2 finery, ornamentation;
maèsi to make up with bridal cosmetics;
pepaès to adorn o.s.;
paèsan wearing bridal make-up.

paésan *reg* grave-marker (*var of* maésan).

paéthé *reg* famine, time of scarcity before harvest.

paga kitchen shelf or rack for earthenware and crockery.

pagajih silt or sediment (of river).

pagak stump (of branch). *See also* pragak.

pagang, magang 1 to wait for (*see also* adhang); 2 to be an apprentice.

pagas, magas to cut back, prune.

pageblug disastrous epidemic.

pagéné why? how (come)? (*var of* yagéné). *See also* généya.

pager 1 fence, outside wall; 2 shield of spells to protect from black magic; - bata *or* - témbok brick wall; - gaplok bamboo fence used as a support for climbing vines;
mager *or* mageri 1 to surround with a fence; 2 *fig* to limit s.o.'s wishes; 3 to set up a shield of spells;

pager mangan tandur(an) *prov* to do harm to s.t. entrusted to one's care; **ngrusak pager ayu** *idiom* to engage in illicit sex with another's wife.

pagir *reg* ridge (of mountain).

pago *reg* low wooden bench.

pagol, I magol fail;
    magoli to hinder, block;
    magolaké to cause to fail;
    pagolan hindrance, obstacle;
    II, **magol-magol** to sway the hips provocatively.

pagon 1 *reg* steady;
    magon to stand firm;
    magoni to fix, fasten, to secure.

pagowong a sudden darkness during the day.

pagupon dovecote. *See also* **gupu.**

paguron 1 instruction in higher wisdom; 2 residence of the teacher.

pagut, magut *lit* to step forward; **- jurit** *or* **- yuda** to wage war.

pahal *reg* livelihood, job.

pahala merit, reward for moral conduct, benefit reaped.

paham 1 understanding; 2 to understand, knowledgeable; 3 body of knowledge or thought; 4 view, concept, doctrine;
    mahami to understand;
    mahamaké to explain;
    pahaman opinion.

pahang name of the 16th **wuku.**

pahat I, mahat *reg* to tap (sap of tree).
    II, **mahat** to distil;
    pahatan 1 distilled; 2 distillation.

paheman *lit* council, board.

paidah *var of* **paédah.**

paido *ng,* **paiben** *kr,* **maido 1** to express doubt or disbelief; 2 to disparage, belittle;
    paidon 1 one whose word is doubted; 2 one who is disparaged.

paidon *see* **idu.**

paiguh effort, exertion (*var of* **pangiguh**).

See also **iguh.**

paila *reg* 1 famine; 2 time of scarcity before harvest.

pailit bankrupt;
    mailitaké to cause to be bankrupt.

Paing a day of the five-day week.

pait I bitter; **- getir; - madu** very sweet: even honey is more bitter;
    maiti to embitter;
    maitaké to make s.t. more bitter than before;
    paitan various drinks (folk medicine) that are bitter.
    II, **paitan** financial capital (*var of* **pawitan**);
    maiti to finance an enterprise.

paja, ora paja-paja not at all.

pajar 1 bright, light (*kr for* **padhang**); 2 to cheer up; 3 daybreak, dawn;
    majaraké to cheer s.o. up.

pajeg *ng,* **paos** *kr,* 1 tax; 2 rental money for land;
    majegi 1 to levy a tax on s.t.; 2 to pay taxes for; to pay up (one's taxes or lease money); 3 to dock s.o.'s profit;
    majegaké to lease out (land);
    pamajeg rental terms;
    pamajegan leased-out land.

pajeng I to be in demand (*kr for* **payu I**). II (*kr for* **paju**).

paju 1 (**pajeng** *opt kr*) angle, corner; 2 metal wedge for splitting wood;
    maju *or* **majokaké** to split (wood) with a wedge.

pajut *lit* lamp, light.

pak I 1 father (*shtf of* **bapak**); 2 *adr, title* father; older or higher-status male; **-dhé, - tuwa** (**sepuh** *kr*) uncle (parent's older brother); **-lik** (**- alit** *kr*) uncle (parent's younger brother); **pakné** term by which a wife addresses her husband if they have children;
    ngepak to treat or regard s.o. as one's father;
    pakpakan brothel boss.

II 1 bundle, package; 2 pack;
ngepak to pack;
ngepaki to make into a bundle.
III, pak gadhé *reg* pawnshop.
IV, pak glèdhèg *reg* small cart with iron wheels.
pakah *or* makah (of main stem) having a branch.
pakakas *var of* bekakas.
pakal I boat caulking;
makal to caulk, apply putty or caulking.
II *reg* livelihood, job.
pakan *or* pakanan animal food;
makan 1 to take effect; 2 *fig* to consume, take a lot of (time, money);
makani to feed (an animal);
makakaké to 1 to feed s.t. to (an animal); 2 to cause s.t. to take effect.
pakang *reg* a thick branch.
pakangkang *var of* pekangkang.
pakathik 1 servant (*e.g.* grasscutter for horses); 2 follower.
pakatul *var of* bekatul.
pakéan 1 suit (jacket and trousers); 2 horse harness.
pakèhan *see* pakéan.
pakèkèh *see* pèkèh, pekèkèh.
pakèl I variety of mango, 'horse-mango'.
II *reg* armpit.
pakéling *lit* mindful. *See also* éling.
pakem 1 summary, concise version of a story used as a guide by a dhalang; 2 a handbook containing outlines of such stories; - balungan story in skeletal form; - gancaran story in scenario form; - padhalangan story in script form showing dialogue, narration, and music for a shadow-play.
pakemit I fee for guard duty. *See also* kemit.
II, pakemitan *reg* charm, talisman.
paken nail (*reg kr for* paku).
pakèn *see* kèn, kon.
pakenceng *see* kenceng.

pakeneng *var of* bekeneng.
pakèngkèng *var of* pekèngkèng.
pakenira you, your (Basa Kadhaton; used by royalty to subordinates). *See also* manira.
pakepel *reg* food presented to a social superior when ritual feast is being held.
pakéring *lit* respect. *See also* éring.
pakerti character, nature.
pakès *reg* salt warehouse.
pakèwed *kr for* pakéwuh.
pakéwuh *ng*, pakèwed *kr*, 1 (to have) difficulty; 2 (to feel) uncomfortable, uneasy, awkward, ill at ease;
makéwuhi *or* makéwuhaké 1 to cause difficulty for; 2 to cause to feel discomfort; 3 embarrassing;
pakéwuhan shy, timid, uncomfortable with people.
See also éwuh.
pakéyan *see* pakéan.
pakhis *var of* pakès.
pakir *var of* fakir.
pakis fern, bracken; -aji a variety of fern.
pakiwèn *reg kr for* pakuwon. *See also* kuwu.
paklaring (paklantun *kr*) explanation, declaration, certificate.
paklèkèk tax on slaughtered animals.
pakolèh *ng*, pikantuk *kr*, 1 gain; to gain; 2 to produce good results; 3 use, results;
makolèhi productive, lucrative;
pakolèhan valuable result.
See also olèh.
pakolih *var of* pakolèh.
pakon *see* kon, akon.
pakongkong *see* pekongkong.
pakpung *chld* to have a bath.
pakra, ora pakra not good-looking at all.
paksa *var of* peksa.
paksi bird (*lit, var of* peksi).
paku (iron or copper) nail; - idep small nail; - jamur *or* - jamuran drawing-pin; - kelingan rivet;

maku *or* makoni to nail s.t. down;
pakon *or* pakonan nailed down tightly.

pakudhung copy of official decree.

pakungkung *see* pekungkung.

pakupon dovecote (*var of* gupon).

pal I 1 measure of distance: 1,507
metres; 2 marker placed at one-pal
intervals along a road.
II, ngepal convinced that s.t. undesirable will take place.

pala I *lit* fruit; - gumantung fruits that
grow on trees; - kependhem edible
roots - kesimpar fruits that grow at
ground level; - kirna fruits (cultivated) from long-lived trees; - kitri fruits
from orchard trees; -wija *or* - wiji crop
other than rice planted in a field.
II nutmeg.
III, mala *lit* to chastise.

palacidra *lit* 1 untrue, false; 2 falseness,
treachery.

paladho *see* paladhu.

paladhu a time of floods. *See also* ladhu
I.

palagara a gift presented to a social superior when a ritual feast is being held.

palah *reg* even, moreover, beyond that
(*var of* malah).

palak, ngèlmu - astronomy (*var of* falak).

palakerti *lit* accessory.

palaki wedding;
malakèkaké to marry off a daughter.
See also laki.

palaku I *reg* village messenger.
II (palampah *kr*) *lit* request; malaku
to request;
malakoni to ask s.o. to do s.t.

palakrama *lit* 1 greeting, salutation; 2
marriage, wedding.

palakrami *var of* palakrama.

palal *lit* grace, favour (of God).

palamarta *var of* paramarta.

palana saddle.

palang *ng*, pambeng *kr*, 1 obstacle,
object placed crosswise to s.t.; 2
bridge hand-rail;
malang to lie crosswise;
malangi to impede;
malangaké to use as a barrier;
malang-mégung 1 to lie across; 2
unlucky, unfortunate;
kepalang obstructed, impeded;
kepalang tanggung not worth the
trouble;
pepalang obstacle, hindrance;
palangan 1 railing, armrest; 2 hindrance.

palanggatan *lit* retreat, secret room.

palanyahan *see* lanyah.

palar, malar *reg* to take, fetch;
malari *reg* to ask for help;
palar-pinulir to help each other.

palastha *lit* 1 finished; 2 completed.

palastra *lit* dead; to die.

palawija I crops planted as second crop
in dry season.
II misshapen servants maintained in
the royal palace.

palaur *var of* plaur.

palem palm tree.

palèn 1 *reg* a small-scale peddler; 2 small
second-hand articles sold by peddlers
in the marketplace.

paleng *reg* headache.

palestha *see* palastha.

pali, pepali *lit* prohibitions (from ancestors on their descendants).

palibaya *lit* colleague, brother; you, your.

palih half (*kr for* paro).

palikrama *lit* honour, respect, esteem.

palimirma *lit* pity, mercy.

paling most.

palir a long dent or scratch mark on a
surface;
malir to scratch a long mark on s.t.;
paliran 1 a long scratch mark; 2 *reg*
small path.

paliwara *lit* 1 news; 2 messenger; 3
female servant.

paljayan *reg* brothel.

palowanu *lit* throne.

palsu false, fake;
 malsu to counterfeit, falsify.

palu hammer, mallet;
 malu to hammer.

palud cork; the tree the bark of which produces cork.

paluh muddy swampy ground;
 maluh full of mud;
 kepaluh stuck in the mud.

palung a variety of sea fish.

palunturan *var of* pluntur I.

palupi *lit* 1 example; 2 letter, document.

paluwanu *var of* palowanu.

palwa *lit* boat, ship.

palwaga *lit* monkey.

pama *shtf of* upama.

pamadé *lit* middle, middlemost.

pamah, mamah to chew, bite on.

paman uncle (parent's younger brother).

pamarta, Sang - the Saviour.

pamasa *lit* king, monarch.

pambayun I *lit* the eldest (of children).
 II *lit* breast.

pamekak *see* mekak.

pamèr to show off;
 mamèri to show to s.o.;
 mamèraké to show s.t.;
 pamèran exhibition, show.

pami *shtf of* upami.

pamidhangan shoulder (*k.i. for* pundhak).

pamili relatives, family.

pamit 1 permission to leave or be absent; 2 to apply for leave;
 mamiti to take leave of s.o.;
 mamitaké to say goodbye on behalf of s.o.; to have s.o. say goodbye or give notice of not being able to come;
 pamitan 1 to take leave; 2 to say goodbye to each other.

pamong one who cares for, watches over, provides for another.

pamor 1 blending, alloy; 2 pattern on a kris blade achieved by forging different metals.

pamrih the hope of reward, expectation of a return for o.s.;
 sepi ing pamrih (ramé ing gawé) *expr* devoid of self-interest (devoted to work).

pamugari *lit* leader, commander.

pamuk *lit* commander, war chief.

pan I pan, baking pan;
 ngepan to bake in a pan;
 pangepan act of baking.
 II *reg* to catch on, get it (*also* empan).
 III *lit* for, as (*also* apan, mapan I).
 IV *reg* but.

pana *lit* to be right, clear.

panah *ng*, jemparing *kr*, arrow;
 manah to shoot at with a bow and arrow;
 manahi to shoot an arrow repeatedly;
 manahaké to shoot an arrow for s.o.; to shoot s.t. out like an arrow;
 panahan archery;
 pamanah act or way of shooting with a bow and arrow;
 sapamanah the distance of a bowshot.

panakawan 1 follower, servant; 2 (in wayang) a follower of the hero who advises, noted for humour (*also* punakawan);
 manakawan to be or act as a panakawan.

panambang I suffix.
 II craft used for ferrying;
 panambangan ferry, crossing.
 See also tambang I.

panampan serving tray, platter (*k.i. for* talam).

pananggap I gently sloping roof section below the steeply ascending portion above.
 II tax collector. *See also* tanggap I.

panas *ng*, bentèr *kr* 1 hot (as opposed to cold); 2 feverish; 3 magically dangerous; bringing misfortune; - tis (to

have) malaria; **dhuwit** - cursed
money; - **atèn** envious;
manas to sunbathe;
manasi 1 to get hot under the collar; **2**
to heat s.t.; to anger s.o.;
manasaké to heat s.t.; - **ati** annoying,
exasperating; - **kuping** to anger/offend
s.o.;
panasan 1 to sun o.s.; **2** sunny place;
3 to get on people's nerves;
pepanas to stay out in the sun;
kepanasan to stay in the sun too long;
manasatèni 1 to irritate, get on s.o.'s
nerves; **2** to envy s.o. or s.t.
panasar I tobacco quid (*k.i. for* **susur**).
II, panasaran angered (but suppressed), embittered; **2** anxious to do
or find out s.t.
panasbaran hot-tempered, hotheaded.
panasbranan *var of* **panasbaran**.
panca *lit* five.
pancabakah *lit* to have a disagreement.
pancabaya *lit* all kinds of dangers.
pancad, mancad to stand/step up onto;
pancadan s.t. to stand/step up on; a
stepping-stone.
pancah, mancahi to contradict, answer
back.
pancak, mancak to catch with both
hands;
pancakan *reg* **1** newly arrived; **2** ceremony for a baby, attended by small
children, at which the child's future
is foretold symbolically. *See also* **bancak**.
pancakara *lit* to fight, struggle; battle.
pancal, mancal 1 to kick accidentally;
- **donya** to die; **2** to divorce one's husband by repaying the bride-price;
- **kemul** to fall asleep;
kepancal 1 to get kicked; **2** to get left
behind, miss one's transportation.
pancaniti *lit* royal audience-hall.
pancar, mancar to shine with radiant
beauty;

mancaraké to broadcast;
pamancar a broadcast, act of broad-
casting.
pancaroba 1 a great storm; **2** transition
period, period of life *etc*.
pancas, mancas to cut s.t. through with a
single stroke;
mancasi to settle (a matter);
mancasaké to cut s.t. for s.o.;
pancasan decision.
pancèn *ng*, **panci** *kr*, certainly, really, for
a fact;
pancèna *or* **pancèné** it is true.
pancer I 1 tap-root; **2** line of descent
(male, female).
II direction, destination;
mancer to point the direction.
III original form.
panci I cooking pan.
II 1 portion, share; **2** one's lot.
III for a fact (*kr for* **pancèn**).
pancik, mancik to stand on (in order to
reach higher);
pancikan s.t. to step up on.
pancing 1 fishing rod; **2** fish-hook.
mancing 1 to fish, angle; **2** to provoke,
start s.t.;
mancingaké 1 to use s.t. for bait; **2** to
fish for s.o.;
pancingan 1 bait; **2** fishing-place; **3** to
fish around;
pancingen to have a very painful sore
throat;
pamancing bait.
panclas *var of* **pancas**.
pancrut, mancrut to spurt, squirt;
pating pancrut *pl* to spatter.
pancur, mancur to flow downward, to
stream out;
pancuran fountain, spring.
pancuran kapit sendhang girl-boy-
girl sibling combination.
pandak, ora pandak unable to stand,
endure s.t.
pandam *lit* light, lamp.

pandara *var of* **bandara, bendara**.

pandek *reg* 1 fixed; 2 regular porter.

pandelar 1 candlestick; 2 standard-lamp.

pandelep *or* **mak pandelep** *repr* a quick disappearance or concealment;
  mandelep 1 to disappear, conceal o.s.; 2 recessed, set inward.

pandelik *see* **pendelik**.

pandelo *see* **pendelo**.

pandeng gaze, scrunity;
  mandeng to look at directly/fixedly;
  pandengan 1 to try to outstare; 2 view, opinion;
  pandeng-pandengan to stare at each other;
  pamandeng way of looking;
  sapamandeng a long distance, as far as one can see.

pandhak 1 short (*var of* **pendhèk**); 2 dwarf.

pandhan 1 pandanus tree; 2 fragrant pandanus leaf as cooking ingredient;
  pandhanan pandanus thicket.

pandhapa *see* **pendhapa**.

pandharat I a rope for tying up or leading cattle (*var of* **kendharat**).
  II one who serves when a ceremony is held.

pandhatos *reg kr* two-wheeled ox-cart.

Pandhawa 1 descendant of Pandhu, collective name of the five brothers of the wayang purwa repertoire; 2 five brothers.

pandhé 1 blacksmith; 2 skilled; 3 an expert, specialist;
  mandhé 1 to be or become a blacksmith; 2 to forge (metal);
  pandhéan place where a blacksmith works, smithy.

pandhéga, mandhégani to be the leader of.

pandhékar champion of a cause, skilled fighter.

pandhekel *see* **pendhekel**.

pandhekuk pancake.

pandhel pennant, banner.

pandhelong *see* **pendhelong**.

pandhelus *see* **pendhelus**.

pandhem *var of* **bandhem**.

pandhemèn (excavated) foundations.

pandhes 1 cut off just above the roots; 2 cut short (hair).

pandhèsèl *see* **pendhèsèl**.

pandhi I, mandhi to hold (a weapon) at shoulder height.
  II an expert (*var of* **pandhé**);

pandhikil *see* **pendhikil**.

pandhing *var of* **tandhing** I.

pandhiran *reg* to converse together.

pandhisil *see* **pendhisil**.

pandhita 1 holy hermit, great teacher, pundit; 2 Protestant preacher; - endhog *or* - antelu a false hermit;
  mandhita to be or become a holy hermit;
  kapandhitan wisdom, higher knowledge.

pandhok *reg* location, where s.t. is.

pandhokol *var of* **pendhokol**.

pandhosa *var of* **bandhosa**.

pandhu boy scout.

pandhuk *reg* to meet each other.

pandhukul *var of* **pendhukul**.

pandika *lit* words, what s.o. says. *See also* **ngendika**.

pandiringan *see* **pendiringan**.

pandom 1 (*or* **pandoman**) compass; 2 hands of a timepiece. *See also* **dom**.

pandon 1 effect; 2 practice; 3 end, ultimate fate. *See also* **don**.

panduk, kapanduk *lit* affected by s.t.; to come into contact with, be attached.

pandum fate, lot, allotment;
  mandumi to share, apportion;
  panduman portion, (one's) proper share.
  See also **dum**.

pandung I thief (*kr for* **maling**).
  II to fail to recognise (*kr for* **pangling**).

pané *reg* large flat bowl for cooking.

panèk *var of* pènèk.

panekar policeman; errand-runner.

panèket *title of a low-ranking official. See also* sèket.

panekuk pancake.

panembrama choral song for welcoming an honoured guest, accompanied by gamelan music.

panèn harvest;
maneni to take the harvest from (a field);
panènan to take in the harvest.

panèwu administrative officer having authority over village leaders;
kapanèwon 1 territory over which the above officer has jurisdiction; 2 residence of the above official.

pang branch;
ngepang to grow or put out branches.

pangan *ng,* (tedha *kr,* dhaharan *k.i.*) food, s.t. to eat;
mangan 1 to eat; 2 to consume;
prov akèh mangan uyah to be rich in experience;
mangan-mèngèn to keep on stuffing o.s.;
mangani to eat constantly;
pamangan act or way of eating;
memangan 1 to eat frequently; 2 act of eating;
panganan food, refreshment, s.t. to eat.

pangantèn 1 bride, groom; 2 pertaining to weddings;
pangantènan 1 to hold a wedding ceremony; 2 to play weddings, have a pretend wedding (children).

pangaron earthenware pot. *See also* karu.

pangaruh influence;
mengaruhi to influence.

pangéran 1 the Lord, God; 2 title for sons of monarchs, prince; - adipati anom crown prince; pangéran adipati arya title of the Mangkunagara and Paku Alam;

mangéran to serve s.o. as one's lord.

pangèstu blessing, good wishes, prayers;
mangèstu *lit* - pada to make a humble gesture of obeisance;
mangèstoni to bestow one's blessings on s.o.;
mangèstokaké *lit,* ngèstokaké to obey; to carry out (an order);
pangèstuné thanks to s.o.'s blessing.

panggah 1 to stand firm; 2 remaining as before, enduring, still going strong.

panggalih 1 heart, feelings (*k.i. for* ati I); 2 inner feeling (*k.i. for* batin);
manggalih to think about, consider. *See also* galih II.

panggang, manggang to roast, toast, grill;
panggangan 1 roasted meat dishes; 2 griller.

panggawa *var of* punggawa.

panggel 1 short and thick (neck); 2 double chin.

panggeng *reg* constant, remaining as before.

panggih to meet (*kr for* temu I);
pinanggih to meet (*kr for* kepethuk, *see* pethuk II).

panggil a request for s.t.;
panggilan notice, notification, document;
pepanggil *lit* a request for s.t.

panggok I *reg* hut on poles (in a ricefield).
II, manggoki to check (the progress of), retard.

panggul, manggul to carry on the shoulder.

panggung 1 stage, raised platform; 2 grandstand; 3 scaffolding;
panggungan platform built on piles, lookout tower;
manggung to appear on stage.

pangkal, mangkali to obstruct;
pangkalan obstruction.

pangkarag *or* mak pangkarag *repr* hair standing on end.

pangkat I 1 rank, position, status; 2 grade in school; 3 degree, power; **pamangkatan** ordinal number. II departure; **mangkat** to depart, leave.

pangkelang *see* **pangkeleng, pangkelung**.

pangkeleng, **pangkelang-pangkeleng** stiff, hard.

pangkeluk a bend; **mangkeluk** bent, crooked, warped.

pangkelung, **pangkelang-pangkelung** to keep bending or swaying.

pangkèng *reg* bedroom.

pangkered *or* **mak pangkered** *repr* shrinking; **mangkered** to shrink (in fear); **pangkeredan** to keep shrinking; **pating pangkered** *pl* feeling cowed.

pangking *var of* **pangkèng**.

pangkirig *or* **mak pangkirig** *repr* hair standing on end for a moment; **mangkirig** (of hair) standing on end; *fig* scared stiff.

pangkling *var of* **pangling**.

pangkring, **mangkring** to perch, alight, sit in a high place; **pangkringan** bird's perch.

pangku I to sit on s.o.'s lap; **mangku 1** to take on one's lap; **2** to take care, take charge of; **pangkon 1** lap; **2** sitting on s.o.'s lap; **3** occasion where the bride and the groom sit on the lap of the bride's father during the wedding ceremony. II, **pangkon** a Javanese script sign used for cutting off a vowel; **mangku** to cut off a vowel by using the above sign. III, **sapangkon** one set of gamelan instruments.

pangkul, **mangkul** *reg* **1** to carry; **2** to embrace s.o. by placing one's hands on their shoulders.

pangkur a certain classical verse form.

pangling to fail to recognise; **ora pang-ling** not to fail to recognise, definitely remember the face; **manglingi** so beautiful as to be unrecognisable; **panglingan** not good at remembering faces.

panglong later in the month than the full moon; waning moon.

pangon shepherd, herdsman. *See also* **angon**.

pangot a small curved knife with sharpened outer edge.

pangsi Chinese silk.

pangsit a variety of meatball or ravioli.

pangulu chief religious official in the community; - **banyu** village official in charge of irrigation; - **hakim** religious official who officiates at weddings; **pangulon** place where the above official resides or officiates.

pangur **1** chiselling tool; **2** tooth-file; evenly filed (of teeth); **mangur** to file (teeth); **panguran** (of teeth) filed.

paningset (*k.i. for* **sabuk**) sash.

panja I dibble; **manja** to plant using a dibble. II spur on a cock's foot (*reg kr for* **jalu**); **manja** to strike with the spur.

panjait *see* **penjait**.

panjak gamelan musician.

panjalin (**panjatos** *k.i.*) rattan.

panjang I long (*kr for* **dawa**); **dadi panjanging kidung** *idiom* famous, renowned. II - **putra** large oval-shaped plate; - **ilang** disposable bowl woven of young coconut leaves. III, **panjangan** *reg* gift of honour.

panjara *or* **panjaran** jail, prison (*var of* **kunjara**); **manjara** to put s.o. in prison.

panjat, **manjat** to slope, slant; **panjatan** a slope.

panjel *reg* substitute.

panjelut *see* penjelut.

panjenengan I reign, rule.

II you, your (*k.i. for* kowé); panjenen-gané (*kr* panjenenganipun) he, she (*k.i.* for dhèwèké); panjenengan dalem you (to nobles).

III walking stick (*k.i. for* teken).

panjer I down payment;

manjeri to pay (as) a deposit.

II, glittering star;

manjer 1 to keep (an oil lamp) burn-ing all night; 2 to keep s.t. up; - laya-ngan to keep a kite flying; - gendéra to put out the flag;

panjeran 1 night light; 2 flagpole;

lintang panjer ésuk (panjer rina) morning star;

lintang panjer soré evening star.

panji I flag, banner.

II a certain aristocratic title;

kepanjèn this aristocrat's residence.

III a legendary prince, the hero of a genre of stories.

panjidhor Turkish drum. *See also* jédhor I, jidhur.

panjing *lit* entering;

manjing 1 to enter; 2 to go to work; 3 to fit well together; 4 to be included in, considered as; 5 to accept, embrace (religion); wis manjing wektuné it is the right time for (prayer);

manjingi to enter s.t. *See also* anjing.

panjor *lit* basic principle.

panjoto, manjoto having a bump or bulge;

pating panjoto having many swellings or bulges.

panjrah spread; spreading (*var of* anjrah).

panjut *lit* lamp, light.

panjutu *var of* panjoto.

panili vanilla; the plant from the flowers of which this is extracted.

panitra secretary.

panitya committee.

panon 1 *lit* face; 2 eye, vision, sight. *See also* ton.

pantalon long trousers;

pantalonan to put on or wear long trousers.

pantar, pantaran about the same age (as).

pantèk 1 bamboo or wooden nails or dowels; 2 wedge driven into a space to make s.t. fit tighter;

mantèk to equip (a loose fitting) with such a wedge; to drive a wedge into;

pantèkan fitted with a wedge.

pantes appropriate, deserving, suitable;

mantesi to make attractive/becoming;

sarwa mantesi to form an attractive whole;

memantes to fix s.t. up;

sapantesé what is appropriate or suit-able.

pantha group, team; portion, share;

mantha *or* mantha-mantha to divide into groups;

pepanthan divided into groups, arranged in sections.

pantheng, mantheng 1 to pull s.t. taut or straight; 2 to require a total effort.

panti 1 house, residence; 2 institution, home.

pantun *kr*, pari *ng* rice (plant).

papa misery and suffering, poverty, mis-fortune; - cintraka misfortune,

papag, mapag 1 to pick up, call for; 2 to meet from opposite directions;

mapagaké 1 to go to meet; 2 to have s.o. go to meet;

kepapag to meet and pass (s.t. going in the opposite direction);

papagan a meeting from different directions.

papah I centre stalk of a leaf;

mapah 1 resembling a leaf stalk; 2 to make use of a leaf stalk.

II, mapah to support s.o. walking.

papak 1 blunt (rather than pointed or tapering); **2** dull (of objects; of wits); **3** level, even (with);
mapak level, of equal height;
mapaki to make level/even; to trim s.t. evenly.

papali *see* **pali**.

papan I 1 place, position; **2** the appropriate circumstances, the right place and time;
mapan 1 to take one's place, get into position; **2** to settle s.w.; **3** apt, to the point; - **turu** to go to bed;
mapanaké to put s.t. in place.
II board, plank, shelf.

papar flat, level;
mapar *or* **mapari** to flatten;
paparan (of area) flattened.

papas *var of* **papras**.

papat *ng*, **sekawan** *kr*, four;
mapat four each;
mapati to form a group of four;
papat-papat by fours;
kapat 1 four times; fourth in a series; **2** 4th period of the Javanese agricultural year (19 September– 13 October).

papin *reg* to miss s.t. desired.

papinder *var of* **padpinder**.

papon container for slaked lime. *See also* **apu**.

papral broken off, hanging by a thread;
mapral *or* **maprali** to break (the branches) off.

papras, mapras to cut off, trim, prune;
kepapras cut off unintentionally.

para I marker of group or collectivity;
para ningrat the nobility.
II mara to divide; **pinara** divided by…; *lit* **pinara sasra** divided into a thousand parts.
III mara 1 to approach; **2** come on! *See also* **paran**.
IV *reg* bamboo rack.
V trader (*esp* in jewels).

parab, marabi to (nick)name s.o.;
paraban nickname, epithet;
peparab by the name of.

paracampah scornful, contumelious.

paracidra falseness, perfidy.

parag, keparag 1 to get attacked by a destructive force; **2** (of plants) infested with a disease.

parah I, peparah *or* **parah-parah** to consider s.t. according to the circumstances.
II variety of basket used for measuring a quantity of fruits *etc*.

parak I, marak to sit humbly before a high-status person to pay one's respects;
pinarak to sit (*k.i. for* **lungguh**);
keparak 1 female palace retainer who sits beside the monarch; **2** to be approached or visited.
II *var of* **parag**.

parakirna *lit* fruit trees.

parakrama *lit* **1** wedding; **2** compliment.

paramakawi 1 man of letters; **2** literary scholar.

paramarta *lit* noble, good.

paramasastra grammar, grammatical system of a language.

parampara *var of* **paranpara**.

paran *ng*, **purug** *kr*, **1** way, course, destination; **2** away from home, abroad;
marani 1 to approach; **2** to go and get s.t. at a particular place, fetch;
marakaké 1 to bring about, cause; **2** to escort, convey;
keparan to lose touch, get separated; - **tutuh** to get blamed (for s.t. that has happened);
saparan-paran, saparané everywhere, in any direction.
See also **para III**.

parandéné nevertheless.

parang I knife, chopper, cleaver;
marang to chop with a knife.
II cliff.

III batik patterns with wavy diagonal pattern;

parang-parangan the group of **parang** patterns (reserved for nobility).

parangmuka *lit* enemy.

paranyai maidservant to an aristocratic family.

paranpara spokesman, chairman.

parapaben *kr for* **parapadu**.

parapadu *lit* to quarrel.

paras I a pinch (small quantity of leaves).

II (to have) a haircut (*k.i. for* **cukur**); **marasi** 1 to cut off s.o.'s hair; 2 to cut off the end of a young coconut; **parasan** with the top cut off.

parasdya *lit* meaning, intention; undertaking.

parastra *lit* dead; to die.

parat, keparat damn you!

paratantang *lit* combative, desirous of fighting.

paratra *lit* dead; to die.

parawadul to tell tales; **parawadulan** a tattletale.

parawanten *reg* offering.

pardi *var of* **perdi**.

pardika I *lit* explanation of meaning.

II, **mardika** free, not in service to s.o. else; **pardikan** (of land) free, unencumbered by taxes.

paré a certain vine; the fruits of this vine; - **anom** green and yellow (colours of flags or ornaments).

parek close, nearby; **marek** to have an audience (with) (*var of* **parak** I); **mareki** to approach; **parekan** a group of female servants in the palace.

parem a soothing analgesic mixture of aromatic herbs applied to the body; **maremi** to apply the above to (s.o.); **pareman** to rub with such a mixture.

paremas *lit* adorned with gold (cloth).

pareng 1 to have or be given permission; 2 (*or* **kepareng**) to say goodbye; to ask permission to leave (*kr for* **pamit**).

paréntah an order, command; to tell s.o. to do s.t.; - **ageng** the governing council of the sultanate; **maréntah** 1 to govern, have authority over; 2 to order, give an instruction; **maréntahaké** to command s.t. to s.o.; **pamaréntah** government. *See also* **préntah**.

parepat servant (*var of* **prepat**).

parèsan *reg* 1 jail, prison; 2 prisoner.

pari *ng*, **pantun** *kr*, rice plant (growing, or harvested but still in the ear); - **gadhung** rice grown in a field during the dry season; - **gaga** rice grown in a dry field; - **génjah** quick-growing rice: first harvest taken from the ricefields cultivated during the dry season; - **jero** slow-growing rice, *i.e.* the choicest rice, which takes over six months to mature; - **wuluh** unhusked rice grains.

paribasa, paribasan 1 proverb, saying, expression; 2 practically speaking; it could be said that...

paribawa *lit* influence; authority.

parid, paridan halyard.

parijatha a shrub bearing yellow berries, eaten by pregnant women in order to bear a beautiful child.

parikan a form of traditional poetry (often sung), each verse of which consists of two couplets; the first suggests the second by sound or other similarity.

parikena, sembrana - to say s.t. in jest but be taken seriously.

parikedah *kr for* **parikudu**.

parikrama with impeccable manners.

parikudu *ng*, **parikedah** *kr*, to have a longing or compulsion (to).

paril, maril *reg* to predestine (fate).

pariman *or* papariman *lit* to beg alms, ask charity.

parimana *lit* boundary, border.

parimarma pity, compassion.

parimirma *var of* palimirma.

paring to give (*k.i. for* awèh, wènèh); -
dalem a gift from a social superior;
maringi to grant s.o. (of lower status) s.t.;
maringaké to grant s.t.;
peparing, paringan a grant, gift, s.t. bestowed by a superior.

paringkelan astrological system of reck-oning by days of the six-day week. *See also* ringkel II.

paripaben *kr for* paripadu.

paripadu (paripaben *kr*) to quarrel. *See also* padu.

paripaos *subst kr for* paribasa.

paripeksa *var of* parikudu.

paripolah actions, behaviour;
saparipolahé whatever one does. *See also* polah.

paripurna 1 finished, over; 2 complete, plenary.

paris I shield, buckler.
II, marisi to cut off the end of a young coconut;
parisan having the top cut off. *See also* paras II.

pariwara I *lit* announcement.
II *lit* follower, adherent.

pariwarta news. *See also* warta.

pariwisata 1 tourism; 2 touring.

parji *lit* female genitals.

parkir, markir to park (a vehicle); parki-ran parking-place.

parman grace (of God).

parnèl flannel.

paro *ng*, palih *kr*, 1 half; 2 one half each;
maro to split in half;
marokaké 1 to split for s.o.; 2 to have s.o. share the work and profit, *esp* of a ricefield;
paron 1 half-and-half; 2 (*or* paron-paron) to share and share alike;
separo one half;
separo-separo vaguely, not entirely.

paroki parish.

paron anvil.

parosa, marosa 1 to force; 2 to rape. *Also* prosa.

parot, maroti to put away.

Parsi Iran (*var of* Pèrsi).

parswa *lit* slope (of mountain).

parti *var of* perti.

partikelir private;
partikeliran (of civilian) plain clothes. *Also* patikelir.

partisara certificate.

paru beef lung (fried as chips);
paru-paru human lung.

parud *see* parut.

paruk *reg* earthenware water container.

parung I ravine, gorge.
II curved portion of a kris blade.

parusa *var of* parosa.

parut grater;
marut to grate;
marutaké to grate for s.o.;
keparut scratched when grating;
pamarut act or way of grating;
parutan grated.

parwata *lit* mountain.

pas 1 to fit, be the right size; 2 exact, exactly; just right;
ngepas 1 to try clothes on; 2 to fit (of clothes); 3 right on time;
ngepasaké to make s.t. just right.

pasa *ng*, siyam *kr*, 1 to fast; 2 9th month of the Islamic calendar: the Fasting Month, Ramadhan;
masani to fast for (a certain purpose);
masakaké to fast for s.o.'s good for-tune.

pasagi *var of* pesagi.

pasah I 1 carpenter's plane; 2 (kethik *k.i.*) tooth-file;
masah 1 to plane (wood); 2 (*or* masahi) to file;

pasahan 1 planed; 2 filed.
II ora - unharmed, unaffected.
III divorce pronounced by the official on behalf of a woman.
pasaja *var of* **prasaja**.
pasaji offering. *See* **saji**.
pasagi *see* **pesagi**.
pasak I *see* **pasah III**.
II 1 compact, tight; 2 strong, remaining as before.
pasal paragraph, article (of a document).
pasang I 1 to put in place, set up; 2 ; - **angkuh** to put on airs; - **graita** (- **cipta**) to apply the mind, understand; - **liring** to cast glances at; - **rakit** (- **wangun**) build, construction; - **semu**; - **ulat** to put on an expression;
masang 1 to install in or on; 2 to turn on; 3 to fasten, pin, post; 4 to stake one's money; 5 to set (the fare);
masangi 1 to equip s.t. with; 2 to catch in a trap;
masangaké 1 to install, fit; 2 apply;
pasangan 1 arrangement, placing; 2 trap; 3 gambling; 4 certain Javanese script characters used for indicating consonant clusters; 5 brickwork for a house foundation; 6 ox yoke;
pamasang (action of) putting s.t. in place.
II pair; **sepasang** a pair, a couple.
III rising tide.
pasanggiri *lit* 1 a prize contest; 2 to hold a contest over.
pasar *ng*, **peken** *kr*, 1 market(place); 2 five-day week; - **malem** night fair, bazaar;
masar to do business at the market as a seller;
masaraké to market s.t.;
pasaran 1 (the group of) market days; **dina** - day of the five-day week; 2 market day (in a particular community); 3 to play markets; 4 ceremony for a child five days after birth; 5 market price.

pascima *lit* west.
pasèh (of speech) fluent, eloquent.
paséhat fine reading from the Quran.
pasek, compact, tight (*var of* **pasak II**);
masek *reg* 1 to clog; clogged; 2 to press, pack down; 3 to bury; 4 *cr* to kill.
pasèk godless, impious, ungodly.
pasékat *var of* **paséhat**.
paser a dart;
maser to throw a dart (at);
paseran dart game.
pasèran *reg* a large box with a rolling lid for drying coffee beans.
pasèt facet (of precious stone).
pasetrèn I ricefield on a riverside.
II female genitals. *See also* **setri**.
pasih fluent, eloquent (*var of* **pasèh**).
pasik *var of* **pasèk**.
pasikon (*k.i. of* **wedhung**) a cleaver-like knife worn with court dress.
pasir sand;
masir 1 resembling sand in texture; 2 (of **salak** fruit) (fine) granular;
pasiran place covered with sand;
pasir awukir *lit* seashore and mountains.
pasirah poll-tax.
pasisir 1 beach, shoreline; 2 coastal area; 3 (*or* **tanah pesisir**) northern territory of Java along the coast;
pasisiran 1 coastal territory; 2 pertaining to Javanese custom and culture outside the Principalities (Surakarta and Yogyakarta).
pasiyar 1 trip, journey; 2 to take a trip, to go for a ride, excursion. *See also* **besiyar**, **pesiyar**.
pasiyun pensioned, retired (*var of* **pènsiyun**).
Paskah Easter; **paskahan** 1 to celebrate Easter; 2 to go on Easter holidays.
paso *reg* a large earthenware bowl.
pasog *see* **pasok**.
pasok to hand over a payment, pay tribute;

masok 1 to make a deposit; 2 to turn over money one has taken to the proprietor of the business; to pay a rental fee; 3 to put in storage;

masoki 1 to hand over (a payment); 2 to supply with merchandise;

masokaké 1 to make a payment for; 2 to deposit s.t.;

pasokan 1 deposit; 2 rental fee (for taxi drivers *etc*);

pemasok 1 depositor; 2 purveyor, supplier.

paspis *or* paspus non-stop smoking.

pasrah I to give up, return, yield up; - bongkokan to surrender unconditionally; - ngalah to submit to God's will;

masrahi 1 to entrust to, turn over to; 2 to hand over to s.o.;

masrahaké to entrust s.t., give over, delegate;

pasrah jiwa raga *or* pasrah pati urip to surrender unconditionally.

pasrangkara *lit* friendly talk.

pasthi *var of* pesthi.

pastil *var of* pastèl, pasty.

pastur Catholic priest;

pasturan presbytery.

pasu I bridge of the nose.

II *reg* false, counterfeit (*var of* palsu).

pasukan group of soldiers, military unit.

pasung I nosebone, base of the nose.

II a variety of cake.

pasuryan (*k.i. for* rai) face.

pat *ng* four (*shtf of* papat); -belas fourteen; -likur twenty-four;

patang four (*as modifier*); patang atus 400; patang èwu 4,000; kapat tengah three and a half.

pata *reg* curse. *See also* supata.

patah I bridesmaid.

II, matah to assign a task (to);

kapatah *or* kapatahan to be assigned a task.

III, patahé naturally, by its very nature.

IV *lit* broken.

patala *lit* one of the regions under the earth (*also* pratala).

patangaring partition inside a Javanese house separating bedrooms.

patar I a big file (for smoothing horns *etc*);

matar to file with such a tool.

II, pataran *reg* footholds or stepping-place cut into a coconut palm trunk. *See also* tatar.

patarana *lit* seat, place to sit.

patarangan nesting-place, *esp* for poultry;

matarangan to go to the nest in preparation for laying an egg. *See also* tarang.

patèk, ora patèk not very (*coll var of* pati II).

patékah the first chapter in the Quran, al-Fatihah.

pater *see* geter.

patèn *see* pati I.

patété *var of* petété.

patètèng *var of* petètèng.

pathak I *cr* head.

II, mathak to hurl s.t. at.

pathangkrèk *var of* pethangkrèk.

pathangkrik *var of* pethangkrik.

pathangkring *var of* pethangkring.

pathangkrok *var of* pethangkrok.

pathangkrong *var of* pethangkrong.

pathangkruk *var of* pethangkruk.

pathanthang *var of* pethanthang.

pathathus *var of* pethathus.

pathek *reg* stake, boundary-marker (*var of* pathok).

pathèk frambesia.

pathekel *var of* pethekel.

pathengkreng *var of* pethengkreng.

pathèngkrèng *var of* pethèngkrèng.

pathéngkol *var of* pethéngkol.

paththentheng *var of* pethentheng.

pathènthèng *var of* pethènthèng.

pathet 1 key or mode of gamelan music; 2 that part of a shadow-play in which a certain mode of music is played; **3** (*or* **pathetan**) a melody which brings out the character of a given **pathet** (also called **lagon**);

mathet 1 to dampen the vibration of a gamelan instrument with the hand after striking the notes; **2** to tone down, restrain;

pamathet act or way of damping the vibration of a gamelan instrument.

pathéthah *var of* **pethéthah**.

pathethek *var of* **pethethek**.

pathèthèk *var of* **pethèthèk**.

pathi 1 starch, flour; **2** essence;

mathi to make s.t. into flour/starch.

pathingkrang *var of* **pethingkrang**.

pathingkrik *var of* **pethingkrik**.

pathingkring *var of* **pethingkring**.

pathinthing *var of* **pethinthing**.

pathis *reg var of* **mathis**.

pathithil *var of* **pethithil**.

pathok stake, pole driven into the ground as a sign of s.t.; **-bangkrong** (**- bangkrung**) fixed, unchangeable;

mathok to mark s.t. off with stakes;

mathoki to set up regulations or criteria for;

pathokan 1 boundary marker; **2** regulations.

pathokol *var of* **pethokol**.

pathol I *reg* the leader of the gang.

II, mathol *reg* to peck (at).

pathola a fine soft silk material.

pathothok *var of* **pethothok**.

pathu, mathu to hit another spinning top with one's own;

pathon to play this game.

pathuk sharp bend in a river.

pathungkruk *var of* **pethangkruk**.

pathungkrung *var of* **pethungkrung**.

pathunthung *var of* **pethunthung**.

pati I *ng*, **pejah** *kr*, **séda** *k.i.* death; **- geni 1** without festivities (*e.g.* wedding); **2** very strict (austerities); **- raga** mortification of the flesh; **- urip** life and death;

mati dead; to die;

matèni 1 to kill; **2** to put out (fire), turn off (light);

matèkaké 1 to allow to die; **2** to cause s.t. to be dead;

patèn 1 having ceased to function; **2** sign in Javanese script that functions to remove a final vowel;

patèn-patèn s.o. who can be sacrified (in achieving a certain aim);

matèn hard to keep alive.

II *ng*, **patos** *kr*, **ora pati**, **ora patia** not very. *See also* **kepati**.

patih, pepatih 1 prime minister, king's chief councillor; **2** an official under a regent.

patihah *var of* **patékah**.

patikah *var of* **patékah**.

patik I *reg var of* **pating**.

II *lit* servant (of king); **-bra** I, me, your servant;

III, pinatik *lit* bedecked (with precious gems).

patikelir private (*var of* **partikelir**);

patikeliran informal.

patil I stinger of a fish;

matil 1 to sting;

patilan stung.

II, matil to breed or mate (animals);

matilaké to have (an animal) mate with another;

patilan male animal used for breeding purposes.

pating particle which precedes a word referring to a visual or auditory or action effect and gives it a plural connotation (the effect is repeated or continuous, the performers are multiple, or both), in addition to a degree of confusion or disorder; **- clurut** to keep darting about; **- kroncal** to keep jerking.

patinggi *reg* village chief (*also* **petinggi**).

patitis 1 correct; **2** plain, obvious;

matitisaké to demonstrate beyond doubt.

See also **titis** I.

patlikur twenty-four. *See also* **likur**.

patlop pencil (*var of* **potelod**).

patlum cartridge (*var of* **patrum**).

patohan 1 hard to be defeated; 2 distinguished.

patontong *var of* **petontong**.

patos, boten patos not very (*kr for* **pati**).

patoto *var of* **petoto**.

patotong *var of* **petotong**.

patra 1 *lit* leaf; 2 letter, document.

patrap behaviour; way of doing;
   matrapi to inflict (punishment) on;
   matrapaké 1 to apply s.t. (to); 2 to inflict (a punishment);
   kapatrapan to have (a penalty) inflicted on one;
   patrapan penalty.

patrasèli parsley.

patrem a small dagger.

patri solder;
   matri to solder s.t.;
   matrèkaké to have s.t. soldered;
   patrèn soldered.

patrol patrol;
   matroli to patrol (a place);
   patrolan place for patrolmen; sentry-box.

patroli *var of* **patrol**.

patros *subst kr for* **patri**.

patrum cartridge.

patrun dress pattern.

patuh regular assignment;
   matuh to have a regular assignment;
   matuhaké to assign s.o. a regular task.

patuk a beak;
   matuk 1 to peck; 2 to grab with the beak;
   matukaké to peck at with s.t.;
   patuk-patukan to peck each other.

patung I, **patungan** joint venture; to go in together in a money venture;
   matungi to participate in a venture.
   II statue, sculpture;
   matung to sculpt.

patungkas message, instruction. *See also* **tungkas**.

patut I 1 in harmony, in agreement; 2 right and proper, decent;
   matut (*or* **mematut** *lit*) 1 tune (musical instruments); 2 to come to an agreement;
   patuté rightly, fittingly.
   II, **patutan** (a child) begotten (by…). *See also* **atut**.

patuwas payment or compensation for one's time and trouble (*var of* **pituwas**). *See also* **tuwas**.

patwa pronouncement (by a jurist) (*var of* **fatwa**).

pawaka *lit* fire.

pawana *lit* wind.

pawar *reg* village messenger. *See also* **uwar**.

pawèstri *lit* woman; female;
   pawèstrèn 1 place reserved for women, *e.g.* in a mosque; 2 (*or* **pawèstrènan**) female genitals (*kr for* **pawadonan**, *see* **wadon**).

pawit, mawiti to finance;
   pawitan financial capital.

pawitra *lit* holy, clean, pure.

pawon kitchen. *See also* **awu** I.

pawong (*or* **pawongan**) servant; - **mitra** *or* - **sanak** close friend. *See also* **wong** I.

paya means; device;
   maya 1 to try to find a way to do s.t.; 2 to seek, look for (*var of* **ngupaya**, *see* **upaya**).

payadan pretext, excuse (*var of* **pawadan**, *see* **awad**).

payah *reg* weary;
   mayahaké tiring, causing weariness.

payang boat used for deep-sea fishing.

paying, poyang-paying confused, not sure what to do;
   poyang-payingan 1 to go this way and that in confusion or uncertainty; 2 to be in a restless, confused state.

payo I *lit* come on! *See also* **ayo**.

II, **payo-payo** *coll* trouble, s.t. going on.

payoman *lit* 1 shade, shady place; 2 protection, shelter. *See also* **ayom**.

payon I roof.

II *see* **payu** II.

payu I *ng*, **pajeng** *kr*, 1 to get sold; 2 *fig* to be in demand;

mayokaké 1 to succeed in selling; 2 to sell for s.o. else (on commission); 3 (of currency) to put into circulation;

kepayon sold out;

pepayon proceeds from selling;

sapayuné *or* **sapayu-payuné** at whatever price it fetches.

II, **mayu** *reg* to cover. *See also* **payon**.

payudara *lit* breast.

payug, mayug to lean, list;

mayug-mayug *or* **moyag-mayug** to wobble, shake;

mayugaké to lean s.t. (on, against etc).

payun, payunan I *lit* in front. *See* **ayun** III.

II swing, cradle. *See* **ayun** I.

payung *ng, kr,* (**songsong** *k.i.*) parasol, sunshade, umbrella; - **agung** large ceremonial umbrella; - **kalong** *or* - **lawa** *or* - **motha** black umbrella;

mayung to overshadow like a parasol;

mayungi to shield s.o. from sun or rain with an umbrella;

mayungaké to use s.t. to screen or protect overhead;

payungan *or* **pepayung** to use an umbrella; to have s.t. as an umbrella.

payus pale due to illness or fright.

pé I ray (variety of fish).

II, **ngepé** *or* **ngepèni** to put s.t. in the sun or fresh air; to spread out in the sun to dry;

ngepèkaké to dry s.t. in the sun on behalf of s.o.;

pangepé act of sunning or airing s.t.;

pangepèn place for drying or airing things. *See also* **pépé**.

péang *or* **péyang** (of head) with a bump, irregular shape.

peca *reg var of* **weca**.

pecah 1 to break (off, out); broken, smashed; 2 divided; - **nalaré** to get a clear understanding; - **pamoré** to reveal one's adult features (growing girl);

mecah 1 to break (open, out); 2 to break (into, through) s.t.;

mecahi to break (several things);

mecahaké 1 to break s.t. unintentionally; 2 to solve (problems);

pecahan 1 fraction; 2 a fragment;

pecah-pecah breaking here and there.

pecak I length of the foot as a unit of measurement;

mecaki to measure by pacing; to pace off (a distance);

sapecak one pace; (one's) every step.

II mixture of salt, tamarind and other ingredients for rubbing into meat before cooking.

pécak *reg* blind (*var of* **picak**).

pecal *reg* ricefield.

pecalang police officer (in village).

pecat, mecat to discharge, dismiss; - **nyawané** *cr* dead.

mecati moribund;

pecat-pecat off and on; spottily.

pécé one-eyed; blind in one eye.

pecéca-pecécé *see* **pecécé**.

pecécé, mecécé to swagger, strut;

pecéca-pecécé to keep swaggering, acting in a jaunty way.

pecèh *reg* having conjunctivitis.

pecel salad made from parboiled vegetables served with hot peanut sauce.

pecèl, mecèl to cut, chop;

mecèli to chop (wood) into small pieces;

mecèlaké 1 to chop (wood) for s.o. else; 2 to use s.t. as a chopper;

pecèlan cut-up pieces.

pècèl *reg var of* pecèl.

pecenceng, pecencengan to argue heatedly, act vehemently.

pecengès *or* **mak pecengès** *repr* a sudden jeering laugh;
  pecengas-pecengès to keep jeering.

pecengis *var of* pecengès.

pecerèn drain, gutter.

pèci black velvet, rimless cap.

pecical-pecicil *see* pecicil.

pecicil, mecicil to stare glassily; *fig repr* striving without success.
  pecicilan *or* **pecical-pecicil** to stare about in a rude way.

pecil *reg* child, kid.

pecing I bad smell (s.t. gone off).
  II, mecing to ask for a share of the profit;
  pecingan one's share of the profit on goods sold.

pècis *var of* pèci.

pecoco *var of* pecucu.

pecoh to fight, peck each other (cocks);
  mecohi to attack, peck at (another cock).

pecok, mecoki to cut off (leaves, branches, with knife).

pécok sickle;
  mécok to lop off with a sickle.

pecongol *var of* pencongol.

pecot *reg* to come loose; to come off/out (*var of* pocot, copot).

pecothot, mecothot to emerge suddenly, burst out;
  pating pecothot *pl* as above.

pecoto to swell up;
  pating pecoto *pl* as above.

pecroh *var of* pecoh.

pecruk cormorant.

pecuca-pecucu *see* pecucu.

pecucu, mecucu with lips thrust forward;
  mecucokaké to thrust forward (the lips);

pecuca-pecucu to keep pouting.

pecuh semen, ejaculate (*also* pejuh).

pecuk 1 pickaxe; **2** (*or* **pecruk**) cormorant.

pecus, ora - unable.

pecut a whip;
  mecut *or* **mecuti** to whip; *fig* to inspire, motivate.

peda fish preserved in salt.

pédah *var of* paédah.

pedhak I, medhak to get off; to descend (*k.i. for* medhun).
  II *lit* near, close.
  medhaki to get nearer; to approach;
  kepedhak 1 court servant; lady-in-waiting of the queen; **2** beloved. *See also* cedhak.

pédhak *reg* near, close.

pedhang 1 (sabet *k.i.*) sword; **2** counting unit for long thin objects; **- larakan** sabre; **- suduk** (stabbing) sword;
  medhang 1 to cut with a sword; **2** resembling a sword;
  pedhangan *or* **pedhang-pedhangan 1** to strike each other with a sword; **3** toy sword.

pedhati *reg* two-wheeled ox-drawn cart.

pedhatos *reg kr for* pedhati.

pedhaya *reg* a classical court dance performed by females (*var of* bedhaya).

pedhek *reg var of* cedhak.

pèdhek *reg var of* cedhak.

pedhes 1 hot, spicy; **2** to sting, feel a stinging sensation; **3** sharp, biting (words); **- perih** oppressive difficulties;
  medhesi to make (food) hot;
  medhesaké to make hotter (than before);
  pedhesan *or* **pepedhes** hot food.

pèdhes, mèdhes *reg* to press, oppress, squash flat.

pedhèt calf (young of the sapi).

pèdhèt, pèdhèten to suffer from a twisted, scarred eyelid.

pedhidhing *var of* **bedhidhing**.

pedhot broken off, interrupted;

medhot to break off, interrupt;

medhoti to cut off (rope, wire, thread *etc*);

medhotaké 1 to break s.t. unintentionally; to break off; 2 to cause to be discontinued;

pedhotan 1 a broken-off piece; 2 caesura in the singing of Javanese verse, indicated by pauses in breathing;

kapedhotan broken ; - **katresnan** broken-hearted;

pedhot-pedhot broken into short lengths;

pedhat-pedhot repeatedly broken;

pedhot ambekané breathless; exhausted.

pedhut fog, mist.

pédok, pédokan area reserved for women. *See also* **wédok**.

pédon *reg* corner. *See also* **padon, padu II**.

pega smoke, steam;

megani to give off smoke/steam.

pegat 1 broken off; 2 cut off; 3 divorced; **ora - , tan -** *lit* constant(ly);

pegat-pegat (of speech) broken, halting;

megat to divorce (one's spouse);

megati to block the passage of;

megataké to cause s.o. to be divorced;

pegatan 1 to be divorced; 2 a divorce.

pegawan *var of* **begawan**.

pegel 1 stiff and sore from strain or exertion; 2 annoyed, fed up; 3 weary, exhausted;

megelaké exasperating, irritating;

pegelan easily fed up.

pegeng, megeng to hold the breath.

pèges cut slantwise;

mèges to cut or slice slantwise.

kepèges to get slashed;

pègèsan act of slashing; a slash mark.

pégin *reg* still, remaining (in a certain condition).

pégo to speak Javanese with a regional accent;

pégon 1 the form of language spoken in the border between Javanese and Sundanese regions (*see also* **pégo**); 2 Javanese language written with Arabic script.

pégos, mégos 1 slantwise, on the diagonal; 2 to cut slantwise (*var of* **pègès**).

pegot *reg* broken, interrupted (*var of* **pedhot**);

megot to break, interrupt.

pégung *see* **plégung**.

pèh I bladder.

II just because (of s.t. irrelevant) (*shtf of* **dupèh**).

III *reg* ditch, gutter.

IV *reg* weak, slack.

V, **pèhan** one who gets the blame.

péhak side (*e.g.* of an argument);

méhak to side (with), take s.o.'s part.

Pèhcun Chinese Water Festival (beginning of June).

pèi a game played with Chinese cards (*kertu cilik*).

pejah 1 death; dead (*kr for* **pati** I); 2 dead; to die (*kr for* **mati**).

pejang, mejang *reg* to grasp s.t.; to hold tightly.

pèjèt, mèjèt to press or exert pressure, *esp* with the thumb;

pèjètan push-button.

pejrah, mejrah *reg* to deal with (things) little by little.

pejuh semen (*var of* **pecuh**).

pek *or* **mak pek** *repr* a slap;

pèk I *or* **mak pèk** *repr* falling.

II, **ngepèk** 1 to take, take away, fetch; 2 to adopt (child);

pèk-pèkan (an) adopted (child);

ngepèkaké to take s.t. on behalf of s.o. else.

III, **pèké** *reg* 1 let (it go!); 2 so that.

péka I (*or* pepéka) negligent, inattentive. II trick, deceit (*var of* paéka);

pekah 1 basic necessities of life; 2 money given to one's wife for household expenses.

pekak, mekak to check, restrain; pamekak 1 act of restraining; 2 waist (*k.i. for* bangkèkan).

pekakas tool(s), equipment (*var of* bekakas).

pekangkang, mekangkang having the legs spread; mekangkangaké to spread (the legs) apart; pekangkangan to keep the legs spread apart in a rude way;

pekara *var of* perkara.

pekatul *var of* bekatul.

pekawis *var of* perkawis.

pèkèh, mèkèh to carry (a child) on one's hip; mèkèh-mèkèh *or* mékah-mèkèh to walk with a waddle.

pekek *var of* pekak.

pekèkèh, mekèkèh to be seated improperly, with the legs apart; pekakah-pekèkèh to walk with the legs wide apart.

pekelur attorney, lawyer (*var of* pokrul).

peken market(place) (*kr for* pasar).

pekeneng *see* bekeneng.

pekengkeng *see* bekengkeng.

pekèngkèng *see* bekèngkèng.

pekenira you. *See also* pakenira.

pekèt 1 the watch, guard duty; 2 to be on guard duty (*var of* pikèt).

pekèwed *kr for* pekéwuh.

pekéwuh *see* pakéwuh.

pekih 1 s.o. learned in Islamic law; 2 Islamic law.

pekik *lit* handsome.

peking I a kind of small rice-bird with high-pitched call; peking abuntut merak to make a mountain out of a molehill.

II small metallophone consisting of six or seven bronze keys on a wooden frame; meking to play such an instrument.

pekir *var of* fakir.

peklantun *kr for* peklaring.

peklaring statement (in court case).

pékoh (to walk when in pain) with the legs sore and bent.

pekok *reg* blockhead, dullard, duffer.

pékong *var of* tepékong.

pekongkong, mekongkong to sit (improperly) with the legs spread.

pékrak-pékrok *reg* imperfect, unsound.

pekrok, mekrok (of flowers) to open out; mekrokaké to open out s.t.; to cause to be opened out.

peksa 1, meksa to force, compel; 2 still, even so; - wani over-bold, reckless; meksakaké to force s.t.; kepeksa forced, compelled; peksan 1 coercion; 2 forced; pameksa a warrant for search or arrest.

peksi bird (*kr for* manuk).

pekul, mekul *lit* to embrace.

pekungkung, mekungkung to sit, squat in a hunched position, with bent back.

pèl I floor-cleaning mop or rag; ngepèl to clean the floor with the above. II blotting-paper.

pela *var of* rempela.

péla woven fibre sash.

péla-pèlu I *reg* a certain fly that swarms around livestock; horsefly. II *reg* slime, mucus.

pélad *reg* speech defect (inability to pronounce rolled *R*) (*var of* célad).

pelag *reg* cross-beam joist; melagaké to put such a joist on; kepelag obstructed, impeded.

pélag *lit* handsome.

pélah *var of* péla.

pelak I, melak *reg* to quicken one's pace (*var of* gelak).

II small edible sea fish (young of the kakap).

pelana *lit* elephant saddle.

pélas I steamed dish of soybeans and grated coconut wrapped with banana leaf.

II *reg* addition, supplement.

III *reg* trivial, trifling.

pelat 1 record, disc; 2 metal sheet.

peleg *reg* chock-full, crammed.

pèleh rim (of wheel).

pelek I, melek *var of* melak, *see* pelak I.

II *reg* the end (of time).

pelem mango.

pèlem film.

peleng focal point of concentration or attention;

meleng to concentrate or focus the attention on; to meditate by concentrating;

pamelengan a place for meditating.

pèlèt I, lenga - a kind of magic oil used to make a person fall in love;

mèlèti to rub with magic oil (as above).

II, mèlèt to stick out the tongue. *See also* èlèt, èlèd.

peli *cr* penis, dick.

pélih *reg var of* pilih.

pelik I spark, sparkle, flicker;

pepelik a sparkling ear ornament;

melik to sparkle;

pelik-pelik that which sparkles;

sapelik 1 one spark; 2 a tiny bit.

II melik to look for metals, *esp* gold, in the earth or in a river;

pelikan obtained by mining;

pamelikan a mine.

peling brand new, very good.

péling (*or* pepéling) *ng*, pènget (*or* pepènget) *kr*, a reminder, warning. *See also* éling.

pelit stingy, tight-fisted.

pélo hard to understand, defective (speech of child, toothless person);

mélo to affect a speech defect;

mélokaké to pronounce words with a defect.

pélog seven-note gamelan scale;

mélog to play in this scale;

mélogaké to change the scale into the above.

peloh *var of* peluh.

péloh limp, flaccid;

pélah-péloh pliant.

pelok I mango stone (seed).

II, melok conspicuous, striking;

melok-melok (of powder on the face) blatant, eye-catching.

pelong, melong *or* melong-melong 1 (of eyes) wide open; 2 (of pattern) big, wide.

pélor bullet.

pélot (of blades) bent out of shape, twisted.

pelpèn fountain pen (*var of* pulpèn).

pèlpulisi rural constabulary.

peluh impotent (of penis).

peluk, meluk to embrace;

sapeluk an armful, as much as the arms can clasp.

pelung a blue coot.

pelur a tiled or cement floor.

pelus 1 a certain freshwater eel; 2 a kind of leech or snail; 3 *cr* penis, dick.

péma by all means; (with negative) by no means (*subst kr for* poma).

pémah tame; to feel at home (*kr for* pomah).

pembayun (*k.i. for* susu) breast. *Also* prembayun.

pèmès folding pocket knife, penknife.

pémut a reminder, a warning (*kr for* péling, *var of* pènget). *See also* émut.

pèn pen;

ngepèn to write with a pen.

pena *reg* you, your.

pénah quill.

penak rice wrapped into a packet;

menaki to wrap rice into a packet;

sapenak one rice packet.

pénak comfortable, pleasant (*var of* **kepénak**).

pénakan nephew, niece (*var of* **kepénakan**).

pénal grazed, scraped, injured on the head.

pénang *reg* brood (of chickens).

penapa what (*var of* **punapa**). *Also* **menapa**.

penapi *var of* **penapa**.

penat *reg* exhausted, tired.

penatos *subst kr for* **penatu**.

penatu 1 laundryman; (*or* **penaton**) laundry shop; 2 (*or* **penaton**) laundry to be washed;
menatu to do laundry as one's trade;
menatokaké to have clothes laundered at a shop.

penatus *reg* village chief.

pencak self-defence system and stylised art form;
mencak to engage in **pencak**;
mencak-mencak furious, enraged.

pencalang *var of* **pacalang**.

pencar to spread, get disseminated;
mencar to go in various directions;
mencaraké to scatter/disseminate s.t.

pencelat, mencelat to bound, get ejected or thrown about;
mencelataké to eject, throw off;
pating pencelat to come out in all directions.

pencelèk, mencelèk to be fully exposed (head of the penis);
mencelèkaké to expose by retracting the foreskin.

pèncèng 1 inclining to one side; 2 (of head) deformed;
mèncèng 1 crooked, lopsided, off-centre; 2 incompatible, inharmonious; 3 slanted, skewed;
mèncèngaké to make s.t. lopsided;
méncang-mèncèng not in a straight line, contorted.

pencengès *repr* a sneer;
mencengès to sneer.

pencengis *var of* **pencengis**.

pencereng an intent stare; **pating -** *pl* staring fixedly;
mencereng to stare fixedly;
mencerengi to stare at fixedly.

pencèrèt, mencèrèt gleaming, shining.

pencèt, mencèt 1 to squeeze; 2 to push (button).

pencil, mencil to stay far from everything;
kepencil secluded, isolated.

pencilak, mencilak *or* **pencilakan** to move about in an uncontrolled way.

pencilat *var of* **pencilak**.

pencinat *reg var of* **pencilak**.

pencing 1 a bribe; 2 a share of one's profit;
mencing *or* **mencingi** 1 to bribe; 2 to share one's profit.

pencingil, mencingil standing out prominently (of small or slim things).

pencir I, **mencir** *reg* to knock s.o.'s head slightly.
II, **menciri** to add to.

pencit I the very top, the tip or peak;
mencit at the very top; *fig* to the limit.
II *reg* young mango.

penclok, menclok to chop, hack.

pénclok, ménclok to perch, alight;
pénclokan a perch(ing place).

pencok *var of* **penclok**.

péncok *var of* **pénclok**.

pencolot *or* **mak pencolot** *repr* a bounding jump;
mencolot to jump;
mencoloti to leap at, leap over s.t.;
pencolotan 1 to jump about; 2 a jumping game;
pating pencolot *pl* to keep jumping about.

péncong off-centre, off-target;
méncong to go off-centre;
méncongaké to cause s.t. to be off-centre or off-target;

méncang-méncong not in a straight line, contorted.

pencongat, mencongat to extend outward; pating pencongat pl extending outward (of s.t. long and spiky).

pencongol or mak pencongol repr a sudden appearance;
mencongol to stand way out, appear suddenly.

pencono var of pecoto.

péncor reg 1 lame; 2 crooked (hands, legs).

pencorong, mencorong 1 to shine, send out beams; 2 showy, conspicuous, eye-catching;
pating pencorong pl shining round about.

pencorot, mencorot to glitter, gleam, shine;
pating pencorot pl glittering, gleaming.

pencrit reg young mango (var of pencit II).

pencu 1 protruding knob of gamelan gong; 2 with pyramid-shaped roof (house);
mencu (of roofs) shaped as above.

penculat, menculat to leap;
pating penculat pl to pop up everywhere.

pencungat var of pencongat.

pencungul, mencungul to put in an appearance, show up;
pating pencungul pl coming into view.

pencurat, mencurat to spurt up;
pating pencurat pl squirting out.

péndah lit tan - , lir - like, as; as if, as though.

pendara I reg master, mistress (var of bendara).
II reg ladies' wide wrapped sash worn with traditional Javanese dress.

pendèl, mendèl or mendèli to attack, fly at.

pèndel lavender.

pendelik, mendelik to stare at with a menacing look; to look at with big eyes;
pating pendelik or pendelikan pl staring with wide eyes.

pendelo, mendelo to stare wide-eyed.

pendeng, mendeng to concentrate or focus the attention on.

pèndèng pressed flat, flattened;
mèndèng to flatten s.t.

pendhak 1 each, every; 2 in a ...'s time (when the unit of time is completed);
- pisan the first death anniversary; - pindho the second death anniversary;
mendhak or mendhaki to commemorate a death anniversary;
pendhak-pendhak every time.

pendhalit var of penthalit.

pendhalung, pendhalungan to talk in an impolite, careless way.

pendhapa a large square pavilion or hall which forms part of the front of a traditional Javanese house of a person of rank (or of an institution), featuring a raised floor, open sides and an elaborate roof, and used for receptions or performances.

pendharat var of kendharat.

pendhatos subst kr for pedhati.

pendhéga var of pandhéga.

pendhèk ng, andhap kr short.

pèndhèk var of pendhèk;
pèndhèké or pèndhèkèn or pèndhèknèn reg 1 short but to the point; 2 be that as it may.

pendhekel, mendhekel swollen;
pating pendhekel bulging with muscles.

pendhelis var of pendhilis.

pendhelong repr to give way (under a weight).

pendhelus repr showing as round glossy surfaces.

pendhem underground; baris - undercover movement of armed forces;

bètèng - bunker, underground fortification; kacang - peanut;

mendhem to bury; - kula to conceal one's true position, be in disguise;

mendhemaké to bury on behalf of s.o. else;

kapendhem buried, underground;
pala - edible roots;

pendheman underground, buried;

mendhem jero, mikul dhuwur (idiom) to reflect honour on one's parents.

pendhèsèl var of pendhisil.

pendhet, mendhet to take (kr for jupuk).

pendhikil var of pendhisil.

pendhil reg earthenware or copper utensil for cooking rice (var of kendhil).

pendhilis, mendhilis forming a small lump;
pating pendhilis lumpy, bumpy (with small bumps).

pendhisil, mendhisil knobby, knotty;
pating pendhisil full of knobs.

pendhok ng, kandelan kr, decorative metal plating on a kris sheath; - bléwah an opened out plating on a kris sheath; - bunton a closed plating on a kris sheath;
golèk pendhok to help people in order to get praised for it.

pendhokol, mendhokol 1 swollen, bulging; 2 affronted;
pating pendhokol pl bumpy, having many bulges.

pendhosol, mendhosol forming a hump;
pating pendhosol pl showing humps or bulges.

pendhukul, mendhukul bumpy, protruding;
pating pendhukul pl bulging out.

pendhulus or mak pendhulus repr a sudden appearance (of smooth rounded object);
mendhulus to show up suddenly;
pating pendhulus pl, repr the sight of

many bald heads in a crowd.

pendhusul var of pendhosol.

pending woman's belt of metal plates.

pendir, mendir to assign s.o. a heavy job.

pendirang, pendirangan to dart glances about nervously.

pendiring, mendiring horrified, terrified.

pendul I or mendul (of eyes) swollen, bulging.
II, menduli reg to break open, dig over (dry earth).

pened lit 1 in good order; 2 fine, beautiful.

penek reg, var of penak.

pènèk, mènèk or mènèki to climb;
mènèkaké 1 to help s.o. climb; 2 to climb a tree for s.o.;
pènèkan 1 to make a habit of climbing up; 2 act or way of climbing.

penèker marble(s) (var of kenèker).

pener ng, leres kr, in a straight line, right on (a certain spot);
meneri coinciding with, right on/at;
meneraké to head s.t. forward; to aim a certain spot;
kapener related in a certain way;
peneran 1 coincidentally; 2 luckily, by chance. See also bener.

penet I, menet to squeeze, press, knead;
menetaké to press s.t. on.
II see pened.

penèt var of pènèt.

pènèt, mènèt to squash, flatten.

penèwu var of panèwu.

peng I, or mak peng repr a ringing (in the head, from a bump or loud noise).
II, ngepeng to apply o.s. to s.t. completely;
peng-pengan 1 serious, keen, enthusiastic; 2 excellent, the best, top-notch. See also mempeng.

pengak an irritating bad smell.

pengar a sharp odour, e.g. of vinegar.

pengaron a wide earthenware pot. See also karu.

pèngès, mèngès to cut, slash;
kepèngès to get cut (off).

pènget 1 commemoration; 2 (or
pepènget) warning (kr for péling);
mèngeti to commemorate, celebrate
(an occasion);
pèngetan commemoration, celebration;
pepènget warning.
See also ènget.

penggak, menggak to restrain;
pamenggak restraint.

penggalih heart, feelings (k.i. for ati). See
also galih.

penggang var of benggang.

penggel, menggel to cut off, cut into
pieces.

pènggèl, sapènggèl reg (of steamed rice)
one bowl (inverted, like pudding
mould).

penggik, menggik narrowed in the middle; (of waist) slim.

péngin or kepéngin to want, desire;
méngini or ménginaké 1 tempting,
appealing; 2 to desire s.t.;
meméngin to make s.o. want s.t.;
pénginan 1 covetous; 2 (or pepéngi-
nan) what is needed or desired.

penging, menging to forbid.

péngkal I a diacritic sign in Javanese script showing a y after a consonant;
méngkal to apply this sign.
II, méngkal (of horses) to kick with
the hind legs.

pengkang, mengkang to make a space
between things.

pengkarag repr hair rising from fear (var
of pengkorog).

pengkelang-pengkeleng (of faeces or
words) stiff, hard.

pengkeluk or mak pengkeluk repr bending, leaning over;
mengkeluk to bend, lean;
mengkelukaké to bend s.t.;

pating pengkeluk pl bending, drooping.

pengkelung, mengkelung to bend; bent
(var of pentelung).

pengker 1 back, rear (kr for buri); 2
kapengker last, past, the previous (kr
for pungkur).

pengkered or mak pengkered repr
shrinking;
mengkered to shrink; fig to shrink in
fear;
pengkeredan to keep shrinking in fear;
pating pengkered pl shrinking in fear.

pengki rubbish basket.

pengkirig or mak pengkirig repr hair
standing on end;
mengkirig (of hair) standing on end;
fig scared stiff.

pengkok, mengkoki to catch s.o. in the
act;
kepengkok to get caught.

péngkol, méngkol to turn, branch off;
péngkolan a bend in the road, curve.

pengkorog or mak pengkorog repr hair
rising;
mengkorog scared stiff.

péngkrang reg lame, crippled.

pengkred var of pengkered.

pengkuh solid, firm, strong;
mengkuhi or mengkuhaké to make
s.t. more solid.

pengkuk var of bengkuk.

pènglèh reg hanging loose, limp, flaccid.

péngo, péngo-péngo reg to turn the head
repeatedly;
méngo to swivel the head; to glance to
one side;
ménga-méngo to keep turning the
head.

pengong var of pengung.

péngos, méngos 1 slantwise, on the diagonal; 2 to turn the head aside (var of
mléngos, see pléngos).

péngot reg a knife with a curving blade.
See also pangot.

penguk musty, stale-smelling (food).

pengulu *var of* pangulu.

pengung dim-witted.

pengur *var of* penguk.

pengus *var of* penguk.

pèni fine, splendid, valuable

pèni-pèni fine things, treasures.

peniti 1 safety pin; 2 decorative pin, brooch.

penjait tailor. *See* jait.

penjalin rattan;

menjalin 1 resembling rattan; 2 to apply rattan to.

penjatos *subst kr for* penjalin.

penjawat *lit* wing.

penjelut, menjelut *or* pating penjelut completely out of sorts (physically or emotionally).

penjété, menjété forming a bulge or a swelling;

pating penjété *pl* having many swellings or bulges.

pénjol a bump or swelling of irregular shape.

penjorang, penjorangan *reg* mischievous, inconsiderate.

penjoto *var of* penjété.

penjuluk, menjuluk 1 raised, pulled up; 2 to lie with the head higher up on the pillows;

menjulukaké to move s.t. up higher, upwards.

penjutu *var of* penjoto.

pènmès folding pocket knife, penknife (*also* pèmès).

pènsiyun pension;

pènsiyunan pensioned, retired;

mènsiyun to retire s.o. on a pension.

pental, mental 1 springy; 2 to bounce back; 3 unaffected, unbeaten;

kepental flung away, flung off.

pentas, mentas 1 to come ashore, out of the water; 2 already married off; 3 just now;

pentasan shore.

See also entas.

pentèl *reg* 1 nipple; 2 dummy (*var of* penthil).

pentelung *repr* suddenly bending;

mentelung to bend, sway, *e.g.* of a branch in the wind;

mentelungaké to bend s.t., cause to bend.

penthalèt *var of* penthalit.

penthalit, menthalit to grasp or clamp with the legs;

penthalitan to clamber everywhere;

pating penthalit topsy-turvy.

penthang the Cross;

menthang 1 to stretch out, extend; 2 to crucify;

pamenthang 1 act or way of stretching out; 2 crucifixion.

penthangul, penthangulan shameless.

penthélang, penthélangan mischievous, naughty.

pentheleng *repr* widening of the eyes;

mentheleng 1 to stare wide-eyed; 2 to glare in anger;

menthelengi to glower at;

menthelengaké to open the eyes wide;

penthelengan *or* pentheleng-penthelengan to look at each other angrily;

penthelang-pentheleng to keep staring wide-eyed.

penthelèt, menthelèt (of the belly) flat, tight;

menthelètaké to flatten (the stomach); to tighten and pull in (the stomach muscles).

penthèng the Cross (*var of* penthang);

menthèng to stretch (a limb) out from the body;

menthèng-kèlèk with hands on hips in a defiant attitude.

penthèngèl, menthèngèl to stretch up the head;

penthéngal-penthèngèl to keep stretching the head up or out.

penthengil *or* mak penthengil *repr* the

sudden appearance of s.t. small;

menthengil in (plain) sight;

pating penthengil to appear everywhere (little things).

penthèr I 1 cleared up after rain (sky); **2** brightened up (face);

menthèraké to put on a happy face, make s.o.'s face appear happy.

II, menthèr to expand;

menthèraké to open out, broaden. *See also* **pethèr**.

penthès, menthès to drill strictly. *See also* **pethès**.

penthèt I a variety of bird.

II, menthèt *reg* to snap the fingers (at).

penthéyat *see* **penthèyèt**.

penthèyèt, penthéyat-penthèyèt *or* **penthèyètan 1** laboured, difficult (of the stance or walking pace of a heavily burdened person);

penthéyot *var of* **penthèyèt**.

penthil *ng, kr,* **mundri** *k.i.,* nipple;

menthil to give suck.

penthingil, menthingil to be in view (of small things); to show a little part;

pating penthingil *pl* just coming into view everywhere, budding.

penthiyèt *var of* **penthèyèt**.

penthol, menthol knobby;

pentholan 1 knob, bulb; **2** leader of a gang.

pentholos, mentholos round and shaved bare;

pating pentholos *pl* (of heads) round and bare.

penthong, penthongan *reg, var of* **kenthongan**.

pénthong, ménthong pigeon-toed, crooked, deformed (hand, foot).

penthongol, menthongol to stick out the head;

pating penthongol *pl* to stick up everywhere.

penthung stick, club, cudgel;

menthung to club;

menthungi to club repeatedly;

kepenthung to get clubbed;

penthung-penthungan to club each other.

penthungul, menthungul to emerge, pop up, rise to the surface;

pating penthungul *pl* to pop up everywhere.

pentil fruit bud.

pèntil valve, tube used for inflating s.t., e.g. ball, tyre.

penting *reg* important.

pentiyung, mentiyung bent low (under a heavy weight);

mentiyungaké to bend s.t., cause to bend;

pating pentiyung *pl* to bend low, bow.

pentul, mentul *or* **mentul-mentul** to bounce, spring;

mentulaké to bounce s.t.; to cause to bounce or spring.

penuh *lit* in great numbers;

menuhi abundant.

penunuk, menunuk lying in a heap;

pating penunuk lying in little hills, heaps.

penyak, menyak to step on s.t.;

kepenyak to step on s.t. inadvertently.

penyanyak, penyanyakan to go past impolitely.

penyet crushed, flattened;

menyet 1 to crush fine; **2** squeeze, flatten, pinch hard.

penyèt *var of* **penyet**.

pènyèt *var of* **penyet**.

penyinyang *see* **penyinying**.

penyinying, penyinyang-penyinying hesitant, wary, chary.

penyok, menyok to step on s.t. dirty;

menyokaké to bring into contact with s.t. unpleasant;

kepenyok to step in s.t. dirty by accident.

pényok having a dent in it;

ményokaké to cause to be dented;
pényak-pényok full of dents.

penyon, ora penyon *reg* unable.

penyonyo, menyonyo to have a bump on
the head;
pating penyonyo covered with bumps.

penyu 1 turtle; 2 tortoiseshell.

penyuk *var of* penyok.

pep, ngepep to seal off from the air.

pepak complete, full, all there;
mepaki to add s.t. to the contents of,
to complete, supplement s.t.;
pepakan completely stocked, containing everything.

pepali *var of* papali. *See* pali.

pépé to lie in the sun;
mépé to dry s.t. in the sun;
pamépé act of sun-drying or airing
things;
pépéan, péméan *reg* 1 washing, things
(to be) dried in the sun; 2 drying-
place, clothesline. *See also* pé II.

pèpèd, mèpèd 1 pressed/pushed close,
right up against; 2 pressed to the limit;
mèpèdi to press against, push onto;
mèpèdaké to push s.t. against s.t.;
pèpèd-pèpèdan to push each other;
kepèpèd hard pressed.

pepeg, mepeg to keep in check, bridle,
curb.

pèpèh, mèpèh to flatten, beat (gold
plate).

pepek *var of* pepak.

pepéka *see* péka I.

pèpèl *var of* pipil.

peper 1 (of a knife) blunt; 2 (of magical
power) ineffectual;
meper to blunt, take the edge off;
meperaké to cause the power to be
ineffectual.

pèpèr to wipe o.s. (without water) after
defecating.

pepes limp, lacking strength;
mepesaké to deprive s.o. (magically)
of their strength.

pèpès *or* pèpèsan fish wrapped in a
banana leaf and cooked;
mèpès to prepare this food. *See also*
pès II.

pepet I 1 blocked; clogging; 2 crowded;
mepeti to block;
kepepetan blocked.
II the sign in Javanese script for indicating the mute *e* or schwa.

pèpèt *see* pèpèd.

pepethan *see* petha.

pèprèk, mèprèki *reg* to flatten bamboo
section for fences, floor *etc.*

pèprèl broken off;
mèprèl to break off easily;
mèprèli to remove the outer part
from.

pèr a spring (in a car *etc*);
ngepèr springy.

pera (of rice) dry, grainy, gritty.

perak *lit* near, close to;
merak to approach; mrak-ati attractive, charming;
meraki to approach s.t.;
perakan short distance.

pérak I silver;
sepérak *reg* one rupiah.
II, pérakan *reg* divorced;
mérak to divorce one's wife.

péran *title for males of the nobility* (*shtf of*
pangéran).

perang 1 battle, combat; 2 to fight;
merangi to fight against; - tatal to
withdraw the agreement;
merangaké to manipulate puppets in
a battle scene;
keperang to get cut;
perangan to wage war, fight. *See also*
prang I.

pérang, mérang to divide;
mérang-mérang to divide up;
kapérang divided into;
pérangan section, part;
sapérangan a part.

peras *reg* an offering.

perbal 1 official report; 2 charge, summons;
merbal to process a criminal charge.

perban bandage;
merban to bandage, dress a wound;
perbanan bandaged.

perbatang *reg* fallen tree.

perbawa *var of* prabawa.

perbeng, perbeng-perbeng to go red in the face (about to cry, angry).

perbot potter's wheel.

percados to believe, rely on, trust (*subst kr for* percaya).

percanten *subst kr for* percaya.

percat-percèt *see* percèt.

percaya *ng*, pitados *kr*, to believe, rely on, trust;
mercayakaké to entrust s.t. to;
kapercayan faith, belief, confidence. *See also* pitaya.

percet *or* mak precet (of chicken) *repr* excreting droppings; *cr repr* giving birth.

percèt *or* mak percèt *repr* leaving suddenly.

percil a baby frog (young of the kodhok). *Also* precil.

percumah 1 useless, in vain; 2 for nothing, gratis.

perdapa *var of* pradapa.

perdeng, perdeng-perdeng to feel strained in the stomach.

perdi, merdi to exert o.s., strive; to try to increase one's skill.

perdika *var of* pardika II.

perdondi 1 dispute, difference of opinion; 2 to quarrel, argue.

perduli to care, heed, be concerned;
merduli *or* merdulèkaké to heed, care about;
perdulèn *or* perdulènan (one who is) concerned.

peré 1 free; 2 broke (without money); 3 unhampered.

péré, péré-péré *reg* 1 worthless; 2 a waste.

pered not slippery, providing traction.

pèrèd, pèrèdan *reg* to wear a headcloth with the border showing.

perèh *var of* perih.

perek *reg* near, close to (*var of* perak).

pèrek *reg, var of* perek.

peremas *var of* paremas.

pereng burnt, scorched, blackened.

pèrèng slope (of mountain), incline;
mèrèng to slope, slant;
pepèrèng a range of sloping hills; a series of slopes or inclines.

perep, merepi *lit* to approach s.t. *See also* prepek.

peres I, meres 1 to squeeze out, milk; 2 to force o.s. to make a big effort; 3 to extort.
II (*k.i. of* wuwung) to take a splash-bath.

pèrès a levelled-off container-full;
sapèrès one such container-full;
mèrès to measure (dry materials) with a level container;
pèrèsan a cylindrical container used as a measure.

peret *see* pered.

pèrèt I (of pottery work) earthenware refiner.
II (of cow, horse *etc*) a white blaze on the nose up to the forehead.
III *var of* pèrèd.

pergedèl rissole (*var of* bergedèl).

pergigah-pergigih eager to act.

pergogok *var of* bergogok, begogok.

pergok, mergoki to catch s.o. at s.t. wrong or improper;
kepergok to get caught.

pergul, mergul to gild s.t.;
pergulan gilt.

perguwa *reg* big and tall like a giant.

peri fairy, nymph.

perih smarting, stinging, painful. *See also* prihatin.

perjaka *var of* prajaka.

perjanji *var of* prajanji.

perjit, merjit-merjit to divide up into little bits.

perjiwat, perjiwatan *lit* to make love.

perjaya, merjaya to beat, defeat, to kill.

perkakah, merkakah spreading out in a disorderly way;
pating perkakah spreading out wide to the side (branches).

perkangkang *see* pekangkang.

perkara *ng*, perkawis *kr*, 1 matter, case; 2 problem, trouble; 3 lawsuit, case;
merkara to bring a case to court;
merkarakaké to bring s.o. to court;
perkaran to litigate, be involved in litigation. *Also* prakara.

perkatak, merkatak 1 to have a skin rash; 2 to produce crackling or tearing sounds;
pating perkatak 1 *pl*, *repr* crackling sounds; 2 *pl*, *describing a skin rash*.

perkèkèh *var of* pekèkèh.

perkeneng *var of* pekeneng.

perkengkeng *var of* pekengkeng.

perkèngkèng *var of* pekèngkèng.

perkènten *subst kr for* perkéwuh.

perketek *or* mak perketek *repr* cracking or crackling sounds;
merketek to crack, crackle, snap.

perkèwed *var of* pakèwed.

perkéwuh *var of* pakéwuh.

perkinding, merkinding to feel a shudder of revulsion.

perkinting *var of* perkinding.

perkis cute.

perkisong percussion cap.

perkitik *see* merkitik.

perklaring declaration, certificate.

perkongkong *var of* pekongkong.

perkonyoh, merkonyoh burned, blistered;
pating perkonyoh *pl repr* burning or blistering of the skin.

perkosa, merkosa to act violently, exert force.

perkotok, merkotok having a severe skin irritation;

pating perkotok *pl* broken in many places (skin).

perkul a variety of adze.

perkungkung *var of* pekungkung.

perkunyuh *var of* perkonyoh.

perkutuk, merkutuk I to keep talking.
II having a severe skin rash.

perkutut a kind of dove, prized for its soft, melodious cooing.

perkuwu *reg* village chief. *See also* kuwu.

perlak 1 protective rubber sheet for a bed; 2 protective canvas cover.

perlambang symbol, symbolic representation;
merlambangi *or* merlambangaké to represent symbolically. *See also* pralambang.

perlaya *var of* pralaya.

perlèng prolonged, extended;
merlèng to prolong, extend.

perlik, merlik to twinkle;
pating perlik *pl* twinkling everywhere.

perlok, pating perlok *pl* sparkling, glittering.

perlop 1 leave, furlough; 2 on leave;
merlopaké to give s.o. furlough, leave.

perlos, merlos to discharge (on completion of service).

perlu 1 compulsory; 2 necessary; 3 urgent, pressing; a need;
merlokaké 1 to need s.t.; 2 to deem necessary; 3 to require, make compulsory; 4 to consider important; 5 to find a way to (do);
kaperluan 1 a necessity; 2 a purpose, interests; 3 requirement.

perlup I engaged to be married.
II loose, worn (screw).

permadani carpet.

permana sharp, clear (vision). *See also* pramana II.

permati excellent, top-rate.

permèn 1 peppermints; 2 sweets (in general).

permili *reg var of* pamili.

permingsi *reg, see* permisi.

permisi (to ask for) permission to go.

permomong, pating permomong glowing everywhere (fires).

permumuh, pating permumuh reddish and infected-looking (sores).

pernah 1 position, location; 2 family relationship; 3 settled, at home;
mernahaké 1 to place s.t. s.w.; 2 to explain a family relationship;
kapernah 1 located; 2 related as, in the relationship of.

pernèl flannel.

pernèng, mernèng to shine, gleam;
pernèng-pernèng glittering and gleaming.

pernès I *or* pernèsan appealing and light-hearted (narrative);
pernèsan *or* pepernèsan 1 designed to appeal, make o.s. attractive; 2 joking, flirtatious, playful (talk).
II prickling, tickling, rollicking.
III *or* pernèsan *reg* prying, inquisitive.

perngangah, merngangah to glow red (fire);
pating perngangah *pl* glowing everywhere;
merngangahaké to cause to glow.

perngèngèh *var of* perngèngès.

pernis varnish;
mernis 1 to apply varnish to; 2 to shine (like varnish).
pernisan varnished.

pernyènyèng, pernyènyèngan naughty, cheeky, boastful.

péron (railway) platform.

pérong, mérong to gash, streak s.t.;
mérong-mérong streaky; full with messy streaks.

pérot (of mouth) awry, twisted to one side;
mérot to twist the mouth or lips to one side;
méroti to tease s.o. by twisting the mouth or lips;

mérotaké to twist the lips as a teasing or disdainful gesture;
mérat-mérot to keep twisting the lips.

perpat *way* group of four clown-servants to a warrior.

perpek *see* prepek.

perplèster nurse.

persaben 1 to warn, admonish; 2 *reg* to ask for leave. *See also* prasaben.

persah sandy, gritty; not clean enough.

persaja *var of* prasaja.

persak *var of* persah.

persanakan 1 relatives; 2 to be (each other's) relative, friend.

persandha *reg* mark, token.

persapa *var of* prasapa.

persekot advanced money, advance;
mersekoti to provide with an advance.

persèn I to be present.
II tip, present to a subordinate;
mersèni to give a tip to.
III percent;
persènan percentage.

Pèrsi Persian.

persikan dressing table with a centre mirror.

persil 1 bale, bundle; 2 a parcel of agricultural land held by long-lease tenure.

persis exactly, precisely, a perfect fit.

perslah report.

persudi, mersudi, marsudi to exert one's best efforts toward (a goal);
pamersudi efforts to reach a goal.

pertal, mertal to translate;
pertalan translation.

pertéla *var of* pratéla.

perti, merti *or* mertèni to care for; - désa *var of* bersih désa.

pertingkah *var of* pratingkah.

pertingsing, kakèhan - excessively demanding or pretentious.

pertiwi *lit* earth.

peru gall (*var of* amperu).

perung missing an ear;

merung to cut off s.o.'s ear.

perut creased, wrinkled (ear).

perwandé *reg* inevitable.

perwandos *reg kr for* perwandé.

perwasa *var of* prawasa.

perwinci *reg var of* princi.

pès I bubonic plague.

II ngepès, mèpès to cook fish wrapped in banana leaves.

pesa *inf var of* peksa.

pesagi four-sided, square, rectangular; - dawa (- panjang *kr*) *or* - mbata (- mbanon *kr*) rectangular; -gésot *or* - miring lozenge-shape, diamond-shape; - kubuk cubic;

pesagèn a square, rectangle.

pesaja *var of* prasaja.

pesat 1 spring; 2 flying away with a spring, elasticity;

mesat to speed off, fly away (as a result of released tension, *e.g.* arrow).

pèsèk flat (nose);

mèsèkaké to make flat.

pesen to order;

mesen to put in an order for s.t.;

pesenan 1 an order, commission; 2 message.

peseng *reg* to install (*var of* pasang).

pèsèr ¹/₂ cent of the colonial period.

pesi I bird (*var of* peksi, *kr for* manuk).

II a part of kris which is covered in the wooden handle, pin.

pesindhèn *see* sindhèn.

pesing 1 smelling of urine; 2 the set of clothes presented by a man to his prospective bride's grandparents on their betrothal.

pesisir shore, coast; coastal region;

pesisiran shoreline, coastal territory. *See also* pasisir.

pesiyar 1 trip, journey; 2 to take a trip, excursion.

pesmèn I seedbed, nursery.

II trimmings, braid. *See also* semi.

péso table knife; - cukur razor.

pésok having a dent in it, dented;

mésokaké to cause a dent.

pésta festivity, a large dinner party.

pestangan *reg* handkerchief.

pesthi predestined fate;

mesthi inevitable;

mesthèkaké 1 to fix, set, determine; 2 to check, make sure of;

pinesthi predestined;

pepesthèn that which is predestined or inevitable.

pestil I pasty.

II pastels.

pestrèn ricefield on river flats.

pestul pistol (*var of* pistul).

pesu, mesu to exert one's utmost effort;

pamesu exertion.

pesud cloth used for wiping dirt;

mesud to wipe (up) or sponge with a cloth.

pesus *var of* pusus.

pet *or* mak pet *repr* sudden darkness;

pet-petan to have things go dark before the eyes (about to faint). *See also* byar I.

pèt I kerosene (*shtf of* pétroli).

II officer's cap.

III *reg var of* pèk II.

petak, metak to bury (*subst kr for* ngubur, *see* kubur).

pétak compartment, partitioned-off space;

métak-métak to divide up into compartments, partition up.

pétan *ng, kr*, ulik *k.i.* to hunt lice in s.o.'s hair;

métani 1 to hunt lice or pick lice from s.o.'s hair; 2 *fig* to search out (flaws); engage in nit-picking.

pétang calculation (*kr for* pétung). *See also* étang.

pétar, métar to shell with cannon shots.

petasan *reg* firecrackers.

peté a variety of bean with pungent odour, eaten raw and cooked.

petek to have a massage (*k.i. for* pijet).

petel, metel *or* metelaké to press forcibly.

peteng 1 dark; 2 obscure, undercover, gloomy; - dhedhet pitch dark, - ndumuk irung *expr* so dark you can't see your hand in front of you;
metengi 1 to darken s.t.; 2 to cut off a view;
metengaké to make darker;
petengan 1 (in the) darkness; 2 moonless nights;
kepetengan 1 to be overtaken by darkness; 2 to have one's view obstructed;
pepeteng the dark; darkness (physical, intellectual, spiritual).

peténtang-petèntèng arrogant, cocksure.

petéta-petété *var of* peténtang-petèntèng.

petétang-petètèng *var of* peténtang-petèntèng.

petha *or* pepethan 1 *reg* shape; 2 imagination, visualisation; 3 idea, notion, concept; 4 mode of action;
metha to picture, imagine.

pethak white (*kr for* putih).

pethakil, methakil to act boisterously;
pethakilan to clamber about.

pethal 1 severed, separated; 2 loose, detached;
methal, methali to separate, sever;
methalaké to break off (friendship);
pethalan broken piece.

pethangkrèk, methangkrèk to sit perched in a high place, *e.g.* on a branch (impolite);
pating pethangkrèk *pl as above*.

pethangkrik *var of* pethangkrèk.

pethangkring *var of* pethangkrèk.

pethangkrok *var of* pethangkrèk.

pethangkrong *var of* pethangkrèk.

pethangkruk *var of* pethangkrèk.

pethanthang, methanthang to sit with the legs spread apart (impolite);
pating pethanthang *pl as above*.

pethar *var of* pethèr.

pethat I 1 to separate o.s.; 2 to cease (rain during the wet season);
methataké 1 to separate s.t.; 2 to spread (the legs) wide apart.
II comb (*k.i. for* jungkat).

pethathak, methathak seated with the legs spread (impolite);
pating pethathak *pl* as above;
methathakaké to spread (the legs) while sitting.

pethathus, pating pethathus with an undershot jaw and jutting chin.

pethèk a guess;
methèk to guess (the answer to), predict;
methèkaké to tell s.o.'s fortune, make predictions about s.t.;
pamethèk act or way of telling fortunes.

pèthèk I wooden or bamboo clamp.
II a small fish, dried and salted.
III, mèthèk (of ladies' hairstyle) spread wide.
IV, mèthèk to hold up (a kite) before s.o. lets it fly.

pethekel, pating - bulging with muscles.

pethel industrious, hard-working.

pethèl carpenter's adze;
methèl *or* methèli to work (wood) with an adze.

pèthèl broken off;
mèthèli to break or snap s.t. off with the fingers;
mèthèlaké to cause to be broken.
See also prèthèl.

pethèngèl *var of* penthèngèl.

pethengil *var of* penthengil.

pethéngkol, methéngkol gnarled (muscles, tree branches *etc*);
pating pethéngkol *pl as above*.

pethengkreng, methengkreng to sit silent and motionless;
pating pethengkreng *pl as above*.

pethèngkrèng, methèngkrèng to perch in a high place;

methèngkrèngaké to put s.t. in a high place;

pating pethèngkrèng *pl* perching in a high place.

pethengkruk, methengkruk to sit silent and motionless;

pating pethengkruk *pl as above.*

pethengkuk, methengkuk to bend the back while sitting;

pating pethengkuk *or* pethengkukan *pl* as above.

pethenguk, pating pethenguk *pl* to sit around idly.

pethentheng, methentheng braced with anger or effort;

pethenthengan to argue heatedly;

pating pethentheng *pl* made taut, tightened, strained.

pethènthèng, methènthèng with hands on hips in a defiant or challenging pose;

pating pethènthèng *pl as above.*

pethèr, methèr to turn outwards, separate;

methèraké to bend, turn outwards.

pethès, methès to drill strictly.

pethèsèl, methèsèl wiry.

pethèt I, pethètan ornamental plants.

II, methèti to snap the finger lightly against (a songbird) to induce it to sing.

III, methèt *or* methèti to graft a cutting (onto).

IV *var of* pethat II.

pethéthah-pethèthèh *see* pethèthèh.

pethèthèh, methèthèh to stand wide-legged with knees bent;

pethéthah-pethèthèh to walk wide-legged with knees bent, *e.g.* when in pain.

pethethek, methethek 1 forming a small heap; 2 (of cooked food) not nice for eating (left too long).

pethèthèk, methèthèk sitting improperly with the legs apart;

pating pethèthèk *pl as above.*

pethi case, chest, box, trunk;

pethèn 1 by the boxful; 2 a small box or trunk.

pethik, methik 1 to pick (out), pluck; 2 to select, extract, quote;

methiki to pick many things;

methikaké to pick for s.o.;

pethikan 1 that which is picked; 2 quotation, excerpt.

pethil I to fall off;

methil 1 *var of* methik; 2 to remove s.t. from a larger part;

methili to pull to pieces with the fingers;

pethilan a fragment taken from a classical dance drama; - buwengan segment of a circle.

II small wooden hammer;

methil to hit with a hammer.

pething, pethingan *or* pepethingan of the highest quality, first-rate, choice.

pethingkrang, methingkrang sitting improperly with the legs raised.

pethingkrik, methingkrik sitting in a high-up position.

pethingkring *var of* pethingkrik.

pethinthing, methinthing tight-fitting;

pating pethinthing *pl as above.*

pethit a tapering point, top point; - naga tip of a dragon's tail;

methit (to come) to a top point.

pethithil, methithil excessively stingy.

pethok I proof, receipt.

II, methoki to hit (a wedge).

III, pethokan *reg* pressed coconut oil.

péthok I *reg* dull (of blade).

II, méthok en face, seen from the front.

pethokol *var of* pethekel.

pethol, metholi to break up clods in a field in preparation for planting.

pethola a snack made from rice flour, eaten with brown sugar and coconut milk.

pethongkrong, methongkrong to sit up high with the legs drawn up (improper);

pating pethongkrong *pl as above*.

pethot *var of* **bethot**.

péthot *or* **méthot** to bend, become crooked;

méthotaké to cause to be bent.

pethothok, methothok to squat on the haunches with the legs apart (improper);

pating pethothok *pl as above*.

pethuk I *var of* **pethok**.

II 1 to agree on, reach agreement; **2** *or* **kepethuk** to meet;

methuk to pick up, fetch;

methuki 1 to pick up repeatedly; **2** to meet, (go to) see;

methukaké to go to meet s.o. who is arriving;

pethukan 1 to meet and pass from opposite directions; **2** pick-up service.

III *reg*, **methuk** to pack;

pethukan package.

pethungkruk, methungkruk sitting with hunched back;

pating pethungkruk *pl as above*.

pethungkrung *var of* **pethungkruk**.

pethunthung, methunthung swollen;

pating pethunthung swollen in many places;

pethunthang-pethunthung puffed up, arrogant, conceited.

pethut *lit* outlaw leader, head of the gang.

pethuthuk, methuthuk to form a heap;

methuthukaké to pile things up, accumulate things;

pating pethuthuk *pl* forming a series of heaps.

petinggi *var of* **patinggi**.

petis fish or shrimp extract (black paste used in cooking);

metis to make the above.

petitis 1 accurate; **2** plain, obvious, clear;

metitisaké to observe, examine closely, accurately. *See also* **patitis**.

petok 1 to cackle; (*or* **papetok**) a cackle; **2** *fig* to chatter;

petok-petok to keep cackling.

petontong, metontong protruding outward (of long objects);

pating petontong *pl as above*.

pétor *reg* assistant resident.

petoto *or* **mak petoto** *repr* a sudden bulging;

metoto to bulge.

petotong *var of* **petontong**.

petrèk, petrèk-petrèk to keep shrieking (woman).

petri, metri *or* **memetri** to take scrupulous care of, cherish (old traditions).

pètroli kerosene.

petung a variety of large, thick bamboo.

pétung *ng*, **pétang** *kr*, (*or* **pétungan**) **1** calculation; **2** excessively careful with one's money;

métung 1 to calculate, *esp* numerologically; **2** to take into account; **3** to consider as belonging to;

pétungan number value of days *etc* used in numerological calculations;

kepétung to be considered or taken into account.

See also **étung**.

péyat-péyot *see* **péyot**.

pèyèk peanut biscuit fried in spiced rice flour. *Also* **rempèyèk**.

peyik *reg var of* **piyik**.

péyok I dented;

méyokaké to make a dent in.

II méyak-méyok to wobble unsteadily (*see also* **pléyok**).

péyor I wobbly, infirm.

II *reg* tiger cub (young of the **macan**).

péyot 1 very old, senile; **2** dull;

péyat-péyot 1 full of dents, bumps; **2** (*or* **méyat-méyot**) rickety, decrepit.

piadu *lit* to quarrel, dispute.

piagem royal decree or deed conferring

land or high office upon the recipient.

piala 1 evil; 2 crime, misdeed, felony. *See also* **ala**.

piandel 1 belief, superstition; 2 one who can be depended on. *See also* **andel**.

pianggep opinion, thought, attitude. *See also* **anggep**.

piangkah intention, expectation, goal. *See also* **angkah**.

piangkuh arrogance, conceit. *See also* **angkuh**.

pianjur advice, suggestion. *See also* **anjur** II.

piarsa, **miarsa** *lit* to hear;
miarsakaké to listen to;
kapiarsa to be heard;
pamiarsa listener, audience.

piatu orphan(ed).

piatur advice, respectful submission. *See also* **atur** I.

piawon *kr for* **piala**. *See also* **ala**.

picak blind;
micak 1 to feign blindness; 2 *cr* to have a nap;
micaki *or* **micakaké** 1 to blind s.o.; 2 to humiliate s.o. by treating them as they did not exist or were not there.

picé *reg var of* **pécé**.

picek *var of* **picak**.

picis I 1 money; 2 *reg* a ten-cent piece;
picisan ten-cent pieces;
pamicis 1 tax; 2 tax-collector.
II **micis** to put to death by cutting off the flesh bit by bit.

pidak, **midak** to step, put the foot on s.t.;
kepidak to get stepped on;
pidakan pedal, s.t. to step on;
pidak pedarakan (people) of the lowest social stratum, kind.

pidana punishment, chastisement; - **pati** death penalty;
midana to inflict a penalty on (a criminal).

pidek *var of* **pidak**.

pideksa well-built (physique).

pidhanget, **midhanget** to hear (*k.i. for* **krungu**, *see* **rungu**).

pidih I, **midih** to press with a thumb;
pidihan a pressing of the thumb.
II cosmetic mixture of wax, coconut oil and a certain leaf for blackening eyebrows;
midih *or* **pidihan** to use such a cosmetic mixture.

pidik, **pidikan** *lit* a place for prayer and meditation.

pidosa sin. *See also* **dosa**.

piduwung regret, remorse. *See also* **duwung** II.

pigegel *reg* memory, remembrance, souvenir.

piguna use, utility, benefit;
migunani useful, beneficial;
migunakaké to use, make use of.
See also **guna** I.

pigurah picture (hung on wall as decoration).

pih ditch, small stream (*var of* **pèh** III).

pihak side, party;
mihak to take sides.

pijar I *reg* impossible, unthinkable.
II *reg* constantly, incessantly (*var of* **pijeri**).

pijer I (to do s.t.) uninterruptedly, without distraction.
II a kind of resin used for soldering.
III hammer-scale, slivers of iron.
IV a kind of small grasshopper.

pijet, **petek** *k.i.*, to have a massage;
mijet to pinch, squeeze, knead;
mijeti to massage;
mijetaké to have s.o. massage one;
pijetan 1 push button; 2 massage given, act or way of kneading; 3 a small sweet yellow fruit that grows in clusters.

piji, **miji** *lit* 1 to select s.o., call s.o. singly; 2 to assign s.o. a task;
mijèkaké 1 to distinguish, give preference over another; 2 to put s.o. under one's direct orders.

pijig *reg var of* piji.

pijir, mijir to count s.t. correctly. *See also* ijir.

pik I *coll var of* dhisik.

II *coll var of* ping.

III *reg var of* mung.

IV, ngepik-pik to touch, get at, take s.t. (wrongfully).

pikajeng (*kr for* pikarep).

pikalah loss. *See also* kalah.

pikandel, pikandelan 1 trust, belief; 2 to believe. *See also* andel.

pikangsal *kr for* pikolèh.

pikantuk 1 to gain, get (*kr for* olèh); 2 accomplishment (*kr for* pikolèh).

pikarep, pikarepan wish, intention, purport. *See also* karep.

pikat decoy bird;

mikat to trap by using a decoy bird.

piké piqué (fabric).

pikekah *kr for* pikukuh.

piker *reg* to have crooked fingers (*var of* ciker).

pikèt 1 the watch, guard duty; 2 *fig* to visit one's girlfriend;

mikèti to guard s.t.

pikir *ng*, manah *kr*, galih *k.i.*, 1 opinion, idea; 2 thought;

mikir 1 to think (about); 2 to be concerned, worried;

mikir-mikir to think things over;

mikiri to give thought, give consideration to;

mikiraké to think or be concerned about;

kepikir in one's thoughts;

mikir-mikir to think over; to try to think of s.t.;

pikiran 1 *var of* pikir; 2 intelligence, mind; 3 concern, anxiety;

mikiran full of ideas, brainy;

pamikir 1 thought; 2 object of one's thoughts, result of one's thinking.

piklah *reg* please yourself!

pikolèh accomplishment, gain, result.

See also olèh.

pikrama 1 marriage; 2 to marry;

mikramakaké to marry off.

See also krama.

pikudhung copy of a decree document.

pikukuh certificate.

pikul *ng*, rembat *kr*, 1 a long pole carried over one shoulder with carrying baskets suspended fore and aft; 2 a unit of weight: *ca* 62 kg;

mikul to carry with the above equipment;

mikuli to carry (many things);

mikulaké to have s.o. carry (as above);

pikulan a long pole used for carrying as above.

pikun absent-minded or dull-witted in one's old age.

pikut, mikut to capture, captivate;

kepikut to get captured.

pikuwat strengthening, reinforcement. *See also* kuwat.

pil pill, tablet.

pilag beautiful (form) (*lit, var of* pélag).

pilah classified, separate;

milah *or* milah-milah to classify, sort, divide up;

milahaké to differentiate, classify.

pilakon destiny, the way things go. *See also* laku.

pilala, milala 1 to value highly; 2 to give preference to;

pilalan s.t. chosen or selected.

pilalah, milalah to content o.s. with.

pilalu *var of* pilalah.

pilampu *var of* pilalah. *See also* lampu II.

pilang a certain tall tree.

pilar, milar to split lengthwise (bamboo);

pilaran split lengthwise.

pilara *ng*, pisakit *kr*, act of causing or inflicting physical pain; physical torture;

milara to torture, inflict pain on.

See also **lara** I.

pilas, milasi to give an extra, on top of a purchase;

pilasan an extra, bonus.

pilèh reg var of **pilih**.

pileg 1 (to have/get) a cold; 2 cr gonorrhea.

pilèk reg, cr child.

pilenggah kr for **pilungguh**.

piler, pileren sickly, weak-looking (chickens, fig of people).

piles, miles 1 to hold (rope etc) firmly and twist it; 2 to knead (clay etc).

pilih to make a choice; - **kasih** to play favorites, give preferential treatment (to); - **tandhing** outstanding, superior; ora - without distinction;

milih to choose, elect, appoint;

milihi to sort out, select;

milihaké to select for s.o.;

kepilih to get chosen/elected;

pilihan 1 (having been) selected; 2 selected or outstanding (person), chosen ones; 3 choice, selection;

pamilih act or way of choosing;

pilih-pilih to make choices;

pilih-pilih tebu to make an unpredictable choice.

piling, pilingan temple (side of forehead).

pilis I a herbal paste applied to the forehead to relieve pain or restore health;

milisi to apply the above.

II bonus, s.t. extra thrown in.

pilong reg blind.

pilulus, pilulusan permit. See also **lulus**.

pilungguh, pilenggah kr, k.i., 1 residence; 2 a gift presented to s.o. in authority. See also **lungguh**.

piluta, miluta to try to win over;

kapiluta won over; to succumb, yield;

pamiluta a means winning or captivating.

pimpin, mimpin to lead, guide, preside (over), chair;

pimpinan 1 director, head; 2 guidance, leadership;

pamimpin leader, guide.

pinang reg betel nut.

pinangka place of origin;

minangka (serving) as, for;

minangkani to serve, satisfy a need, comply with a request.

pinarak 1 to sit (k.i. for **lungguh**); 2 to receive in audience.

pinasthika lit most excellent, extremely good.

pincang lame, crippled;

pincangan to feign lameness.

pincuk container for carrying food made by folding a banana leaf and pinning it with a sharpened palm leaf rib;

mincuk 1 to eat from the above container; 2 to fold a banana leaf as above;

pincukan (food) served in such a container.

pindeng, mindeng to concentrate on doing s.t., focus the attention on.

pinder I, **minder** to cause to be numb (var of **plinder**).

II, **minder** to look at fixedly; - **liring** to keep watching fixedly.

pindha lit like, as, resembling;

mindhakaké to illustrate s.t. figuratively;

pepindhan 1 a figure of speech; 2 to represent figuratively;

mindha-mindha to imitate, assume the guise of.

pindhah to move, change residence;

mindhah to shift, change;

mindhahaké to transfer s.t.; to shift s.t. to;

pindhahan 1 act or process of moving; 2 changed, shifted.

pindhang a process for preparing eggs or fish using salt and certain spices; a dish prepared in this way;

mindhang to prepare (food) as above.

pindho *ng*, kaping kalih *kr*, twice; (for) the second time; (the) second (one); mindhoni to do s.t. for a second time; mindhogawèni to do s.t. again because it was not done properly the first time; mindho, mindhoan third cousin; kapindho 1 the second one; 2 repeated for the second time; pindhon 1 redone (batik); 2 second-hand.

pindi, mindi 1 to comb (cotton before spinning); 2 to examine carefully, keep after s.o. with questions.

ping (*or* kaping) 1 (number of) times; 2 *ordinal marker*; 3 multiplication sign; ngeping to multiply; ngepingaké to multiply by; ping-pingan multiplication.

pingé *lit* white.

pinggah means, way for stepping up or down (*kr for* punggah).

pinggan bowl or plate of earthenware or porcelain.

pinggang *lit* waist.

pinggel I, minggel *reg* to divide into pieces (*var of* punggel). II *lit* bracelet (*var of* binggel).

pingget (to have) a mark on the skin where s.t. has pressed against it; minggeti to leave a mark on the skin; minggetaké to cause to have a mark on the skin; pinggetan sensitive, easily hurt.

pingging *lit* stupid, ignorant.

pinggir edge, side; minggir to go to(ward) the edge; minggiraké to send, move s.t. to the side or edge; pinggiran 1 at the edge/side; 2 outside territory; kepinggiren *or* keminggiren too far toward the edge.

pingil I behaviour, attitude. II calculation, divination.

pingit, mingit to seclude (a marriageable girl) at home; pingitan a girl of marriageable age who is secluded in the house.

pingkel, kepingkel-pingkel (to laugh) heartily, double up with laughter.

pingkus, mingkus shrunken (*var of* pringkus).

pingseng 1 with sunken (diseased) nose; 2 to talk through the nose.

pingul *lit* white.

pinihan seedbed, nursery. *See also* winih.

pinikolot *reg var of* pinituwa.

pinisepuh *kr for* pinituwa.

pinituwa *ng*, pinisepuh *kr*, one's elders; one's older-generation relatives. *See also* tuwa.

piniwayah *reg var of* pinituwa.

pinjal flea.

pinjem, pinjeman *reg* a loan, debt.

pinjung, pinjungan (of girls or women) to wear the kain high enough to cover the breasts (after taking a bath).

pinta, minta *or* meminta *lit* to make a demand or request; paminta act of requesting/demanding; papintan a request, demand.

pinten how many? what amount? (*kr for* pira); -banggi luckily (*kr for* pirangbara).

pinter bright, clever, educated, skilled; minteri 1 to be too clever for; 2 to play a trick on s.o.; minteraké to develop one's ability, sharpen one's mind; kapinteran cleverness, skill; kuminter to pretend one is clever, assume an air of cleverness.

pinti *reg* fishing line.

pinton sample of merchandise; mintoni *or* mintonaké to show s.t. and ask for assessment.

pintu *reg* door; - aèr sluice gate; - angin porthole, vent; - monyèt folding doors.

pinuju in the middle of (do)ing; to happen to be (do)ing;

kapinujon by chance, coincidentally.

pinunjul outstanding (person); excellent. *See also* punjul.

pipa 1 pipe, tube; 2 chimney, funnel;

mipa to smoke a pipe.

pipi *ng, kr*, pangarasan *k.i.* cheek.

pipih I *or* pipihan cloth used as a sanitary napkin.

II mipih to beat out (metal).

pipik I, mipik to buy up a large quantity at once;

mipikaké to buy up for s.o.

II, mipik to choose, select, pick out.

pipil, mipil 1 to pick off one by one; 2 *fig* to do little by little;

pipilan 1 (corn kernels) which have been plucked off; 2 kernel remover (tool); 3 (in gamelan music) a certain rhythmic pattern played on the bonang.

pipir *reg* side; near to.

pipis I, mipis to grind on a square stone pestle;

pipisan square stone pestle on which herbs *etc* are ground fine by rolling a cylindrical implement (gandhik) over them.

II leaf-wrapped boiled cake.

III (*pron as:* pipi:s) *chld* 1 urine; 2 to urinate.

pipit close together with no space intervening;

mipit to press close together;

pipit adu cukit *expr* densely covered with houses.

pir spring (*var of* pèr).

pira *ng*, pinten *kr*, how many? what amount?;

mira how much apiece?;

sapira how much (of s.t. not specified in units);

piraa no matter how much;

pirang how much? how many? (*as modifier*);

pira-pira 1 no matter how much; 2 luckily;

pirang-pirang a lot (of);

sapirang-pirang in large quantities;

pirabara *or* pirangbara happily and unexpectedly.

pirak *reg* apart, separate(d);

mirak 1 to separate; 2 to divorce (one's spouse);

pirakan divorced.

piranti *ng*, pirantos *kr*, equipment, instrument, apparatus;

miranti equipped, ready;

mirantèni to equip s.t.; to furnish as equipment.

pirasat 1 sign, omen; 2 physiognomy, character-reading by studying the face;

mirasati to prophesy the future, give an omen.

piré, miré to avoid meeting with, sidestep, get out of the way;

mirèkaké to get s.t. out of the way.

pirena contentment. *See also* rena II.

pirid, mirid 1 to trace; 2 to refer; 3 to take s.t. as an example;

miridi to pay full attention to;

piridan *or* pepiridan 1 example, model; 2 instance taken as an example.

pirik, mirik *reg* to set one's eye on, have in mind.

piring dish, plate;

piringan 1 on dishes; 2 plate-shaped.

pirit *see* pirid.

pirma, sympathy, pity;

mirma to feel solicitous toward;

mirmakaké to suggest, give a good piece of advice. *See also* palimirma.

piroga *lit* illness. *See also* roga.

pirsa 1 to see (*k.i. for* weruh); 2 to know, to understand (*k.i. for* sumurup, ngerti);

mirsa 1 to know about; 2 to witness;

mirsani 1 to look at; 2 to see, watch;
mirsakaké to show, let see;
pamirsa 1 vision; 2 spectator, viewer (TV). *See also* priksa.

pirukun harmony, concord, agreement;
pirukunan to live in harmony, cooperate;
mirukunaké to bring peace about, restore to harmony.
See also rukun.

pirung, pirung-pirung *reg* luckily.

pirus turquoise (stone).

pis I (*pron as:* pi:s) *excl uttered when s.o. sneezes* ('Bless you!').
II *chld* 1 urine; 2 to urinate. *See also* pipis III.

pisah 1 apart, separate(d); 2 divorced; -kebo to live apart (but not divorced);
misah 1 to separate (out), separate o.s. from; 2 to divorce (one's spouse); 3 to break up a fight, separate (fighters);
misahi to separate;
misahaké 1 to separate s.t.; 2 to cause to divorce;
pisahan *or* pepisahan 1 separation, parting; 2 separated; to part from each other;
pamisah partition, divider.

pisaid testimony, declaration.

pisak flat (nose) (*var of* pèsèk).

pisakit physical torture (*kr for* pilara).

pisalin *ng*, pisantun *kr*, new suit of clothes (as a gift). *See also* salin.

pisan 1 once; the first time; 2 at the same time, as well, on top of it; 3 altogether;
misan related as a second cousin;
misani to do successfully at once;
misanaké to do at the same time;
kapisan first; first time;
kapisanan in the same instant;
sepisan one time, once;
sepisanan first one; (for) the first time;
aja pisan-pisan don't ever (do);

ora pisan-pisan never; by no means.

pisang banana (*kr for* gedhang).

pisarat means, condition, prerequirement. *See also* sarat III.

piser I bullet.
II, miser to twirl, twist.

pisin *reg* saucer.

pising *var of* pisin.

piskucing touch-me-not (medicinal plant). *Also* kumis-kucing.

piso *var of* péso.

pispot chamber pot.

pista *var of* pésta.

pistul pistol, revolver;
mistul to shoot with a pistol;
mistulaké to fire a pistol;
pistul-pistulan 1 to shoot at each other; 2 toy pistol.

pisuh abusive words;
misuh to curse, use bad language in anger;
misuhi to swear at, heap abuse on;
misuh-misuh to yell abusively;
pisuhan swear-word.

pisuka heart's desire, what makes s.o. happy. *See also* suka.

pisungsung a gift presented to a person socially superior or s.o. in authority;
misungsungaké to present a gift (to a social superior).

pit I Chinese brush pen.
II (*pron as:* pi:t) bicycle;
ngepit to ride a bike;
pit-pitan to go for a bike ride.

pita 1 ribbon; 2 tape.

pitados to believe (*kr for* percaya).

pitajeng to believe (*subst kr for* percaya).

pitak horsefly, gadfly.

pitakon *ng*, pitakèn *kr*, 1 to ask a question; 2 (*or* pitakonan) a question. *See also* takon.

pitakèn *kr for* pitakon.

pitambet *subst kr for* pitambuh.

pitambuh 1 ignorant; 2 feigning ignorance or lack of interest;

mitambuhi to pretend not to know or care about; to ignore.
See also tambuh.

pitawa pronouncement (of Islamic jurist).

pitaya *ng*, pitados *kr*, to believe (in), have confidence (in);
mitaya to trust, rely upon;
mitayani trustworthy; worthy of confidence;
mitayakaké to entrust s.t. to;
kapitayan 1 confidence, faith; 2 belief.

pitedah direction, advice (*kr for* pituduh).

pitedhan a gift (*kr for* pawèwèh). *See also* tedha III.

pitek *var of* pitak.

pitekur 1 to engage in meditation; 2 to pray in commemoration of a dead person.

pitembung a request;
pitembungan usage, expression, phrase.
See also tembung I.

pitenah slander;
mitenah to slander s.o., accuse s.o. slanderously.

pitepang *kr for* pitepung.

pitepung, pitepungan *ng*, pitepangan *kr* to (get to) know, become acquainted;
mitepungaké to introduce (people to each other).
See also tepung.

piterang, miterang to ask for information, try to get elucidation.

pithat, mithat to classify, sort;
mithati to select, choose the good ones from;
pithatan what has been selected.

pithes, mithes *or* mithesi to pinch or squeeze (louse *etc*) with a thumbnail;
mithesaké to squeeze for s.o.

pithet I (to have) a scar from a wound (*var of* bithet, githet).
II, mithet to pinch (a nose) with fingers.

pithi I tikus - small mouse.
II one of the small playing-cards (*kertu cilik*).
III a small basket of bamboo.

pithil to become detached;
mithili to detach, break off;
mithilaké to detach accidentally;
pithilan a piece of s.t. detached.

pithing I crab (*var of* kepithing).
II, mithing 1 to grip, clasp, hug tightly; 2 to hold s.o.'s head in the crook of one's arm;
pithingan 1 to wrestle; 2 way of wrestling;
pithing-pithingan to wrestle with each other.

pitho *reg cr* blind.

pithong *var of* pitho.

pithut almond-eyed (*var of* cithut).

pitik *ng*, ayam *kr*, chicken; - iwèn poultry; - walik a variety of chicken with the feathers 'back-to-front';
pitik trondhol dibubuti wuluné *expr* a poor man who is swamped with expenses or who is robbed of all his belongings;
pitik trondhol saba ing lumbung *expr* a poor man entrusted with money.

pitnah *var of* pitenah.

pitobat repentance, contrition. *See also* tobat.

pitonton, mitontonaké to display, exhibit. *See also* ton, tonton.

pitrah compulsory gift to the poor (in Islam) given at the close of the Fasting Month;
mitrahi to give rice or cash (as obligatory alms) at end of the Fasting Month. *See also* fitrah.

pitroli kerosene.

pitu seven;
mitu seven each;
mitoni to hold a ceremony for a woman in the seventh month of pregnancy;

kapitu 1 7th month of the Javanese year; **2** (for) the seventh time, seventh in a series.

pituduh *ng*, **pitedah** *kr*, **1** advice; **2** indication, demonstration;
　mituduhi to advise;
　mituduhaké to guide, advise, point out (the right thing). *See also* **tuduh**.

pituhu, mituhu, mituhoni to be true to, adhere loyally to;
　pituhon true, loyal (by nature).

pitulas seventeen;
　pitulasan to celebrate the proclamation of independence of the Republic of Indonesia on 17 August.
　See also **pitu**.

pitulung *or* **pitulungan** help, assistance;
　mitulungi to come to s.o.'s help or rescue.
　See also **tulung**.

pituna loss, harm;
　mitunani to bring about, inflict a loss;
　kapitunan 1 hardship; **2** to suffer a setback, undergo hardship/loss.
　See also **tuna**.

pitung- seven (*as modifier*); **-atus** 700; **-èwu** 7,000.

pitungkas (final) instructions; parting words;
　mitungkasi to give final instructions, advice.

piturut obedient;
　miturut 1 to obey; **2** (to go) according to, in obedience with;
　mituruti to act in accordance with;
　sapituruté in the same way; and so on.
　See also **turut**.

pitutur 1 (words of) advice; **2** admonition, caution;
　mituturi to instruct, admonish.
　See also **tutur I**.

pituwa chairman, presiding officer;
　mituwani to preside over, to chair.
　See also **tuwa**.

pituwah I pronouncement (of Islamic jurist).
　II compensation for one's time and trouble (*var of* **pituwas**).
　III *reg* **1** souvenir; **2** heirloom, revered heritage from one's ancestors.

pituwas compensation for services.

pituwi *var of* **pituwin**.

pituwin *lit* and, also.

piunjuk *lit* s.t. respectfully presented, conveyed.

piutang debt. *See also* **utang**.

piwadul malicious gossip. *See also* **wadul**.

piwales 1 retribution; **2** revenge. *See also* **wales**.

piwelas compassion, pity. *See also* **welas I**.

piweling a (last) message, instruction. *See also* **weling I**.

piwulang instruction, teachings. *See also* **wulang**.

piyagah, miyagah to do s.t. by guesswork, work at random. *See also* **wiyagah**.

piyah *excl of disbelief, disparagement*.

piyak 1 opening up, parting; **2** to stand aside;
　miyak 1 to open s.t. up, push apart; **2** *fig* to reveal (a secret); **3** to part (hair);
　miyaki to open s.t. up repeatedly;
　piyakan with a part (hair).

piyambak 1 alone; **2** (by) oneself (*kr for* **dhéwé**).

piyapat character-reading by studying the face, physignomy.

piyara, miyara to raise, breed, tend.

piyarsa, miyarsa *lit* to hear;
　miyarsakaké to listen to;
　kapiyarsa audible;
　pamiyarsa listener, hearer.
　See also **piarsa**.

piyas *reg* to go pale.

piyatu orphan.

piyayi *var of* **priyayi**.

piyé *inf var of* kepriyé.

piyek I, miyek to crush utterly, squash the life out of s.t.

II, piyek-piyek *var of* piyik-piyik.

piyèk, piyèk-piyèk *reg var of* piyik-piyik.

piyik baby chick, baby dove;

piyik-piyik (*pron as:* piyi:k-piyi:k) *repr* the cheeping of baby chicks.

piyon pawn (chess piece).

piyul violin;

miyul to play a violin.

placek *reg* a row of poles in a field (for spacing plants).

pladhu *reg* a time of floods (*var of* paladhu).

plag *repr* drumbeats.

plaga *lit* monkey (*var of* plawaga).

plahara *var of* prahara.

plajeng running pace (*kr for* playu).

plak I *or* mak plak *repr* the sound of a slap (*var of* plek);

ngaplak to make a 'plak, plak' sound on a drum.

plak-plek to keep slapping. *See also* plek I.

II, plak glèdhèg *reg* small cart with iron wheels.

III *reg* precisely, just like (*var of* plek II).

IV, ngaplak to come walking up quickly.

plakang *or* plakangan *reg* groin, inner part of the thigh (*var of* lakang, wlakang).

plaken, mlakeni *reg* to ask for.

plaksana, mlaksana to force, punish s.o. as a warning for other people.

plaksègel receipt stamp or seal.

plaksik, pating plaksik *reg* messy, in disorder.

plaku *see* palaku II.

plala *var of* pilala.

plalah *var of* pilalah.

plalu *var of* pilalu.

plamar rope stretched to mark a boundary that is not to be crossed. *See also* kamar.

plampit, plampitan *reg* oil-press.

plampu *var of* pilampu.

plana saddle;

mlanani to saddle;

planan saddled.

planangan male parts, penis. *See also* lanang.

planca *reg* bench (to lie or to sit on).

plancoh *reg* a stake used for supporting a tree or for mooring a boat.

plancong, mlancong to go s.w. for enjoyment or sightseeing;

plancongan 1 to keep visiting places; 2 a place visited by a traveller.

plancur, pating plancur *pl* to stream out, flow upward.

plandang, mlandang to attract attention, strike.

plander, mlander to change (writing), make a correction.

plandhèn *reg* 1 sail-pulley; 2 ready to sail, ready for sea.

plandhungan scrotum (*k.i. for* konthol).

plang 1 sign, signboard; 2 shelf (in book case);

ngeplang to give a sign, hand signal;

ngeplangi to signal to.

planggang *var of* planggrang I, II.

plangger, mlanggeri to apply rules (to), furnish regulation (for);

planggeran, ora - unregulated.

planggrang I , mlanggrang to roast, grill;

mlanggrangaké to place s.t. on a surface over a fire;

planggrangan a roasting-grill.

II mlanggrangaké to hang up, put on a rack (*e.g.* to dry).

planggrok, mlanggrok to rest along the way;

planggrokan a place to rest along the way.

planggrong, planggrongan platform built on piles (for hunting).

plangi bandanna cloth, coloured by the tie-and-dye process, used as a sash or breastcloth.

plangka (of animal's coats) spotted, piebald.

plangkah a gift to an older unmarried sibling, made by a younger sibling when marrying first.

plangkan 1 wooden drum standard; **2** umbrella rack; **3** throne, low table.

plangki or **plangkèn** palanquin.

plangkring, mlangkring 1 to perch, alight; to sit in a high place; **2** fig to jack up the price (to a patently interested customer);

plangkringan a bird's perch.

plangkrong, mlangkrong sitting on a high-up tree branch;

pating plangkrong pl as above.

plangkruk var of **plangkrong**.

plang-pleng repr leaving precipitately. See also **pleng**.

planthang, mlanthang to ride (a bicycle) by sitting on the bar rather than back on the seat;

planthangan 1 crossbar; **2** horizontally placed pole (e.g. for drying clothes) (see also **klanthang**); **3** measuring-staff.

planthas var of **plonthos**.

planthing, planthingan mischievous, impolite.

planthir, mlanthir to plough the first furrow (also as irrigation ditch);

planthiran the first furrow.

planthur, mlanthur to spout up, stream out;

pating planthur pl as above.

plantrah var of **plantrang**.

plantrang, mlantrang to go s.w. other than one's intended destination, wander off;

mlantrangaké to take s.o. too far;

mlantrang-mlantrang to wander around;

keplantrang to get off the track.

planjer gland;

mlanjer or **planjeren** having a painful swelling in the neck or groin (due to infection in another place).

planyahan whore, prostitute.

plapah reg spices, s.t. added during preparation of food to improve the taste.

plapat reg sign, omen;

mlapat or **mlapati** to be an omen of.

plara var of **pilara**.

plarah, mlarah reg to feel, pass the hand over.

plarang, mlarangi to pay a high price for.

plas or **mak plas** rep a sudden departure;

plas-plasan hard to get hold of, coming for a moment then heading off again.

plasa a variety of tree the leaves of which are used for wrapping food.

plat 1 zinc plating; **2** record; **3** car number-plate.

plathas or **plathasan** reg to go out for a stroll.

plathok, mlathok or **mlathoki** to chop up into pieces (with a sharp instrument);

keplathok to get chopped accidentally (finger or toe).

plathuk or **plathukan 1** trigger; **2** hammer for cocking a gun;

mlathuk to cock (a pistol).

plathus, plathusé reg sequel, continuation; the next, the following.

platok reg a variety of bird (var of **platuk**).

platuk I a certain bird; - **bawang** woodpecker-like bird;

mlatuk to peck with the beak;

mlatuki to keep pecking.

II var of **plathuk**.

III var of **plathok**.

IV, mlathuk cr (of a man) to have intercourse with s.o.

platun 1 platoon; 2 corporal.

plaur, diplaur *pass* would rather have (s.t. bad) happen than.

plawaga *lit* monkey.

plawah, plawahan a deep hole dug in the ground for rubbish.

plawangan 1 doorway; 2 doorkeeper. *See also* lawang.

plawongan *var of* plawungan.

plawungan rack for holding weapons (spear, kris). *See also* lawung I.

playangan postman. *See also* layang I.

playu, *ng*, plajeng *kr* a running pace;
mlayu to run (off, away);
mlayoni to run to s.o.;
mlayokaké to run off with s.t. belonging to s.o. else;
mlayu-mlayu to keep running around;
keplayu defeated, routed;
playon to run around.

plebuhan *reg* rubbish dump. *See also* lebuh.

pleca-plecu *see* plecu.

plecas-plecus boasting, big talk.

plecèk, mlecèk to draw back (the foreskin);
mlecèkaké to cause to draw back.

plecèt, mlecèt to do an about-turn, leave without a word.

plècèt, mlècèt skinned, bruised;
mlècèti to remove the outer layer from, peel, shell.

plecis *or* mak plecis *repr* 1 to appear unexpectedly; 2 to turn out to be a false hope.

plecit, mlecit to chase.

plecu, mlecu to pout, have the lips thrust forward;
pleca-plecu to keep pouting.

plecus I *var of* plecis.
II, plecusan *reg* to chatter idly.

plecut *var of* plencut II.

pledhang-pledhing *see* pledhing.

plédhang *reg* a wandering tinker.

pledhing, mledhing to show the buttocks openly while on all fours;

mledhingi 1 to humiliate s.o. by showing the buttocks; 2 *fig* to humiliate s.o. publicly;
pledhang-pledhing to keep showing the buttocks.

plegak-pleguk to stutter and stammer.

plégung, mlégungaké to have/let (cattle) rest in a shady place;
plégungan a place for cattle (buffaloes) to rest, lie (under a tree).

plek I *or* mak plek *repr* a sound of slap, a blow of the hand;
plak-plek *repr* repeated slaps or splatting sounds;
II just like, coinciding with;
ngepleki to look just like; coinciding with;
ngeplekaké to make s.t. coincide with.

plèk I (*or* mak plèk) 1 *repr* coming to, and remaining in, contact; 2 *repr* a slap or blow (*var of* plek I);
ngeplèk 1 to slap s.o. on the back; 2 to produce clop-clop sounds.
II dirty mark, spot, stain;
ngeplèk to get stained, get dirty marks.
III ngeplèk 1 to sit up late doing s.t.; 2 to gamble.
IV ngeplèk to trace (an outline, using thin paper).

plekah a crack, split;
mlekah to crack, split open;
mlekahi to crack/split s.t.;
pating plekah splitting open everywhere.

plekak-plekèk *or* plekak-plekuk to feel nauseated.

plekara *var of* perkara.

plekat I *reg* broad grassy area in front of a regent's residence, square.
II proclamation, publication.

plékat sarong with striped or check pattern.

plekèk, mlekèk 1 wide open; 2 *cr*

exposed (woman); 3 split open (fruit); mlekèkaké to open (a fruit) by pressing it with the hands.

plèkèk, mlèkèk to slaughter (by cutting the throat). *See also* klèkèk.

plekèt *reg* the watch, guard duty (*var of* pikèt).

plekik (*pron as:* pleki:k), plekiken 1 to swallow s.t. the wrong way; 2 to hiccup.

plekok *var of* plèkèk.

plekrok, mlekrok to open out;
   pating plekrok *pl repr* bursting out everywhere (flowers in bloom). *See also* pekrok.

pleksana *var of* plaksana.

plekuk, mlekuk 1 bent; 2 (of road) narrow and sharply curved.

plelang-pleleng *see* pleleng.

pleleng, mleleng to stare long and unblinkingly;
   plelang-pleleng to keep staring as above.

plèlèr clothing given to a servant. *See also* lèlèr III.

plembas-plembis *or* plembas-plembus to keep changing one's mind, unable to stick to one's word.

plembir *var of* plombir I, II.

plembung, mlembung inflated, swollen, puffed up;
   mlembungaké to inflate;
   plembungan 1 balloon; 2 crop (of a bird);
   pating plembung *pl* inflated;
   plembung anginen (of stomach) to feel bloated.

plempas-plempus to tell fibs, tell a different story to different people.

plempeng pipe, water supply.

plèmpèng, mlèmpèng 1 to go sideways; 2 to go away.

plempuh, mlempuh swollen;
   pating plempuh *pl* swollen in many places.

plempung, mlempung swollen, puffed;
   pating plempung having many swellings on the skin.

plencang-plencing *see* plencing I.

pléncang-plèncèng *see* plèncèng.

plencar, mlencar to spread, get disseminated;
   pating plencar *pl* scattered everywhere. *See also* pencar.

plencat *or* plencat-plencat *or* mlencat-mlencat *or* pating plencat to jump back and forth; - kidang here and there, now and then, sporadic;
   plencat-plencut 1 to keep on doing s.t. different, heading off s.w. else; 2 shifty, unreliable.

plèncèng , mlèncèng off the mark;
   mlèncèngaké to miss deliberately;
   plèncèngan in an off-target direction;
   pléncang-plèncèng to keep missing, (do) in a zigzag path.

plencing I (*pron as:* plenci:ng) *or* mak plencing *repr* walking off suddenly, without saying anything;
   plencang-plencing to keep walking off.
   II, plencingan *reg* to cycle around.
   III baby rhinoceros (young of the warak).
   IV flower of the kapok tree.

pléncong *var of* plèncèng.

plencut I, mlencut, mlencuti (of riceplants in a field) with ears beginning to appear.
   II, pating plencut to jump out in all directions.

plendak-plendèk *or* mlendak-mlendèk (to do s.t.) with reluctance, disliking;
   mak plendèk suddenly unable to go on, out of revulsion.

plendak-plenduk to act hastily.

plender, mlender to have to bear the whole burden, do the whole job alone.

plendhing *var of* blendhing.

plendhung, mlendhung *var of* plembung.

plendir *var of* plender.

pléndo, mak pléndo *repr* giving out, suddenly breaking down;
 mléndo 1 to have no effect (bad tools); 2 to be useless, of no value (promise).

plendreng *var of* plender.

plenek, saplenek a little heap of s.t.

pleneng, sapleneng a little mound of s.t.

plenet *or* mak plenet *repr* squirting, squeezing;
 mlenet to press, squeeze;
 keplenet to get squeezed;
 plenetan tool for pressing or mashing.

plenèt *var of* plenet.

plènèt *var of* plenet.

pleng I *or* mak pleng *repr* a sudden departure;
 plang-pleng *repr* leaving precipitately.
 II ces pleng just right, having the desired result;
 ngeplengi to be exactly like.

plengah-plengèh *see* plengèh.

plengak-plengok to keep staring in surprise.

plengang-plengong dumb-looking.

plengèh *or* mak plengèh *repr* a sudden smile;
 mlengèh to smile broadly;
 plengah-plengèh to keep smiling.

plèngèh *var of* plengèh.

plenggang-plenggong *see* plenggong.

plenggong, mlenggong to stare in bewilderment;
 pating plenggong *pl* to stare in bewilderment;
 plenggongan gaping with surprise, taken aback;
 plenggang-plenggong to keep staring stupidly or vacantly, sit looking bewildered.

plénggrong *var of* planggrong.

plengkang, mlengkang to do the splits, sit with the legs stretched straight in opposite directions;

keplengkang to inadvertently do the splits.

pléngkrang, mléngkrang to sit with the legs up;
 mléngkrangaké to put (the feet) up high on the desk while sitting.

plengkuk, mlengkuk to bend; bent;
 mlengkukaké to bend s.t.

plengkung arch, vault, archway;
 mlengkung curved, arc-shaped;
 mlengkungaké to curve s.t., shape into an arc.

pléngo *or* mak pléngo *repr* a turn of a head;
 mléngo to turn the head. *See also* méngo.

plengong *var of* penggong.

pléngos *repr* turning the head aside (in dislike);
 mléngos to turn the head aside;
 mléngas-mléngos to keep averting the face.

plèngsèng, plèngsèngan sloping bank lined with cement, to divert rainwater from a building.

plèngsèr ½ cent (*var of* pèsèr).

plenguk, mlenguk to sit motionless;
 pating plenguk standing around, hanging around.

plenik dot, speck, fleck;
 mlenik to form little dots;
 plenik-plenik full of little dots.

plenis, mlenis shiny and cute-looking (small things);
 pating plenis *pl as above*.

plenok a rounded heap or mound;
 mlenok mound-shaped;
 pating plenok *pl* in mounds, in small heaps.

plèntèk, mlèntèk *reg* to ask left and right, look everywhere for s.t.

plenthas-plenthus *see* plenthus.

plénthas, mlénthas to shave completely bald;
 keplénthas to have a part of the hair cut inadvertently.

plenthèt, mlenthèt (of the belly) concave, flat;
   mlenthètaké to flatten, pull in (the stomach).

plenthi *or* **mak plenthi** *repr* swelling, puffing;
   mlenthi bloated;
   mlenthèkaké to swell s.t. up.

plenthing a small swelling;
   mlenthing to be(come) swollen;
   plenthingen to suffer from little pussy blisters.

plenthong I electric light bulb.
   II, **mlenthong** muddy;
   keplenthong to get stuck in a muddy place.

plenthu, mlenthu to be bloated, bulge;
   mlenthokaké to puff up, distend (the stomach);
   pating plenthu *pl* bulging, protruding;
   plenthon s.t. puffed up.

plenthuk *var of* **plenthu**.

plenthung a large swelling, blister;
   mlenthung to be puffed out, swollen;
   pating plenthung full of swellings, blisters.

plenthus (*pron as:* penthu:s) *or* **mak plenthus** puffing out suddenly;
   mlenthus puffed up, swelling out;
   mlenthusaké to cause s.t. to swell;
   plenthas-plenthus 1 swelled up with pride or self-importance; 2 *reg* choked with emotion.

plentong *var of* **blentong**.

plenuk a heap or mound;
   mlenuk mound-shaped;
   pating plenuk *pl* in mounds, in small heaps.

plenyak-plenyèk *see* **plenyèk**.

plenyek *var of* **plenyèk**.

plenyèk *or* **mak plenyèk** *repr* stepping into s.t. large and soft;
   mlenyèk 1 to step on s.t. soft; 2 (to become) soft and mushy;

keplenyèk to step on s.t. soft and mushy inadvertently;
   plenyak-plenyèk (to eat) without enjoyment, pick at one's food.

plenyok, mlenyok (to become) soft and mushy (*var of* **plenyèk**);
   keplenyok to step on s.t. soft and mushy (*var of* **keplenyèk**).

plep, ngeplep to get/keep selfishly or dishonestly. *See also* **emplep**.

plepah bamboo split open and beaten flat (material for fences, floors *etc*) (*reg kr for* **plupuh**).

plepak-plepek *see* **plepek**.

plepak-plepuk bubbling (of boiling water).

plepas-plepus *reg var of* **plempas-plempus**.

plèpèd any tool used for pressing, a press;
   mlèpèd to push, press.

plepek I, **plepek-plepek** *or* **plepak-plepek** to have difficulty breathing (blocked nose, with heavy cold);
   keplepek *or* **keplepeken** suffocated, stifled, to suffer from a blocked nose.
   II **mlepek** oversupplied with fluid, flooded;
   mlepeki to oversupply with fluid;
   mlepekaké to immerse s.t. in liquid;
   var of **blebeg**.

pleper *repr* sudden flight of a bird;
   pleper-pleper *or* **plepar-pleper** to flutter around.

plepuh *var of* **plempuh**.

plepuk, plepuk-plepuk *or* **plepak-plepuk** bubbling (boiling water).

pléra-pléré *see* **pléré**.

plerak-pleruk *see* **pleruk**.

plérak-plérok *see* **plérok**.

pléran *reg* field ready to be planted. *See also* **lèr** II.

pléré, mléré 1 to slip, slide down, away; 2 to play on a slide, slippery dip;
   kepléré to slide down unintentionally;

pléra-pléré to slide from side to side.

plered see **pleret**.

plèrèd I, **plèrèdan** embankment, dam.
II children's slide;
mlèrèd to slope. See also **plorod**.
III hot coconut milk drink with small round glutinous riceballs in it.

plèrèh or **mak plèrèh** appearing in a sudden red splotch;
mlèrèh, **abang** - blood-red.

plerek, **mlerek** to scowl, wear a displeased look.

pleret or **mak pleret** repr a sudden dimming;
mleret to dim, become gloomy;
mleretaké to make s.t. dim/gloomy.
See also **bleret**.

pléro var of **plérok**.

plérok, **mlérok** to turn away with a sidelong glance (out of aversion, contempt, shame);
mléroki to turn away from s.o. thus;
plérak-plérok to keep looking about furtively;
plérokan a furtive sidelong glance.

pleruk, **mleruk**, **plerak-pleruk** to peep up furtively (out of shyness, shame);
mleruki to peep at s.o. thus.

ples I or **mak ples** repr a sudden departure (var of **plas**).
II precisely, just like. See also **cèples**.

plès I or **mak plès** repr a slap.
II reg bottle.

plesat flying away suddenly;
mlesat to jump out, be thrown out;
pating plesat to shoot out in all directions.

plèsèd, **mlèsèd** off-target, wide of the mark;
mlèsèdi to cause to slip or skid;
mlèsèdaké 1 (or **mlèsèdi**) to cause to slip or skid; 2 to mislead, lead astray; 3 to play with or on words (by punning);
keplèsèd to skid, slip inadvertently;

plèsèdan 1 to slip and slide for fun; 2 punning, engaging in wordplay.

plèsèh, **mlèsèh** or **pating plèsèh** scattered, lying on the ground.

plèsèt see **plèsèd**.

plesir amusement, pleasure;
plesir-plesir or **plesiran** 1 to go s.w. for pleasure; 2 to go sightseeing;
mlesiraké to take s.o. for a pleasure trip.

plesta reg over, finished.

plestèr or **plestèran** concrete floor;
mlestèr to cover a floor with concrete.

plèster an adhesive plaster;
mlèster to cover with a plaster;
plèsteran to wear a plaster.

pléta-plété see **plété**.

plété, **mlété** or **pléta-plété** 1 arrogant; 2 to chatter.

pleter, **mleter** 1 reg to pursue; 2 to run after, chase, drive hard, keep at it.

plethèk or **mak plethèk** repr breaking open;
mlethèk 1 (of glass, cup etc) to crack; 2 to break open; 3 (of the sun) to rise;
mlethèkaké to cause to crack;
plethèkan a cracked part.

plethes, **mlethes** to crush, squash flat (under a big weight).

plèthès var of **plethes**.

plethet or **mak plethet** repr pressing, squeezing;
mlethet (or **mlethetaké**) to press, squeeze, crush;
mletheti to squeeze s.t. repeatedly;
keplethet pressed by s.t. heavy inadvertently.

plèthèt var of **plethet**.

plethik (pron as: **plethi:k**) repr a small cracking sound.

plethis (pron as: **plethi:s**) or **mak plethis** repr a sudden breaking, coming off;
mlethis (of small things) to break, crack, burst.

plethok *or* mak plethok *repr* cracking or bursting open;

mlethok to break with a cracking sound.

plethor *or* mak plethor *repr* cracking (of firecracker *etc*).

plethos *or* mak plethos *repr* cracking, crunching;

mlethos to pop, crack.

pléthot, mléthot crooked, bent, twisted, going the wrong way;

pating pléthot *pl as above*.

plethus *var of* plethos.

pletik 1 a spark; 2 (*pron as:* pleti:k) *or* mak pletik *repr* a spark shooting; 3 white flecks on the black part of the eye;

mletik 1 to sparkle; 2 to have white flecks on the black part of the eye, suffer from cataract;

mletiki to shoot sparks.

pleton I platoon.

II concrete (*var of* beton II).

plétra-plétré *see* plétré.

plétré *or* mak plétré *repr* slipping down;

mlétré to slip down(ward);

mlètrèkaké to make s.t. slip down, to slide s.t. down;

plétra-plétré to keep slipping down.

pletuk, mletuk *or* pating pletuk flecked with white (hair).

pletun *var of* pleton I.

plèwèh, mlèwèh with a wide opening, to open too wide;

plèwèhan the act of opening too wide (*e.g.* mouth).

plèwèk *var of* plèwèh.

pléyat-pléyot *see* pléyot.

plèyèk, mlèyèk askew, awry, out of shape.

pléyok *see* pléyot.

pléyot, mléyot to stand at an angle, be bent;

pléyat-pléyot *or* mléyat-mléyot 1 to wobble unsteadily; 2 *fig* hesitant, uncertain.

plikan 1 mine; 2 obtained by mining (*var of* pelikan). *See also* pelik II.

pliket sticky;

mliketi to stick to.

plikpliker nurse.

plikplok a toy trumpet.

plilah *or* plilahan permission (*var of* palilah). *See also* lilah.

plilak-plilik *see* plilik.

plilik (*pron as:* plili:k), mlilik to stare wide-eyed;

mliliki to stare at s.o. with anger;

plilikan *or* plilak-plilik to keep staring wide-eyed.

plilis, mlilis *reg* to twist (fibres) into rope.

plilit, mlilit to twist, twine; - wetengé to have griping pains in the stomach;

plilitan to wriggle, squirm;

pating plilit *repr* to have stomach cramps.

plim 1 wooden or marble trim around the bottom of the room-wall, skirting-board; 2 plinth.

plimping, mlimpingi 1 to provide with a folded or woven hem (mat, basket); 2 to convey s.t. indirectly, make an insinuation;

plimpingan 1 edge, folded or woven hem; 2 insinuation, innuendo, sarcastic remarks.

plincut, plincutan shy, timid, embarrassed (*var of* klincut, klicut).

plinder, mlinder to press down firmly on one spot;

keplinder to suffer pain due to pressure on part of the body.

plindhes, mlindhes to run over, knock down;

keplindhes crushed, run over (by a car *etc*), to get struck.

plindhukan a hideout. *See also* lindhuk.

plindhungan a refuge. *See also* lindhung.

pling, ngepling-pling *reg* to pamper.

plingak-plinguk *see* plinguk.

plinguk, plingukan *or* plingak-plinguk to look around in confusion or bewilderment (searching for s.t.).

plinthas *var of* plénthas.

plinthat-plinthut *see* plinthut.

plintheng catapult;
mlintheng to shoot (at) with a catapult;
plinthengan 1 catapult; 2 shot with a catapult.

plinthut, plinthutan lacking firm loyalties, not adhering to one's word;
plinthat-plinthut now this way, now that; swaying with the wind, following whatever opinion is dominant.

plintir, mlintir to spin, twirl;
plintiran spun, twirled.

plipid, mlipid *or* mlipidi to hem s.t.;
plipidan a hem.

plipir, mlipir 1 (to go) along the edge, to skirt around; 2 circumspect, polite (speech);
mlipir-mlipir to go along the edge of, walk on the side of the road;
plipiran the side of the path.

plipis I, mlipis 1 to flatten, make smooth by pressing (clothes); 2 elegant, accomplished, refined; 3 to speak Krama fluently and correctly.
II, plipisan temples (side of the forehead).

plirak-plirik *see* plirik.

plirid, mlirid to pull s.t. while squeezing it with the fingers.

plirik, mlirik to glance fitfully or nervously (showing the whites of the eyes);
plirak-plirik (of eyes) to shift from side to side;
plirik-plirikan to gaze at each other. *See also* lirik I.

pliser curly, kinky.

plisir decorative edging, trimming (attached under eaves *etc*);
mlisir *or* mlisiri to edge s.t. with trimming.

plistur *reg var of* plitur.

plithes, mlithes to run over (*var of* plindhes).

plitur varnish, french polishing;
mlitur to apply varnish to;
plituran varnished.

pliyas, pliyasan a magical means of warding off danger.

plocot, mlocot 1 to peel, have open blisters (skin); 2 to fade (colours); 3 not to keep (promise);
mlocot *or* mlocoti to remove the outer layer from.

plodra-plodro to keep slipping, falling down.

plok I *or* mak plok 1 *repr* s.t light falling; 2 *repr* putting food into the mouth;
plok-plokan to gobble up.
II, saplok *or* saploké since.
III, plok-plokan to get the shudders, shakes. *See also* koplok III.
IV, plok-plokan to bang (a blown-up paper bag).

plokat *reg* avocado.

plok-plik children's paper trumpet.

plola-plolo *see* plolo.

plolo *or* mak plolo (of eyes) *repr* a sudden bulging;
mlolo (to stare) wide-eyed, bulge (eyes);
plola-plolo 1 to stare wide-eyed; 2 *fig* to look stupid.

plombir I 1 seal; 2 tax sticker for a vehicle;
mlombir to apply a seal, tax sticker.
II filling;
mlombir to fill (a tooth cavity);
plombiran filling (of tooth).

plompang-plompong *see* plompong.

plompong I, mlompong with mouth gaping;
pating plompong *pl* open-mouthed (lost for words);
plompang-plompong *fig* stupid-looking;

plompongan *reg* a round opening (of tube, pipe).

II one of the small playing-cards (*kertu cilik*).

plonco one who is about to get a new status, novice, neophyte;

mlonco to initiate.

ploncon I a rack for storing lances or spears.

II a wooden form for holding or shaping headdresses (**blangkon**).

plong *or* mak **plong** *repr* **1** sudden relief from tension; **2** empty; **3** *intsfr* utterly empty;

ngeplongi to make a hole in;

ngeplongaké to put through a slot, post (a letter);

plong-plongan an opening.

plonga-plongo *see* **plongo**.

plongak-plongok *see* **plongok**.

plongo, mlongo to gape open-mouthed;

plonga-plongo 1 to have the mouth hanging open; **2** *fig* stupid-looking.

plongoh, mlongoh with open mouth (naive, *e.g.* babies).

plongok *var of* **plongo**.

plongor, mlongor-mlongoraké to speak to s.o. harshly, complain loudly about.

plonos, mlonos (to look) big and round and smooth;

pating plonos *pl as above*.

plontho *reg* whore, prostitute.

plonthos bald, shaved clean;

mlonthos to shave one's head clean;

plonthosan 1 (of head) shaved clean; **2** *reg* to wear batik headdress without an extending outward point.

plonyo eau-de-cologne (*var of* **klonyo**).

plonyoh, mlonyoh burned, scalded, peeling from a burned place (skin).

plopor a pioneer;

mlopori to lead the way, pioneer (a movement *etc*).

plopos, ploposan big talk, boasting, bragging.

plorak-plorok *see* **plorok**.

plorod, mlorod to slide down;

mlorad-mlorod to keep slipping down;

mlorodaké 1 to shift s.t. downward; **2** to hand down (a used article);

keplorod to slide down accidentallly;

plorodan s.t used for sliding, a slide. *See also* **lorod**.

plorok, mlorok to cast a sharp look, glare (angry, direct);

plorak-plorok *or* **mlorak-mlorok** to keep casting sharp looks, keep glaring.

plosnong *or* mak **plosnong** *repr* a sudden escape from grasp.

plota-ploto *see* **ploto**.

plothot, mlothot *or* **mlothoti** to squeeze (the contents) out;

mlothotaké to squeeze out for s.o.;

plothotan squeezer;

keplothot to get the insides squeezed out.

ploto, mloto *or* **plota-ploto** to tell tall tales.

plotra-plotro *see* **plotro**.

plotro *or* mak **plotro** *repr* slipping down suddenly;

mlotro to slip down(ward);

mlotrokaké to slip s.t. down;

plotra-plotro to keep slipping down.

plotrok *var of* **plotro**.

ployok, pating ployok ramshackle, tumbledown.

plucu *or* mak **plucu** *repr* a sudden escape from grasp.

pluk I (*pron as:* plu:k) *or* mak **pluk** *repr* a slap (on the face);

plak-pluk *repr* slapping a face repeatedly.

II, pluk-plukan groove, notch.

plukok, plukokan to feel nauseated, vomit.

plumpung 1 a variety of tall reed; **2** isabel (brownish-yellow, colour of horses).

plunan cousin (*var of* pulunan).

pluncar, pating pluncar to glisten, glitter.

plung (*pron as:* plu:ng) *or* mak plung *repr* s.t small falling into liquid;
plang-plung *repr* dropping small things repeatedly into liquid.

plungsung, mlungsungi to cast the skin, slough (snake);
plungsungan skin shed by a reptile. *See also* wlungsung.

pluntah, mluntah to pour out (thick liquid).

plunther, mlunther to curl;
pating plunther curling, in curls.

pluntir, mluntir to twist tightly (together) (*var of* puntir);
kepluntir twisted accidentally.

pluntur I cord used for hanging various gamelan instruments.
II traditional medicine prepared for a woman after giving birth.

plupuh 1 split-bamboo section for walls, fences; 2 bamboo bed or floor covering;
mlupuh to make s.t. from bamboo sections; to cover the floor with the above.

pluru bullet.

plurud I, mlurud to pull (rope *etc*) while squeezing it with the fingers. *See also* plirid.
II, keplurud to slide down(ward). *See also* plorod.

pluruh, pluruhan garbage pit.

plus *or* mak plus *repr* piercing.

plusat-plusut *see* plusut.

plusut *or* mak plusut *repr* slipping free;
mlusut to slip free;
plusat-plusut to keep slipping.

pluta *gram* contraction, shortening a word by eliminating a vowel (*e.g.* semu: smu; kalayan: klayan);
mluta to reduce (a word) as above;
plutan first-syllable vowel which is removed.

pluthas-pluthus *see* pluthus.

pluthus, mluthus completely naked, unclothed.

pluwang noose.

pluwèk, mluwèk gaping open;
mluwèkaké to open s.t. (up, out).

pluwer, mluwer curled up;
pating pluwer curling in all directions.

pluwi blotting-paper.

pluwit 1 a whistle (device); 2 whistle (sound).

pluwok *var of* pluwèk.

poak *reg* bald, hairless.

pocar-pacir *reg* in total confusion, in disarray.

pocèl with a bit broken off;
mocèli to pick little bits off s.t.

poci (tea)pot.

pocok I, mocok 1 *lit* to cut; 2 to discharge, dismiss.
II, mocok *or* mocoki to do s.o. else's job on a temporary basis;
mocokaké to have s.o. work by the day;
pocokan temporary fill-in work.

pocol, pocolan *reg* to engage in wayward or disgraceful behaviour.

pocong I buttock (*k.i. for* bokong).
II 1 harvested rice tied in bundles; 2 unit of weight (of raw rice);
mocong 1 to wrap (a corpse, preparatory to burial); 2 to bundle harvested rice;
pocongan 1 winding-sheet; 2 corpse wrapped in a winding-sheet.

pocot *var of* copot.

pocuk *reg var of* pucuk.

pocung *reg var of* pucung III.

podhang the golden oriole. *See also* kepodhang.

podhèn *reg* remainder, excess.

podheng pudding.

podhi loose, not set (precious stones).

poèl 1 *cr* toothless, old; 2 to change teeth (of horses).

pog *var of* pok II.

pogog I, pogogan a tree trunk growing without branches.

II a certain type of male dancer's headdress.

pogok *see* mogok.

pogot *reg* strong, robust.

pogramah programme.

pog-pogan I *reg* the last one.

II s.t. used for daily needs, everyday clothes.

poh I *reg* (pelem *kr*) mango.

II *var of* puh.

pohot *reg* molasses.

pohung cassava.

pojar *lit* 1 what s.o. says; 2 *reg* information, announcement;

mojar to say, speak;

pojaran utterance.

pojok *or* pojokan corner, angle; - bener *or* - jejeg right angle; - lancip *or* - lincip acute angle; - majupat square; - miring non-rectangular parallelogram; - telu triangle; - tempak obtuse angle;

mojok in(to) a corner;

mojokaké to corner s.o., put s.t. in a corner;

kepojok pushed in a corner, cornered.

pok I *or* mak pok *repr* s.t. flat dropping.

II, the very end;

ngepok (to cut) at the very bottom;

pok-pokan finally; at the end;

pok-puneng *reg* completely finished, nothing left.

pokah lopped off; - bung a kind of rot (in sugarcane);

mokahaké to lop off.

pokak I *var of* pokah.

II a hot drink spiced with ginger.

pokal I banana shoot (for transplanting).

II 1 idea; 2 a tricky idea.

pokèk *reg* (of trousers) short.

pokik *or* mokik *cr* dead; to die.

pokil 1 a small gain, advantage; 2 to be out for any small gain;

mokil-mokilaké to make efforts to gain s.t. for s.o.

pokir, pokiran *reg* profile (of face).

poklèk broken, snapped;

moklèk to break;

moklèki to break s.t. off, snap s.t. off;

moklèkaké to break s.t. unintentionally.

poklot *reg* pencil (*var of* potelod).

poko *cr* dead.

pokok 1 essence, the essential, main thing, part; 2 business capital;

mokoki 1 to back (a business venture) financially; 2 to be the main or responsible person behind (s.t.);

pokoké in essence, essentially, the main thing is…

pokol 1 trunk of a tree; 2 knot in wood.

pokping mentholated stick for use as a nasal decongestant.

pokrol *var of* pokrul.

pokrul lawyer, attorney; - bambu a bush lawyer (not properly qualified); - jéndral Attorney General;

mokrul to act in the capacity of lawyer;

mokruli to take legal action on behalf of (a client);

mokrulaké to have (a lawyer) act for one.

pokung cassava (*reg var of* pohung).

pol I to the limit;

ngepol *or* ngepolaké to (do) to the limit;

pol-polan as much as (one) can.

II *reg* paying off a debt.

pola design, pattern;

mola to follow a pattern.

polah 1 action, motion; 2 to move (about);

molah to act, move (about);

molahaké to move or handle s.t.;

polahan way of acting or moving.

polatan facial expression. *See also* **ulat**.

poldhan paid off;

moldhani to pay off (a debt);

moldhanaké to pay off a debt (for s.o. else).

polèng check (pattern).

polèt epaulette.

polih *lit* to get, receive, accept (*var of* **olèh**).

polir tin-foil (of a looking-glass);

polo I 1 *cr* head; 2 *cr* brain.

II 1 house top, ridgepole; 2 *fig* household, roof (*var of* **molo** I).

polok ankle.

polong I a kind of bean.

II a small fruit tasting like cloves.

polor core (of tree, soft wood).

polos 1 (of fabric) plain, unfigured; 2 simple, without guile.

poluk *reg var of* **puluk**.

poma by all means; (with negative) by no means;

poma-poma to impress it on s.o. that they must...;

poma dipoma by all means; (with negatives) by no means.

pomah *ng*, **pémah** *kr*, 1 tame, domesticated; 2 to feel at home;

pomahan 1 a house lot; 2 tamed, domesticated by nature.

See also **omah**.

pompa a pump;

mompa to pump;

mompakaké to pump for s.o.; to have s.t. pumped.

pompan (that which can be) pumped; **bal** - soccer ball. *Also* **kompa**.

pon I a day of the five-day week.

II unit of weight: pound;

pon-ponan by the pound.

ponakan cousin, niece (*var of* **keponakan**).

ponang *lit* the (*article*) (*var of* **punang**).

poncol *or* **poncolan** protrusion, protruding corner;

moncol 1 to stick out, protrude; 2 outstanding, eminent; 3 in(to) the corner.

poncot 1 *var of* **poncol**; 2 the very end.

pondhamèn foundation.

pondhèh 1 *reg* intimate, trusted (friend); 2 to have had enough of.

pondhemèn *var of* **pondhamèn**.

pondhoh I sweet edible inner leaves of the coconut palm.

II, **mondhoh** to pierce the ears of newborn babies and insert white thread strung with medicinal roots (to avert bad luck).

pondhok I 1 a small crude hut; 2 *fig* my humble home; - **dhèmpèl**, - **karang**, - **rompok**, - **tèmpèl** inhabitant of a house built on s.o. else's land; - **gamblok** *or* - **glongsor** *or* - **karang** *or* - **kringkel** *or* - (k)**ringkuk** *or* -**slosor** *or* - **slusup** *or* - **sumpel** *or* - **tlosor** someone who lives in (has neither house nor yard);

mondhok to live in a rented room away from home;

mondhoki to rent a room in (s.o.'s house);

mondhokaké 1 to board s.o; 2 to have s.o. live in another's home as a paying guest;

pondhokan 1 a place to stay when away from home, lodgings, rented room; 2 a boarding school where students study the Quran.

II a packet wrapped with banana leaf; **mondhok** to wrap (food) in banana leaves.

pondhol, **pondholan** cloth knot at the back of a fabric headdress (**blangkon**, **iket**) (*var of* **mondholan**).

pondhong, **mondhong** 1 to carry in the arms against the chest; 2 to carry one's bride at a wedding ceremony;

pondhongan 1 act of carrying s.t. in the arms against the chest; 2 ceremony in which one carries the bride on the arm.

ponès *var of* **ponis**.

pong I *repr* a sound of a small bronze gong.

II empty and puffy (soybean cake).

III, **pong-pongan** sea snail.

pongah *reg* stupid, ignorant;

mongah to make s.o. look foolish.

pongah-pangih *or* **pongah-pangihan** *lit* to toss and turn in one's bed.

ponggé durian pit.

ponggok *reg* to stall, fail, stop.

ponggol a small bowl used for measuring a quantity of steamed rice;

saponggol one bowl (of steamed rice).

pongkang *var of* **pongkrang**.

pongkong, pongkongan very old person.

pongkor *reg* bamboo cylinder used for tapping palm juice.

pongkrang, gerang pongkrang *or* **pongkrangan** (to engage in) silly antics.

pongo I *var of* **plongo**.

II, **mongo-mongo** to suck and blow air because of a feeling of hotness in the mouth.

pongol 1 a large protruding object; 2 cape;

mongol to stick out, protrude (large object).

pongor, mongor-mongor *or* **mongor-mongoraké** to really tell s.o. off.

pongpok *reg* a certain weave for bamboo wall panels.

ponis sentence, judgement.

ponjèn bag used for storing herbs and drugs;

monjèni to store herbs and drugs in such a bag.

ponjol *var of* **pénjol**.

pontèn fountain.

ponthang variegated, with bands of different colours.

ponthèng *reg var of* **ponthang**.

ponyol portruding edge or frame.

po-o mentholated stick for curing headache.

po-ot *reg* molasses.

poping *var of* **pokping**.

popo, mopo to rebel, resist, refuse (to do s.t.).

popog, popogan *reg* village head.

popoh I strong, muscular.

II, **kepopoh** *or* **kepopohan** to have a task to perform, have responsibility fall on one.

popok I nappy;

mopoki to put a nappy on;

popokan wrapped with a nappy (baby).

II 1 ointment of power mixed with water, poultice; 2 mud, plastered on ricefield dykes;

mopok 1 to apply such an ointment; 2 to plaster dykes with mud;

mopoki to add s.t. extra to;

mopokaké to apply s.t. as an ointment.

III to slump (*var of* **poprok**).

popol I mopol to cut short (hair).

II **mopol** 1 to be half rotten (cloth, thread); 2 to collapse, fall apart.

popor rifle butt;

mopor to hit with a rifle butt.

poprok I 1 to slump, lie weakly from exhaustion; 2 collapsed, fallen in; 3 bankrupt (*see also* **bobrok**);

poprokan ricefield abandoned by the former owner.

II, **moprok** to pile up, in big heaps. *See also* **mupruk**.

poprol *var of* **popol II**.

por I 1 (to the) utmost, (to) the limit or end; 2 (*or* **ngepor**) excellent, incomparable;

por-poran to one's utmost capacity;

ngepor *or* **ngeporaké** to (do) to the limit;

saporé to one's capacity.

II a pole of a weaving loom, against which the weaver leans.

III *or* **kaporan** exhausted. *See also* **apor**.

pora, poran *reg* let it be, leave it…

porang a kind of intestinal parasite in buffaloes;

porangen to suffer from the above.

poret port wine.

porod decreased, diminished, reduced;

morod 1 to decrease, diminish; 2 to withdraw, leave before the end;

morodi 1 to gnaw at, bite into; 2 to steal;

morodaké 1 to sell for a reduced price; 2 to remove s.t. for s.o. during sale;

porodan 1 loss; 2 at a loss, for a reduced price.

porok 1 fork; 2 bicycle fork.

porong I 1 burned black; 2 with black spots;

morong to make black spots (on rattan) by touching with a burning object.

II teapot (European style).

III the train of a sash hanging from the hip (wayang figure of warrior).

poros bundle, bunch;

moros to bundle;

porosan in bundles;

saporos (of betel leaves) one bunch.

porot blowpipe (used by goldsmiths);

morot to use a blowpipe, purify (gold) by blowing.

portepèl portfolio.

pos 1 mail, post; 2 post of duty; 3 a unit of distance: a stage, 5 *pal* or *ca* 7.5 km; 4 way station, post house where travellers rest; - **pakèt** parcel post; - **wesel** postal money order;

ngepos to stop and rest at a post house;

ngeposaké 1 to mail (a letter); 2 to send s.t. through the mail;

pos-posan a post house.

posah-pasihan to act, talk fondly to each other (*esp* newlyweds). *See also* **asih**.

posing *reg* to feel dizzy.

posit *cr* dead, to die.

poso I moso-moso to speak angrily, snarl. *See also* **oso**.

II *cr* dead, to die.

posol *reg* young maize.

posong *reg* a hoop-net for catching prawns.

pot I (or **epot**) 1 to cease; 2 at an end, over; 3 elapsed, used up;

ngepoti to omit, pass over, neglect;

ngepotaké to break s.t. off, cause s.t. to cease, be omitted;

pot-potan completely at an end; **ora pot-pot** non-stop.

II 1 pot, flowerpot, chamber pot; 2 *or* **pot-potan** (to play) a certain game of marbles; 3 gambling stakes, a bet;

pot-potan various kinds of pots.

potang 1 a loan; 2 moneylender; 3 foreclosure on a loan; 4 to put s.o. in one's debt; - **kabecikan** to owe a favour;

motangi to lend to s.o.;

motangaké 1 to lend for interest; 2 to sell on credit; 3 to extend (a favour) to;

potangan borrowed for interest, taken on credit;

kapotangan to be endebted (to s.o.).

potéhi Chinese glove-puppet theatre.

potelod pencil;

potelodan (written, drawn) in pencil.

potha, motha-motha to pester, molest (a woman).

pothah, mothah to nag, whine (to get s.t.);

pamothah nagging, whining.

pothar-pathir *reg* 1 scattered; 2 confused.

pothèk *reg var of* **pothèl**.

pothèl broken off, snapped;

mothèl to break off, remove from the stalk;

mothèlaké to break off s.t. unintentionally.

pothèng divided into pieces;
  mothèng to dismember, cut up;
  mothèng-mothèng to dismember, cut into pieces.

pothès *var of* **pothèl**.

pothèt *reg* a little runt, shrimp, squirt.

potho 1 a certain cattle disease; 2 the spirit that causes this disease.

pothok 1 strong, sturdy; 2 *reg* (of price) fixed.

pothol broken, snapped, come off;
  motholi 1 to snap s.t.; 2 to fall off;
  motholaké to snap s.t. unintentionally.

potlop *var of* **potelod**.

poto, moto to take a photograph.

potok, motok (of broken objects) to join, knit (of bones);
  potokan *reg* made of pieces fitted together (kris sheath).

potong 1 (to have/get) a haircut; 2 a cut-off piece; 3 style, cut;
  motong to cut (out, off, down), cut s.o.'s hair;
  motongi to cut out (clothing);
  motongaké to have s.o.'s hair cut;
  kepotong to get cut;
  potongan 1 a cut off piece; a scrap; 2 a deduction; 3 style, fashion, cut.

potrèk 1 camera; 2 photograph, picture, snapshot; 3 to have one's picture taken;
  motrèk *or* **motrèki** to take a picture (of);
  potrèk-potrèkan to take pictures repeatedly, here and there.

potrèt *var of* **potrèk**.

powak *reg* bald, hairless.

powan cow's milk.

powèl *var of* **poèl**.

powotan *reg* simple, makeshift bridge. *See also* **wot** I.

poyan *reg* 1 to come and talk about s.t.; 2 to ask permission to leave.

poyang-payingan to move this way and that in confusion or uncertainty.

poyok, moyoki 1 to mock, ridicule, make fun of; 2 to apply a nickname to s.o.;
  poyokan 1 mockery, ridicule; 2 a teasing nickname;
  poyok-poyokan 1 to mock each other; 2 to call each other nicknames.

pra *lit, marker of group or collectivity (var of* **para** I).

praba 1 glow, ray of light; 2 wing-like ornament on the back of certain wayang puppets and dancers' costumes.

prabancana *lit* wind.

prabangkara *lit* sun.

prabasuyasa *lit* palace, court (*var of* **prabayasa**).

prabata *lit* mountain.

prabatang *var of* **perbatang**.

prabawa 1 awesomeness, splendour, majesty; 2 authority;
  mrabawani to exert authority or influence (over).

prabayasa *lit* palace, court.

prabayeksa a large hall in the palace.

prabéda *lit* difference. *See also* **béda** I.

prabéya expense, cost.

prabot I 1 equipment, tools, instruments; 2 harness; 3 materials; 4 village official;
  mrabot 1 fully equipped; 2 fully decked out (in costume);
  mraboti to equip s.o.;
  prabotan furniture.
  II custom, habit.

prabu king, monarch;
  mrabu *or* **mraboni** kingly;
  kaprabon 1 kingship, the throne; 2 (things) pertaining to royalty.

prabusèt passion-flower.

pracados *var of* **percados**.

pracalita *lit* flash of lightning.

pracandha *lit* storm, gale.

pracang I, **mracang** to sell spices.
  II, **mracangaké** to have (outside workers) harvest rice;

pracangan rice crop harvested by these workers.

pracaya to believe, rely on, trust (*var of* **percaya**).

pracéka, mracéka to (try to) conjure up an idea in the imagination, think up; **pracékan** invention, composition.

pracihna sign, indication, mark; **mracihnani** to indicate, be a sign of. *See also* **cihna**.

pracik bird snare.

pracima *lit* west.

pracondhang, kapracondhang *lit* defeated.

prada *ng*, **praos** *kr*, gold leaf, gilding; **mrada** to gild; **pradan** gilded.

pradana *lit* leader, person in authority.

pradangga *lit* musical instruments; gamelan ensemble.

pradanggapati *lit* sun.

pradapa *lit* young, fresh leaves.

pradata 1 civil (as opposed to criminal); **2** civil court.

pradhah I 1 generous; **2** *reg* controller of a halting-place; **mradhahi 1** to treat s.o. generously; **2** to face (adversity) with a stout heart. **II, mradhah** to convict, find guilty; **kepradhah** to be held responsible.

pradikan freed from payment of taxes (in villages) as result of assuming some burden or responsibility.

pradin *reg* finished, over.

pradipta *lit* light, lamp.

pradon, praduan *lit* bedchamber, (royal) bed.

pradondi difference of opinion, dispute (*var of* **perdondi**).

pradul *reg* **1** a tattletale; **2** to tattle (*var of* **wadul**).

praèn, praènan features, countenance. *See also* **rai**.

pragad, mragad to slaughter.

pragak forked tree trunk (as prop).

pragalba *lit* **1** fierce, furious, wild; **2** tiger.

pragas *var of* **pagas**.

pragedèl *var of* **bregedèl**.

pragèn little box for storing salt and spices in the kitchen.

pragéné *reg* when, if.

pragola ruket *lit* duel.

praguwa *reg* huge, gigantic.

pragi *reg* tool, equipment, tackle.

prah *repr* falling carelessly.

prahara wind and rain storm.

prahoto truck.

prahpun how? (*subst kr for* **kepriyé**).

prail, mrail to divide inheritance (according to Islamic law).

praja 1 kingdom, realm; **2** residence of a king, court; **3** capital city (as opposed to the countryside); **praja dhéwé** to have one's own household; **njaga praja** *idiom* to take care of the good reputation of one's family.

prajaka *lit* messenger.

prajanji promise.

prajaya *var of* **perjaya**.

praji *reg* village midwife.

prajurit 1 soldier, troops; **2** corps of palace soldiers, each with its own uniform *etc*; **prajuritan 1** (attired in) the costume of a warrior; **2** the dance movement or style of a warrior; **kaprajuritan 1** the rank of **prajurit**; **2** (things) pertaining to a warrior.

prak I *or* **mak prak** *repr* a cracking sound; **prak-prakan** to produce cracking sounds repeatedly. **II** *lit* near, close by. *See also* **perak**.

prakampa 1 earthquake; **2** shaken, stirred up.

prakampita *var of* **prakampa**.

prakara *var of* **perkara**.

prakarsa initiative; **mrakarsani** to initiate.

prakasa *lit* well-known, famous.

prakati attractive, charming (*var of* mrak-ati). *See* perak.

prakawis *var of* perkara, prakara.

prakempa *see* prakampa.

prakeneng *var of* perkeneng.

prakosa mighty, powerful, strong. *See also* perkosa.

praksana *lit* 1 telescope; 2 microscope.

praktèk practice;
    mraktèkaké to practise s.t., put s.t. into practice, apply.

pralabda *see* pralebda.

pralambang 1 symbol, sign; 2 allegory; 3 prophecy;
    mralambangi to make hidden allusions to.

pralambi *var of* pralampita.

pralampita *lit* 1 sample, example; 2 allusion; lesson.

pralaya *lit* dead; to die.

pralebda *lit* expert, skilled, practised. *Also* lebda.

praléna *lit* dead; to die (*var of* pralina);
    pralénan an organisation to collect money for assisting a family in which a death has occurred.

praliman 1 a fifth; 2 five-way intersection. *See also* lima.

pralina *lit* dead; to die.

pramana I (*also* premana, permana) I 1 (in Javanese philosophy) the bearer of the life of the individual (distinct from the soul); 2 sign of life, heartbeat.
    II 1 clear and evident; 2 precise, accurate;
    mramanakaké 1 to make clear; 2 to have s.t. done accurately; 3 to observe exactly.

pramanem, sidhem - *lit* quiet; soundless.

pramasastra grammar. *See also* paramasastra.

pramati *var of* permati.

prambayun *var of* pembayun.

pramèsthi the supreme god, Bathara Guru.

pramèswari queen, a king's most senior wife.

praméya *lit* excellent, incomparable.

pramila therefore (*kr for* mula). *See also* mila.

pramoda *lit* chief, principal; king.

prampang I feverish, oppressively hot.
    II full of holes, damaged, moth-eaten.

prampuhan to turn up in large numbers.

pramudita, jagat - *lit* the whole world.

pramugara male steward.

pramugari 1 leader; 2 stewardess.

pramuka 1 the first, leader; 2 Boy or Girl Scout.

prana I *lit* heart, innermost feelings;
    mranani 1 to hit the exact spot; to the point (words); 2 attractive, charming, appealing;
    kepranan 1 mortally wounded, stricken; 2 strongly attracted, enchanted.
    II *lit* breath, breathing.
    III, clitoris (*k.i. of* itil).
    IV *See* rana.

pranaja *lit* chest, breast.

pranakan 1 of mixed descent; 2 *reg* womb; 3 long-sleeved cloth jacket worn by officials at court.

pranata I act of arranging; - mangsa the Javanese agricultural (solar) calendar;
    mranata to arrange;
    pranatan rule, regulations.
    II *lit* respectful greeting.

pranawa *lit* 1 bright; 2 watchful, on the alert.

prandang, mrandangi *reg* to join in working on s.t.

prandéné *see* parandéné.

pranèl flannel.

pranem a sixth. *See also* nem.

prang I *see* perang; prang kembang, gagal terms for certain parts of a wayang performance;
    paprangan *lit* battle, battlefield.
    II *or* mak prang *repr* (falling) with a clang (metal object).

pranggal I, **mranggal** 1 to hit on the head; 2 to nag, argue over;
　pranggalan to hit each other on the head.
　II, **mranggal** to prune.

pranggul, **mrangguli** to encounter s.t., come across, come upon;
　kepranggul to encounter by chance.

prangkat set of objects;
　saprangkat a set (of gamelan instruments).

prangko postage stamp;
　mrangkoni to put a stamp on.

prangkul, **saprangkul** an armful: as much as the arms can clasp.

prangwedani a carpet, floor rug (floral or embroidered with gold).

pranili *reg var of* **panili**.

praniti *lit* investigation, observation.

pranji or **pranjèn** *reg* chicken coop, henhouse.

prantas, **mrantasi** to see s.t. through to the finish.

pranti *var of* **piranti**

prantos *var of* **pirantos**.

prantun, **prantunan** 1 snack bar; 2 cabinet for displaying knick-knacks.

praoto *see* **prahoto**.

praos gold leaf, gilding (*kr for* **prada**).

prapal, **mrapal** to cut short, cut back (branches, grass).

prapanca *lit* confused.

prapas, **prapasan** shortcut.

prapat I *ng*, **prasekawan** *kr* quarter;
　mrapat 1 to divide into quarters; 2 a quarter each; 3 to lie in a cross-shape; 4 to draw a cross;
　prapatan intersection, crossroads;
　saprapat one-fourth, a quarter.
　II, **parepat** *lit* servant, follower.
　III surrounding villages;
　mrapataké to submit to a committee from the surrounding villages.

prapèn fireplace, place for an open fire, a blacksmith's forge. *See also* **api**.

prapiton a seventh. *See also* **pitu**.

prapta *lit* 1 arrival; 2 to come, arrive.

prapti *var of* **prapta**.

prasa *ng*, **praos** *kr*, *reg* feeling, thought.

prasaben I, **mrasabeni** to warn, admonish. *See also* **persaben**.
　II every, each. *See* **saben**.

prasada *lit* building, temple, hall, palace.

prasaja plain, unaffected, unadorned;
　mrasajani 1 to act in a frank way; 2 to tell the truth frankly (to);
　prasajan frank, candid.

prasama *lit* alike; the same.

prasami *var of* **prasama**.

prasanak, **prasanakan** relatives. *See also* **sanak**.

prasangan a ninth. *See also* **sanga**.

prasapa *lit* curse, oath;
　mrasapani to put a curse on;
　mrasapakaké to wish (s.t. bad on s.o.). *See also* **sapa II**.

prasasat *lit* like, as; as if, as though.

prasasta *lit* well-known, famous, praised.

prasasti ancient inscription (on copper plates or stone).

prasatya *var of* **prasetya**.

prasé, **mangsa prasé** rutting season.

prasèn zodiac beaker.

prasetya 1 loyal, faithful, obedient; 2 to vow loyalty. *See also* **setya**.

prasida *lit* 1 to go through, ahead; 2 to succeed in (do)ing. *See also* **sida**.

prasman, **prasmanan** buffet (dinner; the guests serve themselves and then sit down).

prasmèn passementerie, lace, galloon.

prasu *reg* false, fake.

prasudi *see* **persudi**.

prastawa *lit* I to have clear insight;
　mrastawakaké to examine closely.
　II happening, event.

pratala *lit* one of the regions under the earth. *Also* **patala**.

pratama *lit* the first, number one, the best.

pratandha 1 mark, indication;
  mratandhani 1 to mark s.t.; 2 to show,
  indicate;
  mratandhakaké to show, indicate.
  See also tandha I.
pratanggakara *lit* sun.
pratanggapati *lit* sun.
pratapan *see* pertapan. *See also* tapa.
pratéla to inform, announce;
  mratélani to inform s.o.;
  mratélakaké to convey, mention;
  pratélan information, list. *See also* téla.
pratelon, pratigan *kr* T-intersection;
  sapratelon one-third.
  See also telu.
pratigan *kr for* pratelon.
pratignya *lit* 1 vow; 2 to make a vow.
pratikel 1 way, means; 2 advice; 3 rule,
  regulation;
  mratikeli to use s.t. as a means for
  avoiding bad influence;
  mratikelaké 1 to make s.t. happen,
  provide a means for; 2 to explain, set
  out (how s.t. works).
pratima *lit* 1 statue, sculpture; 2 doll.
pratinggi *reg* village head (*var of* petinggi).
pratingkah 1 actions, behaviour; 2 odd
  quirk, whim.
pratingkes *lit* skilful, dextrous.
pratingsing *see* pertingsing.
pratipa *lit* gale.
pratisara *see* partisara.
pratistha *lit* to stay, sit, occupy a place.
pratitis *see* patitis, *also* titis I.
pratiwa *lit* troop commander, war chief.
pratiwi *lit* earth.
pratok, mratoki *reg* to wait for.
pratola, kendhi - a kind of waterpot.
pratuwin *lit* and. *Also* tuwin.
prau *ng*, baita *kr* ship, boat;
  mrau to go sailing, travel by ship or
  boat;
  mraoni 1 to use a boat (for); 2 to
  transport by boat;

mraokaké to transport by boat;
praon to go boating for pleasure;
prau-praunan toy boat, boat model.
praupan *lit* 1 facial features; 2 washbasin. *See also* raup.
prawa *var of* purwa.
prawan 1 virgin; 2 young girl of marriageable age; 3 unmarried servant
  girl; - kencur *or* - sunthi girl entering
  puberty, physically immature girl; -
  tuwa spinster;
  mrawani 1 to act like a young girl; 2
  to take a virgin.
prawantu *reg* since, in view of the fact
  that.
prawara *lit* 1 soldier; 2 ladies-in-waiting
  of a queen.
prawasa, mrawasa *lit* 1 to use force
  against, torture; 2 to rape;
  mrawasa-pinrawasa to use force
  against each other, push each other
  around.
prawata *lit* mountain.
prawédyarini *lit* midwife.
prawira mighty, powerful, courageous;
  kaprawiran courage, might, bravery.
prawita *lit* to become the pupil of a holy
  man. *See also* puruhita.
praya I *lit* intention, wish.
  II *lit* gleam, splendour.
prayagung *var of* priyagung.
prayayi *var of* priyayi.
prayang, prayangan inhabitants of the
  spirit world;
  mrayang to wander, roam (spirits).
prayantun *kr for* prayayi.
prayatna *var of* prayitna.
prayig, pating prayig *pl* to shake, wobble.
prayitna cautious, carefully;
  mrayitnani to watch out for, be careful about;
  kaprayitnan care, caution.
prayojana *lit* intention, aim.
prayoga *ng*, prayogi *kr*, 1 advisable, recommended; 2 good, acceptable;

mrayogani to agree to, approve s.t.;

mrayogakaké to advise, recommend;

pamrayoga advice, recommendation;

saprayogané whatever is advisable, what is appropriate.

prayogi *kr for* **prayoga**.

prayut *var of* **brayut**.

pré leek. *See also* **prèh** I.

prebel *var of* **brebel**.

prèbel kindergarten.

prebeng *var of* **perbeng, prembeng**.

prècèh *reg* to have inflamed eyelids.

prècèl, mrècèli to cut up, cut into little pieces.

precet *or* **mak precet** *repr* a sudden emergence or ejection.

precèt *or* **mak precèt** *repr* a sudden departing without saying anything.

prècèt I, **mrècèt** clean and fine-looking.

II *var of* **plècèt**.

precil *see* **percil**.

predeng, predeng-predeng to feel the abdominal muscles contract (giving birth, going to the toilet);

mredeng to press (demands, questions).

pregedèl *see* **pergedèl**.

prègès eaten bare by insects (trees, plants).

pregok *see* **pergok**.

prégolan gatehouse. *See also* **régol**.

prèh I a variety of fig tree (*also* **prih** II).

II *var of* **pré**.

prèhpun how (*reg kr for* **kepriyé**).

prèi 1 free, at leisure; 2 free of restraint or constraint; 3 disengaged (gear);

mrèi to absent o.s. from the normal activity;

mrèkaké 1 to give s.o. time off; 2 to disengage (gear);

prèèn vacation, having free time.

prèjèl *var of* **projol**.

prèjèng, mrèjèngi to square (wood) by chopping with an adze along the side;

prèjèngan 1 shape; 2 profile.

prejit *see* **perjit**.

prek *or* **mak prek** *repr* a sudden weakening or collapse; 2 *repr* the sound of s.t. smashing;

prak-prek frail, sickly.

prèk I (*or* **mak prèk**) *repr* the sound of s.t. breaking.

II nonsense! shut up!

prékal-prékol curved, crooked, bent.

prekara *see* **perkara**.

prekis *reg* small and attractive.

prekul *reg* small axe.

prekutut *see* **perkutut**.

prel *or* **mak prel** *repr* breaking to pieces, falling apart.

prèl *var of* **prel**.

prelu *see* **perlu**.

prem *lit* to sleep;

papreman bed. *See also* **merem, rem** I.

préma, préman 1 exempt (from duties); 2 discharged (soldier); 3 private (not official); 4 dressed in civilian clothes; 5 private (not public); 6 *reg* day labourer.

premana *see* **permana**.

premanem *see* **pramanem**.

premati *see* **permati**.

prembak-prembik *see* **prembik**.

prembayun *see* **pembayun**.

prembé 1 second-hand shop; 2 dealer in smuggled opium.

prembèh *var of* **prembik**.

prembeng-prembeng red in the face, *e.g.* when on the verge of crying. *See also* **mrembeng**.

prembik, mrembik, prembik-prembik *or* **prembak-prembik** about to cry, beginning to cry softly, whimper, sniffle.

prémi bonus.

prempang-prempeng *see* **prempeng**.

prempeng *or* **mak prempeng** *repr* a sudden impact on the senses or sensitivities;

mrempeng to flush in anger;

prempang-prempeng to keep flushing.

prempul *repr* welling up suddenly;
  mrempul 1 to well up; 2 to swell;
  pating prempul *pl* 1 full of bumps; 2 bubbling, foamy, frothy.

prenah *see* pernah.

prenca spread out, one here and one there;
  mrenca to spread out, set at a distance from each other;
  prenca-prenca spread over a wide area.

prencil, mrencil isolated, secluded (*see also* pencil);
  pating prencil *pl as above*.

prencu, pating prencu protruding in many places.

prending, mrending *or* pating prending badly frayed (rope).

prenjak a variety of warbler.

prenès *see* pernès.

préné *see* sepréné.

préngas-prèngès *see* prèngès.

prengat-prengut *see* prengut.

prèngès *or* mak prèngès *repr* a sudden grinning;
  mrèngès to grin broadly showing the teeth;
  préngas-prèngès *or* prèngèsan to be all smiles, keep grinning.

prenget, prenget-prenget to be feverish.

prènget *var of* pèngèt. *See also* ènget.

prenggak-prengguk to keep grumbling, growling.

prénggok, pating prénggok to turn this way and that.

prengit (of sweat) to smell rank.

prengkel, mrengkel 1 to have a lump or callus; 2 *fig* resentful;
  pating prengkel *pl* lumpy, calloused.

prengus strong, smelling bad (animal odour).

prengut, mrengut to scowl, look sullen;
  mrenguti to scowl at;
  prengat-prengut to keep scowling.

préntah an order, command; to tell s.o. to do s.t.; **Préntah Ageng** High Council, Council of State (in the Sultanate);
  mréntah 1 to have an authority over, govern; 2 to give instructions;
  mréntahi to give instructions to many people;
  mréntahaké to order, command s.t.;
  papréntahan *or* pamaréntah government. *See also* paréntah.

prèntèk, mrèntèk *or* mrèntèki to spread over, encroach on (fire);
  mrèntèk-mrèntèk to keep spreading.

prenthel, mrenthel 1 to be lumpy (full of bits, not smooth); 2 to tighten the belt, economise;
  pating prenthel all in little lumps.

prentheng, pating prentheng *pl* with tensed muscles.

prenthil, mrenthil to form a knobby protuberance;
  pating prenthil *pl* in the form of many small knobby shapes.

prenthol, mrenthol to form knob-shaped protuberances;
  pating prenthol *pl as above*.

prenthul, mrenthul to form good-sized knob-shaped protuberances;
  pating prenthul *pl as above*.

prentul 1 a small swelling; 2 (*or* mak prentul) *repr* welling up/out;
  mrentul to have many small swellings;
  pating prentul 1 to swell in many places; 2 to keep welling up.

prep *var of* pep.

prepat *lit* servant, follower.

prepek, mrepeki *lit* to approach.

prepet 1 *or* mak prepet *repr* suddenly feeling faint, suddenly going dark;
  mrepet to go dark;
  prepet-prepet 1 to become dark; 2 to start to feel faint.

II mrepet to be pressing, urgent.

prèpèt *var of* brèbèt.

prépun how? (*reg kr for* kepriyé.

pres *or* mak pres *repr* breaking, smashing (glass);

pras-pres to break frequently.

près a press, equipment for pressing s.t.;
ngeprès to press with pressing equipment;
près-prèsan 1 way of pressing; 2 pressed; 3 s.t. used for pressing.

présa *see* pirsa.

presah *var of* presak.

presak 1 coarse sand; 2 sandy, not washed properly (food).

presan cow's milk (*md for* susu).

presèn *see* persèn.

presis *var of* persis.

pret *or* mak pret 1 *repr* ejection of air through the compressed lips with a sharp report as an expression of disdain; 2 *repr* fabric tearing;
ngepreti 1 to express disdain for s.o. by making the above sound; 2 *fig* to belittle, look down on;
prat-pret *repr* repeating the above sound.

prèt 1 *repr* trumpet tootings; 2 *repr* breaking wind;
prat-prèt *or* prèt-prètan to break wind repeatedly.

pretek, mretek to urge the matter further, to pursue one's point.

pretèk, pating pretèk *repr* (of hens) cackling.

prèthèl to become detached;
mrèthèli 1 to detach themselves; 2 to break (things) off, pull apart;
prèthèlan chip, fragment of broken object.

préthot *var of* pléthot.

pretok *repr* a hen's clucking (*var of* petok).

préwangan a medium (possessed by a spirit for the purpose of finding cures).

préwé *reg* how? (*var of* priyé).

priangga *see* priyangga.

pribadi self, one's own self;
kapribadèn personality.

pribé (*or* pribèn *or* kepribèn) how? *See also* kepriyé.

pribèn *see* pribé.

pribu, mribu *reg* to attack, assault.

pribumi, wong - native, person born in the place.

prigé *reg* how? *See also* kepriyé.

prigel skilful, dextrous;
kaprigelan skill, dexterity.

prigèn *var of* prigé.

prigi *reg* a little dam made up of piled stones.

prigis eaten bare, denuded.

prih I *lit* to hurt, sting. *See also* perih.
II a variety of fig tree.

prihatin, *kr* prihatos 1 concerned, anxious, prayerful; 2 to undertake austerities for a particular purpose;
mrihatini to be concerned about, share in s.o.'s troubles;
mrihatinaké worrying, causing concern.

prihpun *var of* pripun.

prikadèl rissole.

prikanca colleague, co-worker. *See also* kanca.

priki *see* sepriki.

priksa 1 to know, understand (*k.i. for* ngerti); 2 to see; to know (*k.i. for* weruh);
mriksa to examine, investigate;
mriksani to see, watch (*k.i. for* ndeleng, nonton);
mriksakaken 1 to have s.o. examine(d) or investigate(d); 2 to show s.t.;
kapriksan to be found out (*k.i. for* kaweruhan);
pamriksa 1 act or way of examining/investigating; 2 spectator. *See also* pirsa.

pril *or* mak pril *repr* a small piece breaking (off).

priman *var of* préman.

primbetan *reg kr for* primbon.

primbon Javanese almanac, compendium of astrological knowledge.

primé (*or* primèn *or* keprimèn) how? *reg var of* kepriyé.

primèn *see* primé.

primpen, mrimpeni to put away, store carefully.

primpi, mrimpèni to appear to s.o. in a dream. *See also* impi.

princi, mrinci 1 to classify; 2 to specify (the details of);

princèn *or* peprincèn classification, specifications.

prinding *see* mrinding.

pring *ng*, deling *kr*, bamboo plant; bamboo stalk; - ampèl a variety of fine bamboo; - gadhing yellowish decorative bamboo; - ori thorn bamboo; - petung a certain large and thick bamboo plant; - wuluh a certain slender bamboo plant;

papringan bamboo grove.

pringas-pringis *see* pringis.

pringetan *reg* celebration, commemoration.

pringga *lit* trouble, danger, difficulty;

mringga to be afraid, show fear;

mringgani 1 frightening, dangerous; 2 to be on one's guard;

mringgakaké to take precautions against.

pringgitan *see* ringgit.

pringis, mringis to bare the teeth;

pringisan to grin from pain;

pringas-pringis to keep clenching the teeth, grin wryly.

pringkel, pringkelan unlucky times reckoned according to a cycle of six days. *See also* ringkel.

pringkil *or* pringkilan a small lump;

mringkil to form a lump;

pringkilen to suffer from a small painful swelling.

pringkus, mringkus to shrink, shrivel;

mringkusaké to make s.t. smaller.

pringsilan testicles.

printis I, mrintis (to have or get) little pimples;

pating printis covered with pimples.

II mrintis to make gains (*e.g.* in weight, wealth).

pripéan brother- or sister-in-law's sibling; *or* spouse's brother- or sister-in-law. *See also* ipé.

pripih I, mripih to calm down, cheer up, comfort s.o.

II jimat - amulet, good luck charm.

pripit, pripitan wooden trim around the bottom of a wall.

pripun how? (*md for* kepriyé).

pris prize, reward;

pris-prisan lottery.

prit I *See* emprit.

II (*pron as:* pri:t) *or* mak prit *repr* the sound of a whistle;

prat-prit to keep blowing a whistle.

prithil to fall off (little bits);

mrithili 1 to fall off (many little bits); 2 to break off;

mrithilaké to cause to be broken;

prithilan a little bit broken off.

prithut, mrithut *or* pating prithut wrinkled, full of creases.

prituwin *lit* also, and. *See also* tuwin.

priwé (*or* priwèn *or* kepriwèn) how? *See also* kepriyé.

priya *lit* a man; male; priya-wanita *lit* men and women.

priyagung a high official.

priyambada sweet, seductive words;

mriyambada to address with sweet, seductive words.

priyambak *var of* piyambak.

priyang, mriyang to have a fever;

priyang-priyang shivery, feverish.

priyangga *lit* oneself.

priyantun *kr for* priyayi.

priyat *reg* finished, done with, over.

priyayi *ng*, priyantun *kr*, 1 official, person of high status person (in the official hierarchy); 2 respected person, member of the upper class;
  mriyayi *or* mriyayèni to behave like a gentleman, in a gentlemanly way.
priyé how? (*shtf of* kepriyé)
priyembada *see* priyambada.
priyoga *var of* prayoga.
priyogi *var of* prayogi.
priyos I *reg* pepper (*kr for* mrica).
  II, mriyos to inspect (*md for* mriksa, *see* priksa).
priyuk *reg* rice cooking pot.
probol *var of* projol.
procot *or* mak procot *repr* emergence at birth;
  mrocot to slip out;
  keprocot to slip out accidentally (birth, *fig* one's words).
prodong, prodong-prodong I to work assidously (at).
  II *reg* to go away whining.
prog *or* mak prog *repr* s.t. being set or dropped heavily.
  prag-prog *repr* sounds of heavy footsteps.
progèl, progèl-progèl to keep wriggling;
  pating progèl *pl* to wriggle, squirm everywhere.
progoh an arm's length (unit of measure);
  saprogoh one arm's length.
progol *var of* pronggol.
progos *var of* prègès.
projol, mrojol to slip out through an opening;
  mrojolaké to allow to emerge or slip out;
  keprojolan to have s.t. slip out accidentally;
  mrojol ing akerep *idiom* exceptional, extraordinary;
  mrojol selaning garu *idiom* 1 to succesfully complete a difficult or dan-

gerous activity; 2 to stand out above others.
prok *or* mak prok *repr* sitting down suddenly.
prol I a variety of cake (made from fermented cassava).
  II *or* mak prol *repr* s.t. breaking apart;
  pral-prol to break apart easily.
prombèng, prombèngan second-hand market. *See* rombèng.
promosi 1 promotion; 2 to get promoted; 3 advertising; 4 defence of a doctoral thesis.
prompang having missing teeth (comb, saw);
  mrompang *or* mrompangi to chop off/away;
  pating prompang missing cogs, teeth everywhere.
prondhan nightwatchman's post. *See* rondha.
pronggol, mronggoli to trim (branches).
prongkal large lump;
  mrongkal in (the form of) a large lump;
  prongkalan *or* prongkal-prongkol in lumps.
prongkol *var of* prongkal.
prongos projecting (upper teeth);
  mrongos bucktoothed.
prop 1 pith (helmet); 2 cork, plug.
prosa, mrosa 1 to force; 2 to rape. *See also* perkosa.
prot *or* mak prot *repr* popping, bursting.
protès 1 a protest; 2 (*or* mrotès) to protest (against).
prothol *var of* pothol.
protong, protong-protong to go away whining (*var of* prodong II).
prucah *see* prutah.
prucah-prucèh *reg* worthless.
prucat-prucut *see* prucut.
prucul lacking horns.
prucut *or* mak prucut *repr* a sudden release from one's grasp;

mrucut to get released from one's grasp, slip through the fingers;

mrucuti to have a tendency to slip from one's grasp (slippery object);

mrucutaké to release (one's grasp);

keprucut to lose one's hold;

prucat-prucut to keep slipping through the fingers.

prugul var of prunggul.

prugus var of prègès.

pruk or mak pruk crash! smash!

prukah reg lavish (feast).

prumpung yellowish (colour of horse) (var of plumpung).

prunan nephew, niece (child of one's younger sibling). See also pulun, pulunan.

pruncah, mruncah reg to break to pieces.

prundhan var of prondhan.

prung or mak prung repr a sudden departure, whisking away.

prunggu bronze.

prunggul, mrunggul or mrungguli to cut, prune, trim.

prungsang feeling hot, feverish.

prungu, prungon what is heard;

mrungoni to communicate supernaturally;

keprungu to be heard;

keprungon sense of hearing. See also rungu.

pruntah, pruntahan garbage pit. See runtah.

prunthel, mrunthel tangled, twisted;

pating prunthel or prunthel-prunthel in curls, kinky, twisted.

pruntus, mruntus to form small specks or dots (e.g. goose pimples, skin rash);

pating pruntus or pruntus-pruntus covered with little bumps.

prupuh, mrupuh to prune (a tree).

pruput I, mruput 1 early in the morning; 2 to undertake s.t. early in the morning.

II, mruput reg to seize, grab and hold;

pruputan reg what one picks up.

prus I or mak prus repr breaking.

II reg precisely, just like.

prusa see prosa.

prusah reg languid, sluggish.

prusi 1 verdigris; 2 an ointment made from verdigris for healing sores.

pruslin porcelain.

prusuh I see mrusuh.

II, mrusuhi to pound (rice) to remove the husks.

prut or mak prut repr popping; bursting (var of prot).

prutah, mrutah to cut into pieces.

pruthul var of puthul.

pruwa reg var of purwa.

pruwita see puruhita.

pu ancient title for outstanding artists, craftsmen, poets etc. See also empu I.

pucak summit, pinnacle.

pucang areca tree;

mucang reg to chew betel.

pucat, mucat to undress, remove (clothing).

pucet pale, wan.

pucuk 1 point, tip, top, summit; 2 beginning;

mucuk 1 point-shaped; 2 to raise to the top;

mucuki to begin, initiate.

pucung I a certain tree (the seeds, called kluwak, are poisonous).

II bapak - a certain small red beetle.

III a certain Javanese verse form;

mucung to sing verse in the metre Pucung.

pudhak 1 a certain cake of rice flour and brown sugar.

II pandanus flower;

pudhak sinumpet or pudhak sinupit a certain way of folding one's kain.

pudhat var of pundhat.

pudhot reg widower.

pudyastuti lit prayer, wish, hope.

pugag, **mugag** *reg* to remove the tip (from). *See also* **pogog I**.

pugal hard to domesticate.

pugas *reg* finished.

pugel cut, severed;

mugel *or* **mugeli** to cut, sever.

puger, **pugeran** rule(s), regulation(s). *See also* **uger**.

puges *reg*, **muges** 1 to cut off at the roots; 2 to settle once and for all.

puguh 1 firm, determined; 2 to stand one's ground; 3 to persevere, push on regardless.

pugut I harvesting knife;

mugut 1 to cut off at the tip; 2 *reg* to give s.o. his earned portion of the harvest (**bawon**).

II without a point, broken (needle).

puh, **ngepuh** 1 to squeeze, wring liquid from; 2 to milk;

puhan cow's milk (*var of* **powan**, **puwan**); **klapa** - a mature coconut the water of which has a milky appearance; **puh-puhan** 1 for squeezing; 2 to be squeezed;

pangepuh act of wringing or squeezing. *See also* **apuh**.

puhara, **puwara** *lit* finally, as the ultimate result.

puhawang *lit* ship's captain, master of a ship.

puhung *see* **pohung**.

puja worship; - **brata** *or* - **krama** *or* -**stuti** *lit* reverence, worship;

muja to praise, worship, adore;

memuja to worship, praise;

pujan 1 created by praying; 2 object of worship;

pepujan *lit* one who is esteemed;

pamuja act of praising;

pamujan place of worship.

pujangga a master of the literary art, poet;

kapujanggan 1 mastery of letters; 2 the art of literature.

pujastuti *var of* **pudyastuti**.

puji 1 prayer, wish, hope; 2 praise, worship;

muji 1 to hope, pray; 2 to praise, worship;

mujèkaké to wish/pray for s.t.;

muji-muji to pray repeatedly;

pujian 1 act of praying; 2 object of worship;

pamuji act of praying/wishing.

puk I *mak* **puk** *repr* falling with a plop.

II **ngepuk-puk** to pat (with the flat of the hand).

III **ngepuk** to chop or saw wood into blocks.

pukah *var of* **pokah**.

pukang I thigh (of animal).

II *see* **tukang II**.

pukat avocado.

puket, **muket** to tie up, bundle.

puki *reg cr* female genitals.

pukir *var of* **pungkir**.

pukrul *var of* **pokrul**.

pukul I hour; o'clock (*kr for* **jam**).

II, **pukul besi** hammer;

mukul to strike with a hammer.

pukulun *lit* my lord, lady.

pul I pole (of earth).

II gong stroke (*shtf of* **kempul**).

pulang *lit* **I** to recover.

II stained, smeared.

III to mingle (with), be united; - **asmara** *or* - **hyun** *or* - **gati** *or* - **lulut** *or* - **raras** *or* - **resmi** *or* - **sari** to make love.

pulanggeni *lit* incense.

pulas paint;

mulas to paint, apply a colour;

pulasan 1 covered with a layer of colour; 2 *fig* false, outward appearance.

pulasara, **mulasara** 1 to look after, care for; 2 to support; 3 to work on.

pulasari a creeper the bark of which has a medicinal use.

pulawaras a certain medicinal herb.

pulé a certain tall tree with soft wood, the bark of which is used in medicines.

pulèh *reg var of* **pulih**.

pulen 1 (of cooked rice) sticky (not loose); 2 thick and creamy.

pules I deep, sound (sleep).

II **mules** 1 to twist together; 2 to have stomach cramps;

mules-mules to keep pressing (with a request).

pulet, mulet to entwine;

pepuletan intertwined.

puli a ball made from mashed rice.

pulih I to recover, to regain a former condition; - **getih** 1 to get even; 2 without profit or loss;

mulihaké to restore s.t. to its original condition;

pulihan in the process of recovering;

pamulihan recovery, restoration to normal;

pepulih 1 retribution; 2 what one gives back; 3 *lit* revenge (for a crime);

pepulihan to reconcile.

II, **pulihan** *reg* accretion of land, deposition.

pulir, mulir to pinch and twist. *See also* **ulir**.

pulisi police; policeman;

mulisèkaké to notify the police;

kapulisèn police office, police force.

pulitik politics.

pulo island;

kapuloan archipelago.

pulpèn fountain pen.

pulu, kembang - safflower (used for yellow dye).

puluh I, *ng*, **dasa** *kr* the tens digit;

puluhan (**dasanan** *kr*) 1 10-rupiah note; 2 tens;

sepuluh ten.

II *ng*, *kr*, although; otherwise.

III **puluh-puluh** *ng*, *kr*; - **kepriyé manèh** what else can we do?

puluk *or* **pulukan** a handful of food;

muluk to eat (rice) with the fingers.

pulun *or* **pulunan** *or* **kapulunan** nephew, niece (child of one's younger brother or sister).

pulung I falling star, which descends on s.o. destined to receive a high position.

II, **mulung** 1 to tie harvested rice into a bundle; 2 *or* **mulungi** to bring things in after drying outside in the sun.

III *or* **pulung ati** the portion of the body below the heart and ribs; *fig* the heart as the seat of emotions.

pulur I *reg* knot in wood.

II, **puluran** *reg* refreshment, delicacy.

pulus *coll* money.

pulut sticky sap from certain fruits (used as birdlime);

mulut 1 to smear with sticky sap; 2 to trap (birds, small animals) with sticky sap; 3 *coll* to try to talk s.o. round, win over.

pumpa see **pompa**.

pumpet clogged, stopped up (*var of* **bumpet**).

pumpung *or* **mumpung** while one has the opportunity;

mumpung-mumpung *or* **mumpang-mumpung** to make the most of the opportunity.

pun I *familiar title used before a name or name substitute*: *kr* for **si**.

II finished (*shtf of* **sampun**, *md for* **wis**).

III don't (*shtf of* **sampun**), *md for* **aja**).

IV *shtf of* **dipun-** (*kr for* prefix **di-**).

punagi (to make) a vow (*k.i. for* **kaul**, **nadar**, **ujar**);

munagèni to vow to do s.t. if prayer is granted;

punagènan to vow together.

punah *lit* wiped put, gone, destroyed utterly;

munah to destroy;

pamunah 1 act or way of destroying; **2** destroyer.

punakawan *var of* **panakawan**.

punakèplèk lowly, poor servant.

punang *lit* the (*article*) (*also* **ponang**).

punapa (*also pron as:* **menapa**, *kr of* **apa**) **1** what? **2** ... or anything.

punapi *lit var of* **punapa**.

punar boiled in coconut milk and coloured with turmeric (rice for ritual meal).

punas *reg* paid in full. *See also* **lunas**.

puncak *var of* **pucak**.

puncet the top part of a ritual rice cone (**tumpeng**).

puncit top, tip, peak (*var of* **pencit**);
muncit to move to the top;
puncitan the banana at the bottom (small) end of the bunch.

puncu, **I muncu** to point (a sharp weapon).
II puncon *or* **pepuncon** peak (of a mountain).

pundelik *see* **pendelik**.

pundhah *reg* a kind of squirrel.

pundhak *ng, kr*, **pamidhangan** *k.i.* shoulder;
mundhak 1 to carry on the shoulder; **2** to walk supporting o.s. on someone else's shoulder;
pundhak nraju mas *idiom* fine firmly squared shoulders.

pundhamèn *see* **pondhamèn**.

pundhat, **mundhati** to pay off, settle (debt);
pundhatan final, full payment.

pundhèh *var of* **pondhèh**, **pundhuh**.

pundhèn *see* **pundhi**.

pundhes all gone, cleaned out, extinct.

pundhi I, **mundhi** *or* **mundhi-mundhi** *or* **memundhi 1** to hold s.t. above the head (as mark of respect); **2** to honour, hold in esteem;
pundhèn, **pepundhèn 1** an object of the highest reverence (person or

place); **2** spot in a village where offerings are placed (grave of founder, residence of guardian spirit).
II *reg* lead sinker for a fishnet.

pundhong a variety of grass.

pundhuh I 1 accustomed to; **2** well acquainted with.
II hunter.

pundhung I 1 (*or* **pundhungan**) mound of earth, heap of sand; **2** little hill;
mundhung *or* **mundhung-mundhung** piled up, existing in abundance. *See also* **undhung**.
II a tree with sour fruit.

pundhut, **mundhut 1** to ask for (from an inferior) (*k.i. for* **njaluk**); **2** to get, take (possession of) (*k.i. for* **njupuk**, **ngepèk**); **3** to buy (*k.i. for* **tuku**); - **ngampil** to borrow; - **priksa** to ask;
kapundhut to die, *i.e.* to be taken by God;
pundhutan 1 (*or* **pepundhutan**) thing requested (*k.i. for* **jalukan**); **2** purchases made (*k.i. for* **tukon**); **3** *lit* entertainment, refreshment (for guests).

pundi 1 where? **2** which (one)? (*kr for* **endi**).

pundoh *reg* to feel at home.

punel *var of* **pulen**.

pung *repr* a sound of a small gong;
pang-pung repeated small gong beats.

punggah *ng*, **pinggah** *kr*, **munggahi** to reach, come up to (e.g. flood);
punggahan 1 road to the top; **2** raising, promotion; **3** the observance of the day before the beginning of the Fasting Month (for purification). *See also* **unggah**.

punggal *var of* **punggel**.

punggawa 1 court official, grandee; **2** officer, functionary; **3** employee.

punggel, **munggel 1** to cut off; **2** to interrupt;
kepunggel to get broken off;

punggelan 1 s.t. cut off; **2 punggelan(ing rembug)** decision reached, conclusion;
pamunggel interruption.
pungges snapped;
mungges to snap, break off.
punggung *lit* stupid.
punggur, munggur to top, poll (tree).
punggut *var of* pugut.
pungkas the end, limit, extremity;
mungkasi **1** to bring to a complete end; **2** to finish up or off;
pungkasan **1** the end; **2** final;
pamungkas *lit* the last, youngest.
pungkir, mungkir *or* **mungkiri** to deny, disavow.
pungkruk I, mungkruk to lie in an untidy heap;
mungkrukaké to heap, pile things up.
II excited, with happy feelings.
pungkur *ng,* **pengker** *kr,* the back (part);
mungkur **1** past, overdue; **2** to turn one's back; **3** to refuse to cooperate;
mungkuraké **1** to turn one's back toward, have one's back to; **2** to pass by, have s.t. behind one;
kepungkur past, last, previous, ago;
pungkuran **1** back (body part); **2** (*or* pepungkuran) backyard. *See also* ungkur.
punglor a certain bird with green wings and a yellow head.
punglu a small round pellet used as a blown missile.
pungpung *var of* pumpung.
pungseng, mungseng 1 to rotate; **2** to search everywhere for s.t. *See also* puseng II.
pungser I 1 navel; **2** centre (*var of* puser).
II, mungser to spin rapidly (top);
mungseraké to cause to hum, whirl, spin rapidly.
pungun, pungun-pungun *lit* in a daze, stunned (with sadness, grief).

pungut, mungut to levy, assess (a tax *etc*);
pungutan assessment.
punika (*also pron as:* **menika**) **1** this (thing, place, time) (*kr for* iki); **2** that (thing, place, time) (*kr for* kuwi, kaé);
sapunika now.
puniki *lit var of* punika.
puniku *lit var of* punika.
punis sentence, punishment; judge's verdict (*var of* ponis).
punjer 1 tap-root; **2** root, deepest part.
punji, munji to carry s.o. on the shoulders or neck;
punjèn riding on s.o.'s shoulders.
punjul 1 outstanding; **2** in excess;
munjuli **1** to exceed, surpass; **2** to add (an amount) to;
pinunjul outstanding, superior;
punjulan **1** excess, surplus; **2** an extra, given 'into the bargain';
punjul ing apapak *lit* superior, outstanding.
punjung *lit* high, honoured, noble;
munjung to give food to an elder, or superior, as a token of respect and gratitude;
punjungan gift as a token of respect to an elder or superior.
punten *reg* excuse me! pardon? (*shtf for* pangapunten);
punten dalem sèwu I don't know (*k.a. for* embuh).
punther bent or withered at the tip through inhibited growth (*var of* puther).
punthes all gone;
munthes *or* munthesi to take all of s.t. *See also* pundhes.
punthuk mound, hill, peak;
munthuk **1** mound-shaped; **2** to rise, swell;
punthukan s.t. resembling a hill.
punting *reg* with too small legs and too big body.

puntir, muntir 1 to twist tightly, twine (rope); 2 twisted, warped; 3 recalcitrant, uncooperative. *See also* pluntir, untir.

puntiyanak a malicious supernatural being that is the spirit of a woman who died in childbirth and appears as a beautiful young woman with a hole in her back.

puntu, muntu 1 to twine; 2 to plait; 3 to think over seriously;
pepunton 1 subject of careful thought; 2 decision, conclusion.

punuk hump on the back;
punuken to have such a hump, humpbacked.

pupak *ng, kr,* daut (*or* dhaut) *k.i.* 1 to become detached from the body; 2 (of children's teeth) to come loose, fall out; - puser 1 (of the umbilical cord) to drop off; 2 rites marking this event in the life of a newborn infant;
mupak *or* mupaki to extract a tooth (of child).

pupu I *ng, kr,* wentis *k.i.* thigh; - gendhing chicken leg, drumstick.
II, mupu 1 to adopt; 2 to levy, collect (tax); 3 to pluck, pick (flowers);
pupon adopted in babyhood;
pamupu act or procedure of adopting.

pupug broken on the top, topless;
mupug *reg* to break the top of s.t.;
pupugan 1 used scraps of thatch; 2 blunt, worn (of a pointed object).
See also popog.

pupuh I 1 metre (in poetry); 2 canto.
II *lit* 1 club, bludgeon; 2 prang - a fierce hand-to-hand fight;
mupuh to strike, attack;
kapupuh defeated (in battle).
III eyewash;
mupuhi to wash the eyes.

pupuk I a poultice of pounded herbs, placed on a child's fontanel to ward off illness;

mupuki *or* mupukaké to apply a poultice to (as above);
pupukan to have such a poultice on one's head;
pupuk bawang a poultice of onions, *idiom* one who cannot contribute a full share to a joint endeavour (*usu* of a small child in a game with older people).
II plump, buxom, well-fleshed.

pupul *lit* gathered together, assembled.

pupung *var of* pumpung.

pupur *ng, kr,* tasik *k.i.* scented white rice powder used as a cosmetic;
mupuri to powder s.o.;
mupuraké to apply powder to;
pupuran to have or put powder on one's face;
pupur sadurungé benjut *prov* look before you leap: take preventive measures;
pupur sawisé benjut *prov* to lock the stable door after the horse has bolted.

pupus I the new leaf unfolding in the crown of a tree, top of a plant.
II *reg* dead, to die.
III, mupus to resign o.s. to the inevitable.
IV the top, hawser of a seine-net;
mupus to pull in a netful of fish.

puput I *ng, kr,* daut (*or* dhaut) *k.i.* 1 the falling off of an infant's umbilical cord; to have the cord drop off; - puser 1 cord-dropping; 2 cord-dropping ceremony;
muputi to hold a ceremony for (an infant) on this occasion;
puputan ceremony marking the falling off of the cord.
II right to the end, to come to an end, be over;
muput throughout; sawengi - the whole night.

pur I 1 a tie (score); all even; 2 forward (soccer player, position; *var of* por);
ngepuraké to make even, square a debt.

pura I palace.

II forgiveness (*var of* **apura**).

III a steamed fluffy powdered cassava with brown sugar and grated coconut.

purak I, **murak** to cut (an animal carcass) to pieces and share it out.

II, **purak-purak** *reg* to pretend, not be in earnest.

puran *reg* the half of a slaughtered animal, a side.

purantara *lit* royal palace.

purasani, wesi - high-quality iron or steel used for making krises, royal carriage *etc.*

puraya *lit* royal palace.

purba I, **murba** to rule over, be in command of; -**wasésa** *or* -**wisésa** authority, control, mastery.

II ancient; - **kala** ancient times.

purdrah lecture, presentation.

purek *reg* too short.

pureng, mureng to scowl, look very angry;

purengen to suffer from a fit of anger, be furious.

pures all gone, used up.

puret I dim, blurry, unclear.

II stunted, not growing properly (plants).

puri I palace.

II, *see* **wuri** II.

purih I, **murih** 1 for the purpose of; to intend for (a purpose); 2 to strive to do, obtain. *See also* **amrih, kapurih**.

II leg of beef or mutton.

purik 1 to sulk, not talk (offended at unjust treatment); 2 to run away, leave (one's home, husband, in anger);

muriki to avoid, leave s.o. (in anger);

purikan 1 not on speaking terms, avoiding each other; 2 easily offended, touchy.

puring a certain ornamental garden plant; croton plant.

puringis *see* **pringis**.

purna *lit* 1 recovered; 2 complete; whole; finished; 3 (of the moon) full. *See also* **paripurna**.

purnama full moon.

purohita *var of* **puruhita**.

puru, lara - a certain skin disease; **lemah** - red ochre.

purug way, course (*kr for* **paran**).

puruhita *lit* 1 a learned holy man; 2 to be a student of a learned holy man.

purun 1 to be willing (*kr for* **gelem**).

purus urinary canal at the perineum.

purusa *gram* person; **utama**- first person, **madyama**- second person, **pratama**- third person.

purusotama *lit* hero, distinguished person.

purut, jeruk - a certain small aromatic lemon with crinkly skin.

purwa 1 *lit* beginning; 2 *gram* initial (letter, syllable); 3 ancient; -**kala** ancient times; -**kandha** ancient story; 4 *lit* east;

murwa *or* **murwani** 1 to begin, initiate; 2 to create;

purwa madya wasana the facts from the beginning [the middle] to the end, *i.e.* the whole story;

ora éling purwa-daksina *idiom* completely confused.

purwaka *lit* preface, introduction, introductory remarks;

murwakani to provide with an introduction.

purwakanthi (in classical Javanese poetry) repetition of sounds (alliteration, assonance).

pus I *rpr* a puff of blown-out breath; **pas-pus** to chain smoke.

II puss, puss!

pusa *reg* unproductive (ricefield).

pusak crown of the head.

pusaka 1 heirloom, revered object (*e.g.* kris, spear) passed down from one's ancestors; 2 inheritance (*k.i. for*

warisan); **3** (ricefield) owned by one family through the generations (rather than being communal property);
musakani to pass down to;
musakakaké to pass s.t. down to one's descendants.

pusang *lit* bewildered, dazed.

pusara *lit* **1** string, rope, cord; **2** -**ning praja** the reins of government.

pusek, pusekan *lit* confused, bewildered, groggy.

puseng I *var of* **pusing**.
II, museng to search all around for.

puser I (**nabi** *or* **tuntunan** *k.i.*) umbilical cord.
II centre, middle point; **pusering tanah Jawa** the centre of Java (Mataram);
muser to turn, spin fast;
puseran ring (in wood, water).
puser III a kind of caterpillar.

pusing confused, bewildered.

puspa *lit* flower; - **kajang** *or* **pajang** a boa constrictor; -**lémbong** a certain plant with an edible tuberous root; -**njali** name of a classical verse form; - **nyidra** a decorative plant with red and yellow flowers.

puspita *lit* flower.

pustaka *lit* book, letter, document;
kapustakan literature.

pusthi I, musthi *lit* to grasp a weapon (while fighting).
II, musthi *lit* to concentrate the attention on.

pusthika *var of* **musthika**.

pusuh, pusuhan a roll of cleaned cotton (ready for spinning).

pusus, musus 1 to keep turning s.t. round, revolve; **2** to roll between the palms;
mususi to clean rice for cooking by washing and stirring with the hand;
pususan water in which s.t. has been washed as above;
pamusus 1 act of cleaning rice in this

way; **2** act of rolling s.t. between the hands.

putat a variety of tree.

putèh white (*reg var of* **putih**).

putek in a quandary, unable to cope.

puter I puter-puter to do the rounds, travel around;
muter 1 to turn to face the other way; **2** to wander about; **3** to turn s.t. round; wind (clock), show (film);
muteri to go around s.t.;
muteraké to lend (money) for interest;
puteran a device for winding.
II dove, kept in a cage.

puthel broken on the tip;
muthel to cut off at the tip.

puther bent, withered (branch, finger).

puthes *var of* **punthes**.

puthu cylindrical dumpling of rice flour in a sauce of salted coconut milk with a lump of brown sugar in the centre;
puthon (of gold or silver piece) half-cylindrical.

puthul to break off;
muthuli 1 to break off; **2** to fall off;
muthulaké to cause s.t. to be broken.

puthuk *reg* hill, mound. *See also* **punthuk**.

puthun, muthun-muthun to spoil, overindulge (a child). *See also* **uthun**.

puthut pupil or disciple of a holy man or hermit.

putih *ng*, **pethak** *kr* **1** white; **2** pure; - **memplak** *or* - **mulus** pure white;
mutih 1 to eat only unspiced food (rice, cassava, potato) as a form of fasting or self-denial; **2** to bleach; **3** to clean (a kris) with lemon juice;
mutihi *or* **mutihaké** to have s.t. made white, make whiter (than before);
putihan 1 whites, linen; **2** egg white;
mutihan 1 pious Muslims; **2** district where these live.

putra 1 child, offspring (*k.i. for* **anak**); **2**

child, young person (*k.i. for* **bocah**); **peputra** to have as child; **peputran** puppet;

mutrani 1 to beget offspring; 2 to renew by making a copy (*esp* regalia); **putran** *way* puppet depicting a prince; **kaputran** prince's residence.

putraka *lit* grandchild.

putri 1 female (*k.i. for* **wadon**); 2 princess;

mutrèni womanly, feminine;

kaputrèn apartments of the princesses within the palace;

putrèn 1 young corn; 2 *way* puppet depicting a princess.

putu *ng*, *kr*, **wayah** *k.i.* grandchild.

putung broken (stick, bone);

mutung 1 to break s.t.; 2 to sulk, become sullen, withdraw (from criticism);

mutungaké to break s.t. accidentally;

mutungan 1 prone to be resentful of criticism; 2 to break easily;

keputungan to sulk, become sullen.

putus 1 detached, broken off; 2 brought to completion; 3 expert; erudite; 4 to win a prize, *esp* in a lottery;

mutus *or* **mutusi** *or* **mutusaké** to decide;

putusan *or* **kaputusan** decision.

puwa, **puwa-puwa** arbitrary, tyrannical, merciless.

puwadhé dais on which the bridal couple sits.

puwan cow's milk (*var of* **powan**).

puwanten *kr for* **puwara**.

puwara *ng*, **puwanten** *kr* 1 last, final; 2 in the end, finally.

puwas *reg* satisfied with one's lot.

puwasa *lit var of* **pasa**.

puwer leg of meat (beef, lamb *etc*).

puwung, **muwung** to put up with s.t., make do with s.t.;

puwungan inclined to accept what life offers; easily satisfied.

puyeng to have a headache (*kr for* **ngelu**, **mumet**).

puyer medication in powdered form.

puyuh I female quail (*var of* **gemak**).

II fierce squall, windstorm.

puyuhan urine bladder.

pyah *or* **mak pyah** *repr* falling and splattering.

pyah-pyoh *repr* splashing about in water.

pyayama *lit* to speak respectfully.

pyak *see* **piyak**.

pyambak *see* **piyambak**.

pyan ceiling.

pyang-pyangan I *repr* clattering.

II to enjoy going places.

pyantun *see* **priyantun**.

pyarsa *see* **piyarsa**.

pyek *or* **mak pyek** *repr* s.t. soft plopping down.

pyèng *or* **mak pyèng** *repr* metal object (*e.g.* enamel plate, spoon) falling.

pyoh *or* **mak pyoh** *repr* sloshing (*e.g.* a bucket of water) over s.t.

pyok *or* **mak pyok** *repr* s.t. small dropping (*e.g.* an egg).

pyuk *or* **mak pyuk** *repr* stepping in a puddle.

pyung *or* **mak pyung** *repr* s.t. flying away at speed.

pyur I *repr* spraying, sprinkling;

ngepyuri to sprinkle, strew (*e.g.* rice for the chickens).

II, **pyur-pyuran** to pound, throb (heart, with emotion).

R

ra no; not (*shtf of* ora).

rabah, rabah-rabah crockery, earthenware, pots (*see also* grabah).

rabas, ngrabas *reg* to clear, cut down.

rabasa, ngrabasa to ravage, overpower.

rabat marked-down price; discount.

rabèk *var of* rawèk.

rabèt *var of* rawèk.

rabi 1 wife; 2 to take a wife;
ngrabi *or* ngrabèni to marry s.o.;
ngrabèkaké to arrange for (a boy's) marriage; rabèn to marry a lot.

rabingulakir 4th month of the Islamic calendar.

rabingulawal 3rd month of the Islamic calendar.

rabuk fertiliser;
ngrabuk *or* ngrabuki to fertilise, apply fertiliser to;
rabukan fertilised.

racak 1 usual, common(place); 2 equal;
racak-racak on the whole, by and large;
ngracak 1 occurring commonly; 2 equally distributed; 3 to judge s.t. from the available data; 4 to make equal, distribute evenly;
ngracakaké to distribute evenly;
racakan considering everything;
racaké usually, ordinarily.

racek a type of worm that affects the stomach or eyes;
raceken affected with this worm.

racik I prepared in measured quantities (ingredients);
racik-racik to keep mixing (medicines);
ngracik 1 to measure out (portions, ingredients); 2 to lay out (a meal); 3 to prepare, mix (prescription, sauce);
racikan 1 prepared, measured out; 2 mixture, preparation (foods, ready to cook); 3 a set of clothes.
II finger, toe (*reg k.i. for* driji).

racuk *see* tracuk.

racun poison;
ngracun *or* ngracuni to poison s.o. or s.t.;
ngracunaké 1 to use s.t. as poison; 2 to poison s.o. on behalf of another;
keracunan 1 poisoned; 2 displaying symptoms of having been poisoned.

racut I ngracut 1 to gather up; 2 to sum up.
II 1 to release from a setting; 2 to undress, strip.

rad council, board.

rada *ng*, radi *kr*, somewhat; quite; rada-rada *coll* 'a bit off', a bit on the … side.

radèn (*abbr:* R.) *title applied to male royal descendants of middle rank*; - adipati *title for Patih of Surakarta or Yogyakarta*; - adipati arya *honorary title for government regent*; - ajeng (*abbr:* R.A.) *title for an unmarried female aristocrat*; - ayu (*abbr:* R.Aj.) *title for a married female aristocrat*; - mas (*abbr:* R.M.) *male nobility title*; - ngabèhi *title for a married male or female aristocrat*; - ngantèn *title for a married woman of medium-low status*; - rara (*abbr:* R.R.) *title for an unmarried high-status girl.*

radi somewhat, quite (*kr for* rada).

radiktya *var of* radité.

radin (*or* wradin) even(ly distributed, spread) (*kr for* rata).

radité (*or* dité) *lit* Sunday.

raditya 1 *lit* sun; 2 *var of* radité.

rados, radosan main road (*alternate kr, rural var of* ratan).

radya royal; -pustaka royal library.

radyan *lit var of* radèn.

raga I body; jiwa - body and soul;
ngraga sukma to assume an immaterial form through mortifying the flesh.
II basketwork.

ragab *reg* glad, happy.

ragad (*or* wragad) expense(s), cost;
ngragadi to finance, bear the expenses of.

ragaina a certain purple flower.

ragan, ragan-ragan *lit* coquettish, flirtatious. *See also* wiraga.

ragang, I ngragangi to make a frame for s.t.;
ragangan frame, skeleton.
II rumagang to come forward to undertake a task, to set to work (a number of people).

ragas bare, leafless (tree);
ragasan in skeletal form, reduced to a skeleton.

ragem *reg* 1 to agree, match; 2 to find pleasure in.

ragi I yeast;
ngragèni to add yeast to.
II seasoned and fried coconut (used also as a base for other dishes).
III (*subst kr of* rada).

ragil (*or* wragil, wuragil) last-born, youngest child in a family; - kuning *name of a character from folklore; pet name sometimes given to a fair-complexioned, sweet-tempered youngest child*; - urip youngest living child.

rago, raga-rago *reg* hesitant, uncertain.

ragrag *reg* style. *See also* gagrag I.

ragu ragout.

ragum *var of* ragem.

rah I, ngerah 1 to aim for/at; 2 to reach out for s.t.;
rah-rahan the way to reach;
pangerah goal aimed at, intention, expectation. *See also* arah I.
II blood (*kr for* getih).

rahab 1 lusty, with a good appetite; 2 well-disposed;
ngrahabi 1 appetising; 2 to enjoy heartily (meal);
rumahab displaying an inclination, willingness.

rahadèn *var of* radèn.

rahadyan *lit var of* radèn.

rahajeng in good health and spirits (*subst kr for* rahayu).

raharja healthy, prosperous;
karaharjan prosperity, welfare.

rahayu 1 in good health and spirits; 2 secure, tranquil;
karahayon 1 good health; 2 freedom from difficulties.

rahina *var of* raina.

rahmat God's mercy; mulih ing rahmat-ullah to return to God's mercy, die;
ngrahmati to bring good fortune.

rahsa *lit* 1 secret, hidden meaning; 2 semen.

rahuru turmoil, chaotic situation (*var of* dahuru).

rai *ng, kr*, pasuryan *or* wadana *k.i.*, 1 human face; 2 front, facade, surface; 3 page; - gedhèg insensitive, shameless;
raimu *term of abuse*: you fool!
ngraèni 1 to draw a face of s.t.; 2 to make flat surfaces on;
raèn, reraèn 1 likeness or imitation of human face; 2 surface;
praèn, praènan features, countenance.

raina day, daylight (as opposed to night);
karainan 1 (too) late (in the morning); 2 *way* past dawn (of improperly timed shadow-play performances); 3 to sleep in. *See also* rina.

raja 1 king; 2 gedhang - a variety of banana; 3 compounding element: - brana treasure, jewels; -darbé possessions, belongings; -kaya cattle; livestock; -mala a variety of banana; - keputrèn attire worn by a princess or bride; -pati a crime carrying a death penalty; **-pèni** treasure, valuables; **- putra** prince; **-putri** princess; **-singa** syphilis; **-siwi**, **-sunu** prince; **-swala** (of girls) of marriageable age (already menstruating); **-werdi** bluish enamel used for jewelry. *See also* **krajan**.

rajab *var of* **rejeb**.

rajag leaking badly, full of leaks;
   ngrajagi to put water all over (s.t.);
   rajagan a bad leak, place where the rain pours in.

rajah I 1 magical drawing; **2** lines on the palm of the hand;
   ngrajah to interpret palm lines; **- tangan** to engage in palmistry.
   II *lit* passion, lust.

rajah-tamah *lit* passion and ignorance.

rajam, **ngrajam** to stone s.o. to death.

rajamal *lit* worldly possessions.

rajang, **ngrajang** *or* **ngrajangi** to slice (*e.g.* tobacco);
   rajangan in slices, sliced.

rajata *lit* silver.

rajatadi *lit* treasure, valuables.

rajeg fence; wooden fence; **- wesi** iron fence;
   ngrajegi to fence s.t. in, enclose with a fence.

rajèh, **rojah-rajèh** in shreds; torn to ribbons.

rajin 1 industrious, dilligent; **2** neat, orderly, tidy.

rajug, **ngrajug** *reg* shocked, startled.

rajung, **rajungan** a small sea crab.

rajut 1 net(ting), hair net; **2** knitted purse, bag;
   ngrajut 1 to make netting; **2** to knit.

rak I 1 no, not; **2** *particle inviting agreement or confirmation*: isn't it? *etc*; (*in final position*: **rakan**).
   II rack, shelf.

raka older brother (*k.i. for* **kakang**); **- dalem** his majesty's older brother; your (royal) older brother; (**ing**)**kang -** (your, her) husband.

rakangat essential unit of Islamic prayer ritual, consisting of bows and prostrations performed a prescribed number of times.

rakatha *lit* crab.

raké *reg* you.

raket I close, intimate;
   ngraketi to adhere closely to, stick to;
   ngraketaké 1 to bring together again (after disagreement); **2** to attach firmly;
   reraketan to be intimate, good friends with;
   rumaket close, intimate. *See also* **kraket**.
   II raketan *k.i.* herbal medication rubbed on the stomach;
   ngraketi to apply this.

rakèt bat, racket.

raki *reg* you (*var of* **raké**).

rakit set, pair, team;
   ngrakit 1 to assemble; **2** to arrange;
   ngrakiti 1 to lay out; **2** to hitch up (a horse); **3** to arrange;
   ngrakitaké to yoke up (a pair of farm animals);
   rakitan 1 yoked; **2** (forming) a set *or* pair; **3** layout, arrangement;
   sarakit a pair.

raksa *var of* **reksa**.

raksasa male ogre.

raksasi female ogre.

rakud, **ngrakud** to carry off, seize.

rakup, **ngrakup** *or* **ngrakupi** to gather *or* rake together with the arms.

rakus 1 to eat greedily; **2** to like anything, indiscriminately.

rakyat the people, the public.

ralat error, misprint;
   ngralat to make corrections (in a text).

ram I brushwood;
   ram-raman a makeshift dam made from brushwood.
   II 1 window; **2** picture-frame.

rama I 1 father; older and/or higher-ranking male (*k.i. for* **bapak**) **2** Roman Catholic priest; - **ibu** parents; **Rama Kawula** the Lord's Prayer.

II name of the hero of the **Serat** -, a Javanese version of the Indian epic Ramayana.

ramad *see* **ramat**.

Ramadan 9th month of the Islamic calendar, the Fasting Month.

ramah friendly, easy to talk to; - **tamah** to hold an informal meeting.

ramak father (*inf var of* **rama**).

ramal, ngramal 1 to predict, portend; **2** to prophesy;

ngramalaké to predict or portend s.t.;

ramalan 1 prediction, prognosis; **2** prophecy.

ramat 1 fibrous tissue (of plant); **2** spider web.

rambah, - menèh again, another time;

rambah ping pindho twice;

rambah-rambah repeatedly; again and again;

ngrambahi to do s.t. another time;

marambah-rambah to (do) again and again;

rambahan 1 time (occasion); **2** repetition.

rambak I edible beef hide, often fried as chips or used in sauces.

II tree root growing on the surface of the ground.

ramban to pick edible leaves for use in cooking or as animal fodder;

(re)rambanan edible leaves and herbs.

rambang I, ngrambang 1 to stand s.t. in a container of water; **2** to bathe (the eyes) in a dish of water; **3** to wash down (a fighting cock or cricket) by pouring water over it.

II degree, power (in mathematics);

ngrambangaké to raise (a number) to a power.

rambas *or* **ngrambas** to ooze, seep, soak through.

rambat, ngrambati 1 to creep or climb on(to); **2** to spead outward or into;

ngrambataké to train (a vine) up a supporting pole;

mrambat 1 to creep, crawl; **2** to edge toward;

rambat-rambat to crawl everywhere, be at the crawling stage;

rambatan 1 to creep; **2** a support for a climbing plant.

rambet, ngrambet *reg* to clear (land) of weeds.

rambit *or* **rambit-rambit** thorny shrubs, bushes.

rambon I a variety of fine fragrant tobacco.

II crossbreed between a domestic cow and a wild ox.

rambu, ngrambu to go in search of, trace, track down, investigate.

rambut (*k.i.* **rikma, réma**) hair on the head;

ngrambut resembling hair, hairy;

ngrambuti to have hairline cracks (glassware);

rumambut in the fine thread stage (boiling syrup);

rambutan *see* **rambutan**. *See also* **mrambut**.

rambutan a tree and its 'hairy' fruit.

ramé noisy, bustling, alive with activity, making commotion;

ngramé to live in the community with all its bustle;

ngramèni 1 to disturb with noise and commotion; **2** to stir up, throw into commotion;

ngramèkaké to enliven, bring action to;

keramèn too noisy, excessively bustling;

keraméan 1 festival, celebration; **2** bustle, commotion of normal life and activity;

ramé-ramé (to hold) a celebration, festival or any noisy gathering;

ramèn-ramèn (noisy) celebration *or* party.

ramelan *var of* **ramadan**.

rames, sega - rice combined with several other foods arranged around it, a combination of foods served on one plate; **ngramesi** to combine (foods).

rami the ramie or rhea ('china grass'), a shrub producing a fibre used for making string and cloth.

ramon I s.t. used to keep o.s. afloat in water.

II, ngramon 1 to torture s.o. together; **2** to rob; **dadi ramon** (a woman) to be forced to submit to maltreatment or violation by many. *See also* **ramu**.

rampa, ngrampa *or* **ngrerampa 1** (of many) to carry, support; **2** to gather round and offer help.

rampad, rampadan *or* **rerampadan** dishes served up and placed ready for a meal (mainly meat); **ngrampad** to lay out foods on separate plates (on table, mat).

rampag *var of* **rampak**.

rampak all the same, with none differing from the others.

rampal broken off, knocked out (tooth); **ngrampal, ngrampali** to break off, knock out.

rampang *reg* crosspiece between wagon shafts.

rampas, ngrampas *or* **ngrampasi 1** to plunder; **2** to prune; **3** *reg* to pick (the last, best leaves of tobacco plants).

rampèk I a style of wearing the **dodot** employed by palace troops.

II ngrampèk *or* **ngrampèk-rampèk** to play up to, appeal to, strengthen bonds of affection with; **rampèk-rampèk kethèk** to get into trouble by joining s.o. with a shady reputation.

rampes, ngrampes to slice, cut into pieces.

rampès I *reg* finished.

II, ngrampès to pay attention, take notice of.

rampet *reg* rope used for carrying s.t. by hanging it over the shoulder.

rampid I 1 close by; **2** tight.

II, ngrampid 1 to creep up on; **2** to attack, board (a ship); **3** to plunder.

ramping 1 slim, slender; **2** thin, lean; **3** correct, without faults; **4** fine, polished (language); **ngrampingaké** to make fine, polished.

rampog, ngrampog to attack (in numbers, with weapons); **rampogan** *or* **prampogan** *way* a wayang puppet depicting an army armed with pikes.

rampung over, finished, settled, completed, done with; **ngrampungi 1** to finish off; **2** to kill; **3** to decide, settle (case); **ngrampungaké** to finish, complete (work); **karampungan 1** decision; **2** sentence.

ramu, ngramu *or* **ngreramu** to seize, snatch; **ramon** to get seized, robbed.

ramud *reg* finished, completed.

ramuh, ngramuhi 1 to take liberties with, violate; **2** to rape.

ramut, ngramuti *reg* to keep, care for, make a hobby of.

ramyang, ramyang-ramyang *or* **ngramyang** *or* **rumamyang 1** hazy, dimly visible; **2** vague, obscure.

ran name (*shtf of* **aran**).

rana I *ng*, **rika** *kr* to that place; **rana-rana** to wander around; **rana-réné** (**rika-riki** *kr*) here and there; **mranakaké** to put s.t in *or* move s.t. toward that place. *See also* **mrana**.

II **rana**, **ranangga**, **rananggana** *lit* battle, battlefield.

III screen. *See also* **warana**.

rancag I quick;

ngrancag to speed up, expedite;

rancagan 1 to make haste to get s.t. finished; 2 in short.

II (of horses) lame.

rancah, **ngrancahi** to harrow (a field) for the first time. *See also* **gaga**.

rancak I a piece of wood;

ngrancak 1 to cut *or* break (wood); 2 to cut into small bits.

II a set of gamelan instruments;

rancakan a rack for **bonangs** (gamelan instruments).

rancana I, **ngrancana** 1 to design, to plan; 2 to place in order, arrange. *Also* **rencana** I.

II, **pangrancana** *or* **godha rancana** *lit* trouble, vexation, temptation. *Also* **rencana** II.

rancang, **ngrancang** 1 to set up, assemble; 2 to design, draw; 3 to estimate, budget;

rancangan plan, proposal, programme.

rancas, **ngrancas** *or* **ngrancasi** to trim, prune.

randha 1 widow or divorced woman with children; 2 missing its counterpart (cup without saucer).

randhat slow, behind;

ngrandhataké to slow down, delay. *See also* **rendhet**.

randhi I spotted deer.

II multicoloured fabric.

randhing, **ngrandhing** to set up, assemble a house-frame (provisionally).

randhu kapok tree; kapok seeds, from which kapok is collected; - **alas** wild kapok tree; - **kuning** kapok wood (used for kris sheaths).

rang I a tiny worm that penetrates the soles of the feet of those who have to stand in water;

rangen to be affected by this.

II order, ranking.

rangah *or* **rangah-rangah** sharply pointed (teeth).

rangap *var of* **rangah**.

rangas (*or* **wrangas**) a certain red ant or termite.

rangdha *lit, var of* **randha**.

rangga a low ranking court official.

ranggah branching widely, spreading (horns, antlers).

ranggèh, **ngranggèh** to reach out for s.t., stretch the hand out to take s.t.;

ngranggèhaké to reach for s.t. high for s.o.;

kranggèhan reaching up with the hand.

ranggèn hut for keeping watch in the fields (*kr for* **ranggon**).

ranggi a low-ranking court official (*kr for* **rangga**).

ranggon hut for keeping watch in the fields;

ngranggon 1 to live in a hut in the fields; 2 incurable; endemic;

kethèk saranggon *idiom* a group of people who have the same character and behaviour.

rangin, **ngrangin** *or* **ngrerangin** (to be heard) soft and sweet (of gamelan music in the distance).

rangka I wooden sheath (of kris, pike, sword);

ngrangkani 1 to provide (a kris) with a sheath; 2 *fig* to handle s.o.'s behaviour;

ngrangkakaké 1 to sheathe (a kris); 2 to stab s.o. to death with a kris;

ngrangkani kudhi to handle a difficult person. *See also* **wrangka**.

II frame; skeleton.

rangkad *reg* to run away with a lover;

ngrangkadaké to abduct.

rangkah 1 thorny hedge; 2 border, barrier (of city).

rangkang, ngrangkang to crawl (on all fours) (var of brangkang);
rangkang-rangkang to keep crawling with difficulty.

rangké chain, garland;
ngrangké or ngrangkèni to add, join, make a chain.

rangkep double;
ngrangkep 1 to double as; to double up; ngrangkepi 1 to add another one; 2 to wear double layers;
ngrangkepaké to put s.t. over s.t. else;
rangkepan 1 (clothing) worn as an additional layer; 2 s.t. double, duplicate.

rangkèt, ngrangkèt to beat with a stick as punishment.

rangki var of rangké.

rangkok hornbill.

rangkud, ngrangkud or ngrangkudi to gather up and take away.

rangkul, ngrangkul 1 to embrace s.o. by throwing arms around; 2 fig to associate with s.o. closely;
rangkulan or rerangkulan to embrace each other;
saprangkul an armful; as much as the arms can clasp.

rangkulu reg pillow (var of karangulu, see karang II).

rangkung I (or ngrangkung) lit tall and slender.
II, ngrangkung to squat down, crouch.

rangkus, ngrangkus 1 to shackle, tie up; 2 to hold two things (reins etc) in one hand.

rangram reg brushwood.

rangrang a large red tree ant. See also kangrang, ngangrang.

rangsang I desire, drive;
ngrangsangi exciting, stimulating;
rangsangan stimulus.
II ngrangsang to storm, attack, try to seize.

rangseg, ngrangseg 1 to push backward; 2 to attack, strike.

rangsèh, rangsèhan to hold a discussion. See also srasèhan.

rangsel var of ransel.

rangsir var of langsir.

rangsuk var of rasuk.

rangsum a ration of food;
ngrangsum to give out rations;
rangsuman food given as a ration.

rangu I, rangu-rangu doubtful, hesitant, unable to make up one's mind.
II, lit ngrerangu to yearn.

ranjam I, ngranjam to stone to death (var of rajam).
II bed.

ranjang bedstead, esp of metal.

ranjap, ngranjap 1 to stab, cut into from all sides; 2 to cut up a slaughtered beast and share out the meat;
ranjapan an animal that is slaughtered and divided up.

ranji, reg ngranji to assign a job to s.o.;
ranjèn work assigned for s.o.;
ranjiné reg actually, should, ought to.

ranjing I var of randhing.
II, ngranjingi (of spirit) to possess s.o.;
keranjingan 1 possessed (by a spirit); 2 wild about, addicted to.

ranju reg mantrap.

ransel knapsack, rucksack.

ranta, karanta-ranta to grieve, be in a sorrowful, dejected mood.

rantab, rantab-rantab to lie about in large quantities;
ngrantabi to fall on and cover (small, fine objects).

rantak, mrantak or rantak-rantak to begin to appear everywhere.

rantam, ngrantam to make provision, set up a plan for;
rantaman 1 plan of action, proposal; 2 estimate, budget.

rantang set of stacked containers for transporting food;

ngrantang to have a standing order for meals delivered in such containers;

rantangan system of getting one's food delivered on a standing basis.

rantap *var of* rèntèp.

rantas 1 broken off; 2 frayed;

ngrantas to break s.t. off;

ngrantasaké to cause s.t. to be frayed;

rantasan broken off; s.t. broken off.

ranté 1 chain; 2 necklace;

ngranté to put chains on; to attach with a chain.

ranten *lit* younger sibling.

ranti a tree bearing a small, bitter fruit;

suwé mijet wohing ranti *prov* very easy, a cinch.

ranting, rontang-ranting tattered, ragged.

rantun I, ngrantun 1 laid out in readiness; 2 to lay out, prepare;

pangrantunan a place for laying out or preparing a meal.

II ngrantun to pursue, go in search of.

ranu *lit* 1 (mountain) lake; 2 water.

raos *kr for* rasa.

rapah dry leaves, twigs, brush.

rapak I a divorce petition originating with the wife.

II dried-out sugarcane leaves.

rapal (Arabic) text (of prayer, magical formula);

ngrapal to utter such a text.

rapat a meeting;

ngrapataké to bring up or discuss s.t. at a meeting.

rapèh neat, orderly (*reg var of* rapih II).

rapèk I *var of* rampèk.

II, ngrapèk *or* ngrapèk-rapèk to appeal for sympathy (*var of* rampèk II).

rapèl, ngrapèl to receive back pay;

rapélan back pay.

rapèn dry grass (remains of cattle fodder).

rapet 1 tightly closed; 2 close, next to;

ngrapeti 1 to cover s.t. tightly; 2 to move closer;

ngrapetaké 1 to draw s.t. close; 2 to join up, push together.

rapi orderly, neat, tidy.

rapih I no longer angry;

ngrapih to calm s.o. down.

II neat, orderly.

rapoh *var of* rapuh.

rapor school report.

rapot *var of* rapor.

rapu calmed down, no longer upset;

ngrapu *or* ngrerapu to calm s.o.;

ngraponi to (try to) quieten s.o.

rapuh I *lit* tired, wearied;

rapuhan, jamu - a medicine to relieve fatigue.

II *reg* split, cracked.

rara young girl (*var of* lara).

rarab to fall, sprinkle down (of s.t. fine);

ngrarabi to sprinkle on;

keraraban to get sprinkled.

rarah, rarahan litter, rubbish (*var of* larahan, *see* larah II).

raras *lit* harmonious, pleasant;

rumaras fine, beautiful;

ngraras *or* ngraras-raras to think over, consider. *See also* laras II.

raré *lit, var of* laré.

raryan *lit* to stop, take a rest. *See also* lèrèn.

rarywa *var of* raré.

rarywan *var of* raryan.

ras 1 race, ethnic origin; 2 pedigreed, thoroughbred (horse, dog).

rasa *ng*, raos *kr*, 1 taste; 2 sensation; 3 meaning, sense;

ngrasa to feel, sense;

ngrasani to talk about s.o. (behind their back);

ngrasakaké 1 to taste, sample; 2 to feel, experience, take note of;

rasanan *or* rerasanan 1 to talk, chat; 2 gossip, food for conversation;

krasa to have (a certain) taste or feeling;

pangrasa feeling; idea;

rasa pangrasa 1 feeling, interpretation, idea; 2 the inner feeling of the heart;

krasan to feel at home;

ngrasanaké to cause to feel at home;

rumasa *or* **rumangsa** (**rumaos** *kr*) 1 thought; 2 to have feeling;

ngrumangsani to be aware, realise, see in true perspective;

rumangsanan a feeling of pride or superiority;

mirasa tasty, delicious;

surasa meaning, content, connotation;

nyurasa to get the meaning, sense the connotation;

panyurasa grasp or insight into meanings contained in texts, messages *etc.*

rasamala a tall forest tree producing a gum used in incense.

rasé civet cat.

raseksa *var of* **raksasa**.

raseksi *var of* **raksasi**.

rasmi *formal var of* **resmi** II.

rasuk, **ngrasuk** 1 to accept fully (religion); 2 to intrude, marry s.o. one should not, *e.g.* one's sister-in-law or one's adopted daughter;

ngrasuk busana to get dressed;

ngrasuki 1 to dress s.o. in a dress or shirt (*kr for* **nglambèni**, *see* **klambi**); 2 to possess s.o.;

ngrasukaké to cause s.t. to penetrate;

rumasuk to enter and penetrate (flavour, medicine);

mrasuk to permeate completely;

rasukan article of clothing for the upper part of the body (*kr for* **klambi**);

kerasukan possessed (by a spirit).

rasul apostle;

rasulullah the Apostle of God;

ngrasulaké to hold a ceremony of thanksgiving;

rasulan a ceremony of thanksgiving.

raswa *lit, var of* **rasa**.

rat *lit* world; the whole world; **rat Jawa** the whole of Java.

rata *ng*, **radin** *kr* (*or* **wradin**) even(ly) distributed or spread;

rata-rata 1 on the average, mean; 2 approximately, roughly; 3 comparatively;

ngrata 1 to level s.t.; 2 to distribute evenly;

ngratani 1 to treat all the same; 2 to reach all points;

ngratakaké 1 to cause to be even; 2 to spread s.t. around.

ratak *reg* let it be, I don't care.

ratan *ng*, **margi** *or* **radosan** *kr* main road.

ratap cry, complaint, lamentation.

rateng cooked, done, ready to eat;

ngratengi to heat food, prepare (a meal) by heating it;

ratengan *or* **reratengan** various sorts of cooked food.

rati *lit* moon (*var of* **ratih** II).

ratib the repetition of religious formulas as a mystical exercise;

ratiban to recite these formulas (*e.g. Hua Allah,* 'He is God', *or Allahu akbar,* 'God is Great').

ratih I the Goddess of Love.

II moon.

ratna *var of* **retna**.

ratri *lit* night. *Also* **latri**.

ratu 1 king, queen, monarch; 2 chess king; 3 one of the small playing-cards (*kertu cilik*);

ngratoni to reign over, rule over;

ratu-ratuning *or* **reratuning** *lit* the most, the best;

reraton 1 characteristic ornaments and dress of royalty (in drama); 2 to form a group under a leader (in children's games); 3 to flock together in one place (birds).

See also **kraton**.

ratum *reg* new sugarcane sprout.

ratus incense, various fragrant substances mixed in a powdered form;
ngratus *or* ngratusi to apply the above, by burning under clothes.

ratya *lit* king;
karatyan palace, court.

rauk, ngrauk 1 to gather up/in with the hands; 2 *var of* ngrawuk.

raup 1 (suryan *k.i.*) to wash one's face; 2 the amount one can hold in the cupped hands;
ngraupi to wash s.o.'s face;
ngraupaké to wash (one's, s.o.'s) face with; - tangan to pass one's hands over one's face after prayer;
praupan (pasuryan *k.i.*) 1 facial features; 2 washbasin;
ngraup pada to 'kiss the feet', i.e. display respect or esteem (for).

rauru *var of* dauru.

raut, ngrauti to whittle, trim, sharpen (pencil *etc*);
rautan (pencil) sharpener.

rawa 1 swamp; 2 shallow lake;
rawan swampy area.

rawat I nurse;
ngrawat 1 to nurse; 2 (*or* ngrawati) to keep, put away carefully.
II, rawat-rawat faintly audible, faintly visible.

rawé I a creeper the hairy pods of which cause itching;
ngrawé to scatter the hairs of the rawé on.
II rawé-rawé hanging in a fringe, in strands, strings;
rawé-rawé rantas, malang-malang putung *prov* no matter what the problems, we will overcome them.

rawèh *coll* prohibited, not allowed (*shtc of* ora awèh).

rawèk, rowak-rawèk in tatters, frayed, torn to shreds.

rawi I *lit* sun.

II swamp, lake (*subst kr for* rawa).

rawing, rowang-rawing badly damaged (of metal objects), with big notches.

rawis 1 a hanging wisp; 2 moustache (*k.i. for* brengos);
ngrawis (of hair) thin, not luxuriant.
II, ngrawis to slice, shred;
rawisan 1 in slices; 2 sliced, shredded.

rawit I lombok - small, very hot chili.
II, ngrawit very fine and smooth;
karawitan gamelan music.

rawon a clear brown beef soup;
ngrawon to make (meat) into the above.

rawuh to come, arrive (*k.i. for* teka);
ngrawuhi to call on s.o.;
karawuhan 1 visited by a guest; 2 entered by a spirit;
rawuhan a visit from a respected person;
sugeng rawuh welcome!

rawuk, ngrawuk to scratch, claw;
ngrawuki to keep scratching s.o.;
ngrawukaké to scratch on behalf of s.o.;
rawuk-rawukan to scratch each other.

raya I great, large, important;
ngrayakaké to celebrate.
II, keraya-raya to go to a lot of trouble for, to.

rayagung *reg* Besar, the 12th month of the Islamic calendar.

rayah, ngrayah (*or* ngrayahi) to grab at, snatch, plunder, raid;
rayahan loot, s.t. grapped.

rayang I a variety of caterpillar.
II, ngrayang-ruyung to carry out (work) cooperatively.

rayap termite; - bala termites that guard the queen and the colony;
ngrayap to behave like a colony of termites;
kumrayap to swarm like termites.

rayat 1 wife (*md for* bojo); 2 family; one's household; 3 the people, the public (*var of* rakyat).

rayi younger sibling (*k.i. for* **adhi**); **ingkang** - (your, his) wife.

rayud, ngrayud 1 to bundle or bunch together; 2 to claim (ownership of); to acknowledge as one's own.

rayuk, ngrayuk to take (away) *esp* by force or without permission.

rayung I a variety of long, fine, soft reed; **ngrayung** long and slender (fingers). II, **ngrayung, rayung-rayung** scarcely audible (a cry).

réak-réok *see* **réok**.

réang *reg* I, me.

rebab two-stringed bowed lute; **ngrebab** to play this instrument; **pangrebab** 1 act or way of playing this instrument; 2 player of this instrument.

rebah to fall; fallen (*kr for* **rubuh**).

rebat *kr for* **rebut**.

rebatang *lit* fallen tree trunk.

rebda, ngrebda to grow, increase.

rèbed *reg var of* **ribed**.

rèbèk matané *reg* to have sore, inflamed eyes.

rèbèl to fall, drop off; **ngrèbèli** to drop things on, scatter bits on; **rèbèlan** what has fallen off.

rèbèt, ngrèbètaké to leave a bit over for s.o. else; **rèbètan** 1 (a bit) left over; 2 'an afterthought' (youngest child).

rèbewès driver's license.

Rebo Wednesday; - **wekasan** the last Wednesday in the month of Sapar.

rebon a certain small river shrimp.

rebu dust (*var of* **lebu** I).

rebut *ng*, **rebat** *kr*, to compete for s.t.; - **bener** to argue each other; - **ngarep** to elbow each other trying to get in front; - **dhucung** to try to get ahead of each other; - **cukup** to make a long story short...; **ngrebut** to seize for o.s.;

rebutan 1 rivalry; 2 object competed for; 3 to struggle for possession of; **ngrebut kemiri kopong** *prov* 1 to quarrel over s.t. trivial; 2 to yearn for s.t. of little value.

rèbyèg (with) much fuss and trouble, much ado.

reca statue.

recaci *reg* clasp, buckle.

recapada *lit* earth, place of human habitation (*var of* **marcapada**).

rècèh I (coins) of small denomination, small change. II over-familiar, talkative. III messy, wet; **ngrècèhi** to make (the floor) messy, wet. IV of inferior quality (batik).

recek *var of* **resek**.

reda *var of* **rebda**.

redana money (*subst kr for* **dhuwit**)

redatin *var of* **rudatin**.

redatos *kr for* **rudatin**.

redhem *reg* to be motionless, keep still.

rédhu *var of* **ridhu**.

redi mountain (*kr for* **gunung**).

Redité Sunday (*var of* **Raditya**).

reg *repr* a violent jerk; **rag-reg** to keep jerking violently.

règ, règ-règan to fidget, squirm, move about nervously.

rega *ng*, **regi** *kr*, 1 price, cost, value; - **mati** fixed price; 2 to cost; **ngregani** to put a price on; **reregan** market prices, price level; **ana rega, ana rupa** *prov* what you see is what you get.

regadag *or* **mak regadag** *repr* a hard or quick tug.

regag *reg* unable to decide.

regak, regak-regak *reg* in a quandary.

régang *reg* rack for drying tobacco leaves.

regas *reg* crumbly, friable, brittle.

régé 1 a low round flat basket woven of palm leaf ribs; 2 a short coconut leaf rib broom;

règèn woven bamboo container.

reged dirty;
ngregedi to dirty s.t., defile, befoul;
regedan or rereged 1 dirt; 2 waste matter, muck; 3 *fig* scum.

regedeg or mak regedeg *repr* a sudden arrival of a lot of people or things.

regèdèg or mak regèdèg *repr* a rasping, scraping sound.

regejeg, regejegan (to have) a noisy quarrel, to bicker, squabble.

règèl to fall off, fallen; sapu - 1 a palm leaf spine broom (sapu lidhi) that has been worn down by use (short, stiff and good for cleaning); 2 *fig* an older man still in good shape;
ngrègèli to let (various things) slip from one's grasp.

regem 1 a small vice; 2 small pliers, tweezers;
ngregem to squeeze, clutch, hold firmly;
regeman a firm hold.

regemeng, ngregemeng or regemeng-regemeng to loom up in the twilight.

regeng, katon - to give an impression of bustle, stir, liveliness;
ngregengaké to make s.t. lively;
regeng-regeng or regeng-regengan s.t. lively.

règèng, règèng-règèng just back on one's feet (after illness).

regep, ngregep I *lit* to take up, take hold of (a weapon).
II, ngregep to receive cordially, heartily, warmly;
rumegep to be very attentive, show much concern.

règès leafless (*var of* ragas).

regéyong, ngregéyong to hang heavily, dangle;
regéyongan dangling.

regi price, cost (*kr for* rega).

regiyeg *repr* an effort to lift a heavy burden;

ngregiyeg to carry a heavy burden.

regiyeng *var of* regiyeg.

régoh lame (gait), with weak legs.

régol 1 outer gateway of a traditional-style house; 2 name of one of the clowns, servant of Gunungsari, in the wayang gedhog repertoire.

regu I (or wregu) a small palm with a slender hardwood trunk.
II 1 taciturn, disdainful; 2 serious, sober.

régu, ngrégoni to hinder, obstruct, disturb.

regudug *repr* stampeding, dragging s.t. heavy over the ground.

regul (or wergul) a marten-like animal.

regung, ngregung or regung-regung luxuriant, flourishing (plants).

regunuk, ngregunuk looming ominously, ghostly-looking;
regunuk-regunuk to move in the dark with an ominous or ghostly look.

rèh, erèh 1 actions, proceedings, how things are done; 2 rule, regulation, ordering, disposition; 3 (under the) authority, area of; 4 (in the) case of;
ngerèh to command;
ngerèhaké to govern, hold sway over;
kerèh, kaerèh subordinated;
rèh-rèhan a subordinate (person or territory);
rèhné, sarèhné since, in view of the fact that, seeing that.

reja flourishing, prosperous, thriving;
ngrejakaké to bring prosperity to.

rejasa I a tree with red flowers.
II *lit* solder (mixture of tin and gluga).

Rejeb 7th month of the Islamic calendar;
rejeban a thanksgiving ceremony held during Rejeb.

rejeg, ngrejeg 1 to compel, force; 2 to seize.

rèjèg *var of* rajag.

rejèh *reg* prosperous, lively, festive.

rejek, ngrejek to crush, break to pieces.

rejeki 1 daily food, necessities of life; 2 good fortune;
ngrejekèni 1 to bring one's daily bread; 2 to bring good fortune;
karejekèn to enjoy an abundance of good things.

rejeng, ngrejeng to dispute, snatch away;
rerejengan to keep pulling each other back and forth.

rèjèng rocks in a ravine.

réjog reg lame because of one non-functioning leg.

rèk I 1 or mak rèk repr a scraping sound;
rak-rèk scraping repeatedly;
2 match, lighter;
ngerèk to produce a light;
ngerèki to light s.t. with a match;
ngerèkaké to light a match.
II reg child (shtf of arèk).

réka 1 invention; 2 (ingenious) means; 3 reg plan; 4 to do tricky things;
réka-réka 1 to have a cunning idea; 2 to pretend;
ngréka to invent, make up, think out;
ngréka-réka to (try to) conjure up an idea or picture in the imagination;
ngrékani to find, think up a means for;
ngrékakaké to take suitable measures for;
rékan imitation, fake.

rékadaya a plan, plot, scheme;
ngrékadaya to (try to) hit on an idea;
pangrékadaya act of plotting.

rekah I cracked.
II ill at ease (kr for rikuh).
III or rumekah to spread wide, become more and more (branches of trees).

rékal folding book-rest.

rekangat essential unit of prayer ritual, consisting of bows and prostrations performed a prescribed number of times.

rekaos kr for rekasa.

rekasa ng, rekaos kr, difficult, to have a hard time, suffer from hardships;
rekasa uripé to live in difficult circumstances (poverty);
ngrekasakaké to make trouble for.

rékat inf var of rikat I.

rekatak or mak rekatak repr a ripping sound.

reké lit see reko.

rèken, ngrèken to set a value (on); to reckon s.t. (at);
rèkenan way of settling expenses with each other.

rékening bill presented for payment.

rèkèp reg proper, neat.

rekès a request, letter of request or application;
ngrekès to put in a request or application (for).

rèket var of rakèt.

reketek or mak reketek 1 repr a tug, jerk; 2 repr wood or bamboo cracking.

rekètèk or mak rekètèk repr a tearing sound.

rèki small but cute.

rekitik repr a light cracking sound.

réklame advertisement.

reko lit now, then.

reksa, ngreksa to guard, watch over;
rumeksa lit, var of ngreksa;
reksan that which is guarded or watched over.

reksaka lit keeper, guard, watchman.

reksasa see raksasa.

reksasi see raksasi.

reksi var of resi I.

rèkstok horizontal bar (used in gymnastics).

rekta lit red.

rèktor university rector, vice-chancellor.

rekutuk repr a loud cracking sound.

rekyana patih lit title for a prime minister.

rem I, ngeremaké to close (the eyes);

merem 1 closed (eyes); 2 indifferent, taking no notice of others;

meram-merem 1 to keep blinking the eyes; 2 to pretend to have the eyes closed;

rem-rem ayam *idiom* dozing.

II, angrem *or* ngengremi to sit on (eggs);

ngengremaké to have (eggs) hatched;

ngrem-ngreman used for breeding.

rèm brakes;

ngerèm to apply brakes;

ngerèmaké to brake s.t.

réma hair of the head (*k.i. for* rambut).

rémah house (*reg kr for* romah).

remaja adolescent;

remaja putra/putri teenage boy/girl.

remak *var of* remek.

rématik rheumatism.

rembag words, talk (*kr for* rembug I).

rémbak to demolish (*kr for* rombak).

rembaka, ngrembaka to flourish, grow luxuriantly (crop, social activities).

rémban *reg* recovered (from illness).

rembang 1 ready to cut (sugarcane); 2 cutting time;

ngrembang to cut (sugarcane);

pangrembangan time for cutting sugarcane.

rembat shoulder pole (*kr for* pikul).

rèmbèl, - utangé deep in debt.

remben slow, undecided, hesitant.

rembeng a large basket.

rembes, ngrembes *or* mrembes 1 to ooze, seep; 2 *fig* to infiltrate;

rembesan oozing liquid, seepage;

rembesing madu *idiom* of noble blood.

rèmbès running, watery (eyes).

rembet, rembetan old clothes, rags, scraps.

rèmbèt, mrèmbèt to spread;

ngrèmbèti to spread to.

rembug I *ng*, rembag *kr* 1 topic of discussion; 2 advice, counsel; 3 opinion, proposal;

ngrembug to discuss, talk about;

ngrembugi to advise s.o., give s.o. one's opinion;

ngrembugaké to negotiate on behalf of s.o.;

rembugan 1 topic of discussion; 2 to engage in discussion;

pirembug, pirembugan consultation, deliberation;

sarembug in agreement.

II powder puff;

ngrembug to powder one's face.

rembulan moon. *See also* bulan, candra I.

rembulung the sago palm.

rembus *var of* rembes.

rembuwas-rembuwis to keep turning up to have a look.

rembuyuk, ngrembuyuk with luxuriant foliage.

rembuyung, ngrembuyung thick, dense, luxuriant.

rembuyut, ngrembuyut producing large quantities of fruit.

rembyah, ngrembyah 1 luxuriant, ubiquitous; 2 to flutter loosely;

rembyah-rembyah to keep waving.

rémbyak, ngrémbyak *or* rémbyak-rémbyak hanging down (long hair).

rembyang *var of* rembyah.

rémbyong, ngrémbyong to decorate with hanging foliage.

rembyung *var of* rembuyung.

remed broken into little pieces;

ngremed to wring, to twist, squeeze, crumple;

ngremedi *or* ngremed-remed to keep crumpling.

rèmèh insignificant, of little worth, trivial;

ngrèmèhaké to treat with contempt, look down on, consider of no importance.

remek broken into pieces;

ngremek to break into pieces, smash s.t.;

623

remekan smashed fragments.

remen 1 to take pleasure in (*kr for* **dhemen**); **2** pleased; to like (*kr for* **seneng**); **remenan 1** to be lovers; **2** s.t. one is fond of, hobby (*kr for* **senengan**).

remeng, remeng-remeng dim, vague, obscure.

remes, ngremes to squeeze, knead.

remet *see* **remed**.

remih, ngremih *or* **ngreremih** to woo, flatter.

remik, remikan *reg* chip snacks.

reming-reming turning yellow (stage in growth of rice plants).

remis I a variety of mussel.

II ½ cent (during the colonial period).

remit 1 (*or* **ngremit**) intricate, delicate, detailed; **2** wily, secretive, subtle.

rémong *var of* **rimong**.

rémot *reg* decayed, in a shambles.

rempag *reg* in agreement.

rempah 1 fried balls of mincemeat and grated coconut; **2** (*or* **rempah-rempah**) *reg* spices.

rempak broken to pieces (*var of* **remak**).

rempayak, ngrempayak luxuriant, covered with foliage.

remped bushy, overgrown.

rempeg *var of* **rampak**.

rempek *var of* **rampak**.

rèmpèl *var of* **rampal**.

rempela giblets.

rempelas 1 a certain tree with rough-textured leaves; **2** sandpaper; **ngrempelas** to sandpaper s.t.

rempelu gall; **ngrempelu, ora nyana ora -** to have no inkling; **ora duwé rempelu** to have no brains.

rempèyèk peanut biscuit fried in spiced rice flour. *Also* **pèyèk**.

rempit hidden, undercover, secret.

rempiyag *see* **rempiyeg**.

rempiyeg, ngrempiyeg aching in muscles and joints;

rempiyag-rempiyeg (to walk) slowly and painfully, as when convalescent.

rémpo feeble with old age.

rémpoh *var of* **rémpo**.

rempon *or* **rerempon** *lit* to cut each other to bits.

rempoyok, ngrempoyok *or* **rempoyokan** producing (large) foliage in great abundance.

rempu broken to pieces; **rempu-rempu** bruised and battered.

rempug *reg* even, all the same, with none differing from the others.

rempuh *var of* **rempu**.

rempuyuk *var of* **rembuyuk**.

rempyo *var of* **rompyo**.

remu, remu-remu beginning to ripen.

remujung a certain plant the leaves of which are used for treating kidney complaints (*also called* **kumis kucing**).

remuk broken into little pieces; **ngremuk** to break into pieces, crush, destroy; **remukan** little broken pieces.

remus, ngremus to eat s.t. crunchy. *See also* **kremus, kermus**.

remyeng *var of* **ramyang**.

rèn *see* **ri I, eri**.

rena I a certain small centipede.

II pleased, contented (*k.i. for* **bungah, seneng**); **ngrenani** to take pleasure in, cherish, enjoy; **karenan** pleased, delighted; **pirena** joy.

III *inf var of* **warna**.

réna *lit* mother.

renak-renuk to have a quiet, confidential talk.

rencah *reg var of* **rancah**.

rencak, ngrencak to divide up, split (*e.g.* loot).

rencaka *lit* trouble, anxiety; **ngrencaka** to cause trouble, anxiety.

rencana I plan, planning;
ngrencanakaké to plan s.t.
II, (or pangrencana) lit temptation.

rencang I completely recovered (esp after giving birth).
II reg widely spaced, at a distance from each other.

réncang 1 friend, companion (kr for kanca); 2 (domestic) helper; to help (kr for réwang); 3 servant (kr for batur I); 4 placenta.

rèncèk twigs, branches for firewood;
ngrèncèki to chop off twigs from branches;
rèncèkan cut firewood.

rencem 1 bruised inside; 2 having prickly skin sensations.

rèncèt fuss, bother.

réncog lame from weariness (animal).

rénda lace edging, crocheting;
ngrénda to crochet, make lace.

rèndèng leaves of the peanut plant (used as animal fodder).

rendhah low, humble.

rèndhèl one after another, in large numbers.

rendhem, ngrendhem to immerse, soak;
rendheman 1 act of soaking; 2 what is soaked.

rèndhèn foliage.

rendheng rainy season, west monsoon;
rendhengan (a crop) planted during the rainy season.

rendhet slow, sluggish, slack;
ngrendheti or ngrendhetaké to cause to be slow or slack.

rèndhèt, ngrèndhèt 1 to scratch (thorns); 2 - ati to treat s.o. meanly, hurt s.o.'s feelings;
kerèndhèt-rèndhèt to get scratched or pricked.

réndhon slow, sluggish;
reréndhonan slowly.

réné ng riki kr to this place, hither;
réna-réné to come here frequently;

mrènèkaké to bring s.t. here. See also mréné.

renes to be well off.

reng repr the sound of an engine revving.

rèng slat, batten to which roofing is attached; paku - roofing nail.

rengak-rengik see rengik.

rengat 1 a break, crack; 2 cracked, chapped.

rèngèd, ngrèngèd to have an arrogant manner;
rèngèd-rèngèd reg to be rowdy, hold a noisy gathering.

rengeng, rengeng-rengeng a soft singing or humming voice;
ngrengeng-rengengi or ngrengeng-rengengaké to sing softly to or for s.o.

rèngès reg to sit, stand in a row, rows.

renget clothes moth.

rengga, ngrengga to decorate;
ngrenggani to decorate, adorn; lit fig - praja to reign;
rinengga decorated;
renggan 1 a person to be looked after; 2 (or rerenggan) adornment.

renggang parted, separated, distant, estranged;
ngrenggangi to withdraw from (a friend);
ngrenggangaké 1 to pull s.t. apart; 2 to cause s.t. to be separated;
renggang gula kumepyur pulut prov (of friendship) intimate, close.

rengged reg messy, littered.

renggep way adroit (esp in manipulating puppets);
ngrenggep to grip, hold, handle.

rengges I, ngrengges to persuade, urge;
renggesan persuasive talk.
II, ngrengges to burn (a field) clean.

renggéto, ngrenggéto heavily laden, having to deal with a heavy burden.

renggi or rerenggi lit doubt, suspicion.

rengginang a fried sweet cake of glutinous rice.

renggiyek, ngrenggiyek heavy, burdensome.

rénggong, rénggong-rénggong or rerénggongan to stagger under a heavy burden.

renggos, renggos-renggos panting, out of breath. *See also* krenggos.

rénggot, rénggot-rénggot or rerénggotan to reel, sway, stagger (with sleep).

renggoto *var of* renggéto.

renggunuk *var of* regunuk.

renggut, ngrenggut to rip, jerk; to pull out.

rengih, ngrengih or ngrerengih to moan, groan, weep in pain;
rengih-rengih to plead pitifully, implore, beseech.

rengik, rengak-rengik to whine, whimper. *Also* ringik.

rengit a kind of small fly.

rengka 1 a crack, split, schism; 2 to split;
ngrengka or ngrengkani to split or crack s.t.;
ngrengkakaké to cause s.t. to split.

réngkad-réngkod to do grudgingly, go away in resentment.

rengkah *var of* rekah III.

réngkak-réngkok to keep twisting and turning the head (out of aversion).

rengkang (*or* wrengkang) obstinate, self-willed, headstrong.

rengked closely spaced;
ngrengkedi or ngrengkedaké to space closely;
kerengkeden too closely spaced.

rengkèg trouble, nuisance.

rèngkèk-rèngkèk to walk with a bent back.

rèngkèl, ngrèngkèl stubborn, obstinate.

rengkeng I (*or* wrengkeng) *var of* rengkang.
II, rengkeng-rengkeng (to get up) with difficulty (because of stiff muscles).

rengkèt, rengkèt-rengkèt squeaking or creaking sounds, *e.g.* of a bed. *See also* krengkèt.

rengkik, rengkik-rengkik slight, slender; thin, slim.

réngkod I, réngkad-réngkod to squeak, creak.
II *var of* rantang.

réngkok, réngkak-réngkok *see* réngkak.

réngkol, réngkol-réngkol full of twistings and turnings.

rengkong *reg* carrying-pole.

réngkong curved, crooked, bent (*var of* béngkong).

réngkot I *see* réngkod.
II a portable set of pots for carrying food.

rengkuh, ngrengkuh 1 to regard, think of (as); 2 to treat as;
pangrengkuh manner of treating;
rumengkuh to be kindly, cordial (toward s.o.).

rengkuk bowed down by a heavy burden.

rengkulu pillow (*var of* rangkulu).

rengos, rengos-rengos to gasp (for breath), pant.

rengreng stately, grand, dignified (*var of* ngengreng).

rèngrèng, ngrèngrèng 1 to draft (a document *etc*); 2 to draw a pattern outline onto fabric being worked in batik;
rèngrèngan 1 a rough (first) draft; 2 an outline.

réngsé *reg* finished, done with.

rèngsel *var of* rangsel.

rengu angry, sullen, resentful.

rèni *lit* woman, girl.

renik, renik-renik 1 cute, fine (ringlet); 2 cunning, subtlety.

renjah, ngrenjah to trample, crush underfoot.

renjak *var of* renjah.

rentah to fall (down, off, apart) (*kr for* runtuh).

rènte *var of* rènten.

rèntèg to drop off (*reg var of* rontog).

rèntèk with a serrated border.

rènten interest on money loaned;

ngrènteni to pay interest on;

ngrèntenaké to lend money at interest.

renteng *see* **ruwed**.

rèntèng strung together, forming a line or row;

rèntèng-rèntèng *or* **réntang-rèntèng** strung together;

ngrèntèng *or* **ngrèntèngi** to string together, form into a line.

rèntenir moneylender, loanshark.

rèntèp (*or* **rèntèp-rèntèp**) lined up in orderly rows.

rèntès to tell clearly;

ngrèntèsaké to explain s.t. clearly.

rentet closely spaced, tight.

rèntèt *var of* **rèntèng**.

rénto feeble with old age (*var of* **réto**).

renuk, renak-renuk to discuss in low voices.

renyah 1 crisp, crunchy; 2 (of voice) soft, sweet, clear.

renyak crushed, bruised;

ngrenyak to crush.

renyek *var of* **renyak**.

renyep soft and pleasant (music).

rényom *reg* talkative, to like talking.

renyuh *reg* brittle, fragile.

renyuk full of creases or wrinkles;

ngrenyuk to crease, wrinkle.

réok *see* **réyok**.

rep *or* **mak rep** *repr* going out (of fire, lamp).

repa *see* **rerepa**.

repak *var of* **rupak**.

rèpèh 1 not steep, easy to pass; 2 shallow, easy to cross (river).

rèpèk *or* **rerèpèk** to gather dry twigs (as firewood).

repèpèh, ngrepèpèh to sit cross-legged with bowed head;

repèpèh-repèpèh to approach humbly with bowed head.

repet, repet-repet the time just before sunrise, dawn, half-light.

repetisi a test (schoolwork); - **jèneral** dress rehearsal.

repi, rerepèn 1 short song, sung poetry (sung from memory); 2 letter;

ngrerepi to accompany with song;

ngrerepèkaké to sing for s.o.

repih, ngrepih *or* **ngrerepih** to calm or soothe s.o.

repit *var of* **rempit**.

répo feeble with old age (*var of* **réto**).

répoh *var of* **répo**.

repot a report;

ngrepotaké to report.

répot 1 busy, (hard-)pressed; 2 **aja répot-répot!** don't go to too much trouble!;

ngrépoti to be a burden to, cause inconvenience to s.o.;

ngrépotaké to cause a fuss, make difficulties for;

karépotan trouble, weighty responsibility.

rereb *var of* **lereb**.

rèrèh 1 to become calm; 2 to rest;

ngrèrèh to calm down;

ngrèrèhi to calm s.o.

rerem *lit* 1 to calm, quieten down; 2 to stand still, rest. *See also* **lerem**.

rèrèn to rest, take a break (*var of* **lèrèn**).

rerepa, ngrerepa 1 to speak sweetly (in an effort to please); 2 to ask humbly.

res (*or* **res-res**) dirt, grit;

ngeres 1 gritty to the touch; 2 grating to the ear; 3 heart-rending;

ngeres-eresi causing anguish.

rès I confinement, incarceration;

ngerès 1 to keep confined; 2 to punish. II cutting off (in circumcising);

ngerès to cut off (in circumcising).

resa *inf var of* **reksa**.

resados *reg kr for* **resaya**.

resah messy, disturbed (*kr for* **rusuh**).

resak damaged, out of order (*reg kr for* **rusak**).

resaya, ngresaya to ask s.o. for help;

pangresaya a request for help.

resban *var of* resbang

resbang bench for sitting (park bench-style piece of furniture).

reseh *reg* dirty, shabby.

resek dirty, untidy;
resekan rubbish, junk, clutter.

resep I ngresepi to enjoy, take delight in;
ngresepaké 1 pleasing (*esp* to the eye); 2 lovely, charming.
II, ngresep *or* rumesep to enter, seep in.

resèp 1 recipe; 2 medical prescription.

resèrse, resèrsir detective.

resi I hermit, ascetic holy man; -wara revered holy man.
II receipt.

résidhèn Resident (administrator);
karésidhènan residency, territory under the authority of a Resident;
residhènan the house, office of a Resident.

resik 1 clean, pure; 2 in order, fixed up; 3 net, clear;
resik-resik *or* reresik to do the cleaning;
ngresiki *or* ngresikaké to clean s.t. (up, out);
resikan 1 cleanly (by nature); 2 decent, proper.

resiya secret.

resmi I official, formal;
ngresmèkaké 1 to formalise; 2 to inaugurate, open officially.
II *lit* beauty; saresmi to enjoy the delights of love together;
ngresmèni to make love to.

Respati *lit* Thursday.

resrespoh a kind of small worm.

rèstan remains, remnants.

resu receipt.

resula I the sago palm.
II, ngresula to sigh, complain;
ngresulani to complain about.

rèt diamonds (playing-card suit).

reta *var of* rekta.

réta *var of* kréta.

rété baby crocodile (young of the baya). *See also* krété.

rètèp *var of* rèntèp.

reti *ng*, retos *kr*, *reg* meaning.

réting *reg* neat, pretty.

retna 1 diamond, precious gem, jewel; 2 *lit* girl, princess.

rètnong a kind of cicada that makes a loud chirping sound at the end of the wet season (contracted from cenggèrètnong).

réto *reg* feeble with old age.

retos *reg* meaning (*kr for* reti).

retu *or* reretu chaos, turmoil, disturbance.

réwa, réwa-réwa to pretend.

réwah *reg* difficulty, obstacle.

réwanda *lit* monkey.

réwang *ng*, réncang *kr*, 1 servant, (domestic) helper, companion; 2 to help s.o., *esp* with preparations for a celebration;
ngréwangi 1 to help s.o.; 2 to take steps, make efforts (in a certain direction, to achieve s.t.).

rèwed, ngrèwedi to disturb, bother.

rèweg *var of* rèwed.

rèwèl fussy, demanding, hard to handle.

rèwèng, ngrèwèng *or* ngrerèwèng *or* ngréwang-rèwèng to drag, tug, pull s.t. back and forth, from side to side.

rèwès, ngrèwès to heed, pay attention to.

réwo, réwo-réwo unkempt, slovenly (appearance).

réwok, ngréwok *or* réwok-réwok shaggy, bushy.

réwot *reg* in a difficult situation, having one's troubles;
ngréwoti to disturb, hamper.

réyab, réyab-réyab to sway, sweep (long hair).

réyang *reg* I, me.

rèyèng, ngrèyèng-rèyèng to beat up, assault (in a group).

réyog various performances, the best known that of Ponorogo, which features an enormous monster mask (**singabarong**) with peacock plumes; ngréyog to conduct this performance.

réyoh, ngréyoh to disparage, treat with contempt.

réyok I old, worn out, broken down; réyak-réyok on the verge of collapse. II *reg* scoop; ngréyok to take a big scoop of s.t.

réyong, reréyongan *or* réyang-réyong to drag the legs, trail along (walking wearily).

réyot shaky, wobbly, ready to collapse.

ri, eri I 1 thorn; 2 bone of a fish; ngeri 1 resembling a thorn, sharp, prickly; 2 (of writing) spiky; rèn, rènrènan a thorny place. II *lit* at, on, in.

riba usury, interest on money loaned.

ribed 1 in a difficult or unpleasant situation; 2 in distress; ngribedi 1 to disturb, hamper; 2 to cause s.o. distress; reribed 1 disturbance, obstacle; 2 unpleasantness, distress, difficulty. *See also* rubed.

ribèn *reg* leave it, I don't care! *See also* karebèn.

ribeng *lit* at one's wits' end.

ribig generally agreed, unanimous.

ribit *see* kribit.

ribug old and weak (gamecock).

ribut I 1 busy, rushed; 2 making a noise, disturbance; ngributi to disturb s.o. at work; ngributaké to cause a noisy disturbance. II angin ribut gale.

ricik I *reg* 1 to divide up; 2 to calculate; ricikan (extra) parts, requirements (for work, machine, game). II udan ricik-ricik soft, rustling rain. *See also* kricik.

ridhong, ridhong-ridhong to wear a cloth over the shoulders against the cold.

ridhu (*or* reridhu) disturbance, trouble, annoyance; ngridhoni 1 to disturb, bother, annoy; 2 to torment, plague.

rigal *var of* rigol.

rigèl *var of* rigol.

rigen skilful, resourceful, shrewd; ngrigen 1 to devise, form a plan; 2 to organise, regulate, put in order; ngrigenaké to take appropriate measures for.

rigèn flat woven bamboo tray.

rigih, rigih-rigih hesitant to touch s.t.

rigol *reg* to fall off (fruit).

rigrig *reg* to come loose, fall off.

rih, ngerih-rih 1 to calm (an angry person); to comfort (a sad person); 2 to persuade, coax. *See also* arih II.

rihadi *var of* riyadi.

rijal strange noises heard in the dead of night; **rijal al-ghaib** the 'Hidden Beings' who control human destinies.

rijig 1 neat and clean; 2 neatly arranged, well laid out.

rijol *reg* exchange item, replacement. *See also* ijol.

rijug to limp because one leg is shorter.

rik (*pron as:* ri:k) I (*or* mak rik) *repr* a scraping sound; ngerik (of cricket) to chirp.

rika I, ngrika in that place (*kr for* kana, rana); mrika to that place. II *reg* you, your.

rikala *lit* (at a past time) when.

rikat I fast, quick; ngrikataké to accelerate; rikatan *or* rikat-rikatan, *or* rerikatan in haste; sarikat-rikaté 1 no matter how fast; 2 as fast as possible. II rikat-rikat *reg* to pack up, clean up;

ngrikati to pack up (merchandise).

riki here; to this place (*kr for* kéné, réné).

rikma hair (*k.i. for* rambut). *See also* réma.

rikné *reg* because, in view of the fact that.

rikrik I to keep (doing) patiently.

II, ngrikrik *reg* to clear (land) of weeds.

riku there, that place (*kr of* kono);
ngriku in that place;
mriku to that place, thither (*kr of* rono).

rikuh *ng*, rekah *kr*, ill at ease, awkward, embarrassed;
rikah-rikuh to feel intensely uncomfortable;
ngrikuhi *or* ngrikuhaké to make s.o. uncomfortable, embarrass;
rikuhan awkward by nature.

ril rail, railway track.

rila wholeheartedly willing or in agreement; - legawa wholeheartedly willing;
ngrilani 1 to give permission; 2 to consent gladly;
ngrilakaké (to give, give up) willingly or with all one's heart.

rim I ream (500 sheets) of paper.

II leather belt.

III *var of* rèm.

rimab *reg* feverish (*kr for* rumab).

rimah house (*reg kr for* omah).

rimang I *lit* lovesick(ness), amorous feelings, sad or wistful longing.

II *reg* blurred, hazy.

rimat to care for (*root form: kr for* rumat).

rimba *lit* forest.

rimbag *gram* derived form;
ngrimbag to affix (a word);
rimbagan 1 an affix; 2 process of affixation; 3 affixed.

rimbas, ngrimbas to square wood with an adze.

rimis, rimis-rimis light rain (*var of* grimis). *See also* riwis.

rimong a cloth used for wrapping o.s. in, cloak.

rimpang branch of a tuber.

rimpil to crumble, break off;
ngrimpili to pick, pluck off.

rimpung lame.

rimpus, ngrimpus to tie together (feet).

rimuk, ngrimuk to persuade, talk s.o. into;
pangrimuk persuasion.

rina *ng*, rinten *kr*, 1 day (as contrasted with night); 2 rina wengi day and night. *See also* dina, raina.

rincag lame (because one leg is shorter than the other).

rinci, I ngrinci 1 to classify; 2 to specify (the details of);
rincèn detail, classification, specification.
See also princi.

II *reg* a kind of large basket.

rincik I fuss, ado.

II *var of* rinci.

rindhèk slow (*reg, var of* rindhik).

rindhik 1 slow; 2 soft, low (sound);
ngrindhikaké 1 to cause to be slow; 2 to make softer;
rindhik asu digitik *prov* quick as a flash.

rindhil to come pouring out one after the other.

rinding Jew's harp;
ngrinding 1 to play a Jew's harp; 2 to try to talk s.o. round.

ringa *lit* reringa, ringa-ringa cautious, wary, circumspect.

ringan *reg* light, easy.

ringas 1 wild, untamed; 2 lively, active; 3 sharp, alert, clever.

ringen gymnastic rings.

ringga hesitant, fearful.

ringgeng *reg* iron gamelan instruments.

ringgi, saringgi 1 sheaf (or 5 bundles) of newly harvested rice.

ringgit I shadow-play puppet (*kr for* **wayang**);

pringgitan, paringgitan section of a traditional house (between the **pendhapa** and the main section) where shadow-plays are performed.

II 2½ rupiahs.

ringih, ringih-ringih jagged, with sharp points.

ringik, ngringik *or* **ringik-ringik** to whine, whimper, complain.

ringin (*or* **wringin**) banyan tree; - **kurung** fenced banyan trees in the square on the north and south of the palaces. *See also* **waringin**.

ringkel I, **ngringkel, ringkelan** (to lie, sleep) curled up.

II time of evil portent reckoned astrologically by the days of the six-day week; - **jalma** a day of evil portent for human beings;

paringkelan system of reckoning by days of the six-day week.

ringkes concise, compact;

ngringkes to make concise, compact;

ngringkesi 1 (*or* **ringkes-ringkes**) to pack up, tidy up; 2 to simplify;

ngringkesaké to make concise, make s.t. occupy less space, shorten;

ringkesan shortened, simplified form;

ringkesé in short, to put it briefly.

ringkih weak, feeble, lacking strength (firmness, stamina);

ngringkihaké to weaken, make weak.

ringkot *var of* **réngkot**.

ringkud, ngringkud to gather up and pack away.

ringkuk, ngringkuk 1 to be bent over (under a burden); 2 *fig* confined to a prison.

ringkus, ngringkus to catch by binding the limbs;

mringkus 1 bent over; stooped; 2 to shrink, curl up.

ringong *lit* I, me.

ringring, ngringringi to calm s.o. down.

ringut, ringuten mad, raving, furious.

rini *lit* woman, girl.

rinjing large bamboo basket.

rintang, rintangan obstacle, hindrance.

rinten day (as contrasted with night) (*kr for* **rina**).

rintih, ngrintih *or* **ngrerintih** to moan, weep in pain.

rintik, rintik-rintik I with infrequent drops, drizzling (rain).

II with a serrated border (*var of* **rèntèk**).

rintip (*or* **rintip-rintip**) lined up, in a row. *Also* **rèntèp**.

rintis, ngrintis to pioneer, lead the way;

rintisan pioneering action.

rinto *var of* **réto**.

ripah *see* **gemah**.

ripak narrow, restricted, confined (*reg kr for* **rupak**).

ripik (*or* **ripik-ripik**) to fetch sticks and twigs, *esp* for kindling;

ripikan kindling wood.

ripta, ngripta to compose, write, create;

riptan *or* **reriptan** poetic writing, musical composition;

pangripta composer, author.

ripu *lit* enemy.

ripuh *reg* troublesome.

ripuk, ripak-ripuk *reg* soaking wet.

ririh 1 to calm down, control one's anger; 2 *lit* (of sounds) soft, low. *See also* **lirih**.

ririp hurt, injured, wounded.

riris, udan - *lit* light rain.

ris 1 boundary line marked with a rope (*see also* **aris** II); 2 *reg* low boundary wall;

ngerisi 1 to mark a boundary line with a rope; 2 to build a boundary wall.

risak damaged, out of order, not functioning (*kr for* **rusak**).

risaksana *lit* then, after that.

risalat message, missive, letter.

risang *lit honorific marker for a king*: risang prabu. *See also* sang.

risdhèn *var of* résidhèn.

risi to feel aversion, revulsion, distaste; ngrisèni *or* nggrisèni repulsive, irritating.

risidhèn *var of* résidhèn.

risig *var of* rijig.

risih *var of* risi.

risoles a roll containing meat or chicken.

rispis guilder (during the colonial period).

risuh, ngrisuhi to trouble, pester, plague.

rit I trip, run, journey (bus).
   II, ngeriti to cut grass with a sickle; ngeritaké to cut grass for s.o. with a sickle. *See also* arit I.

ritak let it go; I don't care.

ritèk *var of* ritak.

riti, riti-riti with a serrated border. *See also* rintik II.

ritslèteng zipper.

riwa-riwi to keep going back and forth (*var of* wira-wiri).

riwé sweat (*k.i. for* kringet); riwènen sweating.

riwed, ngriwedi to be a bother to, disturb, interfere with; riwedan pest, nuisance.

riweg *var of* riwed.

riweng at one's wits' end.

riwi *see* riwa-riwi.

riwih, riwih-riwih to trickle down, out.

riwik *var of* riwih.

riwil *var of* rèwèl.

riwis, riwis-riwis the steady rush of rain; ngriwis steady and gentle (rain).

riwug I, riwug-riwug shaggy (hair).
   II, *var of* riwed.

riwuk nuisance; ngriwuki to disturb.

riwus, riwusé *or* riwusnya *lit* after.

riwut *var of* ribut.

riya *title of a man of high nobility* (*also* arya).

riyadi *kr for* riyaya.

riyah, riyah-riyah bright, glowing (colours).

riyaya *ng*, riyadi *kr*, communal feast to celebrate the main Muslim holiday (Lebaran) held at the end of the Fasting Month (Pasa).

riyak *ng*, jlagra *k.i.*, phlegm (from the chest); ngriyaki to expectorate.

riyek, ngriyek-riyek 1 to crunch into pieces; 2 to crumple; riyek menthek joto kemil words repeated over and over in sequence to test one's luck.

riyel, jejel-riyel crowded, teeming with people.

riyep I *var of* liyep.
   II, riyep-riyep *intsfr* bright green. *See also* riyo.

riyin 1 formerly (*md for* biyèn); 2 first, ahead (*md for* dhisik).

riyo, riyo-riyo *intsfr* bright green.

riyon *reg* relaxing and chatting together.

riyug, riyug-riyug *or* riyag-riyug to stumble, totter.

riyuh *reg* noisy, boisterous.

riyuk *reg* tumbledown, ruinous, dilapidated.

riyung, ngriyung *reg* to snatch everything, pocket the lot.

ro *ng*, two (*shtf of* loro); robelah 150; rolas twelve; rolikur twenty-two.

rob to rise (of water level, *e.g.* during a flood, when the tide comes in); karoban to get flooded.

robah, ngrobah to change, alter; robahan a change, difference.

robak-rabèk in tatters, torn to shreds.

robat-rabèt *var of* robak-rabèk.

robaya *lit* I, me, my.

robelah *see* ro.

robèt a torn piece of cloth;

ngrobèt to tear to shreds.

robyok, ngrobyok to take part in profi-
teering.

robyong decorative hanging object;
ngrobyongi or ngrobyong-robyong to
decorate with hanging objects.

rocoh var of trocoh.

rocok var of krocok I.

rod to ebb, recede.

roda, ngroda, ngrodapeksa to force; to
rape;
pangrodapeksa force, violence.

rodha wheel.

rodhong tobacco plant shade/screen.

rodok reg somewhat, quite; (quite) a bit
(var of rada)

rodra lit fierce, wild.

rog, ngerog or ngerog-rog to shake (tree,
to make fruit fall);
rog-rogan shivering, shaking.

roga lit sickness.

rogoh, ngrogoh to reach for s.t., grope,
search (in pocket, bag);
rogoh-rogoh to keep putting the hand
into s.t., grope repeatedly in s.t.

rogol var of rigol.

rogrog to fall down/off (var of gogrog);
udan rogrog asem idiom drizzle.

rogul var of rigol.

roh soul, spirit; Roh Suci the Holy
Ghost.

roham-rahèm reg 1 in disarray, in a mess;
2 smashed to smithereens.

rohani spiritual, of the mind or soul;
karohanian matters pertaining to the
spirit.

rohmat var of rahmat.

rojèng, ngrojèng to steal rice by cutting it
in the field.

rojod var of rujad.

rojoh reg a small mortar for pounding
betel.

rojong, ngrojongi 1 to agree with, side
with, take the part of; 2 to approve of.

rok Western-style dress or skirt;

1 rok-rokan to wear such a dress; 2 reg
to play hide-and-seek.

rokèl reg bumpy, bad (road).

rokok, ses kr, cigarette;
ngrokok 1 to smoke a cigarette; 2 to
smoke s.t.; 3 to be a cigarette addict;
rokokan to have a casual smoke;
rokok-rokokan to sit around smoking
and chatting together;
ngrokok cendhak idiom inquisitive.

rol I role, function.
II a roll(ed-up object);
ngerol to roll s.t. (up).

rolade slices of spiced beef rolled with
egg.

rolah curb, embankment.

rolak var of rolah.

rolis roll-call; ngrolis to call the roll.

roma (reg kr for rambut) hair.

romal reg headcloth.

roman I modern fiction, novel.
II, roman-romanan to have a romantic
relationship.

rombak ng, rémbak kr, ngrombak 1 to
demolish; 2 to dig up (a crop).

rombang-rambing in tatters, torn to
shreds.

rombèng second-hand, used;
ngrombèngaké to sell second-hand
(for s.o.);
rombèngan second-hand (goods).

rombong a kind of large basket.

romé reg lively, busy.

romèd, ngromèd to rant, rave, speak
deliriously.

romèh var of romèd.

romès, ngromès to heed, pay attention
to.

romot reg dirt, rubbish.

rompal knocked out, broken (row of
teeth).

rompang var of rompal.

rompi man's vest (Western-style);

rompod bushy, thickly overgrown. See
also remped.

rompok a small hut.

rompya *var of* rompyoh.

rompyo, ngrompyo-rompyo to edge with a fringe (fancy clothing).

rompyoh, rompyoh-rompyoh to hang in bunches, tresses (leaves, hair).

ron leaf (*kr for* godhong).

roncé, ngroncé *or* ngroncèni to thread, string;

    roncèn a string (beads, flowers).

roncot *reg* to fall apart.

rondha the rounds (nightwatch);

    ngrondhani to do the rounds, keep watch over;

    pangrondhan nightwatchman's post.

rondhé hot ginger-flavoured drink containing small round glutinous rice-balls, sometimes with peanuts and/or palm kernels.

rondhon *reg* leaf.

rong I hole, hollow (used as a home by some creature);

    ngerong 1 to enter a hole; 2 (*or* ngerongi) to live in a hole; 3 to make a hole in s.t.

    II, two (*as modifier*); - puluh 20, - atus 200, - èwu 2,000.

rongèh restless, unable to sit still.

ronggah, ronggah-ronggah broad, chunky (body).

ronggé *reg* ear (of rice, corn);

    ronggèn in (the form of) ears.

ronggèng *reg* dancing-girl (paid by male partners).

ronggos hairy, shaggy, bushy.

ronggot *var of* ronggos.

ronggung jiwan awkward (*shtc of* loro tanggung siji kedawan: two is too short, one is too long).

rongkob thickly overhanging, dense (foliage, forest);

    ngrongkob to overhang thickly.

rongkong 1 rump, rumpbone (of roast fowl); 2 the space between breastbone and tailbone (of fowl); 3 the space between the ribs (human being).

rongsok, rongsokan junk, second-hand goods.

ronjat, ngronjati to leap up and reach for s.t. high (over one's head).

rono ng, riku kr, (*or* mrono) to that place;

    mronokaké to move s.t. toward that place;

    rona-rono to move to that place repeatedly.

rontang-ranting tattered, ragged, in shreds.

rontèk a small banner affixed to a spear just below the point.

rontog to fall, drop off (flowers, leaves, fruit);

    ngrontogi to remove (leaves, fruits);

    ngrontogaké to cause s.t. to fall;

    rontogan fallen;

    rontog atiné heartbroken;

    mangsa rontog autumn.

ronyok, suweng - a type of ear ornament which has a large diamond in the centre and two rows of smaller ones set around it.

ropal a vegetable dye giving a dark brown colour.

ropèk delicate, slightly built.

ropel double(d);

    ngropel to double (things) up.

ropéya, ngropéya *reg* to take care of, pay attention to.

ropoh barricade, barrier;

    ngropohi to barricade, block.

ropyan, ropyan-ropyan to celebrate, feast.

roro *lit* two. *See also* ro, loro.

ros 1 joint, section, internode, segment (bamboo, sugarcane); 2 the main point, essentials (of letter, case);

    ngeros up to or at the joint;

    ngerosi 1 to cut off at the joint; 2 to explain point by point;

    rosan sugarcane (*kr for* tebu);

ros-rosan knuckle, joint.

rosa strong, powerful;
ngrosani 1 to exert force on s.t.; 2 to lend strength to, support strongly;
karosan strength, prowess;
sarosané with all one's strength, to the limit of one's strength.

rosan sugarcane (*kr for* **tebu**). *See also* **ros**.

rosok worn out (from much use, metal objects);
rosokan junk, worn out objects, old iron.

roster I grid, grating, grille.
II roster, schedule, timetable.

rota *lit* fierce; **-denawa** a fierce ogre.

rotan rattan.

rotèng 12½ cents (during the colonial period) (*shtf of* **karo tèng**).

roti bread, cake, biscuit; **- kismis** currant bread; **- panggang** toast.

rotuh *reg var of* **runtuh**.

rowa sizeable, bulky, extensive; **rowan-rowan** elaborate, large-scale (celebration).

rowak-rawèk in tatters, torn to shreds.

rowan *reg* old, worn out (animals for slaughter).

rowang *lit* companion, helper. *See also* **réwang**.

rowé, rowé-rowé hanging loose, trailing.

royah, royah-royah rapacious, wild, indiscriminate.

royak-rayèk ruinous, tumbledown.

royal 1 generous, extravagant; 2 sexually promiscuous;
royal-royalan 1 to splurge; 2 to indulge one's tastes frequently.

royo, royo-royo *intsfr* bright green.

royok, ngroyok 1 to attack in numbers, from all sides; 2 to tackle (a job) together;
royokan 1 to set on s.o. in numbers; 2 to scramble to get s.t. *See also* **kroyok**.

royom *var of* **royong**.

royong *see* **gotong**.

royot subordinate people (*var of* **rayat**).

ru I land measure, a square Rhenish rod, *ca* 14.19 square metres.
II *lit* arrow,

ruba *or* **reruba** a present to appease s.o., bribe;
ngrubani to try to buy over, bribe;
ngrubakaké to give s.t. as a bribe.

rubed *reg* disturbance, obstacle;
ngrubedi to hamper, disturb.

rubéda obstacle, difficulty, misfortune.

rubes *reg* 1 bustling; 2 confused; 3 heavy going (road).

rubiyah *lit* a God-fearing, devout woman, wife.

rubiru *see* **arubiru**.

rubrik 1 category; 2 column (in paper, magazine).

rubuh *ng*, **rebah** *kr*, fallen; to fall flat, collapse;
ngrubuhi to fall on;
ngrubuhaké to cause to collapse, bring about the fall of s.t.;
rubuhan fallen (tree);
rubuh-rubuh gedhang *idiom* to observe and imitate others (*esp* during religious rituals);
ambata rubuh 'like collapsing bricks', tumultuous (of loud applause).

rubuk *reg* 1 equal, shared evenly; 2 worth the trouble.

rubung, ngrubung to gather around;
rubung-rubung to form a crowd.

rucah low, common, insignificant.

rucat taken apart, dismantled;
ngrucat 1 to take apart, dismantle; 2 to break up; 3 to take off (clothes); 4 to dismiss from (office), deprive of (rank, position).

rucek (of writing) scribbled, scrawled.

ruci *reg* fiery, quick-tempered.

rucuh a refreshing drink, made from grated coconut mixed with brown sugar;

ngrucuh to prepare such a drink.

rudah *lit* sad, sorrowful.

rudatin *ng*, rudatos *kr*, sad, sorrowful, worried;

pangrudatin sadness, sorrow, anxiety.

rudatos *kr for* rudatin.

rudet tangled, complicated, confused (*var of* ruwed).

rudhapeksa, ngrudhapeksa to force, compel.

rudira *lit* blood.

rudita *lit* sad, sorrowful.

rujad damaged, useless (because it has fallen apart);

ngrujad to put apart, ruin. *See also* bujad, rucat.

rujag I, ngrujag to hold fast and force to do s.t., rape.

II, ngrujag 1 to draw freehand, without a model; 2 to batik without a pattern;

rujagan s.t. drawn without a pattern.

rujak a salad of chopped unripe fruit with a hot sauce;

ngrujak to make (fruits) into the above;

ngrujaki to contribute to preparing food for a special occasion;

rujakan 1 to prepare and eat rujak together, *i.e.* have a little party; 2 ingredients for the above dish;

rumujak (fruits) just at the right stage (*i.e.* not too ripe);

ngrujak wuni 1 to buy or sell as a group rather than as individual items; 2 to serve a dish consisting of rice with some side dishes on one plate.

ruji 1 window bars; 2 wheel spokes;

rujèn with bars (window).

rujit, ngrujit to cut, slash;

rinujit-rujit deeply hurt.

ruju *reg* youngest child in a family, the last-born. *See also* waruju.

rujuk 1 to agree, consent; 2 to become reconciled after the first (preliminary) stage of divorce;

ngrujuki to agree to. *See also* sarujuk.

rug *lit* to fall down, fall in, collapse.

rugi to suffer a financial loss;

ngrugèkaké to cause s.o. to suffer a loss;

karugian a loss, setback.

rugol *reg* to fall (down, off) (*var of* rigol).

rugrug *reg* to slide, fall down, collapse.

rugul, ngrugul to force, compel.

ruh I to see; to know (*shtf of* weruh).

II, ngeruh-ruhi to greet, speak with/to in a friendly way (*var of* ngaruh-aruhi, *see* aruh).

ruhara *var of* aruara.

ruk (*pron as:* ru:k) *or* mak ruk *repr* scraping out.

rukem a certain tree and its fruits.

ruket 1 closely attached, pressed close together (embrace); 2 prang - hand-to-hand (fighting);

ngruket to associate closely (friends), stick together.

rukma *var of* rukmi.

rukmi *lit* gold.

rukon to join forces, be unanimous, agreed. *See also* gendhon III.

ruksa *lit* damaged, out of order, destroyed.

rukti, ngrukti to make ready, provide;

ngruktèni to provide with, fit out.

rukuh white prayer robe for female Muslims.

rukuk to bow with the hands on the knees (one of the Islamic praying positions).

rukun at peace with one another, reconciled, harmonious;

ngrukunaké to reconcile, restore harmony (between people);

rukunan *or* rerukunan 1 to live in peace and harmony with each other; 2 to come to a mutual agreement.

rum I *lit* fragrant. *See also* arum.

II Roman; angka - Roman numeral.

rumab *reg* 1 fever, feverish; 2 (of an illness) to recur, have a relapse.

rumabasa *lit* to overwhelm.

rumah *reg, var of* **omah**.

rumangsa *ng,* **rumaos** *kr* 1 to be aware; 2 to feel, think;
ngrumangsani to realise, become aware of. *See also* **rasa**.

rumaos (*kr for* **rumangsa**).

rumasa *var of* **rumangsa**.

rumat *ng,* **rimat** *kr,* **ngrumat** to take care of;
ngrumati 1 to look after, tend, provide sustenance for; 2 to keep, put away carefully;
kerumat well cared for, well kept.

rumbah *reg* vegetables.

rumbu, isih rumbu-rumbu not yet completely recovered.

rumbuk *var of* **rumbut**.

rumbut overgrown, full of weeds.

rumembé *lit* to put out buds, sprout.

rumil *reg* to keep nagging.

rumiyin 1 formerly, in the past (*kr for* biyèn); 2 first, ahead (*kr for* **dhisik**).

rumpak destroyed.

rumpek I *var of* **rumpak**.
II *var of* **rupek**.

rumpaka, ngrumpaka *lit* 1 to describe or narrate in poetry; 2 to write, compose poetry;
rumpakan 1 a poetic description; 2 poetry.

rumpi *var of* **rompi**.

rumpil 1 rough, hard to travel (road); 2 difficult, hard to organise.

rumpu bushes or branches used to block a passage;
rumpon fish trap consisting of a pool blocked off with bushes or branches.

rumpuk *reg, var of* **tumpuk**.

rumpung 1 with a piece missing; 2 missing a part of the body.

rumput grass (*kr for* **suket**).

rumuhun *lit* 1 formerly; 2 first. *See also* **rumiyin**.

runcang-runcung *var of* **runtang-runtung**. *See* **runtung**.

runcat *var of* **rucat**.

runcung *var of* **runtung**.

rundah *lit* sad, sorrowful.

rundha *var of* **rondha**.

rundhing, ngrundhing to discuss, negotiate;
ngrundhingaké to negotiate on behalf of s.o.;
rundhingan 1 discussion, negotiation; 2 to discuss, negotiate.

rundhuk, ngrundhuk to sneak up on, catch off-guard.

rungak, rungak-rungak startled and confused.

runggé *var of* **runggi**.

runggi *see* **sanggarunggi**.

runggud *var of* **rungkud**.

rungih, ngrungih pointed, tapering (nose).

rungkad *or* **mrungkad** torn out by the roots, uprooted;
ngrungkad to tear out by the roots.

rungkeb, ngrungkeb (lying) face down;
ngrungkebi 1 to cover s.t. with one's body, lie on; 2 to lie face-down on (*e.g.* feet, as a sign of devotion);
krungkeb to fall flat on one's face.

rungkil bumpy (street).

rungkud thick, dense (undergrowth);
rerungkudan densely overgrown area.

rungkuk, ngrungkuk bent, bowed (the back).

rungkup, ngrungkup (bandits) to take by surprise (at home).

rungrum, ngrungrum to address with sweet words, cajole, coax;
pangrungrum words of endearment, cajolement.

rungseb barely passable.

rungseg *var of* **ruseg**.

rungsit *lit* dangerous, unsafe to walk on, difficult of access. *See also* **rusit**.

rungu *ng,* **pireng** *kr,* **ngrungu** to hear;

ngrungoni to have s.o. hear s.t., communicate s.t. to s.o.;

ngrungokaké to hear or listen (to);

krungu (**mireng** *kr*, **midhanget** *k.i.*) to hear;

rungon to have a keen sense of hearing;

rungon-rungonen to keep hearing over and over in the mind;

pangrungu 1 sense of hearing; 2 what is heard.

runjah, runjah-runjah to jump with joy.

runjak, ngrunjak to jump up in an effort to reach s.t. (*var of* **lunjak**).

runjang, ngrunjang 1 to rush upon, storm; 2 to run counter to.

runjung pointed (roof shape).

runtag 1 a strong shaking (inside s.t.); 2 turbulence, unrest.

runtah 1 dirt on the ground; 2 *reg* spilled or poured out, spilled everywhere;

ngruntahi to spill on s.t.;

ngruntahaké to spill s.t. out, shed s.t.

runtang, runtang-runtung *see* **runtung**.

runtik *lit* enraged.

runting, ngrunting to tear up, mangle.

runtuh *ng*, **rentah** *kr*, to fall (down, off, apart);

ngruntuhi to drop or fall on(to);

ngruntuhaké to drop s.t., cause s.t. to fall, come apart;

runtuhan fallen (*e.g.* fruit);

karuntuhan to be hit by a falling object.

runtung, runtung-runtung *or* **runtang-runtung** *or* **reruntungan** always together, one after the other.

runtut 1 belonging together, matching; 2 **atut** - living together in harmony; 3 harmonious (musical instruments);

ngruntutaké to bring into harmony with each other.

rupa *ng*, **rupi** *kr*, 1 appearance; 2 kind, shape; 3 colour;

rupamu (*term of abuse*) 'you fancy yourself!';

rupa-rupa various, of all kinds;

sarupané all kinds of;

rerupan an unusual, strange shape;

rupa dudu rupa *idiom* a strange-looking object.

rupak narrow, restricted, confined;

ngrupak to limit, restrict;

rupak jagadé *idiom* to see no way out;

rupak segarané *idiom* of limited patience or forgiveness.

rupek *var of* **rupak**.

rupi appearance; kind; colour (*kr for* **rupa**).

rupit small, narrow (path).

rupiyah the rupiah, Indonesian unit of currency;

ngrupiyahaké to change foreign currency into rupiahs;

rupiyahan 1 in the form of 1-rupiah notes; 2 notes in a certain denomination of rupiahs.

rurah, ngrurah *or* **mangrurah** *lit* to destroy, wipe out;

pangrurah weapon for destroying (enemy).

rurek to come to blows.

ruru *var of* **luru II**.

rurub *var of* **lurub**.

ruruh *var of* **luruh I**.

rus rose (flower).

rusak damaged, out of order, not functioning;

ngrusak to damage, ruin;

ngrerusak to lay waste, destroy and plunder;

ngrusaki to do harm to;

ngrusakaké to damage inadvertently;

karusakan 1 damage; 2 to get damaged.

rusban *var of* **resbang**.

ruseg crowded, noisy, disorganised, messy;

ngrusegi to bother, make things unpleasant.

rusiku *lit* resentment, rancour, spite.

rusit *lit* dangerous, unsafe.

rusiya *var of* **resiya**.

rusoh *reg var of* **rusuh**.

rusuh *ng*, **resah** *kr* 1 disturbed, unsafe; 2 untidy;

ngrusuhi to disturb, bother;

rerusuh 1 trouble, disturbance; 2 troublemaker.

rut, ngerut to tie s.t. to;

rut-rutan *or* **pangerut** way of tying.

ruwag, ngruwag *reg* to pull apart;

ruwag-ruwag *reg* 1 broken; 2 disorderly, unruly.

ruwah 1 8th month of the Islamic calendar, in which graveyards are cleaned and offerings made to deceased family members; 2 *reg* anniversary of a death;

ruwahan a ritual meal held during the month of Ruwah.

ruwat, ngruwat to release from a divine punishment (misshapen, demonic form), to exorcise, free from the threat of divine anger;

ruwatan a ceremony (special wayang performance) held as an act of exorcism, to protect a threatened person (*e.g.* an only child).

ruwed tangled, complicated, confused; - **renteng** 1 turbulence, disturbances, problems; 2 stunned, dismayed;

ngruwedi *or* **ngruwedaké** to snarl, complicate, confuse; **ngruwedi ati** to make one's head reel.

ruwèg, ruwèg-ruwèg untidy, unkempt.

ruwil *reg* stingy, miserly.

ruwing kupingé (to hear) buzzing in the ears.

ruwit delicate, exquisite;

ngruwit finely worked, ingenious.

ruwog *var of* **ruwèg**.

ruyung wood of the sugar-palm, *i.e.* commonplace wood, used as a rough building material.

rwa *lit* two.

S

sab I *reg* **1** reason, cause; **2** because. *See also* **sabab**.

II, ngesab *reg* to warm up (steamed rice).

III, ora sabé *reg* dead set against, unwilling.

saba 1 (of animals; *cr* of people) to stray, wander around; **2** to be often found in a place;

nyaba *or* **nyabani** to visit frequently, hang around;

saban *or* **pasaban 1** place where animals are let loose; **2** haunt, place frequented.

sabab 1 reason, cause; **2** because. *Also* **sebab**.

sabak school slate.

Sa'ban 8th month of the Islamic calendar. *See also* **ruwah**.

sabar patient, stoical, tolerant, long-suffering; **-drana** patient by nature; **-subur** all things come to him who waits; **- tawakal 1** resignation; **2** to trust in God who orders everything;

nyabari to be patient with/about;

nyabaraké to keep o.s. under control;

kasabaran patience, self-control.

sabat I close friend, companion.

II the Sabbath.

sabawa *lit* sound, noise, sign of life;

nyabawa to make a noise. *See also* **bawa III**.

sabda *lit* what s.o. says; words, speech;

nabda *lit* to speak;

nyabdani to pronounce (powerful words, blessing) over s.o.; **sadba pandhita ratu** *idiom* a promise that cannot be broken.

sabeg *reg* full, satiated.

saben 1 every, each;

sabené usually; **kaya -** as usual;

saben-saben again and again, every time.

sabet 1 a whip, lash; **2** sword (*k.i. for* **pedhang**);

nyabet to whip;

nyabeti to whip frequently;

nyabetaké to swing s.t. as a whip at/onto;

sabetan *way* manipulation of shadow-play puppets during wayang performance.

sabil, prang - 1 holy war; **2** the struggle to defeat one's passions;

nyabili 1 to become a martyr to, sacrifice o.s. for; **2** to fight down (temptation *etc*).

sabilullah 'God's path'; in God's cause.

sabin ricefield (*kr for* **sawah**).

sablog *var of* **sablug**.

sablug, dandang sablugan a one-piece rice steamer in which rice rests on a perforated metal sheet above the water.

sabran *reg* every, each. *See also* **saben**.

sabrang I 1 the other side (of river, street); **2** overseas, foreign;

nyabrang 1 to go across; **2** across from;

nyabrangi 1 to cross s.t.; **2** to go across s.t.;

nyabrangaké to transport across, help s.o. to go across;

sabrangan 1 the other side; **2** characterised by being foreign;

panyabrangan (*or* **sabrangan**) place for crossing a river, ferry, ford.

II *reg* a variety of cassava.

III *reg* chili pepper.

sabruk pyjamas.

Sabtu Saturday (*var of* **Setu**).

sabuk I *ng, kr,* **paningset** *k.i.* sash, cloth sash worn by males as a part of their Javanese-style dress, or by market sellers to stow money;
nyabuk to put a sash on s.o.;
sabukan to wear a sash.
II a measure of polished rice (5 kati).

sabun soap;
nyabun 1 to wash s.o./s.t. with soap; 2 *fig* to connive with s.o. to do s.t. illegal, bribe;
nyabuni to lather;
sabunan to soap o.s.

sacemit a tiny bit.

sacemlik a little, a bit.

sacléraman *see* **cléram.**

saclèrètan *see* **clèrèt.**

sacretan *see* **cret.**

sacublik *var of* **sacemlik.**

sacumlik *var of* **sacemlik.**

sacumbana *lit* to have sexual intercourse. *See also* **cumbana.**

sacuplik *var of* **sacemlik.**

sad *lit* six.

sada main rib of a palm leaf; - **lanang** magic wand.

sadak a betel leaf rolled into a point containing lime, for chewing (thrown down by both bride and groom at the moment they meet at the wedding ceremony).

sadana *lit* money, property, wealth.

sadariyah Arab man's wear, 'breast-jacket'.

sadarum *lit* all.

sadasa ten (*kr for* **sapuluh**). *See also* **dasa.**

sadat *see* **sahadat.**

sadaya all (*kr for* **kabèh**). *Also* **sedaya.**

sadé to sell (*kr for* **adol, dodol**).

sadhang I fan-palm.
II, nyadhangi to try to restrain, check.

sadhar to realise, be aware;
nyadhari to realise, become aware of;
nyadharaké 1 to remind, warn; 2 to bring back to consciousness, to revive;
kasadharan consciousness, awareness.

sadheg I, sadhegan 1 tobacco mixture; **2** powder (medicine).
II sadhegan chin (*reg k.i. for* **janggut**).

sadhel bicycle seat.

sadhéla a moment, a short while.

sadhèng fan-palm (*var of* **sadhang I**).

sadhèrèk sibling; relative (*kr for* **sadulur**).

sadhiya to prepare, have available;
nyadhiyani to make ready or available for s.o.;
nyadhiyakaké to provide, lay out;
sumadhiya to be in readiness;
sadhiyan 1 stock, supply; 2 available, ready for. *Also* **sedhiya.**

sadho I a kind of two-wheeled horse-drawn cart (dos-à-dos, 'back-to-back').
II, nyadho to plant rice in the dry season;
sadhoan *or* sadhon dry season rice-planting.

sadhu two-wheeled horse-drawn cart (*var of* **sadho I**).

sadhuk I, nyadhuk to kick; **2** *reg* to slap s.o. in the stomach.
II handkerchief (*var of* **sakdhuk**).

sadi rather, somewhat; - **réné** move this way a bit!

sadrah, ora sadrah ing angin *lit* not the slightest.

sadran, nyadran to make offerings at a family ancestral grave during the month of Ruwah; to visit and maintain ancestral graves;
sadranan the offering of flowers and incense at the graves of ancestors;
panyadranan place where such offerings are made.

sadu *lit* virtuous, pure, holy.

sadulur *ng,* **sadhèrèk** *kr,* **1** sibling; **2** relatives; - **suson** half-sibling nursed by the same mother;

nyedulur *or* sumadulur friendly, outgoing;

nyeduluraké to treat or regard s.o. as a relative;

seduluran being close friends;

paseduluran relationship, friendship, brotherhood;

saseduluré together with one's relatives;

sedulur tunggal kringkel/welad children of the same parents.

sadur *reg* replacement, substitute.

saé 1 good, nice, attractive (*kr for* apik); 2 good, advisable (*kr for* becik).

saékong *var of* saéngkong.

saèng, nyaèng-nyaèng *reg* to discriminate between.

saéngga 1 until, up to; 2 with the result that...; 3 *lit* like, as; as if, as though; saénggané if, supposing that.

saéngkong *reg* a variety of cassava.

saèstu *see* èstu.

saga a certain trailing shrub with small round aromatic leaves (sometimes used as tea) and small red-and-black beans; - thuntheng a black variety, having sweet leaves and red-and-black beans.

sagah willing, able (*kr for* saguh).

saged can, to be able (*kr for* bisa).

sagu sago (tree);

sagon a crumbly biscuit of coconut and sago.

saguh *ng*, sagah *kr*, 1 willing, able; 2 to agree to (do s.t.);

nyaguhi to promise, agree to s.t.;

sumaguh to act as though willing to do s.t.;

kasaguhan an agreement, a promise.

sagon coconut biscuit.

sagotra *lit var of* sagotrah.

sagotrah nuclear family: parents with children. *See also* gotrah.

sah I 1 valid, legitimate, legal; 2 paid up, paid in full;

ngesahi 1 to pay up, pay in full; 2 to legalise (one's wife);

ngesahaké to validate.

II separate (*shtf of* pisah).

saha *lit* and, with, as well as.

sahabat a close friend (*var of* sakabat).

sahadat the Islamic profession of faith. *Also* sadat.

sahal *reg* an instant, that very instant, for a moment. *See also* sakal, kal I.

sahbandar harbour master, head of the port authority.

sahid religious martyr.

sahwat sensual pleasure, orgasm.

saiba how! *Also* iba.

saiki *ng*, sapunika *kr*, now;

saiki-saiki right now, at this very moment; saikiné now (not past and not future).

saing, nyaingi to compete with;

nyaingaké to have s.o./s.t. compete;

saingan 1 *reg* to sail out together; 2 competitor; 3 competition.

sait I, nyait *reg* to jerk (at), pull, draw.

II, kesait *reg* 1 wealthy looking; 2 beloved.

sajak 1 aspect, demeanor; 2 to seem, look as if;

sajaké *or* sajakané it seems, apparently, to judge from appearances.

sajeg the course of life; - jumbleg *or* - jumleg *or* - umleg all one's life.

sajeng *reg* palm wine.

saji *ng*, *kr*, saos *k.i.*, nyajèni to make an offering to;

nyajèkaké 1 to place (food) before a guest; 2 to put out (an offering for spirits);

sajèn *or* sesajèn an offering placed for the spirits;

pasaji *lit* offering.

sak I pocket;

ngesaki to put s.t. in a pocket.

II, sak-saké just able to do the most important, basic thing and no more.

III *see* mesakaké.

saka I *ng*, saking *kr*, 1 from; 2 because of; 3 according to; 4 made of; 5 than.
II saka siji one by one; saka sethithik little by little, bit by bit.
III pillar (supporting roof); - guru the four main pillars.
IV (year) of the Saka Era. *See also* sakakala.

sakabat close friend.

sakakala the Saka Era (plus 78 = A.D.), used in Hindu Java and Bali.

sakal immediately.

sakala immediately. *See also* kala I.

sakaliyan as a couple, man and wife together (*kr for* sakloron).

sakalir *lit* all (of).

sakalangkung *lit* exceedingly.

sakamantyan *lit* exceedingly.

sakang *reg* groin, inner part of the thigh. *See also* lakang, wlakang.

sakat *reg* to begin; beginning from...

sakdhuk handkerchief.

sakéca comfortable, pleasant (*kr for* kapénak).

sakédah-sakérah whatever, however one wishes.

sakérah-kérah *var of* sakédah-sakérah.

sakedhap a moment (*kr for* sedhéla). *See also* kedhap I.

sakedhik a little, a few (*kr for* sethithik). *See also* kedhik.

sakembu *reg* to conspire, act in concert.

saking *kr* (saka *ng*) from.

sakit ill; painful (*kr for* lara);
  panyakit *ng*, *kr*, 1 sickness (physical or spiritual); 2 *fig* s.t. that causes serious trouble.

saklah *coll* by God's will. *See also* insya'allah.

sakloron *ng*, sakaliyan *kr* as a couple, man and wife together.

sakojur all, the whole of.

saku pocket (*var of* sak).

sakolah *var of* sekolah.

sakorap very much, a great many.

sakorat *var of* sakorap.

saksana *lit* immediately, after that, and then.

saksat *lit* as if, as though; like, as. *See also* sasat, prasasat.

sakserik 1 offended; 2 to have a grudge against s.o. *See also* serik.

saksi *var of* seksi.

sakti *see* sekti.

sakwèhning *lit* all.

sal I shawl, scarf.
II 1 hospital ward; 2 large hall for gatherings.

Sala informal name of the city of Surakarta (also spelt Solo).

salad (of fire) spreading;
  nyalad to catch on fire;
  nyaladi to ignite s.t., set on fire.

salaga *var of* slaga.

salagéwa *reg*, ora - to not look out, pay heed.

salah I wrong; to do s.t. wrong, make a mistake; - gawé wrongdoing; to do wrong; - kaprah to misuse, *i.e.* use for the wrong purpose; - kedadèn 1 to have a different result from the one hoped for; 2 to change one's shape magically; - mangsa to occur out of season; -paham misunderstood; - tampa to misinterpret, make incorrect inferences; - urat to have a sprained muscle; - wèngwèng to get off the track, not stick to business; - wisel to fail to follow or understand;
  nyalahi to deviate from (proper or expected behaviour);
  nyalahaké to blame, find fault with;
  kasalahan 1 mistake; guilt; to be blamed.
II salah-sawiji, salah-siji one or other (of).

salak a stemless thorny palm producing a fruit with a rough brown skin.

salaka silver (metal). *Also* slaka.

salam I 1 peace (in greetings); **2** a greeting; **- pandonga** (written greetings as conventional openings in letters) my prayers go to you!; **- taklim** (greetings at the end of the letter) respectfully yours;
nyalami to greet (officially), shake the hand of;
salaman or **sesalaman** to shake hands. **II** bay leaf, used in cooking for flavour.

salang I collarbone.
II cradle of crossed ropes by which baskets are attached to a shoulder pole.
III - suduk to stab each other in turn; **- sebat** resembling each other quite a bit; **- sengguh** or **salang surup** misunderstood, mixed up; **- tunjang** to run into each other (in panic, haste).

salap to put s.t. s.w. (root form: kr for sèlèh, dèkèk).

salar, nyalar to inform, tell;
nyalari to give orders to s.o. to buy and pay; to place an order;
salaran 1 levy; **2** market-dues.

salasilah family tree, genealogy.

salat 1 ritual Islamic prayers and actions performed five times daily; **2** to perform such prayers; **- Id** ritual prayer celebrating the end of the Fasting Month.

salawana reg to quarrel, have a conflict.

salawat money given to officials who attend a funeral and offer prayers (see also **slawat**).

salé sun-dried banana slices.

salécun very much, a great many.

salèh saintly.

salep ointment, salve;
nyalep or **nyalepi** to apply ointment to.

salib a cross; **Dalan Salib** the Stations of the Cross;
nyalib to crucify.

salimaha reg clumsy, doltish, bungling.

salin ng, **santun** kr, **1** change, replacement; **2** a change of clothing; **3** to change, replace (clothes, name); **- slaga** to become completely different (behaviour);
salin-sumalin to keep on changing, alternating;
nyalin to translate;
nyalini 1 to change or replace s.t.; **2** to change s.o.'s clothing;
pasalin or **pisalin** new clothing, a change of wardrobe;
solan-salin to keep changing, to change often;
nyolan-nyalini to keep changing or replacing s.t.

salira body (k.i. for **awak**). Also **sarira**, **slira II**.

salit dry, rough (mouth, throat, voice).

salju snow.

salok some of (it, them);
saloké the rest, what remains.

saloka proverb, maxim containing a simile, metaphor (esp as a legal term);
nyalokani to apply a simile/metaphor to;
nyalokakaké to indicate s.t. by use of a simile.

salong var of **salok**.

salu 1 verandah; **2** bench on a verandah.

saluku to sit with the legs stretched straight out (var of **sluku**).

salulut lit to make love; to be united in love.

sama the same, alike (subst kr for **padha**). See also **sami**.

samad I a blessing bestowed with magical powers (var of **sawab**);
nyamadi to confer such a blessing on s.o.
II, nyamadi to influence;
samad-sinamadan to influence each other.

samadya in the middle (of). See also **madya**.

samak I 1 paper or leather cover; **2** leather;

nyamak to process leather, to tan;

nyamaki to put a cover on, equip with a cover, bind (books);

nyamakaké to cover s.t. on;

samakan 1 (of leather) already processed; **2** covered with paper or leather, bound.

II *reg* floor mat.

saman *var of* samang.

samana *see* semana.

samang you; your (*md: var of* sampéyan).

samangké *kr for* samengko.

samengko *ng*, samangké *kr* now, these days.

samangsa 1 when, at the time (of); **2** (*or* samangsa-mangsa) at any time, whenever. *See also* mangsa.

samantara *lit* and then, after that.

samanten *see* semanten.

samaos *reg kr of* samangsa.

samapta *lit* in readiness;

nyamaptakaké to make s.t. ready.

samar 1 vague, obscure, dimly visible; **2** worried, apprehensive;

nyamar 1 to hide, keep under wraps; **2** to disguise o.s.;

nyamari 1 scary, deceptive to the eye; **2** worrying, giving cause for concern;

nyamaraké to worry about;

sinamar *lit* under cover;

sumamar *lit* obscure(d);

samaran 1 concealed, pseudonymic; **2** apprehensive by nature.

sambang I to do the rounds (*e.g.* patrol); to go around and inspect;

nyambangi to do the rounds of (a place).

II 1 an evil spirit that roams about at night and brings stomach cramps; **2** this illness combined with other symptoms *e.g.* - leles *or* - lelet postnatal haemorrhaging; **3** an affliction (illness or *fig*).

sambat 1 complaint, outcry; **2** to complain, wail; - sebut troubles, problems;

nyambat to ask (fellow villagers) to help;

nyambati to ask s.o. for help;

nyambataké to do (a job) with the help of one's neighbours;

sesambat to cry out, wail loudly;

sambatan to help (one's neighbour with work that he could not do alone);

pasambat *lit* complaint;

sambat-sinambat to help one another (as neighbours);

nyambat-nyebuti to seek help from.

sambawa I *lit* proper, right, suitable.

II *gram* subjunctive mood.

sambékala accident.

sambel hot spicy sauce or paste;

nyambel to make (ingredients) into the above;

nyambeli to put hot spicy sauce into;

nyambelaké to make such a sauce for s.o.;

nyambel wijèn *idiom* turning grey, flecked with white (hair).

samben *reg var of* saben.

samber to strike (*root form*); - bledhèg, gelap (oath) may I (you *etc*) be struck by lightning if...!; go to hell!;

-lilèn green scarab, worn as a decorative pin; - mata a small nocturnal flying insect that often strikes people in the eye;

nyamber to strike swiftly, swoop down and seize;

nyamberi to strike swiftly from above repeatedly;

nyamberaké to grab with a forceful swoop on behalf of s.o.;

samberan 1 strike, stroke, act of swooping; **2** chicken (*reg kr for* pitik).

sambet (to make a) connection, continuation (*kr for* sambung);

nyambet to continue;

kesambet 1 afflicted by a sudden illness with no apparent cause; 2 to be entered by an evil spirit; 3 to have a fainting fit.

sambéwara, bakul - wandering trader.

sambi I a variety of tree, also its wood (*var of* **kesambi**).

II, **nyambi** to have a job on the side, do s.t. else while doing s.t.;

sinambi done simultaneously with;

sambèn a job on the side.

sambil I, **sambilan** kris sheath without lacquer or metal cover.

II, **sambilan** wooden pin in a yoke on either side of the animal's neck.

sambit, nyambit *or* **nyambiti** to strike with a whip or missile;

kesambit to get struck by a whip or missile;

sambitan to compete each other (kites).

samblug a variety of rice cooker.

sambogen *var of* **samblug**.

sambong *reg* earth dam built in ricefield to control the flow of water.

sambrug *var of* **samblug**.

sambuk a large whip;

nyambuk to whip, lash; *fig* to spur, exhort;

nyambuki to whip s.t. frequently;

nyambukaké to apply the whip.

sambung *ng*, **sambet** *kr*, (to make a) connection, continuation;

nyambung to continue; - **obor** to preserve family connections, not lose track of relatives; - **watang putung** to reconcile people who are fighting;

nyambungi to continue, add to, go on with (*e.g.* conversation);

nyambungaké to make a connection for s.o.;

sumambung 1 to put in a remark; 2 to join in a conversation; to reply;

sesambungan to associate;

panyambung 1 a joining; 2 *gram* conjunction.

sambut, nyambut 1 *lit* to receive, take; 2 (*kr for* **utang**) to borrow money; 3 (*kr for* **nyilih**) to borrow (things); - **gawé** (*kr* **nyambut damel**) to work, have a job, be employed;

nambut *lit* to take hold of, receive; - **silaning akrama** *lit* to marry.

samèk I *reg* lining, protective underlayer.

II (*or* **sèmèkan**) *reg* breakfast.

samekta ready and waiting;

nyamektani to get ready;

nyamektakaké to get s.t. ready.

saméné as much as this. *See also* **méné**.

samengko *ng*, **samangké** *kr*, now, at present. *See also* **mengko**.

sami alike, the same; *plural marker* (*kr for* **padha**).

samipa *lit* side, vicinity.

samir I a round banana leaf cut to fit in dishes as napkin or mat.

II a fringed silken scarf of various colours worn by palace officials as an emblem of their office.

III curtain.

samirana *lit* wind.

samita *lit var of* **sasmita**.

samiwa *lit var of* **samipa**.

samodra *lit* ocean, sea.

samoha *var of* **semuwa**.

sampad I *lit* complete.

II strap (*e.g.* of sandal).

sampah garbage, waste matter;

nyampah (*or* **nyenyampah**) to reject s.o. from a group.

sampak quick-paced gamelan music to accompany marching or battle scenes;

nyampaki to meet, confront, run into unexpectedly;

sampakan style of presentation in theatre.

sampan boat.

sampar broom, brush; - **angin** leaf of the turi plant;

nyampar 1 to shove with the feet; 2 to skim over or through; - **banyu** *fig* to lease a planted ricefield;

samparan 1 female classical dance garment that touches the ground; 2 leg, foot (*reg k.i. for* **sikil**); 3 broom, brush.

sampé, nyampé to brush against s.t. with the hand or arm;

kesampé to get knocked accidentally.

sampeg *reg var of* **sampet.**

sampèk *reg* until, up to. *See also* **nganti.**

sampéka deceit;

nyampékani to cheat, deceive.

samper, nyamper *or* **nyamperi** *reg* to call on s.o.; to drop in to pick s.o. up.

sampet adequate;

nyampeti to cover adequately, provide for.

sampéyan 1 you; your (*kr for* **kowé**); 2 leg, foot (*k.i. for* **sikil**); - **dalem** you (*addressing a king*).

sampir 1 scarf-like cloth worn over the shoulder (*var of* **samir**); 2 shoulder (*reg k.i. for* **pundhak**);

nyampir to be hanging;

nyampiri 1 to hang (clothing) s.w.; 2 to entrust temporarily to;

nyampiraké 1 to hang (clothing) s.w.; 2 to place (temporarily) under the control of s.o.;

sumampir to be hanging (draped over s.t.);

sampiran clothesline or other line strung for hanging things;

sampir-sampir, sompar-sampir *pl* hanging about.

samplak, nyamplak to slap in the face.

samplok a cake made from cassava flour and sugar.

samplong, nyamplong *reg* 1 to throw s.t.; 2 to strike s.t. against.

sampluk a hit, a slap;

nyampluk 1 to slap in the face (with the back of the hand); 2 to knock (with a swinging motion);

kesampluk to get hit accidentally;

samplukan 1 a hit, a slap; 2 act or way of slapping.

sampun I already, finished (*past tense marker*) (*kr for* **wis**).

II don't! (*kr for* **aja**).

sampur a long scarf worn as part of a classical dance costume.

sampyeng *reg* alive with activity.

sampyoh *var of* **sampyuh.**

sampyuh 1 to clash head-on; 2 to fall down together (fighting).

sampyuk, nyampyuk to splash, splatter;

nyampyukaké to splash s.t. on (s.o.'s face);

kesampyuk to get splashed.

samubarang *ng*, **samukawis** *kr*, everything, anything at all, every kind of.

samudana *lit* a pleasant friendly expression which conceals contrary inner feelings;

nyamudana, namudana *lit* to feign, dissemble.

samudaya *lit* everything.

samukawis *kr for* **samubarang.**

samun 1 lonely, deserted; 2 stealthy, secret, incognito;

nyamun to camouflage or disguise (one's appearance; one's feelings);

sinamun *lit* to be camouflaged;

pasamunan a lonely, deserted place.

samur, nyamur 1 to be in disguise (*see also* **samun**); 2 to make unrecognisable; 3 to distract, cheer up;

namur *lit var of* **nyamur**; - **laku** to be incognito; - **kula** to be incognito as a common person.

samuwa, Pasamuwan Suci, the Holy Church.

sana I *lit* place, position, site; **seni** - art centre, art gallery. *See also* **sasana.**

II a kind of tree with dark, heavy wood used for furniture.

sanadyan even though, although. *Also* **senajan.**

sanak relative, relation; - **kadang** *or* - **sedulur** relative, kinsman;
nyanak 1 to accept or treat s.o. as a relative; 2 to be nice to s.o. with an ulterior motive;
sumanak outgoing, friendly;
sanakan *or* sesanakan 1 to make friends; 2 reconciled; 3 relationship with s.o.; (one's) associate(s);
dudu sanak dudu kadang, yèn mati mèlu kélangan *prov* he's not a relative to me, but his death is a personal loss.

sanalika instantly, suddenly. *See also* nalika.

sanambang *lit* one thousand.

sananta *gram* active propositive form.

sanatku I feel, I think...

sancaya 1 name of the 4th **windu** in the cycle of eight; 2 *lit* a gathering of friends or acquaintances.

sandé I to fail to happen, not go ahead (*kr for* **wurung**).
II sarong (*reg kr for* **sarung**).

sandékala dusk, twilight.

sander, nyander to rush at, charge;
nyanderaké 1 to let run, race; 2 to let loose (*e.g.* dog);
sanderan at the run, with great haste.

sandéya *lit* hesitant, uncertain.

sandha I, nyandhakaké to pawn land;
sandhan to lean against (*var of* **sèndhèn**);
sandhan kayu aking *prov* to lean on a poor family.
II, sandhanen to suffer from a lump in the breast.

sandhal sandals;
sandhalan to put on or wear sandals.

sandhang clothing; - **lawé** a certain black stork; **sandhang-pangan** (necessary, essential) food and clothing;
nyandhang to wear (clothes);
nyandhangi 1 to dress s.o. 2 to supply s.o. with clothing;
sandhangan 1 clothing; 2 diacritical mark in Javanese script; - **wyanjana** diacritical mark indicating certain modification of consonant sound;
panyandhang act or way of wearing. *See also* nandhang.

sandhat straps, shoulder-belt, rope (joining a load to a yoke or pole for carrying);
nyandhat *or* nyandhati to lash, attach to such straps, string s.t. on a rope.

sandhéné *reg* supposing that. *See also* andhé.

sandhik *reg var of* sandhing.

sandhing close by, next to;
nyandhing to be close to, have s.t. next to;
nyandhingi 1 to accompany; 2 *fig* to be married to;
nyandhingaké to put s.t. close to, cause s.t. to be close by;
sumandhing to be alongside or next to, accompanying;
sesandhingan side by side;
sandhing kebo gupak *idiom* to associate with questionable people.

sandhung, nyandhung to stumble on, trip over difficulties;
kesandhung to get tripped (up);
kesondhang-(ke)sandhung 1 to keep stumbling; 2 to encounter a series of difficulties;
kesandhung ing awang-awang *prov* to run into uninvited trouble.

sandhur *reg* a variety of folk performance.

sandi I secret, concealed; - **asma** cryptogram, hidden name; - **lata** a variety of climbing vine; - **sastra** secret alphabet or writing system; - **upaya** underhand ruse, trick; - **upama** *lit* symbolic expression;
nyandi to conceal; to put in a secret form;
sinandi *lit* concealed, cryptic.
II *reg* somewhat, a bit. *See also* sadi.

sandik somewhat, a bit (*var of* **sandi II**).

sandika 1 as you command!; **2** to agree (to);

nyandikani to agree to s.t.; to promise to do as ordered. *Also* **sendika**.

sanéga *lit* ready; to make ready.

sanèhnèh some, certain (ones). *See also* **sawenèh, wenèh**.

sanéngga *or* **sanénggané** *reg* supposing that.

sanépa *or* **sanépan** figure of speech making a contradictory comparison, *e.g.* **pait madu** very sweet (so sweet that honey seems bitter by comparison);

nyanépakaké to use s.t. as a comparison.

sanès 1 different; other (*kr for* **séjé**); **2** not, other than, not the same thing as (*kr for* **dudu**); **3** other (*kr for* **liya**); **sanèsé** *md* sorry! (*said when refusing a beggar*).

sang *honorific marker applied to exalted persons or things*; - **ahulun** *lit* you, your; - **hyang** the gods; - **prabu** his majesty; - **retna** jewel (applied to a beautiful princess).

sanga nine; - **bang** a playing-card (*kertu cilik*) with red marking;

kasanga 1 ninth (in order); 2 the 9th period of the Javanese agricultural year;

sangang nine (with a measure).

sangan *or* **sanganan** food fried without oil, or with hot sand;

nyangan to dry fry food as above.

sangar taboo, to be avoided, magically dangerous.

sangat 1 hour, time of day; **2** auspicious moment.

sanget very *kr for* **banget**.

sangga I *ng*, **sanggi** *kr*

nyangga 1 to hold on the open hand; 2 to hold up, support; 3 to prop up; 4 to bear, endure; - **bokong** (of a wife) to support one's husband;

nyanggakaké to use s.t. as a support;

sanggan, sesanggan 1 support, prop; 2 burden, responsibility.

II a measure of harvested rice, 5 or 6 double sheaves (*ca* 50 **kati**).

sanggama, sanggami *lit* sexual intercourse;

nyanggama, nyanggamani to have intercourse with.

sanggar shrine (high place in house, for keeping sacred objects), place of worship.

sanggarunggi suspicious, mistrustful.

sanggem, nyanggemi to agree, accept (to do s.t.).

sanggi *kr for* **sangga**.

sanggrah, nyanggrahi to lodge s.w.; **sanggrahan, pasanggrahan** lodging, rest-house.

sanggul traditional ladies' hair arrangement, consisting of a smooth bun at the back.

sanggup to promise, be willing; nyanggupi to give a promise, undertake to do s.t.

sangi vow, promise; nyangèni 1 to promise (that s.t. will happen); 2 to make a vow for.

sangit to smell of burning, scorching; sumangit, semangit to have an unpleasant smell of burning. *See also* **walang**.

sangiwèn *reg* formerly, once.

sangka I *var of* **saka** from; sangkan 1 origin; 2 cause, source; sangkan-paraning dumadi the origin and destination of creation.

II a shrub, the leaves of which are used medicinally.

sangkal I handle of an adze; nyangkal putung angular.

II, nyangkal to resist (authority).

sangkelat broadcloth.

sangkep complete, all there; nyangkepi to provide, supply (what is lacking).

sangking *var of* saking.

sangkrah barrier of branches; nyangkrahi to block, barricade.

sangku water bowl, basin.

sangkul, nyangkul gawé to take over part of s.o.'s work, in order to help.

sangkut, nyangkut 1 to twist, coil around (rope); 2 to snag (kite); 3 to involve (in a case); 4 to snare, trap (a woman).

sangli to differ, not match, not fit together.

sangling, nyangling to polish (gold); sinangling *lit* polished.

sanglir I with one testicle small or missing.

II *lit* he (she) who looks like...

sangsalan *coll* excuse, pretext.

sangsam *kr for* menjangan deer.

sangsang, nyangsang, nangsang, to catch on s.t., hang down, be suspended; nyangsangaké, nangsangaké to cause to hang from s.t.; sumangsang to be hanging from s.t.; kesangsang to get caught, snagged on s.t., so that it hangs down; sangsangan 1 *reg* clothesline; 2 necklace (*k.i. for* kalung).

sangsara *lit* misery, sorrow.

sangsaya I more and more. *Also* saya.

II *reg lit* troubles, cares.

sangu s.t. taken on a journey as supplies (*e.g.* food, money); nyangokaké to provide s.t. for the journey; nyangoni to provide s.o. with s.t. for the journey; - slamet may good fortune go with you; sangon, pasangon food, money *etc* taken along as supplies for the journey.

saniki *md for* saiki now.

saniskara *lit* everything, the whole, all.

sanityasa *lit* always, constantly.

sanja to visit, drop in (*esp* at the neighbours');

nyanjani to visit s.o. for a chat; sanjan-sanjanan *or* sanjan-sinanjan to visit each other; kesanja baya to meet with misfortune while away from home.

sanjang 1 to say, tell (*kr for* kandha); 2 advice; to say, tell (*kr for* tutur I).

santa I *lit* inner peace, calm.

II holy; Kangjeng Santa Papa the Holy Father, Pope.

santana *var of* sentana I.

santen coconut milk pressed from shredded coconut flesh; - kanil coconut cream (the thick part of coconut milk that rises to the top); nyanten to extract coconut milk by pressing; nyanteni to add coconut milk to; santenan having coconut milk mixed into it.

santer 1 flowing fast and strongly; 2 energetic, fast; 3 serious (illness); nyanter to do s.t. faster or more strongly.

santhèt a type of black magic.

santi, sesanti to undertake spiritual exercises.

santika *lit* skilled (at handling weapons of war); kasantikan skill (in the use of arms).

santiyo a variety of Chinese silk.

santlap, a scold, yell; nyantlap to scold, yell at; santlap-santlapan to yell at each other.

santog I a variety of mango.

II *reg* to the utmost (*var of* katog).

santosa strong, firm, steadfast; nyantosani to strengthen, support; nyantosakaké to make stronger in order to endure s.t.; to encourage s.o. to be firm; kasantosan strength, firmness, steadfastness, endurance, security.

santri 1 a student of Islam living in a

school; 2 one who adheres strictly to Islamic rules; - **buki** student at traditional Islamic school who is a very strict adherent of Islam;

nyantri to enter the home of one's prospective father-in-law to work as a servant;

nyantrèni to act and dress like a **santri**; **pesantrèn** school where one receives instruction in Islam. *See also* **cantrik**.

santun I 1 change, replacement; **2** to change (clothing) (*kr for* **salin**).

II essence (*kr for* **sari I**).

III betel-chewing ingredient (*subst kr for* **gambir**).

sanubari, ati - inner person, one's inner self, heart.

saong, ora - unwilling, dead set against.

saos I 1 to visit (an exalted person) (*k.a. for* **sowan**); **2** to offer (*root form: k.a. for* **saji**); **saos atur,** - **unjuk** to inform;

nyaosi to serve s.o.;

nyaosaké to offer s.t.

II *reg* only, just (*subst kr for* **baé**). *See also* **besaos**.

III sauce, gravy.

saoto kind of clear soup. *Also* **soto**.

sap a layer in a stack, row;

ngesapi to furnish with layers;

sap-sapan in layers, piled up, in rows, lined up.

sapa I ng, sinten *kr*, **1** who?; **2** whoever, anyone who…; **3** s.o. else; - **baé** *or* - **sing** *or* -**baya** *lit* whoever; anyone who…;

nyapa 1 to address, ask 'who?'; **2** to greet;

sapan-sinapan 1 (of strangers) to strike up a conversation; **2** to speak to each other in greeting;

sapa-sapa everyone; (not) anyone.

II *lit* curse.

sapah *reg* cassava.

Sapar 2nd month of the Islamic calendar;

nyapar to hold a customary celebration in Sapar;

saparan religious festival celebrated during Sapar.

sapata *see* **sepata**.

sapé *reg* because.

sapeket *var of* **supeket**.

sapelik a tiny bit. *See also* **pelik I**.

sapet *reg* reaching as far as.

sapi ng, lembu *kr*, cow, bull, ox.

sapih, nyapih 1 to separate (fighters); **2** to wean;

sapihan weaned.

sapit tongs, pincers;

nyapit to handle with tongs. *See also* **supit**;

saplak exactly (like, fitting).

saplenek one small heap. *See also* **plenek**.

saplenong one small mound. *See also* **plenong**.

saplenuk *var of* **saplenong**.

saploké since, from the time that.

sapon market-dues. *See also* **sapu**.

saprana ng, saprika *kr*, since that time.

sapranggèh the height within reach, as far as one can reach.

sapréné ng, sepriki *kr*, until now;

saprana-sapréné up to the present time, after all this time.

sapta *lit* seven.

saptangan handkerchief (*var of* **saputangan**).

Saptu *var of* **Sabtu**, Saturday.

sapu broom; - **dhendha 1** a fine; **2** retribution; - **kawat** a trusted person, deputy; - **lebu** close to the ground; - **lidhi** a broom of palm spines; - **tangan** handkerchief;

nyapu *or* **nyaponi 1** to sweep; **2** to whack with a broom;

nyapokaké to sweep for s.o.;

sapon 1 sweepings; **2** tax paid by shop owners and market sellers, market-dues;

sinapon *lit* swept away;

pasapon market-tax (for sweeping);

sapu ilang suhé a broom that has come unbound; *fig* a disbanded group.

sapuluh ten. *See also* **puluh**.

saput cloth for applying powder to the face; - **dhengkul** knee-high (water level); - **ésuk** all the morning; - **lemah** dawn;

nyaput or **nyaputi** 1 to apply powder; 2 to cover; 3 to strike, overtake;

nyaputaké to apply powder;

sumaput, semaput to fall in a swoon, faint.

sar *or* **mak sar** *repr* a feeling of shock;

ngesar-sari to throw into confusion;

sar-saran 1 in fear; 2 in confusion.

sara I *lit* arrow.

II *reg* unlucky (*shtf of* **sangsara**).

sarab I (various kinds of) children's illness; - **sawan** convulsions, fit.

II, **nyarab** to snap at and devour.

saradan mannerism, funny habit.

saradhadhu soldier.

saradula *lit* tiger. *See also* **sardula**.

saraf nerve. *See also* **sarap** I.

sarah rubbish, flotsam.

sarak religious rules, prescriptions; **murang** - to deviate from the rules; immoral, wicked.

saran recommendation, suggestion;

nyaranaké to recommend, suggest.

sarana 1 means; 2 by means of, by, with; 3 object used to achieve an end by magical means;

nyaranani to apply a means (*etc*) to. *See also* **serana, srana**.

sarandu, saranduning awak all over the body.

sarang I nest; - **burung** edible birds' nest.

II **sarangan** metal grid separating the upper and lower parts of a rice steamer.

III unable to hold water (ricefield), porous.

saranta *see* **sranta**.

sarap I nerve (*var of* **saraf**).

II, bottom layer, basis (to put s.t. on); - **turu** to get some sleep in advance (before having to sit up late);

nyarap to eat breakfast;

nyarapi to provide s.o. with breakfast;

sarapan 1 breakfast; 2 to eat breakfast.

saras 1 healthy; 2 recovered (*kr for* **waras**).

sarasa of one mind, in harmony. *See also* **rasa**.

saraséhan informal discussion, seminar.

sarasilah family tree, genealogy.

sarat I heavily laden, with a full cargo.

II 1 means, what has to be done to attain an aim; 2 magical charm; 3 fee paid to a **dhukun**;

nyarati to use s.t as means.

III condition, necessary requirement;

nyarataké to make s.t. a necessary condition.

sarawèdi, nyarawèdi to polish gems;

nyarawidèkaké to have a gem polished;

sinarawèdi *lit* cherished.

saraya help, assistance (*var of* **sraya**).

sarayuda *lit* a judicial official sent out to investigate.

sardhèn, sardine(s).

sardhin *var of* **sardhèn**.

sardula *lit* tiger.

saré to sleep, go to bed (*k.i. for* **turu**);

nyaré to stay s.w. overnight (*k.i. for* **nginep**);

nyarèkaké to bury (*k.i. for* **ngubur**);

saréan 1 lying down; 2 taking a rest;

pasaréan 1 (*k.i. for* **paturon**) sleeping-place, bed; 2 (*k.i. for* **kuburan, pakuburan**) grave, graveyard.

sarèh 1 calmed down, quiet; 2 patience, respite;

nyarèh to calm down;

nyarèhi 1 to allow respite; 2 to await calmly;

nyarèhaké 1 to calm s.o.; 2 to allow s.o. time.

sarékat association, union, partnership.

sarem salt (*kr for* uyah).

sarèn congealed animal blood as a food. *See also* sari I.

sareng 1 as soon as, when; 2 together (*kr for* bareng).

saréngat the prescriptions of Islamic law.

saresmi *lit* to enjoy the pleasures of love together.

sari I 1 (santun *kr*) essence, the best part; 2 pollen of plants); - pathi essence; nyarèni to dip (fabric being worked in batik) in sarèn (limewater) to fix dye. II anggarap - to have a menstrual period. III tan asari (tan asantun *kr*) *lit* without delay. IV *var of* sri.

sariah the prescriptions of Islamic law.

sarib to break wind (*k.i. for* entut).

sarik, kesarik to receive supernatural retribution for one's wrongdoing.

sarilak foster brother or sister. *See also* dulur, sadulur.

sarimbit (together) as a couple, *i.e.* husband and wife, together with one's spouse; sarimbitan in pairs.

saring, nyaring *or* nyaringi to filter, strain; nyaringaké to have s.t. filtered; saringan 1 sieve, filter; 2 strained, filtered; 3 container for (filtered) drinking water.

sarip *see* sarib.

sarira body (*k.i. for* awak).

sarjana scholar, specialist in a branch of knowledge; kasarjanan scholarship.

sarju to agree, be in accord with, assent to.

sarkara 1 *lit* sugar; 2 certain verse form (*var of* Dhandhanggula).

saroja water lily, lotus.

saron (various kinds of) gamelan instrument consisting of a number of bronze keys over a wooden frame; - peking a type of small saron; nyaron to play the above instrument.

sarong I a partitioned-off space used *e.g.* as a chicken coop or for storage. II *var of* sarung.

sarpa *lit* serpent.

sarsor *see* sor I.

sarta 1 and; 2 with; nyartani to accompany; sinartan *lit* accompanied by.

saru I indecent, improper, unbecoming, annoying (in behaviour or speech); nyaru to disturb, annoy; - wuwus to disturb (a conversation), interrupt; kesaru to get interrupted. II, nyaru to be in disguise, be incognito.

sarug, nyarug to scuff the feet, kick up dirt *etc* as one walks.

sarujuk to agree, in agreement (about); nyarujuki to agree on/to s.t. *See also* rujuk.

sarung sarong; nyarungi 1 to dress s.o. in a sarong; 2 to wrap in a cloth; 3 to sheath; sarungan 1 to wear a sarong; 2 kris sheath (*kr for* wrangka); 3 case, tube.

sarwa (sarwi *subst kr*) in every respect, altogether, completely.

sarwi while, at the same time.

sasab I cover, covering layer, cloak; nyasabi to cover over, cover up; nasabi dhengkul *prov* to benefit members of one's own family. II *reg* to win.

sasadara *lit* moon.

sasag, nasag (to brush, rub, stroke) the wrong way, against the grain (hair, feathers), back-to-front, contrary.

sasak, nyasak *or* nasak to cross, go through, traverse (the forest *etc*).

sasana *lit* place, location; - inggil an elevated hall in the Kraton.

sasangka *lit* moon.

sasar going the wrong way, abberation, error;

nyasar *or* nasar to take the wrong path, go astray;

nyasaraké to mislead, lead astray;

kesasar to get lost, lose one's way.

sasat as if, as though; like, as. *See also* prasasat.

sasi 1 (wulan *kr*) month; 2 *lit* moon;

sasèn 1 monthly; 2 (*or* sasèn-sasèn) month after month.

sasmaya *lit* beautiful, good.

sasmita 1 facial expression; 2 hint, signal, sign;

nyasmitani to give a hint, signal (to).

sasra *lit* one thousand.

sasrah, nyasrahi to give a present to one's bride on the wedding day;

sasrahan a gift given to the bride's parents by the groom's parents.

sastra 1 writing; 2 literature.

sasur, kapat - 35; kalima - 45 *etc* (*market terms*).

sat 1 dried; 2 to become dry;

ngesataké to drain (a field). *See also* asat.

sata I tobacco (*kr for* tembako).

II *lit* rooster, cock.

III *lit* one hundred.

satak a currency item used during the colonial period, 100 dhuwit.

satang pole, barge-pole;

nyatangi to punt (a boat) with a pole.

satata I all in place, all arranged. *See also* tata.

II *lit* constantly, always.

saté small pieces of meat roasted on skewers, kebabs;

nyaté to make meat into the above.

satemah finally, as a result or consequence. *See also* temah.

sathemlik a small piece. *See also* themlik.

sathemplik *var of* sathemlik.

sathim penis.

sathungan *reg* to join together (to do s.t.).

satiti *var of* setiti.

satmata I 1 visible; 2 keen-sighted (*shtf of* kasat-mata).

II testimony, evidence.

sato animal; - iwèn poultry, fowl; - kéwan (the class of) animals;

saton animal-like creature or figure;

pasatoan a system of reckoning lucky and unlucky days.

satriya 1 nobleman; 2 warrior prince (in wayang);

nyatriya 1 to live the life of a nobleman; 2 to have the characteristics of a nobleman.

sinatriya noble;

kasatriyan 1 pertaining to, having the qualities of a satriya; 2 the residence of a satriya.

satru I 1 enemy, foe; 2 to be at odds with; - bebuyutan traditional enemy, archenemy;

nyatru to be hostile, be at odds with;

nyatroni to be hostile toward, consider as one's enemy;

satron *or* sesatron to be enemies with each other;

satru mungging cangklakan *prov* an enemy close to home (one's own daughter).

II *var of* satu.

satu a cake made from green bean flour.

satuhu really, truly. *See also* tuhu I.

satungan *reg var of* sathungan.

satunggal one (*kr for* siji).

satunggil one (*subst kr for* siji).

satus one hundred;

nyatus 1 one hundred each; 2 by the hundred; 3 (*or* nyatusi) to hold a ceremony on the 100th day after a death;

satusan 1 approximately 100; 2 a 100-rupiah note. *See also* atus.

saudara *lit* 1 sibling; 2 relative; 3 intimate friend (*var of* sudara).

sauga even if.

saum 1 the fast; 2 to fast.

saur I (to eat) a meal before daybreak during the Fasting Month.

II 1 oral reply; 2 repayment; - manuk to answer in unison;

nyaur to repay (a debt);

nyauri *or* sumaur to answer;

nyauraké to repay (a debt) on behalf of s.o.; to use as a repayment;

panyaur payment of (or on) a debt;

sesauran to echo back and forth (sounds, music).

saus sauce, gravy.

saut, nyaut 1 to snatch (up, away) in the hand or mouth in passing; 2 to bite, snap at;

kesaut 1 to be pulled (in); 2 to lay one's hands on.

sauwèn-uwèn *or* sauwèn-iyèn *reg* for a considerable length of time. *See also* uwèn.

sawa I python.

II *lit* corpse.

sawab beneficent influence proceeding from s.o.;

nyawabi to transmit one's power, influence or blessing to s.o.;

kesawaban to be affected by s.o.'s beneficent influence.

sawah *ng*, sabin *kr* dyked ricefield;

- ajangan community-owned ricefield;

- bengkok fields reserved for the use of the headman by way of salary;

- gadhu irrigated field for cultivating rice in the dry season;

sumawah to begin to bubble (hot water);

nyawah 1 to work a ricefield; 2 to live by working ricefields (as occupation);

pasawahan sawah-land, the fields.

Sawal 10th month of the Islamic calendar;

sawalan a celebration held at the conclusion of the Fasting Month (beginning of Sawal).

sawala *var of* suwala.

sawan convulsions, fits (children's disease);

sawanan a medicinal herb used for warding off convulsions;

sawanen to suffer from convulsions.

sawang I 1 caked dirt, soot; 2 cobwebs (in the house);

sawangen covered in dirt, cobwebs.

II to look like, resemble;

nyawang to look at, gaze at (steadily, longingly) from a distance;

sawangen with eyes dimmed (of the dying);

sesawangan 1 view, scenery; 2 to gaze at each other, look each other in the eye.

III sawangan mouth of a river.

IV sawangan a whistle fixed to the tail of a dove which sounds in flight.

sawastu *lit* truly. *See also* saèstu.

sawat stone used as a missile;

nyawat to throw at s.t.;

nyawati to throw at s.t. repeatedly;

nyawataké to throw (a missile) at;

sawat-sawatan to throw at/toward each other.

sawawa *var of* suwawa.

saweg to be (do)ing *etc* (*kr for* lagi).

sawéga *lit* ready, prepared.

sawegung *lit* (in) all.

sawelas eleven. *See also* sewelas.

sawenèh some, certain (ones). *See also* wenèh.

sawer snake (*kr for* ula).

sawetara 1 an interval of time; 2 several, some (number or amount of). *See also* wetara.

sawi the mustard plant (young leaves eaten).

sawiji a certain, one;
  nyawiji to agree, be of one mind;
  nyawijèkaké to unite, bring into agreement;
  sawijining dina one day.
sawit I batik garment with headdress of matching material;
  nyawit to put on or wear the above;
  sawitan 1 an outfit or combination as above; 2 matching wedding batiks of a special pattern, worn by the bride and groom.
  II klapa - oil palm.
sawiyah I the young of a wall lizard (cecak).
  II 1 common, ordinary, everyday; 2 of any kind, of whatever sort;
  nyawiyah or nyawiyah-wiyah to treat unworthily, with contempt;
  sawiyah-wiyah without consideration, impertinent, contemptuous.
sawo a small tree and its fruit; - mateng brown;
  nyawo mateng brown-coloured (skin).
sawon reg wrong (kr for salah).
sawonga anybody at all, everybody. See also wong.
sawud a cake made of shredded cassava and sugar.
sawung I 1 rooster, cock (kr for jago); 2 chicken (reg kr for pitik); - galing 1 an undefeated fighting cock; 2 cock-shaped golden item of regalia carried in procession.
  II, nyawung to carry (a child) on one's arms (rather than using a sling);
  sinawung lit expressed in the form of a song or poem.
sawur small objects (rice, coins etc) scattered before a funeral procession as it makes its way to the cemetery;
  nyawuri to bestrew (s.t.) with small particles, e.g. sand;
  nyawuraké to strew or scatter s.t.;

sumawur scattered, sprinkled.
saya I increasingly, more and more;
  saya-saya all the more. See also sangsaya.
  II snare for trapping birds or fish (shtf of wisaya).
sayab, nyayabi to sneak in s.w. to steal, to rob s.o. by day.
sayad I, nyayadi to remove unusable parts from meat;
  sayadan scraps of unusable meat.
  II, nyayadaké reg to use s.t. as a pretext;
  sayadan reg a pretext.
sayaga lit to dress in one's best clothes, to dress up.
sayah tired, weary;
  nyayah to act as if weary;
  nyayahi tiring, wearisome;
  nyayahaké to make tired;
  sasayahé to the point of exhaustion.
sayak 1 skirt; 2 women's Western-style dress (blouse and skirt);
  nyayaki to dress s.o. in blouse and skirt;
  sayakan wearing such clothing.
sayan var of saya I.
sayang I coppersmith;
  nyayang to work as a coppersmith;
  sayangan the street of the coppersmiths.
  II reg a pity;
  nyayang to show affection toward.
sayembara 1 contest of arms, with as prize being chosen in marriage by a princess (in ancient story); 2 competition.
sayid title given to descendants of the Prophet;
  sayidina title for the Prophet, also for saints.
sayoga suitable, appropriate (var of sayogya).
sayogi kr for sayoga.
sayogya suitable, appropriate; sayogyané it would be a good idea to...;

nyayogyani to agree to, comply with;
nyayogyakaké to recommend, approve.
sayom *reg* in cooperation;
nyayomi to ask people to work together cooperatively.
sayub spoiled, rancid, going off.
sayuk harmonious, united;
nyayukaké to try to get s.o. on one's side, to cooperate.
sayur vegetable dish; - asin pickled vegetables;
nyayur to prepare as a vegetable dish;
sayuran vegetable(s) (*esp* European, boiled).
sayut I, nyayuti to restrain, check.
II *reg* scarf-like batik ladies' wear.
III, nyayut 1 to tie; 2 to wind around; 3 to embrace.
IV *var of* sayuk.
sè I *reg particle used to mark a topic.*
II Chinese surname.
sèb, sèb-sèben to keep burping, to have s.t. repeat (*e.g.* after eating durian).
séba to appear before s.o. (*esp* a king) to show loyalty and offer service;
nyébani to pay a visit to (s.o. of high standing);
nyébakaké to present s.o. to an exalted person;
sinéba *lit* to be paid homage;
paséba *or* piséba a visit (to s.o. high);
paséban audience-hall, place for official sittings. *See also* séwaka.
sebab 1 reason, cause; 2 because (*var of* sabab).
sebah 1 to have an uncomfortable feeling of fullness; 2 fed up, to have had enough;
nyebahi causing the above feelings.
sebal, nyebal to differ from the usual or normal, to form an exception.
sebar, nyebar *or* nyebari 1 to spread, distribute; 2 to disseminate;
nyebaraké 1 to strew, scatter; 2 to distribute;

sumebar spread, scattered.
sebaran s.t. spread.
sebat I to name, mention (*root form: kr for* sebut).
II adoh sebaté karo *idiom* to differ a lot from.
sebda *see* sabda.
sebé long scarf worn by Muslim men.
sebel to have no luck, not get what one wanted;
nyebeli to bring bad luck.
sebelah *reg* next door.
sèben to hire (*reg kr for* séwa).
sebèt torn (off, apart);
nyebèt to tear (off, apart);
sebètan torn scraps.
sèbet I right away; - byar *way* opening phrase uttered by a dhalang.
II a whip, a lash (*reg var of* sabet).
III, sèbetan *reg* (of clothing) just right, not too big and not too small.
sebit *var of* sebèt.
seblak I, nyeblak to beat with s.t. supple;
nyeblakaké to beat out (mat).
II, nyeblakaké to open or extend s.t. wide to the light, sun;
sumeblak 1 wide open; 2 shining, glowing.
seblok *reg var of* seblak I.
sébok *reg* short and stout.
sebrak 1 *repr* tearing; 2 to get torn; to get pulled off/apart;
nyebrak to tear; to pull off/apart.
sébrat, nyébrataké to disown (a relative).
sebrèt *var of* sebrak.
sebrot, nyebrot to snatch.
sebrung *repr* swooping, flying;
sebrang-sebrung to fly away/off; to toss away.
sebut I, (*pron as:* sebu:t) *repr* a whisking motion;
II, nyebut 1 to utter, mention; 2 to refer to by title or rank; 3 (*or* nyebut-nyebut) to cry out in pain or strong emotion;

kasebut mentioned, referred to;

sebutan 1 official title, rank; 2 technical term; 3 what is said about s.o., good or bad reputation.

seca, secan *reg* to make an appointment or date.

sécé *reg* ten cents. *See also* écé I.

sécok *reg* one. *See also* siji.

séda to die, dead (*k.i. for* mati).

sedadal *reg* to keep moving the legs (in a stiff-kneed kicking motion, when swimming).

sedagar merchant (*var of* sudagar).

sedasa ten (*kr for* sepuluh).

sedaya all (*kr for* kabèh).

sedéné 1 and furthermore; 2 as for.

sedhah 1 the betel plant; 2 betel leaves (*kr for* suruh).

sedhakep with arms folded across the chest;

nyedhakepaké to fold the arms as above;

sedhakep awé-awé *prov* to ask s.o. to do wrong with o.s. secretly.

sédhan sedan.

sédhang, nyédhang to fold s.t. in a diagonal line;

sédhangan folded in a diagonal line.

sedhar conscious, aware.

sedhat-sedhèt to ogle frequently.

sedhèdhèk *reg* a little, few. *See also* sethithik.

sedheg *reg* waste, dregs.

sedhekah 1 alms, charitable gift; 2 a ritual meal (slametan); - bumi an annual village celebration;

nyedhekahaké to give s.t. as alms.

sedhéla a moment, short interval;

sedhéla-sedhéla every so often, from moment to moment.

sedhèlèt, sedhélit, sedhélok, sedhélot, sedhèluk, sedhèlut *coll var of* sedhéla.

sedheng 1 enough, just right; 2 (*or* sedhengé) while, during; as long as;

nedheng to be at just the right stage; - birahi of marriageable age;

nedhengi to reach a certain stage;

sedhengan average, medium.

sèdhèng, laku - adultery committed by a wife;

nyèdhèng (of a woman) to commit adultery.

sedhéngah any (one), every (one).

sedhènget *reg* a moment, short interval. *See also* sedhéla.

sedhengklang *reg* sitting on the ground with the arms at the back supporting the body.

sedhep pleasant to the senses, *esp* smell, taste; fresh; - malem a certain flower that gives a pleasing fragrance;

nyedhepi *or* nyedhepaké to give a pleasing, fresh, smell or taste.

sedhépah short but muscular.

sedhepek, sedhépok, sedhéprok to sit suddenly on the floor (out of respect).

sedhèrèk relative, sibling (*kr for* sadulur).

sedhèt I *repr* a quick glance.

II *repr* a sudden pulling out.

sèdhet (of female) well-proportioned, shapely.

sedhidhik *reg* a little, bit, few (*var of* sethithik).

sedhih sad, sorrowful, grieved;

nyedhihi *or* nyedhihaké 1 sorrowful, causing sadness; 2 to sadden, grieve.

sedhil 1 soggy, too moist to burn (of tobacco); 2 to not progress smoothly.

sedhilit, sedhiluk, sedhilut a very short moment (*coll var of* sedhéla).

sedhinga *var of* sedhéngah.

sedhiya *see* sadhiya.

sedhot, nyedhot to suck, inhale, sip from;

nyedhoti to suck s.t. frequently;

nyedhotaké to suck s.t. for s.o.;

sedhotan 1 a straw; 2 (*or* panyedhot) act or way of sucking;

sumedhot to start, feel an inner shock.

sedhuh, nyedhuh to pour hot water on s.t.;

sedhuhan steepings, prepared by pouring hot water on s.t.

sedik var of **sidik**.

sediya var of **sedya**.

sedul, nyedul to poke the finger in a hole.

sedulur see **sadulur**.

sedya plan, intention;

nedya to intend;

sumedya to have the intention to.

seg I or **mak seg** repr sudden inertness.

II or **mak seg** repr a sudden crowded condition;

ngeseg to push, crowd;

ngeseg-segi to cause s.t. to be filled to overflowing;

seg-segan crowding each other. See also **seseg**.

III to be (do)ing (coll for **saweg**, md for **lagi**); - **anu** reg a few days ago.

sèg, sèg-sègan in constant motion, unable to remain still, restless.

sega ng, **sekul** kr, cooked rice; - **golong** rice balls for ceremonial meals; - **gurih** rice cooked in coconut milk; - **kuning** or - **punar** rice boiled in coconut milk and coloured yellow with turmeric; - **wadhang** yesterday's rice fried for breakfast; - **wuduk** rice boiled in coconut milk;

sumega (of a child's age) fond of eating rice.

segah kr for **suguh**.

seganten sea, ocean (kr for **segara**).

segara ng, **seganten** kr, sea, ocean; - **anakan** strait, channel; - **muncar** a round earring set with a circlet of diamonds; - **wedhi** desert.

segawon dog (kr for **asu**).

segèh var of **cegèh**.

sègel a seal;

nyègel 1 to affix a seal (on); 2 to place under seal.

seger fresh, refreshed, buoyant; - **buger** in fine health; - **sumyah** refreshed after having felt weary; - **waras** healthy and strong;

nyegeri or **nyegeraké** to freshen, refresh;

seger-segeran s.t. refreshing.

seglang-seglèng to swing the arms casually while walking.

segok reg var of **sogok**.

segrak sharp, acrid, pungent;

nyegrak or **sumegrak** to have an acrid odour.

segrèk a small saw used by kris makers.

segrok var of **sogrok**.

ségrok repr a sudden sitting.

segu 1 a hiccup, to hiccup; 2 a belch, to belch (k.i. for **glègèken**);

segunen to have the hiccups.

segung a kind of badger that emits a bad smell. Also **senggung**.

sèh title of Muslim scholar.

séhat healthy, hale;

nyéhataké healthful, wholesome;

kaséhatan health, physical welfare.

sejarah 1 genealogy; 2 history; **nyejara- haké** to relate the history of.

séjé, sèjèn reg ng (**sanès** kr) 1 another, s.o. or s.t. else; 2 different from; 3 strange; 4 reg exceptional;

nyèjèkaké to make a difference, keep separate.

sek see **seg**.

seka coll var of **saka**.

sekabat var of **sakabat**.

sekadé var of **sekadi**.

sekadhé var of **sekadi**.

sekadhi var of **sekadi**.

sekadi matching (of clothing).

sekait, sekaitan to form an alliance, conspire.

sekak 1 (to play) chess; 2 check! (called when threatening the opponent's

chess king); - **mat** checkmate;
nyekak to put (the opposing king) in check.

sekakel link.

sekal immediately (*var of* **sakal**).

sekala *see* **sakala, kala I**.

sekalir *see* **sakalir**.

sekalor I a variety of herbal medicine.
II epilepsy without foaming.

sekantuk to have a piece of luck; lucky by nature (*kr for* **sekolèh**).

sekar 1 flower (*kr for* **kembang**); **2** classical verse (*kr for* **tembang I**);
nyekar 1 to place flowers on a grave; **2** to sing classical poetry.

sekarat (to be in) death throes.

sekarep, nyekarep to let s.o. act as they please. *See also* **karep**.

sékat healthy (*var of* **séhat**).

sekati name of a special gamelan orchestra kept at the courts of Surakarta, Yogyakarta and Cirebon, played in the compound of the Great Mosque during Sekatèn week (6–12 Mulud);
sekatèn the festivities leading up to the Garebeg Mulud (on 12 Mulud);
sekatènan to attend the Sekatèn fair.

sekater assessor (of taxes), valuer.

sekathung, nyekathung *reg* to swindle, cheat.

sekawan four (*kr for* **papat**).

sekawit 1 formerly; in the beginning; **2** because (of); **3** (ever) since. *See also* **awit, kawit**.

sekeb, nyekeb to put s.t. into (a container) to ripen;
sekeban a ripe fruit after being put in a storage box for several days.

sekèber 'Gezaghebber' [Authority], former title of a high civil official.

sekéca *see* **sakéca**.

sekedhap *see* **sakedhap**.

sekedhik *see* **sakedhik**.

sèkèk *reg var of* **dèkèk**.

sekéki *reg* now. *See also* **saiki**.

sekel sad, grieving (*k.i. for* **susah**).

sèkèl, sèkèlen *reg* to ache in the joints.

sekembu *reg* to conspire.

sekendi *reg* how much, how many?

sekèng, nyekèng to ostracise, boycott.

sèkèng weak, feeble.

sekènten to feel ill at ease (*subst kr for* **sekéwuh**).

sèkertaris secretary.

sekèsel draught-screen.

sekèt sketch, (sketchy) outline;
nyekèt to sketch, draw (sketch) in outline.

sèket fifty.

sekèthèng, lawang - gateway, main entrance.

sekèwed *kr for* **sekéwuh**.

sekéwuh *ng*, **sekèwed** *kr*, to feel ill at ease. *See also* **éwuh, pakéwuh**.

sekilwak sentinel, sentry.

seking I from (*coll var kr for* **saking**), (*md for* **saka**).
II knife, lancet, fleam.

sekip 1 target, mark; **2** range, practice ground.

sekiyé *reg* now (*var of* **saiki**).

sekiyen *var of* **sekiyé**.

seklangkung *see* **sakalangkung**.

sekloron *see* **sakloron**.

sekoci I sloop, boat.
II bobbin, shuttle.

sekojur *see* **sakojur**.

sekoki *reg* now. *See also* **saiki**.

sekolah 1 to attend school; **2** (*or* **sekolahan**) school; - **dhasar** (*abbr*: **S.D.**) elementary school;
nyekolahaké to send s.o. to school;
sekolahan 1 school (building); **2** educated.

sekolèh *or* **sekolèhan** to have a piece of luck, be lucky by nature;
nyekolèhi worth going after.

sekon a second;
nyekoni to time s.t. in seconds.

sekoneng rabbet, slot, groove.

sekong *reg* small boat with outrigger(s).

sekongkel to plot, conspire;
　sekongkelan 1 conspiracy; 2 to conspire.

sekonyar variety of boat, schooner.

sekop 1 shovel, spade; 2 spades (cards).

sekores suspension (of student, sportsman *etc*);
　nyekores 1 to suspend s.o.; 2 to adjourn (a meeting).

sekoteng a hot ginger-flavoured drink.

sekrap, nyekrap to scratch out.

sekrip writing book, manual of handwriting.

sekrok shovel, spade. *See also* sekop.

sekrop *var of* sekrok.

sekrup screw, bolt;
　nyekrup to fasten with a screw;
　sekrupan fastened with a screw.

seksi 1 witness; 2 testimony;
　nyeksèni to witness, observe;
　nyeksèkaké to cause or allow s.t. to be witnessed;
　paseksèn 1 evidence; 2 fee for acting as a witness. *Also* saksi.

sekti to have magical powers; - mandraguna *lit* endowed with superhuman powers;
　sinekti *lit* endowed with supernatural powers;
　kasektèn magical power. *Also* sakti.

sekuja, nyekuja to let s.o. do anything they please.

sekul cooked rice (*kr for* sega).

sekung I root hair of palm tree used for bird-trapping snare.
　II *lit* sekunging tyas burning desire.

sekuthu 1 allied; 2 plot, conspiracy;
　nyekuthoni to form an alliance.

sekutu *see* sekuthu.

sel *or* mak sel *repr* inserting;
　sel-selan to crowd together; to push against each other.

sèl I (biological) cell.
　II prison cell;

ngesèl to imprison.

sela 1 (*or* sela-sela) a little space between; 2 (to have) a gap, interval; 3 (to have) leisure time;
　nyela *or* nyelani *or* sumela to interrupt, intervene;
　nyelakaké to give priority to (s.t., over another thing in progress);
　nyela-nyela to annoy with repeated interruptions;
　selan a partition;
　kaselan interrupted by.

séla stone (*kr for* watu).

selag *reg* temporary substitute;
　nyelagi to replace temporarily, do s.o. else's work.

selaga *var of* slaga.

selagi, selagia even if it were...; selaginé at the time when..., at the same time (as).

selah *reg var of* sèlèh.

selak on the verge of, about to (in a condition needing urgent action);
　nyelak to make haste to be ready on time;
　sumelak hasty, rushed;
　nyelaki choking, to cause a choking feeling;
　nyelakaké to make haste with s.t.;
　keselak 1 hardly able to wait; 2 to have s.t. go down the wrong way, to choke.

sélak to deny;
　nyélaki to deny s.t.; to renege, go back on.

selaka silver (metal). *See also* salaka, slaka.

sélakarang, sélakarangen to suffer from mange (horses).

sélakrama *var of* silakrama.

selam 1 Muslim; 2 circumcised;
　nyelamaké to have s.o. circumcised.

Sélan Ceylon (*var of* Sélon).

selang I by turns, alternating; - surup a misunderstanding.

II rubber pipe, hose;

nyelang to use a rubber pipe to drain s.t.

III, nyelang *reg* to borrow;

nyelangi *or* nyelangaké to lend s.t. to;

selangan a debt, s.t. borrowed.

IV, sumelang worried.

selapan one 35-day period (combination of five-day and seven-day weeks);

nyelapani to hold a ceremony to mark the (first) 35 days of an infant's life;

selapanan the above ceremony. *See also* lapan.

selap-selip *see* selip III.

selar variety of dried salt fish.

Selasa Tuesday.

selat I salad.

II strait.

sélat *var of* silat.

selawat *see* slawat.

selawé *ng*, selangkung *kr*, 25;

nyelawé 25 at a time; (for) every 25; (*or* nyelawé-nyelawé) 25 each;

selawèn *or* selawéan *or* selawénan 25-rupiah note.

selaya *var of* sulaya.

selé I jelly, jam;

nyelé to make (ingredients) into jelly or jam;

II, nyelé to be unusual, different from others;

selèn odd, not matching, paired wrongly;

saselé 1 one of a pair; 2 *fig* one-sidedness.

selèg *reg var of* selé II.

selèh *reg var of* silih I.

sèlèh 1 to resign; 2 to put s.t. s.w. (*root form: var of* dèkèk);

nyèlèh to put s.t. s.w.;

nyèlèhaké to leave s.t. lying s.w.;

nyèlèhi to put s.t. on;

sumèlèh 1 lying; having been put (down); 2 calm, settled, resigned.

selek *var of* selak.

selèk, nyelèkaké to show up s.o.'s mistake;

keselèk to have one's wrongdoing discovered and censured.

selèn *see* selé II.

seler, nyeler to steal, pinch, pilfer (by day);

seleran s.t. stolen.

selèt *repr* the crack of a whip;

sumelèt stinging, burning (sun's rays).

selikur 21;

selikuran name of a card game.

seling interspersed; - surup to misunderstand, misinterpret;

nyeling to alternate, vary (with);

nyelingi to intersperse with;

selingan 1 interlude, s.t. put in between; 2 variation from routine.

selip I to slip, slide, skid.

II to misunderstand, misinterpret.

III, nyelip *or* sumelip inserted into; stuck in between;

nyelipi *or* nyelipaké to insert s.t. in between;

keselip inserted into s.t. unintentionally;

selipan s.t. inserted in between;

selap-selip inserted, slipped in here and there.

selir *ng*, *kr*, ampil *k.i.* a minor wife, concubine (of aristocrat, royalty);

nyelir 1 to select (the best), give preference to; 2 to take as a minor wife;

sinelir *lit* chosen, favourite.

selira body (*k.i. for* awak). *See also* slira.

sélo *intsfr* two; loro - two and only two.

sélog *reg* variety of edible turnip-like root.

seloh *reg var of* sèlèh.

selon *reg* bamboo tube used as container for spices.

Sélon Ceylon.

Sélong *var of* Sélon;

nyélong to send s.o. into exile (formerly to Ceylon).

selop slipper, sandals with closed toes;
selopan to put on or wear the above.

selot I increasingly, all the more.
II lock (of door);
nyelot to lock (a door);
selotan locked.
III, selot-seloté occasionally.

sèluman var of siluman.

selup sloop.

selur in a row, lined up, one after the other.

selut metal band adorned with jewels around the bottom of a kris handle.

sem lit enchantment, charm. See also sengsem.

semada or semadan reg somewhat, quite; a little.

semadi meditation, clearing the mind with the intention of achieving a religious goal. Also semèdi.

semados kr of semaya.

semagar or semagaran reg to exert o.s. to the limit.

sémah 1 spouse (kr for bojo); 2 household (kr for somah).

semail amulet.

semak, nyemak to follow (a text) closely, as s.o. else reads.

semakéyan var of semangkéyan.

semambu reg rattan walking stick.

semana ng, semanten kr, that much/many; to that extent; dhèk - at that (past) time.

semang I to pretend, feign, make an excuse.
II semang-semang uncertain, concerned; ora - to not bother to (do), not worry about.

semanger reg fine, beautiful, delightful.

semangka water melon.

semangkéyan to pride o.s., boast.

semangkin all the more, increasingly.

semangsa see samangsa, mangsa.

semanten kr for seméné, semono, semana.

semau formerly, in the beginning.

semaput to lose consciousness, faint.

Semar I name of one of the clown-servants to the Pandawas, father of Pétruk, Nalagarèng and Bagong; - mendem snack made from steamed glutinous rice wrapped with omelette;
nyemari 1 resembling Semar (in appearance, character, gait); 2 to play the part of Semar.
II (or semar-semar) prop, support; - tinandhu traditional house with roof supported by four pillars;
nyemari to support with pillars.

semara (var of asmara) romantic love.

semat I to recur (of illness).
II pin of sharpened coconut leaf rib, used for fastening leaf-wrapped packages.

Semawis reg kr for Semarang.

semawon perhaps, possibly, probably (reg var of mbok menawa).

semaya ng, semados kr, to postpone, delay;
nyemayani to promise s.o. (but for a later time);
nyemayakaké to promise s.t. to s.o.;
semayan (to have made) a promise, appointment, date.

sembada appropriate, seemly, fitting, in proportion;
nyembadani 1 to respond adequately; 2 to offer sufficient resistance; 3 to fulfil, satisfy (wish, desires);
kasembadan to be carried out, fulfilled.

sembaga var of sumbaga.

sembagi or sembagèn imported flowered chintz.

sembah 1 a gesture of high esteem made to a superior by holding the hands before the face, palms together, thumbs approaching the nose, and bowing the head slightly; 2 one's respect, one's high regards; - bekti or -

sungkem one's respectful regards;
Sembah Bekti the Hail Mary;
nuwun (expression of) thanks;
nyembah to gesture humbly to s.o. as above;
panembah 1 object of high esteem or worship; 2 the act of making a **sembah**;
panembahan a princely title;
sesembahan an object of high esteem.
sembahyang ritual prayers (in Islam, five times daily);
nyembahyangi or **nyembahyangaké** to say prayers for s.o.;
sembahyangan (Catholic) prayer.
sembarang some, any (at all); someone, anyone (at all);
nyembarangaké to regard s.o. as an ordinary person;
sembarangan 1 (to treat) lightly, not (take) seriously enough; 2 random, no particular one.
sembari reg while.
sembawa var of **sambawa** I.
sembelèh, **nyembelèh** to butcher, slaughter. See also **belèh** II.
sembèn reg var of **sambèn**. See also **sambi** II.
sembèr I raucous, hoarse, cracked (voice).
II crazy about men, nymphomaniac.
sembèrèt, **nyembèrèt** to flow out in a flat jet as through a split, e.g. water from a leaky bucket;
pating sembèrèt pl as above.
sembet or **sesembetan** rags, worn-out clothing, cloth scraps.
sembèt, **nyembèt** to involve, drag s.o.in;
kesembèt to get involved, dragged in.
sembiyang coll var of **sembahyang**.
sembir I a tree, producing the wood from which **gambang** keys are made.
II, **nyembir-nyembir** to make indirect allusions, have a sly dig at s.o.
semboja frangipani, a tree with sweet-

scented flowers, often growing in cemeteries.
sembok coll var of **simbok**.
sémbong folded batik garment worn without train by female court servants;
sémbongan to wear such a garment.
semborol, **semborolan** reg 1 prostitute; 2 inferior quality.
sembrama, lit **nembrama** to welcome guests;
panembrama song for welcoming a guest accompanied by gamelan music.
sembrana 1 nonchalant, careless; 2 rude, lacking respect;
nyembranani to treat s.o. lightly or with disrespect;
sembranan or **sesembranan** 1 nonchalant, careless (by nature); 2 to act in such a way.
sembrèt torn, ripped;
nyembrèt to tear, rip (fabric).
sembuh, **nyembuh** or **nyembuhi** to renew (batik) by rewaxing and redyeing it;
nyembuhaké to have (batik) redyed;
sembuhan batik that has been renewed by being redyed.
sembung reg var of **sambung**.
sembulih compensation;
nyembulihi 1 to make good; 2 to calm (anger).
sembur what is sprayed from the mouth: 1 poison of a snake; 2 chewed incense resin sprayed on the body as medicine or to drive out a spirit;
nyembur to spit or hiss at;
nyemburaké to spray s.t. out;
sumembur to spit, hiss, squirt, spray out;
semburan 1 s.t. which is sprayed out; 2 outpouring, spraying out;
sembur-sembur **adas** idiom with blessing of many people, one's wish may be fulfilled.

semburat 1 tinged with (another colour); 2 tinged with red.

semèdi *var of* semadi.

semekan *or* kasemekan ladies' breast-cloth (*k.i. for* kemben).

sèmèk underlayer, coaster, napkin;
nyèmèki to provide with an underlayer;
sèmèkan supplied with an underlayer.

semekta *var of* samekta.

semelak a drink made from pacé fruit.

semèn cement in powdered form;
nyemèn *or* nyemèni to cement s.t.;
semènan covered with cement.

semendhang, semendhik, semendhing *reg* a little, a bit. *See also* mendhang.

semendhi nearly the same.

seméné *ng*, semanten *kr* this much/many, to this extent;
nyemènèkaké to do s.t. as much as this.

semeng *or* semeng-semeng (to have or get) a fever. *See also* sumeng.

semengké *coll var of* samangké.

semengkin *var of* semangkin.

semengko *var of* samangko.

semènten this much/many (*md for* seméné).

semeper *reg* to drop in, call in.

semerap *var of* sumerep.

semerep *var of* sumerep.

semèt *reg* a little, a bit. *See also* mit.

semi to sprout, shoot, bud forth, blossom;
semèn 1 new leaves, shoots; 2 a class of batik patterns; udan - the first rain after the dry season;
nyemèni to cause to shoot;
pasemèn plants that come up of their own accord.

semil *reg* a little, a bit.

semir 1 polish (for shoes); 2 grease, oil (lubricant);
nyemir 1 to polish; 2 to grease; 3 to bribe, grease s.o.'s palm;
semiran polished.

semita *var of* sasmita.

semiyur *reg* worried, uneasy, apprehensive.

sémog chubby.

semongkel *reg* to plot.

semon *see* semu.

semono *ng*, semanten *kr*, that much/many, to that extent; - uga and so…; and (not) either.

sempad, nyempad 1 to graze, sideswipe; 2 to chide, rebuke; 3 to make indirect criticisms.

sempal broken off, cut off, torn off;
nyempal to break s.t. off;
sempalan 1 a broken off piece; 2 *way* fragment of a story, developed into a separate drama.

semparèt *repr* suddenly running off.

sempèd *var of* sempad. *See also* srèmpèd.

sèmpèr lame, dragging one foot.

sempérat *repr* a quick dash;
nyempérat to sprint.

sempèrèt *var of* sempérat.

sempet to have time (for);
nyempetaké 1 to make use of; 2 to give one's time.

sèmpèt 1 a cloth used for wrapping betel ingredients; 2 *reg* batik garment.

semplah broken, hanging useless.

semplak *var of* sémplak.

sémplak, nyémplak to slap (with the back of the hand).

sémplang *var of* sémplak.

semplé, semplèh, semplèk (*var of* semplah).

semplok broken, snapped off, useless.

semporot, pating semporot to spurt up/out everywhere.

sempoyongan to totter, stagger.

semprang a kind of red and yellow butterfly.

semprat-semprit *see* semprit.

semprat-semprut to keep sniffing; to have a runny nose.

sempring, sempring-sempring to run quickly (insect).

semprit 1 *or* **sempritan** a whistle; **2** to blow one's nose (*k.i. for* **sisi**); **3** a crisp whistle-shaped biscuit;
nyemprit to blow a whistle;
nyempriti to blow a whistle at s.o.;
sempritan whistle (sound);
semprat-semprit to whistle repeatedly.

semprong 1 bamboo tube used to blow on fires to produce flame; **2** glass lamp chimney; **3** binoculars, magnifying glass; **4** a crisp cylinder-shaped snack;
nyemprong 1 to ripen (mangoes) by keeping warm and draught-free; **2** to blow on a fire with a tube; **3** to examine through a magnifying instrument or other cylindrical object;
semprongan (of mangoes) picked while immature and ripened by keeping warm and draught-free.

semprot, nyemprot 1 to spray, squirt, pour from a hole; **2** *coll* to tell off, scold;
nyemproti to squirt or spray onto;
nyemprotaké to squirt or spray s.t. (liquid);
kesemprot to get scolded;
semprotan 1 nozzle, spraying device; **2** telling off, scolding.

semprul 1 tobacco of inferior quality; **2** *excl* 'damn it!'.

semprung *repr* a sudden departure, whizzing off.

sempug dull, blunt.

sempulur prosperity, well-being.

sempyok, nyempyok to splash;
nyempyoki to splash against;
nyempyokaké to splash s.t. against;
kesempyok 1 to get splashed inadvertently; **2** *fig* to get involved in s.o. else's trouble;
sempyokan a splash (of water).

semrawang *var of* **sumrawang**.

semrinthil *var of* **sumrinthil**, *see* **srinthil III**.

semromong to feel hot, glowing, *e.g.* from fever.

semu 1 appearance, what shows through or is visible outwardly of something inward; **2** what can be read on the face; **3** to seem to, have the appearance of; **semuné** it seems that; **4** to have a hint or tinge of (colour);
nyemoni 1 to indicate, give to understand; **2** to insinuate;
pasemon 1 facial expression; **2** hint, signal; **3** allusion, allegory; **lakon pasemon** a wayang story which alludes to real events and characters.

semukirang a certain batik pattern. *See also* **cemukiran**.

semur meat boiled in spiced soy sauce;
nyemur to make the above dish.

semuruh pliable, docile.

semut ant (various kinds);
semuten to have pins and needles.

semuwa decked out, festively attired;
nyemuwakaké 1 to deck out, enliven; **2** *reg* to have s.o. perform in a dance drama;
semuwan *reg* performance of a dance drama held for a special occasion.

sèn cent.

séna *lit* troops, soldiers, army.

senag-senig *see* **senig**.

senagi *reg var of* **senajan**.

senaja *reg var of* **senajan**.

senajan even though, although. *Also* **sanadyan**.

senaos *subst kr for* **senajan**.

senapang rifle.

sénapati commanding general;
nyénapatèni to have command over (troops).

senasa *reg kr for* **sanajan**.

senat-senut *see* **senut**.

sendarèn, sundarèn wind-harp attached to a kite to sound as the kite flies.

sendawa I 1 saltpeter, potassium nitrate; 2 gunpowder.

II a swallow which makes edible nests.

séndhak *reg* whenever, if, supposing that.

sendhakep *var of* sedhakep.

sendhang a natural pool of spring water; sendhang kapit pancuran *idiom* boy-girl-boy sibling combination.

séndhé *or* nyéndhé to lean; nyèndhèni to lean against; nyèndhèkaké to lean s.t. against; sèndhèn leaning, in a leaning position; sèndhènan 1 s.t. for leaning against; 2 to lean against; suméndhé leaning against; pasèndhènan s.t. to lean against.

sendheng bowstring, any stretched cord.

sèndhèr *reg* slanting, slope, aslant.

sendhet sluggish; nyendheti to hold up (progress), slow down.

sendhi *reg* prop, support.

sèndhing Protestant mission.

séndhok spoon; - bèbèk an enamel soup-spoon; nyéndhok to spoon, stir or dish up with a spoon; nyéndhoki to ladle up/out repeatedly; nyéndhokaké to spoon out for s.o.; séndhokan to eat with a spoon.

sendhol, nyendhol *reg* to push s.t. with the head from below (*var of* sundhul).

sendhon *way* mood song chanted by a dalang to set the scene; sesendhonan to sing for one's own amusement.

sendhu in a reproving tone, snappy, curt, brusque; nyendhu to reprove, rebuke, chide; kesendhu to get censured; sesendhon to find fault with each other;

sendhon-waon always finding fault (with).

sendika *var of* sandika.

sendut twitching (in a particular part of the body).

sené *var of* seni II.

senen *lit* 1 ray, beam; 2 gleam.

senèn I Monday; - kemis 1 to fast on Monday and Thursday; 2 poverty-stricken; nyenèn to (do) every Monday.

II, nyenèni to bawl out, tell off.

seneng *ng*, remen *subst kr*, rena *k.i.*, 1 happy, glad, pleased; 2 to like; 3 to (do) habitually or characteristically; nyenengi 1 to like; to love; 2 to like, prefer; nyenengaké 1 to please, bring pleasure to; 2 to amuse, do s.o. a favour; seneng-seneng to enjoy o.s., have a good time; kesenengan 1 hobby, favourite; 2 happiness, contentment, pleasure.

senéngga *reg* if (it were true); let's suppose.

senénjong rice mixed into the accompanying dishes.

senéwen to have a fit of nerves, get uptight.

seng *or* mak seng *describing a bad odour*; sang-seng to give off a disagreeable odour.

sèng I *reg* nyèngi to call, invite to come.

II 1 zinc; 2 corrugated iron (roofing).

sengadi 1 pretence; 2 to pretend.

sengados *subst kr for* sengadi.

sengak sharp, acrid, biting.

sengap, nyengap to snap angrily.

sengar *var of* sengak.

sengara 1 curse; 2 solemn oath; nyengara to swear, take an oath (not to do s.t.); nyengarakaké to reject as an impossibility, out of the question.

sèngèk *reg* fuss, ado.

sengèn, nyengèni *reg* to bawl out, tell off. *See also* senèn II.

sengéngé sun (*var of* srengéngé).

sengèr *var of* cengèr.

séngga *reg* until, up to.

senggak, nyenggaki to punctuate with cries;

senggakan cries or exclamations uttered to accompany classical dance.

senggang 1 leisure; 2 to get over, recover (from illness) (*k.i. for* mari, waras); 3 somewhat lightened, to get some relief (*reg kr for* mayar).

senggani mingling, sounding together.

senggara, nyenggara *lit* to seduce; - macan to seduce forcibly.

senggata *var of* sugata.

senggèh *reg var of* sengguh.

sènggèk *var of* sènggèt.

sènggèt a long pole for picking fruit high up on a tree;

nyènggèt to get s.t. down with a long pole;

nyènggètaké to pick (fruit *etc*) for s.o. with a long pole;

nyènggèt babal, ketiban nangkané *prov* to get more than one expected.

senggih *var of* sengguh.

sengglèng, sengglèng-sengglèng 1 to swing the arms loosly; 2 rickety.

senggoh *var of* sengguh.

sénggol, nyénggol 1 to touch lightly; 2 to bump against; 3 to nudge (with the elbow);

nyénggoli *or* sénggal-sénggol to keep touching/bumping;

sénggolan *or* sénggol-sénggolan to touch each other;

kesénggol to get bumped unintentionally.

senggor *var of* senggur.

sénggot *or* sénggotan equipment for dipping up water from a well, a bamboo lever weighted at one end and holding the bucket at the other;

nyénggot to dip up water with the above.

senggoyongan to stagger, walk unsteadily.

senggoyoran *var of* senggoyongan.

senggrak-senggruk *see* senggruk.

senggrèk *var of* sènggrèk.

sènggrèk *var of* sènggèt.

senggring, senggring-senggring as thin as a rake.

senggrok, nyenggrok to draw in the breath noisily, grunt (pigs);

senggrok-senggrok to keep grunting.

sénggrok, nyénggrok to be stuck, unable to go any further;

nyénggroki to hinder, impede, obstruct.

senggruk, nyenggruk to sniff up or inhale s.t.;

senggruk-senggruk *or* senggrak-senggruk to sob;

senggruken *or* sesenggrukan to keep sobbing, have a fit of sobbing.

sengguh 1 imagined idea; 2 mistaken idea;

nyengguh 1 to think, assume, imagine; 2 to think of, regard (as);

panyengguh assumption, conclusion.

sènggun *reg* supposing.

senggung a kind of badger (*var of* segung).

senggur, senggur-senggur *or* sesengguran *repr* the sound of snoring, purring;

nyenggur 1 to snore; 2 to purr.

senggut, nyenggut to graze;

nyenggutaké to let graze.

sengir 1 having a strong, turpentine-like taste, smell; 2 a variety of mango.

sengit 1 unpleasant, prickly; 2 to detest, loathe;

nyengit *or* nyenyengit nasty, spiteful, sharp;

nyengiti to dislike, hate s.o.;

sumengit 1 annoying in nature; 2 of an age when children like to fight;

sengit-sengitan to hate each other.

sengiyèn *kr, reg* once, formerly. *See also* biyèn.

sengka, nyengka 1 to rise steeply (road); to climb (mountain); 2 to do s.t. to a high degree;
nyengkakaké to hasten, give an extra impetus to;
sumengka rising steeply, going uphill;
sengkan a steep place;
sumengka pangawak braja *lit* (to arrive *etc*) in great haste and without advance notice;
sinengkakaké ingaluhur *lit* promoted to a higher status.

sengkala *var of* sangkala.

sengkalang rim on a wheel. *See also* cengkalang.

sengkang earstuds for pierced ears (*kr for* suweng I).

sengkap *reg* a pronged fishing spear;
nyengkap to catch fish with the above.

sengkek short, thick, stubby.

sengkèk, nyengkèk *reg* to jig, jerk (on bridle to make a horse gallop).

sengkel *var of* sekel.

sengkelang, nyengkelang *reg, var of* sengkelit.

sengkelat *var of* sangkelat.

sengkelit *ng, kr,* **wangking** *k.i.,* **nyengkelit** *or* **nyengkelitaké** to wear (a kris, knife *etc*) stuck in the belt at the back.

sengker, nyengker *or* **nyengkeri** 1 to fence in, enclose; 2 to keep for a special purpose, claim for o.s., mark as reserved;
sengkeran 1 kept in seclusion (bride, before marriage); 2 (bird) cage;
sesengkeran suci (Catholic) Holy Sacrament.

sengkéyangan *var of* sengkèyèngan.

sengkèyèngan to stagger, walk unsteadily.

sengkil 1 hard, tough going; 2 tight (cough).

séngklak *reg* to deny. *See also* sélak.

sengklèh broken, hanging loose;
nyengklèhaké to break s.t. (off).

sèngklèh *var of* sengklèh.

séngkong cassava (*var of* singkong).

sengkoyangan *var of* sengkoyongan.

sengkoyongan to stagger, walk unsteadily.

sengkoyoran *var of* sengkoyongan.

sengkrak, nyengkrak I to pull, tug, jerk. II, **nyengkrak** having an acid odour. *See also* segrak.

sengkrang, sengkrang-sengkrang to have a stinging or burning feeling in many places (*e.g.* from touching stinging nettles);
sumengkrang to sting, burn.

sengkrèk stern, rough (words);
nyengkrèk 1 to jerk sharply (on a bridle); 2 to snap sternly, roughly;
kesengkrèk 1 to get pulled sharply; 2 *fig* to get criticised harshly.

sengkring *var of* sengkrang.

sengkud eager, lively;
nyengkud to apply o.s. (to s.t.) with speed and energy, rush through.

senglé, senglèn odd, paired wrongly (*var of* selé II).

séngok *or* **mak séngok** *repr* a big (sniffing) kiss on the cheek;
nyéngok to kiss s.o.'s cheek;
séngok-séngokan to kiss each other;
séngak-séngok to kiss repeatedly.

sengol snappish, harsh.

séngon a high tree, the wood used in building.

sengsem to take great pleasure in;
nengsemaké of deep interest, very attractive;
kasengsem engrossed in.

sèngslo jumbled, in a mess.

sèngso *var of* sèngslo.

senguk *var of* séngok.

sengur stinking (dead body, rotten fish).

seni I art;

  kasenian art object, work of art.

  II urine (*reg kr for* **uyuh**, *also* **sené**).

senig, senag-senig worried, anxious.

senik I a small basket of woven bamboo with square foot.

  II (*pron as:* **seni:k**), **senak-senik** worried, apprehensive.

seninjong *see* **senénjong**.

senit (*pron as:* **seni:t**), *or* **mak senit** *repr* a stab of pain;

  senit-senit *or* **senat-senit** to throb with pain (*e.g.* an infected finger).

seniyèn *reg* once, formerly. *See also* **biyèn**.

seniyin *var of* **seniyèn**.

senjata 1 gun, rifle (*kr for* **bedhil**); 2 weapon; - **pamungkas** a magical weapon for killing one's enemies; - **pitulung** vital aid, assistance.

sénjing all the morning (*kr for* **sakésuk**). *See also* **énjing**.

sentak *or* **sentakan** angry, impatient words;

  nyentak to speak to angrily, snarl, snap at;

  nyentaki to keep snarling, snapping.

sentana I 1 family, relatives (*kr for* **sedulur**); 2 a child who is taken into a socially high family to become educated and grow up as one of them; 3 retinue and family of a village headman;

  nyentana to live in the home of a socially high family (as above);

  sumentana on friendly terms with aristocrats.

  II cemetery (*reg kr for* **pakuburan**).

sentani *lit* pillow.

sentèg, nyentèg 1 to press down firmly, tighten (weaving, with shuttle); 2 to push into (s.o. else's position);

  sentèg pisan anigasi *idiom* to say or do s.t. only once but effectively.

sènteg *or* **mak sènteg** *repr* the feel of a sudden heavy burden;

  sumènteg burdensome.

sentèleng, I scaffolding.

  II exhibition (*var of* **setèleng**).

sentèlèng *var of* **sentèleng**.

sènter I 1 torch, flashlight;

  nyènter, nyènteri to shine a torch (on).

  II centre line in soccer field; - **pur** centre forward (soccer player or position);

  nyènteri to play centre (in soccer).

senthak-senthuk *see* **senthuk** II.

senthar-senthir to chain-smoke.

sentheng clothesline.

senthèt I *or* **mak senthèt** *repr* sudden heating up;

  nyenthètaké to put s.t. in the hot sun to dry;

  sumenthèt to heat up suddenly (of sun), to turn out hot.

  II *reg* to be cracked (plaster, earthenware).

senthir I, **diyan** - makeshift lamp consisting of an oil-filled bottle or tin and a wick.

  II *repr* a small squirt of urine (children);

  sumenthir to keep trickling or dripping (tap).

senthit I 1 piercing high-pitched sound, whistle; 2 to whistle (train *etc*);

  nyenthit to produce such a sound.

  II, **nyenthit** to keep quiet, make no disclosure;

  nyenthitaké to conceal, withhold;

  senthitan s.t. concealed, embezzled.

senthiyeng *or* **mak senthiyeng** *repr* a sudden, silent departure.

senthiyer *var of* **senthiyeng**.

senthiyot *var of* **senthiyeng**.

senthong a small inner room in traditional Javanese houses; **senthong tengah** innermost room, reserved for sacred purposes.

senthot *or* mak senthot *repr* a sudden runaway.

senthuk I, nyenthuk to sit concentrating on or absorbed in s.t.

II senthuk-senthuk *or* senthak-senthuk to keep sobbing softly.

senthur *repr* a big spurt of urine.

sènti centimetre.

sentika *lit* skilled in handling weapons.

sentil 1 uvula; 2 trigger; 3 tongue (of buckle);

nyentil 1 to pull (trigger); 2 to shoot (a marble) by flipping it with a finger suddenly released from the thumb; 3 to draw s.o.'s attention to s.t. gently.

senting, klambi - *reg* a kind of men's jacket.

sèntir (silk) sash, waistband.

sentlap-sentlup *see* sentlup.

sentlèp *repr* a sharp stinging sensation; nyentlèp to sting, prick.

sentlup *var of* sentrup.

séntol I strong, muscular, tough.

II, séntolan, ora - to not care, not be bothered.

sentolo I *reg* a variety of durian.

II *reg* landing-stage, jetty.

sentolop, lampu - oil lamp in a hanging glass dome.

sentor, nyentor *or* nyentoraké to flush away with water;

kesentor to be caught and carried away (by flowing water).

sentosa *see* santosa.

sentoyang-sentaying *var of* sentoyongan.

sentoyongan to stagger, walk unsteadily (*var of* sempoyongan).

sèntral central, centre.

sentrap-sentrup *see* sentrup.

sentrong *reg* spotlight;

nyentrongi 1 to shed light on; 2 *fig* to highlight, focus attention on;

nyentrongaké to cast light.

sentrup, sentrup-sentrup *or* sentrap-sentrup to keep sniffing, have a runny nose.

sentug *or* mak sentug *repr* a whiff; sumentug to smell disagreeable.

sentut *var of* setut I.

senut (*pron as:* senu:t) *or* mak senut *repr* a stab of pain;

senut-senut *or* senat-senut to throb with pain.

sèp head (of section), boss, manager.

sepa insipid, tasteless.

sépa a comparison (*var of* sanépa).

sepada *ng*, sepaos *kr*, watchful, on the alert (*var of* waspada).

sepah I old (*subst kr for* tuwa). *See also* sepuh I.

sepai sepoy.

sépak a kick;

nyépak to kick (of horse).

sepakat in agreement;

nyepakati to agree to.

sepala, mung - trivial, insignificant.

sepalih one half (*kr for* separo). *See also* palih.

sepan tight-fitting.

sepandri infantryman, foot soldier.

sepangat mediation, intercession (of the Prophet with God) (*var of* supangat).

sepanten *reg* unimportant and trivial.

sepaos 1 a vow, an oath; 2 to swear (*reg kr for* sepata).

separbang savings bank.

separo one half. *See also* paro.

sepasar one five-day or market week;

nyepasari to hold a slametan to mark one five-day week;

sepasaran the above slametan.

sepat a certain edible freshwater fish.

sepata *var of* supata.

sepatu shoes; - jinjit high-heeled shoes; - rodha roller-skates; - sandhal open-toed shoes; - sandhat laced shoes;

sepaton to put on or wear shoes;

nyepatoni to put shoes on s.o.

sepédhah bicycle;

nyepédhah to ride a bicycle;

sepédhahan to go for a bicycle ride.

sepeket to have a friendly relationship (with) (*var of* supeket).

sepèksi rural inspection.

sepèktur rural inspector.

sepèkuk layer cake.

sepèl, nyepèl to spell;
sepèlan spelling.

sepélé, mung - trivial, of no consequence;
nyepèlèkaké to trivialise, treat with contempt.

sepen quiet, lonely, deserted (*kr for* sepi).

sepèn 1 storage cupboard; 2 series of rooms at the back used for storage, servants' quarters *etc. See also* sepi.

sèper I *reg* secretary, clerk (village administrative position).
II, nyèper 1 to group, classify; 2 to regard s.o. as.

sepèrsi asparagus.

sepet I coconut or betel nut fibre.
II 1 tart, sour; 2 disagreeable or wearisome to look at; - madu very sweet-tasting;
nyepeti 1 astringent (taste); 2 offensive (to look at).

sepethik *reg* a tiny bit.

sepethil *var of* sepethik.

sepi quiet, lonely, deserted; - mamring *or* - nyenyet very quiet, utterly still;
nyepi to become desolate;
nenepi to withdraw to a quiet place for meditation;
kesepèn 1 to feel lonely; 2 too lonely;
sepèn 1 storage cupboard; 2 series of rooms at the back used for storage, servants' quarters *etc*);
panepèn sanctuary, place where one meditates in solitude;
sepa-sepi very quiet;
sepi ing pamrih *expr* unselfish, disinterested.

sèpi *lit* magic spell, incantation; - angin incantation for producing powerful wind to chase enemies away.

sepinten *kr for* sepira.

sepir biceps, well-developed muscles.

sepira *ng*, sepinten *kr* how much? (of s.t. not specified in units);
nyepira (to be) how much apiece?;
ora sepiraa not so much, not very.

sepiral spiral.

sepiritus methylated spirits for lamps or medicinal use.

sepisan one time, once. *See also* pisan.

sepisiyal special, out of the ordinary.

sepit *var of* supit.

sepiyun spy.

séplé *coll* trivial, paltry, insignificant.

sèplèk *var of* séplé.

sepon household sponge.

seprana *ng*, seprika *kr*, till that time, as long as that;
seprana-sepréné, ora - 1 up to the present time, still nothing (heard); 2 what's going on?

seprapat one quarter. *See also* prapat I.

sepré bedspread.

seprèi *var of* sepré.

sepréné *ng*, sepriki *kr*, until now;
seprana-sepréné *see* seprana.

seprika till that time (*kr for* seprana).

sepriki till now (*kr for* sepréné).

sepritus *var of* sepiritus.

septa to like, want (*md for* doyan). *See also* seta.

septu *var of* Sabtu.

sepud urgent.

sepuh I old, mature, ripe (*kr for* tuwa);
kasepuhan pertaining to the state of the head of the older generation (King, in contrast to the Crown Prince, kanoman).
II, nyepuhi 1 to harden (steel); 2 to darken (colour of gold); 3 to use fish poison (to catch fish).

sepuluh *ng*, sedasa *kr*, ten;
nyepuluh ten each;
kasepuluh ten times; (for) the 10th time;

sepuluhan ten-rupiah note.

sepundi *coll* how (*kr for* **kepriyé**).

sepur train; - **kluthuk** *or* - **thruthuk** slow local train;

nyepur to go by train;

nyepuri to pay s.o.'s railway ticket;

nyepuraké to send s.t. or s.o. by train;

sepuran money for buying a railway ticket;

sepur-sepuran 1 toy train; **2** to play trains.

sepura forgiveness (*var of* **apura**);

sepurané excuse me! (when denying money to a beggar).

ser *or* **mak ser 1** *repr* spinning, whirling; **2** *repr* a sharp pain; **3** *repr* a quick shift of position.

sèr *or* **mak sèr 1** *repr* water emerging; **2** *repr* smearing.

sérad-sèrèd to borrow clothing and wear it without permission of the owner.

serada *reg* somewhat, quite. *See also* **rada**.

serah, nyerah to surrender;

nyerahi to hand over to s.o.;

nyerahaké to hand over, transfer s.t.

serak I husky, hoarse (of voice);

nyeraki *or* **nyerakaké** to make (the voice) husky/hoarse.

II wad of cloth or fibre used as a filter.

serang, nyerang to attack;

serangan an attack;

panyerang act or way of attacking.

serap 1 to enter; **2** to go down, set (sun) (*kr for* **surup**).

sérap dazzled, temporarily blinded by glare.

serat I 1 fibre; **2** grain (of wood); **3** vein (in leaf); **4** barb (of feather).

II 1 letter; **2** book (*kr for* **layang**);

nyerat 1 to write (*kr for* **nulis**); **2** to make batik (*kr for* **mbathik**).

III comb (*kr for* **jungkat**).

serban turban;

nyerbani to put a turban on s.o.;

serbanan to wear a turban.

serbat a hot drink spiced with ginger.

serbèt 1 serviette, napkin; **2** cloth for cleaning;

nyerbèti to clean s.t. with a cloth;

nyerbètaké to use s.t. as a cloth for cleaning;

serbètan to wipe one's hands with a napkin;

serbèt-serbèt to use a cloth or napkin for cleaning.

serdhadhu soldier. *See also* **saradhadhu**.

serdu *reg* to agree.

seré lemon grass.

sèrèd I the narrow undyed strip at the edge of a piece of batik fabric;

nyèrèdi to leave (the edge) undyed when making batik;

sèrèdan wearing the undyed strip at the front of one's batik along the edge of the folds (**wiron**).

II, nyèrèd to drag s.t. (along);

kesèrèd to get dragged (along).

sereg, nyereg to put pressure on s.o.;

seregan hasty, done under pressure.

sèrèh I to resign, retire.

II, nyèrèhi *reg* to skim s.t. from the surface.

sèrèn 1, semèrèn to stop, take a rest, discontinue an activity; **2** to leave a position, hand over (to s.o. else);

nyèrèni to hand over (to s.o.);

nyèrèkaké to lay down, hand over s.t.

sereng I stern, harsh, angry, displeased.

II liquid squeezed from lemon peel;

nyereng *or* **nyerengaké** to squirt s.o. with lemon peel juice.

sèrèng squinting, unable to see properly.

serep 1 to enter; **2** sunset, to set (*var of* **serap**). *See also* **surup**.

sèrep *or* **sèrepan** a spare (part *etc*);

nyèrepi to substitute (s.t.) with a spare.

seret 1 choked (voice); **2** tight (of money), hard to get;

nyereti 1 to stick or get stuck, *esp* in

the throat; 2 (*or* **nyeretaké**) to make tight, screw up tight.

serèt, nyerèt to smoke opium;
serètan opium-smoking equipment;
panyerèt act of smoking opium;
panyerètan opium den.

sèrèt *see* **sèrèd I, II**.

serga *coll* the late (deceased) (*var of* **swarga**).

sergi *coll* the late (deceased) (*var of* **swargi**).

serik offended, irritated;
nyeriki *or* **nyerikaké 1** to irritate, annoy s.o.; **2** to make s.o. offended; **3** offensive;
serikan, serik-atèn touchy, easily offended;
serik-serikan, seserikan to have a grudge against each other.

sering often;
sering-sering quite often (*kr for* **kerep**). *See also* **asring**.

serit I a fine-toothed comb for removing lice from hair;
nyeriti to comb the lice from s.o.'s hair;
seritan to comb o.s. with the above.
II young cucumber.

serju *var of* **sarju**.

serkah *reg* greedy.

sèrkulèr a circular (letter).

séro I a type of fish trap consisting of a palisade in the sea;
nyéro to catch fish with the above trap.
II financial share in a business.

serog *see* **srog**.

sérok a long-handled dipper;
nyérok to scoop up;
nyéroki to scoop up repeatedly.

sérong 1 diagonal, slantwise; **2** to commit adultery;
nyérong 1 to set s.t. in a diagonal position; **2** to saw, cut at an angle.

serop *see* **sérop**.

sérop *or* **mak sérop 1** *repr* kissing s.o.'s cheek; **2** *repr* slurping;
nyérop 1 to kiss s.o.'s cheek; **2** to slurp noisily;
nyéropi to scoop s.t. from the surface;
sérap-sérop to keep slurping.

serot, nyerot 1 to sip, suck; **2** to absorb;
serotan drinking straw;
panyerot act or way of sucking/absorbing (*var of* **sedhot**).

serpis tea service.

sersan sergeant.

serseg *lit var of* **seseg**.

serta *var of* **sarta**.

sertipikat certificate.

sertu *var of* **satru**.

seru 1 loud; **2** forceful;
nyeroni to make s.t. loud(er) or strong(er);
nyerokaké to do s.t. hard, forcefully;
keseron excessively loud or forceful;
panyeru *gram* exclamation. *Also* **sru**.

sérub a blindfold;
nyérub to blindfold;
séruban blindfolded.

sérum serum;
nyérum to inoculate s.o. with serum.

serung thorny branches wrapped around a coconut palm to prevent it being climbed.

sérung *reg* variety of rice (late ripening).

seruni a certain flower (*var of* **sruni I**).

serwa *var of* **sarwa**.

ses I a smoke (*kr for* **udud, rokok**); (*or* **ngeses**) to smoke.
II *repr* a sibilant sound;
ngeses to produce a sibilant sound;
ngesas-ngeses to inhale and exhale audibly through the teeth.

sesa, kesesa in a hurry (*kr for* **kesusu**, *see* **susu II**).

sésa I, sésa-sésa to depend (on), be up (to).
II tanpa sésa *lit* leaving none, with none remaining.

sesah (not) need to, (not) necessary (*var of* **sisah**).

sesak 1 to have too little space; **2** tight, hard to breathe.

seseg *var of* **sesak**.

sèsèk I woven bamboo panel or mat.
II n(y)èsèk *reg* to cross straight through, traverse.
III boiled corn scraped from the cob and mixed with grated coconut and salt.

sesel, n(y)esel to push in;
n(y)eseli to insert into;
n(y)eselaké to insert s.t. into;
seselan **1** that which is inserted into s.t.; **2** *gram* infix.

sesep, n(y)esep to suck (*kr for* n(y)usu);
n(y)esepi to suckle (*kr for* n(y)usoni);
sesepan an infant still being breastfed (*kr for* **suson**, *see* **susu I**).

seser I (to rotate) fast.
II *or* **seseran** a style of ring in spiral shape.
III, keseser beaten back, defeated.

sèsèr scoop-net of woven bamboo.

sèsèt to come off, peel off;
nyèsèt *or* nyèsèti to tear, pull off (skin, bark).

sesi *coll var of* **seksi**.

sester 1 nurse; **2** Catholic nun (*var of* **suster**).

sèstu *coll var of* **saèstu**.

sésuk *ng*, **mbénjing-énjing** *kr*, tomorrow;
- embèn day after tomorrow; - ésuk tomorow morning;
sésuk-sésuk at some (indefinite) future time.

sesuker *see* **suker**.

sèt maggot;
sèten infested with maggots.

seta to like, want (*md for* **doyan**).

séta *lit* white.

setabel gunner, artillery;
setabelan quarters of the artillery.

setajab efficacious (*var of* **mustajab**).

setagèn a broad band of woven material worn by women wound many times around the waist.

setaking 1 a strike; **2** to strike.

setal horse stable.

setali *ng*, **setangsul** *kr*, **1** 25 cents (during the colonial period); **2** formerly used unit of weight for gold;
setalèn *or* setalènan 25-cent coin;
nyetalènan 25 cents each; worth 25 cents;
setali telung wang *idiom* no different; six of one and half a dozen of the other.

setalpèn pen nib.

setaman, kembang - water and flower mixture used ceremonially.

setambul stage production somewhat resembling a Western-style musical comedy.

sétan devil, evil spirit; - **alas 1** an evil spirit of the forest; **2** *term of abuse*.
nyétani to incite s.o. to quarrel.

setana *reg* cemetery.

setandar 1 standard; **2** bicycle stand.

setang bicycle handlebars.

setangan handkerchief (*var of* **saputangan**).

setanplat bus station.

setap staff.

setasiyun station.

setat list, record, register.

setater starter.

setatsiyun *var of* **setasiyun**.

setèl 1 a matching set; **2** to harmonise, go well (with);
nyetèl **1** to switch on (radio); **2** to match; **3** to adjust;
setèlan (wearing) a suit (coat and trousers).

setèleng 1 exposition, exhibition; **2** military emplacement.

setèm true (of pitch);
nyetèm **1** to tune (an instrument); **2** to decide by majority vote;

setèman voting;

setèm-setèman to vote for s.t.

setengah 1 a half; **2** partly, somewhat. *See also* **tengah**.

sétham-séthom to keep popping s.t. into the mouth with a spoon.

séthap-séthop *var of* **sétham-séthom**.

sethemlik *var of* **sathemplik**.

sethemlok *var of* **sathemlok**.

sethemplik *var of* **sathemplik**.

sèthèp dry dirt in the eye (after sleeping);

sèthèpen to have eye-dirt. *See also* **sithip**.

sethi *reg* of course, certainly (*var of* **mesthi**).

sethithik *ng*, **sekedhik** *kr* **1** a little, a bit, a few; **2** partly, somewhat;

sethithiké *or* **sethithik-sethithiké** at least;

sethithik-sethithik 1 little by little; **2** very little;

ora sethithik a great many, a good deal.

setijab efficacious.

setik stitching; - **balik** a hem;

nyetik to hem (a garment).

setilah I *reg* manner, way, custom.

II (to be in) death throes.

setin I satin.

II a marble.

setinggar *lit* gun, rifle.

setingkul coal.

setip rubber eraser;

nyetip to erase.

setipar prayer asking for forgiveness (*var of* **istipar**).

setir steering wheel;

nyetir *or* **nyetiri** to drive (a car), steer.

setiti careful, accurate, scrupulous.

setiwel tall boots (*esp* riding boots);

setiwelan to put on or wear boots.

setiyar to seek (help, remedy), try to do s.t. about;

nyetiyaraké to try to find s.t. to help, seek a remedy on behalf of.

setlika iron (for pressing clothes) (*var of* **setrika**).

setolep electric torch (*var of* **sentolop**).

setolup *var of* **sentolop**.

setop to stop;

setopan bus-stop, stopping-place.

setoplès a glass jar with airtight stopper, used for storing biscuits.

setor *or* **nyetor** *or* **nyetoraké 1** to pay a rental fee; **2** to deposit (money in the bank);

setoran 1 rental fee (taxi, pedicab *etc*); **2** deposit.

setori *ng*, **setonten** *kr* a quarrel; to quarrel, bicker.

setoter a kind of European card game;

setoteran to play this game.

sétra *lit* (*or* **pasétran**) place where corpses are disposed of;

nyétrakaké to dispose of (corpses).

setral 1 ray, beam (of light), gleam; **2** radius (of a circle).

setrali a variety of oil lamp.

setrap punishment;

nyetrap to punish s.o.

setrèk I, **setrèkan** performance of music for strings.

II, **nyetrèk** to drag (log) from the forest using oxen.

setrèn ricefield near a riverbank.

setrèng strict, stern, harsh.

setri 1 female (*md for* **wadon**); **2** wife (*md for* **bojo**).

setrik a bow knot, hair ribbon;

nyetriki to put a ribbon in s.o.'s hair;

setrikan to wear a hair ribbon.

setrika iron (for pressing clothes);

nyetrika to iron, press;

nyetrikakaké 1 to iron for s.o.; **2** to have s.t. ironed;

setrikan clothes for ironing, ironed clothes.

setrikel 1 *reg* to stumble, trip (horse); **2** to lose a lot of money, founder (business).

setrilam *reg var of* setrali.

setriman steersman.

setring *reg* reins.

setrip 1 dash, hyphen; 2 stripe, marking line;
    nyetrip to mark with dash or line;
    nyetripi to make lines on;
    setripan *or* setrip-setrip with stripes.

setripu *reg* thong sandals. *See also* cripu.

setroli *var of* setrali.

setrolup glass dome in which an oil lamp is hung.

setrongking hurricane lamp, pressure lamp.

setruksi instruction.

setrum electric current, power.

setrup syrup (of fruit juice and sugar, mixed with water).

Setu Saturday. *See also* Sabtu.

setuju in agreement;
    nyetujoni to reach an agreement (about).

setum 1 steam; 2 steam engine; 3 steam roller;
    nyetum 1 to steam; 2 to flatten with a steam roller.

setun actually (it) should have, but... (*var of* destun).

setunggal 1 one (*kr for* siji); 2 a certain (*kr for* sawiji). *See also* tunggal.

setunggil *subst kr for* setunggal.

setup 1 a drink made by boiling fruit with sugar and water; 2 vegetable in coconut milk sauce;
    nyetup to stew, boil (fruit, vegetables).

setut I belt, sash;
    nyetuti to put a belt on s.o.
    II, nyetut to overtake, pass.
    III prop, strut.

setya loyal, faithful, obedient; - tuhu faithful and loyal;
    nyetyani to be loyal/obedient to;
    kasetyan loyalty, allegiance.

séwa, nyéwa to rent, hire;

nyéwakaké to rent s.t. out;
    séwan 1 rent money; 2 rented, for rent.

séwak, nyéwak *reg* to divide (a ricefield) up into parts.

séwaka (*also* séwa, siwi, siwaka) service, homage, obedience;
    sinéwaka, siniwaka to sit in state, to hold audience (of a king, whereby the subjects sit before him in token of their loyalty and service);
    paséwakan place where the subjects sit, audience-hall. *See also* séba.

séwal to come off as a result of damage (*var of* siwal I).

sèwèk *reg* batik garment, kain.

sewelas eleven. *See also* welas II.

seweng *reg* empty, vacant, unoccupied, uninhabited. *See also* suwung.

sèwèr *reg* ripped, torn (*var of* siwir);
    nyèwèr *reg* to tear to pieces.

sèwèt *var of* sèwèk.

sewidak sixty.

sewiwi wing (*var of* suwiwi).

séwot furious.

sèwu 1 one thousand; 2 *lit* a very large number;
    nyèwu 1 by the thousand; a thousand at a time; 2 to hold a commemorative ceremony on the 1,000th day after s.o.'s death;
    panèwu title of an official of medium rank. *See also* èwu.

séyat-séyot *reg* (to do s.t.) briskly, quickly, deftly.

sèyèg wobbly, unsteady, rickety.

séyok, nyéyoki to grab by the handful.

séyos *reg* different (*kr for* séjé).

si I 1 *deprecatory person marker, used before the names of those with whom the speaker and interlocutor are intimate, e.g.* simbok (our) *Mum,* simbah (our) *Grandma;* 2 *particle used before a noun referring to a particular person in a category.*
    II *emphatic particle, e.g.* dhèké ora

sinau si! but he didn't study, did he!

sibar ointment to be rubbed on the chest, neck *etc*;

nyibari to apply the above.

sibat *inf var of* musibat.

sibin to take a quick bath by splashing the body and then going over it with a cloth.

siblon *reg* slapping the surface of water rhythmically for fun. *See also* ciblon.

sibrat *var of* sébrat.

sibu mother (*var of* ibu).

sicok *reg* one (*var of* sithok).

sida *ng*, **siyos** *kr*, 1 to succeed in (do)ing; 2 to go ahead (as planned); - guri a small plant the flowers of which are used for treating bee stings; - luhur a batik design of diagonally placed rows of circles: used for bridal batiks; - mukti a bridal batik design; - wurung to finally not go through;

nyidakaké to carry out (an intention); sidané as it finally turned out.

sidadal *var of* sedadal.

sidhakep with the arms folded across the chest (*var of* sedhakep);

nyidhakepaké to fold the arms as above.

sidhang sitting, session;

nyidhangaké to take before a court, hear (a case) in court.

sidhat, nyidhat to take a short cut;

sidhatan a short cut.

sidhekah *var of* sedhekah.

sidheku *var of* sedheku.

sidhekul *var of* sidheku.

sidhekung *var of* sidheku.

sidhekus *var of* sidheku.

sidhem *lit* - premanem soundless, with nothing to be heard;

nyidhem to keep s.t. quiet, hush up.

sidhep, nyidhep to take to be, consider as.

sidhum shaded, shady, sheltered;

nyidhum to take shelter;

kesidhumen excessively shady, over-protected;

panyidhuman 1 protection; 2 protector.

sidik 1 truthful; 2 clairvoyant, to know before being told;

nyidiki *or* nyidikaké to look into, attempt to confirm.

sidikara *lit*, nyidikara to utter prayers, magical spells over (for).

siduwa to sit cross-legged with the elbows resting on the knees.

sigar cut in half, cracked, split; - jambé (*or* jambé sinigar) (of lips) beautifully proportioned, of equal thickness; - semangka cut precisely in half;

nyigar to split, cleave, cut through lengthwise;

nyigari to split s.t. repeatedly;

nyigaraké to split s.t. for s.o.;

sinigar split, cut in half;

sigaran 1 cut open; 2 a split, crack, cut;

sasigar one half; karo sigar one and a half; telu sigar two and a half *etc*.

sigeg 1 finished, over; end; 2 (of streets) not through, (coming to) a dead end; 3 *gram* closed (of syllables);

nyigeg to cut off, discontinue;

sinigeg (of part of a story) brought to an end; sinigeg genti kocapa *way* (in narrative) 'let us change the subject to...';

panyigeg a means of closing (syllables).

sigi I threads at the end of a fabric (cut off).

II, nyigèni to keep an eye on s.o. (out of suspicion).

sigid *reg* mosque.

sigit *lit* very handsome (young man).

sigra I 1 a sneeze; 2 to sneeze (*k.i. for* wahing).

II *lit* quickly, at once.

sigrak bursting with energy and buoyant health.

sigreng charismatic, with a forceful personality, influential.

sigrong wide and dark (ravine).

sigug stiff, rigid.

sih I 1 love, loving kindness; **2** favour;
ngasih-asih to try to win favour;
sih-sinihan to love each other;
sih-sihen biased, partisan;
pasihan **1** in the state of newfound romantic love (just married); **2** loved one;
pangasih **1** s.t. used to win favour; **2** aji - a magical spell used to win a girl's love. *See also* **asih, kasih.**
II *inf var of* **isih.**
III shoo! **ngesihi** to shoo away.

sihir black magic, witchcraft;
nyihir to practise black magic on s.o.

siji *ng*, **satunggal** *kr*, one;
n(y)iji one each;
n(y)iji-n(y)iji one by one, one at a time.

sik 1 first, beforehand (*shtf of* **dhisik**); **2** just a minute! (*shtf of* **mengko dhisik**).

sikak *reg* shoo!

sikang *var of* **singkang.**

sikara, nyikara to molest, harm, maltreat.

sikat I 1 a brush; **2** *reg* a comb (of bananas);
nyikat to brush;
nyikati to brush s.t. repeatedly;
sikatan to brush the teeth.
II sikatan a small bird of the wagtail family.

sikep I, nyikep to grapple (fighters);
sikepan **1** an embrace; **2** a type of formal jacket.
II an armed man, retainer (liable to service).
III attitude, way of thinking.

siki I *lit* one.
II now (*coll var of* **saiki**).

sikiah a kind of Chinese card game.

sikik *reg var of* **dhisik.**

sikil *ng*, **suku** *kr*, **sampéyan** *k.i.* leg, foot;
nyikili to put the leg in front of s.o. impolitely;
sikilan leg (of furniture).

sikir *var of* **sihir.**

sikon set-square. *See also* **siku.**

siksa punishment, chastisement;
nyiksa **1** to punish, chastise; **2** to torment, maltreat (*e.g.* animal).

siku 1 a right-angle; **2** to form a right-angle (with), be perpendicular (to); **3** set-square (implement for checking rightangles); **4** elbow (*k.i. for* **sikut**).

sikut *ng*, *kr*, **siku** *k.i.* elbow;
nyikut **1** to nudge with the elbow; **2** *fig* to deceive, cheat; - bathi to reject;
sikut-sikutan **1** to nudge each other; **2** *fig* to deceive each other.

sil, sil-silan agitated, restless (child).

sila I (to sit) cross-legged; - panggung to sit with crossed legs and the knees pulled up (woman); - tumpang to sit cross-legged with the right leg over the left; - timpuh to sit with knees drawn up alongside the body, to squat on crossed ankles (woman);
pasilan a place to sit.
II nambut silaning akrama *lit* to enter into matrimony.

silad, nyilad *or* **nyiladi** to trim (bamboo) into slivers;
siladan slivers resulting from trimming a split length of bamboo.

siladri *lit* mountain.

silah *or* **silah-silah** each one separately;
nyilah-nyilah to treat each one separately, one by one.

silak wide open, clear (free of obstructions, *e.g.* brushwood, rubbish);
nyilakaké **1** to open up wide; **2** to sweep away, sweep clean;
sumilak wide open, clear, clean, unobstructed.

silakrama *lit* good manners, courtesy;

nilakrama to receive courteously, welcome politely.

silang *reg var of* **selang** III.

silar *var of* **singlar**.

silat traditional self-defence arts.

silaturahmi to express respect and ask forgiveness of others at the end of the Fasting Month.

silem 1 to become submerged; 2 to disappear from sight;
nyilem to dive;
nyilemi to dive into, dive for;
nyilemaké to submerge s.t.

silep I submerged, sunken, out of sight;
nyilep to hide, keep back;
nyilepaké to submerge, plunge, dip s.t.;
kesilep 1 accidentally submerged in water; 2 *fig* thrown into the shade (reputation).
II banana leaves used to cover half-cooked rice, then covered with a lid;
nyilep to cook rice to the stage when it can be covered by **silep**;
nyilepi to cover with **silep**.

silib stealthy, furtive, secret, unnoticed;
nyilibi to be secretive toward, do s.t. without s.o.'s knowledge;
nyilibaké to keep s.t. secret, to outwit, trick.

silih I, *ng*, **sambut** *kr*, **ampil** *k.i.*, **nyilih** to borrow;
nyilihi to lend to, loan to;
nyilihaké 1 to lend s.t.; 2 to borrow s.t. on behalf of s.o.;
silihan 1 borrowed; 2 s.t. borrowed;
silih-silihan *or* silih-sinilih to lend to each other, borrow back and forth.
II, **sesilih** *lit* 1 name; 2 bearing the name.
III *lit* mutually, to (with) each other.

silir I (of breezes) soft, gentle;
silir-silir to go out and get some fresh air;
nyilir to winnow (rice) by pouring from a height, so that the wind blows the chaff away;
nyilir-nyiliraké to put s.t. in the fresh air (to cool or dry);
kasilir *or* kasiliran to get blown on;
sumilir blowing softly.
II (of balance scales) tilting slightly in one direction or the other.
III court official in charge of the palace lamps.
IV (of outer skin) thin (*e.g.* of onion).

silit 1 anus; 2 bottom of utensil, pan *etc*;
- kodhok coccyx;
nyiliti to insult, humiliate.

silo blinded by glare, dazzled.

siluk dark, thickly overgrown.

siluman 1 invisible; 2 spirits, invisible beings;
nyiluman to remain invisible.

silwak sentinel, sentry.

sima tiger (*kr for* **macan**).

simah *var of* **sémah**.

simak I *var of* **semak**.
II *reg* mother.

simbah grandmother, grandfather (familiar term of reference). *See also* **embah**.

simbar hair on the chest; - menjangan a kind of parasitic plant found on tree trunks, staghorn fern.

simbat, **nyimbat** *reg* 1 to borrow for a short time; 2 to ask for help for a moment.

simbing, **nyimbing** *or* **nyimbing-nyimbing** to look around furtively.

simbok mother (familiar term of reference). *See also* **embok**, **bok** I.

simbul symbol.

simbun *reg* a variety of cotton fabric.

simbungan lengthwise accordion folds formed in a ceremonial kain with a train. *See also* **sémbong**.

simet a tiny bit. *See also* **imet**.

simik *reg var of* **dhisik**.

simil sea-mail.

simin *reg var of* **dhisik**.

simpang, nyimpang 1 to take a side-road; 2 to deviate from (the rules);
nyimpangi to (move aside and) make away for;
simpangan 1 fork or branch in a road; 2 to step aside for each other when passing in the street.

simpar var of sémpar.

simpé iron tyre which encircles a wooden wheel.

simpen, nyimpen to store, put away;
nyimpeni to store things;
nyimpenaké to store s.t. for s.o.;
sumimpen stored, put away, saved;
simpenan 1 savings, goods put away; 2 storage place; 3 mistress, a secret wife;
panyimpen way of saving, storing.

simping I a kind of oyster shell resembling mother-of-pearl.
II, nyimping way to arrange (puppets) ready for use by sticking them into a banana log with their rods;
simpingan arrangement of puppets in banana logs on either side of the screen ready for the puppet-master to use, from tall at the outside to short next to the screen.
III var of sumping.

simpir var of sèmpèr.

sinang lit bright red.

sinaos even though (kr for senajan).

sinapan gun, flintlock.

sinar light, ray, beam (var of sunar).

sinau to study, learn;
nyinau to study/learn s.t.;
nyinaokaké to send s.o. to study;
pasinaon school, place of study.

sindap dandruff.

sinder inspector, supervisor.

sindhat worms (in meat, plants) (see also singgat).

sindhèn a female vocalist who sings in the gamelan orchestra;
nyindhèn to be a professional female singer;

nyindhèni to sing with (gamelan music).
Also pesindhèn.

sindhet or sindhetan 1 knot; 2 tangled rope, thread;
nyindhet or nyindhetaké to knot s.t. together.

sindhir or nyindhiri to make allusions to, drop hints about;
sindhiran 1 teasing allusion; 2 satire.

sindhung, - riwut lit fierce storm, gale, tempest.

sindhutan reg a variety of bean (see also peté).

sindik hinge pin;
nyindik to put a pin (into a hinge);
nyindiki to furnish (a hinge) with a pin;
sindikan locked with a pin.

sindikara var of sidikara.

sindu lit water, river.

sindur white-bordered red sash tied at the rear (worn at weddings).

sinèh var of jenèh.

sinemèni see udan.

sinep reg quiet, silent;
nyinep to hush up, keep s.t. quiet.

sing I ng, ingkang kr, relative pronoun: who, which, that (various grammatical functions, nominalising: the… one; indicating a modal imperative, e.g. sing ati-ati! be careful! etc).
II from (see also saking).
III Banyuwangi reg not.

singa lion; -barong a monster mask used in certain performances; - nabda lit lion's roar; -nagara executioner; -pati king of the beasts.

singangsana var of singasana.

singasana throne.

singat horn, antler (kr for sungu).

singeb blanket (k.i. for kemul).

singed var of singid.

singel headcloth;

nyingeli to furnish s.o. with a head-cloth;

singelan to wear a headcloth.

singèn formerly, in the past (reg var of biyèn).

singer 1 impressive, awe-inspiring; 2 reg dangerous (place, inhabited by spirits).

singgah, nyinggahi to evade;

nyinggahaké 1 to move s.t. out of the way; 2 to put away, store;

singgah-singgah, sesinggah incanta-tion to avoid dangers.

singgan-singgun, ora - without fear, not anxious about what others will think.

singgang rice plant growing after har-vest.

singgasana throne (var of singasana).

singgat worms in rotting fruit; - betatung moving about rapidly, hyperactive;

nyinggati to shred (coconut) into worm-like pieces.

singgel single.

singget, nyingget to divide up (house) with partitions;

singgetan partitions.

singgih, kasinggihan indeed, it is true that... (kr for bener).

singgul finely pounded herbs applied to child's forehead in order to ward off illness.

singid, nyingidaké to hide, keep out of sight, conceal;

singidan or sesingidan to hide, stay out of sight, lie in wait.

singik reg var of dhisik.

singin reg var of dhisik.

singir (Islamic) religious verses;

singiran to chant verses.

singit haunted, spooky, dangerous.

singkab I side of the chest near the armpit.

II, nyingkab to open (curtain), lift the cover, reveal.

singkal I 1 mouldboard (above the ploughshare); 2 a large plough;

nyingkal reg to plough;

singkalan furrow.

II reg outer end of a bunch of bananas.

singkang, nyingkang-nyingkang to cast out, drive away, banish.

singkat brief, concise;

nyingkat to shorten, abbreviate;

singkatan abbreviation.

singkèk a full-blood Chinese.

singkel sad, grieving. See also sekel.

singkik dangerous, unsafe.

singkin reg more and more, all the more.

singkir, nyingkir 1 to step aside; 2 to avoid;

nyingkiri to avoid s.t.;

nyingkiraké 1 to set on one side; 2 to banish;

sumingkir to get out of the way.

singkong reg cassava.

singkrèh reg var of singkrih.

singkrih var of singkir.

singkur, nyingkur or nyingkuri or nyingkuraké to ignore, reject, turn one's back on;

kesingkur ignored, avoided;

panyingkur act of rejecting or avoid-ing.

singlar 1 to avoid, dodge; 2 to answer evasively.

singlèt T-shirt.

singlo var of singlu.

singlon or sesinglon 1 pseudonym, assumed name; 2 to use a pseudonym.

singlu eerie, gloomy (because of silence and loneliness).

singluk var of singlu.

singlur reg exchange item, replacement;

nyingluri to exchange (one thing) for (another);

nyingluraké to exchange, replace.

singsal or kesingsal 1 to fly away or be thrown where s.t. ought not to be; 2 to get lost, misplaced.

singsèh Chinese apothecary.

singset 1 tight, taut; 2 firm, compact;

n(y)ingseti to make tight(er);
paningset 1 a gift given by a boy's
father to the girl's father as a pledge of
betrothal; 2 sash (*k.i. for* sabuk).

singsèk *var of* singsèh.

singsot to whistle;
nyingsoti to whistle at/to s.o.;
singsat-singsot to keep whistling.

singu, singunen to feel sick, dizzy on
seeing s.t., *e.g.* looking down from a
height.

singub 1 dark, gloomy; 2 the ceiling
above the four pillars in a Javanese
house.

siniwaka *lit see* séwaka.

sinjang ankle-length batik garment (*kr
for* jarik).

sinom I a popular classical verse form;
nyinom to sing such a verse.
II 1 *lit* young shoots; 2 young leaves
of the tamarind tree;
sinoman in rural society, an association of unmarried boys and girls,
whose task it is to serve guests with
food and drink on formal occasions.
III *lit* a fringe worn by girls across the
forehead at the hairline.

sinta name of the 1st wuku week.

sinten who? (*kr for* sapa).

sinthing I kite-tail.
II crazy.

sinthir I makeshift oil lamp (*var of* senthir).
II with out-turned eyeballs.

sintrèn folk magic show.

sintru I movable decorative screen used
as a partition.
II *reg* 1 quiet, lonely; 2 sombre,
gloomy.

sinuhun, ingkang - His Highness (the
late) Susuhunan of Surakarta, or
Sultan of Yogyakarta.

sinuwun, ingkang - His Highness the
Susuhunan of Surakarta, or Sultan of
Yogyakarta.

sinwam *lit* young shoots (*see also* sinom
II).

sinyo European boy, young master.

sipat I 1 attribute of God; 2 character,
nature.
II (forming) a straight line; (*or* sipatan)
string used for marking a straight line; -
banyu level, horizontal; - gantung perpendicular, perfectly vertical; - kuping
swift; (to run) like the wind;
nyipat 1 to align; 2 to make a straight
line with a string;
nyipataké 1 to align s.t.; 2 to direct a
tongue of flame at (of goldsmiths
working gold);
III, nyipati to witness, observe.
IV eye-black, kohl.

sipeng *or* nyipeng to stay s.w. overnight,
lodge (*kr for* nginep).

sipi, tan sipi *or* tan sinipi *lit* great;
exceedingly.

sipik *reg var of* dhisik.

sipil I unimportant, of no consequence.
II civil.

sipilis syphilis.

sipin *reg var of* dhisik.

sipir prison guard.

sipwa abacus (*var of* cipowah).

sir I 1 idea, opinion; 2 duwé - to have
ideas about, be interested in (wanting
to do, get s.t.);
ngesir *or* ngesiri to have in mind,
have one's eye on;
sir-siran 1 s.o. you have your eye on;
2 to be very keen on each other;
sasiré whatever one pleases.
II (*pron as:* si:r) *or* mak sir *repr* a sudden feeling of apprehension, fear;
sir-siran apprehensive, anxious.
III (*pron as:* si:r) *or* mak sir *repr* a
sound of hissing.

sira *lit* 1 you (court idiom, used by royalty to officials); 2 he, she.

sirah 1 head (*kr for* endhas); 2 head (for
counting people); 3 source (of a large

river); 4 units column (in a year);

sesirah 1 first payment on a debt; 2 title (of an article or book); entitled.

siram to take a bath (*k.i.* for **adus**).

sirap wooden roofing shingle;

nyirap to shingle (a roof).

sirat I ray, beam;

sumirat to shine.

II, **nyirati** to sprinkle/splatter with water on;

sirat-sirat to keep sprinkling or splattering with water;

sumirat to splash, spray, splatter.

sirem *lit* dim, obscure (*var of* **surem**).

sirep 1 back to normal, calm once again; 2 **aji** - a magic spell to make the inhabitants of the house fall into a deep sleep; **wayah** - **bocah** the time of night when children quieten down for the night; - **jalma** *or* - **wong** the time when everybody else quietens down for the night;

nyirep *or* **nyirepi** 1 to put out (fire *etc*); 2 to put s.o. under a magic spell (as above);

nyirepaké 1 to put out (a lamp, fire); 2 to calm down (the situation).

sirig, nyirig to prance like a horse;

sirig-sirig to keep prancing.

sirih I *reg* calm, self-controlled.

II *or* **sesirih** (*var of* **sesirik**) to impose moderation (in eating *etc*) on o.s.

sirik to be avoided, abstained from;

nyirik to avoid, abstain from;

sesirik not to eat certain foods as a form of self-denial;

sirikan 1 thing (to be) avoided; 2 prohibition (*e.g.* on eating certain things).

siring I 1 side, flank; 2 slanting, sloping.

II 1 border; 2 from outside (the city); 3 *lit* opponent.

sirkaya *var of* **srikaya**.

sirna *lit* gone, wiped out;

nyirnakaké to kill, eliminate, stamp out.

sirsak soursop (tree and fruit).

sirsat *var of* **sirsak**.

siru banana-leaf spoon (*var of* **suru** I).

siruk, nyiruk to dive, swoop (of kite);

nyirukaké to cause to dive/swoop.

sirung 1 dark, heavily shaded; 2 (of eyes) narrowed to cut down on glare; 3 having eyebrows that meet above the nose (angry);

nyirungi to cause (the eyes) to narrow.

sis *repr* sound of hissing.

sisa 1 residue, remainder; 2 remnant;

nyisa left over;

nyisani to leave the remainder for s.o.;

nyisakaké to set aside for later;

sisan 1 remainder; 2 leftovers from a meal.

sisah 1 sad, grieving (*kr for* **susah**); 2 (not) need to, not necessary (*kr for* **susah**).

sisan 1 altogether, (in) all; 2 at once, at the same time; 3 once and for all. *See also* **pisan**.

sisèt to come off, peel off (*var of* **sèsèt**).

sisi *ng*, *kr*, **semprit** *k.i.*, to blow one's nose;

n(y)isèni 1 to help (a child) blow its nose; 2 to blow snot onto;

n(y)isèkaké to blow s.t. from the nose.

sisig 1 (**lathi** *or* **lelathi** *kr*) with blackened teeth; 2 a quid of tobacco chewed with betel;

nyisig *or* **nyisigi** to blacken one's teeth.

sisih side, part, direction;

n(y)isih to move aside; 'sih! stand aside, make way!;

n(y)isihi 1 to stand by s.o.; 2 to avoid by moving aside;

n(y)isihaké to move s.t. aside;

sisihan spouse.

sisik 1 fish scale(s); 2 snake skin; - **melik** evidence, trace;

n(y)isiki 1 to remove the scales from; 2 to smooth by scraping;
  sisik-sisik to smooth bamboo with a knife.

sisil, n(y)isil to nibble, peck;
  sisilan s.t. to be nibbled; act or way of nibbling.

sisip 1 wrong, mistake; 2 to miss (one's aim *etc*); - sembiré it could easily happen that... (s.t. goes wrong);
  n(y)isip to miss a target.

sisir 1 a comb of bananas; 2 *reg* a comb; 3 a covered verandah;
  n(y)isir *or* n(y)isiri 1 to scrape off with a sharp knife; 2 to plough a dry field for a second time.

sisrik, n(y)isrik to smooth the ridges of (bamboo) at the joints.

siswa student, pupil.

sisya *lit, var of* siswa.

sit (*pron as:* si:t) *or* mak sit *repr* a whizzing past.

sitangsu *lit* moon.

sitaresmi *lit* moon.

sitèn I a regional official (*from* asistèn);
  sitènan residence or office of the above.

siter a zither-like musical instrument;
  nyiter to play the siter;
  siteran 1 music played on the siter; 2 a group of siter-players and singers who go from house to house playing for money.

sithèng ½ cent during the colonial period.

sithik a few, a little (*coll var of* sethithik).

sithil *reg var of* sithik.

sithip dried dirt in the corner of the eye (after sleep).

sithok one (*reg var of* siji).

sitingarah *var of* istingarah.

siti earth, soil, land (*kr for* lemah); -nggil main audience hall on the northern side of the palace.

sitipayah a living, a livelihood.

sitok *var of* sithok.

sitrun lemon.

situ, situ-situ in haste.

situn olive, olive tree. *See also* jaétun.

siwa uncle/aunt (parent's older sibling). *See also* uwa I.

siwah different, changed.

siwak *reg var of* siwa.

siwaka *see* séwaka.

siwal I to come off as a result of damage. II, siwalan fan palm, also its edible fruit.

siwar 1 bristles on a swine's jaw; 2 whiskers of a cat; 3 fins next to a fish's gills.

siwat-siwut (of work) rough and ready.

siweg *reg* to be (do)ing (*var of* saweg).

siwèl to come off, chipped off.

siwer I rope;
  nyiwer 1 to bind; 2 to confiscate; 3 to keep in seclusion.
  II 1 light-coloured (eyes, blue or grey, of Europeans); 2 short-sighted.

siwi I *lit* child, son;
  sesiwi to have a son.
  II *see* séwaka.

siwil I offshoot, protuberance; driji - a sixth finger (*var of* sriwil).
  II *var of* siwèl.

siwir *var of* suwir.

siwo, nyiwo *or* nyenyiwo *reg, lit* to disturb, upset, interfere with.

siwur ladle, water-dipper (often of coconut shell).

siya *or* siya-siya cruel, contemptuous, pitiless;
  nyiya-nyiya to treat cruelly, persecute.

siyaga prepared, equipped;
  nyiyagani all ready for s.t.;
  nyiyagakaké to equip, put into a state of readiness for s.t.

siyah *reg* for all that; nevertheless.

siyal 1 bad luck; 2 unlucky.

siyam to fast (*kr for* pasa).

siyang the middle part of the day (*kr for* awan).

siyar, nyiyaraké to broadcast, announce;
siyaran a broadcast.

siyas a variety of horse-drawn carriage.

siyasat I *lit* firm treatment, punishment, chastisement;
nyiyasat to punish severely, chastise, torture.
II strategy, stratagem, plan of action.

Siyem Siam.

siyèn formerly, in the past (*subst kr, var of* **rumiyin**).

siyos to succeed in (do)ing (*kr for* **sida**).

siyub *reg* shady, sheltered (*var of* **éyub**).

siyung I 1 canine tooth; fang, tusk; **2** clove (of garlic);
nyiyung 1 to bare the teeth; **2** *fig* to make a show of force; **3** to bite with the canines/fangs;
siyungan 1 having canine teeth; **2** in cloves, sections.
II a wild béyo. *See also* **ciyung**.

siyut *or* **mak siyut** *repr* a whizzing, swishing sound;
sumiyut 1 to produce a whistling sound; **2** to lean, sway, be about to fall over (*e.g.* sleepy);
siyat-siyut to whiz repeatedly.

skak 1 (to play) chess; **2** check! *Also* **sekak**.

skop spade(s) playing-card suit. *Also* **sekop**.

skrip writing book, manual of handwriting. *Also* **sekrip**.

slabar *reg* news;
nylabari to tell, let know.

slaber, nylaber to swab, mop.

slabruk pyjamas.

sladhah lettuce, salad.

sladhang, pating - (of long objects) lying this way and that;
nyladhang 1 to carry s.t. crosswise; **2** to shoot (a marble) with a two-handed technique;
nyladhangaké 1 to lay (flat or length-ways) across s.t.; **2** to place high up between two points.

sladri *var of* **slèdri**.

slaga flower bud.

slagang, slagrang *see* **sladhang**.

slaka silver (metal).

slakang *or* **slakangan** groin, inner part of the thigh. *See also* **lakang, wlakang**.

slakup *var of* **tlakup**.

slaman-slumun slippery, unreliable, unprincipled (*var of* **sluman-slumun**).

slamber, seslamberan *or* **pating slamber** swooping everywhere.

slambruh *reg* similar to each other, hard to distinguish.

slambu *reg* mosquito net.

slambur, nylamburi *reg* to sow mixed seeds in a field;
slamburan mixed seeds for sowing.

slamet *ng*, **wilujeng** *kr*, **sugeng** *k.i.*, well, safe and sound, secure;
nylameti to hold a **slametan** for;
nylametaké 1 to keep s.o. safe, well, secure; **2** to save (the life of); **3** to hold a ceremony on behalf of s.o.;
slametan (to hold) a ritual communal meal, at which prayers are recited and food offered, for the purpose of ensuring safety;
kaslametan safety, welfare.

slampar a rope ring used for climbing trees.

slamper *var of* **slampar**.

slampir, nylampiri *or* **nylampiraké 1** to place (a garment over s.o.'s shoulders); **2** to hang (garments) on a line;
pating slampir hanging all over the place. *See also* **sampir**.

slamur, nylamur 1 to (try to) take one's mind off s.t.; **2** to change the subject;
keslamur to get one's thoughts diverted, distracted.

slandhok *reg var of* **slondhok**.

slang rubber tubing, hose.

slangan *reg* it is not necessary, no need to.

slanggap, nylanggapi to strike up a conversation with;
slanggapan conversation.

slanggat var of slanggap.

slanggrang var of slagrang.

slangkrah var of sangkrah.

slangsang a container made from banana leaves.

slarak var of slorok.

Slasa Tuesday (var of Selasa).

slasab var of slesep, tlesep.

slasah, nlasah to trace, track. See also tlasah.

slasak var of sasak.

slasar, nlasari 1 to supply s.t. with a base or underlayer; 2 to move the hand under s.t. in search of (an object). See also tlasar.

slasih I basil (flower, herb) (var of tlasih).
II, pating slasih scattered, in disorder.

slaton reg quick-tempered, fierce, vicious.

slawat money given to those who attend a funeral and offer prayers;
slawatan religious songs (with Arabic text) sung in chorus by men to the accompaniment of tambourines (terbang).

slawir, nylawir to flap loosely;
nylawiraké to wave s.t.;
pating slawir flapping loosely (e.g. coconut leaves, streamers).

slebar, pating slebar spread about everywhere. See also sebar.

slébok wide and low (basket).

slébor mudguard.

slébrak saddle-blanket.

slebrèh, pating slebrèh pl to hang untidily in tatters.

slèdèr or slèdèran careless, lax, negligent.

slèdri celery.

slégrang, slégrang-slégrang tall and strong (shape of the body).

slègreng or mak slègreng repr doing s.t. (entering, sitting) brazenly, without asking permission.

slègrèng I crossbar.
II var of slègreng.

slekak too narrow, tight (collar).

slekek var of slekak.

sléko reg village gateway.

slelep or nylelep to dive;
nylelepaké to push s.t. under water. See also slulup.

slémar a bamboo layer on a floor for sitting.

slémbat, nylémbataké to move s.t. along, pass on (job to s.o. else). See also lémbat.

slembrah, pating slembrah sloppy or careless in one's dress and grooming.

slembrèh var of slembrah.

slembur, pating slembur pl to spray, spit.

slemet I vermin which come out of the ground and attack rice plants. Also sremet.
II, slemet-slemet or slemat-slemet to have a nagging, gnawing pain in the stomach.

slémpang bandolier, strap over the shoulder;
slémpangan to wear a bandolier.

slémpat, slémpatan to skin stones on water, play ducks-and-drakes.

slempèd reg var of slempit.

slempit, nylempit to be hidden in, between (e.g. folds, pages);
nylempiti or nylempitaké to slip s.t. into;
keslempit to get concealed among other things;
sumlempit inserted (into), tucked in;
slempitan pushed into a small space between other things.

slemprit var of semprit;
pating slemprit pl to be blowing whistles everywhere.

slénca different from usual, different from before, divergent, aberrant.

slendep, pating slendep having pricking skin sensations (in the stomach).

slènder 1 cylinder (car-engine part); 2 steamroller;
nylènder to roll (a road *etc*) with a steamroller.

sléndhang a cloth worn over one shoulder or diagonally across the body (used for carrying);
nyléndhangi to put a sléndhang on s.o.'s shoulder;
nyléndhangaké to use s.t. as a sléndhang;
sléndhangan to wear a sléndhang.

sléndho, sléndhok s.t. worn around the neck;
nyléndhokaké to wind (a cloth *etc*) around the neck.

sléndro the five-note scale in Javanese music *esp* gamelan;
nyléndro to play (a note of) this scale.

slenèh, nylenèh to deviate from the usual run, be out of the ordinary, weird.

slenget *repr* burning heat;
sumlenget burning, biting (heat).

slénggrang-slènggreng (to take s.t. away) without permission from the owner.

slenggring, pating slenggring *pl* emaciated, very thin.

slenggrok, pating slenggrok *pl* to draw in the breath noisily, sniffle.

slenggruk, pating slenggruk *pl* to sob repeatedly. *See also* senggruk.

slenggur, pating slenggur *pl* to snore repeatedly. *See also* senggur.

sléngkrah, pating sléngkrah *pl* in disorder.

slengkrang, pating slengkrang *pl* stabs of pain, stinging pains all over.

sléngkrang *repr* putting the feet up (rudely) while sitting.

slengkring, pating slengkring *pl* to feel pinpricks of pain.

slengseng, nylengseng to search all around.

sléngso *reg* in disorder, in a mess.

slenter *var of* slenther.

slénthak, nylénthak (of horses) to kick with a rear leg;
nylénthaki to kick repeatedly.

slenthang-slenthing *see* slenthing.

slenthar-slenthir a little at a time; bit by bit.

slénthar, pating slénthar *pl* all awry.

slenthem I a gamelan instrument with metal keys;
nylenthem to play such an instrument.
II, slentham-slenthem to do s.t. quietly or without anyone's knowledge.

slenther *or* mak slenther *repr* a precipitate or unannounced departure.

slenthik a snap by bending the finger with nail against thumb and then releasing it suddenly;
nylenthik 1 to flick s.o. on the ear with the finger as above (as punishment); 2 to reprimand; 3 to snap with the rear legs (fighting-crickets).

slenthing *or* mak slenthing *repr* a whiff of s.t. disagreeable;
slenthingan *or* slenthang-slenthing rumour.

slenthir, slenthar-slenthir *or* pating slenthir puffing (smoke) on all sides, one after the other.

slep *or* mak slep *repr* slipping into a place unobtrusively, ducking in.

slepa a pouch of woven leaves *etc* for betel, cigarettes, tobacco.

slépé a buckle of gold or silver attached to a belt (èpèk), worn by girls for certain ceremonial occasions or for the classical dance.

slepek cramped, narrow, constricted;
nylepek to have too little time (to, for);
nylepeki to cause a feeling of being trapped, pressed;

keslepek 1 to be tight (breath, space); 2 to be pressed for time.

slepi *or* slepèn cigarette case of woven palm leaves.

slera slat to reinforce a woven bamboo wall.

slèrèk, nylèrèk to slide aside over s.t. else;

nylèrèki *or* nylèrèkaké to slide s.t.

slesep, n(y)lesepi *or* n(y)lesepaké to slip s.t. into;

sumlesep to go in, find (its) way into;

keslesep to get slipped in between s.t. by accident.

slesih accurate, detailed, complete (*var of* tlesih).

slètel spanner.

slethem, sletheman *reg* on the quiet, unobserved.

sléwah 1 of two colours; 2 different, contrasting.

sléwang-slèwèng *see* slèwèng.

sléwar *repr* a sudden turn, leaving its proper path.

sléwar-slèwèr *see* slèwèr.

slèwèh, slèwèhan *reg* a ditch, channel.

slèwèng, nylèwèng 1 to stray, wander, leave the straight and narrow; 2 to commit adultery;

nylèwèngaké to divert, deflect s.t. from its proper purpose;

slèwèngan to be unfaithful in an amorous relationship;

sléwang-slèwèng to wander here and there, stray from the objective.

slèwèr, slèwèran *or* sléwar-slèwèr to wave, hang loose, flutter.

sléyar-sléyor *see* sléyor.

sléyat-sléyot *var of* sléyar-sléyor.

sléyor, sléyoran *or* sléyar-sléyor weak(ened), infirm.

slibik, nylibik *reg* 1 to sneak up on; 2 to deceive s.o.

slibuk, nylibukaké to pass s.t. off as genuine.

slidhik, nylidhik *or* nylidhiki to investigate.

sligi 1 a kind of spear; 2 a short stick, sharp at both ends, used in weaving.

slikur *see* selikur.

slilit food caught between the teeth;

nyliliti 1 (of fibrous food) likely to catch in the teeth; 2 annoying, irritating;

sliliten *or* kesliliten to get food caught in the teeth;

ora dadi slilit *idiom* a small, unsatisfying amount of food.

slimpang *reg var of* slémpang.

slimpé, nylimpé to slip away (without being noticed);

slimpéan to sneak up on. *See also* limpé.

slimpet *var of* slimpé.

slimur, nylimur to chase away s.o.'s sadness;

keslimur 1 to get one's thoughts diverted; 2 to have such a good time that one forgets one's troubles.

slimut *reg* blanket.

slinder *var of* slènder.

slindhit, slindhitan 1 winding tortuously; 2 children's game played by running around in patterned circles;

pating slindhit with twists and turns in all directions.

slingker *or* mak slingker *repr* a sudden swerve;

nylingker to change direction suddenly.

slingkuh to do s.t. on the sly;

nylingkuhaké to take s.t. stealthily, embezzle;

slingkuhan (to do) in a secretive or underhand manner.

slingkur *var of* singkur.

slingsing, slingsingan to miss each other, pass without noticing, not meet up. *Also* tlingsing.

slingso *var of* sléngso.

slinthat-slinthut *see* slinthut.

slinthut, slinthutan *or* slinthat-slinthut in secret, on the sly;
nylinthutaké to conceal temporarily (s.t. one is planning to carry off later).

slintru *reg var of* sintru.

slira I iguana.
II (*also* salira) body (*k.i. for* awak); suduk - to commit suicide;
sliramu *or* slirané *or* keng slira (*k.i.*) you.

sliri, pating sliri, slira-sliri to keep going past, back and forth.

sliring *var of* slingsing.

slisib *var of* tlisib.

slisih to disagree, not coincide.

slisik I *repr* a harsh hissing.
II to preen the feathers with the beak; n(y)lisik *or* n(y)lisiki 1 to preen the feathers with the beak; 2 to investigate, look into.

slisip *var of* slesep.

slisir *or* nlisir to be off-target, miss the mark.

slisuh I *lit* exhausted.
II messy, lying in disorder.

slitha-slithi to keep wriggling, squirming, fidgeting.

sliwah *var of* sléwah.

sliwar-sliwer *see* sliwer.

sliwer, sliweran *or* sliwar-sliwer to flit, dart, weave this way and that;
pating sliwer *pl as above.*

sliwing *reg var of* slèwèng.

slobok, nyloboki to put (fingers, hands) into (an opening);
nylobokaké to put s.t. into an opening, hole.

slodha-slodho *see* slodho.

slodho *reg, repr* bursting into a place where one does not belong;
slodha-slodho to keep on intruding.

slogrong *or* mak slogrong *repr* quick growth, shooting up (*e.g.* child).

slohak-slohok to talk rudely.

sloka *var of* saloka.

slokan *reg* ditch, channel.

sloki glass of liquor.

slomod, nylomod to touch with a burning object;
keslomod to come into accidental contact with a burning object.

slomprèt 1 trumpet, bugle; 2 shawm, oboe; 3 *term of abuse*: 'you bastard!'; 4 trumpeter;
nylomprèt to play a trumpet;
slomprètan 1 a toy trumpet; 2 to play trumpetting; 3 *coll* to muck around; 4 place where the royal trumpeters live.

slondhoh, nylondhoh *or* nylondhohi to accommodate o.s. to, compromise, yield for the sake of peace.

slondhok 1 metal ring for holding s.t.; 2 a belt buckle;
nylondhokaké to thread s.t. through an opening.

slondom *reg* variety of spade.

slondop *var of* slondom.

slongop, slongopan to keep yawning.

slonjor to extend one's legs (while sitting on the ground);
nylonjoraké to stretch the legs out.

slonong *or* mak slonong *repr* a sudden move, reaching out rudely;
nylonong to go through (in, out) without permission;
slonang-slonong *or* pating slonong shooting forward rudely everywhere.

slonthong, slonthongan 1 s.t. hollow, empty or emptied of its contents; 2 hollow bamboo water pipe; 3 letterbox.

slop slippers, sandals with closed toes. *Also* selop.

slorok a panel that slides over s.t.;
nyloroki to equip with a sliding panel;
nylorokaké to slide s.t. over s.t. else;
slorokan 1 a drawer; 2 kris cover.

slosor *var of* tlosor.

slotho *reg* cigarette case made from woven palm leaves.

slubuk, nylubukaké 1 to pass s.t. off as; 2 to persuade s.o. to do wrong.

sludhah, nyludhah *reg* (of refreshments served to a guest) to keep on coming.

sludhing *var of* **slundhing**.

slugrak-slugruk to keep reaching up for s.t. in a rude way.

sluku to sit with the legs stretched straight out before one;

sluku-sluku bathok opening words of a children's song chanted while sitting as above.

slukup a variety of cap.

slulup to go under water;

nylulup to submerge o.s.;

nylulupi to submerge s.t.;

nylulupaké to hold s.o.'s head under water.

sluman-slumun slippery, unreliable, unprincipled.

slumbat a bar for removing the outer husk of coconuts;

nylumbat to remove the outer husk from a coconut using such a bar.

slumpring *reg* sheath growing out from a bamboo stalk joint. *See also* **clumpring**.

slundap-slundup *see* **slundup**.

slundep, nylundepi to pierce with a sharp pointed object.

slundhing, nylundhingi 1 to substitute for; 2 to act in the capacity of, change with;

slundhingan a substitute, replacement.

slundup, nylundup to enter illicitly;

nylundupi 1 to stab s.t. into; 2 to smuggle s.t./s.o.;

nylundupaké 1 to insert; 2 to smuggle s.t./s.o.;

slundupan smuggled;

slundap-slundup *pl* to enter and leave;

pating slundup to go in and out everywhere.

slungsum, nylungsumi to patch, to mend s.t. by replacing materials;

slungsuman material used to repair or replace s.t. broken.

slup (*pron as:* **slu:p**) *or* **mak slup** *repr* quick immersion.

slura-sluru to keep getting s.t. wrong, in haste or confusion.

slurup *reg* to submerge, dive, go under water.

slusub *repr* entering and hiding;

n(y)lusub to enter in between;

nylusubi to enter, slip into;

nylusubaké to insert s.t.;

keslusuben to get entered by s.t. sharp;

slusuban *or* **slusab-slusub** to go into and out of;

pating slusub *pl* taking quick cover.

slusur *var of* **tlusur**.

slutha-sluthu *see* **sluthu**.

sluthak-sluthuk *var of* **slutha-sluthu**.

sluthu *or* **mak sluthu** *repr* a sudden bursting in;

nyluthu to enter s.o.'s place without permission;

slutha-sluthu to keep entering s.o.'s room without permission or forewarning.

sluwang, pating sluwang fluttering or waving motions.

sluwat, nyluwat (of s.t. long and sharp) to project outward and upward;

pating sluwat full of sharp spiky projections.

sluwir, pating sluwir in rags, shreds.

smara *lit* romantic love. *See also* **asmara**.

smaradana *var of* **asmaradana**.

so a certain tree (**mlinjo**) bearing edible leaves and seeds.

soal problem, matter, question; **- jawab** question and answer;

nyoal *or* **nyoalaké** to cause problems (for).

sob 1 at a low level (water); **2** at ebb tide.

sobat close friend;

nyobat to get close to; to regard as a close friend.

sobèk *reg* **1** ripped; **2** unlucky.

sobong *reg* **1** a small inner room; **2** house (humble).

sobrah 1 fringe-like tree root; **2** bride's fringed ornament on the head.

sobyung a children's singing game.

soca I *see* **sotya**.

II 1 knot (in wood, bamboo); **2** shortcoming, fault.

sodhèr *var of* **soldir**.

sodhog, nyodhog to prod;

nyodhogi to prod s.t. repeatedly;

nyodhogaké to move s.t. by prodding or pushing hard at it;

sodhogan act or way of prodding.

sodok *reg* somewhat.

sodor jousting lance with tassel instead of an iron point;

nyodor to prod with the above;

sodoran 1 to joust; **2** to play tilt-at-the-ring.

soé *reg* **1** bored, fed up; **2** unlucky.

sog I, ngesog to put down, set down;

ngesogaké to set s.t. down.

II ngesog-sog to give s.o. a scalp massage (treatment for headache).

soga 1 a tree the bark of which produces a reddish-brown dye; **2** this dye, used in making batik;

nyoga to dye (batik) with the above;

sogan 1 fabric dyed with the above; **2** reddish-brown in colour.

sogat *reg* s.t. offered to a guest (*kr for* **suguh**).

sogèl *reg* early-ripening variety of rice.

soglèng, soglèngan (of tobacco plant) a sprout growing between the leaf and the stalk;

nyoglèngi to remove the sprout (of tobacco plant).

sogok 1 long stick used for prodding; **2**

key; - **untu** toothpick; - **upil** a certain Yogya style of jacket;

nyogok 1 to prod, poke; **2** to unlock a door; **3** *fig* to bribe s.o.;

nyogoki to keep prodding;

sogokan 1 a bribe; **2** bribery.

sogol, sogolan a sucker, new shoot/bud.

sogrok *var of* **sogok**.

sojah a Chinese gesture of high esteem by bowing the head and placing two fists together on the chest.

sojar *reg* to tell, speak about.

sok I *ng*, **kala-kala** *kr*, **1** sometimes, often; **2** (don't) ever; **3** even if (*with* -a); **sok-sok** once in a while, every so often.

II, *or* **mak sok** *repr* pouring out, spilling;

ngesoki to pour into/onto s.t.;

ngesok *or* **ngesokaké** to pour s.t. (out);

kesokan to get poured on.

soka a flowering tree (*see also* **angsoka**).

soké *reg* in order to, so that.

soklat 1 chocolate; **2** brown;

nyoklat to colour/dye s.t. brown;

nyoklataké to have s.t. coloured/dyed brown.

sokong, nyokong 1 to support financially; **2** to contribute support;

sokongan financial support, contribution.

sokoteng *var of* **sekoteng**.

soksi *reg* key (*var of* **sosi**).

sokur 1 thank God!; it is good (that...); **2** gratitude; **3** let it be a lesson; - **bagé** (**sèwu**) **1** thank God!; **2** may it happen that;

nyokuraké to rub it in, (to say) 'I told you so!' *Also* **sukur**.

sol I uprooted (by wind);

ngesol to uproot;

ngesolaké to cause to uproot;

kasol to get uprooted.

II, ngesol to push aside with the elbow;

sol-solan to elbow each other, try to push each other aside.
III (shoe) sole;
ngesol to repair shoes.
solah actions, motions; behaviour, conduct; - bawa or - jantra or - tingkah behaviour, actions;
nyolahaké to move (around); to make motions with.
solan-salin see salin.
solat var of salat.
soldir solder;
nyoldir to solder s.t.;
solèd 1 flat kitchen tool resembling a pancake turner; 2 (slang) kris; - patri soldering iron;
nyolèd to turn or manipulate (food) with a pancake turner.
Solo var of Sala.
solok, solokan a ditch, channel. See also slokan.
solor reg aerial roots (var of sulur).
solot reg 1 to work assiduously; 2 courageous, bold.
solung reg firstborn child (var of sulung).
soma lit 1 moon; 2 Monday.
somah ng, sémah kr, 1 spouse; 2 household, family.
somba see sumba.
sombèng reg torn, ripped.
sombong snobbish, arrogant;
nyombong to boast;
nyombongaké to boast about s.t.
sompang, sesompang reg a small inner room.
sompèl chipped, with a piece missing.
sompèt reg a bag of woven straw material.
sompil 1 a variety of freshwater snail; 2 conical sweet made from rice. Also sumpil.
sompok 1 narrow, cramped; 2 very limited (time); 3 reg a small hut.
sona lit dog.

sondèl reg ora - no way!
sondher without.
sondhèr scarf worn around the waist in classical dance;
sesondhèran to put on or wear this scarf.
sondhol, nyondhol to push, press, nudge;
nyondhol-nyondhol to keep pushing or poking;
kesondhol to get pushed from behind or one side.
sondhong reg long bamboo pole with a small basket on the end for picking fruit from the tree.
song hollow or opening in a riverbank, cliffside, valley wall etc;
ngesong forming a hollow of this type.
songa silk thread.
songar, sesongaran boastful; to show off.
songgèk var of sènggèt.
songgèt var of sènggèt.
songglèng, songglèngan new shoot (of tobacco plant).
songgo reg basket-like woven bamboo stand for holding a water carafe.
songgom var of songgo.
songkèl crowbar-like prying tool, used with a wedge for leverage;
nyongkèl 1 to pry, exert leverage; 2 to open s.t. (with the above equipment).
songkèt fabric interwoven with gold thread;
nyongkèt to produce this fabric.
songkil reg var of songkèl.
songkob, nyongkobaké to let the hair hang down over one's forehead.
songkok 1 black velvet three-cornered hat (warrior's formal costume); 2 a half-hat (front of crown and visor);
songkokan to put on or wear such headgear.
songkol, nyongkol to punch;
songkolan to have a fist fight, punch each other.

songkop woven bamboo implement (*var of* sosog).

songkrah *reg* turbulent.

songkro an old dump, wreck.

songol snappish, harsh (*var of* sengol).

songot *reg* strong, muscular, tough.

songsong umbrella, parasol (*k.i. for* payung).

sontak *reg* broken to pieces, crushed.

sontan-santun *see* santun I.

sonten late afternoon, early evening (*kr for* soré).

sontèng, nyontèng to hit hard.

sonthèk *var of* sontèng.

sontok, nyontok to push, shove.

sontong a kind of squid.

sontrot fibrous threads running down the centre of a cassava root or mango; nyontrot full of fibres.

sonya *lit* quiet, lonely, deserted (*var of* sunya).

sonyaruri *lit* the realm of the spirits.

sonyok, nyonyok to poke (*e.g.* with fingers, in the face).

sop I soup.

II at a low level, at ebb tide.

sopak *or* sopakan false part added on; nyopak *or* nyopaki to add (a false piece) to.

sopal ornamental ring of a spear.

sopan polite, well-mannered.

sopana *lit* way, means of reaching s.t.

sopi strong drink.

sopir driver, chauffeur; nyopir to be(come) a driver; nyopiri to drive (a vehicle); sopiran 1 driver's seat, position; 2 manner, act of driving.

sor I *or* mak sor *repr* a rapid flow; ngesori to pour into/onto; ngesoraké to pour s.t.; sar-sor to keep pouring.

II 1 under, below; 2 inferior; ngesoraké to look down on; sor-soran a subordinate.

sora 1 loud; 2 aloud.

sorah image, likeness, comparison; sesorah (to give) a speech, lecture; nyorahaké to deliver a speech about.

soré *ng*, sonten *kr*, the late afternoon, early evening period; nyorèni to arrive before dark; kesorèn 1 too late (in the afternoon); 2 too early (in the evening); soré-sorénan late in the afternoon-evening period; sasoré bendhé throughout the evening.

sorèng, kumidhi - a show demonstrating various skills.

sori *lit* queen.

soro *var of* soroh.

sorog a key; nyorog to lock with a key; sorogan a drawer.

soroh *or* nyorohaké to hand over, offer, let s.o. have; - amuk in an enraged or violent condition.

sorok long-handled shovel of wood or bamboo; nyorok *or* nyoroki to shovel s.t. with the above.

sorot I ray, beam; nyorot to shine light; nyoroti to shine light on; nyorotaké to flash; sumorot to shine, flash; sorotan a flash.

II, nyorotaké to let (irrigation water) into a field; sorotan fields that get their water by irrigation.

sos *or* mak sos *repr* a swishing sound; ngesos to produce such a sound; ngesosaké to discharge (air, gas).

sosi a key.

sosial 1 social; 2 having a social conscience.

sosis sausage; nyosis to make sausages.

soso *reg* brusque; to act roughly and hurriedly.

sosog I implement of woven bamboo on a handle, shaped for holding various objects;

nyosog 1 to use the above implement; 2 *fig* to scold.

II, **nyosog** 1 to push, prod.

III to put s.t. down.

sosoh, n(y)osoh to pound a second time (to remove the inner membrane from rice).

sosol brusque;

kesosolen to make a slip of the tongue;

kamisosolen to have difficulty speaking because of strong emotion.

sosor, nyosor to attack with the beak;

kesosor to get pecked by a goose or duck.

sosot angry words;

nyosot-nyosotaké to keep pressing s.o. with angry words, scold.

sosrob, nyosrob 1 to slurp; 2 *cr* to drink.

sosrok a broad short-handled dustpan used *esp* for scooping up dirt or manure;

nyosrok to scoop s.t. up with the above;

sot a curse, malediction;

ngesotaké to put a curse on s.o.

sota *lit* feeling.

sotah *reg* willing and eager.

soté *reg* all the more (so), to say nothing of.

sotèn *var of* soté.

sothal-sathil 1 in rags, all worn out; 2 very poor.

sothil a pancake turner-like kitchen implement.

sotho a punch with the fist;

nyotho to punch with the fist.

soto a kind of clear soup (*var of* saoto).

sotong octopus, squid.

sotya *lit* 1 human eye; 2 *or* sesotya jewel, gems.

so'un 1 shiny bean noodle; 2 rice sticks used in soup.

sowak, nyowak to spread s.t. apart, *esp* to enlarge the field of vision.

sowal stripped. *See also* sowèl.

sowan to visit (one who is socially superior);

nyowani to visit (s.o. high);

nyowanaké to present s.o. (to an exalted person);

pasowanan place where visits to exalted persons take place.

sowang I, **sowangan** small whistle attached to a pigeon's tail. *See also* sawangan IV.

II, **sowang-sowang** *or* sesowangan each (separately, for him/herself).

sowé *reg* unlucky, bad luck.

sowèl stripped (*var of* sowal).

soyi clown, jokes.

spion spy. *Also* spiyun.

spirtus *var of* sepiritus.

spiyun spy.

sporet sports, athletics.

sraba *lit* voice;

tanpa sraba-sraba without notice, without saying anything.

srabat *reg* a prayer for warding off misfortune.

srabèd, srabèdan *lit* wicked desires.

srabi pancake eaten with a coconut, sugar and milk syrup;

nyrabi to make such pancakes.

srabud, srabudan 1 not particular, not fussy; 2 suitable for anything, ready for any kind of work.

srada *reg* somewhat, quite.

sradan *reg, var of* srada.

sradi *reg, kr for* srada.

srag-srog *see* srog.

srah to surrender, give up;

ngesrahi *or* ngesrahaké to turn s.t. over (to s.o.);

sasrahan name of a gift from the bridegroom to the bride three or five days before the wedding consisting of kitchenware *etc.*

srakah greedy.

srakat, kesrakat poor and needy.

srama 1 a present to a superior; 2 a gift to the landlord.

srambah, nyrambahi 1 to affect widely; 2 to spread out, cover;
sumrambah to spread far and wide;
kesrambah accessible, available, used generally.

srambi front porch, vestibule of a mosque.

srambu *reg* mosquito net.

srambung, pating srambung all joining up. *See also* **sambung.**

srampad I a rope ring used for climbing trees.
II, **nyrampad** to graze, scrape;
srampadan act of grazing.

srampang, nyrampang to throw (a missile) at;
srampangan careless, haphazard.

srana medium, tool, means (*var of* **sarana**).

srandhal sandals, thongs, flip-flops (*var of* **sandhal**).

srandhul a type of folk drama.

srandu I all over (the body) (*var of* **sarandu**).
II, **nyrandu** to interfere with, annoy, pester.

srang, nrang *lit* to attack;
srang-srangan hurried, hasty.

srang-srèng *see* **srèng.**

srani Christian;
nyranèkaké to convert s.o. to Christianity.

sranta, ora - impatient. *See also* **sranti.**

sranthal *or* **mak sranthal** *repr* scurrying away;
nyranthal to dash, sprint;
sumranthal to run fast.

sranthil, nyranthil penniless;
pating sranthil in rags, all worn out.

sranti *ng*, **srantos** *kr*, **ora** - impatient;
nyranti *or* **nyrantèkaké** 1 to wait for s.t. in patience; 2 to leave s.t. alone, allow s.t. to wait;
srantèn patient by nature.

srantos patient, willing to wait (*kr for* **sranti**).

srapah *reg* cassava.

srapat, nyrapat to graze, glance;
srapatan a glance.

srasah 1 covering, overlay; 2 inlay, mosaic; 3 paving;
nyrasah 1 to cover with a layer of s.t.; 2 to inlay; 3 to pave.

srasèh, srasèhan, sarasèhan an informal discussion;
nyrasèhaké to discuss s.t.

srat-srit *see* **srit.**

srati *ng*, **sratos** *kr*, 1 *lit* charioteer; 2 mahout;
nyratèni 1 to drive, control; 2 to get on well with, know how to please;
sratènan act or way of managing, serving.

srathil, srothal-srathil *var of* **sranthil.**

sraton *reg* wild, quick-tempered.

sratos *kr for* **srati.**

srawa *lit* voice (*var of* **sraba**).

srawang, sumrawang transparent.

srawat, nyrawat *reg* to throw s.t. at. *See also* **sawat.**

srawé, srawéan to keep waving, fluttering.

srawung *or* **sesrawungan** to associate with, become acquainted with;
srawungan acquaintance, association (with);
pasrawungan acquaintance, association with s.o.

srawut, sumrawut disorderly, chaotic, disorganised.

sraya 1 help, assistance; 2 a cooperative effort;
nyraya to ask for help;
nyrayakaké to have s.o. help with s.t.

srebed, sumrebed 1 to blow softly, waft; 2 to swish, rustle;
  srebed-srebed 1 the sound of a gentle breeze; 2 the soft swishing of a kain as one walks.

sred or mak sred repr a sudden stop, a sudden getting stuck.

sreg 1 well-fitting, comfortable, easy; 2 or mak sreg repr the feel of settling into place comfortably.

srèg repr a rustling sound produced by small movements;
  srag-srèg to keep producing such a sound.

sregep industrious, diligent;
  nyregep to increase one's industriousness;
  nyregepi to apply o.s. diligently to;
  nyregepaké to cause s.o. to apply themselves diligently;
  kasregepan industriousness, diligence.

srèi malicious, jealous, selfish.

srèk or mak srèk repr scratching, scraping.

srékal or srékalan a kind of wordplay based on puns or over-literal interpretation;
  nyrékal to talk (to) with the above type of wordplay;
  srékal-srékalan to engage in such wordplay with one another.

srékat var of sarékat.

srèkèng, pating srèkèng weak everywhere, in every way.

srémbong, pating srémbong sloppy, full of creases (not tight, clothing).

sremet vermin (var of slemet).

sreming, krungu sreming-sreming to hear a vague rumour that...

srempal, pating srempal all tattered and torn.

srémpang bandolier;
  srémpangan to wear a bandolier.

srèmpèd, nyrèmpèd 1 to graze, brush against s.t.; 2 to allude to, refer to;
  nyrèmpèdaké to cause s.t. to graze;
  kesrèmpèd to get grazed;
  srèmpèdan 1 abrasion; 2 allusion, reference.

srempeng, nyrempeng to do in earnest, keep right on at the job.

srempil, nyrempili to take little pieces away from s.t., bit by bit;
  srempilan a small piece taken away, broken off.

sremplah, pating sremplah (of clothing) tattered, hanging in rags.

sreng lit stern, harsh, angry.

srèng or mak srèng repr sizzling;
  srang-srèng to keep sizzling.

sréngat var of saréngat.

srengen ng, kr, duka k.i. angry;
  nyrengeni to speak to s.o. angrily.

srengéngé sun.

srenggala lit dog.

srenggara lit amorous feelings, love;
  nyrenggara lit to inspire love; - macan to force, rape.

srenggut var of senggut.

sréngkad-sréngkod crusty, testy, peevish.

srenit (pron as sreni:t), srenit-srenit or pating srenit to throb with pain. See also senit.

srenteg 1 (of females) well-proportioned; 2 straight and proper (of women's stance).

srenten bridge (supporting the strings of a rebab).

srenthit, pating srenthit pl producing piercing high-pitched sounds.

srenti to come one after the other, not at the same time.

srentos reg kr for srenti.

srenut, pating srenut to throb with pain (var of srenit). See also senut.

srep I cold. See also asrep.
  II var of serep.

srepan lucky in getting what one tries for.

srepeg, srepegan a class of fast gamelan melody accompanying fights.

srepek *var of* **slepek**.

srepet *repr* a sudden dimming of the vision;
sumrepet (of vision) to become dim (about to faint).

srèpèt *repr* unsheathing a kris;
nyrèpèt to draw a kris from its sheath swiftly.

srèsèh friendly, cordial (reception of guest).

sresep, n(y)resep to penetrate;
sumresep to enter, seep in.

sréwat-sréwot to act impetuously, be in a rush, in a big hurry.

srèwèh, pating srèwèh to flow everywhere;
srèwèhan a little stream of water (*esp* irrigating a field).

sréyag-srèyèg weak, without energy, near collapse.

sri I 1 *lit* shining ray or beam; **2** glorious; **3** *title for a royal personage*; - **Sultan** the Sultan of Yogyakarta.
II Dèwi - the goddess of rice; - **Sedana** Sri and Sedana, a mythological couple associated with agriculture.

sriawan a particular herbal medicine for intestinal disorders.

sribid, nyribid *or* **sumribid** *or* **sribid-sribid** to blow gently (wind).

sribombok a certain water bird.

srig, srig-srigan to fidget, move restlessly (rather than sitting poised and quiet).

srigadhing a certain flowering plant.

srigak bursting with energy and health (*var of* **sigrak**).

sriging *reg* a variety of small fish trap.

srigsig *var of* **srisig**.

srigunting a black insect-eating songbird with a scissor-shaped tail.

srik (*pron as:* **sri:k**) *or* **mak srik** *repr* a scooping motion.

srikat *var of* **sarikat**.

srikat-srikut *see* **srikut**.

srikawin money given to the bride by the groom's parents, bride-price.

srikaya sweetsop, custard-apple (tree and fruit) (*also* **sirkaya**).

srikep, nyrikep to catch (birds) at night, using torches.

srikut, srikutan busily engaged (using the hands).

srilak, sedulur - sibling nursed by the same mother.

srilik *reg* to pay attention, keep an eye out.

srimanganti a particular courtyard and pavilion within the Kraton.

srimpak *reg* a doorstep, threshold.

srimped, nyrimped to entangle, enwine s.t.;
kesrimped to get entangled, ensnarled.

srimpi a certain court dance performed by females;
nyrimpi, srimpèn to perform this dance.

srimpung, nyrimpung to tie the feet together loosely, hobble;
kesrimpung to get entangled, tied up.

srindhit, srindhitan a variety of small green parrot.

sring *reg* often, sometimes.

srinthil I remains of smoked opium in pipe.
II goat droppings.
III *repr* scurrying (of small animal);
sumrinthil eager, ready and waiting, joining in gladly.

sripah, kesripahan to have a death in the family, suffer a bereavement.

sripanganti *var of* **srimanganti**.

sripenganti *var of* **srimanganti**.

sriping *var of* **criping**.

sripit I (*pron as:* **sripi:t**) *repr* a brisk, easy motion;
sripit-sripit *or* **sripat-sripit 1** (walking) with short steps while wearing a tight skirt.

II 1 **nyripit** to sip (*var of* **sruput**); 2 to brush the surface of s.t. lightly.

srisig a certain step in classical dance used to progress sideways by moving only the feet.

srit (*pron as:* **sri:t**) *or* **mak srit** *repr* a shrill sound;

srat-srit to screech repeatedly.

sriti a variety of swallow, the house-marten.

sriwed to hang around or move about s.w.;

sumriwed to move about in profusion;

pating sriwed moving about in large numbers and all directions, teeming, swarming.

sriwil offshoot, protuberance; - **kutil** a certain wild tree with leaves with wart-shaped welts;

nyriwil 1 to touch lightly with the finger; 2 to take (a bit of food) on the fingertip;

sriwilan 1 offshoot; 2 scraps, parings.

sriwing, nyriwing to blow softly;

sumriwing to have a refreshing feel (of a gentle breeze);

kesriwing touched by a soft flow of air;

sriwing-sriwing 1 faint, indistinct, far-off (sound); 2 (it is) rumoured.

sriwut, sriwutan *or* **pating sriwut** rushing about busily and confusedly.

sriyaban *reg cr* to wander about, hang around.

sriyat, nyriyati to make an offering for warding off misfortune;

sriyatan an offering for warding off misfortune.

srobod *reg* thick, dense (undergrowth).

srobot, nyrobot to snatch, grab;

srobotan snatched.

srodog I, **nyrodog** 1 stiff, standing out; 2 sticking straight out (hair).

II, **nyrodog** to push, butt (*var of* **srudug**).

srog *or* **mak srog** *repr* brushing, grazing, scuffing (the feet);

ngesrogaké to put s.t. (in a place) roughly;

srag-srog *repr* repeated brushing, grazing, scuffing.

srok *or* **mak srok** *repr* the act of sitting down with a bump.

srombong *reg var of* **srumbung**.

srompod I undergrowth, weeds.

II *reg* eager, willing to take on anything.

srondhol, nyrondhol to push, press, nudge;

kesrondhol to get pushed;

srondholan a forceful push. *See also* **sondhol**.

sronèn *reg var of* **srunèn**.

sronggot, nyronggot 1 to root with the snout (pig, boar); 2 to butt with the tusks.

sropot *var of* **sruput**.

srothal-srathil *see* **srathil**.

srotong I pipe, for tobacco or opium.

II octopus, squid (*var of* **sotong**).

srowal-srowol cheeky, rude, insolent.

srowod, nyrowod *or* **pating srowod** full of fibres (*e.g.* mango).

srowok, nyrowok *reg* to butt with the horns.

srowol, nyrowoli to speak familiarly to;

srowal-srowol cheeky, rude, insolent.

srowong, pating srowong (*e.g.* of bamboo wall) full of holes, letting the light through.

sru *lit* 1 loud; 2 strong.

sruba, nyruba to receive with honour, pile compliments on.

srubud, srubud-srubud 1 *repr* sound of a rushing wind; 2 *repr* a fast long-striding walking pace;

sumrubud in a rush.

srudag-srudug *see* **srudug**.

srudhah *reg var of* **sludhah**.

srudug, nyrudug to butt with the head;

srudag-srudug rude.

srugal-srugul *reg* rude.

srumbat *var of* slumbat.

srumbung a cylindrical, bottomless container of woven bamboo with various uses (*e.g.* protecting plants, raising capacity of baskets);
nyrumbung *or* nyrumbungi to equip s.t. with the above.

srundèng shredded coconut fried either with or without oil.

srundha *reg* outrider;
nyrundha 1 to ride (a horse) in front; 2 to tow (boats).

srundhul *var of* sundhul.

srunèn Madurese gamelan orchestra.

srunggan *reg* mix of many kinds of seeds.

sruni I an oboe or shawm (East Java and Madura).
II a certain flower.

srunthul (*pron as:* srunthu:l) *or* mak srunthul *repr* a quick dash;
nyrunthul to dash, sprint;
sumrunthul to run fast;
srunthal-srunthul to keep running back and forth.

srupat-sruput *see* sruput.

sruput (*pron as:* srupu:t) *or* mak sruput *repr* sipping or sucking sound;
nyruput to sip or suck audibly;
srupat-sruput to sip repeatedly.

sruti *lit* 1 cautious; 2 (with) precautions.

srutu I cigar;
nyrutu to smoke a cigar.
II, nyrutu 1 to walk stiffly or without looking up; 2 to act without consulting.

sruwa I *reg* palm fibres, used for making a brush-tipped pen.
II malicious, jealous, selfish (*reg var of* srèi).

sruwal *ng, kr,* lancingan *k.i.,* trousers.

sruwang-sruwing *see* sruwing.

sruwé I sound, voice.
II, nyruwé 1 to pay attention to, con-

cern o.s. with; 2 to offer criticism, comment on.

sruwed, pating sruwed *pl* milling around, moving to and fro, with hustle and bustle.

sruwèk, pating sruwèk in rags, torn to shreds.

sruweng, pating sruweng to make a swishing or buzzing sound everywhere;
sumruweng to buzz, rush, ring (ears).

sruwi, sruwi-sruwi totally, altogether, in every respect.

sruwil, pating sruwil in shreds.

sruwing, sruwing-sruwing *or* sruwang-sruwing (to hear) vague rumours.

sruwud *var of* srowod.

sruwung *var of* sruweng.

stagèn long wide ladies' sash wound around the waist to hold the kain in place (also after pregnancy to support the body). *Also* setagèn.

stan 1 booth, stand; 2 score.

stèleng 1 installation, camp; 2 position, to take up a position. *See also* setèleng.

stèr star (of film).

stingkul *var of* setingkul.

stoplès stoppered glass jar for storing food.

strèng strict, firm.

strip strip, stripe, striped. *See also* setrip.

sual matter, question (*var of* soal).

suba, suba-suba, nyuba(-nyuba) to receive, welcome with honour.

subal 1 stuffing; 2 hairpiece worn by a short-haired girl to form Javanese-style hair-do (gelung); 3 s.t. of inferior quality mixed in with high-quality goods;
nyubal *or* nyubali to mix lower-quality stuff in with (material of high quality).

subasita etiquette, rules of behaviour.

sublug *or* sublugan a one-piece rice steamer in which rice rests on a perforated metal sheet above the water. *See also* **sablug**.

subuh dawn, time for the early morning prayer (about 5 a.m.).

subur I prosperous, flourishing;
nyuburaké to cause s.t. to flourish.
II, nyubur to gild.

subya, nyubya-nyubya to respect, honour, esteem.

suci 1 holy, sacred; **2** pure, without moral blemish; **3** (of a woman) pure, without menstrual periods; **Kitab -** the Holy Scriptures, Bible;
sesuci to bathe, wash o.s.;
nyucèni to wash and cleanse (a corpse) before burial;
nyucèkaké to purify, make clean;
sumuci-suci to engage in or commit o.s. to holy practices;
kasucian *or* **kasucèn** purity, virginity.

suda to decrease, diminish;
nyuda 1 to decrease, lessen s.t.; **2** to cut back, cut down on; curtail (production *etc*);
nyudakaké to cut down, diminish;
kesuda to have s.t. substracted from it, be reduced by;
sudan subtraction (arithmetical process).

sudagar large-scale merchant, businessman;
nyudagar *or* **sudagaran** to engage in business, practise trade.

sudama *lit* star.

sudara *lit* sibling, kinsman;
nyudara to treat or consider s.o. as one's relative; **-wèdi** *or* **-werdi** *or* **-werti** *lit* sibling, relative; intimate friend.

sudarma *lit* **1** noble, virtuous; **2** father;
kasudarman 1 virtue, generosity, charity; **2** acknowledged as father.

sudarsana *lit* model, example;
sinudarsana taken as an example or model.

sudhah, nyudhah *reg* to unload, unpack (*e.g.* goods from a ship, out of a box).

sudhang *var of* **sundhang I**.

sudhat *var of* **sudhèt**.

sudhèt, nyudhèt 1 to cut open, through (flesh); **2** to break through (channel, to divert water);
sudhètan 1 an open flesh wound; **2** diversion (of a stream).

sudhi a container for offerings, made from a banana leaf folded and held with a bamboo pin.

sudhing *reg* dead set against.

sudhiya *var of* **sadhiya**.

sudhung 1 lair of wild pigs; **2** polite self-deprecating term for one's own house.

sudi 1 willing to (do); **2** to acquiesce, be agreeable.

sudibya most excellent, illustrious, august;
kasudibyan excellence, illustriousness. *See also* **dibya**.

sudik *see* **sudi**.

suding *reg* to point with the index finger.

sudira *lit* brave, bold;
kasudiran bravery, courage, boldness.

sudra low, humble.

suduk, - salira to stab o.s., commit suicide;
nyuduk to stab;
nyuduki to stab repeatedly;
nyudukaké to stab with (a weapon);
sudukan act or way of stabbing;
suduken to get a stitch in the side;
suduk-sudukan to stab each other.

sugal stern, harsh, severe.

sugat *reg var of* **sugata**.

sugata 1 (*or* **pasugatan**) refreshments served to guests (*k.i. for* **suguh**); **2** a formal welcome;
nyugata to serve (guests).

sugeng 1 well, safe, secure (*k.i. for* **slamet**); **2** life; to live (*k.i. for* **urip**); **- dhahar** enjoy your meal, please! **-**

rawuh welcome; - **tindak** have a good trip!;

kasugengan well-being, security.

sugih 1 rich; 2 *fig* to have a wealth of;

nyugihi *or* **nyugihaké** to make s.o. rich;

sumugih to act as though one were rich.

sugik *reg var of* **sudi**.

sugu 1 a piece of bamboo used for rubbing wooden objects smooth; 2 a kind of knife used for tapping **arèn** palms;

nyugu to rub smooth;

nyugoni to stoke a fire by pushing firewood deeper into it;

nyugokaké to feed (wood) into the fire.

suguh *or* **suguhan** *ng*, **segah** *or* **segahan** *kr*, **sugata** *or* **pasugatan** *k.i.*, food and drink offered to a guest;

nyuguh *or* **nyuguhi** to serve s.o.;

nyuguhaké to serve s.t.

sugun, **sugun-sugun** very busy (in welcoming a guest).

sugreng dark and frightening (forest).

sugri *reg* all, everything.

suh I band, binding, hoop (*esp* of broom);

ngesuhi 1 to bind (a broom); 2 *fig* to act in the capacity of guardian to members of a group.

II shoo!

suhul to concentrate, pay full attention to, be completely occupied with.

suhun *var of* **suwun**;

nyuhun-nyuhun to hold in great respect;

susuhunan title of the ruler of Surakarta.

sujalma *lit* human being.

sujana I learned.

II suspicious;

nyujanani to suspect s.o.; to have misgivings about;

sujanan suspicious by nature.

sujanma *var of* **sujalma**.

sujarah I *var of* **sejarah**.

II *reg* pilgrimage. *See also* **jiyarah**.

suji 1 quill, needle; 2 embroidery; **pan-cak** - fence;

nyujèni to place (meat chunks) on a skewer;

sujèn 1 skewer; 2 on a skewer.

sujud prostration, one of the positions for Islamic prayer: kneeling with forehead to the floor;

sujudan knee (*subst kr for* **dhengkul**);

pasujudan prayer mat.

suk I *ng*, **bénjing** *kr*, next, the coming (*shtf of* **bésuk**).

II, **ngesuk** to push aside, shove around;

suk-sukan pushing/crowding each other.

suka I gay, happy, having pleasure; **-lila** *or* **-rila** with all one's heart; **-pari** - to have a good time; - **(pi)rena** happy, happiness; - **rila sokur** happy and thankful;

sukan *or* **kasukan** to play cards for gambling (*reg kr for* **main**).

II 1 to give (*kr for* **wènèh**); 2 to put s.t. s.w. (*root form: kr for* **dèlèh**).

sukak I to enjoy o.s.

II **sukak-sukak** often, sometimes.

sukan I *see* **suka**.

II reluctant, unwilling (*var of* **sungkan**).

sukarsa *lit* glad, happy, overjoyed.

sukci *lit, var of* **suci**.

sukarta *see* **sukerta**.

suker 1 difficulties, trouble; 2 dirty, impure; 3 to have a menstrual period; - **sakit** illness and difficulties;

sesuker excrement;

nyukeri 1 to soil, befoul; 2 to sully s.o.'s name.

sukerta s.t. that plagues, torments or hinders; **wong** - a person born in ominous circumstances for whom a ceremony including a shadow-play performance must be held as protection; n(y)ukertani to hinder, disturb.

suket *ng*, **rumput** *kr*, grass;

suketan *or* pasuketan grassy place.

suklé searchlight.

suklih *var of* suklé.

sukma 1 soul, life; 2 spiritual, immaterial. *See also* suksma.

sukra *lit* 1 the planet Venus; 2 Friday.

suksès successful; a success.

suksma *lit* 1 spiritual, immaterial; 2 the Immaterial; 3 soul, life (of human being); **hyang** - God, the Universal Soul;

manuksma, nyuksma 1 to enter into an invisible form; 2 to be incarnated; 3 to absorb the essence (of a message).

suku 1 leg, foot (*kr for* sikil); 2 a diacritical mark denoting the vowel U in Javanese script; 3 *reg* one-half rupiah;

nyuku to affix the above diacritic to (a letter);

sukon 1 marked with the above diacritic; 2 worth half a rupiah;

suku jaja, teken janggut *idiom* to make the utmost effort.

sukun breadfruit.

suk'un Chinese vermicelli. *See also* so'un, su'un.

sukup crowded, jam-packed.

sukur *var of* sokur.

sul shoe sole;

ngesul to sole s.t.;

sulsulan s.t. soled.

sula *lit* spear.

sulah *lit* sharp-pointed weapon.

sulak I chicken-feather duster;

nyulaki to dust with a feather duster.

II 1 light, rays shining on s.t.; 2 reflected light; 3 a tinge, touch (of colour).

sulaksana a good omen.

sulam material used to repair or replace s.t. broken;

nyulam 1 to embroider; 2 (*or* nyulami) to patch, mend s.t. by replacing broken materials with new ones; 3 to replace plants that have died;

sulaman 1 embroidery, embroidered goods; 2 s.t. mended by replacing materials.

sulang I (*or* sesulang) the facts of the case, how it really happened;

nyulangaké to convey the whole circumstances (of a case).

II new growth of a plant (sugarcane, after first cutting).

sulanten *md for* sulaya.

sulap I sleight-of-hand;

nyulap 1 to do a magic trick; 2 to transform by sleight-of-hand;

sulapan sleight-of-hand trick or performance.

II 1 unable to see clearly because of a bright light; 2 blinded, enchanted.

sulaya 1 in disagreement; 2 to quarrel, have a conflict;

nyulayani 1 to be at odds with, disagree with; 2 to fail to live up to one's agreement;

pasulayan conflict, disagreement.

sulbi *lit* womb, uterus.

suldhat soldier.

suled, nyuled to light, ignite.

sulek *reg* restricted, confining (space).

sulih, sesulih 1 a representative, substitute, stand-in; 2 *gram* pronoun;

nyulihi to represent, to act in place of or on behalf of;

nyulihaké to delegate, to have s.o. act as representative.

suling I bamboo flute (end-blown, four finger-holes for Sléndro and five or six for Pélog);

nyuling to play the flute;

panyuling act or way of playing the flute.

II, nyuling to distil;

panyulingan a distillery.

sulistya *lit* handsome, charming, beautiful;

kasulistyan beauty, charm.

sulit difficult, complicated;

nyuliti *or* **nyulit-nyuliti** to cause difficulties;

nyulitaké to cause difficulties for;

kasulitan trouble, difficulty.

sultan sultan, monarch;

kasultanan sultanate.

suluh I 1 torch; 2 *reg* firewood; 3 (or **sesuluh**) information, advice;

nyuluhi 1 to light s.t. with a torch; 2 to cast a light upon s.t.;

kesuluhan lit with a torch.

II pale golden (colour of skin, ripening bananas);

suluhan a banana ripened on the tree (not artificially).

III sleep in the corner of the eyes;

suluhan 1 inner corner of the eye; 2 a join in masonry or floor tiles.

suluk I (*or* **sulukan**) *way* 1 mood song sung by a puppet-master to set the scene in a wayang performance; 2 to sing a mood song;

nyuluki to introduce a scene as above.

II a category of poem in **macapat** metres, containing mystical Islamic themes.

sulung small flying ant which comes out at night.

sulur aerial roots.

sum hem of a garment, seam;

ngesum to hem, seam.

suma flower (*shtf of* **kusuma**).

sumados *var of* **semados**.

sumagar, **sumagaran** 1 (to work) assiduously (at); 2 industrious, serious.

sumakéyan boastful.

sumandhi *reg* compared with, rather than.

sumangga 1 as you wish; 2 please (go ahead); 3 come on!;

nyumanggakaké 1 to leave s.t. up to s.o.; 2 to entrust, put s.t. in the hands of.

sumangkéyan *var of* **sumakéyan**.

sumangkin all the more, increasingly.

sumaput *var of* **semaput**.

sumar *lit* to spread, waft (fragrance).

sumarah to submit, be obedient (to the will of).

sumarma *lit* to pity, have feelings of compassion.

sumarmi *var of* **sumarma**.

sumawana *lit* and furthermore.

sumba *or* **kesumba** safflower.

sumbaga *lit* famous, glorious.

sumbalinga *reg* it could happen that.

sumbang (*or* **sumbangan**) 1 a contribution, donation; 2 support; 3 gift, present;

nyumbang 1 to contribute, donate; 2 to support;

nyumbangaké to contribute s.t.;

pasumbang donation, support.

sumbar 1 a boast, a jeer; 2 to boast, jeer, swagger;

sumbar-sumbar to defy, challenge;

sesumbar to boast, show off;

nyumbari to challenge, jeer at;

nyumbaraké to boast about.

sumbat I all even, without profit or loss. II worthwhile, worth the trouble (*var of* **sumbut**).

sumber 1 spring; 2 source, origin;

nyumber 1 to produce water; 2 watery, soggy, to have water in it; 3 spring-like; forming a spring;

sumberan swampy, soggy.

sumbi a small stick covered with cotton used for pulling s.t. taut when weaving.

sumbit *reg* a long pole with a fork at the end used for picking fruits.

sumbu I wick; fuse;

sumbon opening for inserting a fuse (in a firecracker, old-style gun *etc*).

II, **sumbon** *reg* to have good luck, get a good catch (*e.g.* of fish).

sumbul *reg* rice serving-basket with a cover.

sumbung famous, widely known.

sumbut worthwhile, worth the trouble;
nyumbutaké to make s.t. worth the trouble.

sumed, nyumed to light, ignite;
sumedan a burning taper.

sumèdi *var of* **semèdi, semadi**.

sumèh friendly, smiling;
nyumèhi to treat s.o. pleasantly;
nyumèhaké to make (one's expression) friendly.

sumek having a musty odour.

sumeksa *lit* to press, urge, insist.

sumekta *var of* **samekta**.

sumelang worried, uneasy, apprehensive;
nyumelangi worrisome, causing apprehension;
nyumelangaké to fear, worry about;
sumelangan tending to worry too much or be overanxious.

sumelèt burning, stinging (heat of the sun).

sumené to delay;
nyumenèkaké to wait for, delay, postpone s.t.

sumeng hot, glowing, feverish.

sumer *var of* **sumar**.

sumerap *var of* **sumerep**.

sumerep 1 to see; 2 to know (*kr for* **weruh**).

sumet *see* **sumed**.

sumitra 1 *lit* a good friend; 2 tiger. *See also* **mitra**.

sumlenger, sumlengeren astonished, dazed, dumbfounded.

sumongah arrogant, boastful.

sumpah 1 an oath; 2 to swear, take an oath;
nyumpah to administer an oath to;
nyumpahi to put a curse on s.o.;
panyumpahan 1 a swearing-in; 2 an oath sworn by s.o.

sumpek crowded, jammed, stuffed, choked, suffocated;
nyumpeki to crowd, jam, throng to.

sumpel *var of* **sumpet**.

sumpena *var of* **supena**.

sumpet stopper, cork;
nyumpet *or* **nyumpeti** to stop up, close off;
kesumpetan stuck or caught so as to block s.t.

sumpil a small shellfish.

sumping an ear ornament worn as part of the costume for a classical dance;
nyumpingi *or* **nyumpingaké** to put the above on s.o.'s ear;
sumpingan to put on or wear the above ornament.

sumpit *reg* cigarette case of woven material.

sumpung lacking a body part that projects (finger, toe, nose), maimed;
nyumpungaké to maim in this way.

sumpyuh downhearted, dejected.

sumrah *reg* feeling refreshed.

sumrawang transparent.

sumreg lively, noisy.

sumrepet to have everything go dark before the eyes (on the verge of losing consciousness).

sumub steam from boiling water;
kesumuban to get scalded by steam.

sumuk hot and sticky;
nyumuki to make one feel hot and sweaty;
kesumuken 1 to be too hot; 2 to suffer from sticky heat.

sumung hot, glowing, feverish (*var of* **sumeng**).

sumungah *var of* **sumongah**.

sumur well; - **bandhung** a large well; - **gumuling** underground waterway, tunnel (in Taman Sari, Yogyakarta);
nyumur resembling a well, to form a well; - **gumuling** mysterious, inscrutable.

sumurup to know (*var of* **weruh**);
nyumurupaké to let s.o. know;
kasumurupan to be found out, detected, known.

sumyah feeling refreshed.

sumyak *or* **sumyak-sumyak** festive, bustling.

sumyang loud, boisterous.

sumyar I 1 scattered roundabout; **2** (of the face) shining, bright-looking.
II (of a crowd) buzzing, murmuring.
III *lit* heartbroken.

sumyur broken, shattered, smashed.

sumaya *var of* **semaya**.

sun *lit, shtf of* **ingsun**.

sunah meritorious and recommended but not obligatory according to Islamic law.

sunan 1 *title applied to the apostles of Islam in Java (Wali Sanga), and to the ruler of Surakarta*; **2** the ruler of Surakarta;
kasunanan 1 realm of the Sunan; **2** the position of Sunan. *See also* **Susuhunan**.

sunar *lit* light, radiance;
nyunari to give light to, shine on;
sumunar radiant, shining.

sunat meritorious but not obligatory according to Islamic law (*var of* **sunah**);
nyunati 1 to circumcise; **2** (**netesi** *k.i.*) to circumcise (a girl, performed by cutting a **kunir** root);
nyunataké to have (a boy) circumcised;
sunatan 1 circumcision; **2** (**tetesan** *k.i.*) female circumcision;
pasunatan circumcising knife.

sundek *reg* stuffy (*var of* **sumpek**).

sundel prostitute; - **bolong** female ghost with a hole in her back;
nyundel to engage in prostitution.

sundep rice borer (insect);
nyundep to stab, prick, pierce.

sundha one after the other, passing along from one to another (*var of* **tundha II**).

sundhang I *lit* horn of an animal;
nyundhang 1 to butt or gore with the horns.
II, nyundhang to support a woman from behind when she gives birth.

sundhul to reach or come up (to), to touch (s.t. high); - **langit 1** to reach the sky; **2** a small-leafed creeper with small flowers;
nyundhul to push or hit from underneath;
nyundhuli 1 to push or hit from underneath repeatedly; **2** to send a second letter which countermands, adds to *etc*;
kesundhul to get pushed upward;
kesundhulan 1 to get pushed from below; **2** to have become pregnant again before the preceding child is weaned;
pasundhulan crown of the head (*k.i.* for **embun-embunan**, *see* **embun II**);
nyundhul poyuh to move s.t. in a high arc, *esp* to push s.o. in a swing.

sundhung *reg* pole used for carrying grass.

sunduk skewer;
nyunduk *or* **nyunduki** to put things on a skewer;
sundukan 1 skewer; **2** things put on a skewer.

sung *lit* to give;
pasung a gift, offering. *See also* **asung**, **angsung**.

sunga silk thread.

sungap, sungapan estuary, rivermouth.

sungar *var of* **songar**.

sungé *lit* river.

sungga I *reg* booby trap of sharpened bamboo points stuck in the ground.
II, nyungga-nyungga to respect highly, show great esteem for.

sunggal *var of* sugal.

sunggar, nyunggar 1 to comb (the hair above the ears) upwards; 2 to turn over the soil; 3 to egg on, incite (fighting cocks);
sunggaran a certain puffed-out hairstyle.

sunggata *var of* sugata.

sunggèk *reg var of* sènggèk.

sunggi, nyunggi to carry on the head.

sungging, juru - an expert painter;
nyungging 1 to apply decorative painting (to woodwork, puppets); 2 to copy an intricate design exactly;
nyunggingaké to have (a puppet) painted;
sinungging *lit* decorated with painted designs;
sunggingan 1 painted, skilfully decorated; 2 an exact copy.

sungil impassable, difficult or hazardous to negotiate (*e.g.* a mountain pass).

sungkal, nyungkal to break (stones).

sungkan reluctant, unwilling;
sungkanan habitually unwilling.

sungkawa *lit* sad, dejected.

sungkem the attitude of being inclined forward, sloping, touching the ground;
nyungkemi to pay one's respects to s.o. by bowing deeply and touching the head on the lap, knee or foot;
nyungkemaké to have s.o. show esteem and humility as above;
sumungkem *lit* 1 to lay o.s. (before, at the feet); 2 to devote o.s. completely;
sungkeman the ceremony in which the bride and the groom pay respects to the parents as above.

sungku, nyungku to concentrate or focus the attention on;
manungku *lit* to meditate by concentrating.

sunglon I rivermouth, estuary;

II a mould of decorative metal plate on a kris sheath.

sungsang I 1 upside-down; 2 standing on its head; waringin - the name of a song (kidung) of great magical power; n(y)ungsang turned upside-down; - njempalik to work o.s. to the bone, do with all one's might.
II the superb lily (highly poisonous).

sungsat, adoh sungsaté quite different from, far from it.

sungsud *var of* susud.

sungsum 1 bone marrow; 2 *fig* strength.

sungsun 1 layer; 2 storey of a building; - timbun lying in piles;
nyungsun to make (into) layers.

sungsung, nungsung to go to meet; - kabar *or* - warta 1 to try to get news; 2 to ask/check on about the origin of a report;
pasungsung, pisungsung a gift of welcome (honour).

sungu *ng*, singat *kr*, horn, antler;
nyungu to attack with the horns.

sungut 1 insect's feeler/antenna; 2 tendril (of creeper).

suntak, nyuntak to spill or tip s.t. out.

suntek *reg var of* suntak.

Sunten 1st month of the Islamic calendar (*reg kr for* Sura).

sunthi *see* prawan.

suntik injection;
nyuntik 1 to inject; 2 vaccinate, innoculate;
nyuntikaké to inject s.t. into;
suntikan 1 injection; 2 vaccination.

sunting *reg var of* sumping.

suntrut sad, drooping, depressed.

sunu I *lit* child;
sesunu to have a child.
II *lit* ray, beam, radiance;
sumunu to shine.

sunya *lit* quiet, lonely, deserted.

sunyata *lit* true, factual;
kasunyatan truth, fact. *See also* nyata.

sunyuk *var of* **nyunyuk**.

sup *var of* **sop** I.

supadi *lit* in order to, so that.

supados in order to, so that (*kr for* **supaya**).

supadya *var of* **supadi**.

supangat mediation, intercession (of the Prophet with God).

supaos *subst kr for* **supata**.

supata 1 a vow, an oath; 2 to swear (to);
nyupatani to put a curse on s.o. (to the effect that…);
nyupatakaké 1 to have s.o. swear (to); 2 to swear on s.o.'s behalf;
pasupata 1 an oath; 2 a curse.

supaya *ng*, **supados** *kr*, 1 in order to, so that; 2 (to wish, urge *etc*) that…

supé I to forget (*kr for* **lali**).
II, sesupé (*kr for* **ali-ali**) finger-ring.

supek *var of* **sumpek**.

supeket to have a friendly relationship (with).

supena 1 a dream (*kr for* **impèn**); 2 (*or* **nyupena**) to dream (*kr for* **ngimpi**).

supenuh *lit* very full.

supi *lit* mysticism.

supir *var of* **sopir**.

supit 1 pinchers, pinching claws; 2 pincers, tongs; 3 circumcision (*k.i. for* **sunat**); -urang 1 shrimp claw; 2 a flanking battle array;
nyupit to pick up with pincers, tweezers, tongs *etc*;
supitan circumcision (*k.i. for* **sunatan**).

suprandéné nevertheless.

suprèh *reg var of* **suprih**.

suprih in order to, so that.

sur I (*pron as:* **su:r**) *or* **mak sur** *repr* flowing, pouring;
ngesuri to pour onto;
ngesuraké to pour s.t.;
kesuran to get poured on;
sur-suran to keep flowing, pouring.
II, ngesur 1 to push aside; 2 to appro-

priate by pushing s.t. aside;
kesur to get pushed aside.

Sura I 1 Islamic feast-day on 10th Muharram; 2 1st month of the Islamic calendar.
II *lit* 1 hero; 2 heroic.
III *lit* deity.

suradhadhu soldier (*var of* **serdhadhu**).

surah a subdivision or chapter of the Quran.

surak *or* **surak-surak** to cheer;
nyuraki to jeer at, boo.

suralaya *lit* the realm of the deities.

suraloka *var of* **suralaya**.

surambi *var of* **srambi**.

surang, kesurang-surang beset with troubles.

suraos *kr for* **surasa**.

surapsara *lit* deity, heavenly being.

surapsari *lit* heavenly nymph.

surasa *ng*, **suraos** *kr*, contents, meaning, connotation;
nyurasa to get the meaning, sense the connotation;
panyurasa grasp or insight into meanings contained in texts, messages *etc*.

surat 1 letter, document (*var of* **serat**); 2 *var of* **surah**.

surastri *lit* heavenly maiden.

surawadu *lit* heavenly woman.

surem dim, gloomy;
nyuremaké to cause to be dim/gloomy.

surèn red cedar, valued for its timber.

suréndra *lit* the king of the gods.

surèngrana *lit* 1 hero in battle; 2 name of a gamelan melody.

suretna *lit* 1 a fine diamond; 2 a beautiful princess.

suri 1 a weaver's comb; 2 a curved comb worn to hold the hair in place; 3 small comb for removing lice; 4 horse's mane; 5 comb *subst kr for* **jungkat**;
nyurèni to comb s.o.'s hair.

surjan a man's jacket (double-breasted, with high collar).

surtanah a ceremony held for a person who has just died;
 nyurtanah *or* **ngesurtanah** to hold such a ceremony.
surti careful and cautious;
 nyurtèni to take precautions for.
suru I 1 spoon fashioned from a banana leaf; **2** spoon (in general);
 nyuru to eat with a spoon;
 nyuroni to scoop (food) with a spoon repeatedly.
 II a certain thick shrub used for hedges.
surud 1 to ebb, recede; **2** to pass away.
suruh *ng*, **sedhah** *kr*, **1** the betel plant; **2** betel leaves, used for chewing;
 nyuruhi 1 to invite; **2** to ask for help;
 suruhan 1 messenger; **2** certain female servants at court (*also* **sedhahan**).
surung I a certain sea fish.
 II, **nyurung** to push s.t. forward from behind;
 kasurung pushed, shoved;
 surungan pushing;
 surung-surungan to push each other.
surup *ng*, **serap** *kr*, **1** sunset; **2** to enter;
 nyurupi (of spirit) to enter, possess;
 nyurupaké to thread (a needle);
 kesurupan to be possessed (by a spirit);
 sumurup to know, understand;
 nyumurupi to know about, see;
 kasumurupan to be seen.
surya I *lit* sun; **- candra** sun and moon.
 II *or* **pasuryan** face (*k.i. for* **rai**);
 suryan to wash the face (*k.i. for* **raup**).
suryakantha magnifying glass.
sus cream puff.
susah I *ng*, **sisah** *kr*, **sekel** *k.i.*, sad, grieving, sorrowful;
 nyusahi *or* **nyusahaké** to sadden, cause sorrow for;
 kasusahan 1 sorrow, grief, trouble; **2** to experience sorrow.

 II *ng*, **sisah** *kr*, (not) need to, (not) necessary.
susetya faithful and loyal.
susila decent, morally or socially acceptable;
 kasusilan virtue, good morals.
suster 1 nurse; **2** Catholic nun. *Also* **sester**.
susu I 1 (p(r)embayun *k.i.*) breast; **2** milk;
 n(y)usu to suck at the breast;
 nyusoni to breastfeed a baby;
 nyusokaké to have (a baby) fed by s.o.;
 suson not yet weaned (baby).
 II, **kesusu** in a hurry;
 nyusokaké *or* **nyusu-nyusu** to hurry s.o.
susud to lose weight, reduce, diminish, go down (water).
susug long-handled fish trap.
susuh nest, breeding-place;
 n(y)usuh 1 to build a nest; **2** to let things pile up in a mess;
 n(y)usuhi to build a nest in.
Susuhunan title of the ruler of Surakarta.
susuk I 1 pancake turner, spatula; **2** hairpin.
 II change (money);
 nyusuki to give s.o. change;
 nyusukaké to purchase s.t. in order to get small change.
susul, **n(y)usul** to follow s.o. later, to catch up with;
 nyusuli to send a letter after s.o., or after an earlier letter, with additional information;
 nyusulaké to add s.t. later on;
 kesusul to be caught up with.
susun, **nyusun** to arrange and classify, sort out;
 susunan arrangement, deployment.
susung *var of* **sungsung**.
susup, **nyusup 1** to seep in; **2** to work one's way into/through/under;

nyusupi 1 to insert into; 2 to infiltrate;

nyusupaké to push s.t. into/through/under;

kasusupan to get entered.

susur, panasar k.i. a tobacco quid, used to rub over the teeth after chewing betel;

nyusur 1 to chew tobacco; 2 to wax thread to prevent it from snarling;

susuran to chew a tobacco quid.

sut I (pron as: su:t) to play um-ping-sut to decide who wins.

II (pron as: su:t) or mak sut repr a sudden going out/off (light).

suta 1 lit child; 2 si Suta Joe Blow (anybody at all).

sutapa lit holy hermit;

kasutapan an ascetic life, the way of life of a hermit. See also tapa.

suthang 1 a cricket's back legs; 2 cr hand, foot.

suthik unwilling, reluctant.

suthil pancake turner-like kitchen implement.

suthing reg var of suthik.

suthup slant-eyed (Chinese).

suthur var of suthup.

sutra silk fabric.

sutresna very dear (listeners, on radio).

sutri chains forming part of a horse's harness.

su'un var of so'un.

suwa, kalam - brush pen made from palm fibre.

suwab see suwap.

suwadi ng, suwados kr 1 the real (inner, hidden) thing; 2 secret. See also wadi.

suwados kr for suwadi.

suwak, nyuwak to abolish, cancel.

suwal reg var of sruwal.

suwala 1 to argue, disagree; 2 to disobey, resist;

nyuwalani to disobey or defy s.o.

suwalapatra lit letter, document.

suwalik on the contrary, on the other hand. See also walik.

suwan a stick of hard wood for digging in the ground.

suwang, suwangan mouth of a river.

suwaos pinchbeck, a copper-zinc alloy (kr for suwasa).

suwap 1 a mouthful; 2 fig bribe;

nyuwap to bribe s.o.;

nyuwapi 1 to feed s.o. by hand; 2 to bribe;

suwapan 1 act of eating with hand; 2 bribe.

suwarat, nyuwarataké reg to proclaim (a command).

suwari cassowary (var of kaswari).

suwasa ng, suwaos kr, pinchbeck, a gold-coloured copper-zinc alloy; - bubul low quality of this alloy;

suwasan, swasan made of this alloy, fake (cheap jewelry).

suwat-suwut see suwut.

suwau formerly, before now (kr for mauné).

suwawa 1 equal to; 2 fitting, suitable;

nyuwawa to be a match for, be able to equal.

suwawi 1 come on! let's…! (subst kr for ayo); 2 here! take it! (subst kr for nya, nyoh).

suwé ng, dangu kr, (a) long (time); ora - before long;

nyuwé or nyenyuwé to use up time;

nyuwèni or nyuwèkaké to take a long time over;

nyuwèn-nyuwèni to make s.t. last an unnecessarily long time;

kesuwèn too long;

suwé-suwé or suwéning suwé after a while, eventually;

suwéné the (length of) time.

suweg a variety of edible tuber.

suwèk ripped, torn;

nyuwèk to rip, tear;

nyuwèki to keep tearing;

nyuwèkaké to tear s.t. accidentally;
nyuwèk-nyuwèk to tear to pieces;
suwèkan 1 torn; 2 torn scraps of (paper);
sasuwèk a scrap of (paper).
suwel, nyuwel to push, tuck into a pocket or hole;
nyuwelaké to tuck, stuff s.t. away.
suweng I ng, sengkang kr, earstud;
nyuwengi to put earstuds on s.o.;
suwengan or sesuwengan to wear or put on earstuds.
II empty, vacant, unoccupied (reg kr for suwung).
suwèni see udan.
suwidak sixty (var of sewidak).
suwiké green frog's leg soup (Chinese delicacy).
suwing (with) a harelip.
suwir ripped;
nyuwir, nyuwiri 1 to tear; 2 to tear off;
sumiwir torn to shreds.
suwit (pron as: suwi:t) tweet! (sound of whistle);
suwat-suwit to keep blowing a whistle.
suwita or nyuwita to live in the home of a prominent family in order to learn their manners and style of living, and in return to serve them during this period.
suwiwi wing.
suwolo reg var of suwala.
suwot var of suwut.
suwuk I to stop (music);
nyuwuk to (cause to) stop (music);
suwukan 1 a large gong in the gamelan orchestra; 2 beat struck with the large gong to stop the music.
II medical treatment consisting of incantations and blowing on the patient's head;
nyuwuk to blow on s.o.'s head as treatment for an illness;

nyuwukaké to have s.o. treated (as above).
suwun, nyuwun to ask (humbly) (k.a. for njaluk);
nuwun var of nyuwun used in certain phrases;
nenuwun to keep on praying;
kesuwun reg thank-you;
pan(y)uwun or panyuwunan 1 a humble request; 2 a prayer;
kula nuwun hello! anybody home? (at the door);
matur nuwun thank-you.
suwung empty, vacant, unoccupied, uninhabited; - blung completely empty, without a soul in it;
nyuwungaké to vacate, leave empty, evacuate.
suwur rumour, news spread roundabout;
nyuwuraké to spread (news), make known roundabout;
misuwur famous, renowned.
suwut, nyuwut to snatch s.t. away;
suwat-suwut snatching away repeatedly.
suyasa lit building. See also yasa.
suyud devoted, loyal, obedient;
nyuyudi to serve devotedly;
nyuyudaké to cause s.o. to be devoted;
sumuyud obedient.
swabawa I lit sound, noise.
II lit nature, disposition.
swagata lit welcome (to a guest).
swagotra lit one's own family.
swah lit sky, heavens.
swami lit 1 lord, master; 2 husband.
swana I lit dog.
II lit blood.
swandana lit vehicle, chariot.
swanita lit blood.
swayambara var of sayembara.
swanten noise, voice (kr for swara).
swara ng, swanten kr, 1 noise, sound; 2 voice; 3 a voice in s.t., opinion, vote;

4 vowel sound; - **ampang** *gram* unvoiced consonant sound; - **anteb** *gram* voiced consonant sound;

nywara to make a sound, speak;

nywarani to criticise;

nywarakaké to give voice to, express.

swarga 1 (**swargi** *reg kr*) heaven; the realm of God; 2 deceased, the late...;

nywargakaké to take solicitous care of, to pamper;

swarga nunut neraka katut to share the good and the bad (said of a wife).

swargaloka *lit* the realm of the gods.

swargi 1 deceased, the late... (*k.i. for* **jenat**); 2 heaven (*reg kr for* **swarga**).

swasambada self-supporting, self-sufficient.

swasana *lit* atmosphere.

swasta well, safe and sound.

swéda *lit* sweat.

swèmpak swimming costume.

swi *lit* to insist, urge.

swikara *lit* forceful, insistent.

swuh *lit* destroyed, crushed.

sya'ban the 8th month of the Islamic calendar. *See also* **Ruwah**.

syair 1 Indonesian poetry; 2 story related in Malay verse form using one-end-rhyme quatrains.

syaraf *var of* **saraf**, **sarap**.

syarat condition, requirement (*var of* **sarat III**).

syari'at Islamic law (*var of* **saréngat**).

syarif title of a male descendant of Muhammad.

syukur thank God, thanks be to God. *See also* **sokur**, **sukur**.

T

ta 1 *particle, inviting agreement or confirmation*; 2 *particle, adding emphasis.*

ta'at 1 devout; 2 (*or* **na'ati**) to obey.

tab I *see* **ketab**.

II, **ngetab** *or* **tab-taban** to thump, beat fast (the heart). *See also* **tratab**.

tabag rough panel of woven bamboo;
  nabag 1 to make a bamboo panel; 2 to build with bamboo panels.

tabah strong, resilient;
  nabahaké to face up to s.t. with endurance.

tabé *var of* **tabik**.

tabèk *reg var of* **tabik**.

tabel 1 puffy, swollen (face); 2 headstrong.

tabèl table (*e.g.* figures, facts).

tabela box for carrying a body to the cemetery, coffin (*also* **terbela**).

taberi assiduous, diligent;
  naberèni to apply o.s. to s.t. with diligence;
  kataberèn diligence.

tabet remains, trace, mark (*kr for* **tapak**, **tilas**);
  nabet to leave traces;
  nabeti to leave traces on s.t.;
  katabetan bearing traces.

tabib (Arab) physician.

tabik greeting;
  nabiki to greet s.o.;
  tabikan to shake hands, greet each other.

tabit *var of* **tabib**.

tablag *reg var of* **tabag**.

tablas 1 (cut or pierced) all the way through; 2 all used up;
  nablasaké 1 to cut/pierce through; 2 to finish, use all of.

tableg I *reg* dyke, embankment;
  nableg 1 to build a dyke of earth; 2 to fill a hole with earth.

II indifferent, insensitive.

tablèg I *reg var of* **tabag**.

II Islamic preaching (*var of* **tablig**).

tablèt pill.

tablig Islamic preaching.

tablun *reg cr* faeces;
  nablun to defecate.

tabok width of the palm of the hand (used as a measure);
  nabok to slap;
  naboki to slap s.o. repeatedly;
  tabokan act of slapping; (*or* **tabok-tabokan**) to slap each other;
  satabok one palm's width;
  nabok nyilih tangan *idiom* to strike at s.o. through another person.

tabon I the oldest, most senior.

II coconut shell fibre.

tabrak, nabrak 1 to collide with, run into; 2 to catch (thief);
  nabraki *or* **nabrak-nabrak** to repeatedly run into obstacles or hit things;
  nabrakaké to make collide, let s.t. strike;
  ketabrak to get hit, get run into;
  tabrakan 1 a collision; 2 to collide.

tabuh 1 *lit* o'clock; 2 mallet or hammer for striking a percussion instrument;
  nabuh 1 to play a gamelan instrument; 2 *reg* to let off, fire; 3 to question, induce s.o. to talk;
  nabuhi to play music for (s.t., as an accompaniment);
  tabuhan *or* **tetabuhan** 1 percussion instrument; 2 the playing of (gamelan music).

tabur I 1 *reg* small coins ceremonially distributed among the poor; 2 one who is sacrificed. *See also* **tawur**.

II **tabur-tabur** embroidery with silk

and gold thread;

nabur to embroider thus.

tadha iron or wooden peg for holding roof sections in place.

tadhah 1 container for catching s.t. from above; 2 capacity, consumption; - **amin** to hold out the hands and then bring them to the face while saying 'Amin', following prayer; - **duka** to accept deserved blame; - **kringet** 1 singlet; 2 lining; - **udan** 1 ricefield irrigated by rainfall; 2 *reg* top row of bananas of a comb;

nadhah 1 to hold the palms facing up; 2 to receive s.t. in one's hands; 3 *lit* to eat;

nadhahi to catch s.t. coming from above;

nadhahaké to use s.t. for catching s.t. from above;

tadhahan act or way of catching s.t. from above.

tag, ngetag to keep after s.o. to do s.t., to urge on;

tag-tagan one who does things only when urged on repeatedly. *See also* **atag**.

taga, tagané finally.

tagèh a certain freshwater fish.

tagen, nageni to ward off, cope with.

tagih I *var of* **tagèh**.

II, **nagih** 1 to dun, collect one's debts; 2 to demand fulfilment of an agreement;

nagihi 1 to demand payment of a debt; 2 habit-forming;

nagihaké to collect a debt for s.o.;

tagihan a claim;

ketagihan 1 addiction; 2 addicted to.

tagon *or* **tagonan** *reg* fiancé(e);

tetagon *reg* to engage in a love affair.

tah 1 *reg var of* **ta**; 2 *reg var of* **utawa**.

taha thought, guess, opinion;

tumaha hesitant, undecided;

taha-taha to (do) hesitantly because of

a social or moral restraint; **ora** - without fear or hesitation.

tahajud a non-obligatory, nocturnal, time of prayer for Muslims.

tahan to (with)stand, endure;

nahan 1 to restrain; 2 to endure s.t.;

nahan-nahanaké to force o.s. to endure s.t.;

tahanan 1 prisoner; 2 prison, jail; 3 capable of enduring;

tahan-tahanan to try to out-endure each other.

tahang *reg* barrel, keg.

tahayul superstition, superstitious belief (*var of* **takayul**).

tahen *var of* **tahan**.

tahjud *var of* **tahajud**.

tahlil to praise God by chanting the first words of the Islamic profession of faith (**la ilaha illa'llah**) in unison;

nahlilaké to recite this for s.o. (deceased);

tahlilan to perform this recitation.

tahu beancake, beancurd.

tahun *see* **taun**.

tahyat greeting (part of prayer ritual).

tai 1 (**tinja** *kr*) faeces; 2 rust; 3 sawdust, shavings; 4 *term of abuse*: bullshit!; - **manuk** lime (used in betel chewing, term used at night to avoid taboo); - **yèng** a reddish deposit of iron compounds in pools, ricefields *etc*;

nai 1 to rust; 2 to give birth to kittens;

tainen to get rusty.

tetai rust.

tail 1 a measure of weight equal to 16 **kati**; 2 a measure of gold, silver, or opium.

tajab potent, efficacious (*var of* **mustajab**).

tajali manifestation, revelation of truth.

tajap *see* **tajab**.

tajem I 1 in balance (scales); 2 calm, settled (expression); 3 firm, steady (mind).

II sharp, cutting;

najemi 1 to sharpen, hone; 2 to incite, egg on.

tajèn I *see* **taji**.

II labour demanded by the headman from villagers.

taji spur attached to a fighting cock's leg;

naji 1 to strike with a spur; 2 to accuse, charge;

najèni to put a spur on (a fighting cock);

tajèn spurred, equipped with a spur.

tajin water in which rice has been boiled, starch;

najini to skim the liquid from (boiling rice).

taju I *lit* a crown.

II metal wedge for splitting wood (*var of* **paju**);

naju to split (wood) with a metal wedge.

tajug I in the shape of a four-sided pyramid with a levelled-off top (of roofs, polished gems).

II **najug** to accuse, express one's suspicions.

tak *prefix denoting 1st person singular: 1 as agent of passive verb; 2 in propositive* (*also* **dak**).

takad able to endure pain and sorrow;

nakadaké to steel o.s. to endure afflictions.

takal *reg* hoisting device resembling a block-and-tackle.

takayul superstition, superstitious belief.

takbir I the words 'Allahu akbar' (God is the Greatest);

takbiran a meeting for recitation of the above.

II **takbiran** meaning, interpretation (of dream *etc*).

takdir fate, destiny;

nakdiraké to determine the course of destiny;

tinakdir destined.

takèk *var of* **takèn**.

takèn to ask (*kr for* **takon**).

taker a measure of capacity (*e.g.* a pot);

naker to measure (*e.g.* rice);

takeran 1 measurer; 2 amount measured, a measureful; 3 the standard of;

sataker one unit of a measure.

taki, **tetaki** *or* **taki-taki** *lit* to devote o.s. to, concentrate on.

takir 1 small shallow banana leaf container; 2 part of a wooden house frame; - **ponthang** container made from young coconut leaves;

nakir to fashion (banana leaves) into a container;

nakiri to fill such containers with food;

takiran food served in such containers.

taklèk 1 addendum, attachment; 2 conditions attached to an agreement, *esp* marriage contracts so that divorce is effected if the husband fails to return after a certain time *etc*.

taklid 1 to accept on authority; 2 to imitate unthinkingly.

taklim respect, honour, esteem.

takluk *reg* 1 subject; 2 subjection.

takok to ask (*reg var of* **takon**).

takon *ng*, **takèn** *kr*, **ndangu** *or* **mundhut priksa** *k.i.*, **nyuwun priksa** *k.a.* to ask (a question), seek information;

nakoni to question s.o.;

nakokaké 1 to ask (about) s.t.; 2 to ask for (s.o.'s) hand in marriage;

takon-takonan *or* **takon-tinakon** to ask each other questions;

pitakon 1 (*or* **pitakonan**) a question; 2 to ask (a question).

takowah variety of Chinese soup.

takrul to respect, obey (religious duties, laws).

taksaka *lit* snake.

taksi taxi;

naksèkaké 1 to pay s.o.'s taxi fare; 2 to

rent out one's car as a taxi;

taksi-taksinan 1 toy taxi; **2** to travel around by taxi.

taksih still, even now (*kr for* isih).

taksir 1 a cost estimate; **2** to appraise, value;

naksir 1 to estimate the cost of; **2** to look over or size up (s.o. of the opposite sex);

naksiraké to estimate the cost of s.t. on behalf of s.o.;

taksiran estimation, appraisal.

takwa I 1 piety; **2** pious.

II a certain style of Javanese men's jacket;

takwan to put on or wear the above.

takyin certain, sure;

nakyinaké to establish the facts about.

takyun experience, one's own observation.

tal the fan or lontar palm, the leaves formerly used for writing on.

tala honeycomb.

talab *lit* to study religious matter.

talad (there is) plenty of time, no need to hurry.

talah *excl* by God!

talak a form of divorce in which the husband renounces the wife three times before witnesses;

nalak to divorce (one's wife) in this way.

talam serving tray, platter.

talang I bamboo pipe serving as a water conduit; **- catur** an intermediary; **- jiwa** *or* **- pati** to risk one's life for a cause;

nalang 1 to convey (liquid) through a pipe; **2** resembling a pipe;

nalangi to furnish with a pipe;

talang lumrahé teles *idiom* a go-between gets a commission, of course.

II, nalangi to advance money.

talawéngkar *reg* fragment of broken tile, shard of earthenware.

talèdhèk female dancer who performs with a group of street musicians door-to-door or for hire. *See also* **tlèdhèk**.

talèk, nalèk *reg* to ask s.o. for a decision, yes or no.

talenan chopping board for kitchen use. *See also* **telenan**.

taler 1 outline, thread (of story); **2** line of descent; **isih ana taleré** related by blood;

naleraké to follow the line (of story, descent).

tales taro;

nales having the texture of cooked taro: thick, creamy.

tali *ng*, **tangsul** *kr*, string, cord, rope;

nalèni to tie up, bind;

nalèkaké 1 to tie for s.o.; **2** to fasten or secure to s.t.;

talènan 1 act or way of tying; **2** a tied bundle;

setali 25 cents; **- telung wang** *idiom* all the same;

setalèn *or* **nyetalèn** 25 cents each;

talènan 25-cent coin.

talib I *reg* sandbank, shoal.

II nalibaké 1 to fold s.t. around (an object) to cover or conceal it; **2** *fig* to do s.t. under cover or in secret.

talika, nalika *lit* to spy out, investigate;

katalika to appear, turn out to be.

talil *var of* **tahlil**.

talimangsa, katalimangsa past (season), lapsed, expired.

taling Javanese script diacritical mark indicating the vowel *é* or *è*; **-tarung** diacritical marks indicating the vowel *o*.

talinga *lit*, **talingan** ear (*k.i. for* **kuping**).

tallah *var of* **talah**.

taloh *var of* **taluh**.

talok a certain tree.

talu I 1 *way* musical overture of a shadow-play performance; **2** to begin (shadow-play performance);

matalu-talu (to sound) repeatedly.

II **katalu** *lit* defeated.

talub Mongoloid fold.

taluh *reg* 1 to feel at home; 2 bored, fed up;

ketaluhen surfeited, to have had too much of s.t., sick and tired.

talun 1 an unirrigated field abandoned after harvest; 2 an unirrigated mountain field cultivated only every two or three years;

patalunan newly opened up land in the mountains.

tama I excellent, superior (*see also* **utama**).

II, **namakaké** to use (a weapon) to strike;

ketaman to get struck;

tumama 1 to enter, penetrate; 2 to be effective, have the desired effect.

taman 1 ornamental garden; 2 *lit* garden attached to a palace, containing a pool for bathing; - **sari** pleasure park, flower garden;

patamanan 1 horticulture; 2 flower garden, park.

tamat I 1 the end (of a book); 2 finished, read;

tamatan to have finished one's study of the Quran.

II observant;

namataké to look closely at s.t.

tamba *ng*, **jampi** *kr*, medicine, treatment, remedy; - **arip** s.t. to keep one awake; - **kangen** s.t. to remember s.o. by, souvenir;

nambani to treat with medicines, to cure;

nambakaké 1 to use as medicine; 2 to have s.o. treated;

tetamba to take medicine;

mertamba to have medical treatment;

tamba teka, lara lunga medicine comes, illness goes! (*phrase chanted to*

a patient being given medicine).

tambah increasingly, more and more;

nambah to add s.t. to (the others);

nambahi to supplement s.t. with, to add s.t. to;

tambahan 1 an addition, a supplement; 2 in addition (to the rest);

katambahan to get s.t. added (to an existing amount or number).

tambak 1 a pond near the shore where certain sea fish are bred; 2 a dyke, dam, bank;

nambaki 1 to dam; 2 to ward off, hold back.

tambal a mending patch; - **butuh** s.t. for making ends meet; - **sulam** 1 to make small repairs; 2 to patch up a quarrel;

nambal to put a patch on;

nambali to patch s.t. in many places;

nambalaké 1 to have s.t. patched; 2 to patch for s.o.;

tambalan 1 act or way of patching; 2 patched. *See also* **trambal**.

tamban, tamban-tamban at an easy, slow pace; in no hurry.

tambang I thick rope, cable, hawser;

nambang to abandon one's spouse without divorcing her; - **aksi** *lit* to gaze into each other's eyes (lovers);

nambangi to ferry;

nambangaké to take s.o. on a ferry;

panambang, prau - a ferry (boat);

panambangan crossing (place), ferry;

tambangan 1 ferry; 2 boat fare.

II *reg* mine, mining.

tambar 1 *reg* no longer effective; 2 (of rice) not yet completely white (after being pounded).

tambas to leak through, run, blot.

tambel (*or* **tambelan**) s.t. used to fill a need for the time being; - **butuh** money for making ends meet;

nambeli 1 to patch; 2 to fill a need, add what is lacking.

tambem *or* **tambeman** 1 a rifle-prop; 2 a

prop for supporting a carrying-pole.

tambeng headstrong, obstinate, stubborn.

tambet ignorant (*reg kr for* **tambuh**).

tambi 1 wide, flat tree roots growing above the ground; 2 *subst kr for* **tamba**.

tambir 1 broad shallow woven bamboo bowl; 2 wooden or bamboo extension of the deck space of a barge or boat.

tamblag *reg* bamboo panel;
namblag 1 to make a bamboo panel; 2 to build with bamboo panels.

tamblang spotted (*var of* **tamblong**).

tambleg *var of* **tableg** I.

tamblèg bamboo panel (*var of* **tabag**).

tamblong *or* **tamblong-tamblong** spotted, covered with blemishes.

tambon *reg* a small sampan-like boat, canoe.

tambra a kind of carp.

tambuh 1 to not know, not recognise, understand; 2 to act as if one does not know, take no notice, ignore;
tambuh-tambuh indescribable, incalculable;
nambuhi to pretend not to know or care about;
tumambuh to feign ignorance or lack of interest.

tambung *lit* vague, obscure, inconspicuous;
nambung laku to disguise o.s.

tambur 1 (European) drum; 2 drumbeat for reveille and tattoo; 3 one of the Chinese playing-cards (*kertu cilik*);
nambur to beat (a drum);
panambur 1 a drummer; 2 act of drumming; 2 small bullets, buckshot.

tamèng shield;
namèngi to use s.t. as a shield;
tetamèng protector; protection; a shield from harm.

tami I guest (*reg kr for* **tamu**).
II excellent, superior (*kr for* **tama** I).
III to get struck (*kr for* **tama** II).

tampa *ng*, **tampi** *kr*, 1 (*or* **nampa**) to receive, accept; 2 to take, interpret, understand;
nampani to receive, accept, catch;
nampakaké to cause to receive, *i.e.* to hand over, give;
ketampa *or* **ketampan** to get accepted, taken, received;
panampa understanding, grasp.

tampah winnow, wide tray of woven bamboo with a low rim.

tampak, **nampak** to plant (seeds) in a seedbed;
tampakan seedbed.

tampang 1 lead sinker for a fishnet; 2 a roll of tobacco leaves;
satampang one roll of tobacco.

tampar rope made from twisted fibres;
nampar to make (fibres) into rope;
tamparen to suffer from cramp in the calf muscle.

tampek, **nampek** 1 to slap s.o. in the face; 2 (of wind: *fig* of misfortunes) to buffet;
ketampek to get a slap in the face; to get slapped (by the wind).

tampèk flat object for hitting (*var of* **tamplèk**);
nampèk to hit with such an object.

tampel, **nampel** (of leech) to adhere to the body. *See also* **tapel**.

tampèl, **nampèl** to slap s.o. on the hand;
ketampèl to get slapped with the hand unintentionally.

tamper, **uyah** - fine-grained salt.

tampi to receive, accept (*kr for* **tampa**).

tampik, **nampik** to avoid, shun, reject;
tampikan 1 rejection; 2 that which is avoided.

tamping 1 edge, side; 2 shoulder, verge; 3 border (of district); 4 shield, protection (from wind, rain); 5 (*or* **tetamping**) village policeman;
namping 1 to shape by cutting off the corners (eyebrows); 2 to trim the

sides (embankment);

nampingi to protect, shelter (against water flow, wind).

tampir *reg var of* **tambir**.

tamplèk flat object for hitting;

namplèk 1 to hit with such an object; **2 - puluk** *idiom* to treat rudely, bite the hand that feeds one;

tamplèkan 1 *var of* **tamplèk**; **2** to play ball by using flat objects.

tampo an alcoholic beverage made from fermented rice.

tampol, nampol *reg* to cut down (a tree) at the base of a trunk.

tampong, nampong to slap s.o. in the face.

tampu 1 raindrops blowing in; **2** to rain in, blow in (rain);

namponi to rain in on, spatter with raindrops, wet;

ketampon to get spattered with rain water.

tampung protective shield, shelter;

nampung to protect, shelter.

tamsil 1 parable; **2** good example.

tamsir sword, scimitar.

tamtu sure, certain. *See also* **temtu**.

tamu (*kr of* **dhayoh**) guest, visitor;

namoni to visit, go to see;

ketamuan *or* **ketamonan 1** to be visited, to have a guest come; **2** to receive an unwelcome visit;

tetamu 1 guests, visitors; **2** (to pay) a visit;

tetamon to visit back and forth;

patamon place where one visits.

tan *lit* not; **- asari, - asantun** *lit* without delay.

tanah 1 land, country; **2** parcel of land; **3** soil; **- asal** country of origin; **- manca** *or* **- sabrang** foreign land, foreign country; **- wutah getih** (**rah** *kr*) fatherland.

tanajul descent, decline; **- munggah** rise and fall (life, fortune).

tanak well done (of boiled or fried food).

tanana *lit* (there is/are) none, not any.

tanangsub to be connected with.

tanapi *lit* **1** and, also, in addition; **2** but.

tanaya *lit* child, son.

tanbuh *var of* **tambuh**.

tanceb 1 tip of a pointed object used for piercing; **2** place where s.t. is stuck or (*fig*) belongs, stays; **- kayon** *way* the end of a shadow-play, signalled by placing the mountain-like puppet in front of the screen;

nanceb *or* **tumanceb** sticking (into), piercing;

nancebi to pierce s.t.;

nancebaké to stick/stab s.t. (into);

ketanceban to get pierced accidentally;

tancebing langit horizon.

tandang 1 actions, behaviour; **2** to act; **3** to come to the aid (of); **4** *gram* passive propositive form; **- gawé** to work; **- tanduk** behaviour, conduct;

nandangi to undertake, deal with, tackle;

tumandang to set to work, go into action.

tandha I visible sign, mark, indication; **- cap** seal; **- tangan** signature; **- yekti** proof, evidence;

nandha to signify;

nandhani 1 to mark s.t., supply with a sign; **2** to be a sign of, to signify;

nandhakaké to show, indicate;

katandha to be indicated.

II 1 official in charge of the market; **2** a military rank;

ketandhan residence of this market official.

tandhak a professional female dancer who performs as an entertainer and can be paid to dance with a man as his partner;

nandhak to dance with a female dancer (as above);

tandhakan 1 act of dancing (as above); **2** to hold a ceremony or gathering where such dancing is performed.

tandheg, nandheg to leave s.t. for a long time, let it accumulate, allow it to pile up;
ketandhegan utang deep in debt.

tandhes I 1 deep down, to the bottom; **2** strong, firm;
nandhes to mark deeply;
nandhesaké 1 to make a deep mark with; **2** to emphasise.
II *reg* bare (ground).

tandhing I 1 matched (against); **2** equally matched;
nandhingi to equal, be a match for;
nandhingaké to compare, match one against the other;
tandhingan *or* **tetandhingan 1** match, contest; **2** to compete; to fight a duel; **3** proportion, ratio.
II the peg or pin used to attach the blade of a hoe;
nandhing to attach with such a peg.

tandho to lay in supplies;
nandho to store up (*esp* food) for future consumption;
tandhon stored supplies;
panandhon place where supplies are stored;
tumandho laid away, set aside.

tandhu I stretcher-like conveyance for transporting things or persons, litter;
nandhu to carry s.t. on the above.
II nandhu to pawn (one's ricefield) to a debtor with the the crop as payment;
mertandhu to take, hold land (as above).

tandra *lit* and then, after that (*var of* **tandya**).

tanduk I actions, behaviour; **2** manner, etiquette; **3** *gram* active form;
nanduk to try for s.t.;
nanduki to react;

nandukaké to apply, do, practise. *See also* **tindak**.
II (to have) a second helping of food;
nanduki to give s.o. a second helping.

tandur *ng*, **tanem** *kr*, to do the planting;
nandur to plant;
nanduri to plant (a field) with s.t.;
tinandur *lit* to be planted;
tanduran *or* **tetanduran** plants, crop.

tandya *lit* and then, after that.

tanèh as you well know (*var of* **jenèh**).

tanek *var of* **tanak**.

tanem *kr for* **tandur**.

tang I *lit* the, the one which.
II pliers;
ngetang to use pliers, hold or twist s.t. with pliers.

tangala 'may He be exalted' (said after the name of God).

tangan *ng*, *kr*, **asta** (*k.i.*) hand, arm;
nangani 1 to hit s.o. with the hand; **2** to undertake, accomplish;
tanganan 1 imitation hand/arm; **2** arm rest; **3** handle.

tangat *var of* **ta'at**.

tangèh to be far from, remote from realisation.

tangga *ng*, **tanggi** *kr*, neighbour; **- teparo** (**tanggi tepalih** *kr*) one's neighbours; neighbourhood;
nangga to visit the neighbours (habitually);
tetanggan to live near to, be each other's neighbour.

tanggah *var of* **tangguh I**.

tanggal 1 date; **2** beginning of the lunar month; **- nom** the early part of the month, first quarter; **- tuwa** the days of the waning moon;
nanggal sepisan crescent-shaped like the new moon;
tanggalan, pananggalan calendar, almanac;
tumanggal (of the moon) new, waxing.

tanggap I 1 responsive, receptive, attentive; 2 *gram* passive form;
  nanggap to ask and listen carefully to what s.o. says;
  nanggapi to respond or react (to);
  tumanggap responsive, receptive.
II, **nanggap** to ask, call (entertainers) to perform;
  nanggapaké to have entertainers perform for s.o.;
  tanggapan 1 the performance ordered; 2 payment for the performance.

tanggel I, (*or* **nanggel**) to vouch for;
II halfway between (*kr for* **tanggung** II).

tanggem a large bench-vice;
  nanggem to hold or clamp in a vice.

tanggen *reg* dependable, trustworthy (*var of* **tanggon**).

tanggèn *kr for* **tanggon**.

tanggenah, **tinanggenah** to be entrusted with a task, be assigned to do a job.

tanggi neighbour (*kr for* **tangga**).

tanggok *reg* a small cup-shaped container of woven bamboo.

tanggon *ng*, **tanggèn** *kr*, dependable, trustworthy, firm, not yielding to pressure;
  nanggoni to take it upon o.s. (to), presume (to).

tanggor, **nanggor** *or* **nanggori** to collide with, come up against;
  ketanggor to meet up with, collide with inadvertently.

tangguh I 1 dependable; 2 estimate, opinion concerning; 3 characteristics of a kris according to the period of the maker;
  nangguh mangsa to speculate on, try to determine the right time for;
  nangguhi to give a guarantee that s.t. will happen;
  tumangguh to stand firm.
II **nangguh**, **nangguhaké** to postpone, put off.

tanggul embankment, dam;
  nanggul to dam up, hold back;
  nangguli to provide with earthen dams.

tanggulang cross-beam, buttress (to hold s.t. back, also *fig*);
  nanggulangi to combat, ward off, hold back (an attack; *fig* a problem or difficulty).

tanggun *reg* 1 at least s.t., better than nothing; 2 reasonable.

tanggung *ng*, **tanggel** *kr*, I to vouch (for), to accept responsibility (for); - **jawab** to take responsibility for; - **jiwa** life insurance; - **rèntèng** mutual responsibility;
  nanggungi 1 to take responsibility for; 2 to stand surety for;
  tanggungan 1 guarantee, commitment; 2 security, pledge (*e.g.* for a loan); 3 responsibility, obligation.
II *ng*, **tanggel** *kr* half-hearted, only part, not completely, insufficiently;
  nanggung 1 to be partway through; 2 to stop before completion, not last to the end;
  ketanggungan 1 inadequate; 2 to get interrupted partway through;
  mertanggung *or* **mratanggung** halfway in between, half done.

tangi *ng, kr*, **wungu** *k.i.*, to get up (from a lying or sitting position); to wake up;
  nangèkaké 1 to get s.o. up; 2 to lift s.o. from bed; 3 to arouse;
  nenangi 1 to awaken; 2 *fig* to arouse;
  ketangi *lit* aroused;
  tangèn to be easily awakened, a light sleeper.

tangis *ng, kr*, **muwun** *k.i.* crying, weeping;
  nangis to cry, weep;
  nenangis to make cry;
  nangisi 1 to cry about s.t.; 2 to go to s.o. with an urgent request;

nangisan to cry easily, be a cry-baby;
nongas-nangis to keep crying;
tangisan 1 things cried over; 2 to pretend to cry; 3 *or* tangis-tangisan to (all) cry together.

tangkar I breastbone (of slaughtered animal).
II nangkar to multiply (numbers);
nangkaraké 1 to breed (animals); 2 to multiply (numbers);
tinangkar the number being multiplied;
tangkaran 1 multiplication (arithmetical process); 2 product, *i.e.* the result of multiplying two numbers;
tangkar-tumangkar to proliferate, reproduce;
panangkar multiplier.

tangkeb 1 closing from two sides; 2 the two closing leaves of a door;
nangkebi to close over, behind one;
nangkebaké to close (doors, curtains);
tangkeban double-breasted (men's jacket); lawang - swing doors;
tumangkeb to be closed.

tangkep I attitude, manner toward;
tangkepé becik he treats s.o. kindly.
II one of two parts that fit together (*esp* cakes of palm sugar).
III nangkep *reg* 1 to seize, grab; 2 to arrest;
ketangkeb caught, arrested.

tangkil I a certain climbing plant, the wild so or mlinjo.
II, nangkil to attend audience, appear before (the king), pay homage;
tinangkil (of a king) to sit in state, hold audience;
panangkilan hall where royal audiences are held.

tangkis 1 a means of warding off; 2 shield; 3 *reg* embankment;
nangkis to ward off, parry;
tangkisan defence, resistance;
panangkis 1 act of warding off attack;

2 s.t. which wards off.
tangkur I seahorse.
II crocodile's penis (used as a medicine).

tangkuwèh chunks of sweetened squash used in baking.

tangled I to ask (*subst kr for* takon).
II 1 to fight (*kr for* tarung); 2 opinion *reg kr for* tangguh I.

tangsel carpenter's wedge.

tangsi I fields reserved for the village head by way of salary;
tangsèn *reg* 1 agreement (for a particular time); 2 to borrow a house.
II barracks;
tangsèn 1 the spaces in a honeycomb; 2 a building with rooms for housing workers.

tangsil *var of* tamsil.

tangsu *lit* moon (*var of* sitangsu).

tangsul rope, string (*kr for* tali).

tangtang *var of* tantang.

tangting *var of* tanting.

tangtu *var of* tamtu.

tangwun *reg* 1 at least s.t., better than nothing; 2 reasonable.

tani I respectable, virtuous, decent, honourable, honest;
nanèni to have an honest appearance.
II 1 farmer; 2 pertaining to farming;
tetanèn to engage in agriculture;
patanèn 1 agriculture; 2 a small store room in a traditional house.

taning, naning to form into a mound;
naningi *or* naning-naning to gather (food, flowers) into little heaps;
taningan a mound made up of small loose objects heaped together.

tanja I 1 sharp stick for making holes to plant seedlings in; 2 to plant (seedlings);
nanja to make a hole with such a stick;
nanjakaké to use s.t. for making holes.

II having a useful purpose, worth-while;

nanjakaké 1 to put s.t. to its proper use; 2 to specify expenditure;

tumanja put to the right purpose, appropriate.

tanjak I a certain leaping move in the classical dance;

nanjak 1 to perform the above dance movement; 2 to rise sharply;

tanjakan top of the rise, the point at which an upgrade levels off.

II *see* **tanja** I.

tanjang, nanjangi to intersperse plants with new ones.

tanjeb *var of* **tancep**.

tanjèh *var of* **tanjih**.

tanjek I *var of* **tanja, tanjak**.

II *reg* calm, steady.

III *reg* shoot, sprout (with roots).

tanjem, nanjem to pierce, penetrate deeply;

tumanjem to stand vertically, fixed deeply (in the ground).

tanji a musician in a band.

tanjidhor 1 musician; 2 European band music.

tanjidhur *var of* **tanjidhor**.

tanjih, nanjihaké to check, investigate whether s.t. is true or not.

tanjir, nanjir to impale (a severed head) on a stake.

tanjlig *reg* sluice, floodgate.

tanjung a tree with small, white fragrant flowers.

tanpa without, with no…; - **gawé** useless, in vain; - **tandhing** matchless, unsurpassed.

tansah always, constantly.

tansaya *var of* **sangsaya** I.

tansil *var of* **tamsil**.

tansipi *lit* extremely, exceedingly.

tantang, nantang to challenge;

tantangan a challenge;

panantang 1 a challenge; 2 challenger.

tantara *lit* before long, not long after that.

tanting, nanting 1 to estimate the weight of s.t. by holding it in the hand; 2 to sound out (whether s.o. is willing).

tantu *var of* **tamtu**.

tantun to ask about s.o.'s willingness (*kr for* **tari**).

tanwrin *lit* undaunted, unafraid, fearless.

tanwun *lit* certainly, inevitably.

taoco fermented soybean paste with split beans in it, a sauce ingredient.

taogé bean sprout.

taon *ng*, **tatèn** *kr*, familiar, used to;

ketaon accustomed to doing s.t.;

taon-taonan (to have done s.t. only) once or twice.

taoyah a Chinese cake made from soya beans (*var of* **koyah**).

tap I neat arrangement, proper order;

ngetap to pile up neatly;

ngetapaké to arrange neatly;

tap-tapan in layers, in rows. *See also* **trap** I.

II, **ngetap** to drain off (liquid);

tap-tapan drained (oil).

tapa 1 (*also* **tapa-brata**) asceticism, austerities; 2 to practise asceticism by withdrawing from the world and concentrating one's powers through denying the desires of the flesh, in order to obtain a goal, such as being granted a favour by the gods; 3 an ascetic, holy man, hermit;

maratapa, mratapa, mertapa *lit* to practise asceticism;

napani to do **tapa** to obtain s.t.;

napakaké to do **tapa** on behalf of s.o.;

tapan, patapan, pratapan a place where **tapa** is practised, hermitage.

tapak (**tabet** *kr*) footstep, trace, track; - **asma** *k.i.* handwritten signature; - **dara** 1 a certain flower; 2 *way* wooden tripod on which the banana log holding the puppets is placed; - **jalak** an X used as a signature; - **jempol** thumb-print (used as a signature by illiterates); - **tangan 1** handprint; **2** (- **asta** *k.i.*) signature; - **tatu** scar; - **tilas** footprint;

napak 1 to leave a mark; **2** to step; - **tilas** to follow in s.o.'s footsteps; to repeat s.o. else's experience; - **astani** *k.i.* to affix one's signature to;

napaki 1 to leave a mark on; **2** to track down;

napakaké to put (the foot) in or on;

tumapak to start (into), embark upon.

tapakur 1 to be sunk in thought, reflection; **2** to think deeply, pray silently.

tapan I hermitage. *See* **tapa**.

II *reg* word used for stressing order, prohibition.

tapang (*or* **ketapang**) a variety of tree, also its fruits; the Indian almond.

tapas leaf sheath covering the coconut flower and young coconut.

tapé a sweet food made from fermented glutinous rice (or cassava);

napé 1 to make ingredients into the above; **2** fermented like the above.

tapèh *reg var of* **tapih**.

tapèk *or* **tapèkna** *reg* but (*var of* **tapi**).

tapel I 1 metal band for reinforcing box corners; **2** - **tracak** horseshoe; **3** (**raketan** *k.i.*) poultice of herbs used for babies; - **wates** boundary line;

napel 1 to adhere to the body; **2** to solder s.t.;

napeli 1 to reinforce with metal bands; **2** to shoe (a horse); **3** to apply a poultice to;

napelaké to apply (external medication);

tapelan to have a poultice on.

II an image or statue modelled from clay *etc.*

tapèn *see* **tapi I**.

tapet *reg* trace, track, remainder.

tapi I, **napèni** to winnow rice;

tapèn winnowed grains of rice.

II *reg* but. *See also* **tanapi**.

tapih 1 (*ng*, *kr*, **nyamping** *k.i.*) ankle-length batik garment worn by ladies; **2** protective cover;

napihi to dress s.o. in a **tapih**;

tapihan to put on or wear a **tapih**.

tapis 1 thoroughly, omitting nothing; **2** completely finished up;

napisaké to do a job thoroughly, do a complete job on.

taplak tablecloth;

naplaki to cover with a tablecloth.

taplek *reg* sitting motionless.

tapsila *var of* **trapsila**.

tapsir I interpretation or commentary (*esp* Quran); **ngèlmu** - the science of commentary;

napsiri to provide with commentary, explain, interpret.

II napsir to estimate. *See also* **taksir**.

tapsirih cone-shaped brass or silver container for betel leaves.

tapuk I a slap on the mouth;

napuk to slap on the mouth.

II a mask;

napuk to perform a masked dance.

III to begin, to start together;

napukaké to begin to work (an organisation).

tapung, **napungaké** to transfer partly cooked rice into the **kukusan** (steaming basket) to steam it.

tar fancy cake.

tara I between; **dina** - days on which worship is not prescribed; **mangsa** - a period of fine weather in the rainy season; **sasi** - a month when fasting is not prescribed.

II *lit* **1** clean; **2** shining brightly; **3** star; **4** high (note in music).

tarab I 1 menstruation; **2** to menstruate (*k.i. for* **kèl**);

taraban ritual meal held at the time of a girl's first menstruation.

II, **narabaké** to throw a corpse away to be eaten by wild animals.

III **lemah taraban** sandy clay soil.

tarak 1 abstinence from sensual pleasures; 2 to perform austerities;

naraki to perform austerities for s.t.

taramangsa I period between dry and rainy season.

II *lit* **naramangsa** to swallow up, devour.

tarang, narang to hang s.t. up in a high place to preserve it;

tarangan *or* **patarangan** nesting place for poultry, placed high up on a stake;

metarangan 1 (of a hen) to go to the nest to lay; 2 *fig* restless.

taranggana *lit* the stars.

tarap aligned in rows.

tarbuka, ditarbuka atiné (*pass*) to receive clear understanding, be enlightened;

narbukani to interpret the meaning (of a dream).

tarékah way of acting in order to do s.t., what is contrived to achieve s.t.

tarékat the way of the mystic, the religious life, the Path.

tari 1 (**tantun** *kr*) to put a proposition, ask about s.o's willingness;

nari 1 to ask s.o. whether he/she would like to do s.t.; 2, **tarèn, tetarèn** (**taros** *kr*) to consult with; **nari laki** to ask a girl whether she wishes to marry;

narèni to consult s.o.;

panari proposition;

patarèn *or* **patarènan** s.o. whom one can consult, adviser.

tarib protective screen.

tarik, narik 1 to pull, tug, draw; 2 to collect (money);

nariki to keep collecting s.t. from;

narikaké to collect (money, lottery *etc*) on behalf of s.o.;

nenarik to attract, appeal to;

tarikan 1 a trailer; 2 contribution, donation; 3 a pull, tug, jerk; 4 (*or* **tarik-tarikan**) tug-of-war;

panarik 1 act of collecting (money); 2 one who collects money;

ketarik 1 to get pulled, drawn; 2 attracted (to), charmed (by);

norak-narik to pull this way and that;

ketorak-ketarik to get pulled this way and that.

taring rack for kitchen utensils.

tarip rate, fare, price list.

tarka *or* **panarka** suspicion;

narka to suspect;

tinarka *lit* suspected.

tarlèn *lit* none other than.

taroh *see* **taruh**.

taros to ask for permission (*reg kr for* **tari**).

tarpa *lit* without (*var of* **tanpa**).

tart fancy cake. *Also* **tar**.

taru *lit* tree.

tarub 1 a temporary structure erected on the front of a house for wedding festivities; 2 decorations, *usu* for a wedding, of young coconut leaves split lengthwise and hung at the entrance gate;

narub *or* **tetarub** to put up the above;

narubi to attach offerings and young coconut palm leaves to a **tarub**.

taruh, naruh *reg* to place, put on.

taruk *var of* **taruh**.

tarulata *lit* foliage, leaves.

tarum indigo plant.

taruna *lit* 1 young; 2 a young adult;

tumaruna 1 young and firm; 2 to act as a young adult; 3 young and fresh (plants).

tarung *ng*, **tangled** *lit kr*, to fight;

narungi to fight against (an opponent);

narungaké to pit (one fighter) against (another).

taruni *lit var of* **taruna**.

tarwe wheat.

tarwèh non-obligatory night prayers recited in the mosque during the Fasting Month (*also* **trawèh**).

tarwiyah *var of* **tarwèh**.

tas I handbag.

II just now (*shtf of* **mentas**).

tasawuf Islamic mysticism.

tasbèh rosary, prayer-counting beads.

tasblang *reg* clear, understandable.

tasdik clairvoyant (*var of* **kesdik**, **sidik**).

tasih *coll var of* **taksih**.

tasik I *lit* ocean.

II face powder (*k.i. for* **pupur**).

tasiyun station (*var of* **setasiun**).

tas-tès *see* **tès**.

tata (to put) in an orderly arrangement; - **basa** grammar; social styles of speech; - **cara** manners and customs; - **gelar** to spread out, deploy (them)-selves; arrangement, deployment; - **krama** (- **krami** *kr*) etiquette, proper social conduct; - **lair** the external aspects; - **pernah** genealogical relationship; - **praja** public administration; - **rakit** layout, arrangement; - **susila** manners, etiquette; - **tentrem** peace and order; tata-tata to tidy things up; nata *or* natani to arrange, put in order; natani to set up/out s.t. in (a place); natakaké to put s.t in order for s.o.; tumata put in order; tatanan 1 (*or* **pranatan**) regulations, rules; 2 protocol, established custom; panata 1 act or way of arranging; 2 administrator; satata all in place, all arranged.

tatab, natab 1 to bump into, hit (against); 2 to play (gamelan music); ketatab to bump into/against inadvertently; tataban to bump against each other.

tatag confident, composed; natag-natag to brace o.s. for, face confidently;

natag-natagaké to try to make o.s. be confident.

tatah chisel, punch, file; natah to chisel, chisel out; tatahan chiselling, chiselled work (*esp* of puppets); tinatah chiselled; tinatah mendat, jinara mèntèr *idiom* very tough, supernaturally invulnerable.

tatak, nataki to put a coaster under s.t.; tatakan 1 coaster, saucer; 2 concave stone block for cupboard legs, holding water to keep insects at bay.

tatal 1 wood-shaving, chip; 2 tried and tested; tatalan the evidence of what one is worth; ketatalan to have proved s.t. from experience.

tatap *see* **tatab**.

tatapi *reg* but.

tatar footholds or stepping places for climbing (*e.g.* cut in a palm trunk); natar to climb; natari to cut steps; panataran ladder.

tatas 1 (cut) right through; 2 - **titis** accurate, exact; 3 to break (day); - **ésuk** *or* - **raina** daybreak; natas 1 to cut through; 2 throughout; panatas tali a kind of fee on selling a house.

taté *see* **tau**;

naté ever, at any time (*kr for* **tau**).

tating, nating *reg* to sound, test out. *See also* **tanting**.

tatkala *lit* when, at the time.

tatrap 1 well-fitted; 2 *reg* to start to act; tatrapan act or way of carrying out.

tatu a wound; natoni to wound, injure; ketaton injured, to get wounded.

tatur, natur to hold (a child) in a semi-lying back position, with one arm supporting it around the shoulders and the other under the knees so that it can urinate or defecate.

tau *ng*, **naté** *kr*, ever, at any time; - **taté** *lit* to have done many times, to be quite used to.

taun year; - **hijrah** year of the Islamic era; - **Jawa** the Javanese era (inaugurated by Sultan Agung); - **Saka** the Saka era (A.D. minus 78) used in Hindu Java and Bali; - **wastu** 354-day year; - **wuntu** 355-day year;
naun 1 for a year; 2 for years;
taunan 1 yearly; 2 (*or* **tetaunan**) year after year;
setaun one year.

tauco *var of* **taoco**.

tawa I *ng*, **tawi** *kr*, 1 to make an offer; 2 (*or* **tawa-tawa**) to peddle wares;
nawani to offer s.o. s.t.;
nawakaké to offer s.t. for sale or use. II 1 harmless, powerless; 2 insensitive, immune to; 3 fresh (water);
nawa to counteract (poison);
panawa antidote.

tawakal submissive acceptance of God's will.

tawakup religious feelings, reverence for God.

tawan, **nawan** to capture;
tawanan 1 booty; 2 persons carried off as spoils of war, captive;
ketawan to get captured;
tawan kanin *lit* wounded (in battle);
tawan-tawan tangis to come running in tears.

tawang I *lit* sky, the air; **nggayuh** - *prov* to attempt the impossible.
II aspect, appearance;
nawang to stare (at);
nawangaké to look at s.t. (transparent or translucent) in a bright light.

tawap making a circuit of a holy place, *esp* the Kaaba on the pilgrimage to Mecca.

tawar 1 harmless; 2 insipid; 3 fresh (water);
nawar to neutralise, counteract (poison);
panawar antidote. *See also* **tawa II**.

tawas alum crystals.

tawekal *see* **tawakal**.

taweng, **nawengi** to cover up, conceal, shield from view;
katawengan concealed, shielded.

tawi *kr for* **tawa I**.

tawing 1 shield, cover, *esp* as protection against the elements; 2 a certain classical dance movement; - **tangan** to shade the eyes with the hand;
nawingi to protect, shield.

tawon bee, wasp; - **dhowan**, **madu** honey bee; - **suk** hornet that builds a mud nest;
nawon resembling a bee; - **kemit** wasp-waisted (of woman);
tumawon humming like a swarm of bees (*said of a busy marketplace*).

tawu, **nawu** 1 to bail out (water); 2 to drain a pond by bailing to catch fish;
nawoni to reduce the supply of water.

tawur 1 (*or* **tawuran**) to engage in a gang fight; 2 small coins ceremonially distributed among the poor; 3 (human) sacrifice in connection with war;
nawur to attack in a group;
tawuran a general fight, a brawl.

tayeh *reg* strong, sturdy, firm.

tayoh *reg var of* **tayuh I**.

tayoli *reg term of abuse*: scoundrel, rascal.

tayub *or* **tayuban** 1 a Javanese social dance in which professional females dance and from time to time ask spectators to dance with them; 2 to hold such a dance.

tayuh I 1 strong, sturdy, firm; 2 fast (of colours, *i.e.* not subject to fading or running).
II a dream that gives a sign for one's future;

nayuh to try to get a sign in a dream;
nayuhi to appear to s.o. in a dream.

tayum mildew;
tayumen mildewed.

tayung, nayung to walk rhythmically in
the classical dance;
tayungan a walking step in the classical dance.

teba 1 open fields outside a village; 2
area frequented by travellers; ana ing -
to be on the road;
neba 1 to head for the fields to work;
2 (of birds) to settle in a field.

tebah I width of the palm of the hand, as
a unit of measurement;
satebah one palm-width;
nebah to slap with the palm of the hand.
II a beater (usually of rattan);
nebahi or tebah-tebah to beat (a mattress or pillow) to freshen it up.

tebak I a bamboo section to be used in
building a wall;
satebak one such section.
II, nebak 1 to beat s.t. on/against; 2 to
spring on, seize.
III, nebak to clear (land) for cultivating, settling.

tebal, nebal to dig over (the soil).

tebang, nebang to cut (esp sugarcane or
bamboo);
tebangan field from which the sugarcane has been harvested.

tébang, ketébang-ketébang to be seen
approaching in the distance.

tebaruk blessings.

tebas, nebas 1 to buy up (a crop) in the
field, before it is ripe; 2 to buy in
wholesale lots; 3 to contract for an
entire job;
nebasaké to sell in advance (fruits on
the tree, wholesale lots);
tebasan sale with payment in advance;
panebas act of buying (as above).

tebek var of tebak II.

tebela var of tabela.

tebeng overhanging portion of a roof, or
built-out part over a door or window,
as protection against sun and rain;
nebengi to equip (a building) with
such devices.

tèbèng reg structure acting as a protective shelter against the elements.

teberi var of taberi.

tebes, nebes to prune, trim, cut back.

tèbès neat, nicely groomed.

tebih far, distant (kr for adoh, doh).

tebir var of takbir I.

tebiyas reg 1 to get driven out; 2 to deviate from the expected course.

tebiyat character, nature, habit.

tèblèg reg 1 remaining as before, still
going strong; 2 to stand one's ground.

tebok a piece of wood added, nailed on;
nebok to patch with such a piece of
wood.

tébok bowl-shaped container of woven
bamboo.

tebu I (rosan kr) sugarcane;
nebu to plant sugarcane;
tebon 1 corn stalks (fodder); 2 or
panebon land planted with sugarcane.
II, nenebu to do s.t. in turns; - bocah
to carry a child some of the way, then
let it walk.

tebus, nebus 1 to redeem (a pledge); 2 to
buy s.t. back; 3 to pay ransom for;
nebusaké to redeem (a pledge) on
behalf of s.o.;
tebusan 1 ransom; 2 compensation;
panebus 1 redemption; 2 ransom;
3 redeemer; Sang Panebus the
Redeemer;
panebusan 1 redemption; 2 compensation.

tedah to show, point (to/out) (root form:
kr for tuduh).

tedha I to ask for (root form: kr for jaluk).
II food, s.t. to eat (kr for pangan);
nedha to eat (kr for mangan).
III nedhani lit to give (a gift, to an

inferior); **patedhan** a gift.

tedhak 1 to descend, go down (*k.i. for* **medhun**); **2** descendant; **3** to descend genealogically (*k.i. for* **turun**); **4** to copy (*root form: kr for* **turun**); - **sitèn** (to hold) a ceremony marking a child's first contact with the ground at the age of 7 **lapan**;
nedhak to make a copy;
tumedhak to descend, get off (*k.i. for* **medhun**);
panedhak act or way of copying.

tedhas able to pierce, cut, penetrate;
nedhas to have a harmful effect on;
nedhasi able to pierce/cut;
ora tedhas tapak paluning pandhé sisaning gurénda *idiom* magically invulnerable.

tèdhèng I 1 protective cover/shield (against sun, rain, wind); **2** hat brim;
nèdhèngi to cover, protect;
nèdhèngaké to use s.t. as a (protective) cover;
ora tèdhèng aling-aling *idiom* (to speak) frankly, to tell the truth.
II, nèdhèng-nèdhèng to expose, show openly.

tèdhès *reg* all gone, finished, completely exhausted.

tedhi food, s.t. to eat (*md for* **tedha II**).

tédhok bowl-shaped container of woven bamboo (*var of* **tébok**).

tedhuh *reg* **1** cloudy, overcast; **2** (of a storm) to subside.

tedhun, tumedhun to descend (*also* **medhun**);
nedhunaké to lower;
ketedhun 1 to suffer from a hernia or prolapse; **2** to get demoted.

téga 1 to be heartless enough (to…); **2** to behave callously (toward);
négakaké to leave s.o. to their fate.

tegak erect, upright;
negakaké to uphold.

tegal *ng*, **tegil** *kr*, dry agricultural land, used for crops other than rice;
negal 1 to convert (land) to such fields; **2** to plant (crops) in such fields;
tegalan *or* **pategalan** dry farmland (as above).

tegang tight, tense;
negangaké to cause to be tight/tense, full of suspense.

tegar *or* **tetegaran 1** to ride a horse out for pleasure; **2** to allow the horse one is riding to gallop as it pleases;
negar to gallop;
negari to train (a horse) for riding;
negaraké 1 to take a ride on (a horse); **2** to have (a horse) trained or broken in;
panegar professional horse-trainer.

tegayur to keep changing, unsteady.

tégé *reg* deep basket of woven bamboo, used for storing fruits.

tegeg to not shrink from (s.t. shameful);
tegegan unscrupulous, without conscience.

tegel to have the heart (to do s.t. horrid), merciless;
negeli to persist in (an action, without regard for another's feelings);
negel-negelaké to try to bear seeing s.o.'s suffering;
tegelan able to bear to see s.o. suffer.

tègel floor tile;
nègel to lay floor tiles;
tègelan tiled floor.

tegen persistent, assiduous, industrious;
negeni to stick to, persist with (work).

tegeng *var of* **tegang**.

tegep quick, smart, alert.

teger *reg* strong, sturdy, firm.

tegerang a certain wood from which yellow dye (used for batik-work) is extracted.

teges I 1 meaning, significance, sense;
tegesé that is to say; **2** clear, easy to understand;
neges to ask for an explanation;

negesi to explain the meaning (of);
negesaké to interpret the meaning (of);
maneges *lit* to seek a sign or explanation from heaven regarding one's fate;
paneges explaining, interpretation;
neges-neges to inquire repeatedly.
II a small goldsmith's mallet.
III, tegesan cigarette stub.

tègin *reg* still (*var of* isih).

tegor I, negor to cut down at the base of a tree trunk.
II, 1 to speak to s.o. in greeting; 2 to ask s.o. not to (do);
tegoran warning, reprimand.

tégrok to stop and stay s.w.

teguh firm, strong, steadfast (physically, morally); - timbul supernaturally invulnerable and highly esteemed;
neguhi to face s.t. with physical and moral fortitude;
neguhaké to make firm/strong;
kateguhan firmness, strength.

tèh tea;
patèhan 1 tea service; 2 place in the palace where tea is made; 3 tea plantation.

teher, neher *lit* and then, after that.

téja 1 light, ominous red glow (in the sky), rainbow; 2 aura (of a mighty personage).

Téjamaya the abode of Bathara Guru.

teka I *ng*, dhateng *kr*, rawuh *k.i.*, to come, arrive;
nekani 1 to visit, come to; 2 to bring about, cause to happen; 3 to be present at, attend;
nekakaké 1 to cause s.o. to come; to cause s.t. to come about; 2 to accomplish, complete;
neneka to come s.w. for the first time and remain permanently;
katekan 1 to be visited; 2 to be brought to pass;
tekan 1 up to, until; 2 to get to, reach;

tumeka to go to, head for;
satekané upon s.o.'s arrival.
II *emphatic particle* (expressing surprise etc), see kok.
III *reg* from, out of.

tekabul ngèlmu to receive instruction. *See also* kabul.

tekabur 1 arrogance; 2 to boast.

tékad determination, resolve;
nékad to persist in what one has decided to do;
nékadi to persist (in), keep after;
tékad-tékadan to persist wilfully.

tekak I, nekak 1 to strangle s.o.; 2 *fig* to get a stranglehold (on);
II a certain nocturnal bird with an ominous call.

tekan *see* teka.

tékang *lit* (one) who, (that) which.

tekap *lit* 1 because of; 2 up to, until.

tekbir *var of* takbir.

tekdir *var of* takdir.

tekek, nekek to strangle (*var of* tekak I).

tekèk large striped lizard which lives in the roof and makes the sound 'to-kek';
tekèk mati ing uloné *prov* doomed by one's own words.

tekem handful, fistful;
nekem to hold tightly in the hand;
ketekem held firmly, kept under control;
tekeman 1 s.t held in the hand, a handful; 2 grasp, grip, clutch;
satekem a handful of (rice, corn *etc*).

tèken signature;
nèkeni to sign (with one's name).

teken (lantaran *k.i.*) cane, walking stick;
nekeni 1 to use a cane; 2 to give s.o. a helping hand;
tekenan to walk with a walking stick;
teken janggut, suku jaja *prov* by dint of great effort.

tekèng *lit* to come to; until (*shtf of* teka ing).

tekérah idea, scheme (*var of* trékah).

tekes wig made from palm fibres, worn in a certain dance.

teki a certain grass with an edible tuberous root.

tèki, tetèki *or* tèki-tèki *lit* to seclude o.s. to concentrate one's thoughts.

tekik a tree producing a fine hardwood used for kris sheaths.

tekiyar to seek (for help, remedy) (*var of* setiyar).

tekiyur 1 shaky (faith); 2 unfaithful (woman).

teklim *reg var of* taklim.

téko Chinese teapot of red earthenware.

tékong 1 crooked, lopsided; 2 curved, bent (*var of* tikung).

tekor (to show) a deficit.

teksa, neksa to force, compel (*coll var of* peksa).

teksaka *lit* snake (*var of* taksaka).

teksih *coll var of* taksih.

teksila well-mannered (*var of* tapsila).

teksir *var of* taksir.

tèkté key money.

tekuk, nekuk to fold, bend double, turn back;
  ketekuk to get folded by mistake;
  tekukan a fold(ed place);
  panekuk act or way of folding.

tekung, nekung (*or* manekung *lit*) to sit with folded arms meditating;
  tekungan with the arms folded across the chest while meditating.

tékung *reg var of* tikung.

tekwan *lit* and, with; even more, beyond that.

tekyan *var of* tekwan.

tèkyan *reg* to pool capital for a business enterprise, work together cooperatively;

tela a crack in the ground;
  nela to crack, split. *See also* tlanakan.

téla I 1 cassava; 2 sweet potato; - gantung papaya; - gendruwo poisonous cassava;

- kaspé *or* - pohung cassava root; - pendhem sweet potato.

II téla, tetéla, téla-téla 1 clearly visible; 2 obvious, evident;
  nélakaké to indicate, show. *See also* pratéla.

télad, nélad to take as an example, emulate, imitate.

teladha example, model (*var of* tuladha).

telag 1 low on, short of; 2 hard to find (fruits out of season);
  nelag to run out of;
  ketelagan having a shortage of; coming to the end of.

telaga lake (*var of* tlaga).

telah *lit*, (a)nelah to call, name;
  katelah called, generally known as;
  ketelah (ng)anak (of a parent) named after one's child;
  panelah name.

telak 1 soft palate; 2 throat;
  ketelak to get stuck in the throat.

télak 1, télaké it looks or seems (as if); 2 in fact; obviously.

telar 1 large field, uncultivated grassland; 2 swampy area.

telas all gone, used up (*kr for* entèk).

telat (too) late;
  nelat to be late deliberately;
  nelataké to make or set s.t. later, delay;
  ketelatan too late for doing s.t.

telèh *reg var of* telih.

telèk chicken dropping; - léncung moist, foul-smelling chicken droppings;
  nelèk to drop (droppings);
  nelèki to drop (droppings) onto;
  telèkan of the lowest quality, useless;
  kembang - a certain plant the flower of which smells foul.

telenan chopping board for kitchen use. *Also* tlenan.

teleng 1 (innermost) depths, heart; 2 the central point of s.t.; 3 a creeper with blue flowers, the clitoris flower (medicinal uses); **telenging ati** the person (thing) who is deepest in one's heart; **neleng 1** to try to fathom s.o.'s innermost feelings; **2** to centre one's concentration; **3** to go into seriously; to probe (the secrets of);

kateleng ing sih the most favoured one.

tèlèng, olèh - to see a chance.

telep, ketelep unrecovered, irrecoverable.

tèlep or **mak tèlep** repr popping s.t. into the mouth;

tèlap-tèlep to eat hungrily, keep putting food into the mouth.

tèlèr I foul discharge from an infected ear;

tèlèren to have an infected ear.

II 1 sick, exhausted; **2** utterly drunk.

teles wet; **- kebes** soaking wet;

nelesi to wet s.t.;

nelesaké to make s.t. wet;

telesan, patelesan clothing worn while bathing in the open.

telih 1 crop (bird's organ); **2** cr stomach; **3** water reservoir.

telik (or **telik sandi**) spy, secret agent;

nelik to spy on;

telik sandi upaya trick, ruse;

telik mangéndrajala lit spy who destroys the enemy by trickery.

telkim exhortation to the dead, consisting of advice on how to answer the questions of Munkar and Nakir, the Interrogators of the Dead.

telkun turkey (var of **kalkun**).

telnan var of **telenan**.

telu ng, **tiga** kr, three; **- las** 13; **- likur** 23; **nelu** three each;

neloni 1 to form a group of three; **2** to hold a ceremonial feast for a woman in the third month of pregnancy;

nelokaké to multiply by three, make s.t. three;

tetelu (the group or unit of) three;

telu-telu by threes;

telon 1 approximately three; **2** consisting of three; **kembang -** three-coloured, tortoiseshell (colour of cat);

telonan ceremony held for a woman in the third month of pregnancy;

katelu third.

teluh black magic; **- braja** shooting star, fireball (cause of illness);

neluh to cast a spell on;

paneluhan black magic spell.

teluk I bay, inlet.

II to give up, surrender;

nelukaké to conquer, overcome.

telulas thirteen. See also **telu**.

telulikur twenty-three. See also **telu**.

telung ng, **tigang** kr three (as modifier);

nelungdinani to hold a ceremony on the third day after death.

tem, ngetem to apply o.s. seriously to;

tem-teman to do seriously.

temah to produce (a result), end up (in a certain way);

nemah to regard s.t. as one's fate, resign o.s.;

nemahi to experience s.t. as a result;

temahan result, consequence;

satemah finally, as a result.

temaha, nemaha 1 to (do) on purpose, do intentionally; **2** to defy (danger);

temahan wilful, reckless.

temangga reg var of **kemangga**.

temantèn var of **mantèn**.

tembaga ng, **tembagi** kr, copper;

nembaga resembling copper;

tembagan a kind of grass with reddish leaves.

tembajeng reg kr for **tembalo**.

témbak I, némbak to shoot;

témbakan a shot.

II, némbak to choose a number and go and buy a lottery ticket.

tembako ng, **sata** kr tobacco.

tembalo a high tree, the wood of which is used for kris sheaths.

tembalong a kind of large centipede.

tembang I *ng*, sekar *kr* classical verse (recited or sung); - cilik, tengahan, gedhé the 'small', 'middle' and 'great' metres, categories of metre in classical verse;
nembang to sing verse;
nembangi to accompany gamelan music with singing;
nembangaké 1 to sing a classical song; 2 to sing for s.o.'s pleasure.
II, nembang to beat an alarm drum;
tembang rawat-rawat ujaré bakul sinambéwara *prov* unclear news is only rumour, *i.e.* not to be believed.

tembarok *or* tembarokan *reg* anthill, insect nest.

tembaruk *reg* a blessing with magical power.

tembaya, tembayan, patembayan a business relation.

tembayatan mutual help, cooperation.

tembé 1 just, in the process of; 2 just, a moment ago; 3 (ing) tembé buri later, in future; 4 (*or* nembé) just, for the first time;
ketembèn (now) for the first time;
tembéan for the first time (bear young).

tembèk *reg var of* tembé.

tèmbel *or* mak tèmbel 1 *repr* a direct hit; 2 *describing a sudden fortunate event*.

tèmbèl I, nèmbèl to patch (*var of* tambal);
tèmbèlan 1 patch, mended place; 2 act of patching.
II (with a) scar on the face (from skin disease).

tembelang *var of* tembelong.

tembelèk chicken droppings (*var of* telèk).

tembelong, pating tembelong spotted, covered with blemishes.

tèmbèr I rough, rude.
II *reg* 1 powerless; 2 insignificant, trivial.

tembilung a container made from a gourd shell or leaf sheath from the palm tree.

tembing side, border, bank, flank, shore.

tembirang rope used for hoisting and lowering sails.

temblag a layer of soil added to an existing earthen wall or dyke.

tèmblèg, nèmblèg 1 to build a dyke of earth; 2 to fill a hole with earth.

temblog *var of* temblag.

témblok *var of* temblag.

témbo a small sampan-like boat, canoe.

témbok 1 wall, brick or stone wall; 2 built of bricks or stone (in contrast to bamboo panels);
némbok 1 to equip with walls; 2 to build with bricks and mortar; 3 to put wax on cloth in batik-making;
témbokan wax applied to cloth in batik-making.

témbor *reg* 1 brass tray on short legs; 2 basin for washing hands.

témbré of inferior quality, not worth much.

tembung I word(s), what s.o. says;
nembung 1 to say (to), speak (to); 2 to go to s.o. with a polite request;
nembungi to ask s.o. for s.t.;
nembungaké 1 to say/express s.t.; 2 to ask on s.o.'s behalf;
tetembungan *or* pitembungan words, expressions, talk;
pitembung a request;
panembung a request.
II riding whip (*k.i. see* cemethi);
nembung to whip.

tembus to penetrate, perforate, pierce;
nembus to pierce, penetrate;
tembusan 1 the other opening at the far end; 2 tunnel, channel; 3 act of piercing/penetrating; 4 carbon-copy (of document).

temen 1 really, very, decidedly; 2 true, honest; 3 in earnest, serious;

nemen to be serious, in earnest;

nemeni to treat seriously;

tumemen faithful, loyal, serious;

temen-temen to take seriously;

temenan seriously;

katemenan 1 loyalty, honesty; 2 to actually happen, turn out to be true;

satemené really, actually, in fact.

temendhil 1 mouse dirts; 2 goat droppings.

temenggung *title applied to a regent*.

temon found, *see* temu.

tempah compensation (*kr for* tempuh II).

tempak having no sharp angles, blunt, rounded;

nempakaké to make s.t. blunt or rounded, *i.e.* without any sharp angles.

tempaling implement consisting of a basket on a long handle, for catching walang-sangit (a stinking insect).

tempat *reg* capable of helping;

nempati to ask s.o. for help;

nempat-nempataké to help, give assistance.

tempayan large earthenware waterpot.

tempayang *var of* tempayan.

témpé beancake of whole fermented soybeans; - benguk beancake made of benguk beans;

némpé to make (ingredients) into beancake.

tèmpèh winnow (*var of* tampah).

tèmpèl, nèmpèl to adhere, stick;

nèmpèli to stick s.t. with;

nèmpèlaké to attach, affix;

tèmpèlan 1 sticker; 2 attached to s.t.;

ketèmpèlan 1 to get stuck to by s.t.; 2 to bear signs of (good luck); 3 possessed by a spirit;

tumèmpèl to adhere, stick;

tèmpèl-tèmpèlan various things stuck on.

tempélang a packet made by wrapping s.t. (*usu* with banana leaves) by fold-

ing the four corners in and holding them with a bamboo pin;

nempélang to wrap s.t. as above.

tempéling *reg var of* tempiling.

tempérong *reg* a slap in a face;

nempérong to slap s.o.'s face.

tempik *cr* female genitals (little girl).

tempil, nempil to take over part of what s.o. has bought, buy a share;

tempilan that part of a purchase taken over.

tempiling a slap on the side of the head (temple, or head in general);

nempiling to slap s.o. on the side of the head;

tempilingan to slap each other (as above).

tempiyas to spatter, blow in (rain drops).

témplang-tèmpleng to eat hungrily, keep putting food into the mouth.

tèmplèk, nèmplèk to adhere, be attached;

nèmplèki to stick to s.t.;

nèmplèkaké to stick s.t.;

tumèmplèk to be stuck, attached.

templik, nemplik to take away or break off a small piece;

satemplik a little bit, a small piece or part.

témplok *var of* tèmplèk.

témpo 1 time, enough time; 2 time limit; 3 extra time;

némponi to set a time limit (on, for);

témponé the time for s.t.

tempolong cuspidor, spittoon (of wood or earthenware).

témpong, némpong to slap on the cheek.

temporat *reg* misery, suffering.

tempuh I, nempuh 1 to attack in force; 2 to face up to, confront;

tumempuh to undergo; to be subjected to;

katempuh to get hit; attacked by;

panempuh (head on) attack; collision.

II tempuh, tetempuh *ng* (tempah,

tetempah *kr*) compensation;

nempuh to pay for (merchandise) in advance of delivery;

nempuhi to compensate, to pay for the damages;

nempuhaké to have s.o. pay damages;

katempuhan liable for damages.

tempuk *or* tempukan 1 to flow together, join; 2 the time of a celebration;

tempuking nétra *lit* a meeting of the eyes.

tempur I, nempur to buy up dehusked rice;

nempuraké to sell dehusked rice;

tempuran bought rice;

dudu berasé ditempuraké *prov* '(this rice) is not the rice being sold', *i.e.* to interrupt a conversation and make a suggestion that is not to the point.

II, tempuran (of bodies of water) confluence.

temtu 1 certainly, of course; 2 fixed, set; 3 to go through (*reg kr for* sida);

nemtokaké 1 to decide, settle (on); 2 to foreordain, predict;

katemtuan stipulation, provision.

temu I *ng*, panggih *kr*, to meet as bride and groom during the wedding ceremony; - gelang forming a not-quite-closed circle like a bracelet; - pèk finders' keepers; - rosé *fig* suitable, harmonious, to get along well with each other; - taun in a year's time;

nemu to find, come upon;

nemoni 1 to receive (guest); 2 to look for, go to see (a person); 3 to meet with, come up against;

nemokaké 1 to bring together the bride and groom during the wedding ceremony; 2 to find, discover;

ketemu 1 to meet, come together; 2 to find, come across s.t.;

tinemu (pinanggih *kr*) 1 to find, come across; 2 to turn out, end up; - nalar reasonable, sensible;

panemu opinion, point of view;

temon, tetemon 1 found; 2 s.t. found; 3 discovery;

patemon a meeting;

sapatemon, durung - (of a bride and groom) to have not yet been intimate.

II certain roots of the Ginger family, used medicinally, of various sorts: - giring, - ireng; - kuning; - lawak; - poh; - putih;

nemu resembling one of these roots; - giring smooth and light-yellowish coloured (skin).

ten I *coll var of* boten.

II *coll var of* wonten.

tèn *reg* mesh (of a net).

tenaga 1 power, strength; 2 personnel, employee.

tenan true, real;

nenani to take or treat seriously;

tenanan really, seriously.

tenapi *lit* 1 and, also, in addition; 2 but (*var of* tanapi).

tenaya *lit* child, son (*var of* tanaya).

téndha tent, sun shade, hood.

tendhag, ketendhagan (to experience) a shortage.

tendhak *reg* a certain type of fish trap with barred doors.

tendhang, nendhang 1 to kick, bump against; 2 to run into, collide;

nendhangi to kick s.t. repeatedly;

nendhangaké to kick for s.o.;

ketendhang 1 to get kicked or bumped; 2 to get hit by;

tendhangan 1 act or way of kicking; 2 thing kicked or bumped; 3 to kick the ball around;

tendhang-tendhangan to kick or bump into each other.

tendhas *lit* head. *See also* endhas.

tendhog, tendhogan *reg* to bump against.

tened, nened to compress, pack tightly;

ketened to get pressed.

tenèh after all.

tenèn *see* **teni**.

tènes tennis.

teng I 1 to, toward (*md for* **marang**, **menyang**); **2** *coll var of* **wonten**.
II stomach, belly (*shtf of* **weteng**);
ngetengi *cr* to get s.o. pregnant;
tengan foetus (*shtf of* **wetengan**).
III, ngetengaké to cook s.t. until it is done. *See also* **mateng**.

tèng I storage tank.
II military tank (armored vehicle);
tèng-tèngan toy tank.
III, ngetèngi to take in, make smaller (garment).

tenga, nenga *or* **tumenga 1** to look up(ward); **2** *fig* to look to s.o. of power or authority to help.

tengadur *reg* hindrance, obstacle.

tengah 1 (in the) middle, centre; (with)in; **2** centre (soccer player, position); **3** (in) half;
nengah (to move) toward the centre;
nengahi to place between or in the middle of;
nengah-nengahi in the middle of;
nengahaké to put in or move toward the middle;
tengahan 1 (in the) middle part; **2** around the middle, about half; **3** half (as a fraction); **4** ½-rupiah coin; **5** to go halves; **6** a category of classical verse forms;
satengahé in the midst of, surrounded by;
tengah-tengah (in) the very middle part.

tengangé middle of the day (between 11–12 o'clock a.m.), noontide.

tengara a signal given by sound, *e.g.* by ringing a bell, pounding on wood;
nengarani to sound a signal.

tengen right (as opposed to left);
nengen to move to the right;
nengenaké 1 to move s.t. to the right;

2 to consider s.t. essential, give priority to;
ketengen 1 guided; **2** liked, appreciated;
satengené to the right of.

tèngèng 1 to have a stiff neck; **2** to have a crooked neck (so that the head hangs to one side).

tenger mark, sign, label;
nengeri to put a mark(er) on, attach a label to;
tetenger 1 name; **2** label;
ketenger to get noticed;
tetenger *or* **tetengeran 1** (having) a mark or identifying sign; **2** gift given to a bride's family by the groom's family as an engagement or marriage token;
panengeran 1 *lit* distinguishing mark; **2** (*also* **panengran**) *lit* name.

tengga to wait (for); to watch over (*kr for* **tunggu**).

tenggak 1 throat; **2** the tens column (in dates);
nenggak to tilt the head back when drinking; **- waspa** to try to hold back one's tears;
panenggak the second child.

tenggang *reg* intervening space, interspace.

tenggar broad and open, with a view;
nenggar *reg* to hoist (a bird cage) to the top of a pole;
tenggaran an open space.

tenggek *var of* **tenggak**.

tenggel, nenggel 1 to bring s.t. straight down on; **2** to head straight across s.t.;
ketenggel hit squarely.

tenggenah *var of* **tanggenah**.

tengger, tengger-tengger hilly, mountainous, high (land).

tenggèrèng cleared up after rain (sky).

tenggi I to wait (for) (*reg kr for* **tunggu**).
II, tumenggi to curve upward (eyelashes).

tenggik, tenggikan borderline, mark (e.g. to where a pot is filled).

tenggiling anteater (var of trenggiling).

tengginas var of trengginas.

tenggirang to feel better (after illness).

tenggok the neck above the Adam's apple.

ténggok small deep basket of woven bamboo.

tenggulang var of tanggulang.

tengguluk, nengguluk to carry on the shoulder.

tenggun reg 1 at least something; 2 reasonable.

tenggung see temenggung.

tengik I 1 rancid-smelling; 2 of very bad quality.

II, satengik ½-cent coin.

tengkar, nengkaraké to increase the numbers of (plants, animals) by breeding. See also tangkar II.

tèngkèk a large noisy bird, said to feed on dead flesh, considered unlucky.

tengkel piece cut from s.t.;
nengkel to cut a piece from;
nengkeli to cut in pieces;
tengkelan a cut-off piece.

tengker, manengker lit noisy, loud.

tengkulak I one who buys up agricultural products or cattle.

II quiver for arrows.

tengkuwèh a Chinese dish made from sweetened gourd.

téngok, néngok reg to look (in a particular direction), turn the head.

téngos, néngos reg to cut s.t. on the slant;
téngosan slantwise cut piece.

tèngsu lit moon.

tengu a minute reddish mite, causing itching in the genitals of little boys who play in the dirt with no pants on.

teni full dress, full uniform;
tenèn wearing full dress.

ténja reg faeces (var of tinja).

ténong a round covered box of woven bamboo, used esp for keeping pastries or snacks;
ténongan various kind of snacks peddled in such a woven bamboo container.

tenta, ketenta to have fallen into the habit of (do)ing.

tentang, nentang to oppose, fight against.

tentrem tranquil, serene, quiet, peaceful;
nentremaké to make tranquil/serene, bring about peace in/at (a place);
katentreman tranquillity, peace, serenity.

tentu var of temtu.

tenun, nenun to weave;
tenunan 1 woven material, fabric; 2 weaving equipment, loom;
patenunan place (esp factory) where weaving is done.

tenung 1 black magic; 2 reg practitioner of black magic;
nenung to put a spell on.

tepa measure, model; - palupi an example to others; - slira to put o.s. in another's place; - tuladha an example to others;
nepakaké 1 to measure; 2 - awaké dhéwé to consider as if applying to o.s.;
tepa-tepa 1 to keep proportion in mind; 2 to take o.s. as model, imagine how another feels.

tepak I upper part of the back.
II fly-swat;
nepak to slap, swat.
III a disease of rice crops.
IV reg excellent.

tépak wooden tray with containers comprising a set of betel-chewing equipment.

tepakur to be sunk in thought, pray silently (var of tapakur).

tepalih next door (kr for teparo).

tepang to be(come) acquainted (*kr for* **tepung**).

tépang, népang to kick with the side of the foot;
ketépang to get kicked;
tépangan a kick, act or way of kicking.

teparo *ng*, **tepalih** *kr*, **tangga** - next-door neighbours.

tepas portion of a house (*e.g.* a verandah) that is roofed over but not walled in;

tépas I bamboo fan for fanning a fire;
népasi to fan;
tépas-tépas 1 to fan a flame; 2 to keep fanning o.s.
II, **népasi** to peel fibre from a coconut.

tepat exactly right.

tepaut *reg* to differ (in amount).

tepékong image of a deity in a Chinese temple.

tepekur *var of* **tapakur**.

tepes *reg* coconut fibre.

tepès *reg* flat-nosed.

tepet *lit* world; - **suci** the hereafter.

tepi 1 edge, border, boundary; 2 decorative edging, braid;
tepèn to have decorative edging, braid.

tepis, - wiring border, border area, outskirts.

tepiyo a European hat.

téplé roughly woven coconut leaves (for walls, roofs).

teplèk fly-swat.

tèplek *or* **mak tèplek** *repr* s.t. hitting the right spot;
tumèplek (to sit/lie on) comfortably;
téplak-tèplek *pl as above.*

téplok, diyan - kerosene lamp hung on a wall or pillar.

tepo 1 decayed, rotten (wood, fabric); 2 weak with age.

tépo *reg* rice formed into a roll and cooked in a banana leaf wrapper.

tépong hind part (under the tail);
népong to hit (*esp* a horse) on the hind part;

tépos (of buttocks) flat, unrounded;
- **bokongé** 1 to have to stay sitting too long; 2 making no progress;
népos to slap s.o. on the buttocks.

tepsila *var of* **tapsila**.

tepsir *var of* **tapsir**.

tepu *var of* **ketepu**.

tepung *ng*, **tepang** *kr* 1 to (get to) know, be(come) acquainted (with); 2 to match, meet; - **gelang** forming a nearly-closed circle; - **kebo** having a speaking acquaintance (with); - **rembug** to have a discussion with; - **rukun** to become acquainted with one another (of members of a group);
nepungaké to introduce (people);
nepungi 1 to meet people and introduce o.s.; 2 to know, be familiar;
tepungan *or* **tetepungan** 1 to be acquainted with each other; 2 acquaintances, friends;
tepung cukit adu tritis *idiom* crowded together, almost touching (houses).

tepus string used to measure length;
nepus to measure with a measuring string.

ter, ngeteri 1 to take (food) as a present to s.o.'s house; 2 *or* **eter-eter** to distribute food after a **slametan**;
ngeteraké to take, escort, accompany;
ter-teran 1 to take each other home; 2 s.t. delivered.

terag premature; (*or* **keteragan**) to have a miscarriage (*kr for* **kluron**).

terak, nerak 1 to strike, run into; 2 *fig* to fly in the face of; 3 to violate (the law);
neraki to crash repeatedly;
keterak to get struck;
panerak misdemeanor, transgression.

terang 1 clear, cleared up; 2 (of rain) to stop; - **bulan** moonlight;

nerang 1 to request clarification; 2 - **udan** to prevent rain magically;

nerangi to shed light on;

nerangaké 1 to clarify; 2 *gram* to modify;

miterang to ask for an explanation, to find out;

terangé plainly, it is clear that..., by way of clarification;

katerangan 1 information, explanation; 2 *gram* modifier;

terang-terangan frank, open, blunt.

terap *var of* **trap** I.

teras I brand new, never been worn;

neras 1 to use (s.t. new) for the first time; 2 to do the first ploughing of (a ricefield); 3 to peel (fruit) thickly; 4 **prawan, jaka** - virgin;

keterasen too deep (digging, peeling), too much.

II *subst kr for* **terus**.

terbang tambourine;

terbangan 1 to play the tambourine; 2 a performance with chanting and tambourine.

terbela *var of* **tabela**.

terbik, terbik-terbik *reg* (beginning) just here and there, just appearing a little.

terbis steep, hard to scale (ravines, mountainsides).

terbit published;

nerbitaké to publish;

terbitan 1 edition; 2 published;

panerbit publisher;

panerbitan publication.

terbuka *var of* **tarbuka**.

terbumi *reg* traditional ceremony held during the month prior to the Fasting Month.

terceb *see* **cerceb**.

tercek, tercek-tercek *reg* to make a rustling sound (*e.g.* stiff cloth).

tercel *see* **cercel**.

terces, nerces *or* **pating terces** to have a shivery, sensitive feeling in the skin.

terèg 1 to fall, drop off; 2 miscarriage (*var of* **terag**).

tereh *lit* 1 descendant; 2 rain.

tèrèk *reg* an ointment rubbed on the forehead against pain.

tèrèp *reg* in serried rows.

teres, neres to ring-bark a tree that is to be cut, in order to season the timber.

tères *var of* **tèrès**.

tèrès red dye used as food colouring and for colouring the lips;

nèrès to redden (food, lips) with the above.

terganca *reg* to quarrel, have conflict.

teri a certain small edible sea fish.

terik 1 dish made with meat, beancake, or other ingredients cooked in coconut milk and spiced; 2 an edible migratory bird.

terjang *var of* **trajang**.

terjik *reg* scrupulous, accurate.

terka, nerka to suspect.

terkadhang sometimes, now and then.

terkaos difficult (*reg kr for* **rekasa**).

terna *lit* young plant, young foliage.

terni *var of* **terna**.

térob *reg var of* **tarub**.

térok *coll var of* **tiru**.

térong eggplant, aubergine (several varieties); - **glathik** small round eggplant (white or orange).

térop *see* **térob**.

teros, terosé it is said (*md for* **jaré**).

terpas 1 level; 2 a spirit-level; **terpasé** *reg* as far as one can work out.

tersandha I *reg* sign, signal, mark.

II *reg* to lean against.

tertamtu *var of* **tamtu**.

tertep *reg* buckle, clasp.

tertib meticulous, orderly, correct.

tertil accurate, scrupulous.

teruh *var of* **tereh**.

terus 1 penetrating, going right through; 2 straight (on, as before); 3 immediately; 4 to continue;

nerusi to apply (the same batik design) to the other side of the fabric;

nerusaké 1 to continue, keep on with; **2** to forward (mail, message *etc*);

terusan 1 continuing in the same way, a continuation; **2** full length; **3** link between two things; **4** a back or side exit through a wall; **5** having batik pattern applied to both sides of it;

terus-terusan continuously, again and again;

panerus 1 beam of a Javanese-style house connecting the upper and lower parts of the roof; **2** the second **bonang** (or other gamelan instrument) which carries on the melody introduced by the first **bonang** (or others).

terwaca clear(ly visible, audible, comprehensible);

nerwacakaké to make clear, to explain.

terwèlu rabbit. *Also* **truwèlu**.

terwéngkal *reg* potsherd.

terwilun *lit* stupid, dumb.

terwungkal *var of* **terwéngkal**.

tes *coll* just now, a moment ago. *See also* **mentas**.

tès *or* **mak tès** *repr* a drop falling;

tas-tès *repr* continuous dripping;

tès-tèsan to keep dripping. *See also* **tètès**.

tesbèh *var of* **tasbèh**.

tesdik to know in advance, clairvoyant;

nesdikaké to look into, attempt to confirm. *See also* **sidik**.

tèsèk I a certain hardwood tree the wood of which is used for walking sticks.

II *reg* (of nose) flat (*var of* **pèsèk**).

tesih *md for* **isih**; *coll var of* **taksih**.

tesir *var of* **taksir**.

tesmak *ng, kr,* **kaca-tingal** *k.i.* eyeglasses; **- bathok** unable to see what is right in front of one.

tesmèn last will and testament.

tetag up to, as far as (*subst kr for* **tutug**).

tétah, nétah to hold a child by the hands to steady it as it learns to walk.

tetak *ng, kr,* **supit** *k.i.* circumcision;

netaki to circumcise;

netakaké to have (a boy) circumcised;

tetakan circumcision ceremony.

tetapi *reg* but.

teteg I barrier, bar placed across s.t.;

neteg to bar;

netegi to close with a bar.

II stoical;

netegi *or* **netegaké** to steel o.s. to s.t., display fortitude against;

teteg-tetegan to get up the courage to (do) s.t.

III long repeated beating or tapping (*e.g.* of a mosque drum) as a signal;

neteg to beat thus.

tètèh clearly pronounced, understandable;

nètèhaké 1 to pronounce clearly; **2** to explain.

tètèk *chld* breast;

nètèki to give the breast.

tetek, netek to cut off a piece (*e.g.* bamboo);

satetek a cut piece.

tetel a mashed glutinous rice dish;

netel 1 to make (ingredients) into the above dish; **2** to crowd; **3** to stuff o.s. with food;

netelaké to press, cram s.t. (into).

tetéla in fact, obviously. *See also* **téla II**.

tetep 1 steady, unchanging; **2** firm, confirmed;

netep 1 to be firmly closed; **2** to do s.t. firmly;

netepi 1 to adhere to firmly; **2** to fulfil (a promise, responsibility *etc*);

netepaké to make s.t. steady/firm;

katetepan confirmation, authorisation;

tetepan *or* **panetep** act of confirming/establishing.

teter I, neter to keep on urging (with repeated questions).

II *reg* harrow;

neter to harrow.

III a shrub, the leaves of which are used medicinally.

tètèr I a termite-like pest;

tètèren eaten or destroyed by this pest.

II 1 test; 2 evidence;

nètèr to examine, put to the test;

ketètèr to proved by experience.

tetes I 1 able to be cut, pierced by s.t. sharp; 2 *or* tetesan female circumcision (*k.i. for* sunat).

II, netes to hatch;

netesaké to have or allow s.t. to hatch;

tetesan what has hatched out.

tètès 1 a drop; 2 to fall in drops; 3 molasses; 4 to resemble, agree exactly; 5 to come out exactly (prediction);

nètès to fall in drops;

nètèsi 1 to sprinkle on s.t.; 2 agree completely with s.t.;

nètèsaké 1 to sprinkle or drip s.t.; 2 to check whether s.t. agrees;

tètèsan drops (of water);

ketètèsan to get sprinkled;

tumètès to drip steadily.

tewekal *var of* tawakal.

tèyèng I *reg cr* ora - not able to, strong enough to.

II rust;

nèyèng to rust;

tèyèngen rusty.

tèyèr *cr* urine.

thah-thuh always off the mark, getting it wrong.

thak *or* mak thak *repr* a hard object striking a firm surface;

thak-thakan to move about restlessly making a clatter.

thakthik to make noise or clatter.

thakthuh to keep bumping into each other.

thakur, nakur *or* nakuri to paw or claw at;

thakur-thakur to paw repeatedly, dig with the hands or forefeet.

thalang, thalang-thalang (of long things) sticking out at the ends.

thangkring, nangkring *see* pethangkring.

thangkrong, nangkrong *see* pethangkrong.

thanglung, thanglung-thanglung supple, lithe, pliant.

thang-theng to keep wafting across a disagreeable odour (*var of* sang-seng).

tharik, tharik-tharik in neat rows.

thar-thèr *repr* repeated loud reports.

thar-thir (to keep coming up) with trivial little things.

that-thèt *repr* repeatedly trumpeting, whistling.

thathit lightning followed by thunder.

thawé, thawé-thawé to reach out with the hand to grasp s.t.;

kethawéan to keep reaching out the hand;

pating kethawé *pl* with outstretched hands.

thek *or* mak thek 1 *repr* a tapping sound; 2 *repr* a quick action/motion; 3 the sound made with the tongue to urge a horse on; 4 tsk! tsk!; - kliwer everything that happens, the whole situation; - seg *repr* sudden inertness, sudden death;

ngethek to produce a tapping sound;

thak-thek 1 (with) quick actions/motions; 2 to be now on, now off;

sathekan (with) a quick action.

thèk I 1 *repr* the sound produced by striking a bamboo tube; 2 *repr* a tapping or light knocking;

ngethèkaké to turn on (an appliance).

II *coll* belonging to (*var of* duwèk).

thèkèl, kethèkèlan *or* thèkèl-thèkèl to climb with difficulty, to struggle up(ward).

thèkèr, kethèkèran 1 to make one's way

upward with difficulty; **2** *fig* to scrape a living;

thèkèr-thèkèr *or* **nyèkèr-nyèkèr** to scratch for food (of chickens, *fig* of the poor).

théklé 1 (of arms) deformed, *i.e.* short and bent; **2** unlucky.

thèklèk wooden sandal with a rubber toe strap.

theklik (*pron as:* **thekli:k**), **theklik-theklik** *or* **theklak-theklik 1** *repr* a clippity-clop sound; **2** to take a stroll;

ketheklikan *or* **ketheklik-ketheklik** to walk slowly with difficulty.

théklok 1 broken but not detached; **2** sagging with weariness.

thekluk (*pron as:* **theklu:k**) *or* **mak thekluk** *repr* a drowsy nodding;

theklak-thekluk to keep nodding drowsily.

thékor crooked, deformed (hands, feet).

thel *or* **mak thel** *repr* breaking, cutting;

methel to break easily (thread).

thelek, **thelek-thelek** to remain silent and numb as a result of a shattering experience.

theleng 1 (*or* **thetheleng**) pupil of the eye; **2** playing-card spot;

thelengan having round black eyes: the distinguishing characteristic of wayang figures.

thelik (*pron as:* **theli:k**), **thelik-thelik** to sit idly, with nothing to do.

theling-theling to lie alone just staring into space.

thélo a chicken disease;

thélonen suffering from this chicken disease;

thélo-thélo *or* **théla-thélo 1** weak, limp; **2** hopeless, impossible.

thelong, **thelong-thelong** *or* **thelang-thelong** to move the head back and forth while gazing emptily into space.

them *reg* quite satisfied.

thémal-thèmel to eat hungrily, greedily.

themil (*pron as:* **themi:l**), **themil-themil** *or* **themal-themil** to keep nibbling;

nemili to eat continuously;

themilan snacks, nibbles;

kethemil-kethemil *or* **kethemal-kethemil** to eat little by little.

thémla-thémlo to eat hungrily, greedily (*var of* **thémal-thèmel**).

thémol *or* **mak thémol** *repr* pinching, grabbing;

némol to take a bit of s.t.;

thémal-thémol to have a big appetite, take some of everything;

sathémol one large handful taken in the fingers of hand (*e.g.* of rice, from the serving bowl; of flesh, in pinching).

theng *or* **mak theng 1** *describing a bad odour*; **2** *repr* sudden headache.

thèng 1 *repr* a sharp metallic ring; **2** *repr* ting of a clock, bell.

théngal-thèngèl *see* **thèngèl**.

thengar-thenger *see* **thenger**.

thèngèl, **thèngèl-thèngèl** *or* **théngal-thèngèl** to lift the head a little (from a lying position);

nèngèl to stretch the neck and look around;

pating thèngèl *or* **pating thrèngèl** *pl* poking out here and there.

thenger, **thenger-thenger** *or* **thengar-thenger** to remain utterly motionless (*e.g.* loafing; stunned, shocked).

thengik, **thengik-thengik** (to sit) all by o.s.

thengil a hard knobble (*e.g.* bone under the skin), knuckle;

menthengil to stick out (as above).

thengkreng, **nengkreng** *or* **thengkreng-thengkreng** to sit by coolly, silent and motionless.

thènglèng (of the head) tipped to one side;

nènglèng to tip a head to one side;

nènglèngaké to cock (the head).

thengor *var of* thenger.

thèngthèng I, thèngthèngan to tap on s.t. (*e.g.* a pot) to make it sound in order to test whether it is cracked on not.

II thèngthèng, nèngthèngi to earmark (for);

thèngthèngan earmarked.

thenguk, thenguk-thenguk *or* thetheng-uk to sit around idly;

pating threnguk *pl* sitting around loafing;

thenguk-thenguk nemu kethuk *prov* to get a fortune without working to earn it.

ther 1 *repr* s.t. rushing past, pouring out.

thèr 1 *repr* a sudden loud report (whip, fireworks); 2 *repr* water trickling continuously;

thar-thèr *repr* repeated loud reports.

thérok, thérok-thérok thick(ly powdered).

thèthèk I, nèthèk to produce a sharp sound by rapping;

thèthèkan 1 a hollow bamboo tube which produces a sharp sound when rapped with a stick: used by night patrols to sound an alarm, by peddlers to attract customers; 2 a sharp sound produced by rapping s.t. with a stick.

II, thèthèkan *reg* money prepared for paying s.t.

thethel *var of* thèthèl.

thèthèl to become detached, peel off;

nèthèl *or* nèthèli to peel/strip s.t. off;

thèthèlan peeled-off pieces.

théthélilé children's musical instrument, a little saron.

thèthèr I termite-like pest;

thèthèren eaten into, destroyed by this pest.

II, kethèthèran cornered, beaten, unable to cope.

thèwel *or* mak thèwel *repr* a large mouthful (of meat); a large fingerful (of flesh being pinched).

thèwèr, thèwèr-thèwèr to hang limp.

théwul *reg var of* thiwul.

théyol exhausted, tired.

théyot I, théyot-théyot *repr* the croaking of frogs;

II, néyot *reg* to pinch.

thik I *emphatic particle expressing surprise and disapproval, e.g.* thik nggang-go abang! why on earth wear red! (*shtf of* kathik III).

II (*pron as:* thi:k) *or* mak thik *repr* the sound of clinking.

III, thik-thikan to keep fiddling with things.

thikil (of small plants) to grow;

thikilan bud, growing plant. *See also* thukul.

thiklu, thiklu-thiklu bent, stooped with age.

thikluk *var of* thiklu.

thikruk, kethikrukan to make one's way with difficulty.

thil 1 (*pron as:* thi:l) *intsfr* one; 2 *or* mak thil *repr* plucking, breaking off.

thilang a certain bird (*var of* kuthilang).

thilek *var of* thelek.

thileng, thilang-thileng 1 to have large black eyes; 2 unable to close one's eyes.

thili, thili-thili soaking wet.

thilong, thilong-thilong *or* thilang-thilong ignorant, mindless, taken aback.

thilung *see* dhèt.

thimik, thimik-thimik *or* thimak-thimik (to walk) slowly and with short steps, to teeter. *See also* kethimik.

thing I (*pron as:* thi:ng) *repr* a clear high jingling or tinkling;

thing-thing to keep jingling/tinkling.

II jaka thing-thing a confirmed bachelor.

thingik, thingik-thingik *reg* teeny-weeny.

thingil, thingil-thingil (of small objects) to emerge above the surroundings.

thingkrang sitting improperly in an elevated place higher than others;

ningkrangaké to put s.t. in a high place.

See also pethingkrang.

thingkrik var of thingkrang.

thingkring var of thingkrang.

thinik (pron as: thini:k) cute and pretty (little girls).

thinthil chicken liver.

thinthing I, ninthing to test the pitch of a gamelan instrument by tapping on it;

thinthingan a pitch test.

II, ninthing (of clothing) tight.

thiplak a type of sandal.

thipluk, thipluk-thipluk chubby.

thir I (pron as: thi:r) repr a cricket's chirp.

II (or mak thir) repr a flash.

III, ngethir to drip, trickle;

thar-thir a little at a time, bit by bit.

thirik var of tharik.

this (pron as: thi:s), this-thisan to keep trying to touch things, get one's hands on things.

thithik I ng, kedhik kr, a little, a few;

sethithik a little, a few.

II, nithik to strike a light using flint and steel for starting fires;

nithiki to hit or tap (s.t. small);

thithikan flint and steel for lighting fire.

thithil to have a small bit flaked or peeled from it;

nithil to flake or break a small amount from s.t.;

nithili to flake s.t. bit by bit.

thithit repr squeaking, twittering; - thuwit to produce twittering bird-like sounds.

thiwal-thiwul unkempt, untidy (hair).

thiweg, thiweg-thiweg roly-poly, chubby (little girl).

thiwul a steamed porridge of powdered cassava with brown sugar and grated coconut;

niwul to make food as above.

thok I (or thok-thok) only, alone, nothing but.

II or mak thok repr a knock;

ngethok to knock, rap (on);

thak-thok to produce knocking sounds repeatedly.

thokcèr repr starting up instantly (car engine). Also dhogjèr.

thokèr var of cokèr.

thoklèh, nyoklèh to reproach s.o., tease s.o. about s.t. embarrassing.

thoklèk reg var of coklèk.

thoklo turned downwards (horns).

thokol, thokolan bean sprout.

thokor cr foot (var of cokor).

thokrak reg very old, decrepit.

thokthel at a fixed price.

thol repr pecking;

thol-tholan to peck eagerly.

tholang, tholang-tholang sticking out too far (e.g. a long bamboo pole carried on the shoulder);

nolang-nolang to extend outward.

tholé little boy, lad.

thongkrang too short, too small (var of congkrang).

thongkrong, nongkrong to squat, sit around doing nothing;

nongkrongi 1 to squat on s.t.; 2 to hang around at; 3 to occupy, lay claim to;

thongkrongan slang what you drive, car.

thongol, nongol to stick the head out, turn up, pop up;

nongolaké 1 to stick s.t. out; 2 to show (the face, head).

thongthong-sot a certain type of ghost, mentioned in a children's game.

thonthong I, nonthong to remain silent, not speak.

II, bango thonthong a certain large stork with a long beak. See also bango I.

thonthor I reg 1 lampshade; 2 oil lamp with shade.

II, **nonthor** 1 to hold s.t. in the hand but do nothing with it; 2 lazy.

thorok, **thorok-thorok** (of girl) pretty-looking.

thosol *reg* strong, firm, muscular.

thothit a certain game played with the Chinese cards (*kertu cilik*).

thothok I 1 the back of the hand, the top of the foot; 2 hard outer shell (of crab, turtle).

II, **nothok** to knock, hit (with the knuckles);

nothoki to keep knocking;

kethothok to get knocked by accident;

thothokan *or* **thothok-thothokan** to hit each other;

thothok-thothok to knock on, rap (repeatedly).

thothol, **nothol** 1 to peck (at); 2 *fig* to peck away at, embezzle;

notholi to keep pecking (at);

thotholan chicken feed.

thowok, **nini thowok** a puppet made of a coconut shell dipper dressed up which moves when a spirit enters it and is able to pass messages.

thowong I sunken (face).

II *var of* **thowok**.

thoyung ouch! (*var of* **adhuh biyung**).

thral bang! boom!

thrathak, **nrathak** to make a light tapping sound;

pating thrathak *pl* making light, hollow tapping sounds.

threnguk, **pating threnguk** sitting around loafing everywhere. *See also* **thenguk**.

thrèthèl, **nrèthèl** rapid and copious (speech).

thrithik, **nrithik** to touch, handle, finger;

thrithikan act of handling or fingering things.

thrithil *var of* **thrèthèl**.

throngol, **pating throngol** *pl* coming into view. *See also* **thongol**.

thronthong, **nronthong** 1 to have holes in it; 2 to make a hole or opening (in a bamboo wall);

pating thronthong *pl* full of holes.

throthok *repr* a sharp tapping;

throthokan woodpecker.

throthol, **pating throthol** *pl* to peck here and there.

throthuk woodpecker.

thruthuk (of public conveyances) to make frequent stops; **sepur** - stop-train;

nruthuk to call in everywhere.

thruthus, **thruthusan** tearing about in an uncontrolled way (naughty children);

pating thruthus *pl as above*.

thuk 1 *repr* a beat of the bowl-like metal gamelan instrument (**kethuk**); 2 *repr* a knock;

ngethuk to make a knocking sound;

II, 1 **ngethukaké** to match, join, unite; 2 to test whether two things fit together;

thak-thuk to come together, meet each other frequently (*see also* **pethuk** II).

III, **ngethukaké** to prepare and serve up (food).

thuk-athèng to pass the time idly.

thukluk *reg* hill, mound.

thukmis always philandering, infatuated with every pretty face (*shtc from* **bathuk klimis**).

thukul 1 to begin to grow, to sprout; 2 to develop;

nukulaké to give rise to (feelings);

kethukulan 1 to have s.t. growing on it; 2 to get an idea implanted in the mind;

thukulan 1 sprout; 2 to grow easily;

thethukulan 1 plants, vegetation; 2 weeds.

thung I (*pron as:* thu:ng) *or* **mak thung** *repr* gamelan sound;

thang-thung repeated gamelan sounds.

II, **ngethungi** to hold s.t. out toward; to point (a weapon) at s.o.;

ngethungaké to hold (*esp* the hand) up or out toward s.o.

thungkrang *reg* hill, mound.

thungul (*pron as:* thungu:l) mak thungul *repr* s.t. appearing suddenly;

nungul to loom up, come into view;

nungulaké to stick s.t. out.

thur (*pron as:* thu:r) *or* mak thur 1 *repr* a drop of water dripping; 2 *repr* a downward flow;

ngethuri to pour onto s.t. through a spout;

ngethuraké to pour s.t. from a spout.

thus 1 (*pron as:* thu:s) *or* mak thus *repr* bursting open, *e.g.* a fruit when bitten into; 2 *reg* almost! (*expression used in games when an object almost reaches its target, e.g. a marble landing close to the circle*).

thut 1 (*pron as:* thu:t) *or* mak thut *repr* a toot; 2 *repr* a release of wind, fart.

thuthuk object used for hitting;

nuthuk to hit, knock;

nuthuki to knock, rap again and again;

nuthukaké to knock (an implement) against s.t.

kethuthuk to get knocked;

thuthukan *or* panuthuk act or way of knocking;

thuthuk-thuthuk to hit repeatedly;

thuthul *reg var of* thothol.

thuyuk (*pron as:* thuyu:k), thuyuk-thuyuk bent and bowed with age.

thuyul 1 a spirit in the form of a child that can be sent out to gather wealth for its master; 2 a young (apprentice) dancing-girl.

tiba *ng,* dhawah *kr,* 1 to fall, drop; 2 to lapse into (poverty); 3 to fall on, coincide with; 4 to be handed down (order, sentence);

niba to fall deliberately;

nibani to fall or drop on(to);

nibakaké 1 to let s.t. fall; 2 to cause s.t. to fall;

ketiban 1 to get fallen on (by); 2 to have s.t. happen to one;

tumiba (dhumawah *kr*) *lit* to fall, drop;

tiban 1 fallen, come down (from heaven, miraculously); 2 a scapegoat; 3 (one) time;

paniba a fine for accidental injury; - sampir a betrothal gift from prospective groom to bride;

tibané (tibaké *reg*) apparently, as it turns out;

satibané *or* satiba-tibané at the (very) worst.

tidha, tidha-tidha dim, vague, uncertain, obscure.

tidhem pramanem quiet, still, hushed.

tidhur, tidhuran prolonged beating of a mosque drum on certain occasions during the Fasting Month.

tigan egg (*kr for* endhog).

tigas I cut off; - pancing cut off slantwise;

nigas to cut off;

nigasi to decide (a case).

II, tigasan brand new, never used, virgin.

tigung *var of* tikung.

tijab efficacious (*var of* setijab).

tik typewriting;

ngetik to typewrite;

ngetikaké to type for s.o.;

tik-tikan 1 action of typing; 2 typed.

tiké certain leaves dried and finely ground, mixed with opium, for smoking;

patikèn office where opium was sold.

tikel I many times greater; - tekuk manifold, many times as much;

nikel to increase in number;

nikeli to increase the amount of (s.t. one does);

nikelaké to increase s.t. manifold;

matikel-tikel *or* tikel matikel *or* many times as much;

tikelan *or* tetikelan having increased manifold;

ketikel to get multiplied/increased;

ketikel-tikel to increase many times over.

II broken; folded;

nikel to fold; - alis to knit the brows; - asta to fold the hands (in a respectful gesture); - werti a certain motion in the classical dance.

tikep, nikep to catch, grab.

tikèt ticket.

tiksa *var of* tiksna.

tiksna *lit* 1 sharp; 2 sharpness.

tikswa *var of* tiksna.

tikta *lit* bitter (in taste).

tikung, nikung to curve, bend;

tikungan a curve, a bend.

tikus mouse, rat;

tikusan 1 a kind of firework that moves about on the ground as it goes off, jumping-jack; 2 a plant used in folk medicine;

tikus mati ing elèngé *prov* 1 s.o. who has nowhere left to visit because of having many enemies; 2 a criminal caught or killed in his own house.

tilak *reg* trace, remains (*var of* tilas).

tilam 1 mattress, bed; 2 inner layer of clothing.

tilap, nilapaké to leave s.o. alone without their knowledge;

ketilapan to get left alone (by s.o. who goes off without one's knowledge).

tilar 1 to leave (behind) (*kr for* tinggal); 2 to die, dead (*kr for* tinggal donya, mati).

tilas 1 (tabet *kr*) mark, trace, remains; 2 former, ex-;

nilasi to leave a print on s.t.;

patilasan ruins, remains of the past.

tilawat recitation of the Quran.

tilem to sleep, go to bed (*kr for* turu).

tilgram (to send) a telegram;

nilgram to send a telegram (to);

nilgramaké to send by telegraph.

tilgrap telegraph.

tilik *ng*, tuwi *kr*, to pay a visit (to see how s.o. is, *esp* if sick);

niliki 1 to pay a visit to; 2 to approach and scrutinise.

tiling, nilingaké to listen attentively (to, for) in order to understand;

tumiling 1 to bend forward in order to listen closely; 2 to be declining (sun, in the sky).

tilpun 1 telephone; 2 to telephone, be on the phone;

nilpun to telephone s.o.;

tilpun-tilpunan to ring each other on the phone.

tim I steamed;

ngetim to prepare (foods) by steaming them in a closed pot.

II (*pron as:* ti:m) team.

timah I tin.

II, timah-timah *or* tumimah (of wound) healing, becoming well, on the road to recovery.

timaha a certain beautifully speckled wood, used for making kris sheaths and walking sticks.

timang belt buckle;

nimangi to put a buckle on (a belt);

timangan to wear a buckle.

timba bucket for drawing water from a well; - kèrèkan a well-bucket on a pulley;

nimba to draw water from a well;

timbanan bucketful.

timbak *var of* témbak I.

timbal I, nimbali to summon (an inferior) (*k.i. for* undang);

katimbalan to be summoned, called up;

timbalan a call, summons; - dalem a royal summons.

II, tumimbal *or* tetimbalan to pass from one (person or thing) to another;

nimbalaké to pass, hand over s.t. to another.

timbang 1 (rather) than; compared with; 2 in equilibrium; **tanpa** - *lit* incomparable, unmatched;

nimbang 1 to weigh; 2 to consider alternatives, compare (with);

nimbang-nimbang to consider, weigh things up;

timbangan 1 weight; 2 scale, balance, weight used as a counterbalance; 3 counterpart;

katimbang *or* **tinimbang** (rather) than, compared with;

tetimbangan 1 mate, partner; 2 consideration;

timbangané by comparison with, rather than.

timbel 1 lead (metal); 2 tin.

timbil a sty on the eyelid;

timbilen to suffer from a sty.

timbis *var of* **timblis**.

timblis wooden mallet for breaking things up;

nimblis to drop on(to), hit from above;

ketimblis to get dropped on.

timbrah greenish discolouration (oxidation) on copper or brass;

nimbrah stained with the above.

timbreng overcast, clouded over.

timbrung, **nimbrung** 1 to take part in s.t. unasked, interfere; 2 to interrupt.

timbul I 1 to float to the surface; 2 to emerge, appear; 3 to rise;

nimbulaké to cause to emerge, bring forth.

II resistant to attack;

nimbul to strengthen magically, render invulnerable.

timen *coll var of* **temen**.

timpah, **nimpahi** to press (down) on with the leg while sleeping;

ketimpah 1 to get pressed down; 2 to be on the losing side.

timpal I 1 injured to the extent that flesh is detached or cut away; 2 a gaping wound;

nimpal to wound, hack off a piece of flesh.

II, **nimpal** to dispose of one's faeces on a leaf *etc*;

ketimpal-timpal to be in constant difficulty, rejected by everybody.

timplak, **ketimplak-timplak** *see* **ketimpal-timpal**.

timpuh to sit on the ground on one leg with the other to the side; - **alihan** 1 to keep shifting the feet from one side to the other while sitting as above; 2 to switch to another job on the condition that one may return to the original job;

nimpuh to assume this sitting position;

nimpuhaké to place (the legs) in the above sitting position.

timun cucumber (*var of* **ketimun**);

patimunan cucumber patch;

timun mungsuh durèn *prov* a small or weak opponent pitted against a strong, powerful rival; **timun wungkuk jaga imbuh** *prov* to be there only to make up the numbers.

timur I 1 eastern, Oriental; 2 east wind.

II young (*k.i. for* **nom**); **sang Timur** the Holy Child.

tindak I what s.o. does; actions, conduct; - **tanduk** behaviour, conduct;

nindakaké to do, perform, commit (an act);

tumindak 1 action, activity; 2 to act, do.

II to walk (*k.i. for* **mlaku**).

tindha tent, awning (*var of* **téndha**).

tindhes a heavy object used to weight s.t. down;

nindhes 1 to weight s.t. down; 2 *fig* to oppress;

panindhes suppression, oppression.

tindhih 1 chief, leader; 2 *var of* **tindhes**;

nindhihi 1 to lead (a troop); 2 to be on top of; 3 to put s.t. on top of, weight s.t. down with;

ketindhihan to get s.t. put on it;

tindhihen or ketindhihen 1 to mutter in one's sleep during a nightmare; 2 to be disturbed in one's sleep by having cut off the circulation s.w., e.g. the arm, by lying on it.

tindhik hole pierced for earrings;

nindhik to pierce ears;

tindhikan 1 having pierced ears; 2 act or way of piercing ears.

ting I lantern.

II shtf of pating.

tingal 1 a look, a glance; 2 (or paningal) human eye (k.i. for mripat); 3 to look at (root form: kr for deleng); 4 to watch (root form: kr for ton, tonton);

tingalan 1 (celebration of a) birthday (or other special event) (k.i. for weton); 2 mirror (or paningalan) (kr for pengilon); 3 eyeglasses (k.i. for tesmak).

tingar, ningar to steal (cattle).

tingas, ningas to cut on a slant.

tinggal ng, tilar kr, to leave (behind), abandon, neglect; - tatakrama to forget one's manners;

ninggal 1 to leave (behind); 2 departing from, different from;

ninggali 1 to leave behind (money) as a parting gift; 2 to bequeath;

ninggalaké to leave (to or for s.o., esp as a parting gift);

tinggalan s.t. left behind; an inheritance;

tinggal glanggang colong playu idiom to flee the field of battle;

ninggal tapak jero to leave a deep mark.

tinggar reg a kind of gun.

tinggeng I reg immovable, unshakable.

II quiet, gloomy, sombre.

tinggi I or ketinggi bedbug (found in the cracks of chairs, ambèn).

II patinggi reg a village headman.

tinggil, ninggil to drop s.t. hard onto.

tingi a certain bark used for making dyes.

tingkah 1 what s.o. does; actions, behaviour; - laku actions, behaviour; 2 whim, fancy, quirk.

tingkal borax.

tingkas 1 (of rain) to stop, subside; 2 clear, clearly understood; 3 to understand clearly.

tingkat 1 floor, storey; 2 rank; 3 university level, year;

ningkataké to raise the level (of);

tingkatan of a certain rank, at a certain level.

tingkeb, tingkeban ceremony held in the seventh month of (usually the first) pregnancy;

ningkebi to hold the above ceremony for s.o.

tingkem a small woven bamboo basket with a hinged lid;

ningkem to seal, close securely; - wadi to keep a secret;

tingkeman what is sealed or closed securely.

tingkes, reg ningkes or ningkesi to summarise, bring together, collect in compact form;

tingkesan summary, a concise form.

tingling var of tiling.

tinimbang see timbang.

tinja faeces (kr for tai).

tinjo, mertinjo, tetinjo to visit;

ninjo to go to inspect.

tintah (European) ink.

tinting, nintingi to sort by shaking on a winnowing tray in order to remove inferior grains.

tintrim silent, unable to speak from fear.

tip 1 tape recorder; 2 tape;

ngetip to record on tape.

tipak var of tapak.

tipar reg an unirrigated, cultivated field;

nipar to level off, make even (soil).

tipas fan (var of tépas I).

tipes var of tipus.

tipet *reg var of* tapak.

tipis 1 thin (not thick); 2 weak (tea, coffee); 3 slight, little, running low;
nipis to decrease in amount, become less and less;
nipisi *or* nipisaké 1 to make s.t. thin; 2 to reduce, decrease.

tiplak a type of sandal.

tiplèk *reg var of* tiplak.

tipral, niprali *reg* to level, make even.

tipu deceit, trickery;
nipu to trick, deceive.

tipung (*or* ketipung) a small drum in a gamelan orchestra beaten with the fingers.

tipus typhus.

tir I tar;
ngetir to tar (a surface).
II rook, castle, chariot (in chess).

tirah I (*or* tetirah) to go s.w. for the sake of one's health;
nirahaké to have s.o. rest in a health resort;
patirahan health resort.
II left over (*kr for* turah).
III *lit* edge, bank, side.
See also katirah.

tirakat 1 to journey to a holy place (*e.g.* graves of ancestors, saints); 2 to occupy o.s. with meditation at such a place in order to be granted insight *etc*;
nirakati 1 to fast *etc* for (a special goal); 2 to gather and keep watch over s.o. (*e.g.* a sick person) during the night;
tirakatan a gathering for this purpose.

tirem oyster.

tirep *lit* dim, gloomy (sky).

tirig, tirigan *reg* mannerism, idiosyncracy, nervous habit.

tiris *lit* coconut;
tirisan coconut palm.

tirkah *lit* inheritance.

tiros, tirosé it is said (*reg kr for* jaré).

tirta *lit* water; - marta the water of life, drink of the gods.

tiru 1 to resemble; 2 to imitate, copy;
niru to copy, emulate;
nirokaké 1 to imitate/copy s.t.; 2 to act like s.t. (in a funny way);
tetiru *lit var of* niru;
tiron an imitation, fake, copy;
paniru act or way of imitating.

tis *lit* cold, chilly; panas-tis fever. *See also* atis.

tisik a mended place;
nisik to mend, patch;
tisikan 1 mended, darned, patched; 2 act of mending.

tisna *var of* tresna.

tistis *lit* 1 cold, chilly; 2 lonely, silent, sad.

tita 1 *lit* past, ago; 2 wis - more than enough.

titah 1 pronouncement, order; 2 destiny; 3 creation; 4 creature;
nitahaké to create, bring about;
tinitah (pre)destined;
tumitah to take the form of creature, to have an existence in the world;
satitahé according to its own nature;
panitah act of creating or of predetermining.

titi careful, scrupulous, precise;
niti, nitipriksa to investigate, examine;
nitèni *or* nenitèni to observe and remember (the details of);
titèn careful and accurate by nature;
titèn-titènan to observe the details of;
paniti 1 investigation, examination, observation; 2 one who inspects/examines.

titig 1 *reg* identifying sign; 2 *reg* to recover (from), get over.

titih to ride; to be on (top of) (*root form: k.i. for* tunggang);
titihan 1 horse; 2 that which is ridden on, vehicle (*k.i. for* tunggangan);

panitih 1 a rider; 2 that which sits on top.

titik I dot, point, full stop.

II 1 sign, trace (for finding out about s.t.); 2 indication, evidence (whereabouts of stolen goods);

nitik 1 to judge from appearances, read the signs, know the identifying factors; 2 to hunt for a missing person or thing;

katitik as shown or judged from;

titikan distinguishing mark or characteristic.

titimangsa 1 time, season; 2 date;

nitimangsani to date s.t.

titip to ask (s.o.) to (do a favour, run an errand);

nitipi 1 to ask s.o. to (do a favour); 2 to entrust s.o. with;

nitipaké to entrust s.t. to s.o. for a period;

titipan 1 given into s.o.'s care; 2 entrusted goods, deposit; 3 (or **panitipan**) depositing; 4 storage-place;

ketitipan to have s.t. left with one.

titipriksa, nitipriksa to examine, inspect, observe closely.

titir I alarm signal beaten out on drum, gong *etc*;

nitir to sound an alarm;

titiran act of sounding the alarm.

II continuous, constant.

titis I, **patitis** accurate, exact;

panitis 1 one's aim (with a gun); 2 sights (of a gun).

II **titisan** incarnation, rebirth in a new form;

nitis 1 to enter a human body (*referring to a soul beginning a new incarnation*); 2 to change one's form;

panitis incarnation, taking a bodily form;

panitisan the means (or art) of incarnating o.s.

III **nitis** to make Javanese (palm) sugar;

panitisan a mould for making sugar (in the form of a coconut shell).

tiwas 1 to come to grief, have an accident, come off the worse; 2 to fail, do s.t. in vain; - **kebeneran** a pleasant surprise, lucky coincidence; - **tiwus** or - **tuwas** to (do) in vain.

tiwikrama 1 *way* to transform o.s. into a huge giant; 2 *fig* to show off one's power.

tiyam *reg* Chinese small shop, stall.

tiyang I person; adult; someone (*kr for* **wong** I).

II after all (*kr for* **wong** II).

III pole, flagstaff, ship's mast;

niyangi to put a mast on (a ship).

tiyasa *reg var of* **kuwasa**.

tiyèng *reg* 1 rust; 2 rusty.

Tiyonghwa Chinese.

tiyung I a certain bird (*var of* **ciyung**).

II, **niyung** or **tumiyung** 1 bent over, bowed down; 2 to bend low.

tlabung I *reg* a large knife with a bent end.

II *var of* **tladhung**.

tlacak hoof; - **belah** split hooves; - **wungkul** massive hoof. *Also* **tracak**.

tlacap, tlacapan adorned with large gilded stars (court parasols).

tlacar, tlacaran to spread everywhere (roots).

tladha *var of* **tuladha**.

tladhung, nladhung or **nladhungi** (of chicken) to attack, fly at, beat with wings and feet;

panladhung act of attacking.

tlaga lake.

tlagi *subst kr for* **tlaga**.

tlajak *reg* wooden boundary marker.

tlajer main root of a plant (*var of* **lajer**).

tlajug pedestal for an oil lamp. *See also* **ajug-ajug**.

tlakup 1 covering leaf of a flower or bud; 2 (*or* tlakupan) ear-flaps, a hat with ear-flaps;
nlakup *or* nlakupi to cover with (s.t.);
nlakupaké 1 to close tightly, seal; 2 to use as a cover or coating;
katlakup covered over.

tlalang, tlalangan *or* pating tlalang *pl* (of long things) sticking out in all directions.

tlalé elephant's trunk;
nlalé to hold s.t. with the trunk.

tlampik I a black dove with white wing feathers.
II *see* tampik.

tlampok a variety of jambu.

tlanakan womb.

tlandhing bamboo container for catching coconut sap as it drips.

tlanjer *var of* planjer.

tlanjuk *var of* tlanjur.

tlanjur, ketlanjur *reg var of* kebanjur.

tlangkas deft, adroit, agile.

tlangké, aja - do not delay;
nlangké, ora - without delay.

tlangkup *var of* tlakup.

tlangsa, sadness, sorrow;
nlangsa sad, sorrowful.

tlangsang, pating tlangsang *reg* protruding in all directions.

tlangso to let s.t. go too long;
ketlangso excessive, too far.

tlanthang, tlanthangan *reg* to wander about aimlessly.

tlanyak, tlanyak-tlanyak *or* tlanyakan rude, impolite (*var of* tranyak).

tlapak 1 (*or* tlapakan) palm, sole; 2 footprints, tracks.

tlapuk (*or* tlapukan) eyelid.

tlarap, nlarap to swoop.

tlasab, nlasab *reg* 1 to slip, graze sideways; 2 to go in sideways (of a wound);
nlasabaké to put s.t. in sideways.

tlasah I s.t. used as a cover or top;
nlasah to cover with a layer, to floor with.
II nlasah to search, scour.

tlasak, nlasak to make one's way across or through.

tlasar *reg* underlayer;
nlasari 1 to supply s.t. with a base or underlayer; 2 to move the hand under s.t in search of (an object).

tlasih basil (flower, herb). *See also* slasih I.

tlatah area, territory, domain.

tlatèn *ng*, tlatos *kr*, using patience and perseverance in a difficult or tedious task;
nlatèni to stick at s.t. patiently; to (do) s.t. tirelessly;
tlatènan characterised by patience (as above).

tlawah 1 trough, tub; 2 manger, crib.

tlawung, tlawungan a rack for storing spears and similar weapons (*var of* plawungan). *See also* lawung I.

tlèber *reg* to dawdle, be slow, sluggish.

tlebok *var of* tlebuk.

tlebuk (*pron as:* tlebu:k) *or* mak tlebuk *repr* s.t. heavy and ungainly falling.

tlecek, tlecekan to splash around in a muddy place.

tlècèk, nlècèk *or* pating tlècèk scattered untidily.

tlecer bamboo stakes planted in a field and moved by ropes to scare off birds.

tlédhang-tlèdhèng to take a stroll.

tlèdhèk female dancer who performs with a group of street musicians for hire;
nlèdhèk to be(come) a dancer (as above);
tlèdhèkan 1 act of dancing (as above); 2 to hold a gathering with such a dancing performance.

tlèdhès *reg* wiped out, completely gone.

tlédho *var of* tlédhor.

tledhok, tledhok-tledhok *or* tledhak-

tledhok (to speak) calmly and carefully.

tlédhor careless, negligent, slack.

tlégong, tlégongan a curve, a bend.

tlégram *var of* **tilgram**.

tlégrap *var of* **tilgrap**.

tlekim *var of* **telkim**.

tlèktèk *var of* **tlètèk**.

tlekun turkey (*var of* **kalkun**).

tlekung veil worn by women when praying.

tlemak-tlemèk spattered, covered with big spots.

tlembuk *reg* prostitute.

tlèmèk *reg* lining, underlayer. *See also* **lèmèk**.

tlempak a short spear.

tlémpé fine woven bamboo (for walls).

tlenak, pating tlenak *pl* forming little heaps everywhere.

tlenang-tlenong *see* **tlenong**.

tlenceng the wick of an oil lamp.

tlèncèng, nlèncèng crooked, to go off at an angle;
pating tlèncèng *or* **tléncang-tlèncèng** full of twistings and turnings.

tléndho *var of* **tlondho**.

tléndhor careless, negligent, slack (*reg var of* **tlédhor**).

tlenek *var of* **tlenak**.

tlenggak, pating tlenggak *pl* to stand and tilt the head back.

tlengseng, nlengseng to search (for) here and there.

tlenik, pating tlenik covered with small things, *e.g.* embroidered flowers on a shirt.

tlening, nlening to dump or heap things here and there;
tlenang-tlening *or* **pating tlening** scattered about, in disorder;
kakèhan tlening of too many different kinds.

tlénok, pating tlénok *pl* all pretty looking.

tlenong, pating tlenong *pl* forming various heaps;
tlenang-tlenong in different sizes of heap.

tlenyak-tlenyek to take short careful steps.

tlenyèk *var of* **plenyèk**.

tlenyer, nlenyer to walk softly, stealthily.

tlepak *var of* **tlapak**.

tlepak-tlepok *see* **tlepok**.

tlépak tray or box holding containers for ingredients for betel-chewing (*var of* **tépak**).

tlepèk splat! (*repr* s.t. wet or soggy dropping, or s.t. dropping onto a soggy surface).

tlepok *repr* s.t. soft falling and spreading, plop! *e.g.* a cake, cow dung;
tlepak-tlepok *or* **pating tlepok** to keep dropping (as above).

tlepong *var of* **tlépong**.

tlépong *reg var of* **tléthong**.

tlépun *var of* **tilpun**.

tléram *or* **mak tléram** *repr* a flash of light;
satléraman instantaneous, momentary.

tlérap *var of* **tléram**.

tlèrèp *var of* **tlèrèt**.

tlèrèt *var of* **clèrèt**.

tlesep *or* **mak tlesep** *repr* a quick popping into a hole;
nlesep to slip quickly into;
nlesepi *or* **nlesepaké** to slip s.t. quickly into (s.t., *esp* for concealment).

tleser, tleser-tleser to slide quickly.

tlèsèr, nlèsèr 1 to slither over the ground; 2 *cr* unable to think straight.

tlesih accurate, detailed, complete;
nlesih *or* **nlesihaké** to investigate thoroughly;
satlesih-tlesihé as complete as possible.

tletah sap, resin (*kr for* **tlutuh**).

tleteh *lit* dirt, impurity.

tlètèh clearly pronounced, understandable (*var of* **tètèh**).

tlètèk *repr* the emergence of faeces;
  nlètèk 1 to eliminate faeces; 2 to force matter out of a tube.

tlethik 1 *repr* s.t. small and compact dropping; 2 a single or separate drop of rain.

tlethok *repr* clattering (of a hard object falling; of raindrops or hailstones spattering).

tlethong *var of* tléthong.

tléthong animal dung, manure;
  nléthong (of animals) to drop dung;
  nléthongi to drop dung on s.t;
  ketléthongan to get dung on o.s.

tlèyèh *var of* tlèyèk.

tlèyèk to lie down (wearily, exhausted);
  ketlèyèk to be worsted, get the worst of it.

tlika, nlika *reg* to investigate, spy on.

tliktik, nliktik *reg* to inspect, examine.

tlikung, nlikung to shackle, tie up, bind the legs.

tlikur, nlikuri to guard, to take care of.

tlimpé *reg* finely woven bamboo (for walls).

tlingsing, tlingsingan to miss, not connect, not meet up (*var of* slingsing).

tlingus nose hair; - kèlèk underarm hair.

tlisib, tlisiban to miss the point, be wrong.

tlisik to preen the feathers with the beak;
  nlisik *or* nlisiki 1 to preen (bird's feathers); 2 to investigate; 3 to gather fallen sticks for firewood.

tlisir, nlisir I to trace (the thread of);
  nlisiri to trim with fancy edging. *See also* plisir.

tliti *var of* titi.

tlitik, tlitik-tlitik *repr* continuous dripping.

tliwang *reg* to not tally, not agree, deviate.

tliweng, ketliweng 1 to lose one's way, be mistaken, wrong; 2 to be in the dark, confused.

tlobèh too wide.

tlocor, tlocoran *reg* 1 lying sprawled; 2 rude, badly behaved.

tlola-tlolé *see* tlolé.

tlolé *or* mak tlolé *repr* s.t. long and flexible extending;
  nlolé to extend long and flexibly;
  nlolèkaké to extend (s.t. long and flexible);
  tlola-tlolé *or* pating tlolé *pl* as above.

tlolèr *var of* tlolé.

tlolor *var of* tlolé.

tlompak *reg* a water trough for cattle to drink from.

tlompé 1 to delay, dawdle; 2 slow, sluggish;
  ketlompèn to be too late, take too long.

tloncang-tloncong *see* tloncong.

tloncong, tloncongan *or* tloncang-tloncong to loaf around, stroll about aimlessly.

tlondho 1 the young of a cricket that has no wings yet; 2 *fig* young and inexperienced.

tlongtong a cylindrical box.

tlop, ngetlopi *or* ngetlopaké to pay off a debt with goods.

tlorong I, nlorong to throw a spear.
  II, tlorong-tlorong shining; to send out beams of light.

tlosor, nlosor to slide, slither forward, go straight across the ground;
  nlosori to slide forward over s.t.;
  tlosoran to lie stretched out on the ground;
  pating tlosor *pl* lying stretched out all over the ground.

tlotok *or* mak tlotok *repr* dropping dung.

tlowong, nlowong to tunnel through s.t. (*var of* trowong);
  tlowongan tunnel.

tluka *reg var of* truka.

tlukah *reg var of* truka.

tluki hibiscus.

tlumpah *var of* **trumpah** I.

tlundhag wooden block used as a step outside the door.

tlungsung, **pating tlungsung** bustling, rushing busily back and forth.

tlungtik, **nlungtik** *reg* to watch closely, keep track of, inspect.

tlunyak-tlunyuk *see* **tlunyuk**.

tlunyuk, **tlunyukan** *or* **tlunyak-tlunyuk** to keep bursting in rudely.

tlusap-tlusup *see* **tlusup**.

tlusub *see* **tlusup**.

tlusuh, **nlusuh** *or* **nlusuhi** to pound rice to separate the grains from the ears.

tlusup 1 sliver or similar object embedded in the skin; 2 (*pron as:* **tlusu:p**) *repr* quick concealment;
nlusup to enter and become concealed (in);
ketlusupen 1 to get entered surreptitiously; 2 to get a thorn stuck in the skin;
tlusap-tlusup to go in and out, make frequent visits. *See also* **slusub**.

tlusur, **nlusur** *or* **nlusuri** 1 to run the hand over s.t. in search of s.t.; 2 to trace back;
tlusuran feeling, groping (with the hand, in search of s.t.).

tlutuh *ng*, **tletah** *kr* 1 sap, resin; 2 dirt, impurity;
nlutuh to exude sap. *See also* **letuh**, **tleteh**.

tobat 1 to repent (of one's sins), mend one's ways; 2 remorse, contrition; 3 *excl* shame! what a pity!;
mertobat to repent;
nobati to swear off;
nobataké 1 to cause s.o. to repent/reform; 2 awe-inspiring; 3 to drive s.o. to despair;
patobat *or* **pitobat** repentance.

tobil the young of the lizard (**kadhal**).

toblok *reg var of* **tomblok**.

toblos *reg var of* **coblos**.

tobong 1 a large woven bamboo basket; 2 a kiln for processing earthenware, bricks, lime.

todhi, **nodhi** to examine, test, try out.

todhong, **nodhong** 1 to hold s.o. up at gunpoint; 2 *fig* to put s.o. on the spot to give s.t.;
nodhongaké to threaten (s.o. with) a weapon;
todhongan holdup, robbery.

todhos I *reg* piercing tool, awl, punch. II *coll* all gone.

tog, **ngetog** to exert all one's strength;
ngetogaké 1 to leave s.t. alone, let it go; 2 to do s.t. to the full. *See also* **katog**.

togé *var of* **taogé**.

togog a corner fence post;
nogog to sit silently by (not contributing to the conversation *etc*).

tograt *coll* character, second nature.

togting *reg* all gone.

toh I gambling stake; - **nyawa** *or* - **pati** to stake one's life, *fig* to risk everything, devote one's all;
ngetohi to bet s.t., *i.e.* use s.t. as a gambling stake.
See also **totoh**.
II dark birthmark.
III *particle:* 1 come on!; 2 *see* **ta**.

tohid a firm, inner (religious) conviction. *Also* **tokid**.

tohwalèn *reg* long-lasting.

tojèh, **nojèh** *reg* to stab with (a sharp weapon).

tojoh *var of* **jojoh**.

tok I *coll var of* **kok** (*2nd person pronoun agent of passive verb*).
II *lit* palm wine.

toko store, shop;
noko to run a shop.

tokuh *reg* kite string.

tokid *var of* **tohid**.

tolèh, **nolèh** to turn the head (to one side, to the rear), to look around; **ora**

tolèh to not bother with, not think of;
tolah-tolèh *or* **nolah-nolèh** to keep turning the head;

tumolèh to turn the head, to look back;

panolèh a magic charm (**aji**) to make s.o. remember you;

kamitolèhen, kamitolihen to keep thinking (be reminded) of s.o. one has left behind.

tolèk, nolèki *reg* to look for, search.

tolèr a long, thin, flexible object;
tolèr-tolèr (of such an object) extending (outward).
See also **tlolèr.**

toli *reg* and then, after that. *See also* **tuli, nuli.**

tolih *var of* **tolèh.**

tolok *reg* a small basket of woven bamboo.

tolol stupid, ignorant.

tolu the 5th **wuku** of the Javanese calendar.

tom I indigo plant the leaves of which are used for dye;
ngetom to plant indigo;
patoman indigo plantation.

II, tom-tomen to keep seeing s.t. (horrible) in the mind's eye. *See also* **tontonen.**

tomah, nomahaké to make s.o. accustomed.

tomat tomato.

tombé (*or* **ketombé**) dandruff;
tombénen to suffer from dandruff.

tomblok a large rough basket (for carrying sand *etc*).

tombok 1 an additional amount to complete the price; **2** an extra, bonus;
nomboki to add (an amount) to s.t.;
tombokan 1 a payment to make up the full price; **2** additional earnings.

tombol button for mechanical devices, push button switch.

tombong *var of* **tobong.**

tomis a dish of chili, onions, and soy sauce;
nomis to make the above dish.

tomplok, nomplok to pile up.

tomprangan I a homing pigeon competition, on which wagers are sometimes made.

II to lay a bet.

III ketomprangan to make a rhythmical drumming (*e.g.* on a desk, naughty boys in class).

IV name-board (in front of an office, house).

tompo a small woven bamboo basket.

ton *ng*, **tingal** *kr*, **salah ton** to be mistaken (about what one has seen);
non *lit* to see, look at;
tinon *lit* to appear, look, be seen;
tumon *ng*, **ningali** *kr* **1** to (be able to) see; **2** to observe; **3** to have seen.
See also **anon, katon, tonton, tumon.**

tondhé *lit* **tanpa** - incomparable;
nondhé to compare with;
tetondhèn measurement, criterion, example.

tong barrel, keg;
tong-tongan in barrels, by the barrel.

tonggari *reg* night.

tongkèng a creeper with fragrant yellow flowers, the Tonkin creeper.

tongki the female of the **grati**, a variety of duck.

tongkok *reg* crooked, humped, hunchbacked.

tongkol a certain fish of the tuna family.

tongo *var of* **tongong.**

tongong 1 an idiot; **2** stupid, dull-witted;
nongong to gape in astonishment.

tongsèng a dish prepared with grilled pieces of goat's meat.

tongton *see* **tonton.**

tongtongan large fireworks.

tonil stage, play in the Western style.

tonjok, nonjok *or* **nonjoki** to send a gift of food by way of invitation to a ceremony, with the obligation to make a contribution;

tonjokan food sent as above.

tonjol, nonjol to stick out, be conspicuous, prominent;

nonjolaké 1 to push s.t. from underneath or behind; 2 to show s.t. off;

tonjolan protrusion, bump (on the skin).

tonto, ketonto to keep reliving a bad experience.

tontok *reg var of* **tonton**.

tonton *ng*, **tingal** *kr*, **nonton** to watch, observe (what is happening, performance);

nontoni to view one's prospective bride during a visit at her home (in arranged marriages);

nontonaké to show, exhibit, display;

tontonan (**tetingalan** *kr*) a show, performance;

tontonen to keep seeing s.o. (or s.t.) before one's eyes, have hallucinations.

tonyo, nonyo to hit, punch.

tonyok *var of* **tonyo**.

tonyol, nonyol to push forward, stick out;

nonyolaké to draw attention to, push forward;

nonyol-nonyol to interrupt, break in, ignore the proper order.

top *reg var of* **tlop**.

topèng a mask; **wayang** - a form of classical dance drama performed by masked dancers;

nopèng 1 to perform a classical masked dance; 2 to make masks;

nopèngi to put a mask on s.o.'s face;

topèngan 1 to put on or wear a mask; 2 leather blinkers worn by a horse.

topi hat; - **prop** pith helmet, solah topee;

topèn to put on or wear a hat.

toplès *var of* **setoplès**.

topling *reg* woven bamboo basket, for carrying cassava *etc*.

topoh *reg* wet rag, floor cloth.

topong 1 ornamental crown worn by traditional drama dancers; 2 *reg* a certain style of cap.

tor I a children's game.

II, **ngetor** 1 to cut down (trees); 2 to prune or cut branches from (trees).

III, **ngetoraké** to exert o.s. to the limit. *See also* **tog, katog**.

torap, norap *reg* to inundate (a ricefield).

torèh, norèh *reg* to slash into, make a shallow cut;

torèhan 1 a slash, a notch, slicing; 2 a woodcut.

Torèt the Law of Moses, Pentateuch.

torog s.t. added, paid into the bargain;

norogi to make up a deficit.

torong funnel.

toros a cylindrical package for cakes of Javanese sugar.

tos I 1 hard(ness); 2 value.

II *or* **ketos** (*kr for* **ketan**) glutinous rice.

III true, real. *See* **yekti**.

IV **tosé** *md*, **tosipun** (*kr for* **jaré**) it is said, they say.

tosan 1 iron (*kr for* **wesi**); 2 bone (*kr for* **balung**). *See also* **tos** I, **atos** I.

totog, notog 1 to extend o.s. to the utmost; 2 to reach the end;

notogaké to knock against, collide with;

ketotog to get knocked accidentally;

totogan the end of the road.

totoh, notohi to bet s.t., use s.t. as a gambling stake;

notohaké to use s.t. as a gambling stake;

totohan 1 act of betting; 2 gambling stake. *See also* **toh**.

totok full-blooded (Chinese, Dutch).

totol, notol 1 to push s.t. down firmly; 2 to keep on (working, trying), to persist; 3 keen, eager.

totor 1 wood-fire (for warmth); 2 to make a fire;

notor to cut wood to make a fire.

totos *reg* the leader, the top man.

towang vacant, unoccupied.

towok a certain type of spear.

towong *var of* **towang**.

towuk *reg var of* **tuwuk**.

toya 1 water, fluid (*kr for* **banyu**); 2 urine (*kr for* **uyuh**);

toyan *or* tetoyan to urinate (*kr for* **bebanyu, nguyuh**).

toyang seagull.

trabas I 1 porous; 2 wasteful (in housekeeping).

II, **nrabas** 1 to take a shortcut, bypass; 2 to cut a path through s.t.;

trabasan shortcut, bypass.

traca a certain water snail.

tracag, **nracag** to ascend rapidly, swarm up;

pating tracag *pl* ascending rapidly.

tracak I hoof (*var of* **tlacak**).

II, **nracak** 1 to touch s.o. (rudely, intrusively); 2 to behave rudely (*var of* **nranyak**).

tracap, udan - the first heavy rain of the wet season.

tracuk the shaft of a plough or ox-cart, *i.e.* the part hitched to the ox yoke.

trajak a row of stakes (fence, for drying nets *etc*).

trajang 1 a fast forwards movement, gait (of person or horse); 2 actions, way of doing s.t.; 3 attack, charge; 4 violation, transgression (of a prohibition, taboo);

nrajang 1 to attack, strike; 2 to cut across or through; 3 to violate, transgress;

katrajang 1 afflicted, hit; 2 violated, transgressed;

panrajang violation, transgression;

trajang-trajangan to intersect;

nrajang grumbul ana cèlèngé *prov* to embark deliberately on a dangerous course.

trajeg a row of stakes.

traju balance-type scale;

nraju to weigh s.t. in a balance scale; - mas firm, square (shoulders).

trag miscarriage (*var of* **terag**).

trah lineage, descent; **trahing kusuma** of noble descent;

nrahaké to beget, have as descendant; trah-tumerah from generation to generation.

traktir, **nraktir** to buy a treat for, to pay the bill for s.o.;

traktiran treating;

traktir-traktiran to buy treats for each other.

trambal, **pating trambal** full of patches.

trambul, **nrambul** to butt in, join in (an activity) without being asked;

ketrambul to get interrupted.

trami to accept (*reg kr for* **trima**).

trampil skilled, competent, quick, deft.

trancag *var of* **tracag**.

trancam raw vegetable salad with hot grated coconut dressing.

trang I bright, clear (*lit var of* **terang**).

II, **trang-trang** *repr* water dropping onto metal.

tranggana *lit* the stars (*var of* **taranggana**).

tranggal, **nranggal** to attack.

tranjel *var of* **trenjel**.

trantan, **nrantan** to help a child learning to walk by using a **sléndang** under the arms as a restraint;

trantanan to toddle, take first steps (little children).

trantang, **nrantang** full of holes (letting the light through).

tranyak, **nranyak** *or* **tranyakan** rude, impolite.

tranyam, **nranyam** to talk back roughly to.

traos shrimp or fish paste (*kr for* **trasi**).

trap I arrangement, attitude, action;
ngetrap to arrange, put in place;
ngetrapi to put onto/into;
ngetrapaké to apply s.t. (to), put s.t. (in, on);
tumrap 1 regarding, applied to, about, with respect to; **2** placed, arranged, set up;
katrap provided, furnished;
atrap *lit* to arrange;
trap-trapan arrangement, application, way in which things are laid out (put in place, made available *etc*);
pangetrap arrangement, layout, application. *See also* **patrap**.
II trap-trapan 1 steps, stairs; **2** in the form of steps.

trapas *reg* **1** wasteful; **2** used up fast.

trapsila 1 well-mannered; **2** good manners.

tras straight away; straight on (*var of* **teras**, *subst kr for* **terus**).

trasah *var of* **srasah**.

trasèk *reg var of* **trasi**.

trasi *ng*, **traos** *kr*, a paste made from pounded and fermented shrimp or fish, used as an ingredient in cooking to improve the taste.

tratab *or* **mak tratab** *repr* a shock, fright;
nratab, **trataban** to have the heart beating with fright.

tratag a temporary roof joined to a house to provide additional space for a special event or ceremony.

traté lotus; **- bang** red lotus.

trawang, **nrawang** transparent;
trawangan openings to let light and air through.

trawas I, **nrawas** *reg* to place a mark as a claim on land before opening it up for cultivation.
II a herb with medicinal use.

trawèh non-obligatory prayers recited in the mosque at night during the Fasting Month.

trayoli *term of abuse*: scoundrel, rascal.

treceb, **pating -** to have pricking feelings everywhere.

trecek, **nrecek** (of speech) to pour out unclearly;
trecek-trecek *repr* water gushing.

trècès, **nrècès** to drip copiously (of tears, raindrops);
trècèsan *or* **pating trècès** to drip everywhere.

trècèt *reg* handkerchief.

trégal-trègèl *see* **trègèl**.

trègèl, **trègèlan** *or* **trégal-trègèl** to act roughly and indifferently.

trek truck.

trèk *or* **mak trèk** *repr* crackling, clicking.

trékah idea, scheme;
nrékah to think up an idea (for).

trèm tram, light railway.

trembel, **trembel-trembel** compact and well-proportioned (woman's body).

trèmbèl I, **pating trèmbèl** full of patches. *See also* **tèmbèl**.
II, **trèmbèlané** *cr* damn it!

trembesi a certain variety of large rain tree.

tremboso *reg* basket made from woven coconut leaves.

trembusu *var of* **tremboso**.

trémos thermos flask.

trèmplèk, **pating trèmplèk** *pl* adhering to, stuck to. *See also* **tèmplèk**.

trèn I train.
II *reg* space on river banks used for raising crops.
III trend.

trencem, **pating trencem** to have jabbing pains all over the body.

trèncèng no longer raining, cleared up;
mangsa - time when there are no rains.

trenjel a wedge inserted into a loose connection to tighten the fitting;
nrenjel 1 to slip in in front of s.o. else; **2** to tighten a fitting with a wedge.

trenggalang, nrenggalangi to combat, defend against, ward off, hold back (an attack).

trenggalung *reg* a sort of civet cat.

trenggana *var of* **tranggana**.

trenggiling anteater;

nrenggiling resembling an anteater (*also* **tenggiling**).

trengginas quick-moving, quick to act.

trenggos *reg* leather cap.

trenggulang *reg var of* **tanggulang**.

trengguli a variety of Cassia tree.

trenggulun a tree that yields edible fruits.

trenten *reg* in order, orderly.

trenyang *reg* limp, lacking strength.

trenyuh crushed, broken; - **atiné** deeply affected, moved to pity;

nrenyuhaké to affect, arouse pity.

trep 1 positioning (of a building); **2** fitting exactly, just right;

ngetrepi 1 to position (a house); 2 to make fit exactly;

satrep just right.

trèpès flat, unrounded (*esp of* buttocks, breasts).

tréplok, pating tréplok *pl* adhering to, stuck to. *See also* **téplok, témplok**.

trepsila *var of* **trapsila**.

très edging of gold thread on sleeves.

trèsèh *reg* smiling and friendly.

tresna to love, to be attached to; - **asih** love; to love;

nresnani to love, be kindly disposed (of children, parents; without passion);

katresnan love.

treteg *var of* **kreteg I**.

tretep *var of* **kretep**.

trètès, nrètès to bedeck with precious gems;

trètèsan bedecked with gems.

tri *lit* three. *See* **telu**.

tribawana *or* -**buwana** *or* -**loka** *lit* the three worlds.

tricig *var of* **trincig**.

trijil, trijilan inner corner of the eye.

trig, trigtrigan in constant motion, restless, lacking the desirable serene repose;

trigan *reg* a nervous habit, a mannerism.

triganca *reg* **1** a quarrel; **2** to quarrel.

trigu wheat, wheat flour.

triguna *lit* the three qualities, namely goodness (**sattwa**), lust (**rajah**) and ignorance (**tamah**).

triko tricot, a certain kind of striped fabric.

trim tram (*var of* **trèm**).

trima *ng*, **trimah** *kr,***1** to receive; **2** to accept thankfully;

nrima to accept without protest, to resign o.s.;

nrimakaké 1 to resign o.s. to s.t. with an effort; 2 *or* nrimani to give (a woman) as a wife as a favour to an inferior;

nriman inclined by nature to accept what life offers, easy to please;

triman (a woman) given in marriage (as above).

trimah *kr for* **trima**.

trimulya the Trinity.

trin train.

trincig, nrincig to rise steeply (road);

trincig-trincig to ascend rapidly.

trincing slender;

trincing-trincing tall and slender.

trini *lit* three.

trinil a small water bird with long legs and a mincing gait;

trinil-trinil to walk with quick, short steps (a small person).

trinjil *var of* **trijil**.

trintim *var of* **tintrim**.

tripang bêche-de-mer, sea slug.

tris snaffle-bit.

trisig *var of* **srisig**.

trisik *var of* **tisik**.

trisna *var of* **tresna**.

trisula *lit* trident, three-pronged javelin.

tritik I (*or* tritikan) a pattern of dots produced by the tie-dye process, used *esp* for breastcloths.

II *var of* tritis.

tritis (*or* tritisan) the projecting part of a roof where the rain runs off.

tritunggal the Trinity.

triwikrama *way* to display supernatural powers when angered, *esp* by transforming o.s. into a giant.

trobos, nrobos to cut through;
　trobosan a way through or across.

trocob, nrocobi to mix lower-quality stuff in with (material of high quality).

trocoh 1 (of ceilings, roofs) to leak; 2 *fig* to talk obscenely, swear a lot;
　nrocohi to leak onto (s.t. in the house);
　katrocohan to get leaked on.

trog *see* entrog.

trojog, trojogan a certain style of traditional house.

trokah *var of* trokan.

trokan *reg* a newly settled place.

trombol, nrombol (of a group) to intrude by joining in with a crowd and slipping in unnoticed.

tromel metal box, tin, drum.

tromol *var of* tromel.

trondhol plucked, bare of feathers.

tronjol *var of* trombol.

trontong, trontong-trontong 1 to grow light in the east; 2 *fig* to begin to see the light.

tronyok I *reg* small stone tool used for grinding spices.

II, tronyok-tronyok to keep entering in a rude way (*var of* trunyuk).

tronyol *var of* tronjol.

tropong 1 weaving shuttle; 2 binoculars.

tropos *reg var of* kropos.

trosé it is said (*md for* jaré).

trowong, nrowong to tunnel through s.t.;
　trowongan tunnel.

trubuk 1 a shad-like sea fish; 2 salted, fried roe of this fish.

trubus to sprout, put out new shoots or buds;
　nrubus having sprouted or budded, having put out a shoot;
　trubusan a sprout, new shoot, bud.

trucuk I palisade, row of stakes;
　nrucuk *or* tumrucuk 1 (objects) of approximately the same size; 2 (offspring) born in close succession.

II 1 a variety of mushroom; 2 an object shaped like this mushroom.

III *or* trucukan a thrush-like songbird.

trucut, nrucutaké to slip s.t. (into, out of);
　ketrucut 1 to let s.t. slip from one's hands; 2 to go too far, say too much.

truh *lit* raindrops, drizzle.

truk truck (*var of* trek).

truka *or* tetruka to settle an area by opening up new land;
　trukan a newly settled place.

trukbonen to suffer from a venereal swelling in the groin.

trukbyangané *cr excl* damn it! to hell with it!

truksi instruction.

trulèk a variety of plover.

trumané *reg* and furthermore.

trumbakané *cr excl* damn it!

trumbul woven basket without bottom frame.

trumpah I open thong sandal.

II crosspieces at the top and bottom of a wooden or bamboo wall section which hold the wall to the house.

truna *lit* young, young person (*var of* taruna).

truni *var of* truna.

trunjang, pating trunjang *pl* to run into; to knock against. *See also* tunjang I.

trunjel, pating trunjel *pl* to push through from behind (*e.g.* in a crowd). *See also* tunjel.

trungku *reg* jail, prison;
    nrungku to put in jail, imprison.

truntum I a small tree growing on low muddy ground.
    II 1 to bud, sprout; **2** a certain batik design.

truntun, nruntun, tumruntun to continue on in order without a break.

trunyak-trunyuk *see* **trunyuk**.

trunyam *var of* **tranyam**.

trunyuk, trunyukan *or* **trunyuk-trunyuk** *or* **trunyak-trunyuk** to enter in a rude way, *e.g.* by barging in without first announcing one's presence.

trup troop, group.

trus *var of* **terus**.

trusi *reg* verdigris.

trustha *lit* glad, happy, cheerful.

trusthi *var of* **trustha**.

trutul, trutul-trutul *or* **pating trutul** spotted, speckled. *See also* **tutul**.

trutus, nrutus *or* **trutusan** to search everywhere for s.t.

truwaca clear, visible, audible, comprehensible (*var of* **terwaca**).

truwèlu rabbit.

truwilun *var of* **terwilun**.

truwu *reg* in commotion.

tuba a certain plant that is poisonous to fish;
    nuba to fish using **tuba**.

tubras, nubras *or* **nubras-nubras** to bump into things when running away.

tubruk I, nubruk 1 to pounce (on); **2** to bump into, knock against;
    nubrukaké to cause s.t. to bump against s.t.;
    ketubruk 1 to get pounced on; **2** to get bumped into;
    tubrukan to have a collision, collide with each other.
    II kopi - coffee made by pouring boiling water over ground coffee (without filtering).

tudang-tuding *see* **tuding**.

tuding 1 pointer, index finger; **2** puppet's arm stick;
    nuding *or* **nudingi** to point at/out;
    tuding-tuding *or* **tudang-tuding** to keep pointing (at);
    panuding act or way of pointing.

tuduh *ng*, **tedah** *kr* indication, pointer, instruction, direction, admonition;
    nuduhi to show or point out to (s.o.)
    nuduhaké to show or point out to s.t., show s.o. (the way);
    panuduh act or way of pointing out;
    pituduh instruction, admonition.

tudhun *reg* betting stakes, money contributed to a gambling pool.

tudhung 1 woven bamboo headcover; **2** anything used for covering the head as protection against the sun;
    nudhungi to cover the head;
    nudhungaké to use s.t. for covering the head;
    tudhungan to put s.t. on the head for protecting it against the sun.

tug *reg* **1** having arrived at; **2** when it happened that...;
    ngetugaké 1 to finish, bring to an end; **2** to carry over, bring across (to a destination). *See also* **tutug**.

tugar *reg* wooden pole or bar for digging.

tugas duty, responsibility;
    nugasaké to assign a task to.

tugel 1 broken in half; **2** cut off; **3** ploughed a second time crossways;
    nugel to break, cut in two;
    nugeli to break s.t. repeatedly;
    nugelaké to break s.t. accidentally;
    tugelan a broken-off piece;
    satugel one broken-off piece.

tugi the hair at the point of an ear of rice.

tugu a column, pillar set up to mark s.t.

tugur to stand guard, remain at one's post;
    nuguri to watch over or be in attendance at s.t. throughout the night;
    tuguran 1 the act of staying awake all

night in order to watch over s.t.; 2 to be in attendance at s.t. all night long.

tuhu I 1 truly, indeed, to be sure; **2** steadfast, loyal;

nuhoni to be faithful/loyal to, to honour;

katuhon 1 to materialise; **2** by good fortune;

satuhu really, truly;

satuhuné actually, in fact.

II (or **tetuhu**) male nocturnal cuckoo.

tujah I, nujah to step (trample) on with the forelegs (horse);

tujah bumi with white forelegs (horse).

II, nujah 1 to accuse falsely; **2** to slander s.o.

tujes, nujes to stick/prick with a sharp point;

ketujes to get pricked.

tuju 1 a goal that is aimed at; **2** intention, what is meant; **3** direction toward s.t.; **4** a form of magic for causing sickness to another;

nuju 1 in the act of (do)ing; **2** to happen to (do, be doing); **3** to head for, aim toward;

nujoni to fall exactly on (a day);

nujokaké to direct s.t. to(ward);

tumuju intended (for);

katuju 1 directed (toward), **2** intended (for);

panuju 1 objective, goal; **2** (heart's) desire;

nuja-nuju (to happen) now and then;

tujon a children's game using a flat stone for reaching the target;

tujuan destination, target;

tujuné by good luck, fortunately.

tuk a spring (of water), the source of water in a well;

ngetuk to emerge from the ground (spring water).

tukang I 1 worker; **2** one who operates or works at (equipment, materials); **3** one who (does); - **cukur** barber; - **jait** tailor; - **kayu** carpenter; - **sulap** magician;

nukang to work, labour; to do a job, work at a craft;

nukangi to craft s.t.; to repair s.t.;

nenukang to do odd jobs;

tukangan 1 occupation, craft; **2** street where craftsmen live;

patukangan 1 handicraft; **2** craftsmanship.

II sloth (animal).

tukar I, nukaraké to give s.t. in exchange;

ketukar to get exchanged accidentally;

tukar-tukaran to barter.

II, nukari to annoy, irritate;

tukaran or **tukar padu** to quarrel, fight.

tuku ng, **tumbas** kr, **mundhut** k.i. to buy;

nuku to buy s.t.;

nukoni 1 to go to s.o. to buy s.t.; **2** to pay a sum of money to the parents of the bride;

nukokaké to buy for s.o.;

tinuku to be sold;

tetuku or **tuku-tuku** to do shopping;

tukon s.t. has been bought (rather than home-made);

tetukon purchasing, buying;

panuku act of buying;

patukon or **pitukon 1** gift given to one's bride; **2** purchase price.

tukung a variety of chicken with no tail.

tukup, nukup 1 to cover s.t. with a quick movement of the hand; **2** to take by surprise.

tulad, nulad to follow an example;

tetuladan an example to be followed.

tuladha or **tuladhan** an example, instance, model;

nuladha to set an example;

nuladhani to give an example (of).

tulah allowance, bonus.

tulah-sarik curse, malediction.

tulak I to go and return on the same day. **II** a black chicken flecked with white. **III** magical protection; - **sawan** a potion for warding off illness in a child; - **bilahi** or **tanggul** a magical preventive measure;
nulak to take preventive measures against s.t.; to forestall;
panulak act of warding off.
IV, **tulakan** an opening at the edge of a ricefield for letting in water from the channel.

tulalé (elephant) trunk (var of **tlalé**).

tulang I small box used as an arena for cricket fights.
II reg bone.

tular, **nular** (of disease) to spread;
nulari or **nenulari 1** to infect s.o.; **2** to contaminate with s.t.;
nularaké to spread, transmit;
tumular to spread;
tular-tumular or **tular-tularan** to infect each other;
katularan 1 to get infected; **2** (of disease, fire etc) to get spread.

tulèn original, authentic.

tuli ng, **tunten** kr, **nuli** or **tumuli** (**tumunten** kr) and then, thereupon.

tulis ng, **serat** kr, **nulis** to write;
nulisi to write on s.t.;
nulisaké to write for s.o.;
nenulis to write in general;
nulis-nulis or **nulas-nulis** to keep writing, to write repeatedly;
tinulis lit **1** written; **2** fore-ordained.

tultis at close range.

tulung 1 help, assistance; **2** to help; **3** please;
nulung or **nulungi** to help s.o.;
katulungan to be helped;
tetulung 1 help; **2** to lend assistance (in time of danger);
tulung-tulung to call for help;
tulung-tinulung to help each other;

pitulungan help, assistance;
tulung menthung to make a show of helping while actually hindering.

tulup or **tulupan** blowgun;
nulup to shoot pebbles etc with a blowgun.

tulus 1 to go ahead without mishap, be successful; **2** lasting, prosperous; **3** pure, unmixed; **4** sincere, honest, genuine;
nulusaké to allow s.t. to go through without a setback;
katulusan sincerity, genuineness.

tulya lit like, the same as.

tum, **ngetumi** to cook food by wrapping in banana leaves and steaming in a basket.

tuma ng, kr, **itik** k.i. hair louse.

tumama to enter, penetrate. See also **tama II**.

tumambang lit (of sun) to rise, become visible.

tuman to acquire a taste, become accustomed to;
numani causing s.o. to acquire a taste;
nenuman to induce to like s.t.

tumang a supporting piece on the side of a cooking pit to place the pot on.

tumaninah reg peaceful, calm (mind).

tumat var of **tomat**.

tumbak I ng, **waos** kr, k.i. spear, lance;
numbak to stab s.o. with a spear;
numbaki to keep stabbing with a spear;
numbakaké to use s.t. for stabbing as a spear;
tumbakan 1 toy spear; **2** to spear each other;
tumbak-tumbakan 1 to spear each other; **2** a prohibited pattern of marriage whereby two males marry each other's younger sister;
panumbak 1 act of throwing a spear; **2** soldier who carries a spear;
tumbak cucukan tattletale.

II a measure of length, the Rhenish rod = *ca* 3.77 metres.

tumbal (*or* **tetumbal** *lit*) **1** a sacrifice symbolically representing human victims (of flood *etc*) killed to forestall a calamity; **2** ritual held to nullify the bad portent (indicated numerologically) of a coming marriage;
  numbali 1 to sacrifice (a victim); **2** to hold the above ceremony for s.o.

tumbar *or* **tumbar jinten** coriander (*var of* **ketumbar**).

tumbas to buy (*kr for* **tuku**).

tumbeng a wedge (inserted to make s.t. tight, *e.g.* a kris sheath);
  numbeng to insert such a wedge;
  tumbengan an artificial node placed in the resonator of a **gendèr** to adjust the pitch.

tumbleg, numbleg to butt.

tumblog *var of* **tumbleg**.

tumbu 1 a bamboo basket; **2** a rectangular box with a lid.

tumbuk 1 to collide head-on; **2** to coincide (with), be the same (as);
  numbuk to collide with, knock against;
  tumbukan 1 to strike each other; **2** to coincide (with); **3** traditional ceremony held to celebrate s.o.'s eight-year cycle (**windu**) birthday, *e.g.* - **wolu** 64th birthday (8 x 8 years).

tumeg 1 too sweet; **2** full, satiated.

tumendhil mouse droppings.

tumenggung *see* **temenggung**.

tumlawung to echo loudly in the distance.

tumon, numoni to see, watch, witness.
  See also **ton**.

tumoninah *var of* **tumaninah**.

tumpa, tumpa-tumpa (**matumpa-tumpa** *lit*) one on top of the other;
  numpa-numpa forming a pile, all heaped up.

tumpak I, numpak to ride (*kr for, also var of* **nunggang**); to take (a vehicle);

numpaki to ride on;
  numpakaké to have/let s.o. ride;
  tumpakan *or* **tetumpakan** means of transportation, that which is ridden.
  II *lit* Saturday.

tumpal I border (triangular) design on the vertical edge of a kain.
  II *lit* according to s.o. else's will;
  numpal kèli to travel around accompanying s.o., with no destination of one's own.

tumpang I, s.t. put on top of; - **sari 1** part of the roof of a traditional Javanese house; **2** (a piece of land which is) planted with two different crops; - **suh** piled up any way at all; - **tindhih** one on top of the other; **sila** - to sit cross-legged with the right leg over the left (puppet-master fashion) (*see also* **sila**);
  numpang 1 to be on or at the top; **2** to get a ride (from); **3** to move in with s.o. (temporarily), board; **4** to put forward (a question, idea, opinion) merely as an addition;
  numpangi 1 to be on (top of); **2** to put s.t. on (top of); **3** to get board and lodging (from); **4** to get a ride (from);
  numpangaké to put s.t. on (top of);
  tumumpang 1 (resting) on; **2** (of land) lying at a higher level;
  katumpangan to have s.t. on top of it;
  tumpangan a ride.
  II a certain dressing made from soy sauce, coconut milk and chili.

tumpek *var of* **tumplak**.

tumpeng a cone of rice surrounded by vegetables and other dishes prepared for a ritual meal;
  numpeng 1 to prepare the above meal; **2** cone-shaped;
  tumpengan to hold a ceremony with rice cones as above.

tumper 1 a burning stick removed from the fire; **2** an ember;

numper (to act) recklessly, go head-long, out of control;

tumper cinawetan an illegitimate child (considered dangerous).

tumpes done away with; - **tapis** utterly wiped out, altogether destroyed;

numpes to exterminate;

panumpes (act of) doing away with.

tumpi I the node dividing sections of bamboo.

II a certain crisp fried chip made from rice flour.

tumplak (or **tumplak blak**) spilled or poured out all over the place, *e.g.* rice from a tipped-over basket; secrets poured into another's ear; - **punjèn** the final wedding for which parents are responsible, *i.e.* the wedding of their youngest daughter;

numplak to spill/pour (things) by inverting the container.

tumplek *var of* **tumplak**.

tumpling *reg* a rough basket for carrying earth *etc.*

tumpu, numpu 1 to hunt (deer); **2** to trap (fish).

tumpuk in a pile, in large quantities; - **timbun** in piles, in large quantities;

numpuk 1 to pile s.t. up, accumulate things; **2** to hand in (an assignment);

numpuki to pile s.t. on;

numpuk-numpuk or **tetumpukan** (or **matumpuk-tumpuk** *lit*) forming many piles;

tumumpuk piled up;

tumpukan 1 heaped up; **2** piles (of s.t.).

tumpur *lit*, - **lebur** destroyed, wiped out.

tumrap 1 (or **tumrapé**) regarding, applied to, about; **2** placed, located, set up. *See also* **trap**.

tumuli and then, after that (*var of* **nuli**).

tumunten *kr for* **tumuli**.

tumus to flow from one to another (*e.g.* damp, also a mood);

numusi to influence, affect.

tumut to accompany, (do) with (*kr for* **mèlu**);

numutaken to have s.o. accompany or live with s.o. (*kr for* **ngélokaké**, *see* **èlu**).

tuna (**tuni** *subst kr*), a loss, deficiency; to lose; - **dungkap** not exactly, more or less; - **budi** stupid, short of brains; - **karya** unemployed; - **nétra** blind; - **susila** immoral; - **wewéka** careless;

nunani to cause loss to;

nunakaké to sell at a loss;

ketuna to suffer a loss;

kapitunan 1 hardship, loss; **2** to undergo hardship/loss;

tuna satak, bathi sanak *prov* to lose in worldly goods but gain a friend. *See also* **pituna**.

tunang, tunangan 1 fiancé(e); **2** to be engaged.

tunas I, nunasi *reg* to cut down (a tree) at the base of the trunk;

tunasan a sprout that appears at the base of the trunk.

II, tunasan *reg* food left on s.o.'s plate.

tundha I 1 step, stair; **2** - **telu** *etc* with (3) steps, layers over (behind) each other;

tundha-tundha in layers, ranks;

nundha 1 to arrange things in layers; **2** to do, send s.t. a second time.

II, nundha(-nundha) to pass s.t. from one to the other;

nundhakaké 1 to station, hold ready (post horse, runner); **2** to take over (from the previous runner *etc*);

tundhan 1 a relay system for transporting things (porters, runners); **2** relief (horses, runners); **3** stationing (of relief).

tundhes, nundhes to examine s.o. with questions about the real facts.

tundhuk *reg* **1** to bow the head; **2** *fig* to be under s.o.'s thumb;

nundhukaké 1 to bow (the head); 2 to cause s.o. to submit.

tundhun banana stalk with bunches of fruit growing on either side;
tundhunan the bunches on the stalk;
satundhun a stalk of bananas.

tundhung, nundhung to evict, drive out.

tundhon, tundhoné so that finally, as a result.

tunggak I tree stump; - semi 'sprouting stump', name of a style of kris handle;
nunggak to resemble a stump (not move forward); - semi to bear the same title as one of one's forebears, usu father;
ketunggak to trip over a stump (bad omen), hit an obstacle.
II, nunggak to be in arrears;
tunggakan 1 remnant, remaining portion; 2 overdue (debt); 2 - bojo former wife.

tunggal ng, tunggil kr of the same...;
tunggalé of the same sort, group; - ajang co-worker; - banyu having received the same spiritual teachings, having the same spiritual teacher; - kringkel or - welat own brother or sister; - rasa tasting alike;
nunggal 1 to join or group together; 2 to do s.t. together; - turu to sleep together; 3 to form one, abut on each other;
nunggalaké to join, bring together, unite;
manunggal joined, united;
satunggal one (kr for siji);
panunggalan things belonging to the same category; lan sapanunggalané (abbrev lsp) and so forth.

tunggang ng, tumpak kr, titih k.i., tunggang gunung the time just before sunset (when the sun touches the mountains);
nunggang 1 to ride; 2 to take (a vehicle);

nunggangi 1 to ride on; 2 to perch or sit on (top of);
nunggangaké to have/let s.o. ride;
nenunggang to take a vehicle;
tunggangan or tetunggangan means of transportation, that which is ridden.

tunggara reg south-east.

tunggil of the same... (kr for tunggal).

tunggu ng, tengga kr 1 to wait (for); 2 to keep watch over, look after; sing tunggu omah house-minder, caretaker;
nunggu to wait for, look forward to;
nunggoni 1 to wait for; 2 to watch over, look after s.t.; 3 to guard;
nunggokaké to look after on behalf of s.o.;
patunggon 1 act of waiting or watching; 2 waiting-place.

tungguk (caos k.a.) to serve (s.o. of high status) as guard; - kemit 1 a guardian; 2 to guard;
nungguki 1 to guard s.o. ('s place); 2 to take one's turn at serving as guard;
tunggukan 1 act of serving s.o. as guard; 2 place where s.o. serves.

tunggul I lit (or tetunggul) what is most important, the best;
panunggul 1 middle finger; 2 gem set in the centre (of a ring, earring etc); 3 the first or most important thing, the foremost consideration.
II banner, flag.
III reg tree stump.

tungka, nungka to come straight after s.o. or s.t.;
ketungka (an activity) interrupted or overlapped by (another).

tungkak heel;
nungkak 1 to follow on s.o.'s heels; 2 to tread on s.o.'s heels from behind; - krama to ignore the rules of etiquette;
ketungkak 1 to get blocked, tripped (by s.o.'s heels); 2 to receive an unexpected visit when about to leave;
tungkakan heel of shoe or sock.

tungkas message, instruction (*kr for* **wel-ing**). *See also* **pitungkas**.

tungkeb, **nungkeb** 1 to cover with a hollow object (*e.g.* a basket); 2 to surround and capture;
nungkebi to put s.t. (*e.g.* a lid) on s.t.;
nungkebaké to place s.t. face down.

tungkel a large burning stick removed from the fire.

tungku I *reg* hearth, fireplace of stones.
II *lit* **nungku** to concentrate (thoughts).

tungkul, **nungkul** 1 to bow the head; 2 to surrender; - **aris** to submit freely; 3 to attack unexpectedly, catch unawares;
nungkuli 1 to bow the head over s.t.; 2 to observe intently, not take the eyes off s.t.;
nungkulaké 1 to cause to bow, to lower s.t.; 2 to cause s.o. to surrender or bow down to one; 3 to catch unawares;
tumungkul 1 to bow the head; 2 (*also* **temungkul**) bending (stage in the growth of a rice plant);
ketungkul absorbed, engrossed;
panungkul 1 subjection; 2 tribute.

tunglé first day of the six-day week.

tungtum *var of* **tuntum**.

tungtun *var of* **tuntun**.

tungtung *var of* **tuntung**.

tunjang I, **nunjang** I to knock against, run into;
nunjang-nunjang *or* **nunjang-palang** to run all over, bump into things;
ketunjang to get knocked against or run into.
II, **nunjang** to provide financial support for;
tunjangan financial support, bonus.

tunjel, **nunjel** to push s.o. from behind;
ketunjel to get pushed from behind.

tunjem, **nunjem** *or* **tumunjem** thrusting down(ward) strongly;
nunjemaké to thrust or implant s.t. deeply into.

tunjuk, **nunjuk** to appoint, name;

tunjung I 1 lotus (white or blue); 2 a metal knob on the end of a spear shaft (shaped like a lotus bud, for placing in the ground);
nunjung to resemble a lotus;
tunjung tuwuh ingséla *prov* 'a lotus growing on a stone', something that cannot be.
II copper sulphate (put on wounds).

tuntak to spill out;
nuntak to vomit (*kr for* **mutah**).

tuntas 1 squeezed dry (so that there is no more fluid in it); 2 completely used up, exhausted, finished; 3 clearly, completely (expressed, ideas);
nuntasaké 1 to cause to run dry; 2 to carry s.t. out completely, exhaustively.

tuntum healed, closed (wound);
nuntumaké to heal, cure.

tuntun, **nuntun** 1 to guide s.o. or s.t. by the hand *etc*; 2 to give guidance to, lead, instruct;
nuntuni to guide s.o. by giving examples;
tuntunan 1 guidance; 2 umbilical cord (*k.i. for* **puser**);
panuntun 1 leader; 2 guidance.

tuntung 1 tip, point; 2 what is aimed at, goal; 2 a touch of (another flavour);
nuntung to point toward or in the direction of.

tuntut I 1 banana flower; 2 to come into flower (banana).
II, **nuntut** 1 to demand, claim; 2 to prosecute;
tuntutan demand, claim;
panuntut prosecutor.

tunu, **nunu** *lit* to burn, set on fire;
tinunu burned (by fire, also by frost);
tunon burnt;
patunon place for burning.

tupiksa, **nupiksa** *lit* 1 to examine, investigate; 2 to read (letter).

tur I 1 also, in addition; 2 although, even though; - **manèh** furthermore.

II to offer, present. *See also* **atur** I.

turah *ng*, **tirah** (*or* **langkung**) *kr*, left over, remaining;

nurahi *or* **nurahaké** to consume less of s.t. in order to leave some for others;

turahan (that which is) left over;

turah-turah abundant, plentiful, profuse;

saturahé all that is left of s.t.

turangga *lit* horse;

katuranggan interpretation of the character of a woman, horse, cat, dove, cock, from their physical characteristics (good and bad signs).

turas I urine (*k.i. for* **uyuh**);

nurasi to urinate on s.t. (*k.i. for* **nguyuhi**);

turasan, paturasan 1 chamber pot; 2 a place for urinating; 3 **cèrèt** - a kettle with spout, for ablution after urination.

II descendant.

turé (*or* **turéné**) it is said (*md for* **jaré**).

turi a certain flowering tree, the corkwood tree;

- **bang** bitter-tasting red blossoms used in folk medicines.

turida *lit* 1 cares, sadness; 2 longing, heartache.

turné 1 a tour for inspection; 2 to go on a tour of inspection.

turu *ng*, **tilem** *kr*, **saré** *k.i.* 1 to sleep; 2 to go to bed;

nuroni 1 to sleep in/on; 2 to sleep (in the same bed) with;

nurokaké to put s.o. to bed;

nenuru to lull s.o. to sleep;

turon *or* **teturon** *or* **turonan** lying down;

keturon to drop off to sleep accidentally, to doze;

paturon place for sleeping; bed, bedroom;

sapaturon (to sleep) in the same bed.

turuh 1 *reg* to leak, leaky; 2 faded, discoloured; 3 (*or* **turuhan**) water poured over a weapon (used as medicine);

nuruhi *or* **teturuh** to pour a stream of water over s.t.

turuk *cr* female genitals, cunt.

turun I 1 (**tedhak** *k.i.*) to descend genealogically; 2 descendant;

nurun *or* **tumurun** 1 inherited, hereditary; 2 *lit* to go down, descend;

nurunaké 1 to cause s.t. to descend; 2 to transmit to one's descendants;

turun-tumurun from one generation to the next.

II, **tedhak** *kr*, **nurun** to copy, duplicate;

nurunaké to have s.t. copied;

turunan a copy, duplicate.

III to contribute;

nuruni to contribute to;

turunan contribution. *See also* **urun**.

turus I a cutting from which a new plant is raised;

nurus to grow (a plant) from a cutting;

turusan raised from a cutting.

II a kind of fish trap.

turut 1 regular order, proper coherence; 2 along; 3 to go along with; 4 obedient, compliant;

nurut, tumurut to follow, act according to, obey;

nuruti to comply with;

nurutaké to obey, follow;

turutan 1 guide, s.t. followed; 2 textbook for reading Arabic.

tus I hundred (*shtf of* **atus**); **ji-** one per hundred;

tus-tusan hundreds.

II, **ngetus** to drain, drip-dry s.t.;

patusan drain(pipe). *See also* **atus** II.

III, pure (blood, descent, from nobility).

IV (*pron as:* **tu:s**) *excl of reproof.*

tusih (official) supervision.

tuslah 1 extra allowance, wage supplement; **2** extra charge on tickets.

tustha *lit* contented, satisfied.

tusuk a hairpin; - **kondhé** a decorative hairpin for ladies' hair.

tut along, following;
ngetut *or* ngetutaké to follow s.o.;
tut-buri *ng*, tut-wingking *kr*, to follow, walk behind.

tutas *var of* **tuntas**.

tutu *ng*, gentang *kr*, nutu to pound (rice) to remove the grains from the ears (the result is **gabah**);
nutoni to keep pounding;
tuton pounded.

tutug *ng*, **dumugi** *kr*, **tetag** *subst kr* **1** (up) to, as far as; **2** to reach the end; finished, over;
nutug **1** to the end or utmost; **2** to keep on, to resume;
nutugi to fulfil (wishes);
nutugaké to continue, finish off;
tutugé (**sambetipun** *kr*) the continuation of (a serial *etc*).

tutuh *ng*, **tetah** *kr*, nutuh to blame, reprimand;
nutuhaké to blame s.o. when things go wrong;
ketutuh to get the blame when things go wrong;
tutuhan one who gets blamed;
tutuh-tutuhan to blame each other.

tutuk 1 mouth (*k.i. for* **cangkem**); **2** *way* well-spoken (of a **dhalang**).

tutul 1 spot, speckle; **2** spotted, speckled;
nutul to dab (at);
nutuli to dab on;
nutulaké **1** to dab s.t. (into, at); **2** to dip s.t. into;
tutulan a dab.

tutup 1 a cover, means of closing; **2** closed; **3** the close (of); **4** to close, cover; - **kéyong** a certain weave for bamboo wall coverings; - **saji** food cover of woven bamboo or wire;

nutup 1 to close, cover, shut; **2** to keep closed or under cover;

nutupi 1 to close, cover; **2** to cover up;

nutupaké 1 to close s.t.; to close for s.o.; **2** to use as a cover;

tutupan 1 closed, shut; **2** locked, secured;

katutupan covered, closed;

panutup means of covering or closing;

tumutup covered, closed.

tutur I sanjang *or* criyos *kr*, dhawuh *or* ngendika *or* paring priksa *k.i.*; matur *or* ngaturi priksa *or* caos priksa *k.a.* **1** advice; **2** to say (to), tell;
nuturi to tell, advise;
nuturaké to tell (about);
pitutur advice.

II to pick up, find by accident;
nuturi to pick (things) up.

tutus cord made from strands of split bamboo; - **kajang** long, irregular stitching;
nutus to tie s.t. with such cord.

tutut tame, submissive;
nutut to obey, to follow advice;
nututi **1** to follow, chase, (try to) catch up with; **2** to try to recover (losses);
nututaké to tame, make submissive or obedient;
katututan **1** to come across (s.t. one is tracking down) in an unexpected place; **2** to have (one's illness) overcome;
nenutut to tame, make submissive;
nututi barang wis tiba *prov* to lock the stable door after the horse has bolted;
nututi layangan pedhot *prov* to make a futile effort.

tuwa *ng*, **sepuh** *kr* **1** old, senior, mature; **2** ripe, ready to eat, cooked; **3** ripe for harvesting (rice); **4** dark (colours); **bojo** - wife married first; **jeneng** - adult name;

meteng - in the last stages of pregnancy; **wong** - parents; - **nom** young and old; - **buru** hunter; - **pikun** old and senile; - **rawa** fisherman;

tetuwa elder, authority, respected person, leader;

nenuwakaké to regard, acknowledge as an elder *etc*;

nuwani 1 to act in a mature way; 2 to be the eldest (most senior) over;

nuwakaké 1 to make darker; 2 to burnish (gold);

ketuwan too old to use, stale;

ketuwanen too old;

kamituwa a village official, next below the headman;

pinituwa 1 elders; 2 an elder (Christian).

tuwajuh to be certain of one's feelings; to (do) seriously.

tuwagana *var of* **tuwanggana**.

tuwah to grow (*reg kr for* **tuwuh**).

tuwak I a prop, a support;

nuwak to prop s.t. up, support s.t.

II an intoxicating liquor made from fermented coconut juice.

tuwakup 1 faith in God; 2 to submit to God's will.

tuwan *lit* 1 lord, lady; 2 *respectful title applied to European men*; - **besar** boss, head of a plantation; - **tanah** landlord.

tuwang empty, vacant, unoccupied (*var of* **towang**).

tuwanggana elders (of a village or any organisation).

tuwas, patuwas *or* **pituwas** 1 payment or compensation for one's time and trouble. *See also* **tiwas**.

tuwawa village official for irrigation.

tuwek, nuwek to stab with a sharp object.

tuwèk *coll* old (*var of* **tuwa**); - **ngèkèk** very old.

tuwi to visit (*kr for* **tilik**).

tuwilun *reg* stupid, dull-witted.

tuwin *lit* and.

tuwu (*or* **tetuwu**) male nocturnal cuckoo (*var of* **tuhu** II, **tetuhu**).

tuwuh 1 outgrowth, sprout; 2 *fig* descendant; 3 to come into existence, grow;

nuwuhi to plant (an area);

nuwuhaké to grow, raise;

tuwuhan 1 ceremonial decoration for weddings symbolising prosperity and fertility; 2 (*or* **tetuwuhan**) plants, growing things;

katuwuhan grown over.

tuwuk full, satisfied (*kr for* **wareg**).

tuwung putra ceramic bowl, cup.

twin and (*lit var of* **tuwin**).

tyang person, adult; someone (*lit var of* **tiyang**).

tyas *lit* heart, feelings.

Tyonghwa Chinese.

U

ubad-ubed *see* **ubed**.

ubak-ubek *see* **ubek**.

ubak *see* **ubek**.

ubal I, ngubal to twist (strands) into rope;
ubal-ubalan twisted together (strands) to form rope.
II 1 spreading (fire); **2** overflowing (flood);
ubal-ubalan to flare up, spread everywhere;
ngubalaké to cause to flare up;
kobalan to get an abundance of s.t. *See also* **mubal**.

ubang-ubeng *see* **ubeng**.

ubanggi promise, agreement (*kr for* **ubaya**).

ubarampé things needed for a special purpose, requisites, requirements.

ubaya *ng*, **ubanggi** *kr*, **1** promise, agreement (regarding time); **2** summons to appear before a court at a certain time;
ngubayani to agree on a certain time.

ubed 1 wrapped, swathed; **2** shrewd, sharp, astute;
ubed-ubed *or* **ubed-ubedan** to wear or put on (a wrapped clothing item);
ubad-ubed to keep swathing;
ngubedaké 1 to wrap s.t. around; **2** to use (money) efficiently; to invest (money) for profit;
ngubed-ubed *or* **ngubed-ubedi** to wrap s.t. around;
mubed *or* **mubad-mubed** evasive, devious.

ubek I 1 noisy; **2** disharmonious.
II, ngubek to stir, mix;
ubak-ubek to keep moving around in the same general area;
ubek-ubekan to mill around.

ubel, ubel-ubel head scarf, neck cloth;

ngubel-ubeli to wind (such a cloth) around;
ubel-ubelan to wear s.t. wrapped around the neck.

ubeng, ngubengi to surround, encircle, go around s.t.;
ngubengaké to cause to go around;
mubeng to spin, whirl, go around;
ngubeng-ubengaké 1 to make s.t. go round and round; **2** confusing;
ubengan 1 rotation, time around; **2** an evasion, circumlocution;
ubeng-ubengan 1 to run around in circles; **2** to miss each other, cross;
kubeng circumference;
saubengan one time round;
saubengé surrounding;
ubang-ubeng evasive, not to the point.

uber, nguber to chase, pursue, hunt down;
uber-uberan to chase each other.

ubin *var of* **obin II**.

ublak, ngublak to stir rapidly, to beat (eggs);
ublakan 1 beaten, stirred; **2** beater.

ublek *var of* **ublak**.

ublik small oil lamp (*var of* **cublik I**).

ubral *reg var of* **obral**.

ubreg 1 noise, racket; **2** noisy;
ngubreg to ply with questions.

ubres, ngubres to search for everywhere.

ubrus *coll* lieutenant colonel.

ubub, ngububi to blow on, fan (a fire, to make it hotter);
ububan bellows.

ubud *reg* rough (workmanship) (*var of* **obod**).

ubug, ubug-ubug *repr* the roar of wind or flames.

ubung, ngubungi to get in touch with;
ngubungaké to connect, link, bring into contact;

ubungan connection, relationship.

ubur I, ubur-ubur jellyfish.

II ngubur-uburi to smoke (a house) to drive out mosquitoes.

ubut, ubut-ubut *intsfr* early; **ésuk** - very early in the morning. *See also* **umun-umun**.

ubyang-ubyung *see* **ubyung**.

ubyar sparkling lights;

mubyar to sparkle, glitter;

ngubyaraké to cause to sparkle/glitter.

ubyek intense, very lively.

ubyung, ngubyungi to get together, join in with people;

ubyang-ubyung *pl* to move about idly in groups, hang out together.

ucal I *reg kr for* **olah, ulat,** *kr for* **wulang**.

ucap 1 what s.o. says; **2** to say;

ngucap to say, express, speak;

ngucapaké to say, to pronounce, to utter;

kocap to be said, talked about;

kocapa it is told (that); now, it happened that...;

ucapan 1 utterance; **2** pronunciation;

ucap-ucapan 1 topic of conversation; **2** proverb, saying;

pangucap 1 what s.o. says; **2** act of saying or speaking;

pangucapan pronunciation;

pocapan 1 speech; **2** conversation; **3** saying, expression.

ucek, ngucek 1 to rub (*esp* the eyes); **2** *fig* to criticise, pick on;

nguceki to wash (cloth) by rubbing it with the hands;

ucek-ucek to keep rubbing.

ucel, ngucel-ucel to finger, fondle, cuddle.

uceng I a little freshwater fish;

mburu uceng, kélangan deleg *prov* to let trivialities distract one from the essentials.

II flower of the **mlinjo** tree, eaten as a vegetable.

III (*or* **uceng-uceng**) **1** oil-lamp wick; **2** firework fuse.

IV *reg* **1** head of a hamlet (**dhukuh**); **2** village official in charge of distributing irrigation water.

uci, uci-uci a skin disease characterised by pustules.

ucik, ngucik-ucik to demand (what was promised), claim one's rights.

ucir I, ngucir to take to one's heels.

II, ngucir to make a pigtail. *See also* **kucir**.

ucul 1 loose, astray; **2** to get loose;

nguculi 1 to unfasten, free; **2** to remove (clothing);

nguculaké to let s.t. go loose;

uculan wild, unencumbered;

ucul-uculan free, liberated, unencumbered.

ucus *reg* intestine(s). *See also* **usus**.

ucut I, ngucut to strip (leaves from harvested ears of rice). *See also* **uthut**.

II, ngucut to shuffle (cards);

ucutan 1 act or way of shuffling; **2** (of cards) shuffled.

uda I *ng*, *kr*, **lukar** *k.i.* naked (*var of* **wuda**);

ngudani 1 to undress s.o.; **2** *fig* to uncover s.o.'s secret.

II uda-uda at a guess, estimate.

III nguda-uda to moderate, reduce, lessen.

IV *lit* water.

udadi *lit* ocean.

udag, ngudag *or* **ngudag-udag** to chase, run after.

udaka *lit* water.

udakara *ng*, **udakawis** *kr*, approximately;

ngudakara to take a guess at;

pangudakara a guess.

udal, mudal to well up (water, from a spring);

udalan bubbling up, welling up.

udan *ng*, **jawah** *kr*, rain; to rain; - **awu** a rain of ash; - **barat** rain and gale;

- baya pépé, kethèk adus, macan dhédhé, wéwé rain with sunshine; - ès, woh, wuh hail; - sinemèni, suwèni the rush of heavy rain heard in the distance;

ngudani to rain (objects) on;

ngudanaké to fall or pour on from above;

udan-udanan to play in the rain;

ngudan-udanaké to put s.t. out in the rain to wash it;

kodanan to get rained on, caught in the rain.

udanagara social forms, manners, social sensibility.

udani *lit* to know, be aware;

ngudani to know, understand, be aware of s.t.

udara *lit* sky, the air.

udaraga multicoloured cloth sash.

udaraos *kr for* udarasa.

udarasa *ng*, udaraos *kr*, a guess, opinion;

ngudarasa to guess, form an opinion, think.

udarati *lit* ocean, sea.

udasmara *lit*, ngudasmara to think about, think over;

pangudasmara thought, idea, thinking.

udawiyah *var of* adangiyah, adawiyah.

udaya *lit* mountaintop.

udel *ng*, *kr*, nabi *k.i.* navel;

ora duwé udel 1 stupid, brainless; 2 tireless. *See also* wudel.

udhak, ngudhak to stir (with a spoon); ngudhak-udhak to keep stirring.

udhal, ngudhal-udhal 1 to open and spread around the contents of s.t., to unpack, unravel; 2 *fig* to reveal and spread (a secret).

udhang prawn (*reg var of* urang).

udhar *ng*, *kr*, lukar *k.i.* loose, loosened (hair);

ngudhari to loosen, unbind.

udheg, udheg-udheg sixth-generation ancestor or descendant.

udhek I *var of* udhak.

II *var of* uget.

udhel, udhel-udhel too short to use (handle). *See also* uthel.

udheng wrapped headdress (*kr for* iket).

udhet sash worn around the waist by women.

udhèt little freshwater eel (young of the welut).

udhi *reg* betting stakes; money contributed to a gambling pool (*var of* udhu).

udhik I upstream part of a river;

mudhik to go upriver;

ngudhikaké to take (a boat) upriver.

II, udhik-udhik to strew coins (for the poor, children to pick up).

udhil, ora - to be of little use, benefit.

udhip *reg* 1 to live; 2 life (*var of* urip).

udhis, ngudhis-udhis (of insects) to crawl into s.t. (hair, clothes).

udhu betting stakes, money contributed to a gambling pool;

ngudhoni *or* ngudhokaké to place a bet, make a contribution;

udhon accompanied by gambling. *Also* wudhu.

udhun descent;

mudhun 1 to descend; 2 to get off (vehicle);

ngudhuni to descend from, get off s.t.;

ngudhunaké to lower, cause to descend; to help s.o. descend;

udhunan a delivery, an unloading;

udhun-udhunan 1 things unloaded; 2 unloading place. *See also* medhun, tedhun.

udhung *reg* not yet.

udi, ngudi to exert o.s., strive;

pangudi exertion, effort.

udrasa *lit* maca - to weep.

udreg *repr* the stamp of feet;

udreg-udregan to grapple with each other, fight noisily.

udu *reg* not; s.t. other than. *See also* dudu.

udud *ng,* **ses** *kr* 1 s.t. to smoke; 2 to smoke;
    ngudud to smoke s.t.;
    udud-ududan to smoke just to past the time.

uduk fat(ty); **sega** - rice boiled in coconut milk. *See also* **wuduk**.

udun a boil;
    udunen to suffer from boils. *See also* **wudun**.

udung, ngudung resentful.

udur 1 a matter of contention; 2 argument;
    nguduraké to quarrel about;
    udur-uduran to quarrel with each other.

udyana *lit* garden, park.

uga *ng,* **ugi** *kr,* 1 also, too; either; 2 *confirmatory or emphatic function, e.g.* **bisa uga** that's quite possible; **saiki uga** right now, this very minute;
    sauga provided, on condition that.

ugag-ugeg *see* **ugeg**.

ugah *reg var of* **wegah**.

ugal, ugal-ugalan to behave in a cheeky way (*e.g.* naughty boys).

ugal-ugil, ngugal-ugilaké to pull to and fro, wrench.

ugat-uget *see* **uget**.

ugeg, ugag-ugeg to move or rock back and forth, without going forward;
    ngugeg-ugeg to move s.t. back and forth, shake s.t. to make it open.

ugel, ugel-ugel wrist.

ugem, ngugem to predict by astrological calculation;
    ngugemi to rely on, stand by, stick to;
    ugeman *or* **paugeman** handhold, mainstay.

ugeng *reg* to work assiduously (at).

uger 1 s.t. to which s.t. can be bound; 2 basis, basic rule; 3 **layang** - proces-verbal; 4 if, provided; 5 whenever, every time (*kr for* **angger** I);
    nguger to tie s.t. to (a post, stake);

    ngugeri 1 to regulate; 2 to take testimony in court;
    uger-uger pillar, post (to which s.t. is tied);
    ugeran 1 pertaining to court testimony; 2 (*or* **paugeran**) principles, constitution.

uget, uget-uget 1 wrigglers, mosquito larvae; 2 (*or* **ugat-uget**) to wriggle, squirm.

ugi also, too (*kr for* **uga**).

ugrag-ugreg *see* **ugreg**.

ugreg, ugreg-ugreg *or* **ugrag-ugreg** poorly fitting, hard to get in or out;
    ngugreg-ugreg *or* **ngugrag-ugreg** to move s.t. this way and that, *e.g.* in an effort to get it into the proper position, to fiddle, tinker with s.t.

ugung I, **ngugung** to spoil (a child);
    ugungan spoiled, overindulged;
    kogung to get spoiled or overindulged. II not yet (*reg var of* **durung**).

uhut, nguhuti *reg* to restrain.

uja, nguja 1 to spoil (a child); 2 to give in to; 3 let s.o. get away with s.t.;
    ujan spoiled person;
    ujan-ujanan 1 splurging (on o.s.); 2 indulging each other.

ujag, ujag-ujagan *reg* to gad about; dissolute.

ujana *lit* park, garden (*var of* **udyana**).

ujani money paid to a healer for treatment.

ujar 1 what s.o. says or advises; 2 (**punagi** *kr*) a pledge to do s.t. if one's hopes or wishes are granted;
    ngujar-ujari to abuse s.o., scold s.o. roundly;
    kojar *lit* related, told.

ujeg, ngujeg-ujeg to keep after s.o.; to keep asking for s.t.

ujer after all, for a fact (*var of* **jer**).

uji, nguji 1 to assay (gold); 2 to test;
    ujian test, examination.

ujiwat, ngujiwat to look cast a sidelong glance;

ngujiwati to cast a meaningful side-long glance at s.o.

ujub dedication of offerings (at a ritual meal, to the Prophet, saints, guardian spirits);
ngujubaké to dedicate offerings (as above).

ujubriya pride, sinful overestimation of o.s.

ujud form, shape (*var of* **wujud**);
ngujudi 1 to comprise, make up; **2** (*or* **ngujudaké**) to cause to materialise;
maujud to take (the) shape (of);
ujudé the fact of the matter is that...

ujug, ujug-ujug suddenly, unexpectedly.

ujung I peninsula.
II kissing of the knee of a respected older relative (performed on certain special occasions);
ngujungi to pay one's respects as above.
III *lit* tip of pointed weapon.
IV, ujungan mock duel with rattan canes.
V, ujungan leaf (*reg kr for* **godhong**).

ujur I lengthwise dimension;
mujur in a lengthwise position;
ngujuraké to put (lengthwise) in a certain direction or position;
ujur-ujuran alongside each other lengthwise.
II, ngujuri to share one's profits with s.o.;
ujuran a share of one's profits.

ujwala *lit* **1** beam, ray; **2** countenance;
ngujwala 1 surrounded by a halo; **2** radiant, beaming.

ukak *see* **ungkak**.

ukanten *subst kr for* **ukara**.

ukara *gram* sentence.

ukeb *reg var of* **ungkeb**.

ukèh much, many (*inf var of* **akèh**).

ukel 1 (in the shape of) a coil; **2** counting unit for thread, yarn, fibre; **3** depiction of tendrils in batik or carving; **4** ladies' hairstyle (*k.i. for* **gelung**); **- mayang** a curl-shaped gesture in the classical dance; **- pakis 1** a curl, ringlet (ladies' hair); **2** *var of* **ukel mayang**;
ngukel 1 to shape s.t. into a coil; **2** to coil or roll (of thread, rope *etc*);
ukelan 1 roll, coil; **2** in rolls;
ukel-ukel *or* **ukal-ukel** to keep coiling or curling.

ukih (*intsfr of* **akèh**) very much, many.

ukir, ngukir 1 to carve decoratively; **2** *fig* to be the father of;
ukiran 1 (*or* **ukir-ukiran**) carved design; **2** (**jejeran** *k.i.*) kris handle.

ukon a silver 50-cent coin during the colonial period.

ukub 1 scented by burning incense; **2** *reg var of* **ungkeb**;
ngukub to scent clothes (by laying them over an inverted basket under which incense resin is burned).

ukud, adhem ngukud freezing cold.

ukuk, ngukuk to laugh heartily. *See also* **ukung II**.

ukum 1 law, rule(s); **2** punishment, sentence;
ngukum to inflict a penalty;
ukuman punishment;
paukuman sentence, (judicial) punishment;
ukumullah divine retribution.

ukung I *repr* the cooing of a dove (**perkutut**). *See also* **kung II**.
II, ngukung to laugh heartily.

ukur, ngukur to measure;
ukuran 1 unit of measurement; **2** standard, criterion;
saukur what one would expect.

ula *ng*, **sawer** *kr*, snake; **- naga** dragon, serpent;
ngula snakelike;
ula-ula backbone, spinal column;
ulan-ulan snake-shaped;
ngulan-ulan long (of neck);

ula marani gebug (gitik) *prov* in the wrong place at the wrong time, always getting into trouble.

ulad flaring up;

mulad-mulad to burn up, blaze brightly.

ulah 1 way of conducting o.s. or handling s.t.; 2 to practise, strive for; 3 to cook (*var of* olah);

ngulah 1 to occupy s.o. with; 2 to practise, strive for (skill); 3 to prepare, put together.

ulam 1 meat; fish (*kr for* iwak); 2 side dish, foods eaten with rice (*kr for* lawuh).

ulama (*or* ngulama) 1 Islamic scholar, scholar of religion; 2 true dedicated Muslim.

ulan *see* ula.

ulandara, ngulandara to wander, roam, be a vagabond.

ulang I, ngulang to do over, repeat;

ulangan test, examination.

II ulang-ulang, ulangan to drift from place to place, in search of work.

ulap I *lit* fearful (unable to look s.o. in the eye);

ulap-ulap (of dance movement) to look into the distance shading the eyes with the hand. *See also* sulap II.

II, ngulapi to wipe off/away, remove (dirt).

ular, ular-ular I introduction, preparatory remarks;

ngular-ulari to introduce, lead off a discussion.

II sewing thread;

ngular-ulari to sew, mend.

ulas, ngulas to put a cover on s.t.

ulas-ulas s.t. done merely for the sake of appearances.

ulat 1 look, glance; 2 facial expression;

ngulati to look for;

ngulat-ulati to keep an eye on, look out for;

polatan facial expression. *See also* wulat.

uled 1 tough, hard to break or pierce; 2 *fig* not easily discouraged, determined (*also* wuled).

uleg *or* uleg-uleg wooden or stone tool used for grinding spices in a flat stone bowl;

nguleg to grind with the above tool;

ulegan ground-up finely.

ulek I, mulek 1 (of smoke, odour) to hang; 2 to eddy, whirl;

ulekan whirlpool.

II, ngulek-ulek 1 to keep handling or fussing with; 2 *fig* to keep picking on s.o.

ulem I (of voice or sound) deep, clear, resonant.

II ulem-ulem 1 formal (written) invitation to attend a celebration; 2 to send out such invitations;

ngulemi to invite s.o. to attend a celebration;

uleman invited guest.

uleng I ceiling of stacked beams in the roof of a pendhapa.

II to wrestle each other (fighting women);

nguleng 1 to wind the hair around the hand to drag an opponent down; 2 to wrestle;

uleng-ulengan 1 to mill around (crowd); 2 to spread roundabout (perfume, smoke); 3 to tussle, wrestle with each other; 4 indescribably, unbelievably pretty.

uler I caterpillar; - jaran, kambang, kèkèt, kilan various sorts of caterpillars;

nguler resembling a caterpillar; - kambang drifting with the current, not exerting o.s., taking it easy; - kèkèt (of moustaches) thick and bushy; - kilan (of horses) to gallop;

nguleri to deceive, worm one's way in little by little;

uler-uleran a toy caterpillar;
uler-uleren damaged by caterpillars (crops).
II a counting unit for bananas (*var of* **ler**).

ules 1 the colour of an animal's coat (horse, cat *etc*); **2** protective cloth; **3** winding sheet;
ngulesi to cover or wrap with a cloth.

ulet, ngulet to mix, knead together (ingredients, with water);
ulet-uletan to cling to each other;
ulet-uleten to suffer from stomach cramps.

uli, ngulèni 1 to mix, blend, knead together (by squeezing and pinching); **2** (*or* **nguli-uli**) to pinch between thumb and finger;
ulènan blending, act or way of blending;
ula-uli inseparable.

ulig I counting unit for certain round-shaped foods.
I, ngulig *or* **ngulig-ulig 1** to rub the hand over (as treatment); **2** to care for, prepare (fighting cock).

ulih *ng*, **antuk** *kr*, act of returning home;
ngulihi to go back to (s.o. one has left);
ngulihaké 1 to return s.o. to their home or place of origin; **2** to return (a borrowed item);
mulih 1 to go home; **2** to return to place of origin;
ngulih-ulihaké to try to persuade s.o. to go back;
ulih-ulihan back home together, back together (separated spouses).
II ulih-ulih a gift (of food) out of gratitude (for a service, loan, cure).
III *var of* **olèh**.

ulik 1 to pick, pry (*root form: var of* **uthik**); **2** (*or* **ngulik, nguliki** to pick lice from s.o.'s hair (*k.i. for* **pétan**).

uling I a certain large eel.

II shaky, having a strong roll (ship *etc*) (*var of* **oling**);
nguling to roll, pitch, swing.

ulir screw, corkscrew;
ngulir to turn (a screw, valve *etc*); **- budi** to use one's brain, find a way;
uliran 1 screwed on; **2** operated by a rotating knob, valve *etc*;
pangulir tool used for rotating knob *etc*.

uliya *var of* **oliya**.

ulon speaking or singing voice;
tekèk mati ing uloné *prov* doomed by one's own words.

ulu I 1 *lit* head; **2** leader, head; **- ati** heart; **-balang** commander, military head; **- bekti** *lit* gift to a powerful person, tribute; **-guntung** *lit* pupil, disciple;
ulu-ulu village official in charge of irrigation;
ulon-ulon head position (of s.o. who is lying down).
II, ngulu to swallow; **- idu** *fig* to have the mouth watering;
nguloni to swallow;
kolu 1 to get swallowed; **2** able to be swallowed; **3** to find it in one's heart to do s.t.

uluh, pring - a variety of bamboo (*var of* **wuluh I**).

uluk to salute s.o.; **- salam** to greet or welcome s.o.;
muluk 1 to ascend, rise high in the air (bird, kite); **2** (*or* **muluk-muluk**) high-flown; **3** unrealistically high, unattainable (objective);
nguluki to greet or welcome s.o.;
ngulukaké 1 to make/let fly; **2** to salute s.o. with a salvo;
uluk-uluk 1 to send up a salvo (of gunfire, fireworks); **2** the words of a messenger conveying a royal order to the Patih.

ulun *lit* **1** I, me; **2** servant, retainer;
mangulun *lit* to serve, be a subject of.

ulung I hawk, eagle (*var of* **wulung**).
 II 1 to be extended (two hands); **2** to suddenly arrive; **3** long drawn-out (sound); **4 mulung atiné** ready, inclined (to give, concur);
 ngulungi to give, hand over;
 ngulungaké 1 to give, hand over to; **2** to yield, submit;
 ulung-ulungan to exchange, give to each other;
 diulungaké endhasé, digondhèli buntuté *prov* given grudgingly or halfheartedly.
ulupis *var of* **holobis**.
ulur I to extend, get let out (*e.g.* rope);
 ngulur to extend;
 nguluri to provide, feed;
 nguluraké 1 to let out (rope *etc*); **2** to stretch (s.t. elastic); **3** to refer (a lawsuit) to a higher court.
 II, ngulur to plant seed in prepared holes in rows (*e.g.* peanuts);
 nguluri to plant (a field) thus;
 nguluraké to plant (seed) thus.
Uma name of a goddess (Siwa's spouse).
umad-umed *see* **umed**.
umah *var of* **omah**.
umak-umik *see* **umik**.
uman I ngumani to give out, dole out;
 komanan to be given (what others are given), get a share of s.t.
 II, uman-uman *or* **panguman-uman** a tongue-lashing;
 nguman-uman to speak harshly to, blame s.o.
umat group, community, religious community, followers.
umbag boastful.
umbah, ngumbah to wash, launder;
 umbah-umbah 1 to do the washing; **2** to have a menstrual period. *See also* **kumbah**.
umbak wave (*var of* **ombak**).
umbal 1 to hire transport; **2** to take a passage; **3** to work as a labourer;

umbalan 1 price paid for a passage; **2** wage paid for work.
umbang, umbangan *reg* boastful;
 ngumbang-umbangi to show one's dissatisfaction with s.o.
umbar, ngumbar to let loose, leave unattended; **- hawa** to indulge one's passions; **- kunca** to loosen or spread one's kain to facilitate walking; **- suku** to go where the feet take one; **- tangan** to pick pockets;
 umbaran (on the) loose;
 umbar-umbaran to do as one pleases, indulge o.s.
umbara, ngumbara to drift around, wander.
umbé *reg var of* **ombé**.
umbel *ng, kr,* **gadhing** *k.i.* nasal mucus.
umblug 1 foam, froth; **2** to boast about o.s.;
 ngumblug to foam, froth;
 ngumblugaké to boast about s.t., show s.t. off.
umbreng, ngumbreng 1 to make a buzzing or humming sound; **2** to swarm.
umbris *reg* a children's game played with fruit seeds. *See also* **cirak, jirak**.
umbruk 1 heap, pile; **2** a bet placed in the 'kitty';
 ngumbruk *or* **mumbruk** heaped, piled;
 ngumbrukaké to heap (things) up;
 umbrukan *or* **umbruk-umbrukan** *or* **saumbruk-umbruk** in heaps, in piles.
umbuk, umbuk-umbukan heaped, piled. *See also* **umbruk**.
umbul I 1 spring, source of a river; **2** a certain boys' game played by tossing cards in the air;
 ngumbulaké to raise, cause to ascend;
 mumbul to ascend, rise in the air;
 kombul 1 to get carried up in the air; **2** famous, well-known.
 II umbul-umbul Javanese-style flag (strip attached to pole), pennant.

umbut 1 edible rattan shoots; 2 palm pith.

umbyung, ngumbyungi to accompany, join in with.

umé *reg* to swim.

umeb *reg* (of water) to boil. *See also* umob.

umèb *lit* to overwhelm.

umed, umed-umed *or* umad-umed to mouth words, mumble, mutter;
  ngumed-umedaké to move (the mouth) shaping words as if speaking.

umek, umek-umek 1 (of people jabbering) loud, noisy; 2 (of water) sloshing.

umel, ngumel-umeli to scold, grumble at.

umèr soaking wet.

umes damp, moist.

umès *var of* umes.

umet, mumet (puyeng *kr*) 1 to feel headachy, dizzy; 2 *fig* to be bewildered;
  ngumetaké causing dizziness, headache, bewilderment;
  komet bewildered, muddled;
  umet-umetan to have bouts of dizziness.

umi mother.

umik (*pron as:* umi:k), umik-umik *or* umak-umik to form soundless words.

umil *var of* umik.

umis *lit* to flow.

umob boiling (vigorously);
  ngumobaké to cause to boil, bring to a boil.

umok to rise, be at flood level (river).

umor to have a lot of saliva and a feeling of being about to vomit;
  ngumor-umori to cause a feeling of nausea, nauseating.

umos porous (waterpot).

umpah, ngumpah-umpah to speak harshly to.

umpak socle, stone block used as base of a pillar;

umpak-umpak 1 edge of a batik pattern; 2 words of praise introducing a letter; 3 passage at the end of a gamelan melody before going back to the start;
  ngumpak to praise to the sky, flatter;
  ngumpaki to provide with a socle;
  pangumpak-umpak praise, flattery.

umpal I a fishnet float.

II, ngumpal foaming, white-topped (waves);
  mumpal-mumpal turbulent, leaping up (waves).

umpama *see* upama.

umpan bait.

umpang *reg* more than the usual weight.

umpeg, umpeg-umpeg short and fat.

umpel, ngumpel to stick together, form lumps;
  mumpel stuck together in lumps;
  umpel-umpelan jam-packed, tightly pressed together.

umpeng narrow water channel.

umpet, ngumpet *or* umpetan to hide, take cover;
  ngumpetaké to hide s.t.

um-ping-sut a method of choosing who goes first in a game (like 'eeny-meeny, miny-mo').

umplèh *var of* omplèh.

umpleng small oil lamp (*var of* umpling I).

umpling I small oil lamp.

II cone-shaped salty rice cake wrapped in coconut leaf.

III tube-shaped opium container.

umpluk foam, froth;
  mumpluk to foam, froth;
  ngumplukaké to make suds from/with.

umplung cuspidor, spittoon.

umpon fish trap consisting of a small diversion from a river (*var of* rumpon).

umprik to rise (of river level). *See also* umrik.

umpruk *var of* umbruk.

umpuk, ngumpuk-umpuk to pile;

> umpuk-umpukan (to heap) in an untidy pile.

umrang to make a din, great noise.

umreg noisy, bustling, crowded.

umreng *var of* umrang.

umres *var of* ubres.

umrik to rise (of river level) (*var of* umprik).

umuk to boast about o.s. or one's possessions;

> ngumuki to boast about o.s. to s.o.;
>
> ngumukaké to boast about s.t.;
>
> umuk-umukan 1 boasting; 2 to boast to each other, engage in one-upmanship.

umum 1 common; 2 public; 3 the public, the people;

> ngumumi to join in with the others, do like the general run;
>
> ngumumaké to make public; to popularise;
>
> umumé usually, commonly, generally.

umun, umun-umun *intsfr* very early in the morning.

umung *var of* umyung.

umur *ng, kr,* yuswa *k.i.,* 1 (years of) age; 2 life span; 3 to be aged (a number of years); 4 length of time; 5 wis - to be of age, adult;

> umur-umuran 1 approximate age; 2 comparative age;
>
> saumuring jagung 'of the age of maize', a very short time (about three months).

umus *var of* umos.

umyang *var of* umyung.

umyek noisy, bustling.

umyeng *var of* umyung.

umyung loud, tumultuous (great multitude).

umyus *lit* to rustle.

un a measure of opium weight.

una-uni *see* uni.

unakara approximately (*var of* udakara).

unakawis *kr for* unakara.

unandika, ngunandika to say or talk to o.s., to think out loud;

> pangunandika what one says to o.s.

unang *var of* onang.

unangkara *var of* udakara.

unangkawis *kr for* unangkara.

unar *var of* onar.

uncal long narrow sash worn as part of a classical dancer's costume, the end of which is tossed with the hand;

> nguncali to throw at;
>
> nguncalaké to throw s.t;
>
> uncal-uncalan to toss back and forth, throw to each other.

uncang, nguncang *or* manguncang *lit* to fling away;

> panguncang act of flinging away; dadi - getting further and further away.

uncar, muncar 1 to spout, spray into the air (water); 2 to flare up (lamp), shine.

uncé *var of* oncé I.

unceg piercing tool, awl, small drill;

> ngunceg *or* nguncegi to make hole(s) with such an implement.

uncek *see* unceg.

uncel, nguncel *reg* to continue obstinately.

uncet point of a rice cone (tumpeng).

uncis, nguncis pale and emaciated.

uncit, nguncit-uncit to chase s.t./s.o.;

> uncit-uncitan to chase each other.

unclang *var of* onclang.

unclug, ngunclug to walk with quick short steps and downcast eyes.

uncrat, muncrat to splash;

> nguncrati to splash onto, spatter.

uncul, muncul to emerge, appear, turn up;

> ngunculaké 1 to bring to the fore; 2 to bring forward to show to the public.

uncung a peacock chick (young of the merak).

uncuwé pipe for smoking tobacco (*var of* **huncuwé**).

uncuwi *var of* **uncuwé**.

undang *ng*, *kr*, **timbal** *k.i.*, **atur** *k.a.*, **ngundang** 1 to call; 2 to call by name, title; 3 *reg* to invite;

ngundangi 1 to call out s.t.; 2 to summon, call for;

ngundangaké to summon on behalf of s.o.;

undang-undang to keep calling;

kondangan to be invited to attend a ceremony;

undangan *or* **undang-undangan** what s.o. is called.

under, **ngunderi** to encircle;

underan *or* **under-underan** 1 the head of a pimple; 2 the core of s.t.; 3 a circle as middle point of s.t.

undha I, **ngundha** 1 to let fly (bird, kite); 2 to fling in the air (weapon).

II undha-usuk nearly the same, differing little.

undhag, **undhag-undhag** skilled, expert.

undhagi 1 carpenter, woodworker; 2 skilled;

(un)dhagèn the street of the carpenters.

undhak I *ng*, **indhak** *kr*, a rise, an increase;

ngundhaki to increase s.t.;

ngundhakaké 1 to raise s.t.; 2 to promote, advance s.t.;

mundhak 1 to increase, become greater; 2 to rise a rank; 3 otherwise, or else, lest (after warning, prohibition);

undhakan a supplement, an increase;

undhak-undhakan 1 increasing, raising (price, salary *etc*); 2 stairs, stairway; 3 terracing (fields); 4 road edge, shoulder;

kaundhakan 1 to be surpassed; 2 to get overcharged.

II undhakan *lit* horse.

undhamana, **ngundhamana** to reprove, reproach, upbraid.

undhang, **ngundhangi** to issue official information or orders to;

ngundhangaké to order, proclaim;

undhang-undhang regulation, law.

undhat, **ngundhat-undhat** to bring up past mistakes, engage in recriminations.

undher, **ngundher** to remain in the same place, stay put, not go out;

ngundheri to stay around for a purpose.

undhi I, **ngundhi** to decide by lot.

II, **undha-undhi** almost the same, not much different (size, length).

undhig *reg* skilled (in), expert (at).

undhil, **ora ngundhili** to be of no avail, accomplish nothing.

undhuh, **ngundhuh** 1 to convey the bride and groom to the groom's home for a second wedding celebration; **-mantu** to have or acquire a son- or daughter-in-law; 2 (*or* **ngundhuhi**) to pick (fruits *etc*);

ngundhuhaké to pick for s.o.;

undhuhan 1 fruits picked; 2 second wedding celebration;

undhuh-undhuhan act or way of picking.

undhuk the shadow cast by s.t.;

mundhuk-mundhuk to approach bowing low (humbly);

ngundhuk-undhuki to approach s.t. slowly, bowed low;

kundhukan to be in the shadow of s.t.

undhung, **mundhung** *or* **mundhung-mundhung** to exist in abundance;

ngundhung-undhung to amass in abundance, pile up.

undur a backward motion, withdrawal;

undur-undur 1 a certain insect that walks backwards; 2 a type of drill;

ngundur 1 to postpone; 2 to demote, discharge;

ngunduri to back into or away from;
- tuwa to grow old;

ngunduraké 1 to cause to go backwards; 2 to postpone s.t.;

mundur to move backwards, retreat;

kunduran 1 to get backed into by accident; 2 mati - to die in childbirth;

kondur *k.i.* to return home.

uneg (*also* unek), nauseous, queasy;

muneg-muneg on the point of vomiting;

uneg-uneg embittered, bearing a grudge;

nguneg-unegi 1 to cause a feeling of nausea; 2 revolting, nauseating;

panguneg-uneg s.t. that makes one feel annoyed, a cause of ill feeling.

unem spice container.

uneng *var of* oneng.

ungak, ungak-ungak to be on the lookout;

ngungak to look at with craned neck;

ngungak-ungaki to go and look out for s.t., try to see s.t. (in the distance).

ungal I *var of* ungel.

II, mungal protruding (*esp* the chest);

ngungalaké to thrust forward (the chest).

III, mungal to turn up the flame in an oil lamp;

ngungalaké to brighten (an oil lamp).

ungap I *lit* hesitant, doubtful.

II, ngungapi to look out for s.t.;

ngungap-ungapi to go and have a look, check how things are going.

III ungapan estuary, rivermouth (*var of* sungapan).

ungar, ngungari *reg* 1 to start working; 2 to begin s.t.;

ungaran 1 for the first time; 2 fresh, still new.

ungas, ngungasaké to show s.t. off, pride o.s. on;

ngungas-ungas to sniff up, smell;

kongas 1 fragrant; 2 renowned.

ungel sound, noise; what s.o./s.t. says (*kr for* uni).

unggab, ngunggapi to uncover, open. *See also* ungkab.

unggah *ng*, inggah *kr*, a rise;

ngunggahi 1 to climb (on); 2 to top, exceed;

ngunggahaké 1 to bring up higher; 2 to bring in (harvest); 3 to promote; 4 to notify (marriage);

munggah 1 to rise, ascend; 2 to rise in rank; - kaji 1 to make the pilgrimage to Mecca; 2 to go to the pengulu to get married; - papahan to marry the older sister of one's divorced or deceased wife;

unggah-unggahan 1 ascending, going up; 2 promotion time at the end of a school year; 3 bringing up, storing away (harvest); 4 a ritual meal before the beginning of the Fasting Month;

ngunggah-unggahi (of girls) to visit (a man) to propose marriage. *See also* punggah.

unggal *ng*, unggil *reg kr*, every; - dina every day.

unggar, ngunggar 1 to loosen; 2 to release, give vent to.

unggeb, ngunggeb *reg* to store (foods) in covered containers. *See also* ungkeb.

unggon *lit* place. *See also* enggon I.

ungguh manners; - tatakrama etiquette;

mungguh appropriate, fitting;

unggah-ungguh manners, etiquette; - basa the social styles of Javanese speech used according to the social relationships among the speakers, speech level;

ngunggah-ungguhaké to treat s.o. with the proper forms (speech).

unggul superior, outstanding;

ngungguli to exceed;

ngunggulaké to raise, elevate:

munggul superior, outstanding;

kaunggulan supremacy, eminence;

unggulan s.o. or s.t. considered superior;

ngunggul-unggulaké 1 to raise, elevate; **2** to consider superior or exalted;

unggul-unggulan to compete for supremacy.

unggwan *lit* place. *See also* **enggon I**.

unggyan *var of* **unggwan**.

ungik, ungak-ungik to hesitate, waver.

ungkab, ngungkabi 1 (*or* **ungkab-ungkab**) to uncover, open; **2** to show s.t. off, display one's ability;

mungkab gaping wide open.

ungkad, ngungkad 1 to scoop up and turn over; **2** to arouse s.o.'s emotions, incite;

mungkad to lose one's temper;

ungkad-ungkad to open up old sore points;

ungkad-ungkadan *reg* mud lifted from a ditch.

ungkag-ungkeg *see* **ungkeg**.

ungkak, ngungkak to disregard; **- krama** to omit the usual polite forms, not stand on ceremony.

ungkal I, ngungkal to whet, sharpen (knife, on stone). *See also* **wungkal**.

II, ngungkal to lift, shift (heavy object).

ungkang *var of* **ongkang**.

ungkara *lit* prayer.

ungkeb, ngungkebi to cook or store (foods) in covered containers;

ungkeb-ungkeb to cover o.s. with a blanket.

ungkeg, ungkeg-ungkeg *or* **ungkag-ungkeg** a back-and-forth motion in the same spot;

ngungkeg-ungkeg *or* **ungkag-ungkeg** to work s.t. back and forth to dislodge it (*e.g.* stake, nail).

ungker I butterfly cocoon (contents eaten as a delicacy).

II spool of thread.

ungkih, ngungkih 1 to push s.t. aside; **2** to move toward s.t.;

kungkih *or* **kongkih** to pushed from one's place.

ungkil, ngungkil to try to lift, lever up (s.t. heavy, using crowbar).

ungking *reg* to wrestle.

ungkir, ngungkiri to refuse to acknowledge s.t.;

mungkir to deny, disavow.

ungkluk, ngungkluk to walk with a preoccupied air.

ungkrag-ungkreg *see* **ungkreg**.

ungkrah, ngungkrah-ungkrah to disarrange, put into disorder.

ungkred, ngungkred to shrink or decrease s.t.;

mungkred to shrink.

ungkreg, ungkrag-ungkreg to move with difficulty, be in a tight spot;

ngungkrag-ungkreg to move s.t. back and forth. *See also* **ungkeg**.

ungkrik, ngungkrik-ungkrik *reg* to pick at, tamper with s.t.

ungkrug, ngungkrug-ungkrug *reg* to throw up (soil), to put up (barricades).

ungkruk, ngungkruk to sit with bowed head and shoulders.

ungkul, ngungkuli to exceed, surpass;

ngungkulaké to exceed, surpass;

kungkulan exceeded, surpassed.

ungkung odds-on favourite, front runner.

ungkur, ngungkuri 1 to turn one's back on; **2** to have s.t. at one's back or behind one;

ngungkuraké 1 to put s.t. behind; **2** to leave behind, say farewell to;

ungkur-ungkuran 1 to turn their backs on each other; **2** to part and go in opposite directions;

saungkuré after (his) departure, death.

ungrum, ngungrum to address sweetly, court (woman);

pangungrum sweet words. *See also* **rungrum**.

ungseb, ngungseb-ungsebaké to press one's face to the ground;
  kongseb to fall face down.

ungsed, ngungsed 1 to push hard, shove up (in some direction); **2** to persist, press (with questions, demands).

ungsel *var of* **usel**.

ungseng I a fibre brush used for washing dishes.
  II, mungseng to search everywhere.
  III, ungseng-ungseng grease in a fry-ing-pan.

ungser, ngungseraké to spin or twirl s.t.

ungsi, ngungsi 1 to flee; **2** to move away, go s.w. else (out of necessity);
  ngungsèni to flee to;
  ngungsèkaké to remove s.o. from (a threatened area);
  pangungsi a refugee;
  pangungsèn a place of refuge.

ungsil *var of* **usil**.

ungsir *var of* **usir**.

ungsum season *var of* **usum**.

ungup, ngungupaké to reveal just a little of s.t.;
  ungup-ungup to peek, peep;
  mungup to show a little, begin to appear;
  mungup-mungup to peek, peep.

uni I, *ng,* **ungel** *kr,* **1** sound, noise; **2** what s.o. says; **3** content of a letter;
  ngunèkaké 1 to cause s.t. to produce sound; **2** to say or read aloud;
  ngunèk-ngunèkaké to complain loud-ly about, scold s.o.;
  muni 1 to make a sound; **2** to say;
  muni-muni to keep on complaining angrily;
  muna-muni to say over and over;
  unèn-unèn 1 a saying; **2** what s.o. or s.t. says;
  sauni-uniné 1 whatever one says; **2** whatever one feels like babbling.
  II *or* **nguni** *lit* formerly, former time;
  wingi - , *see* **wingi**.

III a certain tree, also the tart fruits that grow in clusters on this tree (*var of* **wuni**).

uning *var of* **uninga**.

uninga (*k.i. of* **weruh**) to know, under-stand;
  nguningani *lit* to be informed about;
  nguningakaké *lit* to inform;
  kauningan *lit* it is known that;
  kauningana *lit* may you be advised that.
  Also **wuninga**.

uniwèh, nguniwèh *lit* and also, especial-ly, in the first place.

unjal, ngunjal 1 to gather materials for a nest (birds); **2 - ambekan** to draw a deep breath.

unjar, ngunjar to let loose, let go free;
  unjaran unshackled (prisoner).

unjel, ngunjel-unjel to jostle, elbow, shove;
  unjel-unjelan jostling each other (crowd).

unjem, konjem siti *lit* to press the head to the ground in respect.

unjlug, ngunjlug to walk on steadily without looking around.

unjug *var of* **unjlug**.

unjuk I *k.a.* what s.o. says (to an exalted person);
  ngunjuki uninga to inform;
  ngunjukaké to offer respectfully;
  munjuk to tell, say, inform (*k.a. for* **kandha**);
  konjuk 1 intended for, submitted to; **2** in the name of (in prayer).
  II to drink (*root form: k.i. for* **ombé**);
  ngunjuk to drink (*k.i. for* **ngombé**);
  ngunjuki to give s.o. a drink.
  III, ngunjukaké to hitch, pull up a bit;
  munjuk to move up higher.

unjung I, ngunjungaké to pile (things) up;
  munjung-munjung heaped up high, overflowing (measure).

II **unjungan** leaf (*reg kr for* **godhong**).

unon 1 remaining as before; **2** regularly irrigated (throughout the year).

unta camel.

untab emerging together (*e.g.* army);
muntab 1 to come pouring out; **2** to lose one's temper.

untal, nguntal *or* **nguntali 1** to swallow whole; **2** *cr* to eat, gobble;
kuntal to get swallowed.

untap, nguntapaké 1 to see off or escort (a departing person); **2** *lit* to kill;
untap-untapan 1 to walk in behind at equal intervals; **2** (to be or do) almost the same, almost simultaneous(ly).

untar pimple, boil (*k.i. for* **wudun**).

untara I *reg ng*, **untawis** *kr*, **1** between, among; **2** approximately (*var of* **antara, watara**);
sauntara some amount or interval of time; quite a while.
II, nguntarani to indicate, show signs of. *See also* **ketara**.
III *lit* **1** north; **2** left (as opposed to right).

untas *reg* (of sounds) loud and clear, to carry far.

untawis *kr for* **untara**.

untek, muntek *or* **untek-untekan** (of insects in a swarm) forming a bunch.

untel, nguntel-untel to rumple, crumple into a ball (clothing, paper *etc*);
muntel 1 to lie rolled up together; **2** to not go out at all; **3** to keep on lying asleep;
untel-untelan rolled up together (*e.g.* asleep).

unthal, unthal-unthalan naughty, mischievous.

unthel, ngunthel-unthel to wind the hair up loosely (not in a tight bun).

unther 1 a curl, tendril (in decorative art); **2** *var of* **undher**.

unthet, ngunthet to withhold;
ngunthetaké 1 to hold s.t. back (so that s.o. else goes short); **2** to not pay the full amount; **3** to not tell the whole story.

unthig *reg* skilful, dextrous.

unthil *reg* bunch, bundle. *See also* **until**.

unthit, ngunthit to tail, shadow, follow s.o.;
ngunthitan to have a tendency to follow (*e.g.* little child its mother).

unthug, ngunthug to walk hurriedly with bowed head.

unthuk 1 a little pile of earth; **2** foam, froth; - **cacing 1** worm castings; **2** a type of pastry made from long thin strips of dough; - **semut** anthill;
ngunthuk mound-shaped;
ngunthuk-unthuk to heap s.t. into a mound;
munthuk foamy, frothy;
unthukan *or* **unthuk-unthukan** mounds.

unthul I an animal serving to encourage others of its kind to fight (only quail and crickets);
ngunthul 1 to be a hanger-on; **2** to follow along after s.o. (*e.g.* a child walking behind its mother);
ngunthuli to use (a cricket, bird) to goad contestants (as above).
II *reg* small two-wheeled cart for transporting freight.

until bunch, bundle (*var of* **unthil, unting**).

unting a bunch (measure of bundled vegetables);
nguntingi to bundle (plants) in bunches;
untingan (tied) in bunches.

untir, untir-untir a snack made from sticky rice flour, twisted and fried;
nguntir to hold s.t. firmly and twist it;
untiran 1 twisting; **2** s.t. twisted. *See also* **puntir**.

untu 1 (**waos** *kr*, **waja** *k.i.*) tooth; **2** cog, serration; **3** rung of ladder; - **gelap 1**

thunderbolt; **2** prehistoric stone implement; - **walang** object in the shape of grasshopper teeth, zigzag; **nguntu** resembling a tooth or cog; **nguntoni** to equip with gears or cogs.

untul young sugar-palm leaf.

untung 1 profit; **2** lucky, by good luck; **nguntungi** *or* **nguntungaké** to be of benefit to; **kauntungan** profit, gain; **untung-untungan** to take a chance, try one's luck.

untup, nguntupaké 1 to let (a little of s.t.) show; **2** to let out a hint of what one is thinking; **muntup-muntup** to peep out, show a little.

untut, nguntuti to eat bit by bit from the open hand (*e.g.* loose grains).

unu, ngunu *reg* to regulate the flow of (irrigation water).

unul, ngunul to walk on quickly, run away.

unur *reg* a rounded mound (*esp* anthill).

unus 1 shape, form (kris blades); **2** *lit* character as seen from facial expression; **ngunus** to unsheathe, draw (a weapon) from its sheath; **unusan** unsheathed weapon.

unwakin *reg* opium den.

unya *lit* sound, voice; **munya** to emit sounds. *See also* **uni I**.

unyag-unyug *see* **unyug**.

unyal, unyal-unyalan fidgety, unable to sit still.

unyar *reg* a small bundle, bunch (as much as can be spanned by thumb and middle finger); **ngunyari** to bind (plants) in bundles.

unyel *var of* **uyel**.

unyeng, munyeng to spin, rotate; **unyeng-unyeng** *ng, kr,* **panengeran** *k.i.* **1** crown of the head; **2** the point on the crown of the head from which the hair growth radiates outward; **3** whorl in an animal's coat (*esp* horse).

unyer, munyer to spin, rotate; **ngunyer-unyer** to keep recurring in the same spot; **ngunyer-unyeraké** to rotate s.t. on its axis.

unyet, ngunyet-unyet to squeeze, crush.

unyik, dadi - to be the loser, the last one (in Javanese card games); **unyikan** to come in last, to get the booby prize.

unyleng *reg* very tasty, delicious.

unyling *var of* **unyleng**.

unyug, unyug-unyug *or* **unyag-unyug** (to walk) in a brash and inconsiderate way; **munyug-munyug** *or* **munyag-munyug** to barge in, to sneak in unannounced.

unyuk *var of* **unyug**.

unyur, ngunyur *or* **unyar-unyur** to go through/in/out without permission.

upa cooked rice grain; **ana dina ana upa** *prov* let tomorrow take care of itself; **ngupa 1** to glue s.t. with cooked rice grains; **2** to eat only white rice (as a form of abstinence); **ngupa-upa 1** to sponge, be a free-loader; **2** to 'tighten the belt', make do with less.

upaboga, ngupaboga to earn one's daily bread, make a living; **pangupaboga** work by which one earns one's living.

upacanten *subst kr for* **upacara**.

upacara 1 insignia pertaining to a high official; **2** formal ceremony; - **kaprabon** regalia (carried in procession); **ngupacarani** to receive or greet s.o. formally.

upacawis *subst kr for* **upacara**.

upadamel *kr for* **upagawé**.

upados *var of* **pados**, *kr for* **golek**, **ngupadosi** to search for.

upadrawa *lit* disaster, calamity;
  ngupadrawa to afflict, inflict a disaster.

upagawé *ng*, **upadamel** *kr*, to take charge of, care for.

upah *var of* **opah**.

upajiwa livelihood, means of support;
  ngupajiwa to earn one's living;
  pangupajiwa livelihood.

upakara 1 fine ornaments; 2 a good deed;
  ngupakara 1 to adorn; 2 to see to, take charge of; 3 to tend, take good care of;
  pangupakara 1 care, maintenance; 2 preparation of a body for burial.

upakarti *lit* things prepared for a ceremony or a special purpose.

upakarya *lit, var of* **upakara**.

upakat *var of* **mupakat**.

upakawis *subst kr for* **upakara**.

upaksama *lit, var of* **aksama**.

upaksi *lit, var of* **uninga**, **priksa**.

upama *ng*, **upami** *kr*, 1 (*or* **sandi-upama**) allegory, symbolic expression; 2 example (for clarification); 3 comparison;
  upamané 1 if, supposing that; 2 for example; **tanpa upama** beyond compare, unequalled;
  ngupamakaké to liken.

upaos *kr for* **upata**.

upapanji in Javanese script, the removal of the mute *e* (**pepet**) by the use of a **pasangan**, so that *e.g.* **pedang** becomes **pdang**.

uparengga *lit* decorations, ornamentation;
  nguparengga to decorate;
  panguparengga act of decorating.

upas I 1 orderly, messenger; - **pos** postman; 2 policeman.
  II 1 poison; 2 poisonous;
  ngupasi to poison s.o.

upasadana *lit* honour, respect, esteem.

upasama *var of* **upasanta**.

upasanta *lit* patient and helpful.

upasraya *lit* aid, help.

upasuba *lit* festive reception, pomp and ceremony.

upat I, **upat-upat** a whipcord.
  II to swear (never to do s.t. again).

upata *var of* **supata**.

upawasa *lit* to fast.

upaya trick, scheme;
  ngupaya 1 to try to find a way to do s.t.; 2 to seek, look for.

upéksa *var of* **upiksa**.

upèksi *var of* **upiksa**.

upekti *var of* **upeti**.

upet a taper (material used for lighting s.t.).

upeti tribute, tax on production (paid to king).

upetya *lit, var of* **upeti**.

upih leaf sheath of the **pinang** (areca) tree.

upiksa *lit* 1 to know, understand; 2 to see.

upil 1 dry snot; 2 dry scab; 3 soot that collects on the wick of an oil lamp;
  ngupil to dry and form a crust;
  ngupili to pick off little bits (*e.g.* snot, scab, kernels from cob).

uplik I small kerosene lamp consisting of a wick in a container of oil.
  II, **nguplik** (of the lips) small and cute.
  III, **nguplik** to stand in a precarious position;
  nguplik-uplik to teeter on the edge, about to fall.

uprek *var of* **upyek**.

upret I, **ngupret** 1 tight (clothing); 2 very short (hair).
  II, **ngupret** *or* **ngupret-upret** to chase, pursue everywhere.

upruk *reg* prostitute, whore.

upsinder supervisor of plantations, schools *etc.*

upsir *var of* **opsir**.

uput, **uput-uput** very early in the morning.

upyek, **upyek-upyekan** to be in uproar,

chattering noisily, making a fuss (*e.g.* about some unusual event).

ura I 1 lying spread out; **2** to fly away, flee in all directions; **3** to break up, come to nothing (*e.g.* discussions); **uran** *reg* loose, come apart.

II, ura-ura to sing for one's own pleasure;

nguran-urani *or* **ngurak-urakaké** to sing to/for s.o.;

uran-uran song(s) sung for pleasure, relaxation.

urab 1 a miscellaneous mixture; **2** a mixture of vegetables; **- sari** a mixture of various kinds of flowers;

ngurab to mix (a variety of things);

urab-uraban cangkemé to abuse obscenely.

urah, urahan noisy, loud, boisterous (*var of* **wurah**).

urag, ngurag (of animals) very old; **mati - to** die of old age.

urak I duty list, roster (for sentry, contained in a tube and handed to the next in turn); **ketiban -** to get one's turn (to go and do s.t.);

pangurakan the northern part of the palace square, where the lists were handed over.

II, ngurak-urak to drive away, evict with angry words.

III (wong) urakan common people, humble folk.

urang shrimp; **- ayu** a certain style of earring; **- watang** a certain crab;

urang-urang the black of the eyes.

urat I 1 blood vessel; **2** muscle; **4** flesh, tissue; **5** leaf vein; **- sarap** nerve.

II genitals (male or female).

III waybread, plantain.

urdah *var of* **hurdah**.

urdenas an orderly.

urdi 1 order; **2** permission.

uré *var of* **oré**.

ureg *var of* **oreg**.

urek s.t. for poking with; **- kuping** earpick;

ngurek-urek to scribble;

ngurek-ureki 1 to poke the finger around in a hole; **2** to scratch, dig a hole in the ground (insects);

urek-urekan scribble.

urèn black mynah bird.

ureng I, ngureng to be deep, eaten away (sore, wound);

ngurengi to burn away stumps (after clearing);

mureng 1 to smoulder under the ash (fire); **2** *fig* to be resentful.

II ureng-ureng a grub in mangoes.

ures, ures-ures *reg* thief.

urèt I a big grub, beetle larva.

II *var of* **urèn**.

uri, nguri-uri to observe, keep up, maintain.

urik I to cheat, to (do) unfairly;

nguriki to cheat s.o. in a game;

urik-urikan to play unfairly.

II, urik-urik scribbling;

ngurik-urik to scribble. *See also* **urek**.

uring, nguring-uring to be angry and grumble at s.o.;

muring-muring grumpy, displeased, in a bad mood;

uring-uringan *or* **uring-uringen** to suffer from bad moods.

urip *ng*, **gesang** *kr*, **1** life; **2** to live, be alive;

nguripi 1 to provide (the essentials of) life to/for; **2** to grant s.o. their life;

nguripaké 1 to restore the life or health of; **2** to enliven, make lively;

uripan to live or grow easily;

urip-urip a dish prepared from **lélé** fish;

urip-uripan barely alive;

panguripan a living, a livelihood;

koripan *lit* life, existence;

ngurip-urip (**nggegesang** *kr*) to nurture, encourage.

uris, nguris emaciated, wasted, in poor shape.

urit, ngurit *or* **nguriti** to plant rice still on the stalk (not loose grains) in a nursery bed;
uritan 1 rice seedling ready for transplanting; **2** ovary, eggs still in the ovary; **3** embryo.

urmat 1 (to show) respect; **2** a military salute; **3** to salute; **kanthi** - honourable (discharge);
ngurmati to honour, pay homage to;
kaurmatan honour, respect, esteem;
pangurmatan way of esteeming. *See also* **kurmat**

urub I flash, flare, flame;
ngurubaké 1 to ignite, cause to burn; **2** to stir up (a fire) to make it burn brightly;
murub 1 to burn, flare up; **2** *fig* to get angry, flare up;
korub to get kindled/ignited;
urub-urub kindling material.
II, ngurubi to cover with a cloth.

urud, murud 1 *lit* to depart; **2** to pass away;
ngurud to grow less (fire);
ngurud-urudi to diminish;
korud *lit* **1** emaciated; **2** - **kamané** to have an involuntary ejaculation of semen.

urug *or* **urug-urug** earth used for levelling or filling;
ngurug to fill in with earth;
ngurugi to cover with earth;
kurugan to get buried or covered with earth by accident;
urugan filled with sand, soil; mound.

uruh dirty foam in river or ditch water;
nguruh *or* **muruh** foamy, frothy, sudsy;
uruh-uruh *or* **uruh-uruhan** dirty matter floating on the surface of water, *esp* after rainfall.

uruk *var of* **wuruk III**.

urun, urun-urun to make a contribution in kind toward the costs of a celebration;
nguruni to contribute to;
ngurunaké to contribute s.t.;
urunan 1 amount contributed; **2** to contribute to an organisation.

urung I 1 pillow case; **2** drum frame over which skins are stretched.
II bamboo pipe for smoking opium.
III not yet (*reg var of* **durung**).
IV, urung-urung covered channel, culvert, pipe.
V, ngurung-urung to escort s.o. by walking on either side.

urup I, ngurupi to swap for (s.t. else), to barter;
ngurupaké to swap;
urup-urup *or* **urup-urupan** (the practice of) barter;
kurup, ora - not worth the trouble.
II (Arabic) letter, character.

urus I, ngurus *or* **ngurusi** to handle, take care of;
ngurusaké to handle an affair on behalf of s.o.;
keurus to get attended to;
urusan affair, matter;
ora urus improper.
II, murus to have diarrhoea;
ngurus-urusi to dose o.s. with castor oil;
urus-urus 1 laxative; **2** to take a laxative.

urut 1 along; **2** in sequence; - **kacang 1** single file; **2** alternating;
ngurut 1 to go through or trace in sequence; **2** to massage with soft pressure;
ngurutaké to arrange (tell) in order;
urutan in sequence; (as) a series;
urut-urutan in sequence, serial(ly), lined up;
sauruté along (the length of).

us *excl of dismay*.

usada *lit* medicine, remedy.

usah, ora - no need to, not necessary (*var of* **susah II**).

usak-usek *see* **usek I**.

usan *reg* to take a break.

usana *lit* end, finally (*var of* **wusana**).

usap *or* **usap-usap** s.t. used for wiping;
- **tangan** handkerchief;
ngusap *or* **ngusapi** to wipe s.t.;
ngusapaké to rub s.t. over.

usar s.t. spread as a coating;
ngusar to coat (with), to spread thinly;
ngusaraké *or* **ngusar-usaraké** to coat (s.t.) with.

usara *lit* dew.

usé *var of* **husé**.

useb *var of* **ungseb**.

useg *see* **usek I**.

usek I (*or* **usek-usek** *or* **usak-usek**) to move restlessly.
II ngusek-usek to keep rubbing;
ngusek-usekaké 1 to rub out (embers of fire); **2** to rub out (with eraser).

usel, ngusel-usel to snuggle up to;
ngusel-uselaké to press s.t. (against s.o.) in a cosy way.

useng I *intsfr* black, jet black.
II *var of* **osèng I**.

user, nguser-useraké to rub s.t. (into), massage with, round and round;
muser to spin, rotate.

usèt, usèt-usèt *repr* surprising, astonishing.

usik whetstone, polisher;
ngusik to polish, scour, smoothe (stone, floor).

usil restless, fidgety (rather than composed and quiet);
ngusil-usil to touch or handle or move things constantly in a nervous, fidgety way.

usim *reg* season (*var of* **usum**).

using *reg* **1** no!; **basa** - the language of Banyuwangi.

usir, ngusir to drive away, chase off.

usreg restless, fidgety;
usreg-usregan restless (situation);
ngusregaké fidgeting, squirming.

usu *var of* **wusu**.

usug, ngusug 1 to apply liniment after having massage; **2** to pick up scattered rice grains by placing a cloth over them.

usuk rafter, roof joist.

usul I a suggestion, proposal;
ngusuli to make a suggestion, offer a proposal;
ngusulaké to suggest or propose s.t. to s.o.
II, (*or* **asal-usul**) origin.

usul-uddin doctrinal theology, 'the roots of the faith'.

usum the season (for…); proper time;
usum-usuman to happen according to season.

usung, ngusung to transport (s.t. heavy) jointly;
ngusungi to carry heavy objects;
ngusungaké to carry s.t. heavy for s.o. else;
usung-usung to lug things from one place to another;
usungan 1 act or way of carrying s.t.; **2** equipment for carrying s.t. heavy;
pangusungan equipment for carrying s.t. heavy;
usung-usung lumbung 1 to move house carrying all one's goods and chattels; **2** to work together contributing to the limits of one's ability.

usup, ngusup-usupi to repair a roof by putting new parts in between.

usur payment for lawsuit.

usus intestine(s); - **buntu** appendix;
ngusus resembling intestines; - **pitik** tangled, snarled;
usus-usus cord, ribbon for closing s.t.

usut, ngusut to investigate;
pangusutan investigating.

uswa *lit* a kiss;
 nguswa to kiss.
uswasa *lit* to breathe; breath.
utah to spill (out) (*var of* **wutah**);
 ngutahi to spill on s.t.;
 ngutahaké to cause s.t. to spill;
 kutah spilled (out);
 kutahan to have s.t. spilled on it;
 utah-utahan vomit.
utak brains. *See also* **utek**.
utama *ng*, **utami** *kr*, 1 good, excellent; 2 superior, prominent;
 ngutamakaké to consider of greatest importance, give priority to;
 kautaman virtue;
 utamané it would be best to...
utamangga *lit* head.
utami *var of* **utama**.
utang *ng*, **sambut** *kr*, 1 (**sambutan** *kr*) a debt, credit; 2 (*or* **ngutang, nyambut** *kr*) to incur a debt; - **budi** to owe a favour or a kindness; - **nyawa** *or* - **pati** to owe one's life;
 ngutangi to lend to;
 ngutangaké 1 to give s.t. as a loan, lend money; 2 to sell s.t. on credit;
 utangan 1 a debt, loan; 2 to borrow habitually;
 utang-utang 1 to borrow here and there; 2 to borrow repeatedly;
 utang-utangan to borrow from each other, be indebted to each other;
 piutang debt;
 kapotangan endebted.
utara I *var of* **untara** III.
 II, **ngutarakaké** to explain, express, tell.
utawa *ng*, **utawi** *kr*, 1 or; 2 and.
utawi *kr for* **utawa**.
utawis *kr for* **utara**; *var of* **untawis**.
utek 1 brain; 2 brains; intelligence.
uter, nguter 1 to shape into a round form; 2 to ball roots for transplanting.
uthak-uthek *see* **uthek** I.
uthal-uthil *see* **uthil** II.

uthek I, **uthek-uthek** *or* **uthak-uthek** to linger, dawdle;
 nguthek *or* **muthek** to stay at home all the time, never stir out of doors.
 II, **nguthek-uthek** to keep touching s.t. with the fingers.
uthel, uthel-uthel short in stature;
 nguthel-uthel too short to handle easily (*e.g.* implement).
uthem, uthem-uthem chubby-looking, round-faced.
utheng, utheng-utheng *reg* taper. *See also* **upet**.
uthi to busy o.s., keep doing things.
uthik, nguthik to pick or pry with a long thin object;
 uthik-uthik *or* **uthak-uthik** to keep picking at;
 nguthik-uthik 1 to arouse, stir up, pester; 2 (*or* **nguthak-uthik**) to keep picking at s.t.;
 panguthik a knife with a curved blade;
 panguthik-uthik act of picking at s.t.
uthil I stingy, close-fisted;
 II *or* **uthil-uthil** *or* **uthal-uthil** to keep touching with a finger.
uthuh, nguthuh 1 to persist; 2 shameless, brazen, to have a nerve.
uthuk I, **uthuk-uthuk** 1 small wooden box; 2 piggy bank;
 nguthuk-uthuk to put away carefully.
 II **ésuk uthuk-uthuk** very early in the morning.
uthun, nguthun-uthun to spoil, overindulge (a child);
uthut, ana uthuté there's some hope that...;
 nguthut 1 to peek slowly at (s.t., *e.g.* a newly dealt playing-card); 2 to pick (*i.e.* steal) s.o. else's rice plants.
utik, ngutik-utik to sift out.
util, ngutil to pick pockets, steal;
 ngutili to steal from s.o.'s pocket;
 ngutilaké to steal on s.o.'s behalf.

utoh *reg var of* utuh.

utpala *lit* blue lotus.

utri I a dish made from steamed cassava and brown sugar.

II a variety of rice plant.

utu, ngutu *reg* to walk quickly without looking to right or left, be determined.

utuh *var of* wutuh.

utun *var of* wutun.

utus to send s.o. to do s.t. (*root form: k.i. for* kongkon).

uwa I aunt, uncle (parent's older sibling only);

nguwa to address s.o. as one's aunt/ uncle;

nguwakaké to treat or consider s.o. as one's aunt/uncle.

II, nguwakaké 1 to let loose; 2 to neglect, be absent from (work).

III, uwa-uwa a gibbon. *See also* wawa I.

uwab steam, water vapour;

nguwab to boil off, evaporate;

nguwabaké to cause to evaporate.

uwak *var of* uwa I.

uwal to be or break free/loose;

nguwalaké 1 to release; 2 to loosen, take off.

uwan grey hair;

uwanen grey-haired. *See also* jambul.

uwang *var of* wang I.

uwar, nguwaraké to tell, reveal, disclose.

uwas *var of* was II.

uwat I labour pains.

II uwat-uwat things used as reinforcement, to strengthen s.t.;

nguwat-uwataké 1 to exert o.s. fully; 2 to tighten one's hold on, hang onto. *See also* kuwat.

uwed 1 string, *esp* that used for spinning a top; 2 busy, industrious, always occupied;

nguwed-uwed to stroke, caress gently with the hand;

nguwedi to wind string around (a top).

uwèg *repr* a duck's quack.

uwèh *reg var of* wènèh.

uwek, nguwek-uwek to scratch, pick (with the fingers).

uwèk, nguwèk-uwèk to tear s.t. into pieces; uwèk-uwèkan torn to pieces. *See also* suwèk.

uwel I membrane surrounding the foetus in the womb.

II uwel-uwel crumpled, shoved in untidily;

nguwel-uwel to wad or crumple s.t. into a ball;

uwel-uwelan mixed up together, confused, swarming, churning;

muwel pushed together in a confused mass.

uwèn, sauwèn-uwèn *or* sauwèn-iyèn for a considerable length of time.

uwer 1 a small piece of rolled leaf used for enlarging a pierced earring hole; 2 *reg* ring-shaped carving on a kris handle;

nguweri to enlarge an earring piercing with a rolled leaf.

uwet *see* uwed.

uwèt *var of* wèt.

uwi yam, various tubers.

uwik *var of* wik.

uwil *var of* wil.

uwis *var of* wis.

uwit *var of* wit.

uwod *var of* wod.

uwoh *var of* woh.

uwok *var of* wok II.

uwol *var of* wol I.

uwong *var of* wong I.

uwor *var of* wor.

uwos *var of* wos II.

uwot *var of* wot I.

uwuh I *var of* wuh.

II, nguwuh *or* nguwuh-uwuh to call (out);

panguwuh 1 act of calling out; 2 *gram* exclamation.

uwuk *reg* to come to nothing;
  nguwukaké to prevent s.t. from happening; to foil, thwart.

uwul *reg* an additional amount;
  nguwul-uwuli to add (to); to increase. *See also* **wuwul**.

uwung, uwung-uwung 1 empty space; 2 the space right under the roof of a building. *See also* **awang**.

uwur, uwur-uwur jellyfish (*var of* **ubur-ubur** I).

uwus *lit* words (spoken by s.o.);
  nguwus-uwus to scold, berate. *See also* **wuwus**.

uyab 1 disturbed, ill at ease; 2 itchy from hair lice;
  nguyab to pull (another woman's hair, in anger);
  nguyabi to mix;
  muyab restless, moody.

uyag-uyug *see* **uyug**.

uyah *ng*, sarem *kr*, salt; - asem salt and tamarind, for seasoning fish or for use as a compress;
  nguyahi to salt s.t.;
  nguyah-asemi 1 to season with salt and tamarind; 2 to praise excessively;
  uyah-uyahan 1 salted; 2 the leaf of a certain shrub used as a medicine for women after giving birth.

uyak *var of* **oyak**.

uyang I hot, feverish, uneasy. *See* **gerah**.
  II **nguyang** to go about buying up rice;
  nguyangaké to sell rice to a dealer.

uyang-uyung *see* **uyung**.

uyar-uyur *see* **uyur**.

uyèb *var of* **uyab**.

uyeg, nguyeg *or* nguyeg-uyeg to run one's hands through s.t. to mix it up well;
  muyeg 1 well-mixed; 2 even (coloured);
  uyeg-uyegan to jostle each other (crowd).

uyel, nguyel *or* nguyel-uyel 1 to keep fiddling with s.t.; 2 to pick on, be mean to;
  uyel-uyelan swarming, teeming (crowd).

uyeng *var of* **unyeng**.

uyer *var of* **unyer**.

uyil *reg* restless, fidgety. *See also* **usil**.

uyoh *reg var of* **uyuh**.

uyu I, uyu-uyu *lit* pupil, disciple of a holy man.
  II, **nguyu-uyu** to play light gamelan melodies;
  uyon-uyon light gamelan melodies.

uyug, uyag-uyug to totter, stagger.

uyuh urine (toya, sené *kr*, turas *k.i.*);
  nguyuh to urinate;
  nguyuhi to urinate on;
  nguyuhan to have to urinate frequently;
  kuyuhan to get urinated on;
  kepoyuh to urinate involuntarily;
  panguyuhan chamber pot;
  puyuhan bladder.

uyuk, uyuk-uyukan to gather around, form a crowd.

uyun, nguyun-uyun 1 to engulf s.t. in a crowd; 2 to protect, safeguard;
  sauyun 1 a clump of sugarcane stalks growing from the same plant; 2 *fig* a group of people with a common goal.

uyung, uyung-uyung *or* uyang-uyung to carry around or back and forth;
  nguyung-uyung *or* **nguyang-uyung** to carry s.t. around with one for fear of losing it.

uyup, nguyup to drink from a bowl or soup plate;
  nguyupaké 1 to have s.o. drink a medicine as above; 2 to give s.o. to drink from a bowl or soup plate;
  uyup-uyup a herbal medicine for mothers who are breastfeeding.

uyur, uyar-uyur to wander around.

W

wa *adr* uncle, aunt (parent's older sibling) (*var of* **uwa**).

waca *ng*, **waos** *kr*, **maca** 1 to read; 2 to recite, chant, sing (poetry);
maca-maca to have a read;
moca-maca to read s.t. repeatedly;
macakaké to read for s.o.;
wacan *or* **wacanan** reading matter;
pamaca act or way of reading.

wacucal (*kr for* **lulang, wlulang**) leather.

wada, mada to criticise;
madani to call s.o. by a teasing nickname;
wadanan teasing nickname;
wadan-wadanan to call each other names.

wadal 1 s.t. offered up or sacrificed for s.t. or s.o. else; 2 to offer s.t. up; 3 to propitiate;
madalaké to use s.t. as a sacrifice.

wadana I 1 face (*k.i. for* **rai**); 2 *lit* face; mouth.
II 1 head of an administrative district;
asistèn - assistant district head; 2 *lit* leader;
kawadanan 1 official residence of a district head; 2 district administered by the above official;
madanani 1 to act as head of a district; 2 to act as a leader of a group.

wadat to stay unmarried, live a celibate life.

wadé 1 batik goods as merchandise; 2 *reg var of* **sadé**;
kawadéan *or* **kuwadéan** 1 trade in cloth; 2 to carry on trade in cloth.

wadéné even so, but still, in spite of (the foregoing) (*var of* **éwadéné**).

wader a freshwater fish; - **bang** goldfish.

wadhag visible, corporeal (as contrasted with non-material, spiritual).

wadhah container, receptacle for keeping things in;
madhahi to put s.t. into a container, where it belongs;
madhahaké to put s.t. into a container for s.o.

wadhang left over from the previous day;
sega - last night's rice served for breakfast;
madhang to eat a meal, *esp* of rice;
madhangan to be always eating, an eater (by nature).

wadhas hard ground. *See also* **padhas**.

wadhé 1 known to many; 2 tasteless, in bad taste; 3 to have an aversion to, be unable to stand;
madhèkaké to reveal a secret, let s.t. become common knowledge.

wadhèh *var of* **wadhé**.

wadhih *var of* **wadhé**.

wadhong wing-like part of classical dancer's costume (*var of* **badhong**).

wadhuk 1 stomach; 2 *cr* belly; 3 dam, reservoir.

wadhuh *excl of astonishment* wow!

wadi *ng*, **wados** *kr*, 1 a secret (s.t. that should be kept hidden); 2 a sore point (which should not be referred to); 3 a deep meaning;
wewadi *lit* 1 a secret; 2 secrecy;
madèni 1 to keep secret from s.o.; 2 to act in a secretive, furtive way;
winadi kept secret, confidential.

wadidang *see* **wedidang**.

wadok *var of* **wadon**.

wadon female;
madon to womanise;
pawadonan, kuwadonan *ng*, **pawèstrèn** *kr*, **badhong** *k.i.*, female genitals. *See also* **wédok**.

wados secret (*kr for* **wadi**).

wadu *lit* soldier(s), troops; - aji king's servant.

wadul 1 a tattletale; 2 to tattle (to);
maduli to tattle to s.o.;
madulaké to tattle s.t. to; to tattle on;
wadulan *or* wewadul 1 to tattle habitually; 2 what s.o. says or tells.

wadung I axe;
madung to cut wood with an axe.
II jack (playing-card).

wadwa *var of* wadya.

wadya soldiers, army; -bala troops, army.

waé *ng*, kémawon *kr*, just, only, *var of* baé.

waérut *reg* arrowroot.

wafat *lit* to die.

Wagé a day of the five-day week.

waged *subst var of* saged.

wagel obstacle to success;
mageli 1 to obstruct; 2 to set a term to;
magel half done, (of fruit) not ripe enough.

wagra *lit* tiger.

wagu 1 ungainly, poorly proportioned; 2 unpleasing, lacking tastefulness.

wagug, wagugen embarrassed, in difficulties.

wah I heavens! my! wow!
II 1 *lit* increase; 2 *reg* and furthermore; wahné moreover, besides.
III *lit* fruit.
IV *lit* flood.

wahana I *lit* vehicle, conveyance.
II interpretation, meaning;
mahanani 1 to interpret, explain the meaning (of a dream); 2 to signify, convey a meaning.

wahaya *reg* danger; dangerous.

wahdaniyat the unity of God.

wahdat celibate.

wahing *ng*, *kr*, sigra *k.i.* 1 a sneeze; 2 to sneeze.

wahini *lit* princess.

wahya *lit* outward, external, visible;

mahyakaké 1 to make manifest; 2 to express;
kawahya expressed, externalised;
winahya expressed outwardly.

wahyu a sign from heaven in the form of a falling star, indicating that the one on whom it falls is destined for high office (village head or king).

waing *var of* wahing.

waja I steel, iron.
II tooth (*k.i. for* untu).

wajah face, appearance.

wajan frying pan.

wajang, majangi to mate with (of animals);
wajangan mating, pairing.

waji *lit* horse.

wajib 1 obligatory; 2 fee paid to a religious official for praying;
majibi to give a responsibility to s.o.;
majibaké to make s.t. compulsory;
kawajiban *or* kuwajiban duty, obligation.

wajik 1 a sweet cake made from glutinous rice; 2 diamonds (playing-card suit); - klethik a stiff coconut sugar pudding;
wajikan 1 to serve wajik for a party; 2 diamond-shaped.

wajir, wajiré *reg* what ought to be done.

wak I aunt, uncle (parent's older sibling). *See also* uwa, uwak.
II body, self (*shtf of* awak).
III, wak-wakan to act in a rowdy way, showing off and creating a nuisance.

wakap religious endowment, *esp* a building or piece of productive land;
makapaké to give (land *etc*) as a wakap.

wakca *var of* weca.

waked *var of* wates.

wakil 1 representative; 2 substitute, deputy;
makili to represent, substitute for, act for;

makilaké to deputise, designate as a substitute;

pawakilan delegation, representative.

wakta, waktanen *lit* let us tell about.

waktu *var of* wektu.

wakul rice-serving basket;

wakulan 1 in a serving basket; 2 by the basket(ful).

wak-wik to move the fingers busily or nervously. *See also* uwik.

wakya *lit* speech, words.

wala I stem from which a bunch of coconuts grows.

II *or* walan gift given to the head of a village.

III, wala-wala kuwata give me strength!

walah I *excl of dismay over s.t. beyond one's control.*

II, kuwalahan *or* kuwalahen to feel unable to cope or carry on.

walahualam who knows! God only knows!

walak, walak-walak to depend on, be according to.

Walanda *ng*, Walandi *kr*, 1 Dutch; 3 European, Western; cara - Dutch (language). *See also* Landa.

walang locust, grasshopper, or similar insect with jointed legs; - ataga *lit* all living creatures; - ati, atèn anxious, concerned; - kadhak a kind of stork; - kapa a kind of flying squirrel; - sayit a kind of beetle; - sangker *lit* difficulty, hindrance; - slenthikan to suffer from stiff hind legs (horse); ora ana - slisik *lit* deathly still.

walat heaven-sent retribution for insulting treatment of parents, teachers or for blasphemy;

malati causing retribution if offended against;

kuwalat *or* kewalat to receive one's retribution; be struck down by a calamity, accursed.

waled I overdue, in arrears;

maled to be behind in payments.

II silt, sediment, alluvium.

walèh I to tell the truth, admit frankly;

malèhaké to confess s.t.;

walèh-walèh apa frankly speaking...; to tell the truth...; as a matter of fact.

waler I (*or* wewaler *or* waleran) prohibition, taboo;

maleri to place a prohibition on, prescribe a limit.

II viscera of slaughtered animals, fish.

wales I 1 retribution, revenge; 2 response, reaction, return;

males 1 to repay; 2 to (do) in retaliation;

malesi to reply to; to return s.t.;

malesaké to avenge;

walesan 1 a reply; 2 s.t. done in return;

wales-walesan 1 reciprocal; 2 to reciprocate;

wales-winales to take revenge on each other;

wewales revenge, retribution;

pamales what one gives back;

piwales return, revenge, retribution.

II, walesan a flexible rod (whip, fishing rod).

walgita *lit* book, letter.

wali I 1 male next of kin legally responsible for a bride, *usu* her father; - hakim person who acts on behalf of the father of a bride; 2 guardian of the bride at a wedding ceremony; 3 (*or* waliyullah) saint, apostle (of Islam in Java); Wali Sanga the nine saints who established Islam in Java;

malèni to act as guardian to (a bride);

kawalian *or* kuwalian, jaman - the time of the Walis.

II *lit, var of* bali;

mawali-wali *lit* again and again.

III a small, sharp-pointed knife (for writing on lontar leaf).

walija *lit* trader.

walih to change one's appearance/shape (*reg var of* **malih II**).

walik on the contrary, the other way round, on the opposite side; - **dadah** massage of a new mother (40 days following the birth, to restore condition); - **dami** to plant a second crop of rice during the dry season;

malik 1 to turn s.t. the other way around or in a different direction; **2** to turn over or upside down; **3** to change, take a different course; **4** to turn around, turn back; - **bumi** to turn traitor; - **tingal** to go back on one's word, shift one's loyalty;

maliki to turn s.t. over repeatedly;

malikaké 1 to reverse s.t. for s.o.; **2** to turn s.t. inside out;

walikan 1 (turned) the other way around; **2** the opposite;

sawaliké the other side, *i.e.* the reverse; **kuwalik** *or* **kewalik** (turned) upside down;

wolak-walik 1 on both sides; **2** the other way around;

molak-malik 1 to turn this way and that; **2** (of things in a series) to go through the same motions, follow each other in a pattern.

walikat scapula, shoulder blade.

walikukun a tall tree, valued for its wood.

walimah a wedding feast recommended by Islamic law, held after the marriage ceremony.

waluh a kind of gourd.

walulang leather (*var of* **lulang**).

walun apron, cloth placed on the lap (*esp* when tending a baby).

walur an edible tuber.

waluya *lit* **1** healthy, well; **2** having recovered or survived; - **jati** as good as an original state;

maluyakaké to restore s.t. to its original state.

wal-wel *see* **wel**.

wana (*kr for* **alas**) **1** forest; **2** *reg* fields, area outside the village (*kr for* **alas**); - **dri** *lit* forest and mountains; **-ntara** *lit* depths of the forest, wilderness; **-wasa 1** thick, dark forest; **2** dwelling in the forest.

wanah *see* **waneh**.

wanara *lit* monkey.

wanari *lit* female monkey.

wancah I, **mancah** to shorten, contract; **wancahan** a shortening, contraction.

II, **mancahi 1** to criticise, find fault with; **2** to defy, challenge, contradict.

wancak I *lit* grasshopper, locust; **mancak** to catch grasshoppers/locusts.

II wancak-suji fencing, fence.

wanci 1 (the right) time (for) (*kr for* **wayah**); **2** time, season (*kr, var of* **mangsa**).

wanda I 1 *lit* body; **2** *way* shape, form (shadow puppets, expressing various moods or emotions of the characters); **3** outward appearance.

II (*pron as:* **wan-da**) *gram* syllable.

wandé I small shop (*kr for* **warung**).

II to fail to occur, not go ahead (*kr for* **wurung**).

wandhan *lit* a dark-skinned, curly-haired race, Papuan.

wandira, **wandéra** *lit* banyan tree, waringin.

wandu I 1 an unfeminine woman; **2** a bisexual person, hermaphrodite.

II wandu-wandawa *lit* relatives.

waneh *lit* to have had enough.

wanèh *lit* **1** other; **2** others.

wang I jaw, jawbone (*also* **uwang**).

II 1 money; **2** former monetary unit, worth 10 doits; - **kunci** down payment on rental or purchase price of a home.

wangan irrigation channel in ricefields.

wangen, **mangeni** to set a time limit (on, for);

wangenan, wewangen time limit.

wangi fragrant;

wangèn that which is fragrant;

wewangi 1 s.t. fragrant; 2 lit name.

wangkal 1 obstinate, self-willed; 2 disobedient;

mangkali to defy, disregard, resist.

wangkang Chinese junk.

wangkawa lit rainbow.

wangké lit corpse.

wangkid I border;

mangkidi to border on.

II wangkidan (reg k.i. for kuluk) a kind of formal headgear, fez.

wangkil a trowel-like tool for weeding;

mangkil to weed with such a tool;

mangkili to remove the weeds from s.t. with the above implement.

wangking I slim-waisted.

II, mangking to wear s.t. in the back of the belt;

wangkingan kris (k.i. for keris).

wangkis, mangkis to stretch a skin over a drum.

wangkit lit able, capable (var of bangkit).

wangkong the area of the buttocks, lower back.

wangkot stubborn, obstinate, rebellious;

mangkoti to disobey s.o.'s order.

wangkring reg var of angkring.

wangkung barrack where the beggars are quartered.

wanglu lit ankle bone.

wangon roof.

wangsa lit 1 relatives, kinsmen, family; 2 descendant.

wangsal I a fishing creel.

II, wangsalan a form of riddle making use of similarities in sound between words;

mangsali to manipulate (words) as above.

wangsit whispered, secret message (warning or instruction), revelation, prompting;

mangsit to whisper s.t. in s.o.'s ear;

wangsitan or wewangsitan to whisper messages to each other, give each other secret orders.

wangsul to return (kr for bali);

mangsuli 1 to repeat (kr for mbalèni); 2 to answer (a question);

wangsulan an answer;

wewangsul gift to a departing guest (var of angsul-angsul);

wongsal-wangsul see bali.

wangun 1 design, shape; 2 appearance, aspect; 3 suitable (to), in keeping (with);

mangun to design, fashion, give shape to;

wanguné it looks as if;

wangunan or wewangunan 1 shape, form, figure; 2 building, structure.

wanguntur or manguntur lit elevated dais, seat (of a king).

wangwa reg a glowing coal.

wangwang I lit hesitant, uncertain.

II, mangwang lit to stare at, watch fixedly;

kewangwang to appear in the mind's eye.

III lit promptly, quickly.

wangwung I empty (shtc of awang-uwung).

II coconut beetle (var of kuwang-wung).

wani ng, wantun kr, 1 to dare, be bold enough to; 2 willing, prepared to; 3 defiant, insolent; 4 coll sexually able (to take on a woman); - angas or - èrès to put up a bold front;

manèni 1 to accept (a challenge); 2 to act impudently or defiantly toward;

memani to egg on, goad;

manèk-manèkaké to steel o.s. (to);

kawanèn or kuwanèn courage, boldness, bravery;

wanèn daring by nature;

kuwanènen foolhardy.

wanita 1 female; 2 woman;
  kawanitan relating to women.
wanodya *lit* female, woman.
wantah 1 pure, with nothing added, in
  its natural state; 2 genuine, sincere,
  open;
  mantahaké to tell simply, plainly;
  wantahan, wewantahan 1 pure, with
  nothing added; 2 origin(al form); 3
  plainly and simply;
  sawantahé in its true form, as in the
  original.
wantèg 1 solid, firm; 2 fast (of colours),
  i.e. not subject to fading or running; 3
  unchanged.
wantèn *reg, var of* wantèg.
wanter 1 brave, steadfast, determined; 2
  fast (*var of* banter);
  kawanteran courage, bravery, determination.
wanthèn *reg* not easily scared.
wanti *ng*, wantos *kr*, wanti-wanti time
  after time;
  manti-manti 1 to keep telling or
  advising s.o.; 2 to (do) again and
  again;
  pamanti-manti act of telling again and
  again.
wantil, wantilan stake to which an elephant is tethered.
wanting I, wewanting to wash the hands
  and dry them by shaking;
  manting 1 to beat (washing); 2 *lit* to
  chastise.
  II, wantingan earthenware flask with
  a neck and spout (*reg kr for* kendhi).
wantos *kr for* wanti.
wantu I, banyu - boiling water kept
  ready to add to that in the rice steamer;
  mawantu-wantu repeatedly;
  mantu to increase;
  mantoni to add s.t. to.
  II watak wantu *see* watak.
wantun *kr of* wani.

wantya *lit, var of* wanti.
wanudya *var of* wanodya.
wanuh to know, be acquainted (with);
  manuh to have become accustomed
  to;
  manuhi to become acquainted with;
  manuhaké 1 to introduce, make
  acquainted with; 2 to accustom or
  habituate s.o. to;
  memanuh to get o.s. used (to);
  wanuhan *or* wewanuhan 1 acquaintance; 2 to become acquainted with;
  kawanuhan an acquaintance.
waon *or* waonan to criticise habitually;
  maoni to criticise, find fault with.
waos I 1 spear (*kr for* tumbak); 2 tooth
  (*kr for* untu); 3 iron, steel (*kr for*
  waja).
  II land measure (*kr for* tumbak).
  III to read (*root form: kr for* waca).
wapat *var of* wafat.
wara I words; mung - baé only words;
  wara-wara 1 public announcement,
  proclamation; 2 to keep saying/telling;
  3 *reg* about, approximately;
  marak-marakaké to go around announcing s.t.
  II *lit, title used before girl's names,
  'lady'*; wara kawuri *lit* widow.
  III *emphatic word, sentence finally, see*
  hara.
  IV *lit* day.
warah I *or* wewarah instruction, guidance, teaching;
  marahi to teach, advise;
  winarah to be given instruction;
  warah-warahan to teach each other.
  II *see* marahi.
warak rhinoceros.
warana 1 screen (to keep s.t. out of
  sight); 2 pretext (words used to hide
  the intention); 3 *lit* substitute, representative. *Also* wrana, rana III.
warandha *lit* an old widow (*var of* randha).

warang I, **marangi** 1 to rub (a kris) with arsenic; 2 to poison s.o. with arsenic; **warangan** 1 arsenic; 2 poisoned with arsenic.

II *reg* the parents of one's son- or daughter-in-law. *See also* **bésan**.

waranggana 1 *lit* heavenly nymph; 2 female singer with gamelan. *See also* **pesindhèn**.

warangka kris sheath. *See also* **wrangka**, **rangka** I.

waras *ng*, **saras** *kr*, 1 (**dhangan** *or* **senggang** *k.i.*) healthy, well; 2 recovered; 3 (of land) untilled, fallow; **ora - ** *cr* not all there (mentally); **marasaké** to cure, heal; **waras-wiris** hale and hearty, in top condition; **kawarasan**, **kuwarasan** *or* **kewarasan** 1 good (physical or mental) health; 2 to feel fit and healthy.

warastra 1 *lit* arrow; 2 *lit* the male organ.

warayang *lit* arrow.

wardah *lit* old (*var of* **werda**).

wardaya *lit* heart.

wardi *var of* **werdi**.

wareg *ng*, **tuwuk** *kr*, full, sated; **maregi** 1 filling; 2 to give s.o. their fill; **maregaké** to do till full (eating); **kuwaregen**, **kewaregen** too full, uncomfortably full.

warèh *var of* **warih**.

warèng I fifth-generation ancestor or descendant.

II crossbreed between a chicken and a bantam rooster.

warga 1 family, relatives; 2 (member) of the same group.

wargi *kr, var for* **warga**.

warid *var of* **wirid**.

warigaluh *lit* fisherman.

warih *lit* water.

waring *reg* shrimp net.

waringin banyan tree (considered to be the abode of a spirit); **- kurung** the two (fenced) sacred banyan trees on the northern square of the palace. *See also* **ringin**, **wringin**.

waris, **ahli -** heir; **maris** *or* **marisi** to inherit; **marisaké** to bequeath; **warisan** inheritance, bequest; **kuwarisan** handed down, inherited, hereditary.

warna *ng*, **warni** *kr*, 1 form, appearance; 2 colour; 3 sort, kind; **marna** 1 to paint, colour; 2 to describe, represent (in a story); **marnani** to apply colour to; **marnakaké** to give form to; **warna-warna** of various kinds; **mawarna-warna** of all kinds; **winarna** *lit* narrated, told; **warnanen**, **kawarnaa** *lit* let us tell of...; **sawarnané** all kinds of.

warni *kr for* **warna**.

warok 1 kind of ascetic expert in martial arts; 2 (*or* **warokan**) tough guy, gang boss.

warsa I *lit* year.

II *lit* rain.

warsita *var of* **wasita**.

warta *ng*, **wartos** *kr*, news; **martani** to give news to; **martakaké** to give news (of); **kawarta** *lit* famous, renowned.

warti *lit, var of* **warta**.

wartos news (*kr for* **warta**).

waru a certain hibiscus tree (the fibres of its bark used for making rope and sacking material).

waruju the youngest child in a family, last-born. *See also* **ragil**, **wuragil**.

warung *ng*, **wandé** *kr*, a small shop, food stall; **marung** to run a **warung**; **warungan** 1 to run a **warung**; 2 to eat out at a **warung**.

was I, was-was apprehensive, on the lookout, hesitant, indecisive.
II, nguwasi to look at;
nguwasaké to watch, keep an eye on (*var of* **ngawasaké**, *see* **awas**).

wasa, wasa-wasa *lit* to use force.

wasana 1 final; **2** the end (*see also* **wusana**);
wasana walang wisma suku asta *prov* to leave s.t. to s.o. else's judgment or discretion.

wasésa I power, authority (*see also* **wisésa I**);
masésa 1 to exercise authority over; **2** to punish, discipline;
kawasésa under the sway of, ruled by.
II *gram* predicate.

wasir I haemorrhoids (*var of* **bawasir**).
II prime minister.

wasis clever, skilful (at s.t.);
kawasisan skill, proficiency, expertise;
winasis skilled (at).

wasit referee.

wasita instruction, guidance, words;
kawasita to be informed.

wasiyat 1 last instructions of the deceased which must be carried out; **2** teachings passed down from the ancestors; **3** heirloom;
masiyati to bequeath s.t. to s.o.

waskitha *lit* possessing clear insight (into hidden matters, the future);
kawaskithan the ability to see or understand clearly, prescience.

waspa tear(s) (*lit, k.i. for* **luh**).

waspada watchful, on the alert;
maspadakaké to look at intently;
kawaspadan watchfulness, alertness.

wasta *kr* **1** name; **2** (*or* **awasta**) named, called;
mastani 1 to call, name; **2** to consider, regard (*kr for* **ngarani**, *see* **aran**).

wastra *lit* clothing, garment.

wastu, taun wastu 354-day year. *See also* **taun**.

wasuh, masuh 1 to wash (clothes, by beating); **2** to purify; **3** to wash face, hands and feet before prayer;
masuhaké to have s.t. washed;
pamasuh 1 the act of washing; **2** s.o. who washes, washerman/woman;
pawasuhan, pamasuhan the place where washing is done.

wat I sa-wat instantly, immediately.
II, wat-wat strengthening, intensification, fortification. *See also* **uwat II, kuwat**.
III 1 labour pains; **2** to push (in giving birth) (*var of* **uwat I**).

watak character, disposition, nature; -**wantu** character;
awatak characterised by;
wataké ordinarily, characteristically;
wewatakan character, characteristic.

watang 1 long pole; **2** horizontal tree trunk; **3** tournament lance;
matang 1 to pole, push forward with a pole; **2** to stab with a lance;
watangan tournament, jousting contest; **balé -** a certain building within the Kraton complex;
matang tuna, numbak luput *prov* to always fail to achieve one's goals. *See also* **matangnya**.

watara *see* **wetara I, II**.

watek *var of* **watak**.

wates 1 border, boundary, limit; **2** up to, as far as;
matesi to set limits, to place a boundary;
watesan 1 boundary marker; **2** limitation, restriction.

watgata *lit* wound;
kawatgata wounded.

watir *ng*, **watos** *kr*, fearful (*shtf of* **kuwatir, kuwatos**);
matiri 1 inspiring fear; **2** dangerous.

wathathithah *excl of anger or defiance or surprise* oho!

wathuh *var of* **wadhuh**.

waton I 1 general rule, criterion, basis; 2 on the basis of; 3 provided, as long as; 4 (- **waé**) just for the sake of it, for no particular reason;
maton logical, factual;
matoni to set up a basis or criterion for;
wewaton 1 criterion, reason, logic; 2 based on.
II side or edge (of a bedstead).

watos fearful (*kr for* **watir**).

watu *ng*, **séla** *kr*, stone, rock; - **api** flint for striking fire; - **beras** light porous rock; - **cendhani** marble; - **gumantung** stalactite; - **item** hard black stone; - **kambang** pumice; - **karang** coral; - **lintang** 1 a certain variety of limestone full of sparkles; 2 a certain variety of gypsum;
matu 1 (to be) as hard as rock; 2 to pave with stones;
watunen to suffer from stones (urinary tract).

watuk *ng*, *kr*, **cekoh** *k.i.* 1 a cough; 2 to cough;
matuki to cause s.o. to cough;
matukaké to cough and spit s.t. up;
watukan susceptible to coughs.

watun, matun to clear (fields) of weeds.

wau the (aforesaid), just now (*kr for* **mau**).

waung *reg var of* **baung**, bear.

wauta *lit* it so happened, in times of old... (beginning of story).

wawa I gibbon.
II, **mawa** 1 to contain, carry; 2 with; 3 to cause, bring about;
kawawa able to carry. *See also* **kuwawa**.

wawah spacious;
mawahi to make room for s.t., leave space.

wawal I 1 broken, pulled apart; 2 a small trowel for weeding; 2 a large crowbar;
mawal to break open (with a crowbar).

II, **mawali** to argue with s.o., contradict, disagree;
wawalan a dispute.

wawan with each other; - **gunem** to carry on a conversation or discussion (with); - **sabda** to have a talk (with); -**cara** 1 an interview; 2 to interview.

wawang *lit*, **mawang** to watch intently, consider;
pamawang view, idea.

wawar I long-haired (tail); **asu** - a kind of wild dog.
II, **mawari** to pick (coconut) from the shell and slice it;
wawaran in slices (coconut);
sawawar one slice of coconut.

wawas, mawas, mawasaké to view attentively;
wawasan view, opinion, judgement;
pamawas view, consideration.

wawuk *var of* **bawuk** II.

wawuh to be friends again, reconciled (after disagreement);
mawuhaké to reconcile.

wayah I *ng*, **wanci** *kr*, 1 time (of day); 2 time (of life);
sawayah-wayah at any time, whenever.
II grandchild (*k.i. for* **putu**).

wayang *ng*, **ringgit** *kr*, 1 puppet used in the shadow-play; 2 shadow-play; - **bèbèr** wayang performance using a picture scroll; - **dupara** a wayang performance depicting episodes from the history of Surakarta; - **Jawa** wayang performance depicting the story of national hero Diponegoro; - **gedhog** shadow-play depicting the adventures of the hero Prince Panji; - **golèk** wayang performance using three-dimensional wooden puppets; - **klithik** *or* - **krucil** wayang performance depicting the tale of Damar Wulan, using flat wooden puppets; - **kulit** shadow-play with leather puppets; - **madya** wayang performance depicting tales from the 'middle' period; - **Ménak** wayang performance depicting the Islamic hero Ménak, using three-dimensional wooden puppets; - **Pancasila** shadow-play depicting the story of the five Pandhawa presented symbolically as the Five Principles of the Republic of Indonesia (*Pancasila*); - **potèhi** Chinese glove-puppet play; - **purwa** classical wayang performance in which the Pandawa cycle and Rama are most important; - **suluh** shadow-play dramatising events of Indonesia's revolutionary struggle; - **thengul** wayang performance using wooden puppets; - **thithi** Chinese shadow-play of Yogyakarta; - **wahana** shadow-play depicting events of the 1920s; - **wong** plays performed as dance drama by human beings;

mayang to perform a shadow-play;

mayangi having a wayang-shape; resembling a wayang figure;

mayangaké to perform s.t. as a wayang show;

wayangan 1 shadow-play performance; 2 to hire a wayang performance;

pawayangan things pertaining to the wayang;

wewayangan shadow, reflection.

wayu old, stale, no longer fresh;

mayokaké to let s.t. stand overnight;

kewayon kept too long.

wayuh 1 a co-wife in a polygamous marriage; 2 to have or take an additional wife;

mayuh to take another wife.

wé I *lit* water;

wé rekta kang muroni *expr* wine (red water that can cause one to get drunk). *See also* **wédang**.

II *inf var of* **baé**.

III *excl of surprise*.

weca 1 declaration; 2 prediction, prophecy;

meca 1 to say straight out, say how it is; 2 to predict, foresee;

mecakaké to reveal (occult matters);

pameca prediction;

wewecan facts imparted in a prophecy.

wecana *lit* 1 words, what s.o. says; 2 to speak.

wecucal leather (*var of* **wacucal, cucal** *kr, see* **wlulang**).

wéda *lit* holy text, words of wisdom.

wedaka *lit* hindrance, obstacle.

wedal I *kr of* **wetu**.

II *inf var of* **wekdal**.

wedana *var of* **wadana** I, II.

wédang 1 (**bentèran** *kr*) boiled (hot) water for making drinks; 2 hot drinks; - **kopi** coffee; - **tèh** tea;

médang to consume a hot drink;

médangi 1 to provide with a hot drink; 2 to pour boiling water on s.t.;

wédangan to have a cup of tea or coffee together;

wédangen to suffer from burning blisters.

wedari *lit* garden, park.

wedel *ng* **celep** *kr*, **medel** to dye with indigo (dark blue);

medelaké to apply indigo dye to s.t.;

wedelan 1 s.t. dyed indigo; 2 indigo dye.

wédha *var of* **wéda**.

wedhak (rice-)powder; - **pupur** face powder;

medhaki to apply powder to;

wedhakan to powder one's face.

wedhal *reg var of* **wedhel**.

wedhar, medhar, medharaké 1 to reveal, disclose; 2 to express, set out;

wedharan explanation, expression.

wedhel (of fish) swimming-bladder;

wedhelan guts (of fish).

wedhi sand; **segara** - desert;

medhi 1 sand-like, crumbly; 2 (of the texture of ripe **salak** fruit) pleasantly crumbly;

wedhèn *or* pawedhèn a sandy place, heap of sand;

wedhi kèngser 1 sand bank; 2 variety of horse movement; 3 variety of dance movement.

wedhon a certain kind of ghost that resembles a corpse wrapped in a shroud; banyu - water in which a corpse has been washed.

wedhung *ng*, pasikon *k.i.*, a cleaver-like knife (worn with court dress).

wedhus *ng*, ménda *kr* goat, sheep; -bérok large goat with a beard; - **Jawa** *or* - gèmbèl ordinary Javanese goat; -gibas fat-tailed sheep; - kendhit sheep with a white stripe around the middle; **wedhus diumbar ing pakacangan** *prov* one who gets the opportunity to enjoy s.t. highly desirable.

wedi *ng*, ajrih *kr*, 1 fear, afraid; 2 awe, respect; - asih (to feel) awe and reverence (toward);

medèni 1 to frighten; 2 frightening;

medèn-medèni, memedèni 1 to threaten; 2 to put the wind up, try to scare s.o.;

memedi a ghost; anything that frightens;

memedèn ricefield scarecrow;

wedèn timid by nature;

wedèn-wedènan 1 to play ghosts; 2 a pretend, make-believe ghost;

wedi rai, wani silit *prov* afraid to come out and fight but brave enough to talk behind s.o.'s back.

wedidang 1 lower part of the leg, between knee and heel; 2 *reg* Achilles heel.

wédok *ng*, èstri *kr*, putri *k.i.* female;

médoki 1 effeminate (men); 2 feminine, ladylike (women);

médokaké to regard (a man) as a female;

wédokan 1 female animal used for breeding purposes; 2 fond of women; 3 nut, female screw. *See also* **wadon**.

wedos *subst kr for* wedi.

wedra *reg* 1 old; 2 parent's elder brother or sister.

wedrah *reg, var of* wedra.

wedrug path worn smooth by many feet.

wédya *lit* physician; -rini *lit* midwife.

wèg *see* wèk II.

wegah averse, unwilling, can't be bothered (doing s.t.);

megahi *or* megahaké causing aversion, bothersome;

wegahan 1 averse to work, lazy; 2 easily revolted.

wegang I *reg var of* wegah.

II a kind of lathe.

wegig 1 *reg* lively; 2 clever; 3 bold; 4 *reg* rude.

wèh I *ng*, suka *kr*, ngewèhi to give to;

ngewèhaké to give s.t. to;

wèwèh to give (things);

pawèh *or* pawèwèh gift;

winèh *lit* to be given s.t.

II *excl expressing surprise (var of* wah I).

wejag *var of* wedrug.

wejah medicine drunk by breastfeeding mothers to ensure enough milk.

wejak, mejak to wring (out), squeeze.

wejang, mejang to advise, instruct;

wejangan 1 advice; 2 speech containing advice.

wejani fee paid to a healer (dhukun);

mejani to make a payment to (a healer).

wejar *var of* wedhar.

wejek *var of* wejak.

wejing, mejing-mejing to tear into little pieces.

wèk I (*or* mak wèk) *repr* ripping.

II *repr* a duck's quack.

III belonging to, the possession of (*shtf of* duwèk).

weka I 1 scale (deposit in a kettle); 2 tartar (deposit on teeth); 3 a deeply
ingrained vice.
II *lit* child, son;
wekan womb.

wéka *or* wewéka care, prudence;
mékani to take care, think of. *See also*
wiwéka.

wekas I (*or* wekasan) 1 the end, limit,
last; 2 in the end, finally;
mekasi 1 to bring to an end, complete;
2 to put an end to life, die;
pamekas 1 the last of a series; 2 the
youngest in the family;
kawekas the last, highest (of all
things), God.
II wekas, wewekas 1 last instructions
(at parting); 2 message, request;
mekas 1 to give advice; 2 to make a
request;
mekasi to ask *or* instruct s.o. (to);
mekasaké to convey s.o.'s request;
kawekas to get sent on an errand;
pamekas 1 message; 2 parting words.

wekca *var of* weca.

wekdal time (*subst kr for* wektu).

wekel diligent, industrious, serious.

wektu *ng*, wekdal *kr*, 1 fixed time (for
the five daily prayers in Islam); 2 time
(of day, for s.t.); 3 at the time when.

wel, wal-wel *repr* eating quickly, hungrily, with enjoyment.

wèl, wèl-wèlan 1 to shiver, tremble,
shake; 2 to have the jitters, to fidget.

wela *reg* 1 (to have) a gap, interval;
melani to interrupt, intervene;
welan fine for overdue payment.

wéla, wéla-wéla clear, distinct; cetha -
very clearly visible, understandable;
wélan *reg* clear, distinct.

welad a sharp sliver of bamboo, used as a
knife for cutting the umbilical cord;
sedulur tunggal welad *idiom* brothers
and sisters of the same father and
mother.

welah I oar;
melahi to propel (a boat) with oars;
welahan act of rowing;
pamelah oarsman, rower.
II a slender bamboo (*kr for* wuluh I).

welak *or* wewelak divine retribution in
the form of a natural disaster, plague.

Welanda *var of* Walanda.

welang, ula - a black-and-white striped
venomous snake.

welar (of chest) broad;
melar to expand, swell, spread.

welas I 1 pity; 2 sympathetic, sorry for;
- asih compassion;
melas *or* memelas 1 inspiring pity; 2
having pity;
melasi to feel sorry for;
melas asih inspiring pity;
kawelas asih *lit* inspiring pity;
kamiwelasen to feel deeply sorry for
or sympathetic to.
II welasan an 11th item into the bargain when buying 10.

weleg, meleg 1 to give guidance in moral
and ethical matters; 2 to stuff, fill
(with food).

welèh misfortune (interpreted as) retribution for one's wrong acts; sinung -
to get one's just deserts;
melèhaké to bring s.o.'s errors to light,
to give the lie to;
kawelèh *or* kuwelèh to have one's
wrongdoing discovered.

welek *reg* smoke swirling in the air.

welèri a kind of grasshopper.

weling I *ng*, tungkas *or* pitungkas *kr*, (a
final) instruction, message (at parting);
meling 1 to give a message; 2 to ask
s.o. to do an errand;
melingaké 1 to convey (an instruction, a message); 2 to send for;
welingan 1 a message, an instruction;
2 an errand (to be) done;
II ula - a certain small venomous
snake.

welirang sulphur;
   melirang to treat (rub) with sulphur.

welit bundles of palm leaves, straw *etc* bound together with strips of bamboo as roofing material;
   melit to make (a roof) with the above.

wéloh *reg var of* **waluh**.

welu 1 pale, dull, not bright (light, colour); 2 listless, slow; 3 unbending (character).

welug *reg* outlaw leader, head of a gang.

welulang *var of* **walulang**. *See also* **lulang**.

welur *reg var of* **selur**.

welurat *reg* poor, beggarly.

welut the common mud eel;
   melut to catch eels, work as an eeler;
   welut didoli udhèt *prov* to boast of one's achievements to others who have greater ones.

wèn *reg, var of* **wèh**.

wenah *var of* **benah**.

wenang I to have an authority, privilege;
   wewenang privilege;
   kawenang to have authority; to have the privilege or right;
   winenang *lit* to have an authority;
   sawenang-wenang arbitrary, having no regard for other's rights;
   kawenangan 1 privilege, right; 2 to take an advantage, benefit o.s.;
   menangaké to give an authority to, grant a privilege to.
   II, **menangi** (**meningi** *kr*) to experience, witness, see (in one's time).

wenara monkey (*var of* **wanara**).

wendéra *lit* a banyan tree.

wendira *var of* **wandéra**

wendra *lit* a unit of 10 million;
   wendran in tens of millions; in huge numbers.

wéndra an edible sea fish.

wenèh, sawenèh some, certain (ones);
   sawenèh-wenèh all, every/any one.

wènèh *ng*, **suka** *kr*, **mènèhi** 1 to give to; 2 to put s.t. s.w.;

mènèhaké 1 to give s.t. to s.o.; 2 to put s.t. s.w.

monah-mènèhi to give repeatedly;
   sawènèhé whatever one gives.

wenes bright and clear.

wenga, menga 1 open; to come open; 2 clear (of the mind); - **sumeblak** wide open;
   mengani 1 to open for; 2 to keep opening, to keep open;
   wengan 1 act of opening; 2 *fig* generous, helpful;
   wewengan peace of mind, understanding, solace. *See also* **enga**.

wengi *ng*, **dalu** *kr* 1 evening, night; 2 late (at night); **tengah** - midnight;
   kewengèn 1 overtaken by night; 2 too late (at night);
   sawengi 1 one night; 2 the whole night;
   wengi-wengi late at night, deep in the night;
   wengi-wenginan rather late at night. *See also* **bengi**.

wengis cruel, heartless.

wengkang, mengkang to bend apart, separate forcibly (*e.g.* split bamboo);
   mengkang-mengkang to move s.t. forcibly this way and that.

wengkel, wengkelan calf of the leg (*k.i. for* **kéntol, kémpol**).

wengkelang hard (of faeces).

wengku frame, edge, border, hoop;
   mengku 1 to rule, have authority over; 2 to care for (wife, child);
   mengkoni 1 to frame s.t.; 2 to have authority over; 3 to surround or enclose (with);
   kawengku 1 dominated, mastered (by); 2 under the control (of);
   pamengku 1 care, attention; 2 patience, indulgence;
   wewengkon domain, area.

wengur disagreeable odour, *e.g.* of a snake or mouse.

wèngwèng *see* salah.

wèni *lit* hair.

wening I 1 clear, pure; 2 free from evil (*lit var of* bening);
meningaké to make clear or pure. *See also* ening.
II, meningi to experience, see (in one's time) (*kr of* menangi). *See also* wenang II.

weninga *var of* wuninga.

wentala, mentala 1 able to bear; 2 heartless enough to;
mentalan heartless by nature.

wentara *var of* wetara.

wèntèh *or* wewèntèhan (to remember, see in a dream) clearly, large as life.

wènten *reg var of* wonten.

wènter a method of dying cloth (using powder in a sachet);
mènter to dye using the above;
wènteran 1 dyed; 2 *fig* not genuine, insincere (conduct).

wentis thigh (*k.i. for* pupu).

wenyet, menyet 1 to crush fine; 2 to press, squeeze. *See also* enyet, penyet.

wèr *or* mak wèr *repr* a whizzing sound.

werak Javanese vinegar (from the juice of the coconut or aren palm, used as a refreshing drink).

werat *reg var of* awrat.

werda, werdha *lit* old (*also* wreda).

werdaya *var of* wardaya.

werdi I meaning conveyed;
merdèni to give the meaning of, explain, comment on.
II, werdèn fecund (animals).

werjit *lit* worm.

wereg *var of* bereg.

wèreg a recruiter of labourers.

wereng 1 small black insect pest that attacks rice crops; 2 *cr* prostitute.

werga *var of* warga.

wergul a marten-like animal (*var of* regul).

werhaspati *lit* Thursday.

weri a nuisance, *e.g.* troublemakers, thieves.

wèri *lit* enemy.

werit 1 mysterious, spooky, scary (place); 2 cryptic, deep; 3 shy, timorous (animals).

werna *var of* warna.

werni *var of* warni.

werta *var of* warta.

wertek, mertek *reg* to drill, train strictly.

wertos *var of* wartos.

weruh *ng*, sumerep *kr*, priksa *or* uninga *k.i.*, 1 to see and recognise, know s.t. (from sight, experience); 2 to understand, perceive; 3 to see (a ghost);
meruhi 1 to show, let s.o. see; 2 diweruhi (*pass*) to be visited by (vision of a deceased person);
meruhaké to tell, inform;
kaweruhan to be seen, caught (at);
kaweruh (*usu pron as:* kawruh) knowledge;
weruh-weruh 1 just come to find out...; 2 all of a sudden. *See also* kawruh.

werut 1 rough, fibrous (wood); 2 wrinkled (skin).

wèsel *var of* wisel.

wesi *ng*, tosan *kr*, iron; - aji sharp weapons of metal (kris, spear; highly revered); - bang red-hot iron; - barut metal band for reinforcing a crate; - brani magnet; - gligèn iron bar;
mesi as hard as iron.

wesiyasat *lit* force, with force.

wesisan *reg* 1 at once; 2 altogether;
mesisan all at once;
mesisani to do s.t. all at once.

wespada *var of* waspada.

westa *var of* wasta.

wèsthi *lit* obstacle, danger.

wèt, ngewèt-wèt *or* nguwèt-wèt to use sparingly, save;
ngewètaké *or* nguwètaké to make s.t. last a long time, preserve, conserve.

See also **awèt**.

wetah intact (*kr for* **wutuh**).

wétan east;

ngétan, mangétan eastwards, to go eastwards;

ngétanaké (*pass* dingétanaké) to move s.t. to the east;

wétanan pertaining to the East, Oriental;

wétan-wétanan the eastern part;

sawétané to the east of;

sapangétan everything located to the east of.

wetara I *ng*, **wetawis** *kr* 1 1 estimate; 2 approximately; sawetara some, a few; metara to estimate as, consider.

II 1 interval; 2 between; ora wetara suwé not long after, before long.

weteh *reg var of* **wutuh**.

weteng *ng, kr*, **padharan** *k.i.* stomach, belly;

meteng *ng*, wawrat *kr*, mbobot, ngandhut *k.i.*, 1 pregnant; 2 swelling (ear of rice); 3 loaded (gun);

metengi *or* ngetengi *cr* to get s.o. pregnant;

metengaké pregnant with, carrying (a child);

wetengan 1 pregnancy; 2 unborn baby, foetus.

wètèng *reg* long bamboo pole.

wéthéthithé *var of* **wathathithah**.

wétikna *var of* **witikna**.

wetu *ng*, **wedal** *kr*, 1 emergence; 2 product; 3 rising (*esp* moon); 4 expenditure;

metu 1 to emerge, come out, leave (a job, school); 2 to follow (a way, road); 3 to be born (as male or female); 4 to appear, be published; 5 to produce a yield (crop);

metoni 1 to travel over (a path); 2 to take the field against; 3 to have a child;

metokaké 1 to bring out; 2 to display; 3 to dismiss (from a job), expel (from school); 4 to spend (money);

pametu 1 product; 2 income;

weton 1 (wedalan *kr*) a product of; 2 (wedalan *kr*, wiyosan *k.i.*) birthday reckoned by combining days from the five-day and seven-day weeks;

wetonan 1 connected with a birthday; 2 ceremony celebrating one's birthday.

wewah to increase (*kr for* **wuwuh**).

wéwé a forest spirit, a female **gendruwo**.

wewedhé *reg* to be in labour, about to give birth.

weweg compact and firm (as contrasted with flabby).

weweh *reg, var of* **wuwuh**.

wèwèh to give gifts;

pawèwèh a gift.

See also **wèh**, **wènèh**.

wewéka *or* **wéwéka** careful, cautious.

wewer, **mewer** *lit* to roll up.

wewes, **mewes** *lit* to put pressure on, force.

wéya *reg* careless, negligent.

wi I *var of* **awi** I.

II *var of* **uwi**.

wiben *reg kr for* **wido**.

wibi *lit* mother.

wicaksana endowed with wisdom.

wicanten 1 talk, discussion (*kr for* **catur**, **ucap**); 2 to speak (*kr for* **celathu**); 3 speech (*kr for* **wicara**).

wicara *ng*, **wicanten** *kr*, speech, conversation;

micara 1 to discuss, treat; 2 to be a good speaker;

pamicara way of speaking.

wicarita *lit* a good narrator.

wicitra *lit* 1 very beautiful; 2 of many kinds.

wida a cosmetic mixture made from flowers and perfume. *See also* **ganda**.

widada *lit* successful, prosperous, safe and sound.

widadara male counterpart of a **widadari**.

widadari nymph, heavenly maiden;
  midadarèni to observe a vigil for the
  bride on the eve of her wedding.

widadi *var of* widada.

widadya *lit var of* widada.

widagda *lit* clever, knowledgeable.

widara the jujube tree and its fruit;
  widaran balls of rice or cassava flour,
  eggs and sugar.

widasari a certain plant and its flower.

widayaka *lit* wise man.

widayat heaven-sent help.

widhag-widhig *see* widhig II.

widhé I 1 fish trap in the form of a barricade of bamboo slats tied together so
  that it can be rolled up; 2 bamboo
  shutters;
  midhé to catch fish with such a trap.
  II widhèn meat bought in the market.

widheng I a certain freshwater crab.
  II, *or* kewidhengan *reg* bewildered,
  confused, forgetful.

widhig I a mat of woven palm leaves.
  II, widhag-widhig, ora nganggo -
  without hesitation.

widhung awkward, clumsy (*var of* kidhung).

widi I *lit* 1 rule, regulation; 2 destiny,
  fate; Hyang Widi God (who ordains
  all);
  midèni to make law, ordain.
  II, midi to choose;
  midèni to check, count again.
  III, midèni to grant permission. *See
  also* idi.

widik, midik-midik to estimate by examining closely.

wido (of a cock) of three different
  colours and with green edges on the
  back feathers.

widya *lit* knowledge, wisdom.

widyadara *var of* widadara.

widyadari *var of* widadari.

widyastuti *lit* blessings, good wishes.

widyuta *lit* lightning, thunder.

wigar I 1 to lose strength or resistance; 2
  to wilt, fade (*e.g.* flowers); 3 to fail
  (plan).
  II *lit* happy, glad.

wigati *ng*, wigatos *kr* 1 important, serious; 2 intent, aim;
  migatèkaké to consider important,
  take an interest in;
  kawigatèn interest, concern.

wigatos *kr for* wigati.

wigena *lit* 1 sad, sorrowful; 2 hindrance,
  obstacle.

wigih, wigih-wigih *or* wigah-wigih to
  feel shy, embarrassed, diffident about
  doing s.t.

wigna *var of* wigena.

wignya I skilled, well versed;
  kawignyan skill, wisdom.
  II, wignyan Javanese script diacritic
  accompanying a consonant character
  to denote syllable-final *h*.

wiguh *var of* wigih.

wiguna *lit* 1 competent; 2 useful, having
  utility.

wija *lit* 1 seed; 2 offspring.

wijah I common, ordinary.
  II wijah-wijah sorted, classified.
  III wijah-wijah *lit* elated, excited.

wijang I 1 distinct, with the elements
  properly sorted out; 2 (of speech)
  clearly enunciated;
  mijang *or* mijang-mijang to keep distinct;
  wijangan a clear distinction.
  II, mijang *reg* to instruct.

wijaya *lit* victory; - kusuma a tree and its
  flower, that blooms on one night of
  the year and is fetched by royal emis-
  saries from islands in the Segara
  Anakan when a new ruler of Surakarta
  ascends the throne;
  kawijayan to capacity to conquer,
  invincibility.

wijèn *see* wiji I.

wiji I 1 seed; 2 descendant; 3 origin;

miji to resemble a seed;

mijèni 1 to sow seeds in; 2 to put sesame seeds in s.t.; 3 to have (descendants);

mijèkaké to have descendants;

wijèn 1 sesame seed; 2 rice for sowing;

pawijènan a plot sown with rice seeds.

II *var of* iji;

sawiji one (*lit, var of* siji).

wijik to wash the hands or feet (*k.i. for* wisuh);

pawijikan a bowl for washing the hands.

wijil *lit* 1 emergence, exit; 2 descendant; 3 product; 4 name of a classical verse form; 5 gateway, exit;

mijil to emerge.

wijir *var of* ijir.

wijuk *reg* to wash one's hands or feet.

wijung a variety of large wild boar.

wik, wik-wik *or* wak-wik to move the fingers busily. *Also* uwik.

wikan *lit* to know;

wikana *or* tan - *reg* I don't know;

mikani to understand, know about.

wikara I *reg* cause.

II *lit* mikara to harm, mistreat.

wiki choosy, hard to please, finicky.

wiku priest, ascetic learned man.

wikrama I *lit* valour.

II *lit* wedding ceremony;

mikramakaké to hold a wedding for (one's daughter). *See also* pikrama.

wil I *lit* demon.

II wil, wal-wil to touch with the fingers repeatedly, move fingers busily (at s.t.). *Also* uwil.

wilah 1 bamboo lath; 2 kris blade; 3 (*or* wilahan) the keys of Javanese musical instruments; 4 interval, tone-step;

milah to steal a kris from the wearer out of its sheath.

wilang *ng*, wical *kr*, milang to count,

enumerate; - kori to go from house to house; - usuk to lie around doing nothing;

milangaké to classify; differentiate;

kawilang counted, considered;

pamilang act or way of counting; an enumeration;

wilangan 1 counting; 2 number.

wilangèn *reg* fortunately; lucky.

wilangon *var of* wilangun.

wilangun *lit* charming, attractive.

wilanten *var of* wlanten.

wilapa *lit* letter, poem, plaint.

wilasa *lit* favour, sympathy, pity;

kawilasan compassion, pity.

Wilatikta *see* Wilwatikta.

wilayat region, district, zone.

wilet 1 well-rounded (argument); 2 pleasant to listen to, elegant (speech); 3 (in gamelan music) a melodic phrase;

milet well mixed;

mileti to entwine, make s.t. more beautiful;

kawiletan moved, charmed by sweet words, entreaties;

mawiletan *lit* entwined together.

wilis I *lit* green, dark green, shiny green.

II *var of* wilang.

wilujeng well, safe and sound (*kr for* slamet).

wilut I *see* idu.

II, milut to twist together.

wilwa I a kind of ghost.

II *lit* a certain bitter fruit with hard skin, the bael. *See also* maja I.

Wilwatikta the kingdom of Majapahit.

wimba I *lit* statue, likeness;

mimba 1 to look like; 2 to imitate, represent.

II emergence (*lit var of* wetu);

wimbaning lèk the time of the new moon.

wimbasara *lit* messenger; policeman.

wimbuh *lit* increase (*see also* imbuh).

windasa *lit* destroyed.

windu I wall, edge of a well;
    mindoni to provide a well with a wall.
  II a period of eight (Javanese) years, in the following cycle: Alip, Ehé, Jimawal, Jé, Dal, Wawu, Jimakir; **windu** in turn run in a cycle of four: Adi, Kunthara, Sangara and Sancaya (each having its own character);
    mindoni to celebrate reaching the age of eight years;
    windon 1 (counting) by the **windu; 2** for many **windu; 3** the celebration of the age of one **windu.**

winga, mawinga-winga *lit* enraged, glowing with anger.

wingi yesterday; - **uni** *reg* in the past, in former times;
    winginé the day before;
    wingènané the day before yesterday;
    wingi-wingi formerly, in the old days.

wingit *var of* **singit.**

wingka I shard of earthenware or roofing tile;
    mingka hardheaded, pigheaded.
  II cake made from sticky rice flour and baked; - **babat** special cake from the town of Babat (Kabupaten Lamongan, East Java).

wingking 1 back, rear; **2** later on, last (time) (*kr for* **buri**).

wingkis, mingkis 1 to roll up (the sleeves); **2** to hitch up, tuck up (clothing);
    wingkisan rolled up sleeves, tucked up clothes.
  II, wingkisan gums (*k.i. for* **gusi**).

wingsil, wingsilan testicles.

wingwal different, divergent; to deviate.

wingwang *var of* **wingwal.**

wingwing slight, slender.

wingwrin *lit* afraid; fear.

winih 1 seed; **2** seedling; **3** breeding animal; **4** cause, origin;
    minihi 1 to sow (ground) with seed; **2** to be the cause of;

    pawinihan seedbed for rice.

wipra *lit* an ascetic, holy man.

wira *lit* courageous, manly.

wiradat wish, intention;
    miradati to seek a means of implementing a wish or intention.

wiraga (deliberately) charming, appealing behaviour;
    miraga to put on attractive or appealing ways;
    miragakaké to adopt (certain characteristics of behaviour);
    kawiragan behaviour which one adopts deliberately, *e.g.* as an impersonation, in depicting a character in a dance-drama.

wiragé *lit* sad, sorrowful, lovesick.

wirama 1 measure, tempo (in music, dance); **2** the appropriate use of words and expressions. *See also* **irama.**

wirandhungan *lit* slow, hesitant, indecisive.

wirang shame, embarrassment, loss of face, humiliation;
    mirangaké *or* **memirang 1** to make embarrassed; **2** embarrassing;
    mirang-mirangaké 1 to put to shame; **2** shameful;
    kawirangan *or* **kewirangan 1** shame; **2** to be put to shame.

wirangrong *lit* **1** suffering from the pangs of love; **2** name of a classical verse form.

wirasa I 1 expression of s.o.'s thoughts, feelings, opinion; **2** sense, meaning, content (of a letter);
    mirasa 1 to express in words, describe; **2** to discuss; **3** to seek the meaning.
  II, mirasa tasty, delicious.

wirasat character-reading by studying the face. *See also* **pirasat.**

wira-wiri to move back and forth restlessly.

wirayat *lit* story, tradition.

wiré *reg* small and neat (figure).

wirèng (or wirèngan) a martial dance.

wirid teachings, guidance;

　mirid to teach, instruct, give guidance.

wiroda *lit* furious, infuriated.

wirodra *var of* wiroda.

wirog, tikus - a field rat.

wirota *lit* violent.

wirotama brave, manly, courageous.

wiru I dried covering of a corn cob (*subst kr for* klobot).

　II (*or* wiron) folds, pleats (accordion-style) at the front of a kain;

　miru *or* mironi to fold, form pleats.

wirya *lit* brave, courageous, noble;

　kawiryan courage, valour.

wiryawan *lit* brave, courageous, noble;

　kawiryawan courage, valour.

wis *ng,* sampun *kr,* 1 already finished, over, done; 2 past tense marker; wis tau (to have) ever (done s.t.); sing wis-wis from before, past; ora wis-wis still not finished, still going; lèk wis! get on with it!;

　nguwisi to put a halt to;

　nguwisaké to finish off;

　sawisé after, afterwards;

　wisan 1 finished, over *etc* (emphatic, sentence-final); 2 - gawé the end of the day's work; the time (*ca* 11 a.m.) when the morning work in the rice-fields is finished.

wisa poison, venom;

　misani to poison.

wisada *lit* medicine (*var of* usada).

wisana *reg* finally (*var of* wusana).

wisata *lit* trip, journey; darma - travel for the purpose of study or for pleasure (*esp* a picnic).

wisaya trap, snare, noose;

　misaya to trap, snare.

wisel 1 postal money order; 2 railway points;

　miseli *or* miselaké to transfer money by postal order.

wisésa I authority, control (*see also* wasésa); Hyang Maha - the Almighty, God.

　II *gram* affix.

wisik, wisikan secret instruction (in wisdom);

　misik 1 in instruct; 2 *cr* to sleep with a woman;

　misiki to whisper s.t. to s.o.

wisma *lit* house.

wisudha 1 graduation; 2 pure, clean;

　misudha to promote, raise to higher rank;

　wisudhan, pamisudhan promotion.

wisuh *ng,* kr, wijik *k.i.,* to wash one's hands or feet;

　wisuhan water or basin for washing the hands or feet.

wisuna *reg* 1 slander, false accusation; 2 (source of) distress.

wiswa *lit* poison. *See also* wisa.

wisya *var of* wiswa.

wit 1 tree; 2 plant; 3 root, origin, cause;

　wit-witan trees, wooded area.

witana *lit* pavilion (for celebrations).

witaradya *lit* royal descent.

wité *reg, var of* witikna.

witikna because, in view of the fact that.

witir, salat - a non-obligatory time of prayer, last at night.

witna *var of* witikna.

wiwaha *lit* 1 wedding, wedding feast;

　miwaha 1 to perform the marriage ceremony for s.o.; 2 to celebrate (an event) with a great feast;

　pawiwahan wedding celebration.

wiwal 1 separating, coming apart; 2 (of mind) unbalanced, crazy;

　miwal to divorce (one's husband);

　pamiwal a sum of money with which a wife can buy a divorce.

wiwara *lit* hole, opening.

wiwéka care, prudence, caution.

wiwi wings (*shtf of* suwiwi).

wiwing slight, slender (*var of* wingwing).

wiwir, miwir to extend or spread s.t. sideways (bird's wings).

wiwit 1 the beginning; 2 to begin; 3 beginning with, from;
miwiti to begin s.t.;
wiwitan 1 (at) the beginning; 2 the first (part); 3 the origin.

wiya careless (var of wéya).

wiyadi lit saddened, grieving, anxious.

wiyaèn pretentious.

wiyaga musician in a gamelan orchestra var of niyaga.

wiyagah to be willing, really want to do s.t.;
miyagah to do s.t. with a real will, genuine desire.

wiyagra lit tiger.

wiyah usual, ordinary; wiyahé usually. See also sawiyah II.

wiyak, miyak 1 to push aside, to open s.t. apart; 2 to disclose (a secret);
kawiyak discovered, revealed.

wiyana lit strong, resistant.

wiyang I reg to go away.
II lit to refuse, be unwilling.

wiyar broad, wide, large, spacious (kr for amba I).

wiyat sky (var of awiyat).

wiyata I lit instruction, teachings;
pawiyatan educational institution.
II, miyatani reliable; adequate, effective.

wiyoga lit sad, sorrowful, troubled;
kawiyogan sadness.

wiyos k.i. for wetu.

wiyung lit frog.

wlagang to grow fast (baby).

wlagar, kawlagar lit burnt bare.
II, wlagaran unsaddled, bareback.

wlaha, mlaha for nothing, without result.

wlahar a flow of hot mud and lava (var of lahar I).

wlajar plough (reg kr for luku).

wlaka lit var of blaka.

wlakang var of lakang.

Wlanda, mlandani to act like a European. See also Landa, Walanda.

wlandang reg boss (in gambling).

Wlandi kr for Wlanda.

wlanjar young childless widow or divorcee (also lanjar, wulanjar).

wlangat reg planks laid above the corpse in the grave.

wlangsang var of langsang.

wlanten, mlanten to whiten, wash (clothes);
pamlanten washerman.

wlija reg peddler.

wlikat var of walikat.

wlingsang a marten-like animal.

wlira in a loom, the bar used to press the weft down. Also lira.

wlirang var of welirang. Also lirang I.

wluku a plough;
mluku to plough;
mlukokaké 1 to plough for s.o.; 2 to have s.o. plough.

wlulang ng, wacucal kr, leather.

wlulèn reg original, authentic, genuine.

wlungsung, mlungsungi 1 to shed the old skin and grow a new one, slough (snake); 2 to provide s.o. with a change of clothing; 3 to have a change of heart;
wlungsungan cast-off skin.

wod 1 root; 2 fundamental concept; 3 gram root, base of a word; 3 root (in maths); woding ati beloved;
ngewod 1 to produce lots of roots; 2 old and gnarled;
wod-wodan thick roots around the base of a tree.

wogan I if.
II or - uler name of the 6th day of the nine-day week.

woh fruit;
awoh to bear fruit;
wohan betel-nut;
woh-wohan various kinds of fruits.

wok I, wokan a shallow hole in the ground (in children's games).

II 1 beard under the chin; 2 hanging roots, of *e.g.* banyan tree.

wol 1 wool.

II *or* **mak wol** *repr* a large pinch of a fat person's flesh.

III short, dwarfish.

woldhèg woollen blanket.

wolu eight; **-las** 18; **-likur** 28; **wolung puluh** 80;

wewolu (group or unit of) eight;

wolu-wolu by eights, eight at a time;

kawolu (*or* **kaping wolu**) 1 eight times; 2 the eighth.

wondéné now as for (*kr for* **déné**).

wong I *ng*, **tiyang** *kr*, **priyantun** *k.i.* 1 person, human being; 2 a successful person; 3 the physical or mental characteristics of a person; 4 someone, anyone; 5 subordinate, follower; **- akèh** public; **- ayu** my dear; **- cilik** common people; **- gedhé** important or high-ranking person; **- lanang** 1 man; 2 husband; **- liya** non-family; **- ora duwé** the have-nots; **- tuwa** 1 old person; 2 parent; **- wadon** woman;

wong-wong people in general;

wong-wongan 1 dummy, fake human being; 2 personal characteristics;

nguwongi 1 to become a responsible human being; 2 to man, provide people for;

nguwongaké to treat s.o. as a human being.

II after all, as.

wonga-wonga *lit* bosom (between the breasts), cleavage.

wongsal-wangsul *see* **wangsul**.

wongwa *reg* glowing coal.

wonten 1 there is/are; to be, exist (*kr for* **ana**); 2 in, on, at (*kr for* **ana ing**, **nèng**).

wor together with, combined;

nguwor *or* **ngewor** to mix;

nguwori to mix s.t. (into s.t. else);

nguworaké to put s.t. in with (s.t. else);

wor-woran mixture;

wor-suh helter-skelter, random, disorganised. *See also* **mor**.

wora-wari hibiscus.

wortel carrot.

wos I essence, contents, gist of the matter.

II uncooked rice (*kr for* **beras**).

wosé shelled kernel or seed; **kacang -** shelled peanuts;

wosèn shelled, peeled, husked.

wot I narrow, makeshift bridge (of tree trunk, bamboo);

nguwot to cross such a bridge;

nguwoti to provide with such a bridge.

II **wotsari**, **wotsantun** *lit* to make a gesture of homage (**sembah**).

III *reg* **mot** to carry, load into. *See also* **momot**.

wowog, **kewowogen**, **kuwowogen**, **kemomogen** staggered, overcome with aversion at the quantity (size) of it, unable to take any more.

wowor, **momor** to mix in;

kawoworan mixed with/into;

woworan 1 ingredient; 2 mixture;

momor sambu *lit* 1 a spy; 2 to spy on. *See also* **wor**.

wra *lit* scattered.

wradin *kr for* **wrata**. *See also* **radin**.

wragad expense, cost (*var of* **ragad**).

wragang I *var of* **wlagang**.

II a kind of palm wine.

wragil *var of* **ragil**, **wuragil**.

wraha *lit* wild boar.

wrana *var of* **warana**, **rana III**.

wrandha *var of* **warandha**, **randha**.

wrangas small red ant.

wrangka 1 *ng*, **sarungan** *kr*, kris sheath; 2 *lit* **-ning ratu** prime minister, the Patih.

wrat heavy; important (*kr for* **bot I**);

ngewrat 1 to hold, contain; 2 to load, accommodate. *See also* **awrat**.

wrata *var of* **rata**.

wratsangka *lit* magnolia.

wratsari *var of* wratsangka.

wrayang *var of* warayang.

wré *lit* monkey.

wreda, wredha *lit* old (*also* werda).

wregu a small palm with a slender hard-wood trunk.

wreksa *lit* tree, wood.

wrena a certain small centipede (*var of* rena I).

wrengkeng stubborn, obstinate, head-strong.

wresni *lit* in-law of the same generation, sibling-in-law.

wretek *var of* wertek.

wresthi *lit* rain.

wrin, tan - *lit* 1 fearless; 2 not to know.

wringin banyan tree (*var of* waringin, ringin).

wringut, wringuten raging, mad with fury.

wruh *lit* to know; to see;
  kawruh knowledge, science, what one has come to know;
  kumawruh conceited, self-opinionated;
  pangawruh knowing, knowledge;
  ngawruhi to come to know about, find out about;
  wruhanamu let me tell you, you should know... *See also* weruh.

wruju *var of* waruju.

wucal *subst kr of* wulang.

wuda (lukar *k.i.*) naked (*var of* uda);
  kawudan 1 bared, made naked; 2 *fig* penniless.

wudel *ng, kr,* nabi *or* tuntunan *k.i.* navel.

wudhar *var of* udhar.

wudhu *var of* udhu.

wudlu *var of* wudu.

wudu to wash the face, hands and feet ritually before praying;
  mudoni to bathe s.o. ritually in prepa-ration for s.t., *esp* a bride (for her wed-ding), a corpse (for burial).

wuduk *lit* fatty, rich; sega - rice boiled in coconut milk. *See also* uduk.

wudul, mudul to push a hole in s.t., chis-el through.

wudun *ng, kr,* untar *k.i.* pimple, boil; - brama boil, carbuncle; - semat a small painful abscess;
  wudunen to have a pimple/boil.

wuh rubbish, litter;
  pawuhan pit for rubbish.

wujang *reg* bachelor (*var of* bujang).

wujil *lit* dwarf.

wujud 1 shape, form, appearance; 2 to be (in the form of); 3 the being, existence (of God);
  mujudi 1 (*or* mujudaké) to compose, make up; 2 to repay a debt in the form of (s.t. precious).

wuk I little girl (*adr, term of endearment: shtf of* bawuk II).
  II, wuk-wukan (of egg) rotten, decayed.

wukir *lit* mountain.

wukon *var of* ukon.

wuku I one of 30 seven-day periods, each with its own name, which make up a 210-day cycle;
  pawukon almanac, astrological reck-oning by wukus.
  II little pip, seed.
  III section of a bamboo or rattan stalk.

wulan 1 month (*kr for* sasi); 2 moon (*kr for* rembulan);
  wulanan 1 monthly, by the month (*kr for* sasèn); 2 to have menstruation.

wulanjar *var of* wlanjar.

wulang (wucal *subst kr*) · instruction, teachings, lesson; - wuruk teachings;
  mulang to teach;
  mulangaké to teach (a lesson);
  pamulang 1 act or way of teaching; 2 teacher, instructor;
  (we)wulangan teaching, instruction;
  pamulangan school, place of learning;
  piwulang instruction.

wulangun *lit* to yearn, be lovesick.

wulat, mulat *lit* to look at, see.

wuled *var of* uled.

wuli ear (of rice and other grains, in counting);
  wulèn 1 ear; **2** still in the ear;
  wulènan by the ear.
wulik *var of* **ulik**.
wulu I fur, feathers, body hair; **-cumbu 1** thumb hair; **2** clown-servant.
  II diacritic in the Javanese script which changes vowel *A* to *I*;
  wulon bearing the vowel *I*.
  III *var of* **wudlu, wudu**.
wuluh I 1 pring - a small variety of bamboo; **2** gun barrel;
  muluh to sand, rub smooth with the rough side of the above bamboo;
  wuluhan pipe, lamp chimney.
  II beras - brown rice (not polished).
  III lintang - name of a constellation, the Pleiades.
wulung I blue-black; **pring** - a blackish coloured bamboo;
  mulung to dye (fabric) blue-black.
  II hawk.
wulus, wulusan *lit* a stream of water.
wulya *lit* having recovered (*var of* **waluya**).
wun *reg*, **tan** - without fail, certainly.
wungkal a flat grindstone. *See also* **ungkal**.
wungkuk bent, crooked, deformed, hunchbacked.
wungkul 1 (of round objects) whole, not yet cut; **2** (of hoofs) whole, not split;
  wungkulan whole (*e.g.* diamond).
wungkus wrapper, *esp* of banana leaves;
  wungkusan 1 a packet wrapped with banana leaf; **2** (food) cooked in a leaf wrapping.
wunglon chameleon *var of* **bunglon**.
wungu I 1 to wake up (*k.i. for* **tangi**); **2** to awaken s.o. (*root form: k.i. for* **gugah**);
  wungon 1 to keep o.s. awake at night (*k.i. for* **lèk-lèkan**); **2** to be a light sleeper (*k.i. for* **tengèn**).

  II 1 purple; **2** a big tree with purple flowers;
  mungu to make s.t. purple;
  mungokaké to have s.t. coloured or dyed purple.
wungwang, bumbung - a bamboo pipe open at both ends.
wungwung *var of* **wuwung**.
wuni a certain tree and its tart fruits.
wuninga to know, understand;
  ngawuningani to be informed about;
  kawuningan it is known (that...);
  kawuningana know! be advised! let me tell you (*k.i. for* **kawruhana**). *Also* **uninga**.
wuntel I wrapping (*var of* **buntel**).
  II *var of* **untel**.
wuntu *var of* **buntu**; **taun** - 355-day year (*see* **taun**).
wunu loose ears, grains of rice that fall out of bundles while being worked on.
wunuh, winunuh *lit* killed.
wunut a variety of tree.
wur the fragrant root of the 'pipe rhubarb' (**klembak**), powdered and used for flavouring cigarette tobacco;
  ngewuri *or* **ngewur-wuri** to scatter/sprinkle s.t. onto;
  ngewuraké *or* **ngewur-wuraké** to scatter/sprinkle s.t. *See also* **wuwur**.
wuragil *var of* **ragil**.
wurah, wurahan *or* **mawurahan** tumultuous.
wurcita *see* **wursita**.
wurda *lit* one hundred thousand million; countless, innumerable.
wurdha *var of* **wurda**.
wuri I *lit* back, rear; **2** later on, in the future;
  wuri-wuri in the future, ultimately, in the end;
  kawuri 1 last, past; **2** left behind.
  II, muri-muri *lit* to honour, respect (example, holy place).
wurik (of hens) speckled.

wursita *lit* speech, words;
  winursita *or* **kawursita** it is told that...
wuru drunk, intoxicated, drugged (*k.i.* for **mendem**); - **getih** out for blood, intoxicated with the heat of the battle;
  muroni to make drunk.
wuruh foam, scum;
  muruh to foam up.
wuruk I 1 wagon-driver, charioteer; **2** *lit* chariot.
  II *lit* calf.
  III teaching, instruction;
  muruki to teach, instruct;
  wurukan *or* **wuruk-wurukan** that which is taught.
wurukung name of the 6th day of the six-day week.
wurung *ng*, **sandé** *or* **wandé** *kr* to fail to happen; **ora** - inevitable; - **bahan** *or* - **dandanan** *or* - **wong** to come to nothing;
  murungaké to prevent s.t. from happening; to foil, thwart;
  murungan to habitually let people down, fail to keep appointments;
  pamurung 1 a factor that prevents s.t. from happening; **2** cancellation of a projected activity.
wuryan, kawuryan *lit* to appear, be seen.
wus *lit, var of* **wis**.
wusana 1 final; **2** the end; **wusanané** finally, in the end;
  kawusanan end, conclusion. *See also* **wasana**.
wusanten *md for* **wusana**.
wusdéné *ng*, **wusdènten** *md*, moreover, furthermore, and what is more.
wusdènten *md for* **wusdéné**.
wusu 1 a bow-shaped tool for cleaning cotton or **kapok**; **2** bent (the back);
  musoni to clean with the above tool.
wuta blind; - **sastra** illiterate;
  muta 1 to go blind; **2** to act as though one were blind; - **tuli 1** to act as a blind and deaf person; **2** *fig* hotheaded.

wutah to spill out; - **getih** native (place, land);
  mutah *ng, kr,* **luntak** *k.i.* to vomit s.t.;
  mutahi to spill onto, to spit on;
  mutahaké to vomit s.t., to spill s.t. (out);
  wutahan 1 s.t. spilled out; **2** an extra plan that has to be abandoned;
  wutah-wutahan vomit.
wuthuh wow! (*var of* **wadhuh**, **wathuh**).
wutuh *ng*, **wetah** *kr*, whole, intact, unbroken (*also* **utuh**);
  mutuhaké 1 to leave, keep whole; **2** to make whole;
  wutuhan in an unbroken condition, whole;
  wutuh-wutuhan completely, throughout, thoroughly.
wutun hardworking, dedicated. *Also* **utun**, **yutun**.
wuwa measuring unit for rice plants: $\frac{1}{2}$ **amet**, or *ca* 77 kg.
wuwu I a certain type of bamboo or wicker fish trap.
  II hawk; - **rawa** a variety of hawk.
wuwuh *ng*, **wewah** *kr*, to increase; to add (to);
  muwuhi to increase s.t.; to add to;
  muwuhaké to add s.t. to;
  wuwuhan an additional amount, contribution;
  wuwuh-wuwuh furthermore, especially.
wuwul *reg* betting stakes, money contributed to a gambling pool.
wuwung rooftop, ridgecap (tile, wood, metal);
  muwung to cover the top of a roof with a cap.
wuwur s.t. to sprinkle;
  muwuri *or* **muwur-muwuri** to scatter/sprinkle s.t. onto;
  muwur-muwuraké to scatter/sprinkle;
  kawuwuran sprinkled with. *See also* **wur**.

wuwus *lit* words, what s.o. says;
   muwus to tell, say;
   kawuwus told, related.
wuyé name of the 22nd **wuku**.
wuyung 1 *lit* bewildered; 2 *lit* sad; sadness;

wuyungan turbulence, tumult, chaos;
   wayang-wuyungan running to and fro in confusion and fear.
wyaèn *see* **wiyaèn**.
wyagah *var of* **wiyagah**.
wyakarana *lit* grammar.

Y

ya *ng* (**inggih** *kr*) 1 yes, yes indeed (it is so); 2 also; 3 *particle with gram function, introducing further specification*; 4 (*sentence-final*) isn't that so? (after question); right, okay? (after order);
   ya iku, **ya kuwi** *ng* (**inggih punika** *kr*) that is, namely;
   ngiyani to say yes to, to agree to. *Also* **iya**.
yab, **yab-yaban** to walk restlessly back and forth, rush around wildly.
yadi *lit* if, when.
yadnya *lit* a sacrifice, offering.
yadyan *lit* if, even though.
yadyastun *lit* even so.
yag, **yag-yagan** to act in unseemly haste, rush around.
yagéné why? how come?
yah I *excl of scepticism, disparagement*.
   II time (*shtf of* **wayah**); **yah éné** *or* **yah méné** at this moment, at such a time as this.
yai *reg var of* **kyai**.
yak I *excl of disbelief* (*var of* **yah**).
   II, **yak-yakan** to keep rushing around; to get in others' way.
yakin 1 to feel sure; 2 certain, in fact, actually;
   ngyakini 1 to accept the truth of, believe in; 2 convincing;
   ngyakinaké 1 to convince; 2 to check the facts about s.t.

yaksa *lit* demon, giant.
yaksi *var of* **yaksa**.
yakti *lit* 1 really, actually; 2 *see* **yati**.
yakut crystal used in jewelry settings.
Yama, **- Dipati** god (king) of the underworld.
yamani *lit* hell, the underworld.
yamyam *lit*, **yamyam tilam kajiwatan** *term of affection*: divine lady of the bedchamber, dearest beloved.
yang *lit* god;
   kayangan heaven, the abode of the gods.
yar yard (measure of length).
yasa 1 *lit* building; 2 to make, create, set up, build;
   ngyasani to build s.t.;
   ngyasakaké 1 to build for s.o.; 2 to have s.t. made/built;
   yasan that which has been made *or* built, *e.g.* **yasan dalem** created by His Majesty;
   yayasan foundation.
yasin, **surah** *or* **surat - the 37th chapter of the Quran (recited for the dying).
yat *reg* intention (*shtf of* **niyat**).
yatallah oh God!
yati, **yatiwara** *lit* pundit, holy man.
yatim fatherless, orphaned; **- piyatu** orphan.
yatin *var of* **yatim**.
yatma, **yatmaka** *lit* soul.

yatna *lit* cautious.

yatra money (*kr for* dhuwit).

ya'uk, ora ya'uk *coll* no way! no good!

yaya *var of* yayah.

yayah I *lit* father; - réna *or* - wibi *lit* parents.

II *lit* like, as.

yayi *lit* 1 younger brother/sister; 2 *adr* wife, younger brother/sister.

yé 1 hurray!; 2 *teasing excl.*

yeg, yeg-yeg *or* yag-yeg *repr* swaying, unsteady. *See also* iyeg II.

yèk *reg var of* yèn.

yéka *lit* that is (*shtf of* ya ika), *also* yèki, yèku.

yeksa *var of* yaksa.

yeksi *var of* yaksi.

yekti *ng*, yektos *kr*, real, actual;
   ngyektèni to notice s.t. particularly, take special note of;
   ngyektèkaké to test the truth of;
   sayekti real(ly), actual(ly), in fact;
   sayektiné as a matter of fact, in fact.

yektos *kr for* yekti.

yem, ngeyem to keep moist, prevent from drying out;
   ngeyem-yemi to bear calmly, patiently, keep calm. *See also* ayem.

yèn *ng*, *kr* (bilih, menawi *kr*) 1 when-(ever), if; 2 that (after words of saying *etc*); 3 as for; 4 or else, for fear that. *See also* nèk I.

yer, yer-yeran dizzy, spinning.

yeti *inf var of* yekti.

yetos *inf var of* yektos.

yeyes, ngyeyes (of rain) incessant.

yi *reg, shtf of* kyai.

ying *reg* (the one) which. *See also* sing.

yitma soul (*var of* yatma).

yitna cautious;
   yitna yuwana, léna sirna *prov* better safe than sorry. *See also* prayitna.

yiyid sticky substance, slime;
   ngyiyid to ooze slime.

yiyis, ngyiyis (of rain) incessant.

yo *ng* come on! *See* ayo.

yod, ngeyod *or* ngeyod-yod to bounce s.t. up and down;
   yod-yodan to bounce up and down.

yodhemporem iodoform.

yodhium iodine.

yog, ngeyog to shake (*var of* rog).

yoga *lit* child (son or daughter);
   kang ayoga father.

yoga-brata, yoga-semèdi *lit* to meditate.

yogi pundit, revered teacher;
   yogiswara a highly revered pundit.

yogya proper, appropriate.

yoh 1 *attention-directing excl*; 2 yes, yep.

yojana *lit* a league (measure of distance).

yok-apa *reg* why, how, how come?

yom, ngeyom 1 to cast shade, create shelter; 2 to take shelter from sun, rain;
   ngeyomi to shade/shelter/protect s.t.;
   yom-yoman that which is shaded *or* sheltered;
   payoman protection, shelter;
   pangayoman 1 a shaded place; 2 protector/shelter.
   See also ayom.

yoni *lit* to have magical power; distinguished, excellent.

yu 1 older sister (*shtf of* bakyu); 2 term for addressing females of lower status.

yud *var of* yod.

yuda *lit* war, battle; - negara 1 administration of the country; 2 etiquette;
   payudan battlefield.

yudasmara *lit* to wage the 'battle of love', i.e. be united sexually.

yuga *lit* age, era.

yujana *var of* yojana.

yuk come on! (*shtf of* ayo).

yukti *lit* suitable, appropriate.

yumana *var of* yuwana.

yumani *var of* yamani.

yun I *lit* 1 to wish to; 2 to be going to. *See also* ayun II, hyun.

II, **ngeyun** to swing;
yun-yunan 1 a swing; 2 to play on a swing. *See also* **ayun** I.

yung *shtf of* **biyung**.

yungta *reg* aunt (parent's older sister) (*shtc from* **biyung anta**).

yunyun, yungyun *var of* **yuyun**.

yur, yur-yuran to sway in the wind.

yuri 1 jury; 2 umpire, referee.

yuswa age (*k.i. for* **umur**).

yuta million;
yutan (numbering in the) millions.

yuton *reg var of* **yutun**.

yutun hardworking, dedicated; **tani** - respectable and hardworking. *See also* **wutun**.

yuwana *lit* healthy, well, safe and sound;
kayuwanan health, well-being, safety.

yuyu river crab; - **rumpung** a river crab that has lost a claw;

yuyu rumpung ing jaladri a certain flat fish;

yuyu rumpung mbarong rongé *prov* one whose home is luxurious beyond his means;

ngyuyu (of livestock) 'as thin as a crab', so thin that the ribs show.

yuyun, kayuyun 1 attracted (by), madly in love (with); 2 *reg* to grieve for (a dead person);

ngyuyuni to charm;

ngyuyunaké attractive.

yuyut *reg* third-generation ancestor or descendant. *See also* **buyut**.

ywa *lit* do not. *See also* **aywa**.

ywang *lit, var of* **hyang, yang**.

Z

zabur, kitab - the Psalms.

zaétun *lit* olive. *Also* **jaétun, jétun**.

zakat *lit* annual religious tithe. *Also* **jakat**.

zaman *lit* time, period, era. *See also* **jaman**.

zamrut *lit* emerald.

zamzam, banyu - *lit* holy water from Mecca.

zat *lit* substance. *See also* **dat**.

ziyarah *lit* pilgrimage. *See also* **jiyarah**.

zina *lit* immorality, vice. *See also* **jina, jinah**.

Other Language Titles from Periplus Editions

Indonesian

Bahasa Indonesia Book One: Introduction to Indonesian Language and Culture
ISBN 0-945971-56-7

Bahasa Indonesia Book Two: Introduction to Indonesian Language and Culture
ISBN 0-945971-57-5

English-Indonesian/Indonesian-English Pocket Dictionary
ISBN 0-945971-66-4

Everyday Indonesian: Phrasebook and Dictionary
ISBN 0-945971-58-3

Practical Balinese
ISBN 962-593-068-X

Practical Indonesian
ISBN 0-945971-52-4

Malay

English-Bahasa Malaysia/Bahasa Malaysia-English Pocket Dictionary
ISBN 0-945971-99-0

Everyday Malay: Phrasebook and Dictionary
ISBN 0-945971-83-4

Upcoming Language Titles from Periplus Editions

Periplus Essential Phrase Books (Asian Languages):

Essential Chinese Phrase Book
ISBN 0-7946-0037-9

Essential Filipino Phrase Book
ISBN 0-7946-0040-9

Essential Indonesian Phrase Book
ISBN 0-7946-0036-0

Essential Korean Phrase Book
ISBN 0-7946-0041-7

Essential Thai Phrase Book
ISBN 0-7946-0039-5

Essential Vietnamese Phrase Book
ISBN 0-7946-0038-7

Periplus Pocket Dictionaries:

Pocket Bahasa Malaysia Dictionary
ISBN 0-7946-0057-3

Pocket Chinese Dictionary
ISBN 0-7946-0043-3

Pocket Filipino Dictionary
ISBN 0-7946-0046-8

Pocket Indonesian Dictionary
ISBN 0-7946-0042-5

Pocket Japanese Dictionary
ISBN 0-7946-0048-4

Pocket Korean Dictionary
ISBN 0-7946-0047-6

Pocket Thai Dictionary
ISBN 0-7946-0045-X

Pocket Vietnamese Dictionary
ISBN 0-7946-0044-1